D0180608

# The Oxford French Minidictionary

## Third Edition, revised

FRENCH–ENGLISH
ENGLISH–FRENCH

FRANÇAIS ANGLAIS
ANGLAIS–FRANÇAIS

OXFORD
UNIVERSITY PRESS

Great Clarendon Street, Oxford OX2 6DP

Oxford University Press is a department of the University of Oxford.
It furthers the University's objective of excellence in research, scholarship,
and education by publishing worldwide in

Oxford New York

Auckland Bangkok Buenos Aires Cape Town Chennai
Dar es Salaam Delhi Hong Kong Istanbul Karachi Kolkata
Kuala Lumpur Madrid Melbourne Mexico City Mumbai Nairobi
São Paulo Shanghai Singapore Taipei Tokyo Toronto

and an associated company in Berlin

Oxford is a registered trade mark of Oxford University Press
in the UK and in certain other countries

Published in the United States
by Oxford University Press Inc., New York



First edition 1986, Second edition 1993, Reissued 1997, Third edition 1999, Revised edition 2002



British Library Cataloguing in Publication Data

Data available

Library of Congress Cataloging in Publication Data

Data available

ISBN 0-19-860467-X

10 9 8 7 6 5 4 3 2 1

Typeset by Tradespools Ltd
Printed in Great Britain by
Charles Letts & Co Ltd
Dalkeith, Scotland

## Contents


| | |
|---|---|
| Introduction | vii |
| The pronunciation of French | xi |
| Abbreviations | xiii |
| **French-English Dictionary** | **1** |
| Phrasefinder | |
| **English-French Dictionary** | **305** |
| French Verbs | 601 |
| Numbers | 603 |


## Table des matières


| | |
|---|---|
| Introduction | ix |
| Prononciation de l'anglais | xii |
| Abréviations | xiii |
| **Dictionnaire français-anglais** | **1** |
| Mini guide de conversation | |
| **Dictionnaire anglais-français** | **305** |
| Verbes irréguliers anglais | 601 |
| Les nombres | 603 |

## Proprietary Terms

This dictionary includes some words which are, or are asserted to be, proprietary terms or trademarks. The presence or absence of such assertions should not be regarded as affecting the legal status of any proprietary name or trademark.

## Les marques déposées

Les mots qui, à notre connaissance, sont considérés comme des marques ou des noms déposés sont signalés dans cet ouvrage par ®. La présence ou l'absence de cette mention ne peut pas être considérée comme ayant valeur juridique.

# The Oxford French Minidictionary

## Revised Edition

Marianne Chalmers

## Third Edition

**Project Direction/ Direction de projet**

Isabelle Stables-Lemoine

**Editors/Rédactrices**

Marianne Chalmers
Rosalind Combley
Catherine Roux
Laura Wedgeworth

**Phrasefinder/Mini guide de conversation**

Hélène Haenen
Neil and Roswitha Morris

**Data-capture/Saisie des données**

Anna Cotgreave
Alison Curr
Sara Hawker
Muriel Ranivoalison
Steven Siddle

**Proofreader/Correctrice**

Genevieve Hawkins

## First and Second Editions

**Editors/Rédacteurs**

Michael Janes
Dora Latiri-Carpenter
Edwin Carpenter

# Introduction

This new edition of the *Oxford French Minidictionary* is designed as an effective and practical reference tool for the student, adult learner, traveller and business professional. It provides **user-friendly treatment** of core vocabulary across a broad spectrum of written and spoken language.

The wordlist has been revised and updated to reflect recent additions to both languages. The central ***Phrasefinder***, a feature normally only found in much larger dictionaries, aims to provide the user with the confidence to **communicate** in the most commonly encountered social situations such as travel, shopping, eating out and organizing leisure activities. In addition, a section at the back of the dictionary is devoted to numbers.

A further valuable feature of the dictionary is the special status given to more complex grammatical words which provide the basic structure of both languages. These ***function words*** are given a special layout to make them instantly accessible and offer clearly presented translation options and examples, with **short usage notes** to warn of possible pitfalls.

**French verbs** in the text are cross-referenced to the appropriate section of the verb tables. Examples of the three main French verb groups, as well as *avoir* and *être*, are conjugated in the most commonly used tenses. A quick **reference guide** giving the English translation of an example verb in the principal tenses has been included, followed by examplified guidance on **how to conjugate a reflexive verb**.

## Easy reference

The dictionary layout has been designed to be **clear**, streamlined and easy to consult. **Bullet points** separate each new part of speech within an entry, making it easy to scan. Nuances of sense or usage are pinpointed by semantic indicators (in condensed type in round brackets) or by typical collocates (*in italics in round brackets*) with which the word frequently occurs, quickly guiding the user to the appropriate translation. Extra help is given in the form of **symbols** to mark the register of language unambiguously. An exclamation mark ! indicates colloquial language and a cross ✖ indicates slang.

Each headword is followed by its **phonetic transcription** between slashes, except in the case of English compound headwords where the pronunciation can be derived from that of each of the component parts. The symbols used for the pronunciation are those of the International Phonetic Alphabet. Any unpredictable plural forms or irregular English conjugations, comparative and superlative forms are also given in brackets.

The *Oxford French Minidictionary* is designed to present essential information in an accessible format, providing the user with a fast track to **clear and effective communication**.

# Introduction

Cette nouvelle édition de l'*Oxford French Minidictionary* a été conçue comme un outil de référence efficace et pratique destiné aux étudiants de tous âges, aux touristes et aux professionnels. Elle offre un **traitement convivial** du vocabulaire de base représentatif de la langue écrite et parlée.

La nomenclature a été révisée et mise à jour de façon à refléter les récents apports de vocabulaire dans les deux langues. La partie centrale intitulée ***Mini guide de conversation***, que l'on ne trouve généralement que dans des dictionnaires de taille plus importante, aidera l'utilisateur à **communiquer** facilement dans les situations de la vie quotidienne les plus courantes telles que le voyage, le shopping, les sorties au restaurant ou les loisirs. En outre, une section sur les **nombres** a été incluse à la fin du dictionnaire.

Le statut particulier qui a été donné aux **mots grammaticaux** les plus complexes, qui forment les structures de base des deux langues, est un atout pour la consultation. Ces mots grammaticaux font en effet l'objet d'une présentation distincte qui les rend rapidement accessibles, les choix de traduction et des exemples étant clairement signalés. De courtes **notes d'usage** indiquent les pièges éventuels. Une liste de **verbes irréguliers anglais** se trouve à la fin de l'ouvrage.

## Une consultation facilitée

La présentation du dictionnaire a été conçue de façon à être **claire**, simplifiée et à faciliter la consultation de l'ouvrage. Des **puces** séparent chaque nouvelle partie du discours à l'intérieur d'une entrée, ce qui facilite leur repérage. Les nuances de sens ou d'usage sont marquées au moyen d'indicateurs sémantiques (en caractères sans serif mis entre parenthèses) ou par des collocateurs types (*en italique mis entre*

*parenthèses*) avec lesquels le mot s'emploie fréquemment, guidant ainsi rapidement l'utilisateur à la traduction appropriée. Une aide supplémentaire est donnée sous forme de **symboles** pour marquer le registre de langue sans ambiguïté: un point d'exclamation ! indique un niveau de langue familier et une croix ✖ indique un niveau de langue argotique.

Chaque entrée est suivie de sa transcription **phonétique** entre deux barres obliques, à l'exception des mots composés anglais dont la prononciation peut être dérivée de celle de chacun des éléments du mot. Les symboles utilisés pour la prononciation sont ceux de l'Alphabet Phonétique International. Les pluriels irréguliers ainsi que les conjugaisons ou les formes du comparatif et du superlatif irrégulières anglaises sont indiqués entre parenthèses.

L'*Oxford French Minidictionary* est fait de telle manière à présenter les informations essentielles dans un format accessible qui donne à l'utilisateur un moyen rapide pour **communiquer de façon claire et efficace**.

# The pronunciation of French

## Vowels

| | | | | | | | |
|---|---|---|---|---|---|---|---|
| a | *as in* | patte | /pat/ | ɑ | *as in* | pâte | /pɑt/ |
| ɑ̃ | | clan | /klɑ̃/ | e | | dé | /de/ |
| ɛ | | belle | /bɛl/ | ɛ̃ | | lin | /lɛ̃/ |
| ə | | demain | /dəmɛ̃/ | i | | gris | /gʀi/ |
| o | | gros | /gʀo/ | ɔ | | corps | /kɔʀ/ |
| ɔ̃ | | long | /lɔ̃/ | œ | | leur | /lœʀ/ |
| œ̃ | | brun | /bʀœ̃/ | ø | | deux | /dø/ |
| u | | fou | /fu/ | y | | pur | /pyʀ/ |

## Semi-Vowels

| | | | |
|---|---|---|---|
| j | *as in* | fille | /fij/ |
| ɥ | | huit | /ɥit/ |
| w | | oui | /wi/ |

## Consonants

*Aspiration of 'h'*

Where it is impossible to make a liason this is indicated by /'/ immediately after the slash e.g. *haine* /'ɛn/.

| | | | | | | | |
|---|---|---|---|---|---|---|---|
| b | *as in* | bal | /bal/ | ŋ | *as in* | camping | /kɑ̃piŋ/ |
| d | | dent | /dɑ̃/ | p | | porte | /pɔʀt/ |
| f | | foire | /fwar/ | ʀ | | rire | /ʀiʀ/ |
| g | | gomme | /gɔm/ | s | | sang | /sɑ̃/ |
| k | | clé | /kle/ | ʃ | | chien | /ʃjɛ̃/ |
| l | | lien | /ljɛ̃/ | t | | train | /tʀɛ̃/ |
| m | | mer | /mɛʀ/ | v | | voile | /vwal/ |
| n | | nage | /naʒ/ | z | | zèbre | /zɛbʀ/ |
| ɲ | | gnon | /ɲɔ̃/ | ʒ | | jeune | /ʒœn/ |

## La prononciation de l'anglais

### Voyelles et diphtongues

| | | | | | | | |
|---|---|---|---|---|---|---|---|
| iː | see | ɔː | saw | eɪ | page | ɔɪ | join |
| ɪ | sit | ʊ | put | əʊ | home | ɪə | near |
| e | ten | uː | too | aɪ | five | eə | hair |
| æ | hat | ʌ | cup | aɪə | fire | ʊə | poor |
| ɑː | arm | ɜː | fur | aʊ | now | | |
| ɒ | got | ə | ago | aʊə | flour | | |

### Consonnes

| | | | | | | | |
|---|---|---|---|---|---|---|---|
| p | pen | tʃ | chin | s | so | n | no |
| b | bad | dʒ | June | z | zoo | ŋ | sing |
| t | tea | f | fall | ʃ | she | l | leg |
| d | dip | v | voice | ʒ | measure | r | red |
| k | cat | θ | thin | h | how | j | yes |
| g | got | ð | then | m | man | w | wet |

## Abbreviations/Abréviations

| | | |
|---|---|---|
| adjective | *a* | adjectif |
| abbreviation | *abbr, abrév* | abréviation |
| adverb | *adv* | adverbe |
| anatomy | *Anat* | anatomie |
| archeology | *Archeol, Archéol* | archéologie |
| architecture | *Archit* | architecture |
| motoring | *Auto* | automobile |
| auxiliary | *aux* | auxiliaire |
| aviation | *Aviat* | aviation |
| botany | *Bot* | botanique |
| commerce | *Comm* | commerce |
| computing | *Comput* | informatique |
| conjunction | *conj* | conjonction |
| cookery | *Culin* | culinaire |
| determiner | *det, dét* | déterminant |
| electricity | *Electr, Électr* | électricité |
| figurative | *fig* | sens figuré |
| geography | *Geog, Géog* | géographie |
| geology | *Geol, Géol* | géologie |
| grammar | *Gram* | grammaire |
| humorous | *hum* | humoristique |
| interjection | *interj* | interjection |
| invariable | *inv* | invariable |
| law | *Jur* | droit |
| linguistics | *Ling* | linguistique |
| literal | *lit* | littéral |
| phrase | *loc* | locution |
| medicine | *Med, Méd* | médecine |
| military | *Mil* | armée |
| music | *Mus* | musique |
| noun | *n* | nom |
| nautical | *Naut* | nautisme |
| feminine noun | *nf* | nom féminin |
| masculine noun | *nm* | nom masculin |
| masculine and feminine noun | *nm,f or nmf or nm/f* | nom masculin et féminin |

| | | |
|---|---|---|
| computing | *Ordinat* | informatique |
| pejorative | *pej, péj* | péjoratif |
| philosophy | *Phil* | philosophie |
| photography | *Photo* | photographie |
| plural | *pl* | pluriel |
| politics | *Pol* | politique |
| possessive | *poss* | possessif |
| past participiple | *pp* | participe passé |
| prefix | *pref, préf* | préfixe |
| preposition | *prep, prép* | préposition |
| present participle | *pres p* | participe présent |
| pronoun | *pron* | pronom |
| psychology | *Psych* | psychologie |
| past | *pt* | prétérit |
| something | *qch* | quelque chose |
| somebody | *qn* | quelqu'un |
| railway | *Rail* | chemin de fer |
| relative pronoun | *rel pron, pron rel* | pronom relatif |
| religion | *Relig* | religion |
| somebody | *sb* | quelqu'un |
| school | *School, Scol* | scolaire |
| sport | *Sport* | sport |
| something | *sth* | quelque chose |
| technology | *Tech* | technologie |
| theatre | *Theat, Théât* | théâtre |
| television | *TV* | télévision |
| university | *Univ* | université |
| American English | *US* | anglais américain |
| auxiliary verb | *v aux* | verbe auxiliaire |
| intransitive verb | *vi* | verbe intransitif |
| reflexive verb | *vpr* | verbe pronominal |
| transitive verb | *vt* | verbe transitif |
| transitive and intransitive verb | *vt/i* | verbe transitif et intransitif |
| translation equivalent | ≈ | équivalent approximatif |
| trademark | ® | marque déposée |
| colloquial | [!] | familier |
| slang | [✖] | argot |

# French–English Dictionary

# Aa

**a** /a/ ⇒AVOIR [5].

**à** /a/ *préposition*

à+le = au
à+les = aux

····➤ (avec verbe de mouvement) to.

····➤ (pour indiquer où l'on se trouve) **~ la maison** at home; **~ Nice** in Nice.

····➤ (âge, date, heure) **~ l'âge de...** at the age of...; **au XIXe siècle** in the 19th century; **~ deux heures** at two o'clock.

····➤ (description) with; **aux yeux verts** with green eyes.

····➤ (appartenance) **~ qui est ce stylo?** whose pen is this?; **c'est ~ vous?** is this yours?

····➤ (avec nombre) **~ 90 km/h** at 90 km per hour; **~ 10 minutes d'ici** 10 minutes from here; **des tomates ~ 3 francs le kilo** tomatoes at 3 francs a kilo; **un timbre ~ 3 francs** a 3-franc stamp; **nous avons fait le travail ~ deux** two of us did the work; **mener 5 ~ 4** to lead 5 (to) 4.

····➤ (avec être) **c'est ~ moi** it's my turn; **je suis ~ vous tout de suite** I'll be with you in a minute; **c'est ~ toi de décider** it's up to you to decide.

····➤ (hypothèse) **~ ce qu'il paraît** apparently; **~ t'entendre** to hear you talk.

····➤ (exclamatif) **~ ta santé!** cheers!; **~ demain/bientôt!** see you tomorrow/soon!

····➤ (moyen) **~ la main** by hand; **~ vélo** by bike; **~ pied** on foot; **chauffage au gaz** gas heating

**abaissement** /abɛsmɑ̃/ *nm* (de taux, de prix) cut; (de seuil) lowering.

**abaisser** /abese/ [1] *vt* lower; (*levier*) pull *ou* push down; (fig) humiliate. □ **s'~** *vpr* go down, drop; (fig) demean oneself; **s'~ à** stoop to.

**abandon** /abɑ̃dɔ̃/ *nm* abandonment; (de personne) desertion; (de course) withdrawal; (naturel) abandon; **à l'~** in a state of neglect.

**abandonner** /abɑ̃dɔne/ [1] *vt* abandon; (*épouse, cause*) desert; (renoncer à) give up, abandon; (céder) give (**à** to); (*course*) withdraw from, (Ordinat) abort. □ **s'~ à** *vpr* give oneself up to.

**abasourdir** /abazuʀdiʀ/ [2] *vt* stun.

**abat-jour** /abaʒuʀ/ *nm inv* lampshade.

**abats** /aba/ *nmpl* offal.

**abattement** /abatmɑ̃/ *nm* dejection; (faiblesse) exhaustion; (Comm) reduction; **~ fiscal** tax allowance.

**abattre** /abatʀ/ [11] *vt* knock down; (*arbre*) cut down; (*animal*) slaughter; (*avion*) shoot down; (affaiblir) weaken; (démoraliser) demoralize; **ne pas se laisser ~** not let things get one down. □ **s'~** *vpr* come down, fall (down).

**abbaye** /abei/ *nf* abbey.

**abbé** /abe/ *nm* priest; (supérieur d'une abbaye) abbot.

**abcès** /apsɛ/ *nm* abscess.

**abdiquer** /abdike/ [1] *vt/i* abdicate.

**abdomen** /abdɔmɛn/ *nm* abdomen.

**abdominal** (*pl* **-aux**) /abdɔminal/ *a* abdominal. **abdominaux** *nmpl* (Sport) stomach exercises.

**abeille** /abɛj/ *nf* bee.

**aberrant, ~e** /abɛʀɑ̃, -t/ *a* absurd.

**abêtir** /abetiʀ/ [2] *vt* turn into a moron.

**abîme** /abim/ *nm* abyss.

**abîmer** /abime/ [1] *vt* damage, spoil. □ **s'~** *vpr* get damaged *ou* spoilt.

**ablation** /ablasjɔ̃/ *nf* removal.

**aboiement** /abwamɑ̃/ *nm* bark, barking; **~s** barking.

**abolir** /abɔliʀ/ [2] *vt* abolish.

**abondance** /abɔ̃dɑ̃s/ *nf* abundance; (prospérité) affluence. **abondant, ~e** *a* abundant, plentiful.

**abonder** /abɔ̃de/ [1] *vi* abound (**en** in); **~ dans le sens de qn** agree wholeheartedly with sb.

**abonné, ~e** /abɔne/ *nm,f* (lecteur) subscriber; (voyageur, spectateur) season-ticket holder.

**abonnement** /abɔnmɑ̃/ *nm* (à un journal) subscription; (de bus, Théât) season-ticket; (au gaz) standing charge.

**abonner (s')** /(s)abɔne/ [1] *vpr* subscribe (**à** to).

**abord** /abɔʀ/ *nm* access; **~s** surroundings; **d'~** first.

**abordable** /abɔʀdabl/ *a* (*prix*) affordable; (*personne*) approachable; (*texte*) accessible.

**aborder** /abɔʀde/ [1] *vt* approach; (*lieu*) reach; (*problème*) tackle. ● *vi* reach land.

**aborigène** /abɔʀiʒɛn/ *nm* aborigine.

**aboutir** /abutiʀ/ [2] *vi* succeed, achieve a result; **~ à** end (up) in, lead to; **n'~ à rien** come to nothing.

**aboutissement** /abutismɑ̃/ *nm* outcome; (de carrière, d'évolution) culmination.

**aboyer** /abwaje/ [31] *vi* bark.

**abrégé** /abʀeʒe/ *nm* summary.

**abréger** /abʀeʒe/ [14] [40] *vt* (*texte*) shorten, abridge; (*mot*) abbreviate, shorten; (*visite*) cut short.

**abreuver** /abʀœve/ [1] *vt* water; (fig) overwhelm (**de** with). □ **s'~** *vpr* drink.

**abréviation** /abʀevjasjɔ̃/ *nf* abbreviation.

**abri** /abʀi/ *nm* shelter; **à l'~** under cover; (en lieu sûr) safe; **à l'~ de** sheltered from; **se mettre à l'~** take shelter.

**abricot** /abʀiko/ *nm* apricot.

**abriter** /abʀite/ [1] *vt* shelter; (recevoir) house. □ **s'~** *vpr* (take) shelter.

**abrupt, ~e** /abʀypt/ *a* steep, sheer; (fig) abrupt.

**abruti, ~e** /abʀyti/ *nm,f* 🄸 idiot.

**absence** /apsɑ̃s/ *nf* absence; **il a des ~s** sometimes his mind goes blank.

**absent, ~e** /apsɑ̃, -t/ *a* (*personne*) absent, away; (*chose*) missing; **il est toujours ~** he's still away; **d'un air ~** absently. ● *nm,f* absentee.

**absenter (s')** /(s)apsɑ̃te/ [1] *vpr* go *ou* be away; (sortir) go out, leave.

**absolu, ~e** /apsɔly/ *a* absolute.

**absorbant, ~e** /apsɔʀbɑ̃, -t/ *a* (*travail*) absorbing; (*matière*) absorbent.

**absorber** /apsɔʀbe/ [1] *vt* absorb; **être absorbé par qch** be engrossed in sth.

**abstenir (s')** /(s)apstəniʀ/ [58] *vpr* abstain; **s'~ de** refrain from.

**abstrait**, **~e** /apstʀɛ, -t/ *a* & *nm* abstract.

**absurde** /apsyʀd/ *a* absurd.

**abus** /aby/ *nm* abuse, misuse; (injustice) abuse; **~ de confiance** breach of trust.

**abuser** /abyze/ [1] *vt* deceive. ● *vi* go too far; **~ de** abuse, misuse; (profiter de) take advantage of; (*alcool*) overindulge in. □ **s'~** *vpr* be mistaken.

**abusif**, **-ive** /abyzif, -v/ *a* excessive; (impropre) wrong; (injuste) unfair.

**académie** /akademi/ *nf* academy; (circonscription) local education authority.

**acajou** /akaʒu/ *nm* mahogany.

**accablant**, **~e** /akablɑ̃, -t/ *a* (*chaleur*) oppressive; (*fait, témoignage*) damning.

**accabler** /akable/ [1] *vt* overwhelm; **~ d'impôts** burden with taxes; **~ d'injures** heap insults upon.

**accéder** /aksede/ [14] *vi* **~ à** (*lieu*) reach; (*pouvoir, trône*) accede to; (*requête*) grant; (Ordinat) access; **~ à la propriété** become a homeowner.

**accélérateur** /akseleʀatœʀ/ *nm* accelerator.

**accélérer** /akseleʀe/ [14] *vt*/*i* accelerate. □ **s'~** *vpr* speed up.

**accent** /aksɑ̃/ *nm* accent; (sur une syllabe) stress, accent; **mettre l'~ sur** stress; **~ aigu/grave/circonflexe** acute/grave/circumflex accent.

**accentuer** /aksɑ̃tɥe/ [1] *vt* (*lettre, syllabe*) accent; (fig) emphasize, accentuate. □ **s'~** *vpr* become more pronounced, increase.

**accepter** /aksɛpte/ [1] *vt* accept; **~ de faire** agree to do.

**accès** /aksɛ/ *nm* access; (porte) entrance; (de fièvre) bout; (de colère) fit; (d'enthousiasme) burst; (Ordinat) access; **les ~ de** (voies) the approaches to; **facile d'~** easy to get to.

**accessoire** /akseswaʀ/ *a* secondary, incidental. ● *nm* accessory; (Théât) prop.

**accident** /aksidɑ̃/ *nm* accident; **~ de train/d'avion** train/plane crash; **par ~** by accident. **accidenté**, **~e** *a* (*personne*) injured (in an accident); (*voiture*) damaged; (*terrain*) uneven, hilly. **accidentel**, **~le** *a* accidental.

**acclamer** /aklame/ [1] *vt* cheer, acclaim.

**accommoder** /akɔmɔde/ [1] *vt* adapt (**à** to); (cuisiner) prepare; (assaisonner) flavour. □ **s'~ de** *vpr* make the best of.

**accompagnateur**, **-trice** /akɔ̃paɲatœʀ, -tʀis/ *nm,f* (Mus) accompanist; (guide) guide; **~ d'enfants** accompanying adult.

**accompagner** /akɔ̃paɲe/ [1] *vt* accompany. □ **s'~ de** *vpr* be accompanied by.

**accomplir** /akɔ̃pliʀ/ [2] *vt* carry out, fulfil. □ **s'~** *vpr* take place, happen; (*vœu*) be fulfilled.

**accord** /akɔʀ/ *nm* agreement; (harmonie) harmony; (Mus) chord; **être d'~** agree (**pour** to); **se mettre d'~** come to an agreement, agree; **d'~!** all right!, OK!

**accorder** /akɔʀde/ [1] *vt* grant; (*couleurs*) match; (Mus) tune; (attribuer) (*valeur, importance*) assign. □ **s'~** *vpr* (se mettre d'accord) agree; (s'octroyer) allow oneself; **s'~ avec** (s'entendre avec) get on with.

**accotement** /akɔtmɑ̃/ *nm* verge; **~ non stabilisé** soft verge.

**accouchement** /akuʃmɑ̃/ *nm* childbirth; (travail) labour.

**accoucher** /akuʃe/ [1] *vi* give birth (**de** to); (être en travail) be in labour. ● *vt* deliver. **accoucheur** *nm* **médecin ~** obstetrician.

**accoudoir** /akudwaʀ/ *nm* armrest.

**accoupler** /akuple/ [1] *vt* (Tech) couple. □ **s'~** *vpr* mate.

**accourir** /akuʀiʀ/ [20] *vi* run up.

**accoutumance** /akutymɑ̃s/ *nf* familiarization; (Méd) addiction.

**accoutumer** /akutyme/ [1] *vt* accustom. □ **s'~** *vpr* get accustomed.

**accro** /akʀo/ *nmf* Ⓘ (drogué) addict; (amateur) fan.

**accroc** /akʀo/ *nm* tear, rip; (fig) hitch.

**accrochage** /akʀɔʃaʒ/ *nm* hanging; hooking; (Auto) collision; (dispute) clash; (Mil) encounter.

**accrocher** /akʀɔʃe/ [1] *vt* (suspendre) hang up; (attacher) hook, hitch; (déchirer) catch; (heurter) hit; (attirer) attract. □ **s'~** *vpr* cling, hang on (**à** to); (se disputer) clash.

**accroissement** /akʀwasmɑ̃/ *nm* increase (**de** in).

**accroître** /akʀwɑtʀ/ [24] *vt* increase. □ **s'~** *vpr* increase.

**accroupir (s')** /(s)akʀupiʀ/ [2] *vpr* squat.

**accru**, **~e** /akʀy/ *a* increased, greater.

**accueil** /akœj/ *nm* reception, welcome.

**accueillant**, **~e** /akœjɑ̃, -t/ *a* friendly, welcoming.

**accueillir** /akœjiʀ/ [25] *vt* receive, welcome; (*film, livre*) receive; (prendre en charge) (*réfugiés, patients*) take care of, cater for.

**accumuler** /akymyle/ [1] *vt* (*énergie*) store up; (*capital*) accumulate. □ **s'~** *vpr* (*neige, ordures*) pile up; (*dettes*) accrue.

**accusation** /akyzasjɔ̃/ *nf* accusation; (Jur) charge; **l'~** (magistrat) the prosecution.

**accusé**, **~e** /akyze/ *a* marked. ● *nm,f* defendant, accused.

**accuser** /akyze/ [1] *vt* accuse (**de** of); (blâmer) blame (**de** for); (Jur) charge (**de** with); (fig) emphasize; **~ réception de** acknowledge receipt of.

**acharné**, **~e** /aʃaʀne/ *a* relentless, ferocious. **acharnement** *nm* (énergie) furious energy; (ténacité) determination.

**acharner (s')** /(s)aʃaʀne/ [1] *vpr* persevere; **s'~ sur** set upon; (poursuivre) hound; **s'~ à faire** (s'évertuer) try desperately; (s'obstiner) keep on doing.

**achat** /aʃa/ *nm* purchase; **~s** shopping; **faire l'~ de** buy; **faire des ~s** do some shopping.

**acheminer** /aʃ(ə)mine/ [1] *vt* dispatch, convey; (*courrier*) handle. □ **s'~ vers** *vpr* head for.

**acheter** /aʃ(ə)te/ [6] *vt* buy; **~ qch à qn** (pour lui) buy sth for sb; (chez lui) buy sth from sb. **acheteur, -euse** *nm,f* buyer; (client de magasin) shopper.

**achèvement** /aʃɛvmɑ̃/ *nm* completion.

**achever** /aʃ(ə)ve/ [6] *vt* finish (off). □ **s'~** *vpr* end.

**acide** /asid/ *a* acid, sharp. ● *nm* acid.

**acier** /asje/ *nm* steel.

**acné** /akne/ *nf* acne.

**acompte** /akɔ̃t/ *nm* deposit, part-payment.

**à-côté** (*pl* **~s**) /akote/ *nm* side issue; **~s** (argent) extras.

**acoustique** /akustik/ *nf* acoustics (+ *sg*). ● *a* acoustic.

**acquéreur** /akeʀœʀ/ *nm* purchaser, buyer.

**acquérir** /akeʀiʀ/ [7] *vt* acquire, gain; (*biens*) purchase, acquire.

**acquis**, **~e** /aki, -z/ *a* acquired; (*fait*) established; **tenir qch pour ~** take sth for granted. ● *nm* experience. **acquisition** *nf* acquisition; purchase.

**acquitter** /akite/ [1] *vt* acquit; (*dette*) settle. □ **s'~ de** *vpr* (*promesse*) fulfil; (*devoir*) discharge.

**âcre** /ɑkʀ/ *a* acrid.

**acrobatie** /akʀɔbasi/ *nf* acrobatics (+ *pl*); **~ aérienne** aerobatics (+ *pl*).

**acte** /akt/ *nm* act, action, deed; (Théât) act; (Jur) deed; **~ de naissance/mariage** birth/marriage certificate; **~s** (compte-rendu) proceedings; **prendre ~ de** note.

**acteur** /aktœʀ/ *nm* actor.

**actif**, **-ive** /aktif, -v/ *a* active; (*population*) working. ● *nm* (Comm) assets; **avoir à son ~** have to one's credit ou name.

**action** /aksjɔ̃/ *nf* action; (Comm) share; (Jur) action; (effet) effect; (initiative) initiative. **actionnaire** *nmf* shareholder.

**activer** /aktive/ [1] *vt* speed up; (*feu*) boost. □ **s'~** *vpr* hurry up; (s'affairer) be very busy.

**activité** /aktivite/ *nf* activity; **en ~** (*volcan*) active; (*fonctionnaire*) working; (*usine*) in operation.

**actrice** /aktʀis/ *nf* actress.

**actualité** /aktɥalite/ *nf* topicality; **l'~** current affairs; **les ~s** news; **d'~** topical.

**actuel**, **~le** /aktɥɛl/ *a* current, present; (d'actualité) topical. **actuellement** *adv* currently, at the present time.

**acupuncture** /akypɔ̃ktyʀ/ *nf* acupuncture.

**adaptateur** /adaptatœʀ/ *nm* (Électr) adapter.

**adapter** /adapte/ [1] *vt* adapt; (fixer) fit. □ **s'~** *vpr* adapt (oneself); (Tech) fit.

**additif** /aditif/ *nm* (note) rider; (substance) additive.

**addition** /adisjɔ̃/ *nf* addition; (au café) bill; (US) check. **additionner** [1] *vt* add; (totaliser) add (up).

**adepte** /adɛpt/ *nmf* follower; (d'activité) enthusiast.

**adéquat**, **~e** /adekwa, -t/ *a* suitable; (suffisant) adequate.

**adhérent**, **~e** /adeʀɑ̃, -t/ *nm,f* member.

**adhérer** /adeʀe/ [14] *vi* adhere, stick (**à** to); **~ à** (*club*) be a member of; (s'inscrire à) join.

**adhésif**, **-ive** /adezif, -v/ *a* adhesive; **ruban ~** sticky tape

**adhésion** /adezjɔ̃/ *nf* membership; (soutien) support.

**adieu** (*pl* **~x**) /adjø/ *interj & nm* goodbye, farewell.

**adjectif** /adʒɛktif/ *nm* adjective.

**adjoint**, **~e** /adʒwɛ̃, -t/ *nm,f* assistant; **~ au maire** deputy mayor. ● *a* assistant.

**adjuger** /adʒyʒe/ [40] *vt* award; (aux enchères) auction. □ **s'~** *vpr* take (for oneself).

**admettre** /admɛtʀ/ [42] *vt* let in, admit; (tolérer) allow; (reconnaître) admit, acknowledge; (*candidat*) pass.

**administrateur**, **-trice** /administʀatœʀ, -tʀis/ *nm,f* administrator, director; (Jur) trustee; **~ de site Internet** Webmaster.

**administratif**, **-ive** /administʀatif, -v/ *a* administrative; (*document*) official. **administration** *nf*

administration; (gestion) management; **l'A~** Civil Service.

**administrer** /administʀe/ [1] *vt* run, manage; (*justice, biens, antidote*) administer.

**admirateur**, **-trice** /admiʀatœʀ, -tʀis/ *nm,f* admirer.

**admiration** /admiʀasjɔ̃/ *nf* admiration.

**admirer** /admiʀe/ [1] *vt* admire.

**admission** /admisjɔ̃/ *nf* admission.

**ADN** *abrév m* (**acide désoxyribonucléique**) DNA.

**adolescence** /adɔlesɑ̃s/ *nf* adolescence. **adolescent**, **~e** *nm,f* adolescent, teenager.

**adopter** /adɔpte/ [1] *vt* adopt. **adoptif**, **-ive** *a* (*enfant*) adopted; (*parents*) adoptive.

**adorer** /adɔʀe/ [1] *vt* love; (plus fort) adore; (Relig) worship, adore.

**adosser** /adɔse/ [1] *vt* lean (**à**, **contre** against). □ **s'~** *vpr* lean back (**à**, **contre** against).

**adoucir** /adusiʀ/ [2] *vt* soften; (*boisson*) sweeten; (*chagrin*) ease. □ **s'~** *vpr* soften; (*chagrin*) ease; (*temps*) become milder. **adoucissant** *nm* (fabric) softener.

**adresse** /adʀɛs/ *nf* address; (habileté) skill; **~ électronique** e-mail address.

**adresser** /adʀese/ [1] *vt* send; (écrire l'adresse sur) address; (*remarque*) address; **~ la parole à** speak to. □ **s'~ à** *vpr* address; (aller voir) (*personne*) go and ask *ou* see; (*bureau*) enquire at; (viser, intéresser) be directed at.

**adroit**, **~e** /adʀwa, -t/ *a* skilful, clever.

**adulte** /adylt/ *nmf* adult. ● *a* adult; (*plante, animal*) fully-grown.

**adultère** /adyltɛʀ/ *a* adulterous. ● *nm* adultery.

**adverbe** /advɛʀb/ *nm* adverb.

**adversaire** /advɛʀsɛʀ/ *nmf* opponent, adversary.

**aérer** /aeʀe/ [1] *vt* air; (*texte*) space out. □ **s'~** *vpr* get some air.

**aérien**, **~ne** /aeʀjɛ̃, -jɛn/ *a* air; (*photo*) aerial; (*câble*) overhead.

**aérobic** /aeʀɔbik/ *nm* aerobics (+ *sg*).

**aérogare** /aeʀɔgaʀ/ *nf* air terminal.

**aéroglisseur** /aeʀɔglisœʀ/ *nm* hovercraft.

**aérogramme** /aeʀɔgʀam/ *nm* airmail letter; (US) aerogram.

**aéronautique** /aeʀɔnotik/ *a* aeronautical. ● *nf* aeronautics (+ *sg*).

**aéroport** /aeʀɔpɔʀ/ *nm* airport.

**aérospatial**, **~e** (*mpl* **-iaux**) /aeʀɔspasjal, -jo/ *a* aerospace.

**affaiblir** /afebliʀ/ [2] *vt* weaken. □ **s'~** *vpr* get weaker.

**affaire** /afɛʀ/ *nf* affair, matter; (Jur) case; (histoire, aventure) affair; (occasion) bargain; (entreprise) business; (transaction) deal; (question, problème) matter; **~s** (Comm) business; (Pol) affairs; (problèmes personnels) business; (effets personnels) things; **c'est mon ~** that's my business; **avoir ~ à** deal with; **ça fera l'~** that will do the job; **ça fera leur ~** that's just what they need; **tirer qn d'~** help sb out of a tight spot; **se tirer d'~** get out of trouble.

**affairé**, **~e** /afeʀe/ *a* busy.

**affaisser (s')** /(s)afese/ [1] *vpr* (*terrain, route*) sink, subside; (*poutre*) sag; (*personne*) collapse.

**affamé**, **~e** /afame/ *a* starving.

**affectation** /afɛktasjɔ̃/ *nf* (nomination) (à une fonction) appointment;

(dans un lieu) posting; (de matériel, d'argent) allocation; (comportement) affectation.

**affecter** /afɛkte/ [1] *vt* (feindre) affect; (toucher, affliger) affect; (destiner) assign; (nommer) appoint, post.

**affectif**, **-ive** /afɛktif, -v/ *a* emotional.

**affection** /afɛksjɔ̃/ *nf* affection; (maladie) complaint.

**affectueux**, **-euse** /afɛktɥø, -z/ *a* affectionate.

**affichage** /afiʃaʒ/ *nm* billposting; (électronique) display.

**affiche** /afiʃ/ *nf* (public) notice; (publicité) poster; (Théât) bill; **être à l'∼** (*film*) be showing; (*pièce*) be on.

**afficher** /afiʃe/ [1] *vt* (*annonce*) put up; (*événement*) announce; (*sentiment*) display; (Ordinat) display.

**affirmatif**, **-ive** /afiʀmatif, -v/ *a* affirmative. **affirmation** *nf* assertion.

**affirmer** /afiʀme/ [1] *vt* assert; (soutenir) maintain.

**affligé**, **∼e** /afliʒe/ *a* distressed; **∼ de** afflicted with.

**affluer** /aflye/ [1] *vi* flood in; (*sang*) rush.

**affolant**, **∼e** /afɔlɑ̃, -t/ *a* alarming.

**affoler** /afɔle/ [1] *vt* throw into a panic. □ **s'∼** *vpr* panic.

**affranchir** /afʀɑ̃ʃiʀ/ [2] *vt* stamp; (à la machine) frank; (*esclave*) emancipate; (fig) free. **affranchissement** *nm* (tarif) postage.

**affreux**, **-euse** /afʀø, -z/ *a* (laid) hideous; (mauvais) awful.

**affrontement** /afʀɔ̃tmɑ̃/ *nm* confrontation.

**affronter** /afʀɔ̃te/ [1] *vt* confront. □ **s'∼** *vpr* confront each other.

**affûter** /afyte/ [1] *vt* sharpen.

**afin** /afɛ̃/ *prép & conj* **∼ de faire** in order to do; **∼ que** so that.

**africain**, **∼e** /afʀikɛ̃, -ɛn/ *a* African. **A∼**, **∼e** *nm, f* African.

**Afrique** /afʀik/ *nf* Africa; **∼ du Sud** South Africa.

**agacer** /agase/ [10] *vt* irritate, annoy.

**âge** /ɑʒ/ *nm* age; (vieillesse) (old) age; **quel ∼ avez-vous?** how old are you?; **∼ adulte** adulthood; **∼ mûr** maturity; **d'un certain ∼** middle-aged.

**âgé**, **∼e** /ɑʒe/ *a* elderly; **∼ de cinq ans** five years old.

**agence** /aʒɑ̃s/ *nf* agency, bureau, office; (succursale) branch; **∼ d'interim** employment agency; **∼ de voyages** travel agency; **∼ publicitaire** advertising agency.

**agenda** /aʒɛ̃da/ *nm* diary; **∼ électronique** electronic organizer.

**agent** /aʒɑ̃/ *nm* agent; (fonctionnaire) official; **∼ (de police)** policeman; **∼ de change** stockbroker; **∼ commercial** sales representative.

**agglomération** /aglɔmeʀasjɔ̃/ *nf* town, built-up area.

**aggraver** /agʀave/ [1] *vt* aggravate, make worse. □ **s'∼** *vpr* get worse.

**agile** /aʒil/ *a* agile, nimble.

**agir** /aʒiʀ/ [2] *vi* act; (se comporter) behave; (avoir un effet) work, take effect. □ **s'∼ de** *vpr* (être nécessaire) **il s'agit de faire** we/you *etc.* must do; (être question de) **il s'agit de faire** it is a matter of doing; **dans ce livre il s'agit de** this book is about; **dont il s'agit** in question; **il s'agit de ton fils** it's about your son; **de quoi s'agit-il?** what is it about?

**agitation** /aʒitasjɔ̃/ *nf* bustle; (trouble) agitation; (malaise social) unrest.

**agité**, **~e** /aʒite/ *a* restless, fidgety; (troublé) agitated; (*mer*) rough.

**agiter** /aʒite/ [1] *vt* (*bras, mouchoir*) wave; (*liquide, boîte*) shake; (troubler) agitate; (discuter) debate. □ **s'~** *vpr* bustle about; (*enfant*) fidget; (*foule, pensées*) stir.

**agneau** (*pl* **~x**) /aɲo/ *nm* lamb.

**agrafe** /agʀaf/ *nf* hook; (pour papiers) staple. **agrafeuse** *nf* stapler.

**agrandir** /agʀɑ̃diʀ/ [2] *vt* enlarge; (*maison*) extend. □ **s'~** *vpr* expand, grow. **agrandissement** *nm* extension; (de photo) enlargement.

**agréable** /agʀeabl/ *a* pleasant.

**agréé**, **~e** /agʀee/ *a* (*agence*) authorized; (*nourrice, médecin*) registered; (*matériel*) approved.

**agréer** /agʀee/ [15] *vt* accept; **~ à** please; **veuillez ~, Monsieur, mes salutations distinguées** (personne non nommée) yours faithfully; (personne nommée) yours sincerely.

**agrégation** /agʀegasjɔ̃/ *nf highest examination for recruitment of teachers*. **agrégé**, **~e** *nm,f* teacher (*who has passed the agrégation*).

**agrément** /agʀemɑ̃/ *nm* charm; (plaisir) pleasure; (accord) assent.

**agresser** /agʀese/ [1] *vt* attack; (pour voler) mug.

**agressif**, **-ive** /agʀesif, -v/ *a* aggressive. **agression** *nf* attack; (pour voler) mugging; (Mil) aggression.

**agricole** /agʀikɔl/ *a* agricultural; (*ouvrier, produit*) farm. **agriculteur** *nm* farmer. **agriculture** *nf* agriculture, farming.

**agripper** /agʀipe/ [1] *vt* grab. □ **s'~** *vpr* cling (**à** to).

**agroalimentaire** /agʀɔalimɑ̃tɛʀ/ *nm* food industry.

**agrumes** /agʀym/ *nmpl* citrus fruit(s).

**ai** /e/ ⇒**avoir** [5].

**aide** /ɛd/ *nf* help, assistance; (en argent) aid; **à l'~ de** with the help of; **venir en ~ à** help; **~ à domicile** home help; **~ familiale** mother's help; **~ sociale** social security; (US) welfare. ● *nmf* assistant. **aide-mémoire** *nm inv* handbook of key facts.

**aider** /ede/ [1] *vt/i* help, assist; (subventionner) aid, give aid to; **~ à faire** help to do. □ **s' ~ de** *vpr* use.

**aïeul**, **~e** /ajœl/ *nm,f* grandparent.

**aigle** /ɛgl/ *nm* eagle.

**aigre** /ɛgʀ/ *a* sour, sharp; (fig) sharp.

**aigrir** /egʀiʀ/ [2] *vt* embitter. □ **s'~** *vpr* turn sour; (*personne*) become embittered.

**aigu**, **~ë** /egy/ *a* (*douleur, problème*) acute; (*objet*) sharp; (*voix*) shrill; (Mus) high(-pitched); (*accent*) acute.

**aiguille** /egɥij/ *nf* needle; (de montre) hand; (de balance) pointer; **~ à tricoter** knitting needle.

**aiguilleur** /egɥijœʀ/ *nm* pointsman; **~ du ciel** air traffic controller.

**aiguiser** /eg(ɥ)ize/ [1] *vt* sharpen; (fig) stimulate.

**ail** (*pl* **~s** *ou* **aulx**) /aj, o/ *nm* garlic.

**aile** /ɛl/ *nf* wing.

**ailier** /elje/ *nm* winger; (US) end.

**aille** /aj/ ⇒ALLER [8].

**ailleurs** /ajœʀ/ *adv* elsewhere, somewhere else; **d'~** besides, moreover; **nulle part ~** nowhere

else; **par ~** moreover, furthermore; **partout ~** everywhere else.

**aimable** /ɛmabl/ *a* kind.

**aimant** /ɛmɑ̃/ *nm* magnet.

**aimer** /eme/ [1] *vt* like; (d'amour) love; **j'aimerais faire** I'd like to do; **~ bien** quite like; **~ mieux** *ou* **autant** prefer.

**aîné**, **~e** /ene/ *a* eldest; (de deux) elder. ● *nm,f* eldest (child); (premier de deux) elder (child); **~s** elders; **il est mon ~** he is older than me *ou* my senior.

**ainsi** /ɛ̃si/ *adv* like this, thus; (donc) so; **et ~ de suite** and so on; **pour ~ dire** so to speak, as it were; **~ que** as well as; (comme) as.

**air** /ɛʀ/ *nm* air; (mine) look, air; (mélodie) tune; **~ conditionné** air-conditioning; **avoir l'~** look, appear; **avoir l'~ de** look like; **avoir l'~ de faire** appear to be doing; **en l'~** (up) in the air; (*promesses*) empty; **prendre l'~** get some fresh air.

**aire** /ɛʀ/ *nf* area; **~ d'atterrissage** landing-strip; **~ de pique-nique** picnic area; **~ de repas** rest area; **~ de services** (motorway) services.

**aisance** /ɛzɑ̃s/ *nf* ease; (richesse) affluence.

**aise** /ɛz/ *nf* joy; **à l'~** (sur un siège) comfortable; (pas gêné) at ease; (fortuné) comfortably off; **mal à l'~** uncomfortable; ill at ease; **aimer ses ~s** like one's creature comforts; **mettre qn à l'~** put sb at ease; **se mettre à l'~** make oneself comfortable.

**aisé**, **~e** /eze/ *a* easy; (fortuné) well-off.

**aisselle** /ɛsɛl/ *nf* armpit.

**ait** /ɛ/ ⇒AVOIR [5].

**ajourner** /aʒuʀne/ [1] *vt* postpone; (*débat, procès*) adjourn.

**ajout** /aʒu/ *nm* addition.

**ajouter** /aʒute/ [1] *vt* add (**à** to); **~ foi à** lend credence to. □ **s'~** *vpr* be added.

**ajuster** /aʒyste/ [1] *vt* adjust; (*cible*) aim at; (adapter) fit; **~ son coup** adjust one's aim.

**alarme** /alaʀm/ *nf* alarm; **donner l'~** raise the alarm.

**alarmer** /alaʀme/ [1] *vt* alarm. □ **s'~** *vpr* become alarmed (**de** at).

**Albanie** /albani/ *nf* Albania.

**alcool** /alkɔl/ *nm* alcohol; (eau de vie) brandy; **~ à brûler** methylated spirit. **alcoolique** *a & nmf* alcoholic. **alcoolisé**, **~e** *a* (*boisson*) alcoholic. **alcoolisme** *nm* alcoholism.

**alcootest** /alkɔtɛst/ *nm* breath test; (appareil) Breathalyser®.

**aléa** /alea/ *nm* hazard. **aléatoire** *a* unpredictable, uncertain; (Ordinat) random.

**alentours** /alɑ̃tuʀ/ *nmpl* surroundings; **aux ~ de** (de lieu) around, (de chiffre, date) about, around.

**alerte** /alɛʀt/ *a* (*personne*) alert; (vif) lively. ● *nf* alert; **~ à la bombe** bomb scare. **alerter** [1] *vt* alert.

**algèbre** /alʒɛbʀ/ *nf* algebra

**Algérie** /alʒeʀi/ *nf* Algeria.

**algue** /alg/ *nf* seaweed; **les ~s** (Bot) algae.

**aliéné**, **~e** /aljene/ *nm,f* insane person.

**aliéner** /aljene/ [14] *vt* alienate; (céder) give up. □ **s'~** *vpr* alienate.

**aligner** /aliɲe/ [1] *vt* (*objets*) line up, make lines of; (*chiffres*) string together; **~ sur** bring into line with. □ **s'~** *vpr* line up; **s'~ sur** align oneself on.

**aliment** /alimɑ̃/ *nm* food.

**alimentaire** /alimɑ̃tɛʀ/ *a* (*industrie*) food; (*habitudes*) dietary; **produits ~s** foodstuffs.

**alimentation** /alimɑ̃tasjɔ̃/ *nf* feeding, supply(ing); (régime) diet; (aliments) food; **magasin d'~** grocery shop *ou* store.

**alimenter** /alimɑ̃te/ [1] *vt* feed; (fournir) supply; (fig) sustain. □ **s'~** *vpr* eat.

**allaiter** /alete/ [1] *vt* (*bébé*) breast-feed; (US) nurse; (*animal*) suckle.

**allée** /ale/ *nf* path, lane; (menant à une maison) drive(way); (dans un cinéma, magasin) aisle; (rue) road; **~s et venues** comings and goings.

**allégé**, **~e** /aleʒe/ *a* diet; (*beurre, yaourt*) low-fat.

**alléger** /aleʒe/ [14] [40] *vt* make lighter; (*fardeau, chargement*) lighten; (fig) (*souffrance*) alleviate.

**allégresse** /alegʀɛs/ *nf* gaiety, joy.

**alléguer** /alege/ [14] *vt* (*exemple*) invoke; (prétexter) allege.

**Allemagne** /almaɲ/ *nf* Germany.

**allemand**, **~e** /almɑ̃, -d/ *a* German. ● *nm* (Ling) German. **A~**, **~e** *nm,f* German.

**aller** /ale/ [8]

● *verbe auxiliaire*

····➤ **je vais l'appeler** I'm going to call him; **j'allais partir** I was about to leave; **va savoir!** who knows?; **~ en s'améliorant** be improving.

● *verbe intransitif*

····➤ (se déplacer) go; **allons-y!** let's go!; **allez!** come on!

····➤ (se porter) **comment allez-vous?, comment ça va?** how are you?; **ça va (bien)** I'm fine; **qu'est-ce qui ne va pas?** what's the matter?; **ça ne va pas la tête?** 🅸 are you mad? 🅸.

····➤ (mettre en valeur) **~ à qn** suit sb; **ça te va bien** it really suits you.

····➤ (convenir) **ça va ma coiffure?** is my hair OK?; **ça ne va pas du tout** that's no good at all.

□ **s'en aller** *verbe pronominal*

····➤ go; **va-t'en!** go away!; **ça ne s'en va pas** (*tache*) it won't come out.

● *nom masculin*

····➤ outward journey; **~ (simple)** single (ticket); (US) one-way (ticket); **~ retour** return (ticket); (US) round trip (ticket); **à l'~** on the way out.

**allergie** /alɛʀʒi/ *nf* allergy. **allergique** *a* allergic (**à** to).

**alliance** /aljɑ̃s/ *nf* alliance; (bague) wedding-ring; (mariage) marriage.

**allier** /alje/ [45] *vt* combine; (Pol) ally. □ **s'~** *vpr* combine; (Pol) form an alliance; (*famille*) become related (**à** to).

**allô** /alo/ *interj* hallo, hello.

**allocation** /alɔkasjɔ̃/ *nf* allowance; **~ chômage** unemployment benefit; **~s familiales** family allowance.

**allonger** /alɔ̃ʒe/ [40] *vt* lengthen; (*bras, jambe*) stretch (out); (coucher) lay down. □ **s'~** *vpr* get longer; (s'étendre) lie down; (s'étirer) stretch (oneself) out.

**allouer** /alwe/ [1] *vt* allocate; (*prêt*) grant.

**allumer** /alyme/ [1] *vt* (*bougie, gaz*) light; (*lampe, appareil*) turn on; (*pièce*) switch the light(s) on in; (fig) arouse. □ **s'~** *vpr* (*lumière, appareil*) come on.

**allumette** /alymɛt/ *nf* match.

**allure** /alyʀ/ *nf* speed, pace; (démarche) walk; (apparence) appear-

ance; **à toute ~** at full speed; **avoir de l'~** have style; **avoir des ~s de** look like; **avoir une drôle d'~** be funny-looking.

**allusion** /alyzjɔ̃/ *nf* allusion (**à** to); (implicite) hint (**à** at); **faire ~ à** allude to; hint at.

**alors** /alɔʀ/ *adv* (à ce moment-là) then; (de ce fait) so; (dans ce cas-là) then; **ça ~!** well!; **et ~?** so what? ● *conj* **~ que** (pendant que) while, (tandis que) when, whereas.

**alouette** /alwɛt/ *nf* lark.

**alourdir** /aluʀdiʀ/ [2] *vt* weigh down; (rendre plus important) increase.

**aloyau** (*pl* **~x**) /alwajo/ *nm* sirloin.

**Alpes** /alp/ *nfpl* **les ~** the Alps.

**alphabet** /alfabɛ/ *nm* alphabet. **alphabétique** *a* alphabetical.

**alphabétiser** /alfabetize/ [1] *vt* teach to read and write.

**alpinist** /alpinist/ *nmf* mountaineer.

**altérer** /alteʀe/ [14] *vt* (*fait, texte*) distort; (abîmer) spoil; (donner soif à) make thirsty. □ **s'~** *vpr* deteriorate.

**alternance** /altɛʀnɑ̃s/ *nf* alternation; **en ~** alternately.

**altitude** /altityd/ *nf* altitude, height.

**amabilité** /amabilite/ *nf* kindness.

**amaigrir** /amegʀiʀ/ [2] *vt* make thin(ner).

**amande** /amɑ̃d/ *nf* almond; (d'un fruit à noyau) kernel.

**amant** /amɑ̃/ *nm* lover.

**amarre** /amaʀ/ *nf* (mooring) rope; **~s** moorings.

**amas** /amɑ/ *nm* heap, pile.

**amasser** /amɑse/ [1] *vt* amass, gather; (empiler) pile up. □ **s'~** *vpr* pile up; (*gens*) gather.

**amateur** /amatœʀ/ *nm* amateur; **~ de** lover of; **d'~** amateur; (péj) amateurish.

**ambassade** /ɑ̃basad/ *nf* embassy. **ambassadeur**, **-drice** *nm,f* ambassador.

**ambiance** /ɑ̃bjɑ̃s/ *nf* atmosphere. **ambiant**, **~e** *a* surrounding.

**ambigu**, **~ë** /ɑ̃bigy/ *a* ambiguous.

**ambitieux**, **-ieuse** /ɑ̃bisjø, -z/ *a* ambitious. **ambition** *nf* ambition.

**ambulance** /ɑ̃bylɑ̃s/ *nf* ambulance.

**ambulant**, **~e** /ɑ̃bylɑ̃, -t/ *a* itinerant, travelling.

**âme** /ɑm/ *nf* soul; **~ sœur** soul mate.

**amélioration** /ameljɔʀasjɔ̃/ *nf* improvement.

**améliorer** /ameljɔʀe/ [1] *vt* improve. □ **s'~** *vpr* improve.

**aménagement** /amenaʒmɑ̃/ *nm* (de magasin) fitting out; (de grenier) conversion; (de territoire) development; (de cuisine) equipping.

**aménager** /amenaʒe/ [40] *vt* (*magasin*) fit out; (transformer) convert; (*territoire*) develop; (*cuisine*) equip.

**amende** /amɑ̃d/ *nf* fine; **faire ~ honorable** make amends.

**amener** /am(ə)ne/ [6] *vt* bring; (causer) bring about; **~ qn à faire** cause sb to do. □ **s'~** *vpr* [E] turn up.

**amer**, **-ère** /amɛʀ/ *a* bitter.

**américain**, **~e** /ameʀikɛ̃, -ɛn/ *a* American. **A~**, **~e** *nm,f* American.

**Amérique** /ameʀik/ *nf* America; **~ centrale/latine** Central/Latin America; **~ du Nord/Sud** North/South America.

**amertume** /amɛʀtym/ *nf* bitterness.

**ami**, **~e** /ami/ *nm,f* friend; (amateur) lover; **un ~ des bêtes** an animal lover. ● *a* friendly.

**amiable** /amjabl/ *a* amicable; **à l'~** (*divorcer*) by mutual consent; (*se séparer*) on friendly terms; (*séparation*) amicable.

**amical**, **~e** (*mpl* **-aux**) /amikal, -o/ *a* friendly.

**amiral** (*pl* **-aux**) /amiʀal, -o/ *nm* admiral.

**amitié** /amitje/ *nf* friendship; **~s** (en fin de lettre) kind regards; **prendre qn en ~** take a liking to sb.

**amnistie** /amnisti/ *nf* amnesty.

**amoindrir** /amwɛ̃dʀiʀ/ [2] *vt* reduce.

**amont**: **en ~** /ɑ̃namɔ̃/ *loc* upstream.

**amorcer** /amɔʀse/ [10] *vt* start; (*hameçon*) bait; (*pompe*) prime; (*arme à feu*) arm.

**amortir** /amɔʀtiʀ/ [2] *vt* (*choc*) cushion; (*bruit*) deaden; (*dette*) pay off; **~ un achat** make a purchase pay for itself.

**amortisseur** /amɔʀtisœʀ/ *nm* shock absorber.

**amour** /amuʀ/ *nm* love; **pour l'~ de** for the sake of.

**amoureux**, **-euse** /amuʀø, -z/ *a* (*personne*) in love; (*relation, regard*) loving; (*vie*) love; **~ de qn** in love with sb. ● *nm,f* lover.

**amour-propre** /amuʀpʀɔpʀ/ *nm* self-esteem.

**amphithéâtre** /ɑ̃fiteɑtʀ/ *nm* amphitheatre; (d'université) lecture hall.

**ampleur** /ɑ̃plœʀ/ *nf* extent, size; (de vêtement) fullness; **prendre de l'~** spread, grow.

**amplifier** /ɑ̃plifje/ [45] *vt* amplify; (fig) expand, develop. □ **s'~** *vpr* (*son*) grow; (*scandale*) intensify.

**ampoule** /ɑ̃pul/ *nf* (électrique) bulb; (sur la peau) blister; (Méd) phial, ampoule.

**amusant**, **~e** /amyzɑ̃, -t/ *a* (*blague*) funny; (*soirée*) enjoyable, entertaining.

**amuse-gueule** /amyzgœl/ *nm inv* cocktail snack.

**amusement** /amyzmɑ̃/ *nm* amusement; (passe-temps) entertainment.

**amuser** /amyze/ [1] *vt* amuse; (détourner l'attention de) distract. □ **s'~** *vpr* enjoy oneself; (jouer) play.

**amygdale** /amidal/ *nf* tonsil.

**an** /ɑ̃/ *nm* year; **avoir dix ~s** be ten years old; **un garçon de deux ~s** a two-year-old boy; **à soixante ~s** at the age of sixty; **les moins de dix-huit ~s** under eighteens.

**analogie** /analɔʒi/ *nf* analogy.

**analogue** /analɔg/ *a* similar, analogous (**à** to).

**analphabète** /analfabɛt/ *a & nmf* illiterate.

**analyse** /analiz/ *nf* analysis; (Méd) test. **analyser** [1] *vt* analyse; (Méd) test.

**ananas** /anana(s)/ *nm* pineapple.

**anarchie** /anaʀʃi/ *nf* anarchy.

**anatomie** /anatɔmi/ *nf* anatomy.

**ancêtre** /ɑ̃sɛtʀ/ *nm* ancestor.

**anchois** /ɑ̃ʃwa/ *nm* anchovy.

**ancien**, **~ne** /ɑ̃sjɛ̃, -jɛn/ *a* old; (de jadis) ancient; (*meuble*) antique; (précédent) former, ex-, old; (dans une fonction) senior; **~ combattant** veteran. ● *nm,f* senior; (par l'âge) elder. **anciennement** *adv* formerly. **ancienneté** *nf* age, seniority.

**ancre** /ɑ̃kʀ/ *nf* anchor; **jeter/lever l'~** cast/weigh anchor.

**andouille** /ɑ̃duj/ *nf* sausage (*filled with chitterlings*); (idiot [I]) fool; **faire l'~** fool around.

**âne** /ɑn/ *nm* donkey, ass; (imbécile [I]) dimwit [I].

**anéantir** /aneɑ̃tiʀ/ [2] *vt* destroy; (exterminer) annihilate; (accabler) overwhelm.

**anémie** /anemi/ *nf* anaemia.

**ânerie** /ɑnʀi/ *nf* stupid remark.

**anesthésie** /anɛstezi/ *nf* (opération) anaesthetic.

**ange** /ɑ̃ʒ/ *nm* angel; **aux ~s** in seventh heaven.

**angine** /ɑ̃ʒin/ *nf* throat infection.

**anglais, ~e** /ɑ̃glɛ, -z/ *a* English. ● *nm* (Ling) English. **A~, ~e** *nm,f* Englishman, Englishwoman.

**angle** /ɑ̃gl/ *nm* angle; (coin) corner.

**Angleterre** /ɑ̃glətɛʀ/ *nf* England.

**anglophone** /ɑ̃glɔfɔn/ *a* English-speaking. ● *nmf* English speaker.

**angoissant, ~e** /ɑ̃gwasɑ̃, -t/ *a* alarming; (effrayant) harrowing.

**angoisse** /ɑ̃gwas/ *nf* anxiety. **angoissé, ~e** *a* anxious. **angoisser** [1] *vi* worry.

**animal** (*pl* **-aux**) /animal, -o/ *nm* animal; **~ familier, ~ de compagnie** pet. ● *a* (*mpl* **-aux**) animal.

**animateur, -trice** /animatœʀ, -tʀis/ *nm,f* organizer, leader; (TV) host, hostess.

**animation** /animasjɔ̃/ *nf* liveliness; (affairement) activity; (au cinéma) animation; (activité dirigée) organized activity.

**animé, ~e** /anime/ *a* lively; (affairé) busy; (*être*) animate.

**animer** /anime/ [1] *vt* liven up; (*débat, atelier*) lead; (*spectacle*) host; (pousser) drive; (encourager) spur on. □ **s'~** *vpr* liven up.

**anis** /ani(s)/ *nm* (Culin) aniseed; (Bot) anise.

**anneau** (*pl* **~x**) /ano/ *nm* ring; (de chaîne) link.

**année** /ane/ *nf* year; **~ bissextile** leap year; **~ civile** calendar year.

**annexe** /anɛks/ *a* (*document*) attached; (*question*) related; (*bâtiment*) adjoining. ● *nf* (bâtiment) annexe; (US) annex; (document) appendix; (électronique) attachment. **annexer** [1] *vt* annex; (*document*) attach.

**anniversaire** /anivɛʀsɛʀ/ *nm* birthday; (d'un événement) anniversary. ● *a* anniversary.

**annonce** /anɔ̃s/ *nf* announcement; (publicitaire) advertisement; (indice) sign.

**annoncer** /anɔ̃se/ [10] *vt* announce; (prédire) forecast; (être l'indice de) herald. □ **s'~** *vpr* (*crise, tempête*) be brewing; **s'~ bien/mal** look good/bad. **annonceur** *nm* advertiser.

**annuaire** /anɥɛʀ/ *nm* year book; **~ (téléphonique)** (telephone) directory.

**annuel, ~le** /anɥɛl/ *a* annual, yearly.

**annulation** /anylasjɔ̃/ *nf* cancellation; (de sanction, loi) repeal; (de mesure) abolition.

**annuler** /anyle/ [1] *vt* cancel; (*contrat*) nullify; (*jugement*) quash; (*loi*) repeal. □ **s'~** *vpr* cancel each other out.

**anodin, ~e** /anɔdɛ̃, -in/ *a* insignificant; (sans risques) harmless, safe.

**anonymat** /anɔnima/ *nm* anonymity; **garder l'~** remain anonymous. **anonyme** *a* anonymous.

**anorexie** /anɔʀeksi/ *nf* anorexia.

**anormal, ~e** (*mpl* **-aux**) /anɔʀmal, -o/ *a* abnormal.

**anse** /ɑ̃s/ *nf* handle; (baie) cove.

**Antarctique** /ɑ̃taʀktik/ *nm* Antarctic.

**antenne** /ɑ̃tɛn/ *nf* aerial; (US) antenna; (d'insecte) antenna; (succursale) agency; (Mil) outpost; **à l'~** on the air; **~ chirurgicale** mobile emergency unit; **~ parabolique** satellite dish.

**antérieur**, **~e** /ɑ̃teʀjœʀ/ *a* previous, earlier; (placé devant) front; **~ à** prior to.

**antiaérien**, **~ne** /ɑ̃tiaeʀjɛ̃, -ɛn/ *a* anti-aircraft; **abri ~** air-raid shelter.

**antiatomique** /ɑ̃tiatɔmik/ *a* **abri ~** nuclear fall-out shelter.

**antibiotique** /ɑ̃tibjɔtik/ *nm* antibiotic.

**anticipation** /ɑ̃tisipasjɔ̃/ *nf* **d'~** (*livre, film*) science fiction; **par ~** in advance.

**anticiper** /ɑ̃tisipe/ [1] *vt* **~ (sur)** anticipate; (effectuer à l'avance) bring forward.

**anticorps** /ɑ̃tikɔʀ/ *nm* antibody.

**antidater** /ɑ̃tidate/ [1] *vt* backdate, antedate.

**antigel** /ɑ̃tiʒɛl/ *nm* antifreeze.

**Antilles** /ɑ̃tij/ *nfpl* **les ~** the West Indies.

**antipathique** /ɑ̃tipatik/ *a* unpleasant.

**antiquaire** /ɑ̃tikɛʀ/ *nmf* antique dealer.

**antiquité** /ɑ̃tikite/ *nf* (objet) antique; **l'A~** antiquity.

**antisémite** /ɑ̃tisemit/ *a* anti-Semitic.

**antiseptique** /ɑ̃tisɛptik/ *a & nm* antiseptic.

**antivol** /ɑ̃tivɔl/ *nm* anti-theft device; (Auto) steering lock.

**anxiété** /ɑ̃ksjete/ *nf* anxiety.

**anxieux**, **-ieuse** /ɑ̃ksjø, -z/ *a* anxious. ● *nm,f* worrier.

**août** /u(t)/ *nm* August.

**apaiser** /apeze/ [1] *vt* calm down; (*colère, militant*) appease; (*douleur*) soothe; (*faim*) satisfy. □ **s'~** *vpr* (*tempête*) die down.

**apathie** /apati/ *nf* apathy. **apathique** *a* apathetic.

**apercevoir** /apɛʀsəvwaʀ/ [52] *vt* see. □ **s'~ de** *vpr* notice; **s'~ que** notice *ou* realize that.

**aperçu** /apɛʀsy/ *nm* (échantillon) glimpse, taste; (intuition) insight.

**apéritif** /apeʀitif/ *nm* aperitif, drink.

**aphte** /aft/ *nm* mouth ulcer.

**apitoyer** /apitwaje/ [31] *vt* move (to pity). □ **s'~** *vpr* **s'~ sur (le sort de) qn** feel sorry for sb.

**aplanir** /aplaniʀ/ [2] *vt* level; (fig) iron out.

**aplatir** /aplatiʀ/ [2] *vt* flatten (out). □ **s'~** *vpr* (s'immobiliser) flatten oneself.

**aplomb** /aplɔ̃/ *nm* balance; (fig) self-confidence; **d'~** (en équilibre) steady; **je ne suis pas bien d'~** [I] I don't feel very well.

**apogée** /apɔʒe/ *nm* peak.

**apologie** /apɔlɔʒi/ *nf* panegyric.

**apostrophe** /apɔstʀɔf/ *nf* apostrophe; (remarque) remark.

**apothéose** /apɔteoz/ *nf* high point; (d'événement) grand finale.

**apparaître** /apaʀɛtʀ/ [18] *vi* appear; **il apparaît que** it appears that.

**appareil** /apaʀɛj/ *nm* device; (électrique) appliance; (Anat) system; (téléphone) phone; (avion) plane; (Culin) mixture; (système administratif) apparatus; **~ (dentaire)** brace; (dentier) dentures; **~ (photo)** camera; **c'est Gabriel à l'~** it's Gabriel on the phone; **~ auditif** hearing aid; **~**

**électroménager** household electrical appliance.

**appareiller** /apaReje/ [1] *vi* (*navire*) cast off, put to sea.

**apparemment** /apaRamɑ̃/ *adv* apparently.

**apparence** /apaRɑ̃s/ *nf* appearance; **en ~** outwardly; (apparemment) apparently.

**apparent**, **~e** /apaRɑ̃, -t/ *a* apparent; (visible) conspicuous.

**apparenté**, **~e** /apaRɑ̃te/ *a* related; (semblable) similar.

**apparition** /apaRisjɔ̃/ *nf* appearance; (spectre) apparition.

**appartement** /apaRtəmɑ̃/ *nm* flat; (US) apartment.

**appartenir** /apaRtəniR/ [58] *vi* belong (**à** to); **il lui appartient de** it is up to him to.

**appât** /apɑ/ *nm* bait; (fig) lure.

**appauvrir** /apovRiR/ [2] *vt* impoverish. □ **s'~** *vpr* become impoverished.

**appel** /apɛl/ *nm* call; (Jur) appeal; (supplique) appeal, plea; (Mil) call-up; (US) draft; **faire ~** appeal; **faire ~ à** (recourir à) call on; (invoquer) appeal to; (évoquer) call up; (exiger) call for; **faire l'~** (Scol) call the register; (Mil) take a roll-call; **~ d'offres** (Comm) invitation to tender; **faire un ~ de phares** flash one's headlights.

**appeler** /aple/ [38] *vt* call; (téléphoner) phone, call; (nécessiter) call for; **en ~ à** appeal to; **appelé à** (destiné) destined for. □ **s'~** *vpr* be called; **il s'appelle Tim** his name is Tim *ou* he is called Tim.

**appellation** /apelasjɔ̃/ *nf* name, designation.

**appendice** /apɛ̃dis/ *nm* appendix. **appendicite** *nf* appendicitis.

**appesantir** /apəzɑ̃tiR/ [2] *vt* weigh down. □ **s'~** *vpr* grow heavier; **s'~ sur** dwell upon.

**appétissant**, **~e** /apetisɑ̃, -t/ *a* appetizing.

**appétit** /apeti/ *nm* appetite; **bon ~!** enjoy your meal!

**applaudir** /aplodiR/ [2] *vt/i* applaud. **applaudissements** *nmpl* applause.

**application** /aplikasjɔ̃/ *nf* (soin) care; (de loi) (respect) application; (mise en œuvre) implementation; (Ordinat) application program.

**appliqué**, **~e** /aplike/ *a* (*travail*) painstaking; (*sciences*) applied; (*élève*) hard-working.

**appliquer** /aplike/ [1] *vt* apply; (*loi*) enforce. □ **s'~** *vpr* apply oneself (**à** to), take great care (**à faire** to do); **s'~ à** (concerner) apply to.

**appoint** /apwɛ̃/ *nm* support; **d'~** extra; **faire l'~** give the correct money.

**apport** /apɔR/ *nm* contribution.

**apporter** /apɔRte/ [1] *vt* bring; (*aide, précision*) give; (causer) bring about.

**appréciation** /apResjasjɔ̃/ *nf* estimate, evaluation; (de monnaie) appreciation; (*jugement*) assessment.

**apprécier** /apResje/ [45] *vt* appreciate; (évaluer) assess; (*objet*) value, appraise.

**appréhender** /apReɑ̃de/ [1] *vt* dread, fear; (arrêter) apprehend.

**apprendre** /apRɑ̃dR/ [50] *vt* learn; (être informé de) hear, learn; (de façon indirecte) hear of; **~ qch à qn** teach sb sth; (informer) tell sb sth; **~ à faire** learn to do; **~ à qn à faire** teach sb to do; **~ que** learn that; (être informé) hear that.

**apprenti**, **~e** /apRɑ̃ti/ *nm,f* apprentice. **apprentissage** *nm* apprenticeship; (d'un sujet) learning.

**apprêter** /apRete/ [1] *vt* prepare; (*bois*) prime; (*mur*) size. □ **s'~ à** *vpr* prepare to.

**apprivoiser** /apʀivwaze/ [1] *vt* tame.

**approbation** /apʀɔbasjɔ̃/ *nf* approval.

**approchant**, **~e** /apʀɔʃɑ̃, -t/ *a* close, similar.

**approcher** /apʀɔʃe/ [1] *vt* (*objet*) move near(er) (**de** to); (*personne*) approach; **~ de** get nearer *ou* closer to. ● *vi* approach. □ **s'~ de** *vpr* approach, move near(er) to.

**approfondir** /apʀɔfɔ̃diʀ/ [2] *vt* deepen; (fig) (*sujet*) go into sth in depth; (*connaissances*) improve.

**approprié**, **~e** /apʀɔpʀije/ *a* appropriate.

**approprier (s')** /(s)apʀɔpʀije/ [45] *vpr* appropriate.

**approuver** /apʀuve/ [1] *vt* approve; (trouver louable) approve of; (soutenir) agree with.

**approvisionner** /apʀɔvizjɔne/ [1] *vt* supply (**en** with); (*compte en banque*) pay money into. □ **s'~** *vpr* stock up.

**approximatif**, **-ive** /apʀɔksimatif, -v/ *a* approximate.

**appui** /apɥi/ *nm* support; (de fenêtre) sill; (pour objet) rest; **à l'~ de** in support of; **prendre ~ sur** lean on.

**appui-tête** (*pl* **appuis-tête**) /apɥitɛt/ *nm* headrest.

**appuyer** /apɥije/ [31] *vt* lean, rest; (presser) press; (soutenir) support, back. ● *vi* **~ sur** press (on); (fig) stress. □ **s'~ sur** *vpr* lean on; (compter sur) rely on.

**après** /apʀɛ/ *prép* after; (au-delà de) after, beyond; **~ avoir fait** after doing; **~ tout** after all; **~ coup** after the event; **d'~** (selon) according to; (en imitant) from; (adapté de) based on. ● *adv* after(wards); (plus tard) later; **le bus d'~** the next bus. ● *conj* **~ qu'il est parti** after he left.

**après-demain** *adv* the day after tomorrow. **après-guerre** (*pl* **~s**) *nm ou f* postwar period. **après-midi** *nm ou f inv* afternoon. **après-rasage** (*pl* **~s**) *nm* aftershave. **après-ski** *nm inv* moonboot. **après-vente** *a inv* after-sales.

**a priori** /apʀijɔʀi/ *adv* (à première vue) offhand, on the face of it; (sans réfléchir) out of hand. ● *nm* preconception.

**à-propos** /apʀɔpo/ *nm* timing, timeliness; (fig) presence of mind.

**apte** /apt/ *a* capable (**à** of); (ayant les qualités requises) suitable (**à** for); (en état) fit (**à** for).

**aptitude** /aptityd/ *nf* aptitude, ability.

**aquarelle** /akwaʀɛl/ *nf* watercolour.

**aquatique** /akwatik/ *a* aquatic; (Sport) water.

**arabe** /aʀab/ *a* Arab; (Ling) Arabic; (*désert*) Arabian. ● *nm* (Ling) Arabic. **A~** *nmf* Arab.

**Arabie** /aʀabi/ *nf* **~ Saoudite** Saudi Arabia.

**arachide** /aʀaʃid/ *nf* groundnut; **huile d'~** groundnut oil.

**araignée** /aʀeɲe/ *nf* spider.

**arbitraire** /aʀbitʀɛʀ/ *a* arbitrary.

**arbitre** /aʀbitʀ/ *nm* referee; (au cricket, tennis) umpire; (expert) arbiter; (Jur) arbitrator. **arbitrer** [1] *vt* (*match*) referee, umpire; (Jur) arbitrate in.

**arbre** /aʀbʀ/ *nm* tree; (Tech) shaft.

**arbuste** /aʀbyst/ *nm* shrub.

**arc** /aʀk/ *nm* (arme) bow; (courbe) curve; (voûte) arch; **~ de cercle** arc of a circle.

**arc-en-ciel** (*pl* **arcs-en-ciel**) /aʀkɑ̃sjɛl/ *nm* rainbow.

**arche** /aʀʃ/ *nf* arch; **~ de Noé** Noah's ark.

**archéologie** /aʀkeɔlɔʒi/ *nf* archaeology.

**archevêque** /aʀʃəvɛk/ *nm* archbishop.

**architecte** /aʀʃitɛkt/ *nmf* architect. **architecture** *nf* architecture.

**Arctique** /aʀktik/ *nm* Arctic.

**ardent**, **~e** /aʀdɑ̃, -t/ *a* burning; (passionné) ardent; (*foi*) fervent. **ardeur** *nf* ardour; (chaleur) heat.

**ardoise** /aʀdwaz/ *nf* slate; **~ électronique** notepad computer.

**arène** /aʀɛn/ *nf* arena; **~s** amphitheatre; (pour corridas) bullring.

**arête** /aʀɛt/ *nf* (de poisson) bone; (bord) ridge.

**argent** /aʀʒɑ̃/ *nm* money; (métal) silver; **~ comptant** cash; **prendre pour ~ comptant** take at face value; **~ de poche** pocket money.

**argenté**, **~e** /aʀʒɑ̃te/ *a* silver(y); (*métal*) (silver-)plated.

**argenterie** /aʀʒɑ̃tʀi/ *nf* silverware.

**Argentine** /aʀʒɑ̃tin/ *nf* Argentina.

**argile** /aʀʒil/ *nf* clay.

**argot** /aʀgo/ *nm* slang.

**argument** /aʀgymɑ̃/ *nm* argument; **~ de vente** selling point. **argumenter** [1] *vi* argue.

**aristocratie** /aʀistɔkʀasi/ *nf* aristocracy.

**arithmétique** /aʀitmetik/ *nf* arithmetic. ● *a* arithmetical.

**armature** /aʀmatyʀ/ *nf* framework; (de tente) frame.

**arme** /aʀm/ *nf* arm, weapon; **~ à feu** firearm; **~s** (blason) coat of arms.

**armée** /aʀme/ *nf* army; **~ de l'air** Air Force; **~ de terre** Army.

**armer** /aʀme/ [1] *vt* arm; (*fusil*) cock; (*navire*) equip; (renforcer) reinforce; (Photo) wind on. □ **s'~ de** *vpr* arm oneself with.

**armoire** /aʀmwaʀ/ *nf* cupboard; (penderie) wardrobe; (US) closet; **~ à pharmacie** medicine cabinet.

**armure** /aʀmyʀ/ *nf* armour.

**arnaque** /aʀnak/ *nf* 🄸 swindling; **c'est de l'~** it's a swindle *ou* con 🄸.

**arobas(e)** /aʀɔbas, aʀɔbaz/ *nm* at sign.

**aromate** /aʀɔmat/ *nm* herb, spice.

**aromatisé**, **~e** /aʀɔmatize/ *a* flavoured.

**arôme** /aʀom/ *nm* aroma; (additif) flavouring.

**arpenter** /aʀpɑ̃te/ [1] *vt* pace up and down; (*terrain*) survey.

**arqué**, **~e** /aʀke/ *a* arched; (*jambes*) bandy.

**arrache-pied**, **d'~** /daʀaʃpje/ *loc* relentlessly.

**arracher** /aʀaʃe/ [1] *vt* pull out *ou* off; (*plante*) pull *ou* dig up; (*cheveux, page*) tear *ou* pull out; (par une explosion) blow off; **~ à** (enlever à) snatch from; (fig) force *ou* wrest from. □ **s'~ qch** *vpr* fight over sth.

**arranger** /aʀɑ̃ʒe/ [40] *vt* arrange, fix up; (réparer) put right; (régler) sort out; (convenir à) suit. □ **s'~** *vpr* (se mettre d'accord) come to an arrangement; (se débrouiller) manage.

**arrestation** /aʀɛstasjɔ̃/ *nf* arrest.

**arrêt** /aʀɛ/ *nm* stopping; (de combats) cessation; (de production) halt; (lieu) stop; (pause) pause; (Jur) ruling; **aux ~s** (Mil) under arrest; **à l'~** (*véhicule*) stationary; (*machine*) idle; **faire un ~** (make a) stop; **sans ~** (sans escale) nonstop; (sans interruption) constantly; **~ maladie** sick leave; **~ de travail** (grève) stoppage; (Méd) sick leave.

**arrêté** /aʀete/ *nm* order; **~ municipal** bylaw.

**arrêter** /aʀete/ [1] *vt* stop; (*date*) fix; (*appareil*) turn off; (renoncer à) give up; (appréhender) arrest. ● *vi* stop. □ **s'~** *vpr* stop; **s'~ de faire** stop doing.

**arrhes** /aʀ/ *nfpl* deposit; **verser des ~** pay a deposit.

**arrière** /aʀjɛʀ/ *a inv* back, rear. ● *nm* back, rear; (football) back; **à l'~** in *ou* at the back; **en ~** behind; (*marcher, tomber*) backwards; **en ~ de** behind. **arrière-boutique** (*pl* **~s**) *nf* back room (of the shop). **arrière-garde** (*pl* **~s**) *nf* rearguard. **arrière-goût** (*pl* **~s**) *nm* after-taste. **arrière-grand-mère** (*pl* **arrière-grands-mères**) *nf* great-grandmother. **arrière-grand-père** (*pl* **arrière-grands-pères**) *nm* great-grandfather. **arrière-pays** *nm inv* backcountry. **arrière-pensée** (*pl* **~s**) *nf* ulterior motive. **arrière-plan** *nm* (*pl* **~s**) background.

**arrimer** /aʀime/ [1] *vt* secure; (*cargaison*) stow.

**arrivage** /aʀivaʒ/ *nm* consignment.

**arrivée** /aʀive/ *nf* arrival; (Sport) finish.

**arriver** /aʀive/ [1] *vi* (*aux être*) arrive, come; (réussir) succeed; (se produire) happen; **~ à** (atteindre) reach; **~ à faire** manage to do; **je n'arrive pas à faire** I can't do; **en ~ à faire** get to the stage of doing; **il arrive que** it happens that; **il lui arrive de faire** he (sometimes) does.

**arriviste** /aʀivist/ *nmf* go-getter, self-seeker.

**arrondir** /aʀɔ̃diʀ/ [2] *vt* (make) round; (*somme*) round off. □ **s'~** *vpr* become round(ed).

**arrondissement** /aʀɔ̃dismɑ̃/ *nm* district.

**arroser** /aʀoze/ [1] *vt* water; (*repas*) wash down (with a drink); (*rôti*) baste; (*victoire*) drink to. **arrosoir** *nm* watering-can.

**art** /aʀ/ *nm* art; (don) knack (**de faire** of doing); **~s et métiers** arts and crafts; **~s ménagers** home economics (+ *sg*).

**artère** /aʀtɛʀ/ *nf* artery; **(grande) ~** main road.

**arthrite** /aʀtʀit/ *nf* arthritis.

**arthrose** /aʀtʀoz/ *nf* osteoarthritis.

**artichaut** /aʀtiʃo/ *nm* artichoke.

**article** /aʀtikl/ *nm* article; (Comm) item, article; **à l'~ de la mort** at death's door; **~ de fond** feature (article); **~s de voyage** travel goods.

**articulation** /aʀtikylasjɔ̃/ *nf* articulation; (Anat) joint.

**articuler** /aʀtikyle/ [1] *vt* articulate; (structurer) structure; (assembler) connect (**sur** to).

**artificiel**, **~le** /aʀtifisjɛl/ *a* artificial.

**artisan** /aʀtizɑ̃/ *nm* artisan, craftsman; **l'~ de** (fig) the architect of.

**artisanal**, **~e** (*mpl* **~aux**) /aʀtizanal/ *a* craft; (*méthode*) traditional; (amateur) home-made; **de fabrication ~e** hand-made, handcrafted.

**artiste** /aʀtist/ *nmf* artist. **artistique** *a* artistic.

**as**[1] /a/ ⇒AVOIR [5].

**as**[2] /ɑs/ *nm* ace.

**ascenseur** /asɑ̃sœʀ/ *nm* lift; (US) elevator.

**ascension** /asɑ̃sjɔ̃/ *nf* ascent; **l'A~** Ascension.

**aseptiser** /asɛptize/ [1] *vt* disinfect; (stériliser) sterilize; **aseptisé** (péj) sanitized.

**asiatique** /azjatik/ *a* Asian. **A∼** *nm/f* Asian.

**Asie** /azi/ *nf* Asia.

**asile** /azil/ *nm* refuge; (Pol) asylum; (pour malades, vieillards) home; **∼ de nuit** night shelter.

**aspect** /aspɛ/ *nm* appearance; (facettes) aspect; (perspective) side; **à l'∼ de** at the sight of.

**asperge** /aspɛʀʒ/ *nf* asparagus.

**asperger** /aspɛʀʒe/ [40] *vt* spray.

**asphyxier** /asfiksje/ [45] *vt* (*personne*) asphyxiate; (*entreprise, réseau*) paralyse. □ **s'∼** *vpr* suffocate; gas oneself; (*entreprise, réseau*) become paralysed.

**aspirateur** /aspiʀatœʀ/ *nm* vacuum cleaner.

**aspirer** /aspiʀe/ [1] *vt* inhale; (*liquide*) suck up. ● *vi* **∼ à** aspire to.

**aspirine®** /aspiʀin/ *nf* aspirin.

**assainir** /asenir/ [2] *vt* clean up.

**assaisonnement** /asɛzɔnmɑ̃/ *nm* seasoning.

**assassin** /asasɛ̃/ *nm* murderer; (Pol) assassin. **assassiner** [1] *vt* murder; (Pol) assassinate.

**assaut** /aso/ *nm* assault, onslaught; **donner l'∼ à, prendre d'∼** storm.

**assemblage** /asɑ̃blaʒ/ *nm* assembly; (combinaison) collection; (Tech) joint.

**assemblée** /asɑ̃ble/ *nf* meeting; (gens réunis) gathering; (Pol) assembly.

**assembler** /asɑ̃ble/ [1] *vt* assemble, put together; (réunir) gather. □ **s'∼** *vpr* gather, assemble.

**asseoir** /aswaʀ/ [9] *vt* sit (down), seat; (*bébé, malade*) sit up; (affermir) establish; (baser) base. □ **s'∼** *vpr* sit (down).

**assez** /ase/ *adv* (suffisamment) enough; (plutôt) quite, fairly; **∼ grand/rapide** big/fast enough (**pour** to); **∼ de** enough; **j'en ai ∼ (de)** I've had enough (of).

**assidu, ∼e** /asidy/ *a* (zélé) assiduous; (régulier) regular; **∼ auprès de** attentive to. **assiduité** *nf* assiduousness, regularity.

**assiéger** /asjeʒe/ [14] [40] *vt* besiege.

**assiette** /asjɛt/ *nf* plate; (équilibre) seat; **∼ anglaise** assorted cold meats; **∼ creuse/plate** soup-/dinner-plate; **ne pas être dans son ∼** feel out of sorts.

**assigner** /asiɲe/ [1] *vt* assign; (*limite*) fix.

**assimilation** /asimilasjɔ̃/ *nf* assimilation; (comparaison) likening, comparison.

**assimiler** /asimile/ [1] *vt* **∼ à** liken to; (classer) class as. □ **s'∼** *vpr* assimilate; (être comparable) be comparable (**à** to).

**assis, ∼e** /asi, -z/ *a* sitting (down), seated. ● ➔ASSEOIR [9].

**assise** /asiz/ *nf* (base) foundation; **∼s** (tribunal) assizes; (congrès) conference, congress.

**assistance** /asistɑ̃s/ *nf* audience; (aide) assistance; **l'A∼ (publique)** welfare services.

**assistant, ∼e** /asistɑ̃, -t/ *nm,f* assistant; (Scol) foreign language assistant; **∼s** (spectateurs) members of the audience; **∼e sociale** social worker; **∼ personnel numérique** personal digital assistant, PDA.

**assister** /asiste/ [1] *vt* assist; **∼ à** attend, be (present) at; (*accident*) witness; **assisté par ordinateur** computer-assisted.

**association** /asɔsjasjɔ̃/ *nf* association.

**associé**, **~e** /asɔsje/ *nm,f* partner, associate. ● *a* associate.

**associer** /asɔsje/ [45] *vt* associate; (mêler) combine (**à** with); **~ qn à** (*projet*) involve sb in; (*bénéfices*) give sb a share of. □ **s'~** *vpr* (*sociétés, personnes*) become associated, join forces (**à** with); (s'harmoniser) combine (**à** with); **s'~ à** (*joie, opinion de qn*) share; (*projet*) take part in.

**assommer** /asɔme/ [1] *vt* knock out; (*animal*) stun; (fig) overwhelm; (ennuyer [I]) bore.

**Assomption** /asɔ̃psjɔ̃/ *nf* Assumption.

**assortiment** /asɔʀtimɑ̃/ *nm* assortment.

**assortir** /asɔʀtiʀ/ [2] *vt* match (**à** with, to); **~ de** accompany with. □ **s'~** *vpr* match; **s'~ à qch** match sth.

**assoupir (s')** /(s)asupiʀ/ [2] *vpr* doze off; (s'apaiser) subside.

**assouplir** /asupliʀ/ [2] *vt* make supple; (fig) make flexible.

**assourdir** /asuʀdiʀ/ [2] *vt* (*personne*) deafen; (*bruit*) muffle.

**assouvir** /asuviʀ/ [2] *vt* satisfy.

**assujettir** /asyʒetiʀ/ [2] *vt* subjugate, subdue; **~ à** subject to.

**assumer** /asyme/ [1] *vt* assume; (*coût*) meet; (accepter) come to terms with, accept.

**assurance** /asyʀɑ̃s/ *nf* (self-) assurance; (garantie) assurance; (contrat) insurance; **~s sociales** social insurance; **~ automobile/maladie** car/health insurance.

**assuré**, **~e** /asyʀe/ *a* certain, assured; (sûr de soi) confident, assured. ● *nm,f* insured party.

**assurer** /asyʀe/ [1] *vt* ensure; (fournir) provide; (exécuter) carry out; (Comm) insure; (stabiliser) steady; (*frontières*) make secure; **~ à qn que** assure sb that; **~ qn de** assure sb of; **~ la gestion/défense de** manage/defend. □ **s'~** *vpr* take out insurance; **s'~ de/que** make sure of/that; **s'~ qch** (se procurer) secure sth. **assureur** *nm* insurer.

**astérisque** /asteʀisk/ *nm* asterisk.

**asthmatique** /asmatik/ *a & nmf* asthmatic.

**asthme** /asm/ *nm* asthma.

**asticot** /astiko/ *nm* maggot.

**astreindre** /astʀɛ̃dʀ/ [22] *vt* **~ qn à qch** force sth on sb; **~ qn à faire** force sb to do.

**astrologie** /astʀɔlɔʒi/ *nf* astrology. **astrologue** *nmf* astrologer.

**astronaute** /astʀɔnot/ *nmf* astronaut.

**astronomie** /astʀɔnɔmi/ *nf* astronomy.

**astuce** /astys/ *nf* smartness; (truc) trick; (plaisanterie) wisecrack.

**astucieux**, **-ieuse** /astysjø, -z/ *a* smart, clever.

**atelier** /atəlje/ *nm* (local) workshop; (de peintre) studio; (séance de travail) workshop.

**athée** /ate/ *nmf* atheist. ● *a* atheistic.

**athlète** /atlɛt/ *nmf* athlete. **athlétisme** *nm* athletics.

**Atlantique** /atlɑ̃tik/ *nm* Atlantic (Ocean).

**atmosphère** /atmɔsfɛʀ/ *nf* atmosphere.

**atomique** /atɔmik/ *a* atomic; (*énergie, centrale*) nuclear.

**atomiseur** /atɔmizœʀ/ *nm* spray.

**atout** /atu/ *nm* trump (card); (avantage) asset.

**atroce** /atʀɔs/ *a* atrocious.

**attabler (s')** /(s)atable/ [1] *vpr* sit down at table.

**attachant**, **~e** /ataʃɑ̃, -t/ *a* charming.

**attache** /ataʃ/ *nf* (agrafe) fastener; (lien) tie.

**attaché**, **~e** /ataʃe/ *a* **être ~ à** (aimer) be attached to. ● *nm,f* (Pol) attaché.

**attacher** /ataʃe/ [1] *vt* tie (up); (*ceinture, robe*) fasten; (*bicyclette*) lock; **~ à** (attribuer à) attach to. ● *vi* (Culin) stick. □ **s'~** *vpr* fasten, do up; **s'~ à** (se lier à) become attached to; (se consacrer à) apply oneself to.

**attaquant**, **~e** /atakɑ̃, -t/ *nm,f* attacker; (au football) striker; (au football américain) forward.

**attaque** /atak/ *nf* attack; **~ (cérébrale)** stroke; **il va en faire une ~** he'll have a fit; **~ à main armée** armed attack.

**attaquer** /atake/ [1] *vt* attack; (*banque*) raid. ● *vi* attack. □ **s'~ à** *vpr* attack; (*problème, sujet*) tackle.

**attardé**, **~e** /ataʀde/ *a* backward; (*idées*) outdated; (en retard) late.

**attarder (s')** /(s)ataʀde/ [1] *vpr* linger.

**atteindre** /atɛ̃dʀ/ [22] *vt* reach; (blesser) hit; (affecter) affect.

**atteint**, **~e** /atɛ̃, -t/ *a* **~ de** suffering from.

**atteinte** /atɛ̃t/ *nf* attack (**à** on); **porter ~ à** attack; (*droit*) infringe.

**atteler** /atle/ [38] *vt* (*cheval*) harness; (*remorque*) couple. □ **s'~ à** *vpr* get down to.

**attelle** /atɛl/ *nf* splint.

**attenant**, **~e** /atnɑ̃, -t/ *a* **~ (à)** adjoining.

**attendant**: **en ~** /ɑ̃natɑ̃dɑ̃/ *loc* meanwhile.

**attendre** /atɑ̃dʀ/ [3] *vt* wait for; (*bébé*) expect; (être le sort de) await; (escompter) expect; **~ que qn fasse** wait for sb to do. ● *vi* wait; (au téléphone) hold. □ **s'~ à** *vpr* expect.

**attendrir** /atɑ̃dʀiʀ/ [2] *vt* move (to pity). □ **s'~** *vpr* be moved to pity.

**attendu[1]** /atɑ̃dy/ *prép* given, considering; **~ que** considering that.

**attendu[2]**, **~e** /atɑ̃dy/ *a* (escompté) expected; (espéré) long-awaited.

**attentat** /atɑ̃ta/ *nm* assassination attempt; **~ (à la bombe)** (bomb) attack.

**attente** /atɑ̃t/ *nf* wait(ing); (espoir) expectations (+ *pl*).

**attenter** /atɑ̃te/ [1] *vi* **~ à** make an attempt on; (fig) violate.

**attentif**, **-ive** /atɑ̃tif, -v/ *a* attentive; (scrupuleux) careful; **~ à** mindful of; (soucieux) careful of.

**attention** /atɑ̃sjɔ̃/ *nf* attention; (soin) care; **~ (à)!** watch out (for)!; **faire ~ à** (écouter) pay attention to; (prendre garde à) watch out for; (prendre soin de) take care of. **faire ~ à faire** be careful to do. **attentionné**, **~e** *a* considerate.

**attentisme** /atɑ̃tism/ *nm* wait-and-see policy.

**atténuer** /atenɥe/ [1] *vt* (*violence*) reduce; (*critique*) tone down; (*douleur*) ease; (*faute*) mitigate. □ **s'~** *vpr* subside.

**atterrir** /ateʀiʀ/ [2] *vi* land. **atterrissage** *nm* landing.

**attestation** /atɛstasjɔ̃/ *nf* certificate.

**attester** /atɛste/ [1] *vt* testify to; **~ que** testify that.

**attirant**, **~e** /atiʀɑ̃, -t/ *a* attractive.

**attirer** /atiʀe/ [1] *vt* draw, attract; (causer) bring. □ **s'~** *vpr* bring upon oneself; (*amis*) win.

**attiser** /atize/ [1] *vt* (*feu*) poke; (*sentiment*) stir up.

**attitré**, **~e** /atitʀe/ *a* accredited; (habituel) usual, regular.

**attitude** /atityd/ *nf* attitude; (maintien) bearing.

**attraction** /atʀaksjɔ̃/ *nf* attraction.

**attrait** /atʀɛ/ *nm* attraction.

**attraper** /atʀape/ [1] *vt* catch; (*corde, main*) catch hold of; (*habitude, accent*) pick up; (*maladie*) catch; **se faire ~** Ⓘ get told off.

**attrayant**, **~e** /atʀɛjɑ̃, -t/ *a* attractive.

**attribuer** /atʀibɥe/ [1] *vt* allocate; (*prix*) award; (imputer) attribute. □ **s'~** *vpr* claim (for oneself). **attribution** *nf* awarding, allocation.

**attrouper (s')** /(s)atʀupe/ [1] *vpr* gather.

**au** /o/ ⇒À.

**aubaine** /obɛn/ *nf* godsend, opportunity.

**aube** /ob/ *nf* dawn, daybreak.

**auberge** /obɛʀʒ/ *nf* inn; **~ de jeunesse** youth hostel.

**aubergine** /obɛʀʒin/ *nf* aubergine; (US) eggplant.

**aucun**, **~e** /okœ̃, okyn/ *a* (dans une phrase négative) no, not any; (positif) any. ● *pron* (dans une phrase négative) none, not any; (positif) any; **~ des deux** neither of the two; **d'~s** some. **aucunement** *adv* not at all, in no way.

**audace** /odas/ *nf* daring; (impudence) audacity.

**audacieux**, **-ieuse** /odasjø, -z/ *a* daring.

**au-delà** /od(ə)la/ *adv* beyond. ● *prép* **~ de** beyond.

**au-dessous** /od(ə)su/ *adv* below. ● *prép* **~ de** below; (couvert par) under.

**au-dessus** /od(ə)sy/ *adv* above. ● *prép* **~ de** above.

**au-devant** /od(ə)vɑ̃/ *prép* **aller ~ de qn** go to meet sb; **aller ~ des désirs de qn** anticipate sb's wishes.

**audience** /odjɑ̃s/ *nf* audience; (d'un tribunal) hearing; (succès, attention) success.

**audimat**® /odimat/ *nm* **l'~** the TV ratings.

**audiovisuel**, **~le** /odjɔvizɥɛl/ *a* audio-visual.

**auditeur**, **-trice** /oditœʀ, -tʀis/ *nm,f* listener.

**audition** /odisjɔ̃/ *nf* hearing; (Théât, Mus) audition.

**auditoire** /oditwaʀ/ *nm* audience.

**augmentation** /ɔgmɑ̃tasjɔ̃/ *nf* increase; **~ (de salaire)** (pay) rise; (US) raise.

**augmenter** /ɔgmɑ̃te/ [1] *vt/i* increase; (*employé*) give a pay rise *ou* raise to.

**augure** /ogyʀ/ *nm* (devin) oracle; **être de bon/mauvais ~** be a good/bad sign.

**aujourd'hui** /oʒuʀdɥi/ *adv* today.

**auparavant** /opaʀavɑ̃/ *adv* (avant) before; (précédemment) previously; (en premier lieu) beforehand.

**auprès** /opʀɛ/ *prép* **~ de** (à côté de) beside, next to; (comparé à) compared with; **s'excuser/se plaindre ~ de** apologize/complain to.

**auquel** /okɛl/ ⇒LEQUEL.

**aura**, **aurait** /oʀa, oʀɛ/ ⇒AVOIR [5].

**aurore** /oʀɔʀ/ *nf* dawn.

**aussi** /osi/ *adv* (également) too, also, as well; (dans une comparaison) as; (si, tellement) so; **~ bien que** as well as. ● *conj* (donc) so, consequently.

**aussitôt** /osito/ *adv* immediately; **~ que** as soon as, the moment; **~ arrivé** as soon as he arrived.

**austère** /ostɛʀ/ *a* austere.

**Australie** /ɔstʀali/ *nf* Australia.

**australien**, **~ne** /ostʀaljɛ̃, ɛn/ *a* Australian. **A~**, **~ne** *nm,f* Australian.

**autant** /otɑ̃/ *adv* (*travailler, manger*) as much (**que** as); **~ (de)** (quantité) as much (**que** as); (nombre) as many (**que** as); (tant) so much, so many; **~ faire** one had better do; **d'~ plus que** all the more than; **en faire ~** do the same; **pour ~** for all that.

**autel** /otɛl/ *nm* altar.

**auteur** /otœʀ/ *nm* author; **l'~ du crime** the perpetrator of the crime.

**authentifier** /otɑ̃tifje/ [45] *vt* authenticate.

**authentique** /otɑ̃tik/ *a* authentic.

**auto** /oto/ *nf* car; **~ tamponneuse** dodgem, bumper car.

**autobus** /otɔbys/ *nm* bus.

**autocar** /otɔkaʀ/ *nm* coach.

**autochtone** /otɔktɔn/ *nmf* native.

**autocollant**, **~e** /otɔkɔlɑ̃, -t/ *a* self-adhesive. ● *nm* sticker.

**autodidacte** /otɔdidakt/ *nmf* self-taught person.

**auto-école** (*pl* **~s**) /otɔekɔl/ *nf* driving school.

**automate** /otɔmat/ *nm* automaton, robot

**automatique** /otɔmatik/ *a* automatic.

**automatisation** /otɔmatizasjɔ̃/ *nf* automation.

**automne** /otɔn/ *nm* autumn; (US) fall.

**automobile** /otɔmɔbil/ *a* motor, car; (US) automobile. ● *nf* (motor) car; **l'~** the motor industry; (Sport) motoring. **automobiliste** *nmf* motorist.

**autonome** /otɔnɔm/ *a* autonomous; (Ordinat) stand-alone.

**autoradio** /otɔʀadjo/ *nm* car radio.

**autorisation** /otɔʀizasjɔ̃/ *nf* permission, authorization; (permis) permit.

**autorisé**, **~e** /otɔʀize/ *a* (*opinions*) authoritative; (approuvé) authorized.

**autoriser** /otɔʀize/ [1] *vt* authorize, permit; (rendre possible) allow (of); (donner un droit) **~ qn à faire** entitle sb to do.

**autoritaire** /otɔʀitɛʀ/ *a* authoritarian.

**autorité** /otɔʀite/ *nf* authority; **faire ~** be authoritative.

**autoroute** /otɔʀut/ *nf* motorway; (US) highway; **~ de l'information** (Ordinat) information superhighway.

**auto-stop** /otɔstɔp/ *nm* hitch-hiking; **faire de l'~** hitch-hike; **prendre qn en ~** give a lift to sb.

**autour** /otuʀ/ *adv* around; **tout ~** all around. ● *prép* **~ de** around.

**autre** /otʀ/ *a* other; **un ~ jour/livre** another day/book; **~ chose/part** something/somewhere else; **quelqu'un/rien d'~** somebody/nothing else; **quoi d'~?** what else?; **d'~ part** on the other hand; (de plus) moreover, besides; **vous ~s Anglais** you English ● *pron* **un ~, une ~** another (one); **l'~** the other (one); **les ~s** the others; (autrui) others; **d'~s** (some) others; **l'un l'~** each other; **l'un et l'~** both of them; **d'un jour à l'~** (bientôt) any day now; **entre ~s** among other things.

**autrefois** /otʀəfwa/ *adv* in the past; (précédemment) formerly.

**autrement** /otʀəmɑ̃/ *adv* differently; (sinon) otherwise; (plus [I]) far more; **~ dit** in other words.

**Autriche** /otʀiʃ/ *nf* Austria.

**autrichien**, **~ne** /otʀiʃjɛ̃, -jɛn/ *a* Austrian. **A~**, **~ne** *nm,f* Austrian.

**autruche** /otʀyʃ/ *nf* ostrich.

**autrui** /otʀɥi/ *pron* others, other people.

**aux** /o/ ⇒À.

**auxiliaire** /oksiljɛʀ/ *a* auxiliary. ● *nmf* (assistant) auxiliary. ● *nm* (Gram) auxiliary.

**auxquels**, **-quelles** /okɛl/ ⇒LEQUEL.

**aval**: **en ~** /ɑ̃naval/ *loc* downstream.

**avaler** /avale/ [1] *vt* swallow.

**avance** /avɑ̃s/ *nf* advance; (sur un concurrent) lead; **~ (de fonds)** advance; **à l'~** in advance; **d'~** already; **en ~** early; (*montre*) fast; **en ~ (sur)** (menant) ahead (of).

**avancement** /avɑ̃smɑ̃/ *nm* promotion.

**avancé**, **~e** /avɑ̃se/ *a* advanced.

**avancer** /avɑ̃se/ [10] *vi* move forward, advance; (*travail*) make progress; (*montre*) be fast; (faire saillie) jut out. ● *vt* move forward; (dans le temps) bring forward; (*argent*) advance; (*montre*) put forward. □ **s'~** *vpr* move forward, advance; (se hasarder) commit oneself.

**avant** /avɑ̃/ *nm* front; (Sport) forward. ● *a inv* front. ● *prép* before; **~ de faire** before doing; **en ~ de** in front of; **~ peu** shortly; **~ tout** above all. ● *adv* (dans le temps) before, beforehand; (d'abord) first; **en ~** (dans l'espace) forward(s); (dans le temps) ahead; **le bus d'~** the previous bus. ● *conj* **~ que** before; **~ qu'il (ne) fasse** before he does.

**avantage** /avɑ̃taʒ/ *nm* advantage; (Comm) benefit.

**avantager** /avɑ̃taʒe/ [40] *vt* favour; (embellir) show off to advantage.

**avantageux**, **-euse** /avɑ̃taʒø, -z/ *a* advantageous, favourable; (*prix*) attractive.

**avant-bras** /avɑ̃bʀa/ *nm inv* forearm.

**avant-centre** (*pl* **avants-centres**) /avɑ̃sɑ̃tʀ/ *nm* centre forward.

**avant-coureur** (*pl* **~s**) /avɑ̃kuʀœʀ/ *a* precursory, foreshadowing.

**avant-dernier**, **-ière** (*pl* **~s**) /avɑ̃dɛʀnje, -jɛʀ/ *a* & *nm,f* last but one.

**avant-goût** (*pl* **~s**) /avɑ̃gu/ *nm* foretaste.

**avant-hier** /avɑ̃tjɛʀ/ *adv* the day before yesterday.

**avant-poste** (*pl* **~s**) /avɑ̃pɔst/ *nm* outpost.

**avant-première** (*pl* **~s**) /avɑ̃pʀəmjɛʀ/ *nf* preview.

**avant-propos** /avɑ̃pʀɔpo/ *nm inv* foreword.

**avare** /avaʀ/ *a* miserly; **~ de** sparing with. ● *nmf* miser.

**avarié**, **~e** /avaʀje/ *a* (*aliment*) spoiled.

**avatar** /avataʀ/ *nm* misfortune.

**avec** /avɛk/ *prép* with. ● *adv* 🅸 with it *ou* them.

**avènement** /avɛnmɑ̃/ *nm* advent; (d'un roi) accession.

**avenir** /avniʀ/ *nm* future; **à l'~** in future; **d'~** with (future) prospects.

**aventure** /avɑ̃tyʀ/ *nf* adventure; (sentimentale) affair. **aventureux**, **-euse** *a* adventurous; (hasardeux) risky.

**avérer** **(s')** /(s)aveʀe/ [14] *vpr* prove (to be).

**averse** /avɛʀs/ *nf* shower.

**avertir** /avɛʀtiʀ/ [2] *vt* inform; (mettre en garde, menacer) warn. **avertissement** *nm* warning.

**avertisseur** /avɛʀtisœʀ/ *nm* alarm; (Auto) horn; ~ **d'incendie** fire-alarm; ~ **lumineux** warning light.

**aveu** (*pl* ~**x**) /avø/ *nm* confession; **de l'**~ **de** by the admission of.

**aveugle** /avœgl/ *a* blind. ● *nmf* blind man, blind woman.

**aviateur**, **-trice** /avjatœʀ, -tʀis/ *nm,f* aviator.

**aviation** /avjasjɔ̃/ *nf* flying; (industrie) aviation; (Mil) air force.

**avide** /avid/ *a* greedy (**de** for); (anxieux) eager (**de** for); ~ **de faire** eager to do.

**avion** /avjɔ̃/ *nm* plane, aeroplane, aircraft; (US) airplane; ~ **à réaction** jet.

**aviron** /aviʀɔ̃/ *nm* oar; **l'**~ (Sport) rowing.

**avis** /avi/ *nm* opinion; (conseil) advice; (renseignement) notification; (Comm) advice; **à mon** ~ in my opinion; **changer d'**~ change one's mind; **être d'**~ **que** be of the opinion that; ~ **au lecteur** foreword.

**avisé**, ~**e** /avize/ *a* sensible; **être bien/mal** ~ **de** be well /ill-advised to.

**aviser** /avize/ [1] *vt* advise, notify. ● *vi* decide what to do. □ **s'**~ **de** *vpr* suddenly realize; **s'**~ **de faire** take it into one's head to do.

**avocat**, ~**e** /avɔka, -t/ *nm,f* barrister; (US) attorney; (fig) advocate; ~ **de la défense** counsel for the defence. ● *nm* (fruit) avocado (pear).

**avoine** /avwan/ *nf* oats (+ *pl*).

**avoir** /avwaʀ/ [5]

● *verbe auxiliaire*

····➤ have; **il nous a appelés hier** he called us yesterday.

● *verbe transitif*

····➤ (possession) have (got).

····➤ (obtenir) get; (au téléphone) get through to.

····➤ (duper) 🄸 have; **on m'a eu!** I've been had!

····➤ ~ **chaud/faim** be hot/hungry.

····➤ ~ **dix ans** be ten years old.

● **avoir à** *verbe + préposition*

····➤ to have to; **j'ai beaucoup à faire** I have a lot to do; **tu n'as qu'à leur écrire** all you have to do is write to them

● **en avoir pour** *verbe + préposition*

····➤ **j'en ai pour une minute** I will only be a minute; **j'en ai eu pour 100 francs** it cost me 100 francs.

● **il y a** *verbe impersonnel*

····➤ there is; (pluriel) there are; **qu'est-ce qu'il y a?** what's the matter?; **il est venu il y a cinq ans** he came here five years ago; **il y a au moins 5 km jusqu'à la gare** it's at least 5 km to the station.

● *nom masculin*

····➤ (dans un magasin) credit note.

····➤ (biens) asset (+ *pl*).

**avortement** /avɔʀtəmɑ̃/ *nm* (Méd) abortion.

**avorter** /avɔʀte/ [1] *vi* (*projet*) abort; **(se faire)** ~ have an abortion.

**avoué**, ~**e** /avwe/ *a* avowed. ● *nm* solicitor; (US) attorney.

**avouer** /avwe/ [1] *vt* (*amour, ignorance*) confess; (*crime*) confess to, admit. ● *vi* confess.

**avril** /avʀil/ *nm* April.

**axe** /aks/ *nm* axis; (essieu) axle; (d'une politique) main line(s), basis; **~ (routier)** main road.

**ayant** /ɛjɑ̃/ ⇒AVOIR [5].

**azote** /azɔt/ *nm* nitrogen.

**azur** /azyʀ/ *nm* sky-blue.

# Bb

**baba** /baba/ *nm* **~ (au rhum)** (rum) baba; **en rester ~** 🄸 be flabbergasted.

**babillard** /babijaʀ/ *nm* **~ électronique** (Internet) bulletin board system, BBS.

**babines** /babin/ *nfpl* **se lécher les ~** lick one's chops.

**babiole** /babjɔl/ *nf* trinket.

**bâbord** /bɑbɔʀ/ *nm* port (side).

**baby-foot** /babifut/ *nm inv* table football.

**bac** /bak/ *nm* (Scol) ⇒BACCALAURÉAT; (bateau) ferry; (récipient) tub; (plus petit) tray.

**baccalauréat** /bakalɔʀea/ *nm* school leaving certificate.

**bâche** /bɑʃ/ *nf* tarpaulin.

**bachelier**, **-ière** /baʃəlje, -jɛʀ/ *nm,f* holder of the *baccalauréat*.

**bachoter** /baʃɔte/ [1] *vi* cram (for an exam).

**bâcler** /bɑkle/ [1] *vt* botch (up).

**bactérie** /bakteʀi/ *nf* bacterium; **~s** bacteria.

**badaud**, **~e** /bado, -d/ *nm,f* onlooker.

**badigeonner** /badiʒɔne/ [1] *vt* whitewash; (barbouiller) daub.

**badiner** /badine/ [1] *vi* banter.

**baffe** /baf/ *nf* 🄸 slap.

**baffle** /bafl/ *nm* speaker.

**bafouiller** /bafuje/ [1] *vt/i* stammer.

**bagage** /bagaʒ/ *nm* bag; (connaissances) knowledge; **~s** luggage; **~ à main** hand luggage.

**bagarre** /bagaʀ/ *nf* fight.

**bagatelle** /bagatɛl/ *nf* trifle; (somme) trifling amount.

**bagnard** /baɲaʀ/ *nm* convict.

**bagnole** /baɲɔl/ *nf* 🄸 car.

**bague** /bag/ *nf* (bijou) ring.

**baguette** /bagɛt/ *nf* stick; (de chef d'orchestre) baton; (chinoise) chopstick; (pain) baguette; **~ magique** magic wand; **~ de tambour** drumstick.

**baie** /bɛ/ *nf* (Géog) bay; (fruit) berry; **~ (vitrée)** picture window; (Ordinat) bay.

**baignade** /bɛɲad/ *nf* swimming.

**baigner** /beɲe/ [1] *vt* bathe; (*enfant*) bath. ● *vi* **~ dans l'huile** swim in grease. ◻ **se ~** *vpr* have a swim. **baigneur**, **-euse** *nm,f* swimmer.

**baignoire** /bɛɲwaʀ/ *nf* bath(tub).

**bail** (*pl* **baux**) /baj, bo/ *nm* lease.

**bâiller** /baje/ [1] *vi* yawn; (être ouvert) gape.

**bailleur** /bajœʀ/ *nm* **~ de fonds** (Comm) sleeping partner.

**bain** /bɛ̃/ *nm* bath; (baignade) swim; **prendre un ~ de soleil** sunbathe; **~ de bouche** mouthwash; **être dans le ~** (fig) be in the swing of things; **se remettre dans le ~** get back into the swing of things; **prendre un ~ de foule** mingle with the crowd.

**bain-marie** (*pl* **bains-marie**) /bɛ̃maʀi/ *nm* double boiler.

**baiser** /beze/ [1] *vt* (*main*) kiss; [✱] screw [✱]. ● *nm* kiss.

**baisse** /bɛs/ *nf* fall, drop; **être en ~** be going down.

**baisser** /bese/ [1] *vt* lower; (*radio, lampe*) turn down. ● *vi* (*niveau*) go down, fall; (*santé, forces*) fail. □ **se ~** *vpr* bend down.

**bal** (*pl* **~s**) /bal/ *nm* dance; (habillé) ball; (lieu) dance-hall, **~ costumé** fancy-dress ball.

**balade** /balad/ *nf* stroll; (en auto) drive.

**balader** /balade/ [1] *vt* take for a stroll. □ **se ~** *vpr* (à pied) (go for a) stroll; (en voiture) go for a drive; (voyager) travel.

**baladeur** /baladœʀ/ *nm* personal stereo.

**balafre** /balafʀ/ *nf* gash; (cicatrice) scar.

**balai** /balɛ/ *nm* broom.

**balance** /balɑ̃s/ *nf* scales (+ *pl*); **la B~** Libra.

**balancer** /balɑ̃se/ [10] *vt* swing, sway; (lancer [!]) chuck [!]; (se débarrasser de [!]) chuck out [!]. ● *vi* sway. □ **se ~** *vpr* swing; sway; **s'en ~** [!] not to give a damn [!].

**balancier** /balɑ̃sje/ *nm* (d'horloge) pendulum; (d'équilibriste) pole.

**balançoire** /balɑ̃swaʀ/ *nf* swing.

**balayage** /balɛjaʒ/ *nm* sweeping; (cheveux) highlights.

**balayer** /baleje/ [31] *vt* sweep (up); (chasser) sweep away; (se débarrasser de) sweep aside.

**balbutiement** /balbysimɑ̃/ *nm* stammering; **les ~s** (fig) the first steps.

**balcon** /balkɔ̃/ *nm* balcony; (Théât) dress circle.

**baleine** /balɛn/ *nf* whale.

**balise** /baliz/ *nf* beacon; (bouée) buoy; (Auto) (road) sign. **baliser** [1] *vt* mark out (with beacons); (*route*) signpost; (*sentier*) mark out.

**balivernes** /balivɛʀn/ *nfpl* nonsense.

**ballant**, **~e** /balɑ̃, -t/ *a* dangling.

**balle** /bal/ *nf* (projectile) bullet; (Sport) ball, (paquet) bale.

**ballerine** /balʀin/ *nf* (danseuse) ballerina; (chaussure) ballet pump.

**ballet** /balɛ/ *nm* ballet.

**ballon** /balɔ̃/ *nm* (Sport) ball; **~ (de baudruche)** balloon; **~ de football** football.

**ballonné**, **~e** /balɔne/ *a* bloated.

**balnéaire** /balneɛʀ/ *a* seaside.

**balourd**, **~e** /baluʀ, -d/ *nm,f* oaf. ● *a* uncouth.

**balustrade** /balystʀad/ *nf* railing.

**ban** /bɑ̃/ *nm* round of applause; **~s** (de mariage) banns; **mettre au ban de** cast out from.

**banal**, **~e** (*mpl* **~s**) /banal/ *a* commonplace, banal.

**banane** /banan/ *nf* banana.

**banc** /bɑ̃/ *nm* bench; (de poissons) shoal; **~ des accusés** dock, **~ d'essai** (test) testing ground.

**bancaire** /bɑ̃kɛʀ/ *a* (*secteur*) banking; (*chèque*) bank.

**bancal**, **~e** (*mpl* **~s**) /bɑ̃kal/ *a* wobbly; (*solution*) shaky.

**bande** /bɑ̃d/ *nf* (groupe) gang; (de papier ) strip; (rayure) stripe; (de film) reel; (pansement) bandage; **~ dessinée** comic strip; **~ (magnétique)** tape; **~ sonore** sound-track.

**bande-annonce** (*pl* **bandes-annonces**) /bɑ̃danɔ̃s/ *nf* trailer.

**bandeau** (*pl* **~x**) /bɑ̃do/ *nm* headband; (sur les yeux) blindfold; **~ publicitaire** (Ordinat) banner.

**bander** /bɑ̃de/ [1] *vt* bandage; (*arc*) bend; (*muscle*) tense; ~ **les yeux à** blindfold.

**banderole** /bɑ̃dʀɔl/ *nf* banner.

**bandit** /bɑ̃di/ *nm* bandit. **banditisme** *nm* crime.

**bandoulière**: **en** ~ /ɑ̃bɑ̃duljɛʀ/ *loc* across one's shoulder.

**banlieue** /bɑ̃ljø/ *nf* suburbs; **de** ~ suburban. **banlieusard**, ~**e** *nm,f* (suburban) commuter.

**bannir** /baniʀ/ [2] *vt* banish.

**banque** /bɑ̃k/ *nf* bank; (activité) banking; ~ **de données** databank.

**banqueroute** /bɑ̃kʀut/ *nf* bankruptcy.

**banquet** /bɑ̃kɛ/ *nm* banquet.

**banquette** /bɑ̃kɛt/ *nf* seat.

**banquier**, **-ière** /bɑ̃kje, -jɛʀ/ *nm,f* banker.

**baptême** /batɛm/ *nm* baptism, christening. **baptiser** [1] *vt* baptize, christen; (nommer) call.

**bar** /baʀ/ *nm* (lieu) bar.

**baragouiner** /baʀagwine/ [1] *vt/i* gabble; (*langue*) speak a few words of.

**baraque** /baʀak/ *nf* hut, shed; (maison Ⓘ) house.

**baratin** /baʀatɛ̃/ *nm* Ⓘ sweet *ou* smooth talk.

**barbare** /baʀbaʀ/ *a* barbaric. ● *nmf* barbarian.

**barbe** /baʀb/ *nf* beard; ~ **à papa** candy-floss; (US) cotton candy; **quelle** ~**!** Ⓘ what a drag! Ⓘ.

**barbelé** /baʀbəle/ *a* **fil** ~ barbed wire.

**barber** /baʀbe/ [1] *vt* Ⓘ bore.

**barboter** /baʀbɔte/ [1] *vi* (dans l'eau) paddle, splash. ● *vt* (voler Ⓘ) pinch.

**barbouiller** /baʀbuje/ [1] *vt* (souiller) smear (**de** with); **tu es tout barbouillé** your face is all dirty; **être barbouillé** feel queazy.

**barbu**, ~**e** /baʀby/ *a* bearded.

**barème** /baʀɛm/ *nm* list, table; (échelle) scale.

**baril** /baʀil/ *nm* barrel; (de poudre) keg.

**bariolé**, ~**e** /baʀjɔle/ *a* multicoloured.

**baromètre** /baʀɔmɛtʀ/ *nm* barometer.

**baron**, ~**ne** /baʀɔ̃, -ɔn/ *nm,f* baron, baroness.

**barque** /baʀk/ *nf* (small) boat.

**barrage** /baʀaʒ/ *nm* dam; (sur route) roadblock.

**barre** /baʀ/ *nf* bar; (trait) line, stroke; (Naut) helm; ~ **de boutons** (Ordinat) toolbar.

**barreau** (*pl* ~**x**) /baʀo/ *nm* bar; (d'échelle) rung; **le** ~ (Jur) the bar.

**barrer** /baʀe/ [1] *vt* block; (*porte*) bar; (rayer) cross out; (Naut) steer. □ **se** ~ *vpr* Ⓘ leave.

**barrette** /baʀɛt/ *nf* (hair) slide.

**barrière** /baʀjɛʀ/ *nf* (porte) gate; (clôture) fence; (obstacle) barrier.

**bar-tabac** (*pl* **bars-tabac**) /baʀtaba/ *nm* café (*selling stamps and cigarettes*).

**bas**, **basse** /bɑ, bɑs/ *a* (*niveau, table*) low; (*action*) base; **au** ~ **mot** at the lowest estimate; **en** ~ **âge** young; ~ **morceaux** (viande) cheap cuts. ● *nm* bottom; (chaussette) stocking; ~ **de laine** (fig) nest-egg. ● *adv* low; **en** ~ down below; (dans une maison) downstairs; **en** ~ **de la page** at the bottom of the page; **plus** ~ further *ou* lower down; **mettre** ~ give birth (to). **bas de casse** *nm inv* lower case. **bas-côté** (*pl* ~**s**) *nm* (de route) verge; (US) shoulder.

**bascule** /baskyl/ *nf* (balance) scales (+ *pl*); **cheval/fauteuil à ~** rocking-horse/-chair.

**basculer** /baskyle/ [1] *vi* topple over; (*benne*) tip up.

**base** /bɑz/ *nf* base; (fondement) basis; (Pol) rank and file; **de ~** basic. **base de données** *nf* database.

**baser** /bɑze/ [1] *vt* base. □ **se ~ sur** *vpr* go by.

**bas-fonds** /bɑfɔ̃/ *nmpl* (eau) shallows; (fig) dregs.

**basilic** /bazilik/ *nm* basil.

**basilique** /bazilik/ *nf* basilica.

**basque** /bask/ *a* Basque. **B~** *nmf* Basque.

**basse** /bɑs/ ⇒BAS.

**basse-cour** (*pl* **basses-cours**) /bɑskuʀ/ *nf* farmyard.

**bassesse** /bɑsɛs/ *nf* baseness; (action) base act.

**bassin** /basɛ̃/ *nm* (pièce d'eau) pond; (de piscine) pool; (Géog) basin; (Anat) pelvis; (plat) bowl; **~ houiller** coalfield.

**bassine** /basin/ *nf* bowl.

**basson** /basɔ̃/ *nm* bassoon.

**bas-ventre** (*pl* **~s**) /bɑvɑ̃tʀ/ *nm* lower abdomen.

**bat** /ba/ ⇒BATTRE [11].

**bataille** /batɑj/ *nf* battle; (fig) fight.

**bâtard**, **~e** /bɑtaʀ, -d/ *a* (*solution*) hybrid. ● *nm,f* bastard.

**bateau** (*pl* **~x**) /bato/ *nm* boat; **~ pneumatique** rubber dinghy. **bateau-mouche** (*pl* **bateaux-mouches**) *nm* sightseeing boat.

**bâti**, **~e** /bɑti/ *a* **bien ~** well-built.

**bâtiment** /bɑtimɑ̃/ *nm* building; (industrie) building trade; (navire) vessel.

**bâtir** /bɑtiʀ/ [2] *vt* build.

**bâton** /bɑtɔ̃/ *nm* stick; **conversation à ~s rompus** rambling conversation; **~ de rouge** lipstick.

**battant** /batɑ̃/ *nm* (vantail) flap; **porte à deux ~s** double door.

**battement** /batmɑ̃/ *nm* (de cœur) beat(ing); (temps) interval; (Mus) beat.

**batterie** /batʀi/ *nf* (Mil, Électr) battery; (Mus) drums; **~ de cuisine** pots and pans.

**batteur** /batœʀ/ *nm* (Mus) drummer; (Culin) whisk.

**battre** /batʀ/ [11] *vt/i* beat; (*cartes*) shuffle; (Culin) whisk; (l'emporter sur) beat; **~ des ailes** flap its wings; **~ des mains** clap; **~ des paupières** blink; **~ en retraite** beat a retreat; **~ la semelle** stamp one's feet; **~ son plein** be in full swing. □ **se ~** *vpr* fight.

**baume** /bom/ *nm* balm.

**bavard**, **~e** /bavaʀ, -d/ *a* talkative. ● *nm,f* chatterbox.

**bavardage** /bavaʀdaʒ/ *nm* chatter, gossip. **bavarder** [1] *vi* chat; (jacasser) chatter, gossip.

**bave** /bav/ *nf* dribble, slobber; (de limace) slime. **baver** [1] *vi* dribble, slobber. **baveux**, **-euse** *a* dribbling; (*omelette*) runny.

**bavoir** /bavwaʀ/ *nm* bib.

**bavure** /bavyʀ/ *nf* smudge; (erreur) blunder; **~ policière** police blunder.

**bazar** /bazaʀ/ *nm* bazaar; (objets [I]) clutter.

**BCBG** *abrév mf* (**bon chic bon genre**) posh.

**BD** *abrév f* (**bande dessinée**) comic strip.

**béant**, **~e** /beɑ̃, -t/ *a* gaping.

**béat**, **~e** /bea, -t/ *a* (hum) blissful; **~ d'admiration** wide-eyed with admiration.

**beau** (**bel** *before vowel or mute h*), **belle** (*mpl* **~x**) /bo, bɛl/ *a* beautiful; (*femme*) beautiful; (*homme*) handsome; (*temps*) fine, nice. ● *nm* beauty. ● *adv* **il fait ~** the weather is nice; **au ~ milieu** right in the middle; **bel et bien** well and truly; **de plus belle** more than ever; **faire le ~** sit up and beg; **on a ~ essayer/insister** however much one tries/insists.

**beaucoup** /boku/ *adv* a lot, very much; **~ de** (nombre) many; (quantité) a lot of; **pas ~ (de)** not many; (quantité) not much; **~ plus/mieux** much more/better; **~ trop** far too much; **de ~** by far.

**beau-fils** (*pl* **beaux-fils**) /bofis/ *nm* (remariage) stepson.

**beau-frère** (*pl* **beaux-frères**) /bofʀɛʀ/ *nm* brother-in-law.

**beau-père** (*pl* **beaux-pères**) /bopɛʀ/ *nm* father-in-law; (remariage) stepfather.

**beauté** /bote/ *nf* beauty; **finir en ~** end magnificently.

**beaux-arts** /bozaʀ/ *nmpl* fine arts.

**beaux-parents** /bopaʀɑ̃/ *nmpl* parents-in-law.

**bébé** /bebe/ *nm* baby. **bébé-éprouvette** (*pl* **bébés-éprouvette**) *nm* test-tube baby.

**bec** /bɛk/ *nm* beak; (de théière) spout; (de casserole) lip; (bouche 🅘) mouth; **~ de gaz** gas street-lamp.

**bécane** /bekan/ *nf* 🅘 bike.

**bêche** /bɛʃ/ *nf* spade.

**bégayer** /begeje/ [31] *vt/i* stammer.

**bègue** /bɛg/ *nmf* stammerer. ● *a* **être ~** stammer.

**bégueule** /begœl/ *a* prudish.

**beige** /bɛʒ/ *a & nm* beige.

**beignet** /bɛɲɛ/ *nm* fritter.

**bel** /bɛl/ ⇒BEAU.

**bêler** /bele/ [1] *vi* bleat.

**belette** /bəlɛt/ *nf* weasel.

**belge** /bɛlʒ/ *a* Belgian. **B~** *nmf* Belgian.

**Belgique** /bɛlʒik/ *nf* Belgium.

**bélier** /belje/ *nm* ram; **le B~** Aries.

**belle** /bɛl/ ⇒BEAU.

**belle-fille** (*pl* **belles-filles**) /bɛlfij/ *nf* daughter-in-law; (remariage) stepdaughter.

**belle-mère** (*pl* **belles-mères**) /bɛlmɛʀ/ *nf* mother-in-law; (remariage) stepmother.

**belle-sœur** (*pl* **belles-sœurs**) /bɛlsœʀ/ *nf* sister-in-law.

**belliqueux, -euse** /belikø, -z/ *a* warlike.

**bémol** /bemɔl/ *nm* (Mus) flat.

**bénédiction** /benediksjɔ̃/ *nf* blessing.

**bénéfice** /benefis/ *nm* (gain) profit; (avantage) benefit.

**bénéficiaire** /benefisjɛʀ/ *nmf* beneficiary.

**bénéficier** /benefisje/ [45] *vi* **~ de** benefit from; (jouir de) enjoy, have.

**bénéfique** /benefik/ *a* beneficial.

**Bénélux** /benelyks/ *nm* Benelux.

**bénévole** /benevɔl/ *a* voluntary.

**bénin, -igne** /benɛ̃, -iɲ/ *a* minor; (*tumeur*) benign.

**bénir** /beniʀ/ [2] *vt* bless. **bénit, ~e** *a* (*eau*) holy; (*pain*) consecrated.

**benjamin, ~e** /bɛ̃ʒamɛ̃, -in/ *nm,f* youngest child.

**benne** /bɛn/ *nf* (de grue) scoop; **~ à ordures** (camion) waste disposal truck; (conteneur) skip; **~ (basculante)** dump truck.

**béquille** /bekij/ *nf* crutch; (de moto) stand.

**berceau** (*pl* **~x**) /bɛʀso/ *nm* (de bébé, civilisation) cradle.

**bercer** /bɛʀse/ [10] *vt* (balancer) rock; (apaiser) lull; (leurrer) delude.

**béret** /beʀɛ/ *nm* beret.

**berge** /bɛʀʒ/ *nf* (bord) bank.

**berger**, **-ère** /bɛʀʒe, -ɛʀ/ *nm,f* shepherd, shepherdess.

**berne**: **en ~** /ɑ̃bɛʀn/ *loc* at half-mast.

**berner** /bɛʀne/ [1] *vt* fool.

**besogne** /bəzɔɲ/ *nf* task, job.

**besoin** /bəzwɛ̃/ *nm* need; **avoir ~ de** need; **au ~** if need be; **dans le ~** in need.

**bestiole** /bɛstjɔl/ *nf* [I] bug.

**bétail** /betaj/ *nm* livestock.

**bête** /bɛt/ *a* stupid. ● *nf* animal; **~ noire** pet hate; **~ sauvage** wild beast; **chercher la petite ~** be over-fussy.

**bêtise** /betiz/ *nf* stupidity; (action) stupid thing.

**béton** /betɔ̃/ *nm* concrete; **~ armé** reinforced concrete; [illegible] (alibi) concrete; (*argument* [I]) water-tight. **bétonnière** *nf* concrete mixer.

**betterave** /bɛtʀav/ *nf* beet; **~ rouge** beetroot.

**beugler** /bøgle/ [1] *vi* bellow; (*radio*) blare out.

**beur** /bœʀ/ *nmf & a* [I] second-generation North African living in France.

**beurre** /bœʀ/ *nm* butter. **beurré**, **~e** *a* buttered; [I] drunk. **beurrier** *nm* butter-dish.

**bévue** /bevy/ *nf* blunder.

**biais** /bjɛ/ *nm* (moyen) way; **par le ~ de** by means of; **de ~**, **en ~** at an angle; **regarder qn de ~** look sideways at sb.

**bibelot** /biblo/ *nm* ornament.

**biberon** /bibʀɔ̃/ *nm* (feeding) bottle; **nourrir au ~** bottle-feed.

**bible** /bibl/ *nf* bible; **la B~** the Bible.

**bibliographie** /biblijɔgʀafi/ *nf* bibliography.

**bibliothécaire** /biblijɔtekɛʀ/ *nmf* librarian.

**bibliothèque** /biblijɔtɛk/ *nf* library; (meuble) bookcase.

**bic**® /bik/ *nm* biro®.

**bicarbonate** /bikaʀbɔnat/ *nm* **~ (de soude)** bicarbonate (of soda).

**biceps** /bisɛps/ *nm* biceps.

**biche** /biʃ/ *nf* doe; **ma ~** darling.

**bichonner** /biʃɔne/ [1] *vt* pamper.

**bicyclette** /bisiklɛt/ *nf* bicycle.

**bide** /bid/ *nm* (ventre [I]) paunch; (échec [I]) flop.

**bidet** /bidɛ/ *nm* bidet.

**bidon** /bidɔ̃/ *nm* can; (plus grand) drum; (ventre [I]) belly; **c'est du ~** [I] it's a load of hogwash [I]. ● *a inv* [I] phoney.

**bidonville** /bidɔ̃vil/ *nf* shanty town.

**bidule** /bidyl/ *nm* [I] thing.

**Biélorussie** /bjelɔʀysi/ *nf* Byelorussia.

**bien** /bjɛ̃/ *adv* well; (très) quite, very; **~ des** (nombre) many; **tu as ~ de la chance** you are very lucky; **j'aimerais ~** I would like to; **ce n'est pas ~ de** it is not nice to; **~ sûr** of course. ● *nm* good; (patrimoine) possession; **~s de consommation** consumer goods. ● *a inv* good; (passable) all right; (en forme) well; (à l'aise) comfortable; (beau) attractive; (respectable) nice, respectable. ● *conj* **~ que** (al-)though; **~ que ce soit** although it is. **bien-aimé**, **~e** *a & nm,f* beloved. **bien-être** *nm* well-being.

**bienfaisance** /bjɛ̃fəzɑ̃s/ *nf* charity; **fête de ~** charity event. **bienfaisant**, **~e** *a* beneficial.

**bienfait** /bjɛ̃fɛ/ *nm* (kind) favour; (avantage) beneficial effect. **bienfaiteur**, **-trice** *nm,f* benefactor.

**bien-pensant**, **~e** /bjɛ̃pɑ̃sɑ̃, -t/ *a* right-thinking.

**bienséance** /bjɛ̃seɑ̃s/ *nf* propriety.

**bientôt** /bjɛ̃to/ *adv* soon; **à ~** see you soon.

**bienveillance** /bjɛ̃vɛjɑ̃s/ *nf* kind(li)ness.

**bienvenu**, **~e** /bjɛ̃vny/ *a* welcome. ● *nm,f* **être le ~, être la ~e** be welcome.

**bienvenue** /bjɛ̃vny/ *nf* welcome; **souhaiter la ~ à** welcome.

**bière** /bjɛʀ/ *nf* beer; (cercueil) coffin; **~ blonde** lager; **~ brune** ≈ stout; **~ pression** draught beer.

**bifteck** /biftɛk/ *nm* steak.

**bifurquer** /bifyʀke/ [1] *vi* branch off, fork.

**bigarré**, **~e** /bigaʀe/ *a* motley.

**bigoudi** /bigudi/ *nm* curler.

**bijou** (*pl* **~x**) /biʒu/ *nm* jewel; **~x en or** gold jewellery. **bijouterie** *nf* (boutique) jewellery shop; (Comm) jewellery. **bijoutier**, **-ière** *nm,f* jeweller.

**bilan** /bilɑ̃/ *nm* outcome; (d'une catastrophe) (casualty) toll; (Comm) balance sheet; **faire le ~ de** assess; **~ de santé** check-up.

**bile** /bil/ *nf* bile; **se faire de la ~** [I] worry.

**bilingue** /bilɛ̃g/ *a* bilingual.

**billard** /bijaʀ/ *nm* billiards (+ *pl*); (table) billiard-table.

**bille** /bij/ *nf* (d'enfant) marble; (de billard) billiard-ball.

**billet** /bijɛ/ *nm* ticket; (lettre) note; (article) column; **~ (de banque)** (bank) note; **~ de 50 francs** 50-franc note.

**billetterie** /bijɛtʀi/ *nf* cash dispenser.

**billion** /biljɔ̃/ *nm* billion; (US) trillion.

**bimensuel**, **~e** /bimɑ̃sɥɛl/ *a* fortnightly, bimonthly. ● *nm* fortnightly magazine.

**binette** /binɛt/ *nf* hoe; (visage) face; (Internet) smiley.

**biochimie** /bjɔʃimi/ *nf* biochemistry.

**biodégradable** /bjɔdegʀadabl/ *a* biodegradable.

**biographie** /bjɔgʀafi/ *nf* biography.

**biologie** /bjɔlɔʒi/ *nf* biology. **biologique** *a* biological; (*produit*) organic.

**bis** /bis/ *nm & interj* encore.

**biscornu**, **~e** /biskɔʀny/ *a* crooked; (bizarre) cranky [I].

**biscotte** /biskɔt/ *nf* continental toast.

**biscuit** /biskɥi/ *nm* biscuit; (US) cookie; **~ salé** cracker; **~ de Savoie** sponge-cake.

**bise** /biz/ *nf* [I] kiss; (vent) north wind.

**bison** /bizɔ̃/ *nm* buffalo.

**bisou** /bizu/ *nm* [I] kiss.

**bistro(t)** /bistʀo/ *nm* [I] café, bar.

**bit** /bit/ *nm* (Ordinat) bit.

**bitume** /bitym/ *nm* asphalt.

**bizarre** /bizaʀ/ *a* odd, strange. **bizzarerie** *nf* peculiarity.

**blafard**, **~e** /blafaʀ, -d/ *a* pale.

**blague** /blag/ *nf* [I] joke; **sans ~!** no kidding! [I].

**blaguer** /blage/ [1] [I] *vi* joke.

**blaireau** (*pl* **~x**) /blɛʀo/ *nm* shaving-brush; (animal) badger.

**blâmer** /blame/ [1] *vt* criticize.

**blanc**, **blanche** /blɑ̃, blɑ̃ʃ/ *a* white; (*papier, page*) blank. ● *nm* white; (espace) blank; **~ d'œuf** egg white; **~ de poireau** white part of the leek; **~ (de poulet)** chicken breast; **le ~** (linge) whites; **laisser en ~** leave blank. **B~**, **Blanche** *nm,f* white man, white woman. **blanche** *nf* (Mus) minim.

**blanchiment** /blɑ̃ʃimɑ̃/ *nm* (d'argent) laundering.

**blanchir** /blɑ̃ʃiʀ/ [2] *vt* whiten; (*personne*: fig) clear; (*argent*) launder; (Culin) blanch; **~ (à la chaux)** whitewash. ● *vi* turn white.

**blanchisserie** /blɑ̃ʃisʀi/ *nf* laundry.

**blason** /blazɔ̃/ *nm* coat of arms.

**blasphème** /blasfɛm/ *nm* blasphemy.

**blé** /ble/ *nm* wheat.

**blême** /blɛm/ *a* pallid.

**blessant**, **~e** /blesɑ̃, -t/ *a* hurtful.

**blessé**, **~e** /blese/ *nm,f* casualty, injured person.

**blesser** /blese/ [1] *vt* injure, hurt; (par balle) wound; (offenser) hurt. □ **se ~** *vpr* injure *ou* hurt oneself. **blessure** *nf* wound.

**bleu**, **~e** /blø/ *a* blue; (Culin) very rare; **~ marine/turquoise** navy blue/turquoise; **avoir une peur ~e** be scared stiff. ● *nm* blue; (contusion) bruise; **~ (de travail)** overalls (+ *pl*).

**bleuet** /bløɛ/ *nm* cornflower.

**blindé**, **~e** /blɛ̃de/ *a* armoured; (fig) immune (**contre** to); **porte ~e** security car. ● *nm* armoured car, tank.

**blinder** /blɛ̃de/ [1] *vt* armour; (fig) harden.

**bloc** /blɔk/ *nm* block; (de papier) pad; **serrer à ~** tighten hard; **en ~** (matériau) in a block; (nier) outright.

**blocage** /blɔkaʒ/ *nm* (des prix) freeze, freezing; (des roues) locking; (Psych) block.

**bloc-notes** (*pl* **blocs-notes**) /blɔknɔt/ *nm* note-pad.

**blocus** /blɔkys/ *nm* blockade.

**blond**, **~e** /blɔ̃, -d/ *a* fair, blond. ● *nm,f* fair-haired man, fair-haired woman.

**bloquer** /blɔke/ [1] *vt* block; (*porte, machine*) jam; (*roues*) lock; (*prix, crédits*) freeze. □ **se ~** *vpr* jam; (*roues*) lock; (*freins*) jam; (*ordinateur*) crash; **bloqué par la neige** snowbound.

**blottir (se)** /(sə)blɔtiʀ/ [2] *vpr* snuggle, huddle (**contre** against).

**blouse** /bluz/ *nf* overall. **blouse blanche** *nf* white coat.

**blouson** /bluzɔ̃/ *nm* jacket, blouson.

**bluffer** /blœfe/ [1] *vt/i* bluff.

**bobine** /bɔbin/ *nf* (de fil, film) reel; (Électr) coil.

**bobo** /bobo/ *nm* [I] sore, cut; **avoir ~** have a pain.

**bocal** (*pl* **-aux**) /bɔkal, -o/ *nm* jar.

**bœuf** (*pl* **~s**) /bœf, bø/ *nm* bullock; (US) steer; (viande) beef; **~s** oxen.

**bogue** /bɔg/ *nm* (Ordinat) bug.

**bohème** /bɔɛm/ *a & nmf* bohemian.

**boire** /bwaʀ/ [12] *vt/i* (*personne, plante*) drink; (*argile*) soak up; **~ un coup** [I] have a drink.

**bois** /bwa/ ⇒BOIRE [12]. ● *nm* (matériau, forêt) wood; **de ~**, **en ~** wooden. ● *nmpl* (de cerf) antlers.

**boiseries** /bwazʀi/ *nfpl* panelling.

**boisson** /bwasɔ̃/ *nf* drink.

**boit** /bwa/ ⇒BOIRE [12].

**boîte** /bwat/ *nf* box; (de conserves) tin, can; (entreprise [I]) firm; **en ~** tinned, canned; **~ à gants** glove compartment; **~ aux lettres** letter-

box; ~ **aux lettres électronique**, **blé** mailbox; ~ **de nuit** night-club; ~ **postale** post-office box; ~ **de vitesses** gear box.

**boiter** /bwate/ [1] *vi* limp. **boiteux**, **-euse** *a* lame; (*raisonnement*) shaky.

**boîtier** /bwatje/ *nm* case.

**bol** /bɔl/ *nm* bowl; ~ **d'air** a breath of fresh air; **avoir du** ~ 🄸 be lucky.

**bolide** /bɔlid/ *nm* racing car.

**Bolivie** /bɔlivi/ *nf* Bolivia.

**bombardement** /bɔ̃baʀdəmɑ̃/ *nm* bombing; shelling.

**bombarder** /bɔ̃baʀde/ [1] *vt* bomb; (par obus) shell; ~ **qn de** (fig) bombard sb with. **bombardier** *nm* (Aviat) bomber.

**bombe** /bɔ̃b/ *nf* bomb; (atomiseur) spray, aerosol.

**bombé**, ~**e** /bɔ̃be/ *a* rounded; (*route*) cambered.

**bon**, **bonne** /bɔ̃, bɔn/ *a* good; (qui convient) right; ~ **à**/**pour** (approprié) fit to/for; **bonne année** happy New Year; ~ **anniversaire** happy birthday; ~ **appétit**/**voyage** enjoy your meal/trip; **bonne chance**/**nuit** good luck/night; ~ **sens** common sense; **bonne femme** (péj) woman; **de bonne heure** early; **à quoi** ~? what's the point? ● *adv* **sentir** ~ smell nice; **tenir** ~ stand firm; **il fait** ~ the weather is mild. ● *interj* right, well. ● *nm* (billet) voucher, coupon; ~ **de commande** order form; **pour de** ~ for good. **bonne** *nf* (domestique) maid.

**bonbon** /bɔ̃bɔ̃/ *nm* sweet; (US) candy.

**bonbonne** /bɔ̃bɔn/ *nf* demijohn; (de gaz) cylinder.

**bond** /bɔ̃/ *nm* leap; **faire un** ~ (de surprise) jump.

**bonde** /bɔ̃d/ *nf* plug; (trou) plughole.

**bondé**, ~**e** /bɔ̃de/ *a* packed.

**bondir** /bɔ̃diʀ/ [2] *vi* leap; (de surprise) jump.

**bonheur** /bɔnœʀ/ *nm* happiness; (chance) (good) luck; **au petit** ~ haphazardly; **par** ~ luckily.

**bonhomme** (*pl* **bonshommes**) /bɔnɔm, bɔ̃zɔm/ *nm* fellow; ~ **de neige** snowman. ● *a inv* goodhearted.

**bonifier (se)** /(sə)bɔnifje/ [45] *vpr* improve.

**bonjour** /bɔ̃ʒuʀ/ *nm & interj* hallo, hello, good morning *ou* afternoon.

**bon marché** /bɔ̃maʀʃe/ *a inv* cheap. ● *adv* cheap(ly).

**bonne** /bɔn/ ⇒BON.

**bonne-maman** (*pl* **bonnes-mamans**) /bɔnmamɑ̃/ *nf* 🄸 granny.

**bonnement** /bɔnmɑ̃/ *adv* **tout** ~ quite simply.

**bonnet** /bɔnɛ/ *nm* hat; (de soutien-gorge) cup; ~ **de bain** swimming cap. **bonneterie** *nf* hosiery.

**bonsoir** /bɔ̃swaʀ/ *nm* good evening; (en se couchant) good night.

**bonté** /bɔ̃te/ *nf* kindness.

**bonus** /bɔnys/ *nm* (Auto) no-claims bonus.

**boots** /buts/ *nmpl* ankle boots.

**bord** /bɔʀ/ *nm* edge; (rive) bank; **à** ~ **(de)** on board; **au** ~ **de la mer** at the seaside; **au** ~ **des larmes** on the verge of tears; ~ **de la route** roadside.

**bordeaux** /bɔʀdo/ *a inv* maroon. ● *nm inv* Bordeaux.

**bordel** /bɔʀdɛl/ *nm* brothel; (désordre 🄸) shambles.

**border** /bɔʀde/ [1] *vt* line, border; (*tissu*) edge; (*personne*, *lit*) tuck in.

**bordereau** (*pl* ~**x**) /bɔʀdəʀo/ *nm* (document) slip.

**bordure** /bɔʀdyʀ/ *nf* border; **en ~ de** on the edge of.

**borgne** /bɔʀɲ/ *a* one-eyed.

**borne** /bɔʀn/ *nf* boundary marker; (pour barrer le passage) bollard; **~ (kilométrique)** ≈ milestone; **~s** limits.

**borné**, **~e** /bɔʀne/ *a* (*esprit*) narrow; (*personne*) narrow-minded.

**borner (se)** /(sə)bɔʀne/ [1] *vpr* confine oneself (**à** to).

**bosniaque** /bɔsnjak/ *a* Bosnian. **B~** *nmf* Bosnian.

**Bosnie** /bɔsni/ *nf* Bosnia.

**bosse** /bɔs/ *nf* bump; (de chameau) hump; **avoir la ~ de** [!] have a gift for; **avoir roulé sa ~** have been around. **bosselé**, **~e** *a* dented; (*terrain*) bumpy.

**bosser** /bɔse/ [1] *vi* [!] work (hard).

**bossu**, **~e** /bɔsy/ *a* hunchbacked. ● *nm,f* hunchback.

**botanique** /bɔtanik/ *nf* botany ● *a* botanical.

**botte** /bɔt/ *nf* boot; (de fleurs, légumes) bunch; (de paille) bundle, bale; **~s de caoutchouc** wellingtons.

**botter** /bɔte/ [1] *vt* [!] **ça me botte** I like the idea.

**bottin®** /bɔtɛ̃/ *nm* phone book.

**bouc** /buk/ *nm* (billy-)goat; (barbe) goatee; **~ émissaire** scapegoat.

**boucan** /bukɑ̃/ *nm* [!] din.

**bouche** /buʃ/ *nf* mouth; (lèvres) lips; **~ bée** open-mouthed; **~ d'égout** manhole; **~ d'incendie** (fire) hydrant; **~ de métro** entrance to the underground *ou* subway (US). **bouche-à-bouche** *nm inv* mouth-to-mouth resuscitation. **bouche-à-oreille** *nm inv* word of mouth.

**bouché**, **~e** /buʃe/ *a* (*profession, avenir*) oversubscribed; (stupide; péj) stupid.

**bouchée** /buʃe/ *nf* mouthful.

**boucher[1]** /buʃe/ [1] *vt* block; (*bouteille*) cork. □ **se ~** *vpr* get blocked; **se ~ le nez** hold one's nose.

**boucher[2]**, **-ère** /buʃe, -ɛʀ/ *nm,f* butcher. **boucherie** *nf* butcher's (shop); (carnage) butchery.

**bouchon** /buʃɔ̃/ *nm* stopper; (en liège) cork; (de stylo, tube) cap; (de pêcheur) float; (embouteillage) traffic jam; **~ de cérumen** plug of earwax.

**boucle** /bukl/ *nf* (de ceinture) buckle; (de cheveux) curl; (forme) loop; **~ d'oreille** earring. **bouclé**, **~e** *a* (*cheveux*) curly.

**boucler** /bukle/ [1] *vt* fasten; (enfermer [!]) shut up; (encercler) seal off; (*budget*) balance; (terminer) finish off. ● *vi* curl.

**bouclier** /buklije/ *nm* shield.

**bouddhiste** /budist/ *a & nmf* Buddhist.

**bouder** /bude/ [1] *vi* sulk. ● *vt* stay away from.

**boudin** /budɛ̃/ *nm* black pudding.

**boue** /bu/ *nf* mud.

**bouée** /bwe/ *nf* buoy; **~ de sauvetage** lifebuoy.

**boueux**, **-euse** /buø, -z/ *a* muddy.

**bouffe** /buf/ *nf* [!] food, grub.

**bouffée** /bufe/ *nf* puff, whiff; (d'orgueil) fit; **~ de chaleur** (Méd) hot flush.

**bouffi**, **~e** /bufi/ *a* bloated.

**bouffon**, **~ne** /bufɔ̃, -ɔn/ *a* farcical. ● *nm* buffoon.

**bougeoir** /buʒwaʀ/ *nm* candlestick.

**bougeotte** /buʒɔt/ *nf* **avoir la ~** [!] have the fidgets.

**bouger** /buʒe/ [40] *vt/i* move. □ **se ~** *vpr* [!] move.

**bougie** /buʒi/ *nf* candle; (Auto) spark(ing)-plug.

**bouillant**, **~e** /bujɑ̃, -t/ *a* boiling; (très chaud) boiling hot.

**bouillie** /buji/ *nf* (pour bébé) baby cereal; (péj) mush; **en ~** crushed, mushy.

**bouillir** /bujiʀ/ [13] *vi* boil; (fig) seethe; **faire ~** boil.

**bouilloire** /bujwaʀ/ *nf* kettle.

**bouillon** /bujɔ̃/ *nm* (de cuisson) stock; (potage) broth.

**bouillonner** /bujɔne/ [1] *vi* bubble.

**bouillotte** /bujɔt/ *nf* hot-water bottle.

**boulanger**, **-ère** /bulɑ̃ʒe, -ɛʀ/ *nm,f* baker. **boulangerie** *nf* bakery. **boulangerie-pâtisserie** *nf* bakery (*selling cakes and pastries*).

**boule** /bul/ *nf* ball; **~s** (jeu) boules; **jouer aux ~s** play boules; **une ~ dans la gorge** a lump in one's throat; **~ de neige** snowball.

**bouleau** (*pl* **~x**) /bulo/ *nm* (silver) birch.

**boulet** /bulɛ/ *nm* (de forçat) ball and chain; **~ (de canon)** canonball; **~ de charbon** coal nut.

**boulette** /bulɛt/ *nf* (de pain, papier) pellet; (bévue) blunder; **~ de viande** meat ball.

**boulevard** /bulvaʀ/ *nm* boulevard.

**bouleversant**, **~e** /bulvɛʀsɑ̃, -t/ *a* deeply moving. **bouleversement** *nm* upheaval. **bouleverser** [1] *vt* turn upside down; (*pays, plans*) disrupt; (émouvoir) upset.

**boulimie** /bulimi/ *nf* bulimia.

**boulon** /bulɔ̃/ *nm* bolt.

**boulot**, **~te** /bulo, -ɔt/ *a* (rond Ⓘ) dumpy. ● *nm* (travail Ⓘ) work.

**boum** /bum/ *nm & interj* bang. ● *nf* (fête Ⓘ) party.

**bouquet** /bukɛ/ *nm* (de fleurs) bunch, bouquet; (d'arbres) clump; **c'est le ~!** Ⓘ that's the last straw!

**bouquin** /bukɛ̃/ *nm* Ⓘ book. **bouquiner** [1] *vt/i* Ⓘ read. **bouquiniste** *nmf* second-hand bookseller.

**bourbier** /buʀbje/ *nm* mire; (fig) tangle.

**bourde** /buʀd/ *nf* blunder.

**bourdon** /buʀdɔ̃/ *nm* bumble-bee. **bourdonnement** *nm* buzzing.

**bourg** /buʀ/ *nm* (market) town (centre), village centre.

**bourgeois**, **~e** /buʀʒwa, -z/ *a & nm,f* middle-class (person); (péj) bourgeois. **bourgeoisie** *nf* middle class(es).

**bourgeon** /buʀʒɔ̃/ *nm* bud.

**bourgogne** /buʀgɔɲ/ *nm* Burgundy.

**bourlinguer** /buʀlɛ̃ge/ [1] *vi* Ⓘ travel about.

**bourrage** /buʀaʒ/ *nm* **~ de crâne** brainwashing.

**bourratif**, **-ive** /buʀatif, -v/ *a* stodgy.

**bourreau** (*pl* **~x**) /buʀo/ *nm* executioner; **~ de travail** (fig) workaholic.

**bourrelet** /buʀlɛ/ *nm* weatherstrip, draught excluder; (de chair) roll of fat.

**bourrer** /buʀe/ [1] *vt* cram (**de** with); (*pipe*) fill; **~ de** (*nourriture*) stuff with; **~ de coups** thrash; **~ le crâne à qn** brainwash sb.

**bourrique** /buʀik/ *nf* donkey; Ⓘ pig-headed person.

**bourru**, **~e** /buʀy/ *a* gruff.

**bourse** /buʀs/ *nf* purse; (subvention) grant; **la B~** the Stock Exchange.

**boursier**, **-ière** /buʀsje, -jɛʀ/ *a* (*valeurs*) Stock Exchange. ● *nm,f* grant holder.

**boursoufler** /buʀsufle/ [1] *vt* (visage) cause to swell; (peinture) blister.

**bousculade** /buskylad/ *nf* crush; (précipitation) rush. **bousculer** [1] *vt* (pousser) jostle; (presser) rush; (renverser) knock over.

**bousiller** /buzije/ [1] *vt* [I] wreck.

**boussole** /busɔl/ *nf* compass.

**bout** /bu/ *nm* end; (de langue, bâton) piece; (morceau) bit; **à ~** exhausted; **à ~ de souffle** out of breath; **à ~ portant** point-blank; **au ~ de** (après) after; **venir à ~ de** (finir) manage to finish; **d'un ~ à l'autre** throughout; **au ~ du compte** in the end; **~ filtre** filter-tip.

**bouteille** /butɛj/ *nf* bottle; **~ d'oxygène** oxygen cylinder.

**boutique** /butik/ *nf* shop; (de mode) boutique.

**bouton** /butɔ̃/ *nm* button; (sur la peau) spot, pimple; (pousse) bud; (de porte, radio) knob; **~ de manchette** cuff-link. **boutonner** [1] *vt* button (up). **boutonnière** *nf* buttonhole. **bouton-pression** (*pl* **boutons-pression**) *nm* press-stud; (US) snap.

**bouture** /butyʀ/ *nf* cutting.

**bovin**, **~e** /bɔvɛ̃, -in/ *a* bovine. **bovins** *nmpl* cattle (*pl*).

**box** (*pl* **~ ou boxes**) /bɔks/ *nm* lock-up garage; (de dortoir) cubicle; (d'écurie) (loose) box; (Jur) dock.

**boxe** /bɔks/ *nf* boxing.

**boyau** (*pl* **~x**) /bwajo/ *nm* gut; (corde) catgut; (galerie) gallery; (de bicyclette) tyre; (US) tire.

**boycotter** /bɔjkɔte/ [1] *vt* boycott.

**BP** *abrév f* (**boîte postale**) PO Box.

**bracelet** /bʀaslɛ/ *nm* bracelet; (de montre) watchstrap.

**braconnier** /bʀakɔnje/ *nm* poacher.

**brader** /bʀade/ [1] *vt* sell off. **braderie** *nf* clearance sale.

**braguette** /bʀagɛt/ *nf* fly.

**braille** /bʀaj/ *nm & a* Braille.

**brailler** /bʀɑje/ [1] *vt/i* bawl.

**braise** /bʀɛz/ *nf* embers (+ *pl*).

**braiser** /bʀeze/ [1] *vt* (Culin) braise.

**brancard** /bʀɑ̃kaʀ/ *nm* stretcher; (de charrette) shaft.

**branche** /bʀɑ̃ʃ/ *nf* branch.

**branché**, **~e** /bʀɑ̃ʃe/ *a* [I] trendy.

**branchement** /bʀɑ̃ʃmɑ̃/ *nm* connection. **brancher** [1] *vt* (*prise*) plug in; (à un réseau) connect.

**brandir** /bʀɑ̃diʀ/ [2] *vt* brandish.

**branler** /bʀɑ̃le/ [1] *vi* be shaky.

**braquer** /bʀake/ [1] *vt* (*arme*) aim; (*regard*) fix; (*roue*) turn; (*banque*: [I]) hold up; **~ qn contre** turn sb against. ● *vi* (Auto) turn (the wheel). □ **se ~** *vpr* dig one's heels in.

**bras** /bʀa/ *nm* arm; (de rivière) branch; (Tech) arm; **~ dessus ~ dessous** arm in arm; **~ droit** (fig) right-hand man; **~ de mer** sound; **en ~ de chemise** in one's shirt-sleeves. ● *nmpl* (fig) labour, hands.

**brasier** /bʀɑzje/ *nm* blaze.

**brassard** /bʀasaʀ/ *nm* armband.

**brasse** /bʀas/ *nf* breast-stroke; **~ papillon** butterfly (stroke).

**brasser** /bʀase/ [1] *vt* mix; (*bière*) brew; (*affaires*) handle a lot of. **brasserie** *nf* brewery; (café) brasserie.

**brave** /bʀav/ *a* (bon) good; (valeureux) brave. **braver** [1] *vt* defy.

**bravo** /bʀavo/ *interj* bravo. ● *nm* cheer.

**bravoure** /bʀavuʀ/ *nf* bravery.

**break** /bʀɛk/ *nm* estate car; (US) station-wagon.

**brebis** /bʀəbi/ *nf* ewe.

**brèche** /bʀɛʃ/ *nf* gap, breach; **être sur la ~** be on the go.

**bredouille** /bʀəduj/ *a* empty-handed.

**bredouiller** /bʀəduje/ [1] *vt/i* mumble.

**bref, brève** /bʀɛf, -v/ *a* short, brief. ● *adv* in short; **en ~** in short.

**Brésil** /bʀezil/ *nm* Brazil.

**Bretagne** /bʀətaɲ/ *nf* Brittany.

**bretelle** /bʀətɛl/ *nf* (de sac, maillot) strap; (d'autoroute) access road; **~s** (pour pantalon) braces; (US) suspenders.

**breton, ~ne** /bʀətɔ̃, -ɔn/ *a & nm* (Ling) Breton. **B~, ~ne** *nm,f* Breton.

**breuvage** /bʀœvaʒ/ *nm* beverage.

**brève** /bʀɛv/ ⇒BREF.

**brevet** /bʀəvɛ/ *nm* **~ (d'invention)** patent; (diplôme) diploma.

**breveté, ~e** /bʀəvte/ *a* patented.

**bribes** /bʀib/ *nfpl* scraps.

**bricolage** /bʀikɔlaʒ/ *nm* do-it-yourself (jobs).

**bricole** /bʀikɔl/ *nf* trifle.

**bricoler** /bʀikɔle/ [1] *vi* do DIY; (US) fix things, tinker with.

**bricoleur, -euse** /bʀikɔlœʀ, -øz/ *nm,f* handyman, handywoman.

**bride** /bʀid/ *nf* bridle.

**bridé, ~e** /bʀide/ *a* **yeux ~s** slanting eyes.

**brider** /bʀide/ [1] *vt* (*cheval*) bridle; (fig) keep in check.

**brièvement** /bʀijɛvmɑ̃/ *adv* briefly.

**brigade** /bʀigad/ *nf* (de police) squad; (Mil) brigade; (fig) team. **brigadier** *nm* (de gendarmerie) sergeant.

**brigand** /bʀigɑ̃/ *nm* robber.

**brillant, ~e** /bʀijɑ̃, -t/ *a* (*couleur*) bright; (luisant) shiny; (remarquable) brilliant. ● *nm* (éclat) shine; (diamant) diamond.

**briller** /bʀije/ [1] *vi* shine.

**brimade** /bʀimad/ *nf* vexation.

**brimer** [1] *vt* bully, harass; **se sentir brimé** feel put down.

**brin** /bʀɛ̃/ *nm* (de muguet) sprig; (d'herbe) blade; (de paille) wisp; **un ~ de** (un peu) a bit of.

**brindille** /bʀɛ̃dij/ *nf* twig.

**brioche** /bʀijɔʃ/ *nf* brioche, sweet bun; (ventre 🅘) paunch.

**brique** /bʀik/ *nf* brick.

**briquet** /bʀikɛ/ *nm* (cigarette-) lighter.

**brise** /bʀiz/ *nf* breeze.

**briser** /bʀize/ [1] *vt* break. ▫ **se ~** *vpr* break.

**britannique** /bʀitanik/ *a* British. **B~** *nmf* Briton; **les B~s** the British.

**brocante** /bʀɔkɑ̃t/ *nf* bric-à-brac trade; (marché) flea market.

**broche** /bʀɔʃ/ *nf* brooch; (Culin) spit; **à la ~** spit-roasted.

**broché, ~e** /bʀɔʃe/ *a* paperback.

**brochet** /bʀɔʃɛ/ *nm* pike.

**brochette** /bʀɔʃɛt/ *nf* skewer.

**brochure** /bʀɔʃyʀ/ *nf* brochure, booklet.

**broder** /bʀɔde/ [1] *vt/i* embroider.

**broderie** *nf* embroidery.

**broncher** /bʀɔ̃ʃe/ [1] *vi* **sans ~** without turning a hair.

**bronchite** /bʀɔ̃ʃit/ *nf* bronchitis.

**bronze** /bʀɔ̃z/ *nm* bronze.

**bronzé, ~e** /bʀɔ̃ze/ *a* (sun-) tanned.

**bronzer** /bʀɔ̃ze/ [1] *vi* (*personne*) get a (sun-)tan.

**brosse** /bʀɔs/ *nf* brush; **~ à dents** toothbrush; **~ à habits** clothes brush; **en ~** (*coiffure*) in a crew cut.

**brosser** /bʀɔse/ [1] *vt* brush; (fig) paint. □ **se** ~ *vpr* **se** ~ **les dents/les cheveux** brush one's teeth/hair.

**brouette** /bʀuɛt/ *nf* wheelbarrow.

**brouhaha** /bʀuaa/ *nm* hubbub.

**brouillard** /bʀujaʀ/ *nm* fog.

**brouille** /bʀuj/ *nf* quarrel.

**brouiller** /bʀuje/ [1] *vt* (*vue*) blur; (*œufs*) scramble; (*amis*) set at odds; ~ **les pistes** cloud the issue. □ **se** ~ *vpr* (*ciel*) cloud over; (*amis*) fall out.

**brouillon**, ~**ne** /bʀujɔ̃, -ɔn/ *a* untidy. ● *nm* (rough) draft.

**brousse** /bʀus/ *nf* **la** ~ the bush.

**brouter** /bʀute/ [1] *vt/i* graze.

**broyer** /bʀwaje/ [31] *vt* crush; (moudre) grind.

**bru** /bʀy/ *nf* daughter-in-law.

**bruine** /bʀɥin/ *nf* drizzle.

**bruissement** /bʀɥismɑ̃/ *nm* rustling.

**bruit** /bʀɥi/ *nm* noise; ~ **de couloir** (fig) rumour.

**bruitage** /bʀɥitaʒ/ *nm* sound effects.

**brûlant**, ~**e** /bʀylɑ̃, -t/ *a* burning (hot); (*sujet*) red-hot; (*passion*) fiery.

**brûlé** /bʀyle/ *nm* burning; **ça sent le** ~ I can smell something burning. ● ⇒BRÛLER [1].

**brûler** /bʀyle/ [1] *vt/i* burn; (*essence*) use (up); (*cierge*) light (à to); ~ **un feu (rouge)** jump the lights; ~ **d'envie de faire** be longing to do. □ **se** ~ *vpr* burn oneself.

**brûlure** /bʀylyʀ/ *nf* burn; ~**s d'estomac** heartburn.

**brume** /bʀym/ *nf* mist. **brumeux**, **-euse** *a* misty; (*esprit*) hazy.

**brun**, ~**e** /bʀœ̃, -yn/ *a* brown, dark. ● *nm* brown. ● *nm,f* dark-haired person. **brunir** [2] *vi* turn brown; (bronzer) get a tan.

**brushing** /bʀœʃiŋ/ *nm* blow-dry.

**brusque** /bʀysk/ *a* (*personne*) abrupt; (*geste*) violent; (soudain) sudden.

**brusquer** /bʀyske/ [1] *vt* be abrupt with; (précipiter) rush.

**brut**, ~**e** /bʀyt/ *a* (*diamant*) rough; (*champagne*) dry; (*pétrole*) crude; (Comm) gross.

**brutal**, ~**e** (*mpl* **-aux**) /bʀytal, -o/ *a* brutal. **brutalité** *nf* brutality.

**brute** /bʀyt/ *nf* brute.

**Bruxelles** /bʀysɛl/ *npr* Brussels.

**bruyant**, ~**e** /bʀɥijɑ̃, -t/ *a* noisy.

**bruyère** /bʀyjɛʀ/ *nf* heather.

**bu** /by/ ⇒BOIRE [12].

**bûche** /byʃ/ *nf* log; ~ **de Noël** Christmas log; **ramasser une** ~ [!] fall.

**bûcher** /byʃe/ [1] *vt/i* [!] slog away (at) [!]. ● *nm* (supplice) stake.

**bûcheron** /byʃʀɔ̃/ *nm* lumberjack.

**budget** /bydʒɛ/ *nm* budget. **budgétaire** *a* budgetary.

**buée** /bɥe/ *nf* condensation.

**buffet** /byfɛ/ *nm* sideboard; (table garnie) buffet.

**buffle** /byfl/ *nm* buffalo.

**buisson** /bɥisɔ̃/ *nm* bush.

**buissonnière** /bɥisɔnjɛʀ/ *af* **faire l'école** ~ play truant.

**bulbe** /bylb/ *nm* bulb.

**bulgare** /bylgaʀ/ *a & nm* Bulgarian. **B**~ *nmf* Bulgarian.

**Bulgarie** /bylgaʀi/ *nf* Bulgaria.

**bulldozer** /byldozɛʀ/ *nm* bulldozer.

**bulle** /byl/ *nf* bubble.

**bulletin** /byltɛ̃/ *nm* bulletin, report; (Scol) report; ~ **d'information** news bulletin; ~ **météorologique**

weather report; ~ **(de vote)** ballot-paper; ~ **de salaire** pay-slip.

**buraliste** /byʀalist/ *nmf* tobacconist.

**bureau** (*pl* ~**x**) /byʀo/ *nm* office; (meuble) desk; (comité) board; ~ **d'études** design office; ~ **de poste** post office; ~ **de tabac** tobacconist's (shop); ~ **de vote** polling station.

**bureaucrate** /byʀokʀat/ *nmf* bureaucrat. **bureaucratie** *nf* bureaucracy. **bureaucratique** *a* bureaucratic.

**bureautique** /byʀotik/ *nf* office automation.

**burlesque** /byʀlɛsk/ *a* (*histoire*) ludicrous; (*film*) farcical.

**bus** /bys/ *nm* bus.

**buste** /byst/ *nm* bust.

**but** /by(t)/ *nm* target; (dessein) aim, goal; (football) goal; **avoir pour** ~ **de** aim to; **de** ~ **en blanc** point-blank; **dans le** ~ **de** with the intention of; **aller droit au** ~ go straight to the point.

**butane** /bytan/ *nm* butane, Calor gas®.

**buté,~e** /byte/ *a* obstinate.

**buter** /byte/ [1] *vi* ~ **contre** knock against; (*problème*) come up against. ● *vt* antagonize. □ **se** ~ *vpr* (s'entêter) become obstinate.

**buteur** /bytœʀ/ *nm* (au football) striker.

**butin** /bytɛ̃/ *nm* booty, loot.

**butte** /byt/ *nf* mound; **en** ~ **à** exposed to.

**buvard** /byvaʀ/ *nm* blotting-paper.

**buvette** /byvɛt/ *nf* (refreshment) bar.

**buveur, -euse** /byvœʀ, -øz/ *nm,f* drinker.

# Cc

**c'** /s/ ⇒CE.

**ça** /sa/

● *pronom démonstratif*

····➤ (sujet) it; that; ~ **flotte** it floats; ~ **suffit!** that's enough!; ~ **y est!** that's it!; ~ **sent le brûlé** there's a smell of burning; ~ **va?** how are things?

····➤ (objet) (proche) this; (plus éloigné) that; **c'est** ~ that's right.

····➤ (dans expressions) **où** ~**?** where?; **quand** ~**?** when?; **et avec** ~**?** anything else?

**çà** /sa/ *adv* ~ **et là** here and there.

**cabane** /kaban/ *nf* hut; (à outils) shed.

**cabaret** /kabaʀɛ/ *nm* cabaret.

**cabillaud** /kabijo/ *nm* cod.

**cabine** /kabin/ *nf* (à la piscine) cubicle; (de bateau) cabin; (de camion) cab; (d'ascenseur) cage; ~ **d'essayage** fitting room; ~ **de pilotage** cockpit; ~ **de plage** beach hut; ~ **(téléphonique)** phone booth, phone box.

**cabinet** /kabinɛ/ *nm* (de médecin) surgery; (US) office; (d'avocat) office; (clientèle) practice; (cabinet collectif) firm; (Pol) Cabinet; (pièce) room; ~**s** (toilettes) toilet; (US) bathroom; ~ **de toilette** bathroom.

**câble** /kɑbl/ *nm* cable; (corde) rope; (TV) cable TV. **câbler** *vt* [1] cable; (TV) install cable television in.

**cabosser** /kabɔse/ [1] *vt* dent.

**cabotage** /kabɔtaʒ/ *nm* coastal navigation.

**cabrer** (**se**) /(sə)kabʀe/ [1] *vpr* (*cheval*) rear; **se ~ contre** rebel against.

**cabriole** /kabʀijɔl/ *nf* **faire des ~s** caper about.

**cacahuète** /kakawɛt/ *nf* peanut.

**cacao** /kakao/ *nm* cocoa.

**cachalot** /kaʃalo/ *nm* sperm whale.

**cache** /kaʃ/ *nm* mask. ● *nf* hiding place; **~ d'armes** arms cache.

**cache-cache** /kaʃkaʃ/ *nm inv* hide-and-seek.

**cache-nez** /kaʃne/ *nm inv* scarf.

**cacher** /kaʃe/ [1] *vt* hide, conceal (à from). □ **se ~** *vpr* hide; (se trouver caché) be hidden.

**cachet** /kaʃɛ/ *nm* (de cire) seal; (à l'encre) stamp; (de la poste) postmark; (comprimé) tablet; (d'artiste) fee; (chic) stylo, cachet.

**cachette** /kaʃɛt/ *nf* hiding-place; **en ~** in secret.

**cachot** /kaʃo/ *nm* dungeon.

**cachottier**, **-ière** /kaʃɔtjɛ, -jɛʀ/ *a* secretive.

**cacophonie** /kakɔfɔni/ *nf* cacophony.

**cactus** /kaktys/ *nm* cactus.

**cadavérique** /kadaveʀik/ *a* (*teint*) deathly pale.

**cadavre** /kadavʀ/ *nm* corpse; (de victime) body.

**caddie** /kadi/ *nm* (de supermarché)® trolley; (au golf) caddie.

**cadeau** (*pl* **~x**) /kado/ *nm* present, gift; **faire un ~ à qn** give sb a present.

**cadenas** /kadna/ *nm* padlock

**cadence** /kadɑ̃s/ *nf* rhythm, cadence; (de travail) rate; **en ~** in time; (*marcher*) in step.

**cadet**, **~te** /kadɛ, -t/ *a* youngest; (entre deux) younger. ● *nm, f* youngest (child); younger (child).

**cadran** /kadʀɑ̃/ *nm* dial; **~ solaire** sundial.

**cadre** /kɑdʀ/ *nm* frame; (lieu) setting; (milieu) surroundings; (limites) scope; (contexte) framework; **dans le ~ de** (à l'occasion de) on the occasion of; (dans le contexte de) in the framework of. ● *nm* (personne) executive; **les ~s** the managerial staff.

**cadrer** /kadʀe/ [1] *vi* **~ avec** tally with. ● *vt* (*photo*) centre.

**cafard** /kafaʀ/ *nm* (insecte) cockroach; **avoir le ~** [!] be down in the dumps.

**café** /kafe/ *nm* coffee; (bar) café; **~ crème** espresso with milk; **~ en grains** coffee beans; **~ au lait** white coffee.

**cafetière** /kaftjɛʀ/ *nf* coffee pot; **~ électrique** coffee machine.

**cage** /kaʒ/ *nf* cage; **~ d'ascenseur** lift shaft; **~ d'escalier** stairwell; **~ thoracique** rib cage.

**cageot** /kaʒo/ *nm* crate.

**cagibi** /kaʒibi/ *nm* storage room.

**cagneux**, **-euse** /kaɲø, -z/ *a* **avoir les genoux ~** be knock-kneed.

**cagnotte** /kaɲɔt/ *nf* kitty.

**cagoule** /kagul/ *nf* hood; (passe-montagne) balaclava.

**cahier** /kaje/ *nm* notebook; (Scol) exercise book; **~ de textes** homework notebook; **~ des charges** (Tech) specifications (+ *pl*).

**cahot** /kao/ *nm* bump, jolt. **cahoteux**, **-euse** *a* bumpy.

**caïd** /kaid/ *nm* [!] big shot.

**caille** /kɑj/ *nf* quail.

**cailler** /kɑje/ [1] *vi* curdle; **ça caille** Ⓘ it's freezing. ▫ **se ~** *vpr* (*sang*) clot; (*lait*) curdle. **caillot** *nm* (blood) clot.

**caillou** (*pl* **~x**) /kaju/ *nm* stone; (galet) pebble.

**caisse** /kɛs/ *nf* crate, case; (tiroir, machine) till; (guichet) cash desk; (au supermarché) check-out; (bureau) office; (Mus) drum; **~ enregistreuse** cash register; **~ d'épargne** savings bank; **~ de retraite** pension fund. **caissier, -ière** *nm,f* cashier.

**cajoler** /kaʒɔle/ [1] *vt* coax.

**calcaire** /kalkɛʀ/ *a* (*sol*) chalky; (*eau*) hard.

**calciné, ~e** /kalsine/ *a* charred.

**calcul** /kalkyl/ *nm* calculation; (Scol) arithmetic; (différentiel) calculus; **~ biliaire** gallstone.

**calculatrice** /kalkylatʀis/ *nf* calculator. **calculer** [1] *vt* calculate. **calculette** *nf* (pocket) calculator.

**cale** /kal/ *nf* wedge; (pour roue) chock; (de navire) hold; **~ sèche** dry dock.

**calé, ~e** /kale/ *a* Ⓘ clever.

**caleçon** /kalsɔ̃/ *nm* boxer shorts (+ *pl*); underpants (+ *pl*); (de femme) leggings.

**calembour** /kalɑ̃buʀ/ *nm* pun.

**calendrier** /kalɑ̃dʀije/ *nm* calendar; (fig) schedule, timetable.

**calepin** /kalpɛ̃/ *nm* notebook.

**caler** /kale/ [1] *vt* wedge. ● *vi* stall; (abandonner Ⓘ) give up.

**calfeutrer** /kalføtʀe/ [1] *vt* (*fissure*) stop up; (*porte*) draught proof.

**calibre** /kalibʀ/ *nm* calibre; (d'un œuf, fruit) grade.

**calice** /kalis/ *nm* (Relig) chalice; (Bot) calyx.

**califourchon**: **à ~** /akalifuʀʃɔ̃/ *loc* astride.

**câlin, ~e** /kɑlɛ̃, -in/ *a* (*regard, ton*) affectionate; (*personne*) cuddly.

**calmant** /kalmɑ̃/ *nm* sedative.

**calme** /kalm/ *a* calm. ● *nm* peace; calm; (maîtrise de soi) composure; **du ~!** calm down!

**calmer** /kalme/ [1] *vt* (*personne*) calm down; (*situation*) defuse; (*douleur*) ease; (*soif*) quench. ▫ **se ~** *vpr* (*personne, situation*) calm down; (*agitation, tempête*) die down; (*douleur*) ease.

**calomnie** /kalɔmni/ *nf* (*orale*) slander; (écrite) libel. **calomnier** [45] *vt* slander; libel. **calomnieux, -ieuse** *a* slanderous; libellous.

**calorie** /kalɔʀi/ *nf* calorie.

**calque** /kalk/ *nm* tracing; **(papier) ~** tracing paper; (fig) exact copy.

**calquer** /kalke/ [1] *vt* trace; (fig) copy; **~ qch sur** model sth on.

**calvaire** /kalvɛʀ/ *nm* (croix) Calvary; (fig) suffering.

**calvitie** /kalvisi/ *nf* baldness.

**camarade** /kamaʀad/ *nmf* friend; (Pol) comrade; **~ de jeu** playmate. **camaraderie** *nf* friendship.

**cambouis** /kɑ̃bwi/ *nm* dirty oil.

**cambrer** /kɑ̃bʀe/ [1] *vt* arch. ▫ **se ~** *vpr* arch one's back.

**cambriolage** /kɑ̃bʀijɔlaʒ/ *nm* burglary. **cambrioler** [1] *vt* burgle. **cambrioleur, -euse** *nm,f* burglar.

**camelot** /kamlo/ *nm* Ⓘ street vendor.

**camelote** /kamlɔt/ *nf* Ⓘ junk.

**caméra** /kameʀa/ *nf* (cinéma, télévision) camera.

**caméscope®** /kameskɔp/ *nm* camcorder.

**camion** /kamjɔ̃/ *nm* lorry, truck. **camion-citerne** (*pl* **camions-citernes**) *nm* tanker. **camion-**

**nage** *nm* haulage. **camionnette** *nf* van. **camionneur** *nm* lorry *ou* truck driver; (entrepreneur) haulage contractor.

**camisole** /kamizɔl/ *nf* ~ **(de force)** straitjacket.

**camoufler** /kamufle/ [1] *vt* camouflage.

**camp** /kɑ̃/ *nm* camp; (Sport, Pol) side.

**campagnard**, **~e** /kɑ̃paɲaʀ, -d/ *a* country. ● *nm,f* countryman, countrywoman.

**campagne** /kɑ̃paɲ/ *nf* country; countryside; (Mil, Pol) campaign.

**campement** /kɑ̃pmɑ̃/ *nm* camp, encampment.

**camper** /kɑ̃pe/ [1] *vi* camp. ● *vt* (esquisser) sketch. □ **se ~** *vpr* plant oneself. **campeur**, **-euse** *nm,f* camper.

**camping** /kɑ̃piŋ/ *nm* camping; **faire du ~** go camping; **(terrain de) ~** campsite. **camping-car** (*pl* **~s**) *nm* camper-van; (US) motorhome. **camping-gaz®** *nm inv* (réchaud) camping stove.

**Canada** /kanada/ *nm* Canada.

**canadien**, **~ne** /kanadjɛ̃, -ɛn/ *a* Canadian. **C~**, **~ne** *nm,f* Canadian. **canadienne** *nf* (veste) fur-lined jacket, (tente) ridge tent.

**canaille** /kanɑj/ *nf* rogue.

**canal** (*pl* **-aux**) /kanal, -o/ *nm* (artificiel) canal; (bras de mer) channel; (Tech, TV) channel; (moyen) channel; **par le ~ de** through. **canalisation** *nf* (tuyaux) mains (+ *pl*). **canaliser** [1] *vt* (*eau*) canalize; (fig) channel.

**canapé** /kanape/ *nm* sofa.

**canard** /kanaʀ/ *nm* duck; (journal 🅸) rag.

**canari** /kanaʀi/ *nm* canary.

**cancans** /kɑ̃kɑ̃/ *nmpl* 🅸 gossip.

**cancer** /kɑ̃sɛʀ/ *nm* cancer; **le C~** Cancer. **cancéreux**, **-euse** *a* cancerous. **cancérigène** *a* carcinogenic.

**cancre** /kɑ̃kʀ/ *nm* dunce.

**candeur** /kɑ̃dœʀ/ *nf* ingenuousness.

**candidat**, **~e** /kɑ̃dida, -t/ *nm,f* (à un examen, Pol) candidate; (à un poste) applicant, candidate (**à** for).

**candidature** /kɑ̃didatyʀ/ *nf* application; (Pol) candidacy; **poser sa ~ à un poste** apply for a job.

**candide** /kɑ̃did/ *a* ingenuous.

**cane** /kan/ *nf* (female) duck. **caneton** *nm* duckling.

**canette** /kanɛt/ *nf* (bouteille) bottle; (boîte) can.

**canevas** /kanva/ *nm* canvas; (ouvrage) tapestry; (plan) framework, outline.

**caniche** /kaniʃ/ *nm* poodle.

**canicule** /kanikyl/ *nf* scorching heat; (vague de chaleur) heatwave.

**canif** /kanif/ *nm* penknife.

**canine** /kanin/ *nf* canine (tooth).

**caniveau** (*pl* **~x**) /kanivo/ *nm* gutter.

**cannabis** /kanabis/ *nm* cannabis.

**canne** /kan/ *nf* (walking) stick; **~ à pêche** fishing rod; **~ à sucre** sugar cane.

**cannelle** /kanɛl/ *nf* cinnamon.

**cannibale** /kanibal/ *a & nmf* cannibal.

**canoë** /kanɔe/ *nm* canoe; (Sport) canoeing.

**canon** /kanɔ̃/ *nm* (big) gun; (ancien) cannon; (d'une arme) barrel; (principe, règle) canon.

**canot** /kano/ *nm* dinghy, (small) boat; **~ de sauvetage** lifeboat; **~ pneumatique** rubber dinghy. **canotier** *nm* boater.

**cantatrice** /kɑ̃tatʀis/ *nf* opera singer.

**cantine** /kɑ̃tin/ *nf* canteen.

**cantique** /kɑ̃tik/ *nm* hymn.

**cantonner** /kɑ̃tɔne/ [1] *vt* (Mil) billet. □ **se ~ dans** *vpr* confine oneself to.

**canular** /kanylaʀ/ *nm* hoax.

**caoutchouc** /kautʃu/ *nm* rubber; (élastique) rubber band; **~ mousse** foam rubber.

**cap** /kap/ *nm* cape, headland; (direction) course; (obstacle) hurdle; **franchir le ~ de la cinquantaine** pass the fifty mark; **mettre le ~ sur** steer a course for.

**capable** /kapabl/ *a* capable (**de** of); **~ de faire** able to do, capable of doing.

**capacité** /kapasite/ *nf* ability; (contenance, potentiel) capacity.

**cape** /kap/ *nf* cape; **rire sous ~** laugh up one's sleeve.

**capillaire** /kapilɛʀ/ *a* (*lotion, soins*) hair; **(vaisseau) ~** capillary.

**capitaine** /kapitɛn/ *nm* captain.

**capital**, **~e** (*mpl* **-aux**) /kapital, -o/ *a* key, crucial, fundamental; (*peine, lettre*) capital. ●*nm* (*pl* **-aux**) (Comm) capital; (fig) stock; **capitaux** (Comm) capital; **~-risque** venture capital; **~-risqueur** venture capitalist. **capitale** *nf* (ville, lettre) capital.

**capitalisme** /kapitalism/ *nm* capitalism.

**capitonné**, **~e** /kapitɔne/ *a* padded.

**capituler** /kapityle/ [1] *vi* capitulate.

**caporal** (*pl* **-aux**) /kapɔʀal, -o/ *nm* corporal.

**capot** /kapo/ *nm* (Auto) bonnet; (US) hood.

**capote** /kapɔt/ *nf* (Auto) hood; (US) top; (préservatif [I]) condom.

**capoter** /kapɔte/ [1] *vi* overturn; (fig) collapse.

**câpre** /kɑpʀ/ *nf* (Culin) caper.

**caprice** /kapʀis/ *nm* whim; (colère) tantrum; **faire un ~** throw a tantrum. **capricieux**, **-ieuse** *a* capricious; (*appareil*) temperamental.

**Capricorne** /kapʀikɔʀn/ *nm* **le ~** Capricorn.

**capsule** /kapsyl/ *nf* capsule; (de bouteille) cap.

**capter** /kapte/ [1] *vt* (*eau*) collect; (*émission*) get; (*signal*) pick up; (fig) win, capture.

**captif**, **-ive** /kaptif, -v/ *a & nm,f* captive.

**captiver** /kaptive/ [1] *vt* captivate.

**capturer** /kaptyʀe/ [1] *vt* capture.

**capuche** /kapyʃ/ *nf* hood. **capuchon** *nm* hood; (de stylo) cap.

**car** /kaʀ/ *conj* because, for. ●*nm* coach; (US) bus.

**carabine** /kaʀabin/ *nf* rifle.

**caractère** /kaʀaktɛʀ/ *nm* (lettre) character; (nature) nature; **~s d'imprimerie** block letters; **avoir bon/mauvais ~** be good-natured/bad-tempered; **avoir du ~** have character.

**caractériel**, **~le** /kaʀakteʀjɛl/ *a* (*trait*) character; (*enfant*) disturbed.

**caractériser** /kaʀakteʀize/ [1] *vt* characterize. □ **se ~ par** *vpr* be characterized by. **caractéristique** *a & nf* characteristic.

**carafe** /kaʀaf/ *nf* carafe.

**Caraïbes** /kaʀaib/ *nfpl* **les ~** the Caribbean.

**carambolage** /kaʀɑ̃bɔlaʒ/ *nm* pile-up.

**caramel** /kaʀamɛl/ *nm* caramel; (bonbon) toffee.

**carapace** /kaʀapas/ *nf* shell.

**caravane** /kaʀavan/ *nf* (Auto) caravan; (US) trailer; (convoi) caravan.

**carbone** /kaʀbɔn/ *nm* carbon; **(papier) ~** carbon (paper). **carboniser** [1] *vt* burn (to ashes).

**carburant** /kaʀbyʀɑ̃/ *nm* (motor) fuel.

**carburateur** /kaʀbyʀatœʀ/ *nm* carburettor; (US) carburetor.

**carcan** /kaʀkɑ̃/ *nm* constraints (+ *pl*).

**carcasse** /kaʀkas/ *nf* (squelette) carcass; (armature) frame; (de voiture) shell.

**cardiaque** /kaʀdjak/ *a* heart. ● *nmf* heart patient

**cardinal**, **~e** (*mpl* **-aux**) /kaʀdinal, -o/ *a & nm* cardinal.

**Carême** /kaʀɛm/ *nm* **le ~** Lent.

**carence** /kaʀɑ̃s/ *nf* shortcomings (+ *pl*); inadequacy; (Méd) deficiency; (absence) lack

**caresse** /kaʀɛs/ *nf* caress; (à un animal) stroke. **caresser** [1] *vt* caress, stroke; (*espoir*) cherish.

**cargaison** /kaʀgɛzɔ̃/ *nf* cargo.

**cargo** /kaʀgo/ *nm* cargo boat.

**caricature** /kaʀikatyʀ/ *nf* caricature.

**carie** /kaʀi/ *nf* (trou) cavity; **la ~ (dentaire)** tooth decay.

**carillon** /kaʀijɔ̃/ *nm* chimes (+ *pl*).

**caritatif**, **-ive** /kaʀitatif, -v/ *a* **association caritative** charity.

**carnage** /kaʀnaʒ/ *nm* carnage.

**carnassier**, **-ière** /kaʀnasje, -jɛʀ/ *a* carnivorous.

**carnaval** (*pl* **~s**) /kaʀnaval/ *nm* carnival.

**carnet** /kaʀnɛ/ *nm* notebook; (de tickets, timbres) book; **~ d'adresses** address book; **~ de chèques** chequebook.

**carotte** /kaʀɔt/ *nf* carrot.

**carpe** /kaʀp/ *nf* carp.

**carré**, **~e** /kaʀe/ *a* (forme, mesure) square; (fig) straightforward; **un mètre ~** one square metre. ● *nm* square; (de terrain) patch.

**carreau** (*pl* **~x**) /kaʀo/ *nm* (window) pane; (par terre, au mur) tile; (dessin) check; (aux cartes) diamonds (+ *pl*); **à ~x** (*tissu*) check(ed); (*papier*) squared.

**carrefour** /kaʀfuʀ/ *nm* crossroads (+ *sg*).

**carrelage** /kaʀlaʒ/ *nm* tiling; (sol) tiles.

**carrément** /kaʀemɑ̃/ *adv* (complètement) completely; (*stupide, dangereux*) downright; (*dire*) straight out; **elle a ~ démissionné** she went straight ahead and resigned.

**carrière** /kaʀjɛʀ/ *nf* career; (terrain) quarry.

**carrossable** /kaʀɔsabl/ *a* suitable for vehicles.

**carrosse** /kaʀɔs/ *nm* (horse-drawn) coach.

**carrosserie** /kaʀɔsʀi/ *nf* (Auto) body(work).

**carrure** /kaʀyʀ/ *nf* shoulders; (fig) necessary qualities, calibre.

**cartable** /kaʀtabl/ *nm* satchel.

**carte** /kaʀt/ *nf* card; (Géog) map; (Naut) chart; (au restaurant) menu; **~s** (jeu) cards; **à la ~** (*manger*) à la carte; (*horaire*) personalized; **donner ~ blanche à** give a free hand to; **~ de crédit** credit card; **~ de fidélité** loyalty card; **~ grise** (car) registration document; **~ d'identité** identity card; **~ magnétique** swipe card; **~ de paiement** debit card, **~ postale** postcard; **~ à puce** smart card; **~ de séjour**

resident's permit; ~ **des vins** wine list; ~ **de visite** (business) card.

**cartilage** /kaʀtilaʒ/ *nm* cartilage.

**carton** /kaʀtɔ̃/ *nm* cardboard; (boîte) (cardboard) box; ~ **à dessin** portfolio; **faire un** ~ Ⓘ do well.

**cartonné**, ~**e** /kaʀtɔne/ *a* **livre** ~ hardback.

**cartouche** /kaʀtuʃ/ *nf* cartridge; (de cigarettes) carton. **cartouchière** *nf* cartridge-belt.

**cas** /kɑ/ *nm* case; **au** ~ **où** in case; ~ **urgent** emergency; **en aucun** ~ on no account; **en** ~ **de** in the event of, in case of; **en tout** ~ in any case; (du moins) at least; **faire** ~ **de** set great store by; ~ **de conscience** moral dilemma.

**casanier**, **-ière** /kazanje, -jɛʀ/ *a* home-loving.

**cascade** /kaskad/ *nf* waterfall; (au cinéma) stunt; (fig) spate, series (+ *sg*).

**cascadeur**, **-euse** /kaskadœʀ, -øz/ *nm,f* stuntman, stuntwoman.

**case** /kɑz/ *nf* hut; (de damier) square; (compartiment) pigeon-hole; (sur un formulaire) box.

**caser** /kaze/ [1] *vt* Ⓘ (mettre) put; (loger) put up; (dans un travail) find a job for; (marier: péj) marry off.

**caserne** /kazɛʀn/ *nf* barracks; ~ **de sapeurs-pompiers** fire station.

**casier** /kɑzje/ *nm* pigeon-hole, compartment; (à bouteilles, chaussures) rack; ~ **judiciaire** criminal record.

**casque** /kask/ *nm* (de motard) crash helmet; (de cycliste) cycle helmet; (chez le coiffeur) (hair-)drier; ~ **(à écouteurs)** headphones; ~ **anti-bruit** ear defenders; ~ **de protection** safety helmet.

**casquette** /kaskɛt/ *nf* cap.

**cassant**, ~**e** /kɑsɑ̃, -t/ *a* brittle; (brusque) curt.

**cassation** /kasasjɔ̃/ *nf* **cour de** ~ appeal court.

**casse** /kɑs/ *nf* (objets) breakages; (lieu) breaker's yard; **mettre à la** ~ scrap.

**casse-cou** /kɑsku/ *nmf inv* dare-devil.

**casse-croûte** /kɑskʀut/ *nm inv* snack.

**casse-noix** /kɑsnwa/ *nm inv* nut-crackers (+ *pl*).

**casse-pieds** /kɑspje/ *nmf inv* Ⓘ pain (in the neck) Ⓘ.

**casser** /kɑse/ [1] *vt* break; (annuler) annul; ~ **les pieds à qn** Ⓘ annoy sb. ● *vi* break. □ **se** ~ *vpr* break; (partir Ⓘ) be off Ⓘ.

**casserole** /kasʀɔl/ *nf* saucepan.

**casse-tête** /kɑstɛt/ *nm inv* (problème) headache; (jeu) brain teaser.

**cassette** /kasɛt/ *nf* casket; (de magnétophone) cassette, tape; (de vidéo) video tape; ~ **audionumérique** digital audio tape.

**cassis** /kasi(s)/ *nm inv* blackcurrant.

**cassure** /kasyʀ/ *nf* break.

**castor** /kastɔʀ/ *nm* beaver.

**castration** /kastʀasjɔ̃/ *nf* castration.

**catalogue** /katalɔg/ *nm* catalogue.

**catalyseur** /katalizœʀ/ *nm* catalyst; (Auto) catalytic convertor.

**catastrophe** /katastʀɔf/ *nf* disaster, catastrophe. **catastrophique** *a* catastrophic.

**catch** /katʃ/ *nm* (all-in) wrestling.

**catéchisme** /kateʃism/ *nm* catechism.

**catégorie** /kategɔʀi/ *nf* category.

**catégorique** *a* categorical.

**cathédrale** /katedʀal/ *nf* cathedral.

**catholique** /katɔlik/ *a* Catholic; **pas très ~** a bit fishy.

**catimini**: **en ~** /ɑ̃katimini/ *loc* on the sly.

**cauchemar** /kɔʃmaʀ/ *nm* nightmare.

**cause** /koz/ *nf* cause; (raison) reason; (Jur) case; **à ~ de** because of; **en ~** (en jeu, concerné) involved; **pour ~ de** on account of; **mettre en ~** implicate; **remettre en ~** call into question.

**causer** /koze/ [1] *vt* cause; (discuter de [T]) **~ travail** talk shop; **~ de** talk about. ● *vi* chat. **causerie** *nf* talk.

**causette** /kozɛt/ *nf* (Internet) chat; **faire la ~** have a chat.

**caution** /kosjɔ̃/ *nf* surety; (Jur) bail; (appui) backing; (garantie) deposit; **libéré sous ~** released on bail. **cautionner** [1] *vt* guarantee; (soutenir) back.

**cavalcade** /kavalkad/ *nf* stampede, rush.

**cavalier**, **-ière** /kavalje, -jɛʀ/ *a* offhand; **allée cavalière** bridle path. ● *nm,f* rider; (pour danser) partner. ● *nm* (aux échecs) knight.

**cave** /kav/ *nf* cellar. ● *a* sunken.

**caveau** (*pl* **~x**) /kavo/ *nm* vault.

**caverne** /kavɛʀn/ *nf* cave.

**CCP** *abrév m* (**compte chèque postal**) post office account.

**CD** *abrév m* (**compact disc**) CD.

**CD-ROM** *abrév m inv* (**compact disc read only memory**) CD-ROM.

**ce**, **c'**, **cet**, **cette** (*pl* **ces**) /sə, s, sɛt, se/

c' before e. **cet** before vowel or mute h.

● **ce**, **cet**, **cette** (*pl* **ces**) *adjectif démonstratif*

····➤ this; (plus éloigné) that; **ces** these; (plus éloigné) those; **cette nuit** (passée) last night; (à venir) tonight.

● **ce**, **c'** *pronom démonstratif*

····➤ **c'est** it's *ou* it is; **c'est un policier** he's a policeman; **~ sont eux qui l'ont fait** THEY did it; **qui est-~?** who is it?

····➤ **ce que/qui** what; **~ que je ne comprends pas** what I don't understand; **elle est venue, ~ qui est étonnant** she came, which is surprising; **~ que tu as de la chance!** how lucky you are!; **tout ~ que je sais** all I know; **tout ~ qu'elle trouve/peut** everything she finds/can.

**CE** *abrév f* (**Communauté européenne**) EC.

**ceci** /səsi/ *pron* this.

**cécité** /sesite/ *nf* blindness.

**céder** /sede/ [14] *vt* give up; **~ le passage** give way; (vendre) sell. ● *vi* (se rompre) give way; (se soumettre) give in.

**cédérom** /sedeʀɔm/ *nm* CD-ROM.

**cédille** /sedij/ *nf* cedilla.

**cèdre** /sɛdʀ/ *nm* cedar.

**CEI** *abrév f* (**Communauté des États indépendants**) CIS.

**ceinture** /sɛ̃tyʀ/ *nf* belt; (taille) waist; **~ de sauvetage** lifebelt; **~ de sécurité** seatbelt.

**cela** /səla/ *pron* it, that; (pour désigner) that; **~ va de soi** it is obvious; **~ dit/fait** having said/done that.

**célèbre** /selɛbʀ/ *a* famous. **célébrer** [14] *vt* celebrate. **célébrité** *nf* fame; (personne) celebrity.

**céleri** /sɛlʀi/ *nm* (en branches) celery. **céleri-rave** (*pl* **céleris-raves**) *nm* celeriac.

**célibat** /seliba/ *nm* celibacy; (état) single status.

**célibataire** /selibatɛʀ/ *a* single. ● *nm* bachelor. ● *nf* single woman.

**celle, celles** /sɛl/ ⇒CELUI.

**cellulaire** /selylɛʀ/ *a* cell; **emprisonnement ~** solitary confinement; **fourgon** *ou* **voiture ~** prison van; **téléphone ~** cellular phone.

**cellule** /selyl/ *nf* cell; **~ souche** stem cell.

**celui, celle** (*pl* **ceux, celles**) /səlɥi, sɛl, sø/ *pron* the one; **~ de mon ami** my friend's; **~-ci** this (one); **~-là** that (one); **ceux-ci** these (ones); **ceux-là** those (ones).

**cendre** /sɑ̃dʀ/ *nf* ash.

**cendrier** /sɑ̃dʀije/ *nm* ashtray.

**censé, ~e** /sɑ̃se/ *a* **être ~ faire** be supposed to do.

**censeur** /sɑ̃sœʀ/ *nm* censor; (Scol) administrator in charge of discipline.

**censure** /sɑ̃syʀ/ *nf* censorship. **censurer** [1] *vt* censor; (critiquer) censure.

**cent** /sɑ̃/ *a* (a) hundred; **20 pour ~** 20 per cent. ● *n* (quantité) hundred; **~ un** a hundred and one; (centième d'euro) cent.

**centaine** /sɑ̃tɛn/ *nf* hundred; **une ~ (de)** (about) a hundred.

**centenaire** /sɑ̃tnɛʀ/ *nm* (anniversaire) centenary.

**centième** /sɑ̃tjɛm/ *a & nmf* hundredth.

**centimètre** /sɑ̃timɛtʀ/ *nm* centimetre; (ruban) tape-measure.

**central, ~e** (*mpl* **-aux**) /sɑ̃tʀal, -o/ *a* central. ● *nm* (*pl* **-aux**) **~ (téléphonique)** (telephone) exchange. **centrale** *nf* power-station.

**centre** /sɑ̃tʀ/ *nm* centre; **~ d'appel** call centre; **~ commercial** shopping centre; (US) mall; **~ de formation** training centre; **~ hospitalier** hospital. **centrer** [1] *vt* centre. **centre-ville** (*pl* **centres-villes**) *nm* town centre.

**centuple** /sɑ̃typl/ *nm* **le ~ de** a hundred times; **au ~** a hundredfold.

**cep** /sɛp/ *nm* vine stock.

**cépage** /sepaʒ/ *nm* grape variety.

**cèpe** /sɛp/ *nm* cep.

**cependant** /səpɑ̃dɑ̃/ *adv* however.

**céramique** /seʀamik/ *nf* ceramic; (art) ceramics (+ *sg*).

**cercle** /sɛʀkl/ *nm* circle; (cerceau) hoop; (association) society, club; **~ vicieux** vicious circle.

**cercueil** /sɛʀkœj/ *nm* coffin.

**céréale** /seʀeal/ *nf* cereal; **~s** (Culin) (breakfast) cereal.

**cérébral, ~e** (*mpl* **-aux**) /seʀebʀal, -o/ *a* cerebral, intellectual.

**cérémonie** /seʀemɔni/ *nf* ceremony; **sans ~s** (*repas*) informal; (*recevoir*) informally.

**cerf** /sɛʀ/ *nm* stag.

**cerfeuil** /sɛʀfœj/ *nm* chervil.

**cerf-volant** (*pl* **cerfs-volants**) /sɛʀvɔlɑ̃/ *nm* kite.

**cerise** /s(ə)ʀiz/ *nf* cherry. **cerisier** *nm* cherry tree.

**cerner** /sɛʀne/ [1] *vt* surround; (*question*) define; **avoir les yeux cernés** have rings under one's eyes.

**certain, ~e** /sɛʀtɛ̃, -ɛn/ *a* certain; (sûr) certain, sure (**de** of; **que** that); **d'un ~ âge** no longer young; **un ~ temps** some time. **certainement** *adv* (probablement) most probably;

(avec certitude) certainly. **certains, -es** *pron* some people.

**certes** /sɛʀt/ *adv* (sans doute) admittedly; (bien sûr) of course.

**certificat** /sɛʀtifika/ *nm* certificate.

**certifier** /sɛʀtifje/ [45] *vt* certify; ~ **qch à qn** assure sb of sth; **copie certifiée conforme** certified true copy.

**certitude** /sɛʀtityd/ *nf* certainty.

**cerveau** (*pl* ~**x**) /sɛʀvo/ *nm* brain.

**cervelle** /sɛʀvɛl/ *nf* (Anat) brain; (Culin) brains.

**ces** /se/ ⇒CE.

**césarienne** /sezaʀjɛn/ *nf* Caesarean (section).

**cesse** /sɛs/ *nf* **n'avoir de** ~ **que** have no rest until; **sans** ~ constantly, incessantly.

**cesser** /sese/ [1] *vt* stop; ~ **de faire** stop doing. ● *vi* cease; **faire** ~ put an end to.

**cessez-le-feu** /seselfø/ *nm inv* ceasefire.

**cession** /sɛsjɔ̃/ *nf* transfer.

**c'est-à-dire** /setadiʀ/ *conj* that is (to say).

**cet, cette** /sɛt/ ⇒CE.

**ceux** /sø/ ⇒CELUI.

**chacun,** ~**e** /ʃakœ̃, yn/ *pron* each (one), every one; (tout le monde) everyone; ~ **d'entre nous** each (one) of us.

**chagrin** /ʃagʀɛ̃/ *nm* sorrow; **avoir du** ~ be sad.

**chahut** /ʃay/ *nm* row, din.

**chahuter** /ʃayte/ [1] *vi* make a row. ● *vt* (*enseignant*) be rowdy with; (*orateur*) heckle.

**chaîne** /ʃɛn/ *nf* chain; (de télévision) channel; ~ **(d'assemblage)** assembly line; ~**s** (Auto) snow chains; ~ **de montagnes** mountain range; ~ **de montage/fabrication** assembly/production line; ~ **hi-fi** hi-fi system; ~ **laser** CD player; **en** ~ (*accidents*) multiple; (*réaction*) chain. **chaînette** *nf* (small) chain. **chaînon** *nm* link.

**chair** /ʃɛʀ/ *nf* flesh; **bien en** ~ plump; **en** ~ **et en os** in the flesh; ~ **à saucisses** sausage meat; **la** ~ **de poule** goose pimples. ● *a inv* **(couleur)** ~ flesh-coloured.

**chaire** /ʃɛʀ/ *nf* (d'église) pulpit; (Univ) chair.

**chaise** /ʃɛz/ *nf* chair; ~ **longue** deckchair.

**châle** /ʃɑl/ *nm* shawl.

**chaleur** /ʃalœʀ/ *nf* heat; (moins intense) warmth; (d'un accueil, d'une couleur) warmth. **chaleureux, -euse** *a* warm.

**chalumeau** (*pl* ~**x**) /ʃalymo/ *nm* blowtorch.

**chalutier** /ʃalytje/ *nm* trawler.

**chamailler (se)** /(sə)ʃamaje/ [1] *vpr* squabble.

**chambre** /ʃɑ̃bʀ/ *nf* (bed)room; (Pol, Jur) chamber; **faire** ~ **à part** sleep in separate rooms; ~ **à air** inner tube; ~ **d'amis** spare *or* guest room; ~ **de commerce (et d'industrie)** Chamber of Commerce; ~ **à coucher** bedroom; ~ **à un lit/deux lits** single/twin room; ~ **pour deux personnes** double room; ~ **forte** strong-room; ~ **d'hôte** bed and breakfast, B and B. **chambrer** [1] *vt* (*vin*) bring to room temperature.

**chameau** (*pl* ~**x**) /ʃamo/ *nm* camel.

**chamois** /ʃamwa/ *nm* chamois.

**champ** /ʃɑ̃/ *nm* field; ~ **de bataille** battlefield; ~ **de courses** racecourse; ~ **de tir** firing range.

**champêtre** /ʃɑ̃pɛtʀ/ *a* rural.

**champignon** /ʃɑ̃piɲɔ̃/ *nm* mushroom; (moisissure) fungus; **~ de Paris** button mushroom.

**champion**, **~ne** /ʃɑ̃pjɔ̃, -ɔn/ *nm,f* champion. **championnat** *nm* championship.

**chance** /ʃɑ̃s/ *nf* (good) luck; (possibilité) chance; **avoir de la ~** be lucky; **quelle ~!** what luck!

**chanceler** /ʃɑ̃sle/ [38] *vi* stagger; (fig) falter, waver.

**chancelier** /ʃɑ̃səlje/ *nm* chancellor.

**chanceux**, **-euse** /ʃɑ̃sø, -z/ *a* lucky.

**chandail** /ʃɑ̃daj/ *nm* sweater.

**chandelier** /ʃɑ̃dəlje/ *nm* candlestick.

**chandelle** /ʃɑ̃dɛl/ *nf* candle; **dîner aux ~s** candlelight dinner.

**change** /ʃɑ̃ʒ/ *nm* (foreign) exchange; (taux) exchange rate.

**changement** /ʃɑ̃ʒmɑ̃/ *nm* change; **~ de vitesse** (dispositif) gears.

**changer** /ʃɑ̃ʒe/ [40] *vt* change; **~ qch de place** move sth; (échanger) change (**pour**, **contre** for); **~ de nom/voiture** change one's name/car; **~ de place/train** change places/trains; **~ de direction** change direction; **~ d'avis** *ou* **d'idée** change one's mind; **~ de vitesse** change gear. □ **se ~** *vpr* change, get changed.

**chanson** /ʃɑ̃sɔ̃/ *nf* song.

**chant** /ʃɑ̃/ *nm* singing; (chanson) song; (Relig) hymn.

**chantage** /ʃɑ̃taʒ/ *nm* blackmail.

**chanter** /ʃɑ̃te/ [1] *vt* sing; **si cela vous chante** 🄸 if you feel like it. ● *vi* sing; **faire ~** (délit) blackmail. **chanteur**, **-euse** *nm,f* singer.

**chantier** /ʃɑ̃tje/ *nm* building site; **~ naval** shipyard; **mettre en ~** get under way, start.

**chaos** /kao/ *nm* chaos.

**chaparder** /ʃapaʀde/ [1] *vt* 🄸 pinch 🄸, filch.

**chapeau** (*pl* **~x**) /ʃapo/ *nm* hat; **~!** well done!

**chapelet** /ʃaplɛ/ *nm* rosary; (fig) string.

**chapelle** /ʃapɛl/ *nf* chapel.

**chapelure** /ʃaplyʀ/ *nf* (Culin) breadcrumbs.

**chaperonner** /ʃapʀɔne/ [1] *vt* chaperone.

**chapiteau** (*pl* **~x**) /ʃapito/ *nm* marquee; (de cirque) big top; (de colonne) capital.

**chapitre** /ʃapitʀ/ *nm* chapter; (fig) subject.

**chaque** /ʃak/ *a* every, each.

**char** /ʃaʀ/ *nm* (Mil) tank; (de carnaval) float; (charrette) cart; (dans l'antiquité) chariot.

**charabia** /ʃaʀabja/ *nm* 🄸 gibberish.

**charade** /ʃaʀad/ *nf* riddle.

**charbon** /ʃaʀbɔ̃/ *nm* coal; **~ de bois** charcoal.

**charcuterie** /ʃaʀkytʀi/ *nf* pork butcher's shop; (aliments) (cooked) pork meats. **charcutier**, **-ière** *nm,f* pork butcher.

**chardon** /ʃaʀdɔ̃/ *nm* thistle.

**charge** /ʃaʀʒ/ *nf* load, burden; (Mil, Électr, Jur) charge; (responsabilité) responsibility; **avoir qn à ~** be responsible for; **~s** expenses; (de locataire) service charges; **être à la ~ de** (*personne*) be the responsibility of; (*frais*) be payable by; **~s sociales** social security contributions; **prendre en ~** take charge of.

**chargé**, **~e** /ʃaʀʒe/ *a* (*véhicule*) loaded; (*journée, emploi du temps*)

busy; (*langue*) coated. ● *nm,f* ~ **de mission** head of mission; ~ **d'affaires** chargé d'affaires, ~ **de cours** lecturer.

**chargement** /ʃaʀʒəmɑ̃/ *nm* loading; (objets) load.

**charger** /ʃaʀʒe/ [40] *vt* load; (Ordinat, Photo) load; (attaquer) charge; (*batterie*) charge; ~ **qn de** (*fardeau*) weigh sb down with; (*tâche*) entrust sb with; ~ **qn de faire** make sb responsible for doing. ● *vi* (attaquer) charge. □ **se** ~ **de** *vpr* take charge *ou* care of.

**chariot** /ʃaʀjo/ *nm* (à roulettes) trolley; (US) cart; (charrette) cart.

**charitable** /ʃaʀitabl/ *a* charitable.

**charité** /ʃaʀite/ *nf* charity; **faire la** ~ **à** give (money) to.

**charlatan** /ʃaʀlatɑ̃/ *nm* charlatan.

**charmant**, **~e** /ʃaʀmɑ̃, -t/ *a* charming.

**charme** /ʃaʀm/ *nm* charm; (qui envoûte) spell. **charmer** [1] *vt* charm. **charmeur**, **-euse** *nm,f* charmer.

**charnel**, **~le** /ʃaʀnɛl/ *a* carnal.

**charnière** /ʃaʀnjɛʀ/ *nf* hinge; **à la** ~ **de** at the meeting point between.

**charnu**, **~e** /ʃaʀny/ *a* plump, fleshy.

**charpente** /ʃaʀpɑ̃t/ *nf* framework; (carrure) build.

**charpentier** /ʃaʀpɑ̃tje/ *nm* carpenter.

**charrette** /ʃaʀɛt/ *nf* cart.

**charrue** /ʃaʀy/ *nf* plough.

**chasse** /ʃas/ *nf* hunting; (au fusil) shooting; (poursuite) chase; (recherche) hunt(ing); ~ **(d'eau)** (toilet) flush; ~ **sous-marine** harpoon fishing.

**chasse-neige** /ʃasnɛʒ/ *nm inv* snowplough.

**chasser** /ʃase/ [1] *vt* hunt; (au fusil) shoot; (faire partir) chase away; (*odeur, employé*) get rid of. ● *vi* go hunting; (au fusil) go shooting.

**chasseur**, **-euse** /ʃasœʀ, -øz/ *nm,f* hunter. ● *nm* bellboy; (US) bellhop; (avion) fighter plane.

**châssis** /ʃɑsi/ *nm* frame; (Auto) chassis.

**chasteté** /ʃastəte/ *nf* chastity.

**chat**[1] /ʃa/ *nm* cat; (mâle) tomcat.

**chat**[2] /tʃæt/ *nm* (Internet) chat.

**châtaigne** /ʃɑtɛɲ/ *nf* chestnut. **châtaignier** *nm* chestnut tree. **châtain** *a inv* chestnut (brown).

**château** (*pl* **~x**) /ʃɑto/ *nm* castle; (manoir) manor; ~ **d'eau** water tower; ~ **fort** fortified castle.

**châtiment** /ʃɑtimɑ̃/ *nm* punishment.

**chaton** /ʃatɔ̃/ *nm* (chat) kitten.

**chatouillement** /ʃatujmɑ̃/ *nm* tickling. **chatouiller** [1] *vt* tickle. **chatouilleux**, **-euse** *a* ticklish; (susceptible) touchy.

**châtrer** /ʃɑtʀe/ [1] *vt* castrate; (*chat*) neuter.

**chatte** /ʃat/ *nf* female cat.

**chaud**, **~e** /ʃo, -d/ *a* warm; (brûlant) hot; (vif: fig) warm. ● *nm* heat; **au** ~ in the warm(th); **avoir** ~ be warm; be hot; **il fait** ~ it is warm; it is hot; **pour te tenir** ~ to keep you warm. **chaudement** *adv* warmly; (*disputé*) hotly.

**chaudière** /ʃodjɛʀ/ *nf* boiler.

**chaudron** /ʃodʀɔ̃/ *nm* cauldron.

**chauffage** /ʃofaʒ/ *nm* heating; ~ **central** central heating.

**chauffard** /ʃofaʀ/ *nm* (péj) reckless driver.

**chauffer** /ʃofe/ [1] *vt/i* heat (up); (*moteur, appareil*) overheat. □ **se** ~ *vpr* warm oneself (up).

**chauffeur** /ʃofœʀ/ *nm* driver; (aux gages de qn) chauffeur.

**chaume** /ʃom/ *nm* (de toit) thatch.

**chaussée** /ʃose/ *nf* road(way).

**chausse-pied** (*pl* **~s**) /ʃospje/ *nm* shoehorn.

**chausser** /ʃose/ [1] *vt* (*chaussures*) put on; (*enfant*) put shoes on (to). ● *vi* **~ bien** (aller) fit well; **~ du 35** take a size 35 shoe. ▫ **se ~** *vpr* put one's shoes on.

**chaussette** /ʃosɛt/ *nf* sock.

**chausson** /ʃosɔ̃/ *nm* slipper; (de bébé) bootee; **~ de danse** ballet shoe; **~ aux pommes** apple turnover.

**chaussure** /ʃosyʀ/ *nf* shoe; **~ de ski** ski boot; **~ de marche** hiking boot.

**chauve** /ʃov/ *a* bald.

**chauve-souris** (*pl* **chauves-souris**) /ʃovsuʀi/ *nf* bat.

**chauvin, ~e** /ʃovɛ̃, -in/ *a* chauvinistic. ● *nm,f* chauvinist.

**chavirer** /ʃaviʀe/ [1] *vt* (*bateau*) capsize; (*objets*) tip over.

**chef** /ʃɛf/ *nm* leader, head; (supérieur) boss, superior; (Culin) chef; (de tribu) chief; **architecte en ~** chief *ou* head architect; **~ d'accusation** (Jur) charge; **~ d'équipe** foreman; (Sport) captain; **~ d'État** head of State; **~ de famille** head of the family; **~ de file** (Pol) leader; **~ de gare** stationmaster; **~ d'orchestre** conductor; **~ de service** department head; **~ de train** guard; (US) conductor.

**chef-d'œuvre** (*pl* **chefs-d'œuvre**) /ʃɛdœvʀ/ *nm* masterpiece.

**chef-lieu** (*pl* **chefs-lieux**) /ʃɛfljø/ *nm* county town, administrative centre.

**chemin** /ʃəmɛ̃/ *nm* road; (étroit) lane; (de terre) track; (pour piétons) path; (passage) way; (direction, trajet) way; **avoir du ~ à faire** have a long way to go; **~ de fer** railway; **par ~ de fer** by rail; **~ de halage** towpath; **~ vicinal** country lane.

**cheminée** /ʃəmine/ *nf* chimney; (intérieure) fireplace; (encadrement) mantelpiece; (de bateau) funnel.

**cheminot** /ʃəmino/ *nm* railwayman; (US) railroad man.

**chemise** /ʃəmiz/ *nf* shirt; (dossier) folder; (de livre) jacket; **~ de nuit** nightdress. **chemisette** *nf* short-sleeved shirt. **chemisier** *nm* blouse.

**chêne** /ʃɛn/ *nm* oak.

**chenil** /ʃəni(l)/ *nm* (pension) kennels (+ *sg*).

**chenille** /ʃənij/ *nf* caterpillar; **véhicule à ~s** tracked vehicle.

**cheptel** /ʃɛptɛl/ *nm* livestock.

**chèque** /ʃɛk/ *nm* cheque; **~ sans provision** bad cheque; **~ de voyage** traveller's cheque. **chéquier** *nm* chequebook.

**cher, chère** /ʃɛʀ/ *a* (coûteux) dear, expensive; (aimé) dear; (dans la correspondance) dear. ● *adv* (*coûter, payer*) a lot (of money); (en importance) dearly. ● *nm,f* **mon ~, ma chère** my dear.

**chercher** /ʃɛʀʃe/ [1] *vt* look for; (*aide, paix, gloire*) seek; **aller ~** go and get *ou* fetch, go for; **~ à faire** attempt to do; **~ la petite bête** be finicky.

**chercheur, -euse** /ʃɛʀʃœʀ, -øz/ *nm,f* research worker.

**chèrement** /ʃɛʀmɑ̃/ *adv* dearly.

**chéri, ~e** /ʃeʀi/ *a* beloved. ● *nm,f* darling.

**chérir** /ʃeʀiʀ/ [2] *vt* cherish.

**chétif, -ive** /ʃetif, -v/ *a* puny.

**cheval** (*pl* **-aux**) /ʃəval, -o/ *nm* horse; **à ~** on horseback; **à ~ sur**

astride, straddling; **faire du ~** ride, go horse-riding.

**chevalerie** /ʃəvalʀi/ *nf* chivalry.

**chevalet** /ʃəvalɛ/ *nm* easel; (de menuisier) trestle.

**chevalier** /ʃəvalje/ *nm* knight.

**chevalière** /ʃəvaljɛʀ/ *nf* signet ring.

**cheval-vapeur** (*pl* **chevaux-vapeur**) /ʃəvalvapœʀ/ *nm* horse-power.

**chevaucher** /ʃəvoʃe/ [1] *vt* sit astride. □ **se ~** *vpr* overlap.

**chevelu, ~e** /ʃəvly/ *a* (péj) long-haired; (Bot) hairy.

**chevelure** /ʃəvlyʀ/ *nf* hair.

**chevet** /ʃəvɛ/ *nm* **au ~ de** at the bedside of; **livre de ~** bedside book.

**cheveu** (*pl* **~x**) /ʃəvø/ *nm* (poil) hair; **~x** (chevelure) hair; **avoir les ~x longs** have long hair.

**cheville** /ʃəvij/ *nf* ankle; (fiche) peg, pin; (pour mur) (wall) plug.

**chèvre** /ʃɛvʀ/ *nf* goat.

**chevreuil** /ʃəvʀœj/ *nm* roe (deer); (Culin) venison.

**chevron** /ʃəvʀɔ̃/ *nm* (poutre) rafter; **à ~s** herringbone.

**chez** /ʃe/ *prep* (au domicile de) at the house of; (parmi) among; (dans le caractère ou l'œuvre de) in; **aller ~ qn** go to sb's house; **~ le boucher** at *ou* to the butcher's; **~ soi** at home; **rentrer ~ soi** go home. **chez-soi** *nm inv* home.

**chic** /ʃik/ *a inv* smart; (gentil) kind. ● *nm* style; **avoir le ~ pour** have a knack for; **~ (alors)!** great!

**chicane** /ʃikan/ *nf* double bend; **chercher ~ à qn** pick a quarrel with sb.

**chiche** /ʃiʃ/ *a* mean (**de** with); **~ que je le fais!** Ⓘ I bet you I can do it.

**chichis** /ʃiʃi/ *nmpl* Ⓘ fuss.

**chicorée** /ʃikɔʀe/ *nf* (frisée) endive; (à café) chicory.

**chien** /ʃjɛ̃/ *nm* dog; **~ d'aveugle** guide dog; **~ de garde** watch-dog. **chienne** *nf* dog, bitch.

**chiffon** /ʃifɔ̃/ *nm* rag; (pour nettoyer) duster; **~ humide** damp cloth. **chiffonner** [1] *vt* crumple; (préoccuper Ⓘ) bother.

**chiffre** /ʃifʀ/ *nm* figure; (numéro) number; (code) code; **~s arabes/romains** Arabic/Roman numerals; **~s (statistiques)** statistics; **~ d'affaires** turnover.

**chiffrer** /ʃifʀe/ [1] *vt* put a figure on, assess; (*texte*) encode. □ **se ~ à** *vpr* come to.

**chignon** /ʃiɲɔ̃/ *nm* bun, chignon.

**Chili** /ʃili/ *nm* Chile.

**chimère** /ʃimɛʀ/ *nf* fantasy.

**chimie** /ʃimi/ *nf* chemistry. **chimique** *a* chemical. **chimiste** *nmf* chemist.

**chimpanzé** /ʃɛ̃pɑ̃ze/ *nm* chimpanzee.

**Chine** /ʃin/ *nf* China.

**chinois, ~e** /ʃinwa, -z/ *a* Chinese. ● *nm* (Ling) Chinese. **C~, ~e** *nm, f* Chinese.

**chiot** /ʃjo/ *nm* pup(py).

**chipoter** /ʃipɔte/ [1] *vi* (manger) pick at one's food; (discuter) quibble.

**chips** /ʃips/ *nf inv* crisp; (US) chip.

**chirurgie** /ʃiʀyʀʒi/ *nf* surgery; **~ esthétique** plastic surgery. **chirurgien** *nm* surgeon.

**chlore** /klɔʀ/ *nm* chlorine.

**choc** /ʃɔk/ *nm* (heurt) impact, shock; (émotion) shock; (collision) crash; (affrontement) clash; (Méd) shock; **sous le ~** in shock.

**chocolat** /ʃɔkɔla/ *nm* chocolate; (à boire) drinking chocolate; **~ au lait** milk chocolate; **~ chaud** hot

chocolate; ~ **noir** plain *ou* dark chocolate.

**chœur** /kœʀ/ *nm* (antique) chorus; (chanteurs, nef) choir; **en** ~ in chorus.

**choisir** /ʃwaziʀ/ [2] *vt* choose, select.

**choix** /ʃwa/ *nm* choice, selection; **fromage ou dessert au** ~ a choice of cheese or dessert; **de** ~ choice; **de premier** ~ top quality.

**chômage** /ʃomaʒ/ *nm* unemployment; **au** ~, **en** ~ unemployed; **mettre en** ~ **technique** lay off.

**chômeur**, **-euse** /ʃomœʀ, -øz/ *nm,f* unemployed person; **les** ~**s** the unemployed.

**choquer** /ʃɔke/ [1] *vt* shock; (commotionner) shake.

**choral**, ~**e** (*mpl* ~**s**) /kɔʀal/ *a* choral. **chorale** *nf* choir, choral society.

**chorégraphie** /kɔʀegʀafi/ *nf* choreography.

**choriste** /kɔʀist/ *nmf* (à l'église) chorister; (à l'opéra) member of the chorus *ou* choir.

**chose** /ʃoz/ *nf* thing; **(très) peu de** ~ nothing much; **pas grand** ~ not much.

**chou** (*pl* ~**x**) /ʃu/ *nm* cabbage; ~ **(à la crème)** cream puff; ~ **de Bruxelles** Brussels sprout; **mon petit** ~ Ⓘ my dear.

**chouchou**, ~**te** /ʃuʃu, -t/ *nm,f* (de professeur) pet; (du public) darling.

**choucroute** /ʃukʀut/ *nf* sauerkraut.

**chouette** /ʃwɛt/ *nf* owl. ● *a* Ⓘ super.

**chou-fleur** (*pl* **choux-fleurs**) /ʃuflœʀ/ *nm* cauliflower.

**choyer** /ʃwaje/ [31] *vt* pamper.

**chrétien**, ~**ne** /kʀetjɛ̃, -jɛn/ *a* & *nm,f* Christian.

**Christ** /kʀist/ *nm* **le** ~ Christ.

**chrome** /kʀom/ *nm* chromium, chrome.

**chromosome** /kʀɔmozom/ *nm* chromosome.

**chronique** /kʀɔnik/ *a* chronic. ● *nf* (rubrique) column; (nouvelles) news; (annales) chronicle.

**chronologique** /kʀɔnɔlɔʒik/ *a* chronological.

**chronomètre** /kʀɔnɔmɛtʀ/ *nm* stopwatch. **chronométrer** [14] *vt* time.

**chrysanthème** /kʀizɑ̃tɛm/ *nm* chrysanthemum.

**chuchoter** /ʃyʃɔte/ [1] *vt/i* whisper.

**chut** /ʃyt/ *interj* shh, hush.

**chute** /ʃyt/ *nf* fall; (déchet) offcut; ~ **(d'eau)** waterfall; ~ **de pluie** rainfall; ~ **des cheveux** hair loss; ~ **des ventes** drop in sales; ~ **de 5%** 5% drop. **chuter** [1] *vi* fall.

**Chypre** /ʃipʀ/ *nf* Cyprus.

**ci** /si/ *adv* here; ~**-gît** here lies; **cet homme-**~ this man; **ces maisons-**~ these houses.

**ci-après** /siapʀɛ/ *adv* below.

**cible** /sibl/ *nf* target.

**ciboulette** /sibulɛt/ *nf* (Culin) chives (+ *pl*).

**cicatrice** /sikatʀis/ *nf* scar.

**cicatriser** /sikatʀize/ [1] *vt* heal. □ **se** ~ *vpr* heal.

**ci-dessous** /sidəsu/ *adv* below.

**ci-dessus** /sidəsy/ *adv* above.

**cidre** /sidʀ/ *nm* cider.

**ciel** (*pl* **cieux**, **ciels**) /sjɛl, sjø/ *nm* sky; (Relig) heaven; **cieux** (Relig) heaven.

**cierge** /sjɛʀʒ/ *nm* (church) candle.

**cigale** /sigal/ *nf* cicada.

**cigare** /sigaʀ/ *nm* cigar.

**cigarette** /sigaʀɛt/ *nf* cigarette.

**cigogne** /sigɔɲ/ *nf* stork.

**ci-joint** /siʒwɛ̃/ *adv* enclosed.

**cil** /sil/ *nm* eyelash.

**cime** /sim/ *nf* peak, tip.

**ciment** /simɑ̃/ *nm* cement.

**cimetière** /simtjɛʀ/ *nm* cemetery, graveyard; ~ **de voitures** breaker's yard.

**cinéaste** /sineast/ *nmf* film-maker.

**cinéma** /sinema/ *nm* cinema; (US) movie theater. **cinémathèque** *nf* film archive; (salle) film theatre. **cinématographique** *a* cinema.

**cinéphile** /sinefil/ *nmf* film lover.

**cinglant**, **~e** /sɛ̃glɑ̃, -t/ *a* (*vent*) biting; (*remarque*) scathing.

**cinglé**, **~e** /sɛ̃gle/ *a* [I] crazy.

**cinq** /sɛ̃k/ *a & nm* five.

**cinquante** /sɛ̃kɑ̃t/ *a & nm* fifty.

**cinquième** /sɛ̃kjɛm/ *a & nmf* fifth.

**cintre** /sɛ̃tʀ/ *nm* coat-hanger; (Archit) curve.

**cirage** /siʀaʒ/ *nm* polish.

**circoncision** /siʀkɔ̃sizjɔ̃/ *nf* circumcision.

**circonflexe** /siʀkɔ̃flɛks/ *a* circumflex.

**circonscription** /siʀkɔ̃skʀipsjɔ̃/ *nf* district; ~ **électorale** constituency; (US) district; (de conseiller, maire) ward.

**circonscrire** /siʀkɔ̃skʀiʀ/ [30] *vt* (*incendie, épidémie*) contain; (*sujet*) define.

**circonspect**, **~e** /siʀkɔ̃spɛkt/ *a* circumspect.

**circonstance** /siʀkɔ̃stɑ̃s/ *nf* circumstance; (situation) situation; (occasion) occasion; **~s atténuantes** mitigating circumstances.

**circuit** /siʀkɥi/ *nm* circuit; (trajet) tour, trip.

**circulaire** /siʀkylɛʀ/ *a & nf* circular.

**circulation** /siʀkylasjɔ̃/ *nf* circulation; (de véhicules) traffic.

**circuler** /siʀkyle/ [1] *vi* (se répandre, être distribué) circulate; (aller d'un lieu à un autre) get around; (en voiture) travel; (*piéton*) walk; (être en service) (*bus, train*) run; **faire ~** (*badauds*) move on; (*rumeur*) spread.

**cire** /siʀ/ *nf* wax.

**ciré** /siʀe/ *nm* oilskin.

**cirer** /siʀe/ [1] *vt* polish.

**cirque** /siʀk/ *nm* circus; (arène) amphitheatre; (désordre: fig) chaos; **faire le ~** [I] make a racket [I].

**ciseau** (*pl* **~x**) /sizo/ *nm* chisel; **~x** scissors.

**ciseler** /sizle/ [6] *vt* chisel.

**citadelle** /sitadɛl/ *nf* citadel.

**citadin**, **~e** /sitadɛ̃, -in/ *nm,f* city-dweller. ● *a* city.

**citation** /sitasjɔ̃/ *nf* quotation; (Jur) summons.

**cité** /site/ *nf* city; (logements) housing estate; **~ universitaire** (university) halls of residence.

**citer** /site/ [1] *vt* quote, cite; (Jur) summon.

**citerne** /sitɛʀn/ *nf* tank.

**citoyen**, **~ne** /sitwajɛ̃, -ɛn/ *nm,f* citizen.

**citron** /sitʀɔ̃/ *nm* lemon; ~ **vert** lime. **citronnade** *nf* lemon squash, (still) lemonade.

**citrouille** /sitʀuj/ *nf* pumpkin.

**civet** /sivɛ/ *nm* stew; ~ **de lièvre** jugged hare.

**civière** /sivjɛʀ/ *nf* stretcher.

**civil**, **~e** /sivil/ *a* civil; (non militaire) civilian; (poli) civil. ● *nm* civilian; **dans le ~** in civilian life; **en ~** in plain clothes.

**civilisation** /sivilizasjɔ̃/ *nf* civilization.

**civiliser** /sivilize/ [1] *vt* civilize. □ **se ~** *vpr* become civilized.

**civique** /sivik/ *a* civic.

**clair**, **~e** /klɛʀ/ *a* clear; (éclairé) light, bright; (*couleur*) light; **le plus ~ de** most of. ● *adv* clearly; **il faisait ~** it was already light. ● *nm* **~ de lune** moonlight; **tirer une histoire au ~** get to the bottom of things. **clairement** *adv* clearly.

**clairière** /klɛʀjɛʀ/ *nf* clearing.

**clairsemé**, **~e** /klɛʀsəme/ *a* sparse.

**clamer** /klame/ [1] *vt* proclaim.

**clameur** /klamœʀ/ *nf* clamour.

**clan** /klɑ̃/ *nm* clan.

**clandestin**, **~e** /klɑ̃dɛstɛ̃, -in/ *a* secret; (*journal*) underground; (*immigration, travail*) illegal; **passager ~** stowaway.

**clapier** /klapje/ *nm* (rabbit) hutch.

**clapoter** /klapɔte/ [1] *vi* lap.

**claquage** /klakaʒ/ *nm* strained muscle; **se faire un ~** pull a muscle.

**claque** /klak/ *nf* slap.

**claquer** /klake/ [1] *vi* bang; (*porte*) slam, bang; (*fouet*) crack; (se casser Ⓘ) conk out; (mourir Ⓘ) snuff it Ⓘ; **~ des doigts** snap one's fingers; **~ des mains** clap one's hands; **il claque des dents** his teeth are chattering. ● *vt* (*porte*) slam, bang; (dépenser Ⓘ) blow; (fatiguer Ⓘ) tire out.

**claquettes** /klakɛt/ *nfpl* tap dancing.

**clarifier** /klaʀifje/ [45] *vt* clarify.

**clarinette** /klaʀinɛt/ *nf* clarinet.

**clarté** /klaʀte/ *nf* light, brightness; (netteté) clarity.

**classe** /klas/ *nf* class; (salle: Scol) classroom; (cours) class, lesson; **aller en ~** go to school; **faire la ~** teach; **~ ouvrière/moyenne** working/middle class.

**classement** /klasmɑ̃/ *nm* classification; (d'élèves) grading; (de documents) filing; (rang) place, grade; (de coureur) placing.

**classer** /klase/ [1] *vt* classify; (par mérite) grade; (*papiers*) file; (Jur) (*affaire*) close. □ **se ~** *vpr* rank.

**classeur** /klasœʀ/ *nm* (meuble) filing cabinet; (chemise) file; (à anneaux) ring binder.

**classification** /klasifikasjɔ̃/ *nf* classification.

**classique** /klasik/ *a* classical; (de qualité) classic; (habituel) classic, standard. ● *nm* classic; (auteur) classical author.

**clavecin** /klavsɛ̃/ *nm* harpsichord.

**clavicule** /klavikyl/ *nf* collarbone.

**clavier** /klavje/ *nm* keyboard; **~ numérique** keypad.

**clé**, **clef** /kle/ *nf* key; (outil) spanner; (Mus) clef; **~ anglaise** (monkey-)wrench; **~ de contact** ignition key; **~ à molette** adjustable spanner; **~ de voûte** keystone; **prix ~s en main** (de voiture) on-the-road price. ● *a inv* key.

**clémence** /klemɑ̃s/ *nf* (de climat) mildness; (indulgence) leniency.

**clergé** /klɛʀʒe/ *nm* clergy.

**clérical**, **~e** (*mpl* **-aux**) /kleʀikal, -o/ *a* clerical.

**clic** /klik/ *nm* (Ordinat) click.

**cliché** /kliʃe/ *nm* cliché; (Photo) negative.

**client**, **~e** /klijɑ̃, -t/ *nm,f* customer; (d'un avocat) client; (d'un médecin) patient; (d'hôtel) guest; (de taxi) passenger.

**clientèle** /klijɑ̃tɛl/ *nf* customers, clientele; (d'un avocat) clients, practice; (d'un médecin) patients, practice; (soutien) custom.

**cligner** /kliɲe/ [1] *vi* **~ des yeux** blink; **~ de l'œil** wink.

**clignotant** /kliɲɔtɑ̃/ *nm* (Auto) indicator, turn.

**clignoter** /kliɲɔte/ [1] *vi* blink; (*lumière*) flicker; (comme signal) flash.

**climat** /klima/ *nm* climate.

**climatisation** /klimatizasjɔ̃/ *nf* air-conditioning.

**clin d'œil** /klɛ̃dœj/ *nm* wink; **en un ~** in a flash.

**clinique** /klinik/ *a* clinical. ● *nf* (private) clinic.

**clinquant, ~e** /klɛ̃kɑ̃, -t/ *a* showy.

**clip** /klip/ *nm* video.

**cliquer** /klike/ [1] *vi* (Ordinat) click (**sur** on).

**cliqueter** /klikte/ [38] *vi* (*couverts*) clink; (*clés, monnaie*) jingle; (*ferraille*) rattle. **cliquetis** *nm* clink(ing), jingle, rattle.

**clivage** /klivaʒ/ *nm* divide.

**clochard, ~e** /klɔʃaʀ, -d/ *nm,f* tramp.

**cloche** /klɔʃ/ *nf* bell; (imbécile [!]) idiot; **~ à fromage** cheese-cover.

**cloche-pied: à ~** /aklɔʃpje/ **sauter à ~** hop on one leg.

**clocher** /klɔʃe/ *nm* bell tower; (pointu) steeple; **de ~** parochial.

**cloison** /klwazɔ̃/ *nf* partition; (fig) barrier.

**cloître** /klwatʀ/ *nm* cloister. **cloîtrer (se)** [1] *vpr* shut oneself away.

**clonage** /klonaʒ/ *nm* cloning.

**cloner** /klone/ [1] *vt* clone.

**cloque** /klɔk/ *nf* blister.

**clos, ~e** /klo, -z/ *a* closed.

**clôture** /klotyʀ/ *nf* fence; (fermeture) closure; (de magasin, bureau) closing; (de débat, liste) close; (en Bourse) close of trading. **clôturer** [1] *vt* enclose, fence in; (*festival, séance*) close.

**clou** /klu/ *nm* nail; (furoncle) boil; (de spectacle) star attraction; **les ~s** (passage) pedestrian crossing; (US) crosswalk.

**clouer** /klue/ [1] *vt* nail down; (fig) pin down; **être cloué au lit** be confined to one's bed; **~ le bec à qn** shut sb up.

**clouté, ~e** /klute/ *a* studded; **passage ~** pedestrian crossing; (US) crosswalk.

**coaliser (se)** /(sə)kɔalize/ [1] *vpr* join forces.

**coalition** /kɔalisjɔ̃/ *nf* coalition.

**cobaye** /kɔbaj/ *nm* guinea-pig.

**cocaïne** /kɔkain/ *nf* cocaine.

**cocasse** /kɔkas/ *a* comical.

**coccinelle** /kɔksinɛl/ *nf* ladybird; (US) ladybug.

**cocher** /kɔʃe/ [1] *vt* tick (off), check. ● *nm* coachman.

**cochon, ~ne** /kɔʃɔ̃, -ɔn/ *nm,f* (personne [!]) pig. ● *a* [!] filthy. ● *nm* pig. **cochonnerie** *nf* (saleté [!]) filth; (marchandise [!]) rubbish, junk.

**cocon** /kɔkɔ̃/ *nm* cocoon.

**cocotier** /kɔkɔtje/ *nm* coconut palm.

**cocotte** /kɔkɔt/ *nf* (marmite) casserole; **~ minute®** pressure-cooker; **ma ~** [!] my dear.

**cocu, ~e** /kɔky/ *nm,f* [!] deceived husband, deceived wife.

**code** /kɔd/ *nm* code; **~s** dipped headlights; **se mettre en ~s** dip one's headlights; **~ (à) barres** bar code; **~ confidentiel (d'identification)** PIN number; **~ postal** post code; (US) zip code; **~ de la route** Highway Code. **coder** [1] *vt* code, encode.

**coéquipier, -ière** /kɔekipje, -jɛʀ/ *nm,f* team mate.

**cœur** /kœʀ/ *nm* heart; (aux cartes) hearts (+ *pl*); ~ **d'artichaut** artichoke heart; ~ **de palmier** palm heart; **à** ~ **ouvert** (*opération*) open-heart; (*parler*) freely; **avoir bon** ~ be kind-hearted; **de bon** ~ willingly; (*rire*) heartily; **par** ~ by heart; **avoir mal au** ~ feel sick *ou* nauseous; **je veux en avoir le** ~ **net** I want to be clear in my own mind (about it).

**coffre** /kɔfʀ/ *nm* chest; (pour argent) safe; (Auto) boot; (US) trunk. **coffre-fort** (*pl* **coffres-forts**) *nm* safe.

**coffret** /kɔfʀɛ/ *nm* casket, box; (de livres, cassettes) boxed set.

**cogner** /kɔɲe/ [1] *vt/i* knock. □ **se** ~ *vpr* knock oneself; **se** ~ **la tête** bump one's head.

**cohabitater** /kɔabite/ [1] *vi* live together.

**cohérent**, ~**e** /kɔeʀɑ̃, -t/ *a* coherent; (homogène) consistent.

**cohue** /kɔy/ *nf* crowd.

**coi**, ~**te** /kwa, -t/ *a* silent.

**coiffe** /kwaf/ *nf* headgear.

**coiffer** /kwafe/ [1] *vt* do the hair of; (*chapeau*) put on; (surmonter) cap; ~ **qn d'un chapeau** put a hat on sb; **coiffé de** wearing; **être bien/mal coiffé** have tidy/untidy hair. □ **se** ~ *vpr* do one's hair.

**coiffeur**, **-euse** /kwafœʀ, -øz/ *nm,f* hairdresser. **coiffeuse** *nf* dressing-table.

**coiffure** /kwafyʀ/ *nf* hairstyle; (métier) hairdressing; (chapeau) hat.

**coin** /kwɛ̃/ *nm* corner; (endroit) spot; (cale) wedge; **au** ~ **du feu** by the fireside; **dans le** ~ locally; **du** ~ local.

**coincer** /kwɛ̃se/ [10] *vt* jam; (caler) wedge; (attraper 🅸) catch. □ **se** ~ *vpr* get jammed.

**coïncidence** /kɔɛ̃sidɑ̃s/ *nf* coincidence.

**coing** /kwɛ̃/ *nm* quince.

**coït** /kɔit/ *nm* intercourse.

**col** /kɔl/ *nm* collar; (de bouteille) neck; (de montagne) pass; ~ **blanc** white-collar worker; ~ **roulé** polo-neck; (US) turtle-neck; ~ **de l'utérus** cervix; **se casser le** ~ **du fémur** break one's hip.

**colère** /kɔlɛʀ/ *nf* anger; (accès) fit of anger; **en** ~ angry; **se mettre en** ~ lose one's temper; **faire une** ~ throw a tantrum.

**coléreux**, **-euse** /kɔleʀø, -z/ *a* quick-tempered.

**colin** /kɔlɛ̃/ *nm* (merlu) hake; (lieu noir) coley.

**colique** /kɔlik/ *nf* diarrhoea; (Méd) colic.

**colis** /kɔli/ *nm* parcel.

**collaborateur**, **-trice** /kɔlabɔʀatœʀ, -tʀis/ *nm,f* collaborator; (journaliste) contributor; (collègue) colleague.

**collaboration** /kɔlabɔʀasjɔ̃/ *nf* collaboration (**à** on); (à ouvrage, projet) contribution (**à** to).

**collaborer** /kɔlabɔʀe/ [1] *vi* collaborate (**à** on); ~ **à** (*journal*) contribute to.

**collant**, ~**e** /kɔlɑ̃, -t/ *a* (moulant) skin-tight; (poisseux) sticky. ● *nm* (bas) tights; (US) panty hose.

**colle** /kɔl/ *nf* glue; (en pâte) paste; (problème 🅸) poser; (Scol 🅸) detention.

**collecter** /kɔlɛkte/ [1] *vt* collect.

**collectif**, **-ive** /kɔlɛktif, -v/ *a* collective; (*billet, voyage*) group.

**collection** /kɔlɛksjɔ̃/ *nf* collection; (ouvrages) series (+ *sg*); (du même auteur) set. **collectionner** [1] *vt* collect. **collectionneur**, **-euse** *nm,f* collector.

**collectivité** /kɔlɛktivite/ *nf* community; ~ **locale** local authority.

**collège** /kɔlɛʒ/ *nm* secondary school (*up to age 15*); (US) junior high school; (assemblée) college. **collégien**, **~ne** *nm,f* schoolboy, schoolgirl.

**collègue** /kɔlɛg/ *nmf* colleague.

**coller** /kɔle/ [1] *vt* stick; (avec colle liquide) glue; (*affiche*) stick up; (mettre [!]) stick; (par une question [!]) stump; (Scol [!]) **se faire ~** get a detention; **je me suis fait ~ en maths** I failed *ou* flunked maths. ● *vi* stick (**à** to); (être collant) be sticky; ~ **à** (convenir à) fit, correspond to.

**collet** /kɔlɛ/ *nm* (piège) snare; ~ **monté** prim and proper; **mettre la main au ~ de qn** collar sb.

**collier** /kɔlje/ *nm* necklace; (de chien) collar.

**colline** /kɔlin/ *nf* hill.

**collision** /kɔlizjɔ̃/ *nf* (choc) collision; (lutte) clash; **entrer en ~ (avec)** collide (with).

**collyre** /kɔliʀ/ *nm* eye drops (+ *pl*).

**colmater** /kɔlmate/ [1] *vt* plug, seal.

**colombe** /kɔlɔ̃b/ *nf* dove.

**Colombie** /kɔlɔ̃bi/ *nf* Colombia.

**colon** /kɔlɔ̃/ *nm* settler.

**colonel** /kɔlɔnɛl/ *nm* colonel.

**colonie** /kɔlɔni/ *nf* colony; ~ **de vacances** children's holiday camp.

**colonne** /kɔlɔn/ *nf* column; ~ **vertébrale** spine; **en ~ par deux** in double file.

**colorant** /kɔlɔʀɑ̃/ *nm* colouring.

**colorier** /kɔlɔʀje/ [45] *vt* colour (in).

**colosse** /kɔlɔs/ *nm* giant.

**colza** /kɔlza/ *nm* rape(-seed).

**coma** /kɔma/ *nm* coma; **dans le ~** in a coma.

**combat** /kɔ̃ba/ *nm* fight; (Sport) match; **~s** fighting. **combatif**, **-ive** *a* eager to fight; (*esprit*) fighting.

**combattre** /kɔ̃batʀ/ [11] *vt/i* fight.

**combien** /kɔ̃bjɛ̃/ *adv* ~ **(de)** (quantité) how much; (nombre) how many; (temps) how long; ~ **il a changé!** (comme) how he has changed!; ~ **y a-t-il d'ici à ...?** how far is it to ...?; **on est le ~ aujourd'hui?** what's the date today?

**combinaison** /kɔ̃binɛzɔ̃/ *nf* combination; (de femme) slip; (bleu de travail) boiler suit; (US) overalls; ~ **d'aviateur** flying-suit; ~ **de plongée** wetsuit.

**combine** /kɔ̃bin/ *nf* trick; (fraude) fiddle; (intrigue) scheme.

**combiné** /kɔ̃bine/ *nm* (de téléphone) receiver, handset.

**combiner** /kɔ̃bine/ [1] *vt* (réunir) combine; (calculer) devise; ~ **de faire** plan to do.

**comble** /kɔ̃bl/ *a* packed. ● *nm* height; **~s** (mansarde) attic, loft; **c'est le ~!** that's the (absolute) limit!

**combler** /kɔ̃ble/ [1] *vt* fill; (*perte, déficit*) make good; (*désir*) fulfil; ~ **qn de cadeaux** lavish gifts on sb.

**combustible** /kɔ̃bystibl/ *nm* fuel.

**comédie** /kɔmedi/ *nf* comedy; (histoire [!]) fuss; ~ **musicale** musical; **jouer la ~** put on an act. **comédien**, **~ne** *nm,f* actor, actress.

**comestible** /kɔmɛstibl/ *a* edible.

**comète** /kɔmɛt/ *nf* comet.

**comique** /kɔmik/ *a* comical, funny; (*genre*) comic. ● *nm* (acteur) comic; (comédie) comedy; (côté drôle) comical aspect.

**commandant** /kɔmɑ̃dɑ̃/ *nm* commander; (dans l'armée de terre) major; ~ **(de bord)** captain; ~ **en chef** Commander-in-Chief.

**commande** /kɔmɑ̃d/ *nf* (Comm) order; (Tech) control; **~s** (d'avion) controls.

**commandement** /kɔmɑ̃dmɑ̃/ *nm* command; (Relig) commandment.

**commander** /kɔmɑ̃de/ [1] *vt* command; (acheter) order; (*étude, œuvre d'art*) commission; **~ à** (maîtriser) control; **~ à qn de** command sb to. ● *vi* be in command.

**comme** /kɔm/ *adv* **~ c'est bon!** it's so good!; **~ il est mignon!** isn't he sweet! ● *conj* (dans une comparaison) as; (dans une équivalence, illustration) like; (en tant que) as; (puisque) as, since; (au moment où) as; **vif ~ l'éclair** as quick as a flash; **travailler ~ sage-femme** work as a midwife; **~ ci ~ ça** so-so; **~ il faut** properly; **~ pour faire** as if to do; **jolie ~ tout** as pretty as anything; **qu'est-ce qu'il y a ~ légumes?** what is there in the way of vegetables?

**commencer** /kɔmɑ̃se/ [10] *vt/i* begin, start; **~ à faire** begin *ou* start to do.

**comment** /kɔmɑ̃/ *adv* how; **~?** (répétition) pardon?; (surprise) what?; **~ est-il?** what is he like?; **le ~ et le pourquoi** the whys and wherefores.

**commentaire** /kɔmɑ̃tɛʀ/ *nm* comment; (d'un texte, événement) commentary. **commentateur, -trice** *nm,f* commentator.

**commenter** /kɔmɑ̃te/ [1] *vt* comment on; (*film, visite*) provide a commentary for; (radio, TV) commentate.

**commérages** /kɔmeʀaʒ/ *nmpl* gossip.

**commerçant, ~e** /kɔmɛʀsɑ̃, -t/ *a* (*rue*) shopping; (*personne*) business-minded. ● *nm,f* shopkeeper.

**commerce** /kɔmɛʀs/ *nm* trade, commerce; (magasin) business; **faire du ~** be in business; **~ électronique** e-commerce.

**commercial, ~e** (*mpl* **-iaux**) /kɔmɛʀsjal, -jo/ *a* commercial. **commercialiser** [1] *vt* market.

**commettre** /kɔmɛtʀ/ [42] *vt* commit.

**commis** /kɔmi/ *nm* (de magasin) assistant; (de bureau) clerk.

**commissaire** /kɔmisɛʀ/ *nm* commissioner; (Sport) steward; **~ (de police)** (police) superintendent. **commissaire-priseur** (*pl* **commissaires-priseurs**) *nm* auctioneer.

**commissariat** /kɔmisaʀja/ *nm* **~ (de police)** police station.

**commission** /kɔmisjɔ̃/ *nf* commission; (course) errand; (message) message; **~s** shopping.

**commode** /kɔmɔd/ *a* handy, convenient; (facile) easy; **il n'est pas ~** he's a difficult customer. ● *nf* chest (of drawers). **commodité** *nf* convenience.

**commotion** /kɔmosjɔ̃/ *nf* **~ (cérébrale)** concussion.

**commun, ~e** /kɔmœ̃, -yn/ *a* common; (*effort, action*) joint; (*frais, pièce*) shared; **en ~** jointly; **avoir** *ou* **mettre en ~** share; **le ~ des mortels** ordinary mortals. **communal, ~e** (*mpl* **-aux**) *a* of the commune, local.

**communauté** /kɔmynote/ *nf* community.

**commune** /kɔmyn/ *nf* (circonscription, collectivité) commune.

**communicatif, -ive** /kɔmynikatif, -v/ *a* (*personne*) talkative; (*gaieté*) infectious.

**communication** /kɔmynikasjɔ̃/ *nf* communication; (téléphonique) call; **~s** (relations) communications

(+ *pl*); **voies** *ou* **moyens de ~** communications (+ *pl*).

**communier** /kɔmynje/ [45] *vi* (Relig) receive communion; (fig) commune.

**communiqué** /kɔmynike/ *nm* statement; (de presse) communiqué.

**communiquer** /kɔmynike/ [1] *vt* pass on, communicate; (*date, décision*) announce. ● *vi* communicate. □ **se ~ à** *vpr* spread to.

**communiste** /kɔmynist/ *a & nmf* communist.

**commutateur** /kɔmytatœʀ/ *nm* (Électr) switch.

**compagne** /kɔ̃paɲ/ *nf* companion.

**compagnie** /kɔ̃paɲi/ *nf* company; **tenir ~ à** keep company; **en ~ de** together with; **~ aérienne** airline.

**compagnon** /kɔ̃paɲɔ̃/ *nm* companion.

**comparable** /kɔ̃paʀabl/ *a* comparable (**à** to). **comparaison** *nf* comparison; (littéraire) simile.

**comparaître** /kɔ̃paʀɛtʀ/ [18] *vi* (Jur) appear (**devant** before).

**comparatif**, **-ive** /kɔ̃paʀatif, -v/ *a & nm* comparative.

**comparer** /kɔ̃paʀe/ [1] *vt* compare (**à** with). □ **se ~** *vpr* compare oneself; (être comparable) be comparable.

**compartiment** /kɔ̃paʀtimɑ̃/ *nm* compartment.

**comparution** /kɔ̃paʀysjɔ̃/ *nf* (Jur) appearance.

**compas** /kɔ̃pa/ *nm* (pair of) compasses; (boussole) compass.

**compassion** /kɔ̃pasjɔ̃/ *nf* compassion.

**compatible** /kɔ̃patibl/ *a* compatible.

**compatir** /kɔ̃patiʀ/ [2] *vi* sympathize; **~ à** share in.

**compatriote** /kɔ̃patʀijɔt/ *nmf* compatriot.

**compensation** /kɔ̃pɑ̃sasjɔ̃/ *nf* compensation. **compenser** [1] *vt* compensate for, make up for.

**compère** /kɔ̃pɛʀ/ *nm* accomplice.

**compétence** /kɔpetɑ̃s/ *nf* competence; (fonction) domain, sphere; **entrer dans les ~s de qn** be in sb's domain. **compétent**, **~e** *a* competent.

**compétition** /kɔ̃petisjɔ̃/ *nf* competition; (sportive) event; **de ~** competitive.

**complaire (se)** /(sə)kɔ̃plɛʀ/ [47] *vpr* **se ~ dans** delight in.

**complaisance** /kɔ̃plɛzɑ̃s/ *nf* kindness; (indulgence) indulgence.

**complément** /kɔ̃plemɑ̃/ *nm* supplement; (Gram) complement; **~ (d'objet)** (Gram) object; **~s d'information** further information. **complémentaire** *a* complementary; (*renseignements*) supplementary.

**complet**, **-ète** /kɔ̃plɛ, -t/ *a* complete; (*train, hôtel*) full. ● *nm* suit.

**compléter** /kɔ̃plete/ [14] *vt* complete; (agrémenter) complement. □ **se ~** *vpr* complement each other.

**complexe** /kɔ̃plɛks/ *a* complex. ● *nm* (sentiment, bâtiments) complex.

**complexé**, **~e** /kɔ̃plekse/ *a* **être ~** have a lot of hang-ups.

**complice** /kɔ̃plis/ *nm* accomplice.

**compliment** /kɔ̃plimɑ̃/ *nm* compliment; **~s** (félicitations) compliments, congratulations.

**compliquer** /kɔ̃plike/ [1] *vt* complicate. □ **se ~** *vpr* become complicated.

**complot** /kɔ̃plo/ *nm* plot.

**comportement** /kɔ̃pɔʀtəmɑ̃/ *nm* behaviour; (de joueur, voiture) performance.

**comporter** /kɔ̃pɔʀte/ [1] *vt* (être composé de) comprise; (inclure) include; (*risque*) entail. ▫ **se ~** *vpr* behave; (*joueur, voiture*) perform.

**composant** /kɔ̃pozɑ̃/ *nm* component.

**composé, ~e** /kɔ̃poze/ *a* composite; (*salade*) mixed; (guindé) affected. ● *nm* compound.

**composer** /kɔ̃poze/ [1] *vt* make up, compose; (*chanson, visage*) compose; (*numéro*) dial; (*page*) typeset. ● *vi* (transiger) compromise. ▫ **se ~ de** *vpr* be made up *ou* composed of. **compositeur, -trice** *nm, f* (Mus) composer.

**composter** /kɔ̃pɔste/ [1] *vt* (*billet*) punch.

**compote** /kɔ̃pɔt/ *nf* stewed fruit; **~ de pommes** stewed apples.

**compréhensible** /kɔ̃pʀeɑ̃sibl/ *a* understandable; (intelligible) comprehensible.

**compréhensif, -ive** /kɔ̃pʀeɑ̃sif, -v/ *a* understanding.

**compréhension** /kɔ̃pʀeɑ̃sjɔ̃/ *nf* understanding, comprehension.

**comprendre** /kɔ̃pʀɑ̃dʀ/ [50] *vt* understand; (comporter) comprise, be made up of. ▫ **se ~** *vpr* (*personnes*) understand each other; **ça se comprend** that is understandable.

**compresse** /kɔ̃pʀɛs/ *nf* compress.

**comprimé** /kɔ̃pʀime/ *nm* tablet.

**comprimer** /kɔ̃pʀime/ [1] *vt* compress; (réduire) reduce.

**compris, ~e** /kɔ̃pʀi, -z/ *a* included; (d'accord) agreed; **~ entre** (contained) between; **service (non) ~** service (not) included; **tout ~** (all) inclusive; **y ~** including.

**compromettre** /kɔ̃pʀɔmɛtʀ/ [42] *vt* compromise. **compromis** *nm* compromise.

**comptabilité** /kɔ̃tabilite/ *nf* accountancy; (comptes) accounts; (service) accounts department.

**comptable** /kɔ̃tabl/ *a* accounting. ● *nmf* accountant.

**comptant** /kɔ̃tɑ̃/ *adv* (*payer*) (in) cash; (*acheter*) for cash.

**compte** /kɔ̃t/ *nm* count; (facture, comptabilité) account; (nombre exact) right number; **~ bancaire, ~ en banque** bank account; **prendre qch en ~, tenir ~ de qch** take sth into account; **se rendre ~ de** realize; **demander/rendre des ~s** ask for/give an explanation; **à bon ~** cheaply; **s'en tirer à bon ~** get off lightly; **travailler à son ~** be self-employed; **faire le ~ de** count; **pour le ~ de** on behalf of; **sur le ~ de** about; **au bout du ~** all things considered; **~ à rebours** countdown.

**compte-gouttes** /kɔ̃tgut/ *nm inv* (Méd) dropper; **au ~** (fig) in dribs and drabs.

**compter** /kɔ̃te/ [1] *vt* count; (prévoir) allow, reckon on; (facturer) charge for; (avoir) have; (classer) consider; **~ faire** intend to do. ● *vi* (calculer, importer) count; **~ avec** reckon with; **~ parmi** (figurer) be considered among; **~ sur** rely on, count on.

**compte(-)rendu** /kɔ̃tʀɑ̃dy/ *nm* report; (de film, livre) review.

**compteur** /kɔ̃tœʀ/ *nm* meter; **~ de vitesse** speedometer.

**comptine** /kɔ̃tin/ *nf* nursery rhyme.

**comptoir** /kɔ̃twaʀ/ *nm* counter; (de café) bar.

**comte** /kɔ̃t/ *nm* count.

**comté** /kɔ̃te/ *nm* county.

**comtesse** /kɔ̃tɛs/ *nf* countess.

**con**, **~ne** /kɔ̃, kɔn/ *a* ☒ bloody stupid ☒. ● *nm,f* ☒ bloody fool ☒.

**concentrer** /kɔ̃sɑ̃tʀe/ [1] *vt* concentrate. □ **se ~** *vpr* be concentrated.

**concept** /kɔ̃sɛpt/ *nm* concept.

**concerner** /kɔ̃sɛʀne/ [1] *vt* concern; **en ce qui me concerne** as far as I am concerned.

**concert** /kɔ̃sɛʀ/ *nm* concert; **de ~** in unison.

**concerter** /kɔ̃sɛʀte/ [1] *vt* organize, prepare. □ **se ~** *vpr* confer.

**concession** /kɔ̃sesjɔ̃/ *nf* concession; (terrain) plot.

**concevoir** /kɔ̃svwaʀ/ [52] *vt* (imaginer, engendrer) conceive; (comprendre) understand; (élaborer) design.

**concierge** /kɔ̃sjɛʀʒ/ *nmf* caretaker.

**concilier** /kɔ̃silje/ [45] *vt* reconcile. □ **se ~** *vpr* (s'attirer) win (over).

**concis**, **~e** /kɔ̃si, -z/ *a* concise.

**conclure** /kɔ̃klyʀ/ [16] *vt* conclude; **~ à** conclude in favour of. ● *vi* **~ en faveur de/contre** find in favour of/against. **conclusion** *nf* conclusion.

**concombre** /kɔ̃kɔ̃bʀ/ *nm* cucumber.

**concordance** /kɔ̃kɔʀdɑ̃s/ *nf* agreement.

**concourir** /kɔ̃kuʀiʀ/ [20] *vi* compete. ● *vt* **~ à** contribute towards.

**concours** /kɔ̃kuʀ/ *nm* competition; (examen) competitive examination; (aide) help; (de circonstances) combination.

**concret**, **-ète** /kɔ̃kʀɛ, -t/ *a* concrete.

**concrétiser** /kɔ̃kʀetize/ [1] *vt* give concrete form to. □ **se ~** *vpr* materialize.

**conçu**, **~e** /kɔ̃sy/ *a* **bien/mal ~** well/badly designed.

**concubinage** /kɔ̃kybinaʒ/ *nm* cohabitation; **vivre en ~** live together, cohabit.

**concurrence** /kɔ̃kyʀɑ̃s/ *nf* competition; **faire ~ à** compete with; **jusqu'à ~ de** up to a limit of.

**concurrencer** /kɔ̃kyʀɑ̃se/ [10] *vt* compete with.

**concurrent**, **~e** /kɔ̃kyʀɑ̃, -t/ *nm,f* competitor; (Scol) candidate. ● *a* rival.

**condamnation** /kɔ̃danasjɔ̃/ *nf* condemnation; (peine) sentence; **~ centralisée des portières** central locking. **condamné**, **~e** *nm,f* condemned man, condemned woman. **condamner** [1] *vt* (censurer, obliger) condemn; (Jur) sentence; (*porte*) block up.

**condition** /kɔ̃disjɔ̃/ *nf* condition; **~s** (prix) terms; **à ~ de** *ou* **que** provided (that); **sans ~** unconditional(ly); **sous ~** conditionally.

**conditionnel**, **~le** /kɔ̃disjɔnɛl/ *a* conditional. ● *nm* conditional (tense).

**conditionnement** /kɔ̃disjɔnmɑ̃/ *nm* conditioning; (emballage) packaging.

**condoléances** /kɔ̃dɔleɑ̃s/ *nfpl* condolences.

**conducteur**, **-trice** /kɔ̃dyktœʀ, -tʀis/ *nm,f* driver.

**conduire** /kɔ̃dɥiʀ/ [17] *vt* take (**à** to); (guider) lead; (Auto) drive; (*affaire*) conduct; **~ à** (faire aboutir) lead to. ● *vi* drive. □ **se ~** *vpr* behave.

**conduit** /kɔ̃dɥi/ *nm* duct.

**conduite** /kɔ̃dɥit/ *nf* conduct, behaviour; (Auto) driving; (tuyau) pipe;

**voiture avec ~ à droite** right-hand drive car.

**confection** /kɔ̃fɛksjɔ̃/ *nf* making; **de ~** ready-made; **la ~** the clothing industry.

**conférence** /kɔ̃feʀɑ̃s/ *nf* conference; (exposé) lecture; **~ au sommet** summit meeting. **conférencier, -ière** *nm,f* lecturer.

**confesser** /kɔ̃fese/ [1] *vt* confess. □ **se ~** *vpr* go to confession.

**confiance** /kɔ̃fjɑ̃s/ *nf* trust; **avoir ~ en** trust.

**confiant, ~e** /kɔ̃fjɑ̃, -t/ *a* (assuré) confident; (sans défiance) trusting.

**confidence** /kɔ̃fidɑ̃s/ *nf* confidence.

**confidentiel, ~le** /kɔ̃fidɑ̃sjɛl/ *a* confidential.

**confier** /kɔ̃fje/ [45] *vt* **~ à qn** entrust sb with; **~ un secret à qn** tell sb a secret. □ **se ~ à** *vpr* confide in.

**confiner** /kɔ̃fine/ [1] *vt* confine; **~ à** border on. □ **se ~** *vpr* confine oneself (**à, dans** to).

**confirmation** /kɔ̃fiʀmasjɔ̃/ *nf* confirmation. **confirmer** [1] *vt* confirm.

**confiserie** /kɔ̃fizʀi/ *nf* sweet shop; **~s** confectionery.

**confisquer** /kɔ̃fiske/ [1] *vt* confiscate.

**confit, ~e** /kɔ̃fi, -t/ *a* candied; (*fruits*) crystallized. ● *nm* **~ de canard** confit of duck.

**confiture** /kɔ̃fityʀ/ *nf* jam.

**conflit** /kɔ̃fli/ *nm* conflict.

**confondre** /kɔ̃fɔ̃dʀ/ [3] *vt* confuse, mix up; (étonner) confound. □ **se ~** *vpr* merge; **se ~ en excuses** apologize profusely.

**conforme** /kɔ̃fɔʀm/ *a* **être ~ à** comply with; (être en accord) be in keeping with.

**conformer** /kɔ̃fɔʀme/ [1] *vt* adapt. □ **se ~ à** *vpr* conform to.

**conformité** /kɔ̃fɔʀmite/ *nf* compliance, conformity; **agir en ~ avec** act in accordance with.

**confort** /kɔ̃fɔʀ/ *nm* comfort; **tout ~** with all mod cons. **confortable** *a* comfortable.

**confrère** /kɔ̃fʀɛʀ/ *nm* colleague.

**confronter** /kɔ̃fʀɔ̃te/ [1] *vt* confront; (*textes*) compare. □ **se ~ à** *vpr* be confronted with.

**confus, ~e** /kɔ̃fy, -z/ *a* confused; (gêné) embarrassed.

**congé** /kɔ̃ʒe/ *nm* holiday; (arrêt momentané) time off, leave; (avis de départ) notice; **en ~** on holiday *ou* leave; **~ de maladie/maternité** sick/maternity leave; **jour de ~** day off; **prendre ~ de** take one's leave of.

**congédier** /kɔ̃ʒedje/ [45] *vt* dismiss.

**congélateur** /kɔ̃ʒelatœʀ/ *nm* freezer.

**congeler** /kɔ̃ʒle/ [6] *vt* freeze.

**congère** /kɔ̃ʒɛʀ/ *nf* snowdrift.

**congrès** /kɔ̃gʀɛ/ *nm* conference; (Pol) congress.

**conjoint, ~e** /kɔ̃ʒwɛ̃, -t/ *nm,f* spouse. ● *a* joint.

**conjonctivite** /kɔ̃ʒɔ̃ktivit/ *nf* conjunctivitis.

**conjoncture** /kɔ̃ʒɔ̃ktyʀ/ *nf* situation; (économique) economic climate.

**conjugaison** /kɔ̃ʒygɛzɔ̃/ *nf* conjugation.

**conjugal, ~e** (*mpl* **-aux**) /kɔ̃ʒygal, -o/ *a* conjugal, married.

**conjuguer** /kɔ̃ʒyge/ [1] *vt* (Gram) conjugate; (*efforts*) combine. □ **se**

~ *vpr* (Gram) be conjugated; (*facteurs*) be combined.

**conjurer** /kɔ̃ʒyʀe/ [1] *vt* (éviter) avert; (implorer) beg.

**connaissance** /kɔnɛsɑ̃s/ *nf* knowledge; (personne) acquaintance; **~s** (science) knowledge; **faire la ~ de** meet; (apprécier une personne) get to know; **perdre/reprendre ~** lose/regain consciousness; **sans ~** unconscious.

**connaisseur** /kɔnɛsœʀ/ *nm* expert, connoisseur.

**connaître** /kɔnɛtʀ/ [18] *vt* know; (*difficultés, faim, succès*) experience; **faire ~** make known. □ **se ~** *vpr* (se rencontrer) meet; **s'y ~ en** know (all) about.

**connecter** /kɔnɛkte/ [1] *vt* connect; **être/ne pas être connecté** be on-/off-line. □ **se ~ à** *vpr* (Ordinat) log on to.

**connerie** /kɔnʀi/ *nf* ⊠ **faire une ~** do something stupid; **dire des ~s** talk rubbish.

**connu, ~e** /kɔny/ *a* well-known.

**conquérant, ~e** /kɔ̃keʀɑ̃, -t/ *nm,f* conqueror.

**conquête** /kɔ̃kɛt/ *nf* conquest.

**consacrer** /kɔ̃sakʀe/ [1] *vt* devote; (Relig) consecrate; (sanctionner) sanction. □ **se ~ à** *vpr* devote oneself to.

**conscience** /kɔ̃sjɑ̃s/ *nf* conscience; (perception) awareness; (de collectivité) consciousness; **avoir/prendre ~ de** be/become aware of; **perdre/reprendre ~** lose/regain consciousness; **avoir bonne/mauvaise ~** have a clear/guilty conscience.

**conscient, ~e** /kɔ̃sjɑ̃, -t/ *a* conscious; **~ de** aware *ou* conscious of.

**conseil** /kɔ̃sɛj/ *nm* (piece of) advice; (assemblée) council, committee; (séance) meeting; (personne) consultant; **~ d'administration** board of directors; **~ en gestion** management consultant; **~ des ministres** Cabinet; **~ municipal** town council.

**conseiller**[1] /kɔ̃seje/ [1] *vt* advise; **~ à qn de** advise sb to; **~ qch à qn** recommend sth to sb.

**conseiller**[2], **-ère** /kɔ̃seje, -jɛʀ/ *nm,f* adviser, counsellor; **~ municipal** town councillor; **~ d'orientation** careers adviser.

**consentement** /kɔ̃sɑ̃tmɑ̃/ *nm* consent.

**conséquence** /kɔ̃sekɑ̃s/ *nf* consequence; **en ~** (comme il convient) accordingly; **en ~ (de quoi)** as a result of which.

**conséquent, ~e** /kɔ̃sekɑ̃, -t/ *a* consistent, logical; (important) substantial; **par ~** consequently, therefore.

**conservateur, -trice** /kɔ̃sɛʀvatœʀ, -tʀis/ *a* conservative. ● *nm,f* (Pol) conservative; (de musée) curator. ● *nm* preservative.

**conservation** /kɔ̃sɛʀvasjɔ̃/ *nf* preservation; (d'espèce, patrimoine) conservation.

**conservatoire** /kɔ̃sɛʀvatwaʀ/ *nm* academy.

**conserve** /kɔ̃sɛʀv/ *nf* tinned *ou* canned food; **en ~** tinned, canned; **boîte de ~** tin, can.

**conserver** /kɔ̃sɛʀve/ [1] *vt* keep; (en bon état) preserve; (Culin) preserve. □ **se ~** *vpr* (Culin) keep.

**considérer** /kɔ̃sideʀe/ [14] *vt* consider; (respecter) esteem; **~ comme** consider to be.

**consigne** /kɔ̃siɲ/ *nf* (de gare) left-luggage office; (US) baggage checkroom; (somme) deposit; (ordres) orders; **~ automatique** left-luggage lockers; (US) baggage lockers.

**consistance** /kɔ̃sistɑ̃s/ *nf* consistency; (fig) substance, weight.
**consistant**, **~e** *a* solid; (épais) thick.

**consister** /kɔ̃siste/ [1] *vi* **~ en/dans** consist of/in; **~ à faire** consist in doing.

**consoler** /kɔ̃sɔle/ [1] *vt* console. □ **se ~** *vpr* find consolation; **se ~ de qch** get over sth.

**consolider** /kɔ̃sɔlide/ [1] *vt* strengthen; (fig) consolidate.

**consommateur**, **-trice** /kɔ̃sɔmatœʀ, -tʀis/ *nm,f* (Comm) consumer; (dans un café) customer.

**consommation** /kɔ̃sɔmasjɔ̃/ *nf* consumption; (accomplissement) consummation; (boisson) drink; **de ~** (Comm) consumer.

**consommer** /kɔ̃sɔme/ [1] *vt* consume, use; (manger) eat; (boire) drink; (*mariage*) consummate. □ **se ~** *vpr* (être mangé) be eaten; (être utilisé) be used.

**consonne** /kɔ̃sɔn/ *nf* consonant.

**constat** /kɔ̃sta/ *nm* (official) report; **~ (à l')amiable** accident report drawn up by those involved.

**constatation** /kɔ̃statasjɔ̃/ *nf* observation, statement of fact.
**constater** [1] *vt* note, notice; (certifier) certify.

**consternation** /kɔ̃stɛʀnasjɔ̃/ *nf* dismay.

**constipé**, **~e** /kɔ̃stipe/ *a* constipated; (fig) uptight.

**constituer** /kɔ̃stitɥe/ [1] *vt* (composer) make up, constitute; (organiser) form; (être) constitute; **constitué de** made up of. □ **se ~** *vpr* **se ~ prisonnier** give oneself up.

**constitution** /kɔ̃stitysjɔ̃/ *nf* formation, setting up; (Pol, Méd) constitution.

**constructeur** /kɔ̃stʀyktœʀ/ *nm* manufacturer, builder.

**construction** /kɔ̃stʀyksjɔ̃/ *nf* building; (structure, secteur) construction; (fabrication) manufacture.

**construire** /kɔ̃stʀɥiʀ/ [17] *vt* build; (*système, phrase*) construct.

**consulat** /kɔ̃syla/ *nm* consulate.

**consultation** /kɔ̃syltasjɔ̃/ *nf* consultation; (réception: Méd) surgery; (US) office; **heures de ~** surgery *ou* office (US) hours.

**consulter** /kɔ̃sylte/ [1] *vt* consult. ● *vi* (*médecin*) hold surgery, see patients. □ **se ~** *vpr* consult together.

**contact** /kɔ̃takt/ *nm* contact; (toucher) touch; **au ~ de** on contact with; (*personne*) by contact with, by seeing; **mettre/couper le ~** (Auto) switch on/off the ignition; **prendre ~ avec** get in touch with.
**contacter** [1] *vt* contact.

**contagieux**, **-ieuse** /kɔ̃taʒjø, -z/ *a* contagious.

**conte** /kɔ̃t/ *nm* tale; **~ de fées** fairy tale.

**contempler** /kɔ̃tɑ̃ple/ [1] *vt* contemplate.

**contemporain**, **~e** /kɔ̃tɑ̃pɔʀɛ̃, -ɛn/ *a & nm,f* contemporary.

**contenance** /kɔ̃t(ə)nɑ̃s/ *nf* (volume) capacity; (allure) bearing; **perdre ~** lose one's composure.

**contenir** /kɔ̃t(ə)niʀ/ [58] *vt* contain; (avoir une capacité de) hold. □ **se ~** *vpr* contain oneself.

**content**, **~e** /kɔ̃tɑ̃, -t/ *a* pleased, happy (**de** with); **~ de faire** pleased *ou* happy to do.

**contenter** /kɔ̃tɑ̃te/ [1] *vt* satisfy. □ **se ~ de** *vpr* content oneself with.

**contenu** /kɔ̃t(ə)ny/ *nm* (de récipient) contents (+ *pl*); (de texte) content.

**conter** /kɔ̃te/ [1] *vt* tell, relate.

**contestation** /kɔ̃tɛstasjɔ̃/ *nf* dispute; (opposition) protest.

**contester** /kɔ̃tɛste/ [1] *vt* question, dispute; (s'opposer) protest against. ● *vi* protest.

**conteur**, **-euse** /kɔ̃tœʀ, -øz/ *nm,f* storyteller.

**contigu**, **~ë** /kɔ̃tigy/ *a* adjacent (**à** to).

**continent** /kɔ̃tinɑ̃/ *nm* continent.

**continu**, **~e** /kɔ̃tiny/ *a* continuous.

**continuer** /kɔ̃tinɥe/ [1] *vt* continue. ● *vi* continue, go on; **~ à** *ou* **de faire** carry on *ou* go on *ou* continue doing.

**contorsionner** (**se**) /(se)kɔ̃tɔʀsjɔne/ [1] *vpr* wriggle.

**contour** /kɔ̃tuʀ/ *nm* outline, contour; **~s** (d'une route) twists and turns, bends.

**contourner** /kɔ̃tuʀne/ [1] *vt* go round, by-pass; (*difficulté*) get round.

**contraceptif**, **-ive** /kɔ̃tʀasɛptif, -v/ *a* contraceptive. ● *nm* contraceptive. **contraception** *nf* contraception.

**contracter** /kɔ̃tʀakte/ [1] *vt* (*maladie*) contract; (*dette*) incur; (*muscle*) tense; (*assurance*) take out. □ **se ~** *vpr* contract.

**contractuel**, **~le** /kɔ̃tʀaktɥɛl/ *nm,f* (agent) traffic warden.

**contradictoire** /kɔ̃tʀadiktwaʀ/ *a* contradictory; (*débat*) open.

**contraignant**, **~e** /kɔ̃tʀɛɲɑ̃, -t/ *a* restricting.

**contraindre** /kɔ̃tʀɛ̃dʀ/ [22] *vt* force, compel (**à faire** to do).

**contrainte** /kɔ̃tʀɛ̃t/ *nf* constraint.

**contraire** /kɔ̃tʀɛʀ/ *a* opposite; **~ à** contrary to. ● *nm* opposite; **au ~** on the contrary; **au ~ de** unlike.

**contrarier** /kɔ̃tʀaʀje/ [45] *vt* annoy; (*projet, volonté*) frustrate; (chagriner) upset.

**contraste** /kɔ̃tʀast/ *nm* contrast.

**contrat** /kɔ̃tʀa/ *nm* contract.

**contravention** /kɔ̃tʀavɑ̃sjɔ̃/ *nf* (parking) ticket; **en ~** in breach (**à** of).

**contre** /kɔ̃tʀ(ə)/ *prép* against; (en échange de) for; **par ~** on the other hand; **tout ~** close by. **contre-attaque** (*pl* **~s**) *nf* counter-attack. **contre-attaquer** [1] *vt* counter-attack. **contre-balancer** [10] *vt* counterbalance.

**contrebande** /kɔ̃tʀəbɑ̃d/ *nf* contraband; **faire la ~ de** smuggle.

**contrebas**: **en ~** /ɑ̃kɔ̃tʀəbɑ/ *loc* below.

**contrebasse** /kɔ̃tʀəbɑs/ *nf* double bass.

**contrecœur**: **à ~** /akɔ̃tʀəkœʀ/ *loc* reluctantly.

**contrecoup** /kɔ̃tʀəku/ *nm* effects, repercussions.

**contredire** /kɔ̃tʀədiʀ/ [37] *vt* contradict. □ **se ~** *vpr* contradict oneself.

**contrée** /kɔ̃tʀe/ *nf* region; (pays) land.

**contrefaçon** /kɔ̃tʀəfasɔ̃/ *nf* (objet imité, action) forgery.

**contre-indiqué**, **~e** /kɔ̃tʀɛ̃dike/ *a* (Méd) contra-indicated; (déconseillé) not recommended.

**contre-jour**: **à ~** /akɔ̃tʀəʒuʀ/ *loc* against the light.

**contrepartie** /kɔ̃tʀəpaʀti/ *nf* compensation; **en ~** in exchange, in return.

**contreplaqué** /kɔ̃tʀəplake/ *nm* plywood.

**contresens** /kɔ̃tʀəsɑ̃s/ *nm* misinterpretation; (absurdité) nonsense; **à ~** the wrong way.

**contretemps** /kɔ̃tʀətɑ̃/ *nm* hitch; **à ~** (fig) at the wrong time.

**contribuable** /kɔ̃tʀibɥabl/ *nmf* taxpayer.

**contribuer** /kɔ̃tʀibɥe/ [1] *vt* contribute (**à** to, towards).

**contrôle** /kɔ̃tʀol/ *nm* (maîtrise) control; (vérification) check; (des prix) control; (poinçon) hallmark; (Scol) test; **~ continu** continuous assessment; **~ des changes** exchange control; **~ des naissances** birth control; **~ de soi-même** self-control; **~ technique (des véhicules)** MOT (test).

**contrôler** /kɔ̃tʀole/ [1] *vt* (vérifier) check; (surveiller, maîtriser) control. □ **se ~** *vpr* control oneself.

**contrôleur, -euse** /kɔ̃tʀolœʀ, -øz/ *nm,f* inspector.

**convaincre** /kɔ̃vɛ̃kʀ/ [59] *vt* convince; **~ qn de faire** persuade sb to do.

**convalescence** /kɔ̃valesɑ̃s/ *nf* convalescence; **être en ~** be convalescing.

**convenable** /kɔ̃vnabl/ *a* (correct) decent, proper; (approprié) suitable; (acceptable) reasonable, acceptable.

**convenance** /kɔ̃vnɑ̃s/ *nf* **à ma ~** to my satisfaction; **les ~s** conventions.

**convenir** /kɔ̃vniʀ/ [58] *vt/i* be suitable; **~ à** suit; **~ que** admit that; **~ de qch** (avouer) admit sth; (s'accorder sur) agree on sth; **~ de faire** agree to do; **il convient de** it is advisable to; (selon les bienséances) it would be right to.

**convention** /kɔ̃vɑ̃sjɔ̃/ *nf* agreement, convention; (clause) article, clause; **~s** (convenances) convention; **de ~** conventional; **~ collective** industrial agreement.

**convenu, ~e** /kɔ̃vny/ *a* agreed.

**conversation** /kɔ̃vɛʀsasjɔ̃/ *nf* conversation.

**convertir** /kɔ̃vɛʀtiʀ/ [2] *vt* convert (**à** to; **en** into). □ **se ~** *vpr* be converted, convert.

**conviction** /kɔ̃viksjɔ̃/ *nf* conviction; **avoir la ~ que** be convinced that.

**convivial, ~e** (*mpl* **-iaux**) /kɔ̃vivjal, -jo/ *a* convivial; (Ordinat) user-friendly.

**convocation** /kɔ̃vɔkasjɔ̃/ *nf* (Jur) summons; (d'une assemblée) convening; (document) notification to attend.

**convoi** /kɔ̃vwa/ *nm* convoy; (train) train; **~ (funèbre)** funeral procession.

**convoquer** /kɔ̃vɔke/ [1] *vt* (*assemblée*) convene; (*personne*) summon; **être convoqué pour un entretien** be called for interview.

**coopération** /koɔpeʀasjɔ̃/ *nf* cooperation; (Mil) civilian national service abroad.

**coordination** /koɔʀdinasjɔ̃/ *nf* coordination. **coordonnées** *nfpl* coordinates; (adresse) address and telephone number.

**copain** /kɔpɛ̃/ *nm* friend; (petit ami) boyfriend.

**copie** /kɔpi/ *nf* copy; (Scol) paper; **~ d'examen** exam paper *ou* script; **~ de sauvegarde** back-up copy.

**copier** /kɔpje/ [45] *vt/i* copy; **~ sur** (Scol) copy *ou* crib from.

**copieux, -ieuse** /kɔpjø, -z/ *a* copious.

**copine** /kɔpin/ *nf* friend; (petite amie) girlfriend.

**coq** /kɔk/ *nm* cockerel.

**coque** /kɔk/ *nf* shell; (de bateau) hull.

**coquelicot** /kɔkliko/ *nm* poppy.

**coqueluche** /kɔklyʃ/ *nf* whooping cough.

**coquet**, **~te** /kɔkɛ, -t/ *a* flirtatious; (élégant) pretty; (*somme* 🅸) tidy.

**coquetier** /kɔktje/ *nm* eggcup.

**coquillage** /kɔkijaʒ/ *nm* shellfish; (coquille) shell.

**coquille** /kɔkij/ *nf* shell; (faute) misprint; **~ Saint-Jacques** scallop.

**coquin**, **~e** /kɔkɛ̃, -in/ *a* mischievous. ● *nm, f* rascal.

**cor** /kɔʀ/ *nm* (Mus) horn; (au pied) corn.

**corail** (*pl* **-aux**) /kɔʀaj, -o/ *nm* coral.

**corbeau** (*pl* **~x**) /kɔʀbo/ *nm* (oiseau) crow.

**corbeille** /kɔʀbɛj/ *nf* basket; **~ à papier** waste-paper basket.

**corbillard** /kɔʀbijaʀ/ *nm* hearse.

**cordage** /kɔʀdaʒ/ *nm* rope; **~s** (Naut) rigging.

**corde** /kɔʀd/ *nf* rope; (d'arc, de violon) string; **~ à linge** washing line; **~ à sauter** skipping-rope; **~ raide** tightrope; **~s vocales** vocal cords.

**cordon** /kɔʀdɔ̃/ *nm* string, cord; **~ de police** police cordon.

**cordonnier** /kɔʀdɔnje/ *nm* cobbler.

**Corée** /kɔʀe/ *nf* Korea.

**coriace** /kɔʀjas/ *a* tough.

**corne** /kɔʀn/ *nf* horn.

**corneille** /kɔʀnɛj/ *nf* crow.

**cornemuse** /kɔʀnəmyz/ *nf* bagpipes (+ *pl*).

**corner** /kɔʀne/ [1] *vt* (*page*) turn down the corner of; **page cornée** dog-eared page. ● *vi* (Auto) hoot, honk.

**cornet** /kɔʀnɛ/ *nm* (paper) cone; (crème glacée) cornet, cone.

**corniche** /kɔʀniʃ/ *nf* cornice; (*route*) cliff road.

**cornichon** /kɔʀniʃɔ̃/ *nm* gherkin.

**corporel**, **~le** /kɔʀpɔʀɛl/ *a* bodily; (*châtiment*) corporal.

**corps** /kɔʀ/ *nm* body; (Mil) corps; **combat ~ à ~** hand-to-hand combat; **~ électoral** electorate; **~ enseignant** teaching profession.

**correct**, **~e** /kɔʀɛkt/ *a* proper, correct; (exact) correct.

**correcteur**, **-trice** /kɔʀɛktœʀ, -tʀis/ *nm, f* (d'épreuves) proofreader; (Scol) examiner; **~ liquide** correction fluid; **~ d'orthographe** spellchecker.

**correction** /kɔʀɛksjɔ̃/ *nf* correction; (d'examen) marking, grading; (punition) beating.

**correspondance** /kɔʀɛspɔ̃dɑ̃s/ *nf* correspondence; (de train, d'autobus) connection; **vente par ~** mail order; **faire des études par ~** do a correspondence course.

**correspondant**, **~e** /kɔʀɛspɔ̃dɑ̃, -t/ *a* corresponding. ● *nm, f* correspondent; penfriend; (au téléphone) **votre ~** the person you are calling.

**correspondre** /kɔʀɛspɔ̃dʀ/ [3] *vi* (s'accorder, écrire) correspond; (*chambres*) communicate. ● *v + prép* **~ à** (être approprié à) match, suit; (équivaloir à) correspond to. □ **se ~** *vpr* correspond.

**corrida** /kɔʀida/ *nf* bullfight.

**corriger** /kɔʀiʒe/ [40] *vt* correct; (*devoir*) mark, grade, correct; (punir) beat; (guérir) cure.

**corsage** /kɔʀsaʒ/ *nm* bodice; (chemisier) blouse.

**corsaire** /kɔʀsɛʀ/ *nm* pirate.

**Corse** /kɔʀs/ *nf* Corsica. ● *nmf* Corsican. **corse** *a* Corsican.

**corsé**, **~e** /kɔʀse/ *a* (*vin*) full-bodied; (*café*) strong; (scabreux) racy; (*problème*) tough.

**cortège** /kɔʀtɛʒ/ *nm* procession; **~ funèbre** funeral procession.

**corvée** /kɔʀve/ *nf* chore.

**cosmonaute** /kɔsmɔnot/ *nmf* cosmonaut.

**cosmopolite** /kɔsmɔpɔlit/ *a* cosmopolitan.

**cosse** /kɔs/ *nf* (de pois) pod.

**cossu**, **~e** /kɔsy/ *a* (*gens*) well-to-do; (*demeure*) opulent.

**costaud**, **~e** /kɔsto, -d/ ⊡ *a* strong. ● *nm* strong man.

**costume** /kɔstym/ *nm* suit; (Théât) costume.

**cote** /kɔt/ *nf* (classification) mark; (en Bourse) quotation; (de cheval) odds (**de** on); (de candidat, acteur) rating; **~ d'alerte** danger level; **avoir la ~** be popular.

**côte** /kot/ *nf* (littoral) coast; (pente) hill; (Anat) rib; (Culin) chop; **~ à ~** side by side; **la C~ d'Azur** the (French) Riviera.

**côté** /kote/ *nm* side; (direction) way; **à ~** nearby; **voisin d'à ~** next-door neighbour; **à ~ de** next to; (comparé à) compared to; **à ~ de la cible** wide of the target; **aux ~s de** by the side of; **de ~** (regarder) sideways; (*sauter*) to one side; **mettre de ~** put aside; **de ce ~** this way; **de chaque ~** on each side; **de tous les ~s** on every side; (partout) everywhere; **du ~ de** (vers) towards; (dans les environs de) near.

**côtelette** /kotlɛt/ *nf* chop.

**coter** /kɔte/ [1] *vt* (Comm) quote; **coté en Bourse** listed on the Stock Exchange; **très coté** highly rated.

**cotiser** /kɔtize/ [1] *vi* pay one's contributions (**à** to); (à un club) pay one's subscription. □ **se ~** *vpr* club together.

**coton** /kɔtɔ̃/ *nm* cotton; **~ hydrophile** cotton wool.

**cou** /ku/ *nm* neck.

**couchant** /kuʃɑ̃/ *nm* sunset.

**couche** /kuʃ/ *nf* layer; (de peinture) coat; (de bébé) nappy; (US) diaper; **~s** (Méd) childbirth; **~s sociales** social strata.

**coucher** /kuʃe/ [1] *vt* put to bed; (loger) put up; (étendre) lay down; **~ (par écrit)** set down. ● *vi* sleep. □ **se ~** *vpr* go to bed; (s'étendre) lie down; (*soleil*) set. ● *nm* **~ (de soleil)** sunset; **au ~ du soleil** at sunset.

**couchette** /kuʃɛt/ *nf* (de train) couchette; (Naut) berth.

**coude** /kud/ *nm* elbow; (de rivière, chemin) bend; **~ à ~** side by side.

**cou-de-pied** (*pl* **cous-de-pied**) /kudpje/ *nm* instep.

**coudre** /kudʀ/ [19] *vt/i* sew.

**couette** /kwɛt/ *nf* duvet, continental quilt.

**couler** /kule/ [1] *vi* flow, run; (*fromage, nez*) run; (*fuir*) leak; (*bateau*) sink; (*entreprise*) go under; **faire ~ un bain** run a bath. ● *vt* (*bateau*) sink; (*sculpture, métal*) cast. □ **se ~** *vpr* slip (**dans** into).

**couleur** /kulœʀ/ *nf* colour; (peinture) paint; (aux cartes) suit; **~s** (teint) colour; **de ~** (*homme, femme*) coloured; **en ~s** (*télévision, film*) colour.

**couleuvre** /kulœvʀ/ *nf* grass snake.

**coulisse** /kulis/ *nf* (de tiroir) runner; **à ~** (*porte, fenêtre*) sliding; **~s** (Théât) wings; **dans les ~s** (fig) behind the scenes.

**couloir** /kulwaʀ/ *nm* corridor; (Sport) lane; **~ de bus** bus lane.

**coup** /ku/ *nm* blow; (choc) knock; (Sport) stroke; (de crayon, chance, cloche) stroke; (de fusil, pistolet) shot; (fois) time; (aux échecs) move; **donner un ~ de pied/poing à** kick/punch; **à ~ sûr** definitely; **après ~**

after the event; **boire un ~** ⓘ have a drink; **~ sur ~** in rapid succession; **du ~** as a result; **d'un seul ~** in one go; **du premier ~** first go; **sale ~** dirty trick; **sous le ~ de la fatigue/colère** out of tiredness/anger; **sur le ~** instantly; **tenir le ~** hold out; **manquer son ~** ⓘ blow it ⓘ; **~ de chiffon** wipe (with a rag); **~ de coude** nudge; **~ de couteau** stab; **~ d'envoi** kick-off; **~ d'État** (Pol) coup; **~ de feu** shot; **~ de fil** ⓘ phone call; **~ de filet** haul, (fig) police raid; **~ de foudre** love at first sight; **~ franc** free kick; **~ de frein** sudden braking; **~ de grâce** coup de grâce; **~ de main** helping hand; **~ d'œil** glance; **~ de pied** kick; **~ de poing** punch; **~ de soleil** sunburn; **~ de sonnette** ring (on a bell); **~ de téléphone** (telephone call; **~ de tête** wild impulse; **~ de théâtre** dramatic event; **~ de tonnerre** thunderclap; **~ de vent** gust of wind.

**coupable** /kupabl/ *a* guilty. ● *nmf* culprit.

**coupe** /kup/ *nf* cup; (de champagne) goblet; (à fruits) dish; (de vêtement) cut; (dessin) section; **~ de cheveux** haircut.

**couper** /kupe/ [1] *vt* cut; (*arbre*) cut down; (arrêter) cut off; (*voyage*) break up; (*appétit*) take away; (*vin*) water down; **~ par** take a short cut via; **~ la parole à qn** cut sb short. ● *vi* cut. □ **se ~** *vpr* cut oneself; **se ~ le doigt** cut one's finger; (*routes*) intersect; **se ~ de** cut oneself off from.

**couple** /kupl/ *nm* couple; (d'animaux) pair.

**coupure** /kupyʀ/ *nf* cut; (billet de banque) note; (de presse) cutting; (pause, rupture) break; **~ (de courant)** power cut.

**cour** /kuʀ/ *nf* (court)yard; (du roi) court; (tribunal) court; **~ (de récréation)** playground; **~ martiale** court-martial; **faire la ~ à** court.

**courageux, -euse** /kuʀaʒø, -z/ *a* courageous.

**couramment** /kuʀamɑ̃/ *adv* frequently; (*parler*) fluently.

**courant, ~e** /kuʀɑ̃, -t/ *a* standard, ordinary; (en cours) current. ● *nm* current; (de mode, d'idées) trend; **~ d'air** draught; **dans le ~ de** in the course of; **être/mettre au ~ de** know/tell about; (à jour) be/bring up to date on.

**courbature** /kuʀbatyʀ/ *nf* ache; **avoir des ~s** be stiff, ache.

**courber** /kuʀbe/ [1] *vt* bend.

**coureur, -euse** /kuʀœʀ, -øz/ *nm,f* (Sport) runner; **~ automobile** racing driver; **~ cycliste** racing cyclist. ● *nm* womanizer.

**courgette** /kuʀʒɛt/ *nf* courgette; (US) zucchini.

**courir** /kuʀiʀ/ [20] *vi* run; (se hâter) rush; (*nouvelles*) go round; **~ après qn/qch** chase after sb/sth. ● *vt* (*risque*) run; (*danger*) face; (*épreuve sportive*) run *ou* compete in; (fréquenter) do the rounds of; (*filles*) chase (after).

**couronne** /kuʀɔn/ *nf* crown; (de fleurs) wreath.

**couronnement** /kuʀɔnmɑ̃/ *nm* coronation, crowning; (fig) crowning achievement.

**courrier** /kuʀje/ *nm* post, mail; (à écrire) letters; **~ du cœur** problem page; **~ électronique** e-mail.

**cours** /kuʀ/ *nm* (leçon) class; (série de leçons) course; (prix) price; (cote) (de valeur, denrée) price; (de devises) exchange rate; (déroulement, d'une rivière) course; (allée) avenue; **au ~**

**de** in the course of; **avoir ~** (*monnaie*) be legal tender; (fig) be current; (Scol) have a lesson; **~ d'eau** river, stream; **~ du soir** evening class; **~ particulier** private lesson; **~ magistral** (Univ) lecture; **en ~** current; (*travail*) in progress; **en ~ de route** along the way.

**course** /kuʀs/ *nf* running; (épreuve de vitesse) race; (activité) racing; (entre rivaux: fig) race; (de projectile) flight; (voyage) journey; (commission) errand; **~s** (achats) shopping; (de chevaux) races; **faire la ~ avec qn** race sb.

**coursier, -ière** /kuʀsje, -jɛʀ/ *nm,f* messenger.

**court, ~e** /kuʀ, -t/ *a* short. ● *adv* short; **à ~ de** short of; **pris de ~** caught unawares. ● *nm* **~ (de tennis)** (tennis) court.

**courtier, -ière** /kuʀtje, -jɛʀ/ *nm,f* broker.

**courtiser** /kuʀtize/ [1] *vt* woo, court.

**courtois, ~e** /kuʀtwa, -z/ *a* courteous. **courtoisie** *nf* courtesy.

**cousin, ~e** /kuzɛ̃, -in/ *nm,f* cousin; **~ germain** first cousin.

**coussin** /kusɛ̃/ *nm* cushion.

**coût** /ku/ *nm* cost; **le ~ de la vie** the cost of living.

**couteau** (*pl* **~x**) /kuto/ *nm* knife; **~ à cran d'arrêt** flick knife.

**coûter** /kute/ [1] *vt/i* cost; **coûte que coûte** at all costs; **au prix coûtant** at cost (price).

**coutume** /kutym/ *nf* custom.

**couture** /kutyʀ/ *nf* sewing; (métier) dressmaking; (points) seam. **couturier** *nm* fashion designer. **couturière** *nf* dressmaker.

**couvée** /kuve/ *nf* brood.

**couvent** /kuvɑ̃/ *nm* convent.

**couver** /kuve/ [1] *vt* (*œufs*) hatch; (*personne*) overprotect, pamper; (*maladie*) be coming down with, be sickening for. ● *vi* (*feu*) smoulder; (*mal*) be brewing.

**couvercle** /kuvɛʀkl/ *nm* (de marmite, boîte) lid; (qui se visse) screw-top.

**couvert, ~e** /kuvɛʀ, -t/ *a* covered (**de** with); (habillé) covered up; (*ciel*) overcast. ● *nm* (à table) place setting; (prix) cover charge; **~s** (couteaux etc.) cutlery; **mettre le ~** lay the table; (abri) cover; **à ~** (Mil) under cover; **à ~ de** (fig) safe from.

**couverture** /kuvɛʀtyʀ/ *nf* cover; (de lit) blanket; (toit) roofing; (dans la presse) coverage; **~ chauffante** electric blanket.

**couvre-feu** (*pl* **~x**) /kuvʀəfø/ *nm* curfew.

**couvre-lit** (*pl* **~s**) /kuvʀəli/ *nm* bedspread.

**couvrir** /kuvʀiʀ/ [21] *vt* cover. □ **se ~** *vpr* (s'habiller) wrap up; (se coiffer) put one's hat on; (*ciel*) become overcast.

**covoiturage** /kɔvwatyʀaʒ/ *nm* car sharing.

**cracher** /kʀaʃe/ [1] *vi* spit; (*radio*) crackle. ● *vt* spit (out); (*fumée*) belch out.

**crachin** /kʀaʃɛ̃/ *nm* drizzle.

**craie** /kʀɛ/ *nf* chalk.

**craindre** /kʀɛ̃dʀ/ [22] *vt* be afraid of, fear; (être sensible à) be easily damaged by.

**crainte** /kʀɛ̃t/ *nf* fear (**pour** for); **de ~ de/que** for fear of/that. **craintif, -ive** *a* timid.

**crampon** /kʀɑ̃pɔ̃/ *nm* (de chaussure) stud.

**cramponner (se)** /(sə)kʀɑ̃pɔne/ [1] *vpr* **se ~ à** cling to.

**cran** /kʀɑ̃/ *nm* (entaille) notch; (trou) hole; (courage [I]) guts [I], courage; ~ **de sûreté** safety catch.

**crâne** /kʀɑn/ *nm* skull.

**crapaud** /kʀapo/ *nm* toad.

**craquer** /kʀake/ [1] *vi* crack, snap; (*plancher*) creak; (*couture*) split; (fig) (*personne*) break down; (céder) give in. ● *vt* (*allumette*) strike; (*vêtement*) split.

**crasse** /kʀas/ *nf* grime.

**cravache** /kʀavaʃ/ *nf* (horse) whip.

**cravate** /kʀavat/ *nf* tie.

**crayon** /kʀɛjɔ̃/ *nm* pencil; ~ **de couleur** coloured pencil; ~ **à bille** ballpoint pen; ~ **optique** light pen.

**créateur**, **-trice** /kʀeatœʀ, -tʀis/ *a* creative. ● *nm,f* creator, designer.

**crèche** /kʀɛʃ/ *nf* day nursery, crèche; (Relig) crib.

**crédit** /kʀedi/ *nm* credit; (somme allouée) funds; **à** ~ on credit; **faire** ~ give credit (**à** to).

**créer** /kʀee/ [15] *vt* create; (*produit*) design, (*société*) set up.

**crémaillère** /kʀemajɛʀ/ *nf* **pendre la** ~ have a house-warming party.

**crème** /kʀɛm/ *a inv* cream. ● *nm* **(café)** ~ espresso with milk. ● *nf* cream; (dessert) cream dessert; ~ **anglaise** egg custard; ~ **fouettée** whipped cream; ~ **pâtissière** confectioner's custard. **crémerie** *nf* dairy. **crémeux**, **-euse** *a* creamy. **crémier**, **-ière** *nm,f* dairyman, dairywoman.

**créneau** (*pl* ~**x**) /kʀeno/ *nm* (trou, moment) slot, window; (dans le marché) gap; **faire un** ~ parallel-park.

**crêpe** /kʀɛp/ *nf* (galette) pancake. ● *nm* (tissu) crêpe; (matière) crêpe (rubber).

**crépitement** /kʀepitmɑ̃/ *nm* crackling; (d'huile) sizzling.

**crépuscule** /kʀepyskyl/ *nm* twilight, dusk.

**cresson** /kʀesɔ̃/ *nm* (water)cress.

**crête** /kʀɛt/ *nf* crest; (de coq) comb.

**crétin**, ~**e** /kʀetɛ̃, -in/ *nm,f* [I] moron [I].

**creuser** /kʀøze/ [1] *vt* dig; (évider) hollow out; (fig) go into in depth. □ **se** ~ *vpr* (*écart*) widen; **se** ~ **(la cervelle)** [I] rack one's brains.

**creux**, **-euse** /kʀø, -z/ *a* hollow; (*heures*) off-peak. ● *nm* hollow; (de l'estomac) pit; **dans le** ~ **de la main** in the palm of the hand.

**crevaison** /kʀəvɛzɔ̃/ *nf* puncture.

**crevasse** /kʀəvas/ *nf* crack; (de glacier) crevasse; (de la peau) chap.

**crevé**, ~**e** /kʀəve/ *a* [I] worn out.

**crever** /kʀəve/ [1] *vt* burst; (pneu) puncture, burst; (exténuer [I]) exhaust; (œil) put out. ● *vi* (*pneu, sac*) burst; (mourir [I]) die.

**crevette** /kʀəvɛt/ *nf* ~ **grise** shrimp; ~ **rose** prawn.

**cri** /kʀi/ *nm* cry; (de douleur) scream, cry; **pousser un** ~ cry out, scream.

**criard**, ~**e** /kʀijaʀ, -d/ *a* (*couleur*) garish; (*voix*) shrill.

**crier** /kʀije/ [45] *vi* (fort) shout, cry (out); (de douleur) scream; (grincer) creak. ● *vt* (*ordre*) shout (out).

**crime** /kʀim/ *nm* crime; (meurtre) murder.

**criminel**, ~**le** /kʀiminɛl/ *a* criminal. ● *nm,f* criminal; (assassin) murderer.

**crinière** /kʀinjɛʀ/ *nf* mane.

**crise** /kʀiz/ *nf* crisis; (Méd) attack; (de colère) fit; ~ **cardiaque** heart

attack; ~ **de foie** bilious attack; ~ **de nerfs** hysterics (+ *pl*).

**crisper** /kRispe/ [1] *vt* tense; (énerver Ⓘ) irritate. □ **se** ~ *vpr* tense; (*mains*) clench.

**critère** /kRitɛR/ *nm* criterion.

**critique** /kRitik/ *a* critical. ● *nf* criticism; (article) review; (*commentateur*) critic; **la** ~ (personnes) the critics. **critiquer** [1] *vt* criticize.

**Croate** /kRɔat/ *a* Croetian. **C~** *nmf* Croetian.

**Croatie** /kRɔasi/ *nf* Croatia.

**croche** /kRɔʃ/ *nf* quaver.

**croche-pied** (*pl* ~**s**) /kRɔʃpje/ *nm* Ⓘ **faire un** ~ **à** trip up.

**crochet** /kRɔʃɛ/ *nm* hook; (détour) detour; (signe) (square) bracket; (tricot) crochet; **faire au** ~ crochet.

**crochu**, ~**e** /kRɔʃy/ *a* hooked.

**crocodile** /kRɔkɔdil/ *nm* crocodile.

**croire** /kRwaR/ [23] *vt* believe (**à, en** in); (estimer) think, believe (**que** that). ● *vi* believe.

**croisade** /kRwazad/ *nf* crusade.

**croisement** /kRwazmɑ̃/ *nm* crossing; (fait de passer à côté de) passing; (carrefour) crossroads.

**croiser** /kRwaze/ [1] *vi* (*bateau*) cruise. ● *vt* cross; (*passant, véhicule*) pass; ~ **les bras** fold one's arms; ~ **les jambes** cross one's legs; (*animaux*) crossbreed. □ **se** ~ *vpr* (*véhicules, piétons*) pass each other; (*lignes*) cross. **croisière** *nf* cruise.

**croissance** /kRwasɑ̃s/ *nf* growth.

**croissant**, ~**e** /kRwasɑ̃, -t/ *a* growing. ● *nm* crescent; (pâtisserie) croissant.

**croix** /kRwa/ *nf* cross; ~ **gammée** swastika; **C~-Rouge** Red Cross.

**croquant**, ~**e** /kRɔkɑ̃, -t/ *a* crunchy.

**croque-monsieur** /kRɔkməsjø/ *nm inv* toasted ham and cheese sandwich.

**croque-mort** (*pl* ~**s**) /kRɔkmɔR/ *nm* Ⓘ undertaker.

**croquer** /kRɔke/ [1] *vt* crunch; (dessiner) sketch; **chocolat à** ~ plain chocolate. ● *vi* be crunchy.

**croquis** /kRɔki/ *nm* sketch.

**crotte** /kRɔt/ *nf* dropping.

**crotté**, ~**e** /kRɔte/ *a* muddy.

**crottin** /kRɔtɛ̃/ *nm* (horse) dropping.

**croupir** /kRupiR/ [2] *vi* stagnate.

**croustillant**, ~**e** /kRustijɑ̃, -t/ *a* crispy; (*pain*) crusty; (fig) spicy.

**croûte** /kRut/ *nf* crust; (de fromage) rind; (de plaie) scab; **en** ~ (Culin) in pastry.

**croûton** /kRutɔ̃/ *nm* (bout de pain) crust; (avec potage) croûton.

**CRS** *abrév m* (**Compagnie républicaine de sécurité**) French riot police; **un** ~ *a member of the French riot police.*

**cru¹** /kRy/ ⇨CROIRE [23].

**cru²**, ~**e** /kRy/ *a* raw; (*lumière*) harsh; (*propos*) crude. ● *nm* vineyard; (vin) vintage wine.

**crû** /kRy/ ⇨CROÎTRE [24].

**cruauté** /kRyote/ *nf* cruelty.

**cruche** /kRyʃ/ *nf* jug, pitcher.

**crucial**, ~**e** (*mpl* **-iaux**) /kRysjal, -jo/ *a* crucial.

**crudité** /kʀydite/ *nf* (de langage) crudeness; **~s** (Culin) raw vegetables.

**crue** /kʀy/ *nf* rise in water level; **en ~** in spate.

**crustacé** /kʀystase/ *nm* shellfish.

**cube** /kyb/ *nm* cube. ● *a* (*mètre*) cubic.

**cueillir** /kœjiʀ/ [25] *vt* pick, gather; (*personne* [I]) pick up.

**cuiller**, **cuillère** /kɥijɛʀ/ *nf* spoon, **~ à soupe** soup spoon; (mesure) tablespoonful.

**cuir** /kɥiʀ/ *nm* leather; **~ chevelu** scalp.

**cuire** /kɥiʀ/ [17] *vt* cook; **~ (au four)** bake. ● *vi* cook; **faire ~** cook.

**cuisine** /kɥizin/ *nf* kitchen; (art) cookery, cooking; (aliments) food; **faire la ~** cook.

**cuisiner** /kɥizine/ [1] *vt* cook; (interroger [I]) grill. ● *vi* cook.

**cuisinier**, **-ière** /kɥizinje, -jɛʀ/ *nm,f* cook. **cuisinière** *nf* (appareil) cooker, stove.

**cuisse** /kɥis/ *nf* thigh; (de poulet) thigh; (de grenouille) leg.

**cuisson** /kɥisɔ̃/ *nf* cooking.

**cuit**, **~e** /kɥi, -t/ *a* cooked; **bien ~** well done *ou* cooked; **trop ~** overdone.

**cuivre** /kɥivʀ/ *nm* copper; **~ (jaune)** brass; **~s** (Mus) brass.

**cul** /ky/ *nm* (derrière [X]) backside, bottom, arse [X]

**culbuter** /kylbyte/ [1] *vi* (*personne*) tumble; (*objet*) topple (over). ● *vt* knock over.

**culminer** /kylmine/ [1] *vi* reach its highest point *ou* peak.

**culot** /kylo/ *nm* (audace [I]) nerve, cheek; (Tech) base.

**culotte** /kylɔt/ *nf* (de femme) pants (+ *pl*), knickers (+ *pl*); (US) panties (+ *pl*); **~ de cheval** riding breeches; **en ~ courte** in short trousers.

**culpabilité** /kylpabilite/ *nf* guilt.

**culte** /kylt/ *nm* cult, worship; (religion) religion; (office protestant) service.

**cultivateur**, **-trice** /kyltivatœʀ, -tʀis/ *nm,f* farmer.

**cultiver** /kyltive/ [1] *vt* cultivate; (*plantes*) grow.

**culture** /kyltyʀ/ *nf* cultivation; (de plantes) growing; (agriculture) farming; (éducation) culture; (connaissances) knowledge; **~s** (terrains) lands under cultivation; **~ physique** physical training.

**culturel**, **~le** /kyltyʀɛl/ *a* cultural.

**cumuler** /kymyle/ [1] *vt* accumulate; (*fonctions*) hold concurrently.

**cure** /kyʀ/ *nf* (course of) treatment.

**curé** /kyʀe/ *nm* (parish) priest.

**cure-dent** (*pl* **~s**) /kyʀdɑ̃/ *nm* toothpick.

**curer** /kyʀe/ [1] *vt* clean. □ **se ~** *vpr* **se ~ les dents/ongles** clean one's teeth/nails.

**curieux**, **-ieuse** /kyʀjø, -z/ *a* curious. ● *nm,f* (badaud) onlooker.

**curiosité** /kyʀjozite/ *nf* curiosity; (objet) curio; (spectacle) unusual sight.

**curriculum vitae** /kyʀikylɔm vite/ *nm inv* curriculum vitae; (US) résumé.

**curseur** /kyʀsœʀ/ *nm* cursor.

**cutané**, **~e** /kytane/ *a* skin.

**cuve** /kyv/ *nf* vat; (à mazout, eau) tank.

**cuvée** /kyve/ *nf* (de vin) vintage.

**cuvette** /kyvɛt/ *nf* bowl; (de lavabo) (wash)basin; (des cabinets) pan, bowl.

**CV** *abrév m* (**curriculum vitae**) CV.

**cyberbranché**, **~e** /sibɛʀbʀɑ̃ʃe/ *a* cyberwired.

**cybercafé** /sibɛʀkafe/ *nm* cybercafe.

**cyberespace** /sibɛʀsɛpas/ *nm* cyberspace.

**cybernaute** /sibɛʀnot/ *nmf* Netsurfer.

**cybernétique** /sibɛʀnetik/ *nf* cybernetics (+ *pl*).

**cyclisme** /siklism/ *nm* cycling.

**cycliste** /siklist/ *nmf* cyclist. ● *nm* cycling shorts. ● *a* cycle.

**cyclone** /siklon/ *nm* cyclone.

**cygne** /siɲ/ *nm* swan.

**cynique** /sinik/ *a* cynical. ● *nm* cynic.

# Dd

**d'**/d/ ⇒DE.

**d'abord** /dabɔʀ/ *adv* first; (au début) at first.

**dactylo** /daktilo/ *nf* typist. **dactylographier** [45] *vt* type.

**dada** /dada/ *nm* hobby-horse.

**daim** /dɛ̃/ *nm* (fallow) deer; (cuir) suede.

**dallage** /dalaʒ/ *nm* paving. **dalle** *nf* slab.

**daltonien**, **~ne** /daltɔnjɛ̃, -ɛn/ *a* colour-blind.

**dame** /dam/ *nf* lady; (cartes, échecs) queen; **~s** (jeu) draughts; (US) checkers.

**damier** /damje/ *nm* draughtboard; (US) checker-board; **à ~** chequered.

**damner** /dane/ [1] *vt* damn.

**dandiner (se)** /(sə)dɑ̃dine/ [1] *vpr* waddle.

**Danemark** /danmaʀk/ *nm* Denmark.

**danger** /dɑ̃ʒe/ *nm* danger; **en ~** in danger; **mettre en ~** endanger.

**dangereux, -euse** /dɑ̃ʒ(ə)ʀø, -z/ *a* dangerous.

**danois**, **~e** /danwa, -z/ *a* Danish. ● *nm* (Ling) Danish. **D~**, **~e** *nm,f* Dane.

**dans** /dɑ̃/ *prép* in; (mouvement) into; (à l'intérieur de) inside, in; **être ~ un avion** be on a plane; **~ dix jours** in ten days' time; **boire ~ un verre** drink out of a glass; **~ les 10 francs** about 10 francs.

**danse** /dɑ̃s/ *nf* dance; (art) dancing.

**danser** /dɑ̃se/ [1] *vt/i* dance. **danseur, -euse** *nm,f* dancer.

**darne** /daʀn/ *nf* steak (of fish).

**date** /dat/ *nf* date; **~ limite** deadline; **~ limite de vente** sell-by date; **~ de péremption** use-by date.

**dater** /date/ [1] *vt/i* date; **à ~ de** as from.

**datte** /dat/ *nf* (fruit) date.

**daube** /dob/ *nf* casserole.

**dauphin** /dofɛ̃/ *nm* (animal) dolphin.

**davantage** /davɑ̃taʒ/ *adv* more; (plus longtemps) longer; **~ de** more; **je n'en sais pas ~** that's as much as I know.

**de**, **d'** /də, d/

d' before vowel or mute h.

● *préposition*

····➤ of; **le livre ~ mon ami** my

friend's book; **un pont ~ fer** an iron bridge.

····▸ (provenance) from.

····▸ (temporel) from; **~ 8 heures à 10 heures** from 8 till 10.

····▸ (mesure, manière) **dix mètres ~ haut** ten metres high; **pleurer ~ rage** cry with rage.

····▸ (agent) by; **un livre ~ Marcel Aymé** a book by Marcel Aymé.

● **de**, **de l'**, **de la**, **du**, (*pl* **des**) *déterminant*

····▸ some; **du pain** (some) bread; **des fleurs** (some) flowers; **je ne bois jamais ~ vin** I never drink wine.

de + le = du
de + les = des

**dé** /de/ *nm* (à jouer) dice, (à coudre) thimble; **~s** (jeu) dice.

**débâcle** /debɑkl/ *nf* (Géog) breaking up; (Mil) rout.

**déballer** /debale/ [1] *vt* unpack; (révéler) spill out.

**débarbouiller** /debaʀbuje/ *vt* wash the face of. ▫ **se ~** *vpr* wash one's face.

**débarcadère** /debaʀkadɛʀ/ *nm* landing-stage.

**débardeur** /debaʀdœʀ/ *nm* (vêtement) tank top.

**débarquement** /debaʀkəmɑ̃/ *nm* disembarkation. **débarquer** [1] *vt/i* disembark, land; (arriver 🅸) turn up.

**débarras** /debaʀa/ *nm* junk room; **bon ~!** good riddance!

**débarrasser** /debaʀase/ [1] *vt* clear (**de** of); **~ qn de** relieve sb of; (*défaut, ennemi*) rid sb of. ▫ **se ~ de** *vpr* get rid of.

**débat** /deba/ *nm* debate.

**débattre** /debatʀ/ [11] *vt* debate. ● *vi* **~ de** discuss. ▫ **se ~** *vpr* struggle (to get free).

**débauche** /deboʃ/ *nf* debauchery; (fig) profusion.

**débaucher** /deboʃe/ [1] *vt* (licencier) lay off; (distraire) tempt away.

**débile** /debil/ *a* weak; 🅸 stupid. ● *nmf* moron 🅸.

**débit** /debi/ *nm* (rate of) flow; (élocution) delivery; (de compte) debit; **~ de tabac** tobacconist's shop; **~ de boissons** bar.

**débiter** /debite/ [1] *vt* (*compte*) debit; (fournir) produce; (vendre) sell; (dire: péj) spout; (couper) cut up.

**débiteur**, **-trice** /debitœʀ, -tʀis/ *nm,f* debtor. ● *a* (*compte*) in debit.

**déblayer** /debleje/ [31] *vt* clear.

**déblocage** /deblɔkaʒ/ *nm* (de prix) deregulating. **débloquer** [1] *vt* (*prix, salaires*) unfreeze.

**déboiser** /debwaze/ [1] *vt* clear (of trees).

**déboîter** /debwate/ [1] *vi* (*véhicule*) pull out. ● *vt* (*membre*) dislocate.

**débordement** /debɔʀdəmɑ̃/ *nm* (de joie) excess.

**déborder** /debɔʀde/ [1] *vi* overflow. ● *vt* (dépasser) extend beyond; **~ de** (*joie etc.*) be brimming over with.

**débouché** /debuʃe/ *nm* opening; (carrière) prospect; (Comm) outlet; (sortie) end, exit.

**déboucher** /debuʃe/ [1] *vt* (*bouteille*) uncork; (*évier*) unblock. ● *vi* come out (**de** from); **~ sur** (*rue*) lead into.

**débourser** /debuʀse/ [1] *vt* pay out.

**debout** /dəbu/ *adv* standing; (levé, éveillé) up; **être ~**, **se tenir ~** be

standing, stand; **se mettre ~** stand up.

**déboutonner** /debutɔne/ [1] *vt* unbutton. □ **se ~** *vpr* unbutton oneself; (*vêtement*) come undone.

**débrancher** /debʀɑ̃ʃe/ [1] *vt* (*prise*) unplug; (*système*) disconnect.

**débrayer** /debʀeje/ [31] *vi* (Auto) declutch; (faire grève) stop work.

**débris** /debʀi/ *nmpl* fragments; (détritus) rubbish (+ *sg*); debris.

**débrouillard, ~e** /debʀujaʀ, -d/ *a* 🅸 resourceful.

**débrouiller** /debʀuje/ [1] *vt* disentangle; (*problème*) solve. □ **se ~** *vpr* manage.

**début** /deby/ *nm* beginning; **faire ses ~s** (en public) make one's début; **à mes ~s** when I started out. **débutant, ~e** *nm,f* beginner. **débuter** [1] *vi* begin; (dans un métier etc.) start out.

**déca** /deka/ *nm* 🅸 decaf.

**deçà**: **en ~** /ɑ̃dəsɑ/ *loc* this side. ● *prép* **en ~ de** this side of.

**décacheter** /dekaʃte/ [6] *vt* open.

**décade** /dekad/ *nf* ten days; (décennie) decade.

**décadent, ~e** /dekadɑ̃, -t/ *a* decadent.

**décalage** /dekalaʒ/ *nm* (écart) gap; **~ horaire** time difference. **décaler** [1] *vt* shift.

**décalquer** /dekalke/ [1] *vt* trace.

**décamper** /dekɑ̃pe/ [1] *vi* clear off.

**décanter** /dekɑ̃te/ *vt* allow to settle. □ **se ~** *vpr* settle.

**décapant** /dekapɑ̃/ *nm* chemical agent; (pour peinture) paint stripper. ● *a* (*humour*) caustic.

**décapotable** /dekapɔtabl/ *a* convertible.

**décapsuleur** /dekapsylœʀ/ *nm* bottle-opener.

**décédé, ~e** /desede/ *a* deceased.

**décéder** [14] *vi* die.

**déceler** /desle/ [6] *vt* detect; (démontrer) reveal.

**décembre** /desɑ̃bʀ/ *nm* December.

**décemment** /desamɑ̃/ *adv* decently. **décence** *nf* decency. **décent, ~e** *a* decent.

**décennie** /deseni/ *nf* decade.

**décentralisation** /desɑ̃tʀalizasjɔ̃/ *nf* decentralization. **décentraliser** [1] *vt* decentralize.

**déception** /desɛpsjɔ̃/ *nf* disappointment.

**décerner** /desɛʀne/ [1] *vt* award.

**décès** /desɛ/ *nm* death.

**décevant, ~e** /des(ə)vɑ̃, -t/ *a* disappointing. **décevoir** [52] *vt* disappoint.

**déchaîner** /deʃene/ [1] *vt* (*enthousiasme*) rouse. □ **se ~** *vpr* go wild.

**décharge** /deʃaʀʒ/ *nf* (de fusil) discharge; **~ électrique** electric shock; **~ publique** municipal dump.

**décharger** /deʃaʀʒe/ [40] *vt* unload; **~ qn de** relieve sb from. □ **se ~** *vpr* (*batterie, pile*) go flat.

**déchausser (se)** /(sə)deʃose/ [1] *vpr* take off one's shoes; (*dent*) work loose.

**dèche** /dɛʃ/ *nf* 🅸 **dans la ~** broke.

**déchéance** /deʃeɑ̃s/ *nf* decay.

**déchet** /deʃɛ/ *nm* (reste) scrap; (perte) waste; **~s** (ordures) refuse.

**déchiffrer** /deʃifʀe/ [1] *vt* decipher.

**déchiqueter** /deʃikte/ [38] *vt* tear to shreds.

**déchirement** /deʃiʀmɑ̃/ *nm* heartbreak; (conflit) split.

**déchirer** /deʃiʀe/ [1] *vt* (par accident) tear; (lacérer) tear up; (arracher) tear off *ou* out; (diviser) tear apart. □ **se** ~ *vpr* tear. **déchirure** *nf* tear.

**décibel** /desibɛl/ *nm* decibel.

**décidément** /desidemɑ̃/ *adv* really.

**décider** /deside/ [1] *vt* decide on; (persuader) persuade; ~ **que/de** decide that/to; ~ **de qch** decide on sth. □ **se** ~ *vpr* make up one's mind (**à** to).

**décimal**, **~e** (*mpl* **~aux**) /desimal, -o/ *a & nf* decimal.

**décisif**, **-ive** /desizif, -v/ *a* decisive.

**décision** /desizjɔ̃/ *nf* decision.

**déclaration** /deklaʀasjɔ̃/ *nf* declaration; (commentaire politique) statement; ~ **d'impôts** tax return.

**déclarer** /deklaʀe/ [1] *vt* declare; (*naissance*) register; **déclaré coupable** found guilty; ~ **forfait** (Sport) withdraw. □ **se** ~ *vpr* (*feu*) break out.

**déclencher** /deklɑ̃ʃe/ [1] *vt* (Tech) set off; (*conflit*) spark off; (*avalanche*) start; (*rire*) provoke. □ **se** ~ *vpr* (Tech) go off. **déclencheur** *nm* (Photo) shutter release.

**déclic** /deklik/ *nm* click.

**déclin** /deklɛ̃/ *nm* decline.

**déclinaison** /deklinɛzɔ̃/ *nf* (Ling) declension.

**décliner** /dekline/ [1] *vt* (refuser) decline; (dire) state; (Ling) decline.

**décocher** /dekɔʃe/ [1] *vt* (*coup*) fling; (*regard*) shoot.

**décollage** /dekɔlaʒ/ *nm* take-off.

**décoller** /dekɔle/ [1] *vt* unstick. ● *vi* (*avion*) take off. □ **se** ~ *vpr* come off.

**décolleté**, **~e** /dekɔlte/ *a* low-cut ● *nm* low neckline.

**décolorer** /dekɔlɔʀe/ [1] *vt* fade; (*cheveux*) bleach. □ **se** ~ *vpr* fade.

**décombres** /dekɔ̃bʀ/ *nmpl* rubble.

**décommander** /dekɔmɑ̃de/ [1] *vt* cancel.

**décomposer** /dekɔ̃poze/ [1] *vt* break up; (*substance*) decompose. □ **se** ~ *vpr* (pourrir) decompose.

**décompte** /dekɔ̃t/ *nm* deduction; (détail) breakdown.

**décongeler** /dekɔ̃ʒle/ [6] *vt* thaw.

**déconseillé**, **~e** /dekɔ̃sɛje/ *a* not recommended, inadvisable.

**déconseiller** /dekɔ̃sɛje/ [1] *vt* ~ **qch à qn** advise sb against sth.

**décontracté**, **~e** /dekɔ̃tʀakte/ *a* relaxed.

**déconvenue** /dekɔ̃vny/ *nf* disappointment.

**décor** /dekɔʀ/ *nm* (paysage) scenery; (de cinéma, théâtre) set; (cadre) setting; (de maison) décor.

**décoratif**, **-ive** /dekɔʀatif, -v/ *a* decorative.

**décorateur**, **-trice** /dekɔʀatœʀ, -tʀis/ *nm,f* (de cinéma) set designer. **décoration** *nf* decoration. **décorer** [1] *vt* decorate.

**décortiquer** /dekɔʀtike/ [1] *vt* shell; (fig) dissect.

**découdre (se)** /(sə)dekudʀ/ [19] *vpr* come unstitched.

**découler** /dekule/ [1] *vi* ~ **de** follow from.

**découper** /dekupe/ [1] *vt* cut up; (*viande*) carve; (détacher) cut out.

**découragement** /dekuʀaʒmɑ̃/ *nm* discouragement.

**décourager** /dekuʀaʒe/ [40] *vt* discourage. □ **se** ~ *vpr* become discouraged.

**décousu**, **~e** /dekuzy/ *a* (*vêtement*) which has come unstitched; (*idées*) disjointed.

**découvert**, **~e** /dekuvɛʀ, -t/ *a* (*tête*) bare; (*terrain*) open. ● *nm* (de compte) overdraft; **à ~** exposed; (fig) openly.

**découverte** /dekuvɛʀt/ *nf* discovery; **à la ~ de** in search of.

**découvrir** /dekuvʀiʀ/ [21] *vt* discover; (voir) see; (montrer) reveal. □ **se ~** *vpr* (se décoiffer) take one's hat off; (*ciel*) clear.

**décrasser** /dekʀase/ [1] *vt* clean.

**décrépit**, **~e** /dekʀepi, -t/ *a* decrepit. **décrépitude** *nf* decay.

**décret** /dekʀɛ/ *nm* decree. **décréter** [14] *vt* order; (dire) declare.

**décrié**, **~e** /dekʀije/ *a* criticized.

**décrire** /dekʀiʀ/ [30] *vt* describe.

**décroché**, **~e** /dekʀɔʃe/ *a* (*téléphone*) off the hook.

**décrocher** /dekʀɔʃe/ [1] *vt* unhook; (obtenir ⓘ) get. ● *vi* (abandonner ⓘ) give up; **~ (le téléphone)** pick up the phone.

**décroître** /dekʀwatʀ/ [24] *vi* decrease.

**déçu**, **~e** /desy/ *a* disappointed.

**décupler** /dekyple/ [1] *vt/i* increase tenfold.

**dédaigner** /dedeɲe/ [1] *vt* scorn.

**dédain** /dedɛ̃/ *nm* scorn.

**dédale** /dedal/ *nm* maze.

**dedans** /dədɑ̃/ *adv & nm* inside; **en ~** on the inside.

**dédicacer** /dedikase/ [10] *vt* dedicate; (signer) sign.

**dédier** /dedje/ [45] *vt* dedicate.

**dédommagement** /dedɔmaʒmɑ̃/ *nm* compensation. **dédommager** [40] *vt* compensate (**de** for).

**déduction** /dedyksjɔ̃/ *nf* deduction; **~ d'impôts** tax deduction.

**déduire** /dedɥiʀ/ [17] *vt* deduct; (conclure) deduce.

**déesse** /deɛs/ *nf* goddess.

**défaillance** /defajɑ̃s/ *nf* (panne) failure; (évanouissement) blackout. **défaillant**, **~e** *a* (*système*) faulty; (*personne*) faint.

**défaire** /defɛʀ/ [33] *vt* undo; (*valise*) unpack; (démonter) take down. □ **se ~** *vpr* come undone; **se ~ de** rid oneself of.

**défait**, **~e** /defɛ, -t/ *a* (*cheveux*) ruffled; (*visage*) haggard; (*nœud*) undone. **défaite** *nf* defeat.

**défaitiste** /defetist/ *a & nmf* defeatist.

**défalquer** /defalke/ [1] *vt* (*somme*) deduct.

**défaut** /defo/ *nm* fault, defect; (d'un verre, diamant, etc.) flaw; (pénurie) shortage; **à ~ de** for lack of; **pris en ~** caught out; **faire ~** (*argent etc.*) be lacking; **par ~** (Jur) in one's absence; **~ de paiement** non-payment.

**défavorable** /defavɔʀabl/ *a* unfavourable.

**défavoriser** /defavɔʀize/ [1] *vt* discriminate against.

**défectueux**, **-euse** /defɛktɥø, -z/ *a* faulty, defective.

**défendre** /defɑ̃dʀ/ [3] *vt* defend; (interdire) forbid; **~ à qn de** forbid sb to. □ **se ~** *vpr* defend oneself; (se protéger) protect oneself; (se débrouiller) manage; **se ~ de** (refuser) refrain from.

**défense** /defɑ̃s/ *nf* defence; **~ de fumer** no smoking; (d'éléphant) tusk. **défenseur** *nm* defender. **défensif**, **-ive** *a* defensive.

**déferler** /defɛʀle/ [1] *vi* (*vagues*) break; (*violence*) erupt.

**défi** /defi/ *nm* challenge; (provocation) defiance; **mettre au ~** challenge.

**déficience** /defisjɑ̃s/ *nf* deficiency. **déficient**, **~e** *a* deficient.

**déficit** /defisit/ *nm* deficit. **déficitaire** *a* in deficit.

**défier** /defje/ [45] *vt* challenge; (braver) defy.

**défilé** /defile/ *nm* procession; (Mil) parade; (fig) (continual) stream; (Géog) gorge; **~ de mode** fashion parade.

**défiler** /defile/ [1] *vi* march; (*visiteurs*) stream; (*images*) flash by; (*chiffres, minutes*) add up. ▫ **se ~** *vpr* [I] sneak off.

**défini**, **~e** /defini/ *a* (Ling) definite.

**définir** /definiʀ/ [2] *vt* define.

**définitif**, **-ive** /definitif, -v/ *a* final, definitive; **en définitive** in the end.

**définition** /definisjɔ̃/ *nf* definition; (de mots croisés) clue.

**définitivement** /definitivmɑ̃/ *adv* definitively, permanently.

**déflagration** /deflagʀasjɔ̃/ *nf* explosion.

**déflation** /deflasjɔ̃/ *nf* deflation. **déflationniste** *a* deflationary.

**défoncé**, **~e** /defɔ̃se/ *a* (*terrain*) full of potholes; (*siège*) broken; (*drogué*: [I]) high.

**défoncer** /defɔ̃se/ [10] *vt* (*porte*) break down; (*mâchoire*) break. ▫ **se ~** *vpr* [I] to give one's all.

**déformation** /defɔʀmasjɔ̃/ *nf* distortion. **déformer** [1] *vt* put out of shape; (*faits, pensée*) distort.

**défouler (se)** /(sə)defule/ [1] *vpr* let off steam.

**défrayer** /defʀeje/ [31] *vt* (payer) pay the expenses of; **~ la chronique** be the talk of the town.

**défricher** /defʀiʃe/ [1] *vt* clear.

**défroisser** /defʀwase/ [1] *vt* smooth out.

**défunt**, **~e** /defœ̃, -t/ *a* (mort) late. ● *nm,f* deceased.

**dégagé**, **~e** /degaʒe/ *a* (*ciel*) clear; (*front*) bare; **d'un ton ~** casually.

**dégagement** /degaʒmɑ̃/ *nm* clearing; (football) clearance.

**dégager** /degaʒe/ [40] *vt* (exhaler) give off; (désencombrer) clear; (faire ressortir) bring out; (*ballon*) clear. ▫ **se ~** *vpr* free oneself; (*ciel, rue*) clear; (*odeur*) emanate.

**dégarnir (se)** /(sə)degaʀniʀ/ [2] *vpr* clear, empty; (*personne*) be going bald.

**dégâts** /degɑ/ *nmpl* damage (+ *sg*).

**dégel** /deʒɛl/ *nm* thaw. **dégeler** [6] *vi* thaw (out).

**dégénéré**, **~e** /deʒeneʀe/ *a* & *nm,f* degenerate.

**dégivrer** /deʒivʀe/ [1] *vt* (Auto) de-ice; (*réfrigérateur*) defrost.

**déglinguer** /deglɛ̃ge/ [I] [1] *vt* bust. ▫ **se ~** *vpr* break down.

**dégonflé**, **~e** /degɔ̃fle/ *a* (*pneu*) flat; (lâche [I]) yellow [I].

**dégonfler** /degɔ̃fle/ [1] *vt* deflate. ● *vi* (*blessure*) go down. ▫ **se ~** *vpr* [I] chicken out.

**dégouliner** /deguline/ [1] *vi* trickle.

**dégourdi**, **~e** /deguʀdi/ *a* smart.

**dégourdir** /deguʀdiʀ/ [2] *vt* (*membre, liquide*) warm up. ▫ **se ~** *vpr* **se ~ les jambes** stretch one's legs.

**dégoût** /degu/ *nm* disgust.

**dégoûtant**, **~e** /degutɑ̃, -t/ *a* disgusting.

**dégoûter** /degute/ [1] *vt* disgust; **~ qn de qch** put sb off sth.

**dégradant**, **~e** /degʀadɑ̃, -t/ *a* degrading.

**dégradation** /degʀadasjɔ̃/ *nf* damage; **commettre des ~s** cause damage.

**dégrader** /degʀade/ [1] *vt* (abîmer) damage. ▫ **se ~** *vpr* (se détériorer) deteriorate.

**dégrafer** /degʀafe/ [1] *vt* unhook.

**degré** /dəgʀe/ *nm* degree; (d'escalier) step.

**dégressif, -ive** /degʀesif, -v/ *a* graded; **tarif ~** tapering charge.

**dégrèvement** /degʀɛvmɑ̃/ *nm* **~ fiscal** *ou* **d'impôts** tax reduction.

**dégringolade** /degʀɛ̃gɔlad/ *nf* tumble.

**dégrossir** /degʀɔsiʀ/ [2] *vt* (*bois*) trim; (*projet*) rough out.

**déguerpir** /degɛʀpiʀ/ [2] *vi* clear off.

**dégueulasse** /degœlas/ *a* ▣ disgusting, lousy.

**dégueuler** /degœle/ [1] *vt* ▣ throw up.

**déguisement** /degizmɑ̃/ *nm* (de carnaval) fancy dress; (pour duper) disguise.

**déguiser** /degize/ [1] *vt* dress up; (pour duper) disguise. □ **se ~** *vpr* (au carnaval etc.) dress up; (pour duper) disguise oneself.

**déguster** /degyste/ [1] *vt* taste, sample; (savourer) enjoy.

**dehors** /dəɔʀ/ *adv* **en ~ de** outside; (hormis) apart from; **jeter/mettre ~** throw/put out. ● *nm* outside. ● *nmpl* (aspect de qn) exterior.

**déjà** /deʒa/ *adv* already; (avant) before, already.

**déjeuner** /deʒœne/ [1] *vi* have lunch; (le matin) have breakfast. ● *nm* lunch; **petit ~** breakfast.

**delà** /dəla/ *adv & prép* **au ~ (de)**, **par ~** beyond.

**délai** /delɛ/ *nm* time-limit; (attente) wait; (sursis) extension (of time); **sans ~** immediately; **dans un ~ de 2 jours** within 2 days; **finir dans les ~s** finish within the deadline; **dans les plus brefs ~s** as soon as possible.

**délaisser** /delese/ [1] *vt* (négliger) neglect.

**délassement** /delasmɑ̃/ *nm* relaxation.

**délation** /delasjɔ̃/ *nf* informing.

**délavé, ~e** /delave/ *a* faded.

**délayer** /deleje/ [31] *vt* mix (with liquid); (*idée*) drag out.

**délecter (se)** /(sə)delɛkte/ [1] *vpr* **se ~ de** delight in.

**délégué, ~e** /delege/ *nm,f* delegate.

**délibéré, ~e** /delibeʀe/ *a* deliberate; (résolu) determined.

**délicat, ~e** /delika, -t/ *a* delicate; (plein de tact) tactful. **délicatesse** *nf* delicacy; (tact) tact. **délicatesses** *nfpl* (kind) attentions.

**délice** /delis/ *nm* delight. **délicieux, -ieuse** *a* (au goût) delicious; (charmant) delightful.

**délier** /delje/ [45] *vt* untie; (délivrer) free. □ **se ~** *vpr* come untied.

**délimiter** /delimite/ [1] *vt* determine, demarcate.

**délinquance** /delɛ̃kɑ̃s/ *nf* delinquency. **délinquant, ~e** *a & nm,f* delinquent.

**délirant, ~e** /deliʀɑ̃, -t/ *a* delirious; (frénétique) frenzied; 🄸 wild.

**délire** /deliʀ/ *nm* delirium; (fig) frenzy. **délirer** [1] *vi* be delirious (**de** with); 🄸 be off one's rocker 🄸.

**délit** /deli/ *nm* offence.

**délivrance** /delivʀɑ̃s/ *nf* release; (soulagement) relief; (remise) issue.

**délivrer** [1] *vt* free, release; (*pays*) liberate; (remettre) issue.

**déloyal, ~e** (*mpl* **-aux**) /delwajal, -jo/ *a* disloyal; (*procédé*) unfair.

**deltaplane** /dɛltaplan/ *nm* hang-glider.

**déluge** /delyʒ/ *nm* downpour; **le D~** the Flood.

**démagogie** /demagɔʒi/ *nm* demagogy. **démagogue** *nmf* demagogue.

**demain** /dəmɛ̃/ *adv* tomorrow.

**demande** /dəmɑ̃d/ *nf* request; **~ d'emploi** job application; **~ en mariage** marriage proposal.

**demander** /dəmɑ̃de/ [1] *vt* ask for; (*chemin, heure*) ask; (nécessiter) require; **~ que/si** ask that/if; **~ qch à qn** ask sb sth; **~ à qn de** ask sb to; **~ en mariage** propose to. □ **se ~** *vpr* **se ~ si/où** wonder if/where.

**demandeur**, **-euse** /dəmɑ̃dœʀ, -øz/ *nm,f* **~ d'emploi** job seeker; **~ d'asile** asylum-seeker.

**démangeaison** /demɑ̃ʒezɔ̃/ *nf* itch(ing).

**démanteler** /demɑ̃tle/ [6] *vt* break up.

**démaquillant** /demakijɑ̃/ *nm* make-up remover. **démaquiller (se)** [1] *vpr* remove one's make-up.

**démarchage** /demaʀʃaʒ/ *nm* door-to-door selling.

**démarche** /demaʀʃ/ *nf* walk, gait; (procédé) step.

**démarcheur**, **-euse** /demaʀʃœʀ, -øz/ *nm,f* (door-to-door) canvasser.

**démarrage** /demaʀaʒ/ *nm* start.

**démarrer** /demaʀe/ [1] *vi* (*moteur*) start (up); (partir) move off; (fig) get moving. ● *vt* Ⅱ get moving.

**démarreur** /demaʀœʀ/ *nm* starter.

**démêlant** /demelɑ̃/ *nm* conditioner. **démêler** [1] *vt* disentangle.

**déménagement** /demenaʒmɑ̃/ *nm* move; (transport) removal.

**déménager** /demenaʒe/ [40] *vi* move (house). ● *vt* (*meubles*) remove.

**déménageur** /demenaʒœʀ/ *nm* removal man.

**démence** /demɑ̃s/ *nf* insanity.

**démener (se)** /(sə)demne/ [6] *vpr* move about wildly; (fig) put oneself out.

**dément**, **~e** /demɑ̃, -t/ *a* insane. ● *nm,f* lunatic.

**démenti** /demɑ̃ti/ *nm* denial.

**démentir** /demɑ̃tiʀ/ [46] *vt* deny; (contredire) refute; **~ que** deny that.

**démerder (se)** /(sə)demɛʀde/ [1] *vpr* ⊠ manage.

**démettre** /demɛtʀ/ [42] *vt* (*poignet etc.*) dislocate; **~ qn de** relieve sb of. □ **se ~** *vpr* resign (**de** from).

**demeure** /dəmœʀ/ *nf* residence; **mettre en ~ de** order to.

**demeurer** /dəmœʀe/ [1] *vi* live; (rester) remain.

**demi**, **~e** /dəmi/ *a* half(-). ● *nm,f* half. ● *nm* (bière) (half-pint) glass of beer; (football) half-back. ● *adv* **à ~** half; (*ouvrir, fermer*) half-way; **à la ~e** at half past; **une heure et ~e** an hour and a half; (à l'horloge) half past one; **une ~-journée/-livre** half a day/pound. **demi-cercle** (*pl* **~s**) *nm* semicircle. **demi-finale** (*pl* **~s**) *nf* semifinal. **demi-frère** (*pl* **~s**) *nm* half-brother, stepbrother. **demi-heure** (*pl* **~s**) *nf* half-hour, half an hour. **demi-litre** (*pl* **~s**) *nm* half a litre. **demi-mesure** (*pl* **~s**) *nf* half-measure. **à demi-mot** *adv* without having to express every word. **demi-pension** *nf* half-board. **demi-queue** *nm* boudoir grand piano. **demi-sel** *a inv* slightly salted. **demi-sœur** (*pl* **~s**) *nf* half-sister, stepsister.

**démission** /demisjɔ̃/ *nf* resignation.

**demi-tarif** (*pl* **~s**) /dəmitaʀif/ *nm* half-fare.

**demi-tour** (*pl* **~s**) /dəmituʀ/ *nm* about turn; (Auto) U-turn; **faire ~** turn back.

**démocrate** /demɔkʀat/ *nmf* democrat. ● *a* democratic. **démocratie** *nf* democracy.

**démodé**, **~e** /demɔde/ *a* old-fashioned.

**demoiselle** /dəmwazɛl/ *nf* young lady; (célibataire) single lady; **~ d'honneur** bridesmaid.

**démolir** /demɔliʀ/ [2] *vt* demolish.

**démon** /demɔ̃/ *nm* demon; **le D~** the Devil. **démoniaque** *a* fiendish.

**démonstration** /demɔ̃stʀasjɔ̃/ *nf* demonstration; (de force) show.

**démonter** /demɔ̃te/ [1] *vt* take apart, dismantle; (*installation*) take down; (fig) disconcert. □ **se ~** *vpr* come apart.

**démontrer** /demɔ̃tʀe/ [1] *vt* demonstrate; (indiquer) show.

**démoraliser** /demɔʀalize/ [1] *vt* demoralize.

**démuni**, **~e** /demyni/ *a* impoverished; **~ de** without.

**démunir** /demyniʀ/ [2] *vt* **~ de** deprive of. □ **se ~ de** *vpr* part with.

**dénaturer** /denatyʀe/ [1] *vt* (*faits*) distort.

**dénigrement** /denigʀəmɑ̃/ *nm* denigration.

**dénivellation** /denivɛlasjɔ̃/ *nf* (pente) slope.

**dénombrer** /denɔ̃bʀe/ [1] *vt* count.

**dénomination** /denɔminasjɔ̃/ *nf* designation.

**dénommé**, **~e** /denɔme/ *nm,f* **le ~ X** the said X.

**dénoncer** /denɔ̃se/ [10] *vt* denounce. □ **se ~** *vpr* give oneself up. **dénonciateur**, **-trice** *nm,f* informer.

**dénouement** /denumɑ̃/ *nm* outcome; (Théât) dénouement.

**dénouer** /denwe/ [1] *vt* undo. □ **se ~** *vpr* (*nœud*) come undone.

**dénoyauter** /denwajote/ [1] *vt* stone.

**denrée** /dɑ̃ʀe/ *nf* **~ alimentaire** foodstuff.

**dense** /dɑ̃s/ *a* dense. **densité** *nf* density.

**dent** /dɑ̃/ *nf* tooth; **faire ses ~s** teethe; **~ de lait** milk tooth; **~ de sagesse** wisdom tooth; (de roue) cog. **dentaire** *a* dental.

**denté**, **~e** /dɑ̃te/ *a* (*roue*) toothed

**dentelé**, **~e** /dɑ̃tle/ *a* jagged.

**dentelle** /dɑ̃tɛl/ *nf* lace.

**dentier** /dɑ̃tje/ *nm* dentures (+ *pl*), false teeth (+ *pl*).

**dentifrice** /dɑ̃tifʀis/ *nm* toothpaste.

**dentiste** /dɑ̃tist/ *nmf* dentist.

**dentition** /dɑ̃tisjɔ̃/ *nf* teeth, dentition.

**dénudé**, **~e** /denyde/ *a* bare.

**dénué**, **~e** /denɥe/ *a* **~ de** devoid of.

**dénuement** /denymɑ̃/ *nm* destitution.

**déodorant** /deɔdɔʀɑ̃/ *nm* deodorant.

**dépannage** /depanaʒ/ *nm* repair; (Ordinat) troubleshooting. **dépanner** [1] *vt* repair; (fig) help out. **dépanneuse** *nf* breakdown lorry.

**dépareillé**, **~e** /depaʀeje/ *a* odd, not matching.

**départ** /depaʀ/ *nm* departure; (Sport) start; **au ~ de Nice** from Nice; **au ~** (d'abord) at first.

**département** /depaʀtəmɑ̃/ *nm* department.

**dépassé**, **~e** /depɑse/ *a* outdated.

**dépasser** /depɑse/ [1] *vt* go past, pass; (*véhicule*) overtake; (excéder) exceed; (*rival*) surpass; **ça me dépasse** [I] it's beyond me. ● *vi* stick out.

**dépaysement** /depeizmɑ̃/ *nm* change of scenery; (désagréable) disorientation.

**dépêche** /depɛʃ/ *nf* dispatch.

**dépêcher** /depeʃe/ [1] *vt* dispatch. □ **se** ~ *vpr* hurry (up).

**dépendance** /depɑ̃dɑ̃s/ *nf* dependence; (à une drogue) dependency; (bâtiment) outbuilding.

**dépendre** /depɑ̃dʀ/ [3] *vt* take down. ● *vi* depend (**de** on); ~ **de** (appartenir à) belong to.

**dépens** /depɑ̃/ *nmpl* **aux** ~ **de** at the expense of.

**dépense** /depɑ̃s/ *nf* expense; expenditure.

**dépenser** /depɑse/ [1] *vt/i* spend; (*énergie etc.*) use up. □ **se** ~ *vpr* get some exercise.

**dépérir** /depeʀiʀ/ [2] *vi* wither.

**dépêtrer (se)** /(sə)depetʀe/ [1] *vpr* get oneself out (**de** of).

**dépeupler** /depœple/ [1] *vt* depopulate. □ **se** ~ *vpr* become depopulated.

**déphasé**, ~**e** /defɑze/ *a* [I] out of step.

**dépilatoire** /depilatwaʀ/ *a & nm* depilatory.

**dépistage** /depistaʒ/ *nm* screening. **dépister** [1] *vt* detect; (*criminel*) track down.

**dépit** /depi/ *nm* resentment; **par** ~ out of pique; **en** ~ **de** despite; **en** ~ **du bon sens** in a very illogical way. **dépité**, ~**e** *a* vexed.

**déplacé**, ~**e** /deplase/ *a* (*remarque*) uncalled for.

**déplacement** /deplasmɑ̃/ *nm* (voyage) trip.

**déplacer** /deplase/ [10] *vt* move. □ **se** ~ *vpr* move; (voyager) travel.

**déplaire** /deplɛʀ/ [47] *vi* ~ **à** (irriter) displease; **ça me déplaît** I don't like it.

**déplaisant**, ~**e** /deplɛzɑ̃, -t/ *a* unpleasant, disagreeable.

**dépliant** /deplijɑ̃/ *nm* leaflet.

**déplier** /deplije/ [45] *vt* unfold.

**déploiement** /deplwamɑ̃/ *nm* (démonstration) display; (militaire) deployment.

**déplorable** /deplɔʀabl/ *a* deplorable. **déplorer** [1] *vt* (trouver regrettable) deplore; (*mort*) lament.

**déployer** /deplwaje/ [31] *vt* (*ailes, carte*) spread; (*courage*) display; (*armée*) deploy.

**déportation** /depɔʀtasjɔ̃/ *nf* (en 1940) internment in a concentration camp.

**déposer** /depoze/ [1] *vt* put down; (laisser) leave; (*passager*) drop; (*argent*) deposit; (*plainte*) lodge; (*armes*) lay down. ● *vi* (Jur) testify. □ **se** ~ *vpr* settle.

**dépositaire** /depozitɛʀ/ *nmf* (Comm) agent.

**déposition** /depozisjɔ̃/ *nf* (Jur) statement.

**dépôt** /depo/ *nm* (entrepôt) warehouse; (d'autobus) depot; (particules) deposit; (garantie) deposit; **laisser en** ~ give for safe keeping; ~ **légal** formal deposit of a publication with an institution.

**dépouille** /depuj/ *nf* skin, hide; ~ **(mortelle)** mortal remains.

**dépouiller** /depuje/ [1] *vt* (*courrier*) open; (*scrutin*) count; (écorcher) skin; ~ **qn de** strip sb of.

**dépourvu**, ~**e** /depuʀvy/ *a* ~ **de** devoid of; **prendre au** ~ catch unawares.

**déprécier** /depʀesje/ [45] *vt* depreciate. □ **se** ~ *vpr* depreciate.

**déprédations** /depʀedasjɔ̃/ *nfpl* damage (+ *sg*).

**dépression** /depʀesjɔ̃/ *nf* depression; ~ **nerveuse** nervous breakdown.

**déprimer** /depʀime/ [1] *vt* depress.

**depuis** /dəpɥi/

● *préposition*

····➤ (point de départ) since; ~ **quand attendez-vous?** how long have you been waiting?

····➤ (durée) for; ~ **toujours** always; ~ **peu** recently.

● *adverbe*

····➤ since; **il a eu une attaque le mois dernier, ~ nous sommes inquiets** he had a stroke last month and we've been worried ever since.

● **depuis que** *conjonction*

····➤ since, ever since; **Sophie a beaucoup changé depuis que Camille est née** Sophie has changed a lot since Camille was born.

**député** /depyte/ *nm* ≈ Member of Parliament.

**déraciné, -e** /deʀasine/ *nm, f* rootless person.

**déraillement** /deʀajmɑ̃/ *nm* derailment.

**dérailler** /deʀaje/ [1] *vi* be derailed; (fig 🅘) be talking nonsense; **faire ~** derail. **dérailleur** *nm* (de vélo) derailleur.

**déraisonnable** /deʀɛzɔnabl/ *a* unreasonable.

**dérangement** /deʀɑ̃ʒmɑ̃/ *nm* bother; (désordre) disorder, upset; **en ~** out of order; **les ~s** the fault reporting service.

**déranger** /deʀɑ̃ʒe/ [40] *vt* (gêner) bother, disturb; (dérégler) upset, disrupt. ◻ **se ~** *vpr* (aller) go; (fig) put oneself out; **ça te dérangerait de...?** would you mind...?

**dérapage** /deʀapaʒ/ *nm* skid. **déraper** [1] *vi* skid; (fig) (*prix*) get out of control.

**déréglé, ~e** /deʀegle/ *a* (*vie*) dissolute; (*estomac*) upset; (*mécanisme*) (that is) not running properly.

**dérégler** /deʀegle/ [14] *vt* make go wrong. ◻ **se ~** *vpr* go wrong.

**dérision** /deʀizjɔ̃/ *nf* mockery; **tourner en ~** ridicule.

**dérive** /deʀiv/ *nf* **aller à la ~** drift.

**dérivé** /deʀive/ *nm* by-product.

**dériver** /deʀive/ [1] *vi* (*bateau*) drift; ~ **de** stem from.

**dermatologie** /dɛʀmatɔlɔʒi/ *nf* dermatology.

**dernier, -ière** /dɛʀnje, -jɛʀ/ *a* last; (*nouvelles, mode*) latest; (*étage*) top. ● *nm, f* last (one); **ce ~** the latter; **le ~ de mes soucis** the least of my worries.

**dernièrement** /dɛʀnjɛʀmɑ̃/ *adv* recently.

**dérober** /deʀɔbe/ [1] *vt* steal. ◻ **se ~** *vpr* slip away; **se ~ à** (*obligation*) shy away from.

**dérogation** /deʀɔgasjɔ̃/ *nf* special authorization.

**déroger** /deʀɔʒe/ [40] *vi* ~ **à** depart from.

**déroulement** /deʀulmɑ̃/ *nm* (d'une action) development.

**dérouler** /deʀule/ [1] *vt* (*fil etc.*) unwind. ◻ **se ~** *vpr* unwind; (avoir lieu) take place; (*récit, paysage*) unfold.

**déroute** /deʀut/ *nf* (Mil) rout.

**dérouter** /deʀute/ [1] *vt* disconcert.

**derrière** /dɛʀjɛʀ/ *prép & adv* behind. ● *nm* back, rear; (postérieur 🅘)

behind [I]; **de ~** (*fenêtre*) back, rear; (*pattes*) hind.

**des** /de/ ⇒DE.

**dès** /dɛ/ *prép* (right) from; **~ lors** from then on; **~ que** as soon as.

**désabusé**, **~e** /dezabyze/ *a* disillusioned.

**désaccord** /dezakɔʀ/ *nm* disagreement.

**désaffecté**, **~e** /dezafɛkte/ *a* disused.

**désagréable** /dezagʀeabl/ *a* unpleasant.

**désagrément** /dezagʀemɑ̃/ *nm* annoyance, inconvenience.

**désaltérer (se)** /(sə)dezalteʀe/ [14] *vpr* quench one's thirst.

**désamorcer** /dezamɔʀse/ [10] *vt* (*situation, obus*) defuse.

**désapprobation** /dezapʀɔbasjɔ̃/ *nf* disapproval. **désapprouver** [1] *vt* disapprove of.

**désarçonner** /dezaʀsɔne/ [1] *vt* throw.

**désarmement** /dezaʀməmɑ̃/ *nm* (Pol) disarmament.

**désarroi** /dezaʀwa/ *nm* distress.

**désastre** /dezastʀ/ *nm* disaster. **désastreux**, **-euse** *a* disastrous.

**désavantage** /dezavɑ̃taʒ/ *nm* disadvantage. **désavantager** [40] *vt* put at a disadvantage.

**désaveu** (*pl* **~x**) /dezavø/ *nm* denial. **désavouer** [1] *vt* deny.

**descendance** /dɛsɑ̃dɑ̃s/ *nf* descent; (enfants) descendants (+ *pl*). **descendant**, **~e** *nm,f* descendant.

**descendre** /desɑ̃dʀ/ [3] *vi* (*aux être*) go down; (venir) come down; (*passager*) get off *ou* out; (*nuit*) fall; **~ à pied** walk down; **~ par l'ascenseur** take the lift down; **~ de** (être issu de) be descended from; **~ à l'hôtel** go to a hotel; **~ dans la rue** (Pol) take to the streets. ● *vt* (*aux avoir*) (*escalier etc.*) go *ou* come down; (*objet*) take down; (abattre [I]) shoot down.

**descente** /desɑ̃t/ *nf* descent; (à ski) downhill; (raid) raid; **dans la ~** going downhill; **~ de lit** bedside rug.

**descriptif**, **-ive** /dɛskʀiptif, -v/ *a* descriptive. **description** *nf* description.

**désemparé**, **~e** /dezɑ̃paʀe/ *a* distraught.

**désendettement** /dezɑ̃dɛtmɑ̃/ *nm* reduction of the debt.

**déséquilibré**, **~e** /dezekilibʀe/ *a* unbalanced; [I] crazy. ● *nm,f* lunatic. **déséquilibrer** [1] *vt* throw off balance.

**désert**, **~e** /dezɛʀ, -t/ *a* deserted. ● *nm* desert.

**déserter** /dezɛʀte/ [1] *vt/i* desert. **déserteur** *nm* deserter.

**désertique** /dezɛʀtik/ *a* desert.

**désespérant**, **~e** /dezɛspeʀɑ̃, -t/ *a* utterly disheartening.

**désespéré**, **~e** /dezɛspeʀe/ *a* in despair; (*état, cas*) hopeless; (*effort*) desperate.

**désespérer** /dezɛspeʀe/ [14] *vt* drive to despair. ● *vi* despair, lose hope; **~ de** despair of. ■ **se ~** *vpr* despair.

**désespoir** /dezɛspwaʀ/ *nm* despair; **en ~ de cause** as a last resort.

**déshabillé**, **~e** /dezabije/ *a* undressed. ● *nm* négligee.

**déshabiller** /dezabije/ [1] *vt* undress. □ **se ~** *vpr* get undressed.

**désherbant** /dezɛʀbɑ̃/ *nm* weedkiller.

**déshérité**, **~e** /dezeʀite/ *a* (*région*) deprived; (*personne*) the underprivileged.

**déshériter** /dezeʀite/ [1] *vt* disinherit.

**déshonneur** /dezɔnœʀ/ *nm* disgrace.

**déshonorer** /dezɔnɔʀe/ [1] *vt* dishonour.

**déshydrater** /dezidʀate/ [1] *vt* dehydrate. □ **se ~** *vpr* get dehydrated.

**désigner** /deziɲe/ [1] *vt* (montrer) point to *ou* out; (élire) appoint; (signifier) designate.

**désillusion** /dezilyzjɔ̃/ *nf* disillusionment.

**désinence** /dezinɑ̃s/ *nf* (Gram) ending.

**désinfectant** /dezɛ̃fɛktɑ̃/ *nm* disinfectant. **désinfecter** [1] *vt* disinfect.

**désintéressé**, **~e** /dezɛ̃teʀese/ *a* (*personne, acte*) selfless.

**désintéresser** (**se**) /(sə)dezɛ̃teʀese/ [1] *vpr* **se ~ de** lose interest in.

**désintoxiquer** /dezɛ̃tɔksike/ [1] *vt* detoxify; **se faire ~** to undergo detoxification.

**désinvolte** /dezɛ̃vɔlt/ *a* casual. **désinvolture** *nf* casualness.

**désir** /deziʀ/ *nm* wish, desire; (convoitise) desire.

**désirer** /deziʀe/ [1] *vt* want; (sexuellement) desire; **vous désirez?** what would you like?

**désireux**, **-euse** /deziʀø, -z/ *a* **~ de faire** anxious to do.

**désistement** /dezistəmɑ̃/ *nm* withdrawal.

**désobéir** /dezɔbeiʀ/ [2] *vi* **~ (à)** disobey. **désobéissant**, **~e** *a* disobedient.

**désobligeant**, **~e** /dezɔbliʒɑ̃, -t/ *a* disagreeable, unkind.

**désodorisant** /dezɔdɔʀizɑ̃/ *nm* air freshener.

**désodoriser** /dezɔdɔʀize/ [1] *vt* freshen up.

**désœuvré**, **~e** /dezœvʀe/ *a* at a loose end. **désœuvrement** *nm* lack of anything to do.

**désolation** /dezɔlasjɔ̃/ *nf* distress.

**désolé**, **~e** /dezɔle/ *a* (au regret) sorry; (*région*) desolate.

**désoler** /dezɔlɛ̃/ [1] *vt* distress. □ **se ~** *vpr* be upset (**de qch** about sth).

**désopilant**, **~e** /dezɔpilɑ̃, -t/ *a* hilarious.

**désordonné**, **~e** /dezɔʀdɔne/ *a* untidy; (*mouvements*) uncoordinated.

**désordre** /dezɔʀdʀ/ *nm* untidiness; (Pol) disorder; **en ~** untidy.

**désorganiser** /dezɔʀganize/ [1] *vt* disorganize.

**désorienter** /dezɔʀjɑ̃te/ [1] *vt* disorient.

**désormais** /dezɔʀmɛ/ *adv* from now on.

**desquels**, **desquelles** /dekɛl/ ⇒LEQUEL.

**dessécher** /deseʃe/ [1] *vt* dry out. □ **se ~** *vpr* dry out, become dry; (*plante*) wither.

**dessein** /desɛ̃/ *nm* intention; **à ~** intentionally.

**desserrer** /deseʀe/ [1] *vt* loosen; **il n'a pas desserré les dents** he never once opened his mouth. □ **se ~** *vpr* come loose.

**dessert** /desɛʀ/ *nm* dessert; **en ~** for dessert.

**desservir** /desɛʀviʀ/ [46] *vt*/*i* (débarrasser) clear away; (*autobus*) serve.

**dessin** /desɛ̃/ *nm* drawing; (motif) design; (discipline) art; (contour) outline; **professeur de ~** art teacher;

~ **animé** (cinéma) cartoon; ~ **humoristique** cartoon.

**dessinateur**, **-trice** /desinatœʀ, -tʀis/ *nm,f* artist; (industriel) draughtsman.

**dessiner** /desine/ [1] *vt/i* draw; (fig) outline. □ **se** ~ *vpr* appear, take shape.

**dessoûler** /desule/ [1] *vt/i* sober up.

**dessous** /dəsu/ *adv* underneath. ● *nm* underside, underneath. ● *nmpl* underwear; **les ~ d'une histoire** what is behind a story; **du** ~ bottom; (*voisins*) downstairs; **en** ~, **par-**~ underneath. **dessous-de-plat** *nm inv* (heat-resistant) table-mat. **dessous-de-table** *nm inv* backhander. **dessous-de-verre** *nm inv* coaster.

**dessus** /dəsy/ *adv* on top (of it), on it. ● *nm* top; **du** ~ top; (*voisins*) upstairs, **avoir le** ~ get the upper hand. **dessus-de-lit** *nm inv* bedspread.

**déstabiliser** /destabilize/ [1] *vt* destabilize, unsettle.

**destin** /dɛstɛ̃/ *nm* (sort) fate; (avenir) destiny.

**destinataire** /dɛstinatɛʀ/ *nmf* addressee.

**destination** /dɛstinasjɔ̃/ *nf* destination; (fonction) purpose; **vol à ~ de** flight to.

**destinée** /dɛstine/ *nf* destiny.

**destiner** /dɛstine/ [1] *vt* ~ **à** intend for; (vouer) destine for; **le commentaire m'est destiné** this comment is aimed at me; **être destiné à faire** be intended to do; (obligé) be destined to do. □ **se ~ à** *vpr* (*carrière*) intend to take up.

**destituer** /dɛstitɥe/ [1] *vt* discharge.

**destructeur**, **-trice** /dɛstʀyktœʀ, -tʀis/ *a* destructive. **destruction** *nf* destruction.

**désuet**, **-ète** /dezɥɛ, -t/ *a* outdated.

**détachant** /detaʃɑ̃/ *nm* stain remover.

**détacher** /detaʃe/ [1] *vt* untie; (ôter) remove, detach; (déléguer) second. □ **se** ~ *vpr* come off, break away; (*nœud etc.*) come undone; (ressortir) stand out.

**détail** /detaj/ *nm* detail; (de compte) breakdown; (Comm) retail; **au** ~ (*vendre etc.*) retail; **de** ~ (*prix etc.*) retail; **en** ~ in detail; **entrer dans les** ~**s** go into detail.

**détaillant**, ~**e** /detajɑ̃, -t/ *nm,f* retailer.

**détaillé**, ~**e** /detaje/ *a* detailed.

**détailler** /detaje/ [1] *vt* (*rapport*) detail; ~ **ce que qn fait** scrutinize what sb does.

**détaler** /detale/ [1] *vi* [I] bolt.

**détartrant** /detartrɑ̃/ *nm* descaler.

**détecter** /detɛkte/ [1] *vt* detect. **détecteur** *nm* detector.

**détective** /detɛktiv/ *nm* detective.

**déteindre** /detɛ̃dʀ/ [22] *vi* (dans l'eau) run (**sur** on to); (au soleil) fade; ~ **sur** (fig) rub off on.

**détendre** /detɑ̃dʀ/ [3] *vt* slacken; (*ressort*) release; (*personne*) relax. □ **se** ~ *vpr* (*ressort*) slacken; (*personne*) relax. **détendu**, ~**e** *a* (calme) relaxed.

**détenir** /det(ə)niʀ/ [58] *vt* hold; (*secret, fortune*) possess.

**détente** /detɑ̃t/ *nf* relaxation; (Pol) détente; (saut) spring; (gâchette) trigger; **être lent à la** ~ [I] be slow on the uptake.

**détenteur**, **-trice** /detɑ̃tœʀ, -tʀis/ *nm,f* holder.

**détention** /detɑ̃sjɔ̃/ *nf* detention; ~ **provisoire** custody.

**détenu**, ~**e** /detny/ *nm,f* prisoner.

**détergent** /deteʀʒɑ̃/ *nm* detergent.

**détérioration** /deteʀjɔʀasjɔ̃/ *nf* deterioration; (dégât) damage.

**détériorer** /deteʀjɔʀe/ [1] *vt* damage. □ **se** ~ *vpr* deteriorate.

**détermination** /deteʀminasjɔ̃/ *nf* determination. **déterminé**, ~**e** *a* (résolu) determined; (précis) definite. **déterminer** [1] *vt* determine.

**déterrer** /deteʀe/ [1] *vt* dig up.

**détestable** /detɛstabl/ *a* (*caractère, temps*) foul.

**détester** /detɛste/ [1] *vt* hate. □ **se** ~ *vpr* hate each other.

**détonation** /detɔnasjɔ̃/ *nf* explosion, detonation.

**détour** /detuʀ/ *nm* (crochet) detour; (fig) roundabout means; (virage) bend.

**détournement** /detuʀnəmɑ̃/ *nm* hijack(ing); (de fonds) embezzlement.

**détourner** /detuʀne/ [1] *vt* (*attention*) divert; (*tête, yeux*) turn away; (*avion*) hijack; (*argent*) embezzle. □ **se** ~ **de** *vpr* stray from.

**détraquer** /detʀake/ [1] *vt* make go wrong; (*estomac*) upset. □ **se** ~ *vpr* (*machine*) go wrong.

**détresse** /detʀɛs/ *nf* distress; **dans la** ~, **en** ~ in distress.

**détritus** /detʀity(s)/ *nmpl* rubbish (+ *sg*).

**détroit** /detʀwa/ *nm* strait.

**détromper** /detʀɔ̃pe/ [1] *vt* set straight. □ **se** ~ *vpr* **détrompe-toi!** you'd better think again!

**détruire** /detʀɥiʀ/ [17] *vt* destroy.

**dette** /dɛt/ *nf* debt.

**deuil** /dœj/ *nm* (période) mourning; (décès) bereavement; **porter le** ~ be in mourning; **faire son** ~ **de qch** give sth up as lost.

**deux** /dø/ *a & nm* two; ~ **fois** twice; **tous (les)** ~ both. **deuxième** *a & nmf* second. **deux-pièces** *nm inv* (maillot de bain) two-piece; (logement) two-room flat. **deux-points** *nm inv* (Gram) colon. **deux-roues** *nm inv* two-wheeled vehicle.

**dévaliser** /devalize/ [1] *vt* rob, clean out.

**dévalorisant**, ~**e** /devalɔʀizɑ̃, -t/ *a* demeaning.

**dévaloriser** /devalɔʀize/ [1] *vt* (*monnaie*) devalue. □ **se** ~ *vpr* (*personne*) put oneself down.

**dévaluation** /devalɥasjɔ̃/ *nf* devaluation.

**dévaluer** /devalɥe/ [1] *vt* devalue. □ **se** ~ *vpr* devalue.

**devancer** /dəvɑ̃se/ [10] *vt* be *ou* go ahead of; (arriver) arrive ahead of; (prévenir) anticipate.

**devant** /d(ə)vɑ̃/ *prép* in front of; (distance) ahead of; (avec mouvement) past; (en présence de) in front of; (face à) in the face of; **avoir du temps** ~ **soi** have plenty of time. ● *adv* in front; (à distance) ahead; **de** ~ front. ● *nm* front; **prendre les** ~**s** take the initiative.

**devanture** /dəvɑ̃tyʀ/ *nf* shop front; (vitrine) shop window.

**développement** /devlɔpmɑ̃/ *nm* development; (de photos) developing.

**développer** /devlɔpe/ [1] *vt* develop. □ **se** ~ *vpr* (*corps, talent*) develop; (*entreprise*) grow, expand.

**devenir** /dəvniʀ/ [58] *vi* (*aux être*) become; **qu'est-il devenu?** what has become of him?

**dévergondé**, **~e** /devɛʀgɔ̃de/ *a & nm,f* shameless (person).

**déverser** /devɛʀse/ [1] *vt* (*liquide*) pour; (*ordures, pétrole*) dump. □ **se ~** *vpr* (*rivière*) flow; (*égout, foule*) pour.

**dévêtir** /devetiʀ/ [61] *vt* undress. □ **se ~** *vpr* get undressed.

**déviation** /devjasjɔ̃/ *nf* diversion.

**dévier** /devje/ [45] *vt* divert; (*coup*) deflect. ● *vi* (*ballon, balle*) veer; (*personne*) deviate.

**devin** /dəvɛ̃/ *nm* soothsayer.

**deviner** /dəvine/ [1] *vt* guess; (apercevoir) distinguish.

**devinette** /dəvinɛt/ *nf* riddle.

**devis** /dəvi/ *nm* estimate, quote.

**dévisager** /devizaʒe/ [40] *vt* stare at.

**devise** /dəviz/ *nf* motto; **~s** (monnaie) (foreign) currency.

**dévisser** /devise/ [1] *vt* unscrew.

**dévitaliser** /devitalize/ [1] *vt* (*dent*) carry out root canal treatment on.

**dévoiler** /devwale/ [1] *vt* reveal.

---

**devoir** /dəvwaʀ/ [26]

● *verbe auxiliaire*

····➤ **~ faire** (obligation, hypothèse) must do; (nécessité) have got to do; **je dois dire que...** I have to say that...; **il a dû partir** (nécessité) he had to leave; (hypothèse) he must have left.

····➤ (prévision) **je devais lui dire** I was to tell her; **elle doit rentrer bientôt** she's due back soon.

····➤ (conseil) **tu devrais** you should.

● *verbe transitif*

····➤ (*argent, excuses*) owe; **combien je vous dois?** (en achetant) how much is it?

□ **se devoir** *verbe pronominal*

····➤ **je me dois de le faire** it's my duty to do it.

● *nom masculin*

····➤ duty; **faire son ~** do one's duty.

····➤ (Scol) **~** (**surveillé**) test; **les ~s** homework (+ *sg*); **faire ses ~s** do one's homework.

---

**dévorer** /devɔʀe/ [1] *vt* devour.

**dévot**, **~e** /devo, -ɔt/ *a* devout.

**dévoué**, **~e** /devwe/ *a* devoted. **dévouement** *nm* devotion.

**dévouer** (**se**) /(sə)devwe/ [1] *vpr* devote oneself (**à** to); (se sacrifier) sacrifice oneself.

**dextérité** /dɛksteʀite/ *nf* skill.

**diabète** /djabɛt/ *nm* diabetes. **diabétique** *a & nmf* diabetic.

**diable** /djɑbl/ *nm* devil.

**diagnostic** /djagnɔstik/ *nm* diagnosis. **diagnostiquer** [1] *vt* diagnose.

**diagonal**, **~e** (*mpl* **-aux**) /djagɔnal, -o/ *a* diagonal. **diagonale** *nf* diagonal; **en ~e** diagonally.

**diagramme** /djagʀam/ *nm* diagram; (graphique) graph.

**dialecte** /djalɛkt/ *nm* dialect.

**dialogue** /djalɔg/ *nm* dialogue. **dialoguer** [1] *vi* have talks, enter into a dialogue.

**diamant** /djamɑ̃/ *nm* diamond.

**diamètre** /djamɛtʀ/ *nm* diameter.

**diapositive** /djapozitiv/ *nf* slide.

**diarrhée** /djaʀe/ *nf* diarrhoea.

**dictateur** /diktatœʀ/ *nm* dictator.

**dicter** /dikte/ [1] *vt* dictate. **dictée** *nf* dictation.

**dictionnaire** /diksjɔnɛʀ/ *nm* dictionary.

**dicton** /diktɔ̃/ *nm* saying.

**dièse** /djɛz/ *nm* (Mus) sharp.

**diesel** /djezɛl/ *nm & a inv* diesel.

**diète** /djɛt/ *nf* restricted diet.

**diététicien**, **~ne** /djetetisjɛ̃, -ɛn/ *nm,f* dietician.

**diététique** /djetetik/ *nf* dietetics. ● *a* **produit** *ou* **aliment ~** dietary product; **magasin ~** health food shop *ou* store.

**dieu** (*pl* **~x**) /djø/ *nm* god; **D~** God.

**diffamation** /difamasjɔ̃/ *nf* slander; (par écrit) libel. **diffamer** [1] *vt* slander; (par écrit) libel.

**différé**: **en ~** /ɑ̃difeʀe/ *loc* (*émission*) pre-recorded.

**différemment** /difeʀamɑ̃/ *adv* differently.

**différence** /difeʀɑ̃s/ *nf* difference; **à la ~ de** unlike.

**différencier** /difeʀɑ̃sje/ [45] *vt* differentiate. ◻ **se ~** *vpr* differentiate oneself; **se ~ de** (différer de) differ from.

**différend** /difeʀɑ̃/ *nm* difference (of opinion).

**différent**, **~e** /difeʀɑ̃, -t/ *a* different (**de** from).

**différer** /difeʀe/ [14] *vt* postpone. ● *vi* differ (**de** from).

**difficile** /difisil/ *a* difficult; (exigeant) fussy. **difficilement** *adv* with difficulty.

**difficulté** /difikylte/ *nf* difficulty; **faire des ~s** raise objections.

**diffus**, **~e** /dify, -z/ *a* diffuse.

**diffuser** /difyze/ [1] *vt* (*émission*) broadcast; (*nouvelle*) spread; (*lumière, chaleur*) diffuse; (Comm) distribute. **diffusion** *nf* broadcasting; diffusion; distribution.

**digérer** /diʒeʀe/ [14] *vt* digest; (endurer Ⓘ) stomach. **digeste** *a* digestible.

**digestif**, **-ive** /diʒɛstif, -v/ *a* digestive. ● *nm* after-dinner liqueur.

**digital**, **~e** (*mpl* **-aux**) /diʒital, -o/ *a* digital.

**digne** /diɲ/ *a* (noble) dignified; (approprié) worthy; **~ de** worthy of; **~ de foi** trustworthy.

**digue** /dig/ *nf* dyke; (US) dike.

**dilater** /dilate/ [1] *vt* dilate. ◻ **se ~** *vpr* dilate; (*estomac*) distend.

**dilemme** /dilɛm/ *nm* dilemma.

**dilettante** /diletɑ̃t/ *nmf* amateur.

**diluant** /dilɥɑ̃/ *nm* thinner.

**diluer** /dilɥe/ [1] *vt* dilute.

**dimanche** /dimɑ̃ʃ/ *nm* Sunday.

**dimension** /dimɑ̃sjɔ̃/ *nf* (taille) size; (mesure) dimension; (aspect) dimension.

**diminuer** /diminɥe/ [1] *vt* reduce, decrease; (*plaisir, courage*) dampen; (dénigrer) diminish. ● *vi* (se réduire) decrease; (faiblir) (*bruit, flamme*) die down; (*ardeur*) cool. **diminutif** *nm* diminutive; (surnom) pet name. **diminution** *nf* decrease (**de** in); (réduction) reduction; (affaiblissement) diminishing.

**dinde** /dɛ̃d/ *nf* turkey.

**dîner** /dine/ [1] *vi* have dinner. ● *nm* dinner.

**dingue** /dɛ̃g/ *a* Ⓘ crazy.

**dinosaure** /dinozɔʀ/ *nm* dinosaur.

**diphtongue** /diftɔ̃g/ *nf* diphthong.

**diplomate** /diplɔmat/ *nmf* diplomat. ● *a* diplomatic. **diplomatique** *a* diplomatic.

**diplôme** /diplom/ *nm* certificate, diploma; (Univ) degree. **diplômé**, **~e** *a* qualified.

**dire** /diʀ/ [27] *vt* say; (*secret, vérité, heure*) tell; (penser) think; **~ que** say that; **~ à qn que** tell sb that; **~ à qn de** tell sb to; **ça me dit de faire** I feel like doing; **on dirait que** it would seem that, it seems that; **dis/dites donc!** hey! ◻ **se ~** *vpr*

(*mot*) be said; (penser) tell oneself; (se prétendre) claim to be. ● *nm* **au ~ de, selon les ~s de** according to.

**direct**, **~e** /diʀɛkt/ *a* direct. ● *nm* (train) express train; **en ~** (*émission*) live.

**directeur**, **-trice** /diʀɛktœʀ, -tʀis/ *nm,f* director; (chef de service) manager, manageress; (de journal) editor; (d'école) headteacher; (US) principal; **~ de banque** bank manager; **~ commercial** sales manager; **~ des ressources humaines** human resources manager.

**direction** /diʀɛksjɔ̃/ *nf* (sens) direction; (de société) management; (Auto) steering; **en ~ de** (going) to.

**dirigeant**, **~e** /diʀiʒɑ̃, -t/ *nm,f* (Pol) leader; (Comm) manager. ● *a* (*classe*) ruling.

**diriger** /diʀiʒe/ [40] *vt* (*service, école, parti, pays*) run; (*entreprise, usine*) manage; (*travaux*) supervise; (*véhicule*) steer; (*orchestre*) conduct; (braquer) aim; (tourner) turn. □ **se ~** *vpr* (s'orienter) find one's way; **se ~ vers** head for, make for.

**dis** /di/ ⇒DIRE [27].

**discernement** /disɛʀnəmɑ̃/ *nm* discernment.

**disciplinaire** *a* disciplinary. **discipline** *nf* discipline.

**discontinu**, **~e** /diskɔ̃tiny/ *a* intermittent.

**discordant**, **~e** /diskɔʀdɑ̃, -t/ *a* discordant.

**discothèque** /diskɔtɛk/ *nf* record library; (boîte de nuit) disco(thèque).

**discours** /diskuʀ/ *nm* speech; (propos) views.

**discret**, **-ète** /diskʀɛ, -t/ *a* discreet.

**discrétion** /diskʀesjɔ̃/ *nf* discretion; **à ~** (*vin*) unlimited; (*manger, boire*) as much as one desires.

**discrimination** /diskʀiminasjɔ̃/ *nf* discrimination. **discriminatoire** *a* discriminatory.

**disculper** /diskylpe/ [1] *vt* exonerate. □ **se ~** *vpr* vindicate oneself.

**discussion** /diskysjɔ̃/ *nf* discussion; (querelle) argument.

**discutable** /diskytabl/ *a* debatable; (critiquable) questionable.

**discuter** /diskyte/ [1] *vt* discuss; (contester) question. ● *vi* (parler) talk; (répliquer) argue; **~ de** discuss.

**disette** /dizɛt/ *nf* food shortage.

**disgrâce** /disgʀɑs/ *nf* disgrace.

**disgracieux**, **-ieuse** /disgʀasjø, -z/ *a* ugly, unsightly.

**disjoindre** /disʒwɛ̃dʀ/ [22] *vt* take apart. □ **se ~** *vpr* come apart.

**disloquer** /dislɔke/ [1] *vt* (*membre*) dislocate; (*machine*) break (apart). □ **se ~** *vpr* (*parti, cortège*) break up; (*meuble*) come apart.

**disparaître** /dispaʀɛtʀ/ [10] *vi* disappear; (mourir) die; **faire ~** get rid of. **disparition** *nf* disappearance; (mort) death.

**disparate** /dispaʀat/ *a* ill-assorted.

**disparu**, **~e** /dispaʀy/ *a* missing. ● *nm,f* missing person; (mort) dead person.

**dispensaire** /dispɑ̃sɛʀ/ *nm* clinic.

**dispense** /dispɑ̃s/ *nf* exemption.

**dispenser** /dispɑ̃se/ [1] *vt* exempt (de from). □ **se ~ de** *vpr* avoid.

**disperser** /dispɛʀse/ [1] *vt* (éparpiller) scatter; (répartir) disperse. □ **se ~** *vpr* disperse.

**disponibilité** /dispɔnibilite/ *nf* availability. **disponible** *a* available.

**dispos**, **~e** /dispo, -z/ *a* **frais et ~** fresh and alert.

**disposé**, **~e** /dispoze/ *a* **bien/mal ~** in a good/bad mood; **~ à** prepared to; **~ envers** disposed towards.

**disposer** /dispoze/ [1] *vt* arrange; **~ à** (engager à) incline to. ● *vi* **~ de** have at one's disposal. □ **se ~ à** *vpr* prepare to.

**dispositif** /dispozitif/ *nm* device; (ensemble de mesures) operation.

**disposition** /dispozisjɔ̃/ *nf* arrangement, layout; (tendance) tendency; **~s** (humeur) mood; (préparatifs) arrangements; (mesures) measures; (aptitude) aptitude; **mettre à la ~ de** place *ou* put at the disposal of.

**disproportionné**, **~e** /dispʀɔpɔʀsjɔne/ *a* disproportionate; **~ à** out of proportion with.

**dispute** /dispyt/ *nf* quarrel.

**disputer** /dispyte/ [1] *vt* (*match*) play; (*course*) run in; (*prix*) fight for; (gronder Ⓘ) tell off. □ **se ~** *vpr* quarrel; (se battre pour) fight over; (*match*) be played.

**disquaire** /diskɛʀ/ *nmf* record dealer.

**disque** /disk/ *nm* (Mus) record; (Sport) discus; (cercle) disc, disk; (Ordinat) disk; **~ compact** compact disc; **~ dur** hard disk; **~ optique compact** CD-ROM; **~ souple** floppy disk.

**disquette** /diskɛt/ *nf* floppy disk, diskette; **~ de sauvegarde** back-up disk.

**disséminer** /disemine/ [1] *vt* spread, scatter.

**dissertation** /disɛʀtasjɔ̃/ *nf* essay, paper.

**disserter** /disɛʀte/ [1] *vi* **~ sur** speak about; (par écrit) write about.

**dissident**, **~e** /disidɑ̃, -t/ *a & nm, f* dissident.

**dissimulation** /disimylasjɔ̃/ *nf* concealment; (fig) deceit.

**dissimuler** /disimyle/ [1] *vt* conceal (**à** from). □ **se ~** *vpr* conceal oneself.

**dissipé**, **~e** /disipe/ *a* (*élève*) unruly.

**dissiper** /disipe/ [1] *vt* (*fumée, crainte*) dispel; (*fortune*) squander; (*personne*) distract. □ **se ~** *vpr* disappear; (*élève*) grow restless.

**dissolvant** /disɔlvɑ̃/ *nm* solvent; (pour ongles) nail polish remover.

**dissoudre** /disudʀ/ [53] *vt* dissolve. □ **se ~** *vpr* dissolve.

**dissuader** /disɥade/ [1] *vt* dissuade (**de** from).

**dissuasion** /disɥazjɔ̃/ *nf* dissuasion; **force de ~** deterrent force.

**distance** /distɑ̃s/ *nf* distance; (écart) gap; **à ~** at *ou* from a distance.

**distancer** /distɑ̃se/ [10] *vt* outdistance.

**distendre** /distɑ̃dʀ/ [3] *vt* (*estomac*) distend; (*corde*) stretch.

**distinct**, **~e** /distɛ̃(kt), -ɛ̃kt/ *a* distinct.

**distinctif**, **-ive** /distɛ̃ktif, -v/ *a* (*trait*) distinctive; (*signe, caractère*) distinguishing.

**distinction** /distɛ̃ksjɔ̃/ *nf* distinction; (récompense) honour.

**distinguer** /distɛ̃ge/ [1] *vt* distinguish.

**distraction** /distʀaksjɔ̃/ *nf* absent-mindedness; (passe-temps) entertainment, leisure; (détente) recreation.

**distraire** /distʀɛʀ/ [29] *vt* amuse; (rendre inattentif) distract; **~ qn de qch** take sb's mind off sth. □ **se ~** *vpr* amuse oneself.

**distrait**, **~e** /distʀɛ, -t/ *a* absent-minded; (*élève*) inattentive.

**distrayant**, **~e** /distʀɛjɑ̃, -t/ *a* entertaining.

**distribuer** /distʀibɥe/ [1] *vt* hand out, distribute; (répartir) distribute; (*tâches, rôles*) allocate; (*cartes*) deal; (*courrier*) deliver.

**distributeur** /distʀibytœʀ/ *nm* (Auto, Comm) distributor; **~ (automatique)** vending-machine; **~ de billets (de banque)** cash dispenser. **distribution** *nf* distribution; (du courrier) delivery; (acteurs) cast; (secteur) retailing.

**district** /distʀikt/ *nm* district.

**dit**[1], **dites** /di, dit/ ⇒DIRE [27].

**dit**[2], **~e** /di, dit/ *a* (décidé) agreed; (surnommé) known as.

**diurne** /djyʀn/ *a* diurnal; (*activité*) daytime.

**divagations** /divagasjɔ̃/ *nfpl* ravings.

**divergence** /divɛʀʒɑ̃s/ *nf* divergence. **divergent**, **~e** *a* divergent. **diverger** [40] *vi* diverge.

**divers**, **~e** /divɛʀ, -s/ *a* (varié) diverse; (différent) various; (*frais*) miscellaneous; **dépenses ~es** sundries. **diversifier** [45] *vt* diversify.

**diversité** /divɛʀsite/ *nf* diversity, variety.

**divertir** /divɛʀtiʀ/ [2] *vt* amuse, entertain. □ **se ~** *vpr* amuse oneself; (passer du bon temps) enjoy oneself. **divertissement** *nm* amusement, entertainment.

**dividende** /dividɑ̃d/ *nm* dividend.

**divin**, **~e** /divɛ̃, -in/ *a* divine. **divinité** *nf* divinity.

**diviser** /divize/ [1] *vt* divide. □ **se ~** *vpr* become divided; **se ~ par sept** be divisible by seven. **division** *nf* division.

**divorce** /divɔʀs/ *nm* divorce.

**divorcé**, **~e** /divɔʀse/ *a* divorced. ● *nm,f* divorcee.

**divorcer** /divɔʀse/ [10] *vi* **~ (d'avec)** divorce.

**dix** /dis/ (/di/ *before consonant*, /diz/ *before vowel*) *a & nm* ten.

**dix-huit** /dizɥit/ *a & nm* eighteen.

**dixième** /dizjɛm/ *a & nmf* tenth.

**dix-neuf** /diznœf/ *a & nm* nineteen.

**dix-sept** /disɛt/ *a & nm* seventeen.

**docile** /dɔsil/ *a* docile.

**docteur** /dɔktœʀ/ *nm* doctor.

**doctorat** /dɔktɔʀa/ *nm* doctorate, PhD.

**document** /dɔkymɑ̃/ *nm* document. **documentaire** *a & nm* documentary.

**documentaliste** /dɔkymɑ̃talist/ *nmf* information officer; (Scol) librarian.

**documentation** /dɔkymɑ̃tasjɔ̃/ *nf* information, literature; **centre de ~** resource centre.

**documenté**, **~e** /dɔkymɑ̃te/ *a* well-documented.

**documenter** /dɔkymɑ̃te/ [1] *vt* provide with information. □ **se ~** *vpr* collect information.

**dodo** /dodo/ *nm* **faire ~** (langage enfantin) sleep.

**dodu**, **~e** /dɔdy/ *a* plump.

**dogmatique** /dɔgmatik/ *a* dogmatic. **dogme** *nm* dogma.

**doigt** /dwa/ *nm* finger; **un ~ de** a drop of; **montrer qch du ~** point at sth; **à deux ~s de** a hair's breadth away from; **~ de pied** toe. **doigté** *nm* (Mus) fingering, touch; (diplomatie) tact.

**dois**, **doit** /dwa/ ⇒DEVOIR [26].

**doléances** /dɔleɑ̃s/ *nfpl* grievances.

**dollar** /dɔlaʀ/ *nm* dollar.

**domaine** /dɔmɛn/ *nm* estate, domain; (fig) domain, field.

**domestique** /dɔmɛstik/ *a* domestic. ● *nmf* servant. **domestiquer** [1] *vt* domesticate.

**domicile** /dɔmisil/ *nm* home; **à ~** at home; (*livrer*) to the home.

**domicilié, ~e** /dɔmisilje/ *a* resident; **être ~ à Paris** live *ou* be resident in Paris.

**dominant, ~e** /dɔminɑ̃, -t/ *a* dominant. **dominante** *nf* dominant feature.

**dominer** /dɔmine/ [1] *vt* dominate; (surplomber) tower over, dominate; (*sujet*) master; (*peur*) overcome. ● *vi* dominate; (*équipe*) be in the lead; (prévaloir) stand out.

**domino** /dɔmino/ *nm* domino.

**dommage** /dɔmaʒ/ *nm* (tort) harm; **~(s)** (dégâts) damage; **c'est ~** it's a pity *ou* shame; **quel ~** what a pity *ou* shame. **dommages-intérêts** *nmpl* (Jur) damages.

**dompter** /dɔ̃te/ [1] *vt* tame. **dompteur, -euse** *nm,f* tamer.

**DOM-TOM** /dɔmtɔm/ *abrév mpl* (**départements et territoires d'outre-mer**) French overseas departments and territories.

**don** /dɔ̃/ *nm* (cadeau, aptitude) gift. **donateur, -trice** *nm,f* donor. **donation** *nf* donation.

**donc** /dɔ̃k/ *conj* so, then; (par conséquent) so, therefore; **quoi ~?** what did you say?; **tiens ~!** fancy that!

**donjon** /dɔ̃ʒɔ̃/ *nm* (tour) keep.

**donné, ~e** /dɔne/ *a* (fixé) given; (pas cher [I]) dirt cheap; **étant ~ que** given that.

**donnée** /dɔne/ *nf* (élément d'information) fact; **~s** data.

**donner** /dɔne/ [1] *vt* give; (*vieilles affaires*) give away; (distribuer) give out; (*fruits, résultats*) produce; (*film*) show; (*pièce*) put on; **ça donne soif/faim** it makes one thirsty/hungry; **~ qch à réparer** take sth to be repaired; **~ lieu à** give rise to. ● *vi* **~ sur** look out on to; **~ dans** tend towards. □ **se ~ à** *vpr* devote oneself to; **se ~ du mal** go to a lot of trouble (**pour faire** to do).

---

**dont** /dɔ̃/

● *pronom*

- (personne) **la fille ~ je te parlais** the girl I was telling you about; **l'homme ~ la fille a dit...** the man whose daughter said...
- (chose) which, **l'affaire ~ il parle** the matter which he is referring to; **la manière ~ elle parle** the way she speaks; **ce ~ il parle** what he's talking about.
- (provenance) from which.
- (parmi lesquels) **deux personnes ~ toi** two people, one of whom is you; **plusieurs thèmes ~ l'identité et le racisme** several topics including identity and racism.

---

**dopage** /dɔpaʒ/ *nm* (de cheval) doping; (d'athlète) illegal drug-use.

**doper** /dɔpe/ [1] *vt* dope. □ **se ~** *vpr* take drugs.

**doré, ~e** /dɔʀe/ *a* (couleur d'or) golden; (qui rappelle de l'or) gold; (avec de l'or) gilt; **la jeunesse ~e** gilded youth.

**dorénavant** /dɔʀenavɑ̃/ *adv* henceforth.

**dorer** /dɔʀe/ [1] *vt* gild; (Culin) brown.

**dormir** /dɔʀmiʀ/ [46] *vi* sleep; (être endormi) be asleep; **~ debout** be asleep on one's feet; **une histoire à ~ debout** a cock-and-bull story.

**dortoir** /dɔʀtwaʀ/ *nm* dormitory.

**dorure** /dɔʀyʀ/ *nf* gilding.

**dos** /do/ *nm* back; (de livre) spine; **à ~ de** riding on; **au ~ de** (*chèque*) on the back of; **de ~** from behind; **~ crawlé** backstroke.

**dosage** /dozaʒ/ *nm* (mélange) mixture; (quantité) amount, proportions. **dose** *nf* dose. **doser** [1] *vt* measure out; (contrôler) use in a controlled way.

**dossier** /dɔsje/ *nm* (documents) file; (Jur) case; (de chaise) back; (TV, presse) special feature.

**dot** /dɔt/ *nf* dowry.

**douane** /dwan/ *nf* customs.

**douanier, -ière** /dwanje, -jɛʀ/ *a* customs. ● *nm* customs officer.

**double** /dubl/ *a & adv* double. ● *nm* (copie) duplicate; (sosie) double; **le ~ (de)** twice as much *ou* as many (as); **le ~ messieurs** the men's doubles.

**double-cliquer** /dublklike/ [1] *vt* double-click.

**doubler** /duble/ [1] *vt* double; (dépasser) overtake; (*vêtement*) line; (*film*) dub; (*classe*) repeat; (*cap*) round. ● *vi* double.

**doublure** /dublyʀ/ *nf* (étoffe) lining; (acteur) understudy.

**douce** /dus/ ⇒DOUX.

**doucement** /dusmɑ̃/ *adv* gently; (sans bruit) quietly; (lentement) slowly.

**douceur** /dusœʀ/ *nf* (mollesse) softness; (de climat) mildness; (de personne) gentleness; (friandise) sweet; (US) candy; **en ~** smoothly.

**douche** /duʃ/ *nf* shower.

**doucher (se)** /duʃe/ [1] *vpr* have *ou* take a shower.

**doudoune** /dudun/ *nf* 🄸 down jacket.

**doué, ~e** /dwe/ *a* gifted; **~ de** endowed with.

**douille** /duj/ *nf* (Électr) socket.

**douillet, ~te** /dujɛ, -t/ *a* cosy, comfortable; (*personne*: péj) soft.

**douleur** /dulœʀ/ *nf* pain; (chagrin) sorrow, grief. **douloureux, -euse** *a* painful.

**doute** /dut/ *nm* doubt; **sans ~** no doubt; **sans aucun ~** without doubt.

**douter** /dute/ [1] *vt* **~ de** doubt; **~ que** doubt that. ● *vi* doubt. □ **se ~ de** *vpr* suspect; **je m'en doutais** I thought so.

**douteux, -euse** /dutø, -z/ *a* dubious, doubtful.

**Douvres** /duvʀ/ *npr* Dover.

**doux, douce** /du, dus/ *a* (moelleux) soft; (sucré) sweet; (clément, pas fort) mild; (pas brusque, bienveillant) gentle.

**douzaine** /duzɛn/ *nf* about twelve; (douze) dozen; **une ~ d'œufs** a dozen eggs.

**douze** /duz/ *a & nm* twelve. **douzième** *a & nmf* twelfth.

**doyen, ~ne** /dwajɛ̃, -ɛn/ *nm,f* dean; (en âge) most senior person.

**dragée** /dʀaʒe/ *nf* sugared almond.

**draguer** /dʀage/ [1] *vt* (*rivière*) dredge; (*filles* 🄸) chat up.

**drainer** /dʀene/ [1] *vt* drain.

**dramatique** /dʀamatik/ *a* dramatic; (tragique) tragic. ● *nf* (television) drama.

**dramatiser** /dʀamatize/ [1] *vt* dramatize.

**dramaturge** /dʀamatyʀʒ/ *nmf* dramatist.

**drame** /dʀam/ *nm* (genre) drama; (pièce) play; (événement tragique) tragedy.

**drap** /dʀa/ *nm* sheet; (tissu) (woollen) cloth.

**drapeau** (*pl* **~x**) /dʀapo/ *nm* flag.

**drap-housse** (*pl* **draps-housses**) /dʀaus/ *nm* fitted sheet.

**dressage** /dʀɛsaʒ/ *nm* training; (compétition équestre) dressage.

**dresser** /dʀese/ [1] *vt* put up, erect; (*tête*) raise; (*animal*) train; (*liste, plan*) draw up; ~ **l'oreille** prick up one's ears. □ **se** ~ *vpr* (*bâtiment*) stand; (*personne*) draw oneself up. **dresseur**, **-euse** *nm,f* trainer.

**dribbler** /dʀible/ [1] *vi* (Sport) dribble.

**drive** /dʀajv/ *nm* (Ordinat) drive.

**drogue** /dʀɔg/ *nf* drug; **la** ~ drugs.

**drogué**, ~**e** /dʀɔge/ *nm,f* drug addict.

**droguer** /dʀɔge/ [1] *vt* (*malade*) drug heavily; (*victime*) drug. □ **se** ~ *vpr* take drugs.

**droguerie** /dʀɔgʀi/ *nf* hardware shop. **droguiste** *nmf* owner of a hardware shop.

**droit**, ~**e** /dʀwa, -t/ *a* (contraire de gauche) right; (non courbe) straight; (loyal) upright; **angle** ~ right angle. ● *adv* straight. ● *nm* right; ~**(s)** (taxe) duty; **le** ~ (Jur) law; **avoir** ~ **à** be entitled to; **avoir le** ~ **de** be allowed to; **être dans son** ~ be in the right; ~ **d'auteur** copyright; ~ **d'inscription** registration fee; ~**s d'auteur** royalties.

**droite** /dʀwat/ *nf* (contraire de gauche) right; **à** ~ on the right; (direction) (to the) right; **la** ~ the right (side); (Pol) the right (wing); (*ligne*) straight line. **droitier**, **-ière** *a* right-handed.

**drôle** /dʀol/ *a* (amusant) funny; (bizarre) funny, odd. **drôlement** *adv* funnily; (très 🅘) really.

**dru**, ~**e** /dʀy/ *a* thick; **tomber** ~ fall thick and fast.

**drugstore** /dʀœgstɔʀ/ *nm* drugstore.

**du** /dy/ ⇨DE.

**dû**, **due** /dy/ *a* due. ● *nm* due; (argent) dues; ~ **à** due to. ● ⇨DEVOIR [26].

**duc**, **duchesse** /dyk, dyʃɛs/ *nm,f* duke, duchess.

**duo** /dɥo/ *nm* (Mus) duet; (fig) duo.

**dupe** /dyp/ *nf* dupe.

**duplex** /dyplɛks/ *nm* split-level apartment; (US) duplex; (émission) link-up.

**duplicata** /dyplikata/ *nm inv* duplicate.

**duquel** /dykɛl/ ⇨LEQUEL.

**dur**, ~**e** /dyʀ/ *a* hard; (sévère) harsh, hard; (*viande*) tough; (*col, brosse*) stiff; ~ **d'oreille** hard of hearing. ● *adv* hard. ● *nm,f* tough nut 🅘; (Pol) hardliner.

**durable** /dyʀabl/ *a* lasting.

**durant** /dyʀɑ̃/ *prép* (au cours de) during; (avec mesure de temps) for; ~ **des heures** for hours; **des heures** ~ for hours and hours.

**durcir** /dyʀsiʀ/ [2] *vt* harden. ● *vi* (*terre*) harden; (*ciment*) set; (*pain*) go hard. □ **se** ~ *vpr* harden.

**durée** /dyʀe/ *nf* length; (période) duration; **de courte** ~ short-lived; **pile longue** ~ long-life battery.

**durer** /dyʀe/ [1] *vi* last.

**dureté** /dyʀte/ *nf* hardness; (sévérité) harshness.

**duvet** /dyvɛ/ *nm* down; (sac) sleeping-bag.

**dynamique** /dinamik/ *a* dynamic.

**dynamite** /dinamit/ *nf* dynamite.

**dynamo** /dinamo/ *nf* dynamo.

# Ee

**eau** (*pl* **~x**) /o/ *nf* water; **~ courante** running water; **~ de mer** seawater; **~ de source** spring water; **~ douce/salée** fresh/salt water; **~ de pluie** rainwater; **~ potable** drinking water; **~ de Javel** bleach; **~ minérale** mineral water; **~ gazeuse** sparkling water; **~ plate** still water; **~ de toilette** eau de toilette; **~x usées** dirty water; **~x et forêts** forestry commission (+ *sg*); **tomber à l'~** (fig) fall through; **prendre l'~** take in water. **eau-de-vie** (*pl* **eaux-de-vie**) *nf* brandy.

**ébahi**, **~e** /ebai/ *a* dumbfounded.

**ébauche** /eboʃ/ *nf* (dessin) sketch; (fig) attempt.

**ébéniste** /ebenist/ *nm* cabinet-maker.

**éblouir** /ebluiʀ/ [2] *vt* dazzle.

**éboueur** /ebwœʀ/ *nm* dustman.

**ébouillanter** /ebujɑ̃te/ [1] *vt* scald.

**éboulement** /ebulmɑ̃/ *nm* landslide.

**ébouriffé**, **~e** /ebuʀife/ *a* dishevelled.

**ébrécher** /ebʀeʃe/ [14] *vt* chip.

**ébruiter** /ebʀɥite/ [1] *vt* spread about. □ **s'~** *vpr* get out.

**ébullition** /ebylisjɔ̃/ *nf* boiling; **en ~** boiling.

**écaille** /ekaj/ *nf* (de poisson) scale; (de peinture, roc) flake; (matière) tortoiseshell.

**écarlate** /ekaʀlat/ *a* scarlet.

**écarquiller** /ekaʀkije/ [1] *vt* **~ les yeux** open one's eyes wide.

**écart** /ekaʀ/ *nm* gap; (de prix) difference; (embardée) swerve; **~ de conduite** lapse in behaviour; **être à l'~** be isolated; **se tenir à l'~ de** stand apart from; (fig) keep out of the way of.

**écarté**, **~e** /ekaʀte/ *a* (*lieu*) remote; **les jambes ~es** (with) legs apart; **les bras ~s** with one's arms out.

**écarter** /ekaʀte/ [1] *vt* (séparer) move apart; (*membres*) spread; (*branches*) part; (éliminer) dismiss; **~ qch de** move sth away from; **~ qn de** keep sb away from. □ **s'~** *vpr* (s'éloigner) move away; (quitter son chemin) move aside; **s'~ de** stray from.

**ecchymose** /ekimoz/ *nf* bruise.

**écervelé**, **~e** /esɛʀvəle/ *a* scatter-brained. ● *nm,f* scatterbrain.

**échafaudage** /eʃafodaʒ/ *nm* scaffolding; (amas) heap.

**échalote** /eʃalɔt/ *nf* shallot.

**échancré**, **~e** /eʃɑ̃kʀe/ *a* low-cut.

**échange** /eʃɑ̃ʒ/ *nm* exchange; **en ~ (de)** in exchange (for). **échanger** [40] *vt* exchange (**contre** for).

**échangeur** /eʃɑ̃ʒœʀ/ *nm* (Auto) interchange.

**échantillon** /eʃɑ̃tijɔ̃/ *nm* sample.

**échappatoire** /eʃapatwaʀ/ *nf* way out.

**échappement** /eʃapmɑ̃/ *nm* exhaust.

**échapper** /eʃape/ [1] *vi* **~ à** escape; (en fuyant) escape (from); **~ des mains de** slip out of the hands of; **ça m'a échappé** (fig) it just slipped out; **l'~ belle** have a narrow *ou* lucky escape. □ **s'~** *vpr* escape.

**écharde** /eʃaʀd/ *nf* splinter.

**écharpe** /eʃaʀp/ *nf* scarf; (de maire) sash; **en ~** (*bras*) in a sling.

**échasse** /eʃɑs/ *nf* stilt.

**échauffement** /eʃofmɑ̃/ *nm* (Sport) warm-up.

**échauffer** /eʃofe/ [1] *vt* heat; (fig) excite. □ **s'~** *vpr* warm up.

**échéance** /eʃeɑ̃s/ *nf* due date (for payment); (délai) deadline; (obligation) (financial) commitment.

**échéant**: **le cas ~** /ləkazeʃeɑ̃/ *loc* if need be.

**échec** /eʃɛk/ *nm* failure; **~s** (jeu) chess; **~ et mat** checkmate.

**échelle** /eʃɛl/ *nf* ladder; (dimension) scale.

**échelon** /eʃlɔ̃/ *nm* rung; (hiérarchique) grade; (niveau) level.

**échevelé**, **~e** /eʃəvle/ *a* dishevelled.

**écho** /eko/ *nm* echo; **~s** (dans la presse) gossip.

**échographie** /ekɔgʀafi/ *nf* (ultrasound) scan.

**échouer** /eʃwe/ [1] *vi* (*bateau*) run aground; (ne pas réussir) fail; **~ à un examen** fail an exam. ● *vt* (*bateau*) ground. □ **s'~** *vpr* run aground.

**échu**, **~e** /eʃy/ *a* (*délai*) expired.

**éclabousser** /eklabuse/ [1] *vt* splash.

**éclair** /eklɛʀ/ *nm* (flash of) lightning; (fig) flash; (gâteau) éclair. ● *a inv* (*visite*) brief.

**éclairage** /eklɛʀaʒ/ *nm* lighting.

**éclaircie** /eklɛʀsi/ *nf* sunny interval.

**éclaircir** /eklɛʀsiʀ/ [2] *vt* lighten; (*mystère*) clear up. □ **s'~** *vpr* (*ciel*) clear; (*mystère*) become clearer. **éclaircissement** *nm* clarification.

**éclairer** /ekleʀe/ [1] *vt* light (up); (*personne*) (fig) enlighten; (*situation*) throw light on. ● *vi* give light. □ **s'~** *vpr* become clearer.

**éclaireur**, **-euse** /eklɛʀœʀ, -øz/ *nm,f* (boy) scout, (girl) guide.

**éclat** /ekla/ *nm* fragment; (de lumière) brightness; (splendeur) brilliance; **~ de rire** burst of laughter.

**éclatant**, **~e** /eklatɑ̃, -t/ *a* brilliant; (*soleil*) dazzling.

**éclater** /eklate/ [1] *vi* burst; (exploser) go off; (*verre*) shatter; (*guerre*) break out; (*groupe*) split up; **~ de rire** burst out laughing.

**éclipse** /eklips/ *nf* eclipse.

**éclosion** /eklozjɔ̃/ *nf* hatching, opening.

**écluse** /eklyz/ *nf* (de canal) lock.

**écœurant**, **~e** /ekœʀɑ̃, -t/ *a* (*gâteau*) sickly; (fig) disgusting. **écœurer** [1] *vt* sicken.

**éco-guerrier**, **-ière** (*pl* **éco-guerriers**, **-ières**) /ekogɛʀje, ɛʀ/ *nmf* eco-warrior.

**école** /ekɔl/ *nf* school; **~ maternelle/primaire/secondaire** nursery/primary/secondary school; **~ normale** teachers' training college. **écolier**, **-ière** *nm,f* schoolboy, schoolgirl.

**écologie** /ekɔlɔʒi/ *nf* ecology. **écologique** *a* ecological, green. **écologiste** *nmf* (chercheur) ecologist; (dans l'âme) environmentalist; (Pol) Green.

**économie** /ekɔnɔmi/ *nf* economy; (discipline) economics; **~s** (argent) savings; **une ~ de** (gain) a saving of. **économique** *a* (Pol) economic; (bon marché) economical.

**économiser** /ekɔnɔmize/ [1] *vt/i* save.

**écorce** /ekɔʀs/ *nf* bark; (de fruit) peel.

**écorcher** /ekɔʀʃe/ [1] *vt* (*genou*) graze; (*animal*) skin. □ **s'~** *vpr*

graze oneself. **écorchure** *nf* graze.

**écossais**, **~e** /ekɔsɛ, -z/ *a* Scottish. **É~**, **~e** *nm,f* Scot.

**Écosse** /ekɔs/ *nf* Scotland.

**écoulement** /ekulmɑ̃/ *nm* flow.

**écouler** /ekule/ [1] *vt* dispose of, sell. □ **s'~** *vpr* (*liquide*) flow; (*temps*) pass.

**écourter** /ekuʀte/ [1] *vt* shorten.

**écoute** /ekut/ *nf* listening; **à l'~ (de)** listening in (to); **heures de grande ~** prime time; **~s téléphoniques** phone tapping.

**écouter** /ekute/ [1] *vt* listen to. ● *vi* listen; **~ aux portes** eavesdrop. **écouteur** *nm* earphones (+ *pl*); (de téléphone) receiver.

**écran** /ekʀɑ̃/ *nm* screen; **~ total** sun-block.

**écraser** /ekʀɑze/ [1] *vt* crush; (*piéton*) run over; (*cigarette*) stub out. □ **s'~** *vpr* crash (**contre** into).

**écrémé**, **~e** /ekʀeme/ *a* skimmed; **demi-~** semi-skimmed.

**écrevisse** /ekʀəvis/ *nf* crayfish.

**écrier (s')** /(s)ekʀije/ [45] *vpr* exclaim.

**écrin** /ekʀɛ̃/ *nm* case.

**écrire** /ekʀiʀ/ [30] *vt/i* write; (orthographier) spell. □ **s'~** *vpr* (*mot*) be spelt.

**écrit** /ekʀi/ *nm* document; (examen) written paper; **par ~** in writing.

**écriteau** (*pl* **~x**) /ekʀito/ *nm* notice.

**écriture** /ekʀityʀ/ *nf* writing; **~s** (Comm) accounts.

**écrivain** /ekʀivɛ̃/ *nm* writer.

**écrou** /ekʀu/ *nm* (Tech) nut.

**écrouler (s')** /(s)ekʀule/ [1] *vpr* collapse.

**écru**, **~e** /ekʀy/ *a* (*couleur*) natural; (*tissu*) raw.

**écueil** /ekœj/ *nm* reef; (fig) danger.

**éculé**, **~e** /ekyle/ *a* (*soulier*) worn at the heel; (fig) well-worn.

**écume** /ekym/ *nf* foam; (Culin) scum.

**écumer** /ekyme/ [1] *vt* skim. ● *vi* foam.

**écureuil** /ekyʀœj/ *nm* squirrel.

**écurie** /ekyʀi/ *nf* stable.

**écuyer**, **-ère** /ekɥije, -jɛʀ/ *nm,f* (horse) rider.

**eczéma** /ɛgzema/ *nm* eczema.

**EDF** *abrév f* (**Électricité de France**) *French electricity board.*

**édifice** /edifis/ *nm* building.

**édifier** /edifje/ [45] *vt* construct; (porter à la vertu) edify.

**Édimbourg** /edɛ̃buʀ/ *npr* Edinburgh.

**édit** /edi/ *nm* edict.

**éditer** /edite/ [1] *vt* publish; (annoter) edit. **éditeur**, **-trice** *nm,f* publisher; (réviseur) editor.

**édition** /edisjɔ̃/ *nf* (activité) publishing; (livre, disque) edition.

**éditique** /editik/ *nf* electronic publishing.

**éditorial**, **~e** (*pl* **-iaux**) /editɔʀjal, -jo/ *a & nm* editorial.

**édredon** /edʀədɔ̃/ *nm* eiderdown.

**éducateur**, **-trice** /edykatœʀ, -tʀis/ *nm,f* youth worker.

**éducatif**, **-ive** /edykatif, -v/ *a* educational.

**éducation** /edykasjɔ̃/ *nf* (façon d'élever) upbringing; (enseignement) education; (manières) manners; **~ physique** physical education.

**éduquer** /edyke/ [1] *vt* (élever) bring up; (former) educate.

**effacé**, **~e** /efase/ *a* (modeste) unassuming.

**effacer** /efase/ [10] *vt* (gommer) rub out; (à l'écran) delete; (*souvenir*)

erase. □ **s'~** *vpr* fade; (s'écarter) step aside.

**effarer** /efaʀe/ [1] *vt* alarm; **être effaré** be astounded.

**effaroucher** /efaʀuʃe/ [1] *vt* scare away.

**effectif**, **-ive** /efɛktif, -v/ *a* effective. ● *nm* (d'école) number of pupils; **~s** numbers. **effectivement** *adv* effectively; (en effet) indeed.

**effectuer** /efɛktɥe/ [1] *vt* carry out, make.

**efféminé**, **~e** /efemine/ *a* effeminate.

**effervescent**, **~e** /efɛʀvesɑ̃, -t/ *a* **comprimé ~** effervescent tablet.

**effet** /efɛ/ *nm* effect; (impression) impression; **~s** (habits) clothes, things; **sous l'~ d'une drogue** under the influence of drugs; **en ~** indeed; **faire de l'~** have an effect, be effective; **faire bon/mauvais ~** make a good/bad impression; **ça fait un drôle d'~** it feels strange.

**efficace** /efikas/ *a* effective; (*personne*) efficient. **efficacité** *nf* effectiveness; (de personne) efficiency.

**effleurer** /efløʀe/ [1] *vt* touch lightly; (*sujet*) touch on; **ça ne m'a pas effleuré** it did not cross my mind.

**effondrement** /efɔ̃dʀəmɑ̃/ *nm* collapse. **effondrer (s')** [1] *vpr* collapse.

**efforcer (s')** /(s)efɔʀse/ [10] *vpr* try (hard) (**de** to).

**effort** /efɔʀ/ *nm* effort.

**effraction** /efʀaksjɔ̃/ *nf* **entrer par ~** break in.

**effrayant**, **~e** /efʀɛjɑ̃, -t/ *a* frightening; (fig) frightful.

**effrayer** /efʀeje/ [31] *vt* frighten; (décourager) put off. □ **s'~** *vpr* be frightened.

**effréné**, **~e** /efʀene/ *a* wild.

**effriter (s')** /(s)efʀite/ [1] *vpr* crumble.

**effroi** /efʀwa/ *nm* dread.

**effronté**, **~e** /efʀɔ̃te/ *a* cheeky. ● *nm,f* cheeky boy, cheeky girl.

**effroyable** /efʀwajabl/ *a* dreadful.

**égal**, **~e** (*mpl* **-aux**) /egal, -o/ *a* equal; (*surface, vitesse*) even. ● *nm,f* equal; **ça m'est/lui est ~** it is all the same to me/him; **sans ~** matchless; **d'~ à ~** between equals. **également** *adv* equally; (aussi) as well. **égaler** [1] *vt* equal.

**égaliser** /egalize/ [1] *vt/i* (Sport) equalize; (niveler) level out; (*cheveux*) trim.

**égalitaire** /egalitɛʀ/ *a* egalitarian.

**égalité** /egalite/ *nf* equality; (de surface) evenness; **être à ~** be level.

**égard** /egaʀ/ *nm* consideration; **~s** respect (+ *sg*); **par ~ pour** out of consideration for; **à cet ~** in this respect; **à l'~ de** with regard to; (envers) towards.

**égarer** /egaʀe/ [1] *vt* mislay; (tromper) lead astray. □ **s'~** *vpr* get lost; (se tromper) go astray.

**égayer** /egeje/ [31] *vt* (*personne*) cheer up; (*pièce*) brighten up.

**église** /egliz/ *nf* church.

**égoïsme** /egɔism/ *nm* selfishness, egoism.

**égoïste** /egɔist/ *a* selfish. ● *nmf* egoist.

**égorger** /egɔʀʒe/ [40] *vt* slit the throat of.

**égout** /egu/ *nm* sewer.

**égoutter** /egute/ [1] *vt* drain. □ **s'~** *vpr* (*vaisselle*) drain; (*lessive*) drip dry. **égouttoir** *nm* draining-board.

**égratigner** /egʀatiɲe/ [1] *vt* scratch. **égratignure** *nf* scratch.

**Égypte** /eʒipt/ *nf* Egypt.

**éjecter** /eʒɛkte/ [1] *vt* eject.

**élaboration** /elabɔʀasjɔ̃/ *nf* elaboration. **élaborer** [1] *vt* elaborate.

**élan** /elɑ̃/ *nm* (animal) moose; (Sport) run-up; (vitesse) momentum; (fig) surge.

**élancé**, **~e** /elɑ̃se/ *a* slender.

**élancement** /elɑ̃smɑ̃/ *nm* twinge.

**élancer (s')** /(s)elɑ̃se/ [10] *vpr* leap forward, dash; (*arbre, édifice*) soar.

**élargir** /elaʀʒiʀ/ [2] *vt* (*route*) widen; (*connaissances*) broaden. □ **s'~** *vpr* (*famille*) expand; (*route*) widen; (*écart*) increase; (*vêtement*) stretch.

**élastique** /elastik/ *a* elastic. ● *nm* elastic band; (tissu) elastic.

**électeur**, **-trice** /elɛktœʀ, -tʀis/ *nm,f* voter. **élection** *nf* election. **électoral**, **~e** (*mpl* **-aux**) *a* (*réunion*) election. **électorat** *nm* electorate, voters (+ *pl*).

**électricien**, **~ne** /elɛktʀisjɛ̃, ɛn/ *nm,f* electrician. **électricité** *nf* electricity.

**électrifier** /elɛktʀifje/ [45] *vt* electrify.

**électrique** /elɛktʀik/ *a* electric; (*installation*) electrical.

**électrocuter** /elɛktʀɔkyte/ [1] *vt* electrocute.

**électroménager** /elɛktʀɔmenaʒe/ *nm* **l'~** household appliances (+ *pl*).

**électron** /elɛktʀɔ̃/ *nm* electron. **électronicien**, **~ne** *nm,f* electronics engineer.

**électronique** /elɛktʀɔnik/ *a* electronic. ● *nf* electronics.

**élégance** /elegɑ̃s/ *nf* elegance. **élégant**, **~e** *a* elegant.

**élément** /elemɑ̃/ *nm* element; (meuble) unit. **élémentaire** *a* elementary.

**éléphant** /elefɑ̃/ *nm* elephant.

**élevage** /ɛlvaʒ/ *nm* (stock-)breeding.

**élévation** /elevasjɔ̃/ *nf* rise; (hausse) rise; (plan) elevation; **~ de terrain** rise in the ground.

**élève** /elɛv/ *nmf* pupil.

**élevé**, **~e** /ɛlve/ *a* high; (noble) elevated; **bien ~** well-mannered.

**élever** /ɛlve/ [6] *vt* (lever) raise; (*enfants*) bring up, raise; (*animal*) breed. □ **s'~** *vpr* rise; (dans le ciel) soar up; **s'~ à** amount to. **éleveur**, **-euse** *nm,f* (stock-) breeder.

**éligible** /eliʒibl/ *a* eligible.

**élimination** /eliminasjɔ̃/ *nf* elimination.

**éliminatoire** /eliminatwaʀ/ *a* qualifying. ● *nf* (Sport) heat.

**éliminer** /elimine/ [1] *vt* eliminate.

**élire** /eliʀ/ [39] *vt* elect.

**elle** /ɛl/ *pron* she; (complément) her; (chose) it. **elle-même** *pron* herself; itself. **elles** *pron* they; (complément) them. **elles-mêmes** *pron* themselves.

**élocution** /elɔkysjɔ̃/ *nf* diction.

**éloge** /elɔʒ/ *nm* praise; **faire l'~ de** praise; **~s** praise (+ *sg*).

**éloigné**, **~e** /elwaɲe/ *a* distant; **~ de** far away from; **parent ~** distant relative.

**éloigner** /elwaɲe/ [1] *vt* take away *ou* remove (**de** from); (*danger*) ward off; (*visite*) put off. □ **s'~** *vpr* go *ou* move away (**de** from); (affectivement) become estranged (**de** from).

**élongation** /elɔ̃gasjɔ̃/ *nf* strained muscle.

**éloquent**, **~e** /elɔkɑ̃, -t/ *a* eloquent.

**élu**, **~e** /ely/ *a* elected. ● *nm,f* (Pol) elected representative.

**élucider** /elyside/ [1] *vt* elucidate.

**éluder** /elyde/ [1] *vt* evade.

**émacié**, **~e** /emasje/ *a* emaciated.

**e-mail** /imɛl/ *nm* e-mail; **envoyer un ~ à qn** e-mail sb.

**émail** (*pl* **-aux**) /emaj, -o/ *nm* enamel.

**émanciper** /emɑ̃sipe/ [1] *vt* emancipate. □ **s'~** *vpr* become emancipated.

**émaner** /emane/ [1] *vi* emanate.

**emballage** /ɑ̃balaʒ/ *nm* (dur) packaging; (souple) wrapping.

**emballer** /ɑ̃bale/ [1] *vt* pack; (en papier) wrap; **ça ne m'emballe pas** 🅸 I'm not really taken by it. □ **s'~** *vpr* (*moteur*) race; (*cheval*) bolt; (*personne*) get carried away; (*prices*) shoot up.

**embarcadère** /ɑ̃barkadɛr/ *nm* landing-stage.

**embarcation** /ɑ̃barkasjɔ̃/ *nf* boat.

**embardée** /ɑ̃barde/ *nf* swerve.

**embarquement** /ɑ̃barkəmɑ̃/ *nm* (de passagers) boarding; (de fret) loading.

**embarquer** /ɑ̃barke/ [1] *vt* take on board; (*frêt*) load; (emporter 🅸) cart off. ● *vi* board. □ **s'~** *vpr* board; **s'~ dans** embark upon.

**embarras** /ɑ̃bara/ *nm* (gêne) embarrassment; (difficulté) difficulty.

**embarrasser** /ɑ̃barase/ [1] *vt* (encombrer) clutter (up); (fig) embarrass. □ **s'~ de** *vpr* burden oneself with.

**embauche** /ɑ̃boʃ/ *nf* hiring.

**embaucher** [1] *vt* hire, take on.

**embaumer** /ɑ̃bome/ [1] *vt* (*pièce*) fill; (*cadavre*) embalm. ● *vi* be fragrant.

**embellir** /ɑ̃belir/ [2] *vt* make more attractive; (*récit*) embellish.

**embêtant**, **~e** /ɑ̃bɛtɑ̃, -t/ *a* 🅸 annoying.

**embêter** /ɑ̃bete/ [1] *vt* bother. □ **s'~** *vpr* be bored.

**emblée**: **d'~** /dɑ̃ble/ *loc* right away.

**emblème** /ɑ̃blɛm/ *nm* emblem.

**emboîter** /ɑ̃bwate/ [1] *vt* fit together; **~ le pas à qn** (imiter) follow suit. □ **s'~** *vpr* fit together; **(s')~ dans** fit into.

**embonpoint** /ɑ̃bɔ̃pwɛ̃/ *nm* stoutness.

**embourber (s')** /(s)ɑ̃burbe/ [1] *vpr* get stuck in the mud; (fig) get bogged down.

**embouteillage** /ɑ̃butɛjaʒ/ *nm* traffic jam.

**emboutir** /ɑ̃butir/ [2] *vt* (Auto) crash into.

**embraser (s')** /(s)ɑ̃braze/ [1] *vpr* catch fire.

**embrasser** /ɑ̃brase/ [1] *vt* kiss; (adopter, contenir) embrace. □ **s'** *vpr* kiss.

**embrayage** /ɑ̃brɛjaʒ/ *nm* clutch.

**embrayer** [31] *vi* engage the clutch.

**embrouiller** /ɑ̃bruje/ [1] *vt* confuse; (*fils*) tangle. □ **s'~** *vpr* become confused.

**embryon** /ɑ̃brijɔ̃/ *nm* embryo.

**embûches** /ɑ̃byʃ/ *nfpl* traps.

**embuer (s')** /(s)ɑ̃bɥe/ [1] *vpr* mist up.

**embuscade** /ɑ̃byskad/ *nf* ambush.

**émeraude** /ɛmrod/ *nf* emerald.

**émerger** /emɛrʒe/ [40] *vi* emerge; (fig) stand out.

**émeri** /ɛmri/ *nm* emery.

**émerveillement** /emɛʀvɛjmɑ̃/ *nm* amazement, wonder.

**émerveiller** /emɛʀveje/ [1] *vt* fill with wonder. □ **s'~** *vpr* marvel at.

**émetteur** /emɛtœʀ/ *nm* transmitter.

**émettre** /emɛtʀ/ [42] *vt* (*son*) produce; (*message*) send out; (*timbre, billet*) issue; (*opinion*) express.

**émeute** /emøt/ *nf* riot.

**émietter** /emjete/ [1] *vt* crumble. □ **s'~** *vpr* crumble.

**émigrant**, **~e** /emigʀɑ̃, -t/ *nm,f* emigrant. **émigration** *nf* emigration. **émigrer** [1] *vi* emigrate.

**émincer** /emɛ̃se/ [10] *vt* cut into thin slices.

**éminent**, **~e**/eminɑ̃, -t/ *a* eminent.

**émissaire** /emisɛʀ/ *nm* emissary.

**émission** /emisjɔ̃/ *nf* (programme) programme; (de chaleur, gaz) emission; (de timbre) issue.

**emmagasiner** /ɑ̃magazine/ [1] *vt* store.

**emmanchure** /ɑ̃mɑ̃ʃyʀ/ *nf* armhole.

**emmêler** /ɑ̃mele/ [1] *vt* tangle. □ **s'~** *vpr* get mixed up.

**emménager** /ɑ̃menaʒe/ [40] *vi* move in; **~ dans** move into.

**emmener** /ɑ̃mne/ [6] *vt* take; (comme prisonnier) take away.

**emmerder** /ɑ̃mɛʀde/ [1] ⊠ *vt* **~ qn** get on sb's nerves. □ **s'~** *vpr* be bored.

**emmitoufler** /ɑ̃mitufle/ [1] *vt* wrap up warmly. □ **s'~** *vpr* wrap oneself up warmly.

**émoi** /emwa/ *nm* turmoil; (plaisir) excitement.

**émotif**, **-ive** /emɔtif, -v/ *a* emotional. **émotion** *nf* emotion; (peur) fright. **émotionnel**, **~le** *a* emotional.

**émousser** /emuse/ [1] *vt* blunt.

**émouvant**, **~e** /emuvɑ̃, -t/ *a* moving.

**empailler** /ɑ̃paje/ [1] *vt* stuff.

**empaqueter** /ɑ̃pakte/ [38] *vt* package.

**emparer (s')** /(s)ɑ̃paʀe/ [1] *vpr* **s'~ de** get hold of.

**empêchement** /ɑ̃pɛʃmɑ̃/ *nm* avoir un ~ to be held up.

**empêcher** /ɑ̃peʃe/ [1] *vt* prevent; **~ de faire** prevent *ou* stop (from) doing; **(il) n'empêche que** still. □ **s'~** *vpr* **il ne peut pas s'en ~** he cannot help it.

**empereur** /ɑ̃pʀœʀ/ *nm* emperor.

**empester** /ɑ̃pɛste/ [1] *vt* stink out; (*essence*) stink of. ● *vi* stink.

**empêtrer (s')** /(s)ɑ̃petʀe/ [1] *vpr* become entangled.

**empiéter** /ɑ̃pjete/ [14] *vi* **~ sur** encroach upon.

**empiffrer (s')** /(s)ɑ̃pifʀe/ [1] *vpr* ⊡ stuff oneself.

**empiler** /ɑ̃pile/ [1] *vt* pile up. □ **s'~** *vpr* pile up.

**empire** /ɑ̃piʀ/ *nm* empire.

**emplacement** /ɑ̃plasmɑ̃/ *nm* site.

**emplâtre** /ɑ̃plɑtʀ/ *nm* (Méd) plaster.

**emploi** /ɑ̃plwa/ *nm* (travail) job; (embauche) employment; (utilisation) use; **un ~ de chauffeur** a job as a driver; **~ du temps** timetable. **employé**, **~e** *nm,f* employee.

**employer** /ɑ̃plwaje/ [31] *vt* (*personne*) employ; (utiliser) use. □ **s'~** *vpr* be used; **s'~ à** devote oneself to. **employeur**, **-euse** *nm,f* employer.

**empoigner** /ɑ̃pwaɲe/ [1] *vt* grab. □ **s'~** *vpr* come to blows.

**empoisonnement** /ɑ̃pwazɔnmɑ̃/ *nm* poisoning.

**empoisonner** /ɑ̃pwazɔne/ [1] *vt* poison; (embêter [I]) annoy. □ **s'~** *vpr* to poison oneself.

**emporter** /ɑ̃pɔʀte/ [1] *vt* take (away); (entraîner) sweep away; (arracher) tear off. □ **s'~** *vpr* lose one's temper; **l'~** get the upper hand (**sur** of); **plat à ~** take-away.

**empoté**, **~e** /ɑ̃pɔte/ *a* clumsy.

**empreinte** /ɑ̃pʀɛ̃t/ *nf* mark; **~ (digitale)** fingerprint; **~ de pas** footprint.

**empressé**, **~e** /ɑ̃pʀese/ *a* eager, attentive.

**empresser (s')** /(s)ɑ̃pʀese/ [1] *vpr* **s'~ de** hasten to; **s'~ auprès de** be attentive to.

**emprise** /ɑ̃pʀiz/ *nf* influence.

**emprisonnement** /ɑ̃pʀizɔnmɑ̃/ *nm* imprisonment. **emprisonner** [1] *vt* imprison.

**emprunt** /ɑ̃pʀœ̃/ *nm* loan; **faire un ~** take out a loan.

**emprunté**, **~e** /ɑ̃pʀœ̃te/ *a* awkward.

**emprunter** /ɑ̃pʀœ̃te/ [1] *vt* borrow (**à** from); (*route*) take; (fig) assume.

**emprunteur**, **-euse** *nm, f* borrower.

**ému**, **~e** /emy/ *a* moved; (intimidé) nervous.

**émule** /emyl/ *nmf* imitator.

**en** /ɑ̃/

⇨ Pour les expressions comme **en principe**, **en train de**, **s'en aller**, etc. ⇒**principe**, **train**, **aller**, etc.

● *préposition*

····➤ (lieu) in.

····➤ (avec mouvement) to.

····➤ (temps) in.

····➤ (manière, état) in; **~ faisant** by *ou* while doing; **je t'appelle ~ rentrant** I will call you when I get back.

····➤ (en qualité de) as.

····➤ (transport) by.

····➤ (composition) made of; **table ~ bois** wooden table.

● *pronom*

····➤ **~ avoir/vouloir** have/want some; **ne pas ~ avoir/vouloir** not have/want any; **j'~ ai deux** I've got two; **prends-~ plusieurs** take several; **il m'~ reste un** I have one left; **j'~ suis content** I am pleased with him/her/it/them; **je m'~ souviens** I remember it.

····➤ **~ êtes-vous sûr?** are you sure?

**encadrement** /ɑ̃kadʀəmɑ̃/ *nm* framing; (de porte) frame. **encadrer** [1] *vt* frame; (entourer d'un trait) circle; (superviser) supervise.

**encaisser** /ɑ̃kese/ [1] *vt* (*argent*) collect; (*chèque*) cash; (*coups* [I]) take.

**encart** /ɑ̃kaʀ/ *nm* **~ publicitaire** (advertising) insert.

**en-cas** /ɑ̃kɑ/ *nm* (stand-by) snack.

**encastré**, **~e** /ɑ̃kastʀe/ *a* built-in.

**encaustique** /ɑ̃kɔstik/ *nf* wax polish.

**enceinte** /ɑ̃sɛ̃t/ *af* pregnant; **~ de 3 mois** 3 months pregnant. ● *nf* enclosure; **~ (acoustique)** speaker.

**encens** /ɑ̃sɑ̃/ *nm* incense.

**encercler** /ɑ̃sɛʀkle/ [1] *vt* surround.

**enchaînement** /ɑ̃ʃɛnmɑ̃/ *nm* (suite) chain; (d'idées) sequence.

**enchaîner** /ɑ̃ʃene/ [1] *vt* chain (up); (*phrases*) link (up). ● *vi* continue. □ **s'~** *vpr* follow on.

**enchanté**, **~e** /ɑ̃ʃɑ̃te/ *a* (ravi) delighted. **enchanter** [1] *vt* delight; (ensorceler) enchant.

**enchère** /ɑ̃ʃɛʀ/ *nf* bid; **mettre** *ou* **vendre aux ~s** sell by auction.

**enchevêtrer** /ɑ̃ʃəvetʀe/ [1] *vt* tangle. □ **s'~** *vpr* become tangled.

**enclave** /ɑ̃klav/ *nf* enclave.

**enclencher** /ɑ̃klɑ̃ʃe/ [1] *vt* engage.

**enclin**, **~e** /ɑ̃klɛ̃, -in/ *a* **~ à** inclined to.

**enclos** /ɑ̃klo/ *nm* enclosure.

**enclume** /ɑ̃klym/ *nf* anvil.

**encoche** /ɑ̃kɔʃ/ *nf* notch.

**encolure** /ɑ̃kɔlyʀ/ *nf* neck.

**encombrant**, **~e** /ɑ̃kɔ̃bʀɑ̃, -t/ *a* cumbersome.

**encombre** /ɑ̃kɔ̃bʀ/ *nm* **sans ~** without any problems.

**encombrement** /ɑ̃kɔ̃bʀəmɑ̃/ *nm* (Auto) traffic congestion; (volume) bulk.

**encombrer** /ɑ̃kɔ̃bʀe/ [1] *vt* clutter (up); (obstruer) obstruct. □ **s'~ de** *vpr* burden oneself with.

**encontre**: **à l'~ de** /alɑ̃kɔ̃tʀədə/ *loc* against.

**encore** /ɑ̃kɔʀ/ *adv* (toujours) still; (de nouveau) again; (de plus) more; (aussi) also; **~ plus grand** even larger; **~ un café** another coffee; **pas ~** not yet; **si ~** if only; **et puis quoi ~?** 🄸 what next?

**encouragement** /ɑ̃kuʀaʒmɑ̃/ *nm* encouragement. **encourager** [40] *vt* encourage.

**encourir** /ɑ̃kuʀiʀ/ [20] *vt* incur.

**encrasser** /ɑ̃kʀase/ [1] *vt* clog up (with dirt).

**encre** /ɑ̃kʀ/ *nf* ink. **encrier** *nm* ink-well.

**encyclopédie** /ɑ̃siklɔpedi/ *nf* encyclopaedia.

**endettement** /ɑ̃dɛtmɑ̃/ *nm* debt.

**endetter** /ɑ̃dɛte/ [1] *vt* put into debt. □ **s'~** *vpr* get into debt.

**endiguer** /ɑ̃dige/ [1] *vt* dam; (fig) curb.

**endimanché**, **~e** /ɑ̃dimɑ̃ʃe/ *a* in one's Sunday best.

**endive** /ɑ̃div/ *nf* chicory.

**endoctriner** /ɑ̃dɔktʀine/ [1] *vt* indoctrinate.

**endommager** /ɑ̃dɔmaʒe/ [40] *vt* damage.

**endormi**, **~e** /ɑ̃dɔʀmi/ *a* asleep; (apathique) sleepy.

**endormir** /ɑ̃dɔʀmiʀ/ [46] *vt* send to sleep; (médicalement) put to sleep; (duper) dupe (**avec** with). □ **s'~** *vpr* fall asleep.

**endosser** /ɑ̃dɔse/ [1] *vt* (*vêtement*) put on; (assumer) take on; (Comm) endorse.

**endroit** /ɑ̃dʀwa/ *nm* place; (de tissu) right side; **à l'~** the right way round; **par ~s** in places.

**enduire** /ɑ̃dɥiʀ/ [17] *vt* coat. **enduit** *nm* coating.

**endurance** /ɑ̃dyʀɑ̃s/ *nf* endurance. **endurant**, **~e** *a* tough.

**endurcir** /ɑ̃dyʀsiʀ/ [2] *vt* strengthen. □ **s'~** *vpr* become hard(ened).

**endurer** /ɑ̃dyʀe/ [1] *vt* endure.

**énergétique** /enɛʀʒetik/ *a* energy; (*food*) high-calorie. **énergie** *nf* energy; (Tech) power. **énergique** *a* energetic.

**énervant**, **~e** /enɛʀvɑ̃, -t/ *a* irritating, annoying.

**énerver** /enɛʀve/ [1] *vt* irritate. □ **s'~** *vpr* get worked up.

**enfance** /ɑ̃fɑ̃s/ *nf* childhood; **la petite ~** infancy.

**enfant** /ɑ̃fɑ̃/ *nmf* child. **enfantillage** *nm* childishness. **enfantin**, **~e** *a* simple, easy; (puéril) childish; (*jeu, langage*) children's.

**enfer** /ɑ̃fɛʀ/ *nm* (Relig) Hell; (fig) hell.

**enfermer** /ɑ̃fɛʀme/ [1] *vt* shut up. □ **s'~** *vpr* shut oneself up.

**enfiler** /ɑ̃file/ [1] *vt* (*aiguille*) thread; (*vêtement*) slip on; (*rue*) take.

**enfin** /ɑ̃fɛ̃/ *adv* (de soulagement) at last; (en dernier lieu) finally; (résignation, conclusion) well; **~ presque** well nearly.

**enflammé**, **~e** /ɑ̃flame/ *a* (Méd) inflamed; (*discours*) fiery; (*lettre*) passionate.

**enflammer** /ɑ̃flame/ [1] *vt* set fire to. □ **s'~** *vpr* catch fire.

**enfler** /ɑ̃fle/ [1] *vt* (*histoire*) exaggerate. ● *vi* (*partie du corps*) swell (up); (*mer*) swell; (*rumeur, colère*) spread. □ **s'~** *vpr* (*colère*) mount; (*rumeur*) grow.

**enfoncer** /ɑ̃fɔ̃se/ [10] *vt* (*épingle*) push *ou* drive in; (*chapeau*) push down; (*porte*) break down. ● *vi* sink. □ **s'~** *vpr* sink (**dans** into).

**enfouir** /ɑ̃fwiʀ/ [2] *vt* bury.

**enfourcher** /ɑ̃fuʀʃe/ [1] *vt* mount.

**enfreindre** /ɑ̃fʀɛ̃dʀ/ [22] *vt* infringe, break.

**enfuir** (**s'**) /(s)ɑ̃fɥiʀ/ [35] *vpr* run away.

**enfumé**, **~e** /ɑ̃fyme/ *a* filled with smoke.

**engagé**, **~e** /ɑ̃gaʒe/ *a* committed.

**engagement** /ɑ̃gaʒmɑ̃/ *nm* (promesse) promise; (Pol, Comm) commitment.

**engager** /ɑ̃gaʒe/ [40] *vt* (lier) bind, commit; (embaucher) take on; (commencer) start; (introduire) insert; (investir) invest. □ **s'~** *vpr* (promettre) commit oneself; (commencer) start; (*soldat*) enlist; (*concurrent*) enter; **s'~ à faire** undertake to do; **s'~ dans** (*voie*) enter.

**engelure** /ɑ̃ʒlyʀ/ *nf* chilblain.

**engendrer** /ɑ̃ʒɑ̃dʀe/ [1] *vt* (causer) generate.

**engin** /ɑ̃ʒɛ̃/ *nm* device; (véhicule) vehicle; (missile) missile.

**engloutir** /ɑ̃glutiʀ/ [2] *vt* swallow (up).

**engouement** /ɑ̃gumɑ̃/ *nm* passion.

**engouffrer** /ɑ̃gufʀe/ [1] *vt* ⊡ gobble up. □ **s'~ dans** *vpr* rush in.

**engourdir** /ɑ̃guʀdiʀ/ [2] *vt* numb. □ **s'~** *vpr* go numb.

**engrais** /ɑ̃gʀɛ/ *nm* manure; (chimique) fertilizer.

**engrenage** /ɑ̃gʀənaʒ/ *nm* gears (+ *pl*); (fig) spiral.

**engueuler** /ɑ̃gœle/ [1] ⊠ *vt* shout at. □ **s'~** *vpr* have a row.

**enhardir** (**s'**) /(s)ɑ̃aʀdiʀ/ [2] *vpr* become bolder.

**énième** /ɛnjɛm/ *a* umpteenth.

**énigmatique** /enigmatik/ *a* enigmatic. **énigme** *nf* enigma; (devinette) riddle.

**enivrer** /ɑnivʀe/ [1] *vt* intoxicate. □ **s'~** *vpr* get intoxicated.

**enjambée** /ɑ̃ʒɑ̃be/ *nf* stride. **enjamber** [1] *vt* step over; (*pont*) span.

**enjeu** (*pl* **~x**) /ɑ̃ʒø/ *nm* stake.

**enjoué**, **~e** /ɑ̃ʒwe/ *a* cheerful.

**enlacer** /ɑ̃lase/ [10] *vt* entwine.

**enlèvement** /ɑ̃lɛvmɑ̃/ *nm* (de colis) removal; (d'ordures) collection; (rapt) kidnapping.

**enlever** /ɑ̃lve/ [6] *vt* remove (**à** from); (*vêtement*) take off; (*tache, organe*) take out, remove; (kidnapper) kidnap; (gagner) win.

**enliser** (**s'**) /(s)ɑ̃lize/ [1] *vpr* get bogged down.

**enneigé**, **~e** /ɑ̃neʒe/ *a* snow-covered.

**ennemi**, **~e** /ɛnmi/ *a & nm* enemy; **~ de** (fig) hostile to.

**ennui** /ɑ̃nɥi/ *nm* problem; (tracas) boredom; **s'attirer des ~s** run into trouble.

**ennuyer** /ɑ̃nɥije/ [31] *vt* bore; (irriter) annoy; (préoccuper) worry; **si cela ne t'ennuie pas** if you don't mind. ▫ **s'~** *vpr* get bored.

**ennuyeux**, **-euse** /ɑ̃nɥijø, -z/ *a* boring; (fâcheux) annoying.

**énoncé** /enɔ̃se/ *nm* wording, text; (Gram) utterance.

**énoncer** /enɔ̃se/ [10] *vt* express, state.

**enorgueillir (s')** /(s)ɑ̃nɔʀgœjiʀ/ [2] *vpr* **s'~ de** pride oneself on.

**énorme** /enɔʀm/ *a* enormous.

**enquête** /ɑ̃kɛt/ *nf* (Jur) investigation, inquiry; (sondage) survey; **mener l'~** lead the inquiry. **enquêter** [1] *vi* **~ (sur)** investigate. **enquêteur**, **-euse** *nm,f* investigator.

**enquiquinant**, **~e** /ɑ̃kikinɑ̃, -t/ *a* 🅘 irritating.

**enraciné**, **~e** /ɑ̃ʀasine/ *a* deep-rooted.

**enragé**, **~e** /ɑ̃ʀaʒe/ *a* furious; (*chien*) rabid; (fig) fanatical.

**enrager** /ɑ̃ʀaʒe/ [40] *vi* be furious; **faire ~ qn** annoy sb.

**enregistrement** /ɑ̃ʀ(ə)ʒistʀəmɑ̃/ *nm* recording; (des bagages) check-in. **enregistrer** [1] *vt* (Mus, TV) record; (mémoriser) take in; (*bagages*) check in.

**enrhumer (s')** /(s)ɑ̃ʀyme/ [1] *vpr* catch a cold.

**enrichir** /ɑ̃ʀiʃiʀ/ [2] *vt* enrich. ▫ **s'~** *vpr* grow rich(er). **enrichissant**, **~e** *a* (*expérience*) rewarding.

**enrober** /ɑ̃ʀɔbe/ [1] *vt* coat (**de** with).

**enrôler** /ɑ̃ʀole/ [1] *vt* recruit. ▫ **s'~** *vpr* enlist, enrol.

**enroué**, **~e** /ɑ̃ʀwe/ *a* hoarse.

**enrouler** /ɑ̃ʀule/ [1] *vt* wind, wrap. ▫ **s'~** *vpr* wind; **s'~ dans une couverture** roll oneself up in a blanket.

**ensanglanté**, **~e** /ɑ̃sɑ̃glɑ̃te/ *a* bloodstained.

**enseignant**, **~e** /ɑ̃sɛɲɑ̃, -t/ *nm,f* teacher. ● *a* teaching.

**enseigne** /ɑ̃sɛɲ/ *nf* sign.

**enseignement** /ɑ̃sɛɲəmɑ̃/ *nm* (profession) teaching; (instruction) education.

**enseigner** /ɑ̃seɲe/ [1] *vt*/*i* teach; **~ qch à qn** teach sb sth.

**ensemble** /ɑ̃sɑ̃bl/ *adv* together. ● *nm* group; (Mus) ensemble; (vêtements) outfit; (cohésion) unity; (maths) set; **dans l'~** on the whole; **d'~** (idée) general; **l'~ de** (totalité) all of, the whole of.

**ensevelir** /ɑ̃səvliʀ/ [2] *vt* bury.

**ensoleillé**, **~e** /ɑ̃sɔleje/ *a* sunny.

**ensorceler** /ɑ̃sɔʀsəle/ [38] *vt* bewitch.

**ensuite** /ɑ̃sɥit/ *adv* next, then; (plus tard) later.

**ensuivre (s')** /(s)ɑ̃sɥivʀ/ [57] *vpr* follow; **et tout ce qui s'ensuit** and all the rest of it.

**entaille** /ɑ̃taj/ *nf* cut; (profonde) gash; (encoche) notch.

**entamer** /ɑ̃tame/ [1] *vt* start; (inciser) cut into; (ébranler) shake.

**entasser** /ɑ̃tɑse/ [1] *vt* (*livres*) pile; (*argent*) hoard; (*personnes*) cram (**dans** into). ▫ **s'~** *vpr* (*objets*) pile up (**dans** into); (*personnes*) squeeze (**dans** into).

**entendement** /ɑ̃tɑ̃dmɑ̃/ *nm* understanding; **ça dépasse l'~** it's beyond belief.

**entendre** /ɑ̃tɑ̃dʀ/ [3] *vt* hear; (comprendre) understand; (vouloir dire) mean; ~ **parler de** hear of; ~ **dire que** hear that. □ **s'~** *vpr* (être d'accord) agree; **s'~ (bien)** get on (**avec** with); **cela s'entend** of course.

**entendu**, **~e** /ɑ̃tɑ̃dy/ *a* (convenu) agreed; (*sourire, air*) knowing; **bien ~** of course; **(c'est) ~!** all right!

**entente** /ɑ̃tɑ̃t/ *nf* understanding; **bonne ~** good relationship.

**enterrement** /ɑ̃tɛʀmɑ̃/ *nm* funeral.

**enterrer** /ɑ̃teʀe/ [1] *vt* bury.

**en-tête** /ɑ̃tɛt/ *nm* heading; **à ~** headed.

**entêté**, **~e** /ɑ̃tete/ *a* stubborn. **entêtement** *nm* stubbornness. **entêter (s')** [1] *vpr* persist (**à**, **dans** in).

**enthousiasme** /ɑ̃tuzjasm/ *nm* enthusiasm. **enthousiasmer** [1] *vt* fill with enthusiasm. **enthousiaste** *a* enthusiastic.

**enticher (s')** /(s)ɑ̃tiʃe/ [1] *vpr* **s'~ de** become infatuated with.

**entier**, **-ière** /ɑ̃tje, -jɛʀ/ *a* whole; (absolu) absolute; (entêté) unyielding. ● *nm* whole; **en ~** entirely.

**entonnoir** /ɑ̃tɔnwaʀ/ *nm* funnel; (trou) crater.

**entorse** /ɑ̃tɔʀs/ *nf* sprain; (fig) **~ à** (*loi*) infringement of.

**entortiller** /ɑ̃tɔʀtije/ [1] *vt* wind, wrap (**autour** around); (duper Ⓘ) get round.

**entourage** /ɑ̃tuʀaʒ/ *nm* circle of family and friends; (bordure) surround.

**entouré**, **~e** /ɑ̃tuʀe/ *a* (*personne*) supported.

**entourer** /ɑ̃tuʀe/ [1] *vt* surround (**de** with); (réconforter) rally round; **~ qch de mystère** shroud sth in mystery.

**entracte** /ɑ̃tʀakt/ *nm* interval.

**entraide** /ɑ̃tʀɛd/ *nf* mutual aid. **entraider (s')** [1] *vpr* help each other.

**entrain** /ɑ̃tʀɛ̃/ *nm* zest, spirit.

**entraînement** /ɑ̃tʀɛnmɑ̃/ *nm* (Sport) training.

**entraîner** /ɑ̃tʀene/ [1] *vt* (emporter) carry away; (provoquer) lead to; (Sport) train; (actionner) drive. □ **s'~** *vpr* train. **entraîneur** *nm* trainer.

**entrave** /ɑ̃tʀav/ *nf* hindrance. **entraver** [1] *vt* hinder.

**entre** /ɑ̃tʀ(ə)/ *prép* between; (parmi) among(st); **~ autres** among other things; **l'un d'~ nous/eux** one of us/them.

**entrebâillé**, **~e** /ɑ̃tʀəbɑje/ *a* ajar, half open.

**entrechoquer (s')** /(s)ɑ̃tʀəʃɔke/ [1] *vpr* knock against each other.

**entrecôte** /ɑ̃tʀəkot/ *nf* rib steak.

**entrecouper** /ɑ̃tʀəkupe/ [1] *vt* **~ de** intersperse with.

**entrecroiser (s')** /(s)ɑ̃tʀəkʀwaze/ [1] *vpr* (routes) intertwine.

**entrée** /ɑ̃tʀe/ *nf* entrance; (vestibule) hall; (accès) admission, entry; (billet) ticket; (Culin) starter; (Ordinat) **tapez sur E~** press Enter; **'~ interdite'** 'no entry'

**entrejambes** /ɑ̃tʀəʒɑ̃b/ *nm* crotch.

**entremets** /ɑ̃tʀəmɛ/ *nm* dessert.

**entremise** /ɑ̃tʀəmiz/ *nf* intervention; **par l'~ de** through.

**entreposer** /ɑ̃tʀəpoze/ [1] *vt* store.

**entrepôt** /ɑ̃tʀəpo/ *nm* warehouse.

**entreprenant**, **~e** /ɑ̃tʀəpʀənɑ̃, -t/ *a* (actif) enterprising; (séducteur) forward.

**entreprendre** /ɑ̃tʀəpʀɑ̃dʀ/ [50] *vt* start on, undertake; (*personne*)

buttonhole; ~ **de faire** undertake to do.

**entrepreneur** /ɑ̃tʀəpʀənœʀ/ *nm* (de bâtiment) contractor; (chef d'entreprise) firm manager.

**entreprise** /ɑ̃tʀəpʀiz/ *nf* (projet) undertaking; (société) firm, business, company.

**entrer** /ɑ̃tʀe/ [1] *vi* (*aux être*) go in, enter; (venir) come in, enter; ~ **dans** go *ou* come into, enter; (*club*) join; ~ **en collision** collide (**avec** with); **faire** ~ (*personne*) show in; **laisser** ~ let in; ~ **en guerre** go to war. ● *vt* (*données*) enter.

**entre-temps** /ɑ̃tʀətɑ̃/ *adv* meanwhile.

**entretenir** /ɑ̃tʀət(ə)niʀ/ [58] *vt* (*appareil*) maintain; (*vêtement*) look after; (alimenter) (*feu*) keep going; (*amitié*) keep alive; ~ **qn de** converse with sb about. ◻ **s'**~ *vpr* speak (**de** about; **avec** to). **entretien** *nm* maintenance; (discussion) talk; (pour un emploi) interview.

**entrevoir** /ɑ̃tʀəvwaʀ/ [63] *vt* make out; (brièvement) glimpse.

**entrevue** /ɑ̃tʀəvy/ *nf* meeting.

**entrouvert**, ~**e** /ɑ̃tʀuvɛʀ, -t/ *a* ajar, half-open.

**énumération** /enymeʀasjɔ̃/ *nf* enumeration. **énumérer** [14] *vt* enumerate.

**envahir** /ɑ̃vaiʀ/ [2] *vt* invade, overrun; (*douleur, peur*) overcome.

**enveloppe** /ɑ̃vlɔp/ *nf* envelope; (emballage) wrapping; ~ **budgétaire** budget. **envelopper** [1] *vt* wrap (up); (fig) envelop.

**envergure** /ɑ̃vɛʀgyʀ/ *nf* wingspan; (importance) scope; (qualité) calibre.

**envers** /ɑ̃vɛʀ/ *prép* toward(s), to. ● *nm* (de tissu) wrong side; **à l'**~ (*tableau*) upside down; (devant derrière) back to front; (*chaussette*) inside out.

**envie** /ɑ̃vi/ *nf* urge; (jalousie) envy; **avoir** ~ **de qch** feel like sth; **avoir** ~ **de faire** want to do; (moins urgent) feel like doing; **faire** ~ **à qn** make sb envious.

**envier** /ɑ̃vje/ [45] *vt* envy. **envieux**, **-ieuse** *a* envious.

**environ** /ɑ̃viʀɔ̃/ *adv* about.

**environnant**, ~**e** /ɑ̃viʀɔnɑ̃, -t/ *a* surrounding.

**environnement** /ɑ̃viʀɔnmɑ̃/ *nm* environment.

**environs** /ɑ̃viʀɔ̃/ *nmpl* vicinity; **aux** ~ **de** (*lieu*) in the vicinity of; (*heure*) round about.

**envisager** /ɑ̃vizaʒe/ [40] *vt* consider; (imaginer) envisage; ~ **de faire** consider doing.

**envoi** /ɑ̃vwa/ *nm* dispatch; (paquet) consignment; **faire un** ~ send; **coup d'**~ (Sport) kick-off.

**envoler (s')** /(s)ɑ̃vɔle/ [1] *vpr* fly away; (*avion*) take off; (*papiers*) blow away.

**envoyé**, ~**e** /ɑ̃vwaje/ *nm, f* envoy; ~ **spécial** special correspondent.

**envoyer** /ɑ̃vwaje/ [32] *vt* send; (lancer) throw.

**éolienne** /eɔljɛn/ *nf* windmill; **ferme d'**~**s** windfarm.

**épais**, ~**se** /epɛ, -s/ *a* thick. **épaisseur** *nf* thickness.

**épaissir** /epesiʀ/ [2] *vt/i* thicken. ◻ **s'**~ *vpr* thicken; (*mystère*) deepen.

**épanoui**, ~**e** /epanwi/ *a* (*personne*) beaming, radiant.

**épanouir (s')** /(s)epanwiʀ/ [2] *vpr* (*fleur*) open out; (*visage*) beam; (*personne*) blossom. **épanouissement** *nm* (éclat) blossoming.

**épargne** /epaʀɲ/ *nf* savings.

**épargner** /epaʀɲe/ [1] *vt/i* save; (ne pas tuer) spare; ~ **qch à qn** spare sb sth.

**éparpiller** /epaʀpije/ [1] *vt* scatter. □ **s'~** *vpr* scatter; (*fig*) dissipate one's efforts.

**épars**, **~e** /epaʀ, -s/ *a* scattered.

**épatant**, **~e** /epatɑ̃, -t/ *a* 🅸 amazing.

**épaule** /epol/ *nf* shoulder.

**épave** /epav/ *nf* wreck.

**épée** /epe/ *nf* sword.

**épeler** /ɛple/ [6] *vt* spell.

**éperdu**, **~e** /epɛʀdy/ *a* wild, frantic.

**éperon** /epʀɔ̃/ *nm* spur.

**éphémère** /efemɛʀ/ *a* ephemeral.

**épi** /epi/ *nm* (de blé) ear; (mèche) tuft of hair; ~ **de maïs** corn cob.

**épice** /epis/ *nf* spice. **épicé**, **~e** *a* spicy.

**épicerie** /episʀi/ *nf* grocery shop; (produits) groceries. **épicier**, **-ière** *nm,f* grocer.

**épidémie** /epidemi/ *nf* epidemic.

**épiderme** /epidɛʀm/ *nm* skin.

**épier** /epje/ [45] *vt* spy on.

**épilepsie** /epilɛpsi/ *nf* epilepsy. **épileptique** *a & nmf* epileptic.

**épiler** /epile/ [1] *vt* remove unwanted hair from; (*sourcils*) pluck.

**épilogue** /epilɔg/ *nm* epilogue; (fig) outcome.

**épinard** /epinaʀ/ *nm* **~s** spinach (+ *sg*).

**épine** /epin/ *nf* thorn, prickle; (d'animal) prickle, spine; ~ **dorsale** backbone. **épineux**, **-euse** *a* thorny.

**épingle** /epɛ̃gl/ *nf* pin; ~ **de nourrice**, ~ **de sûreté** safety-pin.

**épisode** /epizɔd/ *nm* episode; **à ~s** serialized.

**épitaphe** /epitaf/ *nf* epitaph.

**épluche-légumes** /eplyʃlegym/ *nm inv* (potato) peeler.

**éplucher** /eplyʃe/ [1] *vt* peel; (examiner: fig) scrutinize.

**épluchure** /eplyʃyʀ/ *nf* **~s** peelings.

**éponge** /epɔ̃ʒ/ *nf* sponge. **éponger** [40] *vt* (*liquide*) mop up; (*surface, front*) mop; (fig) (*dettes*) wipe out.

**épopée** /epɔpe/ *nf* epic.

**époque** /epɔk/ *nf* time, period; **à l'~** at the time; **d'~** period.

**épouse** /epuz/ *nf* wife.

**épouser** /epuze/ [1] *vt* marry; (*forme, idée*) adopt.

**épousseter** /epuste/ [38] *vt* dust.

**épouvantable** /epuvɑ̃tabl/ *a* appalling.

**épouvantail** /epuvɑ̃taj/ *nm* scarecrow.

**épouvante** /epuvɑ̃t/ *nf* terror. **épouvanter** [1] *vt* terrify.

**époux** /epu/ *nm* husband; **les ~** the married couple.

**éprendre** (**s'**) /(s)epʀɑ̃dʀ/ [50] *vpr* **s'~ de** fall in love with.

**épreuve** /epʀœv/ *nf* test; (Sport) event; (malheur) ordeal; (Photo, d'imprimerie) proof, **mettre à l'~** put to the test.

**éprouver** /epʀuve/ [1] *vt* (ressentir) experience, (affliger) distress; (tester) test.

**éprouvette** /epʀuvɛt/ *nf* test tube.

**EPS** *abrév f* (**éducation physique et sportive**) PE.

**épuisé**, **~e** /epɥize/ *a* exhausted; (*livre*) out of print. **épuisement** *nm* exhaustion.

**épuiser** /epɥize/ [1] *vt* (fatiguer, user) exhaust. □ **s'~** *vpr* become exhausted.

**épuration** /epyʀasjɔ̃/ *nf* purification; (Pol) purge. **épurer** [1] *vt* purify; (Pol) purge.

**équateur** /ekwatœʀ/ *nm* equator.

**équilibre** /ekilibʀ/ *nm* balance; **être** *ou* **se tenir en ~** (*personne*) balance; (*objet*) be balanced. **équilibré**, **~e** *a* well-balanced.

**équilibrer** /ekilibʀe/ [1] *vt* balance. □ **s'~** *vpr* balance each other.

**équilibriste** /ekilibʀist/ *nmf* acrobat.

**équipage** /ekipaʒ/ *nm* crew.

**équipe** /ekip/ *nf* team; **~ de nuit/jour** night/day shift.

**équipé**, **~e** /ekipe/ *a* equipped; **cuisine ~e** fitted kitchen.

**équipement** /ekipmɑ̃/ *nm* equipment; **~s** (installations) amenities, facilities.

**équiper** /ekipe/ [1] *vt* equip (**de** with). □ **s'~** *vpr* equip oneself.

**équipier**, **-ière** /ekipje, -jɛʀ/ *nm,f* team member.

**équitable** /ekitabl/ *a* fair.

**équitation** /ekitasjɔ̃/ *nf* (horse-) riding.

**équivalence** /ekivalɑ̃s/ *nf* equivalence. **équivalent**, **~e** *a* equivalent.

**équivaloir** /ekivalwaʀ/ [60] *vi* **~ à** be equivalent to.

**équivoque** /ekivɔk/ *a* equivocal; (louche) questionable. ● *nf* ambiguity.

**érable** /eʀabl/ *nm* maple.

**érafler** /eʀafle/ [1] *vt* scratch. **éraflure** *nf* scratch.

**éraillé**, **~e** /eʀɑje/ *a* (*voix*) raucous.

**ère** /ɛʀ/ *nf* era.

**éreintant**, **~e** /eʀɛ̃tɑ̃, -t/ *a* exhausting. **éreinter (s')** [1] *vpr* wear oneself out.

**ériger** /eʀiʒe/ [40] *vt* erect. □ **s'~ en** *vpr* set (oneself) up as.

**éroder** /eʀɔde/ [1] *vt* erode. **érosion** *nf* erosion.

**errer** /ɛʀe/ [1] *vi* wander.

**erreur** /ɛʀœʀ/ *nf* mistake, error; **dans l'~** mistaken; **par ~** by mistake; **~ judiciaire** miscarriage of justice.

**erroné**, **~e** /ɛʀɔne/ *a* erroneous.

**érudit**, **~e** /eʀydi, -t/ *a* scholarly. ● *nm,f* scholar.

**éruption** /eʀypsjɔ̃/ *nf* eruption; (Méd) rash.

**es** /ɛ/ ⇒ÊTRE [4].

**escabeau** (*pl* **~x**) /ɛskabo/ *nm* step-ladder.

**escadron** /ɛskadʀɔ̃/ *nm* (Mil) company.

**escalade** /ɛskalad/ *nf* climbing; (Pol, Comm) escalation. **escalader** [1] *vt* climb.

**escale** /ɛskal/ *nf* (d'avion) stopover; (port) port of call; **faire ~ à** (*avion, passager*) stop over at; (*navire, passager*) put in at.

**escalier** /ɛskalje/ *nm* stairs (+ *pl*); **~ mécanique** *ou* **roulant** escalator.

**escalope** /ɛskalɔp/ *nf* escalope.

**escargot** /ɛskaʀgo/ *nm* snail.

**escarpé**, **~e** /ɛskaʀpe/ *a* steep.

**escarpin** /ɛskaʀpɛ̃/ *nm* court shoe; (US) pump.

**escient**: **à bon ~** /abɔnesjɑ̃/ *loc* wisely.

**esclandre** /ɛsklɑ̃dʀ/ *nm* scene.

**esclavage** /ɛsklavaʒ/ *nm* slavery. **esclave** *nmf* slave.

**escompte** /ɛskɔ̃t/ *nm* discount. **escompter** [1] *vt* expect; (Comm) discount.

**escorte** /ɛskɔʀt/ *nf* escort.

**escrime** /ɛskʀim/ *nf* fencing.

**escroc** /ɛskʀo/ *nm* swindler.

**escroquer** /ɛskʀɔke/ [1] *vt* swindle; ~ **qch à qn** swindle sb out of sth. **escroquerie** *nf* swindle.

**espace** /ɛspas/ *nm* space; ~**s verts** gardens and parks.

**espacer** /ɛspase/ [10] *vt* space out. ▫ **s'**~ *vpr* become less frequent.

**espadrille** /ɛspadʀij/ *nf* rope sandal.

**Espagne** /ɛspaɲ/ *nf* Spain

**espagnol**, ~**e** /ɛspaɲɔl/ *a* Spanish. ● *nm* (Ling) Spanish. **E**~, ~**e** *nm,f* Spaniard.

**espèce** /ɛspɛs/ *nf* kind, sort; (race) species; **en** ~**s** (*argent*) in cash; ~ **d'idiot!** 🄸 you idiot! 🄸.

**espérance** /ɛspeʀɑ̃s/ *nf* hope.

**espérer** /ɛspeʀe/ [14] *vt* hope for; ~ **faire/que** hope to do/that. ● *vi* hope.

**espiègle** /ɛspjɛgl/ *a* mischievous.

**espion**, ~**ne** /ɛspjɔ̃, -ɔn/ *nm,f* spy. **espionnage** *nm* espionage, spying. **espionner** [1] *vt* spy (on).

**espoir** /ɛspwaʀ/ *nm* hope; **reprendre** ~ feel hopeful again.

**esprit** /ɛspʀi/ *nm* (intellect) mind; (humour) wit; (fantôme) spirit; (ambiance) atmosphere; **perdre l'**~ lose one's mind; **reprendre ses** ~**s** come to; **faire de l'**~ try to be witty.

**esquimau**, ~**de** (*mpl* ~**x**) /ɛskimo, -d/ *nm, f* Eskimo.

**esquinter** /ɛskɛ̃te/ [1] *vt* 🄼 ruin.

**esquisse** /ɛskis/ *nf* sketch; (fig) outline.

**esquiver** /ɛskive/ [1] *vt* dodge. ▫ **s'**~ *vpr* slip away.

**essai** /esɛ/ *nm* (épreuve) test, trial; (tentative) try; (article) essay; (au rugby) try; ~**s** (Auto) qualifying round (+ *sg*); **à l'**~ on trial.

**essaim** /esɛ̃/ *nm* swarm.

**essayage** /esɛjaʒ/ *nm* fitting; **salon d'**~ fitting room.

**essayer** /eseje/ [31] *vt/i* try; (*vêtement*) try (on); (*voiture*) try (out); ~ **de faire** try to do.

**essence** /esɑ̃s/ *nf* (carburant) petrol; (nature, extrait) essence; ~ **sans plomb** unleaded petrol.

**essentiel**, ~**le** /esɑ̃sjɛl/ *a* essential. ● *nm* **l'**~ the main thing; (quantité) the main part.

**essieu** (*pl* ~**x**) /esjø/ *nm* axle.

**essor** /esɔʀ/ *nm* expansion, **prendre son** ~ expand.

**essorage** /esɔʀaʒ/ *nm* spin-drying. **essorer** [1] *vt* (*linge*) spin-dry; (en tordant) wring.

**essoreuse** /esɔʀøz/ *nf* spin-drier; ~ **à salade** salad spinner.

**essoufflé**, ~**e** /esufle/ *a* out of breath.

**essuie-glace** /esɥiglas/ *nm inv* windscreen wiper.

**essuie-mains** /esɥimɛ̃/ *nm inv* hand-towel.

**essuie-tout** /esɥitu/ *nm inv* kitchen paper.

**essuyer** /esɥije/ [31] *vt* wipe; (subir) suffer. ▫ **s'**~ *vpr* dry *ou* wipe oneself.

**est**[1] /ɛ/ ➙ ÊTRE [4].

**est**[2] /ɛst/ *nm* east. ● *a inv* east; (partie) eastern, (direction) easterly.

**estampe** /ɛstɑ̃p/ *nf* print.

**esthète** /ɛstɛt/ *nmf* aesthete.

**esthéticienne** /ɛstetisjɛn/ *nf* beautician.

**esthétique** /ɛstetik/ *a* aesthetic.

**estimation** /ɛstimasjɔ̃/ *nf* (de coûts) estimate; (valeur) valuation.

**estime** /ɛstim/ *nf* esteem.

**estimer** /ɛstime/ [1] *vt* (*tableau*) value; (calculer) estimate; (respecter) esteem; (considérer) consider (**que** that).

**estival**, **~e** (*mpl* **-aux**) /ɛstival, -o/ *a* summer. **estivant**, **~e** *nm,f* summer visitor.

**estomac** /ɛstɔma/ *nm* stomach.

**estomaqué**, **~e** /ɛstɔmake/ *a* [I] stunned.

**Estonie** /ɛstɔni/ *nf* Estonia.

**estrade** /ɛstʀad/ *nf* platform.

**estragon** /ɛstʀagɔ̃/ *nm* tarragon.

**estropié**, **~e** /ɛstʀɔpje/ *nm,f* cripple. ● *a* crippled.

**estuaire** /ɛstɥɛʀ/ *nm* estuary.

**et** /e/ *conj* and; **~ moi?** what about me?; **~ alors?** so what?

**étable** /etabl/ *nf* cow-shed.

**établi**, **~e** /etabli/ *a* established; **un fait bien ~** a well-established fact. ● *nm* work-bench.

**établir** /etabliʀ/ [2] *vt* establish; (*liste, facture*) draw up; (*personne, camp, record*) set up. □ **s'~** *vpr* (*personne*) settle; **s'~ à son compte** set up on one's own.

**établissement** /etablismɑ̃/ *nm* (entreprise) organization; (institution) establishment; **~ scolaire** school.

**étage** /etaʒ/ *nm* floor, storey; (de fusée) stage; **à l'~** upstairs; **au premier ~** on the first floor.

**étagère** /etaʒɛʀ/ *nf* shelf; (meuble) shelving unit.

**étain** /etɛ̃/ *nm* pewter.

**étais**, **était** /etɛ/ ⇒ÊTRE [4].

**étalage** /etalaʒ/ *nm* display; (vitrine) shop-window; **faire ~ de** flaunt. **étalagiste** *nmf* window-dresser.

**étaler** /etale/ [1] *vt* spread; (*journal*) spread (out); (*pâte*) roll out; (exposer) display; (*richesse*) flaunt. □ **s'~** *vpr* (prendre de la place) spread out; (tomber [I]) fall flat; **s'~ sur** (*paiement*) be spread over.

**étalon** /etalɔ̃/ *nm* (cheval) stallion; (modèle) standard.

**étanche** /etɑ̃ʃ/ *a* watertight; (*montre*) waterproof.

**étancher** /etɑ̃ʃe/ [1] *vt* (*soif*) quench.

**étang** /etɑ̃/ *nm* pond.

**étant** /etɑ̃/ ⇒ÊTRE [4].

**étape** /etap/ *nf* stage; (lieu d'arrêt) stopover; (fig) stage.

**état** /eta/ *nm* state; (liste) statement; (métier) profession; **en bon/mauvais ~** in good/bad condition; **en ~ de** in a position to; **en ~ de marche** in working order; **faire ~ de** (citer) mention; **être dans tous ses ~s** be in a state; **~ civil** civil status; **~ des lieux** inventory of fixtures. **État** *nm* State.

**état-major** (*pl* **états-majors**) /etamaʒɔʀ/ *nm* (officiers) staff (+ *pl*).

**États-Unis** /etazyni/ *nmpl* **~ (d'Amérique)** United States (of America).

**étau** (*pl* **~x**) /eto/ *nm* vice.

**étayer** /eteje/ [31] *vt* prop up.

**été**[1] /ete/ ⇒ÊTRE [4].

**été**[2] /ete/ *nm* summer.

**éteindre** /etɛ̃dʀ/ [22] *vt* (*feu*) put out; (*lumière, radio*) turn off. □ **s'~** *vpr* (*feu, lumière*) go out; (*appareil*) go off; (mourir) die. **éteint**, **~e** *a* (*feu*) out; (*volcan*) extinct.

**étendard** /etɑ̃daʀ/ *nm* standard.

**étendre** /etɑ̃dʀ/ [3] *vt* (*nappe*) spread (out); (*bras, jambes*) stretch (out); (*linge*) hang out; (agrandir) extend. □ **s'~** *vpr* (s'allonger) lie down; (se propager) spread; (*plaine*) stretch; **s'~ sur** (*sujet*) dwell on.

**étendu**, **~e** /etɑ̃dy/ *a* extensive. **étendue** *nf* area; (d'eau) stretch; (importance) extent.

**éternel**, **~le** /etɛʀnɛl/ *a* (*vie*) eternal; (fig) endless.

**éterniser (s')** /(s)etɛʀnize/ [1] *vpr* (durer) drag on.

**éternité** /etɛʀnite/ *nf* eternity.

**éternuement** /etɛʀnymɑ̃/ *nm* sneeze. **éternuer** [1] *vi* sneeze.

**êtes** /ɛt/ ⇒ÊTRE [4].

**éthique** /etik/ *a* ethical. ● *nf* ethics (+ *sg*).

**ethnie** /ɛtni/ *nf* ethnic group. **ethnique** *a* ethnic.

**étincelant**, **~e** /etɛ̃slɑ̃, -t/ *a* sparkling. **étinceler** [38] *vi* sparkle. **étincelle** *nf* spark.

**étiqueter** /etikte/ [38] *vt* label. **étiquette** *nf* label; (protocole) etiquette.

**étirer** /etiʀe/ [1] *vt* stretch. □ **s'~** *vpr* stretch.

**étoffe** /etɔf/ *nf* fabric.

**étoffer** /etɔfe/ [1] *vt* expand. □ **s'~** *vpr* fill out.

**étoile** /etwal/ *nf* star; **à la belle ~** in the open; **~ filante** shooting star; **~ de mer** starfish.

**étonnant**, **~e** /etɔnɑ̃, -t/ *a* (curieux) surprising; (formidable) amazing. **étonnement** *nm* surprise; (plus fort) amazement.

**étonner** /etɔne/ [1] *vt* amaze. □ **s'~** *vpr* be amazed (**de** at).

**étouffant**, **~e** /etufɑ̃, -t/ *a* stifling.

**étouffer** /etufe/ [1] *vt/i* suffocate, (*sentiment, révolte*) stifle; (*feu*) smother; (*bruit*) muffle; **on étouffe** it is stifling. □ **s'~** *vpr* suffocate; (en mangeant) choke.

**étourderie** /etuʀdəʀi/ *nf* thoughtlessness; (acte) careless mistake.

**étourdi**, **~e** /etuʀdi/ *a* absent-minded. ● *nm,f* scatterbrain.

**étourdir** /etuʀdiʀ/ [2] *vt* stun; (fatiguer) make sb's head spin. **étourdissant**, **~e** *a* stunning.

**étourneau** (*pl* **~x**) /etuʀno/ *nm* starling.

**étrange** /etʀɑ̃ʒ/ *a* strange.

**étranger**, **-ère** /etʀɑ̃ʒe, -ɛʀ/ *a* (inconnu) strange, unfamiliar; (d'un autre pays) foreign. ● *nm,f* foreigner; (inconnu) stranger; **à l'~** abroad; **de l'~** from abroad.

**étrangler** /etʀɑ̃gle/ [1] *vt* strangle; (*col*) throttle. □ **s'~** *vpr* choke.

---

**être** /ɛtʀ/ [4]

● *verbe auxiliaire*

····➤ (du passé) have; **elle est partie/venue hier** she left/came yesterday.

····➤ (de la voix passive) be.

● *verbe intransitif* (*aux avoir*)

····➤ be; **~ médecin** be a doctor; **je suis à vous** I'm all yours; **j'en suis à me demander si...** I'm beginning to wonder whether...; **qu'en est-il de...?** what's the news about...?

····➤ (appartenance) be, belong to.

····➤ (heure, date) be; **nous sommes le 3 mars** it's March 3.

····➤ (aller) be; **je n'y ai jamais été** I've never been; **il a été le voir** he went to see him.

····➤ **c'est** it is *or* it's; **c'est moi qui l'ai fait** I did it; **est-ce que tu veux du thé?** do you want some tea?

● *nom masculin*

····➤ being; **~ humain** human being.

····➤ (personne) person; **un ~ cher** a loved one.

---

**étreindre** /etʀɛ̃dʀ/ [22] *vt* embrace. **étreinte** *nf* embrace.

**étrennes** /etʀɛn/ *nfpl* (New Year's) gift (+ *sg*); (argent) money.

**étrier** /etʀije/ *nm* stirrup.

**étriqué**, **~e** /etʀike/ *a* tight.

**étroit**, **~e** /etRwa, -t/ *a* narrow; (*vêtement*) tight; (*liens, surveillance*) close; **à l'~** cramped. **étroitement** *adv* closely. **étroitesse** *nf* narrowness.

**étude** /etyd/ *nf* study; (enquête) survey; (bureau) office; **(salle d')~** (Scol) prep room; **à l'~** under consideration; **faire des ~s (de)** study; **il n'a pas fait d'~s** he didn't go to university; **~ de marché** market research.

**étudiant**, **~e** /etydjɑ̃, -t/ *nm,f* student.

**étudier** /etydje/ [45] *vt/i* study.

**étui** /etɥi/ *nm* case.

**étuve** /etyv/ *nf* steam room.

**eu**, **~e** /y/ ⇒AVOIR [5].

**euro** /øRo/ *nm* euro.

**Europe** /øRɔp/ *nf* Europe.

**européen**, **~ne** /øRɔpeɛ̃, -eɛn/ *a* European. **E~**, **~ne** *nm,f* European.

**euthanasie** /øtanazi/ *nf* euthanasia.

**eux** /ø/ *pron* they; (complément) them. **eux-mêmes** *pron* themselves.

**évacuation** /evakɥasjɔ̃/ *nf* evacuation; (d'eaux usées) discharge. **évacuer** [1] *vt* evacuate.

**évadé**, **~e** /evade/ *a* escaped. ● *nm,f* escaped prisoner. **évader (s')** [1] *vpr* escape.

**évaluation** /evalɥasjɔ̃/ *nf* assessment. **évaluer** [1] *vt* assess.

**évangile** /evɑ̃ʒil/ *nm* gospel; **l'É~** the Gospel.

**évanouir (s')** /(s)evanwiR/ [2] *vpr* faint; (disparaître) vanish.

**évaporation** /evapɔRasjɔ̃/ *nf* evaporation. **évaporer (s')** [1] *vpr* evaporate.

**évasif**, **-ive** /evazif, -v/ *a* evasive.

**évasion** /evazjɔ̃/ *nf* escape.

**éveil** /evɛj/ *nm* awakening; **en ~** alert.

**éveillé**, **~e** /eveje/ *a* awake; (intelligent) alert.

**éveiller** /eveje/ [1] *vt* awake(n); (susciter) arouse. ▫ **s'~** *vpr* awake.

**événement** /evɛnmɑ̃/ *nm* event.

**éventail** /evɑ̃taj/ *nm* fan; (gamme) range.

**éventrer** /evɑ̃tRe/ [1] *vt* (*sac*) rip open.

**éventualité** /evɑ̃tɥalite/ *nf* possibility; **dans cette ~** in that event.

**éventuel**, **~le** /evɑ̃tɥɛl/ *a* possible. **éventuellement** *adv* possibly.

**évêque** /evɛk/ *nm* bishop.

**évertuer (s')** /(s)evɛRtɥe/ [1] *vpr* **s'~ à** struggle hard to.

**éviction** /eviksjɔ̃/ *nf* eviction.

**évidemment** /evidamɑ̃/ *adv* obviously; (bien sûr) of course.

**évidence** /evidɑ̃s/ *nf* obviousness; (fait) obvious fact; **être en ~** be conspicuous; **mettre en ~** (fait) highlight. **évident**, **~e** *a* obvious, evident.

**évier** /evje/ *nm* sink.

**évincer** /evɛ̃se/ [10] *vt* oust.

**éviter** /evite/ [1] *vt* avoid (**de faire** doing); **~ qch à qn** (*dérangement*) save sb sth.

**évocateur**, **-trice** /evɔkatœR, -tRis/ *a* evocative. **évocation** *nf* evocation.

**évolué**, **~e** /evɔlɥe/ *a* highly developed.

**évoluer** /evɔlɥe/ [1] *vi* evolve; (*situation*) develop; (se déplacer) glide. **évolution** *nf* evolution; (d'une situation) development.

**évoquer** /evɔke/ [1] *vt* call to mind, evoke.

**exacerber** /ɛgzasɛRbe/ [1] *vt* exacerbate.

**exact**, **~e** /ɛgza(kt), -akt/ *a* (précis) exact, accurate; (juste) correct; (*personne*) punctual. **exactement** *adv* exactly. **exactitude** *nf* exactness; punctuality.

**ex æquo** /ɛgzeko/ *adv* **être ~** tie (**avec qn** with sb).

**exagération** /ɛgzaʒeʀasjɔ̃/ *nf* exaggeration. **exagéré**, **~e** *a* excessive.

**exagérer** /ɛgzaʒeʀe/ [14] *vt/i* exaggerate; (abuser) go too far.

**exalté**, **~e** /ɛgzalte/ *nm,f* fanatic. **exalter** [1] *vt* excite; (glorifier) exalt.

**examen** /ɛgzamɛ̃/ *nm* examination; (Scol) exam. **examinateur**, **-trice** *nm,f* examiner. **examiner** [1] *vt* examine.

**exaspération** /ɛgzaspeʀasjɔ̃/ *nf* exasperation. **exaspérer** [14] *vt* exasperate.

**exaucer** /ɛgzose/ [10] *vt* grant; (*personne*) grant the wish(es) of.

**excédent** /ɛksedɑ̃/ *nm* surplus; **~ de bagages** excess luggage; **~ de la balance commerciale** trade surplus. **excédentaire** *a* excess, surplus.

**excéder** /ɛksede/ [14] *vt* (dépasser) exceed; (agacer) irritate.

**excellence** /ɛksɛlɑ̃s/ *nf* excellence. **excellent**, **~e** *a* excellent. **exceller** [1] *vi* excel (**dans** in).

**excentricité** /ɛksɑ̃tʀisite/ *nf* eccentricity. **excentrique** *a & nmf* eccentric.

**excepté**, **~e** /ɛksɛpte/ *a & prép* except.

**excepter** /ɛksɛpte/ [1] *vt* except.

**exception** /ɛksɛpsjɔ̃/ *nf* exception; **à l'~ de** except for; **d'~** exceptional; **faire ~** be an exception. **exceptionnel**, **~le** *a* exceptional. **exceptionnellement** *adv* exceptionally.

**excès** /ɛksɛ/ *nm* excess; **~ de vitesse** speeding.

**excessif**, **-ive** /ɛksesif, -v/ *a* excessive.

**excitant**, **~e** /ɛksitɑ̃, -t/ *a* stimulating; (palpitant) exciting. ● *nm* stimulant.

**exciter** /ɛksite/ [1] *vt* excite; (irriter) get excited. □ **s'~** *vpr* get excited.

**exclamer (s')** /(s)ɛksklame/ [1] *vpr* exclaim.

**exclure** /ɛksklyʀ/ [16] *vt* exclude; (expulser) expel; (empêcher) preclude.

**exclusif**, **-ive** /ɛksklyzif, -v/ *a* exclusive.

**exclusion** /ɛksklyzjɔ̃/ *nf* exclusion.

**exclusivité** /ɛkslyzivite/ *nf* (Comm) exclusive rights (+ *pl*); **projeter en ~** show exclusively.

**excursion** /ɛkskyʀsjɔ̃/ *nf* excursion; (à pied) hike.

**excuse** /ɛkskyz/ *nf* excuse; **~s** apology (+ *sg*); **faire des ~s** apologize.

**excuser** /ɛkskyze/ [1] *vt* excuse; **excusez-moi** excuse me. □ **s'~** *vpr* apologize (**de** for).

**exécrable** /ɛgzekʀabl/ *a* dreadful. **exécrer** [14] *vt* loathe.

**exécuter** /ɛgzekyte/ [1] *vt* carry out, execute; (Mus) perform; (tuer) execute.

**exécutif**, **-ive** /ɛgzekytif, -v/ *a & nm* (Pol) executive.

**exécution** /egzekysjɔ̃/ *nf* execution; (Mus) performance.

**exemplaire** /ɛgzɑ̃plɛʀ/ *a* exemplary. ● *nm* copy.

**exemple** /ɛgzɑ̃pl/ *nm* example; **par ~** for example; **donner l'~** set an example.

**exempt**, **~e** /ɛgzɑ̃, -t/ *a* **~ de** exempt (**de** from).

**exempter** /ɛgzɑ̃te/ [1] *vt* exempt (**de** from). **exemption** *nf* exemption.

**exercer** /ɛgzɛʀse/ [10] *vt* exercise; (*influence, contrôle*) exert; (former) train, exercise; **~ un métier** have a job; **~ le métier de...** work as a... □ **s'~** *vpr* practise.

**exercice** /ɛgzɛʀsis/ *nm* exercise; (de métier) practice; **en ~** in office; (*médecin*) in practice.

**exhaler** /ɛgzale/ [1] *vt* emit.

**exhaustif**, **-ive** /ɛgzostif, -v/ *a* exhaustive.

**exhiber** /ɛgzibe/ [1] *vt* exhibit.

**exhorter** /ɛgzɔʀte/ [1] *vt* exhort (**à** to).

**exigeant**, **~e** /ɛgziʒɑ̃, -t/ *a* demanding; **être ~ avec qn** demand a lot of sb. **exigence** *nf* demand. **exiger** [40] *vt* demand.

**exigu**, **~ë** /ɛgzigy/ *a* tiny.

**exil** /ɛgzil/ *nm* exile. **exilé**, **~e** *nm,f* exile.

**exiler** /ɛgzile/ [1] *vt* exile. □ **s'~** *vpr* go into exile.

**existence** /ɛgzistɑ̃s/ *nf* existence. **exister** [1] *vi* exist.

**exode** /ɛgzɔd/ *nm* exodus.

**exonérer** /egzɔneʀe/ [14] *vt* exempt (**de** from).

**exorbitant**, **~e** /ɛgzɔʀbitɑ̃, -t/ *a* exorbitant.

**exorciser** /ɛgzɔʀsize/ [1] *vt* exorcize.

**exotique** /ɛgzɔtik/ *a* exotic.

**expansé**, **~e** /ɛkspɑ̃se/ *a* (Tech) expanded.

**expansif**, **-ive** /ɛkspɑ̃sif, -v/ *a* expansive. **expansion** *nf* expansion.

**expatrié**, **~e** /ɛkspatʀije/ *nm,f* expatriate.

**expectative** /ɛkspɛktativ/ *nf* **être dans l'~** wait and see.

**expédient** /ɛkspedjɑ̃/ *nm* expedient; **vivre d'~s** live by one's wits; **user d'~s** resort to expedients.

**expédier** /ɛkspedje/ [45] *vt* send, dispatch; (*tâche* Ⓘ) polish off. **expéditeur**, **-trice** *nm,f* sender.

**expéditif**, **-ive** /ɛkspeditif, -v/ *a* quick.

**expédition** /ɛkspedisjɔ̃/ *nf* (envoi) dispatching; (voyage) expedition.

**expérience** /ɛkspeʀjɑ̃s/ *nf* experience; (scientifique) experiment.

**expérimental**, **~e** (*mpl* **-aux**) /ɛkspeʀimɑ̃tal, o/ *a* experimental. **expérimentation** *nf* experimentation. **expérimenté**, **~e** *a* experienced. **expérimenter** [1] *vt* test, experiment with.

**expert**, **~e** /ɛkspɛʀ, -t/ *a* expert. ● *nm* expert; (d'assurances) adjuster. **expert-comptable** (*pl* **experts-comptables**) *nm* accountant.

**expertise** /ɛkspɛʀtiz/ *nf* valuation; (de dégâts) assessment. **expertiser** [1] *vt* value; (*dégâts*) assess.

**expier** /ɛkspje/ [45] *vt* atone for.

**expiration** /ɛkspiʀasjɔ̃/ *nf* expiry.

**expirer** /ɛkspiʀe/ [1] *vi* breathe out; (finir, mourir) expire.

**explicatif**, **-ive** /ɛksplikatif, -v/ *a* explanatory.

**explication** /ɛksplikasjɔ̃/ *nf* explanation; (fig) discussion; **~ de texte** (Scol) literary commentary.

**explicite** /ɛksplisit/ *a* explicit.

**expliquer** /ɛksplike/ [1] *vt* explain. □ **s'~** *vpr* explain oneself; (discuter) discuss things; (être explicable) be understandable.

**exploit** /ɛksplwa/ *nm* exploit.

**exploitant**, **~e** /ɛksplwatɑ̃, -t/ *nm,f* **~ (agricole)** farmer.

**exploitation** /ɛksplwatasjɔ̃/ *nf* exploitation; (d'entreprise) running; (ferme) farm.

**exploiter** /ɛksplwate/ [1] *vt* exploit; (*ferme*) run; (*mine*) work.

**explorateur**, **-trice** /ɛksplɔʀatœʀ, -tʀis/ *nm,f* explorer. **exploration** *nf* exploration. **explorer** [1] *vt* explore.

**exploser** /ɛksploze/ [1] *vi* explode; **faire ~** explode; (*bâtiment*) blow up.

**explosif**, **-ive** /ɛksplozif, -v/ *a & nm* explosive. **explosion** *nf* explosion.

**exportateur**, **-trice** /ɛkspɔʀtatœʀ, -tʀis/ *nm,f* exporter. ● *a* exporting. **exportation** *nf* export. **exporter** [1] *vt* export.

**exposant**, **~e** /ɛkspozɑ, -t/ *nm,f* exhibitor.

**exposé**, **~e** /ɛkspoze/ *nm* talk (**sur** on); (d'une action) account; **faire l'~ de la situation** give an account of the situation. ● *a* **~ au nord** facing north.

**exposer** /ɛkspoze/ [1] *vt* display, show; (expliquer) explain; (soumettre, mettre en danger) expose (**à** to); (*vie*) endanger. □ **s'~ à** *vpr* expose oneself to.

**exposition** /ɛkspozisjɔ̃/ *nf* (d'art) exhibition; (de faits) exposition; (géographique) aspect.

**exprès**[1] /ɛkspʀɛ/ *adv* specially; (délibérément) on purpose.

**exprès**[2], **-esse** /ɛkspʀɛs/ *a* express.

**express** /ɛkspʀɛs/ *a & nm inv* **(café) ~** espresso; **(train) ~** fast train.

**expressif**, **-ive** /ɛkspʀesif, -v/ *a* expressive. **expression** *nf* expression.

**exprimer** /ɛkspʀime/ [1] *vt* express. □ **s'~** *vpr* express oneself.

**expulser** /ɛkspylse/ [1] *vt* expel; (*locataire*) evict; (*joueur*) send off. **expulsion** *nf* (d'élève) expulsion; (de locataire) eviction; (d'immigré) deportation.

**exquis**, **~e** /ɛkski, -z/ *a* exquisite.

**extase** /ɛkstɑz/ *nf* ecstasy.

**extasier (s')** /(s)ɛkstɑzje/ [45] *vpr* **s'~ sur** be ecstatic about.

**extensible** /ɛkstɑ̃sibl/ *a* (*tissu*) stretch.

**extension** /ɛkstɑ̃sjɔ̃/ *nf* extension; (expansion) expansion.

**exténuer** /ɛkstenɥe/ [1] *vt* exhaust.

**extérieur**, **~e** /ɛksteʀjœʀ/ *a* outside; (*signe, gaieté*) outward; (*politique*) foreign. ● *nm* outside, exterior; (de personne) exterior; **à l'~ (de)** outside. **extérioriser** [1] *vt* show, externalize.

**extermination** /ɛkstɛʀminasjɔ̃/ *nf* extermination. **exterminer** [1] *vt* exterminate.

**externe** /ɛkstɛʀn/ *a* external. ● *nmf* (Scol) day pupil.

**extincteur** /ɛkstɛ̃ktœʀ/ *nm* fire extinguisher.

**extinction** /ɛkstɛ̃ksjɔ̃/ *nf* extinction; **avoir une ~ de voix** have lost one's voice.

**extorquer** /ɛkstɔʀke/ [1] *vt* extort.

**extra** /ɛkstʀa/ *a inv* first-rate. ● *nm inv* (repas) (special) treat.

**extraction** /ɛkstʀaksjɔ̃/ *nf* extraction.

**extrader** /ɛkstʀade/ [1] *vt* extradite.

**extraire** /ɛkstʀɛʀ/ [29] *vt* extract. **extrait** *nm* extract.

**extraordinaire** /ɛkstʀaɔʀdinɛʀ/ *a* extraordinary.

**extravagance** /ɛkstʀavagɑ̃s/ *nf* extravagance. **extravagant**, **~e** *a* extravagant.

**extraverti**, ~**e** /ɛkstʀavɛʀti/ *nm,f* extrovert.

**extrême** /ɛkstʀɛm/ *a & nm* extreme. **extrêmement** *adv* extremely.

**Extrême-Orient** /ɛkstʀɛmɔʀjɑ̃/ *nm* Far East.

**extrémiste** /ɛkstʀemist/ *nmf* extremist.

**extrémité** /ɛkstʀemite/ *nf* end; (mains, pieds) extremity.

**exubérance** /ɛgzybeʀɑ̃s/ *nf* exuberance. **exubérant**, ~**e** *a* exuberant.

# Ff

**F** *abrév f* (**franc, francs**) franc, francs.

**fabricant**, ~**e** /fabʀikɑ̃, -t/ *nm,f* manufacturer. **fabrication** *nf* making; manufacture.

**fabrique** /fabʀik/ *nf* factory. **fabriquer** [1] *vt* make; (industriellement) manufacture; (fig) make up.

**fabuler** /fabyle/ [1] *vi* fantasize.

**fabuleux**, **-euse** /fabylø, -z/ *a* fabulous.

**fac** /fak/ *nf* [I] university.

**façade** /fasad/ *nf* front; (fig) façade.

**face** /fas/ *nf* face; (d'un objet) side; **en** ~ **(de)**, **d'en** ~ opposite; **en** ~ **de** (fig) faced with; ~ **à** facing; (fig) faced with; **faire** ~ **à** face. **face-à-face** *nm inv* (débat) one-to-one debate.

**fâcher** /fɑʃe/ [1] *vt* anger; **fâché** angry; (désolé) sorry. □ **se** ~ *vpr* get angry; (se brouiller) fall out.

**facile** /fasil/ *a* easy; (*caractère*) easygoing.

**facilité** /fasilite/ *nf* easiness; (aisance) ease; (aptitude) ability; ~**s** (possibilités) facilities, opportunities; ~**s d'importation** import opportunities; ~**s de paiement** easy terms.

**faciliter** /fasilite/ [1] *vt* facilitate, make easier.

**façon** /fasɔ̃/ *nf* way; (de vêtement) cut; **de cette** ~ in this way; **de** ~ **à** so as to; **de toute** ~ anyway; ~**s** (chichis) fuss; **faire des** ~**s** stand on ceremony; **sans** ~**s** (*repas*) informal; (*personne*) unpretentious. **façonner** [1] *vt* shape; (faire) make.

**fac-similé** (*pl* ~**s**) /faksimile/ *nm* facsimile.

**facteur**, **-trice** /faktœʀ, -tʀis/ *nm,f* postman, postwoman. ● *nm* (élément) factor.

**facture** /faktyʀ/ *nf* bill; (Comm) invoice; ~ **détaillée** itemized bill. **facturer** [1] *vt* invoice. **facturette** *nf* credit card slip.

**facultatif**, **-ive** /fakyltatif, -v/ *a* optional.

**faculté** /fakylte/ *nf* faculty; (possibilité) power; (Univ) faculty.

**fade** /fad/ *a* insipid.

**faible** /fɛbl/ *a* weak; (*espoir, quantité, écart*) slight; (*revenu, intensité*) low; ~ **d'esprit** feeble-minded. ● *nm* (personne) weakling; (penchant) weakness. **faiblesse** *nf* weakness. **faiblir** [2] *vi* weaken.

**faïence** /fajɑ̃s/ *nf* earthenware.

**faillir** /fajiʀ/ [2] *vi* **j'ai failli acheter** I almost bought.

**faillite** /fajit/ *nf* bankruptcy; (fig) collapse.

**faim** /fɛ̃/ *nf* hunger; **avoir** ~ be hungry; **rester sur sa** ~ (fig) be left wanting more.

**fainéant**, ~**e** /feneɑ̃, -t/ *a* idle. ● *nm,f* idler.

**faire** /fɛʀ/ [33]

⇨ Pour les expressions comme **faire attention**, **faire la cuisine**, etc. ⇒**attention**, **cuisine**, etc.

● *verbe transitif*

····➤ (préparer, créer) make; **~ une tarte/une erreur** make a tart/a mistake.

····➤ (se livrer à une activité) do; **~ du droit** do law; **~ du foot/du violon** play football/the violin; **qu'est-ce qu'elle fait?** (dans la vie) what does she do?; (en ce moment précis) what is she doing?

····➤ (dans les calculs, mesures, etc.) **10 et 10 font 20** 10 and 10 make 20; **ça fait 25 francs** that's 25 francs; **~ 60 kilos** weigh 60 kilos; **il fait 1,75 m** he's 1.75 m tall.

····➤ (dans les expressions de temps) **ça fait une heure que j'attends** I have been waiting for an hour.

····➤ (imiter) **~ le clown** act the clown; **faire le malade** pretend to be ill.

····➤ (parcourir) **~ 10 km** do *ou* cover 10 km; **~ les musées** go round the museums.

····➤ (entraîner, causer) **ça ne fait rien** it doesn't matter; **l'accident a fait 8 morts** 8 people died in the accident.

····➤ (dire) say; **'excusez-moi', fit-elle** 'excuse me', she said.

● *verbe auxiliaire*

····➤ **(faire** + infinitif + qn) make; **~ pleurer qn** make sb cry.

····➤ **(faire** + infinitif + qch) have, get; **~ réparer sa voiture** have *ou* get one's car mended.

····➤ **(ne faire que** + infinitif) (continuellement) **ne ~ que pleurer** do nothing but cry; (seulement) **je ne fais qu'obéir** I'm only following orders.

● *verbe intransitif*

····➤ (agir) do, act; **~ vite** act quickly; **fais comme tu veux** do as you please; **fais comme chez toi** make yourself at home.

····➤ (paraître) look; **~ joli** look pretty; **ça fait cher** it's expensive.

····➤ (en parlant du temps) **il fait chaud/gris** it's hot/overcast.

□ **se faire** *verbe pronominal*

····➤ (obtenir, confectionner) make; **se ~ des amis** make friends; **se ~ un thé** make (oneself) a cup of tea.

····➤ **(se faire** + infinitif) **se ~ gronder** be scolded; **se ~ couper les cheveux** have one's hair cut.

····➤ (devenir) **il se fait tard** it's getting late.

····➤ (être d'usage) **ça ne se fait pas** it's not the done thing.

····➤ (emploi impersonnel) **comment se fait-il que tu sois ici?** how come you're here?

····➤ □ **se faire à** get used to; **je ne m'y fais pas** I can't get used to it.

····➤ □ **s'en faire** worry; **ne t'en fais pas** don't worry.

**!** Lorsque **faire** remplace un verbe plus précis, on traduira quelquefois par ce dernier: **faire une visite** *pay a visit*, **faire un nid** *build a nest*.

**faire-part** /fɛʀpaʀ/ *nm inv* announcement.

**fais** /fɛ/ ⇒FAIRE [33].

**faisan** /fəzɑ̃/ *nm* pheasant.

**faisceau** (*pl* **~x**) /fɛso/ *nm* (rayon) beam; (fagot) bundle.

**fait**, **~e** /fɛ, fɛt/ *a* done; (*fromage*) ripe; **~ pour** made for; **tout ~** ready made; **c'est bien ~ pour toi** it serves you right. ● *nm* fact; (événement) event; **au ~ (de)** informed (of); **de ce ~** therefore; **du ~ de** on

account of; ~ **divers** (trivial) news item; ~ **nouveau** new development; **prendre qn sur le** ~ catch sb in the act. ● ⇒FAIRE [33].

**faite** /fɛt/ *nm* top; (fig) peak.

**faites** /fɛt/ ⇒FAIRE [33].

**falaise** /falɛz/ *nf* cliff.

**falloir** /falwaʀ/ [34] *vi* **il faut qch/qn** we/you *etc.* need sth/so; **il lui faut du pain** he needs bread; **il faut rester** we/you *etc.* have to *ou* must stay; **il faut que j'y aille** I have to *ou* must go; **il faudrait que tu partes** you should leave; **il aurait fallu le faire** we/you *etc.* should have done it; **comme il faut** (*manger, se tenir*) properly; (*personne*) respectable, proper. □ **s'en** ~ *vpr* **il s'en est fallu de peu qu'il gagne** he nearly won; **il s'en faut de beaucoup que je sois** I am far from being.

**falsifier** /falsifje/ [45] *vt* falsify; (*signature, monnaie*) forge.

**famé**, ~**e** /fame/ *a* **mal** ~ disreputable, seedy.

**fameux**, **-euse** /famø, -z/ *a* famous; (excellent 🅘) first-rate.

**familial**, ~**e** (*mpl* **-iaux**) /familjal, -jo/ *a* family.

**familiale** /familjal/ *nf* estate car; (US) station wagon.

**familiariser** /familjaʀize/ [1] *vt* familiarize (**avec** with). □ **se** ~ *vpr* familiarize oneself.

**familier**, **-ière** /familje, -jɛʀ/ *a* familiar; (amical) informal.

**famille** /famij/ *nf* family; **en** ~ with one's family.

**famine** /famin/ *nf* famine.

**fanatique** /fanatik/ *a* fanatical. ● *nmf* fanatic.

**fanfare** /fɑ̃faʀ/ *nf* brass band; (musique) fanfare.

**fantaisie** /fɑ̃tezi/ *nf* imagination, fantasy; (caprice) whim; **(de)** ~ (*boutons etc.*) fancy. **fantaisiste** *a* unorthodox; (*personne*) eccentric.

**fantasme** /fɑ̃tasm/ *nm* fantasy.

**fantastique** /fɑ̃tastik/ *a* fantastic.

**fantôme** /fɑ̃tom/ *nm* ghost; **cabinet(-)**~ (Pol) shadow cabinet.

**faon** /fɑ̃/ *nm* fawn.

**FAQ** *abrév f* (**Foire aux questions**) (Internet) FAQ, Frequently Asked Questions.

**farce** /faʀs/ *nf* (practical) joke; (Théât) farce; (hachis) stuffing.

**farcir** /faʀsiʀ/ [2] *vt* stuff.

**fard** /faʀ/ *nm* make-up; ~ **à paupières** eye-shadow; **piquer un** ~ blush.

**fardeau** (*pl* ~**x**) /faʀdo/ *nm* burden.

**farfelu**, ~**e** /faʀfəly/ *a* & *nmf* eccentric.

**farine** /faʀin/ *nf* flour. **farineux**, **-euse** *a* floury. **farineux** *nmpl* starchy food.

**farouche** /faʀuʃ/ *a* shy; (peu sociable) unsociable; (violent) fierce.

**fascicule** /fasikyl/ *nm* (brochure) booklet; (partie d'un ouvrage) fascicule.

**fasciner** /fasine/ [1] *vt* fascinate.

**fascisme** /faʃism/ *nm* fascism.

**fasse** /fas/ ⇒FAIRE [33].

**fast-food** /fastfud/ *nm* fast-food place.

**fastidieux**, **-ieuse** /fastidjø, -z/ *a* tedious.

**fatal**, ~**e** (*mpl* ~**s**) /fatal/ *a* inevitable; (mortel) fatal. **fatalité** *nf* (destin) fate.

**fatigant**, ~**e** /fatigɑ̃, -t/ *a* tiring; (ennuyeux) tiresome.

**fatigue** /fatig/ *nf* fatigue, tiredness.

**fatigué**, ~**e** /fatige/ *a* tired.

**fatiguer** /fatige/ [1] *vt* tire; (*yeux, moteur*) strain. ● *vi* (*moteur*) labour. □ **se ~** *vpr* get tired, tire (**de** of).

**faubourg** /fobuʀ/ *nm* suburb.

**faucher** /foʃe/ [1] *vt* (*herbe*) mow; (voler 🅃) pinch; **~ qn** (*véhicule, tir*) mow sb down.

**faucon** /fokɔ̃/ *nm* falcon, hawk.

**faudra, faudrait** /fodʀa, fodʀɛ/ ⇒FALLOIR [34].

**faufiler (se)** /(sə)fofile/ [1] *vpr* edge one's way, squeeze.

**faune** /fon/ *nf* wildlife, fauna.

**faussaire** /fosɛʀ/ *nmf* forger.

**fausse** /fos/ ⇒FAUX[2].

**fausser** /fose/ [1] *vt* buckle; (fig) distort; **~ compagnie à qn** give sb the slip.

**faut** /fo/ ⇒FALLOIR [34].

**faute** /fot/ *nf* mistake; (responsabilité) fault; (délit) offence; (péché) sin; **en ~** at fault; **~ de** for want of; **~ de quoi** failing which; **sans ~** without fail; **~ de frappe** typing error; **~ de goût** bad taste; **~ professionnelle** professional misconduct.

**fauteuil** /fotœj/ *nm* armchair; (de président) chair; (Théât) seat; **~ roulant** wheelchair.

**fautif, -ive** /fotif, -v/ *a* guilty; (faux) faulty. ● *nm,f* guilty party.

**fauve** /fov/ *a* (couleur) fawn, tawny. ● *nm* wild cat.

**faux[1]** /fo/ *nf* scythe.

**faux[2], fausse** /fo, fos/ *a* false; (falsifié) fake, forged; (*numéro, calcul*) wrong; (*voix*) out of tune; **c'est ~!** that is wrong!; **~ témoignage** perjury; **faire ~ bond à qn** stand sb up; **fausse couche** miscarriage; **~ frais** incidental expenses. ● *adv* (*chanter*) out of tune. ● *nm* forgery. **faux-filet** (*pl* **~s**) *nm* sirloin.

**faveur** /favœʀ/ *nf* favour; **de ~** (*régime*) preferential; **en ~ de** in favour of.

**favorable** /favɔʀabl/ *a* favourable.

**favori, ~te** /favɔʀi, -t/ *a & nmf* favourite. **favoriser** [1] *vt* favour.

**fax** /faks/ *nm* fax. **faxer** [1] *vt* fax.

**fébrile** /febʀil/ *a* feverish.

**fécond, ~e** /fekɔ̃, -d/ *a* fertile. **féconder** [1] *vt* fertilize. **fécondité** *nf* fertility.

**fédéral, ~e** (*mpl* **-aux**) /fedeʀal, -o/ *a* federal. **fédération** *nf* federation.

**fée** /fe/ *nf* fairy. **féerie** *nf* magical spectacle. **féerique** *a* magical.

**feindre** /fɛ̃dʀ/ [22] *vt* feign; **~ de** pretend to.

**fêler** /fele/ [1] *vt* crack. □ **se ~** *vpr* crack.

**félicitations** /felisitasjɔ̃/ *nfpl* congratulations (**pour** on). **féliciter** [1] *vt* congratulate (**de** on).

**félin, ~e** /felɛ̃, -in/ *a & nm* feline.

**femelle** /fəmɛl/ *a & nf* female.

**féminin, ~e** /feminɛ̃, -in/ *a* feminine; (*sexe*) female; (*mode, équipe*) women's. ● *nm* feminine. **féministe** *nmf* feminist.

**femme** /fam/ *nf* woman; (épouse) wife; **~ au foyer** housewife; **~ de chambre** chambermaid; **~ de ménage** cleaning lady.

**fémur** /femyʀ/ *nm* thigh-bone.

**fendre** /fɑ̃dʀ/ [3] *vt* (couper) split; (fissurer) crack. □ **se ~** *vpr* crack.

**fenêtre** /fənɛtʀ/ *nf* window.

**fenouil** /fənuj/ *nm* fennel.

**fente** /fɑ̃t/ *nf* (ouverture) slit, slot; (fissure) crack.

**féodal, ~e** (*mpl* **-aux**) /feɔdal, -o/ *a* feudal.

**fer** /fɛʀ/ *nm* iron; ~ **(à repasser)** iron; ~ **à cheval** horseshoe; ~ **de lance** spearhead; ~ **forgé** wrought iron.

**fera**, **ferait** /fəʀa, fəʀɛ/ ⇒FAIRE [33].

**férié**, ~**e** /feʀje/ *a* **jour** ~ public holiday.

**ferme** /fɛʀm/ *nf* farm; (maison) farm(house). ● *a* firm. ● *adv* (*travailler*) hard.

**fermé**, ~**e** /fɛʀme/ *a* closed; (*gaz, radio*) off.

**fermenter** /fɛʀmɑ̃te/ [1] *vi* ferment.

**fermer** /fɛʀme/ [1] *vt/i* close, shut; (cesser d'exploiter) close *ou* shut down; (*gaz, robinet*) turn off. □ **se** ~ *vpr* close, shut.

**fermeté** /fɛʀməte/ *nf* firmness.

**fermeture** /fɛʀmətyʀ/ *nf* closing; (dispositif) catch; ~ **annuelle** annual closure; ~ **éclair®** zip(-fastener); (US) zipper.

**fermier**, **-ière** /fɛʀmje, -jɛʀ/ *a* farm. ● *nm* farmer. **fermière** *nf* farmer's wife

**féroce** /feʀɔs/ *a* ferocious.

**ferraille** /fɛʀɑj/ *nf* scrap-iron.

**ferrer** /fɛʀe/ [1] *vt* (*cheval*) shoe.

**ferroviaire** /fɛʀɔvjɛʀ/ *a* rail(way).

**ferry** /fɛʀi/ *nm* ferry.

**fertile** /fɛʀtil/ *a* fertile; ~ **en** (fig) rich in. **fertiliser** [1] *vt* fertilize. **fertilité** *nf* fertility.

**fervent**, ~**e** /fɛʀvɑ̃, -t/ *a* fervent. ● *nm,f* enthusiast (**de** of).

**fesse** /fɛs/ *nf* buttock. **fessée** *nf* spanking, smack.

**festin** /fɛstɛ̃/ *nm* feast.

**festival** (*pl* ~**s**) /fɛstival/ *nm* festival.

**fêtard**, ~**e** /fɛtaʀ, -d/ *nm,f* Ⓘ party animal.

**fête** /fɛt/ *nf* holiday; (religieuse) feast; (du nom) name-day; (réception) party; (en famille) celebration; (foire) fair; (folklorique) festival; ~ **des Mères** Mother's Day; ~ **foraine** fun-fair; **faire la** ~ live it up; **les** ~**s (de fin d'année)** the Christmas season. **fêter** [1] *vt* celebrate; (*personne*) give a celebration for.

**fétiche** /fetiʃ/ *nm* fetish; (fig) mascot.

**feu**[1] (*pl* ~**x**) /fø/ *nm* fire; (lumière) light; (de réchaud) burner; **à** ~ **doux**/**vif** on a low/high heat; ~ **rouge**/**vert**/**orange** red/green/amber light; **aux** ~**x, tournez à droite** turn right at the traffic lights; **avez-vous du** ~**?** (pour cigarette) have you got a light?; **au** ~**!** fire!; **mettre le** ~ **à** set fire to; **prendre** ~ catch fire; **jouer avec le** ~ play with fire; **ne pas faire long** ~ not last; ~ **d'artifice** firework display; ~ **de joie** bonfire; ~ **de position** sidelight.

**feu**[2] /fø/ *a inv* (mort) late.

**feuillage** /fœjaʒ/ *nm* foliage.

**feuille** /fœj/ *nf* leaf; (de papier) sheet; (formulaire) form; ~ **d'impôts** tax return; ~ **de paie** payslip.

**feuilleté**, ~**e** /fœjte/ *a* **pâte** ~**e** puff pastry. ● *nm* savoury pasty.

**feuilleter** /fœjte/ [1] *vt* leaf through.

**feuilleton** /fœjtɔ̃/ *nm* (à suivre) serial; (histoire complète) series.

**feutre** /føtʀ/ *nm* felt; (chapeau) felt hat; (crayon) felt-tip (pen).

**fève** /fɛv/ *nf* broad bean.

**février** /fevʀije/ *nm* February.

**fiable** /fjabl/ *a* reliable.

**fiançailles** /fjɑ̃saj/ *nfpl* engagement.

**fiancé**, ~**e** /fjɑ̃se/ *a* engaged. ● *nm* fiancé. **fiancée** *nf* fiancée. **fiancer (se)** [10] *vpr* become engaged (**avec** to).

**fibre** /fibʀ/ *nf* fibre; ~ **de verre** fibreglass.

**ficeler** /fisle/ [38] *vt* tie up.

**ficelle** /fisɛl/ *nf* string.

**fiche** /fiʃ/ *nf* (index) card; (formulaire) form, slip; (Électr) plug.

**ficher**[1] /fiʃe/ [1] *vt* (enfoncer) drive (**dans** into).

**ficher**[2] /fiʃe/ [1] ⓘ *vt* (faire) do; (donner) give; (mettre) put; ~ **le camp** clear off. □ **se** ~ **de** *vpr* make fun of; **il s'en fiche** he couldn't care less.

**fichier** /fiʃje/ *nm* file.

**fichu**, ~**e** /fiʃy/ *a* ⓘ (mauvais) rotten; (raté) done for; **mal** ~ terrible.

**fictif**, **-ive** /fiktif, -v/ *a* fictitious. **fiction** *nf* fiction.

**fidèle** /fidɛl/ *a* faithful. ● *nmf* (client) regular; (Relig) believer; ~**s** (à l'église) congregation. **fidélité** *nf* fidelity.

**fier**[1], **fière** /fjɛʀ/ *a* proud (**de** of).

**fier**[2] (**se**) /(sə)fje/ [45] *vpr* **se** ~ **à** trust.

**fierté** /fjɛʀte/ *nf* pride.

**fièvre** /fjɛvʀ/ *nf* fever; **avoir de la** ~ have a temperature; ~ **aphteuse** *nf* foot-and-mouth disease. **fiévreux**, **-euse** *a* feverish.

**figer** /fiʒe/ [40] *vi* (*graisse*) congeal; (*sang*) clot; **figé sur place** frozen to the spot. □ **se** ~ *vpr* (*personne, sourire*) freeze; (*graisse*) congeal; (*sang*) clot.

**figue** /fig/ *nf* fig.

**figurant**, ~**e** /figyʀɑ̃, -t/ *nm,f* (au cinéma) extra.

**figure** /figyʀ/ *nf* face; (forme, personnage) figure; (illustration) picture.

**figuré**, ~**e** /figyʀe/ *a* (*sens*) figurative.

**figurer** /figyʀe/ [1] *vi* appear. ● *vt* represent. □ **se** ~ *vpr* imagine.

**fil** /fil/ *nm* thread; (métallique, électrique) wire; (de couteau) edge; (à coudre) cotton; **au** ~ **de** with the passing of; **au** ~ **de l'eau** with the current; ~ **de fer** wire; **au bout du** ~ ⓘ on the phone.

**file** /fil/ *nf* line; (voie: Auto) lane; ~ **(d'attente)** queue; (US) line; **en** ~ **indienne** in single file.

**filer** /file/ [1] *vt* spin; (suivre) shadow; ~ **qch à qn** ⓘ slip sb sth. ● *vi* (*bas*) ladder, run; (*liquide*) run; (aller vite ⓘ) speed along, fly by; (partir ⓘ) dash off; (disparaître ⓘ) ~ **entre les mains** slip through one's fingers; ~ **doux** do as one's told.

**filet** /filɛ/ *nm* net; (d'eau) trickle; (de viande) fillet; ~ **(à bagages)** (luggage) rack; ~ **à provisions** string bag (*for shopping*).

**filiale** /filjal/ *nf* subsidiary (company).

**filière** /filjɛʀ/ *nf* (official) channels; (de trafiquants) network; **passer par** *ou* **suivre la** ~ (*employé*) work one's way up.

**fille** /fij/ *nf* girl; (opposé à fils) daughter. **fillette** *nf* little girl.

**filleul** /fijœl/ *nm* godson.

**filleule** /fijœl/ *nf* god-daughter.

**film** /film/ *nm* film; ~ **d'épouvante/muet/parlant** horror/silent/talking film; ~ **dramatique** drama. **filmer** [1] *vt* film.

**filon** /filɔ̃/ *nm* (Géol) seam; (travail lucratif ⓘ) money spinner; **avoir trouvé le bon** ~ be onto a good thing.

**fils** /fis/ *nm* son.

**filtre** /filtʀ/ *nm* filter. **filtrer** [1] *vt/i* filter; (*personne*) screen.

**fin**[1] /fɛ̃/ *nf* end; **à la** ~ finally; **en** ~ **de compte** all things considered; ~ **de semaine** weekend; **mettre** ~ **à** put an end to; **prendre** ~ come to an end.

**fin²**, **~e** /fɛ̃, in/ *a* fine; (*tranche, couche*) thin; (*taille*) slim; (*plat*) exquisite; (*esprit, vue*) sharp; **~es herbes** mixed herbs. ● *adv* (*couper*) finely.

**final**, **~e** (*mpl* **-aux**) /final, -o/ *a* final.

**finale** /final/ *nm* (Mus) finale. ● *nf* (Sport) final; (Gram) final syllable. **finalement** *adv* finally; (somme toute) after all. **finaliste** *nmf* finalist.

**finance** /finɑ̃s/ *nf* finance. **financer** [10] *vt* finance.

**financier**, **-ière** /finɑ̃sje, -jɛʀ/ *a* financial. ● *nm* financier.

**finesse** /finɛs/ *nf* fineness; (de taille) slimness; (acuité) sharpness; **~s** (de langue) niceties.

**finir** /finiʀ/ [2] *vt/i* finish, end; (arrêter) stop; (manger) finish (up); **en ~ avec** have done with; **~ par faire** end up doing; **ça va mal ~** it will turn out badly.

**finlandais**, **~e** /fɛ̃lɑ̃dɛ, -ɛz/ *a* Finnish. **F~**, **~e** *nm,f* Finn.

**Finlando** /fɛ̃lɑ̃d/ *nf* Finland.

**finnois**, **~e** /finwa/ *a* Finnish. ● *nm* (Ling) Finnish.

**firme** /fiʀm/ *nf* firm.

**fisc** /fisk/ *nm* tax authorities. **fiscal**, **~e** (*mpl* **-aux**) *a* tax, fiscal. **fiscalité** *nf* tax system.

**fissure** /fisyʀ/ *nf* crack.

**fixe** /fiks/ *a* fixed; (stable) steady; **à heure ~** at a set time; **menu à prix ~** set menu. ● *nm* basic pay.

**fixer** /fikse/ [1] *vt* fix; **~ (du regard)** stare at; **être fixé** (*personne*) have made up one's mind. ◻ **se ~** *vpr* (s'attacher) be attached; (s'installer) settle down.

**flacon** /flakɔ̃/ *nm* bottle.

**flagrant**, **~e** /flagʀɑ̃, -t/ *a* flagrant, blatant; **en ~ délit** in the act.

**flair** /flɛʀ/ *nm* (sense of) smell; (fig) intuition.

**flamand**, **~e** /flamɑ̃, -d/ *a* Flemish. ● *nm* (Ling) Flemish. **F~**, **~e** *nm,f* Fleming.

**flamant** /flamɑ̃/ *nm* flamingo.

**flambeau** (*pl* **~x**) /flɑ̃bo/ *nm* torch.

**flambée** /flɑ̃be/ *nf* blaze; (fig) explosion.

**flamber** /flɑ̃be/ [1] *vi* blaze; (*prix*) shoot up. ● *vt* (*aiguille*) sterilize; (*volaille*) singe.

**flamme** /flam/ *nf* flame; (fig) ardour; **en ~s** ablaze.

**flan** /flɑ̃/ *nm* custard tart.

**flanc** /flɑ̃/ *nm* side; (d'animal, d'armée) flank.

**flâner** /flɑne/ [1] *vi* stroll. **flânerie** *nf* stroll.

**flanquer** /flɑ̃ke/ [1] *vt* flank; (jeter [!]) chuck; (donner [!]) give; **~ à la porte** kick out.

**flaque** /flak/ *nf* (d'eau) puddle; (de sang) pool.

**flash** (*pl* **~es**) /flaʃ/ *nm* (Photo) flash; (information) news flash; **~ publicitaire** commercial.

**flatter** /flate/ [1] *vt* flatter. ◻ **se ~ de** *vpr* pride oneself on.

**flatteur**, **-euse** /flatœʀ, -øz/ *a* flattering. ● *nm, f* flatterer.

**fléau** (*pl* **~x**) /fleo/ *nm* (désastre) scourge; (personne) pest.

**flèche** /flɛʃ/ *nf* arrow; (de clocher) spire; **monter en ~** spiral; **partir en ~** shoot off.

**flécher** /fleʃe/ [14] *vt* mark *ou* signpost (with arrows). **fléchette** *nf* dart.

**fléchir** /fleʃiʀ/ [2] *vt* bend; (*personne*) move, sway. ● *vi* (faiblir) weaken; (*prix*) fall; (*poutre*) sag, bend.

**flemme** /flɛm/ *nf* Ⓘ laziness; **j'ai la ~ de faire** I can't be bothered doing.

**flétrir (se)** /(sə)fletʀiʀ/ [2] *vpr* (*plante*) wither; (*fruit*) shrivel; (*beauté*) fade.

**fleur** /flœʀ/ *nf* flower; **à ~ de terre/d'eau** just above the ground/water; **à ~s** flowery; **~ de l'âge** prime of life; **en ~s** in flower.

**fleurir** /flœʀiʀ/ [2] *vi* flower; (*arbre*) blossom; (fig) flourish. ● *vt* decorate with flowers. **fleuriste** *nmf* florist.

**fleuve** /flœv/ *nm* river.

**flic** /flik/ *nm* Ⓘ cop.

**flipper** /flipœʀ/ *nm* pinball (machine).

**flirter** /flœʀte/ [1] *vi* flirt.

**flocon** /flɔkɔ̃/ *nm* flake.

**flore** /flɔʀ/ *nf* flora.

**florissant**, **~e** /flɔʀisɑ̃, -t/ *a* flourishing.

**flot** /flo/ *nm* flood, stream; **être à ~** be afloat; **les ~s** the waves.

**flottant**, **~e** /flɔtɑ̃, -t/ *a* (*vêtement*) loose; (indécis) indecisive.

**flotte** /flɔt/ *nf* fleet; (pluie Ⓘ) rain; (eau Ⓘ) water.

**flottement** /flɔtmɑ̃/ *nm* (incertitude) indecision.

**flotter** /flɔte/ [1] *vi* float; (*drapeau*) flutter; (*nuage, parfum, pensées*) drift; (pleuvoir Ⓘ) rain. **flotteur** *nm* float.

**flou**, **~e** /flu/ *a* out of focus; (fig) vague.

**fluctuer** /flyktɥe/ [1] *vi* fluctuate.

**fluet**, **~te** /flyɛ, -t/ *a* thin.

**fluide** /flɥid/ *a & nm* fluid.

**fluor** /flyɔʀ/ *nm* (pour les dents) fluoride.

**fluorescent**, **~e** /flyɔʀɛsɑ̃, -t/ *a* fluorescent.

**flûte** /flyt/ *nf* flute; (verre) champagne glass.

**fluvial**, **~e** (*mpl* **-iaux**) /flyvjal, -jo/ *a* river.

**flux** /fly/ *nm* flow; **~ et reflux** ebb and flow.

**FM** *abrév f* (**frequency modulation**) FM.

**fœtus** /fetys/ *nm* foetus.

**foi** /fwa/ *nf* faith; **être de bonne/mauvaise ~** be acting in good/bad faith; **ma ~!** well (indeed)!

**foie** /fwa/ *nm* liver.

**foin** /fwɛ̃/ *nm* hay.

**foire** /fwaʀ/ *nf* fair; **faire la ~** Ⓘ live it up.

**fois** /fwa/ *nf* time; **une ~** once; **deux ~** twice; **à la ~** at the same time; **des ~** (parfois) sometimes; **une ~ pour toutes** once and for all.

**fol** /fɔl/ ⇒FOU.

**folie** /fɔli/ *nf* madness; (bêtise) foolish thing, folly; **faire une ~, faire des ~s** be extravagant.

**folklore** /fɔlklɔʀ/ *nm* folklore. **folklorique** *a* folk; Ⓘ eccentric.

**folle** /fɔl/ ⇒FOU.

**foncé**, **~e** /fɔ̃se/ *a* dark.

**foncer** /fɔ̃se/ [10] *vt* darken. ● *vi* (s'assombrir) darken; (aller vite Ⓘ) dash along; **~ sur** Ⓘ charge at.

**foncier**, **-ière** /fɔ̃sje, -jɛʀ/ *a* fundamental; (Comm) real estate.

**fonction** /fɔ̃ksjɔ̃/ *nf* function; (emploi) position; **~s** (obligations) duties; **en ~ de** according to; **~ publique** civil service; **voiture de ~** company car. **fonctionnaire** *nmf* civil servant. **fonctionnement** *nm* working.

**fonctionner** /fɔ̃ksjɔne/ [1] *vi* work; **faire ~** work.

**fond** /fɔ̃/ *nm* bottom; (de salle, magasin, etc.) back; (essentiel) basis; (contenu) content; (plan) background; (Sport) long-distance run-

ning; **à ~** thoroughly; **au ~** basically; **de ~** (*bruit*) background; **de ~ en comble** from top to bottom; **au** *ou* **dans le ~** really; **~ de teint** foundation, make-up base.

**fondamental**, **~e** (*mpl* **-aux**) /fɔ̃damɑ̃tal, -o/ *a* fundamental.

**fondateur**, **-trice** /fɔ̃datœʀ, -tʀis/ *nm,f* founder. **fondation** *nf* foundation.

**fonder** /fɔ̃de/ [1] *vt* found; (baser) base (**sur** on); **(bien) fondé** well-founded. □ **se ~ sur** *vpr* be guided by, be based on.

**fonderie** /fɔ̃dʀi/ *nf* foundry.

**fondre** /fɔ̃dʀ/ [3] *vt/i* melt; (dans l'eau) dissolve; (mélanger) merge; **faire ~** melt; dissolve; **~ en larmes** burst into tears; **~ sur** swoop on. □ **se ~** *vpr* merge.

**fonds** /fɔ̃/ *nm* fund; **~ de commerce** business. ● *nmpl* (capitaux) funds.

**fondu**, **~e** /fɔ̃dy/ *a* melted; (métal) molten.

**font** /fɔ̃/ ⇒FAIRE [33].

**fontaine** /fɔ̃tɛn/ *nf* fountain; (source) spring.

**fonte** /fɔ̃t/ *nf* melting; (fer) cast iron; **~ des neiges** thaw.

**foot** /fut/ *nm* [!] football.

**football** /futbɔl/ *nm* football.

**footing** /futiŋ/ *nm* jogging.

**forain** /fɔʀɛ̃/ *nm* fairground entertainer; **marchand ~** stall-holder.

**forçat** /fɔʀsa/ *nm* convict.

**force** /fɔʀs/ *nf* force; (physique) strength; (hydraulique etc.) power; **~s** (physiques) strength; **à ~ de** by sheer force of; **de ~**, **par la ~** by force; **~ de dissuasion** deterrent; **~ de frappe** strike force, deterrent; **~ de l'âge** prime of life; **~s de l'ordre** police (force); **~s de marché** market forces.

**forcé**, **~e** /fɔʀse/ *a* forced; (inévitable) inevitable; **c'est ~ qu'il fasse** [!] he's bound to do. **forcément** *adv* necessarily; (évidemment) obviously.

**forcené**, **~e** /fɔʀsəne/ *a* frenzied. ● *nm,f* maniac.

**forcer** /fɔʀse/ [10] *vt* force (**à faire** to do); (*voix*) strain; **~ la dose** [!] overdo it. ● *vi* force; (exagérer) overdo it. □ **se ~** *vpr* force oneself.

**forer** /fɔʀe/ [1] *vt* drill.

**forestier**, **-ière** /fɔʀɛstje, -jɛʀ/ *a* forest. ● *nm,f* forestry worker.

**forêt** /fɔʀɛ/ *nf* forest.

**forfait** /fɔʀfɛ/ *nm* (Comm) (prix fixe) fixed price; (offre promotionnelle) package. **forfaitaire** *a* (*prix*) fixed.

**forger** /fɔʀʒe/ [40] *vt* forge; (inventer) make up.

**forgeron** /fɔʀʒəʀɔ̃/ *nm* blacksmith.

**formaliser (se)** /(sə)fɔʀmalize/ [1] *vpr* take offence (**de** at).

**formalité** /fɔʀmalite/ *nf* formality.

**format** /fɔʀma/ *nm* format. **formater** [1] *vt* (Ordinat) format.

**formation** /fɔʀmasjɔ̃/ *nf* formation; (professionnelle) training; (culture) education; **~ permanente** *ou* **continue** continuing education.

**forme** /fɔʀm/ *nf* form; (contour) shape, form; **~s** (de femme) figure; **être en ~** be in good shape, be on form; **en ~ de** in the shape of; **en bonne et due ~** in due form.

**formel**, **~le** /fɔʀmɛl/ *a* formal; (catégorique) positive.

**former** /fɔʀme/ [1] *vt* form; (instruire) train. □ **se ~** *vpr* form.

**formidable** /fɔʀmidabl/ *a* fantastic.

**formulaire** /fɔRmylɛR/ *nm* form.

**formule** /fɔRmyl/ *nf* formula; (expression) expression; (feuille) form; **~ de politesse** polite phrase, letter ending. **formuler** [1] *vt* formulate.

**fort**, **~e** /fɔR, -t/ *a* strong; (grand) big; (*pluie*) heavy; (*bruit*) loud; (*pente*) steep; (*élève*) clever; **au plus ~ de** at the height of; **c'est une ~e tête** she/he's headstrong. ● *adv* (*frapper*) hard; (*parler*) loud; (très) very; (beaucoup) very much. ● *nm* (atout) strong point; (Mil) fort.

**fortifiant** /fɔRtifjɑ̃/ *nm* tonic. **fortifier** [45] *vt* fortify.

**fortune** /fɔRtyn/ *nf* fortune; **de ~** (improvisé) makeshift; **faire ~** make one's fortune.

**forum** /fɔRɔm/ *nm* forum; **~ de discussion** (Internet) newsgroup.

**fosse** /fos/ *nf* pit; (tombe) grave; **~ d'orchestre** orchestra pit; **~ septique** septic tank.

**fossé** /fose/ *nm* ditch; (fig) gulf; **~ numérique** digital divide.

**fossette** /fosɛt/ *nf* dimple.

**fossile** /fosil/ *nm* fossil.

**fou** (**fol** *before vowel or mute h*), **folle** /fu, fɔl/ *a* mad; (*course, regard*) wild; (énorme [I]) tremendous; **~ de** crazy about; **le ~ rire** the giggles. ● *nm* madman; (bouffon) jester. **folle** *nf* madwoman.

**foudre** /fudR/ *nf* lightning.

**foudroyant**, **~e** /fudRwajɑ̃, -t/ *a* (*mort, maladie*) violent.

**foudroyer** /fudRwaje/ [31] *vt* (*orage*) strike; (*maladie etc.*) strike down; **~ qn du regard** look daggers at sb.

**fouet** /fwɛ/ *nm* whip; (Culin) whisk.

**fougère** /fuʒɛR/ *nf* fern.

**fougue** /fug/ *nf* ardour. **fougueux**, **-euse** *a* ardent.

**fouille** /fuj/ *nf* search; (Archéol) excavation.

**fouiller** /fuje/ [1] *vt/i* search; (creuser) dig; **~ dans** (*tiroir*) rummage through.

**fouillis** /fuji/ *nm* jumble.

**foulard** /fulaR/ *nm* scarf.

**foule** /ful/ *nf* crowd; **une ~ de** (fig) a mass of.

**foulée** /fule/ *nf* stride; **il l'a fait dans la ~** he did it while he was at *ou* about it.

**fouler** /fule/ [1] *vt* (*raisin*) press; (*sol*) set foot on; **~ qch aux pieds** trample sth underfoot; (fig) ride roughshod over sth. □ **se ~** *vpr* **se ~ le poignet/le pied** sprain one's wrist/foot; **ne pas se ~** [I] not strain oneself.

**four** /fuR/ *nm* oven; (de potier) kiln; (Théât) flop; **~ à micro-ondes** microwave oven; **~ crématoire** crematorium.

**fourbe** /fuRb/ *a* deceitful.

**fourche** /fuRʃ/ *nf* fork; (à foin) pitchfork. **fourchette** *nf* fork; (Comm) bracket, range.

**fourgon** /fuRgɔ̃/ *nm* van.

**fourmi** /fuRmi/ *nf* ant; **avoir des ~s** have pins and needles.

**fourmiller** /fuRmije/ [1] *vi* swarm (**de** with).

**fourneau** (*pl* **~x**) /fuRno/ *nm* stove.

**fourni**, **~e** /fuRni/ *a* (épais) thick.

**fournir** /fuRniR/ [2] *vt* supply, provide; (*client*) supply; (*effort*) put in; **~ à qn** supply sb with. □ **se ~ chez** *vpr* shop at.

**fournisseur** /fuRnisœR/ *nm* supplier; **~ d'accès à l'Internet** Internet service provider.

**fourniture** /fuRnityR/ *nf* supply.

**fourrage** /fuRaʒ/ *nm* fodder.

**fourré**, **~e** /fuʀe/ *a* (*vêtement*) fur-lined; (*gâteau etc.*) filled (*with jam, cream, etc.*). ● *nm* thicket.

**fourre-tout** /fuʀtu/ *nm inv* (sac) holdall.

**fourreur** /fuʀœʀ/ *nm* furrier.

**fourrière** /fuʀjɛʀ/ *nf* (lieu) pound.

**fourrure** /fuʀyʀ/ *nf* fur.

**foutre** /futʀ/ [3] *vt* ⊠ = **ficher**[2] [1].

**foutu**, **~e** /futy/ *a* ⊠ = **fichu.**

**foyer** /fwaje/ *nm* home; (âtre) hearth; (club) club; (d'étudiants) hostel; (Théât) foyer; (Photo) focus; (centre) centre.

**fracas** /fʀaka/ *nm* din; (de train) roar; (d'objet qui tombe) crash. **fracassant**, **~e** *a* (bruyant) deafening; (violent) shattering.

**fraction** /fʀaksjɔ̃/ *nf* fraction.

**fracture** /fʀaktyʀ/ *nf* fracture; **~ du poignet** fractured wrist.

**fragile** /fʀaʒil/ *a* fragile; (*peau*) sensitive; (*cœur*) weak. **fragilité** *nf* fragility.

**fragment** /fʀagmɑ̃/ *nm* bit, fragment. **fragmenter** [1] *vt* split, fragment.

**fraîchement** /fʀɛʃmɑ̃/ *adv* (récemment) freshly; (avec froideur) coolly. **fraîcheur** *nf* coolness; (nouveauté) freshness. **fraîchir** [2] *vi* freshen, become colder.

**frais**[1], **fraîche** /fʀɛ, -ʃ/ *a* fresh; (*temps, accueil*) cool; (*peinture*) wet; **~ et dispos** fresh; **il fait ~** it is cool. ● *adv* (récemment) newly, freshly. ● *nm* **mettre au ~** put in a cool place; **prendre le ~** get some fresh air.

**frais**[2] /fʀɛ/ *nmpl* expenses; (droits) fees; **aux ~ de** at the expense of; **faire des ~** spend a lot of money; **~ généraux** (Comm) overheads, running expenses; **~ de scolarité** school fees.

**fraise** /fʀɛz/ *nf* strawberry. **fraisier** *nm* strawberry plant; (gâteau) strawberry gateau.

**framboise** /fʀɑ̃bwaz/ *nf* raspberry. **framboisier** *nm* raspberry bush.

**franc**, **franche** /fʀɑ̃, -ʃ/ *a* frank; (*regard*) frank, candid; (*cassure*) clean; (net) clear; (libre) free; (véritable) downright. ● *nm* franc.

**français**, **~e** /fʀɑ̃sɛ, -z/ *a* French. ● *nm* (Ling) French. **F~**, **~e** *nm,f* Frenchman, Frenchwoman.

**France** /fʀɑ̃s/ *nf* France.

**franchement** /fʀɑ̃ʃmɑ̃/ *adv* frankly; (nettement) clearly; (tout à fait) really.

**franchir** /fʀɑ̃ʃiʀ/ [2] *vt* (*obstacle*) get over; (*distance*) cover; (*limite*) exceed; (traverser) cross.

**franchise** /fʀɑ̃ʃiz/ *nf* (qualité) frankness; (Comm) franchise; (exemption) exemption; **~ douanière** exemption from duties.

**franc-maçon** (*pl* **francs-maçons**) /fʀɑ̃masɔ̃/ *nm* Freemason. **franc-maçonnerie** *nf* Freemasonry.

**franco** /fʀɑ̃ko/ *adv* postage paid.

**francophone** /fʀɑ̃kɔfɔn/ *a* French-speaking. ● *nmf* French speaker.

**franc-parler** /fʀɑ̃paʀle/ *nm inv* outspokenness.

**frange** /fʀɑ̃ʒ/ *nf* fringe.

**frappe** /fʀap/ *nf* (de texte) typing.

**frappé**, **~e** /fʀape/ *a* chilled.

**frapper** /fʀape/ [1] *vt/i* strike; (battre) hit, strike; (*monnaie*) mint; (à la porte) knock, bang; **frappé de panique** panic-stricken.

**fraternel**, **~le** /fʀatɛʀnɛl/ *a* brotherly. **fraternité** *nf* brotherhood.

**fraude** /fʀod/ *nf* fraud; (à un examen) cheating; **passer qch en ~** smuggle sth in. **frauder** [1] *vt/i* cheat. **frauduleux, -euse** *a* fraudulent.

**frayer** /fʀeje/ [31] *vt* open up. □ **se ~** *vpr* **se ~ un passage** force one's way (**à travers, dans** through).

**frayeur** /fʀɛjœʀ/ *nf* fright.

**fredonner** /fʀədɔne/ [1] *vt* hum.

**free-lance** /fʀilɑ̃s/ *a & nmf* freelance.

**freezer** /fʀizœʀ/ *nm* freezer.

**frein** /fʀɛ̃/ *nm* brake; **mettre un ~ à** curb; **~ à main** hand brake.

**freiner** /fʀene/ [1] *vt* slow down; (modérer, enrayer) curb. ● *vi* (Auto) brake.

**frêle** /fʀɛl/ *a* frail.

**frelon** /fʀəlɔ̃/ *nm* hornet.

**frémir** /fʀemiʀ/ [2] *vi* shudder, shake; (*feuille, eau*) quiver.

**frêne** /fʀɛn/ *nm* ash.

**frénésie** /fʀenezi/ *nf* frenzy. **frénétique** *a* frenzied.

**fréquemment** /fʀekamɑ̃/ *adv* frequently. **fréquence** *nf* frequency. **fréquent, ~e** *a* frequent. **fréquentation** *nf* frequenting.

**fréquentations** /fʀekɑ̃tasjɔ̃/ *nfpl* acquaintances; **avoir de mauvaises ~** keep bad company.

**fréquenter** /fʀekɑ̃te/ [1] *vt* frequent; (*école*) attend; (*personne*) see.

**frère** /fʀɛʀ/ *nm* brother.

**fret** /fʀɛt/ *nm* freight.

**friand, ~e** /fʀijɑ̃, -d/ *a* **~ de** very fond of.

**friandise** /fʀijɑ̃diz/ *nf* sweet; (US) candy; (gâteau) cake.

**fric** /fʀik/ *nm* Ⓘ money.

**friction** /fʀiksjɔ̃/ *nf* friction; (massage) rub-down.

**frigidaire®** /fʀiʒidɛʀ/ *nm* refrigerator.

**frigo** /fʀigo/ *nm* Ⓘ fridge. **frigorifique** *a* (*vitrine etc.*) refrigerated.

**frileux, -euse** /fʀilø, -z/ *a* sensitive to cold.

**frime** /fʀim/ *nf* Ⓘ **c'est de la ~** it's all pretence; **pour la ~** for show.

**frimousse** /fʀimus/ *nf* face.

**fringale** /fʀɛ̃gal/ *nf* Ⓘ ravenous appetite.

**fringant, ~e** /fʀɛ̃gɑ̃, -t/ *a* dashing.

**fringues** /fʀɛ̃g/ *nfpl* Ⓘ gear.

**friper** /fʀipe/ [1] *vt* crumple, crease. □ **se ~** *vpr* crumple, crease.

**fripon, ~ne** /fʀipɔ̃, -ɔn/ *nm,f* rascal. ● *a* mischievous.

**fripouille** /fʀipuj/ *nf* rogue.

**frire** /fʀiʀ/ [56] *vt/i* fry; **faire ~** fry.

**frise** /fʀiz/ *nf* frieze.

**friser** /fʀize/ [1] *vt/i* (*cheveux*) curl; (*personne*) curl the hair of; **frisé** curly.

**frisson** /fʀisɔ̃/ *nm* (de froid) shiver; (de peur) shudder. **frissonner** [1] *vi* shiver; shudder.

**frit, ~e** /fʀi, -t/ *a* fried.

**frite** /fʀit/ *nf* chip; **avoir la ~** Ⓘ feel good.

**friteuse** /fʀitøz/ *nf* chip pan; (électrique) (deep) fryer.

**friture** /fʀityʀ/ *nf* fried fish; (huile) (frying) oil *ou* fat.

**frivole** /fʀivɔl/ *a* frivolous.

**froid, ~e** /fʀwa, -d/ *a & nm* cold; **avoir/prendre ~** be/catch cold; **il fait ~** it is cold. **froidement** *adv* coldly; (*calculer*) coolly. **froideur** *nf* coldness.

**froisser** /fʀwase/ [1] *vt* crumple; (fig) offend. □ **se ~** *vpr* crumple; (fig) take offence; **se ~ un muscle** strain a muscle.

**frôler** /fʀole/ [1] *vt* brush against, skim; (fig) come close to.

**fromage** /fʀɔmaʒ/ *nm* cheese.

**fromager**, **-ère** /fʀɔmaʒe, -ɛʀ/ *a* cheese. ● *nm,f* (fabricant) cheese-maker; (marchand) cheesemonger.

**froment** /fʀɔmɑ̃/ *nm* wheat.

**froncer** /fʀɔ̃se/ [10] *vt* gather; **~ les sourcils** frown.

**front** /fʀɔ̃/ *nm* forehead; (Mil, Pol) front; **de ~** at the same time; (de face) head-on; (côte à côte) abreast; **faire ~ à** face up to. **frontal**, **~e** (*mpl* **-aux**) *a* frontal; (Ordinat) front-end.

**frontalier**, **-ière** /fʀɔ̃talje, -jɛʀ/ *a* border; **travailleur ~** commuter from across the border.

**frontière** /fʀɔ̃tjɛʀ/ *nf* border, frontier.

**frottement** /fʀɔtmɑ̃/ *nm* rubbing; (Tech) friction. **frotter** [1] *vt/i* rub; (*allumette*) strike.

**frottis** /fʀɔti/ *nm* **~ vaginal** cervical smear.

**frousse** /fʀus/ *nf* [I] fear; **avoir la ~** [I] be scared.

**fructifier** /fʀyktifje/ [45] *vi* **faire ~** put to work.

**fructueux**, **-euse** /fʀyktɥø, -z/ *a* fruitful.

**frugal**, **~e** (*mpl* **-aux**) /fʀygal, -o/ *a* frugal.

**fruit** /fʀɥi/ *nm* fruit; **des ~s** (some) fruit; **~s de mer** seafood. **fruité**, **~e** *a* fruity.

**frustrant**, **~e** /fʀystʀɑ̃, -t/ *a* frustrating. **frustrer** [1] *vt* frustrate.

**fuel** /fjul/ *nm* fuel oil.

**fugitif**, **-ive** /fyʒitif, -v/ *a* (*passager*) fleeting. ● *nm,f* fugitive.

**fugue** /fyg/ *nf* (Mus) fugue; **faire une ~** run away.

**fuir** /fɥiʀ/ [35] *vi* flee, run away; (*eau, robinet, etc.*) leak. ● *vt* (quitter) flee; (éviter) shun.

**fuite** /fɥit/ *nf* flight; (de liquide, d'une nouvelle) leak; **en ~** on the run; **mettre en ~** put to flight; **prendre la ~** take flight.

**fulgurant**, **~e** /fylgyʀɑ̃, -t/ *a* (*vitesse*) lightning.

**fumé**, **~e** /fyme/ *a* (*poisson, verre*) smoked.

**fumée** /fyme/ *nf* smoke; (vapeur) steam.

**fumer** /fyme/ [1] *vt/i* smoke.

**fumeur**, **-euse** /fymœʀ, -øz/ *nm,f* smoker; **zone non-~s** no smoking area.

**fumier** /fymje/ *nm* manure.

**funambule** /fynɑ̃byl/ *nmf* tight-rope walker.

**funèbre** /fynɛbʀ/ *a* funeral; (fig) gloomy.

**funérailles** /fyneʀɑj/ *nfpl* funeral.

**funéraire** /fyneʀɛʀ/ *a* funeral.

**funeste** /fynɛst/ *a* fatal.

**fur**: **au ~ et à mesure** /ofyʀeaməzyʀ/ *loc* as one goes along, progressively; **au ~ et à mesure que** as.

**furet** /fyʀɛ/ *nm* ferret.

**fureur** /fyʀœʀ/ *nf* fury; (passion) passion; **avec ~** furiously; passionately; **mettre en ~** infuriate; **faire ~** be all the rage.

**furieux**, **-ieuse** /fyʀjø, -z/ *a* furious.

**furoncle** /fyʀɔ̃kl/ *nm* boil.

**furtif**, **-ive** /fyʀtif, -v/ *a* furtive.

**fuseau** (*pl* **~x**) /fyzo/ *nm* ski trousers; (pour filer) spindle; **~ horaire** time zone.

**fusée** /fyze/ *nf* rocket.

**fusible** /fyzibl/ *nm* fuse.

**fusil** /fyzi/ *nm* rifle, gun; (de chasse) shotgun; ~ **mitrailleur** machine-gun.

**fusion** /fyzjɔ̃/ *nf* fusion; (Comm) merger. **fusionner** [1] *vt/i* merge.

**fut** /fy/ ⇒ÊTRE [5].

**fût** /fy/ *nm* (tonneau) barrel; (d'arbre) trunk.

**futé**, ~**e** /fyte/ *a* cunning.

**futile** /fytil/ *a* futile.

**futur**, ~**e** /fytyʀ/ *a* future; ~**e femme/maman** wife-/mother-to-be. ● *nm* future.

**fuyant**, ~**e** /fɥijɑ̃, -t/ *a* (*front, ligne*) receding; (*personne*) evasive.

**fuyard**, ~**e** /fɥijaʀ, -d/ *nm,f* runaway.

# Gg

**gabardine** /gabaʀdin/ *nf* raincoat.

**gabarit** /gabaʀi/ *nm* size; (patron) template; (fig) calibre.

**gâcher** /gɑʃe/ [1] *vt* (gâter) spoil; (gaspiller) waste.

**gâchette** /gɑʃɛt/ *nf* trigger.

**gâchis** /gɑʃi/ *nm* waste.

**gaffe** /gaf/ *nf* Ⓘ blunder; **faire** ~ be careful (à of).

**gage** /gaʒ/ *nm* security; (de bonne foi) pledge; (de jeu) forfeit; ~**s** (salaire) wages; **en** ~ **de** as a token of; **mettre en** ~ pawn; **tueur à** ~**s** hired killer.

**gageure** /gaʒyʀ/ *nf* challenge.

**gagnant**, ~**e** /gaɲɑ̃, -t/ *a* winning. ● *nm,f* winner.

**gagne-pain** /gaɲpɛ̃/ *nm inv* job.

**gagner** /gaɲe/ [1] *vt* (*match, prix*) win; (*argent, pain*) earn; (*terrain*) gain; (*temps*) save; (atteindre) reach; (convaincre) win over; ~ **sa vie** earn one's living. ● *vi* win; (fig) gain.

**gai**, ~**e** /ge/ *a* cheerful; (ivre) merry. **gaiement** *adv* cheerfully. **gaieté** *nf* cheerfulness.

**gain** /gɛ̃/ *nm* (salaire) earnings; (avantage) gain; (économie) saving; ~**s** (Comm) profits; (au jeu) winnings.

**gaine** /gɛn/ *nf* (corset) girdle; (étui) sheath.

**galant**, ~**e** /galɑ̃, -t/ *a* courteous; (amoureux) romantic.

**galaxie** /galaksi/ *nf* galaxy.

**gale** /gal/ *nf* (de chat etc.) mange.

**galère** /galɛʀ/ *nf* (navire) galley; **c'est la** ~! Ⓘ what an ordeal!

**galérer** /galeʀe/ [14] *vi* Ⓘ (peiner) have a hard time.

**galerie** /galʀi/ *nf* gallery; (Théât) circle; (de voiture) roof-rack; ~ **marchande** shopping arcade.

**galet** /galɛ/ *nm* pebble.

**galette** /galɛt/ *nf* flat cake; ~ **des Rois** Twelfth Night cake.

**Galles** /gal/ *nfpl* **le pays de** ~ Wales.

**gallois**, ~**e** /galwa, -z/ *a* Welsh. ● *nm* (Ling) Welsh. **G**~, ~**e** *nm,f* Welshman, Welshwoman.

**galon** /galɔ̃/ *nm* braid; (Mil) stripe; **prendre du** ~ be promoted.

**galop** /galo/ *nm* canter; **aller au** ~ canter; **grand** ~ gallop; ~ **d'essai** trial run. **galoper** [1] *vi* (*cheval*) canter; (au grand galop) gallop; (*personne*) run.

**galopin** /galɔpɛ̃/ *nm* Ⓘ rascal.

**gambader** /gɑ̃bade/ [1] *vi* leap about.

**gamelle** /gamɛl/ *nf* (de soldat) mess kit; (d'ouvrier) lunch-box.

**gamin**, **~e** /gamɛ̃, -in/ *a* childish; (*air*) youthful. ● *nm,f* Ⓘ kid.

**gamme** /gam/ *nf* (Mus) scale; (série) range; **haut de ~** up-market, top of the range; **bas de ~** down-market, bottom of the range.

**gang** /gɑ̃g/ *nm* Ⓘ gang.

**ganglion** /gɑ̃glijɔ̃/ *nm* ganglion.

**gangster** /gɑ̃gstɛʀ/ *nm* gangster; (escroc) crook.

**gant** /gɑ̃/ *nm* glove; **~ de ménage** rubber glove; **~ de toilette** face-flannel, face-cloth.

**garage** /gaʀaʒ/ *nm* garage. **garagiste** *nmf* garage owner; (employé) car mechanic.

**garant**, **~e** /gaʀɑ̃, -t/ *nm,f* guarantor. ● *a* **se porter ~ de** vouch for.

**garanti**, **~e** /gaʀɑ̃ti/ *a* guaranteed.

**garantie** /gaʀɑ̃ti/ *nf* guarantee; **~s** (de police d'assurance) cover. **garantir** [2] *vt* guarantee; (protéger) protect (**de** from).

**garçon** /gaʀsɔ̃/ *nm* boy; (jeune homme) young man; (célibataire) bachelor; **~ (de café)** waiter; **~ d'honneur** best man. **garçonnière** *nf* bachelor flat.

**garde**[1] /gaʀd/ *nf* guard; (d'enfants, de bagages) care; (service) guard (duty); (infirmière) nurse; **de ~** on duty; **~ à vue** (police) custody; **mettre en ~** warn; **prendre ~** be careful (**à** of); **(droit de) ~** custody (**de** of).

**garde**[2] /gaʀd/ *nm* guard; (de propriété, parc) warden; **~ champêtre** village policeman; **~ du corps** bodyguard.

**garde-à-vous** /gaʀdavu/ *nm inv* (Mil) **se mettre au ~** stand to attention.

**garde-chasse** (*pl* **~s**) /gaʀdəʃas/ *nm* gamekeeper.

**garde-manger** /gaʀdmɑ̃ʒe/ *nm inv* meat safe; (placard) larder.

**garder** /gaʀde/ [1] *vt* (conserver, maintenir) keep; (*vêtement*) keep on; (surveiller) look after; (défendre) guard; **~ le lit** stay in bed. ◻ **se ~** *vpr* (*denrée*) keep; **se ~ de faire** be careful not to do.

**garderie** /gaʀdəʀi/ *nf* day nursery.

**garde-robe** (*pl* **~s**) /gaʀdəʀɔb/ *nf* wardrobe.

**gardien**, **~ne** /gaʀdjɛ̃, -ɛn/ *nm,f* (de locaux) security guard; (de prison, réserve) warden; (d'immeuble) caretaker; (de musée) attendant; (de zoo) keeper; (de traditions) guardian; **~ de but** goalkeeper; **~ de la paix** policeman; **~ de nuit** night watchman; **gardienne d'enfants** childminder.

**gare** /gaʀ/ *nf* (Rail) station; **~ routière** coach station; (US) bus station. ● *interj* **~ (à toi)** watch out!

**garer** /gaʀe/ [1] *vt* park. ◻ **se ~** *vpr* park; (s'écarter) move out of the way.

**gargouille** /gaʀguj/ *nf* water-spout; (sculptée) gargoyle. **gargouiller** [1] *vi* gurgle; (*stomach*) rumble.

**garni**, **~e** /gaʀni/ *a* (*plat*) served with vegetables; **bien ~** (rempli) well-filled.

**garnir** /gaʀniʀ/ [2] *vt* (remplir) fill; (décorer) decorate; (couvrir) cover; (doubler) line; (Culin) garnish. **garniture** *nf* (légumes) vegetables; (ornement) trimming; (de voiture) trim.

**gars** /gɑ/ *nm* Ⓘ lad; (adulte) guy, bloke.

**gas-oil** /gɑzwal/ *nm* diesel (oil).

**gaspillage** /gaspijaʒ/ *nm* waste. **gaspiller** [1] *vt* waste.

**gastrique** /gastʀik/ *a* gastric.

**gastronome** /gastʀɔnɔm/ *nmf* gourmet.

**gâteau** (*pl* **~x**) /gɑto/ *nm* cake; **~ sec** biscuit; (US) cookie; **un papa ~** a doting dad.

**gâter** /gɑte/ [1] *vt* spoil. □ **se ~** *vpr* (*viande*) go bad; (*dent*) rot; (*temps*) get worse.

**gâterie** /gɑtʀi/ *nf* little treat.

**gâteux**, **-euse** /gɑtø, -z/ *a* senile.

**gauche** /goʃ/ *a* left; (maladroit) awkward. ● *nf* left; **à ~** on the left; (direction) (to the) left; **la ~** the left (side); (Pol) the left (wing).

**gaucher**, **-ère** /goʃe, -ɛʀ/ *a* left-handed.

**gaufre** /gofʀ/ *nf* waffle. **gaufrette** *nf* wafer.

**gaulois**, **~e** /golwa, -z/ *a* Gallic; (fig) bawdy. **G~**, **~e** *nm,f* Gaul.

**gaver** /gave/ [1] *vt* force-feed; (fig) cram. □ **se ~ de** *vpr* gorge oneself with; (fig) devour.

**gaz** /gɑz/ *nm inv* gas; **~ d'échappement** exhaust fumes; **~ lacrymogène** tear-gas.

**gaze** /gɑz/ *nf* gauze.

**gazer** /gɑze/ [1] *vi* 🅸 **ça gaze?** how's things?

**gazette** /gazɛt/ *nf* newspaper.

**gazeux**, **-euse** /gɑzø, -z/ *a* (boisson) fizzy; (*eau*) sparkling.

**gazoduc** /gazɔdyk/ *nm* gas pipeline.

**gazon** /gɑzɔ̃/ *nm* lawn, grass.

**gazouiller** /gazuje/ [1] *vi* (*oiseau*) chirp; (*bébé*) babble.

**GDF** *abrév m* (**Gaz de France**) *French gas board.*

**géant**, **~e** /ʒeɑ̃, -t/ *a* giant. ● *nm* giant. **géante** *nf* giantess.

**geindre** /ʒɛ̃dʀ/ [22] *vi* groan, moan.

**gel** /ʒɛl/ *nm* frost; (produit) gel; (Comm) freeze; **~ coiffant** hair gel.

**gelée** /ʒ(ə)le/ *nf* frost; (Culin) jelly; **~ blanche** hoarfrost.

**geler** /ʒəle/ [6] *vt/i* freeze; **on gèle** (on a froid) it's freezing; **il** *ou* **ça gèle** (il fait froid) it's freezing.

**gélule** /ʒelyl/ *nf* (Méd) capsule.

**Gémeaux** /ʒemo/ *nmpl* Gemini.

**gémir** /ʒemiʀ/ [2] *vi* groan.

**gênant**, **~e** /ʒɛnɑ̃, -t/ *a* embarrassing; (irritant) annoying; (incommode) cumbersome.

**gencive** /ʒɑ̃siv/ *nf* gum.

**gendarme** /ʒɑ̃daʀm/ *nm* policeman, gendarme. **gendarmerie** *nf* police force; (local) police station.

**gendre** /ʒɑ̃dʀ/ *nm* son-in-law.

**gène** /ʒɛn/ *nm* gene.

**gêne** /ʒɛn/ *nf* discomfort; (confusion) embarrassment; (dérangement) trouble, inconvenience; (pauvreté) poverty.

**gêné**, **~e** /ʒene/ *a* embarrassed; (désargenté) short of money.

**généalogie** /ʒenealɔʒi/ *nf* genealogy.

**gêner** /ʒene/ [1] *vt* bother, disturb; (troubler) embarrass; (entraver) block; (faire mal) hurt.

**général**, **~e** (*mpl* **-aux**) /ʒeneʀal, -o/ *a* general; **en ~** in general. ● *nm* (*pl* **-aux**) general.

**généralement** /ʒeneʀalmɑ̃/ *adv* generally.

**généraliser** /ʒeneʀalize/ [1] *vt* make general. ● *vi* generalize. □ **se ~** *vpr* become widespread *ou* general.

**généraliste** /ʒeneʀalist/ *nmf* general practitioner, GP.

**généralité** /ʒeneʀalite/ *nf* general point.

**génération** /ʒeneʀasjɔ̃/ *nf* generation.

**généreux**, **~euse** /ʒeneʀø, -z/ *a* generous.

**générique** /ʒeneʀik/ *nm* (au cinéma) credits. ● *a* generic.

**générosité** /ʒeneʀozite/ *nf* generosity.

**génétique** /ʒenetik/ *a* genetic. ● *nf* genetics.

**Genève** /ʒənɛv/ *npr* Geneva.

**génial**, **~e** (*mpl* **-iaux**) /ʒenjal, -jo/ *a* brilliant; (fantastique Ⓘ) fantastic.

**génie** /ʒeni/ *nm* genius; **~ civil** civil engineering.

**génital**, **~e** (*mpl* **-aux**) /ʒenital, -o/ *a* genital.

**génocide** /ʒenɔsid/ *nm* genocide.

**génoise** /ʒenwaz/ *nf* sponge (cake).

**génome** /ʒenom/ *nm* genome.

**génothèque** /ʒenɔtɛk/ *nf* gene bank.

**genou** (*pl* **~x**) /ʒənu/ *nm* knee; **être à ~x** be kneeling.

**genre** /ʒɑ̃ʀ/ *nm* sort, kind; (Gram) gender; (allure) **avoir bon/mauvais ~** to look nice/disreputable; (comportement) **c'est bien son ~** it's just like him/her.

**gens** /ʒɑ̃/ *nmpl* people.

**gentil**, **~le** /ʒɑ̃ti, -j/ *a* kind, nice; (sage) good. **gentillesse** *nf* kindness. **gentiment** *adv* kindly.

**géographie** /ʒeɔgʀafi/ *nf* geography.

**geôlier**, **-ière** /ʒolje, -jɛʀ/ *nm,f* gaoler, jailer.

**géologie** /ʒeɔlɔʒi/ *nf* geology.

**géomètre** /ʒeɔmɛtʀ/ *nm* surveyor.

**géométrie** /ʒeɔmetʀi/ *nf* geometry. **géométrique** *a* geometric.

**gérance** /ʒeʀɑ̃s/ *nf* management.

**gérant**, **~e** /ʒeʀɑ̃, -t/ *nm,f* manager, manageress; **~ d'immeuble** landlord's agent.

**gerbe** /ʒɛʀb/ *nf* (de fleurs) bunch, bouquet; (d'eau) spray; (de blé) sheaf.

**gercer** /ʒɛʀse/ [10] *vt* chap; **avoir les lèvres gercées** have chapped lips. ● *vi* become chapped. **gerçure** *nf* crack, chap.

**gérer** /ʒeʀe/ [14] *vt* manage, run; (traiter: fig) (*crise, situation*) handle.

**germe** /ʒɛʀm/ *nm* germ; **~s de soja** bean sprouts.

**germer** /ʒɛʀme/ [1] *vi* germinate.

**gestation** /ʒɛstɑsjɔ̃/ *nf* gestation.

**geste** /ʒɛst/ *nm* gesture.

**gesticuler** /zɛstikyle/ [1] *vi* gesticulate.

**gestion** /ʒɛstjɔ̃/ *nf* management. **gestionnaire** *nmf* administrator.

**ghetto** /gɛto/ *nm* ghetto.

**gibier** /ʒibje/ *nm* (animaux) game.

**giboulée** /ʒibule/ *nf* shower.

**gicler** /ʒikle/ [1] *vi* squirt; **faire ~** squirt.

**gifle** /ʒifl/ *nf* slap in the face. **gifler** [1] *vt* slap.

**gigantesque** /ʒigɑ̃tɛsk/ *a* gigantic.

**gigot** /ʒigo/ *nm* leg (of lamb).

**gigoter** /ʒigɔte/ [1] *vi* wiggle; (nerveusement) fidget.

**gilet** /ʒilɛ/ *nm* waistcoat; (cardigan) cardigan; **~ de sauvetage** life-jacket.

**gingembre** /ʒɛ̃ʒɑ̃bʀ/ *nm* ginger.

**girafe** /ʒiʀaf/ *nf* giraffe.

**giratoire** /ʒiʀatwaʀ/ *a* **sens ~** roundabout.

**girofle** /ʒiʀɔfl/ *nm* **clou de ~** clove.

**girouette** /ʒiʀwɛt/ *nf* weathercock, weathervane.

**gisement** /ʒizmɑ̃/ *nm* deposit.

**gitan**, **~e** /ʒitɑ̃, -an/ *nm,f* gypsy.

**gîte** /ʒit/ *nm* (maison) home; (abri) shelter; **~ rural** holiday cottage.

**givre** /ʒivʀ/ *nm* frost; (sur pare-brise) ice.

**givré**, **~e** /ʒivʀe/ *a* 🅸 crazy.

**glace** /glas/ *nf* ice; (crème) ice-cream; (vitre) window; (miroir) mirror; (verre) glass.

**glacé**, **~e** /glase/ *a* (*vent, accueil*) icy; (*hands*) frozen; (*gâteau*) iced.

**glacer** /glase/ [10] *vt* freeze; (*gâteau, boisson*) chill; (pétrifier) chill. ▫ **se ~** *vpr* freeze.

**glacier** /glasje/ *nm* (Géog) glacier; (vendeur) ice-cream seller. **glacière** *nf* coolbox. **glaçon** *nm* ice-cube.

**glaïeul** /glajœl/ *nm* gladiolus.

**glaise** /glɛz/ *nf* clay.

**gland** /glɑ̃/ *nm* acorn; (ornement) tassel.

**glande** /glɑ̃d/ *nf* gland.

**glander** /glɑ̃de/ [1] *vi* 🅸 laze around.

**glaner** /glane/ [1] *vt* glean.

**glauque** /glok/ *a* (fig) murky; (*street*) squalid.

**glissade** /glisad/ *nf* (jeu) slide; (dérapage) skid.

**glissant**, **~e** /glisɑ̃, -t/ *a* slippery.

**glissement** /glismɑ̃/ *nm* sliding; gliding; (fig) shift; **~ de terrain** landslide.

**glisser** /glise/ [1] *vi* slide; (être glissant) be slippery; (sur l'eau) glide; (déraper) slip; (*véhicule*) skid. ● *vt* (*objet*) slip (**dans** into); (*remarque*) slip in. ▫ **se ~** *vpr* slip (**dans** into).

**glissière** /glisjɛʀ/ *nf* slide; **porte à ~** sliding door; **~ de sécurité** (Auto) crash-barrier; **fermeture à ~** zip.

**global**, **~e** (*mpl* **-aux**) /glɔbal, -o/ *a* (entier, général) overall. **globalement** *adv* as a whole.

**globe** /glɔb/ *nm* globe; **~ oculaire** eyeball; **~ terrestre** globe.

**globule** /glɔbyl/ *nm* (du sang) corpuscle.

**gloire** /glwaʀ/ *nf* glory, fame.

**glorieux**, **-ieuse** *a* glorious. **glorifier** [45] *vt* glorify.

**glose** /gloz/ *nf* gloss.

**glossaire** /glɔsɛʀ/ *nm* glossary.

**gloussement** /glusmɑ̃/ *nm* chuckle; (de poule) cluck.

**glouton**, **~ne** /glutɔ̃, -ɔn/ *a* gluttonous. ● *nm,f* glutton.

**gluant**, **~e** /glyɑ̃, -t/ *a* sticky.

**glucose** /glykoz/ *nm* glucose.

**glycérine** /gliseʀin/ *nf* glycerin(e).

**GO** *abrév fpl* (**grandes ondes**) long wave.

**goal** /gol/ *nm* 🅸 goalkeeper.

**gobelet** /gɔblɛ/ *nm* cup; (en verre) tumbler.

**gober** /gɔbe/ [1] *vt* swallow (whole); **je ne peux pas le ~** 🅸 I can't stand him.

**goéland** /gɔelɑ̃/ *nm* (sea)gull.

**gogo**: **à ~** /agɔgo/ *loc* 🅸 galore, in abundance.

**goinfre** /gwɛ̃fʀ/ *nm* (glouton 🅸) pig. **goinfrer (se)** [1] *vpr* 🅸 stuff oneself (**de** with).

**golf** /gɔlf/ *nm* golf; (terrain) golf course.

**golfe** /gɔlf/ *nm* gulf.

**gomme** /gɔm/ *nf* rubber; (US) eraser; (résine) gum. **gommer** [1] *vt* rub out.

**gond** /gɔ̃/ *nm* hinge; **sortir de ses ~s** 🅸 go mad.

**gondoler (se)** /(sə)gɔ̃dɔle/ [1] *vpr* (*bois*) warp; (*métal*) buckle.

**gonflé**, **~e** /gɔ̃fle/ *a* swollen; **il est ~** 🅸 he's got a nerve.

**gonflement** /gɔ̃fləmɑ̃/ *nm* swelling.

**gonfler** /gɔ̃fle/ [1] *vt* (*ballon, pneu*) pump up, blow up; (augmenter) increase; (exagérer) inflate. ● *vi* swell.

**gorge** /gɔʀʒ/ *nf* throat; (poitrine) breast; (vallée) gorge.

**gorgée** /gɔʀʒe/ *nf* sip, gulp.

**gorger** /gɔʀʒe/ [40] *vt* fill (**de** with); **gorgé de** full of. ▫ **se ~** *vpr* gorge oneself (**de** with).

**gorille** /gɔʀij/ *nm* gorilla; (garde [I]) bodyguard.

**gosier** /gozje/ *nm* throat.

**gosse** /gɔs/ *nmf* [I] kid.

**gothique** /gɔtik/ *a* Gothic.

**goudron** /gudʀɔ̃/ *nm* tar. **goudronner** [1] *vt* tarmac.

**gouffre** /gufʀ/ *nm* abyss, gulf.

**goujat** /guʒa/ *nm* lout, boor.

**goulot** /gulo/ *nm* neck; **boire au ~** drink from the bottle.

**goulu, ~e** /guly/ *a* gluttonous. ● *nm,f* glutton.

**gourde** /guʀd/ *nf* (à eau) flask; (idiot [I]) fool.

**gourer (se)** /(sə)guʀe/ [1] *vpr* [I] make a mistake.

**gourmand, ~e** /guʀmɑ̃, -d/ *a* greedy. ● *nm,f* glutton.

**gourmandise** /guʀmɑ̃diz/ *nf* greed; **~s** sweets.

**gourmet** /guʀmɛ/ *nm* gourmet.

**gourmette** /guʀmɛt/ *nf* chain bracelet.

**gousse** /gus/ *nf* **~ d'ail** clove of garlic.

**goût** /gu/ *nm* taste; (gré) liking; **prendre ~ à** develop a taste for; **avoir bon ~** (*aliment*) taste nice; (*personne*) have good taste; **donner du ~ à** give flavour.

**goûter** /gute/ [1] *vt* taste; (apprécier) enjoy; **~ à** *ou* **de** taste. ● *vi* have tea. ● *nm* tea, snack.

**goutte** /gut/ *nf* drop; (Méd) gout. **goutte-à-goutte** *nm inv* drip. **goutter** [1] *vi* drip.

**gouttière** /gutjɛʀ/ *nf* gutter.

**gouvernail** /guvɛʀnaj/ *nm* rudder; (barre) helm.

**gouvernement** /guvɛʀnəmɑ̃/ *nm* government.

**gouverner** /guvɛʀne/ [1] *vt/i* govern; (dominer) control. **gouverneur** *nm* governor.

**grâce** /gʀɑs/ *nf* (charme) grace; (faveur) favour; (volonté) grace; (Jur) pardon; (Relig) grace; **~ à** thanks to; **rendre ~(s) à** give thanks to.

**gracier** /gʀasje/ [45] *vt* pardon.

**gracieusement** /gʀasjøzmɑ̃/ *adv* gracefully; (gratuitement) free (of charge).

**gracieux, -ieuse** /gʀasjø, -z/ *a* graceful.

**grade** /gʀad/ *nm* rank; **monter en ~** be promoted.

**gradin** /gʀadɛ̃/ *nm* tier, step; **en ~s** terraced; **les ~s** terraces.

**gradué, ~e** /gʀadɥe/ *a* graded, graduated; **verre ~** measuring jug.

**graffiti** /gʀafiti/ *nmpl* graffiti.

**grain** /gʀɛ̃/ *nm* grain; (Naut) squall; **~ de beauté** beauty spot; **~ de café** coffee bean; **~ de poivre** peppercorn; **~ de raisin** grape.

**graine** /gʀɛn/ *nf* seed.

**graisse** /gʀɛs/ *nf* fat; (lubrifiant) grease. **graisser** [1] *vt* grease. **graisseux, -euse** *a* greasy.

**grammaire** /gʀam(m)ɛʀ/ *nf* grammar.

**gramme** /gʀam/ *nm* gram.

**grand, ~e** /gʀɑ̃, -d/ *a* big, large; (haut) tall; (intense, fort) great; (brillant) great; (principal) main; (plus âgé) big, elder; (adulte) grown-up; **au ~ air** in the open air; **au ~ jour** in broad daylight; (fig) in the open; **en ~e partie** largely; **~e banlieue** outer suburbs; **~ ensemble** housing estate; **~es lignes** (Rail) main lines; **~**

**magasin** department store; **~e personne** grown-up; **~ public** general public; **~e surface** hypermarket; **~es vacances** summer holidays. ● *adv* (*ouvrir*) wide; **~ ouvert** wide open; **voir ~** think big. ● *nm,f* (adulte) grown-up; (enfant) big boy, big girl; (Scol) senior.

**Grande-Bretagne** /gʀɑ̃dbʀətaɲ/ *nf* Great Britain.

**grand-chose** /gʀɑ̃ʃoz/ *pron* **pas ~** not much, not a lot.

**grandeur** /gʀɑ̃dœʀ/ *nf* greatness; (dimension) size; **folie des ~s** delusions of grandeur.

**grandir** /gʀɑ̃diʀ/ [2] *vi* grow; (*bruit*) grow louder. ● *vt* (*talons*) make taller; (*loupe*) magnify.

**grand-mère** (*pl* **grands-mères**) /gʀɑ̃mɛʀ/ *nf* grandmother.

**grand-père** (*pl* **grands-pères**) /gʀɑ̃pɛʀ/ *nm* grandfather.

**grands-parents** /gʀɑ̃paʀɑ̃/ *nmpl* grandparents.

**grange** /gʀɑ̃ʒ/ *nf* barn.

**granulé** /gʀanyle/ *nm* granule.

**graphique** /gʀafik/ *a* graphic; (Ordinat) graphics; **informatique ~** computer graphics. ● *nm* graph.

**graphologie** /gʀafɔlɔʒi/ *nf* graphology.

**grappe** /gʀap/ *nf* cluster; **~ de raisin** bunch of grapes.

**gras**, **~se** /gʀɑ, -s/ *a* (gros) fat; (*aliment*) fatty; (*surface, peau, cheveux*) greasy; (épais) thick; (*caractères*) bold; **faire la ~se matinée** sleep late. ● *nm* (Culin) fat.

**gratifiant**, **~e** /gʀatifjɑ̃, -t/ *a* gratifying; (*travail*) rewarding.

**gratifier** /gʀatifje/ [45] *vt* favour, reward (**de** with).

**gratin** /gʀatɛ̃/ *nm* gratin (*baked dish with cheese topping*); (élite Ⓘ) upper crust.

**gratis** /gʀatis/ *adv* free.

**gratitude** /gʀatityd/ *nf* gratitude.

**gratte-ciel** /gʀatsjɛl/ *nm inv* skyscraper.

**gratter** /gʀate/ [1] *vt/i* scratch; (avec un outil) scrape; **ça me gratte** Ⓘ it itches. ▫ **se ~** *vpr* scratch oneself; **se ~ la tête** scratch one's head.

**gratuiciel** /gʀatɥisjɛl/ *nm* (Internet) freeware.

**gratuit**, **~e** /gʀatɥi, -t/ *a* free; (*acte*) gratuitous. **gratuitement** *adv* free (of charge).

**grave** /gʀav/ *a* (*maladie, accident, problème*) serious; (solennel) grave; (*voix*) deep; (*accent*) grave. **gravement** *adv* seriously; gravely.

**graver** /gʀave/ [1] *vt* engrave; (sur bois) carve.

**gravier** /gʀavje/ *nm* **du ~** gravel.

**gravité** /gʀavite/ *nf* gravity.

**graviter** /gʀavite/ [1] *vi* revolve.

**gravure** /gʀavyʀ/ *nf* engraving; (de tableau, photo) print, plate.

**gré** /gʀe/ *nm* (volonté) will; (goût) taste; **à son ~** (*agir*) as one likes; **de bon ~** willingly; **bon ~ mal ~** like it or not; **je vous en saurais ~** I'd be grateful for that.

**grec**, **~que** /gʀɛk/ *a* Greek. ● *nm* (Ling) Greek. **G~**, **~que** *nm,f* Greek.

**Grèce** *nf* /gʀɛs/ Greece.

**greffe** /gʀɛf/ *nf* graft; (d'organe) transplant. **greffer** [1] *vt* graft; transplant.

**greffier**, **-ière** /gʀefje, -jɛʀ/ *nm,f* clerk of the court.

**grêle** /gʀɛl/ *a* (maigre) spindly; (*voix*) shrill. ● *nf* hail.

**grêler** /gʀele/ [1] *vi* hail; **il grêle** it's hailing. **grêlon** *nm* hailstone.

**grelot** /gʀəlo/ *nm* (little) bell.

**grelotter** /gʀəlɔte/ [1] *vi* shiver.

**grenade** /gʀənad/ *nf* (fruit) pomegranate; (explosif) grenade.

**grenat** /gʀəna/ *a inv* dark red.

**grenier** /gʀənje/ *nm* attic; (pour grain) loft.

**grenouille** /gʀənuj/ *nf* frog.

**grès** /gʀɛ/ *nm* sandstone; (poterie) stoneware.

**grésiller** /gʀezije/ [1] *vi* sizzle; (*radio*) crackle.

**grève** /gʀɛv/ *nf* (rivage) shore; (cessation de travail) strike; **faire ~, être en ~** be on strike; **se mettre en ~** go on strike. **gréviste** *nmf* striker.

**gribouiller** /gʀibuje/ [1] *vt/i* scribble.

**grief** /gʀijɛf/ *nm* grievance.

**grièvement** /gʀijɛvmɑ̃/ *adv* seriously.

**griffe** /gʀif/ *nf* claw; (de couturier) label; **coup de ~** scratch.

**griffé, ~e** /gʀife/ *a* (*vêtement, article*) designer.

**griffer** /gʀife/ [1] *vt* scratch, claw.

**grignoter** /gʀiɲɔte/ [1] *vt/i* nibble.

**gril** /gʀil/ *nm* (de cuisinière) grill; (plaque) grill pan.

**grillade** /gʀijad/ *nf* (viande) grill.

**grillage** /gʀijaʒ/ *nm* wire netting.

**grille** /gʀij/ *nf* railings; (portail) (metal) gate; (de fenêtre) bars; (de cheminée) grate; (fig) grid. **grille-pain** *nm inv* toaster.

**griller** /gʀije/ [1] *vt* (*pain*) toast; (*viande*) grill; (*ampoule*) blow; (*feu rouge*) go through; (*appareil*) burn out. ● *vi* (*ampoule*) blow; (Culin) **faire ~** (*viande*) grill; (*pain*) toast.

**grillon** /gʀijɔ̃/ *nm* cricket.

**grimace** /gʀimas/ *nf* (funny) face; (de douleur, dégoût) grimace; **faire des ~s** make faces; **faire la ~** pull a face, grimace.

**grimper** /gʀɛ̃pe/ [1] *vt* climb. ● *vi* climb; **~ sur** *ou* **dans un arbre** climb a tree.

**grincement** /gʀɛ̃smɑ̃/ *nm* creak(ing).

**grincer** /gʀɛ̃se/ [10] *vi* creak; **~ des dents** grind one's teeth.

**grincheux, -euse** /gʀɛ̃ʃø, -z/ *a* grumpy.

**grippe** /gʀip/ *nf* influenza, flu.

**grippé, ~e** /gʀipe/ *a* **être ~** have (the) flu; (*mécanisme*) be seized up *ou* jammed.

**gris, ~e** /gʀi, -z/ *a* grey; (saoul) tipsy.

**grivois, ~e** /gʀivwa, -z/ *a* bawdy.

**grog** /gʀɔg/ *nm* hot toddy.

**grogner** /gʀɔɲe/ [1] *vi* (*animal*) growl, (*personne*) grumble.

**grognon** /gʀɔɲɔ̃/ *a m* grumpy.

**groin** /gʀwɛ̃/ *nm* snout.

**gronder** /gʀɔ̃de/ [1] *vi* (*tonnerre, volcan*) rumble, (*chien*) growl; (*conflit*) be brewing. ● *vt* scold.

**groom** /gʀum/ *nm* bellboy.

**gros, ~se** /gʀo, -s/ *a* big, large; (gras) fat; (important) big; (épais) thick; (lourd) heavy; (*buveur, fumeur*) heavy; **~ bonnet** 🅸 bigwig; **~ lot** jackpot; **~ mot** swear word; **~ plan** close-up; **~se caisse** bass drum; **~ titre** headline. ● *nm, f* fat man, fat woman. ● *adv* (*écrire*) big; (*risquer, gagner*) a lot. ● *nm* **le ~ de** the bulk of; **de ~** (Comm) wholesale; **en ~** roughly; (Comm) wholesale.

**groseille** /gʀozɛj/ *nf* redcurrant; **~ à maquereau** gooseberry.

**grossesse** /gʀosɛs/ *nf* pregnancy.

**grosseur** /gʀosœʀ/ *nf* (volume) size; (enflure) lump.

**grossier, -ière** /gʀosje, -jɛʀ/ *a* (sans finesse) coarse, rough; (rudimentaire) crude; (vulgaire) coarse;

(impoli) rude; (*erreur*) gross. **grossièrement** *adv* (sommairement) roughly; (vulgairement) coarsely. **grossièreté** *nf* coarseness; crudeness; rudeness; (mot) rude word.

**grossir** /gʀosiʀ/ [2] *vt* (faire augmenter) increase, boost; (agrandir) enlarge; (exagérer) exaggerate; ~ **les rangs** *ou* **la foule** swell the ranks. • *vi* (*personne*) put on weight; (augmenter) grow.

**grossiste** /gʀosist/ *nmf* wholesaler.

**grosso modo** /gʀosomodo/ *adv* roughly.

**grotesque** /gʀɔtɛsk/ *a* grotesque; (ridicule) ludicrous.

**grotte** /gʀɔt/ *nf* cave; grotto.

**grouiller** /gʀuje/ [1] *vi* swarm; ~ **de** be swarming with.

**groupe** /gʀup/ *nm* group; (Mus) group, band; ~ **électrogène** generating set; ~ **scolaire** school; ~ **de travail** working party.

**groupement** /gʀupmɑ̃/ *nm* grouping.

**grouper** /gʀupe/ [1] *vt* put together. □ **se** ~ *vpr* group (together).

**grue** /gʀy/ *nf* (machine, oiseau) crane.

**gruyère** /gʀyjɛʀ/ *nm* gruyère (cheese).

**gué** /ge/ *nm* ford; **passer** *ou* **traverser à** ~ ford.

**guenon** /gənɔ̃/ *nf* female monkey.

**guépard** /gepaʀ/ *nm* cheetah.

**guêpe** /gɛp/ *nf* wasp.

**guère** /gɛʀ/ *adv* **ne** ~ hardly; **il n'y a** ~ **d'espoir** there is no hope; **elle n'a** ~ **dormi** she didn't sleep much, she hardly slept.

**guérilla** /geʀija/ *nf* guerrilla warfare; (groupe) guerillas.

**guérir** /geʀiʀ/ [2] *vt* (*personne, maladie, mal*) cure (**de** of); (*plaie, membre*) heal. • *vi* get better; (*blessure*) heal; ~ **de** recover from. **guérison** *nf* curing; healing; (de personne) recovery.

**guerre** /gɛʀ/ *nf* war; **en** ~ at war; **faire la** ~ wage war (**à** against); ~ **civile** civil war; ~ **mondiale** world war.

**guerrier, -ière** /gɛʀje, -jɛʀ/ *a* warlike. • *nm, f* warrior.

**guet** /gɛ/ *nm* watch; **faire le** ~ be on the watch. **guet-apens** (*pl* **guets-apens**) *nm* ambush.

**guetter** /gete/ [1] *vt* watch; (attendre) watch out for.

**gueule** /gœl/ *nf* mouth; (figure ⊡) face; **ta** ~! ⊠ shut up!; ~ **de bois** ⊡ hangover.

**gueuleton** /gœltɔ̃/ *nm* ⊡ blowout, slap-up meal.

**gui** /gi/ *nm* mistletoe.

**guichet** /giʃɛ/ *nm* window, counter; (de gare) ticket-office; (Théât) box-office; **jouer à** ~**s fermés** (*pièce*) be sold out; ~ **automatique** cash dispenser.

**guide** /gid/ *nm* guide. • *nf* (fille scout) girl guide.

**guider** /gide/ [1] *vt* guide.

**guidon** /gidɔ̃/ *nm* handlebars.

**guignol** /giɲɔl/ *nm* puppet; (personne) clown; (spectacle) puppet-show.

**guillemets** /gijmɛ/ *nmpl* quotation marks, inverted commas; **entre** ~ in inverted commas.

**guillotine** /gijɔtin/ *nf* guillotine.

**guimauve** /gimov/ *nf* marshmallow; **c'est de la** ~ ⊡ it's slushy *ou* schmaltzy ⊡.

**guindé**, ~**e** /gɛ̃de/ *a* stiff, formal; (*style*) stilted.

**guirlande** /giʀlɑ̃d/ *nf* garland; tinsel.

**guitare** /gitaʀ/ *nf* guitar.

**gym** /ʒim/ *nf* gymnastics; (Scol) physical education, PE.

**gymnase** /ʒimnɑz/ *nm* gym(nasium). **gymnastique** *nf* gymnastics.

**gynécologie** /ʒinekɔlɔʒi/ *nf* gynaecology.

**habile** /abil/ *a* skilful, clever.

**habillé**, **~e** /abije/ *a* (*vêtement*) smart; (*soirée*) formal.

**habillement** /abijmɑ̃/ *nm* clothing.

**habiller** /abije/ [1] *vt* dress (**de** in); (équiper) clothe; (recouvrir) cover (**de** with). ◻ **s'~** *vpr* get dressed; (élégamment) dress up.

**habit** /abi/ *nm* (de personnage) outfit; (de cérémonie) tails; **~s** clothes.

**habitant**, **~e** /abitɑ̃, -t/ *nm,f* (de maison, quartier) resident; (de pays) inhabitant.

**habitat** /abita/ *nm* (mode de peuplement) settlement; (conditions) housing.

**habitation** /abitasjɔ̃/ *nf* (logement) house.

**habité**, **~e** /abite/ *a* (*terre*) inhabited.

**habiter** /abite/ [1] *vi* live. ● *vt* live in.

**habitude** /abityd/ *nf* habit; **avoir l'~ de** be used to; **d'~** usually; **comme d'~** as usual.

**habitué**, **~e** /abitɥe/ *nm,f* (client) regular.

**habituel**, **~le** /abitɥɛl/ *a* usual. **habituellement** *adv* usually.

**habituer** /abitɥe/ [1] *vt* **~ qn à** get sb used to. ◻ **s'~ à** *vpr* get used to.

**hache** /'aʃ/ *nf* axe.

**haché**, **~e** /'aʃe/ *a* (viande) minced; (phrases) jerky.

**hacher** /'aʃe/ [1] *vt* mince; (au couteau) chop.

**hachis** /'aʃi/ *nm* minced meat; (US) ground meat; **~ Parmentier** ≈ *shepherd's pie.*

**hachisch** /'aʃiʃ/ *nm* hashish.

**hachoir** /'aʃwaʀ/ *nm* (appareil) mincer; (couteau) chopper; (planche) chopping board.

**haie** /'ɛ/ *nf* hedge; (de personnes) line; **course de ~s** hurdle race.

**haillon** /'ɑjɔ̃/ *nm* rag.

**haine** /'ɛn/ *nf* hatred.

**haïr** /'aiʀ/ [36] *vt* hate.

**hâlé** /'ɑle/ *a* (sun-)tanned.

**haleine** /alɛn/ *nf* breath; **travail de longue ~** long job.

**haleter** /'alte/ [6] *vi* pant.

**hall** /'ol/ *nm* hall; (de gare) concourse.

**halle** /'al/ *nf* market hall; **~s** covered market.

**halte** /'alt/ *nf* stop; **faire ~** stop. ● *interj* stop; (Mil) halt.

**haltère** /altɛʀ/ *nm* dumbbell; **faire des ~s** to do weightlifting.

**hameau** (*pl* **~x**) /'amo/ *nm* hamlet.

**hameçon** /amsɔ̃/ *nm* hook.

**hanche** /'ɑ̃ʃ/ *nf* hip.

**handicap** /'ɑ̃dikap/ *nm* handicap. **handicapé**, **~e** *a & nm,f* disabled (person).

**hangar** /'ãgaR/ *nm* shed; (pour avions) hangar.

**hanter** /'ãte/ [1] *vt* haunt.

**hantise** /'ãtiz/ *nf* dread; **avoir la ~ de** dread.

**haras** /'aRɑ/ *nm* stud-farm.

**harasser** /'aRase/ [1] *vt* exhaust.

**harcèlement** /'aRsɛlmã/ *nm* **~ sexuel** sexual harassment.

**harceler** /'aRsəle/ [6] *vt* harass.

**hardi**, **~e** /'aRdi/ *a* bold.

**hareng** /'aRã/ *nm* herring.

**hargne** /'aRɲ/ *nf* (aggressive) bad temper.

**haricot** /'aRiko/ *nm* bean; **~ vert** French bean; (US) green bean.

**harmonie** /aRmɔni/ *nf* harmony. **harmonieux**, **-ieuse** *a* harmonious.

**harmoniser** /aRmɔnize/ [1] *vt* harmonize. □ **s'~** *vpr* harmonize.

**harnacher** /'aRnaʃe/ [1] *vt* harness.

**harnais** /'aRnɛ/ *nm* harness.

**harpe** /'aRp/ *nf* harp.

**harpon** /'aRpɔ̃/ *nm* harpoon.

**hasard** /'azaR/ *nm* chance; (coïncidence) coincidence; **les ~s de** the fortunes of; **au ~** (choisir etc.) at random; (flâner) aimlessly. **hasardeux**, **-euse** *a* risky.

**hasarder** /'azaRde/ [1] *vt* risk; (remarque) venture.

**hâte** /'ɑt/ *nf* haste; **à la ~**, **en ~** hurriedly; **avoir ~ de** look forward to.

**hâter** /'ɑte/ [1] *vt* hasten. □ **se ~** *vpr* hurry (**de** to).

**hâtif**, **-ive** /'ɑtif, -v/ *a* hasty; (précoce) early.

**hausse** /'os/ *nf* rise (**de** in); **~ des prix** price rise; **en ~** rising.

**hausser** /'ose/ [1] *vt* raise; (épaules) shrug.

**haut**, **~e** /'o, 'ot/ *a* high; (de taille) tall; **à voix ~e** aloud; **~ en couleur** colourful; **plus ~** higher up; (dans un texte) above; **en ~ lieu** in high places. ● *adv* high; **tout ~** out loud. ● *nm* top; **des ~s et des bas** ups and downs; **en ~** (regarder) up; (à l'étage) upstairs; **en ~ (de)** at the top (of).

**hautbois** /'obwa/ *nm* oboe.

**haut-de-forme** /'odfɔRm/ (*pl* **hauts-de-forme**) *nm* top hat.

**hauteur** /'otœR/ *nf* height; (colline) hill; (arrogance) haughtiness; **être à la ~** be up to it; **à la ~ de** (*ville*) near; **être à la ~ de la situation** be equal to the situation.

**haut-le-cœur** /'olkœR/ *nm inv* nausea.

**haut-parleur** (*pl* **~s**) /'opaRlœR/ *nm* loudspeaker.

**havre** /'ɑvR/ *nm* haven (**de** of).

**hayon** /'ɑjɔ̃/ *nm* (Auto) hatchback.

**hebdomadaire** /ɛbdɔmadɛR/ *a & nm* weekly.

**hébergement** /ebɛRʒəmã/ *nm* accommodation.

**héberger** /ebɛRʒe/ [40] *vt* (*ami*) put up; (*réfugiés*) take in.

**hébreu** (*pl* **~x**) /ebRø/ *am* Hebrew. ● *nm* (Ling) Hebrew; **c'est de l'~!** it's all Greek to me!

**Hébreu** (*pl* **~x**) /ebRø/ *nm* Hebrew; **les ~x** the Hebrews.

**hécatombe** /ekatɔ̃b/ *nf* slaughter.

**hectare** /ɛktaʀ/ *nm* hectare (= 10,000 square metres).

**hélas** /'elɑs/ *interj* alas. ● *adv* sadly.

**hélice** /elis/ *nf* propeller.

**hélicoptère** /elikɔptɛʀ/ *nm* helicopter.

**helvétique** /ɛlvetik/ *a* Swiss.

**hématome** /ematom/ *nm* bruise.

**hémorragie** /emɔʀaʒi/ *nf* haemorrhage.

**hémorroïdes** /emɔʀɔid/ *nfpl* piles, haemorrhoids.

**hennir** /'eniʀ/ [2] *vi* neigh.

**hépatite** /epatit/ *nf* hepatitis.

**herbe** /ɛʀb/ *nf* grass; (Méd, Culin) herb; **en ~** in the blade; (fig) budding.

**héréditaire** /eʀeditɛʀ/ *a* hereditary.

**hérédité** /eʀedite/ *nf* heredity.

**hérisser** /'eʀise/ [1] *vt* bristle; **~ qn** (fig) ruffle sb. ▫ **se ~** *vpr* bristle.

**hérisson** /'eʀisɔ̃/ *nm* hedgehog.

**héritage** /eʀitaʒ/ *nm* inheritance; (spirituel) heritage.

**hériter** /eʀite/ [1] *vt/i* inherit (**de** from); **~ de qch** inherit sth. **héritier**, **-ière** *nm,f* heir, heiress.

**hermétique** /ɛʀmetik/ *a* airtight; (fig) unfathomable.

**hernie** /'ɛʀni/ *nf* hernia.

**héroïne** /eʀɔin/ *nf* (femme) heroine; (drogue) heroin.

**héroïque** /eʀɔik/ *a* heroic.

**héros** /'eʀo/ *nm* hero.

**hésiter** /ezite/ [1] *vi* hesitate (**à** to); **j'hésite** I'm not sure.

**hétérogène** /eteʀɔʒɛn/ *a* heterogeneous.

**hétérosexuel**, **~le** /eteʀosɛksɥɛl/ *nm/f & a* heterosexual.

**hêtre** /'ɛtʀ/ *nm* beech.

**heure** /œʀ/ *nf* time; (soixante minutes) hour; **quelle ~ est-il?** what time is it?; **il est dix ~s** it is ten o'clock; **à l'~** (*venir, être*) on time; **à l'~**, **en ~** by the hour; **toutes les deux ~s** every two hours; **~ de pointe** rush-hour; **~ de cours** (Scol) period; **~ indue** ungodly hour; **~s creuses** off-peak periods; **~s supplémentaires** overtime.

**heureusement** /œʀøzmɑ̃/ *adv* fortunately, luckily.

**heureux**, **-euse** /œʀø, -z/ *a* happy; (chanceux) lucky, fortunate.

**heurt** /'œʀ/ *nm* collision; (conflit) clash; **sans ~** smoothly.

**heurter** /'œʀte/ [1] *vt* (cogner) hit; (*mur*) bump into, hit; (choquer) offend. ▫ **se ~ à** *vpr* bump into, hit; (fig) come up against.

**hexagone** /ɛgzagɔn/ *nm* hexagon; **l'~** France.

**hiberner** /ibɛʀne/ [1] *vi* hibernate.

**hibou** (*pl* **~x**) /'ibu/ *nm* owl.

**hier** /jɛʀ/ *adv* yesterday; **~ soir** last night, yesterday evening.

**hiérarchie** /'jeʀaʀʃi/ *nf* hierarchy.

**hilare** /ilaʀ/ *a* (*visage*) merry; **être ~** be laughing.

**hindou**, **~e** /ɛ̃du/ *a & nm,f* Hindu. **H~**, **~e** *nm,f* Hindu.

**hippique** /ipik/ *a* equestrian; **le concours ~** showjumping.

**hippodrome** /ipɔdʀom/ *nm* racecourse.

**hippopotame** /ipɔpɔtam/ *nm* hippopotamus.

**hirondelle** /iʀɔ̃dɛl/ *nf* swallow.

**hisser** /'ise/ [1] *vt* hoist, haul. □ **se ~** *vpr* heave oneself up.

**histoire** /istwaʀ/ *nf* (récit) story; (étude) history; (affaire) business; **~(s)** (chichis) fuss; (ennuis) trouble. **historique** *a* historical.

**hiver** /ivɛʀ/ *nm* winter. **hivernal**, **~e** (*mpl* **-aux**) *a* winter; (glacial) wintry.

**H.L.M.** *abbrév m ou f* (**habitation à loyer modéré**) block of council flats; (US) low-rent apartment building.

**hocher** /'ɔʃe/ [1] *vt* **~ la tête** (pour dire oui) nod; (pour dire non) shake one's head.

**hochet** /'ɔʃɛ/ *nm* rattle.

**hockey** /'ɔkɛ/ *nm* hockey; **~ sur glace** ice hockey.

**hollandais**, **~e** /'ɔlɑ̃dɛ, -z/ *a* Dutch. ● *nm* (Ling) Dutch. **H~**, **~e** *nm,f* Dutchman, Dutchwoman.

**Hollande** /'ɔlɑ̃d/ *nf* Holland.

**homard** /'ɔmaʀ/ *nm* lobster.

**homéopathie** /ɔmeɔpati/ *nf* homoeopathy.

**homicide** /ɔmisid/ *nm* homicide; **~ involontaire** manslaughter.

**hommage** /ɔmaʒ/ *nm* tribute; **~s** (salutations) respects; **rendre ~ à** pay tribute to.

**homme** /ɔm/ *nm* man; (espèce) man(kind); **~ d'affaires** businessman; **~ de la rue** man in the street; **~ d'État** statesman; **~ politique** politician.

**homogène** /ɔmɔʒɛn/ *a* homogeneous.

**homonyme** /ɔmɔnim/ *nm* (personne) namesake.

**homosexualité** /ɔmɔsɛksɥalite/ *nf* homosexuality.

**homosexuel**, **~le** /ɔmɔsɛksɥɛl/ *a & nm,f* homosexual.

**Hongrie** /'ɔ̃gʀi/ *nf* Hungary.

**hongrois**, **~e** /'ɔ̃gʀwa, -z/ *a* Hungarian. ● *nm* (Ling) Hungarian. **H~**, **~e** *nm,f* Hungarian.

**honnête** /ɔnɛt/ *a* honest; (juste) fair. **honnêteté** *nf* honesty.

**honneur** /ɔnœʀ/ *nm* honour; (mérite) credit; **d'~** (*invité, place*) of honour; **en l'~ de** in honour of; **en quel ~?** Ⓘ why?; **faire ~ à** (*équipe, famille*) bring credit to.

**honorable** /ɔnɔʀabl/ *a* honourable; (convenable) respectable.

**honoraire** /ɔnɔʀɛʀ/ *a* honorary. **honoraires** *nmpl* fees.

**honorer** /ɔnɔʀe/ [1] *vt* honour; (faire honneur à) do credit to.

**honte** /'ɔ̃t/ *nf* shame; **avoir ~** be ashamed (**de** of); **faire ~ à** make ashamed. **honteux**, **-euse** *a* (*personne*) ashamed (**de** of); (*action*) shameful.

**hôpital** (*pl* **-aux**) /ɔpital, -o/ *nm* hospital.

**hoquet** /'ɔkɛ/ *nm* **le ~** (the) hiccups.

**horaire** /ɔʀɛʀ/ *a* hourly. ● *nm* timetable; **~s libres** flexitime.

**horizon** /ɔʀizɔ̃/ *nm* horizon; (Fig) outlook.

**horizontal**, **~e** (*mpl* **-aux**) /ɔʀizɔ̃tal, -o/ *a* horizontal.

**horloge** /ɔʀlɔʒ/ *nf* clock.

**hormis** /'ɔʀmi/ *prép* save.

**hormonal**, **~e** (*mpl* **-aux**) /ɔʀmɔnal, -o/ *a* hormonal, hormone.

**hormone** /ɔʀmɔn/ *nf* hormone.

**horreur** /ɔʀœʀ/ *nf* horror; **avoir ~ de** hate.

**horrible** /ɔʀibl/ *a* horrible.

**horrifier** /ɔʀifje/ [45] *vt* horrify.

**hors** /'ɔʀ/ *prép* **~ de** outside, (avec mouvement) out of; **~ d'atteinte** out of reach; **~ d'haleine** out of breath; **~ de prix** extremely expensive; **~**

**pair** outstanding; **~ de soi** beside oneself. **hors-bord** *nm inv* speedboat. **hors-d'œuvre** *nm inv* hors-d'œuvre. **hors-jeu** *a inv* offside. **hors-la-loi** *nm inv* outlaw. **hors-piste** *nm* off-piste skiing. **hors-taxe** *a inv* duty-free.

**horticulteur**, **-trice** /ɔʀtikyltœʀ, -tʀis/ *nm,f* horticulturist.

**hospice** /ɔspis/ *nm* home.

**hospitalier**, **-ière** /ɔspitalje, -jɛʀ/ *a* hospitable; (Méd) hospital. **hospitaliser** [1] *vt* take to hospital. **hospitalité** *nf* hospitality.

**hostile** /ɔstil/ *a* hostile. **hostilité** *nf* hostility.

**hôte** /ot/ *nm* (maître) host; (invité) guest.

**hôtel** /otɛl/ *nm* hotel; **~ (particulier)** (private) mansion; **~ de ville** town hall.

**hôtelier**, **-ière** /otəlje, -jɛʀ/ *a* hotel. ● *nm,f* hotel keeper. **hôtellerie** *nf* hotel business.

**hôtesse** /otɛs/ *nf* hostess; **~ de l'air** stewardess.

**hotte** /'ɔt/ *nf* basket; **~ aspirante** extractor (hood), (US) ventilator.

**houblon** /'ublɔ̃/ *nm* **le ~** hops.

**houille** /'uj/ *nf* coal; **~ blanche** hydroelectric power.

**houle** /'ul/ *nf* swell. **houleux**, **-euse** *a* (*mer*) rough; (*débat*) stormy.

**housse** /'us/ *nf* cover; **~ de siège** seat cover.

**houx** /'u/ *nm* holly.

**huées** /'ɥe/ *nfpl* boos. **huer** [1] *vt* boo.

**huile** /ɥil/ *nf* oil; (personne 🄸) bigwig. **huiler** [1] *vt* oil. **huileux**, **-euse** *a* oily.

**huis** /'ɥi/ *nm* **à ~ clos** in camera.

**huissier** /ɥisje/ *nm* (Jur) bailiff; (portier) usher.

**huit** /'ɥi(t)/ *a* eight; **~ jours** a week; **lundi en ~** a week on Monday. ● *nm* eight. **huitième** *a & nmf* eighth.

**huître** /ɥitʀ/ *nf* oyster.

**humain**, **~e** /ymɛ̃, -ɛn/ *a* human; (compatissant) humane. **humanitaire** *a* humanitarian. **humanité** *nf* humanity.

**humble** /œ̃bl/ *a* humble.

**humeur** /ymœʀ/ *nf* mood; (tempérament) temper; **de bonne/mauvaise ~** in a good/bad mood.

**humide** /ymid/ *a* damp; (*chaleur, climat*) humid; (*lèvres, yeux*) moist. **humidité** *nf* humidity.

**humilier** /ymilje/ [45] *vt* humiliate.

**humoristique** /ymɔʀistik/ *a* humorous.

**humour** /ymuʀ/ *nm* humour; **avoir de l'~** have a sense of humour.

**hurlement** /'yʀləmɑ̃/ *nm* howl(ing). **hurler** [1] *vt/i* howl.

**hutte** /'yt/ *nf* hut.

**hydratant**, **~e** /idʀatɑ̃, -t/ *a* (*lotion*) moisturizing.

**hydravion** /idʀavjɔ̃/ *nm* seaplane.

**hydroélectrique** /idʀɔelɛktʀik/ *a* hydroelectric.

**hydrogène** /idʀɔʒɛn/ *nm* hydrogen.

**hygiène** /iʒjɛn/ *nf* hygiene. **hygiénique** *a* hygienic.

**hymne** /imn/ *nm* hymn; **~ national** national anthem.

**hyperlien** /ipɛʀljɛ̃/ *nm* (Internet) hyperlink.

**hypermarché** /ipɛʀmaʀʃe/ *nm* (supermarché) hypermarket.

**hypertension** /ipɛʀtɑ̃sjɔ̃/ *nf* high blood-pressure.

**hypertexte** /ipɛʀtɛkst/ *nm* (Internet) hypertext.

**hypnotiser** /ipnɔtize/ [1] *vt* hypnotize.

**hypocrisie** /ipɔkʀizi/ *nf* hypocrisy.

**hypocrite** /ipɔkʀit/ *a* hypocritical. ● *nmf* hypocrite.

**hypothèque** /ipɔtɛk/ *nf* mortgage.

**hypothèse** /ipɔtɛz/ *nf* hypothesis.

**hystérie** /isteʀi/ *nf* hysteria.

# Ii

**ici** /isi/ *adv* (dans l'espace) here; (dans le temps) now; **d'~ demain** by tomorrow; **d'~ là** in the meantime; **d'~ peu** shortly; **~ même** in this very place; **jusqu'~** until now; (dans le passé) until then.

**idéal**, **~e** (*mpl* **-aux**) /ideal, -o/ *a* & *nm* ideal. **idéaliser** [1] *vt* idealize.

**idée** /ide/ *nf* idea; (esprit) mind; **avoir dans l'~ de faire** plan to do; **il ne me viendrait jamais à l'~ de faire** it would never occur to me to do; **~ fixe** obsession; **~ reçue** conventional opinion.

**identification** /idɑ̃tifikasjɔ̃/ *nf* identification. **identifier** [45] *vt*, **s'identifier** *vpr* identify (**à** with).

**identique** /idɑ̃tik/ *a* identical.

**identité** /idɑ̃tite/ *nf* identity.

**idéologie** /ideɔlɔʒi/ *nf* ideology.

**idiome** /idjom/ *nm* idiom.

**idiot**, **~e** /idjo, -ɔt/ *a* idiotic. ● *nm,f* idiot. **idiotie** *nf* idiocy; (acte, parole) idiotic thing.

**idole** /idɔl/ *nf* idol.

**if** /if/ *nm* yew.

**ignare** /iɲaʀ/ *a* ignorant. ● *nmf* ignoramus.

**ignoble** /iɲɔbl/ *a* vile.

**ignorance** /iɲɔʀɑ̃s/ *nf* ignorance.

**ignorant**, **~e** /iɲɔʀɑ̃, -t/ *a* ignorant. ● *nm,f* ignoramus.

**ignorer** /iɲɔʀe/ [1] *vt* not know; **je l'ignore** I don't know; (*personne*) ignore.

**il** /il/ *pron* (personne, animal familier) he; (chose, animal) it; (impersonnel) it; **~ est vrai que** it is true that; **~ neige/pleut** it is snowing/raining; **~ y a** there is; (pluriel) there are; (temps) ago; (durée) for; **~ y a 2 ans** 2 years ago; **~ y a plus d'une heure que j'attends** I've been waiting for over an hour.

**île** /il/ *nf* island; **~ déserte** desert island; **~s anglo-normandes** Channel Islands; **~s Britanniques** British Isles.

**illégal**, **~e** (*mpl* **~aux**) /ilegal, -o/ *a* illegal.

**illégitime** /ileʒitim/ *a* illegitimate.

**illettré**, **~e** /iletʀe/ *a* & *nm,f* illiterate.

**illicite** /ilisit/ *a* illicit; (Jur) unlawful.

**illimité**, **~e** /ilimite/ *a* unlimited.

**illisible** /ilizibl/ *a* illegible; (*livre*) unreadable.

**illogique** /ilɔʒik/ *a* illogical.

**illuminé**, **~e** /ilymine/ *a* lit up; (*monument*) floodlit.

**illusion** /ilyzjɔ̃/ *nf* illusion; **se faire des ~s** delude oneself. **illusoire** *a* illusory.

**illustre** /ilystʀ/ *a* illustrious.

**illustré**, **~e** /ilystʀe/ *a* illustrated. ● *nm* comic.

**illustrer** /ilystʀe/ [1] *vt* illustrate. □ **s'~** *vpr* become famous.

**îlot** /ilo/ *nm* islet; (de maisons) block.

**ils** /il/ *pron* they.

**image** /imaʒ/ *nf* picture; (métaphore) image; (reflet) reflection. **imagé**, **~e** *a* full of imagery.

**imaginaire** /imaʒinɛʀ/ *a* imaginary. **imaginatif**, **-ive** *a* imaginative. **imagination** *nf* imagination.

**imaginer** /imaʒine/ [1] *vt* imagine; (inventer) think up. □ **s'~** *vpr* (se représenter) imagine (**que** that); (croire) think (**que** that).

**imbécile** /ɛ̃besil/ *a* idiotic. ● *nmf* idiot.

**imbiber** /ɛ̃bibe/ [1] *vt* soak (**de** with). □ **s'~** *vpr* become soaked (**de** with).

**imbriqué**, **~e** /ɛ̃bʀike/ *a* (lié) interlinked, interlocking; (*tuiles*) overlapping.

**imbu**, **~e** /ɛ̃by/ *a* **~ de** full of.

**imitateur**, **-trice** /imitatœʀ, -tʀis/ *nm,f* imitator; (*comédien*) impersonator. **imiter** [1] *vt* imitate; (*personnage*) impersonate; (*signature*) forge; (faire comme) do the same as.

**immatriculation** /imatʀikylasjɔ̃/ *nf* registration.

**immatriculer** /imatʀikyle/ [1] *vt* register; **se faire ~** register; **faire ~ une voiture** have a car registered.

**immédiat**, **~e** /imedja, -t/ *a* immediate. ● *nm* **dans l'~** for the time being.

**immense** /imɑ̃s/ *a* huge, immense.

**immerger** /imɛʀʒe/ [40] *vt* immerse. □ **s'~** *vpr* immerse oneself (**dans** in).

**immeuble** /imœbl/ *nm* block of flats, building; **~ de bureaux** office building *ou* block.

**immigrant**, **~e** /imigʀɑ̃, -t/ *a* & *nmf* immigrant. **immigration** *nf* immigration. **immigré**, **~e** *a* & *nm,f* immigrant. **immigrer** [1] *vi* immigrate.

**imminent**, **~e** /iminɑ̃, -t/ *a* imminent.

**immobile** /imɔbil/ *a* still, motionless.

**immobilier**, **-ière** /imɔbilje, -jɛʀ/ *a* property; **agence immobilière** estate agent's office, (US) real estate office; **agent ~** estate agent, (US) real estate agent. ● *nm* **l'~** property; (US) real estate.

**immobiliser** /imɔbilize/ [1] *vt* immobilize; (stopper) stop. □ **s'~** *vpr* stop.

**immonde** /imɔ̃d/ *a* filthy.

**immoral**, **~e** (*mpl* **-aux**) /imɔʀal, -o/ *a* immoral.

**immortel**, **~le** /imɔʀtɛl/ *a* immortal.

**immuable** /imɥabl/ *a* unchanging.

**immuniser** /imynize/ [1] *vt* immunize; **immunisé contre** (à l'abri de) immune to. **immunité** *nf* immunity.

**impact** /ɛ̃pakt/ *nm* impact.

**impair**, **~e** /ɛ̃pɛʀ/ *a* (*numéro*) odd. ● *nm* blunder, faux pas.

**imparfait**, **~e** /ɛ̃paʀfɛ, -t/ *a* & *nm* imperfect.

**impasse** /ɛ̃pɑs/ *nf* (rue) dead end; (situation) deadlock.

**impatient**, **~e** /ɛ̃pasjɑ̃, -t/ *a* impatient.

**impatienter** /ɛ̃pasjɑ̃te/ [1] *vt* annoy. □ **s'~** *vpr* get impatient (**contre qn** with sb).

**impayé**, **~e** /ɛ̃peje/ *a* unpaid.

**impeccable** /ɛ̃pekabl/ *a* (propre) impeccable, spotless; (soigné) perfect.

**impensable** /ɛ̃pɑ̃sabl/ *a* unthinkable.

**impératif**, **-ive** /ɛ̃peʀatif, -v/ *a* imperative. ● *nm* (Gram) imperative; (contrainte) imperative; **~s** (exigences) requirements, demands (**de** of).

**impératrice** /ɛ̃peʀatʀis/ *nf* empress.

**impérial**, **~e** (*mpl* **-iaux**) /ɛ̃peʀjal, -jo/ *a* imperial.

**impérieux**, **-ieuse** /ɛ̃peʀjø, -z/ *a* imperious; (pressant) pressing.

**imperméable** /ɛ̃pɛʀmeabl/ *a* impervious (**à** to); (*manteau, tissu*) waterproof. ● *nm* raincoat.

**impersonnel**, **~le** /ɛ̃pɛʀsɔnɛl/ *a* impersonal.

**impertinent**, **~e** /ɛ̃pɛʀtinɑ̃, -t/ *a* impertinent.

**imperturbable** /ɛ̃pɛʀtyʀbabl/ *a* unshakeable, unruffled.

**impétueux**, **-euse** /ɛ̃petɥø, -z/ *a* impetuous.

**impitoyable** /ɛ̃pitwajabl/ *a* merciless.

**implant** /ɛ̃plɑ̃/ *nm* implant.

**implanter** /ɛ̃plɑ̃te/ [1] *vt* establish, set up. □ **s'~** *vpr* become established.

**implication** /ɛ̃plikasjɔ̃/ *nf* (conséquence) implication; (participation) involvement.

**impliquer** /ɛ̃plike/ [1] *vt* (mêler) implicate (**dans** in); (signifier) imply, mean (**que** that); (nécessiter) involve (**de faire** doing).

**implorer** /ɛ̃plɔʀe/ [1] *vt* implore, beg for.

**impoli**, **~e** /ɛ̃pɔli/ *a* impolite, rude.

**importance** /ɛ̃pɔʀtɑ̃s/ *nf* importance; (taille) size; (ampleur) extent; **sans ~** unimportant.

**important**, **~e** /ɛ̃pɔʀtɑ̃, -t/ *a* important; (en quantité) considerable, sizeable, big; (*air*) self-important. ● *nm* **l'~** the important thing.

**importateur**, **-trice** /ɛ̃pɔʀtatœʀ, -tʀis/ *nm,f* importer. ● *a* importing. **importation** *nf* import.

**importer** /ɛ̃pɔʀte/ [1] *vt* (Comm) import. ● *vi* matter, be important (**à** to); **il importe que** it is important that; **n'importe, peu importe** it does not matter; **n'importe comment** anyhow; **n'importe où** anywhere; **n'importe qui** anybody; **n'importe quoi** anything.

**importun**, **~e** /ɛ̃pɔʀtœ̃, -yn/ *a* troublesome. ● *nm,f* nuisance.

**imposer** /ɛ̃poze/ [1] *vt* impose (**à** on); (taxer) tax; **en ~ à qn** impress sb. □ **s'~** *vpr* (*action*) be essential; (se faire reconnaître) stand out; (s'astreindre à) **s'~ de faire** force oneself to do.

**imposition** /ɛ̃pozisjɔ̃/ *nf* taxation; **~ des mains** laying-on of hands.

**impossible** /ɛ̃posibl/ *a* impossible. ● *nm* **faire l'~** do one's utmost.

**impôt** /ɛ̃po/ *nm* tax; **~s** (contributions) tax(ation), taxes; **~ sur le revenu** income tax.

**impotent**, **~e** /ɛ̃pɔtɑ̃, -t/ *a* disabled.

**imprécis**, **~e** /ɛ̃pʀesi, -z/ *a* imprecise.

**imprégner** /ɛ̃pʀeɲe/ [14] *vt* fill (**de** with); (imbiber) impregnate (**de** with). □ **s'~ de** *vpr* (fig) immerse oneself in.

**impression** /ɛ̃pʀesjɔ̃/ *nf* impression; (de livre) printing. **impressionnant** *a* impressive; (choquant) disturbing. **impressionner** [1] *vt* impress; (choquer) disturb.

**imprévisible** /ɛ̃pʀevizibl/ *a* unpredictable.

**imprévu**, **~e** /ɛ̃pʀevy/ *a* unexpected. ● *nm* unexpected incident;

**sauf** ~ unless anything unexpected happens.

**imprimante** /ɛ̃pʀimɑ̃t/ *nf* (Ordinat) printer; ~ **à jet d'encre** ink-jet printer; ~ **(à) laser** laser printer.

**imprimé**, ~**e** /ɛ̃pʀime/ *a* printed. ● *nm* printed form.

**imprimer** /ɛ̃pʀime/ [1] *vt* print; (marquer) imprint. **imprimerie** *nf* (art) printing; (lieu) printing works. **imprimeur** *nm* printer.

**improbable** /ɛ̃pʀɔbabl/ *a* unlikely, improbable.

**impropre** /ɛ̃pʀɔpʀ/ *a* incorrect; ~ **à** unfit for.

**improviste**: **à l'**~ /alɛ̃pʀɔvist/ *loc* unexpectedly.

**imprudence** /ɛ̃pʀydɑ̃s/ *nf* carelessness; (acte) careless action.

**imprudent**, ~**e** /ɛ̃pʀydɑ̃, -t/ *a* careless; **il est** ~ **de** it is unwise to.

**impudent**, ~**e** /ɛ̃pydɑ̃, -t/ *a* impudent.

**impuissant**, ~**e** /ɛ̃pɥisɑ̃, -t/ *a* helpless; (Méd) impotent; ~ **à faire** powerless to do.

**impulsif**, **-ive** /ɛ̃pylsif, -v/ *a* impulsive. **impulsion** *nf* (poussée, influence) impetus; (instinct, mouvement) impulse.

**impur**, ~**e** /ɛ̃pyʀ/ *a* impure.

**imputer** /ɛ̃pyte/ [1] *vt* ~ **à** attribute to, impute to.

**inabordable** /inabɔʀdabl/ *a* (*prix*) prohibitive.

**inacceptable** /inaksɛptabl/ *a* unacceptable.

**inactif**, **-ive** /inaktif, -v/ *a* inactive.

**inadapté**, ~**e** /inadapte/ *a* maladjusted. ● *nm, f* (Psych) maladjusted person.

**inadmissible** /inadmisibl/ *a* unacceptable.

**inadvertance** /inadvɛʀtɑ̃s/ *nf* **par** ~ by mistake.

**inanimé**, ~**e** /inanime/ *a* (évanoui) unconscious; (mort) lifeless; (*matière*) inanimate.

**inaperçu**, ~**e** /inapɛʀsy/ *a* unnoticed.

**inapte** /inapt/ *a* unsuited (**à** to); ~ **à faire** incapable of doing; ~ **au service militaire** unfit for military service.

**inattendu**, ~**e** /inatɑ̃dy/ *a* unexpected.

**inaugurer** /inogyʀe/ [1] *vt* inaugurate.

**incapable** /ɛ̃kapabl/ *a* incapable (**de qch** of sth); ~ **de faire** unable to do, incapable of doing. ● *nmf* incompetent.

**incapacité** /ɛ̃kapasite/ *nf* inability, incapacity; **être dans l'**~ **de faire** be unable to do.

**incarcérer** /ɛ̃kaʀseʀe/ [14] *vt* imprison, incarcerate.

**incarnation** /ɛ̃kaʀnasjɔ̃/ *nf* embodiment, incarnation. **incarné**, ~**e** *a* (*ongle*) ingrowing.

**incassable** /ɛ̃kɑsabl/ *a* unbreakable.

**incendiaire** /ɛ̃sɑ̃djɛʀ/ *a* incendiary; (*propos*) inflammatory. ● *nmf* arsonist.

**incendie** /ɛ̃sɑ̃di/ *nm* fire; ~ **criminel** arson. **incendier** [45] *vt* set fire to.

**incertain**, ~**e** /ɛ̃sɛʀtɛ̃, -ɛn/ *a* uncertain; (*contour*) vague; (*temps*) unsettled. **incertitude** *nf* uncertainty.

**inceste** /ɛ̃sɛst/ *nm* incest.

**incidence** /ɛ̃sidɑ̃s/ *nf* effect.

**incident** /ɛ̃sidɑ̃/ *nm* incident; ~ **technique** technical hitch.

**incinérer** /ɛ̃sineʀe/ [14] *vt* incinerate; (*mort*) cremate.

**inciser** /ɛ̃size/ [1] *vt* make an incision in; (*abcès*) lance. **incisif**, **-ive** *a* incisive. **incision** *nf* incision; (d'abcès) lancing.

**incitation** /ɛ̃sitasjɔ̃/ *nf* (Jur) incitement (**à** to); (encouragement) incentive. **inciter** [1] *vt* incite (**à** to); (encourager) encourage.

**inclinaison** /ɛ̃klinɛzɔ̃/ *nf* incline; (de la tête) tilt.

**inclination** /ɛ̃klinasjɔ̃/ *nf* (penchant) inclination; (geste) (du buste) bow; (de la tête) nod.

**incliner** /ɛ̃kline/ [1] *vt* tilt, lean; (courber) bend; (inciter) encourage (**à** to); **~ la tête** (approuver) nod; (révérence) bow. ● *vi* **~ à** be inclined to. □ **s'~** *vpr* lean forward; (se courber) bow down (**devant** before); (céder) give in, yield (**devant** to); (*chemin*) slope.

**inclure** /ɛ̃klyʀ/ [16] *vt* include; (enfermer) enclose; **jusqu'au lundi inclus** up to and including Monday.

**incohérence** /ɛ̃kɔeʀɑ̃s/ *nf* incoherence; (contradiction) discrepancy. **incohérent**, **~e** *a* incoherent, inconsistent.

**incolore** /ɛ̃kɔlɔʀ/ *a* colourless; (*verre*) clear.

**incommoder** /ɛ̃kɔmɔde/ [1] *vt* inconvenience, bother.

**incompatible** /ɛ̃kɔ̃patibl/ *a* incompatible.

**incompétent**, **~e** /ɛ̃kɔ̃petɑ̃, -t/ *a* incompetent.

**incomplet**, **-ète** /ɛ̃kɔ̃plɛ, -t/ *a* incomplete.

**incompréhension** /ɛ̃kɔ̃pʀeɑ̃sjɔ̃/ *nf* lack of understanding.

**incompris**, **~e** /ɛ̃kɔ̃pʀi, -z/ *a* misunderstood.

**inconcevable** /ɛ̃kɔ̃svabl/ *a* inconceivable.

**incongru**, **~e** /ɛ̃kɔ̃gʀy/ *a* unseemly.

**inconnu**, **~e** /ɛ̃kɔny/ *a* unknown (**à** to). ● *nm,f* stranger. ● *nm* **l'~** the unknown.

**inconscience** /ɛ̃kɔ̃sjɑ̃s/ *nf* unconsciousness; (folie) madness.

**inconscient**, **~e** /ɛ̃kɔ̃sjɑ̃, -t/ *a* unconscious (**de** of); (fou) mad. ● *nm* (Psych) subconscious.

**incontestable** /ɛ̃kɔ̃tɛstabl/ *a* indisputable.

**incontrôlable** /ɛ̃kɔ̃tʀolabl/ *a* unverifiable; (non maîtrisé) uncontrollable.

**inconvenant**, **~e** /ɛ̃kɔ̃vnɑ̃, -t/ *a* improper.

**inconvénient** /ɛ̃kɔ̃venjɑ̃/ *nm* disadvantage, drawback; (objection) objection.

**incorporer** /ɛ̃kɔʀpɔʀe/ [1] *vt* incorporate; (Culin) blend (**à** into); (Mil) enlist.

**incorrect**, **~e** /ɛ̃kɔʀɛkt/ *a* (faux) incorrect; (malséant) improper; (impoli) impolite; (déloyal) unfair.

**incrédule** /ɛ̃kʀedyl/ *a* incredulous.

**incriminer** /ɛ̃kʀimine/ [1] *vt* (*personne*) incriminate; (*conduite, action*) attack.

**incroyable** /ɛ̃kʀwajabl/ *a* incredible.

**incruster** /ɛ̃kʀyste/ [1] *vt* inlay (**de** with).

**incubateur** /ɛ̃kybatœʀ/ *nm* incubator.

**inculpation** /ɛ̃kylpasjɔ̃/ *nf* charge (**de, pour** of). **inculpé**, **~e** *nm,f* accused. **inculper** [1] *vt* charge (**de** with).

**inculquer** /ɛ̃kylke/ [1] *vt* instil (**à** into).

**inculte** /ɛ̃kylt/ *a* uncultivated; (*personne*) uneducated.

**incurver** /ɛ̃kyʀve/ [1] *vt* curve, bend. □ **s'~** *vpr* curve, bend.

**Inde** /ɛ̃d/ *nf* India.

**indécent**, **~e** /ɛ̃desɑ̃, -t/ *a* indecent.

**indécis**, **~e** /ɛ̃desi, -z/ *a* (de nature) indecisive; (temporairement) undecided.

**indéfini**, **~e** /ɛ̃defini/ *a* (Gram) indefinite; (vague) undefined; (sans limites) indeterminate.

**indemne** /ɛ̃dɛmn/ *a* unharmed.

**indemniser** /ɛ̃dɛmnize/ [1] *vt* compensate (**de** for).

**indemnité** /ɛ̃dɛmnite/ *nf* indemnity, compensation; (allocation) allowance; **~s de licenciement** redundancy payment.

**indépendance** /ɛ̃depɑ̃dɑ̃s/ *nf* independence. **indépendant**, **~e** *a* independent.

**indéterminé**, **~e** /ɛ̃detɛʀmine/ *a* unspecified.

**index** /ɛ̃dɛks/ *nm* forefinger; (liste) index.

**indicateur**, **-trice** /ɛ̃dikatœʀ, -tʀis/ *nm, f* (police) informer. ● *nm* (livre) guide, (Tech) indicator.

**indicatif**, **-ve** /ɛ̃dikatif, -v/ *a* indicative (**de** of). ● *nm* (à la radio) signature tune; (téléphonique) dialling code; (Gram) indicative.

**indication** /ɛ̃dikasjɔ̃/ *nf* indication; (renseignement) information; (directive) instruction.

**indice** /ɛ̃dis/ *nm* sign; (dans une enquête) clue; (des prix) index; (évaluation) rating; **~ d'écoute** audience ratings.

**indifférence** /ɛ̃difeʀɑ̃s/ *nf* indifference.

**indifférent**, **~e** /ɛ̃difeʀɑ̃, -t/ *a* indifferent (**à** to); **ça m'est ~** it makes no difference to me.

**indigène** /ɛ̃diʒɛn/ *a & nmf* native, indigenous; (du pays) local. ● *nmf* native.

**indigent**, **~e** /ɛ̃diʒɑ̃, -t/ *a* destitute.

**indigeste** /ɛ̃diʒɛst/ *a* indigestible. **indigestion** *nf* indigestion.

**indigne** /ɛ̃diɲ/ *a* unworthy (**de** of); (*acte*) vile. **indigner** (**s'**) [1] *vpr* become indignant (**de** at).

**indiqué**, **~e** /ɛ̃dike/ *a* (*heure*) appointed; (opportun) appropriate; (conseillé) recommended.

**indiquer** /ɛ̃dike/ [1] *vt* (montrer) show, indicate; (renseigner sur) point out, tell; (déterminer) give, state, appoint; **~ du doigt** point to *ou* out *ou* at.

**indirect**, **~e** /ɛ̃diʀɛkt/ *a* indirect.

**indiscipliné**, **~e** /ɛ̃disipline/ *a* unruly.

**indiscret**, **-ète** /ɛ̃diskʀɛ, -t/ *a* (*personne*) inquisitive; (*question*) indiscreet.

**indiscutable** /ɛ̃diskytabl/ *a* unquestionable.

**indispensable** /ɛ̃dispɑ̃sabl/ *a* indispensable; **il est ~ qu'il vienne** it is essential that he comes.

**individu** /ɛ̃dividy/ *nm* individual.

**individuel**, **~le** /ɛ̃dividɥɛl/ *a* (pour une personne) individual; (qui concerne l'individu) personal; **chambre ~le** single room; **maison ~le** detached house.

**indolore** /ɛ̃dɔlɔʀ/ *a* painless.

**Indonésie** /ɛ̃dɔnezi/ *nf* Indonesia.

**indu**, **~e** /ɛ̃dy/ *a* **à une heure ~e** at some ungodly hour.

**induire** /ɛ̃dɥiʀ/ [17] *vt* infer (**de** from); (inciter) induce (**à faire** to do); **~ en erreur** mislead.

**indulgence** /ɛ̃dylʒɑ̃s/ *nf* indulgence; (de jury) leniency. **indulgent**, **~e** *a* indulgent; (clément) lenient.

**industrialisé**, **~e** /ɛ̃dystʀijalize/ *a* industrialized.

**industrie** /ɛ̃dystʀi/ *nf* industry.

**industriel**, **~le** /ɛ̃dystʀijɛl/ *a* industrial. ● *nm* industrialist.

**inédit**, **~e** /inedi, -t/ *a* unpublished; (fig) original.

**inefficace** /inefikas/ *a* (*remède, mesure*) ineffective; (*appareil, système*) inefficient.

**inégal**, **~e** (*mpl* **-aux**) /inegal, -o/ *a* unequal; (irrégulier) uneven. **inégalable** *a* matchless. **inégalité** *nf* (injustice) inequality; (irrégularité) unevenness; (disproportion) disparity.

**inéluctable** /inelyktabl/ *a* inescapable.

**inepte** /inɛpt/ *a* inept, absurd.

**inerte** /inɛʀt/ *a* inert; (immobile) lifeless; (sans énergie) apathetic. **inertie** *nf* inertia; (fig) apathy.

**inespéré**, **~e** /inɛspeʀe/ *a* unhoped for.

**inestimable** /inɛstimabl/ *a* priceless; (*aide*) invaluable.

**inexact**, **~e** /inɛgza(kt), -kt/ *a* (imprécis) inaccurate; (incorrect) incorrect.

**in extremis** /inɛkstʀemis/ *adv* (par nécessité) as a last resort; (au dernier moment) at the last minute. ● *a* last-minute.

**infaillible** /ɛ̃fajibl/ *a* infallible.

**infâme** /ɛ̃fɑm/ *a* vile.

**infantile** /ɛ̃fɑ̃til/ *a* (puéril) infantile; (*maladie*) childhood; (*mortalité*) infant.

**infarctus** /ɛ̃faʀktys/ *nm* coronary, heart attack.

**infatigable** /ɛ̃fatigabl/ *a* tireless.

**infect**, **~e** /ɛ̃fɛkt/ *a* revolting.

**infecter** /ɛ̃fɛkte/ [1] *vt* infect. □ **s'~** *vpr* become infected. **infectieux**, **-ieuse** *a* infectious. **infection** *nf* infection.

**inférieur**, **~e** /ɛ̃feʀjœʀ/ *a* (plus bas) lower; (moins bon) inferior (**à** to); **~ à** (plus petit que) smaller than; (plus bas que) lower than. ● *nm,f* inferior. **infériorité** *nf* inferiority.

**infernal**, **~e** (*mpl* **-aux**) /ɛ̃fɛʀnal, -o/ *a* infernal.

**infester** /ɛ̃fɛste/ [1] *vt* infest.

**infidèle** /ɛ̃fidɛl/ *a* unfaithful (**à** to). **infidélité** *nf* unfaithfulness; (acte) infidelity.

**infiltrer (s')** /sɛ̃filtʀe/ [1] *vpr* **s'~ (dans)** (*personnes, idées*) infiltrate; (*liquide*) seep through.

**infime** /ɛ̃fim/ *a* tiny, minute.

**infini**, **~e** /ɛ̃fini/ *a* infinite. ● *nm* infinity; **à l'~** endlessly.

**infinité** /ɛ̃finite/ *nf* **l'~** infinity; **une ~ de** an endless number of.

**infinitif** /ɛ̃finitif/ *nm* infinitive.

**infirme** /ɛ̃fiʀm/ *a* disabled. ● *nmf* disabled person. **infirmerie** *nf* sickbay, infirmary. **infirmier** *nm* (male) nurse. **infirmière** *nf* nurse. **infirmité** *nf* disability.

**inflammable** /ɛ̃flamabl/ *a* inflammable.

**inflation** /ɛ̃flasjɔ̃/ *nf* inflation.

**infliger** /ɛ̃fliʒe/ [40] *vt* inflict; (*sanction*) impose.

**influence** /ɛ̃flyɑ̃s/ *nf* influence. **influencer** [10] *vt* influence. **influent**, **~e** *a* influential.

**influer** /ɛ̃flye/ [1] *vi* **~ sur** influence.

**informateur**, **-trice** /ɛ̃fɔʀmatœʀ, -tʀis/ *nm,f* informant; (pour la police) informer.

**informaticien**, **~ne** /ɛ̃fɔʀmatisjɛ̃, -ɛn/ *nm,f* computer scientist.

**information** /ɛ̃fɔRmasjɔ̃/ *nf* information; (Jur) inquiry; **une ~** (some) information; (nouvelle) (some) news; **les ~s** the news.

**informatique** /ɛ̃fɔRmatik/ *nf* computer science; (techniques) information technology. **informatiser** [1] *vt* computerize.

**informer** /ɛ̃fɔRme/ [1] *vt* inform (**de** about, of). □ **s'~** *vpr* enquire (**de** about).

**inforoute** /ɛ̃fɔRut/ *nf* (Ordinat) information highway.

**infortune** /ɛ̃fɔRtyn/ *nf* misfortune.

**infraction** /ɛ̃fRaksjɔ̃/ *nf* offence; **~ à** (*loi, règlement*) breach of.

**infrastructure** /ɛ̃fRastRyktyR/ *nf* infrastructure; (équipements) facilities.

**infructueux, -euse** /ɛ̃fRyktɥø, -z/ *a* fruitless.

**infuser** /ɛ̃fyze/ [1] *vt/i* infuse, brew. **infusion** *nf* herbal tea, infusion.

**ingénier (s')** /(s)ɛ̃ʒenje/ [45] *vpr* **s'~ à** strive to.

**ingénieur** /ɛ̃ʒenjœR/ *nm* engineer.

**ingénieux, -ieuse** /ɛ̃ʒenjø, -z/ *a* ingenious. **ingéniosité** *nf* ingenuity.

**ingénu, ~e** /ɛ̃ʒeny/ *a* naïve.

**ingérence** /ɛ̃ʒeRɑ̃s/ *nf* interference.

**ingérer (s')** /sɛ̃ʒeRe/ [14] *vpr* **s'~ dans** interfere in.

**ingrat, ~e** /ɛ̃gRa, -t/ *a* (*personne*) ungrateful; (*travail*) unrewarding, thankless; (*visage*) unattractive.

**ingrédient** /ɛ̃gRedjɑ̃/ *nm* ingredient.

**ingurgiter** /ɛ̃gyRʒite/ [1] *vt* swallow.

**inhabité, ~e** /inabite/ *a* uninhabited.

**inhabituel, ~le** /inabitɥɛl/ *a* unusual.

**inhumain, ~e** /inymɛ̃, -ɛn/ *a* inhuman.

**inhumation** /inymasjɔ̃/ *nf* burial.

**initial, ~e** (*mpl* **-iaux**) /inisjal, -jo/ *a* initial. **initiale** *nf* initial.

**initialisation** /inisjalizasjɔ̃/ *nf* (Ordinat) formatting. **initialiser** [1] *vt* format.

**initiation** /inisjasjɔ̃/ *nf* initiation; (formation) introduction (**à** to); **cours d'~** introductory course.

**initiative** /inisjativ/ *nf* initiative.

**initier** /inisje/ [45] *vt* initiate (**à** into); (faire découvrir) introduce (**à** to). □ **s'~** *vpr* **s'~ à qch** learn sth.

**injecter** /ɛ̃ʒɛkte/ [1] *vt* inject; **injecté de sang** bloodshot. **injection** *nf* injection.

**injure** /ɛ̃ʒyR/ *nf* insult. **injurier** [45] *vt* insult. **injurieux, -ieuse** *a* insulting.

**injuste** /ɛ̃ʒyst/ *a* unjust, unfair. **injustice** *nf* injustice.

**inné, ~e** /inne/ *a* innate, inborn.

**innocence** /inɔsɑ̃s/ *nf* innocence. **innocent, ~e** *a & nm,f* innocent. **innocenter** [1] *vt* clear, prove innocent.

**innombrable** /inɔ̃bRabl/ *a* countless.

**innovateur, -trice** /inɔvatœR, -tRis/ *nm,f* innovator. **innovation** *nf* innovation. **innover** [1] *vi* innovate.

**inodore** /inɔdɔR/ *a* odourless.

**inoffensif, -ive** /inɔfɑ̃sif, -v/ *a* harmless.

**inondation** /inɔ̃dasjɔ̃/ *nf* flood; (action) flooding.

**inonder** /inɔ̃de/ [1] *vt* flood; (mouiller) soak; (envahir) inundate (**de** with); **inondé de soleil** bathed in sunlight.

**inopiné**, **~e** /inɔpine/ *a* unexpected; (*mort*) sudden.

**inopportun**, **~e** /inɔpɔʀtœ̃, -yn/ *a* inopportune, ill-timed.

**inoubliable** /inublijabl/ *a* unforgettable.

**inouï**, **~e** /inwi/ *a* incredible; (*événement*) unprecedented.

**inox**® /inɔks/ *nm* stainless steel.

**inoxydable** /inɔksidabl/ *a* **acier ~** stainless steel.

**inqualifiable** /ɛ̃kalifjabl/ *a* unspeakable.

**inquiet**, **-iète** /ɛ̃kjɛ, -t/ *a* worried. **inquiétant**, **~e** *a* worrying.

**inquiéter** /ɛ̃kjete/ [14] *vt* worry. □ **s'~** *vpr* worry (**de** about). **inquiétude** *nf* anxiety, worry.

**insaisissable** /ɛ̃sezisabl/ *a* (*personne*) elusive; (*nuance*) indefinable.

**insalubre** /ɛ̃salybʀ/ *a* unhealthy.

**insatisfaisant**, **~e** /ɛ̃satisfəzɑ̃, -t/ *a* unsatisfactory. **insatisfait**, **~e** *a* (mécontent) dissatisfied; (frustré) unfulfilled.

**inscription** /ɛ̃skʀipsjɔ̃/ *nf* inscription; (immatriculation) enrolment.

**inscrire** /ɛ̃skʀiʀ/ [30] *vt* write (down); (graver, tracer) inscribe; (*personne*) enrol; (sur une liste) put down. □ **s'~** *vpr* put one's name down; **s'~ à** (*école*) enrol at; (*club, parti*) join; (*examen*) enter for.

**insecte** /ɛ̃sɛkt/ *nm* insect.

**insécurité** /ɛ̃sekyʀite/ *nf* insecurity.

**insensé**, **~e** /ɛ̃sɑ̃se/ *a* mad.

**insensibilité** /ɛ̃sɑ̃sibilite/ *nf* insensitivity. **insensible** *a* insensitive (**à** to); (graduel) imperceptible.

**insérer** /ɛ̃seʀe/ [14] *vt* insert. □ **s'~** *vpr* be inserted; **s'~ dans** be part of.

**insigne** /ɛ̃siɲ/ *nm* badge; **~s** (d'une fonction) insignia.

**insignifiant**, **~e** /ɛ̃siɲifjɑ̃, -t/ *a* insignificant.

**insinuation** /ɛ̃sinɥasjɔ̃/ *nf* insinuation.

**insinuer** /ɛ̃sinɥe/ [1] *vt* insinuate. □ **s'~** *vpr* (socialement) ingratiate oneself (**auprès de qn** with sb); **s'~ dans** (se glisser) slip into; (*idée, nuance*) creep into.

**insipide** /ɛ̃sipid/ *a* insipid.

**insistance** /ɛ̃sistɑ̃s/ *nf* insistence. **insistant**, **~e** *a* insistent.

**insister** /ɛ̃siste/ [1] *vi* insist (**pour faire** on doing); **~ sur** stress.

**insolation** /ɛ̃sɔlasjɔ̃/ *nf* (Méd) sunstroke.

**insolent**, **~e** /ɛ̃sɔlɑ̃, -t/ *a* insolent.

**insolite** /ɛ̃sɔlit/ *a* unusual.

**insolvable** /ɛ̃sɔlvabl/ *a* insolvent.

**insomnie** /ɛ̃sɔmni/ *nf* insomnia.

**insonoriser** /ɛ̃sɔnɔʀize/ [1] *vt* soundproof.

**insouciance** /ɛ̃susjɑ̃s/ *nf* lack of concern. **insouciant**, **~e** *a* carefree.

**insoutenable** /ɛ̃sutnabl/ *a* unbearable; (*argument*) untenable.

**inspecter** /ɛ̃spɛkte/ [1] *vt* inspect. **inspecteur**, **-trice** *nm,f* inspector. **inspection** *nf* inspection.

**inspiration** /ɛ̃spiʀasjɔ̃/ *nf* inspiration; (respiration) breath.

**inspirer** /ɛ̃spiʀe/ [1] *vt* inspire; **~ la méfiance à qn** inspire distrust in sb. ● *vi* breathe in. □ **s'~ de** *vpr* be inspired by.

**instabilité** /ɛ̃stabilite/ *nf* instability; unsteadiness. **instable** *a* unstable; (*temps*) unsettled.

**installation** /ɛ̃stalasjɔ̃/ *nf* installation; (de local) fitting out; (de locataire) settling in. **installations** *nfpl* facilities.

**installer** /ɛ̃stale/ [1] *vt* install; (*meuble*) put in; (*étagère*) put up; (*gaz, téléphone*) connect; (équiper) fit out. □ **s'~** *vpr* settle (down); (emménager) settle in; **s'~ comme** set oneself up as.

**instance** /ɛ̃stɑ̃s/ *nf* authority; (prière) entreaty; **avec ~** with insistence; **en ~** pending; **en ~ de** in the course of, on the point of.

**instant** /ɛ̃stɑ̃/ *nm* moment, instant; **à l'~** this instant.

**instantané**, **~e** /ɛ̃stɑ̃tane/ *a* instantaneous; (*café*) instant.

**instar**: **à l'~ de** /alɛ̃staʀdə/ *loc* like.

**instaurer** /ɛ̃stoʀe/ [1] *vt* institute.

**instigateur**, **-trice** /ɛ̃stigatœʀ, -tʀis/ *nm,f* instigator.

**instinct** /ɛ̃stɛ̃/ *nm* instinct; **d'~** instinctively. **instinctif**, **-ive** *a* instinctive.

**instituer** /ɛ̃stitɥe/ [1] *vt* establish.

**institut** /ɛ̃stity/ *nm* institute; **~ de beauté** beauty parlour.

**instituteur**, **-trice** /ɛ̃stitytœʀ, -tʀis/ *nm,f* primary-school teacher.

**institution** /ɛ̃stitysjɔ̃/ *nf* institution; (école) private school.

**instructif**, **-ive** /ɛ̃stʀyktif, -v/ *a* instructive.

**instruction** /ɛ̃stʀyksjɔ̃/ *nf* (formation) education; (Mil) training; (document) directive; **~s** (ordres, mode d'emploi) instructions; (Ordinat) (énoncé) instruction; (pas de séquence) statement.

**instruire** /ɛ̃stʀɥiʀ/ [17] *vt* teach, educate; **~ de** inform of. □ **s'~** *vpr* learn, educate oneself; **s'~ de** enquire about. **instruit**, **~e** *a* educated.

**instrument** /ɛ̃stʀymɑ̃/ *nm* instrument; (outil) tool; (moyen: fig) instrument; **~ de gestion** management tool; **~s de bord** (Aviat) controls.

**insu**: **à l'~ de** /alɛ̃sydə/ *loc* without the knowledge of.

**insuffisance** /ɛ̃syfizɑ̃s/ *nf* (pénurie) shortage; (médiocrité) inadequacy. **insuffisant**, **~e** *a* inadequate; (en nombre) insufficient.

**insulaire** /ɛ̃sylɛʀ/ *a* island, ● *nmf* islander.

**insuline** /ɛ̃sylin/ *nf* insulin.

**insulte** /ɛ̃sylt/ *nf* insult. **insulter** [1] *vt* insult.

**insupportable** /ɛ̃sypɔʀtabl/ *a* unbearable.

**insurger (s')** /(s)ɛ̃syʀʒe/ [40] *vpr* rebel.

**intact**, **~e** /ɛ̃takt/ *a* intact.

**intangible** /ɛ̃tɑ̃ʒibl/ *a* intangible; (*principe*) inviolable.

**intarissable** /ɛ̃taʀisabl/ *a* inexhaustible.

**intégral**, **~e** (*mpl* **-aux**) /ɛ̃tegʀal, -o/ *a* complete; (*texte, édition*) unabridged; (*paiement*) full, in full. **intégralement** *adv* in full. **intégralité** *nf* whole.

**intègre** /ɛ̃tɛgʀ/ *a* upright.

**intégrer** /ɛ̃tegʀe/ [14] *vt* integrate. □ **s'~** *vpr* (*personne*) integrate; (*maison*) fit in.

**intégriste** /ɛ̃tegʀist/ *nmf* fundamentalist.

**intégrité** /ɛ̃tegʀite/ *nf* integrity.

**intellect** /ɛ̃telɛkt/ *nm* intellect. **intellectuel**, **~le** *a & nm,f* intellectual.

**intelligence** /ɛ̃teliʒɑ̃s/ *nf* intelligence; (compréhension) understanding; (complicité) agreement; **agir d'~ avec qn** act in agreement with sb. **intelligent**, **~e** *a* intelligent.

**intempéries** /ɛ̃tɑ̃peʀi/ *nfpl* severe weather.

**intempestif, -ive** /ɛ̃tɑ̃pɛstif, -v/ *a* untimely.

**intenable** /ɛ̃tnabl/ *a* unbearable; (*enfant*) impossible.

**intendance** /ɛ̃tɑ̃dɑ̃s/ *nf* (Scol) bursar's office.

**intendant, ~e** /ɛ̃tɑ̃dɑ̃, -t/ *nm* (Mil) quartermaster. ● *nm,f* (Scol) bursar.

**intense** /ɛ̃tɑ̃s/ *a* intense; (*circulation*) heavy. **intensif, -ive** *a* intensive. **intensité** *nf* intensity.

**intenter** /ɛ̃tɑ̃te/ [1] *vt* **~ un procès** *ou* **une action** institute proceedings (**à, contre** against).

**intention** /ɛ̃tɑ̃sjɔ̃/ *nf* intention (**de faire** of doing); **à l'~ de qn** for sb. **intentionnel, ~le** *a* intentional.

**interactif, -ive** /ɛ̃tɛʀaktif, -v/ *a* (*TV, vidéo*) interactive.

**interaction** /ɛ̃tɛʀaksjɔ̃/ *nf* interaction.

**intercaler** /ɛ̃tɛʀkale/ [1] *vt* insert.

**intercéder** /ɛ̃tɛʀsede/ [14] *vi* intercede (**en faveur de** on behalf of).

**intercepter** /ɛ̃tɛʀsɛpte/ [1] *vt* intercept.

**interdiction** /ɛ̃tɛʀdiksjɔ̃/ *nf* ban; **~ de fumer** no smoking.

**interdire** /ɛ̃tɛʀdiʀ/ [37] *vt* forbid; (officiellement) ban, prohibit; **~ à qn de faire** forbid sb to do.

**interdit, ~e** /ɛ̃tɛʀdi, -t/ *a* prohibited, forbidden; (étonné) dumbfounded.

**intéressant, ~e** /ɛ̃teʀɛsɑ̃, -t/ *a* interesting; (avantageux) attractive.

**intéressé, ~e** /ɛ̃teʀese/ *a* (en cause) concerned; (pour profiter) self-interested. ● *nm,f* person concerned.

**intéresser** /ɛ̃teʀese/ [1] *vt* interest; (concerner) concern. □ **s'~ à** *vpr* be interested in.

**intérêt** /ɛ̃teʀɛ/ *nm* interest; (égoïsme) self-interest; **~(s)** (Comm) interest; **vous avez ~ à** it is in your interest to.

**interface** /ɛ̃tɛʀfas/ *nf* (Ordinat) interface.

**intérieur, ~e** /ɛ̃teʀjœʀ/ *a* inner, inside; (*mur, escalier*) internal; (*vol, politique*) domestic; (*vie, calme*) inner. ● *nm* interior; (de boîte, tiroir) inside; **à l'~ (de)** inside; (fig) within. **intérieurement** *adv* inwardly.

**intérim** /ɛ̃teʀim/ *nm* interim; **assurer l'~** deputize (**de** for); **par ~** on an interim basis; **président par ~** acting president; **faire de l'~** temp.

**intérimaire** /ɛ̃teʀimɛʀ/ *a* temporary, interim. ● *nmf* (secrétaire) temp; (médecin) locum.

**interjection** /ɛ̃tɛʀʒɛksjɔ̃/ *nf* interjection.

**interlocuteur, -trice** /ɛ̃tɛʀlɔkytœʀ, -tʀis/ *nm,f* **son ~** the person one is speaking to.

**interloqué, ~e** /ɛ̃tɛʀlɔke/ *a* **être ~** be taken aback.

**intermède** /ɛ̃tɛʀmɛd/ *nm* interlude.

**intermédiaire** /ɛ̃tɛʀmedjɛʀ/ *a* intermediate. ● *nmf* intermediary. ● *nm* **sans ~** without an intermediary, direct; **par l'~ de** through.

**interminable** /ɛ̃tɛʀminabl/ *a* endless.

**intermittence** /ɛ̃tɛʀmitɑ̃s/ *nf* **par ~** intermittently.

**internat** /ɛ̃tɛʀna/ *nm* boarding-school.

**international, ~e** (*mpl* **-aux**) /ɛ̃tɛʀnasjɔnal, -o/ *a* international.

**internaute** /ɛ̃tɛʀnot/ *nmf* (Ordinat) Netsurfer, Internet user.

**interne** /ɛ̃tɛʀn/ *a* internal; (*cours, formation*) in-house. ● *nmf* (Scol) boarder; (Méd) house officer; (US) intern.

**internement** /ɛ̃tɛʀnəmɑ̃/ *nm* (Pol) internment. **interner** [1] *vt* (Pol) intern; (Méd) commit.

**Internet** /ɛ̃tɛʀnet/ *nm* Internet; **sur ~** on the Internet.

**interpellation** /ɛ̃tɛʀpelasjɔ̃/ *nf* (Pol) questioning. **interpeller** [1] *vt* shout to; (apostropher) shout at; (interroger) question.

**interphone** /ɛ̃tɛʀfɔn/ *nm* intercom; (d'immeuble) entry phone.

**interposer (s')** /(s)ɛ̃tɛʀpoze/ [1] *vpr* intervene.

**interprétariat** /ɛ̃tɛʀpʀetaʀja/ *nm* interpreting. **interprétation** *nf* interpretation; (d'artiste) performance. **interprète** *nmf* interpreter; (artiste) performer. **interpréter** [14] *vt* interpret; (jouer) play; (chanter) sing.

**interrogateur, -trico** /ɛ̃tɛʀɔgatœʀ, -tʀis/ *a* questioning. **interrogatif, -ive** *a* interrogative. **interrogation** *nf* question; (action) questioning; (épreuve) test. **interrogatoire** *nm* interrogation. **interroger** [40] *vt* question; (*élève*) test.

**interrompre** /ɛ̃teʀɔ̃pʀ/ [3] *vt* break off, interrupt; (*personne*) interrupt. ❑ **s'~** *vpr* break off. **interrupteur** *nm* switch. **interruption** *nf* interruption; (arrêt) break.

**interurbain, ~e** /ɛ̃tɛʀyʀbɛ̃, -ɛn/ *a* long-distance, trunk.

**intervalle** /ɛ̃tɛʀval/ *nm* space; (temps) interval; **dans l'~** in the meantime.

**intervenir** /ɛ̃tɛʀvəniʀ/ [58] *vi* (agir) intervene (**auprès de qn** with sb); (survenir) occur, take place; (Méd) operate. **intervention** *nf* intervention; (Méd) operation.

**intervertir** /ɛ̃tɛʀvɛʀtiʀ/ [2] *vt* invert; (*rôles*) reverse.

**interview** /ɛ̃tɛʀvju/ *nf* interview. **interviewer** [1] *vt* interview.

**intestin** /ɛ̃tɛstɛ̃/ *nm* intestine.

**intime** /ɛ̃tim/ *a* intimate; (*fête, vie*) private; (*dîner*) quiet. ● *nmf* intimate friend.

**intimider** /ɛ̃timide/ [1] *vt* intimidate.

**intimité** /ɛ̃timite/ *nf* intimacy; (vie privée) privacy.

**intituler** /ɛ̃tityle/ [1] *vt* call, entitle. ❑ **s'~** *vpr* be called *ou* entitled.

**intolérable** /ɛ̃tɔleʀabl/ *a* intolerable. **intolérance** *nf* intolerance. **intolérant, ~e** *a* intolerant.

**intonation** /ɛ̃tɔnasjɔ̃/ *nf* intonation.

**intox** /ɛ̃tɔks/ *nf* Ⓘ brainwashing.

**intoxication** /ɛ̃tɔksikasjɔ̃/ *nf* poisoning; (fig) brainwashing; **~ alimentaire** food poisoning. **intoxiquer** [1] *vt* poison; (fig) brainwash.

**intraitable** /ɛ̃tʀɛtabl/ *a* inflexible.

**Intranet** /ɛ̃tʀanɛt/ *nm* Intranet.

**intransigeant, ~e** /ɛ̃tʀɑ̃ziʒɑ̃, -t/ *a* intransigent.

**intransitif, -ive** /ɛ̃tʀɑ̃zitif, -v/ *a* intransitive.

**intraveineux, -euse** /ɛ̃tʀavɛnø, -z/ *a* intravenous.

**intrépide** /ɛ̃tʀepid/ *a* fearless.

**intrigue** /ɛ̃tʀig/ *nf* intrigue; (scénario) plot.

**intrinsèque** /ɛ̃tʀɛ̃sɛk/ *a* intrinsic.

**introduction** /ɛ̃tʀɔdyksjɔ̃/ *nf* introduction; (insertion) insertion.

**introduire** /ɛ̃tʀɔdɥiʀ/ [17] *vt* introduce, bring in; (insérer) put in, insert; ~ **qn** show sb in. □ **s'~** *vpr* get in; **s'~ dans** get into, enter.

**introuvable** /ɛ̃tʀuvabl/ *a* that cannot be found.

**introverti**, ~**e** /ɛ̃tʀɔvɛʀti/ *nm,f* introvert. ● *a* introverted.

**intrus**, ~**e** /ɛ̃tʀy, -z/ *nm,f* intruder. **intrusion** *nf* intrusion.

**intuitif**, **-ive** /ɛ̃tɥitif, -iv/ *a* intuitive. **intuition** *nf* intuition.

**inusable** /inyzabl/ *a* hard-wearing.

**inusité**, ~**e** /inyzite/ *a* little used.

**inutile** /inytil/ *a* useless; (vain) needless. **inutilement** *adv* needlessly. **inutilisable** *a* unusable.

**invalide** /ɛ̃valid/ *a & nmf* disabled (person).

**invariable** /ɛ̃vaʀjabl/ *a* invariable.

**invasion** /ɛ̃vɑzjɔ̃/ *nf* invasion.

**invectiver** /ɛ̃vɛktive/ [1] *vt* abuse.

**inventaire** /ɛ̃vɑ̃tɛʀ/ *nm* inventory; (Comm) stocklist; **faire l'~** draw up an inventory; (Comm) do a stocktake.

**inventer** /ɛ̃vɑ̃te/ [1] *vt* invent. **inventeur**, **-trice** *nm,f* inventor. **inventif**, **-ive** *a* inventive. **invention** *nf* invention.

**inverse** /ɛ̃vɛʀs/ *a* opposite; (*ordre*) reverse; **en sens** ~ in *ou* from the opposite direction. ● *nm* reverse; **c'est l'~** it's the other way round. **inversement** *adv* conversely. **inverser** [1] *vt* reverse, invert.

**investir** /ɛ̃vɛstiʀ/ [2] *vt* invest. **investissement** *nm* investment.

**investiture** /ɛ̃vɛstityʀ/ *nf* (de candidat) nomination; (de président) investiture.

**invétéré**, ~**e** /ɛ̃veteʀe/ *a* inveterate; (*menteur*) compulsive; (enraciné) deep-rooted.

**invisible** /ɛ̃vizibl/ *a* invisible.

**invitation** /ɛ̃vitasjɔ̃/ *nf* invitation. **invité**, ~**e** *nm,f* guest. **inviter** [1] *vt* invite (à to).

**involontaire** /ɛ̃vɔlɔ̃tɛʀ/ *a* involuntary; (*témoin, héros*) unwitting.

**invoquer** /ɛ̃vɔke/ [1] *vt* call upon, invoke.

**invraisemblable** /ɛ̃vʀɛsɑ̃blabl/ *a* improbable, unlikely; (incroyable) incredible. **invraisemblance** *nf* improbability.

**iode** /jɔd/ *nm* iodine.

**ira**, **irait** /iʀa, iʀɛ/ ⇒ALLER [8].

**Irak** /iʀak/ *nm* Iraq.

**Iran** /iʀɑ̃/ *nm* Iran.

**iris** /iʀis/ *nm* iris.

**irlandais**, ~**e** /iʀlɑ̃dɛ, -z/ *a* Irish. **I~**, ~**e** *nm,f* Irishman, Irishwoman.

**Irlande** /iʀlɑ̃d/ *nf* Ireland.

**ironie** /iʀɔni/ *nf* irony. **ironique** *a* ironic.

**irrationnel**, ~**le** /iʀasjɔnɛl/ *a* irrational.

**irréalisable** /iʀealizabl/ *a* (*idée, rêve*) unachievable; (*projet*) unworkable.

**irrécupérable** /iʀekypeʀabl/ *a* irretrievable; (*capital*) irrecoverable.

**irréel**, ~**le** /iʀeɛl/ *a* unreal.

**irréfléchi**, ~**e** /iʀefleʃi/ *a* thoughtless.

**irrégulier**, **-ière** /iʀegylje, -jɛʀ/ *a* irregular.

**irrémédiable** /iʀemedjabl/ *a* irreparable.

**irremplaçable** /iʀɑ̃plasabl/ *a* irreplaceable.

**irréparable** /iʀepaʀabl/ *a* (*objet*) beyond repair; (*tort, dégâts*) irreparable.

**irréprochable** /iʀepʀɔʃabl/ *a* flawless.

**irrésistible** /iʀezistibl/ *a* irresistible; (drôle) hilarious.

**irrésolu**, **~e** /iʀezɔly/ *a* indecisive; (*problème*) unsolved.

**irrespirable** /iʀɛspiʀabl/ *a* stifling.

**irresponsable** /iʀɛspɔ̃sabl/ *a* irresponsible.

**irrigation** /iʀigasjɔ̃/ *nf* irrigation. **irriguer** [1] *vt* irrigate.

**irritable** /iʀitabl/ *a* irritable.

**irriter** /iʀite/ [1] *vt* irritate. □ **s'~** *vpr* get annoyed (**de** at).

**irruption** /iʀypsjɔ̃/ *nf* **faire ~ dans** burst into.

**Islam** /islam/ *nm* Islam. **islamique** *a* Islamic.

**islandais**, **~e** /islɑ̃dɛ, -z/ *a* Icelandic. ● *nm* (Ling) Icelandic. **I~**, **~e** *nm,f* Icelander.

**Islande** /islɑ̃d/ *nf* Iceland.

**isolant** /izɔlɑ̃/ *nm* insulating material. **isolation** *nf* insulation.

**isolé**, **~e** /izɔle/ *a* isolated. **isolement** *nm* isolation.

**isoler** /izɔle/ [1] *vt* isolate; (Électr) insulate. □ **s'~** *vpr* isolate oneself.

**isoloir** /izɔlwaʀ/ *nm* polling booth.

**Isorel**® /izɔʀɛl/ *nm* hardboard.

**Israël** /isʀaɛl/ *nm* Israel. **israélien**, **~ne** *a* Israeli.

**israélite** /isʀaelit/ *a* Jewish. ● *nmf* Jew.

**issu**, **~e** /isy/ *a* **être ~ de** (*personne*) come from; (résulter de) result *ou* stem from.

**issue** /isy/ *nf* (sortie) exit; (résultat) outcome; (fig) solution; **à l'~ de** at the conclusion of; **~ de secours** emergency exit; **rue** *ou* **voie sans ~** dead end.

**Italie** /itali/ *nf* Italy.

**italien**, **~ne** /italjɛ̃, -ɛn/ *a* Italian. ● *nm* (Ling) Italian. **I~**, **~ne** *nm,f* Italian.

**italique** /italik/ *nm* italics.

**itinéraire** /itineʀɛʀ/ *nm* itinerary, route.

**I.U.T.** *abrév m* (**Institut universitaire de technologie**) university institute of technology.

**I.V.G.** *abrév f* (**interruption volontaire de grossesse**) abortion.

**ivoire** /ivwaʀ/ *nm* ivory.

**ivre** /ivʀ/ *a* drunk. **ivresse** *nf* drunkenness; (fig) exhilaration. **ivrogne** *nmf* drunk(ard).

**j'** /ʒ/ ⇒JE.

**jacinthe** /ʒasɛ̃t/ *nf* hyacinth.

**jadis** /ʒadis/ *adv* long ago.

**jaillir** /ʒajiʀ/ [2] *vi* (*liquide*) spurt (out); (*lumière*) stream out; (apparaître) burst forth, spring out.

**jalonner** /ʒalɔne/ [1] *vt* mark (out).

**jalousie** /ʒaluzi/ *nf* jealousy; (store) (venetian) blind. **jaloux**, **-ouse** *a* jealous.

**jamais** /ʒamɛ/ *adv* ever; **ne ~** never; **il ne boit ~** he never drinks; **à ~** for ever; **si ~** if ever.

**jambe** /ʒɑ̃b/ *nf* leg.

**jambon** /ʒɑ̃bɔ̃/ *nm* ham. **jambonneau** (*pl* **~x**) *nm* knuckle of ham.

**janvier** /ʒɑ̃vje/ *nm* January.

**Japon** /ʒapɔ̃/ *nm* Japan.

**japonais**, **~e** /japɔnɛ, -z/ *a* Japanese. ● *nm* (Ling) Japanese. **J~**, **~e** *nm,f* Japanese.

**japper** /ʒape/ [1] *vi* yap.

**jaquette** /ʒakɛt/ *nf* (de livre, femme) jacket; (d'homme) morning coat.

**jardin** /ʒaʀdɛ̃/ *nm* garden; **~ d'enfants** nursery (school); **~ public** public park. **jardinage** *nm* gardening. **jardiner** [1] *vi* do some gardening, garden. **jardinier**, **-ière** *nm, f* gardener.

**jardinière** /ʒaʀdinjɛʀ/ *nf* (meuble) plant-stand; **~ de légumes** mixed vegetables.

**jarretelle** /ʒaʀtɛl/ *nf* suspender; (US) garter.

**jarretière** /ʒaʀtjɛʀ/ *nf* garter.

**jatte** /ʒat/ *nf* bowl.

**jauge** /ʒoʒ/ *nf* capacity; (de navire) tonnage; (compteur) gauge; **~ d'huile** dipstick.

**jaune** /ʒon/ *a & nm* yellow; (péj) scab; **~ d'œuf** (egg) yolk; **rire ~** give a forced laugh. **jaunir** [2] *vt/i* turn yellow. **jaunisse** *nf* jaundice.

**javelot** /ʒavlo/ *nm* javelin.

**jazz** /dʒaz/ *nm* jazz.

**J.C.** *abrév m* (**Jésus-Christ**) **500 avant/après ~** 500 B.C./A.D.

**je, j'** /ʒə, ʒ/ *pron* I.

**jean** /dʒin/ *nm* jeans; **un ~** a pair of jeans.

**jet**[1] /ʒɛ/ *nm* throw; (de liquide, vapeur) jet; **~ d'eau** fountain.

**jet**[2] /dʒɛt/ *nm* (avion) jet.

**jetable** /ʒətabl/ *a* disposable.

**jetée** /ʒəte/ *nf* pier.

**jeter** /ʒəte/ [38] *vt* throw; (au rebut) throw away; (*regard, ancre, lumière*) cast; (*cri*) utter; (*bases*) lay; **~ un coup d'œil** have *ou* take a look (**à** at). □ **se ~** *vpr* **se ~ contre** crash *ou* bash into; **se ~ dans** (*fleuve*) flow into; **se ~ sur** (se ruer sur) rush at.

**jeton** /ʒətɔ̃/ *nm* token; (pour compter) counter; (au casino) chip.

**jeu** (*pl* **~x**) /ʒø/ *nm* game; (amusement) play; (au casino) gambling; (Théât) acting; (série) set; (de lumière, ressort) play; **en ~** (*honneur*) at stake; (*forces*) at work; **~ de cartes** (paquet) pack of cards; **~ d'échecs** (boîte) chess set; **~ de mots** pun; **~ télévisé** television quiz; **~x de grattage** scratch cards.

**jeudi** /ʒødi/ *nm* Thursday.

**jeun**: **à ~** /aʒœ̃/ *loc* on an empty stomach.

**jeune** /ʒœn/ *a* young; **~ fille** girl; **~ pousse** (Comm) start-up; **~s mariés** newlyweds. ● *nmf* young person; **les ~s** young people.

**jeûne** /ʒøn/ *nm* fast.

**jeunesse** /ʒœnɛs/ *nf* youth; (apparence) youthfulness; **la ~** (jeunes) the young.

**joaillerie** /ʒɔajʀi/ *nf* jewellery; (magasin) jeweller's shop.

**joie** /ʒwa/ *nf* joy.

**joindre** /ʒwɛ̃dʀ/ [22] *vt* join (**à** to); (*mains, pieds*) put together; (*efforts*) combine; (contacter) contact; (dans une enveloppe) enclose. □ **se ~ à** *vpr* join.

**joint**, **~e** /ʒwɛ̃, -t/ *a* (*efforts*) joint; (*pieds*) together. ● *nm* joint; (de robinet) washer.

**joli**, **~e** /ʒɔli/ *a* pretty, nice; (*somme, profit*) nice; **c'est du ~!** (ironique) charming! **c'est bien ~ mais** that is all very well but.

**joncher** /ʒɔ̃ʃe/ [1] *vt* litter, be strewn over; **jonché de** littered with.

**jonction** /ʒɔ̃ksjɔ̃/ *nf* junction.

**jongleur**, **-euse** /ʒɔ̃glœʀ, øz/ *nm,f* juggler.

**jonquille** /ʒɔ̃kij/ *nf* daffodil.

**joue** /ʒu/ *nf* cheek.

**jouer** /ʒwe/ [1] *vt/i* play; (Théât) act; (au casino) gamble; (fonctionner) work; (*film, pièce*) put on; (*cheval*) back; (être important) count; **~ à** (*jeu*, Sport) play; **~ de** (Mus) play; **~ la comédie** put on an act; **bien joué!** well done!

**jouet** /ʒwɛ/ *nm* toy; (personne: fig) plaything; (victime) victim.

**joueur, -euse** /ʒwœʀ, -øz/ *nm,f* player; (parieur) gambler.

**joufflu, ~e** /ʒufly/ *a* chubby-cheeked; (*visage*) chubby.

**jouir** /ʒwiʀ/ [2] *vi* (sexe) come; **~ de** (*droit, avantage*) enjoy; (*bien, concession*) enjoy the use of. **jouissance** *nf* pleasure; (usage) use (**de qch** of sth).

**joujou** (*pl* ~**x**) /ʒuʒu/ *nm* [I] toy.

**jour** /ʒuʀ/ *nm* day; (opposé à nuit) day(time); (lumière) daylight; (aspect) light; (ouverture) gap; **de nos ~s** nowadays; **du ~ au lendemain** overnight; **il fait ~** it is (day)light; **~ chômé** *ou* **férié** public holiday; **~ de fête** holiday; **~ ouvrable, ~ de travail** working day; **mettre à ~** update; **mettre au ~** uncover; **au grand ~** in the open; **donner le ~** give birth; **voir le ~** be born; **vivre au ~ le jour** live from day to day.

**journal** (*pl* **-aux**) /ʒuʀnal, -o/ *nm* (news)paper; (spécialisé) journal; (intime) diary; (à la radio) news; **~ de bord** log-book.

**journalier, -ière** /ʒuʀnalje, -jɛʀ/ *a* daily.

**journalisme** /ʒuʀnalism/ *nm* journalism. **journaliste** *nmf* journalist.

**journée** /ʒuʀne/ *nf* day.

**jovial, ~e** (*mpl* **-iaux**) /ʒɔvjal, -jo/ *a* jovial.

**joyau** (*pl* **~x**) /ʒwajo/ *nm* gem.

**joyeux, -euse** /ʒwajø, -z/ *a* merry, joyful; **~ anniversaire** happy birthday.

**jubiler** /ʒybile/ [1] *vi* be jubilant.

**jucher** /ʒyʃe/ [1] *vt* perch. □ **se ~** *vpr* perch.

**judaïsme** /ʒydaism/ *nm* Judaism.

**judiciaire** /ʒydisjɛʀ/ *a* judicial.

**judicieux, -ieuse** /ʒydisjø, -z/ *a* judicious.

**judo** /ʒydo/ *nm* judo.

**juge** /ʒyʒ/ *nm* judge; (arbitre) referee; **~ de paix** Justice of the Peace; **~ de touche** linesman.

**jugé**: **au ~** /oʒyʒe/ *loc* by guesswork.

**jugement** /ʒyʒmɑ̃/ *nm* judgement; (criminel) sentence.

**juger** /ʒyʒe/ [40] *vt/i* judge; (estimer) consider (**que** that); **~ de** judge.

**juguler** /ʒygyle/ [1] *vt* stamp out; curb.

**juif, -ive** /ʒɥif, -v/ *a* Jewish. ● *nm,f* Jew.

**juillet** /ʒɥijɛ/ *nm* July.

**juin** /ʒɥɛ̃/ *nm* June.

**jumeau, -elle** (*mpl* **~x**) /ʒymo, -ɛl/ *a & nm,f* twin. **jumeler** [38] *vt* (*villes*) twin.

**jumelles** /ʒymɛl/ *nfpl* binoculars.

**jument** /ʒymɑ̃/ *nf* mare.

**junior** /ʒynjɔʀ/ *a & nmf* junior.

**jupe** /ʒyp/ *nf* skirt.

**jupon** /ʒypɔ̃/ *nm* slip, petticoat.

**juré, ~e** /ʒyʀe/ *nm,f* juror. ● *a* sworn.

**jurer** /ʒyʀe/ [1] *vt* swear (**que** that) ● *vi* (pester) swear; (contraster) clash (**avec** with).

**juridiction** /ʒyʀidiksjɔ̃/ *nf* jurisdiction; (tribunal) court of law.

**juridique** /ʒyʀidik/ *a* legal.

**juriste** /ʒyʀist/ *nmf* legal expert.

**juron** /ʒyʀɔ̃/ *nm* swear-word.

**jury** /ʒyʀi/ *nm* (Jur) jury; (examinateurs) panel of judges.

**jus** /ʒy/ *nm* juice; (de viande) gravy; ~ **de fruit** fruit juice.

**jusque** /ʒysk(ə)/ *prép* **jusqu'à** (up) to, as far as; (temps) until, till; (limite) up to; (y compris) even; **jusqu'à ce que** until; **jusqu'à présent** until now; **jusqu'en** until; **jusqu'où?** how far?; ~ **dans,** ~ **sur** as far as.

**juste** /ʒyst/ *a* fair, just; (légitime) just; (correct, exact) right; (vrai) true; (*vêtement*) tight; (*quantité*) on the short side; **le** ~ **milieu** the happy medium. ● *adv* rightly, correctly; (*chanter*) in tune; (seulement, exactement) just; **(un peu)** ~ (*calculer, mesurer*) a bit fine *ou* close; **au** ~ exactly; **c'était** ~ (presque raté) it was a close thing. **justement** *adv* (précisément) precisely; (à l'instant) just; (avec justesse) correctly; (légitimement) justifiably.

**justesse** /ʒystɛs/ *nf* accuracy; **de** ~ just, narrowly.

**justice** /ʒystis/ *nf* justice; (autorités) law; (tribunal) court.

**justifier** /ʒystifje/ [45] *vt* justify. ● *vi* ~ **de** prove. □ **se** ~ *vpr* justify oneself.

**juteux**, **-euse** /ʒytø, -z/ *a* juicy.

**juvénile** /ʒyvenil/ *a* youthful; (*délinquance, mortalité*) juvenile.

# Kk

**kaki** /kaki/ *a inv & nm* khaki.

**kangourou** /kɑ̃guʀu/ *nm* kangaroo.

**karaté** /kaʀate/ *nm* karate.

**kart** /kaʀt/ *nm* go-cart.

**kascher** /kaʃɛʀ/ *a inv* kosher.

**kayak** /kajak/ *nm* kayak.

**képi** /kepi/ *nm* kepi.

**kermesse** /kɛʀmɛs/ *nf* fête.

**kidnapper** /kidnape/ [1] *vt* kidnap.

**kilo** /kilo/ *nm* kilo.

**kilogramme** /kilɔgʀam/ *nm* kilogram.

**kilométrage** /kilɔmetʀaʒ/ *nm* ≈ mileage. **kilomètre** *nm* kilometre.

**kinésithérapeute** /kineziteʀapøt/ *nmf* physiotherapist. **kinésithérapie** *nf* physiotherapy.

**kiosque** /kjɔsk/ *nm* kiosk; ~ **à musique** bandstand.

**kit** /kit/ *nm* kit.

**kiwi** /kiwi/ *nm* kiwi.

**klaxon**® /klaksɔn/ *nm* (Auto) horn. **klaxonner** [1] *vi* sound one's horn.

**Ko** *abrév m* (**kilo-octet**) (Ordinat) KB.

**KO** *abrév m* (**knock-out**) KO Ⓘ.

**K-way**® /kawɛ/ *nm inv* windcheater.

**kyste** /kist/ *nm* cyst.

**l'**, **la** /l, la/ ⇒LE.

**là** /la/

● *adverbe*

····➤ (dans ce lieu) there; (ici) here; (chez soi) in; **c'est** ~ **que** this is where; ~ **où** where; **par** ~ (dans

cette direction) this way; (dans cette zone) around there, **de ~** hence.

····➤ (à ce moment) then; **c'est ~ que** that's when.

····➤ **cet homme-~** that man; **ces maisons-~** those houses.

● *interjection*

····➤ **~! c'est fini** there (now), it's all over!

**là-bas** /labɑ/ *adv* there; (à l'endroit que l'on indique) over there.

**label** /labɛl/ *nm* seal, label.

**laboratoire** /labɔʀatwaʀ/ *nm* laboratory.

**laborieux**, **-ieuse** /labɔʀjø, -z/ *a* laborious; (*personne*) industrious; **classes laborieuses** working classes.

**labour** /labuʀ/ *nm* ploughing; (US) plowing. **labourer** [1] *vt* plough; (US) plow; (déchirer) rip at.

**labyrinthe** /labiʀɛ̃t/ *nm* maze, labyrinth.

**lac** /lak/ *nm* lake.

**lacer** /lase/ [10] *vt* lace up.

**lacet** /lasɛ/ *nm* (de chaussure) (shoe-) lace; (de route) sharp bend.

**lâche** /lɑʃ/ *a* cowardly; (détendu) loose; (sans rigueur) lax. ● *nmf* coward.

**lâcher** /lɑʃe/ [1] *vt* let go of; (laisser tomber) drop; (abandonner) give up; (laisser) leave; (libérer) release; (*flèche, balle*) fire; (*juron, phrase*) come out with; (desserrer) loosen; **~ prise** let go. ● *vi* give way.

**lâcheté** /lɑʃte/ *nf* cowardice.

**lacrymogène** /lakʀimɔʒɛn/ *a* **gaz ~** tear gas.

**lacune** /lakyn/ *nf* gap.

**là-dedans** /lad(ə)dɑ̃/ *adv* (près) in here; (plus loin) in there.

**là-dessous** /lad(ə)su/ *adv* (près) under here; (plus loin) under there.

**là-dessus** /lad(ə)sy/ *adv* (sur une surface) on here; (plus loin) on there; (sur ce) with that; (quelque temps après) after that; **qu'avez-vous à dire ~?** what have you got to say about it?

**ladite** /ladit/ ⇒LEDIT.

**lagune** /lagyn/ *nf* lagoon.

**là-haut** /lao/ *adv* (en hauteur) up here; (plus loin) up there; (à l'étage) upstairs.

**laïc** /laik/ *nm* layman.

**laid**, **~e** /lɛ, lɛd/ *a* ugly; (*action*) vile. **laideur** *nf* ugliness.

**lainage** /lɛnaʒ/ *nm* woollen garment.

**laine** /lɛn/ *nf* wool; **de ~** woollen.

**laïque** /laik/ *a* (*état, loi*) secular; (*habit, personne*) lay; (*école*) nondenominational. ● *nmf* layman, laywoman.

**laisse** /lɛs/ *nf* lead, leash; **tenir en ~** keep on a lead.

**laisser** /lese/ [1] *vt* (déposer) leave, drop off; (confier) leave (**à qn** with sb); (abandonner) leave; (rendre) **~ qn perplexe/froid** leave sb puzzled/cold; **~ qch à qn** (céder, prêter) let sb have sth; (donner) (*choix, temps*) give sb sth. ◻ **se ~** *vpr* **se ~ persuader/insulter** let oneself be persuaded/insulted; **elle ne se laisse pas faire** she won't be pushed around; **laisse-toi faire** leave it to me/him/her *etc.*; **se ~ aller** let oneself go. ● *v aux* **~ qn/qch faire** let sb/sth do; **laisse-moi faire** (ne m'aide pas) let me do it; (je m'en occupe) leave it to me; **laisse faire!** so what! **laisser-aller** *nm inv* carelessness; (dans la tenue) scruffiness. **laissez-passer** *nm inv* pass.

**lait** /lɛ/ *nm* milk; ~ **longue conservation** long-life *ou* UHT milk; **frère/sœur de** ~ foster-brother/-sister. **laitage** *nm* milk product. **laiterie** *nf* dairy. **laiteux**, **-euse** *a* milky.

**laitier**, **-ière** /letje, -jɛʀ/ *a* dairy. ● *nm,f* (livreur) milkman, milkwoman.

**laiton** /lɛtɔ̃/ *nm* brass.

**laitue** /lety/ *nf* lettuce.

**lama** /lama/ *nm* llama.

**lambeau** (*pl* ~**x**) /lɑ̃bo/ *nm* shred; **en** ~**x** in shreds.

**lame** /lam/ *nf* blade; (lamelle) strip; (vague) wave; ~ **de fond** ground swell; ~ **de rasoir** razor blade.

**lamentable** /lamɑ̃tabl/ *a* deplorable. **lamenter (se)** [1] *vpr* moan (**sur** about, over).

**lampadaire** /lɑ̃padɛʀ/ *nm* standard lamp; (de rue) street lamp.

**lampe** /lɑ̃p/ *nf* lamp; (ampoule) bulb; (de radio) valve; ~ **(de poche)** torch; (US) flashlight; ~ **à souder** blowlamp; ~ **de chevet** bedside lamp; ~ **solaire**, ~ **à bronzer** sunlamp.

**lance** /lɑ̃s/ *nf* spear; (de tournoi) lance; (tuyau) hose; ~ **d'incendie** fire hose.

**lancement** /lɑ̃smɑ̃/ *nm* throwing; (de navire, de missile, mise sur le marché) launch.

**lance-missiles** /lɑ̃smisil/ *nm inv* missile launcher.

**lance-pierres** /lɑ̃spjɛʀ/ *nm inv* catapult.

**lancer** /lɑ̃se/ [10] *vt* throw; (avec force) hurl; (*navire, idée, artiste*) launch; (émettre) give out; (*regard*) cast; (*moteur*) start. □ **se** ~ *vpr* (Sport) gain momentum; (se précipiter) rush; **se** ~ **dans** (*explication*) launch into; (*passe-temps*) take up. ● *nm* throw; (action) throwing.

**lancinant**, ~**e** /lɑ̃sinɑ̃, -t/ *a* (*douleur*) shooting; (*problème*) nagging.

**landau** /lɑ̃do/ *nm* pram; (US) baby carriage.

**lande** /lɑ̃d/ *nf* heath, moor.

**langage** /lɑ̃gaʒ/ *nm* language; ~ **machine/de programmation** machine/programming language.

**langouste** /lɑ̃gust/ *nf* spiny lobster. **langoustine** *nf* Dublin Bay prawn.

**langue** /lɑ̃g/ *nf* (Anat) tongue; (Ling) language; **il m'a tiré la** ~ he stuck his tongue out at me; **de** ~ **anglaise** (*personne*) English-speaking; (*journal*) English-language; ~ **maternelle** mother tongue; ~ **vivante** modern language.

**lanière** /lanjɛʀ/ *nf* strap.

**lanterne** /lɑ̃tɛʀn/ *nf* lantern; (électrique) lamp; (de voiture) sidelight.

**lapin** /lapɛ̃/ *nm* rabbit; **poser un** ~ **à qn** 🅸 stand sb up; **le coup du** ~ rabbit punch; (en voiture) whiplash injury.

**lapsus** /lapsys/ *nm* slip (of the tongue).

**laque** /lak/ *nf* lacquer; (pour cheveux) hairspray; (peinture) gloss paint.

**laquelle** /lakɛl/ ⇒LEQUEL.

**lard** /laʀ/ *nm* streaky bacon.

**large** /laʀʒ/ *a* wide, broad; (grand) large; (généreux) generous; **avoir les idées** ~**s** be broad-minded; ~ **d'esprit** broad-minded. ● *adv* (*calculer, mesurer*) on the generous side; **voir** ~ think big. ● *nm* **faire 10 cm de** ~ be 10 cm wide; **le** ~ (mer) the open sea; **au** ~ **de** (Naut) off. **largement** *adv* widely; (*ouvrir*) wide; (amplement) amply; (généreusement) generously; (au moins) easily.

**largesse** /laʀʒɛs/ *nf* generous gift.

**largeur** /laʀʒœʀ/ *nf* width, breadth; **~ d'esprit** broad-mindedness.

**larguer** /laʀge/ [1] *vt* drop; **~ les amarres** cast off.

**larme** /laʀm/ *nf* tear; (goutte [I]) drop; **en ~s** in tears.

**larmoyant, ~e** /laʀmwajɑ̃, -t/ *a* full of tears. **larmoyer** [31] *vi* (*yeux*) water; (pleurnicher) whine.

**larynx** /laʀɛ̃ks/ *nm* larynx.

**las, ~se** /lɑ, lɑs/ *a* weary.

**lasagnes** /lazaɲ/ *nfpl* lasagna.

**laser** /lazɛʀ/ *nm* laser.

**lasser** /lɑse/ [1] *vt* weary. □ **se ~** *vpr* grow tired, get weary (**de** of).

**latéral, ~e** (*mpl* **-aux**) /lateʀal, -o/ *a* lateral.

**latin, ~e** /latɛ̃, -in/ *a* Latin. ● *nm* (Ling) Latin.

**latte** /lat/ *nf* lath; (de plancher) board; (de siège) slat; (de mur, plafond) lath.

**lauréat, ~e** /lɔʀea, -t/ *a* prize-winning. ● *nm, f* prize-winner.

**laurier** /lɔʀje/ *nm* (Bot) laurel; (Culin) bay-leaves.

**lavable** /lavabl/ *a* washable.

**lavabo** /lavabo/ *nm* wash-basin; **~s** toilet(s).

**lavage** /lavaʒ/ *nm* washing; **~ de cerveau** brainwashing.

**lavande** /lavɑ̃d/ *nf* lavender.

**lave** /lav/ *nf* lava.

**lave-glace** (*pl* **~s**) /lavglas/ *nm* windscreen washer.

**lave-linge** /lavlɛ̃ʒ/ *nm inv* washing machine.

**laver** /lave/ [1] *vt* wash; **~ qn de** (fig) clear sb of. □ **se ~** *vpr* wash (oneself); **se ~ les mains** wash one's hands.

**laverie** /lavʀi/ *nf* **~ (automatique)** launderette; (US) laundromat.

**lave-vaisselle** /lavvɛsɛl/ *nm inv* dishwasher.

**laxatif, -ive** /laksatif, -v/ *a & nm* laxative.

**layette** /lɛjɛt/ *nf* baby clothes.

---

**le, la, l'** (*pl* **les**) /lə, la, l, le/

l' before vowel or mute h.

● *déterminant*

....➤ the.

....➤ (notion générale) **aimer la musique** like music; **l'amour** love.

....➤ (possession) **avoir les yeux verts** have green eyes; **il s'est cassé la jambe** he broke his leg.

....➤ (prix) **10 francs ~ kilo** 10 francs a kilo.

....➤ (temps) **~ lundi** on Mondays; **tous les mardis** every Tuesday.

....➤ (avec nom propre) **les Dury** the Durys; **la reine Margot** Queen Margot; **la Belgique** Belgium.

....➤ (avec adjectif) the, **je veux la rouge** I want the red one; **les riches** the rich.

● *pronom*

....➤ (homme) him; (femme) her; (chose, animal) it; (au pluriel) them.

....➤ (remplaçant une phrase) **je te l'avais bien dit** I told you so; **je ~ croyais aussi** I thought so too.

---

**lécher** /leʃe/ [14] *vt* lick; (*flamme*) lick; (*mer*) lap.

**lèche-vitrines** /lɛʃvitʀin/ *nm inv* **faire du ~** go window-shopping.

**leçon** /ləsɔ̃/ *nf* lesson; **faire la ~ à** lecture; **~ particulière** private lesson; **~s de conduite** driving lessons.

**lecteur**, **-trice** /lɛktœʀ, -tʀis/ *nm,f* reader; (Univ) foreign language assistant; ~ **de cassettes** cassette player; ~ **de disquettes** (disk) drive; ~ **laser** CD player; ~ **optique** optical scanner.

**lecture** /lɛktyʀ/ *nf* reading.

**ledit**, **ladite** (*pl* **lesdit(e)s**) /lədi, ladit, ledi(t)/ *a* the aforementioned.

**légal**, **~e** (*mpl* **-aux**) /legal, -o/ *a* legal. **légaliser** [1] *vt* legalize. **légalité** *nf* legality; (loi) law.

**légendaire** /leʒɑ̃dɛʀ/ *a* legendary. **légende** *nf* (histoire, inscription) legend; (de carte) key; (d'illustration) caption.

**léger**, **-ère** /leʒe, -ɛʀ/ *a* light; (*bruit, faute, maladie*) slight; (*café, argument*) weak; (imprudent) thoughtless; (frivole) fickle; **à la légère** thoughtlessly. **légèrement** *adv* lightly; (*agir*) thoughtlessly; (un peu) slightly. **légèreté** *nf* lightness; thoughtlessness.

**légion** /leʒjɔ̃/ *nf* legion.

**législatif**, **-ive** /leʒislatif, -v/ *a* legislative; **élections législatives** general election.

**legislature** /leʒislatyʀ/ *nf* term of office.

**légitime** /leʒitim/ *a* (Jur) legitimate; (fig) rightful; **agir en état de ~ défense** act in self-defence. **légitimité** *nf* legitimacy.

**legs** /lɛg/ *nm* legacy; (d'effets personnels) bequest.

**léguer** /lege/ [14] *vt* bequeath.

**légume** /legym/ *nm* vegetable.

**lendemain** /lɑ̃dmɛ̃/ *nm* **le ~** the next day; (fig) the future; **le ~ de** the day after; **le ~ matin/soir** the next morning/evening; **du jour au ~** from one day to the next.

**lent**, **~e** /lɑ̃, -t/ *a* slow. **lentement** *adv* slowly. **lenteur** *nf* slowness.

**lentille** /lɑ̃tij/ *nf* (Culin) lentil; (verre) lens; **~s de contact** contact lenses.

**léopard** /leɔpaʀ/ *nm* leopard.

**lèpre** /lɛpʀ/ *nf* leprosy.

**lequel**, **laquelle** (*pl* **lesquel(le)s**), **auquel** (*pl* **auxquel(le)s**), **duquel** (*pl* **desquel(le)s**) /ləkɛl, lakɛl, lekɛl, okɛl, dykɛl, dekɛl/

| | |
|---|---|
| à + lequel | = auquel, |
| à + lesquel(le)s | = auxquel(le)s; |
| de + lequel | = duquel, |
| de + lesquel(le)s | = desquel(le)s |

● *pronom*

····➤ (relatif) (personne) who; (complément indirect) whom; (autres cas) which; **l'ami auquel tu as écrit** the friend to whom you wrote; **les voisins chez lesquels Sophie est allée** the neighbours whose house Sophie went to.

····➤ (interrogatif) which; **~ tu veux?** which one do you want?

● *adjectif*

····➤ **auquel cas** in which case.

**les** /le/ ⇒LE.

**lesbienne** /lɛsbjɛn/ *nf* lesbian.

**léser** /leze/ [14] *vt* wrong.

**lésiner** /lezine/ [1] *vi* **ne pas ~ sur** not stint on.

**lesquels**, **lesquelles** /lekɛl/ ⇒LEQUEL.

**lessive** /lesiv/ *nf* (poudre) washing-powder; (liquide) washing liquid; (linge, action) washing.

**leste** /lɛst/ *a* agile, nimble; (grivois) coarse.

**Lettonie** /letɔni/ *nf* Latvia.

**lettre** /lɛtʀ/ *nf* letter; **à la ~, au pied de la ~** literally; **en toutes ~s** in full; **les ~s** (Univ) (the) arts.

**leucémie** /løsemi/ *nf* leukaemia.

**leur** (*pl* ~**s**) /lœʀ/

● *pronom personnel invariable*

····➤ them; **donne-le-~** give it to them; **je ~ fais confiance** I trust them.

● *adjectif possessif*

····➤ their; **~s enfants** their children; **à ~ arrivée** when they arrived.

● **le leur, la leur,** (*pl* **les leurs**) *pronom possessif*

····➤ theirs; **chacun le ~** one each; **je suis des ~s** I am one of them.

**levain** /ləvɛ̃/ *nm* leaven.

**levé, ~e** /ləve/ *a* (debout) up.

**levée** /ləve/ *nf* (de peine, de sanctions) lifting; (de courrier) collection; (de troupes, d'impôts) levying.

**lever** /ləve/ [6] *vt* lift (up), raise; (*interdiction*) lift; (*séance*) close; (*armée, impôts*) levy. ● *vi* (*pâte*) rise. □ **se ~** *vpr* get up; (*soleil, rideau*) rise; (*jour*) break. ● *nm* **au ~** on getting up; **~ du jour** daybreak; **~ de rideau** (Théât) curtain (up); **~ du soleil** sunrise.

**levier** /ləvje/ *nm* lever; **~ de changement de vitesse** gear lever.

**lèvre** /lɛvʀ/ *nf* lip.

**lévrier** /levʀije/ *nm* greyhound.

**levure** /ləvyʀ/ *nf* yeast; **~ chimique** baking powder.

**lexique** /lɛksik/ *nm* vocabulary; (glossaire) lexicon.

**lézard** /lezaʀ/ *nm* lizard.

**lézarde** /lezaʀd/ *nf* crack.

**liaison** /ljɛzɔ̃/ *nf* connection; (transport, Ordinat) link; (contact) contact; (Gram, Mil) liaison; (amoureuse) affair; **être en ~ avec** be in contact with; **assurer la ~ entre** liaise between.

**liane** /ljan/ *nf* creeper.

**Liban** /libɑ̃/ *nm* Lebanon.

**libeller** /libɛle/ [1] *vt* (*chèque*) write; (contrat) draw up; **libellé à l'ordre de** made out to.

**libellule** /libelyl/ *nf* dragonfly.

**libéral, ~e** (*mpl* **-aux**) /libeʀal, -o/ *a* liberal; **les professions ~es** the professions.

**libérateur, -trice** /libeʀatœʀ, -tʀis/ *a* liberating. ● *nm,f* liberator. **libération** *nf* release; (de pays) liberation.

**libérer** /libeʀe/ [14] *vt* (*personne*) free, release; (*pays*) liberate, free; (*bureau, lieux*) vacate; (*gaz*) release. □ **se ~** *vpr* free oneself.

**liberté** /libɛʀte/ *nf* freedom, liberty; (loisir) free time; **être/mettre en ~** be/set free; **~ conditionnelle** parole; **~ provisoire** provisional release (*pending trial*); **~ surveillée** probation; **~s publiques** civil liberties.

**Libertel** /libɛʀtɛl/ *nm* (Internet) Freenet.

**libraire** /libʀɛʀ/ *nmf* bookseller. **librairie** *nf* bookshop.

**libre** /libʀ/ *a* free; (*place, pièce*) vacant, free; (*passage*) clear; (*école*) private (*usually religious*); **~ de qch/de faire** free from sth/to do. **libre-échange** *nm* free trade. **libre-service** (*pl* **libres-services**) *nm* (magasin) self-service shop; (restaurant) self-service restaurant.

**licence** /lisɑ̃s/ *nf* licence; (Univ) degree.

**licencié, ~e** /lisɑ̃sje/ *nm,f* graduate; **~ ès lettres/sciences** Bachelor of Arts/Science.

**licenciements** /lisɑ̃simɑ̃/ *nm* redundancy; (pour faute) dismissal. **licencier** [45] *vt* make redundant; (pour faute) dismiss.

**licorne** /likɔʀn/ *nf* unicorn.

**liège** /ljɛʒ/ *nm* cork.

**lien** /ljɛ̃/ *nm* (rapport) link; (attache) bond, tie; (corde) rope; **~s affectifs/de parenté** emotional/family ties.

**lier** /lje/ [45] *vt* tie (up), bind; (relier) link; (engager, unir) bind; **~ conversation** strike up a conversation; **ils sont très liés** they are very close. □ **se ~ avec** *vpr* make friends with.

**lierre** /ljɛʀ/ *nm* ivy.

**lieu** (*pl* **~x**) /ljø/ *nm* place; **~x** (locaux) premises; (d'un accident) scene; **sur les ~x** at the scene; **au ~ de** instead of; **avoir ~** take place; **donner ~ à** give rise to; **tenir ~ de** serve as; **s'il y a ~** if necessary; **en premier ~** firstly; **en dernier ~** lastly; **~ commun** commonplace; **~ de rencontre** meeting place.

**lièvre** /ljɛvʀ/ *nm* hare.

**lifting** /liftiŋ/ *nm* face-lift.

**ligne** /liɲ/ *nf* line; (trajet) route; (de métro, train) line; (formes) lines; (de femme) figure; **en ~** (joueurs) lined up; (au téléphone) on the phone; (Ordinat) on line; **~ spécialisée** (Internet) dedicated line.

**ligoter** /ligɔte/ [1] *vt* tie up.

**ligue** /lig/ *nf* league. **liguer (se)** [1] *vpr* join forces (**contre** against).

**lilas** /lilɑ/ *nm & a inv* lilac.

**limace** /limas/ *nf* slug.

**limande** /limɑ̃d/ *nf* (poisson) dab.

**lime** /lim/ *nf* file; **~ à ongles** nail file.

**limitation** /limitasjɔ̃/ *nf* limitation; **~ de vitesse** speed limit.

**limite** /limit/ *nf* limit; (de jardin, champ) boundary; **à la ~ de** (fig) verging on, bordering on; **à la ~** if it comes to it, at a pinch; **dans une certaine ~** up to a point; **dans la ~ du possible** as far as possible. ● *a* (*vitesse, âge*) maximum; **cas ~** borderline case; **date ~** deadline; **date ~ de vente** sell-by date.

**limiter** /limite/ [1] *vt* limit; (délimiter) form the border of. □ **se ~** *vpr* limit oneself (**à** to).

**limonade** /limɔnad/ *nf* lemonade.

**limpide** /lɛ̃pid/ *a* limpid, clear.

**lin** /lɛ̃/ *nm* (tissu) linen.

**linge** /lɛ̃ʒ/ *nm* linen; (lessive) washing; (torchon) cloth; **~ (de corps)** underwear. **lingerie** *nf* underwear. **lingette** *nf* wipe.

**lingot** /lɛ̃go/ *nm* ingot.

**linguistique** /lɛ̃gɥistik/ *a* linguistic. ● *nf* linguistics.

**lion** /ljɔ̃/ *nm* lion; **le L~** Leo. **lionceau** (*pl* **~x**) *nm* lion cub. **lionne** *nf* lioness.

**liquidation** /likidasjɔ̃/ *nf* liquidation; (vente) (clearance) sale; **entrer en ~** go into liquidation.

**liquide** /likid/ *a* liquid. ● *nm* **(argent) ~** ready money; **payer en ~** pay cash; **~ de frein** brake fluid.

**liquider** /likide/ [1] *vt* liquidate; (vendre) sell.

**lire** /liʀ/ [39] *vt/i* read. ● *nf* lira.

**lis**[1] /li/ ⇒LIRE[39].

**lis**[2] /lis/ *nm* (fleur) lily.

**lisible** /lizibl/ *a* legible; (*roman*) readable.

**lisière** /lizjɛʀ/ *nf* edge.

**lisse** /lis/ *a* smooth.

**liste** /list/ *nf* list; **~ d'attente** waiting list; **~ électorale** register of voters; **être sur (la) ~ rouge** be ex-directory.

**listing** /listiŋ/ *nm* printout.

**lit** /li/ *nm* bed; **se mettre au ~** get into bed; **~ de camp** camp-bed; **~**

**d'enfant** cot; ~ **d'une personne** single bed; ~ **de deux personnes, grand** ~ double bed.

**literie** /litʀi/ *nf* bedding.

**litière** /litjɛʀ/ *nf* litter.

**litige** /litiʒ/ *nm* dispute.

**litre** /litʀ/ *nm* litre.

**littéraire** /liteʀɛʀ/ *a* literary; (*études, formation*) arts.

**littéral**, ~**e** (*mpl* **-aux**) /liteʀal, -o/ *a* literal.

**littérature** /liteʀatyʀ/ *nf* literature.

**littoral** (*pl* **-aux**) /litɔʀal, -o/ *nm* coast.

**Lituanie** /litɥani/ *nf* Lithuania.

**livide** /livid/ *a* deathly pale.

**livraison** /livʀɛzɔ̃/ *nf* delivery.

**livre** /livʀ/ *nf* (monnaie, poids) pound. ● *nm* book; ~ **de bord** log-book; ~ **de compte** books; ~ **de poche** paperback.

**livrer** /livʀe/ [1] *vt* (Comm) deliver; (abandonner) give over (**à** to); (remettre) (*coupable, document*) hand over (**à** to); **livré à soi-même** left to oneself. □ **se** ~ *vpr* (se rendre) give oneself up (**à** to); **se** ~ **à** (*boisson, actes*) indulge in; (*ami*) confide in.

**livret** /livʀɛ/ *nm* book; (Mus) libretto; ~ **de caisse d'épargne** savings book; ~ **scolaire** school report (book).

**livreur, -euse** /livʀœʀ, -øz/ *nm,f* delivery man, delivery woman.

**local**[1], ~**e** (*mpl* **-aux**) /lɔkal, -o/ *a* local.

**local**[2] (*pl* **-aux**) /lɔkal, -o/ *nm* premises; **locaux** premises.

**localement** /lɔkalmɑ̃/ *adv* locally.

**localiser** /lɔkalize/ [1] *vt* (repérer) locate; (circonscrire) localize.

**locataire** /lɔkatɛʀ/ *nmf* tenant; (de chambre) lodger.

**location** /lɔkasjɔ̃/ *nf* (de maison) renting; (de voiture, de matériel) hire, rental; (de place) booking, reservation; (par propriétaire) renting out; hiring out; **en** ~ (*voiture*) on hire, rented; (*habiter*) in rented accommodation.

**locomotive** /lɔkɔmɔtiv/ *nf* engine, locomotive.

**locution** /lɔkysjɔ̃/ *nf* phrase.

**loft** /lɔft/ *nm* loft (apartment).

**loge** /lɔʒ/ *nf* (de concierge, de franc-maçons) lodge; (d'acteur) dressing-room; (de spectateur) box.

**logement** /lɔʒmɑ̃/ *nm* accommodation; (appartement) flat; (habitat) housing.

**loger** /lɔʒe/ [40] *vt* (*réfugié, famille*) house; (*ami*) put up; (*client*) accommodate. ● *vi* live. □ **se** ~ *vpr* live; **trouver à se** ~ find accommodation; **se** ~ **dans** (*balle*) lodge itself in.

**logiciel** /lɔʒisjɛl/ *nm* software; ~ **contributif** shareware; ~ **d'application** application software; ~ **de groupe** groupware; ~ **de jeux** games software; ~ **de navigation** browser; ~ **public** freeware.

**logique** /lɔʒik/ *a* logical. ● *nf* logic.

**logis** /lɔʒi/ *nm* dwelling.

**logistique** /lɔʒistik/ *nf* logistics.

**loi** /lwa/ *nf* law.

**loin** /lwɛ̃/ *adv* far (away); **au** ~ far away; **de** ~ from far away; (de beaucoup) by far; ~ **de là** far from it; **plus** ~ further; **il revient de** ~ (fig) he had a close shave.

**lointain**, ~**e** /lwɛ̃tɛ̃, -ɛn/ *a* distant. ● *nm* distance; **dans le** ~ in the distance.

**loisir** /lwaziʀ/ *nm* (spare) time; **~s** (temps libre) leisure, spare time; (distractions) leisure activities; **à ~** at one's leisure; **avoir le ~ de faire** have time to do.

**londonien**, **~ne** /lɔ̃dɔnjɛ̃, -ɛn/ *a* London. **L~**, **~e** *nm,f* Londoner.

**Londres** /lɔ̃dʀ/ *npr* London.

**long**, **longue** /lɔ̃, lɔ̃g/ *a* long; **à ~ terme** long-term; **être ~ à faire** be a long time doing. ● *nm* **de ~** (mesure) long; **de ~ en large** back and forth; **(tout) le ~ de** (all) along. ● *adv* **en dire ~ sur qn/qch** say a lot about sb/sth; **en savoir plus ~ sur** know more about.

**longer** /lɔ̃ʒe/ [40] *vt* go along; (limiter) border.

**longitude** /lɔ̃ʒityd/ *nf* longitude.

**longtemps** /lɔ̃tɑ̃/ *adv* a long time; **avant ~** before long; **trop ~** too long; **ça prendra ~** it will take a long time; **prendre plus ~ que prévu** take longer than anticipated.

**longuement** /lɔ̃gmɑ̃/ *adv* (longtemps) for a long time; (en détail) at length.

**longueur** /lɔ̃gœʀ/ *nf* length; **~s** (de texte) over-long parts; **à ~ de journée** all day long; **en ~** lengthwise; **~ d'onde** wavelength.

**lopin** /lɔpɛ̃/ *nm* **~ de terre** patch of land.

**loque** /lɔk/ *nf* **~s** rags; **~ (humaine)** (human) wreck.

**loquet** /lɔkɛ/ *nm* latch.

**lors de** /lɔʀdə/ *prép* (au moment de) at the time of; (pendant) during.

**lorsque** /lɔʀsk(ə)/ *conj* when.

**losange** /lɔzɑ̃ʒ/ *nm* diamond.

**lot** /lo/ *nm* (portion) share; (aux enchères) lot; (Ordinat) batch; (destin) lot; **gagner le gros ~** hit the jackpot.

**loterie** /lɔtʀi/ *nf* lottery.

**lotion** /losjɔ̃/ *nf* lotion.

**lotissement** /lɔtismɑ̃/ *nm* (à construire) building plot; (construit) (housing) development.

**louable** /luabl/ *a* praiseworthy. **louange** *nf* praise.

**louche** /luʃ/ *a* shady, dubious. ● *nf* ladle.

**loucher** /luʃe/ [1] *vi* squint.

**louer** /lwe/ [1] *vt* (approuver) praise (**de** for); (prendre en location) (*maison*) rent; (*voiture, matériel*) hire, rent; (*place*) book, reserve; (donner en location) (*maison*) rent out; (*matériel*) rent out, hire out; **à ~** to let, for rent (US).

**loufoque** /lufɔk/ *a* [I] crazy.

**loup** /lu/ *nm* wolf.

**loupe** /lup/ *nf* magnifying glass.

**louper** /lupe/ [1] *vt* [I] miss; (*examen*) flunk [I].

**lourd**, **~e** /luʀ, -d/ *a* heavy; (*faute*) serious; **~ de dangers** fraught with danger; **il fait ~** it's close *ou* muggy.

**loutre** /lutʀ/ *nf* otter.

**louveteau** (*pl* **~x**) /luvto/ *nm* wolf cub; (scout) Cub (Scout).

**loyal**, **~e** (*mpl* **-aux**) /lwajal, -o/ *a* loyal, faithful; (honnête) fair. **loyauté** *nf* loyalty; fairness.

**loyer** /lwaje/ *nm* rent.

**lu** /ly/ ⇨LIRE [39].

**lubrifiant** /lybʀifjɑ̃/ *nm* lubricant.

**lucide** /lysid/ *a* lucid. **lucidité** *nf* lucidity.

**lucratif**, **-ive** /lykʀatif, -v/ *a* lucrative; **à but non ~** non-profit-making.

**ludiciel** /lydisjɛl/ *nm* (Ordinat) games software.

**lueur** /lɥœʀ/ *nf* (faint) light, glimmer; (fig) glimmer, gleam.

**luge** /lyʒ/ *nf* toboggan.

**lugubre** /lygybʀ/ *a* gloomy.

**lui** /lɥi/

● *pronom*

····➤ (masculin) (sujet) he; **~, il est à l'étranger** he's abroad; **c'est ~!** it's him!; (objet) him; (animal) it; **c'est à ~** it's his; **elle conduit mieux que ~** she's a better driver than he is.

····➤ (féminin) her; **je ~ ai annoncé** I told her.

····➤ (masculin/féminin) **donne-le-~** give it to him/her.

**lui-même** /lɥimɛm/ *pron* himself; (animal) itself.

**luire** /lɥiʀ/ [17] *vi* shine; (reflet humide) glisten; (reflet chaud, faible) glow.

**lumière** /lymjɛʀ/ *nf* light; **~s** (connaissances) knowledge; **faire (toute) la ~ sur une affaire** clear a matter up.

**luminaire** /luminɛʀ/ *nm* lamp.

**lumineux**, **-euse** /lyminø, -z/ *a* luminous; (éclairé) illuminated; (*rayon*) of light; (radieux) radiant; **source lumineuse** light source.

**lunaire** /lynɛʀ/ *a* lunar.

**lunatique** /lynatik/ *a* temperamental.

**lunch** /lœnʃ/ *nm* buffet lunch.

**lundi** /lœ̃di/ *nm* Monday.

**lune** /lyn/ *nf* moon; **~ de miel** honeymoon.

**lunettes** /lynɛt/ *nfpl* glasses; (de protection) goggles; **~ de ski/natation** ski/swimming goggles; **~ noires** dark glasses; **~ de soleil** sun-glasses.

**lustre** /lystʀ/ *nm* (éclat) lustre; (objet) chandelier.

**lutin** /lytɛ̃/ *nm* goblin.

**lutte** /lyt/ *nf* fight, struggle; (Sport) wrestling. **lutter** [1] *vi* fight, struggle; (Sport) wrestle. **lutteur**, **-euse** *nm,f* fighter; (Sport) wrestler.

**luxe** /lyks/ *nm* luxury; **de ~** luxury; (*produit*) de luxe.

**Luxembourg** /lyksɑ̃buʀ/ *nm* Luxemburg.

**luxer (se)** /(sə)lykse/ [1] *vpr* **se ~ le genou** dislocate one's knee.

**luxueux**, **-euse** /lyksɥø, -z/ *a* luxurious.

**lycée** /lise/ *nm* (secondary) school. **lycéen**, **~ne** *nm,f* pupil (at secondary school).

**lyophilisé**, **~e** /ljɔfilize/ *a* freeze-dried.

**lyrique** /liʀik/ *a* (*poésie*) lyric; (passionné) lyrical; **artiste/théâtre ~** opera singer/house.

**lys** /lis/ *nm* lily.

# Mm

**m'** /m/ ⇒ME.

**ma** /ma/ ⇒MON.

**macabre** /makabʀ/ *a* macabre.

**macadam** /makadam/ *nm* Tarmac®.

**macaron** /makaʀɔ̃/ *nm* (gâteau) macaroon; (insigne) badge.

**macédoine** /masedwan/ *nf* mixed diced vegetables; **~ de fruits** fruit salad.

**macérer** /maseʀe/ [14] *vt/i* soak; (dans du vinaigre) pickle.

**mâcher** /mɑʃe/ [1] *vt* chew; **ne pas ~ ses mots** not mince one's words.

**machin** /maʃɛ̃/ *nm* [I] (chose) thing; (dont on ne trouve pas le nom) whatsit [I].

**machinal**, **~e** (*mpl* **-aux**) /maʃinal, -o/ *a* automatic. **machinalement** *adv* mechanically, automatically.

**machination** /maʃinasjɔ̃/ *nf* plot; **des ~s** machinations.

**machine** /maʃin/ *nf* machine; (d'un train, navire) engine; **~ à écrire** typewriter; **~ à laver/coudre** washing-/sewing-machine; **~ à sous** fruit machine; (US) slot-machine. **machine-outil** (*pl* **machines-outils**) *nf* machine tool. **machinerie** *nf* machinery.

**machiniste** /maʃinist/ *nm* (Théât) stage-hand; (conducteur) driver.

**mâchoire** /mɑʃwaʀ/ *nf* jaw.

**mâchonner** /mɑʃɔne/ [1] *vt* chew.

**maçon** /masɔ̃/ *nm* (entrepreneur) builder; (poseur de briques) bricklayer; (qui construit en pierre) mason. **maçonnerie** *nf* (briques) brickwork; (pierres) stonework, masonry; (travaux) building.

**madame** (*pl* **mesdames**) /madam, medam/ *nf* (à une inconnue) (dans une lettre) **M~** Dear Madam; **bonjour, ~** good morning; **mesdames et messieurs** ladies and gentlemen; (à une femme dont on connaît le nom) (dans une lettre) **Chère M~** Dear Mrs *ou* Ms X; **bonjour, ~** good morning Mrs *ou* Ms X; **oui M~ le Ministre** yes Minister; (formule de respect) **oui M~** yes madam.

**mademoiselle** (*pl* **mesdemoiselles**) /madmwazɛl, medmwazɛl/ *nf* (à une inconnue) (dans une lettre) **M~** Dear Madam; **bonjour, ~** good morning; **entrez mesdemoiselles** come in (ladies); (à une jeune fille dont on connaît le nom) (dans une lettre) **Chère M~** Dear Ms *ou* Miss X; **bonjour, ~** good morning Miss *ou* Ms X.

**magasin** /magazɛ̃/ *nm* shop, store; (entrepôt) warehouse; (d'une arme) magazine; **en ~** in stock.

**magazine** /magazin/ *nm* magazine; (émission) programme.

**Maghreb** /magʀɛb/ *nm* North Africa.

**magicien**, **~ne** /maʒisjɛ̃, -ɛn/ *nm,f* magician.

**magie** /maʒi/ *nf* magic. **magique** *a* magic; (mystérieux) magical.

**magistral**, **~e** (*mpl* **-aux**) /maʒistʀal, -o/ *a* masterly; (grand: hum) tremendous; **cours ~** lecture.

**magistrat** /maʒistʀa/ *nm* magistrate.

**magistrature** /maʒistʀatyʀ/ *nf* judiciary; (fonction) public office.

**magner (se)** /(sə)maɲe/ [1] *vpr* [X] get a move on.

**magnétique** /maɲetik/ *a* magnetic. **magnétiser** [1] *vt* magnetize. **magnétisme** *nm* magnetism.

**magnétophone** /maɲetɔfɔn/ *nm* tape recorder; (à cassettes) cassette recorder.

**magnétoscope** /maɲetɔskɔp/ *nm* video recorder.

**magnificence** /maɲifisɑ̃s/ *nf* magnificence. **magnifique** *a* magnificent.

**magot** /mago/ *nm* [I] hoard (of money).

**magouille** /maguj/ *nf* [I] scheming, skulduggery.

**magret** /magʀɛ/ *nm* **~ de canard** duck breast.

**mai** /mɛ/ *nm* May.

**maigre** /mɛgʀ/ *a* thin; (*viande*) lean; (*yaourt*) low-fat; (fig) poor, meagre; **faire ~** abstain from meat.

**maigreur** *nf* thinness; leanness; (fig) meagreness.

**maigrir** /megRiR/ [2] *vi* get thin(ner); (en suivant un régime) slim. ● *vt* make thin(ner).

**maille** /mɑj/ *nf* stitch; (de filet) mesh; **~ qui file** ladder, run; **avoir ~ à partir avec qn** have a brush with sb.

**maillet** /majɛ/ *nm* mallet.

**maillon** /mɑjɔ̃/ *nm* link.

**maillot** /majo/ *nm* (Sport) shirt, jersey; **~ (de corps)** vest; (US) undershirt; **~ (de bain)** (swimming) costume.

**main** /mɛ̃/ *nf* hand; **donner la ~ à qn** hold sb's hand; **se donner la ~** hold hands; **en ~s propres** in person; **en bonnes ~s** in good hands; **~ courante** handrail; **se faire la ~** get the hang of it; **perdre la ~** lose one's touch; **sous la ~** to hand; **vol à ~ armée** armed robbery; **fait (à la) ~** handmade; **haut les ~s!** hands up! **main-d'œuvre** (*pl* **mains-d'œuvre**) *nf* labour; (ouvriers) labour force.

**main-forte** /mɛ̃fɔRt/ *nf inv* **prêter ~ à qn** come to sb's aid.

**maint**, **~e** /mɛ̃, mɛ̃t/ *a* many a (+ *sg*); **~s** many; **à ~es reprises** many times.

**maintenant** /mɛ̃t(ə)nɑ̃/ *adv* now; (de nos jours) nowadays; (l'époque actuelle) today.

**maintenir** /mɛ̃t(ə)niR/ [58] *vt* keep, maintain; (soutenir) support, hold up; (affirmer) maintain; (*decision*) stand by. □ **se ~** *vpr* (*tendance*) persist; (*prix, malade*) remain stable.

**maintien** /mɛ̃tjɛ̃/ *nm* (attitude) bearing; (conservation) maintenance.

**maire** /mɛR/ *nm* mayor.

**mairie** /meRi/ *nf* town hall; (administration) town council.

**mais** /mɛ/ *conj* but; **~ oui** of course; **~ non** of course not.

**maïs** /mais/ *nm* maize, corn; (Culin) sweetcorn.

**maison** /mɛzɔ̃/ *nf* house; (foyer) home; (immeuble) building; **~ (de commerce)** firm; **à la ~** at home; **rentrer** *ou* **aller à la ~** go home; **~ des jeunes (et de la culture)** youth club; **~ de repos** rest home; **~ de convalescence** convalescent home; **~ de retraite** old people's home; **~ mère** parent company. ● *a inv* (Culin) home-made.

**maître**, **-esse** /mɛtR, -ɛs/ *a* (qui contrôle) **être ~ de soi** be one's own master; **~ de la situation** in control of the situation; (principal) (*idée, qualité*) key, main. ● *nm,f* (Scol) teacher; (d'animal) owner, master. ● *nm* (expert, guide) master; (dirigeant) leader; **~ de conférences** senior lecturer; **~ d'hôtel** head waiter; (domestique) butler. **maître-assistant**, **~ e** (*pl* **maîtres-assistants**) *nm,f* lecturer. **maître-chanteur** (*pl* **maîtres-chanteurs**) *nm* blackmailer. **maître-nageur** (*pl* **maîtres-nageurs**) *nm* swimming instructor. **maîtresse** *nf* (amante) mistress.

**maîtrise** /mɛtRiz/ *nf* mastery; (contrôle) control; (Mil) supremacy; (Univ) master's degree; **~ (de soi)** self-control.

**maîtriser** /mɛtRize/ [1] *vt* (*sujet, technique*) master; (*incendie, sentiment, personne*) control. □ **se ~** *vpr* have self-control.

**maïzena®** /maizena / *nf* cornflour.

**majesté** /maʒɛste/ *nf* majesty.

**majestueux**, **-euse** /maʒɛstɥø, z/ *a* majestic.

**majeur**, **~e** /maʒœR/ *a* major, main; (Jur) of age; **en ~e partie**

mostly; la ~e partie de most of. ● *nm* middle finger.

**majoration** /maʒɔʀasjɔ̃/ *nf* increase (de in). **majorer** [1] *vt* increase.

**majoritaire** /maʒɔʀitɛʀ/ *a* majority; être ~ be in the majority. **majorité** *nf* majority; en ~ chiefly.

**Majorque** /majɔʀk/ *nf* Majorca.

**majuscule** /maʒyskyl/ *a* capital. ● *nf* capital letter.

**mal¹** /mal/ *adv* badly; (incorrectement) wrong(ly); **aller** ~ (*personne*) be unwell; (*affaires*) go badly; ~ **entendre/comprendre** not hear/understand properly; ~ **en point** in a bad state; **pas** ~ quite a lot. ● *a inv* bad, wrong; **c'est** ~ **de** it is wrong *ou* bad to; **ce n'est pas** ~ ⓘ it's not bad; **Nick n'est pas** ~ ⓘ Nick is not bad-looking.

**mal²** (*pl* **maux**) /mal, mo/ *nm* evil, (douleur) pain, ache; (maladie) disease; (effort) trouble; (dommage) harm; (malheur) misfortune; **avoir** ~ **à la tête/à la gorge** have a headache/a sore throat; **avoir le** ~ **de mer/du pays** be seasick/homesick; **faire** ~ hurt; **se faire** ~ hurt oneself; **j'ai** ~ it hurts; **faire du** ~ **à** hurt, harm; **se donner du** ~ **pour faire qch** go to a lot of trouble to do sth.

**malade** /malad/ *a* sick, ill; (*bras, œil*) bad; (*plante, poumons, côlon*) diseased; **tomber** ~ fall ill; (*fou* ⓘ) mad. ● *nmf* sick person; (d'un médecin) patient; ~ **mental** mentally ill person.

**maladie** /maladi/ *nf* illness, disease; (manie ⓘ) mania.

**maladif**, **-ive** /maladif, -v/ *a* sickly; (*jalousie, peur*) pathological.

**maladresse** /maladʀɛs/ *nf* clumsiness; (erreur) blunder.

**maladroit**, ~**e** /maladʀwa, -t/ *a* clumsy; (sans tact) tactless.

**malaise** /malɛz/ *nm* feeling of faintness; (gêne) uneasiness; (état de crise) unrest.

**malaisé**, ~**e** /maleze/ *a* difficult.

**Malaisie** /malɛzi/ *nf* Malaysia.

**malaria** /malaʀja/ *nf* malaria.

**malaxer** /malakse/ [1] *vt* (pétrir) knead; (mêler) mix.

**malchance** /malʃɑ̃s/ *nf* misfortune. **malchanceux**, **-euse** *a* unlucky.

**mâle** /mɑl/ *a* male; (viril) manly. ● *nm* male.

**malédiction** /malediksjɔ̃/ *nf* curse.

**maléfice** /malefis/ *nm* evil spell. **maléfique** *a* evil.

**malentendant**, ~**e** /malɑ̃tɑ̃dɑ̃, -t/ *a* hard of hearing.

**malentendu** /malɑ̃tɑ̃dy/ *nm* misunderstanding.

**malfaçon** /malfasɔ̃/ *nf* defect.

**malfaisant**, ~**e** /malfəzɑ̃, -t/ *a* harmful; (*personne*) evil.

**malfaiteur** /malfɛtœʀ/ *nm* criminal.

**malformation** /malfɔʀmasjɔ̃/ *nf* malformation.

**malgré** /malgʀe/ *prép* in spite of, despite; ~ **tout** nevertheless.

**malheur** /malœʀ/ *nm* misfortune; (accident) accident; **par** ~ unfortunately; **faire un** ~ ⓘ be a big hit; **porter** ~ be *ou* bring bad luck.

**malheureusement** /malœʀøzmɑ̃/ *adv* unfortunately.

**malheureux**, **-euse** /malœʀø, -z/ *a* unhappy; (regrettable) unfortunate; (sans succès) unlucky; (insignifiant) paltry, pathetic. ● *nm,f* (poor) wretch.

**malhonnête** /malɔnɛt/ *a* dishonest. **malhonnêteté** *nf* dishonesty.

**malice** /malis/ *nf* mischief; **sans ~** harmless; **avec ~** mischievously. **malicieux**, **-ieuse** *a* mischievous.

**malignité** /maliɲite/ *nf* malignancy. **malin**, **-igne** *a* clever, smart; (méchant) malicious; (*tumeur*) malignant; (difficile [I]) difficult.

**malingre** /malɛ̃gʀ/ *a* puny.

**malle** /mal/ *nf* (valise) trunk; (Auto) boot; (US) trunk.

**mallette** /malɛt/ *nf* (small) suitcase; (pour le bureau) briefcase.

**malmener** /malməne/ [6] *vt* manhandle; (fig) give a rough ride to.

**malnutrition** /malnytʀisjɔ̃/ *nf* malnutrition.

**malodorant**, **~e** /malɔdɔʀɑ̃, -t/ *a* smelly, foul-smelling.

**malpoli**, **~e** /malpɔli/ *a* rude, impolite.

**malpropre** /malpʀɔpʀ/ *a* dirty.

**malsain**, **~e** /malsɛ̃, -ɛn/ *a* unhealthy.

**malt** /malt/ *nm* malt.

**Malte** /malt/ *nf* Malta.

**maltraiter** /maltʀete/ [1] *vt* ill-treat.

**malveillance** /malvɛjɑ̃s/ *nf* malice. **malveillant**, **~e** *a* malicious.

**maman** /mamɑ̃/ *nf* mum(my), mother; (US) mom(my).

**mamelle** /mamɛl/ *nf* teat.

**mamelon** /mamlɔ̃/ *nm* (Anat) nipple; (colline) hillock.

**mamie** /mami/ *nf* [I] granny.

**mammifère** /mamifɛʀ/ *nm* mammal.

**manche** /mɑ̃ʃ/ *nf* sleeve; (Sport, Pol) round. ● *nm* (d'un instrument) handle; **~ à balai** broomstick; (Aviat) joystick. **M~** *nf* **la M~** the Channel; **le tunnel sous la M~** the Channel tunnel.

**manchette** /mɑ̃ʃɛt/ *nf* cuff; (de journal) headline.

**manchot**, **~te** /mɑ̃ʃo, -ɔt/ *nm,f* one-armed person; (sans bras) armless person. ● *nm* (oiseau) penguin.

**mandarine** /mɑ̃daʀin/ *nf* tangerine, mandarin (orange).

**mandat** /mɑ̃da/ *nm* (postal) money order; (Pol) mandate; (procuration) proxy; (de police) warrant; **~ d'arrêt** arrest warrant.

**mandataire** /mɑ̃datɛʀ/ *nm* representative; (Jul) proxy.

**manège** /manɛʒ/ *nm* riding school; (à la foire) merry-go-round; (manœuvre) trick, ploy.

**manette** /manɛt/ *nf* lever; (de jeu) joystick.

**mangeable** /mɑ̃ʒabl/ *a* edible.

**mangeoire** /mɑ̃ʒwaʀ/ *nf* trough; (pour oiseaux) feeder.

**manger** /mɑ̃ʒe/ [40] *vt* eat; (*fortune*) go through; (*profits*) eat away at; (*économies*) use up; (ronger) eat into. ● *vi* eat; **donner à ~ à** feed. ● *nm* food.

**mangue** /mɑ̃g/ *nf* mango.

**maniable** /manjabl/ *a* easy to handle.

**maniaque** /manjak/ *a* fussy. ● *nmf* fusspot; (fou) maniac; (fanatique) fanatic; **un ~ de l'ordre** a stickler for tidiness.

**manie** /mani/ *nf* habit; (marotte) obsession.

**maniement** /manimɑ̃/ *nm* handling. **manier** [45] *vt* handle.

**manière** /manjɛʀ/ *nf* way, manner; **~s** (politesse) manners; (chichis) fuss; **à la ~ de** in the style of; **de ~ à** so as to; **de toute ~** anyway, in any case.

**maniéré**, **~e** /manjeʀe/ *a* affected.

**manif** /manif/ *nf* [I] demo.

**manifestant**, **~e** /manifɛstɑ̃, -t/ *nm,f* demonstrator.

**manifestation** /manifɛstasjɔ̃/ *nf* expression, manifestation; (de maladie, phénomène) appearance; (Pol) demonstration; (événement) event; **~ culturelle** cultural event.

**manifeste** /manifɛst/ *a* obvious. ● *nm* manifesto.

**manifester** /manifɛste/ [1] *vt* show, manifest; (*désir, crainte*) express. ● *vi* (Pol) demonstrate. □ **se ~** *vpr* (*sentiment*) show itself; (apparaître) appear; (répondre à un appel) come forward.

**manigance** /manigɑ̃s/ *nf* little plot. **manigancer** [10] *vt* plot.

**manipulation** /manipylasjɔ̃/ *nf* handling; (péj) manipulation.

**manivelle** /manivɛl/ *nf* handle, crank.

**mannequin** /mankɛ̃/ *nm* (personne) model; (statue) dummy.

**manœuvrer** /manœvʀe/ [1] *vt* manoeuvre; (*machine*) operate. ● *vi* manoeuvre.

**manoir** /manwaʀ/ *nm* manor.

**manque** /mɑ̃k/ *nm* lack (**de** of); (lacune) gap; **~ à gagner** loss of earnings; **en (état de) ~** having withdrawal symptoms.

**manqué**, **~e** /mɑ̃ke/ *a* (*écrivain*) failed, **garçon ~** tomboy.

**manquement** /mɑ̃kmɑ̃/ *nm* **~ à** breach of.

**manquer** /mɑ̃ke/ [1] *vt* miss; (gâcher) spoil; **~ à** (*devoir*) fail in; **~ de** be short of, lack; **il/ça lui manque** he misses him/it; **~ (de) faire** (faillir) nearly do; **ne manquez pas de** be sure to; **~ à sa parole** break one's word. ● *vi* be short *ou* lacking; (être absent) be absent; (en moins, disparu) be missing; **il me manque 20 francs** I'm 20 francs short.

**mansarde** /mɑ̃saʀd/ *nf* attic (room).

**manteau** (*pl* **~x**) /mɑ̃to/ *nm* coat.

**manucure** /manykyʀ/ *nmf* manicurist. ● *nf* (soins) manicure.

**manuel**, **~le** /manɥɛl/ *a* manual. ● *nm* (livre) manual; (Scol) textbook.

**manufacture** /manyfaktyʀ/ *nf* factory; (fabrication) manufacture.

**manufacturer** [1] *vt* manufacture.

**manuscrit**, **~e** /manyskʀi, -t/ *a* handwritten. ● *nm* manuscript.

**mappemonde** /mapmɔ̃d/ *nf* world map; (sphère) globe.

**maquereau** (*pl* **~x**) /makʀo/ *nm* (poisson) mackerel; [I] pimp.

**maquette** /makɛt/ *nf* (scale) model; **~ (de mise en page)** paste-up.

**maquillage** /makijaʒ/ *nm* make-up.

**maquiller** /makije/ [1] *vt* make up; (truquer) doctor, fake. □ **se ~** *vpr* make (oneself) up.

**maquis** /maki/ *nm* (paysage) scrub; (Mil) Maquis, underground.

**maraîcher**, **-ère** /maʀeʃe, -ɛʀ/ *nm,f* market gardener; (US) truck farmer.

**marais** /maʀɛ/ *nm* marsh.

**marasme** /maʀasm/ *nm* slump, stagnation; **dans le ~** in the doldrums.

**marbre** /maʀbʀ/ *nm* marble.

**marc** /maʀ/ *nm* (eau-de-vie) marc; **~ de café** coffee grounds.

**marchand**, **~e** /maʀʃɑ̃, -d/ *a* (*valeur*) market. ● *nm,f* trader; (de charbon, vin) merchant; **~ de couleurs** ironmonger; (US) hardware merchant; **~ de journaux** newsagent; **~ de légumes** greengrocer; **~ de poissons** fishmonger.

**marchander** /marʃɑ̃de/ [1] *vt* haggle over. ● *vi* haggle.

**marchandise** /marʃɑ̃diz/ *nf* goods.

**marche** /marʃ/ *nf* (démarche, trajet) walk; (rythme) pace; (Mil, Mus, Pol) march; (d'escalier) step; (Sport) walking; (de machine) operation, working; (de véhicule) running; **en ~** (*train*) moving; (*moteur, machine*) running; **faire ~ arrière** (*véhicule*) reverse; **mettre en ~** start (up); **se mettre en ~** start moving.

**marché** /marʃe/ *nm* market; (contrat) deal; **faire son ~** do one's shopping; **~ aux puces** flea market; **~ noir** black market.

**marchepied** /marʃəpje/ *nm* (de train, camion) step.

**marcher** /marʃe/ [1] *vi* walk; (poser le pied) tread (**sur** on); (aller) go; (fonctionner) work, run; (prospérer) go well; (*film, livre*) do well; (consentir ⓘ) agree; **faire ~ qn** ⓘ pull sb's leg.

**mardi** /mardi/ *nm* Tuesday; **M~ gras** Shrove Tuesday.

**mare** /mar/ *nf* (étang) pond; (flaque) pool.

**marécage** /marekaʒ/ *nm* marsh; (sous les tropiques) swamp.

**maréchal** (*pl* **-aux**) /mareʃal, -o/ *nm* field marshal.

**maréchal-ferrant** (*pl* **-aux-ferrants**) /mareʃalferɑ̃/ *nm* blacksmith.

**marée** /mare/ *nf* tide; (poissons) fresh fish; **~ haute/basse** high/low tide; **~ noire** oil slick.

**marelle** /marɛl/ *nf* hopscotch.

**margarine** /margarin/ *nf* margarine.

**marge** /marʒ/ *nf* margin; **en ~ de** (à l'écart de) on the fringe(s) of; **~ bénéficiaire** profit margin.

**marginal, ~e** (*mpl* **-aux**) /marʒinal, -o/ *a* marginal. ● *nm,f* drop-out.

**marguerite** /margərit/ *nf* daisy; (qui imprime) daisy-wheel.

**mari** /mari/ *nm* husband.

**mariage** /marjaʒ/ *nm* marriage; (cérémonie) wedding.

**marié, ~e** /marje/ *a* married. ● *nm,f* (bride)groom, bride; **les ~s** the bride and groom.

**marier** /marje/ [45] *vt* marry. □ **se ~** *vpr* get married, marry; **se ~ avec** marry, get married to.

**marin, ~e** /marɛ̃, -in/ *a* sea. ● *nm* sailor.

**marine** /marin/ *nf* navy; **~ marchande** merchant navy. ● *a inv* navy (blue).

**marionnette** /marjɔnɛt/ *nf* puppet; (à fils) marionette.

**maritalement** /maritalmɑ̃/ *adv* (*vivre*) as husband and wife.

**maritime** /maritim/ *a* maritime, coastal; (*agent, compagnie*) shipping.

**marmaille** /marmaj/ *nf* ⓘ brats.

**marmelade** /marməlad/ *nf* stewed fruit; **~ d'oranges** (orange) marmalade.

**marmite** /marmit/ *nf* (cooking-) pot.

**marmonner** /marmɔne/ [1] *vt* mumble.

**marmot** /marmo/ *nm* ⓘ kid.

**Maroc** /marɔk/ *nm* Morocco.

**maroquinerie** /marɔkinri/ *nf* (magasin) leather goods shop.

**marquant, ~e** /markɑ̃, -t/ *a* (remarquable) outstanding; (qu'on n'oublie pas) memorable.

**marque** /mark/ *nf* mark; (de produits) brand, make; (décompte) score; **à vos ~s!** (Sport) on your marks!; **de ~** (Comm) brand name;

(fig) important; ~ **de fabrique** trademark; ~ **déposée** registered trademark.

**marquer** /marke/ [1] *vt* mark; (indiquer) show, say; (écrire) note down; (*point, but*) score; (*joueur*) mark; (influencer) leave its mark on; (exprimer) (*volonté, sentiment*) show. ● *vi* (laisser une trace) leave a mark; (*événement*) stand out; (Sport) score.

**marquis**, ~**e** /marki, -z/ *nm,f* marquis, marchioness.

**marraine** /marɛn/ *nf* godmother.

**marrant**, ~**e** /marɑ̃, -t/ *a* Ⓘ funny.

**marre** /mar/ *adv* **en avoir** ~ Ⓘ be fed up (**de** with).

**marrer (se)** /(sə)mare/ [1] *vpr* Ⓘ laugh, have a (good) laugh.

**marron** /marɔ̃/ *nm* chestnut; (couleur) brown; (coup Ⓘ) thump; ~ **d'Inde** horse chestnut. ● *a inv* brown.

**mars** /mars/ *nm* March.

**marteau** (*pl* ~**x**) /marto/ *nm* hammer; ~ **(de porte)** (door) knocker; ~ **piqueur** *ou* **pneumatique** pneumatic drill; **être** ~ Ⓘ be mad.

**marteler** /martəle/ [6] *vt* hammer; (*poings, talons*) pound; (scander) rap out.

**martial**, ~**e** (*mpl* -**iaux**) /marsjal, -jo/ *a* military; (*art*) martial.

**martien**, ~**ne** /marsjɛ̃, -ɛn/ *a & nm,f* Martian.

**martyr**, ~**e** /martir/ *nm,f* martyr. ● *a* martyred; (*enfant*) battered.

**martyre** /martir/ *nm* (Relig) martyrdom; (fig) agony, suffering.

**martyriser** /martirize/ [1] *vt* (Relig) martyr; (torturer) torture; (*enfant*) batter.

**marxisme** /marksism/ *nm* Marxism. **marxiste** *a & nmf* Marxist.

**masculin**, ~**e** /maskylɛ̃, -in/ *a* masculine; (*sexe*) male; (*mode, équipe*) men's. ● *nm* masculine.

**masochisme** /mazoʃism/ *nm* masochism.

**masochiste** /mazɔʃist/ *nmf* masochist. ● *a* masochistic.

**masque** /mask/ *nm* mask; ~ **de beauté** face pack. **masquer** [1] *vt* (cacher) hide, conceal (**à** from); (*lumière*) block (off).

**massacre** /masakr/ *nm* massacre. **massacrer** [1] *vt* massacre; (abîmer Ⓘ) ruin.

**massage** /masaʒ/ *nm* massage.

**masse** /mas/ *nf* (volume) mass; (gros morceau) lump, mass; (outil) sledgehammer; **en** ~ (*vendre*) in bulk; (*venir*) in force; **produire en** ~ mass-produce; **la** ~ (foule) the masses; **une** ~ **de** Ⓘ masses of; **la** ~ **de** the majority of.

**masser** /mase/ [1] *vt* (assembler) assemble; (pétrir) massage. □ **se** ~ *vpr* (*gens, foule*) mass.

**massif**, **-ive** /masif, -v/ *a* massive; (*or, argent*) solid. ● *nm* (de fleurs) clump; (parterre) bed; (Géog) massif. **massivement** *adv* (en masse) in large numbers.

**massue** /masy/ *nf* club, bludgeon.

**mastic** /mastik/ *nm* putty; (pour trous) filler.

**mastiquer** /mastike/ [1] *vt* (mâcher) chew.

**mat** /mat/ *a* (*couleur*) matt; (*bruit*) dull; (*teint*) olive; **être** ~ (aux échecs) be in checkmate.

**mât** /mɑ/ *nm* mast; (pylône) pole; ~ **de drapeau** flagpole.

**match** /matʃ/ *nm* match; (US) game; **faire** ~ **nul** tie, draw; ~ **aller** first leg; ~ **retour** return match.

**matelas** /matla/ *nm* mattress; ~ **pneumatique** air bed.

**matelassé**, **~e** /matlase/ *a* padded; (*tissu*) quilted.

**matelot** /matlo/ *nm* sailor.

**mater** /mate/ [1] *vt* (*révolte*) put down; (*personne*) bring into line.

**matérialiser (se)** /(sə)mateʀjalize/ [1] *vpr* materialize.

**matérialiste** /mateʀjalist/ *a* materialistic. ● *nmf* materialist.

**matériau** (*pl* **~x**) /mateʀjo/ *nm* material.

**matériel**, **~le** /mateʀjɛl/ *a* material. ● *nm* equipment, materials; **~ informatique** hardware.

**maternel**, **~le** /matɛʀnɛl/ *a* maternal; (comme d'une mère) motherly. **maternelle** *nf* nursery school.

**maternité** /matɛʀnite/ *nf* maternity hospital; (état de mère) motherhood; **de ~** maternity.

**mathématicien**, **~ne** /matematisjɛ̃, -ɛn/ *nm,f* mathematician.

**mathématique** /matematik/ *a* mathematical. **mathématiques** *nfpl* mathematics (+ *sg*).

**maths** /mat/ *nfpl* 🄸 maths (+ *sg*).

**matière** /matjɛʀ/ *nf* matter; (produit) material; (sujet) subject; **en ~ de** as regards; **~ plastique** plastic; **~s grasses** fat content; **~s premières** raw materials.

**matin** /matɛ̃/ *nm* morning; **de bon ~** early in the morning.

**matinal**, **~e** (*mpl* **-aux**) /matinal, -o/ *a* morning; (de bonne heure) early; **être ~** be up early; (d'habitude) be an early riser.

**matinée** /matine/ *nf* morning; (spectacle) matinée.

**matou** /matu/ *nm* tomcat.

**matraque** /matʀak/ *nf* (de police) truncheon; (US) billy (club). **matraquer** [1] *vt* club, beat; (*produit, chanson*) plug.

**matrimonial**, **~e** (*mpl* **-iaux**) /matʀimɔnjal, -jo/ *a* matrimonial; **agence ~e** marriage bureau.

**maturité** /matyʀite/ *nf* maturity.

**maudire** /modiʀ/ [41] *vt* curse.

**maudit**, **~e** /modi, -t/ *a* 🄸 blasted, damned.

**maugréer** /mogʀee/ [15] *vi* grumble.

**mausolée** /mozɔle/ *nm* mausoleum.

**maussade** /mosad/ *a* gloomy.

**mauvais**, **~e** /mɔvɛ, -z/ *a* bad; (erroné) wrong; (malveillant) evil; (désagréable) nasty, bad; (*mer*) rough; **le ~ moment** the wrong time; **~e herbe** weed; **~e langue** gossip; **~e passe** tight spot; **~ traitements** ill-treatment. ● *adv* (*sentir*) bad; **il fait ~** the weather is bad. ● *nm* **le bon et le ~** the good and the bad.

**mauve** /mov/ *a & nm* mauve.

**mauviette** /movjɛt/ *nf* weakling, wimp.

**maux** /mo/ ⇒ MAL².

**maximal**, **~e** (*mpl* **-aux**) /maksimal, -o/ *a* maximum.

**maxime** /maksim/ *nf* maxim.

**maximum** /maksimɔm/ *a* maximum. ● *nm* maximum; **au ~** as much as possible; (tout au plus) at most; **faire le ~** do one's utmost.

**mazout** /mazut/ *nm* (fuel) oil.

**me**, **m'** /mə, m/ *pron* me; (indirect) (to) me; (réfléchi) myself.

**méandre** /meɑ̃dʀ/ *nm* meander.

**mec** /mek/ *nm* 🄸 bloke, guy.

**mécanicien**, **~ne** /mekanisjɛ̃, -jɛn/ *nm,f* mechanic. ● *nm* train driver.

**mécanique** /mekanik/ *a* mechanical; (*jouet*) clockwork; **problème ~** engine trouble. ● *nf* mechanics

(+ *sg*); (mécanisme) mechanism. **mécaniser** [1] *vt* mechanize.

**mécanisme** /mekanism/ *nm* mechanism.

**méchamment** /meʃamɑ̃/ *adv* spitefully. **méchanceté** *nf* nastiness; (action) wicked action.

**méchant**, **~e** /meʃɑ̃, -t/ *a* (cruel) wicked; (désagréable, grave) nasty; (*enfant*) naughty; (*chien*) vicious; (sensationnel ⓘ) terrific. ● *nm,f* (enfant) naughty child.

**mèche** /mɛʃ/ *nf* (de cheveux) lock; (de bougie) wick; (d'explosif) fuse; (outil) drill bit; **de ~ avec** in league with.

**méconnaissable** /mekɔnɛsabl/ *a* unrecognizable.

**méconnaître** /mekɔnɛtʀ/ [18] *vt* misunderstand, misread; (mésestimer) underestimate.

**méconnu**, **~e** /mekɔny/ *a* unrecognized; (*artiste*) neglected.

**mécontent**, **~e** /mekɔ̃tɑ̃, -t/ *a* dissatisfied (**de** with); (irrité) annoyed (**de** at, with). **mécontentement** *nm* dissatisfaction; annoyance. **mécontenter** [1] *vt* dissatisfy; (irriter) annoy.

**médaille** /medaj/ *nf* medal; (insigne) badge; (bijou) medallion. **médaillé**, **~e** *nm,f* medallist.

**médaillon** /medajɔ̃/ *nm* medallion; (bijou) locket.

**médecin** /mɛdsɛ̃/ *nm* doctor.

**médecine** /mɛdsin/ *nf* medicine.

**média** /medja/ *nm* medium; **les ~s** the media.

**médiateur**, **-trice** /medjatœʀ, -tʀis/ *nm,f* mediator.

**médiatique** /medjatik/ *a* (*événement, personnalité*) media.

**médical**, **~e** (*mpl* **-aux**) /medikal, -o/ *a* medical.

**médicament** /medikamɑ̃/ *nm* medicine, drug.

**médico-légal**, **~e** (*mpl* **-aux**) /medikɔlegal, -o/ *a* forensic.

**médiéval**, **~e** (*mpl* **-aux**) /medjeval, -o/ *a* medieval.

**médiocre** /medjɔkʀ/ *a* mediocre, poor. **médiocrité** *nf* mediocrity.

**médire** /mediʀ/ [37] *vi* **~ de** speak ill of, malign.

**médisance** /medizɑ̃s/ *nf* **~(s)** malicious gossip.

**méditer** /medite/ [1] *vi* meditate (**sur** on). ● *vt* contemplate; (*paroles, conseils*) mull over; **~ de** plan to.

**Méditerranée** /meditɛʀane/ *nf* **la ~** the Mediterranean.

**méditerranéen**, **~ne** /meditɛʀaneɛ̃, -ɛn/ *a* Mediterranean.

**médium** /medjɔm/ *nm* (personne) medium.

**méduse** /medyz/ *nf* jellyfish.

**meeting** /mitiŋ/ *nm* meeting.

**méfait** /mefɛ/ *nm* misdeed; **les ~s de** (conséquences) the ravages of.

**méfiance** /mefjɑ̃s/ *nf* suspicion, distrust. **méfiant**, **~e** *a* suspicious, distrustful.

**méfier** (**se**) /(sə)mefje/ [45] *vpr* be wary *ou* careful; **se ~ de** distrust, be wary of.

**mégaoctet** /megaɔktɛ/ *nm* (Ordinat) megabyte.

**mégère** /meʒɛʀ/ *nf* (femme) shrew.

**mégot** /mego/ *nm* cigarette end.

**meilleur**, **~e** /mɛjœʀ/ *a* (comparatif) better (**que** than); (superlatif) best; **le ~ livre** the best book; **mon ~ ami** my best friend; **~ marché** cheaper. ● *nm,f* **le ~**, **la ~e** the best (one). ● *adv* (*sentir*) better; **il fait ~** the weather is better.

**mél** /mel/ *nm* e-mail; **envoyer un ~** send an e-mail.

**mélancolie** /melɑ̃kɔli/ *nf* melancholy.

**mélange** /melɑ̃ʒ/ *nm* mixture, blend.

**mélanger** /melɑ̃ʒe/ [40] *vt* mix; (*thés, parfums*) blend. □ **se ~** *vpr* mix; (*thés, parfums*) blend; (*idées*) get mixed up.

**mélasse** /melas/ *nf* black treacle; (US) molasses.

**mêlée** /mele/ *nf* free for all; (au rugby) scrum.

**mêler** /mele/ [1] *vt* mix (**à** with); (*qualités*) combine; (embrouiller) mix up; **~ qn à** (impliquer dans) involve sb in. □ **se ~** *vpr* mix; combine; **se ~ à** (se joindre à) mingle with; (participer à) join in; **se ~ de** meddle in; **mêle-toi de ce qui te regarde** mind your own business.

**méli-mélo** (*pl* **mélis-mélos**) /melimelo/ *nm* jumble.

**mélo** /melo/ [I] *nm* melodrama. ● *a inv* slushy, schmaltzy [I].

**mélodie** /melɔdi/ *nf* melody. **mélodieux, -ieuse** *a* melodious. **mélodique** *a* melodic.

**mélodramatique** /melɔdʀamatik/ *a* melodramatic. **mélodrame** *nm* melodrama.

**mélomane** /melɔman/ *nmf* music lover.

**melon** /məlɔ̃/ *nm* melon; **(chapeau) ~** bowler (hat).

**membrane** /mɑ̃bʀan/ *nf* membrane.

**membre** /mɑ̃bʀ/ *nm* (Anat) limb; (adhérent) member.

**même** /mɛm/ *a* same; **ce livre ~** this very book; **la bonté ~** kindness itself; **en ~ temps** at the same time. ● *pron* **le ~, la ~** the same (one). ● *adv* even; **à ~** (sur) directly on; **à ~ de** in a position to; **de ~** (aussi) too; (de la même façon) likewise; **de ~ que** just as; **~ si** even if.

**mémé** /meme/ *nf* [I] granny.

**mémo** /memo/ *nm* note, memo.

**mémoire** /memwaʀ/ *nm* (rapport) memorandum; (Univ) dissertation; **~s** (souvenirs écrits) memoirs. ● *nf* memory; **à la ~ de** to the memory of; **de ~** from memory; **~ morte/vive** (Ordinat) ROM/RAM.

**mémorable** /memɔʀabl/ *a* memorable.

**menace** /mənas/ *nf* threat. **menacer** [10] *vt* threaten (**de faire** to do).

**ménage** /menaʒ/ *nm* (couple) couple; (travail) housework; (famille) household; **se mettre en ~** set up house.

**ménagement** /menaʒmɑ̃/ *nm* **avec ~s** gently; **sans ~s** (*dire*) bluntly; (*jeter, pousser*) roughly.

**ménager**[1], **-ère** /menaʒe, -ɛʀ/ *a* household, domestic; **travaux ~s** housework.

**ménager**[2] /menaʒe/ [40] *vt* be gentle with, handle carefully; (utiliser) be careful with; (organiser) prepare (carefully); **ne pas ~ ses efforts** spare no effort.

**ménagère** /menaʒɛʀ/ *nf* housewife.

**ménagerie** /menaʒʀi/ *nf* menagerie.

**mendiant, ~e** /mɑ̃djɑ̃, -t/ *nm,f* beggar.

**mendier** /mɑ̃dje/ [45] *vt* beg for. ● *vi* beg.

**mener** /məne/ [6] *vt* lead; (*entreprise, pays*) run; (*étude, enquête*) carry out; (*politique*) pursue; **~ à** (accompagner à) take to; (faire aboutir) lead to; **~ à bien** see through. ● *vi* lead.

**méningite** /menɛ̃ʒit/ *nf* meningitis.

**menotte** /mənɔt/ *nf* [I] hand; **~s** handcuffs.

**mensonge** /mɑ̃sɔ̃ʒ/ *nm* lie; (action) lying. **mensonger**, **-ère** *a* untrue, false.

**mensualité** /mɑ̃sɥalite/ *nf* monthly payment.

**mensuel**, **~le** /mɑ̃sɥɛl/ *a* monthly. ● *nm* monthly (magazine). **mensuellement** *adv* monthly.

**mensurations** /mɑ̃syʀasjɔ̃/ *nfpl* measurements.

**mental**, **~e** (*mpl* **-aux**) /mɑ̃tal, -o/ *a* mental; **malade ~** mentally ill person; **handicapé ~** mentally handicapped person.

**mentalité** /mɑ̃talite/ *nf* mentality.

**menteur**, **-euse** /mɑ̃tœʀ, -øz/ *nm,f* liar. ● *a* untruthful.

**menthe** /mɑ̃t/ *nf* mint.

**mention** /mɑ̃sjɔ̃/ *nf* mention; (annotation) note; (Scol) grade, **rayer la ~ inutile** delete as appropriate. **mentionner** [1] *vt* mention.

**mentir** /mɑ̃tiʀ/ [46] *vi* lie.

**menton** /mɑ̃tɔ̃/ *nm* chin.

**menu**, **~e** /məny/ *a* (petit) tiny; (fin) fine; (insignifiant) minor. ● *adv* (*couper*) fine. ● *nm* (carte) menu; (repas) meal; (Ordinat) menu; **~ déroulant** pull-down menu.

**menuiserie** /mənɥizʀi/ *nf* carpentry, joinery. **menuisier** *nm* carpenter, joiner.

**méprendre (se)** /(sə)mepʀɑ̃dʀ/ [50] *vpr* **se ~ sur** be mistaken about.

**mépris** /mepʀi/ *nm* contempt, scorn (**de** for); **au ~ de** regardless of.

**méprisable** /mepʀizabl/ *a* contemptible, despicable.

**méprisant**, **~e** /mepʀizɑ̃, -t/ *a* scornful.

**méprise** /mepʀiz/ *nf* mistake.

**mépriser** [1] *vt* scorn, despise.

**mer** /mɛʀ/ *nf* sea; (marée) tide; **en pleine ~** out at sea.

**mercenaire** /mɛʀsənɛʀ/ *nm & a* mercenary.

**mercerie** /mɛʀs(ə)ʀi/ *nf* haberdashery, (US) notions store. **mercier**, **-ière** *nm,f* haberdasher; (US) notions seller.

**merci** /mɛʀsi/ *interj* thank you, thanks (**de**, **pour** for); **~ beaucoup**, **~ bien** thank you very much. ● *nm* thank you. ● *nf* mercy.

**mercredi** /mɛʀkʀədi/ *nm* Wednesday; **~ des Cendres** Ash Wednesday.

**merde** /mɛʀd/ *nf* ⊠ shit ⊠.

**mère** /mɛʀ/ *nf* mother; **~ de famille** mother.

**méridional**, **~e** (*mpl* **-aux**) /meʀidjɔnal, -o/ *a* southern. ● *nm,f* Southerner.

**mérite** /meʀit/ *nm* merit; **avoir du ~ à faire** deserve credit for doing.

**mériter** /meʀite/ [1] *vt* deserve; **~ d'être lu** be worth reading.

**méritoire** /meʀitwaʀ/ *a* commendable.

**merlan** /mɛʀlɑ̃/ *nm* whiting.

**merle** /mɛʀl/ *nm* blackbird.

**merveille** /mɛʀvɛj/ *nf* wonder, marvel; **à ~** wonderfully; **faire des ~s** work wonders.

**merveilleux**, **-euse** /mɛʀvɛjø, -z/ *a* wonderful, marvellous.

**mes** /me/ ⇒MON.

**mésange** /mezɑ̃ʒ/ *nf* tit(mouse).

**mésaventure** /mezavɑ̃tyʀ/ *nf* misadventure; **par ~** by some misfortune.

**mesdames** /medam/ ⇒MADAME.

**mesdemoiselles** /medmwazɛl/ ⇒MADEMOISELLE.

**mésentente** /mezɑ̃tɑ̃t/ *nf* disagreement.

**mesquin**, **~e** /meskɛ̃, -in/ *a* mean-minded, petty; (chiche) mean. **mesquinerie** *nf* meanness.

**mess** /mɛs/ *nm* (Mil) mess.

**message** /mesaʒ/ *nm* message; **un ~ électronique** an e-mail; **~ texte** text message.

**messager**, **-ère** /mesaze, -ɛʀ/ *nm,f* messenger. ● *nm* **~ de poche** pager.

**messagerie** /mesaʒʀi/ *nf* (transports) freight forwarding; (télécommunications) messaging; **~ électronique** electronic mail; **~ vocale** voice mail.

**messe** /mɛs/ *nf* (Relig) mass.

**messieurs** /mesjø/ ⇒MONSIEUR.

**mesure** /məzyʀ/ *nf* measurement; (quantité, unité) measure; (disposition) measure, step; (cadence) time; **en ~** in time; (modération) moderation; **à ~ que** as; **dans la ~ où** in so far as; **dans une certaine ~** to some extent; **en ~ de** in a position to; **sans ~** to excess; **(fait) sur ~** made-to-measure.

**mesuré**, **~e** /məzyʀe/ *a* measured; (atttitude) moderate.

**mesurer** /məzyʀe/ [1] *vt* measure; (juger) assess; (*argent, temps*) ration. ● *vi* **~ 15 mètres de long** be 15 metres long. □ **se ~ avec** *vpr* pit oneself against.

**met** /mɛ/ ⇒METTRE [42].

**métal** (*pl* **-aux**) /metal, -o/ *nm* metal. **métallique** *a* (*objet*) metal; (*éclat*) metallic.

**métallurgie** /metalyʀʒi/ *nf* (industrie) metalworking industry.

**métamorphoser** /metamɔʀfoze/ [1] *vt* transform. □ **se ~** *vpr* be transformed; **se ~ en** metamorphose into.

**métaphore** /metafɔʀ/ *nf* metaphor.

**météo** /meteo/ *nf* (bulletin) weather forecast.

**météore** /meteɔʀ/ *nm* meteor.

**météorologie** /meteɔʀɔlɔʒi/ *nf* meteorology.

**météorologique** /meteɔʀɔlɔʒik/ *a* meteorological; **conditions ~s** weather conditions.

**méthode** /metɔd/ *nf* method; (ouvrage) course, manual. **méthodique** *a* methodical.

**méticuleux**, **-euse** /metikylø, -z/ *a* meticulous.

**métier** /metje/ *nm* job; (manuel) trade; (intellectuel) profession; (expérience) experience, skill; **~ (à tisser)** loom.

**métis**, **~se** /metis/ *a* mixed race. ● *nm,f* person of mixed race.

**métrage** /metʀaʒ/ *nm* length; **court ~** short (film); **long ~** feature-length film.

**mètre** /mɛtʀ/ *nm* metre; (règle) rule; **~ ruban** tape-measure.

**métreur**, **-euse** /metʀœʀ, -øz/ *nm,f* quantity surveyor.

**métrique** /metʀik/ *a* metric.

**métro** /metʀo/ *nm* underground; (US) subway.

**métropole** /metʀɔpɔl/ *nf* metropolis; (pays) mother country. **métropolitain**, **~e** *a* metropolitan.

**mets** /mɛ/ *nm* dish. ● ⇒METTRE [42].

**mettable** /mɛtabl/ *a* wearable.

**metteur** /mɛtœʀ/ *nm* **~ en scène** director.

**mettre** /mɛtʀ/ [42] *vt* put; (*radio, chauffage*) put *ou* switch on; (*réveil*) set; (installer) put in; (revêtir) put on; (porter habituellement) (vêtement, lunettes) wear; (prendre) take; (investir, dépenser) put; (écrire) write, say; **elle a mis deux heures** it took her two hours; **~ la table** lay the

table; ~ **en question** question; ~ **en valeur** highlight; (*terrain*) develop; **mettons que** let's suppose that. ● *vi* ~ **bas** (*animal*) give birth. □ **se** ~ *vpr* (*vêtement, maquillage*) put on; (se placer) (*objet*) go; (*personne*) (debout) stand; (assis) sit; (couché) lie; **se ~ en short** put shorts on; **se ~ debout** stand up; **se ~ au lit** go to bed; **se ~ à table** sit down at table; **se ~ en ligne** line up; **se ~ du sable dans les yeux** get sand in one's eyes; **se ~ au chinois/tennis** take up Chinese/tennis; **se ~ au travail** set to work; **se ~ à faire** start to do.

**meuble** /mœbl/ *nm* piece of furniture; **~s** furniture.

**meublé** /møble/ *nm* furnished flat.

**meubler** /møble/ [1] *vt* furnish; (fig) fill. □ **se** ~ *vpr* buy furniture.

**meugler** /møgle/ [1] *vi* moo.

**meule** /møl/ *nf* millstone; ~ **de foin** haystack.

**meunier**, **-ière** /mønje, -jɛʀ/ *nm,f* miller.

**meurs**, **meurt** /mœʀ/ ⇒MOURIR [43].

**meurtre** /mœʀtʀ/ *nm* murder.

**meurtrier**, **-ière** /mœʀtʀije, -jɛʀ/ *a* deadly. ● *nm,f* murderer, murderess.

**meurtrir** /mœʀtʀiʀ/ [2] *vt* bruise.

**meute** /møt/ *nf* pack of hounds.

**Mexique** /mɛksik/ *nm* Mexico.

**mi-**/mi/ *préf* mid-, half-; **à mi-chemin** half-way; **à mi-pente** half-way up the hill; **à la mi-juin** in mid-June.

**miauler** /mjole/ [1] *vi* miaow.

**micro** /mikʀo/ *nm* microphone, mike; (Ordinat) micro.

**microbe** /mikʀɔb/ *nm* germ.

**microfilm** /mikʀɔfilm/ *nm* microfilm.

**micro-onde** /mikʀoɔ̃d/ *nf* microwave; **un four à ~s** microwave (oven). **micro-ondes** *nm inv* microwave (oven).

**micro-ordinateur** (*pl* **~s**) /mikʀoɔʀdinatœʀ/ *nm* personal computer.

**microphone** /mikʀɔfɔn/ *nm* microphone.

**microprocesseur** /mikʀopʀɔsesœʀ/ *nm* microprocessor.

**microscope** /mikʀɔskɔp/ *nm* microscope.

**midi** /midi/ *nm* twelve o'clock, midday, noon; (déjeuner) lunchtime; (sud) south. **Midi** *nm* **le M~** the South of France.

**mie** /mi/ *nf* soft part (of the loaf); **un pain de ~** a sandwich loaf.

**miel** /mjɛl/ *nm* honey.

**mielleux**, **-euse** /mjɛlø, -z/ *a* unctuous.

**mien**, **~ne** /mjɛ̃, ɛn/ *pron* **le ~**, **la ~ne**, **les ~(ne)s** mine.

**miette** /mjɛt/ *nf* crumb; (fig) scrap; **en ~s** in pieces.

**mieux** /mjø/ *a inv* better (**que** than); **le** *ou* **la** *ou* **les ~** (the) best. ● *nm* best; (progrès) improvement; **faire de son ~** do one's best; **le ~ serait de** the best thing would be to. ● *adv* better; **le** *ou* **la** *ou* **les ~** (de deux) the better; (de plusieurs) the best; **elle va ~** she is better; **j'aime ~ rester** I'd rather stay; **il vaudrait ~ partir** it would be best to leave; **tu ferais ~ de faire** you would do best to do.

**mièvre** /mjɛvʀ/ *a* insipid.

**mignon**, **~ne** /miɲɔ̃, -ɔn/ *a* cute; (gentil) kind.

**migraine** /migʀɛn/ *nf* headache; (plus fort) migraine.

**migration** /migʀasjɔ̃/ *nf* migration.

**mijoter** /miʒɔte/ [1] *vt/i* simmer; (tramer [I]) cook up.

**mil** /mil/ *nm* a thousand.

**milice** /milis/ *nf* militia.

**milieu** (*pl* **~x**) /miljø/ *nm* middle; (environnement) environment; appartenance sociale) background; (groupe) circle; (voie) middle way; (criminel) underworld; **au ~ de** in the middle of; **en plein** *ou* **au beau ~ de** right in the middle (of).

**militaire** /militɛʀ/ *a* military. ● *nm* soldier, serviceman.

**militant, ~e** /militɑ̃, -t/ *nm,f* militant.

**militer** /milite/ [1] *vi* be a militant; **~ pour** militate in favour of.

**mille¹** /mil/ *a & nm inv* a thousand; **deux ~** two thousand; **mettre dans le ~** (fig) hit the nail on the head.

**mille²** /mil/ *nm* **~ (marin)** (nautical) mile.

**millénaire** /milenɛʀ/ *nm* millennium. ● *a* a thousand years old.

**mille-pattes** /milpat/ *nm inv* centipede.

**millésime** /milezim/ *nm* date; (de vin) vintage.

**millet** /mijɛ/ *nm* millet.

**milliard** /miljaʀ/ *nm* thousand million, billion. **milliardaire** *nmf* multimillionaire.

**millième** /miljɛm/ *a & nmf* thousandth.

**millier** /milje/ *nm* thousand; **un ~ (de)** about a thousand.

**millimètre** /milimɛtʀ/ *nm* millimetre.

**million** /miljɔ̃/ *nm* million; **deux ~s (de)** two million. **millionnaire** *nmf* millionaire.

**mime** /mim/ *nmf* mime-artist. ● *nm* (art) mime. **mimer** [1] *vt* mime; (imiter) mimic.

**mimique** /mimik/ *nf* expressions and gestures.

**minable** /minabl/ *a* [I] (*logement*) shabby; (médiocre) pathetic, crummy.

**minauder** /minode/ [1] *vi* simper.

**mince** /mɛ̃s/ *a* thin; (svelte) slim; (faible) (*espoir, majorité*) slim. ● *interj* [I] blast [I], darn it [I]. **minceur** *nf* thinness; slimness.

**mincir** /mɛ̃siʀ/ [2] *vi* get slimmer; **ça te mincit** it makes you look slimmer.

**mine** /min/ *nf* expression; (allure) appearance; **avoir bonne ~** look well; **faire ~ de** make as if to; (exploitation, explosif) mine; (de crayon) lead; **~ de charbon** coal-mine.

**miner** /mine/ [1] *vt* (saper) undermine; (garnir d'explosifs) mine.

**minerai** /minʀɛ/ *nm* ore.

**minéral, ~e** (*mpl* **-aux**) /mineʀal, -o/ *a* mineral. ● *nm* (*pl* **-aux**) mineral.

**minéralogique** /mineʀalɔʒik/ *a* **plaque ~** numberplate; (US) license plate.

**minet, ~te** /minɛ, -t/ *nm,f* (chat [I]) pussy(cat).

**mineur, ~e** /minœʀ/ *a* minor; (Jur) under age. ● *nm,f* (Jur) minor. ● *nm* (ouvrier) miner.

**miniature** /minjatyʀ/ *nf & a* miniature.

**minier, -ière** /minje, -jɛʀ/ *a* mining.

**minimal, ~e** (*mpl* **-aux**) /minimal, -o/ *a* minimal, minimum.

**minime** /minim/ *a* minimal, minor. ● *nmf* (Sport) junior.

**minimum** /minimɔm/ *a* minimum. ● *nm* minimum; **au ~** (pour le moins) at the very least; **en faire un ~** do as little as possible.

**ministère** /ministɛʀ/ *nm* ministry; (gouvernement) government; **~ public** public prosecutor's office. **ministériel, ~le** *a* ministerial, government.

**ministre** /ministʀ/ *nm* minister; (au Royaume-Uni) Secretary of State; (US) Secretary.

**Minitel**® /minitɛl/ *nm* Minitel (*telephone videotext system*).

**minorer** /minɔʀe/ [1] *vt* reduce.

**minoritaire** /minɔʀitɛʀ/ *a* minority; **être ~** be in the minority. **minorité** *nf* minority.

**minuit** /minɥi/ *nm* midnight.

**minuscule** /minyskyl/ *a* minute. ● *nf* (lettre) ~ lower case.

**minute** /minyt/ *nf* minute; **'talons ~'** 'heels repaired while you wait'.

**minuterie** /minytʀi/ *nf* time-switch.

**minutie** /minysi/ *nf* meticulousness.

**minutieux, -ieuse** /minysjø, -z/ *a* meticulous.

**mioche** /mjɔʃ/ *nm,f* [I] kid.

**mirabelle** /miʀabɛl/ *nf* (mirabelle) plum.

**miracle** /miʀɑkl/ *nm* miracle; **par ~** miraculously.

**miraculeux, -euse** /miʀakylø, -z/ *a* miraculous.

**mirage** /miʀaʒ/ *nm* mirage.

**mire** /miʀ/ *nf* (fig) centre of attraction; (TV) test card.

**mirobolant, ~e** /miʀɔbɔlɑ̃, -t/ *a* [I] marvellous.

**miroir** /miʀwaʀ/ *nm* mirror.

**miroiter** /miʀwate/ [1] *vi* shimmer, sparkle.

**mis, ~e** /mi, miz/ *a* **bien ~** well-dressed. ● ⇒METTRE [42].

**mise** /miz/ *nf* (argent) stake; (tenue) attire; **~ à feu** blast-off; **~ au point** adjustment; (fig) clarification; **~ de fonds** capital outlay; **~ en garde** warning; **~ en plis** set; **~ en scène** direction.

**miser** /mize/ [1] *vt* (*argent*) bet, stake (**sur** on). ● *vi* **~ sur** (parier) place a bet on; (compter sur) bank on.

**misérable** /mizeʀabl/ *a* miserable, wretched; (indigent) destitute; (minable) seedy, squalid.

**misère** /mizɛʀ/ *nf* destitution; (malheur) trouble, woe. **miséreux, -euse** *nm,f* destitute person.

**miséricorde** /mizeʀikɔʀd/ *nf* mercy.

**missel** /misɛl/ *nm* missal.

**missile** /misil/ *nm* missile.

**mission** /misjɔ̃/ *nm* mission. **missionnaire** *nmf* missionary.

**missive** /misiv/ *nf* missive.

**mistral** /mistʀal/ *nm* (vent) mistral.

**mitaine** /mitɛn/ *nf* fingerless mitt.

**mite** /mit/ *nf* (clothes-)moth.

**mi-temps** /mitɑ̃/ *nf inv* (arrêt) half-time; (période) half. ● *nm inv* part-time work; **à ~** part-time.

**miteux, -euse** /mitø, -z/ *a* shabby.

**mitigé, ~e** /mitiʒe/ *a* (modéré) lukewarm; (*succès*) qualified.

**mitonner** /mitɔne/ [1] *vt* cook slowly with care; (fig) cook up.

**mitoyen, ~ne** /mitwajɛ̃, -ɛn/ *a* **mur ~** party wall.

**mitrailler** /mitʀɑje/ [1] *vt* machine-gun; (fig) bombard.

**mitraillette** /mitʀɑjɛt/ *nf* submachine gun. **mitrailleuse** *nf* machine gun.

**mi-voix: à ~** /amivwa/ *loc* in a low voice.

**mixeur** /miksœʀ/ *nm* liquidizer, blender; (batteur) mixer.

**mixte** /mikst/ *a* mixed; (*commission*) joint; (*école*) coeducational; (*peau*) combination.

**mobile** /mɔbil/ *a* mobile; (*pièce*) moving; (*feuillet*) loose. ● *nm* (art) mobile; (raison) motive.

**mobilier** /mɔbilje/ *nm* furniture.

**mobilisation** /mɔbilizasjɔ̃/ *nf* mobilization. **mobiliser** [1] *vt* mobilize.

**mobilité** /mɔbilite/ *nf* mobility.

**mobylette®** /mɔbilɛt/ *nf* moped.

**moche** /mɔʃ/ *a* [I] (laid) ugly; (mauvais) lousy.

**modalités** /mɔdalite/ *nfpl* (conditions) terms; (façon de fonctionner) practical details.

**mode** /mɔd/ *nf* fashion; (coutume) custom; **à la ~** fashionable. ● *nm* method, mode; (genre) way; **~ d'emploi** directions (for use).

**modèle** /mɔdɛl/ *a* model. ● *nm* model; (exemple) example; (Comm) (type) model; (taille) size; (style) style; **~ familial** family size; **~ réduit** (small-scale) model.

**modeler** /mɔdle/ [6] *vt* model (**sur** on). □ **se ~ sur** *vpr* model oneself on.

**modem** /mɔdɛm/ *nm* modem.

**modérateur**, **-trice** /mɔdeʀatœʀ, -tʀis/ *a* moderating. **modération** *nf* moderation.

**modéré**, **~e** /mɔdeʀe/ *a & nm, f* moderate.

**modérer** /mɔdeʀe/ [14] *vt* (*propos*) moderate; (*désirs, sentiments*) curb. □ **se ~** *vpr* restrain oneself.

**moderne** /mɔdɛʀn/ *a* modern. **moderniser** [1] *vt* modernize.

**modeste** /mɔdɛst/ *a* modest. **modestie** *nf* modesty.

**modification** /mɔdifikasjɔ̃/ *nf* modification.

**modifier** /mɔdifje/ [45] *vt* change, modify. □ **se ~** *vpr* change, alter.

**modique** /mɔdik/ *a* modest.

**modiste** /mɔdist/ *nf* milliner.

**moduler** /mɔdyle/ [1] *vt* modulate; (adapter) adjust.

**moelle** /mwal/ *nf* marrow; **~ épinière** spinal cord; **~ osseuse** bone marrow.

**moelleux**, **-euse** /mwalø, -z/ *a* soft; (onctueux) smooth.

**mœurs** /mœʀ(s)/ *nfpl* (morale) morals; (usages) customs; (manières) habits, ways.

**moi** /mwa/ *pron* me; (indirect) (to) me; (sujet) I. ● *nm* self.

**moignon** /mwaɲɔ̃/ *nm* stump.

**moi-même** /mwamɛm/ *pron* myself.

**moindre** /mwɛ̃dʀ/ *a* (moins grand) lesser; **le** *ou* **la ~**, **les ~s** the slightest, the least.

**moine** /mwan/ *nm* monk.

**moineau** (*pl* **~x**) /mwano/ *nm* sparrow.

**moins** /mwɛ̃/ *prép* minus; (pour dire l'heure) to; **une heure ~ dix** ten to one. ● *adv* less (**que** than); **le** *ou* **la** *ou* **les ~** the least; **le ~ grand/haut** the smallest/lowest; **~ de** (avec un nom non dénombrable) less (**que** than); **~ de dix francs** less than ten francs; **~ de livres** fewer books; **au ~**, **du ~** at least; **à ~ que** unless; **de ~** less; **de ~ en ~** less and less; **en ~** less; (manquant) missing.

**mois** /mwa/ *nm* month.

**moisi**, **~e** /mwazi/ *a* mouldy. ● *nm* mould; **de ~** (*odeur*) musty. **moisir** [2] *vi* go mouldy. **moisissure** *nf* mould.

**moisson** /mwasɔ̃/ *nf* harvest.

**moissonner** /mwasɔne/ [1] *vt* harvest, reap. **moissonneur**, **-euse** *nm, f* harvester.

**moite** /mwat/ *a* sticky, clammy.

**moitié** /mwatje/ *nf* half; (milieu) halfway mark; **s'arrêter à la ~** stop halfway through; **à ~ vide** half empty; **à ~ prix** (at) half-price; **la ~ de** half (of). **moitié-moitié** *adv* half-and-half.

**mol** /mɔl/ ⇒MOU.

**molaire** /mɔlɛʀ/ *nf* molar.

**molécule** /mɔlekyl/ *nf* molecule.

**molester** /mɔlɛste/ [1] *vt* manhandle, rough up.

**molle** /mɔl/ ⇒MOU.

**mollement** /mɔlmɑ̃/ *adv* softly; (faiblement) feebly. **mollesse** *nf* softness; (faiblesse) feebleness; (apathie) listlessness.

**mollet** /mɔlɛ/ *nm* (de jambe) calf.

**mollir** /mɔliʀ/ [2] *vi* soften; (céder) yield.

**môme** /mom/ *nmf* [I] kid.

**moment** /mɔmɑ̃/ *nm* moment; (période) time; **(petit) ~** short while; **au ~ où** when; **par ~s** now and then; **du ~ où que** (pourvu que) as long as, provided that; (puisque) since; **en ce ~** at the moment.

**momentané**, **~e** /mɔmɑ̃tane/ *a* momentary. **momentanément** *adv* momentarily; (en ce moment) at present.

**momie** /mɔmi/ *nf* mummy.

**mon**, **ma** (**mon** *before vowel or mute h*) (*pl* **mes**) /mɔ̃, ma, mɔ̃n, me/ *a* my.

**monarchie** /mɔnaʀʃi/ *nf* monarchy.

**monarque** /mɔnaʀk/ *nm* monarque.

**monastère** /mɔnastɛʀ/ *nm* monastery.

**monceau** (*pl* **~x**) /mɔ̃so/ *nm* heap, pile.

**mondain**, **~e** /mɔ̃dɛ̃, -ɛn/ *a* society, social.

**monde** /mɔ̃d/ *nm* world; **du ~** (a lot of) people; (quelqu'un) somebody; **le (grand) ~** (high) society; **se faire (tout) un ~ de qch** make a great deal of fuss about sth; **pas le moins du ~** not in the least.

**mondial**, **~e** (*mpl* **-iaux**) /mɔ̃djal, -jo/ *a* world; (*influence*) worldwide. **mondialement** *adv* the world over.

**mondialisation** /mɔ̃djalizasjɔ̃/ *nf* globalization.

**monétaire** /mɔnetɛʀ/ *a* monetary.

**moniteur**, **-trice** /mɔnitœʀ, -tʀis/ *nm,f* instructor; (de colonie de vacances) group leader; (US) (camp) counselor.

**monnaie** /mɔnɛ/ *nf* currency; (pièce) coin; (appoint) change; **faire la ~ de** get change for; **faire de la ~ à qn** give sb change; **menue** *ou* **petite ~** small change.

**monnayer** /mɔneje/ [31] *vt* convert into cash.

**monologue** /mɔnɔlɔg/ *nm* monologue.

**monopole** /mɔnɔpɔl/ *nm* monopoly. **monopoliser** [1] *vt* monopolize.

**monospace** /mɔnɔspas/ *nm* (Auto) people carrier.

**monotone** /mɔnɔtɔn/ *a* monotonous. **monotonie** *nf* monotony.

**Monseigneur** (*pl* **Messeigneurs**) /mɔ̃sɛɲœʀ/ *nm* (à un duc, archevêque) Your Grace; (à un prince) Your Highness.

**monsieur** (*pl* **messieurs**) /məsjø, mesjø/ *nm* (à un inconnu) (dans une lettre) **M~** Dear Sir; **bonjour, ~** good morning; **mesdames et messieurs** ladies and gentlemen; (à un homme dont on connaît le nom) (dans une lettre) **Cher M~** Dear Mr X; **bonjour, ~** good morning Mr X; **M~ le curé** Father X; **oui M~ le ministre** yes Minister; (homme) man; (formule de respect) sir.

**monstre** /mɔ̃stʀ/ *nm* monster. ● *a* [I] colossal.

**monstrueux**, **-euse** /mɔ̃stʀyø, -z/ *a* monstrous. **monstruosité** *nf* monstrosity.

**mont** /mɔ̃/ *nm* mountain; **le ~ Everest** Mount Everest; **être toujours par ~s et par vaux** be always on the move.

**montage** /mɔ̃taʒ/ *nm* (assemblage) assembly; (au cinéma) editing.

**montagne** /mɔ̃taɲ/ *nf* mountain; (région) mountains; **~s russes** roller-coaster. **montagneux**, **-euse** *a* mountainous.

**montant**, **~e** /mɔ̃tɑ̃, -t/ *a* rising; (*col*) high; (*chemin*) uphill. ● *nm* amount; (pièce de bois) upright.

**mont-de-piété** (*pl* **monts-de-piété**) /mɔ̃dpjete/ *nm* pawnshop.

**monte-charge** /mɔ̃tʃaʀʒ/ *nm inv* goods lift.

**montée** /mɔ̃te/ *nf* ascent, climb; (de prix) rise; (de coûts, risques) increase; (côte) hill.

**monter** /mɔ̃te/ [1] *vt* (*aux.* avoir) take up; (à l'étage) take upstairs; (*escalier, rue, pente*) go up; (assembler) assemble; (*tente, échafaudage*) put up; (*col, manche*) set in; (organiser) (*pièce*) stage; (*société*) set up; (*attaque, garde*) mount. ● *vi* (*aux.* être) go *ou* come up; (à l'étage) go *ou* come upstairs; (*avion*) climb; (*route*) go uphill, climb; (augmenter) rise; (*marée*) come up; **~ sur** (*trottoir, toit*) get up on; (*cheval, bicyclette*) get on; **~ à l'échelle/l'arbre** climb the ladder/tree; **~ dans** (*voiture*) get in; (*train, bus, avion*) get on; **~ à bord** climb on board; **~ (à cheval)** ride; **~ à bicyclette/moto** ride a bike/motorbike.

**monteur**, **-euse** /mɔ̃tœʀ, -øz/ *nm,f* (Tech) fitter; (au cinéma) editor.

**montre** /mɔ̃tʀ/ *nf* watch; **faire ~ de** show.

**montrer** /mɔ̃tʀe/ [1] *vt* show (**à** to); **~ du doigt** point to. □ **se ~** *vpr* show oneself; (être) be; (s'avérer) prove to be.

**monture** /mɔ̃tyʀ/ *nf* (cheval) mount; (de lunettes) frames (+ *pl*); (de bijou) setting.

**monument** /mɔnymɑ̃/ *nm* monument; **~ aux morts** war memorial. **monumental** (*mpl* **-aux**) *a* monumental.

**moquer (se)** /(sə)mɔke/ [1] *vpr* **se ~ de** make fun of; **je m'en moque** Ⓘ I couldn't care less. **moquerie** *nf* mockery. **moqueur**, **-euse** *a* mocking.

**moquette** /mɔkɛt/ *nf* fitted carpet; (US) wall-to-wall carpeting.

**moral**, **~e** (*mpl* **-aux**) /mɔʀal, -o/ *a* moral. ● *nm* (*pl* **-aux**) morale; **ne pas avoir le ~** feel down; **avoir le ~** be in good spirits; **ça m'a remonté le ~** it gave me a boost.

**morale** /mɔʀal/ *nf* moral code; (mœurs) morals; (de fable) moral; **faire la ~ à** lecture. **moralité** *nf* (de personne) morals (+ *pl*); (d'action, œuvre) morality; (de fable) moral.

**moralisateur**, **-trice** /mɔʀalizatœʀ, -tʀis/ *a* moralizing.

**morbide** /mɔʀbid/ *a* morbid.

**morceau** (*pl* **~x**) /mɔʀso/ *nm* piece, bit; (de sucre) lump; (de viande) cut; (passage) passage; **manger un ~** Ⓘ have a bite to eat; **mettre en ~x** smash *ou* tear to bits.

**morceler** /mɔʀsəle/ [6] *vt* divide up.

**mordant**, **~e** /mɔʀdɑ̃, -t/ *a* scathing; (*froid*) biting. ● *nm* vigour, energy.

**mordiller** /mɔʀdije/ [1] *vt* nibble at.

**mordre** /mɔʀdʀ/ [3] *vi* bite (**dans** into); ~ **sur** (*ligne*) go over; (*territoire*) encroach on; ~ **à l'hameçon** bite. ● *vt* bite.

**mordu**, ~**e** /mɔʀdy/ [I] *nm,f* fan. ● *a* smitten; ~ **de** crazy about.

**morfondre** (**se**) /(sə)mɔʀfɔ̃dʀ/ [3] *vpr* wait anxiously; (languir) mope.

**morgue** /mɔʀg/ *nf* morgue, mortuary; (attitude) arrogance.

**moribond**, ~**e** /mɔʀibɔ̃, -d/ *a* dying.

**morne** /mɔʀn/ *a* dull.

**morphine** /mɔʀfin/ *nf* morphine.

**mors** /mɔʀ/ *nm* (de cheval) bit.

**morse** /mɔʀs/ *nm* (animal) walrus; (*code*) Morse code.

**morsure** /mɔʀsyʀ/ *nf* bite.

**mort**[1] /mɔʀ/ *nf* death.

**mort**[2], ~**e** /mɔʀ, -t/ *a* dead; ~ **de fatigue** dead tired. ● *nm,f* dead man, dead woman; **les** ~**s** the dead.

**mortalité** /mɔʀtalite/ *nf* mortality; (**taux de**) ~ death rate.

**mortel**, ~**le** /mɔʀtɛl/ *a* mortal; (*accident*) fatal; (*poison, silence*) deadly. ● *nm,f* mortal. **mortellement** *adv* mortally.

**mortifié**, ~**e** /mɔʀtifje/ *a* mortified.

**mort-né**, ~**e** /mɔʀne/ *a* stillborn.

**mortuaire** /mɔʀtɥɛʀ/ *a* (*cérémonie*) funeral.

**morue** /mɔʀy/ *nf* cod.

**mosaïque** /mɔzaik/ *nf* mosaic.

**mosquée** /mɔske/ *nf* mosque.

**mot** /mo/ *nm* word; (lettre, message) note; ~ **d'ordre** watchword; ~ **de passe** password; ~**s croisés** crossword (puzzle).

**motard** /mɔtaʀ/ *nm* biker; (policier) police motorcyclist.

**moteur**, **-trice** /mɔtœʀ, -tʀis/ *a* (Méd) motor; (*force*) driving; **à 4 roues motrices** 4-wheel drive. ● *nm* engine, motor; **barque à** ~ motor launch; ~ **de recherche** (Internet) search engine.

**motif** /mɔtif/ *nm* (raisons) grounds (+ *pl*); (cause) reason; (Jur) motive; (dessin) pattern.

**motion** /mosjɔ̃/ *nf* motion.

**motivation** /mɔtivasjɔ̃/ *nf* motivation. **motiver** [1] *vt* motivate.

**moto** /mɔto/ *nf* motor cycle. **motocycliste** *nmf* motorcyclist.

**motorisé**, ~**e** /mɔtɔʀize/ *a* motorized.

**motrice** /mɔtʀis/ ⇨MOTEUR.

**motte** /mɔt/ *nf* lump; (de beurre) slab; (de terre) clod; ~ **de gazon** turf.

**mou** (**mol** *before vowel or mute h*), **molle** /mu, mɔl/ *a* soft; (*ventre*) flabby; (sans conviction) feeble; (apathique) sluggish, listless. ● *nm* slack; **avoir du** ~ be slack.

**mouchard**, ~**e** /muʃaʀ, -d/ *nm,f* informer; (Scol) sneak.

**mouche** /muʃ/ *nf* fly; (de cible) bull's eye.

**moucher** (**se**) /(sə)muʃe/ [1] *vpr* blow one's nose.

**moucheron** /muʃʀɔ̃/ *nm* midge.

**moucheté**, ~**e** /muʃte/ *a* speckled.

**mouchoir** /muʃwaʀ/ *nm* handkerchief, hanky; ~ **en papier** tissue.

**moue** /mu/ *nf* pout; **faire la** ~ pout.

**mouette** /mwɛt/ *nf* (sea)gull.

**moufle** /mufl/ *nf* (gant) mitten.

**mouillé**, ~**e** /muje/ *a* wet.

**mouiller** /muje/ [1] *vt* wet, make wet; ~ **l'ancre** drop anchor. □ **se** ~ *vpr* get (oneself) wet.

**moulage** /mulaʒ/ *nm* cast.

**moule** /mul/ *nf* (coquillage) mussel. ● *nm* mould; ~ **à gâteau** cake tin;

~ **à tarte** flan dish. **mouler** [1] *vt* mould; (*statue*) cast.

**moulin** /mulɛ̃/ *nm* mill; ~ **à café** coffee grinder; ~ **à poivre** pepper mill; ~ **à vent** windmill.

**moulinet** /mulinɛ/ *nm* (de canne à pêche) reel; **faire des ~s avec qch** twirl sth around.

**moulinette**® /mulinɛt/ *nf* vegetable mill.

**moulu**, **~e** /muly/ *a* ground; (fatigué [I]) worn out.

**moulure** /mulyʀ/ *nf* moulding.

**mourant**, **~e** /muʀɑ̃, -t/ *a* dying. ● *nm,f* dying person.

**mourir** /muʀiʀ/ [43] *vi* (*aux. être*) die; ~ **d'envie de** be dying to; ~ **de faim** be starving; ~ **d'ennui** be dead bored.

**mousquetaire** /muskətɛʀ/ *nm* musketeer.

**mousse** /mus/ *nf* moss; (écume) froth, foam; (de savon) lather; (dessert) mousse; ~ **à raser** shaving foam. ● *nm* ship's boy.

**mousseline** /muslin/ *nf* muslin; (de soie) chiffon.

**mousser** /muse/ [1] *vi* froth, foam; (*savon*) lather.

**mousseux**, **-euse** /musø, -z/ *a* frothy. ● *nm* sparkling wine.

**mousson** /musɔ̃/ *nf* monsoon.

**moustache** /mustaʃ/ *nf* moustache; **~s** (d'animal) whiskers.

**moustique** /mustik/ *nm* mosquito.

**moutarde** /mutaʀd/ *nf* mustard.

**mouton** /mutɔ̃/ *nm* sheep; (peau) sheepskin; (viande) mutton.

**mouvant**, **~e** /muvɑ̃, -t/ *a* changing; (*terrain*) shifting, unstable.

**mouvement** /muvmɑ̃/ *nm* movement; (agitation) bustle; (en gymnastique) exercise; (impulsion) impulse; (tendance) tend, tendency; **en ~** in motion.

**mouvementé**, **~e** /muvmɑ̃te/ *a* eventful.

**moyen**, **~ne** /mwajɛ̃, -ɛn/ *a* average; (médiocre) poor; **de taille moyenne** medium-sized. ● *nm* means, way; **~s** means; (dons) ability; **au ~ de** by means of; **il n'y a pas ~ de** it is not possible to. **Moyen Âge** *nm* Middle Ages (+ *pl*).

**moyennant** /mwajɛnɑ̃/ *prép* (pour) for; (grâce à) with.

**moyenne** /mwajɛn/ *nf* average; (Scol) pass-mark; **en ~** on average; ~ **d'âge** average age. **moyennement** *adv* moderately.

**Moyen-Orient** /mwajɛnɔʀjɑ̃/ *nm* Middle East.

**moyeu** (*pl* **~x**) /mwajø/ *nm* hub.

**mû**, **mue** /my/ *a* driven (**par** by).

**mucoviscidose** /mykɔvisidoz/ *nf* cystic fibrosis.

**mue** /my/ *nf* moulting; (de voix) breaking of the voice.

**muer** /mɥe/ [1] *vi* moult; (*voix*) break. □ **se ~ en** *vpr* change into.

**muet**, **~te** /mɥɛ, -t/ *a* (Méd) dumb; (fig) speechless (**de** with); (silencieux) silent. ● *nm,f* mute.

**mufle** /myfl/ *nm* nose, muzzle; (personne [I]) boor, lout.

**mugir** /myʒiʀ/ [2] *vi* (*vache*) moo; (*bœuf*) bellow; (fig) howl.

**muguet** /mygɛ/ *nm* lily of the valley.

**mule** /myl/ *nf* (female) mule; (pantoufle) mule.

**mulet** /mylɛ/ *nm* (male) mule.

**multicolore** /myltikɔlɔʀ/ *a* multicoloured.

**multimédia** /myltimedja/ *a & nm* multimedia.

**multinational**, ~**e** (*mpl* **-aux**) /myltinasjɔnal, -o/ *a* multinational. **multinationale** *nf* multinational (company).

**multiple** /myltipl/ *nm* multiple. ● *a* numerous, many; (naissances) multiple.

**multiplication** /myltiplikasjɔ̃/ *nf* multiplication.

**multiplicité** /myltiplisite/ *nf* multiplicity.

**multiplier** /myltiplije/ [45] *vt* multiply; (*risques*) increase. □ **se** ~ *vpr* multiply; (*accidents*) be on the increase; (*difficultés*) increase.

**multitude** /myltityd/ *nf* multitude, mass.

**municipal**, ~**e** (*mpl* **-aux**) /mynisipal, -o/ *a* municipal; **conseil** ~ town council. **municipalité** *nf* (ville) municipality; (conseil) town council.

**munir** /myniʀ/ [2] *vt* ~ **de** provide with. □ **se** ~ **de** *vpr* (apporter) bring; (emporter) take.

**munitions** /mynisjɔ̃/ *nfpl* ammunition.

**mur** /myʀ/ *nm* wall; ~ **du son** sound barrier.

**mûr**, ~**e** /myʀ/ *a* ripe; (*personne*) mature.

**muraille** /myʀɑj/ *nf* (high) wall.

**mural**, ~**e** (*mpl* **-aux**) /myʀal, -o/ *a* wall; **peinture** ~**e** mural.

**mûre** /myʀ/ *nf* blackberry.

**mûrir** /myʀiʀ/ [2] *vi* ripen; (*abcès*) come to a head; (*personne, projet*) mature. ● *vt* (*fruit*) ripen; (*personne*) mature.

**murmure** /myʀmyʀ/ *nm* murmur.

**muscade** /myskad/ *nf* **noix** ~ nutmeg.

**muscle** /myskl/ *nm* muscle. **musclé**, ~**e** *a* muscular. **musculaire** *a* muscular.

**musculation** /myskylasjɔ̃/ *nf* bodybuilding.

**musculature** /myskylatyʀ/ *nf* muscles (+ *pl*).

**museau** (*pl* ~**x**) /myzo/ *nm* muzzle; (de porc) snout.

**musée** /myze/ *nm* museum; (de peinture) art gallery.

**muselière** /myzəljɛʀ/ *nf* muzzle.

**musette** /myzɛt/ *nf* haversack.

**muséum** /myzeɔm/ *nm* natural history museum.

**musical**, ~**e** (*mpl* **-aux**) /myzikal, -o/ *a* musical.

**musicien**, ~**ne** /myzisjɛ̃, -ɛn/ *a* musical. ● *nm,f* musician.

**musique** /myzik/ *nf* music; (orchestre) band.

**must** /mœst/ 🅸 *nm* must.

**musulman**, ~**e** /myzylmɑ̃, -an/ *a* & *nm,f* Muslim.

**mutation** /mytasjɔ̃/ *nf* change; (biologique) mutation; (d'un employé) transfer.

**muter** /myte/ [1] *vt* transfer. ● *vi* mutate.

**mutilation** /mytilasjɔ̃/ *nf* mutilation. **mutiler** [1] *vt* mutilate. **mutilé**, ~**e** *nm,f* disabled person.

**mutin**, ~**e** /mytɛ̃, -in/ *a* mischievous. ● *nm* mutineer; (prisonnier) rioter.

**mutinerie** /mytinʀi/ *nf* mutiny; (de prisonniers) riot.

**mutisme** /mytism/ *nm* silence.

**mutuel**, ~**le** /mytɥɛl/ *a* mutual. **mutuelle** *nf* mutual insurance company. **mutuellement** *adv* mutually; (l'un l'autre) each other.

**myope** /mjɔp/ *a* short-sighted. **myopie** *nf* short-sightedness.

**myosotis** /mjozɔtis/ *nm* forget-me-not.

**myrtille** /miʀtij/ *nf* bilberry, blueberry.

**mystère** /mistɛʀ/ *nm* mystery.

**mystérieux, -ieuse** /misteʀjø, -z/ *a* mysterious.

**mystification** /mistifikasjɔ̃/ *nf* hoax.

**mysticisme** /mistisism/ *nm* mysticism.

**mystique** /mistik/ *a* mystic(al). ● *nmf* mystic. ● *nf* mystique.

**mythe** /mit/ *nm* myth. **mythique** *a* mythical.

**mythologie** /mitɔlɔʒi/ *nf* mythology.

# Nn

**n'** /n/ ⇒NE.

**nacre** /nakʀ/ *nf* mother-of-pearl.

**nage** /naʒ/ *nf* swimming; (manière) stroke; **traverser à la ~** swim across; **en ~** sweating.

**nageoire** /naʒwaʀ/ *nf* fin; (de mammifère) flipper.

**nager** /naʒe/ [40] *vt/i* swim. **nageur, -euse** *nm,f* swimmer.

**naguère** /nagɛʀ/ *adv* (autrefois) formerly.

**naïf, -ive** /naif, -v/ *a* naïve.

**nain, ~e** /nɛ̃, nɛn/ *nm,f & a* dwarf.

**naissance** /nɛsɑ̃s/ *nf* birth; **donner ~ à** give birth to; (fig) give rise to.

**naître** /nɛtʀ/ [44] *vi* be born; (résulter) arise (**de** from); **faire ~** (susciter) give rise to.

**naïveté** /naivte/ *nf* naïvety.

**nappe** /nap/ *nf* tablecloth; (de pétrole, gaz) layer; **~ phréatique** ground water.

**napperon** /napʀɔ̃/ *nm* (cloth) tablemat.

**narco-dollars** /naʀkodɔlaʀ/ *nmpl* drug money.

**narcotique** /naʀkɔtik/ *a & nm* narcotic. **narco(-)trafiquant, ~e** (*pl* **~s**) *nm,f* drug trafficker.

**narguer** /naʀge/ [1] *vt* taunt; (*autorité*) flout.

**narine** /naʀin/ *nf* nostril.

**nasal, ~e** (*mpl* **-aux**) /nazal, -o/ *a* nasal.

**naseau** (*pl* **~x**) /nazo/ *nm* nostril.

**natal, ~e** (*mpl* **~s**) /natal/ *a* native.

**natalité** /natalite/ *nf* birth rate.

**natation** /natasjɔ̃/ *nf* swimming.

**natif, -ive** /natif, -v/ *a* native.

**nation** /nasjɔ̃/ *nf* nation.

**national, ~e** (*mpl* **-aux**) /nasjɔnal, -o/ *a* national. **nationale** *nf* A road; (US) highway. **nationaliser** [1] *vt* nationalize.

**nationalité** /nasjɔnalite/ *nf* nationality.

**natte** /nat/ *nf* (de cheveux) plait; (US) braid; (tapis de paille) mat.

**nature** /natyʀ/ *nf* nature; **~ morte** still life; **de ~ à** likely to; **payer en ~** pay in kind. ● *a inv* plain; (*yaourt*) natural; (*thé*) black.

**naturel, ~le** /natyʀɛl/ *a* natural. ● *nm* nature; (simplicité) naturalness; (Culin) **au ~** plain; (*thon*) in brine. **naturellement** *adv* naturally; (bien sûr) of course.

**naufrage** /nofʀaʒ/ *nm* shipwreck; **faire ~** be shipwrecked; (*bateau*) be wrecked.

**nauséabond, ~e** /nozeabɔ̃, -d/ *a* nauseating.

**nausée** /noze/ *nf* nausea.

**nautique** /notik/ *a* nautical; **sports ~s** water sports.

**naval**, **~e** (*mpl* **~s**) /naval/ *a* naval; **chantier ~** shipyard.

**navet** /navɛ/ *nm* turnip; (film: péj) flop; (US) turkey.

**navette** /navɛt/ *nf* shuttle (service); **faire la ~** shuttle back and forth.

**navigateur**, **-trice** /navigatœʀ, -tʀis/ *nm,f* sailor; (qui guide) navigator; (Internet) browser. **navigation** *nf* navigation; (trafic) shipping; (Internet) browsing.

**naviguer** /navige/ [1] *vi* sail; (piloter) navigate; (Internet) browse; **~ dans l'Internet** surf the Internet.

**navire** /naviʀ/ *nm* ship.

**navré**, **~e** /navʀe/ *a* sorry (**de** to).

**ne**, **n'** /nə, n/

n' before vowel or mute h.

● *adverbe*

····➤**je n'ai que 10 francs** I've only got 10 francs.

····➤**tu n'avais qu'à le dire!** you only had to say so!

····➤**je crains qu'il ~ parte** I am afraid he will leave.

! Pour les expressions comme **ne... guère**, **ne... jamais**, **ne... pas**, **ne... plus**, etc. ⇨**guère**, **jamais**, **pas**, **plus**, etc.

**né**, **~e** /ne/ *a* born; **~e Martin** née Martin; (dans composés) **dernier-~** last-born. ● ⇨NAÎTRE [44].

**néanmoins** /neɑ̃mwɛ̃/ *adv* nevertheless.

**néant** /neɑ̃/ *nm* nothingness; **réduire à ~** (*effet, efforts*) negate, nullify; (*espoir*) dash; **'revenus: ~'** 'income: nil'.

**nécessaire** /nesesɛʀ/ *a* necessary. ● *nm* (sac) bag; (trousse) kit; **le ~** (l'indispensable) the necessities *ou* essentials; **faire le ~** do what is necessary.

**nécessité** /nesesite/ *nf* necessity; **de première ~** vital.

**nécessiter** /nesesite/ [1] *vt* necessitate.

**néerlandais**, **~e** /neɛʀlɑ̃dɛ, -z/ *a* Dutch. ● *nm* (Ling) Dutch. **N~**, **~e** *nm,f* Dutchman, Dutchwoman.

**néfaste** /nefast/ *a* harmful (**à** to).

**négatif**, **-ive** /negatif, -v/ *a & nm* negative.

**négligé**, **~e** /negliʒe/ *a* (*travail*) careless; (*tenue*) scruffy. ● *nm* (tenue) negligee.

**négligent**, **~e** /negliʒɑ̃, -t/ *a* careless, negligent.

**négliger** /negliʒe/ [40] *vt* neglect; (ne pas tenir compte de) ignore, disregard; **~ de faire** fail to do. □ **se ~** *vpr* neglect oneself.

**négoce** /negɔs/ *nm* business, trade. **négociant**, **~e** *nm,f* merchant.

**négociation** /negɔsjasjɔ̃/ *nf* negotiation. **négocier** [45] *vt/i* negotiate.

**nègre** /nɛgʀ/ *a* (*musique, art*) Negro. ● *nm* (écrivain) ghost writer.

**neige** /nɛʒ/ *nf* snow. **neiger** [40] *vi* snow.

**nénuphar** /nenyfaʀ/ *nm* water-lily.

**nerf** /nɛʀ/ *nm* nerve; (vigueur) stamina; **être sur les ~s** be on edge.

**nerveux**, **-euse** /nɛʀvø, -z/ *a* nervous; (irritable) nervy; (*centre,*

cellule) nerve; (*voiture*) responsive. **nervosité** *nf* nervousness; (irritabilité) touchiness.

**net**, **~te** /nɛt/ *a* (clair, distinct) clear; (propre) clean; (notable) marked; (soigné) neat; (*prix, poids*) net. ● N~ *nm* (Ordinat) net. ● *adv* (*s'arrêter*) dead; (*refuser*) flatly; (*parler*) plainly; (*se casser*) cleanly; (*tuer*) outright. **nettement** *adv* (*expliquer*) clearly; (*augmenter, se détériorer*) markedly; (indiscutablement) distinctly, decidedly. **netteté** *nf* clearness.

**netéconomie** /nɛtekɔnɔmi/ *nf* e-economy.

**nétiquette** /nɛtikɛt/ *nf* netiquette.

**nettoyage** /nɛtwajaʒ/ *nm* cleaning; **~ à sec** dry-cleaning; **produit de ~** cleaner; **~ ethnique** ethnic cleansing.

**nettoyer** /nɛtwaje/ [31] *vt* clean.

**neuf**[1] /nœf/ (/nœv/ *before vowels and mute h*) *a inv & nm* nine.

**neuf**[2], **-euve** /nœf, -v/ *a* new; **tout ~** brand new. ● *nm* new; **remettre à ~** brighten up; **du ~** a new development; **quoi de ~?** what's new?

**neutre** /nøtʀ/ *a* neutral; (Gram) neuter. ● *nm* (Gram) neuter.

**neuve** /nœv/ ⇒NEUF[2].

**neuvième** /nœvjɛm/ *a & nm, f* ninth.

**neveu** (*pl* **~x**) /nəvø/ *nm* nephew.

**névrose** /nevʀoz/ *nf* neurosis. **névrosé**, **~e** *a & nm,f* neurotic.

**nez** /ne/ *nm* nose; **~ à ~** face to face; **~ retroussé** turned-up nose.

**ni** /ni/ *conj* neither, nor; **~ grand ~ petit** neither big nor small; **~ l'un ~ l'autre ne fument** neither (one nor the other) smokes; **sortir sans manteau ~ chapeau** go without a coat or hat; **elle n'a dit ~ oui ~ non** she didn't say either yes or no.

**niais**, **~e** /njɛ, -z/ *a* silly.

**niche** /niʃ/ *nf* (de chien) kennel; (cavité) niche.

**nicher** /niʃe/ [1] *vi* nest. □ **se ~** *vpr* nest; (se cacher) hide.

**nicotine** /nikɔtin/ *nf* nicotine.

**nid** /ni/ *nm* nest; **faire un ~** build a nest. **nid-de-poule** (*pl* **nids-de-poule**) *nm* pot-hole.

**nièce** /njɛs/ *nf* niece.

**nier** /nje/ [45] *vt* deny.

**nigaud**, **~e** /nigo, -d/ *nm,f* fool.

**nippon**, **~ne** /nipɔ̃, -ɔn/ *a* Japanese. **N~**, **~ne** *nm,f* Japanese.

**niveau** (*pl* **~x**) /nivo/ *nm* level; (compétence) standard; (étage) storey; (US) story; **au ~** up to standard; **mettre à ~** (Ordinat) upgrade; **~ à bulle** (d'air) spirit-level; **~ de vie** standard of living.

**niveler** /nivle/ [6] *vt* level.

**noble** /nɔbl/ *a* noble. ● *nm,f* nobleman, noblewoman. **noblesse** *nf* nobility.

**noce** /nɔs/ *nf* (fête 🄸) party; (invités) wedding guests; **~s** wedding; **faire la ~** 🄸 live it up, party.

**nocif**, **-ive** /nɔsif, -v/ *a* harmful.

**nocturne** /nɔktyʀn/ *a* nocturnal. ● *nm* (Mus) nocturne. ● *nf* (Sport) evening fixture; (de magasin) late-night opening.

**Noël** /nɔɛl/ *nm* Christmas.

**nœud** /nø/ *nm* (Naut) knot; (pour lier) knot; (pour orner) bow; **~s** (fig) ties; **~ coulant** slipknot, noose; **~ papillon** bow-tie.

**noir**, **~e** /nwaʀ/ *a* black; (obscur, sombre) dark; (triste) gloomy. ● *nm* black; (obscurité) dark; **travail au ~** moonlighting. ● *nm,f* (personne) Black.

**noircir** /nwaʀsiʀ/ [2] *vt* blacken; ~ **la situation** paint a black picture of the situation. ● *vi* (*banane*) go black; (*mur*) get dirty; (*métal*) tarnish. □ **se** ~ *vpr* (*ciel*) darken.

**noire** /nwaʀ/ *nf* (Mus) crotchet.

**noisette** /nwazɛt/ *nf* hazelnut; (de beurre) knob.

**noix** /nwa/ *nf* nut; (du noyer) walnut; (de beurre) knob; ~ **de cajou** cashew nut; ~ **de coco** coconut.

**nom** /nɔ̃/ *nm* name; (Gram) noun; **au** ~ **de** on behalf of; ~ **et prénom** full name; ~ **déposé** registered trademark; ~ **de famille** surname; ~ **de jeune fille** maiden name; ~ **de plume** pen name; ~ **propre** proper noun.

**nomade** /nɔmad/ *a* nomadic; (worker, Internet) mobile ● *nmf* nomad.

**nombre** /nɔ̃bʀ/ *nm* number; **au** ~ **de** (parmi) among; (l'un de) one of; **en (grand)** ~ in large numbers; **sans** ~ countless.

**nombreux**, **-euse** /nɔ̃bʀø, -z/ *a* (en grand nombre) many, numerous; (important) large; **de** ~ **enfants** many children; **nous étions très** ~ there were a great many of us.

**nombril** /nɔ̃bʀil/ *nm* navel.

**nomination** /nɔminasjɔ̃/ *nf* appointment.

**nommer** /nɔme/ [1] *vt* name; (élire) (à un poste) appoint; (à un lieu) post. □ **se** ~ *vpr* (s'appeler) be called.

**non** /nɔ̃/ *adv* no; (pas) not; ~ **(pas) que** not that; **il vient,** ~**?** he is coming, isn't he?; **moi** ~ **plus** neither am/do/can/*etc* I. ● *nm inv* no.

**non-** /nɔ̃/ *préf* non-; ~**-fumeur** nonsmoker.

**nonante** /nɔnɑ̃t/ *a & nm* ninety.

**non-sens** /nɔ̃sɑ̃s/ *nm inv* absurdity.

**nord** /nɔʀ/ *a inv* (*façade, côte*) north; (*frontière, zone*) northern. ● *nm* north; **le** ~ **de l'Europe** northern Europe; **vent de** ~ northerly (wind); **aller vers le** ~ go north; **le Nord** the North; **du Nord** northern **nord-est** *nm* north-east

**nordique** /nɔʀdik/ *a* Scandinavian.

**nord-ouest** /nɔʀwɛst/ *nm* northwest.

**normal**, ~**e** (*mpl* **-aux**) /nɔʀmal, -o/ *a* normal. **normale** *nf* normality; (norme) norm; (moyenne) average.

**normand**, ~**e** /nɔʀmɑ̃, -d/ *a* Norman. **N**~, ~**e** *nm,f* Norman.

**Normandie** /nɔʀmɑ̃di/ *nf* Normandy.

**norme** /nɔʀm/ *nf* norm; (de production) standard; ~**s de sécurité** safety standards.

**Norvège** /nɔʀvɛʒ/ *nf* Norway.

**norvégien**, ~**ne** /nɔʀveʒjɛ̃, -ɛn/ *a* Norwegian. **N**~, ~**ne** *nm,f* Norwegian.

**nos** /no/ ⇒NOTRE.

**nostalgie** /nɔstalʒi/ *nf* nostalgia; **avoir la** ~ **de son pays** be homesick. **nostalgique** *a* nostalgic.

**notaire** /nɔtɛʀ/ *nm* notary public.

**notamment** /nɔtamɑ̃/ *adv* notably.

**note** /nɔt/ *nf* (remarque) note; (chiffrée) mark, grade; (facture) bill; (Mus) note; ~ **(de service)** memorandum; **prendre** ~ **de** take note of.

**noter** /nɔte/ [1] *vt* note, notice; (écrire) note (down); (*devoir*) mark; (US) grade; **bien/mal noté** (*employé*) highly/poorly rated.

**notice** /nɔtis/ *nf* note; (mode d'emploi) instructions, directions.

**notifier** /nɔtifje/ [45] *vt* notify (à to).

**notion** /nosjɔ̃/ *nf* notion; **avoir des ~s de** have a basic knowledge of.

**notoire** /nɔtwaʀ/ *a* well-known; (*criminel*) notorious.

**notre** (*pl* **nos**) /nɔtʀ, no/ *a* our.

**nôtre** /notʀ/ *pron* **le** *ou* **la ~, les ~s** ours.

**nouer** /nwe/ [1] *vt* tie, knot; (*relations*) strike up.

**nouille** /nuj/ *nf* (Culin) noodle; **des ~s** noodles, pasta; (idiot Ⓘ) idiot.

**nounours** /nunuʀs/ *nm* Ⓘ teddy bear.

**nourri**, **~e** /nuʀi/ *a* **être logé ~** have bed and board; **~ au sein** breastfed.

**nourrice** /nuʀis/ *nf* childminder.

**nourrir** /nuʀiʀ/ [2] *vt* feed; (*espoir, crainte*) harbour; (*projet*) nurture; (*passion*) fuel. ● *vi* be nourishing. ▫ **se ~** *vpr* eat; **se ~ de** feed on. **nourrissant**, **~e** *a* nourishing.

**nourrisson** /nuʀisɔ̃/ *nm* infant.

**nourriture** /nuʀityʀ/ *nf* food.

**nous** /nu/ *pron* (sujet) we; (complément) us; (indirect) (to) us; (réfléchi) ourselves; (l'un l'autre) each other; **la voiture est à ~** the car is ours. **nous-mêmes** *pron* ourselves.

**nouveau** (**nouvel** *before vowel or mute h*), **nouvelle** (*mpl* **~x**) /nuvo, nuvɛl/ *a* new; **nouvel an** new year; **~x mariés** newly-weds; **~ venu, nouvelle venue** newcomer. ● *nm,f* (élève) new boy, new girl. ● *nm* **du ~** (fait nouveau) a new development; **de ~, à ~** again. **nouveau-né** (*pl* **~s**) *nm* newborn baby.

**nouveauté** /nuvote/ *nf* novelty; (chose) new thing; (livre) new publication; (disque) new release.

**nouvelle** /nuvɛl/ *nf* (piece of) news; (récit) short story; **~s** news.

**Nouvelle-Zélande** /nuvɛlzelɑ̃d/ *nf* New Zealand.

**novembre** /nɔvɑ̃bʀ/ *nm* November.

**noyade** /nwajad/ *nf* drowning.

**noyau** (*pl* **~x**) /nwajo/ *nm* (de fruit) stone; (US) pit; (de cellule) nucleus; (groupe) group; (centre: fig) core.

**noyer** /nwaje/ [31] *vt* drown; (inonder) flood. ▫ **se ~** *vpr* drown; (volontairement) drown oneself; **se ~ dans un verre d'eau** make a mountain out of a molehill. ● *nm* walnut-tree.

**nu**, **~e** /ny/ *a* (*corps, personne*) naked; (*mains, mur, fil*) bare; **à l'œil ~** to the naked eye. ● *nm* nude; **mettre à ~** expose.

**nuage** /nyaʒ/ *nm* cloud.

**nuance** /nyɑ̃s/ *nf* shade; (de sens) nuance; (différence) difference. **nuancer** [10] *vt* (*opinion*) qualify.

**nucléaire** /nykleɛʀ/ *a* nuclear. ● *nm* **le ~** nuclear energy.

**nudisme** /nydism/ *nm* nudism.

**nudité** /nydite/ *nf* nudity; (de lieu) bareness.

**nuée** /nɥe/ *nf* swarm, host.

**nues** /ny/ *nfpl* **tomber des ~** be amazed; **porter qn aux ~** praise sb to the skies.

**nuire** /nɥiʀ/ [17] *vi* **~ à** harm.

**nuisible** /nɥizibl/ *a* harmful (à to).

**nuit** /nɥi/ *nf* night; **cette ~** tonight; (hier) last night; **il fait ~** it is dark; **~ blanche** sleepless night; **la ~, de ~** at night; **~ de noces** wedding night.

**nul**, **~le** /nyl/ *a* (aucun) no; (zéro) nil; (qui ne vaut rien) useless; (non valable)

null; (*contrat*) void; (*testament*) invalid; **match ~** draw; **~ en sciences** no good at science; **nulle part** nowhere; **~ autre** no one else. ● *pron* no one. **nullement** *adv* not at all. **nullité** *nf* uselessness; (personne) nonentity.

**numérique** /nymeʀik/ *a* numerical; (*montre, horloge*) digital.

**numéro** /nymeʀo/ *nm* number; (de journal) issue; (spectacle) act; **~ de téléphone** telephone number; **~ vert** freephone number. **numéroter** [1] *vt* number.

**nuque** /nyk/ *nf* nape (of the neck).

**nurse** /nœʀs/ *nf* nanny.

**nutritif, -ive** /nytʀitif, -v/ *a* nutritious; (*valeur*) nutritional.

# Oo

**oasis** /ɔazis/ *nf* oasis.

**obéir** /ɔbeiʀ/ [2] *vt* **~ à** obey. ● *vi* obey. **obéissance** *nf* obedience. **obéissant, ~e** *a* obedient.

**obèse** /ɔbɛz/ *a* obese.

**objecter** /ɔbʒɛkte/ [1] *vt* object.

**objectif, -ive** /ɔbʒɛktif, -v/ *a* objective. ● *nm* objective; (Photo) lens.

**objection** /ɔbʒɛksjɔ̃/ *nf* objection; **soulever des ~s** raise objections.

**objet** /ɔbʒɛ/ *nm* (chose) object; (sujet) subject; (but) purpose, object; **être** *ou* **faire l'~ de** be the subject of; **~ d'art** objet d'art; **~s trouvés** lost property; (US) lost and found.

**obligation** /ɔbligasjɔ̃/ *nf* obligation; (Comm) bond; **être dans l'~ de** be under obligation to.

**obligatoire** /ɔbligatwaʀ/ *a* compulsory. **obligatoirement** *adv* (par règlement) of necessity; (inévitablement) inevitably.

**obligeance** /ɔbliʒɑ̃s/ *nf* **avoir l'~ de faire** be kind enough to do.

**obliger** /ɔbliʒe/ [40] *vt* compel, force (**à faire** to do); (aider) oblige; **être obligé de** have to (**de** for).

**oblique** /ɔblik/ *a* oblique; **regard ~** sidelong glance; **en ~** at an angle.

**oblitérer** /ɔbliteʀe/ [14] *vt* (*timbre*) cancel.

**obnubilé, ~e** /ɔbnybile/ *a* obsessed.

**obscène** /ɔpsɛn/ *a* obscene.

**obscur, ~e** /ɔpskyʀ/ *a* dark; (confus, humble) obscure; (vague) vague.

**obscurcir** /ɔpskyʀsiʀ/ [2] *vt* make dark; (fig) obscure. □ **s'~** *vpr* (*ciel*) darken.

**obscurité** /ɔpskyʀite/ *nf* dark(ness); (de passage, situation) obscurity.

**obsédant, ~e** /ɔpsedɑ̃, -t/ *a* (*problème*) nagging; (*musique, souvenir*) haunting.

**obsédé, ~e** /ɔpsede/ *nm,f* **~ (sexuel)** sex maniac; **~ du ski/jazz** ski/jazz freak.

**obséder** /ɔpsede/ [14] *vt* obsess.

**obsèques** /ɔpsɛk/ *nfpl* funeral.

**observateur, -trice** /ɔpsɛʀvatœʀ, -tʀis/ *a* observant. ● *nm,f* observer.

**observation** /ɔpsɛʀvasjɔ̃/ *nf* observation; (remarque) remark, comment; (reproche) criticism; (obéissance) observance; **en ~** under observation.

**observer** /ɔpsɛʀve/ [1] *vt* (regarder) observe; (surveiller) watch, observe;

(remarquer) notice, observe; **faire ~ qch** point sth out (**à** to).

**obsession** /ɔpsesjɔ̃/ *nf* obsession.

**obstacle** /ɔpstakl/ *nm* obstacle; (pour cheval) fence, jump; (pour athlète) hurdle; **faire ~ à** stand in the way of, obstruct.

**obstétrique** /ɔpstetʀik/ *nf* obstetrics (+ *sg*).

**obstiné, ~e** /ɔpstine/ *a* stubborn, obstinate.

**obstiner (s')** /(s)ɔpstine/ [1] *vpr* persist (**à** in).

**obstruction** /ɔpstʀyksjɔ̃/ *nf* obstruction; (de conduit) blockage.

**obstruer** /ɔpstʀye/ [1] *vt* obstruct, block.

**obtenir** /ɔptəniʀ/ [58] *vt* get, obtain. **obtention** *nf* obtaining.

**obus** /ɔby/ *nm* shell.

**occasion** /ɔkazjɔ̃/ *nf* opportunity (**de faire** of doing); (circonstance) occasion; (achat) bargain; (article non neuf) second-hand buy; **à l'~** sometimes; **d'~** second-hand. **occasionnel, ~le** *a* occasional.

**occasionner** /ɔkazjɔne/ [1] *vt* cause.

**occident** /ɔksidɑ̃/ *nm* (direction) west; **l'O~** the West.

**occidental, ~e** (*mpl* **-aux**) /ɔksidɑ̃tal, -o/ *a* western. **O~, ~e** (*mpl* **-aux**) *nm,f* westerner.

**occulte** /ɔkylt/ *a* occult.

**occupant, ~e** /ɔkypɑ̃, -t/ *nm,f* occupant. ● *nm* (Mil) forces of occupation.

**occupation** /ɔkypasjɔ̃/ *nf* occupation.

**occupé, ~e** /ɔkype/ *a* busy; (*place, pays*) occupied; (*téléphone*) engaged, busy; (*toilettes*) engaged.

**occuper** /ɔkype/ [1] *vt* occupy; (*poste*) hold; (*espace, temps*) take up. □ **s'~** *vpr* (s'affairer) keep busy (**à faire** doing); **s'~ de** (*personne, problème*) take care of; (*bureau, firme*) be in charge of; (se mêler) **occupe-toi de tes affaires** mind your own business.

**occurrence**: **en l'~** /ɑ̃lɔkyʀɑ̃s/ *loc* in this case.

**océan** /ɔseɑ̃/ *nm* ocean.

**Océanie** /ɔseani/ *nf* Oceania.

**ocre** /ɔkʀ/ *a inv* ochre.

**octante** /ɔktɑ̃t/ *a* eighty.

**octet** /ɔktɛ/ *nm* byte.

**octobre** /ɔktɔbʀ/ *nm* October.

**octogone** /ɔktɔgɔn/ *nm* octagon.

**octroyer** /ɔktʀwaje/ [31] *vt* grant.

**oculaire** /ɔkylɛʀ/ *a* **témoin ~** eyewitness; **troubles ~s** eye trouble.

**oculiste** /ɔkylist/ *nmf* ophthalmologist.

**odeur** /ɔdœʀ/ *nf* smell.

**odieux, -ieuse** /ɔdjø, -z/ *a* odious.

**odorant, ~e** /ɔdɔʀɑ̃, -t/ *a* sweet-smelling.

**odorat** /ɔdɔʀa/ *nm* sense of smell.

**œil** (*pl* **yeux**) /œj, jø/ *nm* eye; **à l'~** [I] for free; **à mes yeux** in my view; **faire de l'~ à** make eyes at; **faire les gros yeux à** glare at; **ouvrir l'~** keep one's eyes open; **~ poché** black eye; **fermer les yeux** shut one's eyes; (fig) turn a blind eye.

**œillères** /œjɛʀ/ *nfpl* blinkers.

**œillet** /œjɛ/ *nm* (plante) carnation; (trou) eyelet.

**œuf** (*pl* **~s**) /œf, ø/ *nm* egg; **~ à la coque/dur/sur le plat** boiled/hard-boiled/fried egg.

**œuvre** /œvʀ/ *nf* (ouvrage, travail) work; **~ d'art** work of art; **~ (de bienfaisance)** charity; **être à l'~** be at work; **mettre en ~** (*réforme,*

moyens) implement; **mise en ~** implementation. ● *nm* (ensemble spécifié) **l'~ entier de Beethoven** the complete works of Beethoven.

**œuvrer** /œvʀe/ [1] *vi* work.

**offense** /ɔfɑ̃s/ *nf* insult.

**offenser** /ɔfɑ̃se/ [1] *vt* offend. □ **s'~** *vpr* take offence (**de** at).

**offensive** /ɔfɑ̃siv/ *nf* offensive.

**offert**, **~e** /ɔfɛʀ, -t/ ⇒OFFRIR [21].

**office** /ɔfis/ *nm* office; (Relig) service; (de cuisine) pantry; **faire ~ de** act as; **d'~** without consultation, automatically; **~ du tourisme** tourist information office.

**officiel**, **~le** /ɔfisjɛl/ *a* official. ● *nm* official.

**officier** /ɔfisje/ [45] *vi* (Relig) officiate. ● *nm* officer.

**officieux**, **-ieuse** /ɔfisjø, -z/ *a* unofficial.

**offre** /ɔfʀ/ *nf* offer; (aux enchères) bid; **l'~ et la demande** supply and demand; **'~s d'emploi'** 'situations vacant'.

**offrir** /ɔfʀiʀ/ [21] *vt* offer (**de faire** to do); (*cadeau*) give; (acheter) buy; **~ à boire à** (chez soi) give a drink to; (au café) buy a drink for. □ **s'~** *vpr* (se proposer) offer oneself (**comme** as); (*solution*) present itself; (s'acheter) treat oneself to.

**ogive** /ɔʒiv/ *nf* **~ nucléaire** nuclear warhead.

**OGM** *abrév m* (**organisme génétiquement modifié**) GMO, genetically modified organism.

**oie** /wa/ *nf* goose.

**oignon** /ɔɲɔ̃/ *nm* (légume) onion; (de fleur) bulb.

**oiseau** (*pl* **~x**) /wazo/ *nm* bird.

**oisif**, **-ive** /wazif, -v/ *a* idle.

**olive** /ɔliv/ *nf & a inv* olive. **olivier** *nm* olive tree.

**olympique** /ɔlɛ̃pik/ *a* Olympic.

**ombrage** /ɔ̃bʀaʒ/ *nm* shade; **prendre ~ de** take offence at. **ombragé**, **~e** *a* shady.

**ombre** /ɔ̃bʀ/ *nf* (pénombre) shade; (contour) shadow; (soupçon: fig) hint, shadow; **dans l'~** (*agir, rester*) behind the scenes; **faire de l'~ à qn** be in sb's light.

**ombrelle** /ɔ̃bʀɛl/ *nf* parasol.

**omelette** /ɔmlɛt/ *nf* omelette.

**omettre** /ɔmɛtʀ/ [42] *vt* omit, leave out.

**omnibus** /ɔmnibys/ *nm* stopping *ou* local train.

**omoplate** /ɔmɔplat/ *nf* shoulder blade.

**on** /ɔ̃/ *pron* (tu, vous) you; (nous) we; (ils, elles) they; (les gens) people, they; (quelqu'un) someone; (indéterminé) one, you; **~ dit** people say, they say, it is said; **~ m'a demandé mon avis** I was asked for my opinion.

**oncle** /ɔ̃kl/ *nm* uncle.

**onctueux**, **-euse** /ɔ̃ktɥø, -z/ *a* smooth.

**onde** /ɔ̃d/ *nf* wave; **~s courtes/longues** short/long wave; **sur les ~s** on the air.

**on-dit** /ɔ̃di/ *nm inv* **les ~** hearsay.

**onduler** /ɔ̃dyle/ [1] *vi* undulate; (*cheveux*) be wavy.

**onéreux**, **-euse** /ɔneʀø, -z/ *a* costly.

**ongle** /ɔ̃gl/ *nm* (finger)nail; **~ de pied** toenail.

**ont** /ɔ̃/ ⇒AVOIR [5].

**ONU** *abrév f* (**Organisation des Nations unies**) UN.

**onze** /ɔ̃z/ *a & nm* eleven. **onzième** *a & nmf* eleventh.

**OPA** *abrév f* (**offre publique d'achat**) takeover bid.

**opéra** /ɔpeʀa/ *nm* opera; (édifice) opera house. **opéra-comique** (*pl* **opéras-comiques**) *nm* light opera.

**opérateur**, **-trice** /ɔpeʀatœʀ, -tʀis/ *nm,f* operator.

**opération** /ɔpeʀasjɔ̃/ *nf* operation; (Comm) deal; (calcul) calculation; ~ **escargot** slow-moving protest convoy.

**opératoire** /ɔpeʀatwaʀ/ *a* (Méd) surgical; **bloc** ~ operating suite.

**opérer** /ɔpeʀe/ [14] *vt* (*personne*) operate on; (exécuter) carry out, make; ~ **qn d'une tumeur** operate on sb to remove a tumour; **se faire** ~ have surgery *ou* an operation. ● *vi* (Méd) operate; (faire effet) work. □ **s'**~ *vpr* (se produire) occur.

**opiniâtre** /ɔpinjɑtʀ/ *a* tenacious.

**opinion** /ɔpinjɔ̃/ *nf* opinion.

**opportuniste** /ɔpɔʀtynist/ *nmf* opportunist.

**opposant**, ~**e** /ɔpozɑ̃, -t/ *nm,f* opponent.

**opposé**, ~**e** /ɔpoze/ *a* (*sens, angle, avis*) opposite; (*factions*) opposing; (*intérêts*) conflicting; **être** ~ **à** be opposed to. ● *nm* opposite; **à l'**~ **de** (contrairement à) contrary to, unlike.

**opposer** /ɔpoze/ [1] *vt* (*objets*) place opposite each other; (*personnes*) match, oppose; (contraster) contrast; (*résistance, argument*) put up. □ **s'**~ *vpr* (*personnes*) confront each other; (*styles*) contrast; **s'**~ **à** oppose.

**opposition** /ɔpozisjɔ̃/ *nf* opposition; **par** ~ **à** in contrast with; **entrer en** ~ **avec** come into conflict with; **faire** ~ **à un chèque** stop a cheque.

**oppressant**, ~**e** /ɔpʀesɑ̃, -t/ *a* oppressive.

**opprimer** /ɔpʀime/ [1] *vt* oppress.

**opter** /ɔpte/ [1] *vi* ~ **pour** opt for.

**opticien**, ~**ne** /ɔptisjɛ̃, -ɛn/ *nm,f* optician.

**optimisme** /ɔptimism/ *nm* optimism.

**optimiste** /ɔptimist/ *nmf* optimist. ● *a* optimistic.

**option** /ɔpsjɔ̃/ *nf* option.

**optique** /ɔptik/ *a* (*verre*) optical. ● *nf* (science) optics (+ *sg*); (perspective) perspective.

**or**[1] /ɔʀ/ *nm* gold; **d'**~ golden; **en** ~ gold; (*occasion*) golden.

**or**[2] /ɔʀ/ *conj* now, well; (indiquant une opposition) and yet.

**orage** /ɔʀaʒ/ *nm* (thunder)storm. **orageux**, **-euse** *a* stormy.

**oral**, ~**e** (*mpl* **-aux**) /ɔʀal, -o/ *a* oral. ● *nm* (*pl* **-aux**) oral.

**orange** /ɔʀɑ̃ʒ/ *a inv* orange; (Aut) (*feu*) amber; (US) yellow. ● *nf* orange. **orangeade** *nf* orangeade. **oranger** *nm* orange tree.

**orateur**, **-trice** /ɔʀatœʀ, -tʀis/ *nm, f* speaker.

**orbite** /ɔʀbit/ *nf* orbit; (d'œil) socket.

**orchestre** /ɔʀkɛstʀ/ *nm* orchestra; (de jazz) band; (parterre) stalls.

**ordinaire** /ɔʀdinɛʀ/ *a* ordinary; (habituel) usual; (*qualité*) standard; (médiocre) very average. ● *nm* **l'**~ the ordinary; (nourriture) the standard fare; **d'**~, **à l'**~ usually. **ordinairement** *adv* usually.

**ordinateur** /ɔʀdinatœʀ/ *nm* computer; ~ **personnel/de bureau** personal/desktop computer; ~ **portable** laptop (computer); ~ **hôte** (Internet) host.

**ordonnance** /ɔʀdɔnɑ̃s/ *nf* (ordre, décret) order; (de médecin) prescription.

**ordonné**, **~e** /ɔʀdɔne/ *a* tidy.

**ordonner** /ɔʀdɔne/ [1] *vt* order (**à qn de** sb to); (agencer) arrange; (Méd) prescribe; (*prêtre*) ordain.

**ordre** /ɔʀdʀ/ *nm* order; (propreté) tidiness; **aux ~s de qn** at sb's disposal; **avoir de l'~** be tidy; **en ~** tidy, in order; **de premier ~** first-rate; **d'~ officiel** of an official nature; **l'~ du jour** (programme) agenda; **mettre de l' ~ dans** tidy up; **jusqu'à nouvel ~** until further notice; **un ~ de grandeur** an approximate idea.

**ordure** /ɔʀdyʀ/ *nf* filth; **~s** (détritus) rubbish; (US) garbage; **~s ménagères** household refuse.

**oreille** /ɔʀɛj/ *nf* ear.

**oreiller** /ɔʀeje/ *nm* pillow.

**oreillons** /ɔʀɛjɔ̃/ *nmpl* mumps.

**orfèvre** /ɔʀfɛvʀ/ *nm* goldsmith.

**organe** /ɔʀgan/ *nm* organ.

**organigramme** /ɔʀganigʀam/ *nm* organization chart; (Ordinat) flowchart.

**organique** /ɔʀganik/ *a* organic.

**organisateur**, **-trice** /ɔʀganizatœʀ, tʀis/ *nm,f* organizer.

**organisation** /ɔʀganizasjɔ̃/ *nf* organization.

**organiser** /ɔʀganize/ [1] *vt* organize. □ **s'~** *vpr* organize oneself, get organized.

**organisme** /ɔʀganism/ *nm* body, organism.

**orge** /ɔʀʒ/ *nf* barley.

**orgelet** /ɔʀʒəlɛ/ *nm* sty.

**orgue** /ɔʀg/ *nm* organ; **~ de Barbarie** barrel-organ. **orgues** *nfpl* organ.

**orgueil** /ɔʀgœj/ *nm* pride. **orgueilleux**, **-euse** *a* proud.

**orient** /ɔʀjɑ̃/ *nm* (direction) east; **l'O~** the Orient.

**oriental**, **~e** (*mpl* **-aux**) /ɔʀjɑ̃tal, -o/ *a* eastern; (de l'Orient) oriental. **O~**, **~e** (*mpl* **-aux**) *nm,f* Asian.

**orientation** /ɔʀjɑ̃tasjɔ̃/ *nf* direction; (tendance politique) leanings (+ *pl*); (de maison) aspect; (Sport) orienteering; **~ professionnelle** careers advice; **~ scolaire** curriculum counselling.

**orienter** /ɔʀjɑ̃te/ [1] *vt* position; (*personne*) direct. □ **s'~** *vpr* (se repérer) find one's bearings; **s'~ vers** turn towards.

**origan** /ɔʀigɑ̃/ *nm* oregano.

**originaire** /ɔʀiʒinɛʀ/ *a* **être ~ de** be a native of.

**original**, **~e** (*mpl* **-aux**) /ɔʀiʒinal, -o/ *a* original; (curieux) eccentric. ● *nm* (œuvre) original. ● *nm,f* eccentric. **originalité** *nf* originality; eccentricity.

**origine** /ɔʀiʒin/ *nf* origin; **à l'~** originally; **d'~** (*pièce, pneu*) original; **être d'~ noble** come from a noble background.

**originel**, **~le** /ɔʀiʒinɛl/ *a* original.

**orme** /ɔʀm/ *nm* elm.

**ornement** /ɔʀnəmɑ̃/ *nm* ornament.

**orner** /ɔʀne/ [1] *vt* decorate.

**orphelin**, **~e** /ɔʀfəlɛ̃, -in/ *nm,f* orphan. ● *a* orphaned. **orphelinat** *nm* orphanage.

**orteil** /ɔʀtɛj/ *nm* toe.

**orthodoxe** /ɔʀtɔdɔks/ *a* orthodox.

**orthographe** /ɔʀtɔgʀaf/ *nf* spelling.

**ortie** /ɔʀti/ *nf* nettle.

**os** /ɔs, o/ *nm inv* bone.

**OS** *abrév m* ⇒OUVRIER SPÉCIALISÉ.

**osciller** /ɔsile/ [1] *vi* sway; (Tech) oscillate; (hésiter) waver; (fluctuer) fluctuate.

**osé**, **~e** /oze/ *a* daring.

**oseille** /ozɛj/ *nf* (plante) sorrel.

**oser** /oze/ [1] *vi* dare.

**osier** /ozje/ *nm* wicker.

**ossature** /ɔsatyʀ/ *nf* skeleton, frame.

**ossements** /ɔsmɑ̃/ *nmpl* bones, remains.

**osseux**, **-euse** /ɔsø, -z/ *a* bony; (Méd) bone.

**otage** /ɔtaʒ/ *nm* hostage.

**OTAN** /ɔtɑ̃/ *abrév f* (**Organisation du traité de l'Atlantique Nord**) NATO.

**otarie** /ɔtaʀi/ *nf* eared seal.

**ôter** /ote/ [1] *vt* remove (**à qn** from sb); (déduire) take away.

**otite** /ɔtit/ *nf* ear infection.

**ou** /u/ *conj* or; **~ bien** or else; **~ (bien)... ~ (bien)...** either... or...; **vous ~ moi** either you or me.

**où** /u/ *pron* where; (dans lequel) in which; (sur lequel) on which; (auquel) at which; **d'~** from which; (pour cette raison) hence; **par ~** through which; **~ qu'il soit** wherever he may be; **juste au moment ~** just as; **le jour ~** the day when. ● *adv* where; **d'~?** where from?

**ouate** /wat/ *nf* cotton wool; (US) absorbent cotton.

**oubli** /ubli/ *nm* forgetfulness; (trou de mémoire) lapse of memory; (négligence) oversight; **tomber dans l'~** sink into oblivion.

**oublier** /ublije/ [45] *vt* forget; (omettre) leave out, forget. □ **s'~** *vpr* (*chose*) be forgotten.

**ouest** /wɛst/ *a inv* (*façade, côte*) west; (*frontière, zone*) western. ● *nm* west; **l'~ de l'Europe** western Europe; **vent d'~** westerly (wind); **aller vers l'~** go west; **l'O~** the West; **de l'O~** western.

**oui** /wi/ *adv & nm inv* yes.

**ouï-dire**: **par ~** /paʀwidiʀ/ *loc* by hearsay.

**ouïe** /wi/ *nf* hearing; (de poisson) gill.

**ouragan** /uʀagɑ̃/ *nm* hurricane.

**ourlet** /uʀlɛ/ *nm* hem.

**ours** /uʀs/ *nm* bear; **~ blanc** polar bear; **~ en peluche** teddy bear.

**outil** /uti/ *nm* tool. **outillage** *nm* tools (+ *pl*). **outiller** [1] *vt* equip.

**outrage** /utʀaʒ/ *nm* (grave) insult.

**outrance** /utʀɑ̃s/ *nf* **à ~** excessively. **outrancier**, **-ière** *a* extreme.

**outre** /utʀ/ *prép* besides. ● *adv* **passer ~** pay no heed; **~ mesure** unduly; **en ~** in addition. **outre-mer** *adv* overseas.

**outrepasser** /utʀəpɑse/ [1] *vt* exceed.

**outrer** /utʀe/ [1] *vt* exaggerate; (indigner) incense.

**ouvert**, **~e** /uvɛʀ, -t/ *a* open; (*gaz, radio*) on. ● ⇒OUVRIR [21].

**ouverture** /uvɛʀtyʀ/ *nf* opening; (Mus) overture; (Photo) aperture; **~s** (offres) overtures; **~ d'esprit** open-mindedness.

**ouvrable** /uvʀabl/ *a* **jour ~** working day; **aux heures ~s** during business hours.

**ouvrage** /uvʀaʒ/ *nm* (travail, livre) work; (couture) (piece of) needlework.

**ouvre-boîtes** /uvʀəbwat/ *nm inv* tin-opener.

**ouvre-bouteilles** /uvʀəbutɛj/ *nm inv* bottle-opener.

**ouvreur**, **-euse** /uvʀœʀ, -øz/ *nm,f* usherette.

**ouvrier**, **-ière** /uvʀije, -jɛʀ/ *nm,f* worker; **~ qualifié/spécialisé** skilled/unskilled worker. ● *a* working-class; (*conflit*) industrial; **syndicat ~** trade union.

**ouvrir** /uvʀiʀ/ [21] *vt* open (up); (*gaz, robinet*) turn on. ● *vi* open (up). □ **s'~** *vpr* open (up); **s'~ à qn** open one's heart to sb.

**ovaire** /ɔvɛʀ/ *nm* ovary.

**ovale** /ɔval/ *a & nm* oval.

**ovni** /ɔvni/ *abrév m* (**objet volant non-identifié**) UFO.

**ovule** /ɔvyl/ *nm* (à féconder) ovum; (gynécologique) pessary.

**oxygène** /ɔksiʒɛn/ *nm* oxygen.

**oxygéner (s')** /(s)ɔksiʒene/ [14] *vpr* get some fresh air.

**ozone** /ozon/ *nf* ozone; **la couche d'~** the ozone layer.

# Pp

**pacifique** /pasifik/ *a* peaceful; (*personne*) peaceable; (Géog) Pacific. **P~** *nm* **le P~** the Pacific.

**pacotille** /pakɔtij/ *nf* junk, rubbish.

**PACS** /paks/ *abrév nm* (**pacte civil de solidarité**) contract of civil union.

**pacser (se)** /pakse/ [1] *vpr* sign a contract of civil union (PACS).

**pagaie** /pagɛ/ *nf* paddle.

**pagaille** /pagaj/ *nf* Ⓘ mess, shambles (+ *sg*).

**page** /paʒ/ *nf* page; **mise en ~** layout; **tourner la ~** turn over a new leaf; **être à la ~** be up to date; **~ d'accueil** (Internet) home page.

**paie** /pɛ/ *nf* pay.

**paiement** /pɛmɑ̃/ *nm* payment.

**païen, ~ne** /pajɛ̃, -ɛn/ *a & nm,f* pagan.

**paillasson** /pajasɔ̃/ *nm* doormat.

**paille** /pɑj/ *nf* straw. ● *a* straw-coloured; **jaune ~** straw yellow.

**paillette** /pajɛt/ *nf* (sur robe) sequin; (de savon) flake.

**pain** /pɛ̃/ *nm* bread; (miche) loaf (of bread); (de savon) bar; **~ d'épices** gingerbread; **~ grillé** toast.

**pair, ~e** /pɛʀ/ *a* (*nombre*) even. ● *nm* (personne) peer; **aller de ~** go together (**avec** with); **au ~** (*jeune fille*) au pair. **paire** *nf* pair.

**paisible** /pezibl/ *a* peaceful.

**paître** /pɛtʀ/ [44] *vi* graze.

**paix** /pɛ/ *nf* peace; **fiche-moi la ~!** Ⓘ leave me alone!

**Pakistan** /pakistɑ̃/ *nm* Pakistan.

**palace** /palas/ *nm* luxury hotel.

**palais** /palɛ/ *nm* palace; (Anat) palate; **~ de Justice** law courts; **~ des sports** sports stadium.

**pâle** /pɑl/ *a* pale.

**Palestine** /palɛstin/ *nf* Palestine.

**palier** /palje/ *nm* (d'escalier) landing; (étape) stage.

**pâlir** /pɑliʀ/ [2] *vt/i* (turn) pale.

**palissade** /palisad/ *nf* fence.

**pallier** /palje/ [45] *vt* compensate for.

**palmarès** /palmaʀɛs/ *nm* list of prize-winners.

**palme** /palm/ *nf* palm leaf; (de nageur) flipper. **palmé, ~e** *a* (*patte*) webbed.

**palmier** /palmje/ *nm* palm (tree).

**palper** /palpe/ [1] *vt* feel.

**palpiter** /palpite/ [1] *vi* (battre) pound; (frémir) quiver.

**paludisme** /palydism/ *nm* malaria.

**pamplemousse** /pɑ̃pləmus/ *nm* grapefruit.

**panaché, ~e** /panaʃe/ *a* (bariolé, mélangé) motley; **glace ~e** mixed-flavour ice cream. ● *nm* shandy.

umes;

pr Paris.

ı, ~ne /paʀizjɛ̃, -ɛn/ *a* arisian; (*banlieue*) Paris. **P~**, **~ne** *nm,f* Parisian.

**parking** /paʀkiŋ/ *nm* car park.

**parlement** /paʀləmɑ̃/ *nm* parliament.

**parlementaire** /paʀləmɑ̃tɛʀ/ *a* parliamentary. ● *nmf* Member of Parliament.

**parlementer** /paʀləmɑ̃te/ [1] *vi* negotiate.

**parler** /paʀle/ [1] *vi* talk (**à** to); **~ de** talk about; **tu parles d'un avantage!** call that a benefit!; **de quoi ça parle?** what is it about? ● *vt* (*langue*) speak; (*politique, affaires*) talk. ◻ **se ~** *vpr* (*personnes*) talk (to each other); (*langue*) be spoken. ● *nm* speech; (dialecte) dialect.

**parmi** /paʀmi/ *prép* among(st).

**paroi** /paʀwa/ *nf* wall; **~ rocheuse** rock face.

**paroisse** /paʀwas/ *nf* parish.

**parole** /paʀɔl/ *nf* (mot, promesse) word; (langage) speech; **demander la ~** ask to speak; **prendre la ~** (begin to) speak; **tenir ~** keep one's word; **croire qn sur ~** take sb's word for it.

**parquet** /paʀkɛ/ *nm* (parquet) floor; **lame de ~** floorboard; **le ~** (Jur) prosecution.

**parrain** /paʀɛ̃/ *nm* godfather; (fig) sponsor.

**parsemer** /paʀsəme/ [6] *vt* strew (**de** with).

**part** /paʀ/ *nf* share, part; **à ~** (de côté) aside; (séparément) separate; (excepté) apart from; **d'une ~** on the one hand; **d'autre ~** on the other hand; (de plus) moreover; **de la ~ de** from; **de toutes ~s** from all sides; **de ~ et d'autre** on both sides; **faire ~ à qn** inform sb (**de** of); **faire la ~ des choses** make allowances; **prendre ~ à** take part in; (*joie, douleur*) share; **pour ma ~** as for me.

**partage** /paʀtaʒ/ *nm* (division) dividing; (répartition) sharing out; **recevoir qch en ~** be left sth in a will.

**partager** /paʀtaʒe/ [40] *vt* divide; (distribuer) share out; (avoir en commun) share. ◻ **se ~ qch** *vpr* share sth.

**partenaire** /paʀtənɛʀ/ *nmf* partner.

**parterre** /paʀtɛʀ/ *nm* flower-bed; (Théât) stalls.

**parti** /paʀti/ *nm* (Pol) party; (décision) decision; (en mariage) match; **~ pris** bias; **prendre ~** get involved; **prendre ~ pour qn** side with sb; **j'en ai pris mon ~** I've come to terms with that.

**partial**, **~e** (*mpl* **-iaux**) /paʀsjal, -jo/ *a* biased.

**participe** /paʀtisip/ *nm* (Gram) participle.

**participant**, **~e** /paʀtisipɑ̃, -t/ *nm,f* participant (**à** in).

**participation** /paʀtisipasjɔ̃/ *nf* participation; (financière) contribution; (d'un artiste) appearance.

**participer** /paʀtisipe/ [1] *vi* **~ à** take part in, participate in; (*profits, frais*) share.

**particule** /paʀtikyl/ *nf* particle.

**particulier**, **-ière** /paʀtikylje, -jɛʀ/ *a* (spécifique) particular; (bizarre) unusual; (privé) private; **rien de ~** nothing special. ● *nm* private individual; **en ~** in particular, particularly. **particulièrement** *adv* particularly.

**partie** /paʀti/ *nf* part; (cartes, Sport) game; (Jur) party; **une ~ de pêche** a

fishing trip; **en ~** partly, in part; **en grande ~** largely; **faire ~ de** be part of; (adhérer à) be a member of; **faire ~ intégrante de** be an integral part of.

**partiel**, **~le** /parsjɛl/ *a* partial. ● *nm* (Univ) exam based on a module.

**partir** /partir/ [46] *vi* (*aux être*) go; (quitter un lieu) leave, go; (*tache*) come out; (*bouton*) come off; (*coup de feu*) go off; (commencer) start; **~ pour le Brésil** leave for Brazil; **~ du principe que** work on the assumption that; **à ~ de** from; **à ~ de maintenant** from now on.

**partisan**, **~e** /partizɑ̃, -an/ *nm,f* supporter. ● *nm* (Mil) partisan; **être ~ de** be in favour of.

**partition** /partisjɔ̃/ *nf* (Mus) score.

**partout** /partu/ *adv* everywhere; **~ où** wherever.

**paru** /pary/ ⇒PARAÎTRE [18].

**parure** /paryr/ *nf* finery; (bijoux) set of jewels; (de draps) set.

**parution** /parysjɔ̃/ *nf* publication.

**parvenir** /parvənir/ [58] *vi* (*aux être*) **~ à** reach; **~ à faire** manage to do; **faire ~** send.

**parvenu**, **~e** /parvəny/ *nm,f* upstart.

---

**pas**[1] /pɑ/

Pour les expressions comme **pas encore**, **pas mal**, etc. ⇒**encore**, **mal**, etc.

● *adverbe*

····➤ not; **ne ~** not; **je ne sais ~** I don't know; **je ne pense ~** I don't think so; **il a aimé, moi ~** he liked it, I didn't; **~ cher/poli** cheap/ impolite.

····➤ **~**, ...

**chance!** tou...

····➤ **on a bien ri,** ...

good laugh, didn't ...

**!** In spoken colloquial French **ne... pas** is often shortened to **pas**. You will often hear **j'ai pas compris** instead of **je n'ai pas compris** (*I didn't understand*). Note that this would not be correct in written French.

---

**pas**[2] /pɑ/ *nm* step; (bruit) footstep; (trace) footprint; (vitesse) pace; **à deux ~ (de)** a step away (from); **marcher au ~** march; **rouler au ~** move very slowly; **à ~ de loup** stealthily; **faire les cent ~** walk up and down; **faire le premier ~** make the first move; **~ de porte** doorstep; **~ de vis** (Tech) thread.

**passage** /pɑsaʒ/ *nm* (traversée) crossing; (visite) visit; (chemin) way, passage; (d'une œuvre) passage; **de ~** (*voyageur*) visiting; (*amant*) casual; **la tempête a tout emporté sur son ~** the storm swept everything away; **~ clouté** pedestrian crossing; **~ interdit** (panneau) no thoroughfare; **~ à niveau** level crossing; **~ souterrain** subway.

**passager**, **-ère** /pɑsaʒe, -ɛr/ *a* temporary. ● *nm,f* passenger; **~ clandestin** stowaway.

**passant**, **~e** /pɑsɑ̃, -t/ *a* (*rue*) busy. ● *nm,f* passer-by. ● *nm* (anneau) loop.

**passe** /pɑs/ *nf* pass; **bonne/ mauvaise ~** good/bad patch; **en ~ de** on the road to.

**passé**, **~e** /pɑse/ *a* (révolu) past; (dernier) last; (fané) faded; **~ de mode** out of fashion. ● *nm* past. ● *prép* after.

n
all

[illegible]/ *nm* passport.

[illegible]ase/ [1] *vi* (*aux être ou* [illegible]) go past, pass; (aller) go; (venir) [illegible]ome; (*temps, douleur*) pass; (*film*) be on; (*couleur*) fade; **laisser ~** let through; (*occasion*) miss; **~ devant** (à pied) walk past; (en voiture) drive past; **~ par** go through; **où est-il passé?** where did he get to?; **~ outre** take no notice; **passons!** let's forget about it!; **passons aux choses sérieuses** let's turn to serious matters; **~ dans la classe supérieure** go up a year; **~ pour un idiot** look a fool. ● *vt* (*aux avoir*) (franchir) pass, cross; (donner) pass, hand; (*temps*) spend; (enfiler) slip on; (*vidéo, disque*) put on; (*examen*) take, sit; (*commande*) place; (faire) **~ le temps** while away the time; **~ l'aspirateur** hoover; **~ un coup de fil à qn** give sb a ring; **je vous passe Mme X** (par le standard) I'll put you through to Mrs X; (en donnant l'appareil) I'll pass you over to Mrs X; **~ qch en fraude** smuggle sth. □ **se ~** *vpr* happen, take place; (s'écouler) go by; **se ~ de** go *ou* do without.

**passerelle** /pɑsʀɛl/ *nf* footbridge; (de navire) gangway; (d'avion) (passenger) footbridge; (Internet) gateway.

**passe-temps** /pɑstɑ̃/ *nm inv* pastime.

**passif**, **-ive** /pasif, -v/ *a* passive. ● *nm* (Comm) liabilities.

**passion** /pɑsjɔ̃/ *nf* passion. **passionnant**, **~e** *a* fascinating.

**passionné**, **~e** /pɑsjɔne/ *a* passionate; **être ~ de** have a passion for.

**passionner** /pɑsjɔne/ [1] *vt* fascinate. □ **se ~ pour** *vpr* have a passion for.

**passoire** /pɑswaʀ/ *nf* (à thé) strainer; (à légumes) colander.

**pastèque** /pastɛk/ *nf* watermelon.

**pasteur** /pastœʀ/ *nm* (Relig) minister.

**pastille** /pastij/ *nf* (médicament) pastille, lozenge.

**patate** /patat/ *nf* 🄸 spud; **~ (douce)** sweet potato.

**patauger** /patoʒe/ [40] *vi* splash about.

**pâte** /pɑt/ *nf* paste; (à gâteau) dough; (à tarte) pastry; (à frire) batter; **~s (alimentaires)** pasta (+ *sg*); **~ à modeler** Plasticine®; **~ d'amandes** marzipan.

**pâté** /pɑte/ *nm* (Culin) pâté; (d'encre) blot; (de sable) sandpie; **~ en croûte** ≈ pie; **~ de maisons** block (of houses).

**pâtée** /pɑte/ *nf* feed, mash.

**patente** /patɑ̃t/ *nf* trade licence.

**paternel**, **~le** /patɛʀnɛl/ *a* paternal. **paternité** *nf* paternity.

**pathétique** /patetik/ *a* moving.

**patience** /pasjɑ̃s/ *nf* patience. **patient**, **~e** *a & nm,f* patient. **patienter** [1] *vi* wait.

**patin** /patɛ̃/ *nm* skate; **~ à roulettes** roller-skate.

**patinage** /patinaʒ/ *nm* skating. **patiner** [1] *vi* skate; (*roue*) spin. **patinoire** *nf* ice rink.

**pâtisserie** /pɑtisʀi/ *nf* cake shop; (gâteau) pastry; (secteur) cake making. **pâtissier**, **-ière** *nm,f* confectioner, pastry-cook.

**patrie** /patʀi/ *nf* homeland.

**patrimoine** /patʀimwan/ *nm* heritage.

**patriote** /patʀijɔt/ *a* patriotic. ● *nmf* patriot.

**patron**, **~ne** /patʀɔ̃, -ɔn/ *nm,f* employer, boss; (propriétaire) owner,

boss; (saint) patron saint. ● *nm* (couture) pattern. **patronal**, **~e** (*mpl* **-aux**) *a* employers'. **patronat** *nm* employers (+ *pl*).

**patrouille** /patʀuj/ *nf* patrol.

**patte** /pat/ *nf* leg; (pied) foot; (de chat) paw; **~s** (favoris) sideburns; **marcher à quatre ~s** walk on all fours; (*bébé*) crawl; **~s de derrière** hind legs.

**paume** /pom/ *nf* (de main) palm.

**paumé**, **~e** /pome/ *nm,f* 🄸 misfit.

**paupière** /popjɛʀ/ *nf* eyelid.

**pause** /poz/ *nf* pause; (halte) break.

**pauvre** /povʀ/ *a* poor. ● *nmf* poor man, poor woman. **pauvreté** *nf* poverty.

**pavé** /pave/ *nm* cobblestone.

**pavillon** /pavijɔ̃/ *nm* (maison) house; (drapeau) flag.

**payant**, **~e** /pɛjɑ̃, -t/ *a* (*hôte*) paying; **c'est ~** you have to pay to get in.

**payer** /peje/ [31] *vt/i* pay; (*service, travail*) pay for; **~ qch à qn** buy sb sth; **faire ~ qn** charge sb; **il me le paiera!** he'll pay for this. □ **se ~** *vpr* **se ~ qch** buy oneself sth; **se ~ la tête de** make fun of.

**pays** /pei/ *nm* country; (région) region; **du ~** local.

**paysage** /peizaʒ/ *nm* landscape.

**paysan**, **~ne** /peizɑ̃, -an/ *nm,f* farmer, country person; (péj) peasant. ● *a* (agricole) farming; (rural) country.

**Pays-Bas** /peibɑ/ *nmpl* **les ~** the Netherlands.

**PCV** *abrév m* (**paiement contre vérification**) **téléphoner en ~** reverse the charges.

**PDG** *abrév m* (**président-directeur général**) chairman and managing director.

**péage** /peaʒ/ *nm* toll; (lieu) tollgate.

**pea**[illegible] hide; [illegible] ther); **~ de** [illegible] **bien/mal dans sa** [illegible] ease with oneself.

**pêche** /pɛʃ/ *nf* (fruit) peach; (activ[illegible]) fishing; (poissons) catch; **~ à la ligne** angling.

**péché** /peʃe/ *nm* sin.

**pêcher** /peʃe/ *vt* (*poisson*) catch; (dénicher 🄸) dig up. ● *vi* fish. **pêcheur** *nm* fisherman; (à la ligne) angler.

**pécuniaire** /pekynjɛʀ/ *a* financial.

**pédagogie** /pedagɔʒi/ *nf* education.

**pédale** /pedal/ *nf* pedal.

**pédalo**® /pedalo/ *nm* pedal boat.

**pédant**, **~e** /pedɑ̃, -t/ *a* pedantic.

**pédestre** /pedɛstʀ/ *a* **faire de la randonnée ~** go walking *ou* hiking.

**pédiatre** /pedjatʀ/ *nmf* paediatrician.

**pédicure** /pedikyʀ/ *nmf* chiropodist.

**peigne** /pɛɲ/ *nm* comb.

**peigner** /peɲe/ [1] *vt* comb; (*personne*) comb the hair of. □ **se ~** *vpr* comb one's hair.

**peignoir** /pɛɲwaʀ/ *nm* dressing-gown.

**peindre** /pɛ̃dʀ/ [22] *vt* paint.

**peine** /pɛn/ *nf* sadness, sorrow; (effort, difficulté) trouble; (Jur) sentence; **avoir de la ~** feel sad; **faire de la ~ à** hurt; **ce n'est pas la ~ de sonner** you don't need to ring the bell; **j'ai de la ~ à le croire** I find it hard to believe; **se donner** *ou* **prendre la ~ de faire** go to the trouble of doing; **~ de mort** death penalty. ● *adv* **à ~** hardly.

**peiner** /pene/ [1] *vi* struggle. ● *vt* sadden.

**peintre** /pɛ̃tʀ/ *nm* painter; ~ **en bâtiment** house painter.

**peinture** /pɛ̃tyʀ/ *nf* painting; (matière) paint; ~ **à l'huile** oil painting.

**péjoratif**, **-ive** /peʒɔʀatif, -v/ *a* pejorative.

**pelage** /pəlaʒ/ *nm* coat, fur.

**pêle-mêle** /pɛlmɛl/ *adv* in a jumble.

**peler** /pəle/ [6] *vt/i* peel.

**pèlerinage** /pɛlʀinaʒ/ *nm* pilgrimage.

**pelle** /pɛl/ *nf* shovel; (d'enfant) spade.

**pellicule** /pelikyl/ *nf* film; ~**s** (cheveux) dandruff.

**pelote** /pəlɔt/ *nf* (of wool) ball.

**peloton** /p(ə)lɔtɔ̃/ *nm* platoon; (Sport) pack; ~ **d'exécution** firing squad.

**pelotonner** (**se**) /(sə)plɔtɔne/ [1] *vpr* curl up.

**pelouse** /p(ə)luz/ *nf* lawn.

**peluche** /p(ə)lyʃ/ *nf* (matière) plush; (jouet) cuddly toy; **en** ~ (*lapin, chien*) fluffy.

**pénal**, ~**e** (*mpl* **-aux**) /penal, -o/ *a* penal. **pénaliser** [1] *vt* penalize. **pénalité** *nf* penalty.

**penchant** /pɑ̃ʃɑ̃/ *nm* inclination; (goût) liking (**pour** for).

**pencher** /pɑ̃ʃe/ [1] *vt* tilt; ~ **pour** favour. ● *vi* lean (over), tilt. ◻ **se** ~ *vpr* lean (forward); **se** ~ **sur** (*problème*) examine.

**pendaison** /pɑ̃dɛzɔ̃/ *nf* hanging.

**pendant**[1] /pɑ̃dɑ̃/ *prép* (au cours de) during; (durée) for; ~ **que** while.

**pendant**[2], ~**e** /pɑ̃dɑ̃, -t/ *a* hanging; **jambes** ~**es** with one's legs dangling. ● *nm* (contrepartie) matching piece (**de** to); ~ **d'oreille** drop ear-ring.

**pendentif** /pɑ̃dɑ̃tif/ *nm* pendant.

**penderie** /pɑ̃dʀi/ *nf* wardrobe.

**pendre** /pɑ̃dʀ/ [3] *vt/i* hang. ◻ **se** ~ *vpr* hang (**à** from); (se tuer) hang oneself.

**pendule** /pɑ̃dyl/ *nf* clock. ● *nm* pendulum.

**pénétrer** /penetʀe/ [14] *vi* ~ (**dans**) enter; **faire** ~ **une crème** rub a cream in. ● *vt* penetrate.

**pénible** /penibl/ *a* (*travail*) hard; (*nouvelle*) painful; (*enfant*) tiresome.

**péniche** /peniʃ/ *nf* barge.

**pénitence** /penitɑ̃s/ *nf* (Relig) penance; (punition) punishment; **faire** ~ repent.

**pénitentiaire** /penitɑ̃sjɛʀ/ *a* (*établissement*) penal.

**pénombre** /penɔ̃bʀ/ *nf* half-light.

**pensée** /pɑ̃se/ *nf* (idée) thought; (fleur) pansy.

**penser** /pɑ̃se/ [1] *vt/i* think; ~ **à** (réfléchir à) think about; (se souvenir de, prévoir) think of; ~ **faire** think of doing; **faire** ~ **à** remind one of.

**pensif**, **-ive** /pɑ̃sif, -v/ *a* pensive.

**pension** /pɑ̃sjɔ̃/ *nf* (Scol) boarding school; (repas, somme) board; (allocation) pension; ~ (**de famille**) guest house; ~ **alimentaire** (Jur) alimony. **pensionnaire** *nmf* (Scol) boarder; (d'hôtel) guest. **pensionnat** *nm* boarding school.

**pente** /pɑ̃t/ *nf* slope; **en** ~ sloping.

**Pentecôte** /pɑ̃tkot/ *nf* **la** ~ Whitsun.

**pénurie** /penyʀi/ *nf* shortage.

**pépin** /pepɛ̃/ *nm* (graine) pip; (ennui Ⓘ) hitch.

**pépinière** /pepinjɛʀ/ *nf* (tree) nursery.

**perçant**, ~**e** /pɛʀsɑ̃, -t/ *a* (*cri*) shrill; (*regard*) piercing.

**perce-neige** /pɛʀsənɛʒ/ *nm or f inv* snowdrop.

**percepteur** /pɛʀsɛptœʀ/ *nm* tax inspector.

**percer** /pɛʀse/ [10] *vt* pierce; (avec perceuse) drill; (*mystère*) penetrate. ● *vi* break through; (*dent*) come through. **perceuse** *nf* drill.

**percevoir** /pɛʀsəvwaʀ/ [52] *vt* perceive; (*impôt*) collect.

**perche** /pɛʀʃ/ *nf* (bâton) pole.

**percher (se)** /(sə)pɛʀʃe/ [1] *vpr* perch.

**percolateur** /pɛʀkɔlatœʀ/ *nm* coffee machine.

**percuter** /pɛʀkyte/ [1] *vt* (*véhicule*) crash into.

**perdant**, **~e** /pɛʀdɑ̃, -t/ *a* losing. ● *nm,f* loser.

**perdre** /pɛʀdʀ/ [3] *vt/i* lose; (gaspiller) waste; **~ ses poils** (*chat*) moult. □ **se ~** *vpr* get lost; (rester inutilisé) go to waste.

**perdrix** /pɛʀdʀi/ *nf* partridge.

**perdu**, **~e** /pɛʀdy/ *a* lost; (*endroit*) isolated; (*balle*) stray; **c'est du temps ~** it's a waste of time.

**père** /pɛʀ/ *nm* father; **~ de famille** father, family man; **~ spirituel** father figure; **le ~ Noël** Santa Claus.

**perfection** /pɛʀfɛksjɔ̃/ *nf* perfection.

**perfectionner** /pɛʀfɛksjɔne/ [1] *vt* (*technique*) perfect; (*art*) refine. □ **se ~** *vpr* improve; **se ~ en anglais** improve one's English.

**perforer** /pɛʀfɔʀe/ [1] *vt* perforate; (*billet, bande*) punch.

**performance** /pɛʀfɔʀmɑ̃s/ *nf* performance.

**perfusion** /pɛʀfysjɔ̃/ *nf* drip; **sous ~** on a drip.

**péridurale** /peʀidyʀal/ *nf* epidural.

**péril** /peʀil/ *nm* peril; **à tes risques et ~s** at your own risk.

**périlleux**, **-euse** /peʀijø, -z/ *a* perilous.

**périmé**, **~e** /peʀime/ *a* (*produit*) past its use-by date; (désuet) outdated.

**période** /peʀjɔd/ *nf* period.

**périodique** /peʀjɔdik/ *a* periodic(al). ● *nm* (journal) periodical.

**péripétie** /peʀipesi/ *nf* (unexpected) event, adventure.

**périphérique** /peʀifeʀik/ *a* peripheral. ● *nm* **(boulevard) ~** ring road.

**périple** /peʀipl/ *nm* journey.

**périr** /peʀiʀ/ [2] *vi* perish, die.

**perle** /pɛʀl/ *nf* (d'huître) pearl; (de verre) bead.

**permanence** /pɛʀmanɑ̃s/ *nf* permanence; (Scol) study room; **de ~** on duty; **en ~** permanently; **assurer une ~** keep the office open.

**permanent**, **~e** /pɛʀmanɑ̃, -t/ *a* permanent; (constant) constant; **formation ~e** continuous education. **permanente** *nf* (coiffure) perm.

**permettre** /pɛʀmɛtʀ/ [42] *vt* allow; **~ à qn de** allow sb to. □ **se ~** *vpr* (*achat*) afford; **se ~ de faire** take the liberty of doing.

**permis**, **~e** /pɛʀmi, -z/ *a* allowed. ● *nm* licence, permit; **~ (de conduire)** driving licence.

**permission** /pɛʀmisjɔ̃/ *nf* permission; **en ~** (Mil) on leave.

**Pérou** /peʀu/ *nm* Peru.

**perpendiculaire** /pɛʀpɑ̃dikylɛʀ/ *a & nf* perpendicular.

**perpétuité** /pɛʀpetɥite/ *nf* **à ~** for life.

**perplexe** /pɛʀplɛks/ *a* perplexed.

**perquisition** /pɛʀkizisjɔ̃/ *nf* (police) search.

**perron** /pɛʀɔ̃/ *nm* (front) steps.

**perroquet** /pɛʀɔkɛ/ *nm* parrot.

**perruche** /peʀyʃ/ *nf* budgerigar.

**perruque** /peʀyk/ *nf* wig.

**persécuter** /pɛʀsekyte/ [1] *vt* persecute.

**persévérance** /pɛʀseveʀɑ̃s/ *nf* perseverance. **persévérer** [14] *vi* persevere.

**persienne** /pɛʀsjɛn/ *nf* (outside) shutter.

**persil** /pɛʀsi/ *nm* parsley.

**persistance** /pɛʀsistɑ̃s/ *nf* persistence. **persistant**, **~e** *a* persistent; (*feuillage*) evergreen.

**persister** /pɛʀsiste/ [1] *vi* persist (**à faire** in doing).

**personnage** /pɛʀsɔnaʒ/ *nm* character; (personne célèbre) personality.

**personnalité** /pɛʀsɔnalite/ *nf* personality.

**personne** /pɛʀsɔn/ *nf* person; **~s** people. ● *pron* nobody, no-one; **je n'ai vu ~** I didn't see anybody.

**personnel**, **~le** /pɛʀsɔnɛl/ *a* personal; (égoïste) selfish. ● *nm* staff.

**perspective** /pɛʀspɛktiv/ *nf* (art, point de vue) perspective; (vue) view; (éventualité) prospect.

**perspicace** /pɛʀspikas/ *a* shrewd. **perspicacité** *nf* shrewdness.

**persuader** /pɛʀsɥade/ [1] *vt* persuade (**de faire** to do).

**persuasif**, **-ive** /pɛʀsɥazif, -v/ *a* persuasive.

**perte** /pɛʀt/ *nf* loss; (ruine) ruin; **à ~ de vue** as far as the eye can see; **~ de** (*temps, argent*) waste of; **~ sèche** total loss; **~s** (Méd) discharge.

**pertinent**, **~e** /pɛʀtinɑ̃, -t/ *a* pertinent.

**perturbateur**, **-trice** /pɛʀtyʀbatœʀ, -tʀis/ *nm,f* disruptive element. **perturbation** *nf* disruption. **perturber** [1] *vt* disrupt; (*personne*) perturb.

**pervers**, **~e** /pɛʀvɛʀ, -s/ *a* (dépravé) perverted; (méchant) wicked.

**pervertir** /pɛʀvɛʀtiʀ/ [2] *vt* pervert.

**pesant**, **~e** /pəzɑ̃, -t/ *a* heavy.

**pesanteur** /pəzɑ̃tœʀ/ *nf* heaviness; **la ~** (force) gravity.

**pesée** /pəze/ *nf* weighing; (effort) pressure.

**pèse-personne** (*pl* **~s**) /pɛzpɛʀsɔn/ *nm* (bathroom) scales.

**peser** /pəze/ [6] *vt/i* weigh; **~ sur** bear upon.

**pessimiste** /pesimist/ *a* pessimistic. ● *nmf* pessimist.

**peste** /pɛst/ *nf* plague; (personne Ⓘ) pest.

**pet** /pɛ/ *nm* Ⓘ fart Ⓘ.

**pétale** /petal/ *nm* petal.

**pétard** /petaʀ/ *nm* banger.

**péter** /pete/ [14] *vi* Ⓘ fart Ⓘ, go bang; (casser) snap.

**pétillant**, **~e** /petijɑ̃, -t/ *a* (*boisson*) sparkling; (*personne*) bubbly.

**pétiller** /petije/ [1] *vi* (*feu*) crackle; (*champagne, yeux*) sparkle; **~ d'intelligence** sparkle with intelligence.

**petit**, **~e** /p(ə)ti, -t/ *a* small; (avec nuance affective) little; (jeune) young, small; (*défaut*) minor; (mesquin) petty; **en ~** in miniature; **~ à ~** little by little; **un ~ peu** a little bit; **~ ami** boyfriend; **~e amie** girlfriend; **~es annonces** small ads; **~e cuillère** teaspoon; **~ déjeuner** breakfast; **~ pois** garden pea. ● *nm,f* little child; (Scol) junior; **~s** (de chat) kittens; (de chien) pups.

**petite-fille** (*pl* **petites-filles**) *nf* granddaughter. **petit-fils** (*pl* **petits-fils**) *nm* grandson.

**pétition** /petisjɔ̃/ *nf* petition.

**petits-enfants** /pətizɑ̃fɑ̃/ *nmpl* grandchildren.

**pétrin** /petʀɛ̃/ *nm* **dans le ~** Ⓘ in a fix Ⓘ.

**pétrir** /petʀiʀ/ [2] *vt* knead.

**pétrole** /petʀɔl/ *nm* oil; **~ brut** crude oil.

**pétrolier, -ière** /petʀɔlje, -jɛʀ/ *a* oil. ● *nm* (navire) oil-tanker.

**peu** /pø/ *adv* **~ (de)** (quantité) little, not much; (nombre) few, not many; **~ intéressant** not very interesting; **il mange ~** he doesn't eat very much. ● *pron* few. ● *nm* little; **un ~ (de)** a little; **à ~ près** more or less; **de ~** only just; **~ à ~** gradually; **~ après/avant** shortly after/before; **~ de chose** not much; **~ nombreux** few; **~ souvent** seldom; **pour ~ que** if.

**peuple** /pœpl/ *nm* people. **peupler** [1] *vt* populate.

**peuplier** /pøplije/ *nm* poplar.

**peur** /pœʀ/ *nf* fear; **avoir ~** be afraid (**de** of); **de ~ de** for fear of; **faire ~ à** frighten. **peureux, -euse** *a* fearful.

**peut** /pø/ ⇒POUVOIR [49].

**peut-être** /pøtɛtʀ/ *adv* perhaps, maybe; **~ qu'il viendra** he might come.

**peux** /pø/ ⇒POUVOIR [49].

**phare** /faʀ/ *nm* (tour) lighthouse; (de véhicule) headlight; **~ antibrouillard** fog lamp.

**pharmacie** /faʀmasi/ *nf* (magasin) chemist's (shop), pharmacy; (science) pharmacy; (armoire) medicine cabinet. **pharmacien, ~ne** *nm, f* chemist, pharmacist.

**phénomène** /fenɔmɛn/ *nm* phenomenon; (personne Ⓘ) eccentric.

**philosophe** /filɔzɔf/ *nmf* philosopher. ● *a* philosophical. **philosophie** *nf* philosophy. **philosophique** *a* philosophical.

**phobie** /fɔbi/ *nf* phobia.

**phonétique** /fɔnetik/ *a* phonetic. ● *nf* phonetics.

**phoque** /fɔk/ *nm* (animal) seal.

**photo** /fɔto/ *nf* photo; (art) photography; **prendre en ~** take a photo of; **~ d'identité** passport photograph.

**photocopie** /fɔtɔkɔpi/ *nf* photocopy. **photocopier** [45] *vt* photocopy.

**photographe** /fɔtɔgʀaf/ *nmf* photographer. **photographie** *nf* photograph; (art) photography. **photographier** [45] *vt* take a photo of.

**phrase** /fʀɑz/ *nf* sentence.

**physicien, ~ne** /fizisjɛ̃, -ɛn/ *nm, f* physicist.

**physique** /fizik/ *a* physical. ● *nm* physique; **au ~** physically. ● *nf* physics (+ *sg*).

**piano** /pjano/ *nm* piano.

**pianoter** /pjanɔte/ [1] *vi* tinkle; **~ sur** (*ordinateur*) tap at.

**PIB** *abrév m* (**produit intérieur brut**) GDP.

**pic** /pik/ *nm* (outil) pickaxe; (sommet) peak; (oiseau) woodpecker; **à ~** (*falaise*) sheer; (*couler*) straight to the bottom; **tomber à ~** Ⓘ come just at the right time.

**pichet** /piʃɛ/ *nm* jug.

**picorer** /pikɔʀe/ [1] *vt/i* peck.

**picotement** /pikɔtmɑ̃/ *nm* tingling. **picoter** [1] *vt* sting; (*yeux*) sting.

**pie** /pi/ *nf* magpie.

**pièce** /pjɛs/ *nf* (d'habitation) room; (de monnaie) coin; (Théât) play; (pour raccommoder) patch; (écrit) document; (morceau) piece; **~ (de théâtre)** play; **dix francs (la) ~** ten francs each; **~ détachée** part; **~ d'identité** identity paper; **~s**

**jointes** enclosures; (courrier électronique) attachments; **~s justificatives** written proof; **~ montée** tiered cake; **~ de rechange** spare part; **un deux-~s** a two-room flat.

**pied** /pje/ *nm* foot; (de meuble) leg; (de lampe) base; (de verre) stem; (d'appareil photo) stand; **être ~s nus** be bare-foot; **à ~** on foot; **au ~ de la lettre** literally; **avoir ~** be able to touch the bottom; **jouer au tennis comme un ~** Ⓘ be hopeless at tennis; **mettre sur ~** set up; **sur un ~ d'égalité** on an equal footing; **mettre les ~s dans le plat** Ⓘ put one's foot in it; **c'est le ~** Ⓘ it's great. **pied-bot** (*pl* **pieds-bots**) *nm* club-foot.

**piédestal** /pjedɛstal/ *nm* pedestal.

**piège** /pjɛʒ/ *nm* trap.

**piéger** /pjeʒe/ [14] [40] *vt* trap; **lettre/voiture piégée** letter/car bomb.

**piercing** /piʀsiŋ/ *nm* body piercing.

**pierre** /pjɛʀ/ *nf* stone; **~ précieuse** precious stone; **~ tombale** tombstone.

**piétiner** /pjetine/ [1] *vi* (avancer lentement) shuffle along; (fig) make no headway; **~ d'impatience** hop up and down with impatience. ● *vt* trample (on).

**piéton** /pjetɔ̃/ *nm* pedestrian.

**pieu** (*pl* **~x**) /pjø/ *nm* post, stake.

**pieuvre** /pjœvʀ/ *nf* octopus.

**pieux, -ieuse** /pjø, -z/ *a* pious.

**pigeon** /piʒɔ̃/ *nm* pigeon.

**piger** /piʒe/ [40] *vt/i* Ⓘ understand.

**pile** /pil/ *nf* (tas) pile; (Électr) battery; **~ ou face?** heads or tails? ● *adv* (*s'arrêter* Ⓘ) dead; **à dix heures ~** Ⓘ at ten on the dot.

**pilier** /pilje/ *nm* pillar.

**pillage** /pijaʒ/ *nm* looting. **pillard, ~e** *nm,f* looter. **piller** [1] *vt* loot.

**pilote** /pilɔt/ *nm* (Aviat, Naut) pilot; (Auto) driver. ● *a* pilot. **piloter** [1] *vt* (Aviat, Naut) pilot; (Auto) drive; (fig) guide.

**pilule** /pilyl/ *nf* pill; **la ~** the pill.

**piment** /pimɑ̃/ *nm* hot pepper; (fig) spice. **pimenté, ~e** *a* spicy.

**pin** /pɛ̃/ *nm* pine.

**pinard** /pinaʀ/ *nm* Ⓘ plonk Ⓘ, cheap wine.

**pince** /pɛ̃s/ *nf* (outil) pliers (+ *pl*); (levier) crowbar; (de crabe) pincer; (à sucre) tongs (+ *pl*); **~ à épiler** tweezers (+ *pl*); **~ à linge** clothes peg.

**pinceau** (*pl* **~x**) /pɛ̃so/ *nm* paintbrush.

**pincée** /pɛ̃se/ *nf* pinch (**de** of).

**pincer** /pɛ̃se/ [10] *vt* pinch; (attraper Ⓘ) catch. □ **se ~** *vpr* catch oneself; **se ~ le doigt** catch one's finger.

**pince-sans-rire** /pɛ̃ssɑ̃ʀiʀ/ *nmf inv* **c'est un ~** he has a deadpan sense of humour.

**pingouin** /pɛ̃gwɛ̃/ *nm* penguin.

**pingre** /pɛ̃gʀ/ *a* stingy.

**pintade** /pɛ̃tad/ *nf* guinea fowl.

**piocher** /pjɔʃe/ [1] *vt/i* dig; (étudier Ⓘ) study hard, slog away (at).

**pion** /pjɔ̃/ *nm* (de jeu) counter; (aux échecs) pawn; (Scol Ⓘ) supervisor.

**pipe** /pip/ *nf* pipe; **fumer la ~** smoke a pipe.

**piquant, ~e** /pikɑ̃, -t/ *a* (*barbe*) prickly; (*goût*) pungent; (*remarque*) cutting. ● *nm* prickle.

**pique** /pik/ *nm* (aux cartes) spades.

**pique-nique** (*pl* **~s**) /piknik/ *nm* picnic.

**piquer** /pike/ [1] *vt* (*épine*) prick; (*épice*) burn, sting; (*abeille, ortie*) sting; (*serpent, moustique*) bite; (enfoncer) stick; (coudre) (machine-) stitch; (*curiosité*) excite; (voler Ⓘ) pinch. ● *vi* (*avion*) dive; (*goût*) be hot. □ **se ~** *vpr* prick oneself.

**piquet** /pikɛ/ *nm* stake; (de tente) peg; (de parasol) pole; ~ **de grève** (strike) picket.

**piqûre** /pikyʀ/ *nf* prick; (d'abeille) sting; (de serpent) bite; (point) stitch; (Méd) injection, jab; **faire une ~ à qn** give sb an injection.

**pirate** /piʀat/ *nm* pirate; ~ **informatique** computer hacker; ~ **de l'air** hijacker.

**pire** /piʀ/ *a* worse (**que** than); **les ~s mensonges** the most wicked lies. ● *nm* **le ~** the worst; **au ~** at worst.

**pis** /pi/ *nm* (de vache) udder. ● *a inv & adv* worse; **aller de mal en ~** go from bad to worse.

**piscine** /pisin/ *nf* swimming-pool; ~ **couverte** indoor swimming pool.

**pissenlit** /pisɑ̃li/ *nm* dandelion.

**pistache** /pistaʃ/ *nf* pistachio.

**piste** /pist/ *nf* track; (de personne, d'animal) track, trail; (Aviat) runway; (de cirque) ring; (de ski) slope; (de danse) floor; (Sport) racetrack; ~ **cyclable** cycle lane.

**pistolet** /pistɔlɛ/ *nm* gun, pistol; (de peintre) spray-gun.

**piteux**, **-euse** /pitø, -z/ *a* pitiful.

**pitié** /pitje/ *nf* pity; **il me fait ~** I feel sorry for him.

**piton** /pitɔ̃/ *nm* (à crochet) hook; (sommet pointu) peak.

**pitoyable** /pitwajabl/ *a* pitiful.

**pitre** /pitʀ/ *nm* clown; **faire le ~** clown around.

**pittoresque** /pitɔʀɛsk/ *a* picturesque.

**pivot** /pivo/ *nm* pivot. **pivoter** [1] *vi* revolve; (*personne*) swing round.

**placard** /plakaʀ/ *nm* cupboard; (affiche) poster. **placarder** [1] *vt* (*affiche*) post up; (*mur*) cover with posters.

**place** /plas/ *nf* place; (espace libre) room, space; (siège) seat, place; (prix d'un trajet) fare; (esplanade) square; (emploi) position; (de parking) space; **à la ~ de** instead of; **en ~, à sa ~** in its place; **faire ~ à** give way to; **sur ~** on the spot; **remettre qn à sa ~** put sb in his place; **ça prend de la ~** it takes up a lot of room; **se mettre à la ~ de qn** put oneself in sb's shoes *ou* place.

**placement** /plasmɑ̃/ *nm* (d'argent) investment.

**placer** /plase/ [10] *vt* place; (*invité, spectateur*) seat; (*argent*) invest. □ **se ~** *vpr* (*personne*) take up a position.

**plafond** /plafɔ̃/ *nm* ceiling.

**plage** /plaʒ/ *nf* beach; ~ **horaire** time slot.

**plagiat** /plaʒja/ *nm* plagiarism.

**plaider** /plede/ [1] *vt/i* plead. **plaidoirie** *nf* (defence) speech. **plaidoyer** *nm* plea.

**plaie** /plɛ/ *nf* wound; (personne 🅘) nuisance.

**plaignant**, **~e** /plɛɲɑ̃, -t/ *nm*, *f* plaintiff.

**plaindre** /plɛ̃dʀ/ [22] *vt* pity. □ **se ~** *vpr* complain (**de** about); **se ~ de** (souffrir de) complain of.

**plaine** /plɛn/ *nf* plain.

**plainte** /plɛ̃t/ *nf* complaint; (gémissement) groan. **plaintif**, **-ive** *a* plaintive.

**plaire** /plɛʀ/ [47] *vi* ~ **à** please; **ça lui plaît** he likes it; **elle lui plaît** he likes her; **ça me plaît de faire** I like *ou* enjoy doing; **s'il vous plaît** please. □ **se ~** *vpr* **il se plaît ici** he likes it here.

**plaisance** /plɛzɑ̃s/ *nf* **la (navigation de) ~** boating.

**plaisant**, **~e** /plɛzɑ̃, -t/ *a* pleasant; (drôle) amusing.

**plaisanter** /plɛzɑ̃te/ [1] *vi* joke. **plaisanterie** *nf* joke. **plaisantin** *nm* joker.

**plaisir** /pleziʀ/ *nm* pleasure; **faire ~ à** please; **pour le ~** for fun *ou* pleasure.

**plan** /plɑ̃/ *nm* plan; (de ville) map; (de livre) outline; **~ d'eau** artificial lake; **~ social** planned redundancy programme; **premier ~** foreground.

**planche** /plɑ̃ʃ/ *nf* board, plank; (gravure) plate; **~ à repasser** ironing-board; **~ à voile** windsurfing board; (Sport) windsurfing.

**plancher** /plɑ̃ʃe/ *nm* floor.

**planer** /plane/ [1] *vi* glide; **~ sur** (*mystère, danger*) hang over.

**planète** /planɛt/ *nf* planet.

**planeur** /planœʀ/ *nm* glider.

**planifier** /planifje/ [45] *vt* plan.

**plant** /plɑ̃/ *nm* seedling; (de légumes) patch.

**plante** /plɑ̃t/ *nf* plant; **~ d'appartement** houseplant; **~ des pieds** sole (of the foot).

**planter** /plɑ̃te/ [1] *vt* (*plante*) plant; (enfoncer) drive in; (*tente*) put up; **rester planté** 🅸 stand still.

**plaque** /plak/ *nf* plate; (de marbre) slab; (insigne) badge; **~ chauffante** hotplate; **~ commémorative** plaque; **~ minéralogique** number-plate; **~ de verglas** patch of ice.

**plaquer** /plake/ [1] *vt* (*bois*) veneer; (aplatir) flatten; (rugby) tackle; (abandonner 🅸) ditch 🅸; **tout ~** chuck it all.

**plastique** /plastik/ *a & nm* plastic; **en ~** plastic.

**plastiquer** /plastike/ [1] *vt* blow up.

**plat**, **~e** /pla, -t/ *a* flat. ● *nm* (Culin) dish; (partie de repas) course; (de la main) flat. ● **à plat** *adv* (*poser*) flat; (*batterie, pneu*) flat; **à ~ ventre** flat on one's face.

**platane** /platan/ *nm* plane tree.

**plateau** (*pl* **~x**) /plato/ *nm* tray; (de cinéma) set; (de balance) pan; (Géog) plateau; **~ de fromages** cheeseboard; **~ de fruits de mer** seafood platter. **plate-bande** (*pl* **plates-bandes**) *nf* flower-bed.

**platine** /platin/ *nm* platinum. ● *nf* (tourne-disque) turntable; **~ laser** compact disc player.

**plâtre** /plɑtʀ/ *nm* plaster; (Méd) (plaster) cast.

**plein**, **~e** /plɛ̃, -ɛn/ *a* full (**de** of); (total) complete. ● *nm* **faire le ~ (d'essence)** fill up (the tank); **à ~** fully; **à ~ temps** full-time; **en ~ air** in the open air; **en ~ milieu/visage** right in the middle/the face; **en ~e nuit** in the middle of the night. ● *adv* **avoir des idées ~ la tête** be full of ideas. **pleinement** *adv* fully.

**pleurer** /plœʀe/ [1] *vi* cry, weep (**sur** over); (*yeux*) water. ● *vt* mourn.

**pleurnicher** /plœʀniʃe/ [1] *vi* 🅸 snivel.

**pleurs** /plœʀ/ *nmpl* tears; **en ~** in tears.

**pleuvoir** /pløvwaʀ/ [48] *vi* rain; (fig) rain *ou* shower down; **il pleut** it is raining; **il pleut à verse** *ou* **des cordes** it is pouring.

**pli** /pli/ *nm* fold; (de jupe) pleat; (de pantalon) crease; (lettre) letter; (habitude) habit; **(faux) ~** crease.

**pliant**, **~e** /plijɑ̃, -t/ *a* folding. ● *nm* folding stool, camp-stool.

**plier** /plije/ [45] *vt* fold; (courber) bend; (soumettre) submit (**à** to). ● *vi*

bend. □ **se** ~ *vpr* fold; **se** ~ **à** submit to.

**plinthe** /plɛ̃t/ *nf* skirting-board.

**plissé**, ~**e** /plise/ *a* (*jupe*) pleated.

**plisser** /plise/ [1] *vt* crease; (*yeux*) screw up.

**plomb** /plɔ̃/ *nm* lead; (fusible) fuse; ~**s** (de chasse) lead shot; **de** *ou* **en** ~ lead. **plombage** *nm* filling.

**plomberie** /plɔ̃bʀi/ *nf* plumbing. **plombier** *nm* plumber.

**plongée** /plɔ̃ʒe/ *nf* diving; **en** ~ (*sous-marin*) submerged.

**plongeoir** /plɔ̃ʒwaʀ/ *nm* diving-board.

**plonger** /plɔ̃ʒe/ [40] *vi* dive; (*route*) plunge. ● *vt* plunge. □ **se** ~ *vpr* plunge into; **se** ~ **dans** (fig) (*lecture*) bury oneself in. **plongeur**, **-euse** *nm,f* diver; (de restaurant) dishwasher.

**plu** /ply/ →PLAIRE [47], PLEUVOIR [48].

**pluie** /plɥi/ *nf* rain; (averse) shower; ~ **battante/diluvienne** driving/torrential rain.

**plume** /plym/ *nf* feather; (pointe) nib.

**plumeau** (*pl* ~**x**) /plymo/ *nm* feather duster.

**plumier** /plymje/ *nm* pencil box.

**plupart**: **la** ~ /laplypaʀ/ *loc* **la** ~ **des** (*gens, cas*) most; **la** ~ **du temps** most of the time; **pour la** ~ for the most part.

**pluriel**, ~**le** /plyʀjɛl/ *a* & *nm* plural.

**plus** /ply, plys, plyz/

● *adverbe de comparaison*

····➤ more (**que** than); ~ **âgé/tard** older/later; ~ **beau** more beautiful; ~ **j'y pense...** the more I think about it...; **deux fois** ~ twice as much; **deux fois** ~ **cher** twice as expensive.

····➤ **le** ~ the most; **le** ~ **grand** the biggest; (de deux) the bigger.

····➤ ~ **de** (*pain*) more; (*dix jours*) more than; **il est** ~ **de 8 heures** it is after 8 o'clock.

····➤ **de** ~ more (**que** than); (en outre) moreover; **les enfants de** ~ **de 10 ans** children over 10 years old; **de** ~ **en** ~ more and more.

····➤ **en** ~ on top of that; **c'est en** ~ it's extra; **en** ~ **de** in addition to.

····➤ ~ **ou moins** more or less.

····➤ **au** ~ **tard** at the latest.

● *adverbe de négation*

····➤ **ne** ~ (*temps*) no longer, not any more; **je n'y vais** ~ I don't go there any longer *ou* any more.

····➤ **ne** ~ **de** (quantité) no more; **il n'y a** ~ **de pain** there is no more bread.

····➤ ~ **que deux jours!** only two days left!

● *préposition & nom masculin*

····➤ (maths) plus.

**plusieurs** /plyzjœʀ/ *a* & *pron* several.

**plus-value** (*pl* ~**s**) /plyvaly/ *nf* (bénéfice) profit.

**plutôt** /plyto/ *adv* rather (**que** than).

**pluvieux**, **-ieuse** /plyvjø, -z/ *a* rainy.

**PME** *abrév f* (**petites et moyennes entreprises**) SME.

**PNB** *abrév m* (**produit national brut**) GNP.

**pneu** (*pl* ~**s**) /pnø/ *nm* tyre. **pneumatique** *a* inflatable.

**poche** /pɔʃ/ *nf* pocket; (sac) bag; ~**s** (sous les yeux) bags.

**pocher** /pɔʃe/ [1] *vt* (*œuf*) poach.

**pochette** /pɔʃɛt/ *nf* (de documents) folder; (sac) bag, pouch; (d'allumettes) book; (de disque) sleeve; (mouchoir) pocket handkerchief.

**poêle** /pwal/ *nf* ~ **(à frire)** frying-pan. ● *nm* stove.

**poème** /pɔɛm/ *nm* poem. **poésie** *nf* poetry; (poème) poem. **poète** *nm* poet. **poétique** *a* poetic.

**poids** /pwa/ *nm* weight; ~ **coq/lourd/plume** bantam weight/heavyweight/featherweight; ~ **lourd** (camion) lorry, juggernaut; (US) truck.

**poignard** /pwaɲaʀ/ *nm* dagger. **poignarder** [1] *vt* stab.

**poigne** /pwaɲ/ *nf* **avoir de la** ~ have a strong grip.

**poignée** /pwaɲe/ *nf* (de porte) handle; (quantité) handful; ~ **de main** handshake.

**poignet** /pwaɲɛ/ *nm* wrist; (de chemise) cuff.

**poil** /pwal/ *nm* hair; (pelage) fur; (de brosse) bristle; ~**s** (de tapis) pile; **à** ~ 🅸 naked; ~ **à gratter** itching powder. **poilu**, ~**e** *a* hairy.

**poinçon** /pwɛ̃sɔ̃/ *nm* awl; (marque) hallmark. **poinçonner** [1] *vt* (*billet*) punch.

**poing** /pwɛ̃/ *nm* fist.

**point** /pwɛ̃/ *nm* (endroit, Sport) point; (marque visible) spot, dot; (de couture) stitch; (pour évaluer) mark; **enlever un** ~ **par faute** take a mark off for each mistake; **à** ~ (Culin) medium; (*arriver*) at the right time; **faire le** ~ take stock; **mettre au** ~ (*photo*) focus; (*technique*) develop; **mettre les choses au** ~ get things clear; **Camille n'est pas encore au** ~ **pour ses examens** Camille is not ready for her exams; **sur le** ~ **de** about to; **au** ~ **que** to the extent that; ~ **(final)** full stop, period; **deux** ~**s** colon; ~ **d'interrogation/d'exclamation** question/exclamation mark; ~**s de suspension** suspension points; ~ **virgule** semicolon; ~ **culminant** peak; ~ **du jour** daybreak; ~ **mort** (Auto) neutral; ~ **de repère** landmark; ~ **de suture** (Méd) stitch; ~ **de vente** point of sale; ~ **de vue** point of view. ● *adv* **(ne)** ~ not.

**pointe** /pwɛ̃t/ *nf* point, tip; (clou) tack; (de grille) spike; (fig) touch (**de** of); **de** ~ (*industrie*) high-tech; **en** ~ pointed; **heure de** ~ peak hour; **sur la** ~ **des pieds** on tiptoe.

**pointer** /pwɛ̃te/ [1] *vt* (cocher) tick off; (diriger) point, aim. ● *vi* (*employé*) (en arrivant) clock in; (en sortant) clock out. □ **se** ~ *vpr* 🅸 turn up.

**pointillé** /pwɛ̃tije/ *nm* dotted line.

**pointilleux**, **-euse** /pwɛ̃tijø, -z/ *a* fastidious, particular.

**pointu**, ~**e** /pwɛ̃ty/ *a* pointed; (aiguisé) sharp.

**pointure** /pwɛ̃tyʀ/ *nf* size.

**poire** /pwaʀ/ *nf* pear.

**poireau** (*pl* ~**x**) /pwaʀo/ *nm* leek.

**poirier** /pwaʀje/ *nm* pear tree.

**pois** /pwa/ *nm* pea; (motif) dot; **robe à** ~ polka dot dress.

**poison** /pwazɔ̃/ *nm* poison.

**poisseux**, **-euse** /pwasø, -z/ *a* sticky.

**poisson** /pwasɔ̃/ *nm* fish; ~ **rouge** goldfish; ~ **d'avril** April fool; **les P**~**s** Pisces. **poissonnerie** *nf* fish shop. **poissonnier**, **-ière** *nm,f* fishmonger.

**poitrine** /pwatʀin/ *nf* chest; (seins) bosom.

**poivre** /pwavʀ/ *nm* pepper. **poivré**, ~**e** *a* peppery. **poivrière** *nf* pepper-pot.

**poivron** /pwavʀɔ̃/ *nm* sweet pepper.

**polaire** /pɔlɛʀ/ *a* polar. ● *nf* (veste) fleece.

**pôle** /pol/ *nm* pole.

**polémique** /pɔlemik/ *nf* debate. ● *a* controversial.

**poli**, **~e** /pɔli/ *a* (*personne*) polite.

**police** /pɔlis/ *nf* (force) police (+ *pl*); (discipline) (law and) order; (d'assurance) policy.

**policier**, **-ière** /pɔlisje, -jɛʀ/ *a* police; (*roman*) detective. ● *nm* policeman.

**polir** /pɔliʀ/ [2] *vt* polish.

**politesse** /pɔlitɛs/ *nf* politeness; (parole) polite remark.

**politicien**, **~ne** /pɔlitisjɛ̃, -ɛn/ *nm,f* (péj) politician.

**politique** /pɔlitik/ *a* political; **homme ~** politician. ● *nf* politics; (ligne de conduite) policy.

**pollen** /pɔlɛn/ *nm* pollen.

**polluant**, **~e** /pɔlɥɑ̃, -t/ *a* polluting. ● *nm* pollutant.

**polluer** /pɔlɥe/ [1] *vt* pollute. **pollution** *nf* pollution.

**polo** /pɔlo/ *nm* (Sport) polo; (vêtement) polo shirt.

**Pologne** /pɔlɔɲ/ *nf* Poland.

**polonais**, **~e** /pɔlɔnɛ, -z/ *a* Polish. ● *nm* (Ling) Polish. **P~**, **~e** *nm,f* Pole.

**poltron**, **~ne** /pɔltʀɔ̃, -ɔn/ *a* cowardly. ● *nm,f* coward.

**polygame** /pɔligam/ *nmf* polygamist.

**polyvalent**, **~e** /pɔlivalɑ̃, -t/ *a* varied; (*personne*) versatile.

**pommade** /pɔmad/ *nf* ointment.

**pomme** /pɔm/ *nf* apple; (d'arrosoir) rose; **~ d'Adam** Adam's apple; **~ de pin** pine cone; **~ de terre** potato; **~s frites** chips; (US) French fries; **tomber dans les ~s** Ⓘ pass out.

**pommette** /pɔmɛt/ *nf* cheekbone.

**pommier** /pɔmje/ *nm* apple tree.

**pompe** /pɔ̃p/ *nf* pump; (splendeur) pomp; **~ à incendie** fire-engine; **~s funèbres** undertaker's (+ *sg*).

**pomper** /pɔ̃pe/ [1] *vt* pump; (copier Ⓘ) copy, crib; **~ l'air à qn** Ⓘ get on sb's nerves.

**pompier** /pɔ̃pje/ *nm* fireman.

**pomponner (se)** /(sə)pɔ̃pɔne/ [1] *vpr* get dolled up.

**poncer** /pɔ̃se/ [10] *vt* sand.

**ponctuation** /pɔ̃ktɥasjɔ̃/ *nf* punctuation.

**ponctuel**, **~le** /pɔ̃ktɥɛl/ *a* punctual.

**pondre** /pɔ̃dʀ/ [3] *vt/i* lay.

**poney** /pɔnɛ/ *nm* pony.

**pont** /pɔ̃/ *nm* bridge; (de navire) deck; (de graissage) ramp; **faire le ~** get an extended weekend; **~ aérien** airlift. **pont-levis** (*pl* **ponts-levis**) *nm* drawbridge.

**populaire** /pɔpylɛʀ/ *a* popular; (*expression*) colloquial; (*quartier*, *origine*) working-class. **popularité** *nf* popularity.

**population** /pɔpylasjɔ̃/ *nf* population.

**porc** /pɔʀ/ *nm* pig; (viande) pork.

**porcelaine** /pɔʀsəlɛn/ *nf* china, porcelain.

**porc-épic** (*pl* **porcs-épics**) /pɔʀkepik/ *nm* porcupine.

**porcherie** /pɔʀʃəʀi/ *nf* pigsty.

**pornographie** /pɔʀnɔgʀafi/ *nf* pornography.

**port** /pɔʀ/ *nm* port, harbour; **à bon ~** safely; **~ maritime** seaport; (transport) carriage; (d'armes) carrying; (de barbe) wearing.

**portable** /pɔʀtabl/ *nm* (Ordinat) laptop (computer); (telephone) mobile (phone).

**portail** /pɔʀtaj/ *nm* gate.

**portatif**, **-ive** /pɔʀtatif, -v/ *a* portable.

**porte** /pɔʀt/ *nf* door; (passage) doorway; (de jardin, d'embarquement) gate; **mettre à la ~** throw out; **~ d'entrée** front door.

**porté, ~e** /pɔʀte/ *a* **~ à** inclined to; **~ sur** keen on.

**porte-avions** /pɔʀtavjɔ̃/ *nm inv* aircraft carrier.

**porte-bagages** /pɔʀtbagaʒ/ *nm inv* (de vélo) carrier.

**porte-bonheur** /pɔʀtbɔnœʀ/ *nm inv* lucky charm.

**porte-clefs** /pɔʀtəkle/ *nm inv* key ring.

**porte-documents** /pɔʀtdɔkymɑ̃/ *nm inv* briefcase.

**portée** /pɔʀte/ *nf* (d'une arme) range; (de voûte) span; (d'animaux) litter; (impact) significance; (Mus) stave; **à ~ de (la) main** within (arm's) reach; **hors de ~ (de)** out of reach (of); **à la ~ de qn** at sb's level.

**porte-fenêtre** (*pl* **portes-fenêtres**) /pɔʀtfənɛtʀ/ *nf* French window.

**portefeuille** /pɔʀtəfœj/ *nm* wallet; (de ministre) portfolio.

**porte-jarretelles** /pɔʀtʒaʀtɛl/ *nm inv* suspender belt.

**portemanteau** (*pl* **~x**) /pɔʀtmɑ̃to/ *nm* coat *ou* hat stand.

**porte-monnaie** /pɔʀtmɔnɛ/ *nm inv* purse.

**porte-parole** /pɔʀtpaʀɔl/ *nm inv* spokesperson.

**porter** /pɔʀte/ [1] *vt* carry; (*vêtement, bague*) wear; (*fruits, responsabilité, nom*) bear; (*coup*) strike; (amener) bring; (inscrire) enter. ● *vi* (*bruit*) carry; (*coup*) hit home; **~ sur** rest on; (concerner) be about. □ **se ~** *vpr* **bien se ~** be *ou* feel well; **se ~ candidat** stand as a candidate.

**porteur, -euse** /pɔʀtœʀ, -øz/ *nm,f* (de nouvelles) bearer; (Méd) carrier. ● *nm* (Rail) porter.

**portier** /pɔʀtje/ *nm* doorman.

**portière** /pɔʀtjɛʀ/ *nf* door.

**porto** /pɔʀto/ *nm* port (wine).

**portrait** /pɔʀtʀɛ/ *nm* portrait. **portrait-robot** (*pl* **portraits-robots**) *nm* identikit®, photofit®.

**portuaire** /pɔʀtɥɛʀ/ *a* port.

**portugais, ~e** /pɔʀtygɛ, -z/ *a* Portuguese. ● *nm* (Ling) Portuguese. **P~, ~e** *nm,f* Portuguese.

**Portugal** /pɔʀtygal/ *nm* Portugal.

**pose** /poz/ *nf* installation; (attitude) pose; (Photo) exposure.

**posé, ~e** /poze/ *a* calm, serious.

**poser** /poze/ [1] *vt* put (down); (installer) install, put in; (*fondations*) lay; (*question*) ask; (*problème*) pose; **~ sa candidature** apply (**à** for). ● *vi* (*modèle*) pose. □ **se ~** *vpr* (*avion, oiseau*) land; (*regard*) fall; (se présenter) arise.

**positif, -ive** /pozitif, -v/ *a* positive.

**position** /pozisjɔ̃/ *nf* position; **prendre ~** take a stand.

**posologie** /pozɔlɔʒi/ *nf* dosage.

**posséder** /pɔsede/ [14] *vt* (*propriété*) own, possess; (*diplôme*) have.

**possessif, -ive** /pɔsesif, -v/ *a* possessive.

**possession** /pɔsesjɔ̃/ *nf* possession; **prendre ~ de** take possession of.

**possibilité** /pɔsibilite/ *nf* possibility.

**possible** /pɔsibl/ *a* possible; **dès que ~** as soon as possible; **le plus tard ~** as late as possible. ● *nm* **le ~** what is possible; **faire son ~** do one's utmost.

**postal, ~e** (*mpl* **-aux**) /pɔstal, -o/ *a* postal.

**poste** /pɔst/ *nf* (service) post; (bureau) post office; ~ **aérienne** airmail; **mettre à la** ~ post; ~ **restante** poste restante. ● *nm* (lieu, emploi) post; (de radio, télévision) set; (téléphone) extension (number); ~ **d'essence** petrol station; ~ **d'incendie** fire point; ~ **de pilotage** cockpit; ~ **de police** police station; ~ **de secours** first-aid post.

**poster**[1] /pɔste/ [1] *vt* (*lettre, personne*) post.

**poster**[2] /pɔstɛʀ/ *nm* poster.

**postérieur**, ~**e** /pɔsteʀjœʀ/ *a* later; (*partie*) back; ~ **à** after. ● *nm* [!] posterior.

**posthume** /pɔstym/ *a* posthumous.

**postiche** /pɔstiʃ/ *a* false.

**postier**, **-ière** /pɔstje, -jɛʀ/ *nm,f* postal worker.

**post-scriptum** /pɔstskʀiptɔm/ *nm inv* postscript.

**postuler** /pɔstyle/ [1] *vt/i* apply (**à** for); (*principe*) postulate.

**pot** /po/ *nm* pot; (en plastique) carton; (en verre) jar; (chance [!]) luck; (boisson [!]) drink; ~ **catalytique** catalytic converter; ~ **d'échappement** exhaust pipe.

**potable** /pɔtabl/ *a* **eau** ~ drinking water.

**potage** /pɔtaʒ/ *nm* soup.

**potager**, **-ère** /pɔtaʒe, -ɛʀ/ *a* vegetable. ● *nm* vegetable garden.

**pot-au-feu** /pɔtofø/ *nm inv* (plat) stew.

**pot-de-vin** (*pl* **pots-de-vin**) /podvɛ̃/ *nm* bribe.

**poteau** (*pl* ~**x**) /pɔto/ *nm* post; (télégraphique) pole; ~ **indicateur** signpost.

**potelé**, ~**e** /pɔtle/ *a* plump.

**potentiel**, ~**le** /pɔtɑ̃sjɛl/ *a* & *nm* potential.

**poterie** /pɔtʀi/ *nf* pottery; (objet) piece of pottery. **potier** *nm* potter.

**potins** /pɔtɛ̃/ *nmpl* gossip (+ *sg*).

**potiron** /pɔtiʀɔ̃/ *nm* pumpkin.

**pou** (*pl* ~**x**) /pu/ *nm* louse.

**poubelle** /pubɛl/ *nf* dustbin.

**pouce** /pus/ *nm* thumb; (de pied) big toe; (mesure) inch.

**poudre** /pudʀ/ *nf* powder; ~ (**à canon**) gunpowder; **en** ~ (*lait*) powdered; (*chocolat*) drinking.

**poudrier** /pudʀije/ *nm* (powder) compact.

**pouf** /puf/ *nm* pouffe.

**poulailler** /pulaje/ *nm* hen house.

**poulain** /pulɛ̃/ *nm* foal; (protégé) protégé.

**poule** /pul/ *nf* hen; (Culin) fowl; (femme [✱]) tart.

**poulet** /pulɛ/ *nm* chicken.

**pouliche** /puliʃ/ *nf* filly.

**poulie** /puli/ *nf* pulley.

**pouls** /pu/ *nm* pulse.

**poumon** /pumɔ̃/ *nm* lung.

**poupe** /pup/ *nf* stern.

**poupée** /pupe/ *nf* doll.

**pour** /puʀ/ *prép* for; (envers) to; (à la place de) on behalf of; (comme) as; ~ **cela** for that reason; ~ **cent** per cent; ~ **de bon** for good; ~ **faire** (in order) to do; ~ **que** so that; ~ **moi** (à mon avis) as for me; **trop poli** ~ too polite to; ~ **ce qui est de** as for; **être** ~ be in favour. ● *nm inv* **le** ~ **et le contre** the pros and cons.

**pourboire** /puʀbwaʀ/ *nm* tip.

**pourcentage** /puʀsɑ̃taʒ/ *nm* percentage.

**pourparlers** /puʀpaʀle/ *nmpl* talks.

**pourpre** /puʀpʀ/ *a* & *nm* crimson; (violet) purple.

**pourquoi** /purkwa/ *conj & adv* why. ● *nm inv* **le ~ et le comment** the why and the wherefore.

**pourra**, **pourrait** /pura, purɛ/ ⇒POUVOIR [49].

**pourri**, **~e** /puri/ *a* rotten. **pourrir** [2] *vt/i* rot. **pourriture** *nf* rot.

**poursuite** /pursɥit/ *nf* pursuit (**de** of); **~s** (Jur) legal action (+ *sg*).

**poursuivre** /pursɥivr/ [57] *vt* pursue; (continuer) continue (with); **~ (en justice)** take to court; (droit civil) sue. ● *vi* continue. □ **se ~** *vpr* continue.

**pourtant** /purtɑ̃/ *adv* yet.

**pourvoir** /purvwar/ [63] *vi* **~ à** provide for; **pourvu de** supplied with.

**pourvu que** /purvyk(ə)/ *conj* (condition) provided (that); (souhait) let us hope (that).

**pousse** /pus/ *nf* growth; (bourgeon) shoot.

**poussé**, **~e** /puse/ *a* (*études*) advanced; (*enquête*) thorough.

**poussée** /puse/ *nf* pressure; (coup) push; (de prix) upsurge; (Méd) attack.

**pousser** /puse/ [1] *vt* push; (*cri*) let out; (*soupir*) heave; (continuer) continue; (exhorter) urge (**à** to); (forcer) drive (**à** to). ● *vi* push; (grandir) grow; **faire ~** (*cheveux*) let grow; (*plante*) grow. □ **se ~** *vpr* move over *ou* up; **pousse-toi!** move over!

**poussette** /pusɛt/ *nf* pushchair.

**poussière** /pusjɛr/ *nf* dust. **poussiéreux**, **-euse** *a* dusty.

**poussin** /pusɛ̃/ *nm* chick.

**poutre** /putr/ *nf* beam; (en métal) girder.

**pouvoir** /puvwar/ [49] *v aux* (possibilité) can, be able; (permission, éventualité) may, can; **il peut/pouvait/pourrait venir** he can/could/might come; **je n'ai pas pu** I couldn't; **j'ai pu faire** (réussi à) I managed to do; **je n'en peux plus** I am exhausted; **il se peut que** it may be that. ● *nm* power; (gouvernement) government; **au ~** in power; **~s publics** authorities.

**prairie** /preri/ *nf* meadow.

**praticien**, **~ne** /pratisjɛ̃, -ɛn/ *nm,f* practitioner.

**pratiquant**, **~e** /pratikɑ̃, -t/ *a* practising. ● *nm,f* churchgoer.

**pratique** /pratik/ *a* practical. ● *nf* practice; (expérience) experience; **la ~ du golf/du cheval** golfing/riding. **pratiquement** *adv* (en pratique) in practice; (presque) practically.

**pratiquer** /pratike/ [1] *vt/i* practise; (Sport) play; (faire) make.

**pré** /pre/ *nm* meadow.

**préalable** /prealabl/ *a* preliminary, prior. ● *nm* precondition; **au ~** first.

**préambule** /preɑ̃byl/ *nm* preamble.

**préavis** /preavi/ *nm* notice.

**précaire** /prekɛr/ *a* precarious. **précarité** *nf* (d'emploi) insecurity.

**précaution** /prekosjɔ̃/ *nf* (mesure) precaution; (prudence) caution.

**précédent**, **~e** /presedɑ̃, -t/ *a* previous. ● *nm* precedent.

**précéder** /presede/ [14] *vt/i* precede.

**précepteur**, **-trice** /preseptœr, -tris/ *nm,f* (private) tutor.

**prêcher** /preʃe/ [1] *vt/i* preach.

**précieux**, **-ieuse** /presjø, -z/ *a* precious.

**précipitamment** /presipitamɑ̃/ *adv* hastily. **précipitation** *nf* haste.

**précipiter** /presipite/ [1] *vt* throw, precipitate; (hâter) hasten. □ **se ~** *vpr* (se dépêcher) rush (**sur**

at, on to); (se jeter) throw oneself; (s'accélérer) speed up.

**précis**, **~e** /pResi, -z/ *a* precise, specific; (*mécanisme*) accurate; **dix heures ~es** ten o'clock sharp. ● *nm* summary.

**préciser** /pResize/ [1] *vt* specify; **précisez votre pensée** could you be more specific. □ **se ~** *vpr* become clear(er). **précision** *nf* precision; (détail) detail.

**précoce** /pRekɔs/ *a* (*enfant*) precocious.

**préconiser** /pRekɔnize/ [1] *vt* advocate.

**précurseur** /pRekyRsœR/ *nm* forerunner.

**prédicateur** /pRedikatœR/ *nm* preacher.

**prédilection** /pRedilɛksjɔ̃/ *nf* preference.

**prédire** /pRediR/ [37] *vt* predict.

**prédominer** /pRedɔmine/ [1] *vi* predominate.

**préface** /pRefas/ *nf* preface.

**préfecture** /pRefɛktyR/ *nf* prefecture; **~ de police** police headquarters.

**préféré**, **~e** /pRefeRe/ *a* & *nm,f* favourite.

**préférence** /pRefeRɑ̃s/ *nf* preference, **de ~** preferably.

**préférentiel**, **~le** /pRefeRɑ̃sjɛl/ *a* preferential.

**préférer** /pRefeRe/ [14] *vt* prefer (**à** to); **~ faire** prefer to do; **je ne préfère pas** I'd rather not; **j'aurais préféré ne pas savoir** I wish I hadn't found out.

**préfet** /pRefɛ/ *nm* prefect; **~ de police** prefect *ou* chief of police.

**préfixe** /pRefiks/ *nm* prefix.

**préhistorique** /pReistɔRik/ *a* prehistoric.

**préjudice** /pReʒydis/ *nm* harm, prejudice; **porter ~ à** harm.

**préjugé** /pReʒyʒe/ *nm* prejudice; **être plein de ~s** be very prejudiced.

**prélasser** (**se**) /(sə)pRelɑse/ [1] *vpr* loll (about).

**prélèvement** /pRelɛvmɑ̃/ *nm* deduction; (de sang) sample. **prélever** [6] *vt* deduct (**sur** from); (*sang*) take.

**préliminaire** /pRelimineR/ *a* & *nm* preliminary; **~s** (sexuels) foreplay.

**prématuré**, **~e** /pRematyRe/ *a* premature. ● *nm* premature baby.

**premier**, **-ière** /pRəmje, -jɛR/ *a* first; (*rang*) front, first; (*enfance*) early; (*nécessité, souci*) prime; (*qualité*) top, prime; **de ~ ordre** first-rate; **~ ministre** Prime Minister. ● *nm,f* first (one). ● *nm* (date) first; (étage) first floor; **en ~** first. **première** *nf* (Rail) first class; (exploit jamais vu) first; (cinéma, Théât) première; (Aut) (vitesse) first (gear). **premièrement** *adv* firstly.

**prémunir** /pRemyniR/ [2] *vt* protect (**contre** against).

**prenant**, **~e** /pRənɑ̃, -t/ *a* (*activité*) engrossing; (*enfant*) demanding.

**prénatal**, **~e** (*mpl* **~s**) /pRenatal/ *a* antenatal.

**prendre** /pRɑ̃dR/ [50] *vt* take; (attraper) catch, get; (acheter) get; (*repas*) have; (engager, adopter) take on; (*poids*) put on; (chercher) pick up; **qu'est-ce qui te prend?** what's the matter with you? ● *vi* (*liquide*) set; (*feu*) catch; (*vaccin*) take. □ **se ~** *vpr* **se ~ pour** think one is; **s'en ~ à** attack; (rendre responsable) blame; **s'y ~** set about (it).

**preneur**, **-euse** /pRənœR, -øz/ *nm,f* buyer; **être ~** be willing to buy; **trouver ~** find a buyer.

**prénom** /pRenɔ̃/ *nm* first name.

**prénommer** /pRenɔme/ [1] *vt* call. □ **se** ~ *vpr* be called.

**préoccupation** /pReɔkypasjɔ̃/ *nf* (souci) worry; (idée fixe) preoccupation.

**préoccuper** /pReɔkype/ [1] *vt* worry; (absorber) preoccupy. □ **se** ~ **de** *vpr* think about.

**préparation** /pReparasjɔ̃/ *nf* preparation. **préparatoire** *a* preparatory.

**préparer** /pRepaRe/ [1] *vt* prepare; (*repas, café*) make; **plats préparés** ready-cooked meals. □ **se** ~ *vpr* prepare oneself (**à** for); (s'apprêter) get ready; (être proche) be brewing.

**préposé**, ~**e** /pRepoze/ *nm,f* employee; (des postes) postman, postwoman.

**préposition** /pRepozisjɔ̃/ *nf* preposition.

**préretraite** /pReRətRɛt/ *nf* early retirement.

**près** /pRɛ/ *adv* near, close; ~ **de** near (to), close to; (presque) nearly; **à cela** ~ except that; **de** ~ closely.

**présage** /pRezaʒ/ *nm* omen.

**presbyte** /pRɛsbit/ *a* long-sighted, far-sighted.

**prescrire** /pRɛskRiR/ [30] *vt* prescribe.

**préséance** /pReseɑ̃s/ *nf* precedence.

**présence** /pRezɑ̃s/ *nf* presence; (Scol) attendance.

**présent**, ~**e** /pRezɑ̃, -t/ *a* present. ● *nm* (temps, cadeau) present; **à** ~ now.

**présentateur**, **-trice** /pResɑ̃tatœR, -tRis/ *nm,f* presenter.

**présentation** /pRezɑ̃tasjɔ̃/ *nf* (de personne) introduction; (exposé) presentation.

**présenter** /pRezɑ̃te/ [1] *vt* present; (*personne*) introduce (**à** to); (montrer) show. ● *vi* ~ **bien** have a pleasing appearance. □ **se** ~ *vpr* introduce oneself (**à** to); (aller) go; (apparaître) appear; (*candidat*) come forward; (*occasion*) arise; **se** ~ **à** (*examen*) sit for; (*élection*) stand for; **se** ~ **bien** look good.

**préservatif** /pRezɛRvatif/ *nm* condom.

**préserver** /pRezɛRve/ [1] *vt* protect.

**présidence** /pRezidɑ̃s/ *nf* (d'État) presidency; (de société) chairmanship.

**président**, ~**e** /pRezidɑ̃, -t/ *nm,f* president; (de société, comité) chairman, chairwoman; ~**-directeur général** managing director.

**présidentiel**, ~**le** /pRezidɑ̃sjɛl/ *a* presidential.

**présider** /pRezide/ [1] *vt* preside.

**présomptueux**, **-euse** /pRezɔ̃ptɥø, -z/ *a* presumptuous.

**presque** /pRɛsk(ə)/ *adv* almost, nearly; ~ **jamais** hardly ever; ~ **rien** hardly anything; ~ **pas (de)** hardly any.

**presqu'île** /pRɛskil/ *nf* peninsula.

**pressant**, ~**e** /pRɛsɑ̃, -t/ *a* pressing, urgent.

**presse** /pRɛs/ *nf* (journaux, appareil) press.

**pressé**, ~**e** /pRese/ *a* in a hurry; (*orange, citron*) freshly squeezed.

**pressentiment** /pRɛsɑ̃timɑ̃/ *nm* premonition. **pressentir** [46] *vt* have a premonition of.

**presser** /pRese/ [1] *vt* squeeze, press; (appuyer sur, harceler) press; (hâter) hasten; (inciter) urge (**de** to). ● *vi* (*temps*) press; (*affaire*) be pressing. □ **se** ~ *vpr* (se hâter) hurry; (se grouper) crowd.

**pressing** /pʀesiŋ/ *nm* (teinturerie) dry-cleaner's.

**pression** /pʀɛsjɔ̃/ *nf* pressure; (bouton) press-stud.

**prestance** /pʀɛstɑ̃s/ *nf* (imposing) presence.

**prestation** /pʀɛstasjɔ̃/ *nf* allowance; (d'artiste) performance.

**prestidigitation** /pʀɛstidiʒitasjɔ̃/ *nf* conjuring.

**prestige** /pʀɛstiʒ/ *nm* prestige. **prestigieux**, **-ieuse** *a* prestigious.

**présumer** /pʀezyme/ [1] *vt* presume; ~ **que** assume that; ~ **de** overrate.

**prêt**, ~**e** /pʀɛ, -t/ *a* ready (**à qch** for sth, **à faire** to do). ● *nm* loan. **prêt-à-porter** *nm inv* ready-to-wear clothes.

**prétendre** /pʀetɑ̃dʀ/ [3] *vt* claim (**que** that); (vouloir) intend; **on le prétend riche** he is said to be very rich. **prétendu**, ~**e** *a* so-called. **prétendument** *adv* supposedly, allegedly.

**prétentieux**, **-ieuse** /pʀetɑ̃sjø, -z/ *a* pretentious.

**prêter** /pʀete/ [1] *vt* lend (**à** to); (*attribuer*) attribute; ~ **son aide à qn** give sb some help; ~ **attention** pay attention; ~ **serment** take an oath. ● *vi* ~ **à** lead to.

**prêteur**, **-euse** /pʀɛtœʀ, -øz/ *nm,f* (money-)lender; ~ **sur gages** pawnbroker.

**prétexte** /pʀetɛkst/ *nm* pretext, excuse.

**prêtre** /pʀɛtʀ/ *nm* priest.

**preuve** /pʀœv/ *nf* proof; **des** ~**s** evidence (+ *sg*); **faire** ~ **de** show; **faire ses** ~**s** prove oneself.

**prévaloir** /pʀevalwaʀ/ [60] *vi* prevail.

**prévenant**, ~**e** /pʀevnɑ̃, -t/ *a* thoughtful.

**prévenir** /pʀevniʀ/ [58] *vt* (menacer) warn; (informer) tell; (*médecin*) call; (éviter, anticiper) prevent.

**préventif**, **-ive** /pʀevɑ̃tif, -v/ *a* preventive.

**prévention** /pʀevɑ̃sjɔ̃/ *nf* prevention; **faire de la** ~ take preventive action; ~ **routière** road safety.

**prévenu**, ~**e** /pʀevny/ *nm,f* defendant.

**prévisible** /pʀevizibl/ *a* predictable. **prévision** *nf* prediction; (météorologique) forecast.

**prévoir** /pʀevwaʀ/ [63] *vt* foresee; (*temps*) forecast; (organiser) plan (for) provide for; (envisager) allow (for); **prévu pour** (*jouet*) designed for; **comme prévu** as planned.

**prévoyance** /pʀevwajɑ̃s/ *nf* foresight. **prévoyant**, ~**e** *a* far-sighted.

**prier** /pʀije/ [45] *vi* pray. ● *vt* pray to; (demander à) ask (**de** to); **je vous en prie** please; (il n'y a pas de quoi) don't mention it.

**prière** /pʀijɛʀ/ *nf* prayer; (demande) request; ~ **de** (vous êtes prié de) will you please.

**primaire** /pʀimɛʀ/ *a* primary.

**prime** /pʀim/ *nf* free gift; (d'employé) bonus; (subvention) subsidy; (d'assurance) premium.

**primé**, ~**e** /pʀime/ *a* prize-winning.

**primeurs** /pʀimœʀ/ *nfpl* early fruit and vegetables.

**primevère** /pʀimvɛʀ/ *nf* primrose.

**primitif**, **-ive** /pʀimitif, -v/ *a* primitive; (d'origine) original. ● *nm,f* primitive.

**primordial**, ~**e** (*mpl* **-iaux**) /pʀimɔʀdjal, -jo/ *a* essential.

**prince** /pRɛ̃s/ *nm* prince. **princesse** *nf* princess. **princier, -ière** *a* princely.

**principal**, ~**e** (*mpl* **-aux**) /pRɛ̃sipal, -o/ *a* main, principal. ● *nm* headmaster; (chose) main thing.

**principe** /pRɛ̃sip/ *nm* principle; **en** ~ in theory; (d'habitude) as a rule.

**printanier, -ière** /pRɛ̃tanje, -jɛR/ *a* spring(-like).

**printemps** /pRɛ̃tɑ̃/ *nm* spring.

**prioritaire** /pRijɔRitɛR/ *a* priority; **être** ~ have priority. **priorité** *nf* priority; (Auto) right of way.

**pris**, ~**e** /pRi, -z/ *a* (*place*) taken; (*personne, journée*) busy; (*nez*) stuffed up; ~ **de** (*peur, fièvre*) stricken with; ~ **de panique** panic-stricken. ● ⇒PRENDRE [50].

**prise** /pRiz/ *nf* hold, grip; (animal attrapé) catch; (Mil) capture; ~ **(de courant)** (mâle) plug; (femelle) socket; ~ **multiple** multiplug adapter; **avoir** ~ **sur qn** have a hold over sb; **aux** ~**s avec** to grips with; ~ **de conscience** awareness; ~ **de contact** first contact, initial meeting; ~ **de position** stand; ~ **de sang** blood test.

**prisé**, ~**e** /pRize/ *a* popular.

**prison** /pRizɔ̃/ *nf* prison, jail; (réclusion) imprisonment. **prisonnier, -ière** *nm,f* prisoner.

**privation** /pRivasjɔ̃/ *nf* deprivation; (sacrifice) hardship.

**privatiser** /pRivatize/ [1] *vt* privatize.

**privé** /pRive/ *a* private. ● *nm* (Comm) private sector; (Scol) private schools (+ *pl*); **en** ~ in private.

**priver** /pRive/ [1] *vt* ~ **de** deprive of. □ **se** ~ **(de)** *vpr* go without.

**privilège** /pRivilɛʒ/ *nm* privilege. **privilégié**, ~**e** *nm,f* privileged person.

**prix** /pRi/ *nm* price; (récompense) prize; **à tout** ~ at all costs; **au** ~ **de** (fig) at the expense of; ~ **coûtant**, ~ **de revient** cost price; **à** ~ **fixe** set price.

**probabilité** /pRɔbabilite/ *nf* probability. **probable** *a* probable, likely. **probablement** *adv* probably.

**probant**, ~**e** /pRɔbɑ̃, -t/ *a* convincing, conclusive.

**problème** /pRɔblɛm/ *nm* problem.

**procédé** /pRɔsede/ *nm* process; (manière d'agir) practice.

**procéder** /pRɔsede/ [14] *vi* proceed; ~ **à** carry out.

**procès** /pRɔsɛ/ *nm* (criminel) trial; (civil) lawsuit, proceedings (+ *pl*).

**processus** /pRɔsesys/ *nm* process; ~ **de paix** peace process.

**procès-verbal** (*pl* **procès-verbaux**) /pRɔsɛvɛRbal, -o/ *nm* minutes (+ *pl*); (contravention) ticket.

**prochain**, ~**e** /pRɔʃɛ̃, -ɛn/ *a* (suivant) next; (proche) imminent; (*avenir*) near. ● *nm* fellow man. **prochainement** *adv* soon.

**proche** /pRɔʃ/ *a* near, close; (avoisinant) neighbouring; (*parent, ami*) close; ~ **de** close *ou* near to; **de** ~ **en** ~ gradually; **dans un** ~ **avenir** in the near future; **être** ~ (imminent) be approaching. ● *nm* close relative; (ami) close friend.

**Proche-Orient** /pRɔʃɔRjɑ̃/ *nm* Near East.

**proclamation** /pRɔklamasjɔ̃/ *nf* declaration, proclamation. **proclamer** [1] *vt* declare, proclaim.

**procuration** /pRɔkyRasjɔ̃/ *nf* proxy.

**procurer** /pRɔkyRe/ [1] *vt* bring (**à** to). □ **se** ~ *vpr* obtain.

**procureur** /pRɔkyRœR/ *nm* public prosecutor.

**prodige** /pʀɔdiʒ/ *nm* (fait) marvel; (personne) prodigy; **enfant/musicien ~** child/musical prodigy. **prodigieux, -ieuse** *a* tremendous, prodigious.

**prodigue** /pʀɔdig/ *a* wasteful; **fils ~** prodigal son.

**producteur, -trice** /pʀɔdyktœʀ, -tʀis/ *a* producing. ● *nm,f* producer. **productif, -ive** *a* productive. **production** *nf* production; (*produit*) product. **productivité** *nf* productivity.

**produire** /pʀɔdɥiʀ/ [17] *vt* produce. □ **se ~** *vpr* (survenir) happen; (*acteur*) perform.

**produit** /pʀɔdɥi/ *nm* product; **~s** (de la terre) produce (+ *sg*); **~ chimique** chemical; **~s alimentaires** foodstuffs; **~ de consommation** consumer goods; **~ intérieur brut** gross domestic product; **~ national brut** gross national product.

**proéminent, ~e** /pʀɔeminɑ̃, -t/ *a* prominent.

**profane** /pʀɔfan/ *a* secular. ● *nmf* lay person.

**proférer** /pʀɔfeʀe/ [14] *vt* utter.

**professeur** /pʀɔfɛsœʀ/ *nm* teacher; (Univ) lecturer; (avec chaire) professor.

**profession** /pʀɔfɛsjɔ̃/ *nf* occupation; **~ libérale** profession.

**professionnel, ~le** /pʀɔfɛsjɔnɛl/ *a* professional; (*école*) vocational. ● *nm,f* professional.

**profil** /pʀɔfil/ *nm* profile.

**profit** /pʀɔfi/ *nm* profit; **au ~ de** in aid of. **profitable** *a* profitable.

**profiter** /pʀɔfite/ [1] *vi* **~ à** benefit; **~ de** take advantage of.

**profond, ~e** /pʀɔfɔ̃, -d/ *a* deep, (*sentiment, intérêt*) profound; (*causes*) underlying; **au plus ~ de** in the depths of. **profondément** *adv* deeply; (*différent, triste*) profoundly; (*dormir*) soundly. **profondeur** *nf* depth.

**progéniture** /pʀɔʒenityʀ/ *nf* offspring.

**progiciel** /pʀɔʒisjɛl/ *nm* (Ordinat) package.

**programmation** /pʀɔgʀamasjɔ̃/ *nf* programming.

**programme** /pʀɔgʀam/ *nm* programme; (Scol) (d'une matière) syllabus; (général) curriculum; (Ordinat) program. **programmer** [1] *vt* (*ordinateur, appareil*) program; (*émission*) schedule. **programmeur, -euse** *nm,f* computer programmer.

**progrès** /pʀɔgʀɛ/ *nm & nmpl* progress; **faire des ~** make progress. **progresser** [1] *vi* progress. **progressif, -ive** *a* progressive. **progression** *nf* progression.

**prohibitif, -ive** /pʀɔibitif, -v/ *a* prohibitive.

**proie** /pʀwa/ *nf* prey; **en ~ à** tormented by.

**projecteur** /pʀɔʒɛktœʀ/ *nm* floodlight; (Mil) searchlight; (cinéma) projector.

**projectile** /pʀɔʒɛktil/ *nm* missile.

**projection** /pʀɔʒɛksjɔ̃/ *nf* projection; (séance) show.

**projet** /pʀɔʒɛ/ *nm* plan; (ébauche) draft; **~ de loi** bill.

**projeter** /pʀɔʒte/ [38] *vt* (prévoir) plan (**de** to); (*film*) project, show; (jeter) hurl, project.

**prolétaire** /pʀɔletɛʀ/ *nmf* proletarian.

**prologue** /pʀɔlɔg/ *nm* prologue.

**prolongation** /pʀɔlɔ̃gasjɔ̃/ *nf* extension; **~s** (football) extra time.

**prolonger** /pʀɔlɔ̃ʒe/ [40] *vt* extend. □ **se ~** *vpr* go on.

**promenade** /pʀɔmnad/ *nf* walk; (à bicyclette, à cheval) ride; (en auto)

drive, ride; **faire une ~** go for a walk.

**promener** /pʀɔmne/ [6] *vt* take for a walk; **~ son regard sur** cast an eye over. □ **se ~** *vpr* walk; **(aller) se ~** go for a walk. **promeneur, -euse** *nm,f* walker.

**promesse** /pʀɔmɛs/ *nf* promise.

**prometteur, -euse** /pʀɔmɛtœʀ, -øz/ *a* promising.

**promettre** /pʀɔmɛtʀ/ [42] *vt/i* promise. ● *vi* be promising. □ **se ~ de** *vpr* resolve to.

**promoteur** /pʀɔmɔtœʀ/ *nm* (immobilier) property developer.

**promotion** /pʀɔmɔsjɔ̃/ *nf* promotion; (Univ) year; (Comm) special offer.

**prompt, ~e** /pʀɔ̃, -t/ *a* swift.

**promu, ~e** /pʀɔmy/ *a* **être ~** be promoted.

**prôner** /pʀone/ [1] *vt* extol.

**pronom** /pʀɔnɔ̃/ *nm* pronoun. **pronominal, ~e** (*mpl* **-aux**) *a* pronominal.

**prononcé, ~e** /pʀɔnɔ̃se/ *a* strong.

**prononcer** /pʀɔnɔ̃se/ [10] *vt* pronounce; (*discours*) make. □ **se ~** *vpr* (*mot*) be pronounced; (*personne*) make a decision (**pour** in favour of). **prononciation** *nf* pronunciation.

**pronostic** /pʀɔnɔstik/ *nm* forecast; (Méd) prognosis.

**propagande** /pʀɔpagɑ̃d/ *nf* propaganda.

**propager** /pʀɔpaʒe/ [40] *vt* spread. □ **se ~** *vpr* spread.

**prophète** /pʀɔfɛt/ *nm* prophet. **prophétie** *nf* prophecy.

**propice** /pʀɔpis/ *a* favourable.

**proportion** /pʀɔpɔʀsjɔ̃/ *nf* proportion; (en mathématiques) ratio; **toutes ~s gardées** relatively speaking. **proportionné, ~e** *a* proportionate (**à** to). **proportionnel, ~le** *a* proportional. **proportionnellement** *adv* proportionately.

**propos** /pʀɔpo/ *nm* intention; (sujet) subject; **à ~** at the right time; (dans un dialogue) by the way; **à ~ de** about; **à tout ~** at every possible occasion. ● *nmpl* (paroles) remarks.

**proposer** /pʀɔpoze/ [1] *vt* suggest, propose; (offrir) offer. □ **se ~** *vpr* volunteer (**pour** to). **proposition** *nf* proposal; (affirmation) proposition; (Gram) clause.

**propre** /pʀɔpʀ/ *a* (non sali) clean; (soigné) neat; (honnête) decent; (à soi) own; (*sens*) literal; **~ à** (qui convient) suited to; (spécifique) particular to. ● *nm* **mettre au ~** write out again neatly; **c'est du ~!** (ironique) well done!

**proprement** /pʀɔpʀəmɑ̃/ *adv* (avec soin) neatly; (au sens strict) strictly; **le bureau ~ dit** the office itself.

**propreté** /pʀɔpʀəte/ *nf* cleanliness.

**propriétaire** /pʀɔpʀijetɛʀ/ *nmf* owner; (Comm) proprietor; (qui loue) landlord, landlady.

**propriété** /pʀɔpʀijete/ *nf* property; (droit) ownership.

**propulser** /pʀɔpylse/ [1] *vt* propel.

**proroger** /pʀɔʀɔʒe/ [40] *vt* (*contrat*) defer; (*passeport*) extend.

**proscrire** /pʀɔskʀiʀ/ [30] *vt* proscribe.

**proscrit, ~e** /pʀɔskʀi, -t/ *a* proscribed. ● *nm,f* (exilé) exile.

**prose** /pʀoz/ *nf* prose.

**prospectus** /pʀɔspɛktys/ *nm* leaflet.

**prospère** /pʀɔspɛʀ/ *a* flourishing, thriving. **prospérer** [14] *vi* thrive, prosper. **prospérité** *nf* prosperity.

**prosterner (se)** /(sə)pRɔstɛRne/ [1] *vpr* prostrate oneself; **prosterné devant** prostrate before.

**prostituée** /pRɔstitɥe/ *nf* prostitute. **prostitution** *nf* prostitution.

**protecteur**, **-trice** /pRɔtɛktœR, -tRis/ *nm,f* protector. ● *a* protective.

**protection** /pRɔtɛksjɔ̃/ *nf* protection.

**protégé**, **~e** /pRɔteʒe/ *nm,f* protégé.

**protéger** /pRɔteʒe/ [40] *vt* protect. □ **se ~** *vpr* protect oneself.

**protéine** /pRɔtein/ *nf* protein.

**protestant**, **~e** /pRɔtɛstɑ̃, -t/ *a & nm, f* Protestant.

**protestation** /pRɔtɛstasjɔ̃/ *nf* protest. **protester** [1] *vt/i* protest.

**protocole** /pRɔtɔkɔl/ *nm* protocol.

**protubérant**, **~e** /pRɔtybeRɑ̃/ *a* protruding.

**proue** /pRu/ *nf* bow, prow.

**prouesse** /pRuɛs/ *nf* feat, exploit.

**prouver** /pRuve/ [1] *vt* prove.

**provenance** /pRɔvnɑ̃s/ *nf* origin; **en ~ de** from.

**provençal**, **~e** (*mpl* **-aux**) /pRɔvɑ̃sal, -o/ *a & nm,f* Provençal.

**provenir** /pRɔvniR/ [58] *vi* **~ de** come from.

**proverbe** /pRɔvɛRb/ *nm* proverb.

**province** /pRɔvɛ̃s/ *nf* province; **de ~** provincial; **la ~** the provinces (+ *pl*). **provincial**, **~e** (*mpl* **-iaux**) *a & nm, f* provincial.

**proviseur** /pRɔvizœR/ *nm* headmaster, principal.

**provision** /pRɔvizjɔ̃/ *nf* supply, store; (sur un compte) credit (balance); (acompte) deposit; **~s** (vivres) food shopping.

**provisoire** /pRɔvizwaR/ *a* provisional.

**provocant**, **~e** /pRɔvɔkɑ̃, -t/ *a* provocative. **provocation** *nf* provocation. **provoquer** [1] *vt* cause; (sexuellement) arouse; (défier) provoke.

**proxénète** /pRɔksenɛt/ *nm* pimp, procurer.

**proximité** /pRɔksimite/ *nf* proximity; **à ~ de** close to.

**prude** /pRyd/ *a* prudish.

**prudemment** /pRydamɑ̃/ *adv* (*conduire*) carefully; (*attendre*) cautiously. **prudence** *nf* caution. **prudent**, **~e** *a* (au volant) careful; (à agir) cautious; (sage) wise.

**prune** /pRyn/ *nf* plum.

**pruneau** (*pl* **~x**) /pRyno/ *nm* prune.

**prunelle** /pRynɛl/ *nf* (pupille) pupil, (fruit) sloe.

**prunier** /pRynje/ *nm* plum tree.

**psaume** /psom/ *nm* psalm.

**pseudonyme** /psødɔnim/ *nm* pseudonym.

**psychanalyse** /psikanaliz/ *nf* psychoanalysis. **psychanalyste** *nmf* psychoanalyst.

**psychiatre** /psikjatR/ *nmf* psychiatrist. **psychiatrie** *nf* psychiatry. **psychiatrique** *a* psychiatric.

**psychique** /psiʃik/ *a* mental, psychological.

**psychologie** /psikɔlɔʒi/ *nf* psychology. **psychologique** *a* psychological. **psychologue** *nmf* psychologist.

**pu** /py/ ⇒POUVOIR [49].

**puant**, **~e** /pɥɑ̃, -t/ *a* stinking.

**pub** /pyb/ *nf* Ⓘ **la ~** advertising; **une ~** an advert.

**puberté** /pybɛRte/ *nf* puberty.

**public**, **-que** /pyblik/ *a* public. ● *nm* public; (assistance) audience;

(Scol) state schools (+ *pl*); **en ~** in public.

**publication** /pyblikasjɔ̃/ *nf* publication.

**publicitaire** /pyblisitɛʀ/ *a* publicity. **publicité** *nf* publicity, advertising; (annonce) advertisement.

**publier** /pyblije/ [45] *vt* publish.

**publiquement** /pyblikmɑ̃/ *adv* publicly.

**puce** /pys/ *nf* flea; (électronique) chip; **marché aux ~s** flea market.

**pudeur** /pydœʀ/ *nf* modesty.

**pudibond**, **~e** /pydibɔ̃, -d/ *a* prudish.

**pudique** /pydik/ *a* modest.

**puer** /pɥe/ [1] *vi* stink. ● *vt* stink of.

**puéricultrice** /pɥeʀikyltʀis/ *nf* pediatric nurse.

**puéril**, **~e** /pɥeʀil/ *a* puerile.

**puis** /pɥi/ *adv* then.

**puiser** /pɥize/ [1] *vt* draw (**dans** from). ● *vi* **~ dans qch** dip into sth.

**puisque** /pɥisk(ə)/ *conj* since, as.

**puissance** /pɥisɑ̃s/ *nf* power; **en ~** potential.

**puissant**, **~e** /pyisɑ̃, -t/ *a* powerful.

**puits** /pɥi/ *nm* well; (de mine) shaft.

**pull(-over)** /pyl(ɔvɛʀ)/ *nm* pullover, jumper.

**pulpe** /pylp/ *nf* pulp.

**pulsation** /pylsasjɔ̃/ *nf* (heart-) beat.

**pulvériser** /pylveʀize/ [1] *vt* pulverize; (*liquide*) spray.

**punaise** /pynɛz/ *nf* (insecte) bug; (clou) drawing-pin.

**punch**[1] /pɔ̃ʃ/ *nm* (boisson) punch.

**punch**[2] /pœnʃ/ *nm* **avoir du ~** have drive.

**punir** /pyniʀ/ [2] *vt* punish. **punition** *nf* punishment.

**pupille** /pypij/ *nf* (de l'œil) pupil. ● *nmf* (enfant) ward.

**pupitre** /pypitʀ/ *nm* (Scol) desk; **~ à musique** music stand.

**pur** /pyʀ/ *a* pure; (*whisky*) neat.

**purée** /pyʀe/ *nf* purée; (de pommes de terre) mashed potatoes (+ *pl*).

**pureté** /pyʀte/ *nf* purity.

**purgatoire** /pyʀgatwaʀ/ *nm* purgatory.

**purge** /pyʀʒ/ *nf* purge. **purger** [40] *vt* (Pol, Méd) purge; (*peine*: Jur) serve.

**purifier** /pyʀifje/ [45] *vt* purify.

**puritain**, **~e** /pyʀitɛ̃, -ɛn/ *nm,f* puritan. ● *a* puritanical.

**pur-sang** /pyʀsɑ̃/ *nm inv* (cheval) thoroughbred.

**pus** /py/ *nm* pus.

**putain** /pytɛ̃/ *nf* ⊠ whore.

**puzzle** /pœzl/ *nm* jigsaw (puzzle).

**P-V** *abrév m* (**procès-verbal**) ticket, traffic fine.

**pyjama** /piʒama/ *nm* pyjamas (+ *pl*); **un ~** a pair of pyjamas.

**pylône** /pilon/ *nm* pylon.

**Pyrénées** /piʀene/ *nfpl* **les ~** the Pyrenees.

**pyromane** /piʀɔman/ *nmf* arsonist.

# Qq

**QG** *abrév m* (**quartier général**) HQ.

**QI** *abrév m* (**quotient intellectuel**) IQ.

**qu'** /k/ ⇒QUE.

**quadriller** /kadʀije/ [1] *vt* (*armée*) take control of; (*police*) spread one's net over; **papier quadrillé** squared paper.

**quadrupède** /kadʀypɛd/ *nm* quadruped.

**quadruple** /kadʀypl/ *a* quadruple. ● *nm* **le ~ de** four times. **quadrupler** [1] *vt*/*i* quadruple.

**quai** /ke/ *nm* (de gare) platform; (de port) quay; (de rivière) bank.

**qualification** /kalifikasjɔ̃/ *nf* qualification; (compétence pratique) skills (+ *pl*).

**qualifié**, **~e** /kalifje/ *a* (diplomé) qualified; (*main-d'œuvre*) skilled.

**qualifier** /kalifje/ [45] *vt* qualify; (décrire) describe (**de** as). □ **se ~** *vpr* qualify (**pour** for).

**qualité** /kalite/ *nf* quality; (titre) occupation; (fonction) position; **en sa ~ de** in his *ou* her capacity as.

**quand** /kɑ̃/ *adv* when; **~ même** all the same. ● *conj* when; (toutes les fois que) whenever; **~ bien même** even if.

**quant à** /kɑta/ *prép* as for.

**quantité** /kɑ̃tite/ *nf* quantity; **une ~ de** a lot of; **des ~s (de)** masses *ou* lots (*of*).

**quarantaine** /kaʀɑ̃tɛn/ *nf* (Méd) quarantine; **une ~ (de)** about forty; **avoir la ~** be in one's forties.

**quarante** /kaʀɑ̃t/ *a* & *nm* forty.

**quart** /kaʀ/ *nm* quarter; (Naut) watch; **onze heures moins le ~** quarter to eleven; **~ (de litre)** quarter litre; **~ de finale** quarter-final; **~ d'heure** quarter of an hour; **~ de tour** ninety-degree turn.

**quartier** /kaʀtje/ *nm* area, district; (zone ethnique) quarter; (de lune, pomme, bœuf) quarter; (d'une orange) segment; **~s** (Mil) quarters; **de ~** local; **~ général** headquarters; **avoir ~ libre** be free.

**quasiment** /kazimɑ̃/ *adv* almost, practically.

**quatorze** /katɔʀz/ *a* & *nm* fourteen.

**quatre** /katʀ(ə)/ *a* & *nm* four. **quatre-vingt(s)** *a* & *nm* eighty. **quatre-vingt-dix** *a* & *nm* ninety.

**quatrième** /katʀijɛm/ *a* & *nmf* fourth. ● *nf* (Auto) fourth gear.

**quatuor** /kwatɥɔʀ/ *nm* quartet.

---

**que**, **qu'** /kə, k/

qu' before vowel or mute h.

● *conjonction*

····➤ that; **je crains ~...** I'm worried that...

····➤ (souhait, volonté) **je veux ~ tu viennes** I want you to come; **~ tu viennes ou non** whether you come or not; **qu'il entre** let him come in.

····➤ (comparaison) than; **plus grand ~ toi** taller than you.

● *pronom interrogatif*

····➤ what; **~ voulez-vous manger?** what would you like to eat?

● *pronom relatif*

····➤ (personne) whom, that; **l'homme ~ j'ai rencontré** the man (whom) I met.

····➤ (chose) that, which; **le cheval ~ Nick m'a offert** the horse (which) Nick gave me.

● *adverbe*

····➤ **~ c'est joli!** it's so pretty!; **~ de monde!** what a lot of people!

---

**Québec** /kebɛk/ *nm* Quebec.

**quel**, **quelle** (*pl* **quel(le)s**) /kɛl/

● *adjectif interrogatif*

····➤ which, what; ~ **auteur a écrit...?** which writer wrote...?; ~ **jour sommes-nous?** what day is it today?

● *adjectif exclamatif*

····➤ what; ~ **idiot!** what an idiot!; **quelle horreur!** that's horrible!

● *adjectif relatif*

····➤ ~ **que soit son âge** whatever his age; **quelles que soient tes raisons** whatever your reasons; ~ **que soit le gagnant** whoever the winner is.

**quelconque** /kɛlkɔ̃k/ *a* any, some; (banal) ordinary; (médiocre) poor, second rate.

**quelque** /kɛlkə/ *a* some; ~**s** a few, some. ● *adv* (environ) about, some; **et** ~ Ⓘ and a bit; ~ **chose** something; (dans les phrases interrogatives) anything; ~ **part** somewhere; ~ **peu** somewhat.

**quelquefois** /kɛlkəfwa/ *adv* sometimes.

**quelques-uns**, **-unes** /kɛlkəzœ̃, -yn/ *pron* some, a few.

**quelqu'un** /kɛlkœ̃/ *pron* someone, somebody; (dans les phrases interrogatives) anyone, anybody.

**querelle** /kəʀɛl/ *nf* quarrel. **quereller (se)** [1] *vpr* quarrel. **querelleur**, **-euse** *a* quarrelsome.

**question** /kɛstjɔ̃/ *nf* question; (affaire) matter, question; **poser une** ~ ask a question; **en** ~ in question; **il est** ~ **de** (cela concerne) it is about; (on parle de) there is talk of; **il n'en est pas** ~ it is out of the question; **pas** ~! no way!

**questionnaire** /kɛstjɔnɛʀ/ *nm* questionnaire.

**questionner** /kɛstjɔne/ [1] *vt* question.

**quête** /kɛt/ *nf* (Relig) collection; (recherche) search; **en** ~ **de** in search of.

**queue** /kø/ *nf* tail; (de poêle) handle; (de fruit) stalk; (de fleur) stem; (file) queue; (US) line; (de train) rear; **faire la** ~ queue (up); (US) line up; ~ **de cheval** pony-tail; **faire une** ~ **de poisson à qn** (Auto) cut in front of sb.

**qui** /ki/

● *pronom interrogatif*

····➤ (sujet) who; ~ **a fait ça?** who did that?

····➤ (complément) whom; **à** ~ **est ce livre?** whose book is this?

● *pronom relatif*

····➤ (personne sujet) who; **c'est Isabelle qui vient d'appeler** it's Isabelle who's just called.

····➤ (autres cas) that, which; **qu'est-ce** ~ **te prend?** what is the matter with you?; **invite** ~ **tu veux** invite whoever you want; ~ **que ce soit** whoever it is, anybody.

**quiche** /kiʃ/ *nf* quiche.

**quiconque** /kikɔ̃k/ *pron* whoever; (n'importe qui) anyone.

**quille** /kij/ *nf* (de bateau) keel; (jouet) skittle.

**quincaillerie** /kɛ̃kɑjʀi/ *nf* hardware; (magasin) hardware shop. **quincaillier**, **-ière** *nm,f* hardware dealer.

**quintal** (*pl* **-aux**) /kɛ̃tal, -o/ *nm* quintal, one hundred kilos.

**quinte** /kɛ̃t/ *nf* ~ **de toux** coughing fit.

**quintuple** /kɛ̃typl/ *a* quintuple. ● *nm* **le ~ de** five times. **quintupler** [1] *vt/i* quintuple, increase fivefold.

**quinzaine** /kɛ̃zɛn/ *nf* **une ~ (de)** about fifteen.

**quinze** /kɛ̃z/ *a & nm inv* fifteen; **~ jours** two weeks.

**quiproquo** /kipʀɔko/ *nm* misunderstanding.

**quittance** /kitɑ̃s/ *nf* receipt.

**quitte** /kit/ *a* quits (**envers** with); **~ à faire** even if it means doing.

**quitter** /kite/ [1] *vt* leave; (*vêtement*) take off; **ne quittez pas!** hold the line, please! □ **se ~** *vpr* part.

**qui-vive** /kiviv/ *nm inv* **être sur le ~** be alert.

**quoi** /kwa/ *pron* what; (après une préposition) which; **de ~ vivre** (assez) enough to live on; **de ~ écrire** something to write with; **~ qu'il dise** whatever he says; **~ que ce soit** anything; **il n'y a pas de ~** my pleasure; **il n'y a pas de ~ s'inquiéter** there's nothing to worry about.

**quoique** /kwak(ə)/ *conj* although, though.

**quota** /kɔta/ *nm* quota.

**quote-part** (*pl* **quotes-parts**) /kɔtpaʀ/ *nf* share.

**quotidien, ~ne** /kɔtidjɛ̃, -ɛn/ *a* daily; (banal) everyday. ● *nm* daily (paper); (vie quotidienne) everyday life. **quotidiennement** *adv* daily.

# Rr

**rabâcher** /ʀabɑʃe/ [1] *vt* keep repeating.

**rabais** /ʀabɛ/ *nm* reduction, discount. **rabaisser** [1] *vt* (déprécier) belittle, (réduire) reduce.

**rabat-joie** /ʀabajwa/ *nm inv* killjoy.

**rabattre** /ʀabatʀ/ [11] *vt* (*chapeau, visière*) pull down, (refermer) shut; (diminuer) reduce; (déduire) take off; (*col, drap*) turn down. □ **se ~** *vpr* (*se refermer*) close; (*véhicule*) cut back in; **se ~ sur** make do with.

**rabot** /ʀabo/ *nm* plane.

**rabougri, ~e** /ʀabugʀi/ *a* stunted.

**racaille** /ʀakɑj/ *nf* rabble.

**raccommoder** /ʀakɔmɔde/ [1] *vt* mend; (*personnes* Ⓘ) reconcile.

**raccompagner** /ʀakɔ̃paɲe/ [1] *vt* see *ou* take back (*home*).

**raccord** /ʀakɔʀ/ *nm* link; (de papier peint) join; (retouche) touch-up. **raccorder** [1] *vt* connect, join.

**raccourci** /ʀakuʀsi/ *nm* short cut; **en ~** in short.

**raccourcir** /ʀakuʀsiʀ/ [2] *vt* shorten. ● *vi* get shorter.

**raccrocher** /ʀakʀɔʃe/ [1] *vt* hang back up; (*passant*) grab hold of; (relier) connect; **~ le combiné** *or* **le téléphone** hang up. ● *vi* hang up. □ **se ~ à** *vpr* cling to; (se relier à) be connected to *ou* with.

**race** /ʀas/ *nf* race; (animale) breed; **de ~** (*chien*) pedigree; (*cheval*) thoroughbred.

**racheter** /ʀaʃte/ [6] *vt* buy (back); (acheter encore) buy more; (*nouvel*

*objet*) buy another; (*société*) buy out; ~ **des chaussettes** buy new socks. □ **se** ~ *vpr* make amends.

**racial**, ~**e** (*mpl* **-iaux**) /Rasjal, -o/ *a* racial.

**racine** /Rasin/ *nf* root; ~ **carrée/cubique** square/cube root.

**racisme** /Rasism/ *nm* racism. **raciste** *a* & *nmf* racist.

**racket** /Rakɛt/ *nm* racketeering.

**raclée** /Rɑkle/ *nf* ⓘ thrashing.

**racler** /Rɑkle/ [1] *vt* scrape. □ **se** ~ *vpr* **se** ~ **la gorge** clear one's throat.

**racolage** /Rakɔlaʒ/ *nm* soliciting.

**raconter** /Rakɔ̃te/ [1] *vt* (*histoire*) tell; (*vacances*) tell about; (*vie, épisode*) describe; ~ **à qn que** tell sb that, say to sb that; **qu'est-ce que tu racontes?** what are you talking about?

**radar** /RadaR/ *nm* radar.

**radeau** (*pl* ~**x**) /Rado/ *nm* raft.

**radiateur** /RadjatœR/ *nm* radiator; (électrique) heater.

**radiation** /Radjasjɔ̃/ *nf* radiation.

**radical**, ~**e** (*mpl* **-aux**) /Radikal, -o/ *a* radical. ● *nm* (*pl* **-aux**) radical.

**radieux**, **-ieuse** /Radjø, -z/ *a* radiant.

**radin**, ~**e** /Radɛ̃, -in/ *a* ⓘ stingy ⓘ.

**radio** /Radjo/ *nf* radio; **à la** ~ on the radio; (radiographie) X-ray.

**radioactif**, **-ive** /Radjɔaktif, -v/ *a* radioactive. **radioactivité** *nf* radioactivity.

**radiocassette** /Radjɔkasɛt/ *nf* radio cassette player.

**radiodiffuser** /Radjɔdifyze/ [1] *vt* broadcast.

**radiographie** /RadjɔgRafi/ *nf* (photographie) X-ray.

**radiomessageur** /Radjɔmesaʒœr/ *nm* pager.

**radis** /Radi/ *nm* radish; **ne pas avoir un** ~ ⓘ be broke.

**radoter** /Radɔte/ [1] *vi* ⓘ talk drivel.

**radoucir (se)** /(sə)RadusiR/ [2] *vpr* (*humeur*) improve; (*temps*) become milder.

**rafale** /Rafal/ *nf* (de vent) gust; (de mitraillette) burst.

**raffermir** /RafɛRmiR/ [2] *vt* strengthen. □ **se** ~ *vpr* become stronger.

**raffiné**, ~**e** /Rafine/ *a* refined. **raffinement** *nm* refinement.

**raffiner** /Rafine/ [1] *vt* refine. **raffinerie** *nf* refinery.

**raffoler** /Rafɔle/ [1] *vt* ⓘ ~ **de** be crazy about ⓘ.

**raffut** /Rafy/ *nm* ⓘ din.

**rafle** /Rɑfl/ *nf* (police) raid.

**rafraîchir** /RafReʃiR/ [2] *vt* cool (down); (*mur*) give a fresh coat of paint to; (*personne, mémoire*) refresh. □ **se** ~ *vpr* (boire) refresh oneself; (*temps*) get cooler. **rafraîchissant**, ~**e** *a* refreshing.

**rafraîchissement** /RafReʃismɑ̃/ *nm* (boisson) cold drink; ~**s** refreshments.

**ragaillardir** /RagajaRdiR/ [2] *vt* ⓘ cheer up.

**rage** /Raʒ/ *nf* rage; (maladie) rabies; **faire** ~ (*bataille, incendie*) rage; (*maladie*) be rife; ~ **de dents** raging toothache. **rageant**, ~**e** *a* infuriating.

**ragots** /Rago/ *nmpl* ⓘ gossip.

**ragoût** /Ragu/ *nm* stew.

**raid** /Rɛd/ *nm* (Mil) raid; (Sport) trek.

**raide** /Rɛd/ *a* stiff; (*côte*) steep; (*corde*) tight; (*cheveux*) straight. ● *adv* (monter, descendre) steeply. **raideur** *nf* stiffness; steepness.

**raidir** /RediR/ [2] *vt* (*corps*) tense. □ **se** ~ *vpr* tense up; (*position*) harden; (*corde*) tighten.

**raie** /Rɛ/ *nf* (ligne) line; (bande) strip; (de cheveux) parting; (poisson) skate.

**raifort** /RɛfɔR/ *nm* horseradish.

**rail** /Rɑj/ *nm* rail, track; **le** ~ (transport) rail.

**raisin** /Rɛzɛ̃/ *nm* **le** ~ grapes; ~ **sec** raisin; **un grain de** ~ a grape.

**raison** /Rɛzɔ̃/ *nf* reason; **à** ~ **de** at the rate of; **avec** ~ rightly; **avoir** ~ be right (**de faire** to do); **avoir** ~ **de qn** get the better of sb; **donner** ~ **à** prove right; **en** ~ **de** because of; ~ **de plus** all the more reason; **perdre la** ~ lose one's mind.

**raisonnable** /Rɛzɔnabl/ *a* reasonable, sensible.

**raisonnement** /Rɛzɔnmɑ̃/ *nm* reasoning; (propositions) argument.

**raisonner** /Rɛzɔne/ [1] *vi* think. ● *vt* (*personne*) reason with.

**rajeunir** /Raʒœniʀ/ [2] *vt* ~ **qn** make sb (look) younger; (moderniser) modernize; (Méd) rejuvenate. ● *vi* (*personne*) look younger.

**rajuster** /Raʒyste/ [1] *vt* straighten; (*salaires*) (re)adjust.

**ralenti**, ~**e** /Ralɑ̃ti/ *a* slow. ● *nm* (au cinéma) slow motion; **tourner au** ~ tick over, idle.

**ralentir** /Ralɑ̃tiR/ [2] *vt/i* slow down. □ **se** ~ *vpr* slow down.

**ralentisseur** /Ralɑ̃tisœR/ *nm* speed ramp.

**râler** /Rɑle/ [1] *vi* groan; (protester **I**) moan.

**rallier** /Ralje/ [45] *vt* rally; (rejoindre) rejoin. □ **se** ~ *vpr* rally; **se** ~ **à** (*avis*) come round to; (*parti*) join.

**rallonge** /Ralɔ̃ʒ/ *nf* (de table) leaf; (de fil électrique) extension lead.

**rallonger** [40] *vt* lengthen; (*séjour, fil, table*) extend.

**rallumer** /Ralyme/ [1] *vt* (*feu*) relight; (*lampe*) switch on again; (ranimer: fig) revive.

**rallye** /Rali/ *nm* rally.

**ramassage** /Ramasaʒ/ *nm* (cueillette) gathering; (d'ordures) collection; ~ **scolaire** school bus service.

**ramasser** /Ramase/ [1] *vt* pick up; (récolter) gather; (recueillir, rassembler) collect. □ **se** ~ *vpr* huddle up, curl up.

**rame** /Ram/ *nf* (aviron) oar; (train) train.

**ramener** /Ramne/ [1] *vt* (rapporter, faire revenir) bring back; (reconduire) take back; ~ **à** (réduire à) reduce to. □ **se** ~ *vpr* **I** turn up; **se** ~ **à** (*problème*) come down to.

**ramer** /Rame/ [1] *vi* row.

**ramollir** /RamɔliR/ [2] *vt* soften. □ **se** ~ *vpr* become soft.

**ramoneur** /RamɔnœR/ *nm* (chimney) sweep.

**rampe** /Rɑ̃p/ *nf* banisters; (pente) ramp; ~ **d'accès** (Auto) slip road; ~ **de lancement** launching pad.

**ramper** /Rɑ̃pe/ [1] *vi* crawl.

**rancard** /Rɑ̃kaR/ *nm* **I** date.

**rancart** /Rɑ̃kaR/ *nm* **mettre** *ou* **jeter au** ~ **I** scrap.

**rance** /Rɑ̃s/ *a* rancid.

**rancœur** /Rɑ̃kœR/ *nf* resentment.

**rançon** /Rɑ̃sɔ̃/ *nf* ransom. **rançonner** [1] *vt* rob, extort money from.

**rancune** /Rɑ̃kyn/ *nf* grudge; **sans** ~! no hard feelings! **rancunier, -ière** *a* vindictive.

**randonnée** /Rɑ̃dɔne/ *nf* walk, ramble; **la** ~ **à cheval** pony trekking; **faire une** ~ go walking *ou* rambling.

**rang** /Rɑ̃/ *nm* row; (hiérarchie, condition) rank; **se mettre en ~** line up; **au premier ~** in the first row; (fig) at the forefront; **de second ~** (péj) second-rate.

**rangée** /Rɑ̃ʒe/ *nf* row.

**rangement** /Rɑ̃ʒmɑ̃/ *nm* (de pièce) tidying (up); (espace) storage space.

**ranger** /Rɑʒe/ [40] *vt* put away; (*chambre*) tidy (up); (disposer) place. ▫ **se ~** *vpr* (*véhicule*) park; (s'écarter) stand aside; (*conducteur*) pull over; (s'assagir) settle down; **se ~ à** (*avis*) accept.

**ranimer** /Ranime/ [1] *vt* revive; (Méd) resuscitate. ▫ **se ~** *vpr* come round.

**rap** /Rap/ *nm* rap (music).

**rapace** /Rapas/ *nm* bird of prey. ● *a* grasping.

**rapatriement** /RapatRimɑ̃/ *nm* repatriation. **rapatrier** [45] *vt* repatriate.

**râpe** /Rɑp/ *nf* (Culin) grater; (lime) rasp.

**râpé**, **~e** /Rɑpe/ *a* (*vêtement*) threadbare; (*fromage*) grated.

**râper** /Rɑpe/ [1] *vt* grate; (*bois*) rasp.

**rapide** /Rapid/ *a* fast, rapid. ● *nm* (train) express (train); (cours d'eau) rapids (+ *pl*). **rapidement** *adv* fast, rapidly. **rapidité** *nf* speed.

**rappel** /Rapɛl/ *nm* recall; (deuxième avis) reminder; (de salaire) back pay; (Méd) booster; (de diplomate) recall; (de réservistes) call-up; (Théât) curtain call.

**rappeler** /Raple/ [38] *vt* (par téléphone) call back; (*réserviste*) call up; (*diplomate*) recall; (évoquer) recall; **~ qch à qn** remind sb of sth. ▫ **se ~** *vpr* remember, recall.

**rappeur, -euse** /RapœR, øz/ *nmf* rapper.

**rapport** /RapɔR/ *nm* connection; (compte-rendu) report; (profit) yield; **~s** (relations) relations; **en ~ avec** (accord) in keeping with; **mettre/se mettre en ~ avec** put/get in touch with; **par ~ à** (comparé à) compared with; (vis-à-vis de) with regard to; **~s (sexuels)** intercourse.

**rapporter** /RapɔRte/ [1] *vt* (ici) bring back; (là-bas) take back, return; (*profit*) bring in; (dire, répéter) report. ● *vi* (Comm) bring in a good return; (moucharder 🄸) tell tales. ▫ **se ~ à** *vpr* relate to.

**rapporteur**, **-euse** /RapɔRtœR, -øz/ *nm,f* (mouchard) tell-tale. ● *nm* protractor.

**rapprochement** /RapRɔʃmɑ̃/ *nm* reconciliation; (Pol) rapprochement; (rapport) connection; (comparaison) parallel.

**rapprocher** /RapRɔʃe/ *vt* move closer (**de** to); (réconcilier) bring together; (comparer) compare; (*date, rendez-vous*) bring forward. ▫ **se ~** *vpr* get *ou* come closer (**de** to); (*personnes, pays*) come together; (s'apparenter) be close (**de** to).

**rapt** /Rapt/ *nm* abduction.

**raquette** /Rakɛt/ *nf* (de tennis) racket; (de ping-pong) bat.

**rare** /RaR/ *a* rare; (insuffisant) scarce. **rarement** *adv* rarely, seldom. **rareté** *nf* rarity; scarcity.

**ras**, **~e** /Rɑ, Rɑz/ *adv* **coupé ~** cut short. ● *a* (*herbe, poil*) short; **à ~ de terre** very close to the ground; **en avoir ~ le bol** 🄸 be really fed up; **~e campagne** open country; **à ~ bord** to the brim.

**raser** /Rɑze/ [1] *vt* shave; (*cheveux, barbe*) shave off; (frôler) skim; (abattre) raze. ▫ **se ~** *vpr* shave.

**rasoir** /RɑzwaR/ *nm* razor. ● *a inv* 🄸 boring.

**rassasier** /Rasazje/ [45] *vt* satisfy, fill up; **être rassasié de** have had enough of.

**rassemblement** /Rasɑ̃bləmɑ̃/ *nm* gathering; (manifestation) rally.

**rassembler** /Rasɑ̃ble/ [1] *vt* gather; (*forces, courage*) summon up; (*idées*) collect. □ **se ~** *vpr* gather.

**rassis**, **~e** /Rasi, -z/ *a* (*pain*) stale.

**rassurer** /RasyRe/ [1] *vt* reassure. □ **se ~** *vpr* reassure oneself; **rassure-toi** don't worry.

**rat** /Ra/ *nm* rat.

**rate** /Rat/ *nf* spleen.

**raté**, **~e** /Rate/ *nm,f* (personne) failure. ● *nm* **avoir des ~s** (*voiture*) backfire.

**râteau** (*pl* **~x**) /Rɑto/ *nm* rake.

**râtelier** /Rɑtəlje/ *nm* hayrack; (dentier [!]) dentures.

**rater** /Rate/ [1] *vt* (*train, rendez-vous, cible*) miss; (gâcher) make a mess of, spoil; (*examen*) fail. ● *vi* fail.

**ratio** /Rasjo/ *nm* ratio.

**rationaliser** /Rasjɔnalize/ [1] *vt* rationalize.

**rationnel**, **~le** /Rasjɔnɛl/ *a* rational.

**rationnement** /Rasjɔnmɑ̃/ *nm* rationing.

**ratisser** /Ratise/ [1] *vt* rake; (fouiller) comb.

**rattacher** /Rataʃe/ [1] *vt* (*lacets*) tie up again; (*ceinture de sécurité, collier*) refasten; (relier) link; (incorporer) join.

**rattrapage** /RatRapaʒ/ *nm* (Comm) adjustment; **cours de ~** remedial lesson.

**rattraper** /RatRape/ [1] *vt* catch; (rejoindre) catch up with; (*retard, erreur*) make up for. □ **se ~** *vpr* catch up; (se dédommager) make up for it; **se ~ à** catch hold of.

**rature** /RatyR/ *nf* deletion.

**rauque** /Rok/ *a* raucous, harsh.

**ravager** /Ravaʒe/ [40] *vt* devastate, ravage.

**ravages** /Ravaʒ/ *nmpl* **faire des ~** wreak havoc.

**ravaler** /Ravale/ [1] *vt* (*façade*) clean; (*colère*) swallow.

**ravi**, **~e** /Ravi/ *a* delighted (**que** that).

**ravin** /Ravɛ̃/ *nm* ravine.

**ravir** /RaviR/ [2] *vt* delight; **~ qch à qn** rob sb of sth.

**ravissant**, **~e** /Ravisɑ̃, -t/ *a* beautiful.

**ravisseur**, **-euse** /RavisœR, -øz/ *nm,f* kidnapper.

**ravitaillement** /Ravitajmɑ̃/ *nm* provision of supplies (**de** to); (denrées) supplies; **~ en essence** refuelling.

**ravitailler** /Ravitaje/ [1] *vt* provide with supplies; (*avion*) refuel. □ **se ~** *vpr* stock up.

**raviver** /Ravive/ [1] *vt* revive; (*feu, colère*) rekindle.

**rayé**, **~e** /Reje/ *a* striped.

**rayer** /Reje/ [31] *vt* scratch; (biffer) cross out; **'~ la mention inutile'** 'delete as appropriate'.

**rayon** /Rɛjɔ̃/ *nm* ray; (étagère) shelf; (de magasin) department; (de roue) spoke; (de cercle) radius; **~ d'action** range; **~ de miel** honeycomb; **~ X** X-ray; **en connaître un ~** [!] know one's stuff [!].

**rayonnement** /Rɛjɔnmɑ̃/ *nm* (éclat) radiance; (influence) influence; (radiations) radiation. **rayonner** [1] *vi* radiate; (de joie) beam; (se déplacer) tour around (*from a central point*).

**rayure** /ʀɛjyʀ/ *nf* scratch; (dessin) stripe; **à ~s** striped.

**raz-de-marée** /ʀɑdmaʀe/ *nm inv* tidal wave; **~ électoral** electoral landslide.

**réacteur** /ʀeaktœʀ/ *nm* jet engine; (nucléaire) reactor.

**réaction** /ʀeaksjɔ̃/ *nf* reaction; **~ en chaîne** chain reaction; **moteur à ~** jet engine.

**réagir** /ʀeaʒiʀ/ [2] *vi* react; **~ sur** have an effect on.

**réalisateur**, **-trice** /ʀealizatœʀ, -tʀis/ *nm,f* (au cinéma) director; (TV) producer.

**réalisation** /ʀealizasjɔ̃/ *nf* (de rêve) fulfilment; (œuvre) achievement; (TV, cinéma) production; **projet en ~** project in progress.

**réaliser** /ʀealize/ [1] *vt* carry out; (*effort, bénéfice, achat*) make; (*rêve*) fulfil; (*film*) direct; (*capital*) realize; (se rendre compte de) realize. □ **se ~** *vpr* be fulfilled.

**réalisme** /ʀealism/ *nm* realism.

**réaliste** /ʀealist/ *a* realistic. ● *nmf* realist.

**réalité** /ʀealite/ *nf* reality.

**réanimation** /ʀeanimasjɔ̃/ *nf* resuscitation; **service de ~** intensive care. **réanimer** [1] *vt* resuscitate.

**réarmement** /ʀeaʀməmɑ̃/ *nm* rearmament.

**rébarbatif**, **-ive** /ʀebaʀbatif, -v/ *a* forbidding, off-putting.

**rebelle** /ʀəbɛl/ *a* rebellious; (*soldat*) rebel; **~ à** resistant to. ● *nmf* rebel.

**rébellion** /ʀebeljɔ̃/ *nf* rebellion.

**rebondir** /ʀəbɔ̃diʀ/ [2] *vi* bounce; rebound; (fig) get moving again.

**rebondissement** /ʀəbɔ̃dismɑ̃/ *nm* (new) development.

**rebord** /ʀəbɔʀ/ *nm* edge; **~ de la fenêtre** window ledge *ou* sill.

**rebours**: **à ~** /aʀəbuʀ/ *loc* (*compter, marcher*) backwards.

**rebrousse-poil**: **à ~** /aʀəbʀuspwal/ *loc* the wrong way; (fig) **prendre qn à ~** rub sb up the wrong way.

**rebrousser** /ʀəbʀuse/ [1] *vt* **~ chemin** turn back.

**rebut** /ʀəby/ *nm* **mettre** *ou* **jeter au ~** scrap.

**rebutant**, **~e** /ʀəbytɑ̃, -t/ *a* off-putting.

**recaler** /ʀəkale/ [1] *vt* ▣ fail; **se faire ~**, **être recalé** fail.

**recel** /ʀəsɛl/ *nm* receiving. **receler** [6] *vt* (*objet volé*) receive; (cacher) conceal.

**récemment** /ʀesamɑ̃/ *adv* recently.

**recensement** /ʀəsɑ̃smɑ̃/ *nm* census; (inventaire) inventory. **recenser** [1] *vt* (*population*) take a census of; (*objets*) list.

**récent**, **~e** /ʀesɑ̃, -t/ *a* recent.

**récépissé** /ʀesepise/ *nm* receipt.

**récepteur** /ʀesɛptœʀ/ *nm* receiver.

**réception** /ʀesɛpsjɔ̃/ *nf* reception; (de courrier) receipt. **réceptionniste** *nmf* receptionist.

**récession** /ʀesesjɔ̃/ *nf* recession.

**recette** /ʀəsɛt/ *nf* (Culin) recipe; (argent) takings; **~s** (Comm) receipts.

**receveur**, **-euse** /ʀəs(ə)vœʀ, -øz/ *nm,f* (de bus) conductor; **~ des contributions** tax collector.

**recevoir** /ʀəs(ə)vwaʀ/ [52] *vt* receive, get; (*client, malade*) see; (*invités*) welcome, receive; **être reçu à un examen** pass an exam.

**rechange**: **de ~** /dəʀəʃɑ̃ʒ/ *loc* (*roue, vêtements*) spare; (*solution*) alternative.

**réchapper** /ʀeʃape/ [1] *vt/i* ~ **de** come through, survive.

**recharge** /ʀəʃaʀʒ/ *nf* (de stylo) refill.

**réchaud** /ʀeʃo/ *nm* stove.

**réchauffement** /ʀeʃofmɑ̃/ *nm* (de température) rise (**de** in); **le ~ de la planète** global warming.

**réchauffer** /ʀeʃofe/ [1] *vt* warm up. □ **se ~** *vpr* warm oneself up; (*temps*) get warmer.

**rêche** /ʀɛʃ/ *a* rough.

**recherche** /ʀəʃɛʀʃ/ *nf* search (**de** for); (raffinement) meticulousness; **~(s)** (Univ) research; **~s** (enquête) investigations; **~ d'emploi** job-hunting.

**recherché**, **~e** /ʀəʃɛʀʃe/ *a* in great demand; (*style*) original, recherché (pej); **~ pour meurtre** wanted for murder.

**rechercher** /ʀəʃɛʀʃe/ [1] *vt* search for.

**rechute** /ʀəʃyt/ *nf* (Méd) relapse; **faire une ~** have a relapse.

**récidiver** /ʀesidive/ [1] *vi* commit a second offence.

**récif** /ʀesif/ *nm* reef.

**récipient** /ʀesipjɑ̃/ *nm* container.

**réciproque** /ʀesipʀɔk/ *a* mutual, reciprocal.

**réciproquement** /ʀesipʀɔkmɑ̃/ *adv* each other; **et ~** and vice versa.

**récit** /ʀesi/ *nm* (compte-rendu) account, story; (histoire) story.

**réciter** /ʀesite/ [1] *vt* recite.

**réclamation** /ʀeklamasjɔ̃/ *nf* complaint; (demande) claim.

**réclame** /ʀeklam/ *nf* advertisement; **faire de la ~** advertise; **en ~** on offer.

**réclamer** /ʀeklame/ [1] *vt* call for, demand. ● *vi* complain.

**reclus**, **~e** /ʀəkly, -z/ *nm,f* recluse. ● *a* reclusive.

**réclusion** /ʀeklyzjɔ̃/ *nf* imprisonment.

**récolte** /ʀekɔlt/ *nf* (action) harvest; (produits) crop, harvest; (fig) crop. **récolter** [1] *vt* harvest, gather; (fig) collect, get.

**recommandation** /ʀekɔmɑ̃dasjɔ̃/ *nf* recommendation.

**recommandé** /ʀəkɔmɑ̃de/ *nm* registered letter; **envoyer en ~** send by registered post.

**recommander** /ʀəkɔmɑ̃de/ [1] *vt* recommend.

**recommencer** /ʀəkɔmɑ̃se/ [10] *vt* (reprendre) begin *ou* start again; (refaire) repeat. ● *vi* start *ou* begin again; **ne recommence pas** don't do it again.

**récompense** /ʀekɔ̃pɑ̃s/ *nf* reward; (prix) award. **récompenser** [1] *vt* reward (**de** for).

**réconcilier** /ʀekɔ̃silje/ [45] *vt* reconcile. □ **se ~** *vpr* become reconciled (**avec** with).

**reconduire** /ʀəkɔ̃dɥiʀ/ [17] *vt* see home; (**à la porte**) show out; (renouveler) renew.

**réconfort** /ʀekɔ̃fɔʀ/ *nm* comfort.

**reconnaissance** /ʀekɔnɛsɑ̃s/ *nf* gratitude; (fait de reconnaître) recognition; (Mil) reconnaissance. **reconnaissant**, **~e** *a* grateful (**de** for).

**reconnaître** /ʀəkɔnɛtʀ/ [18] *vt* recognize; (admettre) admit (**que** that); (Mil) reconnoitre; (*enfant*, *tort*) acknowledge. □ **se ~** *vpr* (s'orienter) know where one is; (l'un l'autre) recognize each other.

**reconstituer** /ʀəkɔ̃stitɥe/ [1] *vt* reconstitute; (*crime*) reconstruct; (*époque*) recreate.

**reconversion** /ʀəkɔ̃vɛʀsjɔ̃/ *nf* (de main-d'œuvre) redeployment.

**recopier** /ʀəkɔpje/ [45] *vt* copy out.

**record** /ʀəkɔʀ/ *nm & a inv* record.

**recouper** /ʀəkupe/ [1] *vt* confirm. □ **se ~** *vpr* check, tally, match up.

**recourbé**, **~e** /ʀəkuʀbe/ *a* curved; (*nez*) hooked.

**recourir** /ʀəkuʀiʀ/ [20] *vi* **~ à** (*expédient, violence*) resort to; (*remède, méthode*) have recourse to.

**recours** /ʀəkuʀ/ *nm* resort; **avoir ~ à** have recourse to, resort to; **avoir ~ à qn** turn to sb.

**recouvrer** /ʀəkuvʀe/ [1] *vt* recover.

**recouvrir** /ʀəkuvʀiʀ/ [21] *vt* cover.

**récréation** /ʀekʀeasjɔ̃/ *nf* recreation; (Scol) break; (US) recess.

**recroqueviller** (**se**) /(sə)ʀəkʀɔkvije/ [1] *vpr* curl up.

**recrudescence** /ʀəkʀydesɑ̃s/ *nf* new outbreak.

**recrue** /ʀəkʀy/ *nf* recruit.

**recrutement** /ʀəkʀytmɑ̃/ *nm* recruitment. **recruter** [1] *vt* recruit.

**rectangle** /ʀɛktɑ̃gl/ *nm* rectangle. **rectangulaire** *a* rectangular.

**rectifier** /ʀɛktifje/ [45] *vt* correct, rectify.

**recto** /ʀɛkto/ *nm* **au ~** on the front of the page.

**reçu**, **~e** /ʀəsy/ *a* accepted; (*candidat*) successful. ● *nm* receipt. ● ⇒RECEVOIR [52].

**recueil** /ʀəkœj/ *nm* collection.

**recueillement** /ʀəkœjmɑ̃/ *nm* meditation.

**recueillir** /ʀəkœjiʀ/ [25] *vt* collect; (prendre chez soi) take in. □ **se ~** *vpr* meditate.

**recul** /ʀəkyl/ *nm* retreat; (éloignement) distance; (déclin) decline; **avoir un mouvement de ~** recoil; **être en ~** be on the decline; **avec le ~** with hindsight.

**reculé**, **~e** /ʀəkyle/ *a* (*région*) remote.

**reculer** /ʀəkyle/ [1] *vt* move back; (*véhicule*) reverse; (différer) postpone. ● *vi* move back; (*voiture*) reverse; (*armée*) retreat; (régresser) fall; (céder) back down; **~ devant** (fig) shrink from. □ **se ~** *vpr* move back.

**récupération** /ʀekypeʀasjɔ̃/ *nf* (de l'organisme, de dette) recovery; (d'objets) salvage.

**récupérer** /ʀekypeʀe/ [14] *vt* recover; (*vieux objets*) salvage. ● *vi* recover.

**récurer** /ʀekyʀe/ [1] *vt* scour; **poudre à ~** scouring powder.

**récuser** /ʀekyze/ [1] *vt* challenge. □ **se ~** *vpr* state that one is not qualified to judge.

**recyclage** /ʀəsiklaʒ/ *nm* (de personnel) retraining; (de matériau) recycling.

**recycler** /ʀəsikle/ [1] *vt* (*personne*) retrain; (*chose*) recycle. □ **se ~** *vpr* retrain.

**rédacteur**, **-trice** /ʀedaktœʀ, -tʀis/ *nm,f* author, writer; (de journal, magazine) editor.

**rédaction** /ʀedaksjɔ̃/ *nf* writing; (Scol) essay, composition; (personnel) editorial staff.

**redevable** /ʀədvabl/ *a* **être ~ à qn de** (*argent*) owe sb; (fig) be indebted to sb for.

**redevance** /ʀədvɑ̃s/ *nf* (de télévision) licence fee; (de téléphone) rental charge.

**rédiger** /ʀediʒe/ [40] *vt* write; (*contrat*) draw up.

**redire** /ʀədiʀ/ [27] *vt* repeat; **avoir** *ou* **trouver à ~ à** find fault with.

**redondant**, **~e** /ʀədɔ̃dɑ̃, -t/ *a* superfluous.

**redonner** /Rədɔne/ [1] *vt* (rendre) give back; (donner davantage) give more; (donner de nouveau) give again.

**redoubler** /Rəduble/ [1] *vt* increase; (*classe*) repeat; ~ **de prudence** be even more careful. ● *vi* (Scol) repeat a year; (s'intensifier) intensify.

**redoutable** /Rədutabl/ *a* formidable.

**redouter** /Rədute/ [1] *vt* dread.

**redressement** /RədRɛsmɑ̃/ *nm* (reprise) recovery; ~ **judiciaire** receivership.

**redresser** /RədRese/ [1] *vt* straighten (out *ou* up); (*situation*) right, redress; (*économie, entreprise*) turn around. □ **se** ~ *vpr* (*personne*) straighten (oneself) up; (se remettre debout) stand up; (*pays, économie*) recover.

**réduction** /Redyksjɔ̃/ *nf* reduction.

**réduire** /RedɥiR/ [17] *vt* reduce (**à** to). □ **se** ~ *vpr* be reduced *ou* cut; **se** ~ **à** (revenir à) come down to.

**réduit**, ~**e** /Redɥi, t/ *a* (*objet*) small-scale; (limité) limited. ● *nm* cubbyhole.

**rééducation** /Reedykasjɔ̃/ *nf* (de handicapé) rehabilitation; (Méd) physiotherapy. **rééduquer** [1] *vt* (*personne*) rehabilitate; (*membre*) restore normal movement to.

**réel**, ~**le** /Reɛl/ *a* real. ● *nm* reality. **réellement** *adv* really.

**réexpédier** /Reɛkspedje/ [45] *vt* forward; (retourner) send back.

**refaire** /RəfɛR/ [33] *vt* do again; (*erreur, voyage*) make again; (réparer) do up, redo.

**réfectoire** /RefɛktwaR/ *nm* refectory.

**référence** /RefeRɑ̃s/ *nf* reference.

**référendum** /RefeRɛ̃dɔm/ *nm* referendum.

**référer** /RefeRe/ [14] *vi* **en** ~ **à** consult. □ **se** ~ **à** *vpr* refer to, consult.

**refermer** /RəfɛRme/ [1] *vt* close (again). □ **se** ~ *vpr* close (again).

**réfléchi**, ~**e** /Refleʃi/ *a* (*personne*) thoughtful; (*verbe*) reflexive.

**réfléchir** /RefleʃiR/ [2] *vi* think (**à**, **sur** about). ● *vt* reflect. □ **se** ~ *vpr* be reflected.

**reflet** /Rəflɛ/ *nm* reflection; (nuance) sheen.

**refléter** /Rəflete/ [14] *vt* reflect. □ **se** ~ *vpr* be reflected.

**réflexe** /Reflɛks/ *a* reflex. ● *nm* reflex; (réaction) reaction.

**réflexion** /Reflɛksjɔ̃/ *nf* (pensée) thought, reflection; (remarque) remark, comment; **à la** ~ on second thoughts.

**refluer** /Rəflye/ [1] *vi* flow back; (*foule*) retreat; (*inflation*) go down.

**reflux** /Rəfly/ *nm* (marée) ebb, tide.

**réforme** /RefɔRm/ *nf* reform. **réformer** [1] *vt* reform; (*soldat*) invalid out.

**refouler** /Rəfule/ [1] *vt* (*larmes*) hold back; (*désir*) repress; (*souvenir*) suppress.

**refrain** /RəfRɛ̃/ *nm* chorus; **le même** ~ the same old story.

**refréner** /RəfRene/ [14] *vt* curb, check.

**réfrigérateur** /RefRiʒeRatœR/ *nm* refrigerator.

**refroidir** /RəfRwadiR/ [2] *vt/i* cool (down). □ **se** ~ *vpr* (*personne, temps*) get cold. **refroidissement** *nm* cooling; (rhume) chill.

**refuge** /Rəfyʒ/ *nm* refuge; (chalet) mountain hut.

**réfugié**, ~**e** /Refyʒje/ *nm,f* refugee. **réfugier (se)** [45] *vpr* take refuge.

**refus** /Rəfy/ *nm* refusal; **ce n'est pas de ~** Ⓘ I wouldn't say no.

**refuser** /Rəfyze/ [1] *vt* refuse (**de** to); (*client, spectateur*) turn away; (recaler) fail; (à un poste) turn down. ◻ **se ~ à** *vpr* (*évidence*) reject; **se ~ à faire** refuse to do.

**regain** /Rəgɛ̃/ *nm* **~ de** renewal *ou* revival of; (Comm) rise.

**régal** (*pl* **~s**) /Regal/ *nm* treat, delight.

**régaler** /Regale/ [1] *vt* **~ qn de** treat sb to. ◻ **se ~** *vpr* (de nourriture) **je me régale** it's delicious.

**regard** /RəgaR/ *nm* (expression, coup d'œil) look; (vue) eye; (yeux) eyes; **~ fixe** stare; **au ~ de** with regard to; **en ~ de** compared with.

**regardant**, **~e** /RəgaRdɑ̃, -t/ *a* **~ avec son argent** careful with money; **peu ~ (sur)** not fussy (about).

**regarder** /RəgaRde/ [1] *vt* look at; (observer) watch; (considérer) consider; (concerner) concern; **~ fixement** stare at; **~ à** think about, pay attention to. ● *vi* look. ◻ **se ~** *vpr* (*soi-même*) look at oneself; (*personnes*) look at each other.

**régate** /Regat/ *nf* regatta.

**régie** /Reʒi/ *nf* **~ d'État** public corporation; (radio, TV) control room; (au cinéma) production; (Théât) stage management.

**régime** /Reʒim/ *nm* (organisation) system; (Pol) regime; (Méd) diet; (de moteur) speed; (de bananes) bunch; **se mettre au ~** go on a diet; **à ce ~** at this rate.

**régiment** /Reʒimɑ̃/ *nm* regiment.

**région** /Reʒjɔ̃/ *nf* region. **régional**, **~e** (*mpl* **-aux**) *a* regional.

**régir** /ReʒiR/ [2] *vt* govern.

**régisseur** /ReʒisœR/ *nm* (Théât) stage manager; **~ de plateau** (TV) floor manager; (au cinéma) studio manager.

**registre** /RəʒistR/ *nm* register.

**réglage** /Reglaʒ/ *nm* adjustment; (de moteur) tuning.

**règle** /Rɛgl/ *nf* rule; (instrument) ruler; **~s** (de femme) period; **en ~** in order.

**réglé**, **~e** /Regle/ *a* (*vie*) ordered; (arrangé) settled; (*papier*) ruled.

**règlement** /Rɛgləmɑ̃/ *nm* (règles) regulations; (solution) settlement; (paiement) payment. **réglementaire** *a* (*uniforme*) regulation. **réglementation** *nf* regulation, rules. **réglementer** [1] *vt* regulate, control.

**régler** /Regle/ [14] *vt* settle; (*machine*) adjust; (programmer) set; (*facture*) settle; (*personne*) settle up with; **~ son compte à** Ⓘ settle a score with.

**réglisse** /Reglis/ *nf* liquorice.

**règne** /Rɛɲ/ *nm* reign; (végétal, animal, minéral) kingdom.

**regret** /RəgRɛ/ *nm* regret; **à ~** with regret.

**regretter** /RəgRete/ [1] *vt* regret; (*personne*) miss; (pour s'excuser) be sorry.

**regrouper** /RəgRupe/ [1] *vt* group *ou* bring together. ◻ **se ~** *vpr* gather *ou* group together.

**régularité** /RegylaRite/ *nf* regularity; (de rythme, progrès) steadiness; (de surface, écriture) evenness.

**régulier**, **-ière** /Regylje, -jɛR/ *a* regular; (*qualité, vitesse*) steady, even; (*ligne, paysage*) even; (légal) legal; (honnête) honest.

**rehausser** /Rəose/ [1] *vt* raise; (faire valoir) enhance.

**rein** /Rɛ̃/ *nm* kidney; **~s** (dos) small of the back.

**reine** /Rɛn/ *nf* queen.

**réinsertion** /ʀeɛ̃sɛʀsjɔ̃/ *nf* reintegration.

**réintégrer** /ʀeɛ̃tegʀe/ [14] *vt* (*lieu*) return to; (Jur) reinstate; (*personne*) reintegrate.

**réitérer** /ʀeiteʀe/ [14] *vt* repeat.

**rejaillir** /ʀəʒajiʀ/ [2] *vi* ~ **sur** splash back onto; ~ **sur qn** (*succès*) reflect on sb.

**rejet** /ʀəʒɛ/ *nm* rejection; **~s** (déchets) waste.

**rejeter** /ʀəʒte/ [38] *vt* throw back; (refuser) reject; (déverser) discharge; ~ **une faute sur qn** shift the blame for a mistake onto sb.

**rejeton** /ʀəʒtɔ̃/ *nm* (enfant Ⓘ) offspring (*inv*).

**rejoindre** /ʀəʒwɛ̃dʀ/ [22] *vt* go back to, rejoin; (rattraper) catch up with; (rencontrer) join, meet up with. □ **se** ~ *vpr* (*personnes*) meet up; (*routes*) join, meet.

**réjoui**, **~e** /ʀeʒwi/ *a* joyful.

**réjouir** /ʀeʒwiʀ/ [2] *vt* delight. □ **se** ~ *vpr* be delighted (**de** at). **réjouissances** *nfpl* festivities. **réjouissant**, **~e** *a* cheering.

**relâche** /ʀəlɑʃ/ *nm* (repos) break, rest; **faire** ~ (Théât) be closed.

**relâcher** /ʀəlɑʃe/ [1] *vt* slacken; (*personne*) release; (*discipline*) relax. □ **se** ~ *vpr* slacken.

**relais** /ʀəlɛ/ *nm* (Sport) relay; (hôtel) hotel; (intermédiaire) intermediary; **prendre le** ~ **de** take over from.

**relancer** /ʀəlɑ̃se/ [10] *vt* boost, revive; (renvoyer) throw back.

**relatif**, **-ive** /ʀəlatif, -v/ *a* relative; ~ **à** relating to.

**relation** /ʀəlasjɔ̃/ *nf* relationship; (ami) acquaintance; (personne puissante) connection; **~s** relations; **~s extérieures** foreign affairs; **en** ~ **avec qn** in touch with sb.

**relativement** /ʀəlativmɑ̃/ *adv* relatively; ~ **à** in relation to.

**relativité** /ʀəlativite/ *nf* relativity.

**relax** /ʀelaks/ *a inv* Ⓘ laid-back.

**relaxer (se)** /(sə)ʀəlakse/ [1] *vpr* relax.

**relayer** /ʀəleje/ [31] *vt* relieve; (*émission*) relay. □ **se** ~ *vpr* take over from one another.

**reléguer** /ʀəlege/ [14] *vt* relegate.

**relent** /ʀəlɑ̃/ *nm* stink; (fig) whiff.

**relève** /ʀəlɛv/ *nf* relief; **prendre** *ou* **assurer la** ~ take over (**de** from).

**relevé**, **~e** /ʀəlve/ *a* spicy. ● *nm* (de compteur) reading; (facture) bill; ~ **bancaire**, ~ **de compte** bank statement; **faire le** ~ **de** list.

**relever** /ʀəlve/ [6] *vt* pick up; (*personne tombée*) help up; (remonter) raise; (*col*) turn up; (*compteur*) read; (*défi*) accept; (relayer) relieve; (remarquer, noter) note; (*plat*) spice up; (rebâtir) rebuild; ~ **de** come within the competence of; (Méd) recover from. □ **se** ~ *vpr* (*personne*) get up (again); (*pays, économie*) recover.

**relief** /ʀəljɛf/ *nm* relief; **mettre en** ~ highlight.

**relier** /ʀəlje/ [45] *vt* link (up) (**à** to); (*livre*) bind.

**religieux**, **-ieuse** /ʀəliʒjø, -z/ *a* religious. ● *nm,f* monk, nun.

**religion** /ʀəliʒjɔ̃/ *nf* religion.

**reliure** /ʀəljyʀ/ *nf* binding.

**reluire** /ʀəlɥiʀ/ [17] *vi* shine.

**remaniement** /ʀəmanimɑ̃/ *nm* revision; ~ **ministériel** cabinet reshuffle.

**remarquable** /ʀəmaʀkabl/ *a* remarkable.

**remarque** /ʀəmaʀk/ *nf* remark; (par écrit) comment.

**remarquer** /Rəmarke/ [1] *vt* notice; (dire) say; **faire ~** point out (**à** to); **se faire ~** draw attention to oneself; **remarque(z)** mind you.

**remblai** /Rɑ̃blɛ/ *nm* embankment.

**remboursement** /Rɑ̃buRsəmɑ̃/ *nm* (d'emprunt, dette) repayment; (Comm) refund.

**rembourser** /Rɑ̃buRse/ [1] *vt* (*dette, emprunt*) repay; (*billet, frais*) refund; (*client*) give a refund to; (*ami*) pay back.

**remède** /Rəmɛd/ *nm* remedy; (médicament) medicine.

**remédier** /Rəmedje/ [45] *vi* **~ à** remedy.

**remerciements** /RəmɛRsimɑ̃/ *nmpl* thanks. **remercier** [45] *vt* thank (**de** for); (licencier) dismiss.

**remettre** /RəmɛtR/ [42] *vt* put back; (*vêtement*) put back on; (donner) hand over; (*devoir, démission*) hand in; (faire fonctionner) switch back on; (restituer) give back; (différer) put off; (ajouter) add; (se rappeler) remember; **~ en cause** *ou* **en question** call into question. □ **se ~** *vpr* (guérir) recover; **se ~ au tennis** take up tennis again; **se ~ au travail** get back to work; **se ~ à faire** start doing again; **s'en ~ à** leave it to.

**remise** /Rəmiz/ *nf* (abri) shed; (rabais) discount; (transmission) handing over; (ajournement) postponement; **~ en cause** *ou* **en question** calling into question; **~ des prix** prizegiving; **~ des médailles** medals ceremony; **~ de peine** remission.

**remontant** /Rəmɔ̃tɑ̃/ *nm* tonic.

**remontée** /Rəmɔ̃te/ *nf* ascent; (d'eau, de prix) rise; **~ mécanique** ski lift.

**remonte-pente** (*pl* **~s**) /Rəmɔ̃tpɑ̃t/ *nm* ski tow.

**remonter** /Rəmɔ̃te/ [1] *vi* go *ou* come (back) up; (*prix, niveau*) rise (again); (revenir) go back (**à** to); **~ dans le temps** go back in time. ● *vt* (*rue, escalier*) go *ou* come (back) up; (relever) raise; (*montre*) wind up; (*objet démonté*) put together again; (*personne*) buck up.

**remontoir** /Rəmɔ̃twaR/ *nm* winder.

**remords** /RəmɔR/ *nm* remorse; **avoir du** *or* **des ~** feel remorse.

**remorque** /RəmɔRk/ *nf* trailer; **en ~** on tow. **remorquer** [1] *vt* tow.

**remous** /Rəmu/ *nm* eddy; (de bateau) backwash; (fig) turmoil.

**rempart** /Rɑ̃paR/ *nm* rampart.

**remplaçant**, **~e** /Rɑ̃plasɑ̃, -t/ *nm,f* replacement; (joueur) reserve, substitute.

**remplacement** /Rɑ̃plasmɑ̃/ *nm* replacement; **faire des ~s** do supply teaching. **remplacer** [10] *vt* replace.

**rempli**, **~e** /Rɑ̃pli/ *a* full (**de** of); (*journée*) busy.

**remplir** /Rɑ̃pliR/ [2] *vt* fill (up); (*formulaire*) fill in *ou* out; (*condition*) fulfil; (*devoir, tâche, rôle*) carry out. □ **se ~** *vpr* fill (up). **remplissage** *nm* filling; (de texte) padding.

**remporter** /Rɑ̃pɔRte/ [1] *vt* take back; (*victoire*) win.

**remuant**, **~e** /Rəmɥɑ̃, -t/ *a* boisterous.

**remue-ménage** /Rəmymenaʒ/ *nm inv* commotion, bustle.

**remuer** /Rəmɥe/ [1] *vt* move; (*thé, café*) stir; (*passé*) rake up. ● *vi* move; (gigoter) fidget. □ **se ~** *vpr* move.

**rémunération** /RemyneRasjɔ̃/ *nf* payment.

**renaissance** /Rənɛsɑ̃s/ *nf* rebirth.

**renard** /ʀənaʀ/ *nm* fox.

**renchérir** /ʀɑ̃ʃeʀiʀ/ [2] *vi* (dans une vente) raise the bidding; ~ **sur** go one better than. ● *vt* increase, put up.

**rencontre** /ʀɑ̃kɔ̃tʀ/ *nf* meeting; (de routes) junction; (Mil) encounter; (match) match; (US) game.

**rencontrer** /ʀɑ̃kɔ̃tʀe/ [1] *vt* meet; (heurter) hit; (trouver) find. □ **se** ~ *vpr* meet.

**rendement** /ʀɑ̃dmɑ̃/ *nm* yield; (travail) output.

**rendez-vous** /ʀɑ̃devu/ *nm* appointment; (d'amoureux) date; (lieu) meeting place; **prendre** ~ **(avec)** make an appointment (with).

**rendormir (se)** /(sə)ʀɑ̃dɔʀmiʀ/ [46] *vpr* go back to sleep.

**rendre** /ʀɑ̃dʀ/ [3] *vt* give back, return; (donner en retour) return; (*monnaie*) give; (*justice*) dispense; (*jugement*) pronounce; ~ **heureux/possible** make happy/possible; (vomir 🄸) vomit; ~ **compte de** report on; ~ **service (à)** help; ~ **visite à** visit. ● *vi* (*terres*) yield; (*activité*) be profitable. □ **se** ~ *vpr* (capituler) surrender; (aller) go (**à** to); **se** ~ **utile** make oneself useful.

**rêne** /ʀɛn/ *nf* rein.

**renfermé**, ~**e** /ʀɑ̃fɛʀme/ *a* withdrawn. ● *nm* **sentir le** ~ smell musty.

**renflé**, ~**e** /ʀɑ̃fle/ *a* bulging.

**renforcer** /ʀɑ̃fɔʀse/ [10] *vt* reinforce.

**renfort** /ʀɑ̃fɔʀ/ *nm* reinforcement; **à grand** ~ **de** with a great deal of.

**renier** /ʀənje/ [45] *vt* (*personne, œuvre*) disown; (*foi*) renounce.

**renifler** /ʀənifle/ [1] *vt/i* sniff.

**renne** /ʀɛn/ *nm* reindeer.

**renom** /ʀənɔ̃/ *nm* renown; (réputation) reputation. **renommé**, ~**e** *a* famous. **renommée** *nf* (célébrité) fame; (réputation) reputation.

**renoncement** /ʀənɔ̃smɑ̃/ *nm* renunciation.

**renoncer** /ʀənɔ̃se/ [10] *vi* ~ **à** (*habitude, ami*) give up, renounce; (*projet*) abandon; ~ **à faire** abandon the idea of doing.

**renouer** /ʀənwe/ [1] *vt* tie up (again); (*amitié*) renew; ~ **avec qn** get back in touch with sb; (après une dispute) make up with sb.

**renouveau** (*pl* ~**x**) /ʀənuvo/ *nm* revival.

**renouveler** /ʀənuvle/ [38] *vt* renew; (réitérer) repeat; (remplacer) replace. □ **se** ~ *vpr* be renewed; (*incident*) recur, happen again.

**renouvellement** /ʀənuvɛlmɑ̃/ *nm* renewal.

**rénovation** /ʀenɔvasjɔ̃/ *nf* (d'édifice) renovation; (d'institution) reform.

**renseignement** /ʀɑ̃sɛɲ(ə)mɑ̃/ *nm* ~**(s)** information; **(bureau des)** ~**s** information desk; **(service des)** ~**s téléphoniques** directory enquiries.

**renseigner** /ʀɑ̃seɲe/ [1] *vt* inform, give information to. □ **se** ~ *vpr* enquire, make enquiries, find out.

**rentabilité** /ʀɑ̃tabilite/ *nf* profitability. **rentable** *a* profitable.

**rente** /ʀɑ̃t/ *nf* (private) income; (pension) annuity. **rentier**, **-ière** *nm,f* person of private means.

**rentrée** /ʀɑ̃tʀe/ *nf* return; (revenu) income; **la** ~ **parlementaire** the reopening of Parliament; **la** ~ **(des classes)** the start of the new school year; **faire sa** ~ make a comeback.

**rentrer** /ʀɑ̃tʀe/ [1] *vi* (*aux être*) go *ou* come back home, return home; (entrer) go *ou* come in; (entrer à nouveau) go *ou* come back in; (*revenu*) come in; (*élèves*) go back (to school); ~ **dans** (heurter) smash

into; **tout est rentré dans l'ordre** everything is back to normal; ~ **dans ses frais** break even. ● *vt* (*aux avoir*) bring in; (*griffes*) draw in; (*vêtement*) tuck in.

**renverser** /ʀɑ̃vɛʀse/ [1] *vt* knock over *ou* down; (*piéton*) knock down; (*liquide*) upset, spill; (mettre à l'envers) turn upside down; (*gouvernement*) overthrow; (inverser) reverse. □ **se** ~ *vpr* (*véhicule*) overturn; (*verre, vase*) fall over.

**renvoi** /ʀɑ̃vwa/ *nm* return; (d'employé) dismissal; (d'élève) expulsion; (report) postponement; (dans un livre, fichier) cross-reference; (rot) burp.

**renvoyer** /ʀɑ̃vwaje/ [32] *vt* send back, return; (*employé*) dismiss; (*élève*) expel; (ajourner) postpone; (référer) refer; (réfléchir) reflect.

**repaire** /ʀəpɛʀ/ *nm* den.

**répandre** /ʀepɑ̃dʀ/ [3] *vt* (liquide) spill; (étendre, diffuser) spread; (*odeur*) give off. □ **se** ~ *vpr* spread; (*liquide*) spill; **se** ~ **en injures** let out a stream of abuse.

**répandu**, ~**e** /ʀepɑ̃dy/ *a* widespread.

**réparateur**, **-trice** /ʀepaʀatœʀ, -tʀis/ *nm* engineer. **réparation** *nf* repair; (compensation) compensation. **réparer** [1] *vt* repair, mend; (*faute*) make amends for; (remédier à) put right.

**repartie** /ʀəpaʀti/ *nf* retort; **avoir de la** ~ always have a ready reply.

**repartir** /ʀəpaʀtiʀ/ [46] *vi* start again; (*voyageur*) set off again; (s'en retourner) go back; (*secteur économique*) pick up again.

**répartir** /ʀepaʀtiʀ/ [2] *vt* distribute; (partager) share out; (étaler) spread. **répartition** *nf* distribution.

**repas** /ʀəpɑ/ *nm* meal.

**repassage** /ʀəpasaʒ/ *nm* ironing.

**repasser** /ʀəpɑse/ [1] *vi* come *ou* go back; ~ **devant qch** go past sth again. ● *vt* (*linge*) iron; (*examen*) retake, resist; (*film*) show again.

**repêcher** /ʀəpeʃe/ [1] *vt* recover, fish out; (*candidat*) allow to pass.

**repentir**[1] /ʀəpɑ̃tiʀ/ *nm* repentance.

**repentir**[2] **(se)** /(sə)ʀəpɑ̃tiʀ/ [2] *vpr* (Relig) repent (**de** of); **se** ~ **de** (regretter) regret.

**répercuter** /ʀepɛʀkyte/ [1] *vt* (*bruit*) send back. □ **se** ~ *vpr* echo; **se** ~ **sur** have repercussions on.

**repère** /ʀəpɛʀ/ *nm* mark; (jalon) marker; (événement) landmark; (référence) reference point.

**repérer** /ʀəpeʀe/ [14] *vt* locate, spot. □ **se** ~ *vpr* get one's bearings.

**répertoire** /ʀepɛʀtwaʀ/ *nm* (artistique) repertoire; (liste) directory; ~ **téléphonique** telephone directory; (personnel) telephone book. **répertorier** [45] *vt* index.

**répéter** /ʀepete/ [14] *vt* repeat; (Théât) rehearse. ● *vi* rehearse. □ **se** ~ *vpr* be repeated; (*personne*) repeat oneself.

**répétition** /ʀepetisjɔ̃/ *nf* repetition; (Théât) rehearsal.

**répit** /ʀepi/ *nm* respite, break.

**replier** /ʀəplije/ [45] *vt* fold (up); (*ailes, jambes*) tuck in. □ **se** ~ *vpr* withdraw (**sur soi-même** into oneself).

**réplique** /ʀeplik/ *nf* reply; (riposte) retort; (objection) objection; (Théât) line; (copie) replica. **répliquer** [1] *vt/i* reply; (riposter) retort; (objecter) answer back.

**répondeur** /ʀepɔ̃dœʀ/ *nm* answering machine.

**répondre** /ʀepɔ̃dʀ/ [3] *vt* (*injure, bêtise*) reply with; ~ **que** answer

*ou* reply that; ~ **à** (être conforme à) answer; (*affection, sourire*) return; (*avances, appel, critique*) respond to; ~ **de** answer for. ● *vi* answer, reply; (être insolent) answer back; (réagir) respond (**à** to).

**réponse** /Repɔ̃s/ *nf* answer, reply; (fig) response.

**report** /RəpɔR/ *nm* (transcription) transfer; (renvoi) postponement.

**reportage** /RəpɔRtaʒ/ *nm* report; (par écrit) article.

**reporter**[1] /RəpɔRte/ [1] *vt* take back; (ajourner) put off; (transcrire) transfer. □ **se** ~ **à** *vpr* refer to.

**reporter**[2] /RəpɔRtœR/ *nm* reporter.

**repos** /Rəpo/ *nm* rest; (paix) peace. **reposant**, ~**e** *a* restful.

**reposer** /Rəpoze/ [1] *vt* put down again; (délasser) rest. ● *vi* rest (**sur** on); **laisser** ~ (*pâte*) leave to stand. □ **se** ~ *vpr* rest; **se** ~ **sur** rely on.

**repousser** /Rəpuse/ [1] *vt* push back; (écarter) push away; (dégoûter) repel; (décliner) reject; (ajourner) postpone, put back. ● *vi* grow again.

**reprendre** /RəpRɑ̃dR/ [50] *vt* take back; (*confiance, conscience*) regain; (*souffle*) get back; (*évadé*) recapture; (recommencer) resume; (redire) repeat; (modifier) alter; (blâmer) reprimand; ~ **du pain** take some more bread; **on ne m'y reprendra pas** I won't be caught out again. ● *vi* (recommencer) resume; (*affaires*) pick up. □ **se** ~ *vpr* (se ressaisir) pull oneself together; (se corriger) correct oneself.

**représailles** /RəpRezaj/ *nfpl* reprisals.

**représentant**, ~**e** /RəpRezɑ̃tɑ̃, -t/ *nm,f* representative.

**représentation** /RəpRezɑ̃tasjɔ̃/ *nf* representation; (Théât) performance.

**représenter** /RəpRezɑ̃te/ [1] *vt* represent; (figures) depict, show; (*pièce de théâtre*) perform. □ **se** ~ *vpr* (s'imaginer) imagine.

**répression** /RepResjɔ̃/ *nf* repression; (d'élan) suppression.

**réprimande** /RepRimɑ̃d/ *nf* reprimand.

**réprimer** /RepRime/ [1] *vt* (*peuple*) repress; (*sentiment*) suppress; (*fraude*) crack down on.

**reprise** /RəpRiz/ *nf* resumption; (Théât) revival; (TV) repeat; (de tissu) darn, mend; (essor) recovery; (Comm) part-exchange, trade-in; **à plusieurs** ~**s** on several occasions.

**repriser** /RəpRize/ [1] *vt* darn, mend.

**reproche** /RəpRɔʃ/ *nm* reproach; **faire des** ~**s à** find fault with.

**reprocher** /RəpRɔʃe/ [1] *vt* ~ **qch à qn** reproach *ou* criticize sb for sth.

**reproducteur**, **-trice** /RepRɔdyktœR, -tRis/ *a* reproductive.

**reproduire** /RəpRɔdɥiR/ [17] *vt* reproduce; (répéter) repeat. □ **se** ~ *vpr* reproduce; (se répéter) recur.

**reptile** /Rɛptil/ *nm* reptile.

**repu**, ~**e** /Rəpy/ *a* satiated, replete.

**républicain**, ~**e** /Repyblikɛ̃, -ɛn/ *a & nm,f* republican.

**république** /Repyblik/ *nf* republic; ~ **populaire** people's republic.

**répudier** /Repydje/ [45] *vt* repudiate; (*droit*) renounce.

**répugnance** /Repyɲɑ̃s/ *nf* repugnance; (hésitation) reluctance; **avoir de la** ~ **pour** loathe. **répugnant**, ~**e** *a* repulsive.

**répugner** /Repyɲe/ [1] *vt* be repugnant to, disgust; ~ **à** (*effort, violence*) be averse to; ~ **à faire** be reluctant to do.

**répulsion** /Repylsjɔ̃/ *nf* repulsion.

**réputation** /ʀepytasjɔ̃/ *nf* reputation.

**réputé**, **~e** /ʀepyte/ *a* renowned (**pour** for); (*école, compagnie*) reputable; **~ pour être** reputed to be.

**requérir** /ʀəkeʀiʀ/ [7] *vt* require, demand.

**requête** /ʀəkɛt/ *nf* request; (Jur) petition.

**requin** /ʀəkɛ̃/ *nm* shark.

**requis**, **~e** /ʀəki, -z/ *a* (exigé) required; (nécessaire) necessary.

**RER** *abrév m* (**réseau express régional**) *Parisian rapid transit rail system.*

**rescapé**, **~e** /ʀɛskape/ *nm,f* survivor. ● *a* surviving.

**rescousse** /ʀɛskus/ *nf* **à la ~** to the rescue.

**réseau** (*pl* **~x**) /ʀezo/ *nm* network; **~ local** local area network, LAN; **le ~ des ~x** (Ordinat) Internet.

**réservation** /ʀezɛʀvasjɔ̃/ *nf* reservation, booking.

**réserve** /ʀezɛʀv/ *nf* reserve; (restriction) reservation, reserve; (indienne) reservation; (entrepôt) store-room; **en ~** in reserve; **les ~s** (Mil) the reserves.

**réserver** /ʀezɛʀve/ [1] *vt* reserve; (*place*) book, reserve. □ **se ~** *vpr* **se ~ qch** save sth for oneself; **se ~ pour** save oneself for; **se ~ le droit de** reserve the right to.

**réservoir** /ʀezɛʀvwaʀ/ *nm* tank; (lac) reservoir.

**résidence** /ʀezidɑ̃s/ *nf* residence; **~ secondaire** second home; **~ universitaire** hall of residence.

**résident**, **~e** /ʀezidɑ̃, -t/ *nm,f* resident; (étranger) foreign resident.

**résider** /ʀezide/ [1] *vi* reside; **~ dans qch** (*difficulté*) lie in.

**résigner (se)** /(sə)ʀeziɲe/ [1] *vpr* **se ~ à faire** resign oneself to doing.

**résilier** /ʀezilje/ [45] *vt* terminate.

**résine** /ʀezin/ *nf* resin.

**résistance** /ʀezistɑ̃s/ *nf* resistance; (fil électrique) element. **résistant**, **~e** *a* tough.

**résister** /ʀeziste/ [1] *vi* resist; **~ à** (*agresseur, assaut, influence, tentation*) resist; (*corrosion, chaleur*) withstand.

**résolu**, **~e** /ʀezɔly/ *a* resolute; **~ à faire** determined to do. ● ⇒RÉSOUDRE [53].

**résolution** /ʀezɔlysjɔ̃/ *nf* (fermeté) resolution; (d'un problème) solving.

**résonner** /ʀezɔne/ [1] *vi* resound.

**résorber** /ʀezɔʀbe/ [1] *vt* reduce. □ **se ~** *vpr* be reduced.

**résoudre** /ʀezudʀ/ [53] *vt* solve; (*crise, conflit*) resolve. □ **se ~ à** *vpr* (se décider) resolve to; (se résigner) resign oneself to.

**respect** /ʀɛspɛ/ *nm* respect. **respectabilité** *nf* respectability.

**respecter** /ʀɛspɛkte/ [1] *vt* respect; **faire ~** (*loi, décision*) enforce.

**respectueux**, **-euse** /ʀɛspɛktɥø, -z/ *a* respectful; **~ de l'environnement** environmentally friendly.

**respiration** /ʀɛspiʀasjɔ̃/ *nf* breathing; (haleine) breath. **respiratoire** *a* respiratory, breathing.

**respirer** /ʀɛspiʀe/ [1] *vi* breathe; (se reposer) catch one's breath. ● *vt* breathe (in); (exprimer) radiate.

**resplendir** /ʀɛsplɑ̃diʀ/ [2] *vi* shine (**de** with). **resplendissant**, **~e** *a* brilliant, radiant.

**responsabilité** /ʀɛspɔ̃sabilite/ *nf* responsibility; (légale) liability.

**responsable** /ʀɛspɔ̃sabl/ *a* responsible (**de** for); **~ de** (chargé de) in charge of. ● *nmf* person in charge; (coupable) person responsible.

**resquiller** /Rɛskije/ [1] *vi* Ⓘ (dans le train) fare-dodge; (au spectacle) get in without paying; (dans la queue) jump the queue.

**ressaisir (se)** /(sə)RəseziR/ [2] *vpr* pull oneself together; (*équipe sportive, valeurs boursières*) make a recovery.

**ressemblance** /Rəsɑ̃blɑ̃s/ *nf* resemblance.

**ressemblant**, **~e** /Rəsɑ̃blɑ̃, -t/ *a* **être ~** (*portrait*) be a good likeness.

**ressembler** /Rəsɑ̃ble/ [1] *vi* **~ à** resemble, look like. □ **se ~** *vpr* be alike; (physiquement) look alike.

**ressentiment** /Rəsɑ̃timɑ̃/ *nm* resentment.

**ressentir** /Rəsɑ̃tiR/ [46] *vt* feel. □ **se ~ de** *vpr* feel the effects of.

**resserrer** /RəseRe/ [1] *vt* tighten; (contracter) compress; (*vêtement*) take in. □ **se ~** *vpr* tighten; (*route*) narrow; (se regrouper) move closer together.

**ressort** /RəsɔR/ *nm* (objet) spring; (fig) energy; **être du ~ de** be the province of; (Jur) be within the jurisdiction of; **en dernier ~** as a last resort.

**ressortir** /RəsɔRtiR/ [46] *vi* go *ou* come back out; (se voir) stand out; (*film, disque*) be re-released; **faire ~** bring out; **il ressort que** it emerges that. ● *vt* take out again; (redire) come out with again; (*disque, film*) re-release.

**ressortissant**, **~e** /RəsɔRtisɑ̃, -t/ *nm,f* national.

**ressource** /RəsuRs/ *nf* resource; **~s** resources; **à bout de ~** at one's wits' end.

**ressusciter** /Resysite/ [1] *vi* come back to life. ● *vt* bring back to life; (fig) revive.

**restant**, **~e** /Rɛstɑ̃, -t/ *a* remaining. ● *nm* remainder.

**restaurant** /Rɛstɔrɑ̃/ *nm* restaurant.

**restauration** /Rɛstɔrasjɔ̃/ *nf* restoration; (hôtellerie) catering.

**restaurer** /Rɛstɔre/ [1] *vt* restore. □ **se ~** *vpr* eat.

**reste** /Rɛst/ *nm* rest; (d'une soustraction) remainder; **~s** remains (**de** of); (nourriture) leftovers; **un ~ de poulet** some left-over chicken; **au ~, du ~** moreover, besides.

**rester** /Rɛste/ [1] *vi* (*aux être*) stay, remain; (subsister) be left, remain; **il reste du pain** there is some bread left (over); **il me reste du pain** I have some bread left (over); **il me reste à** it remains for me to; **en ~ à** go no further than; **en ~ là** stop there.

**restituer** /Rɛstitɥe/ [1] *vt* (rendre) return; (recréer) reproduce; (rétablir) reconstruct.

**restreindre** /RɛstRɛ̃dR/ [22] *vt* restrict. □ **se ~** *vpr* (dans les dépenses) cut back.

**résultat** /Rezylta/ *nm* result.

**résulter** /Rezylte/ [1] *vi* **~ de** result from, be the result of.

**résumé** /Rezyme/ *nm* summary; **en ~** in short; (pour finir) to sum up. **résumer** [1] *vt* summarize.

**résurrection** /RezyRɛksjɔ̃/ *nf* resurrection; (renouveau) revival.

**rétablir** /RetabliR/ [2] *vt* restore; (*personne*) restore to health. □ **se ~** *vpr* (*ordre, silence*) be restored; (guérir) recover. **rétablissement** *nm* restoration; (de malade, monnaie) recovery.

**retard** /RətaR/ *nm* lateness; (sur un programme) delay; (infériorité) backwardness; **avoir du ~** be late; (*montre*) be slow; **en ~** late; (retardé) behind; **en ~ sur l'emploi du temps** behind schedule; **rattraper** *ou* **com-**

**bler son ~** catch up; **prendre du ~** fall behind.

**retardataire** /RətaRdatɛR/ *nmf* latecomer. ● *a* late.

**retarder** /RətaRde/ [1] *vt* **~ qn/qch** delay sb/sth, hold sb/sth up; (par rapport à une heure convenue) make sb/sth late; (*montre*) put back. ● *vi* (*montre*) be slow; (*personne*) be out of touch.

**retenir** /RətniR/ [58] *vt* hold back; (*souffle, attention, prisonnier*) hold; (*eau, chaleur*) retain, hold; (*larmes*) hold back; (garder) keep; (retarder) detain, hold up; (réserver) book; (se rappeler) remember; (déduire) deduct; (accepter) accept. □ **se ~** *vpr* (se contenir) restrain oneself; **se ~ à** hold on to; **se ~ de faire** stop oneself from doing.

**rétention** /Retɑ̃sjɔ̃/ *nf* retention.

**retentir** /Rətɑ̃tiR/ [2] *vi* ring out, resound; **~ sur** have an impact on.

**retentissant**, **~e** *a* resounding.

**retentissement** *nm* (effet) effect.

**retenue** /Rətny/ *nf* restraint; (somme) deduction; (Scol) detention.

**réticent**, **~e** /Retisɑ̃, -t/ *a* (hésitant) hesitant; (qui rechigne) reluctant; (réservé) reticent.

**rétine** /Retin/ *nf* retina.

**retiré**, **~e** /RətiRe/ *a* (*vie*) secluded; (*lieu*) remote.

**retirer** /RətiRe/ [1] *vt* (sortir) take out; (ôter) take off; (*argent, offre, candidature*) withdraw; (écarter) (*main, pied*) withdraw; (*billet, bagages*) collect, pick up; (*avantage*) derive; **~ à qn** take away from sb. □ **se ~** *vpr* withdraw, retire.

**retombées** /Rətɔ̃be/ *nfpl* (conséquences) effects; **~ radioactives** nuclear fall-out.

**retomber** /Rətɔ̃be/ [1] *vi* (faire une chute) fall again; (retourner au sol) land, come down; **~ dans** (*erreur*) fall back into.

**retouche** /Rətuʃ/ *nf* alteration; (de photo, tableau) retouch.

**retour** /RətuR/ *nm* return; **être de ~** be back (**de** from); **~ en arrière** flashback; **par ~ du courrier** by return of post; **en ~** in return.

**retourner** /RətuRne/ [1] *vt* (*aux avoir*) turn over; (*vêtement*) turn inside out; (*maison*) turn upside down; (*lettre, compliment*) return; (émouvoir 🅸) shake, upset. ● *vi* (*aux être*) go back, return. □ **se ~** *vpr* turn round; (dans son lit) twist and turn; **s'en ~** go back; **se ~ contre** turn against.

**retrait** /RətRɛ/ *nm* withdrawal; (des eaux) receding; **être (situé) en ~ (de)** be set back (from).

**retraite** /RətRɛt/ *nf* retirement; (pension) (retirement) pension; (fuite, refuge) retreat; **mettre à la ~** pension off; **prendre sa ~** retire.

**retraité**, **~e** /RətRete/ *a* retired. ● *nm,f* (old-age) pensioner.

**retrancher** /RətRɑ̃ʃe/ [1] *vt* remove; (soustraire) deduct, subtract. □ **se ~** *vpr* (Mil) entrench oneself; **se ~ derrière** take refuge behind.

**retransmettre** /RətRɑ̃smɛtR/ [42] *vt* broadcast.

**rétrécir** /RetResiR/ [2] *vt* make narrower; (*vêtement*) take in. ● *vi* (*tissu*) shrink. □ **se ~** *vpr* (*rue*) narrow.

**rétribution** /RetRibysjɔ̃/ *nf* payment.

**rétroactif**, **-ive** /RetRɔaktif, -v/ *a* retrospective; **augmentation à effet ~** backdated pay rise.

**retrousser** /RətRuse/ [1] *vt* pull up; (*manche*) roll up.

**retrouvailles** /RətRuvɑj/ *nfpl* reunion.

**retrouver** /ʀətʀuve/ [1] *vt* find (again); (rejoindre) meet (again); (*forces, calme*) regain; (*lieu*) be back in; (se rappeler) remember. □ **se ~** *vpr* find oneself (back); (se réunir) meet (again); (être présent) be found; **s'y ~** (s'orienter, comprendre) find one's way; (rentrer dans ses frais 🅘) break even.

**rétroviseur** /ʀetʀɔvizœʀ/ *nm* (Auto) (rear-view) mirror.

**réunion** /ʀeynjɔ̃/ *nf* meeting; (rencontre) gathering; (après une séparation) réunion; (d'objets) collection.

**réunir** /ʀeyniʀ/ [2] *vt* gather, collect; (rapprocher) bring together; (convoquer) call together; (raccorder) join; (*qualités*) combine. □ **se ~** *vpr* meet.

**réussi**, **~e** /ʀeysi/ *a* successful

**réussir** /ʀeysiʀ/ [2] *vi* succeed, be successful; **~ à faire** succeed in doing, manage to do; **~ à un examen** pass an exam; **~ à qn** (*méthode*) work well for sb; (*climat, mode de vie*) agree with sb. ● *vt* (*vie*) make a success of.

**réussite** /ʀeysit/ *nf* success; (jeu) patience.

**revaloir** /ʀəvalwaʀ/ [60] *vt* **je vous revaudrai cela** (en mal) I'll pay you back for this; (en bien) I'll repay you some day.

**revanche** /ʀəvɑ̃ʃ/ *nf* revenge; (Sport) return *ou* revenge match; **en ~** on the other hand.

**rêvasser** /ʀɛvase/ [1] *vi* daydream.

**rêve** /ʀɛv/ *nm* dream; **faire un ~** have a dream.

**réveil** /ʀevɛj/ *nm* waking up, (fig) awakening; (pendule) alarm clock.

**réveillé**, **~e** /ʀeveje/ *a* awake.

**réveiller** /ʀeveje/ [1] *vt* wake (up); (*sentiment, souvenir*) awaken; (*curiosité*) arouse. □ **se ~** *vpr* wake up.

**réveillon** /ʀevɛjɔ̃/ *nm* (Noël) Christmas Eve, (nouvel an) New Year's Eve. **réveillonner** [1] *vi* see Christmas *ou* the New Year in.

**révéler** /ʀevele/ [14] *vt* reveal. □ **se ~** *vpr* be revealed; **se ~ facile** turn out to be easy, prove easy.

**revendeur**, **-euse** /ʀəvɑ̃dœʀ, -øz/ *nm,f* dealer, stockist; **~ de drogue** drug dealer.

**revendication** /ʀəvɑ̃dikasjɔ̃/ *nf* claim. **revendiquer** [1] *vt* claim.

**revendre** /ʀəvɑ̃dʀ/ [3] *vt* sell (again); **avoir de l'énergie à ~** have energy to spare.

**revenir** /ʀəvniʀ/ [58] *vi* (*aux être*) come back, return (**à** to); **~ à** (*activité*) go back to; (se résumer à) come down to; (échoir à) fall to; **~ à 100 francs** cost 100 francs; **~ de** (*maladie, surprise*) get over; **~ sur ses pas** retrace one's steps; **faire ~** (Culin) brown; **ça me revient!** now I remember!; **je n'en reviens pas!** 🅘 I can't get over it!

**revenu** /ʀəvny/ *nm* income; (de l'État) revenue.

**rêver** /ʀeve/ [1] *vt/i* dream (**à** of; **de faire** of doing).

**réverbère** /ʀevɛʀbɛʀ/ *nm* street lamp.

**révérence** /ʀeveʀɑ̃s/ *nf* reverence; (salut d'homme) bow; (salut de femme) curtsy.

**rêverie** /ʀɛvʀi/ *nf* daydream; (activité) daydreaming.

**revers** /ʀəvɛʀ/ *nm* reverse; (de main) back; (d'étoffe) wrong side; (de veste) lapel; (de pantalon) turn-up; (de manche) cuff; (tennis) backhand; (fig) set-back.

**revêtement** /ʀəvɛtmɑ̃/ *nm* covering; (de route) surface; **~ de sol** floor covering. **revêtir** [61] *vt* cover;

(*habit*) put on; (prendre, avoir) assume.

**rêveur**, **-euse** /ʀɛvœʀ, -øz/ *a* dreamy. ● *nm,f* dreamer.

**réviser** /ʀevize/ [1] *vt* revise; (*machine, véhicule*) service. **révision** *nf* revision; service.

**revivre** /ʀəvivʀ/ [62] *vi* come alive again. ● *vt* relive.

**révocation** /ʀevɔkasjɔ̃/ *nf* repeal; (d'un fonctionnaire) dismissal.

**revoir**[1] /ʀəvwaʀ/ [63] *vt* see (again); (réviser) revise.

**revoir**[2] /ʀəvwaʀ/ *nm* **au ~** goodbye.

**révolte** /ʀevɔlt/ *nf* revolt. **révolté**, **~e** *nm,f* rebel.

**révolter** /ʀevɔlte/ [1] *vt* appal, revolt. □ **se ~** *vpr* revolt.

**révolu**, **~e** /ʀevɔly/ *a* past; **avoir 21 ans ~s** be over 21 years of age.

**révolution** /ʀevɔlysjɔ̃/ *nf* revolution. **révolutionnaire** *a & nmf* revolutionary. **révolutionner** [1] *vt* revolutionize.

**revolver** /ʀevɔlvɛʀ/ *nm* revolver, gun.

**révoquer** /ʀevɔke/ [1] *vt* repeal; (*fonctionnaire*) dismiss.

**revue** /ʀəvy/ *nf* (examen, défilé) review; (magazine) magazine; (spectacle) variety show.

**rez-de-chaussée** /ʀedʃose/ *nm inv* ground floor; (US) first floor.

**RF** *abrév f* (**République Française**) French Republic.

**rhinocéros** /ʀinɔseʀɔs/ *nm* rhinoceros.

**rhubarbe** /ʀybaʀb/ *nf* rhubarb.

**rhum** /ʀɔm/ *nm* rum.

**rhumatisme** /ʀymatism/ *nm* rheumatism.

**rhume** /ʀym/ *nm* cold; **~ des foins** hay fever.

**ri** /ʀi/ ⇒RIRE [54].

**ricaner** /ʀikane/ [1] *vi* snigger.

**riche** /ʀiʃ/ *a* rich (**en** in). ● *nmf* rich man, rich woman.

**richesse** /ʀiʃɛs/ *nf* wealth; (de sol, décor) richness; **~s** wealth; (ressources) resources.

**ride** /ʀid/ *nf* wrinkle; (sur l'eau) ripple.

**rideau** (*pl* **~x**) /ʀido/ *nm* curtain; (métallique) shutter; (fig) screen.

**ridicule** /ʀidikyl/ *a* ridiculous. ● *nm* (d'une situation) absurdity; (le grotesque) **le ~** ridicule. **ridiculiser** [1] *vt* ridicule.

**rien** /ʀjɛ̃/ *pron* nothing; (quoi que ce soit) anything; **de ~!** don't mention it!; **~ de bon** nothing good; **elle n'a ~ dit** she didn't say anything; **~ d'autre**/**de plus** nothing else/more; **~ du tout** nothing at all; **~ que** (seulement) just, only; **trois fois ~** next to nothing; **il n'y est pour ~** he has nothing to do with it; **~ à faire!** (c'est impossible) it's no good!; (refus) no way! [I]. ● *nm* **un ~ de** a touch of; **être puni pour un ~** be punished for the slightest thing; **se disputer pour un ~** fight over nothing; **en un ~ de temps** in next to no time.

**rieur**, **-euse** /ʀijœʀ, -øz/ *a* cheerful; (*yeux*) laughing.

**rigide** /ʀiʒid/ *a* rigid.

**rigolade** /ʀigɔlad/ *nf* fun.

**rigoler** /ʀigɔle/ [1] *vi* laugh; (s'amuser) have some fun; (plaisanter) joke.

**rigolo**, **~te** /ʀigɔlo, -ɔt/ *a* [I] funny. ● *nm,f* [I] joker.

**rigoureux**, **-euse** /ʀiguʀø, -z/ *a* rigorous; (*hiver*) harsh; (sévère) strict; (*travail, recherches*) meticulous.

**rigueur** /ʀigœʀ/ *nf* rigour; **à la ~** at a pinch; **être de ~** be obligatory;

**tenir ~ à qn de qch** bear sb a grudge for sth.

**rime** /Rim/ *nf* rhyme.

**rimer** /Rime/ [1] *vi* rhyme (**avec** with); **cela ne rime à rien** it makes no sense.

**rinçage** /Rẽsaʒ/ *nm* rinse; (action) rinsing.

**rincer** /Rẽse/ [10] *vt* rinse.

**riposte** /Ripɔst/ *nf* retort.

**riposter** /Ripɔste/ [1] *vi* retaliate; **~ à** (*attaque*) counter; (*insulte*) reply to. ● *vt* retort (**que** that).

**rire** /RiR/ [54] *vi* laugh (**de** at); (plaisanter) joke; (s'amuser) have fun; **c'était pour ~** it was a joke. ● *nm* laugh; **des ~s** laughter.

**risée** /Rize/ *nf* **la ~ de** the laughing-stock of.

**risque** /Risk/ *nm* risk. **risqué, ~e** *a* risky; (osé) daring.

**risquer** /Riske/ [1] *vt* risk (**de faire** of doing); (être passible de) face; **il risque de pleuvoir** it might rain; **tu risques de te faire mal** you might hurt yourself. □ **se ~ à/dans** *vpr* venture to/into.

**ristourne** /RistuRn/ *nf* discount.

**rite** /Rit/ *nm* rite; (habitude) ritual. **rituel, ~le** *a* & *nm* ritual.

**rivage** /Rivaʒ/ *nm* shore.

**rival, ~e** (*mpl* **-aux**) /Rival, -o/ *a* & *nm,f* rival. **rivaliser** [1] *vi* compete (**avec** with). **rivalité** *nf* rivalry.

**rive** /Riv/ *nf* (de fleuve) bank; (de lac) shore.

**riverain, ~e** /RivRẽ, -ɛn/ *a* riverside. ● *nm,f* riverside resident; (d'une rue) resident.

**rivière** /RivjɛR/ *nf* river.

**riz** /Ri/ *nm* rice. **rizière** *nf* paddy field.

**robe** /Rɔb/ *nf* (de femme) dress; (de juge) robe; (de cheval) coat; **~ de chambre** dressing-gown.

**robinet** /Rɔbinɛ/ *nm* tap; (US) faucet.

**robot** /Rɔbo/ *nm* robot; **~ ménager** food processor.

**robuste** /Rɔbyst/ *a* robust.

**roche** /Rɔʃ/ *nf* rock.

**rocher** /Rɔʃe/ *nm* rock.

**rock** /Rɔk/ *nm* (Mus) rock.

**rodage** /Rɔdaʒ/ *nm* **en ~** (Auto) running in.

**roder** /Rɔde/ [1] *vt* (Auto) run in; **être rodé** (*personne*) have got the hang of things.

**rôder** /Rode/ [1] *vi* roam; (*suspect*) prowl.

**rogne** /Rɔɲ/ *nf* ▣ anger; **en ~** in a temper.

**rogner** /Rɔɲe/ [1] *vt* trim; **~ sur** cut down on.

**rognon** /Rɔɲɔ̃/ *nm* (Culin) kidney.

**roi** /Rwa/ *nm* king; **les R~ mages** the Magi; **la fête des R~** Twelfth Night.

**rôle** /Rol/ *nm* role, part.

**romain, ~e** /Rɔmẽ, -ɛn/ *a* Roman. **R~, ~e** *nm,f* Roman. **romaine** *nf* (laitue) cos.

**roman** /Rɔmɑ̃/ *nm* novel; (genre) fiction.

**romance** /Rɔmɑ̃s/ *nf* ballad.

**romancier, -ière** /Rɔmɑ̃sje, -jɛR/ *nm,f* novelist.

**romanesque** /Rɔmanɛsk/ *a* romantic; (fantastique) fantastic; (*récit*) fictional; **œuvres ~s** novels, fiction.

**romantique** /Rɔmɑ̃tik/ *a* & *nmf* romantic. **romantisme** *nm* romanticism.

**rompre** /Rɔ̃pR/ [3] *vt* break; (*relations*) break off. ● *vi* (se séparer) break up; **~ avec** (*fiancé*) break up with; (*parti*) break away from; (*tradition*) break with. □ **se ~** *vpr* break.

**ronce** /rɔ̃s/ *nf* bramble.

**rond**, **~e** /rɔ̃, -d/ *a* round; (gras) plump; (ivre Ⓘ) drunk. ● *nm* (cercle) ring; (tranche) slice; **en ~** in a circle; **il n'a pas un ~** Ⓘ he hasn't got a penny.

**ronde** /rɔ̃d/ *nf* (de policier) beat; (de soldat, gardien) watch; (Mus) semibreve.

**rondelle** /rɔ̃dɛl/ *nf* (Tech) washer; (tranche) slice.

**rondement** /rɔ̃dmɑ̃/ *adv* promptly; (franchement) frankly.

**rondeur** /rɔ̃dœr/ *nf* roundness; (franchise) frankness; (embonpoint) plumpness.

**rondin** /rɔ̃dɛ̃/ *nm* log.

**rond-point** (*pl* **ronds-points**) /rɔ̃pwɛ̃/ *nm* roundabout, (US) traffic circle.

**ronfler** /rɔ̃fle/ [1] *vi* snore; (*moteur*) purr.

**ronger** /rɔ̃ʒe/ [40] *vt* gnaw (at), (*vers, acide*) eat into. □ **se ~** *vpr* **se ~ les ongles** bite one's nails.

**rongeur** /rɔ̃ʒœr/ *nm* rodent.

**ronronner** /rɔ̃rɔne/ [1] *vi* purr.

**rosbif** /rɔsbif/ *nm* roast beef.

**rose** /roz/ *nf* rose. ● *a* & *nm* pink.

**rosé**, **~e** /roze/ *a* pinkish. ● *nm* rosé.

**roseau** (*pl* **~x**) /rozo/ *nm* reed.

**rosée** /roze/ *nf* dew.

**rosier** /rozje/ *nm* rose bush.

**rossignol** /rɔsiɲɔl/ *nm* nightingale.

**rotatif**, **-ive** /rɔtatif, -v/ *a* rotary.

**roter** /rɔte/ [1] *vi* Ⓘ burp.

**rôti** /rɔti/ *nm* joint; (cuit) roast; **~ de porc** roast pork.

**rotin** /rɔtɛ̃/ *nm* (rattan) cane.

**rôtir** /rɔtir/ [2] *vt* roast.

**rôtissoire** /rɔtiswar/ *nf* roasting spit.

**rotule** /rɔtyl/ *nf* kneecap.

**rouage** /rwaʒ/ *nm* (Tech) wheel; **les ~s** the works; (d'une organisation: fig) wheels.

**roucouler** /rukule/ [1] *vi* coo.

**roue** /ru/ *nf* wheel; **~ dentée** cog(wheel); **~ de secours** spare wheel.

**rouer** /rwe/ [1] *vt* **~ de coups** thrash.

**rouge** /ruʒ/ *a* red; (*fer*) red-hot. ● *nm* red; (vin) red wine; (fard) blusher; **~ à lèvres** lipstick. ● *nmf* (Pol) red. **rouge-gorge** (*pl* **rouges-gorges**) *nm* robin.

**rougeole** /ruʒɔl/ *nf* measles (+ *sg*).

**rouget** /ruʒɛ/ *nm* red mullet.

**rougeur** /ruʒœr/ *nf* redness; (tache) red blotch.

**rougir** /ruʒir/ [2] *vi* turn red; (de honte) blush.

**rouille** /ruj/ *nf* rust. **rouillé**, **~e** *a* rusty.

**rouiller** /ruje/ [1] *vi* rust. □ **se ~** *vpr* get rusty.

**rouleau** (*pl* **~x**) /rulo/ *nm* roll; (outil, vague) roller; **~ à pâtisserie** rolling pin; **~ compresseur** steamroller.

**roulement** /rulmɑ̃/ *nm* rotation; (bruit) rumble; (alternance) rotation; (de tambour) roll; **~ à billes** ball-bearing; **travailler par ~** work in shifts.

**rouler** /rule/ [1] *vt* roll; (*ficelle, manches*) roll up; (*pâte*) roll out; (duper Ⓘ) cheat. ● *vi* (*véhicule, train*) go, travel; (*conducteur*) drive. □ **se ~ dans** *vpr* (*herbe*) roll in; (*couverture*) roll oneself up in.

**roulette** /rulɛt/ *nf* (de meuble) castor; (de dentiste) drill; (jeu) roulette; **comme sur des ~s** very smoothly.

**roulotte** /rulɔt/ *nf* caravan.

**roumain**, **~e** /ʀumɛ̃, -ɛn/ *a* Romanian. **R~**, **~e** *nm,f* Romanian.

**Roumanie** /ʀumani/ *nf* Romania.

**rouquin**, **~e** /ʀukɛ̃, -in/ Ⓘ *a* red-haired. ● *nm,f* redhead.

**rouspéter** /ʀuspete/ [14] *vi* Ⓘ grumble, moan.

**rousse** /ʀus/ ⇒ROUX.

**roussir** /ʀusiʀ/ [2] *vt* scorch. ● *vi* turn brown.

**route** /ʀut/ *nf* road; (Naut, Aviat) route; (direction) way; (voyage) journey; (chemin: fig) path; **en ~** on the way; **en ~!** let's go!; **mettre en ~** start; **~ nationale** trunk road, main road; **se mettre en ~** set out; **il y a une heure de ~** it's an hour's journey.

**routier**, **-ière** /ʀutje, -jɛʀ/ *a* road. ● *nm* long-distance lorry *ou* truck driver; (restaurant) transport café; (US) truck stop.

**routine** /ʀutin/ *nf* routine.

**roux**, **rousse** /ʀu, ʀus/ *a* red, russet; (*personne*) red-haired; (*chat*) ginger. ● *nm,f* redhead.

**royal**, **~e** (*mpl* **-aux**) /ʀwajal, -jo/ *a* royal; (*cadeau*) fit for a king.

**royaume** /ʀwajom/ *nm* kingdom.

**Royaume-Uni** /ʀwajomyni/ *nm* United Kingdom.

**royauté** /ʀwajote/ *nf* royalty.

**RTT** *abrév f* (**réduction du temps de travail**) reduction in working hours.

**ruban** /ʀybɑ̃/ *nm* ribbon; (de chapeau) band; **~ adhésif** sticky tape; **~ magnétique** magnetic tape.

**rubéole** /ʀybeɔl/ *nf* German measles (+ *sg*).

**rubis** /ʀybi/ *nm* ruby; (de montre) jewel.

**rubrique** /ʀybʀik/ *nf* heading; (article) column.

**ruche** /ʀyʃ/ *nf* beehive.

**rude** /ʀyd/ *a* (au toucher) rough; (pénible) tough; (grossier) coarse; (fameux Ⓘ) tremendous.

**rudement** /ʀydmɑ̃/ *adv* (*frapper*) hard; (*traiter*) harshly; (très Ⓘ) really.

**rudimentaire** /ʀydimɑ̃tɛʀ/ *a* rudimentary.

**rue** /ʀy/ *nf* street.

**ruée** /ʀɥe/ *nf* rush.

**ruer** /ʀɥe/ [1] *vi* (*cheval*) buck. □ **se ~** *vpr* rush (**dans** into; **vers** towards); **se ~ sur** pounce on.

**rugby** /ʀygbi/ *nm* rugby.

**rugir** /ʀyʒiʀ/ [2] *vi* roar.

**rugueux**, **-euse** /ʀygø, -z/ *a* rough.

**ruine** /ʀɥin/ *nf* ruin; **en ~(s)** in ruins. **ruiner** [1] *vt* ruin.

**ruisseau** (*pl* **~x**) /ʀɥiso/ *nm* stream; (rigole) gutter.

**rumeur** /ʀymœʀ/ *nf* (nouvelle) rumour; (son) murmur, hum.

**ruminer** /ʀymine/ [1] *vi* (*animal*) ruminate; (méditer) meditate.

**rupture** /ʀyptyʀ/ *nf* break; (action) breaking; (de contrat) breach; (de pourparlers) breakdown; (de relations) breaking off; (de couple, coalition) break-up.

**rural**, **~e** (*mpl* **-aux**) /ʀyʀal, -o/ *a* rural.

**ruse** /ʀyz/ *nf* cunning; **une ~** a trick, a ruse. **rusé**, **~e** *a* cunning.

**russe** /ʀys/ *a* Russian. ● *nm* (Ling) Russian. **R~** *nmf* Russian.

**Russie** /ʀysi/ *nf* Russia.

**rustique** /ʀystik/ *a* rustic.

**rythme** /ʀitm/ *nm* rhythm; (vitesse) rate; (de la vie) pace. **rythmique** *a* rhythmical.

# Ss

**s'** /s/ ⇒SE.

**sa** /sa/ ⇒SON[1].

**SA** *abrév f* (**société anonyme**) PLC.

**sabbatique** /sabatik/ *a* (*année*) sabbatical year.

**sable** /sɑbl/ *nm* sand; **~s mouvants** quicksands. **sabler** *vt* [1] grit.

**sablier** /sablije/ *nm* (Culin) egg-timer.

**sablonneux**, **-euse** /sablɔnø, -z/ *a* sandy.

**sabot** /sabo/ *nm* (de cheval) hoof; (chaussure) clog; (de frein) shoe; **~ de Denver®** (wheel) clamp.

**saboter** /sabɔte/ [1] *vt* sabotage; (bâcler) botch.

**sac** /sak/ *nm* bag; (grand, en toile) sack; **mettre à ~** (*maison*) ransack; (*ville*) sack; **~ à dos** rucksack; **~ à main** handbag; **~ de couchage** sleeping-bag; **mettre dans le même ~** lump together.

**saccadé**, **~e** /sakade/ *a* jerky.

**saccager** /sakaʒe/ [40] *vt* (abîmer) wreck; (*maison*) ransack; (*ville, pays*) sack.

**saccharine** /sakaʀin/ *nf* saccharin.

**sachet** /saʃɛ/ *nm* (small) bag; (d'aromates) sachet; **~ de thé** tea-bag.

**sacoche** /sakɔʃ/ *nf* bag; (de vélo) saddlebag.

**sacre** /sakʀ/ *nm* (de roi) coronation; (d'évêque) consecration. **sacré**, **~e** *a* sacred; (maudit Ⓘ) damned. **sacrement** *nm* sacrament. **sacrer** [1] *vt* crown; consecrate.

**sacrifice** /sakʀifis/ *nm* sacrifice.

**sacrifier** /sakʀifje/ [45] *vt* sacrifice; **~ à** conform to. □ **se ~** *vpr* sacrifice oneself.

**sacrilège** /sakʀilɛʒ/ *nm* sacrilege. ● *a* sacrilegious.

**sadique** /sadik/ *a* sadistic. ● *nmf* sadist.

**sage** /saʒ/ *a* wise; (docile) good, well behaved. ● *nm* wise man.

**sage-femme** (*pl* **sages-femmes**) /saʒfam/ *nf* midwife.

**sagesse** /saʒɛs/ *nf* wisdom.

**Sagittaire** /saʒitɛʀ/ *nm* **le ~** Sagittarius.

**saignant**, **~e** /sɛɲɑ̃, -t/ *a* (Culin) rare.

**saigner** /seɲe/ [1] *vt*/*i* bleed; **~ du nez** have a nosebleed.

**saillant**, **~e** /sajɑ̃, -t/ *a* prominent.

**sain**, **~e** /sɛ̃, sɛn/ *a* healthy; (*moralement*) sane; **~ et sauf** safe and sound.

**saindoux** /sɛ̃du/ *nm* lard.

**saint**, **~e** /sɛ̃, -t/ *a* holy; (bon, juste) saintly. ● *nm,f* saint. **Saint-Esprit** *nm* Holy Spirit. **sainteté** *nf* holiness; (d'un lieu) sanctity. **Sainte Vierge** *nf* Blessed Virgin. **Saint-Sylvestre** *nf* New Year's Eve.

**sais** /sɛ/ ⇒SAVOIR [55].

**saisie** /sezi/ *nf* (Jur) seizure; (Comput) keyboarding; **~ de données** data capture.

**saisir** /seziʀ/ [2] *vt* grab (hold of); (*proie*) seize; (*occasion, biens*) seize; (comprendre) grasp; (frapper) strike; (Ordinat) keyboard, capture;

saisi de (*peur*) stricken by, overcome by. ◻ **se** ~ **de** *vpr* seize. **saisissant**, ~**e** *a* (*spectacle*) gripping.

**saison** /sɛzɔ̃/ *nf* season; **la morte** ~ the off season. **saisonnier**, **-ière** *a* seasonal.

**sait** /sɛ/ ⇒SAVOIR [55].

**salade** /salad/ *nf* (plat) salad; (plante) lettuce. **saladier** *nm* salad bowl.

**salaire** /salɛʀ/ *nm* wages (+ *pl*), salary.

**salarié**, ~**e** /salaʀje/ *a* wage-earning. ● *nm,f* wage earner.

**sale** /sal/ *a* dirty; (mauvais) nasty.

**salé**, ~**e** /sale/ *a* (*goût*) salty; (plat) salted; (opposé à sucré) savoury; (grivois Ⓘ) spicy; (excessif Ⓘ) steep. **saler** [1] *vt* salt.

**saleté** /salte/ *nf* dirtiness; (crasse) dirt; (obscénité) obscenity; ~**(s)** (camelote) rubbish; (détritus) mess.

**salir** /saliʀ/ [2] *vt* (make) dirty; (*réputation*) tarnish. ◻ **se** ~ *vpr* get dirty. **salissant**, ~**e** *a* dirty; (*étoffe*) easily dirtied.

**salive** /saliv/ *nf* saliva.

**salle** /sal/ *nf* room; (grande, publique) hall; (de restaurant) dining room; (Théât, cinéma) auditorium; **cinéma à trois** ~**s** three-screen cinema; ~ **à manger** dining room; ~ **d'attente** waiting room; ~ **de bains** bathroom; ~ **de bavardage**, ~ **de causette** chatroom; ~ **de séjour** living room; ~ **de classe** classroom; ~ **d'embarquement** departure lounge; ~ **d'opération** operating theatre; ~ **des ventes** saleroom.

**salon** /salɔ̃/ *nm* lounge; (de coiffure, beauté) salon; (exposition) show; ~ **de thé** tea-room; ~ **virtuel** chatroom.

**salopette** /salɔpɛt/ *nf* dungarees (+ *pl*); (d'ouvrier) overalls (+ *pl*).

**saltimbanque** /saltɛ̃bɑ̃k/ *nmf* (street) acrobat.

**salubre** /salybʀ/ *a* healthy.

**saluer** /salɥe/ [1] *vt* greet; (en partant) take one's leave of; (de la tête) nod to; (de la main) wave to; (Mil) salute; (accueillir favorablement) welcome.

**salut** /saly/ *nm* greeting; (de la tête) nod; (de la main) wave; (Mil) salute; (rachat) salvation. ● *interj* (bonjour Ⓘ) hello; (au revoir Ⓘ) bye.

**salutation** /salytasjɔ̃/ *nf* greeting.

**samedi** /samdi/ *nm* Saturday.

**SAMU** /samy/ *abrév m* (**Service d'assistance médicale d'urgence**) ≈ mobile accident unit.

**sanction** /sɑ̃ksjɔ̃/ *nf* sanction. **sanctionner** [1] *vt* sanction; (punir) punish.

**sandale** /sɑ̃dal/ *nf* sandal.

**sang** /sɑ̃/ *nm* blood; **se faire du mauvais** ~ *ou* **un** ~ **d'encre** be worried stiff. **sang-froid** *nm inv* self-control. **sanglant**, ~**e** *a* bloody.

**sangle** /sɑ̃gl/ *nf* strap.

**sanglier** /sɑ̃glije/ *nm* wild boar.

**sanglot** /sɑ̃glo/ *nm* sob. **sangloter** [1] *vi* sob.

**sanguin**, ~**e** /sɑ̃gɛ̃, -in/ *a* (*groupe*) blood.

**sanguinaire** /sɑ̃ginɛʀ/ *a* bloodthirsty.

**sanitaire** /sanitɛʀ/ *a* (*directives*) health; (*conditions*) sanitary; (*appareils, installations*) bathroom, sanitary. **sanitaires** *nmpl* bathroom.

**sans** /sɑ̃/ *prép* without; ~ **ça**, ~ **quoi** otherwise; ~ **arrêt** nonstop; ~ **encombre**/**faute**/**tarder** without incident/fail/delay; ~ **fin**/**goût**/**limite** endless/tasteless/limitless;

~ **importance/pareil/précédent/travail** unimportant/unparalleled/unprecedented/unemployed; **j'ai aimé mais ~ plus** it was good, it wasn't great.

**sans-abri** /sɑ̃zabʀi/ *nmf inv* homeless person.

**sans-gêne** /sɑ̃ʒɛn/ *a inv* inconsiderate, thoughtless. ● *nm inv* thoughtlessness.

**sans-papiers** /sɑ̃papje/ *nm inv* illegal immigrant.

**santé** /sɑ̃te/ *nf* health; **à ta** *ou* **votre ~!** cheers!

**saoul, ~e** /su, sul/ ⇒SOÛL.

**sapin** /sapɛ̃/ *nm* fir(tree); **~ de Noël** Christmas tree.

**sarcasme** /saʀkasm/ *nm* sarcasm. **sarcastique** *a* sarcastic.

**sardine** /saʀdin/ *nf* sardine.

**sas** /sɑs/ *nm* (Naut, Aviat) airlock.

**satané, ~e** /satane/ *a* 🄸 damned.

**satellite** /satelit/ *nm* satellite.

**satin** /satɛ̃/ *nm* satin.

**satire** /satiʀ/ *nf* satire.

**satisfaction** /satisfaksjɔ̃/ *nf* satisfaction.

**satisfaire** /satisfɛʀ/ [33] *vt* satisfy. ● *vi* **~ à** fulfil. **satisfaisant, ~e** *a* (acceptable) satisfactory. **satisfait, ~e** *a* satisfied (**de** with).

**saturer** /satyʀe/ [1] *vt* saturate.

**sauce** /sos/ *nf* sauce; **~ tartare** tartar sauce. **saucière** *nf* sauceboat.

**saucisse** /sosis/ *nf* sausage.

**saucisson** /sosisɔ̃/ *nm* (slicing) sausage.

**sauf¹** /sof/ *prép* except; **~ erreur** if I'm not mistaken; **~ imprévu** unless anything unforeseen happens; **~ avis contraire** unless otherwise stated.

**sauf², -ve** /sof, sov/ *a* safe, unharmed.

**sauge** /soʒ/ *nf* (Culin) sage.

**saule** /sol/ *nm* willow; **~ pleureur** weeping willow.

**saumon** /somɔ̃/ *nm* salmon. ● *a inv* salmon-(pink).

**sauna** /sona/ *nm* sauna.

**saupoudrer** /sopudʀe/ [1] *vt* sprinkle (**de** with).

**saut** /so/ *nm* jump; **faire un ~ chez qn** pop round to sb's (place); **le ~** (Sport) jumping; **~ en hauteur/longueur** high/long jump; **~ périlleux** somersault; **au ~ du lit** on getting up.

**sauté, ~e** /sote/ *a & nm* (Culin) sauté.

**saute-mouton** /sotmutɔ̃/ *nm inv* leap-frog.

**sauter** /sote/ [1] *vi* jump; (exploser) blow up; (*fusible*) blow; (se détacher) come off; **faire ~** (détruire) blow up; (*fusible*) blow; (casser) break; **~ à la corde** skip; **~ aux yeux** be obvious; **~ au cou de qn** fling one's arms round sb; **~ sur une occasion** jump at an opportunity. ● *vt* jump (over); (page, classe) skip.

**sauterelle** /sotʀɛl/ *nf* grasshopper.

**sautiller** /sotije/ [1] *vi* hop.

**sauvage** /sovaʒ/ *a* wild; (primitif, cruel) savage; (farouche) unsociable; (illégal) unauthorized. ● *nmf* unsociable person; (brute) savage.

**sauve** /sov/ ⇒SAUF².

**sauvegarder** /sovgaʀde/ [1] *vt* safeguard; (Ordinat) back up.

**sauver** /sove/ [1] *vt* save; (d'un danger) rescue, save; (*matériel*) salvage. □ **se ~** *vpr* (fuir) run away; (partir 🄸) be off. **sauvetage** *nm* rescue. **sauveteur** *nm* rescuer. **sauveur** *nm* saviour.

**savant, ~e** /savɑ̃, -t/ *a* learned; (habile) skilful. ● *nm* scientist.

**saveur** /savœʀ/ *nf* flavour; (fig) savour.

**savoir** /savwaʀ/ [55] *vt* know; **elle sait conduire/nager** she can drive/swim; **faire ~ à qn que** inform sb that; **(pas) que je sache** (not) as far as I know; **à ~** namely. ● *nm* learning.

**savon** /savɔ̃/ *nm* soap; **passer un ~ à qn** 🅘 give sb a telling-off. **savonnette** *nf* bar of soap.

**savourer** /savuʀe/ [1] *vt* savour. **savoureux, -euse** *a* tasty; (fig) spicy.

**scandale** /skɑ̃dal/ *nm* scandal; (tapage) uproar; (en public) noisy scene; **faire ~** shock people; **faire un ~** make a scene. **scandaleux, -euse** *a* scandalous. **scandaliser** [1] *vt* scandalize, shock.

**scander** /skɑ̃de/ [1] *vt* (*vers*) scan; (*slogan*) chant.

**scandinave** /skɑ̃dinav/ *a* Scandinavian. **S~** *nmf* Scandinavian.

**Scandinavie** /skɑ̃dinavi/ *nf* Scandinavia.

**scarabée** /skaʀabe/ *nm* beetle.

**sceau** (*pl* **~x**) /so/ *nm* seal.

**scélérat** /seleʀa/ *nm* scoundrel.

**sceller** /sele/ [1] *vt* seal.

**scène** /sɛn/ *nf* scene; (estrade, art dramatique) stage; **mettre en ~** (*pièce*) stage; (*film*) direct; **mise en ~** direction; **~ de ménage** domestic dispute.

**scepticisme** /sɛptisism/ *nm* scepticism.

**sceptique** /sɛptik/ *a* sceptical. ● *nmf* sceptic.

**schéma** /ʃema/ *nm* diagram. **schématique** *a* schematic; (sommaire) sketchy. **schématiser** [1] *vt* simplify.

**schizophrène** /skizɔfʀɛn/ *a & nmf* schizophrenic.

**sciatique** /sjatik/ *a* (*nerf*) sciatic. ● *nf* sciatica.

**scie** /si/ *nf* saw.

**sciemment** /sjamɑ̃/ *adv* knowingly.

**science** /sjɑ̃s/ *nf* science; (savoir) knowledge.

**science-fiction** /sjɑ̃sfiksjɔ̃/ *nf* science fiction.

**scientifique** /sjɑ̃tifik/ *a* scientific. ● *nmf* scientist.

**scier** /sje/ [45] *vt* saw.

**scintiller** /sɛ̃tije/ [1] *vi* glitter; (*étoile*) twinkle.

**scission** /sisjɔ̃/ *nf* split.

**sclérose** /skleʀoz/ *nf* sclerosis; **~ en plaques** multiple sclerosis.

**scolaire** /skɔlɛʀ/ *a* school. **scolarisé, ~e** *a* going to school. **scolarité** *nf* schooling.

**score** /skɔʀ/ *nm* score.

**scorpion** /skɔʀpjɔ̃/ *nm* scorpion; **le S~** Scorpio.

**scotch** /skɔtʃ/ *nm* (boisson) Scotch (whisky); (ruban adhésif)® Sellotape®.

**scout, ~e** /skut/ *nm & a* scout.

**scrupule** /skʀypyl/ *nm* scruple. **scrupuleux, -euse** *a* scrupulous.

**scruter** /skʀyte/ [1] *vt* examine, scrutinize.

**scrutin** /skʀytɛ̃/ *nm* (vote) ballot; (élections) polls (+ *pl*).

**sculpter** /skylte/ [1] *vt* sculpt, carve. **sculpteur** *nm* sculptor. **sculpture** *nf* sculpture.

**SDF** *abrév mf* (**sans domicile fixe**) homeless person.

**se**, **s'** /sə, s/

**s'** before vowel or mute h.

● *pronom*

····➤ himself, (féminin) herself; (indéfini) oneself; (non humain) itself; (au pluriel) themselves; **~ laver les mains** wash one's hands; (réciproque) each other, one another; **ils se détestent** they hate each other.

**!** The translation of **se** will vary according to which verb it is associated with. You should therefore refer to the verb to find it. For example, **se promener**, **se taire** will be treated respectively under **promener** and **taire**.

**séance** /seɑ̃s/ *nf* session; (Théât, cinéma) show; **~ de pose** sitting; **~ tenante** forthwith.

**seau** (*pl* **~x**) /so/ *nm* bucket, pail.

**sec**, **sèche** /sɛk, sɛʃ/ *a* dry; (*fruits*) dried; (*coup, bruit*) sharp; (*cœur*) hard; (*whisky*) neat. ● *nm* **à ~** (sans eau) dry; (sans argent) broke; **au ~** in a dry place.

**sèche-cheveux** /sɛʃʃəvø/ *nm inv* hairdrier.

**sèchement** /sɛʃmɑ̃/ *adv* drily.

**sécher** /seʃe/ [14] *vt/i* dry; (*cours*: [I]) skip; (ne pas savoir [I]) be stumped. □ **se ~** *vpr* dry oneself. **sécheresse** *nf* (de climat) dryness; (temps sec) drought. **séchoir** *nm* drier.

**second**, **~e** /səgɔ̃, -d/ *a* & *nm,f* second. ● *nm* (adjoint) second in command; (étage) second floor. **secondaire** *a* secondary. **seconde** *nf* (instant) second; (vitesse) second gear.

**seconder** /səgɔ̃de/ [1] *vt* assist.

**secouer** /səkwe/ [1] *vt* shake; (*poussière, torpeur*) shake off. □ **se ~** *vpr* [I] (se dépêcher) get a move on; (réagir) shake oneself up.

**secourir** /səkuʀiʀ/ [20] *vt* assist, help. **secouriste** *nmf* first-aid worker.

**secours** /səkuʀ/ *nm* assistance, help; **au ~!** help!; **de ~** (*sortie*) emergency; (*équipe, opération*) rescue. ● *nmpl* (Méd) first aid.

**secousse** /səkus/ *nf* jolt, jerk; (séisme) tremor.

**secret**, **-ète** /səkʀɛ, -t/ *a* secret. ● *nm* secret; (discrétion) secrecy; **le ~ professionnel** professional confidentiality; **~ de Polichinelle** open secret; **en ~** in secret, secretly.

**secrétaire** /səkʀetɛʀ/ *nmf* secretary; **~ de direction** personal assistant. ● *nm* (meuble) writing-desk; **~ d'État** junior minister.

**secrétariat** /səkʀetaʀja/ *nm* secretarial work; (bureau) secretariat.

**sectaire** /sɛktɛʀ/ *a* sectarian.

**secte** /sɛkt/ *nf* sect.

**secteur** /sɛktœʀ/ *nm* area; (Comm) sector; (circuit: Électr) mains (+ *pl*).

**section** /sɛksjɔ̃/ *nf* section; (Scol) stream; (Mil) platoon. **sectionner** [1] *vt* sever.

**sécuriser** /sekyʀize/ [1] *vt* reassure.

**sécurité** /sekyʀite/ *nf* security; (absence de danger) safety; **en ~** safe, secure. **Sécurité sociale** *nf* social services, social security services.

**sédatif** /sedatif/ *nm* sedative.

**sédentaire** /sedɑ̃tɛʀ/ *a* sedentary.

**séducteur**, **-trice** /sedyktœʀ, -tʀis/ *a* seductive. ● *nm,f* seducer.

**séduction** *nf* seduction; (charme) charm.

**séduire** /sedɥiʀ/ [17] *vt* charm; (plaire à) appeal to; (sexuellement) seduce. **séduisant**, **~e** *a* attractive.

**ségrégation** /segʀegasjɔ̃/ *nf* segregation.

**seigle** /sɛgl/ *nm* rye.

**seigneur** /sɛɲœʀ/ *nm* lord; **le S~** the Lord.

**sein** /sɛ̃/ *nm* breast; **au ~ de** within.

**séisme** /seism/ *nm* earthquake.

**seize** /sɛz/ *a & nm* sixteen.

**séjour** /seʒuʀ/ *nm* stay; (pièce) living room. **séjourner** [1] *vi* stay.

**sel** /sɛl/ *nm* salt; (piquant) spice.

**sélectif**, **-ive** /selɛktif, -v/ *a* selective.

**sélection** /selɛksjɔ̃/ *nf* selection. **sélectionner** [1] *vt* select.

**selle** /sɛl/ *nf* saddle; **~s** (Méd) stools.

**sellette** /sɛlɛt/ *nf* **sur la ~** (*personne*) in the hot seat.

**selon** /səlɔ̃/ *prép* according to; **~ que** depending on whether.

**semaine** /səmɛn/ *nf* week; **en ~** during the week.

**sémantique** /semɑ̃tik/ *a* semantic. ● *nf* semantics.

**semblable** /sɑ̃blabl/ *a* similar (**à** to). ● *nm* fellow (creature).

**semblant** /sɑ̃blɑ̃/ *nm* **faire ~ de** pretend to; **un ~ de** a semblance of.

**sembler** /sɑ̃ble/ [1] *vi* seem (**à** to; **que** that); **il me semble que** it seems to me that.

**semelle** /səmɛl/ *nf* sole; **~ compensée** wedge heel.

**semence** /s(ə)mɑ̃s/ *nf* seed.

**semer** /s(ə)me/ [6] *vt* (*graine, doute*) sow; (jeter, parsemer) strew; (*personne* Ⓘ) lose; **~ la panique** spread panic.

**semestre** /səmɛstʀ/ *nm* half-year; (Univ) semester. **semestriel**, **~le** *a* (revue) biannual; (examen) end-of-semester.

**séminaire** /seminɛʀ/ *nm* (Relig) seminary; (Univ) seminar.

**semi-remorque** /s(ə)miʀ(ə) mɔʀk/ *nm* articulated lorry.

**semis** /s(ə)mi/ *nm* (plant) seedling.

**semoule** /s(ə)mul/ *nf* semolina.

**sénat** /sena/ *nm* senate. **sénateur** *nm* senator.

**sénile** /senil/ *a* senile.

**senior** /senjɔʀ/ *a* (âgé) senior; (mode, publication) for senior citizens. ● *nmf* senior citizen.

**sens** /sɑ̃s/ *nm* (Méd) sense; (signification) meaning, sense; (direction) direction; **à mon ~** to my mind; **à ~ unique** (*rue*) one-way; **ça n'a pas de ~** it doesn't make sense; **~ commun** common sense; **~ giratoire** roundabout; **~ interdit** no-entry sign; (rue) one-way street; **dans le ~ des aiguilles d'une montre** clockwise; **dans le ~ inverse des aiguilles d'une montre** anticlockwise; **~ dessus dessous** upside down; **~ devant derrière** back to front.

**sensation** /sɑ̃sasjɔ̃/ *nf* feeling, sensation; **faire ~** create a sensation. **sensationnel**, **~le** *a* sensational.

**sensé**, **~e** /sɑ̃se/ *a* sensible.

**sensibiliser** /sɑ̃sibilize/ [1] *vt* **~ l'opinion** increase people's awareness (**à qch** to sth).

**sensibilité** /sɑ̃sibilite/ *nf* sensitivity. **sensible** *a* sensitive (**à** to); (appréciable) noticeable. **sensiblement** *adv* noticeably.

**sensoriel**, **~le** /sɑ̃sɔʀjɛl/ *a* sensory.

**sensualité** /sɑ̃sɥalite/ *nf* sensuousness; sensuality. **sensuel, ~le** *a* sensual.

**sentence** /sɑ̃tɑ̃s/ *nf* sentence.

**senteur** /sɑ̃tœʀ/ *nf* scent.

**sentier** /sɑ̃tje/ *nm* path.

**sentiment** /sɑ̃timɑ̃/ *nm* feeling; **faire du ~** sentimentalize; **j'ai le ~ que...** I get the feeling that... **sentimental, ~e** (*mpl* **-aux**) *a* sentimental.

**sentir** /sɑ̃tiʀ/ [46] *vt* feel; (*odeur*) smell; (pressentir) sense; **~ la lavande** smell of lavender; **je ne peux pas le ~** 🅘 I can't stand him. ● *vi* smell. ▫ **se ~** *vpr* **se ~ fier/mieux** feel proud/better.

**séparation** /sepaʀasjɔ̃/ *nf* separation.

**séparatiste** /sepaʀatist/ *a & nmf* separatist

**séparé, ~e** /sepaʀe/ *a* separate; (*conjoints*) separated.

**séparer** /sepaʀe/ [1] *vt* separate; (en deux) split. ▫ **se ~** *vpr* separate, part (**de** from); (se détacher) split; **se ~ de** (se défaire de) part with.

**sept** /sɛt/ *a & nm* seven.

**septante** /sɛptɑ̃t/ *a & nm* seventy.

**septembre** /sɛptɑ̃bʀ/ *nm* September.

**septentrional, ~e** (*mpl* **-aux**) /sɛptɑ̃tʀijɔnal, -o/ *a* northern.

**septième** /sɛtjɛm/ *a & nmf* seventh.

**sépulture** /sepyltyʀ/ *nf* burial; (lieu) burial place.

**séquelles** /sekɛl/ *nfpl* (maladie) aftereffects; (fig) aftermath (+ *sg*).

**séquence** /sekɑ̃s/ *nf* sequence.

**séquestrer** /sekɛstʀe/ [1] *vt* confine (illegally).

**sera, serait** /səʀa, səʀɛ/ ⇒ÊTRE [4].

**serbe** /sɛʀb/ *a* Serbian. **S~** *nmf* Serbian.

**Serbie** /sɛʀbi/ *nf* Serbia.

**serein, ~e** /səʀɛ̃, -ɛn/ *a* serene.

**sérénité** /seʀenite/ *nf* serenity.

**sergent** /sɛʀʒɑ̃/ *nm* sergeant.

**série** /seʀi/ *nf* series (+ *sg*); (d'objets) set; **de ~** (*véhicule etc.*) standard; **fabrication** *ou* **production en ~** mass production.

**sérieusement** /seʀjøzmɑ̃/ *adv* seriously.

**sérieux, -ieuse** /seʀjø, -z/ *a* serious; (digne de confiance) reliable; (*chances, raison*) good. ● *nm* seriousness; **garder son ~** keep a straight face; **prendre au ~** take seriously.

**serin** /səʀɛ̃/ *nm* canary.

**seringue** /səʀɛ̃g/ *nf* syringe.

**serment** /sɛʀmɑ̃/ *nm* oath, (promesse) vow.

**sermon** /sɛʀmɔ̃/ *nm* sermon. **sermonner** [1] *vt* lecture.

**séropositif, -ive** /seʀɔpɔsitif, -v/ *a* HIV positive.

**serpent** /sɛʀpɑ̃/ *nm* snake; **~ à sonnettes** rattlesnake.

**serpillière** /sɛʀpijɛʀ/ *nf* floorcloth.

**serre** /sɛʀ/ *nf* (de jardin) greenhouse; (griffe) claw.

**serré, ~e** /seʀe/ *a* (*habit, nœud, écrou*) tight; (*personnes*) packed, crowded; (*lutte, mailles*) close; (*écriture*) cramped; (*cœur*) heavy.

**serrer** /seʀe/ [1] *vt* (saisir) grip; (presser) squeeze; (*vis, corde, ceinture*) tighten; (*poing, dents*) clench; **~ qn dans ses bras** hug sb; **~ les rangs** close ranks; **~ qn** (vêtement) be tight on sb; **~ qn de près** follow sb closely; **~ la main à** shake hands with. ● *vi* **~ à droite** keep over to

the right. □ **se ~** *vpr* (se rapprocher) squeeze (up) (**contre** against).

**serrure** /seʀyʀ/ *nf* lock. **serrurier** *nm* locksmith.

**servante** /sɛʀvɑ̃t/ *nf* (maid)servant.

**serveur, -euse** /sɛʀvœʀ, -øz/ *nm,f* (homme) waiter; (femme) waitress. ● *nm* (Ordinat) server.

**serviable** /sɛʀvjabl/ *a* helpful.

**service** /sɛʀvis/ *nm* service; (fonction, temps de travail) duty; (pourboire) service (charge); (dans une société) department; **~ (non) compris** service (not) included; **être de ~** be on duty; **pendant le ~** (when) on duty; **rendre ~ à qn** be a help to sb; **~ à thé** tea set; **~ d'ordre** stewards (+ *pl*); **~ après-vente** after-sales service; **~ militaire** military service; **les ~s secrets** the secret service (+ *sg*).

**serviette** /sɛʀvjɛt/ *nf* (de toilette) towel; (cartable) briefcase; **~ (de table)** serviette, napkin; **~ hygiénique** sanitary towel.

**servir** /sɛʀviʀ/ [46] *vt/i* serve; (être utile) be of use, serve; **~ qn (à table)** wait on sb; **ça sert à** (outil, récipient) it is used for; **ça me sert à/de** I use it to/as; **ça ne sert à rien** (*action*) it's pointless; **~ de** serve as, be used as; **~ à qn de guide** act as a guide for sb. □ **se ~** *vpr* (à table) help oneself (**de** to); **se ~ de** use. **serviteur** *nm* servant.

**ses** /se/ ⇒SON[1].

**session** /sesjɔ̃/ *nf* session.

**seuil** /sœj/ *nm* doorstep; (entrée) doorway; (fig) threshold.

**seul, ~e** /sœl/ *a* alone, on one's own; (unique) only; **un ~ exemple** only one example; **pas un ~ ami** not a single friend; **lui ~ le sait** only he knows; **dans le ~ but de** with the sole aim of; **parler tout ~** talk to oneself; **faire qch tout ~** do sth on one's own. ● *nm,f* **le ~, la ~e** the only one. **seulement** *adv* only.

**sève** /sɛv/ *nf* sap.

**sévère** /sevɛʀ/ *a* severe. **sévérité** *nf* severity.

**sévices** /sevis/ *nmpl* physical abuse (+ *sg*).

**sévir** /seviʀ/ [2] *vi* (*fléau*) rage; **~ contre** punish.

**sevrer** /səvʀe/ [6] *vt* wean.

**sexe** /sɛks/ *nm* sex; (organes) genitals (+ *pl*). **sexiste** *a* sexist. **sexualité** *nf* sexuality. **sexuel, ~le** *a* sexual.

**shampooing** /ʃɑ̃pwɛ̃/ *nm* shampoo.

**shérif** /ʃeʀif/ *nm* sheriff.

**short** /ʃɔʀt/ *nm* shorts (+ *pl*).

**si** (**s'** *before il, ils*) /si, s/ *conj* if; (interrogation indirecte) if, whether; **~ on allait se promener?** what about a walk?; **s'il vous** *ou* **te plaît** please; **~ oui** if so; **~ seulement** if only. ● *adv* (tellement) so; (oui) yes; **un ~ bon repas** such a good meal; **~ habile qu'il soit** however skilful he may be; **~ bien que** with the result that.

**sida** /sida/ *nm* (Méd) Aids.

**sidérurgie** /sideʀyʀʒi/ *nf* steel industry.

**siècle** /sjɛkl/ *nm* century; (époque) age.

**siège** /sjɛʒ/ *nm* seat; (Mil) siege; **~ éjectable** ejector seat; **~ social** head office, headquarters (+ *pl*). **siéger** [14] [40] *vi* (assemblée) sit.

**sien, ~ne** /sjɛ̃, -ɛn/ *pron* **le ~, la ~ne, les ~(ne)s** (homme) his; (femme) hers; (chose) its; **les ~s** (famille) one's family.

**sieste** /sjɛst/ *nf* nap, siesta.

**sifflement** /sifləmɑ̃/ *nm* whistling; **un ~** a whistle.

**siffler** /sifle/ [1] *vi* whistle; (avec un sifflet) blow one's whistle; (*serpent, gaz*) hiss. ● *vt* (*air*) whistle; (*chien*) whistle to *ou* for; (*acteur*) hiss.

**sifflet** /siflɛ/ *nm* whistle; **~s** (huées) boos.

**sigle** /sigl/ *nm* acronym.

**signal** (*pl* **-aux**) /siɲal, -o/ *nm* signal; **~ sonore** (de répondeur) tone.

**signalement** /siɲalmɑ̃/ *nm* description.

**signaler** /siɲale/ [1] *vt* indicate; (par une sonnerie, un écriteau) signal; (dénoncer, mentionner) report; (faire remarquer) point out.

**signalisation** /siɲalizasjɔ̃/ *nf* signalling, signposting; (signaux) signals (+ *pl*).

**signataire** /siɲatɛʀ/ *nmf* signatory.

**signature** /siɲatyʀ/ *nf* signature; (action) signing; **~ électronique** digital signature.

**signe** /siɲ/ *nm* sign; (de ponctuation) mark; **faire ~ à qn** wave at sb; (contacter) contact; **faire ~ à qn de** beckon sb to; **faire ~ que non** shake one's head; **faire ~ que oui** nod.

**signer** /siɲe/ [1] *vt* sign. □ **se ~** *vpr* (Relig) cross oneself.

**signet** /siɲɛ/ *nm* (pour livre, Internet) bookmark; **~s favoris** (Internet) hotlist.

**significatif, -ive** /siɲifikatif, -v/ *a* significant.

**signification** /siɲifikasjɔ̃/ *nf* meaning. **signifier** [45] *vt* mean, signify; (faire connaître) make known.

**silence** /silɑ̃s/ *nm* silence; (Mus) rest; **garder le ~** keep silent.

**silencieux, -ieuse** /silɑ̃sjø, -z/ *a* silent. ● *nm* silencer.

**silex** /silɛks/ *nm inv* flint.

**silhouette** /silwɛt/ *nf* outline, silhouette.

**sillon** /sijɔ̃/ *nm* furrow; (de disque) groove.

**sillonner** /sijɔne/ [1] *vt* crisscross.

**similaire** /similɛʀ/ *a* similar. **similitude** *nf* similarity.

**simple** /sɛ̃pl/ *a* simple; (non double) single. ● *nm* **~ dames/messieurs** ladies'/men's singles (+ *pl*). **simple d'esprit** *nmf* simpleton. **simplement** *adv* simply. **simplicité** *nf* simplicity; (naïveté) simpleness.

**simplification** /sɛ̃plifikasjɔ̃/ *nf* simplification. **simplifier** [45] *vt* simplify.

**simpliste** /sɛ̃plist/ *a* simplistic.

**simulacre** /simylakʀ/ *nm* pretence, sham.

**simulation** /simylasjɔ̃/ *nf* simulation. **simuler** [1] *vt* simulate.

**simultané, ~e** /simyltane/ *a* simultaneous.

**sincère** /sɛ̃sɛʀ/ *a* sincere. **sincérité** *nf* sincerity.

**singe** /sɛ̃ʒ/ *nm* monkey; (grand) ape. **singer** [40] *vt* mimic, ape.

**singulier, -ière** /sɛ̃gylje, -jɛʀ/ *a* peculiar, remarkable; (Gram) singular. ● *nm* (Gram) singular.

**sinistre** /sinistʀ/ *a* sinister. ● *nm* disaster; (incendie) blaze; (dommages) damage.

**sinistré, ~e** /sinistʀe/ *a* stricken. ● *nm,f* disaster victim.

**sinon** /sinɔ̃/ *conj* (autrement) otherwise; (sauf) except (**que** that); **difficile ~ impossible** difficult if not impossible.

**sinueux, -euse** /sinɥø, -z/ *a* winding; (fig) tortuous.

**sirène** /siʀɛn/ *nf* (appareil) siren; (femme) mermaid.

**sirop** /siRo/ *nm* (de fruits, Méd) syrup; (boisson) cordial.

**sismique** /sismik/ *a* seismic.

**site** /sit/ *nm* site; **~ touristique** place of interest; **~ Internet** *or* **Web** website.

**sitôt** /sito/ *adv* **~ entré** immediately after coming in; **~ que** as soon as; **pas de ~** not for a while.

**situation** /sitɥasjɔ̃/ *nf* situation; (emploi) job, position; **~ de famille** marital status.

**situé**, **~e** /sitɥe/ *a* situated.

**situer** /sitɥe/ [1] *vt* situate, locate. □ **se ~** *vpr* (se trouver) be situated.

**six** /sis/ (/si/ *before consonant*, /siz/ *before vowel*) *a & nm* six. **sixième** *a & nmf* sixth.

**sketch** (*pl* **~es**) /skɛtʃ/ *nm* (Théât) sketch.

**ski** /ski/ *nm* (matériel) ski; (Sport) skiing; **faire du ~** ski; **~ de fond** cross-country skiing; **~ nautique** water skiing. **skier** [45] *vi* ski.

**slave** /slav/ *a* Slav; (Ling) Slavonic.

**slip** /slip/ *nm* (d'homme) underpants (+ *pl*); (de femme) knickers (+ *pl*); **~ de bain** (swimming) trunks (+ *pl*); (du bikini) bikini bottom.

**slogan** /slɔgɑ̃/ *nm* slogan.

**Slovaquie** /slɔvaki/ *nf* Slovakia.

**Slovénie** /slɔveni/ *nf* Slovenia.

**smoking** /smɔkiŋ/ *nm* dinner jacket.

**SNCF** *abrév f* (**Société nationale des Chemins de fer français**) *French national railway company.*

**snob** /snɔb/ *nmf* snob. ● *a* snobbish. **snobisme** *nm* snobbery.

**sobre** /sɔbR/ *a* sober.

**social**, **~e** (*mpl* **-iaux**) /sɔsjal, -jo/ *a* social.

**socialisme** /sɔsjalism/ *nm* socialism. **socialiste** *nmf & a* socialist.

**société** /sɔsjete/ *nf* society; (entreprise) company; **~ point com** dotcom.

**socle** /sɔkl/ *nm* (de colonne, statue) plinth; (de lampe) base.

**socquette** /sɔkɛt/ *nf* ankle sock.

**soda** /sɔda/ *nm* fizzy drink.

**sœur** /sœR/ *nf* sister.

**soi** /swa/ *pron* oneself; **derrière ~** behind one; **en ~** in itself; **aller de ~** be obvious.

**soi-disant** /swadizɑ̃/ *a inv* so-called. ● *adv* supposedly.

**soie** /swa/ *nf* silk.

**soif** /swaf/ *nf* thirst; **avoir ~** be thirsty; **donner ~** make one thirsty.

**soigné**, **~e** /swaɲe/ *a* (apparence) tidy, neat; (travail) carefully done.

**soigner** /swaɲe/ [1] *vt* (s'occuper de) look after, take care of; (*tenue, style*) take care over; (*maladie*) treat. □ **se ~** *vpr* look after oneself.

**soigneusement** /swaɲøzmɑ̃/ *adv* carefully. **soigneux**, **-euse** *a* careful (**de** about); (ordonné) tidy.

**soi-même** /swamɛm/ *pron* oneself.

**soin** /swɛ̃/ *nm* care; (ordre) tidiness; **~s** care; (Méd) treatment; **avec ~** carefully; **avoir** *ou* **prendre ~ de qn/de faire** take care of sb/to do; **premiers ~s** first aid (+ *sg*).

**soir** /swaR/ *nm* evening; **à ce ~** see you tonight.

**soirée** /swaRe/ *nf* evening; (réception) party.

**soit** /swa/ *conj* (à savoir) that is to say; **~ ... ~** either ... or. ● ⇒ÊTRE [4].

**soixante** /swasɑ̃t/ *a & nm* sixty. **soixante-dix** *a & nm* seventy.

**soja** /sɔʒa/ *nm* (graines) soya beans (+ *pl*); (plante) soya.

**sol** /sɔl/ *nm* ground; (de maison) floor; (terrain agricole) soil.

**solaire** /sɔlɛʀ/ *a* solar; (*huile, filtre*) sun.

**soldat** /sɔlda/ *nm* soldier.

**solde**[1] /sɔld/ *nf* (salaire) pay.

**solde**[2] /sɔld/ *nm* (Comm) balance; **les ~s** the sales; **~s** (écrit en vitrine) sale; **en ~** (acheter) at sale price.

**solder** /sɔlde/ [1] *vt* sell off at sale price; (*compte*) settle. □ **se ~ par** *vpr* (aboutir à) end in.

**sole** /sɔl/ *nf* (poisson) sole.

**soleil** /sɔlɛj/ *nm* sun; (fleur) sunflower; **il y a du ~** it's sunny.

**solennel**, **~le** /sɔlanɛl/ *a* solemn.

**solfège** /sɔlfɛʒ/ *nm* musical theory.

**solidaire** /sɔlidɛʀ/ *a* (*mécanismes*) interdependent; (*collègues*) (mutually) supportive; **être ~ de qn** support sb. **solidarité** *nf* solidarity.

**solide** /sɔlid/ *a* solid; (*personne*) strong. ● *nm* solid.

**solidifier** /sɔlidifje/ [45] *vt* solidify. □ **se ~** *vpr* solidify.

**solitaire** /sɔlitɛʀ/ *a* solitary. ● *nmf* (*personne*) loner. **solitude** *nf* solitude.

**solliciter** /sɔlisite/ [1] *vt* seek; (faire appel à) call upon; **être très sollicité** be very much in demand.

**sollicitude** /sɔlisityd/ *nf* concern.

**solo** /solo/ *nm & a inv* (Mus) solo.

**solution** /sɔlysjɔ̃/ *nf* solution.

**solvable** /sɔlvabl/ *a* solvent.

**solvant** /sɔlvɑ̃/ *nm* solvent.

**sombre** /sɔ̃bʀ/ *a* dark; (triste) sombre.

**sombrer** /sɔ̃bʀe/ [1] *vi* sink (**dans** into).

**sommaire** /sɔmɛʀ/ *a* (*exécution*) summary; (*description*) rough. ● *nm* contents (+ *pl*); **au ~** on the programme.

**sommation** /sɔmasjɔ̃/ *nf* (Mil) warning; (Jur) notice.

**somme** /sɔm/ *nf* sum; **en ~, ~ toute** in short; **faire la ~ de** add (up), total (up). ● *nm* nap.

**sommeil** /sɔmɛj/ *nm* sleep; **avoir ~** be *ou* feel sleepy; **en ~** (*projet*) put on ice. **sommeiller** [1] *vi* doze; (fig) lie dormant.

**sommelier** /sɔməlje/ *nm* wine steward.

**sommer** /sɔme/ [1] *vt* summon.

**sommes** /sɔm/ ⇒ÊTRE [4].

**sommet** /sɔmɛ/ *nm* top; (de montagne) summit; (de triangle) apex; (gloire) height.

**sommier** /sɔmje/ *nm* bed base.

**somnambule** /sɔmnɑ̃byl/ *nm* sleepwalker.

**somnifère** /sɔmnifɛʀ/ *nm* sleeping pill.

**somnolent**, **~e** /sɔmnɔlɑ̃, -t/ *a* drowsy. **somnoler** [1] *vi* doze.

**somptueux**, **-euse** /sɔ̃ptɥø, -z/ *a* sumptuous.

**son**[1], **sa** (**son** *before vowel or mute h*) (*pl* **ses**) /sɔ̃, sa, sɔ̃n, se/ *a* (homme) his; (femme) her; (chose) its; (indéfini) one's.

**son**[2] /sɔ̃/ *nm* (bruit) sound; (du blé) bran; **baisser le ~** turn the volume down.

**sondage** /sɔ̃daʒ/ *nm* **~ (d'opinion)** (opinion) poll.

**sonde** /sɔ̃d/ *nf* (de forage) drill; (Méd) (d'évacuation) catheter; (d'examen) probe.

**sonder** /sɔ̃de/ [1] *vt* (*population*) poll; (explorer) sound; (*terrain*) drill; (*intentions*) sound out.

**songe** /sɔ̃ʒ/ *nm* dream.

**songer** /sɔ̃ʒe/ [40] *vt* ~ **que** think that; ~ **à** think about. **songeur, -euse** *a* pensive.

**sonné, ~e** /sɔne/ *a* (étourdi) groggy; 🅸 crazy.

**sonner** /sɔne/ [1] *vt/i* ring; (*clairon, glas*) sound; (*heure*) strike; (*domestique*) ring for; **midi sonné** well past noon; ~ **de** (*clairon*) sound, blow.

**sonnerie** /sɔnʀi/ *nf* ringing; (de clairon) sounding; (sonnette) bell.

**sonnet** /sɔnɛ/ *nm* sonnet.

**sonnette** /sɔnɛt/ *nf* bell.

**sonore** /sɔnɔʀ/ *a* resonant; (*onde, effets*) sound; (*rire*) resounding.

**sonorisation** /sɔnɔʀizasjɔ̃/ *nf* (matériel) public address system.

**sonorité** /sɔnɔʀite/ *nf* resonance; (d'un instrument) tone.

**sont** /sɔ̃/ ⇒ÊTRE [4].

**sophistiqué, ~e** /sɔfistike/ *a* sophisticated.

**sorcellerie** /sɔʀsɛlʀi/ *nf* witchcraft. **sorcier** *nm* (guérisseur) witch doctor; (maléfique) sorcerer. **sorcière** *nf* witch.

**sordide** /sɔʀdid/ *a* sordid; (lieu) squalid.

**sort** /sɔʀ/ *nm* (destin, hasard) fate; (condition) lot; (maléfice) spell; **tirer (qch) au** ~ draw lots (for sth).

**sortant, ~e** /sɔʀtɑ̃, -t/ *a* (*président etc.*) outgoing.

**sorte** /sɔʀt/ *nf* sort, kind; **de** ~ **que** so that; **en quelque** ~ in a way; **de la** ~ in this way; **faire en** ~ **que** make sure that.

**sortie** /sɔʀti/ *nf* exit; (promenade, dîner) outing; (*déclaration* 🅸) remark; (parution) publication; (de disque, film) release; (d'un ordinateur) output; **~s** (argent) outgoings.

**sortilège** /sɔʀtilɛʒ/ *nm* (magic) spell.

**sortir** /sɔʀtiʀ/ [46] *vi* (*aux être*) go out, leave; (venir) come out; (aller au spectacle) go out; (*livre, film*) come out; (*plante*) come up; ~ **de** (*pièce*) leave; (*milieu social*) come from; (*limites*) go beyond; ~ **du commun ou de l'ordinaire** be out of the ordinary. ● *vt* (*aux avoir*) take out; (*livre, modèle*) bring out; (dire 🅸) come out with; ~ **qn de** get sb out of; **être sorti d'affaire** be in the clear. □ **s'en** ~ *vpr* cope, manage.

**sosie** /sɔzi/ *nm* double.

**sot, ~te** /so, sɔt/ *a* silly.

**sottise** /sɔtiz/ *nf* silliness; (action, remarque) foolish thing; **faire des ~s** be naughty.

**sou** /su/ *nm* 🅸 **~s** money; **sans le** ~ without a penny; **près de ses ~s** tight-fisted.

**soubresaut** /subʀəso/ *nm* (sudden) start.

**souche** /suʃ/ *nf* (d'arbre) stump; (de famille) stock; (de carnet) counterfoil.

**souci** /susi/ *nm* (inquiétude) worry; (préoccupation) concern; (plante) marigold; **se faire du** ~ worry.

**soucier (se)** /(sə)susje/ [45] *vpr* **se** ~ **de** care about. **soucieux, -ieuse** *a* concerned (**de** about).

**soucoupe** /sukup/ *nf* saucer; ~ **volante** flying saucer.

**soudain, ~e** /sudɛ̃, -ɛn/ *a* sudden. ● *adv* suddenly.

**soude** /sud/ *nf* soda.

**souder** /sude/ [1] *vt* weld, solder; **famille très soudée** close-knit family. □ **se** ~ *vpr* (os) knit (together).

**soudoyer** /sudwaje/ [31] *vt* bribe.

**souffle** /sufl/ *nm* (haleine) breath; (respiration) breathing; (explosion) blast; (vent) breath of air; **le** ~ **coupé** out of breath; **à couper le** ~ breathtaking.

**souffler** /sufle/ [1] *vi* blow; (haleter) puff. ● *vt* (*bougie*) blow out; (*pous-*

*sière, fumée*) blow; (*verre*) blow; (par explosion) destroy; (chuchoter) whisper; ~ **la réplique à** prompt. **souffleur**, **-euse** *nm,f* (Théât) prompter.

**souffrance** /sufʀɑ̃s/ *nf* suffering; **en** ~ (*affaire*) pending. **souffrant**, ~**e** *a* unwell.

**souffrir** /sufʀiʀ/ [21] *vi* suffer (**de** from). ● *vt* (endurer) suffer; **il ne peut pas le** ~ he cannot stand *ou* bear him.

**soufre** /sufʀ/ *nm* sulphur.

**souhait** /swɛ/ *nm* wish; **à tes** ~**s!** bless you!; **paisible à** ~ incredibly peaceful. **souhaitable** *a* desirable.

**souhaiter** /swete/ [1] *vt* ~ **qch à qn** wish sb sth; ~ **que/faire** hope that/to do; ~ **la bienvenue à qn** welcome sb.

**soûl**, ~**e** /su, sul/ *a* drunk. ● *nm* **tout son** ~ as much as one can.

**soulagement** /sulaʒmɑ̃/ *nm* relief. **soulager** [40] *vt* relieve.

**soûler** /sule/ [1] *vt* make drunk. □ **se** ~ *vpr* get drunk.

**soulèvement** /sulɛvmɑ̃/ *nm* uprising.

**soulever** /sulve/ [6] *vt* lift, raise; (*question, poussière*) raise; (*enthousiasme*) arouse; (*foule*) stir up. □ **se** ~ *vpr* lift *ou* raise oneself up; (se révolter) rise up.

**soulier** /sulje/ *nm* shoe.

**souligner** /suliɲe/ [1] *vt* underline; (*yeux*) outline; (taille) emphasize.

**soumettre** /sumɛtʀ/ [42] *vt* (assujettir) subject (**à** to); (présenter) submit (**à** to). □ **se** ~ *vpr* submit (**à** to). **soumis**, ~**e** *a* submissive. **soumission** *nf* submission.

**soupape** /supap/ *nf* valve.

**soupçon** /supsɔ̃/ *nm* suspicion; **un** ~ **de** (un peu de) a touch of. **soupçonner** [1] *vt* suspect. **soupçonneux**, **-euse** *a* suspicious.

**soupe** /sup/ *nf* soup.

**souper** /supe/ [6] *vi* have supper. ● *nm* supper.

**soupeser** /supəze/ [1] *vt* judge the weight of; (fig) weigh up.

**soupière** /supjɛʀ/ *nf* (soup) tureen.

**soupir** /supiʀ/ *nm* sigh; **pousser un** ~ heave a sigh.

**soupirer** /supiʀe/ [1] *vi* sigh.

**souple** /supl/ *a* supple; (*règlement, caractère*) flexible. **souplesse** *nf* suppleness; (de règlement) flexibility.

**source** /suʀs/ *nf* (de rivière, origine) source; (eau) spring. **prendre sa** ~ **à** rise in; **de** ~ **sûre** from a reliable source; ~ **thermale** hot spring.

**sourcil** /suʀsi/ *nm* eyebrow.

**sourciller** /suʀsije/ [1] *vi* **sans** ~ without batting an eyelid.

**sourd**, ~**e** /suʀ, -d/ *a* deaf; (*bruit, douleur*) dull; **faire la** ~**e oreille** turn a deaf ear. ● *nm,f* deaf person.

**sourd-muet** (*pl* **sourds-muets**), **sourde-muette** (*pl* **sourdes-muettes**) /suʀmɥɛ, suʀdmɥɛt/ *a* deaf and dumb. ● *nm,f* deaf-mute.

**souricière** /suʀisjɛʀ/ *nf* mousetrap; (fig) trap.

**sourire** /suʀiʀ/ [54] *vi* smile (**à** at); ~ **à** (fortune) smile on. ● *nm* smile; **garder le** ~ keep smiling.

**souris** /suʀi/ *nf* mouse; **des** ~ mice.

**sournois**, ~**e** /suʀnwa, -z/ *a* sly, underhand.

**sous** /su/ *prép* under, beneath; ~ **la main** handy; ~ **la pluie** in the rain; ~ **peu** shortly; ~ **terre** underground.

**sous-alimenté**, **~e** /suzalimɑ̃te/ *a* undernourished.

**souscription** /suskʀipsjɔ̃/ *nf* subscription. **souscrire** [30] *vi* **~ à** subscribe to.

**sous-entendre** /suzɑ̃tɑ̃dʀ/ [3] *vt* imply. **sous-entendu** *nm* innuendo, insinuation.

**sous-estimer** /suzɛstime/ [1] *vt* underestimate.

**sous-jacent**, **~e** /suʒasɑ̃, -t/ *a* underlying.

**sous-marin**, **~e** /sumaʀɛ̃, -in/ *a* underwater; (*plongée*) deep-sea. ● *nm* submarine.

**soussigné**, **~e** /susiɲe/ *a & nm,f* undersigned.

**sous-sol** /susɔl/ *nm* (cave) basement.

**sous-titre** /sutitʀ/ *nm* subtitle.

**soustraction** /sustʀaksjɔ̃/ *nf* (déduction) subtraction.

**soustraire** /sustʀɛʀ/ [29] *vt* (déduire) subtract; (retirer) take away (à from). ◻ **se ~ à** *vpr* escape from.

**sous-traitant** /sutʀɛtɑ̃/ *nm* subcontractor.

**sous-verre** /suvɛʀ/ *nm inv* glass mount.

**sous-vêtement** /suvɛtmɑ̃/ *nm* underwear.

**soute** /sut/ *nf* (de bateau) hold; **~ à charbon** coal-bunker.

**soutenir** /sutniʀ/ [59] *vt* support; (*effort, rythme*) sustain; (résister à) withstand; **~ que** maintain that.

**soutenu**, **~e** /sutny/ *a* (constant) sustained; (style) formal.

**souterrain**, **~e** /sutɛʀɛ̃, -ɛn/ *a* underground. ● *nm* underground passage.

**soutien** /sutjɛ̃/ *nm* support.

**soutien-gorge** (*pl* **soutiens-gorge**) /sutjɛ̃gɔʀʒ/ *nm* bra.

**soutirer** /sutiʀe/ [1] *vt* **~ à qn** extract from sb.

**souvenir**[1] /suvniʀ/ *nm* memory, recollection; (objet) memento; (cadeau) souvenir; **en ~ de** in memory of.

**souvenir**[2] **(se)** /(sə)suvniʀ/ [59] *vpr* **se ~ de** remember; **se ~ que** remember that.

**souvent** /suvɑ̃/ *adv* often.

**souverain**, **~e** /suvʀɛ̃, -ɛn/ *a* sovereign. ● *nm,f* sovereign.

**soviétique** /sɔvjetik/ *a* Soviet.

**soyeux**, **-euse** /swajø, -z/ *a* silky.

**spacieux**, **-ieuse** /spasjø, -z/ *a* spacious.

**sparadrap** /spaʀadʀa/ *nm* (sticking) plaster.

**spatial**, **~e** (*mpl* **-iaux**) /spasjal, -jo/ *a* space.

**speaker**, **~ine** /spikœʀ, -kʀin/ *nm,f* announcer.

**spécial**, **~e** (*mpl* **-iaux**) /spesjal, -jo/ *a* special; (bizarre) odd. **spécialement** *adv* (exprès) specially; (très) especially.

**spécialiser (se)** /səspesjalize/ [1] *vpr* specialize (**dans** in). **spécialiste** *nmf* specialist. **spécialité** *nf* speciality; (US) specialty.

**spécifier** /spesifje/ [45] *vt* specify.

**spécifique** /spesifik/ *a* specific.

**spécimen** /spesimɛn/ *nm* specimen.

**spectacle** /spɛktakl/ *nm* show; (vue) sight, spectacle.

**spectaculaire** /spɛktakylɛʀ/ *a* spectacular.

**spectateur**, **-trice** /spɛktatœʀ, -tʀis/ *nm,f* (Sport) spectator; (témoin oculaire) onlooker; **les ~s** (Théât) the audience (+ *sg*).

**spectre** /spɛktʀ/ *nm* (revenant) spectre; (images) spectrum.

**spéculateur**, **-trice** /spekylatœʀ, -tʀis/ *nm,f* speculator. **spéculation** *nf* speculation. **spéculer** [1] *vi* speculate.

**spéléologie** /speleɔlɔʒi/ *nf* cave exploration, pot-holing.

**spermatozoïde** /spɛʀmatɔzɔid/ *nm* spermatozoon. **sperme** *nm* sperm.

**sphère** /sfɛʀ/ *nf* sphere.

**spirale** /spiʀal/ *nf* spiral.

**spirituel**, **~le** /spiʀitɥɛl/ *a* spiritual; (amusant) witty.

**spiritueux** /spiʀitɥø/ *nm* (alcool) spirit.

**splendeur** /splɑ̃dœʀ/ *nf* splendour. **splendide** *a* splendid.

**sponsoriser** /spɔ̃sɔʀize/ [1] *vt* sponsor.

**spontané**, **~e** /spɔ̃tane/ *a* spontaneous. **spontanéité** *nf* spontaneity.

**sport** /spɔʀ/ *a inv* (*vêtements*) casual. ● *nm* sport; **veste/voiture de ~** sports jacket/car.

**sportif**, **-ive** /spɔʀtif, -v/ *a* (*personne*) sporty; (*physique*) athletic; (*résultats*) sports. ● *nm,f* sportsman, sportswoman.

**spot** /spɔt/ *nm* spotlight; **~ (publicitaire)** ad.

**square** /skwaʀ/ *nm* small public garden.

**squatter** /skwate/ [1] *vt* squat in.

**squelette** /skəlɛt/ *nm* skeleton. **squelettique** *a* skeletal.

**SSII** *abrév f* (**société de services et d'ingénierie informatiques**) computer services company.

**stabiliser** /stabilize/ [1] *vt* stabilize. **stable** *a* stable.

**stade** /stad/ *nm* (Sport) stadium; (phase) stage.

**stage** /staʒ/ *nm* (cours) course; (professionnel) placement. **stagiaire** *nmf* course member; (apprenti) trainee.

**stagner** /stagne/ [1] *vi* stagnate.

**stand** /stɑ̃d/ *nm* stand; (de fête foraine) stall.

**standard** /stɑ̃daʀ/ *nm* switchboard. ● *a inv* standard. **standardiser** [1] *vt* standardize.

**standardiste** /stɑ̃daʀdist/ *nmf* switchboard operator.

**standing** /stɑ̃diŋ/ *nm* status, standing; **de ~** (*hôtel*) luxury.

**starter** /staʀtɛʀ/ *nm* (Auto) choke.

**station** /stasjɔ̃/ *nf* station; (halte) stop; **~ de taxis** taxi rank; **~ balnéaire/de ski** seaside/ski resort; **~ thermale** spa.

**stationnaire** /stasjɔnɛʀ/ *a* stationary.

**stationnement** /stasjɔnmɑ̃/ *nm* parking. **stationner** [1] *vi* park.

**station-service** (*pl* **stations-service**) /stasjɔ̃sɛʀvis/ *nf* service station.

**statique** /statik/ *a* static.

**statistique** /statistik/ *nf* statistic; (science) statistics (+ *sg*). ● *a* statistical.

**statue** /staty/ *nf* statue.

**statuer** /statɥe/ [1] *vi* **~ sur** give a ruling on.

**statut** /staty/ *nm* status. **statutaire** *a* statutory

**sténo** /steno/ *nf* (sténographie) shorthand. **sténodactylo** *nf* shorthand typist. **sténographie** *nf* shorthand.

**stéréo** /steʀeo/ *nf & a inv* stereo.

**stéréotype** /steʀeɔtip/ *nm* stereotype.

**stérile** /steʀil/ *a* sterile.

**stérilet** /steʀilɛ/ *nm* coil, IUD.

**stérilisation** /steʀilizasjɔ̃/ *nf* sterilization. **stériliser** [1] *vt* sterilize.

**stéroïde** /steʀɔid/ *a & nm* steroid.

**stimulant** /stimylɑ̃/ *nm* stimulus; (médicament) stimulant.

**stimulateur** /stimylatœʀ/ *nm* ~ **cardiaque** (Méd) pacemaker.

**stimuler** /stimyle/ [1] *vt* stimulate.

**stipuler** /stipyle/ [1] *vt* stipulate.

**stock** /stɔk/ *nm* stock. **stocker** [1] *vt* stock.

**stoïque** /stɔik/ *a* stoical. ● *nmf* stoic.

**stop** /stɔp/ *interj* stop. ● *nm* stop sign; (feu arrière) brake light; **faire du** ~ ⓘ hitch-hike. **stopper** [1] *vt/i* stop.

**store** /stɔʀ/ *nm* blind; (de magasin) awning.

**strapontin** /stʀapɔ̃tɛ̃/ *nm* folding seat, jump seat.

**stratégie** /stʀateʒi/ *nf* strategy. **stratégique** *a* strategic.

**stress** /stʀɛs/ *nm* stress. **stressant**, ~**e** *a* stressful. **stressé**, ~**e** *a* stressed. **stresser** [1] *vt* put under stress.

**strict** /stʀikt/ *a* strict; (*tenue, vérité*) plain; **le** ~ **minimum** the bare minimum. **strictement** *adv* strictly.

**strident**, ~**e** /stʀidɑ̃, -t/ *a* shrill.

**strophe** /stʀɔf/ *nf* stanza, verse.

**structure** /stʀyktyʀ/ *nf* structure.

**studieux**, **-ieuse** /stydjø, -z/ *a* studious.

**studio** /stydjo/ *nm* (d'artiste, de télévision) studio; (logement) studio flat.

**stupéfaction** /stypefaksjɔ̃/ *nf* amazement. **stupéfait**, ~**e** *a* amazed.

**stupéfiant**, ~**e** /stypefjɑ̃, -t/ *a* astounding. ● *nm* drug, narcotic.

**stupéfier** /stypefje/ [45] *vt* amaze.

**stupeur** /stypœʀ/ *nf* amazement; (Méd) stupor.

**stupide** /stypid/ *a* stupid. **stupidité** *nf* stupidity.

**style** /stil/ *nm* style.

**styliste** /stilist/ *nmf* fashion designer.

**stylo** /stilo/ *nm* pen; ~ **(à) bille** ball-point pen; ~ **(à) encre** fountain pen.

**su** /sy/ ⇒SAVOIR [55].

**suave** /sɥav/ *a* sweet.

**subalterne** /sybaltɛʀn/ *a & nmf* subordinate.

**subconscient** /sypkɔ̃sjɑ̃/ *nm* subconscious.

**subir** /sybiʀ/ [2] *vt* be subjected to; (traitement, expériences) undergo.

**subit**, ~**e** /sybi, -t/ *a* sudden.

**subjectif**, **-ive** /sybʒɛktif, -v/ *a* subjective.

**subjonctif** /sybʒɔ̃ktif/ *nm* subjunctive.

**subjuguer** /sybʒyge/ [1] *vt* (charmer) captivate.

**sublime** /syblim/ *a* sublime.

**submerger** /sybmɛʀʒe/ [40] *vt* submerge; (fig) overwhelm.

**subordonné**, ~**e** /sybɔʀdɔne/ *a & nm,f* subordinate.

**subside** /sybzid/ *nm* grant.

**subsidiaire** /sybzidjɛʀ/ *a* subsidiary; **question** ~ tiebreaker.

**subsistance** /sybzistɑ̃s/ *nf* subsistence. **subsister** [1] *vi* subsist; (durer, persister) exist.

**substance** /sypstɑ̃s/ *nf* substance.

**substantiel**, ~**le** /sypstɑ̃sjɛl/ *a* substantial.

**substantif** /sypstɑ̃tif/ *nm* noun.

**substituer** /sypstitɥe/ [1] *vt* substitute (à for). □ **se** ~ **à** *vpr* (rem-

placer) substitute for. **substitut** *nm* substitute; (Jur) deputy public prosecutor.

**subtil**, **~e** /syptil/ *a* subtle.

**subtiliser** /syptilize/ [1] *vt* **~ qch (à qn)** steal sth.

**subvenir** /sybvəniʀ/ [59] *vi* **~ à** provide for.

**subvention** /sybvɑ̃sjɔ̃/ *nf* subsidy. **subventionner** [1] *vt* subsidize.

**subversif**, **-ive** /sybvɛʀsif, -v/ *a* subversive.

**suc** /syk/ *nm* juice.

**succédané** /syksedane/ *nm* substitute (**de** for).

**succéder** /syksede/ [14] *vi* **~ à** succeed. □ **se ~** *vpr* succeed one another.

**succès** /syksɛ/ *nm* success; **à ~** (film, livre,) successful; **avoir du ~** be a success.

**successeur** /syksesœʀ/ *nm* successor. **successif**, **-ive** *a* successive. **succession** *nf* succession; (Jur) inheritance.

**succinct**, **~e** /syksɛ̃, -t/ *a* succinct

**succomber** /sykɔ̃be/ [1] *vi* die; **~ à** succumb to.

**succulent**, **~e** /sykylɑ̃, -t/ *a* delicious.

**succursale** /sykyʀsal/ *nf* (Comm) branch.

**sucer** /syse/ [10] *vt* suck.

**sucette** /sysɛt/ *nf* (bonbon) lollipop; (tétine) dummy; (US) pacifier.

**sucre** /sykʀ/ *nm* sugar; **~ d'orge** barley sugar; **~ en poudre** caster sugar; **~ glace** icing sugar; **~ roux** brown sugar.

**sucré** /sykʀe/ *a* sweet; (additionné de sucre) sweetened. **sucrer** [1] *vt* sugar, sweeten. **sucreries** *nfpl* sweets.

**sucrier**, **-ière** /sykʀije, -jɛʀ/ *a* sugar. ● *nm* (récipient) sugar-bowl.

**sud** /syd/ *nm* south. ● *a inv* south; (*partie*) southern.

**sud-est** /sydɛst/ *nm* south-east.

**sud-ouest** /sydwɛst/ *nm* south-west.

**Suède** /sɥɛd/ *nf* Sweden.

**suédois**, **~e** /sɥedwa, z/ *a* Swedish. ● *nm* (Ling) Swedish. **S~**, **~e** *nm,f* Swede.

**suer** /sɥe/ [1] *vt/i* sweat; **faire ~ qn** 🅸 get on sb's nerves.

**sueur** /sɥœʀ/ *nf* sweat; **en ~** covered in sweat.

**suffire** /syfiʀ/ [57] *vi* be enough (**à qn** for sb); **il suffit de compter** all you have to do is count; **une goutte suffit** a drop is enough; **~ à** (besoin) satisfy. □ **se ~** *vpr* **se ~ à soi-même** be self-sufficient.

**suffisamment** /syfizamɑ̃/ *adv* sufficiently; **~ de qch** enough of sth. **suffisance** *nf* (vanité) conceit. **suffisant**, **~e** *a* sufficient; (vaniteux) conceited.

**suffixe** /syfiks/ *nm* suffix.

**suffoquer** /syfɔke/ [1] *vt/i* choke, suffocate.

**suffrage** /syfʀaʒ/ *nm* (voix; Pol) vote; (système) suffrage.

**suggérer** /sygʒeʀe/ [14] *vt* suggest. **suggestion** *nf* suggestion.

**suicidaire** /sɥisidɛʀ/ *a* suicidal. **suicide** *nm* suicide. **suicider** (**se**) [1] *vpr* commit suicide.

**suinter** /sɥɛ̃te/ [1] *vi* ooze.

**suis** /sɥi/ ⇒ÊTRE [4], SUIVRE [57].

**Suisse** /sɥis/ *nf* Switzerland. ● *nmf* Swiss. **suisse** *a* Swiss.

**suite** /sɥit/ *nf* continuation, rest; (d'un film) sequel; (série) series; (appartement, escorte) suite; (résultat) consequence; **à la ~**, **de ~** (successivement) in a row; **à la ~ de** (derrière)

behind; **à la ~ de**, **par ~ de** (en conséquence) as a result of; **faire ~ (à)** follow; **par la ~** afterwards; **~ à votre lettre du** further to your letter of the; **des ~s de** as a result of.

**suivant**[1], **~e** /sɥivɑ̃, -t/ *a* following, next. ● *nm,f* following *ou* next person.

**suivant**[2] /sɥivɑ̃/ *prép* (selon) according to.

**suivi**, **~e** /sɥivi/ *a* (*effort*) steady, sustained; (cohérent) consistent; **peu/très ~** (*cours*) poorly/well attended.

**suivre** /sɥivʀ/ [57] *vt/i* follow; (comprendre) follow; **faire ~** (courrier) forward. ◻ **se ~** *vpr* follow each other.

**sujet**, **~te** /syʒɛ, -t/ *a* **~ à** liable *ou* subject to. ● *nm* (d'un royaume) subject; (question) subject; (motif) cause; (Gram) subject; **au ~ de** about.

**super** /sypɛʀ/ *nm* (essence) four-star. ● *a inv* Ⓘ (très) great. ● *adv* Ⓘ ultra, really.

**superbe** /sypɛʀb/ *a* superb.

**supérette** /sypeʀɛt/ *nf* minimarket.

**superficie** /sypɛʀfisi/ *nf* area.

**superficiel**, **~le** /sypɛʀfisjɛl/ *a* superficial.

**superflu** /sypɛʀfly/ *a* superfluous. ● *nm* (excédent) surplus.

**supérieur**, **~e** /sypeʀjœʀ/ *a* (plus haut) upper; (*quantité, nombre*) greater (**à** than); (*études, principe*) higher (**à** than); (meilleur, hautain) superior (**à** to). ● *nm,f* superior. **supériorité** *nf* superiority.

**superlatif**, **-ive** /sypɛʀlatif, -v/ *a* & *nm* superlative.

**supermarché** /sypɛʀmaʀʃe/ *nm* supermarket.

**superposer** /sypɛʀpoze/ [1] *vt* superimpose; **lits superposés** bunk beds.

**superproduction** /sypɛʀpʀɔdyksjɔ̃/ *nf* (film) blockbuster.

**superpuissance** /sypɛʀpɥisɑ̃s/ *nf* superpower.

**superstitieux**, **-ieuse** /sypɛʀstisjø, -z/ *a* superstitious.

**superviser** /sypɛʀvize/ [1] *vt* supervise.

**suppléant**, **~e** /sypleɑ̃, -t/ *nmf* & *a* **(professeur) ~** supply teacher; **(juge) ~** deputy (judge).

**suppléer** /syplee/ [15] *vt* (remplacer) fill in for. ● *vi* **~ à** (compenser) make up for.

**supplément** /syplemɑ̃/ *nm* (argent) extra charge; (de frites, légumes) extra portion; **en ~** extra; **un ~ de** (travail) additional; **payer un ~** pay a supplement. **supplémentaire** *a* extra, additional.

**supplice** /syplis/ *nm* torture.

**supplier** /syplije/ [45] *vt* beg, beseech (**de** to).

**support** /sypɔʀ/ *nm* support; (Ordinat) medium.

**supportable** /sypɔʀtabl/ *a* bearable.

**supporter**[1] /sypɔʀte/ [1] *vt* (*privations*) bear; (*personne*) put up with; (*structure*: Ordinat) support; **il ne supporte pas les enfants/de perdre** he can't stand children/losing.

**supporter**[2] /sypɔʀtɛʀ/ *nm* (Sport) supporter.

**supposer** /sypoze/ [1] *vt* suppose; (impliquer) imply; **à ~ que** supposing that.

**suppression** /sypʀesjɔ̃/ *nf* (de taxe) abolition; (de sanction) lifting; (de mot) deletion. **supprimer** [1] *vt* (*allocation*) withdraw; (*contrôle*) lift; (*train*) cancel; (*preuve*) suppress.

**suprématie** /sypʀemasi/ *nf* supremacy.

**suprême** /sypʀɛm/ *a* supreme.

**sur** /syʀ/ *prép* on, upon; (par-dessus) over; (au sujet de) about, on; (proportion) out of; (mesure) by; **~ la photo** in the photograph; **mettre/jeter ~** put/throw on to; **~ mesure** made to measure; **~ place** on the spot; **~ ce, je pars** with that, I must go; **~ le moment** at the time.

**sûr** /syʀ/ *a* certain, sure; (sans danger) safe; (digne de confiance) reliable; (*main*) steady; (*jugement*) sound; **être ~ de soi** be self-confident; **j'en étais ~!** I knew it!

**surabondance** /syʀabɔ̃dɑ̃s/ *nf* overabundance.

**surcharge** /syʀʃaʀʒ/ *nf* overloading; (poids) excess load. **surcharger** [1] *vt* overload; (*texte*) alter.

**surchauffer** /syʀʃofe/ [1] *vt* overheat.

**surcroît** /syʀkʀwa/ *nm* increase (**de** in); **de ~** in addition.

**surdité** /syʀdite/ *nf* deafness.

**surélever** /syʀelve/ [6] *vt* raise.

**sûrement** /syʀmɑ̃/ *adv* certainly; (sans danger) safely; **il a ~ oublié** he must have forgotten.

**surenchère** /syʀɑ̃ʃɛʀ/ *nf* higher bid. **surenchérir** [2] *vi* bid higher (**sur** than).

**surestimer** /syʀɛstime/ [1] *vt* overestimate.

**sûreté** /syʀte/ *nf* safety; (de pays) security; (d'un geste) steadiness; **être en ~** be safe; **S~ (nationale)** police (+ *pl*).

**surexcité, ~e** /syʀɛksite/ *a* very excited.

**surf** /sœʀf/ *nm* surfing.

**surface** /syʀfas/ *nf* surface; **faire ~** (*sous-marin*, fig) surface; **en ~** on the surface.

**surfait, ~e** /syʀfɛ, -t/ *a* overrated.

**surfer** /sœʀfe/ [1] *vi* go surfing; **~ sur l'Internet** surf the Internet.

**surgelé, ~e** /syʀʒəle/ *a* (deep-) frozen. **aliments ~s** frozen food (+ *sg*).

**surgir** /syʀʒiʀ/ [2] *vi* appear (suddenly); (*difficulté*) crop up.

**sur-le-champ** /syʀləʃɑ̃/ *adv* right away.

**surlendemain** /syʀlɑ̃dmɛ̃/ *nm* **le ~** two days later; **le ~ de** two days after.

**surligneur** /syʀliɲœʀ/ *nm* highlighter (pen).

**surmenage** /syʀmənaʒ/ *nm* overwork.

**surmonter** /syʀmɔ̃te/ [1] *vt* (vaincre) overcome, surmount; (être au-dessus de) surmount, top.

**surnaturel, ~le** /syʀnatyʀɛl/ *a* supernatural.

**surnom** /syʀnɔ̃/ *nm* nickname. **surnommer** [1] *vt* nickname.

**surpeuplé, ~e** /syʀpœple/ *a* overpopulated.

**surplomber** /syʀplɔ̃be/ [1] *vt*/*i* overhang.

**surplus** /syʀply/ *nm* surplus.

**surprenant, ~e** /syʀpʀənɑ̃, -t/ *a* surprising. **surprendre** [50] *vt* (étonner) surprise; (prendre au dépourvu) catch, surprise; (entendre) overhear. **surpris, ~e** *a* surprised (**de** at).

**surprise** /syʀpʀiz/ *nf* surprise.

**surréaliste** /syʀʀealist/ *a* & *nmf* surrealist.

**sursaut** /syʀso/ *nm* start, jump; **en ~** with a start; **~ de** (regain) burst of. **sursauter** [1] *vi* start, jump.

**sursis** /syʀsi/ *nm* reprieve; (Mil) deferment; **deux ans (de prison) avec ~** a two-year suspended sentence.

**surtaxe** /syʀtaks/ *nf* surcharge.

**surtout** /syʀtu/ *adv* especially; (avant tout) above all; **~ pas** certainly not.

**surveillance** /syʀvɛjɑ̃s/ *nf* watch; (d'examen) supervision; (de la police) surveillance. **surveillant, ~e** *nm,f* (de prison) warder; (au lycée) supervisor (in charge of discipline). **surveiller** [1] *vt* watch; (*travaux, élèves*) supervise.

**survenir** /syʀvəniʀ/ [59] *vi* occur, take place; (*personne*) turn up.

**survêtement** /syʀvɛtmɑ̃/ *nm* (Sport) tracksuit.

**survie** /syʀvi/ *nf* survival.

**survivant, ~e** /syʀvivɑ̃, -t/ *a* surviving. ● *nm,f* survivor.

**survivre** /syʀvivʀ/ [63] *vi* survive; **~ à** (*conflit*) survive; (*personne*) outlive.

**survoler** /syʀvɔle/ [1] *vt* fly over; (*livre*) skim through.

**sus**: **en ~** /ɑ̃sys/ *loc* in addition.

**susceptible** /sysɛptibl/ *a* touchy; **~ de faire** likely to do.

**susciter** /sysite/ [1] *vt* (éveiller) arouse; (occasionner) create.

**suspect, ~e** /syspɛ, -ɛkt/ *a* (*individu, faits*) suspicious; (*témoignage*) suspect; **~ de** suspected of. ● *nm,f* suspect. **suspecter** [1] *vt* suspect.

**suspendre** /syspɑ̃dʀ/ [3] *vt* (accrocher) hang (up); (interrompre, destituer) suspend; **suspendu à** hanging from. □ **se ~ à** *vpr* hang from.

**suspens**: **en ~** /ɑ̃syspɑ̃/ *loc* (*affaire*) outstanding; (dans l'indécision) in suspense.

**suspense** /syspɛns/ *nm* suspense.

**suture** /sytyʀ/ *nf* **point de ~** stitch.

**svelte** /svɛlt/ *a* slender.

**S.V.P.** *abrév* (**s'il vous plaît**) please.

**syllabe** /silab/ *nf* syllable.

**symbole** /sɛ̃bɔl/ *nm* symbol. **symboliser** [1] *vt* symbolize.

**symétrie** /simetʀi/ *nf* symmetry.

**sympa** /sɛ̃pa/ *a inv* [I] nice; **sois ~** be a pal.

**sympathie** /sɛ̃pati/ *nf* (goût) liking; (compassion) sympathy; **avoir de la ~ pour** like. **sympathique** *a* nice, pleasant. **sympathisant, ~e** *nm,f* sympathizer. **sympathiser** [1] *vi* get on well (**avec** with).

**symphonie** /sɛ̃fɔni/ *nf* symphony.

**symptôme** /sɛ̃ptom/ *nm* symptom.

**synagogue** /sinagɔg/ *nf* synagogue.

**synchroniser** /sɛ̃kʀɔnize/ [1] *vt* synchronize.

**syncope** /sɛ̃kɔp/ *nf* (Méd) blackout.

**syndic** /sɛ̃dik/ *nm* **~ (d'immeuble)** property manager.

**syndicaliste** /sɛ̃dikalist/ *nmf* (trade-)unionist. ● *a* (trade-) union.

**syndicat** /sɛ̃dika/ *nm* (trade) union; **~ d'initiative** tourist office.

**syndiqué, ~e** /sɛ̃dike/ *a* **être ~** be a (trade-)union member.

**synonyme** /sinɔnim/ *a* synonymous. ● *nm* synonym.

**syntaxe** /sɛ̃taks/ *nf* syntax.

**synthèse** /sɛ̃tɛz/ *nf* synthesis. **synthétique** *a* synthetic.

**synthé(tiseur)** /sɛ̃te(tizœʀ)/ *nm* synthesizer.

**systématique** /sistematik/ *a* systematic.

**système** /sistɛm/ *nm* system; **le ~ D** Ⓘ resourcefulness.

# Tt

**t'** /t/ ⇒TE.

**ta** /ta/ ⇒TON[1].

**tabac** /taba/ *nm* tobacco; (magasin) tobacconist's shop.

**table** /tabl/ *nf* table; **à ~!** dinner is ready!; **~ de nuit** bedside table; **~ des matières** table of contents; **~ à repasser** ironing board; **~ roulante** (tea-)trolley; (US) (serving) cart.

**tableau** (*pl* **~x**) /tablo/ *nm* picture; (peinture) painting; (panneau) board; (graphique) chart; (Scol) blackboard; **~ d'affichage** notice-board; **~ de bord** dashboard.

**tablette** /tablɛt/ *nf* shelf; **~ de chocolat** bar of chocolate.

**tableur** /tablœʀ/ *nm* spreadsheet.

**tablier** /tablije/ *nm* apron; (de pont) platform; (de magasin) shutter.

**tabou** /tabu/ *nm & a* taboo.

**tabouret** /tabuʀɛ/ *nm* stool.

**tache** /taʃ/ *nf* mark, spot; (salissure) stain; **faire ~ d'huile** spread; **~ de rousseur** freckle.

**tâche** /taʃ/ *nf* task, job.

**tacher** /taʃe/ [1] *vt* stain. ☐ **se ~** *vpr* (*personne*) get oneself dirty.

**tâcher** /taʃe/ [1] *vi* **~ de faire** try to do.

**tacheté, ~e** /taʃte/ *a* spotted.

**tact** /takt/ *nm* tact.

**tactique** /taktik/ *a* tactical. ● *nf* (Mil) tactics; **une ~** a tactic.

**taie** /tɛ/ *nf* **~ (d'oreiller)** pillowcase.

**taille** /tɑj/ *nf* (milieu du corps) waist; (hauteur) height; (grandeur) size; **de ~** sizeable; **être de ~ à faire** be up to doing.

**taille-crayons** /tajkʀɛjɔ̃/ *nm inv* pencil-sharpener.

**tailler** /taje/ [1] *vt* cut; (*arbre*) prune; (*crayon*) sharpen; (*vêtement*) cut out. ☐ **se ~** *vpr* ⊠ clear off.

**tailleur** /tajœʀ/ *nm* (costume) woman's suit; (couturier) tailor; **en ~** cross-legged; **~ de pierre** stonecutter.

**taire** /tɛʀ/ [47] *vt* not to reveal; **faire ~** silence. ☐ **se ~** *vpr* be silent *ou* quiet; (devenir silencieux) fall silent.

**talc** /talk/ *nm* talcum powder.

**talent** /talɑ̃/ *nm* talent. **talentueux, -euse** *a* talented, gifted.

**talon** /talɔ̃/ *nm* heel; (de chèque) stub.

**tambour** /tɑ̃buʀ/ *nm* drum; (d'église) vestibule.

**Tamise** /tamiz/ *nf* Thames.

**tampon** /tɑ̃pɔ̃/ *nm* (de bureau) stamp; (ouate) wad, pad; **~ (hygiénique)** tampon.

**tamponner** /tɑ̃pɔne/ [1] *vt* (*document*) stamp; (*véhicule*) crash into; (*plaie*) swab.

**tandem** /tɑ̃dɛm/ *nm* (vélo) tandem; (personnes: fig) duo.

**tandis que** /tɑ̃dik(ə)/ *conj* while.

**tanière** /tanjɛʀ/ *nf* den.

**tant** /tɑ̃/ *adv* (*travailler, manger*) so much; **~ de** (quantité) so much; (nombre) so many; **~ que** as long as; **en ~ que** as; **~ mieux!** all the better!; **~ pis!** too bad!

**tante** /tɑ̃t/ *nf* aunt.

**tantôt** /tɑ̃to/ *adv* sometimes.

**tapage** /tapaʒ/ *nm* din.

**tape** /tap/ *nf* slap. **tape-à-l'œil** *a inv* flashy, tawdry.

**taper** /tape/ [1] *vt* hit; (prendre Ⓘ) scrounge; ~ **(à la machine)** type. ● *vi* (cogner) bang; (*soleil*) beat down; ~ **dans** (puiser dans) dig into; ~ **sur** hit; ~ **sur l'épaule de qn** tap sb on the shoulder. □ **se** ~ *vpr* (*corvée* Ⓘ) get stuck with Ⓘ.

**tapis** /tapi/ *nm* carpet; (petit) rug; ~ **de bain** bathmat; ~ **roulant** (pour objets) conveyor belt; (pour piétons) moving walkway.

**tapisser** /tapise/ [1] *vt* (wall) paper; (fig) cover (**de** with). **tapisserie** *nf* tapestry; (papier peint) wallpaper.

**taquin**, ~**e** /takɛ̃, -in/ *a* fond of teasing. ● *nm,f* tease(r).

**tard** /taʀ/ *adv* late; **au plus** ~ at the latest; **plus** ~ later; **sur le** ~ late in life.

**tarder** /taʀde/ [1] *vi* (être lent à venir) be a long time coming; ~ **(à faire)** take a long time (doing), delay (doing); **sans (plus)** ~ without (further) delay; **il me tarde de** I'm longing to.

**tardif**, **-ive** /taʀdif, -v/ *a* late.

**tare** /taʀ/ *nf* (défaut) defect.

**tarif** /taʀif/ *nm* rate; (de train, taxi) fare; **plein** ~ full price.

**tarir** /taʀiʀ/ [2] *vt/i* dry up. □ **se** ~ *vpr* dry up.

**tarte** /taʀt/ *nf* tart. ● *a inv* (ridicule Ⓘ) ridiculous.

**tartine** /taʀtin/ *nf* slice of bread; ~ **de beurre** slice of bread and butter. **tartiner** [1] *vt* spread.

**tartre** /taʀtʀ/ *nm* (de bouilloire) fur, scale; (sur les dents) tartar.

**tas** /tɑ/ *nm* pile, heap; **un** *ou* **des** ~ **de** Ⓘ lots of.

**tasse** /tɑs/ *nf* cup; ~ **à thé** teacup.

**tasser** /tɑse/ [1] *vt* pack, squeeze; (*terre*) pack (down). □ **se** ~ *vpr* (*terrain*) sink; (se serrer) squeeze up.

**tâter** /tɑte/ [1] *vt* feel; (opinion: fig) sound out. ● *vi* ~ **de** try out.

**tatillon**, ~**ne** /tatijɔ̃, -jɔn/ *a* finicky.

**tâtonnements** /tatɔnmɑ̃/ *nmpl* (essais) trial and error (+ *sg*).

**tâtons**: **à** ~ /atɑtɔ̃/ *loc* **avancer à** ~ grope one's way along.

**tatouage** /tatwaʒ/ *nm* (dessin) tattoo.

**taupe** /top/ *nf* mole.

**taureau** (*pl* ~**x**) /tɔʀo/ *nm* bull; **le T**~ Taurus.

**taux** /to/ *nm* rate.

**taxe** /taks/ *nf* tax.

**taxi** /taksi/ *nm* taxi(-cab); (personne Ⓘ) taxi driver.

**taxiphone**® /taksifɔn/ *nm* pay phone.

**Tchécoslovaquie** /tʃekɔslɔvaki/ *nf* Czechoslovakia.

**tchèque** /tʃɛk/ *a* Czech; **République** ~ Czech Republic. **T**~ *nmf* Czech.

**te**, **t'** /tə, t/ *pron* you; (indirect) (to) you; (réfléchi) yourself.

**technicien**, ~**ne** /tɛknisjɛ̃, -ɛn/ *nm,f* technician.

**technique** /tɛknik/ *a* technical. ● *nf* technique.

**techno** /tɛkno/ *nf* (Mus) techno.

**technologie** /tɛknɔlɔʒi/ *nf* technology.

**teindre** /tɛ̃dʀ/ [22] *vt* dye. □ **se** ~ *vpr* **se** ~ **les cheveux** dye one's hair.

**teint** /tɛ̃/ *nm* complexion.

**teinte** /tɛ̃t/ *nf* shade. **teinter** [1] *vt* (*verre*) tint; (*bois*) stain.

**teinture** /tɛ̃tyʀ/ *nf* (produit) dye.

**teinturier**, **-ière** /tɛ̃tyʀje, -jɛʀ/ *nm,f* dry-cleaner.

**tel**, **~le** /tɛl/ *a* such; **un ~ livre** such a book; **~ que** such as, like; (ainsi que) (just) as; **~ ou ~** such-and-such; **~ quel** (just) as it is.

**télé** /tele/ *nf* 🄸 TV.

**télécharger** /teleʃaʀʒe/ [40] *vt* (Ordinat) download.

**télécommande** /telekɔmɑ̃d/ *nf* remote control.

**télécommunications** /telekɔmynikasjɔ̃/ *nfpl* telecommunications.

**téléconférence** /telekɔ̃feʀɑ̃s/ *nf* teleconferencing.

**télécopie** /telekɔpi/ *nf* fax. **télécopieur** *nm* fax machine.

**téléfilm** /telefilm/ *nm* TV film.

**télégramme** /telegʀam/ *nm* telegram.

**télégraphier** /telegʀafje/ [1] *vt/i* **~ (à)** cable.

**téléguidé**, **~e** /telegide/ *a* radio-controlled.

**téléphérique** /telefeʀik/ *nm* cable car.

**téléphone** /telefɔn/ *nm* (tele-)phone; **~ à carte** cardphone. **téléphoner** [1] *vt/i* **~ (à)** (tele)phone. **téléphonique** *a* (tele)phone.

**téléphonie** /telefɔni/ *nf* telephony; **~ mobile** mobile telephony.

**télé-réalité** /teleʀealite/ *nf* reality TV.

**téléserveur** /telesɛʀvœʀ/ *nm* (Internet) remote server.

**télésiège** /telesjɛʒ/ *nm* chairlift.

**téléski** /teleski/ *nm* ski tow.

**téléspectateur**, **-trice** /telespɛktatœʀ, -tʀis/ *nm,f* viewer.

**télévente** /televɑ̃t/ *nf* telesales (+ *pl*).

**télévisé**, **~e** /televize/ *a* (*débat*) televised; **émission ~e** television programme. **télévision** *nf* television.

**télex** /telɛks/ *nm* telex.

**tellement** /tɛlmɑ̃/ *adv* (tant) so much; (si) so; **~ de** (quantité) so much; (nombre) so many.

**téméraire** /temeʀɛʀ/ *a* reckless.

**témoignage** /temwaɲaʒ/ *nm* testimony, evidence; (récit) account; **~ de** (marque) token of.

**témoigner** /temwaɲe/ [1] *vi* testify (**de** to). ● *vt* (montrer) show; **~ que** testify that.

**témoin** /temwɛ̃/ *nm* witness; (Sport) baton; **être ~ de** witness; **~ oculaire** eyewitness.

**tempe** /tɑ̃p/ *nf* (Anat) temple.

**tempérament** /tɑ̃peʀamɑ̃/ *nm* temperament, disposition.

**température** /tɑ̃peʀatyʀ/ *nf* temperature.

**tempête** /tɑ̃pɛt/ *nf* storm; **~ de neige** snowstorm.

**temple** /tɑ̃pl/ *nm* temple; (protestant) church.

**temporaire** /tɑ̃pɔʀɛʀ/ *a* temporary.

**temps** /tɑ̃/ *nm* (notion) time; (Gram) tense; (étape) stage; **à ~ partiel/plein** part-/full-time; **ces derniers ~** lately; **dans le ~** at one time; **dans quelque ~** in a while; **de ~ en ~** from time to time; **~ d'arrêt** pause; **avoir tout son ~** have plenty of time; (météo) weather; **~ de chien** filthy weather; **quel ~ fait-il?** what's the weather like?

**tenace** /tənas/ *a* stubborn.

**tenaille** /tənaj/ *nf* pincers (+ *pl*).

**tendance** /tɑ̃dɑ̃s/ *nf* tendency; (évolution) trend; **avoir ~ à** tend to.

**tendon** /tɑ̃dɔ̃/ *nm* tendon.

**tendre**[1] /tɑ̃dʀ/ [3] *vt* stretch; (*piège*) set; (*bras*) stretch out;

(*main*) hold out; (*cou*) crane; ~ **qch à qn** hold sth out to sb; ~ **l'oreille** prick up one's ears. ● *vi* ~ **à** tend to.

**tendre²** /tɑ̃dʀ/ *a* tender; (couleur, bois) soft. **tendresse** *nf* tenderness.

**tendu, ~e** /tɑ̃dy/ *a* (*corde*) tight; (*personne, situation*) tense.

**ténèbres** /tenɛbʀ/ *nfpl* darkness (+ *sg*).

**teneur** /tənœʀ/ *nf* content.

**tenir** /təniʀ/ [59] *vt* hold; (*pari, promesse, hôtel*) keep; (*place*) take up; (*propos*) utter; (*rôle*) play; ~ **de** (avoir reçu de) have got from; ~ **pour** regard as; ~ **chaud** keep warm; ~ **compte de** take into account; ~ **le coup** hold out; ~ **tête à** stand up to. ● *vi* hold; ~ **à** be attached to; ~ **à faire** be anxious to do; ~ **bon** stand firm; ~ **dans** fit into; ~ **de qn** take after sb; **tiens!** (surprise) hey! □ **se** ~ *vpr* (debout) stand; (avoir lieu) be held; **se** ~ **à** hold on to; **s'en** ~ **à** (se limiter à) confine oneself to.

**tennis** /tenis/ *nm* tennis; ~ **de table** table tennis. ● *nmpl* (chaussures) sneakers.

**ténor** /tenɔʀ/ *nm* tenor.

**tension** /tɑ̃sjɔ̃/ *nf* tension; **avoir de la** ~ have high blood-pressure.

**tentation** /tɑ̃tasjɔ̃/ *nf* temptation.

**tentative** /tɑ̃tativ/ *nf* attempt.

**tente** /tɑ̃t/ *nf* tent.

**tenter** /tɑ̃te/ [1] *vt* (allécher) tempt; (essayer) try (**de faire** to do).

**tenture** /tɑ̃tyʀ/ *nf* curtain; **~s** draperies.

**tenu, ~e** /təny/ *a* **bien** ~ well kept; ~ **de** required. ● ⇒TENIR [58].

**tenue** /təny/ *nf* (habillement) dress; (de maison) upkeep; (conduite) (good) behaviour; (maintien) posture; ~ **de soirée** evening dress.

**Tergal®** /tɛʀgal/ *nm* Terylene®.

**terme** /tɛʀm/ *nm* (mot) term; (date limite) time-limit; (fin) end; **né avant** ~ premature; **à long/court** ~ long-/short-term; **en bons ~s** on good terms (**avec** with).

**terminaison** /tɛʀminɛzɔ̃/ *nf* (Gram) ending.

**terminal, ~e** (*mpl* **-aux**) /tɛʀminal, -o/ *a* terminal. ● *nm* terminal. **terminale** *nf* (Scol) ≈ sixth form; (US) twelfth grade.

**terminer** /tɛʀmine/ [1] *vt/i* finish; (*discours*) end, finish. □ **se** ~ *vpr* end (**par** with).

**terne** /tɛʀn/ *a* dull, drab.

**ternir** /tɛʀniʀ/ [2] *vt/i* tarnish. □ **se** ~ *vpr* tarnish.

**terrain** /tɛʀɛ̃/ *nm* ground; (parcelle) piece of land; (à bâtir) plot; ~ **d'aviation** airfield; ~ **de camping** campsite; ~ **de golf** golf course; ~ **de jeu** playground; ~ **vague** waste ground.

**terrasse** /tɛʀas/ *nf* terrace; **à la** ~ (d'un café) outside (a café).

**terrasser** /tɛʀase/ [1] *vt* (*adversaire*) knock down; (*maladie*) strike down.

**terre** /tɛʀ/ *nf* (planète, matière) earth; (étendue, pays) land; (sol) ground; **à** ~ (Naut) ashore; **par** ~ (dehors) on the ground; (dedans) on the floor; ~ **(cuite)** terracotta; **la** ~ **ferme** dry land; ~ **glaise** clay. **terreau** (*pl* **~x**) *nm* compost. **terre-plein** (*pl* **terres-pleins**) *nm* platform; (de route) central reservation.

**terrestre** /tɛʀɛstʀ/ *a* (*animaux*) land; (de notre planète) of the Earth.

**terreur** /tɛʀœʀ/ *nf* terror.

**terrible** /tɛʀibl/ *a* terrible; (formidable [I]) terrific.

**terrier** /tɛʀje/ *nm* (trou) burrow; (chien) terrier.

**terrifier** /tɛʀifje/ [45] *vt* terrify.

**territoire** /tɛʀitwaʀ/ *nm* territory.

**terroir** /tɛʀwaʀ/ *nm* land; **du ~** local.

**terroriser** /tɛʀɔʀize/ [1] *vt* terrorize.

**terrorisme** /tɛʀɔʀism/ *nm* terrorism. **terroriste** *nmf* terrorist.

**tertiaire** /tɛʀsjɛʀ/ *a* (*secteur*) service.

**tes** /te/ ⇒TON¹.

**test** /tɛst/ *nm* test.

**testament** /tɛstamɑ̃/ *nm* (Jur) will; (politique, artistique) testament; **Ancien/Nouveau T~** Old/New Testament.

**tétanos** /tetanos/ *nm* tetanus.

**têtard** /tɛtaʀ/ *nm* tadpole.

**tête** /tɛt/ *nf* head; (visage) face; (cheveux) hair; **à la ~ de** at the head of; **à ~ reposée** at one's leisure; **de** (*calculer*) in one's head; **faire la ~** sulk; **tenir ~ à qn** stand up to sb; **il n'en fait qu'à sa ~** he does just as he pleases; **en ~** (Sport) in the lead; **faire une ~** (au football) head the ball; **une forte ~** a rebel; **la ~ la première** head first; **de la ~ aux pieds** from head to toe.

**tête-à-tête** /tɛtatɛt/ *nm inv* tête-à-tête; **en ~** in private.

**tétée** /tete/ *nf* feed.

**tétine** /tetin/ *nf* (de biberon) teat; (sucette) dummy; (US) pacifier.

**têtu, ~e** /tety/ *a* stubborn.

**texte** /tɛkst/ *nm* text; (de leçon) subject; (morceau choisi) passage.

**texteur** /tɛkstœʀ/ *nm* (Ordinat) word-processor.

**textile** /tɛkstil/ *nm & a* textile.

**texto** /tɛksto/ 🅘 *nm* text message.

**TGV** *abrév m* (**train à grande vitesse**) TGV, high-speed train.

**thé** /te/ *nm* tea.

**théâtre** /teɑtʀ/ *nm* theatre; (d'un crime) scene; **faire du ~** act.

**théière** /tejɛʀ/ *nf* teapot.

**thème** /tɛm/ *nm* theme; (traduction: Scol) prose.

**théorie** /teɔʀi/ *nf* theory. **théorique** *a* theoretical.

**thérapie** /teʀapi/ *nf* therapy.

**thermique** /tɛʀmik/ *a* thermal.

**thermomètre** /tɛʀmɔmɛtʀ/ *nm* thermometer.

**thermos**® /tɛʀmos/ *nm ou f* Thermos® (flask).

**thermostat** /tɛʀmɔsta/ *nm* thermostat.

**thèse** /tɛz/ *nf* thesis.

**thon** /tɔ̃/ *nm* tuna.

**thym** /tɛ̃/ *nm* thyme.

**tibia** /tibja/ *nm* shinbone.

**tic** /tik/ *nm* (contraction) tic, twitch; (manie) habit.

**ticket** /tikɛ/ *nm* ticket.

**tiède** /tjɛd/ *a* lukewarm; (*nuit*) warm.

**tiédir** /tjediʀ/ [2] *vt/i* **(faire) ~** warm up.

**tien, ~ne** /tjɛ̃, -ɛn/ *pron* **le ~, la ~ne, les ~(ne)s** yours; **à la ~ne!** cheers!

**tiens, tient** /tjɛ̃/ ⇒TENIR [59].

**tiercé** /tjɛʀse/ *nm* place-betting.

**tiers, tierce** /tjɛʀ, tjɛʀs/ *a* third. ● *nm* (fraction) third; (personne) third party. **tiers-monde** *nm* Third World.

**tige** /tiʒ/ *nf* (Bot) stem, stalk; (en métal) shaft, rod.

**tigre** /tigʀ/ *nm* tiger.

**tigresse** /tigʀɛs/ *nf* tigress.

**tilleul** /tijœl/ *nm* lime tree.

**timbre** /tɛ̃bʀ/ *nm* stamp; (sonnette) bell; (de voix) tone. **timbrer** [1] *vt* stamp.

**timide** /timid/ *a* shy, timid. **timidité** *nf* shyness.

**timoré**, **~e** /timɔʀe/ *a* timorous.

**tintement** /tɛ̃tmɑ̃/ *nm* (de sonnette) ringing; (de clés) jingling.

**tique** /tik/ *nf* tick.

**tir** /tiʀ/ *nm* (Sport) shooting; (action de tirer) firing; (feu, rafale) fire; **~ à l'arc** archery; **~ au pigeon** clay pigeon shooting.

**tirage** /tiʀaʒ/ *nm* (de photo) printing; (de journal) circulation; (de livre) edition; (Ordinat) hard copy; (de cheminée) draught; **~ au sort** draw.

**tire-bouchon** (*pl* **~s**) /tiʀbuʃɔ̃/ *nm* corkscrew.

**tirelire** /tiʀliʀ/ *nf* piggy bank.

**tirer** /tiʀe/ [1] *vt* pull; (*langue*) stick out; (*conclusion, trait, rideaux*) draw; (*coup de feu*) fire; (*gibier*) shoot; (*photo*) print; **~ de** (sortir) take *ou* get out of; (extraire) extract from; (*plaisir, nom*) derive from; **~ parti de** take advantage of; **~ profit de** profit from; **se faire ~ l'oreille** get told off. ● *vi* shoot, fire (**sur** at); **~ sur** (*corde*) pull at; (*couleur*) verge on; **~ à sa fin** be drawing to a close; **~ au clair** clarify; **~ au sort** draw lots (for). □ **se ~** *vpr* 🄸 clear off; **se ~ de** get out of; **s'en ~** (en réchapper) pull through; (réussir 🄸) cope.

**tiret** /tiʀɛ/ *nm* dash.

**tireur** /tiʀœʀ/ *nm* gunman; **~ d'élite** marksman; **~ isolé** sniper.

**tiroir** /tiʀwaʀ/ *nm* drawer. **tiroir-caisse** (*pl* **tiroirs-caisses**) *nm* till, cash register.

**tisane** /tizan/ *nf* herbal tea.

**tissage** /tisaʒ/ *nm* weaving. **tisser** [1] *vt* weave. **tisserand** *nm* weaver.

**tissu** /tisy/ *nm* fabric, material; (biologique) tissue; **un ~ de mensonges** (fig) a pack of lies. **tissu-éponge** (*pl* **tissus-éponge**) *nm* towelling.

**titre** /titʀ/ *nm* title; (diplôme) qualification; (Comm) bond; **~s** (droits) claims; **(gros) ~s** headlines; **à ~ d'exemple** as an example; **à juste ~** rightly; **à ~ privé** in a private capacity; **à double ~** on two accounts; **~ de propriété** title deed.

**tituber** /titybe/ [1] *vi* stagger.

**titulaire** /titylɛʀ/ *a* **être ~** be a permanent staff member; **être ~ de** hold. ● *nmf* (de permis) holder. **titulariser** [1] *vt* give permanent status to.

**toast** /tost/ *nm* (pain) piece of toast; (canapé, allocution) toast.

**toboggan** /tɔbɔgɑ̃/ *nm* (de jeu) slide; (Auto) flyover.

**toi** /twa/ *pron* you; (réfléchi) yourself; **dépêche-~** hurry up.

**toile** /twal/ *nf* cloth; (tableau) canvas; **~ d'araignée** cobweb; **~ de fond** (fig) backdrop; **la ~** (Internet) the Web.

**toilette** /twalɛt/ *nf* (habillement) outfit; **~s** (cabinets) toilet(s); **de ~** (articles, savon) toilet; **faire sa ~** have a wash.

**toi-même** /twamɛm/ *pron* yourself.

**toit** /twa/ *nm* roof; **~ ouvrant** (Auto) sunroof.

**toiture** /twatyʀ/ *nf* roof.

**tôle** /tol/ *nf* (plaque) iron sheet; **~ ondulée** corrugated iron.

**tolérant**, **~e** /tɔleʀɑ̃, -t/ *a* tolerant. **tolérer** [14] *vt* tolerate.

**tomate** /tɔmat/ *nf* tomato.

**tombe** /tɔ̃b/ *nf* grave; (pierre) gravestone.

**tombeau** (*pl* **~x**) /tɔ̃bo/ *nm* tomb.

**tomber** /tɔ̃be/ [1] *vi* (*aux être*) fall; (*fièvre, vent*) drop; **faire ~** knock over; (*gouvernement*) bring down; **laisser ~** (*objet, amoureux*) drop; (*collègue*) let down; (*activité*) give up; **laisse ~!** 🄸 forget it!; **~ à l'eau**

(*projet*) fall through; **~ bien** *ou* **à point** come at the right time; **~ en panne** break down; **~ en syncope** faint; **~ sur** (trouver) run across.

**tombola** /tɔ̃bɔla/ *nf* tombola; (US) lottery.

**tome** /tɔm/ *nm* volume.

**ton**[1], **ta** (**ton** *before vowel or mute h*) (*pl* **tes**) /tɔ̃, ta, tɔ̃n, te/ *a* your.

**ton**[2] /tɔ̃/ *nm* (hauteur de voix) pitch; **d'un ~ sec** drily; **de bon ~** in good taste.

**tonalité** /tɔnalite/ *nf* (Mus) key; (de téléphone) dialling tone; (US) dial tone.

**tondeuse** /tɔ̃døz/ *nf* (à moutons) shears (+ *pl*); (à cheveux) clippers (+ *pl*); **~ à gazon** lawn-mower. **tondre** [3] *vt* (*herbe*) mow; (*mouton*) shear; (*cheveux*) clip.

**tonne** /tɔn/ *nf* tonne.

**tonneau** (*pl* **~x**) /tɔno/ *nm* barrel; (en voiture) somersault.

**tonnerre** /tɔnɛʀ/ *nm* thunder.

**tonton** /tɔ̃tɔ̃/ *nm* [!] uncle.

**tonus** /tɔnys/ *nm* energy.

**torche** /tɔʀʃ/ *nf* torch.

**torchon** /tɔʀʃɔ̃/ *nm* (pour la vaisselle) tea towel.

**tordre** /tɔʀdʀ/ [3] *vt* twist. □ **se ~** *vpr* **se ~ la cheville** twist one's ankle; **se ~ de douleur** writhe in pain; **se ~ (de rire)** split one's sides.

**tordu**, **~e** /tɔʀdy/ *a* twisted, bent; (*esprit*) warped, twisted.

**torpille** /tɔʀpij/ *nf* torpedo.

**torrent** /tɔʀɑ̃/ *nm* torrent.

**torride** /tɔʀid/ *a* torrid; (*chaleur*) scorching.

**torse** /tɔʀs/ *nm* chest; (Anat) torso.

**tort** /tɔʀ/ *nm* wrong; **avoir ~** be wrong (**de faire** to do); **donner ~ à** prove wrong; **être dans son ~** be in the wrong; **faire (du) ~ à** harm; **à ~** wrongly; **à ~ et à travers** without thinking.

**torticolis** /tɔʀtikɔli/ *nm* stiff neck.

**tortiller** /tɔʀtije/ [1] *vt* twist, twirl. □ **se ~** *vpr* wriggle.

**tortionnaire** /tɔʀsjɔnɛʀ/ *nm* torturer.

**tortue** /tɔʀty/ *nf* tortoise; (d'eau) turtle.

**tortueux**, **-euse** /tɔʀtɥø, -z/ *a* (*chemin*) twisting; (*explication*) tortuous.

**torture** /tɔʀtyʀ/ *nf* torture. **torturer** [1] *vt* torture.

**tôt** /to/ *adv* early; **au plus ~** at the earliest; **le plus ~ possible** as soon as possible; **~ ou tard** sooner or later; **ce n'est pas trop ~!** it's about time!

**total**, **~e** (*mpl* **-aux**) /tɔtal, -o/ *a* total. ● *nm* (*pl* **-aux**) total; **au ~** all in all. **totalement** *adv* totally. **totaliser** [1] *vt* total. **totalitaire** *a* totalitarian.

**totalité** /tɔtalite/ *nf* **la ~ de** all of.

**touche** /tuʃ/ *nf* (de piano) key; (de peinture) touch; **(ligne de) ~** (Sport) touchline.

**toucher** /tuʃe/ [1] *vt* touch; (émouvoir) move, touch; (contacter) get in touch with; (*cible*) hit; (*argent*) draw; (*chèque*) cash; (concerner) affect. ● *vi* **~ à** touch; (*question*) touch on; (*fin, but*) approach; **je vais lui en ~ deux mots** I'll talk to him about it. □ **se ~** *vpr* (*lignes*) touch. ● *nm* (sens) touch.

**touffe** /tuf/ *nf* (de poils, d'herbe) tuft; (de plantes) clump.

**toujours** /tuʒuʀ/ *adv* always; (encore) still; (de toute façon) anyway; **pour ~** for ever; **~ est-il que** the fact remains that.

**toupet** /tupɛ/ *nm* (culot [!]) cheek, nerve.

**tour** /tuʀ/ *nf* tower; (immeuble) tower block; (échecs) rook; ~ **de contrôle** control tower. ● *nm* (mouvement, succession, tournure) turn; (excursion) trip; (à pied) walk; (en auto) drive; (artifice) trick; (circonférence) circumference; (Tech) lathe; ~ **(de piste)** lap; **à ~ de rôle** in turn; **à mon ~** when it is my turn; **c'est mon ~ de** it is my turn to; **faire le ~ de** go round; (*question*) survey; **~ d'horizon** survey; **~ de potier** potter's wheel; **~ de taille** waist measurement; (ligne) waistline.

**tourbillon** /tuʀbijɔ̃/ *nm* whirlwind; (d'eau) whirlpool; (fig) swirl.

**tourisme** /tuʀism/ *nm* tourism; **faire du ~** do some sightseeing.

**touriste** /tuʀist/ *nmf* tourist. **touristique** *a* tourist; (*route*) scenic.

**tourmenter** /tuʀmɑ̃te/ *vt* torment. □ **se ~** *vpr* worry.

**tournant**, **~e** /tuʀnɑ̃, -t/ *a* (qui pivote) revolving. ● *nm* bend; (fig) turning-point.

**tourne-disque** (*pl* **~s**) /tuʀnədisk/ *nm* record-player.

**tournée** /tuʀne/ *nf* (de facteur, au café) round; **c'est ma ~** I'll buy this round; (d'artiste) tour.

**tourner** /tuʀne/ [1] *vt* turn; (*film*) shoot, make; **~ le dos à** turn one's back on; **~ en dérision** mock. ● *vi* turn; (*toupie, tête*) spin; (*moteur, usine*) run; **~ autour de** go round; (*personne, maison*) hang around; (*terre*) revolve round; (*question*) centre on; **~ de l'œil** 🅘 faint; **mal ~** (*affaire*) turn out badly. □ **se ~** *vpr* turn.

**tournesol** /tuʀnəsɔl/ *nm* sunflower.

**tournevis** /tuʀnəvis/ *nm* screwdriver.

**tournoi** /tuʀnwa/ *nm* tournament.

**tourte** /tuʀt/ *nf* pie.

**tourterelle** /tuʀtəʀɛl/ *nf* turtle dove.

**Toussaint** /tusɛ̃/ *nf* **la ~** All Saints' Day.

**tousser** /tuse/ [1] *vi* cough.

**tout**, **~e** (*pl* **tous**, **toutes**) /tu, tut/ *nm* (ensemble) whole; **en ~** in all; **pas du ~!** not at all! ● *a* all; (n'importe quel) any; **~ le pays** the whole country, all the country; **~e la nuit/journée** the whole night/day; **~ un paquet** a whole pack; **tous les jours** every day; **tous les deux ans** every deux years; **~ le monde** everyone; **tous les deux, toutes les deux** both of them; **tous les trois** all three (of them). ● *pron* everything; all; anything; **tous** /tus/, **toutes** all; **tous ensemble** all together; **prends ~** take everything; **~ ce que tu veux** everything you want. ● *adv* (très) very; (entièrement) all; **~ au bout/début** right at the end/beginning; **~ en marchant** while walking; **~ à coup** all of a sudden; **~ à fait** quite, completely; **~ à l'heure** in a moment; (passé) a moment ago; **~ au** *ou* **le long de** throughout; **~ au plus/moins** at most/least; **~ de même** all the same; **~ de suite** straight away; **~ entier** whole; **~ neuf** brand new; **~ nu** stark naked. **tout-à-l'égout** *nm inv* main drainage.

**toutefois** /tutfwa/ *adv* however.

**tout(-)terrain** /tuteʀɛ̃/ *a inv* all terrain.

**toux** /tu/ *nf* cough.

**toxicomane** /tɔksikɔman/ *nmf* drug addict.

**toxique** /tɔksik/ *a* toxic.

**trac** /tʀak/ *nm* **le ~** nerves; (Théât) stage fright.

**traçabilité** /tʀasabilite/ *nf* traceability.

**tracas** /tʀaka/ *nm* worry.

**trace** /tʀas/ *nf* (traînée, piste) trail; (d'animal, de pneu) tracks; **~s de pas** footprints.

**tracer** /tʀase/ [10] *vt* draw; (écrire) write; (route) open up.

**trachée-artère** /tʀaʃeaʀtɛʀ/ *nf* windpipe.

**tracteur** /tʀaktœʀ/ *nm* tractor.

**tradition** /tʀadisjɔ̃/ *nf* tradition. **traditionnel, ~le** *a* traditional.

**traducteur, -trice** /tʀadyktœʀ, -tʀis/ *nm,f* translator. **traduction** *nf* translation.

**traduire** /tʀadɥiʀ/ [17] *vt* translate; **~ en justice** take to court.

**trafic** /tʀafik/ *nm* (commerce, circulation) traffic.

**trafiquant, ~e** /tʀafikɑ̃, -t/ *nm,f* trafficker; (d'armes, de drogues) dealer.

**trafiquer** /tʀafike/ [1] *vi* traffic. ● *vt* [I] (moteur) fiddle with.

**tragédie** /tʀaʒedi/ *nf* tragedy. **tragique** *a* tragic.

**trahir** /tʀaiʀ/ [2] *vt* betray. **trahison** *nf* betrayal; (Mil) treason.

**train** /tʀɛ̃/ *nm* (Rail) train; (allure) pace; **aller bon ~** walk briskly; **en ~ de faire** (busy) doing; **~ d'atterrissage** undercarriage; **~ électrique** (jouet) electric train set; **~ de vie** lifestyle.

**traîne** /tʀɛn/ *nf* (de robe) train; **à la ~** lagging behind.

**traîneau** (*pl* **~x**) /tʀɛno/ *nm* sleigh.

**traînée** /tʀɛne/ *nf* (trace) trail; (longue) streak; (femme: péj) slut.

**traîner** /tʀɛne/ [1] *vt* drag (along); **~ les pieds** drag one's feet. ● *vi* (pendre) trail; (rester en arrière) trail behind; (flâner) hang about; (*papiers, affaires*) lie around; **~ (en longueur)** drag on. □ **se ~** *vpr* (par terre) crawl.

**traire** /tʀɛʀ/ [29] *vt* milk.

**trait** /tʀɛ/ *nm* line; (en dessinant) stroke; (caractéristique) feature, trait; **~s** (du visage) features; **avoir ~ à** relate to; **d'un ~** (*boire*) in one gulp; **~ d'union** hyphen; (fig) link.

**traite** /tʀɛt/ *nf* (de vache) milking; (Comm) draft; **d'une (seule) ~** in one go, at a stretch.

**traité** /tʀete/ *nm* (pacte) treaty; (ouvrage) treatise.

**traitement** /tʀɛtmɑ̃/ *nm* treatment; (salaire) salary; **~ de données** data processing; **~ de texte** word processing.

**traiter** /tʀete/ [1] *vt* treat; (*affaire*) deal with; (*données, produit*) process; **~ qn de lâche** call sb a coward. ● *vi* deal (**avec** with); **~ de** (*sujet*) deal with.

**traiteur** /tʀɛtœʀ/ *nm* caterer; (boutique) delicatessen.

**traître, -esse** /tʀɛtʀ, -ɛs/ *a* treacherous. ● *nm,f* traitor.

**trajectoire** /tʀaʒɛktwaʀ/ *nf* path.

**trajet** /tʀaʒɛ/ *nm* (voyage) journey; (itinéraire) route.

**trame** /tʀam/ *nf* (de tissu) weft.

**tramway** /tʀamwɛ/ *nm* tram; (US) streetcar.

**tranchant, ~e** /tʀɑ̃ʃɑ̃, -t/ *a* sharp; (fig) cutting. ● *nm* cutting edge; **à double ~** two-edged.

**tranche** /tʀɑ̃ʃ/ *nf* (rondelle) slice; (bord) edge; (d'âge, de revenu) bracket.

**tranchée** /tʀɑ̃ʃe/ *nf* trench.

**trancher** /tʀɑ̃ʃe/ [1] *vt* cut; (*question*) decide; (contraster) contrast (**sur** with).

**tranquille** /tʀɑ̃kil/ *a* quiet; (*esprit*) at rest; (*conscience*) clear; **être/laisser ~** be/leave in peace; **tiens-**

toi ~! be quiet! **tranquillisant** *nm* tranquillizer. **tranquilliser** [1] *vt* reassure. **tranquillité** *nf* (peace and) quiet; (d'esprit) peace of mind.

**transcription** /tʀɑ̃skipsjɔ̃/ *nf* transcription; (copie) transcript. **transcrire** [30] *vt* transcribe.

**transe** /tʀɑ̃s/ *nf* **en ~** in a trance.

**transférer** /tʀɑ̃sfeʀe/ [14] *vt* transfer.

**transfert** /tʀɑ̃sfɛʀ/ *nm* transfer; **~ d'appel** (au téléphone) call diversion.

**transformation** /tʀɑ̃sfɔʀmasjɔ̃/ *nf* change; transformation.

**transformer** /tʀɑ̃sfɔʀme/ [1] *vt* change; (radicalement) transform; (*vêtement*) alter. □ **se ~** *vpr* change; (radicalement) be transformed; **(se) ~ en** turn into.

**transgénique** /tʀɑ̃sʒenik/ *a* genetically modified.

**transiger** /tʀɑ̃siʒe/ [40] *vi* compromise.

**transiter** /tʀɑ̃zite/ [1] *vt/i* **~ par** pass through.

**transitif, -ive** /tʀɑ̃zitif, -v/ *a* transitive.

**translucide** /tʀɑ̃slysid/ *a* translucent.

**transmettre** /tʀɑ̃smɛtʀ/ [42] *vt* (*savoir, maladie*) pass on; (*ondes*) transmit; (à la radio) broadcast. **transmission** *nf* transmission; (*radio*) broadcasting.

**transparence** /tʀɑ̃spaʀɑ̃s/ *nf* transparency. **transparent, ~e** *a* transparent.

**transpercer** /tʀɑ̃spɛʀse/ [10] *vt* pierce.

**transpiration** /tʀɑ̃spiʀasjɔ̃/ *nf* perspiration. **transpirer** [1] *vi* perspire.

**transplanter** /tʀɑ̃splɑ̃te/ [1] *vt* (Bot, Méd) transplant.

**transport** /tʀɑ̃spɔʀ/ *nm* transport(ation); **durant le ~** in transit; **les ~s** transport (+ *sg*); **les ~s en commun** public transport (+ *sg*).

**transporter** /tʀɑ̃spɔʀte/ [1] *vt* transport; (à la main) carry. **transporteur** *nm* haulier; (US) trucker.

**transversal, ~e** (*mpl* **-aux**) /tʀɑ̃svɛʀsal, -o/ *a* cross, transverse.

**trapu, ~e** /tʀapy/ *a* stocky.

**traumatisant, ~e** /tʀɔmatizɑ̃, -t/ *a* traumatic. **traumatiser** *vt* [1] traumatize. **traumatisme** *nm* trauma.

**travail** (*pl* **-aux**) /tʀavaj, -o/ *nm* work; (emploi, tâche) job; (façonnage) working; **travaux** work (+ *sg*); (routiers) roadworks; **~ à la chaîne** production line work; **travaux dirigés** (Scol) practical; **travaux forcés** hard labour; **travaux manuels** handicrafts; **travaux ménagers** housework.

**travailler** /tʀavaje/ [1] *vi* work; (se déformer) warp. ● *vt* (façonner) work; (étudier) work at *ou* on.

**travailleur, -euse** /tʀavajœʀ, -øz/ *nm,f* worker. ● *a* hardworking.

**travailliste** /tʀavajist/ *a* Labour. ● *nmf* Labour party member.

**travers** /tʀavɛʀ/ *nm* (défaut) failing; **à ~** through; **au ~ (de)** through; **de ~** (*chapeau, nez*) crooked; (*regarder*) askance; **j'ai avalé de ~** it went the wrong way; **en ~ (de)** across.

**traversée** /tʀavɛʀse/ *nf* crossing.

**traverser** /tʀavɛʀse/ [1] *vt* cross; (transpercer) go (right) through; (*période, forêt*) go *ou* pass through.

**traversin** /tʀavɛʀsɛ̃/ *nm* bolster.

**travesti** /tʀavɛsti/ *nm* transvestite.

**trébucher** /tʀebyʃe/ [1] *vi* stumble, trip (over); **faire ~** trip (up).

**trèfle** /tRɛfl/ *nm* (plante) clover; (cartes) clubs.

**treillis** /tReji/ *nm* trellis; (en métal) wire mesh; (tenue militaire) combat uniform.

**treize** /tRɛz/ *a & nm* thirteen.

**tréma** /tRema/ *nm* diaeresis.

**tremblement** /tRɑ̃bləmɑ̃/ *nm* shaking; **~ de terre** earthquake. **trembler** [1] *vi* shake, tremble; (*lumière, voix*) quiver.

**tremper** /tRɑ̃pe/ [1] *vt/i* soak; (plonger) dip; (*acier*) temper; **faire ~** soak; **~ dans** (fig) be mixed up. □ **se ~** *vpr* (se baigner) have a dip.

**tremplin** /tRɑ̃plɛ̃/ *nm* springboard.

**trente** /tRɑ̃t/ *a & nm* thirty; **se mettre sur son ~ et un** dress up; **tous les ~-six du mois** once in a blue moon.

**trépied** /trepje/ *nm* tripod.

**très** /tRɛ/ *adv* very; **~ aimé/estimé** much liked/esteemed.

**trésor** /tRezɔR/ *nm* treasure; **le T~ public** the revenue department.

**trésorerie** /tRezɔRRi/ *nf* (bureaux) accounts department; (du Trésor public) revenue office; (argent) funds (+ *pl*); (gestion) accounts (+ *pl*). **trésorier, -ière** *nm,f* treasurer.

**tressaillement** /tResajmɑ̃/ *nm* quiver; start.

**tresse** /tRɛs/ *nf* braid, plait.

**trêve** /tRɛv/ *nf* truce; (fig) respite; **~ de plaisanteries** that's enough joking.

**tri** /tRi/ *nm* (classement) sorting; (sélection) selection; **faire le ~ de** (classer) sort; (choisir) select; **centre de ~** sorting office.

**triangle** /tRijɑ̃gl/ *nm* triangle.

**tribal, ~e** (*mpl* **-aux**) /tRibal, -o/ *a* tribal.

**tribord** /tRibɔR/ *nm* starboard.

**tribu** /tRiby/ *nf* tribe.

**tribunal** (*mpl* **-aux**) /tRibynal, -o/ *nm* court.

**tribune** /tRibyn/ *nf* (de stade) grandstand; (d'orateur) rostrum; (débat) forum; (d'église) gallery.

**tribut** /tRiby/ *nm* tribute.

**tributaire** /tRibytɛR/ *a* **~ de** dependent on.

**tricher** /tRiʃe/ [1] *vi* cheat. **tricheur, -euse** *nm,f* cheat.

**tricolore** /tRikɔlɔR/ *a* three-coloured; (*écharpe*) red, white and blue; (*équipe*) French.

**tricot** /tRiko/ *nm* (activité) knitting; (pull) sweater; **en ~** knitted; **~ de corps** vest; (US) undershirt. **tricoter** [1] *vt/i* knit.

**trier** /tRije/ [45] *vt* (classer) sort; (choisir) select.

**trimestre** /tRimɛstR/ *nm* quarter; (Scol) term. **trimestriel, ~le** *a* quarterly; (*bulletin*) end-of-term.

**tringle** /tRɛ̃gl/ *nf* rail.

**trinquer** /tRɛ̃ke/ [1] *vi* clink glasses.

**triomphant, ~e** /tRijɔ̃fɑ̃, -t/ *a* triumphant. **triomphe** *nm* triumph. **triompher** [1] *vi* triumph (**de** over); (jubiler) be triumphant.

**tripes** /tRip/ *nfpl* (mets) tripe (+ *sg*); (entrailles 🄸) guts.

**triple** /tRipl/ *a* triple, treble. ● *nm* **le ~** three times as much (**de** as). **triplés, -es** *nm,fpl* triplets.

**tripot** /tRipo/ *nm* gambling den.

**tripoter** /tRipɔte/ [1] *vt* 🄸 (*personne*) grope; (*objet*) fiddle with.

**trisomique** /tRizɔmik/ *a* **être ~** have Down's syndrome.

**triste** /tRist/ *a* sad; (*rue, temps, couleur*) dreary; (lamentable) dreadful. **tristesse** *nf* sadness; dreariness.

**trivial**, **~e** (*mpl* **-iaux**) /tʀivjal, -jo/ *a* coarse.

**troc** /tʀɔk/ *nm* exchange; (Comm) barter.

**trognon** /tʀɔɲɔ̃/ *nm* (de fruit) core.

**trois** /tʀwɑ/ *a & nm* three; **hôtel ~ étoiles** three-star hotel. **troisième** *a & nmf* third.

**trombone** /tʀɔ̃bɔn/ *nm* (Mus) trombone; (agrafe) paperclip.

**trompe** /tʀɔ̃p/ *nf* (d'éléphant) trunk; (Mus) horn.

**tromper** /tʀɔ̃pe/ [1] *vt* deceive, mislead; (déjouer) elude. □ **se ~** *vpr* be mistaken; **se ~ de route/d'heure** take the wrong road/get the time wrong.

**trompette** /tʀɔ̃pɛt/ *nf* trumpet.

**trompeur**, **-euse** /tʀɔ̃pœʀ, -øz/ *a* (*apparence*) deceptive.

**tronc** /tʀɔ̃/ *nm* trunk; (boîte) collection box.

**tronçon** /tʀɔ̃sɔ̃/ *nm* section.

**tronçonneuse** /tʀɔ̃sɔnøz/ *nf* chain saw.

**trône** /tʀon/ *nm* throne. **trôner** [1] *vi* (*vase*) have pride of place (**sur** on).

**trop** /tʀo/ *adv* (*grand, loin*) too; (*boire, marcher*) too much; **~ (de)** (quantité) too much; (nombre) too many; **ce serait ~ beau** one should be so lucky; **de ~, en ~** too much; too many; **il a bu un verre de ~** he's had one too many; **se sentir de ~** feel one is in the way.

**trophée** /tʀɔfe/ *nm* trophy.

**tropical**, **~e** (*mpl* **-aux**) /tʀɔpikal, -o/ *a* tropical. **tropique** *nm* tropic.

**trop-plein** (*pl* **~s**) /tʀoplɛ̃/ *nm* excess; (dispositif) overflow.

**troquer** /tʀɔke/ [1] *vt* exchange; (Comm) barter (**contre** for).

**trot** /tʀo/ *nm* trot; **aller au ~** trot. **trotter** [1] *vi* trot.

**trotteuse** /tʀɔtøz/ *nf* (de montre) second hand.

**trottoir** /tʀɔtwaʀ/ *nm* pavement; (US) sidewalk; **~ roulant** moving walkway.

**trou** /tʀu/ *nm* hole; (moment) gap; (lieu: péj) dump; **~ (de mémoire)** memory lapse; **~ de serrure** keyhole; **faire son ~** carve one's niche.

**trouble** /tʀubl/ *a* (*eau, image*) unclear; (louche) shady. ● *nm* (émoi) emotion; **~s** (Pol) disturbances; (Méd) disorder (+ *sg*).

**troubler** /tʀuble/ [1] *vt* disturb; (*eau*) make cloudy; (inquiéter) trouble. □ **se ~** *vpr* (*personne*) become flustered.

**trouer** /tʀue/ [1] *vt* make a hole *ou* holes in; **mes chaussures sont trouées** my shoes have got holes in them.

**troupe** /tʀup/ *nf* troop; (d'acteurs) company.

**troupeau** (*pl* **~x**) /tʀupo/ *nm* herd; (de moutons) flock.

**trousse** /tʀus/ *nf* case, bag; **aux ~s de** hot on sb's heels; **~ de toilette** toilet bag.

**trousseau** (*pl* **~x**) /tʀuso/ *nm* (de clefs) bunch; (de mariée) trousseau.

**trouver** /tʀuve/ [1] *vt* find; (penser) think; **il est venu me ~** he came to see me. □ **se ~** *vpr* (être) be; (se sentir) feel; **il se trouve que** it happens that; **si ça se trouve** maybe; **se ~ mal** faint.

**truand** /tʀyɑ̃/ *nm* gangster.

**truc** /tʀyk/ *nm* (moyen) way; (artifice) trick; (chose 🅃) thing. **trucage** *nm* (cinéma) special effect.

**truffe** /tʀyf/ *nf* (champignon, chocolat) truffle; (de chien) nose.

**truffer** /tʀyfe/ [1] *vt* (fig) fill, pack (**de** with).

**truie** /tʀɥi/ *nf* (animal) sow.

**truite** /tʀɥit/ *nf* trout.

**truquer** /tʀyke/ [1] *vt* fix, rig; (*photo*) fake; (*résultats*) fiddle.

**tsar** /tsaʀ/ *nm* tsar, czar.

**tu** /ty/ *pron* (parent, ami, enfant) you. ● ⇒TAIRE [47].

**tuba** /tyba/ *nm* (Mus) tuba; (Sport) snorkel.

**tube** /tyb/ *nm* tube.

**tuberculose** /tybɛʀkyloz/ *nf* tuberculosis.

**tuer** /tɥe/ [1] *vt* kill; (d'une balle) shoot, kill; (épuiser) exhaust; ~ **par balles** shoot dead. □ **se** ~ *vpr* kill oneself; (accident) be killed.

**tuerie** /tyʀi/ *nf* killing.

**tue-tête**: **à** ~ /atytɛt/ *loc* at the top of one's voice.

**tuile** /tɥil/ *nf* tile; (malchance 🄸) (stroke of) bad luck.

**tulipe** /tylip/ *nf* tulip.

**tumeur** /tymœʀ/ *nf* tumour.

**tumulte** /tymylt/ *nm* commotion; (désordre) turmoil.

**tunique** /tynik/ *nf* tunic.

**Tunisie** /tynizi/ *nf* Tunisia.

**tunnel** /tynɛl/ *nm* tunnel.

**turbo** /tyʀbo/ *a* turbo. ● *nf* (voiture) turbo.

**turbulent**, ~**e** /tyʀbylɑ̃, t/ *a* boisterous, turbulent.

**turc**, **-que** /tyʀk/ *a* Turkish. ● *nm* (Ling) Turkish. **T**~, **-que** Turk.

**turfiste** /tyʀfist/ *nmf* racegoer.

**Turquie** /tyʀki/ *nf* Turkey.

**tutelle** /tytɛl/ *nf* (Jur) guardianship; (fig) protection.

**tuteur**, **-trice** /tytœʀ, -tʀis/ *nm,f* (Jur) guardian. ● *nm* (bâton) stake.

**tutoiement** /tytwamɑ̃/ *nm* use of the 'tu' form. **tutoyer** [31] *vt* address using the 'tu' form.

**tuyau** (*pl* ~**x**) /tɥijo/ *nm* pipe; (conseil 🄸) tip; ~ **d'arrosage** hosepipe.

**TVA** *abrév f* (**taxe à la valeur ajoutée**) VAT.

**tympan** /tɛ̃pɑ̃/ *nm* ear-drum.

**type** /tip/ *nm* (genre, traits) type; (individu 🄸) bloke, guy; **le** ~ **même de** a classic example of. ● *a inv* typical.

**typique** /tipik/ *a* typical.

**tyran** /tiʀɑ̃/ *nm* tyrant. **tyrannie** *nf* tyranny. **tyranniser** [1] *vt* oppress, tyrannize.

# Uu

**UE** *abrév f* (**Union européenne**) European Union.

**Ukraine** /ykʀɛn/ *nf* Ukraine.

**ulcère** /ylsɛʀ/ *nm* (Méd) ulcer.

**ULM** *abrév m* (**ultraléger motorisé**) microlight.

**ultérieur**, ~**e** /ylteʀjœʀ/ *a* later. **ultérieurement** *adv* later.

**ultime** /yltim/ *a* final.

**un**, **une** /œ̃, yn/

● *déterminant*

···➤ a; (devant voyelle) an; ~ **animal** an animal; ~ **jour** one day; **pas** ~ **arbre** not a single tree; **il fait** ~ **froid!** it's so cold!

● *pronom*

···➤ one; **l'**~ **d'entre nous** one of us; **les** ~**s croient que...** some believe...

···➤ **la une** the front page.

····➤ **j'en veux uno** I want one.

● *adjectif*

····➤ one, a, an; **j'ai ~ garçon et deux filles** I have a *ou* one boy and two girls; **il est une heure** it is one o'clock.

● *nom masculin & féminin*

····➤ **~ par ~** one by one.

**unanime** /ynanim/ *a* unanimous.

**unanimité** /ynanimite/ *nf* unanimity; **à l'~** unanimously.

**uni**, **~e** /yni/ *a* united; (*couple*) close; (*surface*) smooth; (*tissu*) plain.

**unième** /ynjɛm/ *a* -first; **vingt et ~** twenty-first; **cent ~** one hundred and first.

**unifier** /ynifje/ [45] *vt* unify.

**uniforme** /ynifɔʀm/ *nm* uniform. ● *a* uniform. **uniformiser** [1] *vt* standardize. **uniformité** *nf* uniformity.

**unilatéral**, **~e** (*mpl* **-aux**) /ynilateʀal, -o/ *a* unilateral.

**union** /ynjɔ̃/ *nf* union; **l'U~ européenne** the European Union.

**unique** /ynik/ *a* (seul) only; (*prix, voie*) one; (incomparable) unique; **enfant ~** only child; **sens ~** one-way street. **uniquement** *adv* only, solely.

**unir** /yniʀ/ [2] *vt* unite. □ **s'~** *vpr* unite, join.

**unité** /ynite/ *nf* unit; (harmonie) unity.

**univers** /ynivɛʀ/ *nm* universe.

**universel**, **~le** /ynivɛʀsɛl/ *a* universal.

**universitaire** /ynivɛʀsitɛʀ/ *a* (*résidence*) university; (*niveau*) academic. ● *nmf* academic.

**université** /ynivɛʀsite/ *nf* university.

**uranium** /yʀanjɔm/ *nm* uranium.

**urbain**, **~e** /yʀbɛ̃, -ɛn/ *a* urban. **urbanisme** *nm* town planning.

**urgence** /yʀʒɑ̃s/ *nf* (cas) emergency; (de situation, tâche) urgency; **d'~** (*mesure*) emergency; (*transporter*) urgently; **les ~s** casualty (+ *sg*). **urgent**, **~e** *a* urgent.

**urine** /yʀin/ *nf* urine. **urinoir** *nm* urinal.

**urne** /yʀn/ *nf* (*électorale*) ballot box; (vase) urn; **aller aux ~s** go to the polls.

**urticaire** /yʀtikɛʀ/ *nf* hives (+ *pl*), urticar.

**us** /ys/ *nmpl* **les ~ et coutumes** habits and customs.

**usage** /yzaʒ/ *nm* use; (coutume) custom; (de langage) usage; **à l'~ de** for; **d'~** (habituel) customary; **faire ~ de** make use of.

**usagé**, **~e** /yzaʒe/ *a* worn.

**usager** /yzaʒe/ *nm* user.

**usé**, **~e** /yze/ *a* worn (out); (banal) trite.

**user** /yze/ [1] *vt* wear (out). ● *vi* **~ de** use. □ **s'~** *vpr* (*tissu*) wear (out).

**usine** /yzin/ *nf* factory, plant; **~ sidérurgique** ironworks (+ *pl*).

**usité**, **~e** /yzite/ *a* common.

**ustensile** /ystɑ̃sil/ *nm* utensil.

**usuel**, **~le** /yzɥɛl/ *a* ordinary, everyday.

**usure** /yzyʀ/ *nf* (détérioration) wear (and tear).

**utérus** /yteʀys/ *nm* womb, uterus.

**utile** /ytil/ *a* useful.

**utilisable** /ytilizabl/ *a* usable. **utilisation** *nf* use. **utiliser** [1] *vt* use.

**utopie** /ytɔpi/ *nf* Utopia; (idée) Utopian idea. **utopique** *a* Utopian.

**UV**[1] *abrév f* (**unité de valeur**) course unit.

**UV²** *abrév mpl* (**ultraviolets**) ultraviolet rays; **faire des ~** use a sunbed.

# Vv

**va** /va/ ⇒ALLER [8].

**vacance** /vakɑ̃s/ *nf* (poste) vacancy.

**vacances** /vakɑ̃s/ *nfpl* holiday(s); (US) vacation; **en ~** on holiday; **~ d'été, grandes ~** summer holidays. **vacancier, -ière** *nm,f* holidaymaker; (US) vacationer.

**vacant, ~e** /vakɑ̃, -t/ *a* vacant.

**vacarme** /vakaʀm/ *nm* din.

**vaccin** /vaksɛ̃/ *nm* vaccine. **vacciner** [1] *vt* vaccinate.

**vache** /vaʃ/ *nf* cow. ● *a* (méchant 🅸) nasty.

**vaciller** /vasije/ [1] *vi* sway, wobble; (*lumière*) flicker; (hésiter) falter; (*santé, mémoire*) fail.

**vadrouiller** /vadʀuje/ [1] *vi* 🅸 wander about.

**va-et-vient** /vaevjɛ̃/ *nm inv* toing and froing, (de personnes) comings and goings; **faire le ~** go to and fro; (interrupteur) two-way switch.

**vagabond, ~e** /vagabɔ̃, -d/ *nm,f* vagrant.

**vagin** /vaʒɛ̃/ *nm* vagina.

**vague** /vag/ *a* vague. ● *nm* **regarder dans le ~** stare into space; **il est resté dans le ~** he was vague about it. ● *nf* wave; **~ de fond** ground swell; **~ de froid** cold spell; **~ de chaleur** heatwave.

**vaillant, ~e** /vajɑ̃, -t/ *a* brave; (vigoureux) strong.

**vaille** /vaj/ ⇒VALOIR [60].

**vain, ~e** /vɛ̃, vɛn/ *a* vain, futile; **en ~** in vain.

**vaincre** /vɛ̃kʀ/ [59] *vt* defeat; (surmonter) overcome. **vaincu, ~e** *nm,f* (Sport) loser. **vainqueur** *nm* victor; (Sport) winner.

**vais** /vɛ/ ⇒ALLER [8].

**vaisseau** (*pl* **~x**) /vɛso/ *nm* ship; (veine) vessel; **~ spatial** spaceship.

**vaisselle** /vɛsɛl/ *nf* crockery; (à laver) dishes; **faire la ~** do the washing-up, wash the dishes; **liquide ~** washing-up liquid.

**valable** /valabl/ *a* valid; (de qualité) worthwhile.

**valet** /valɛ/ *nm* (aux cartes) jack; **~ (de chambre)** manservant.

**valeur** /valœʀ/ *nf* value; (mérite) worth, value; **~s** (Comm) stocks and shares; **avoir de la ~** be valuable; **prendre/perdre de la ~** go up/down in value; **objets de ~** valuables; **sans ~** worthless.

**valide** /valid/ *a* (*personne*) fit; (*billet*) valid. **valider** [1] *vt* validate.

**valise** /valiz/ *nf* (suit)case; **faire ses ~s** pack (one's bags).

**vallée** /vale/ *nf* valley.

**valoir** /valwaʀ/ [60] *vi* (mériter) be worth; (égaler) be as good as; (être valable) (*règle*) apply; **faire ~** (*mérite, qualité*) emphasize; (*terrain*) cultivate; (*droit*) assert; **se faire ~** put oneself forward; **~ cher/100 francs** be worth a lot/100 francs; **que vaut ce vin?** what's this wine like?; **ne rien ~** be useless *ou* no good; **ça ne me dit rien qui vaille** I don't like the sound of that; **~ la peine** *or* **le coup** 🅸 be worth it; **il vaut/vaudrait mieux faire** it is/would be better to do. ● *vt* **~ qch à qn** (*éloges, critiques*) earn sb sth; (*admiration*) win sb sth. □ **se ~** *vpr* (être équivalents) be as good as each other; **ça se vaut** it's all the same.

**valoriser** /valɔʀize/ [1] *vt* add value to; (*produit*) promote; (*profession*) make attractive; (*région, ressources*) develop.

**valse** /vals/ *nf* waltz.

**vandale** /vɑ̃dal/ *nmf* vandal.

**vanille** /vanij/ *nf* vanilla.

**vanité** /vanite/ *nf* vanity. **vaniteux, -euse** *a* vain, conceited.

**vanne** /van/ *nf* (d'écluse) sluicegate; (propos 🅸) dig 🅸.

**vantard, ~e** /vɑ̃taʀ, -d/ *a* boastful. ● *nm,f* boaster.

**vanter** /vɑ̃te/ [1] *vt* praise. □ **se ~** *vpr* boast (**de** about); **se ~ de faire** pride oneself on doing.

**vapeur** /vapœʀ/ *nf* (eau) steam; (brume, émanation) vapour; **~s** fumes; **à ~** (*bateau, locomotive*) steam; **faire cuire à la ~** steam.

**vaporisateur** /vapɔʀizatœʀ/ *nm* spray, atomizer. **vaporiser** [1] *vt* spray.

**varappe** /vaʀap/ *nf* rock-climbing.

**variable** /vaʀjabl/ *a* variable; (*temps*) changeable.

**varicelle** /vaʀisɛl/ *nf* chickenpox.

**varié, ~e** /vaʀje/ *a* (non monotone, étendu) varied; (divers) various; **sandwichs ~s** a selection of sandwiches.

**varier** /vaʀje/ [45] *vt/i* vary.

**variété** /vaʀjete/ *nf* variety; **spectacle de ~s** variety show.

**vase** /vɑz/ *nm* vase. ● *nf* silt, mud.

**vaseux, -euse** /vɑzø, -z/ *a* (confus 🅸) woolly, hazy.

**vaste** /vast/ *a* vast, huge.

**vaurien, ~ne** /voʀjɛ̃, -ɛn/ *nm,f* good-for-nothing.

**vautour** /votuʀ/ *nm* vulture.

**vautrer (se)** /(sə)votʀe/ [1] *vpr* sprawl; **se ~ dans** (*vice, boue*) wallow in.

**veau** (*pl* **~x**) /vo/ *nm* calf; (viande) veal; (cuir) calfskin.

**vécu, ~e** /veky/ *a* (réel) true, real. ● ⇨VIVRE [62].

**vedette** /vədɛt/ *nf* (artiste) star; **en ~** (*objet*) in a prominent position; (*personne*) in the limelight; **joueur ~** star player; (bateau) launch.

**végétal** (*mpl* **-aux**) /veʒetal, -o/ *a* plant. ● *nm* (*pl* **-aux**) plant.

**végétalien, ~ne** /veʒetaljɛ̃, -ɛn/ *a & nm,f* vegan.

**végétarien, ~ne** /veʒetaʀjɛ̃, -ɛn/ *a & nm,f* vegetarian.

**végétation** /veʒetasjɔ̃/ *nf* vegetation; **~s** (Méd) adenoids.

**véhicule** /veikyl/ *nm* vehicle.

**veille** /vɛj/ *nf* (état) wakefulness; (jour précédent) **la ~ (de)** the day before; **la ~ de Noël** Christmas Eve; **à la ~ de** on the eve of; **la ~ au soir** the previous evening.

**veillée** /veje/ *nf* evening (gathering).

**veiller** /veje/ [1] *vi* stay up; (monter la garde) be on watch. ● *vt* (*malade*) watch over; **~ à** attend to; **~ sur** watch over.

**veilleur** /vɛjœʀ/ *nm* **~ de nuit** night-watchman.

**veilleuse** /vɛjøz/ *nf* night light; (de véhicule) sidelight; (de réchaud) pilot light; **mettre qch en ~** put sth on the back burner.

**veine** /vɛn/ *nf* (Anat) vein; (nervure, filon) vein; (chance 🅸) luck; **avoir de la ~** 🅸 be lucky.

**véliplanchiste** /veliplɑ̃ʃist/ *nmf* windsurfer.

**vélo** /velo/ *nm* bike; (activité) cycling; **faire du ~** go cycling; **~ tout terrain** mountain bike.

**vélomoteur** /velɔmɔtœʀ/ *nm* moped.

**velours** /v(ə)luʀ/ *nm* velvet; **~ côtelé** corduroy.

**velouté**, **~e** /vəlute/ *a* smooth. ● *nm* (Culin) **~ d'asperges** cream of asparagus soup.

**vendanges** /vɑ̃dɑ̃ʒ/ *nfpl* grape harvest.

**vendeur**, **-euse** /vɑ̃dœʀ, -øz/ *nm,f* shop assistant; (marchand) salesman, saleswoman; (Jur) vendor, seller.

**vendre** /vɑ̃dʀ/ [3] *vt* sell; **à ~** for sale. □ **se ~** *vpr* (être vendu) be sold; (trouver acquéreur) sell; **se ~ bien** sell well.

**vendredi** /vɑ̃dʀədi/ *nm* Friday; **V~ saint** Good Friday.

**vénéneux**, **-euse** /venenø, -z/ *a* poisonous.

**vénérer** /veneʀe/ [14] *vt* revere.

**vénérien**, **~ne** /veneʀjɛ̃, -ɛn/ *a* **maladie ~ne** venereal disease.

**vengeance** /vɑ̃ʒɑ̃s/ *nf* revenge, vengeance.

**venger** /vɑ̃ʒe/ [40] *vt* avenge. □ **se ~** *vpr* take *ou* get one's revenge (**de qch** for sth, **de qn** on sb).

**vengeur**, **-eresse** /vɑ̃ʒœʀ, -əʀɛs/ *a* vengeful. ● *nm,f* avenger.

**venimeux**, **-euse** /vənimø, -z/ *a* poisonous, venomous.

**venin** /vənɛ̃/ *nm* venom.

**venir** /vəniʀ/ [58] *vi* (*aux être*) come (**de** from); **faire ~ qn** send for sb, call sb; **en ~ à** come to; **en ~ aux mains** come to blows; **où veut-elle en ~?** what is she driving at?; **il m'est venu à l'esprit** *or* **à l'idée que** it occurred to me that; **s'il venait à pleuvoir** if it should rain; **dans les jours à ~** in the next few days. ● *v aux* **~ de faire** have just done; **il vient/venait d'arriver** he has/had just arrived; **~ faire** come to do; **viens voir** come and see.

**vent** /vɑ̃/ *nm* wind; **il fait du ~** it is windy; **être dans le ~** Ⓘ be trendy.

**vente** /vɑ̃t/ *nf* sale; **~ (aux enchères)** auction; **en ~** on *ou* for sale; **mettre qch en ~** put sth up for sale; **~ de charité** (charity) bazaar; **~ au détail/en gros** retailing/wholesaling; **équipe de ~** sales team.

**ventilateur** /vɑ̃tilatœʀ/ *nm* fan, ventilator. **ventiler** [1] *vt* ventilate.

**ventouse** /vɑ̃tuz/ *nf* suction pad; (pour déboucher) plunger.

**ventre** /vɑ̃tʀ/ *nm* stomach; (d'animal) belly; (utérus) womb; **avoir du ~** have a paunch.

**venu**, **~e** /vəny/ *a* **bien ~** (à propos) apt, timely; **mal ~** badly timed; **il serait mal ~ de faire** it wouldn't be a good idea to do. ● ⇨VENIR [59].

**venue** /vəny/ *nf* coming.

**ver** /vɛʀ/ *nm* worm; (dans la nourriture) maggot; (du bois) woodworm; **~ luisant** glow-worm; **~ à soie** silkworm; **~ solitaire** tapeworm; **~ de terre** earthworm.

**verbal**, **~e** (*mpl* **-aux**) /vɛʀbal, -o/ *a* verbal.

**verbe** /vɛʀb/ *nm* verb.

**verdir** /vɛʀdiʀ/ [2] *vi* turn green.

**véreux**, **-euse** /veʀø, -z/ *a* wormy; (malhonnête) shady.

**verger** /vɛʀʒe/ *nm* orchard.

**verglas** /vɛʀgla/ *nm* black ice.

**véridique** /veʀidik/ *a* true.

**vérification** /veʀifikasjɔ̃/ *nf* check(ing), verification.

**vérifier** /veʀifje/ [45] *vt* check, verify; (confirmer) confirm.

**véritable** /veʀitabl/ *a* true, real; (authentique) real.

**vérité** /veʀite/ *nf* truth; (de tableau, roman) realism; **en ~** in fact, actually.

**vermine** /vɛrmin/ *nf* vermin.

**verni**, **~e** /vɛrni/ *a* (*chaussures*) patent (leather); (chanceux [F]) lucky.

**vernir** /vɛrnir/ [2] *vt* varnish. □ **se ~** *vpr* **se ~ les ongles** apply nail polish.

**vernis** /vɛrni/ *nm* varnish; (de poterie) glaze; **~ à ongles** nail polish.

**verra**, **verrait** /vɛra, vɛrɛ/ ⇒VOIR [64].

**verre** /vɛr/ *nm* glass; (de lunettes) lens; **~ à vin** wine glass; **prendre** *ou* **boire un ~** have a drink; **~ de contact** contact lens; **~ dépoli** frosted glass.

**verrière** /vɛrjɛr/ *nf* (toit) glass roof; (paroi) glass wall.

**verrou** /vɛru/ *nm* bolt; **sous les ~s** behind bars.

**verrouillage** /vɛrujaʒ/ *nm* **~ central** *or* **centralisé (des portes)** central locking.

**verrue** /vɛry/ *nf* wart; **~ plantaire** verruca.

**vers¹** /vɛr/ *prép* towards; (aux environs de) (temps) about; (lieu) near, around; (période) towards; **~ le soir** towards evening.

**vers²** /vɛr/ *nm* (poésie) line of verse.

**versatile** /vɛrsatil/ *a* unpredictable, volatile.

**verse**: **à ~** /avɛrs/ *loc* in torrents.

**Verseau** /vɛrso/ *nm* **le ~** Aquarius.

**versement** /vɛrsəmɑ̃/ *nm* payment; (échelonné) instalment.

**verser** /vɛrse/ [1] *vt*/*i* pour; (*larmes, sang*) shed; (payer) pay. ● *vi* pour; (*voiture*) overturn; **~ dans** (fig) lapse into.

**version** /vɛrsjɔ̃/ *nf* version; (traduction) translation.

**verso** /vɛrso/ *nm* back (of the page); **voir au ~** see overleaf.

**vert**, **~e** /vɛr, -t/ *a* green; (*vieillard*) sprightly. ● *nm* green; **les ~s** the Greens.

**vertèbre** /vɛrtɛbr/ *nf* vertebra; **se déplacer une ~** slip a disc.

**vertical**, **~e** (*mpl* **-aux**) /vɛrtikal, -o/ *a* vertical.

**vertige** /vɛrtiʒ/ *nm* dizziness; **~s** dizzy spells; **avoir le ~** feel dizzy. **vertigineux**, **-euse** *a* dizzy; (très grand) staggering.

**vertu** /vɛrty/ *nf* virtue; **en ~ de** in accordance with. **vertueux**, **-euse** *a* virtuous.

**verveine** /vɛrvɛn/ *nf* verbena.

**vessie** /vesi/ *nf* bladder.

**veste** /vɛst/ *nf* jacket.

**vestiaire** /vɛstjɛr/ *nm* cloakroom; (Sport) changing-room; (US) locker-room.

**vestibule** /vɛstibyl/ *nm* hall; (Théât, d'hôtel) foyer.

**vestige** /vɛstiʒ/ *nm* (objet) relic; (trace) vestige.

**veston** /vɛstɔ̃/ *nm* jacket.

**vêtement** /vɛtmɑ̃/ *nm* article of clothing; **~s** clothes, clothing.

**vétéran** /veterɑ̃/ *nm* veteran.

**vétérinaire** /veterinɛr/ *nmf* vet, veterinary surgeon, (US) veterinarian.

**vêtir** /vetir/ [61] *vt* dress. □ **se ~** *vpr* dress.

**veto** /veto/ *nm inv* veto.

**vêtu**, **~e** /vety/ *a* dressed (**de** in).

**veuf**, **veuve** /vœf, -v/ *a* widowed. ● *nm*,*f* widower, widow.

**veuille** /vœj/ ⇒VOULOIR [64].

**veut**, **veux** /vø/ ⇒VOULOIR [64].

**vexation** /vɛksasjɔ̃/ *nf* humiliation.

**vexer** /vɛkse/ [1] *vt* upset, hurt. □ **se ~** *vpr* be upset, be hurt.

**viable** /vjabl/ *a* viable; (*projet*) feasible.

**viande** /vjɑ̃d/ *nf* meat.

**vibrer** /vibʀe/ [1] *vi* vibrate; **faire ~** (*âme, foules*) stir.

**vicaire** /vikɛʀ/ *nm* curate.

**vice** /vis/ *nm* (moral) vice; (physique) defect.

**vicier** /visje/ [45] *vt* contaminate; (*air*) pollute.

**vicieux, -ieuse** /visjø, -z/ *a* depraved. ● *nm,f* pervert.

**victime** /viktim/ *nf* victim; (d'un accident) casualty.

**victoire** /viktwaʀ/ *nf* victory; (Sport) win. **victorieux, -ieuse** *a* victorious, (*equipe*) winning.

**vidange** /vidɑ̃ʒ/ *nf* emptying; (Auto) oil change; (tuyau) waste pipe *ou* outlet.

**vide** /vid/ *a* empty. ● *nm* (absence, manque) vacuum, void; (espace) space; (trou) gap; (sans air) vacuum; **à ~** empty; **emballé sous ~** vacuum packed; **suspendu dans le ~** dangling in space.

**vidéo** /video/ *a inv* video, **jeu ~** video game. ● *nf* video. **vidéocassette** *nf* video(tape). **vidéoclip** *nm* music video. **vidéoconférence** *nf* videoconferencing, (séance) videoconference. **vidéodisque** *nm* videodisc.

**vide-ordures** /vidɔʀdyʀ/ *nm inv* rubbish chute.

**vidéothèque** /videotɛk/ *nf* video library.

**vider** /vide/ [1] *vt* empty; (*poisson*) gut; (expulser [I]) throw out; **~ les lieux** leave. □ **se ~** *vpr* empty.

**vie** /vi/ *nf* life; (durée) lifetime; **à ~, pour la ~** for life; **donner la ~ à** give birth to; **en ~** alive; **la ~ est chère** the cost of living is high.

**vieil** /vjɛj/ ⇒VIEUX.

**vieillard** /vjɛjaʀ/ *nm* old man.

**vieille** /vjɛj/ ⇒VIEUX.

**vieillesse** /vjɛjɛs/ *nf* old age.

**vieillir** /vjejiʀ/ [2] *vi* grow old, age; (*mot, idée*) become old-fashioned. ● *vt* age. **vieillissement** *nm* ageing.

**viens, vient** /vjɛ̃/ ⇒VENIR [59].

**vierge** /vjɛʀʒ/ *nf* virgin; **la V~** Virgo. ● *a* virgin; (*feuille, cassette*) blank; (*cahier, pellicule*) unused, new.

**vieux** (**vieil** *before vowel or mute h*), **vieille** (*mpl* **vieux**) /vjø, vjɛj/ *a* old. ● *nm,f* old man, old woman; **petit ~** little old man, **les ~** old people; **vieille fille** (péj) spinster; **~ garçon** old bachelor. **vieux jeu** *a inv* old-fashioned.

**vif, vive** /vif, viv/ *a* (animé) lively; (*émotion, vent*) keen; (*froid*) biting; (*lumière*) bright; (*douleur, contraste, parole*) sharp; (*souvenir, style, teint*) vivid; (*succès, impatience*) great; **brûler/enterrer ~** burn/bury alive; **de vive voix** personally. ● *nm* **à ~** (*plaie*) open, **avoir les nerfs à ~** be on edge; **blessé au ~** cut to the quick.

**vigie** /viʒi/ *nf* lookout.

**vigilant, ~e** /viʒilɑ̃, -t/ *a* vigilant.

**vigne** /viɲ/ *nf* (plante) vine; (vignoble) vineyard. **vigneron, ~ne** *nm,f* wine-grower.

**vignette** /viɲɛt/ *nf* (étiquette) label; (Auto) road tax disc.

**vignoble** /viɲɔbl/ *nm* vineyard.

**vigoureux, -euse** /viguʀø, -z/ *a* vigorous, sturdy.

**vigueur** /vigœʀ/ *nf* vigour; **être/entrer en ~** (*loi*) be/come into force; **en ~** current.

**VIH** *abrév m* (**virus immunodéficitaire humain**) HIV.

**vilain**, **~e** /vilɛ̃, -ɛn/ *a* (mauvais) nasty; (laid) ugly. ● *nm,f* naughty boy, naughty girl.

**villa** /villa/ *nf* detached house.

**village** /vilaʒ/ *nm* village.

**villageois**, **~e** /vilaʒwa, -z/ *a* village. ● *nm,f* villager.

**ville** /vil/ *nf* town; (importante) city; **~ d'eaux** spa.

**vin** /vɛ̃/ *nm* wine; **~ d'honneur** reception.

**vinaigre** /vinɛɡʀ/ *nm* vinegar. **vinaigrette** *nf* oil and vinegar dressing, vinaigrette.

**vingt** /vɛ̃/ (/vɛ̃t/ *before vowel and in numbers 22-29*) *a & nm* twenty.

**vingtaine** /vɛ̃tɛn/ *nf* **une ~ (de)** about twenty.

**vingtième** /vɛ̃tjɛm/ *a & nmf* twentieth.

**vinicole** /vinikɔl/ *a* wine(-producing).

**viol** /vjɔl/ *nm* (de femme) rape; (de lieu, loi) violation.

**violemment** /vjɔlamɑ̃/ *adv* violently.

**violence** /vjɔlɑ̃s/ *nf* violence; (acte) act of violence. **violent**, **~e** *a* violent.

**violer** /vjɔle/ [1] *vt* rape; (*lieu, loi*) violate.

**violet**, **~te** /vjɔlɛ, -t/ *a* purple. ● *nm* purple. **violette** *nf* violet.

**violon** /vjɔlɔ̃/ *nm* violin; **~ d'Ingres** hobby.

**violoncelle** /vjɔlɔ̃sɛl/ *nm* cello.

**vipère** /vipɛʀ/ *nf* viper, adder.

**virage** /viʀaʒ/ *nm* bend; (en ski) turn; (changement d'attitude: fig) change of course.

**virée** /viʀe/ *nf* 🅸 trip, tour; (en voiture) drive; (à vélo) ride.

**virement** /viʀmɑ̃/ *nm* (Comm) (credit) transfer; **~ automatique** standing order.

**virer** /viʀe/ [1] *vi* turn; **~ de bord** tack; (fig) do a U-turn; **~ au rouge** turn red. ● *vt* (*argent*) transfer; (expulser 🅸) throw out; (*élève*) expel; (licencier 🅸) fire.

**virgule** /viʀɡyl/ *nf* comma; (dans un nombre) (decimal) point.

**viril**, **~e** /viʀil/ *a* virile.

**virtuel**, **~le** /viʀtɥɛl/ *a* (potentiel) potential; (*mémoire, réalité*) virtual.

**virulent**, **~e** /viʀylɑ̃, -t/ *a* virulent.

**virus** /viʀys/ *nm* virus.

**vis**[1] /vi/ ⇒VIVRE [62], VOIR [63].

**vis**[2] /vis/ *nf* screw.

**visa** /viza/ *nm* visa.

**visage** /vizaʒ/ *nm* face.

**vis-à-vis** /vizavi/ *prép* **~ de** (en face de) opposite; (à l'égard de) in relation to; (comparé à) compared to,beside. ● *nm inv* (personne) person opposite; **en ~** opposite each other.

**visée** /vize/ *nf* aim; **avoir des ~s sur** have designs on.

**viser** /vize/ [1] *vt* (*cible, centre*) aim at; (*poste, résultats*) aim for; (concerner) be aimed at; (*document*) stamp; **~ à** aim at; (*mesure, propos*) be aimed at; **~ à faire** aim to do. ● *vi* aim.

**viseur** /vizœʀ/ *nm* (d'arme) sights (+ *pl*); (Photo) viewfinder.

**visière** /vizjɛʀ/ *nf* (de casquette) peak; (de casque) visor.

**vision** /vizjɔ̃/ *nf* vision.

**visite** /vizit/ *nf* visit; (pour inspecter) inspection; (personne) visitor; **heures de ~** visiting hours; **~ guidée** guided tour; **~ médicale** medical; **rendre ~ à, faire une ~ à** pay a visit; **être en ~ (chez qn)** be

visiting (sb); **avoir de la ~** have visitors.

**visiter** /vizite/ [1] *vt* visit; (*appartement*) view. **visiteur, -euse** *nm,f* visitor.

**visser** /vise/ *vt* screw (on).

**visuel, ~le** /vizɥɛl/ *a* visual. ● *nm* (Ordinat) visual display unit, VDU.

**vit** /vi/ ⇒VIVRE [62], VOIR [63].

**vital, ~e** (*mpl* **-aux**) /vital, -o/ *a* vital.

**vitamine** /vitamin/ *nf* vitamin.

**vite** /vit/ *adv* fast, quickly; (tôt) soon; **~!** quick!; **faire ~** be quick; **au plus ~, le plus ~ possible** as quickly as possible.

**vitesse** /vitɛs/ *nf* speed; (régime: Auto) gear; **à toute ~** at top speed; **en ~** in a hurry, quickly; **boîte à cinq ~s** five-speed gearbox.

**viticole** /vitikɔl/ *a* (*industrie*) wine; (*région*) wine-producing. **viticulteur** *nm* wine-grower.

**vitrage** /vitʀaʒ/ *nm* (vitres) windows; **double ~** double glazing.

**vitrail** (*pl* **-aux**) /vitʀaj, -o/ *nm* stained-glass window.

**vitre** /vitʀ/ *nf* (window) pane; (de véhicule) window.

**vitrine** /vitʀin/ *nf* (shop) window; (meuble) display cabinet.

**vivace** /vivas/ *a* (*plante*) perennial; (durable) enduring.

**vivacité** /vivasite/ *nf* liveliness; (agilité) quickness; (d'émotion, d'intelligence) keenness; (de souvenir, style, teint) vividness.

**vivant, ~e** /vivɑ̃, -t/ *a* (*example, symbole*) living; (en vie) alive, living; (actif, vif) lively. ● *nm* **un bon ~** a bon viveur; **de son ~** in his lifetime; **les ~s** the living.

**vive**[1] /viv/ ⇒VIF.

**vive**[2] /viv/ *interj* **~ le roi!** long live the king!

**vivement** /vivmɑ̃/ *adv* (fortement) strongly; (vite, sèchement) sharply; (avec éclat) vividly; (beaucoup) greatly; **~ la fin!** I'll be glad when it's the end!

**vivier** /vivje/ *nm* fish pond; (artificiel) fish tank.

**vivifier** /vivifje/ [45] *vt* invigorate.

**vivre** /vivʀ/ [63] *vi* live; **~ de** (*nourriture*) live on; **~ encore** be still alive; **faire ~** (*famille*) support. ● *vt* (*vie*) live; (*période, aventure*) live through.

**vivres** /vivʀ/ *nmpl* supplies.

**VO** *abrév f* (**version originale**) **en ~** in the original language.

**vocabulaire** /vɔkabylɛʀ/ *nm* vocabulary.

**vocal, ~e** (*mpl* **-aux**) /vɔkal, -o/ *a* vocal.

**vœu** (*pl* **~x**) /vø/ *nm* (souhait) wish; (promesse) vow; **meilleurs ~x** best wishes.

**vogue** /vɔg/ *nf* fashion, vogue; **en ~** in fashion *ou* vogue.

**voguer** /vɔge/ [1] *vi* sail.

**voici** /vwasi/ *prép* here is, this is; (au pluriel) here are, these are; **me ~** here I am; **~ un an** (temps passé) a year ago; **~ un an que** it is a year since.

**voie** /vwa/ *nf* (route) road; (partie de route) lane; (chemin) way; (moyen) means, way; (rails) track; (quai) platform; **en ~ de** in the process of; **en ~ de développement** (*pays*) developing; **espèce en ~ de disparition** endangered species; **par la ~ des airs** by air; **par ~ orale** orally; **sur la bonne/mauvaise ~** (fig) on the right/wrong track; **montrer la ~** lead the way; **~ de dégagement** slip-road; **~ ferrée** railway; (US) railroad; **V~ lactée** Milky Way; **~ navigable** waterway; **~ publique** public highway; **~ sans issue** (sur

panneau) no through road; (fig) dead end.

**voilà** /vwala/ *prép* there is, that is; (au pluriel) there are, those are; (voici) here is, here are; **le ~** there he is; **~!** right!; (en offrant qch) there you are!; **~ un an** (temps passé) a year ago; **~ un an que** it is a year since; **tu en veux? en ~** do you want some? here you are; **en ~ des histoires!** what a fuss!; **et ~ que** and then.

**voilage** /vwalaʒ/ *nm* net curtain.

**voile** /vwal/ *nf* (de bateau) sail; (Sport) sailing. ● *nm* veil; (tissu léger) net.

**voilé, ~e** /vwale/ *a* (*allusion, femme*) veiled; (flou) hazy.

**voiler** /vwale/ [1] *vt* (dissimuler) veil; (déformer) buckle. ◻ **se ~** *vpr* (devenir flou) become hazy; (se déformer) (*roue*) buckle.

**voilier** /vwalje/ *nm* sailing ship.

**voir** /vwaʀ/ [64] *vt* see; **faire ~ qch à qn** show sth to sb; **laisser ~** show; **avoir quelque chose à ~ avec** have something to do with; **ça n'a rien à ~** that's got nothing to do with it; **je ne peux pas le ~** 🅘 I can't stand him. ● *vi* **y ~** be able to see; **je n'y vois rien** I cannot see; **~ trouble** have blurred vision; **voyons** let's see now; **voyons, soyez sages!** come on now, behave yourselves! ◻ **se ~** *vpr* (dans la glace) see oneself; (être visible) show; (se produire) be seen; (se trouver) find oneself; (se fréquenter, se rencontrer) see each other; (être vu) be seen.

**voire** /vwaʀ/ *adv* or even, not to say.

**voirie** /vwaʀi/ *nf* (service) highway maintenance.

**voisin, ~e** /vwazɛ̃, -in/ *a* (de voisinage) neighbouring; (proche) nearby; (adjacent) next (**de** to); (semblable) similar (**de** to). ● *nm,f* neighbour; **le ~** the man next door, the neighbour. **voisinage** *nm* neighbourhood; (proximité) proximity.

**voiture** /vwatyʀ/ *nf* (motor) car; (wagon) coach, carriage; **en ~!** all aboard!; **~ bélier** ramraiding car; **~ à cheval** horse-drawn carriage; **~ de course** racing car; **~ école** driving school car; **~ d'enfant** pram; (US) baby carriage; **~ de tourisme** saloon car.

**voix** /vwa/ *nf* voice; (suffrage) vote; **à ~ basse** in a whisper.

**vol** /vɔl/ *nm* (d'avion, d'oiseau) flight; (groupe d'oiseaux) flock, flight; (délit) theft; (hold-up) robbery; **~ à l'étalage** shoplifting; **~ à la tire** pickpocketing; **à ~ d'oiseau** as the crow flies; **de haut ~** high-ranking; **~ libre** hang-gliding; **~ à voile** gliding.

**volaille** /vɔlɑj/ *nf* **la ~** (poules) poultry; **une ~** a fowl.

**volant** /vɔlɑ̃/ *nm* (steering-)wheel; (de jupe) flounce; (de badminton) shuttlecock; **donner un coup de ~** turn the wheel sharply.

**volcan** /vɔlkɑ̃/ *nm* volcano.

**volée** /vɔle/ *nf* flight; (oiseaux) flight, flock; (de coups, d'obus, au tennis) volley; **à toute ~** hard; **à la ~** in flight, in mid-air.

**voler** /vɔle/ [1] *vi* (*oiseau*) fly; (dérober) steal (**à** from). ● *vt* steal; **~ qn** rob sb; **il ne l'a pas volé** he deserved it.

**volet** /vɔlɛ/ *nm* (de fenêtre) shutter; (de document) (folded *ou* tear-off) section; **trié sur le ~** hand-picked.

**voleur, -euse** /vɔlœʀ, -øz/ *nm,f* thief; **au ~!** stop thief! ● *a* thieving.

**volley-ball** /vɔlɛbol/ *nm* volleyball.

**volontaire** /vɔlɔ̃tɛʀ/ *a* (délibéré) voluntary; (opiniâtre) determined. ● *nmf* volunteer. **volontairement** *adv* voluntarily; (exprès) intentionally.

**volonté** /vɔlɔ̃te/ *nf* (faculté, intention) will; (souhait) wish; (énergie) willpower; **à ~** (comme on veut) as required; **du vin à ~** unlimited wine; **bonne ~** goodwill; **mauvaise ~** ill will.

**volontiers** /vɔlɔ̃tje/ *adv* (de bon gré) with pleasure, willingly, gladly; (*admettre*) readily.

**volt** /vɔlt/ *nm* volt.

**volte-face** /vɔltəfas/ *nf inv* (fig) U-turn; **faire ~** do a U-turn.

**voltige** /vɔltiʒ/ *nf* acrobatics (+ *pl*).

**volume** /vɔlym/ *nm* volume.

**volumineux**, **-euse** /vɔlyminø, -z/ *a* bulky; (*livre, dossier*) thick.

**volupté** /vɔlypte/ *nf* voluptuousness.

**vomi** /vɔmi/ *nm* vomit.

**vomir** /vɔmiʀ/ [2] *vt* vomit; (fig) belch out. ● *vi* be sick, vomit.

**vomissement** /vɔmismɑ̃/ *nm* vomiting; **~s du matin** morning sickness.

**vont** /vɔ̃/ ⇒ALLER [8].

**vorace** /vɔʀas/ *a* voracious.

**vos** /vo/ ⇒VOTRE.

**votant**, **~e** /vɔtɑ̃, -t/ *nm,f* voter.

**vote** /vɔt/ *nm* (action) voting; (suffrage) vote; **~ d'une loi** passing of a bill; **~ par correspondance/procuration** postal/proxy vote.

**voter** /vɔte/ [1] *vi* vote. ● *vt* vote for; (adopter) pass; (*crédits*) vote.

**votre** (*pl* **vos**) /vɔtʀ, vo/ *a* your.

**vôtre** /votʀ/ *pron* **le** *ou* **la ~**, **les ~s** yours.

**vouer** /vwe/ [1] *vt* (*vie, temps*) dedicate (**à** to); **voué à l'échec** doomed to failure.

**vouloir** /vulwaʀ/ [64] *vt* (exiger) want (**faire** to do); (souhaiter) want; **que veux-tu boire?** what would you like to drink?; **je voudrais bien y aller** I'd really like to go; **je veux bien venir** I'm happy to come; **comme tu voudras** as you wish; (accepter) **veuillez vous asseoir** please sit down; **veuillez patienter** (au téléphone) please hold the line; (signifier) **~ dire** mean; **qu'est-ce que cela veut dire?** what does that mean?; **en ~ à qn** bear a grudge against sb. □ **s'en ~** *vpr* regret; **je m'en veux de lui avoir dit** I really regret having told her.

**voulu**, **~e** /vuly/ *a* (délibéré) intentional; (requis) required.

**vous** /vu/ *pron* (sujet, complément) you; (indirect) (to) you; (réfléchi) yourself; (pluriel) yourselves; (l'un l'autre) each other. **vous-même** *pron* yourself. **vous-mêmes** *pron* yourselves.

**voûte** /vut/ *nf* (plafond) vault; (porche) archway.

**vouvoiement** /vuvwamɑ̃/ *nm* use of the 'vous' form. **vouvoyer** [31] *vt* address using the 'vous' form.

**voyage** /vwajaʒ/ *nm* trip; (déplacement) journey; (par mer) voyage; **~(s)** (action) travelling; **~ d'affaires** business trip; **~ d'études** study trip; **~ de noces** honeymoon; **~ organisé** (package) tour.

**voyager** /vwajaʒe/ [40] *vi* travel.

**voyageur**, **-euse** /vwajaʒœʀ, -øz/ *nm,f* traveller; (passager) passenger; **~ de commerce** travelling salesman.

**voyant**, **~e** /vwajɑ̃, -t/ *a* gaudy. ● *nm* (signal) (warning) light.

**voyelle** /vwajɛl/ *nf* vowel.

**voyou** /vwaju/ *nm* hooligan.

**vrac**: **en** ~ /ɑ̃vʀak/ *loc* (pêle-mêle) haphazardly; (sans emballage) loose; (en gros) in bulk.

**vrai**, **~e** /vʀɛ/ *a* true; (authentique) real. ● *nm* truth; **à ~ dire** to tell the truth; **pour de ~** for real. **vraiment** *adv* really.

**vraisemblable** /vʀɛsɑ̃blabl/ *a* (probable) likely; (*excuse, histoire*) plausible. **vraisemblablement** *adv* probably. **vraisemblance** *nf* likelihood, plausibility.

**vrombir** /vʀɔ̃biʀ/ [2] *vi* roar.

**VRP** *abrév m* (**voyageur représentant placier**) rep, representative.

**VTT** *abrév m* (**vélo tout terrain**) mountain bike.

**vu**, **~e** /vy/ *a* **bien ~** well thought of; **ce serait plutôt mal ~** it wouldn't go down well; **bien ~!** good point! ● *prép* in view of; **~ que** seeing that. ● ⇒VOIR [64].

**vue** /vy/ *nf* (spectacle) sight; (vision) (eye)sight; (panorama, idée, image, photo) view; **avoir en ~** have in mind; **à ~** (*tirer*) on sight; (*payable*) at sight; **de ~** by sight; **perdre de ~** lose sight of; **en ~** (proche) in sight; (célèbre) in the public eye; **en ~ de faire** with a view to doing; **à ~ d'œil** visibly; **avoir des ~s sur** have designs on.

**vulgaire** /vylgɛʀ/ *a* (grossier) vulgar; (ordinaire) common.

**vulnérable** /vylneʀabl/ *a* vulnerable.

# Ww

**wagon** /vagɔ̃/ *nm* (de voyageurs) carriage; (de marchandises) wagon. **wagon-lit** (*pl* **wagons-lits**) *nm* sleeper. **wagon-restaurant** (*pl* **wagons-restaurants**) *nm* restaurant car.

**walkman**® /wokman/ *nm* personal stereo, walkman®.

**waters** /watɛʀ/ *nmpl* toilets.

**watt** /wat/ *nm* watt.

**wc** /(dublə)vese/ *nmpl* toilet (+ *sg*).

**Web** /wɛb/ *nm* Web; **un site ~** a Web site; **une page ~** Web page.

**webcam** /wɛbkam/ *nf* webcam.

**webmestre** /wɛbmɛstʀ/ *nm* webmaster.

**week-end** /wikɛnd/ *nm* weekend.

**whisky** (*pl* **-ies**) /wiski/ *nm* whisky.

**xénophobe** /gzenɔfɔb/ *a* xenophobic. ● *nmf* xenophobe.

**xérès** /gzeʀɛs/ *nm* sherry.

**xylophone** /ksilɔfɔn/ *nm* xylophone.

# Yy

**y** /i/

● *adverbe*

····➤ there; (dessus) on it; (pluriel) on them; (dedans) in it; (pluriel) in them; **j'~ vais** I'm on my way; **n'~ va pas** don't go; **du lait? il n'~ en a pas** milk? there's none; **tu n'~ arriveras jamais** you'll never manage it.

● *pronom*

····➤ **s'~ habituer** get used to it.

····➤ **s'~ attendre** expect it.

····➤ **~ penser** think about it.

····➤ **~ être pour qch** have sth to do with it.

**yaourt** /'jauʀ(t)/ *nm* yoghurt. **yaourtière** *nf* yoghurt-maker.

**yard** /'jaʀd/ *nm* yard (*= 91,44 cm*).

**yen** /'jɛn/ *nm* yen.

**yeux** /jø/ ⇒œil.

**yoga** /'jɔga/ *nm* yoga.

**yougoslave** /'jugɔslav/ *a* Yugoslav. **Y~** *nmf* Yugoslav.

**Yougoslavie** /'jugɔslavi/ *nf* Yugoslavia.

**yo-yo**® /'jojo/ *nm inv* yo-yo®.

# Zz

**zapper** /zape/ [1] *vi* (à la télévision) channel-hop.

**zèbre** /zɛbʀ/ *nm* zebra.

**zèle** /zɛl/ *nm* zeal.

**zéro** /zeʀo/ *nm* nought, zero; (température) zero; (Sport) nil; (tennis) love; (personne) nonentity; **partir de ~** start from scratch; **repartir à ~** start all over again.

**zeste** /zɛst/ *nm* peel; **un ~ de** (fig) a touch of.

**zézayer** /zezeje/ [31] *vi* lisp.

**zigzag** /zigzag/ *nm* zigzag; **en ~** winding.

**zinc** /zɛ̃g/ *nm* (métal) zinc; (comptoir [!]) bar.

**zizanie** /zizani/ *nf* discord; **semer la ~** put the cat among the pigeons.

**zizi** /zizi/ *nm* [!] willy.

**zodiaque** /zɔdjak/ *nm* zodiac.

**zona** /zona/ *nm* (Méd) shingles (+ *sg*)

**zone** /zon/ *nf* zone, area; (banlieue pauvre) slums; **~ bleue** restricted parking zone; **~ euro** euro zone.

**zoo** /zo(o)/ *nm* zoo.

**zoom** /zum/ *nm* zoom lens.

**zut** /zyt/ *interj* [!] damn [!].

# Phrasefinder

| Key phrases | Phrases-clés |
|---|---|
| yes, please | oui, s'il vous plaît |
| no, thank you | non merci |
| sorry | désolé/-e |
| excuse me | excusez-moi |
| you're welcome | de rien |
| hello/goodbye | bonjour/au revoir |
| how are you? | comment allez-vous? |
| nice to meet you | enchanté/-e! |

| Asking questions | Poser des questions |
|---|---|
| do you speak English/French? | parlez-vous anglais/français? |
| what's your name? | comment vous appelez-vous? |
| where are you from? | d'où venez-vous? |
| how much is it? | combien ça coûte? |
| how far is it? | c'est loin d'ici? |
| where is...? | où est...? |
| can I have...? | est-ce que je peux avoir...? |
| would you like...? | voulez-vous...? |

| Statements about yourself | Parler de soi |
|---|---|
| my name is... | je m'appelle... |
| I'm English | je suis anglais/-e |
| I'm French | je suis français/-e |
| I don't speak French/English very well | je ne parle pas très bien français/anglais |
| I'm here on holiday | je suis en vacances ici |
| I live near Sheffield | j'habite près de Sheffield |
| I'm a student | je suis étudiant/-e |

| Emergencies | Urgences |
|---|---|
| can you help me? | pouvez-vous m'aider? |
| I'm lost | je me suis perdu/-e |
| I'm ill | je suis malade |
| call an ambulance | appelez une ambulance |
| watch out! | attention! |

# ❶ Going Places

| On the road | Par la route |
| --- | --- |
| where's the nearest petrol station/filling station (US)? | où se trouve la station-service la plus proche ? |
| what's the best way to get there? | quel est le meilleur chemin pour y aller ? |
| I've got a puncture | j'ai crevé |
| I'd like to hire a bike/car | je voudrais louer un vélo/une voiture |
| I'm looking for somewhere to park | je cherche un endroit pour me garer |
| there's been an accident | il y a eu un accident |
| my car's broken down | ma voiture est en panne |
| the car won't start | la voiture ne démarre pas |

| By rail | Par le train |
| --- | --- |
| where can I buy a ticket? | où est-ce que je peux acheter un billet ? |
| what time is the next train to Paris? | à quelle heure est le prochain train pour Paris ? |
| do I have to change? | est-ce qu'il y a un changement? |
| can I take my bike on the train? | est-ce que je peux prendre mon vélo dans le train ? |
| which platform for the train to Bath? | de quel quai part le train pour Bath ? |
| there's a train to London at 10 o'clock | il y a un train pour Londres à 10 heures |
| a single/return to Nice, please | un aller/aller-retour pour Nice, s'il vous plaît |
| I'd like an all-day ticket | je voudrais un billet valable toute la journée |
| I'd like to reserve a seat | je voudrais réserver une place |

| At the airport | Par avion |
| --- | --- |
| when's the next flight to Paris/Rome? | quand part le prochain avion pour Paris/Rome ? |

| | |
|---|---|
| what time do I have to check in? | à quelle heure est-ce que je dois me présenter à l'enregistrement? |
| where do I check in? | où est le comptoir d'enregistrement? |
| I'd like to confirm my flight | je voudrais confirmer mon vol |
| I'd like a window seat/an aisle seat | je voudrais une place côté fenêtre/côté couloir |
| I want to change/cancel my reservation | je voudrais modifier/annuler ma réservation |

| **Getting there** | **Trouver son chemin** |
|---|---|
| could you tell me the way to the castle? | pourriez-vous m'indiquer la route pour aller au château? |
| how long will it take to get there? | combien de temps est-ce qu'il faut pour y arriver? |
| how far is it from here? | c'est loin d'ici? |
| which bus do I take for the cathedral? | quel bus est-ce que je dois prendre pour aller à la cathédrale? |
| can you tell me where to get off? | pouvez-vous me dire où je dois descendre? |
| how much is the fare to the town centre/center (US)? | quel est le prix d'un billet pour le centre-ville? |
| what time is the last bus? | à quelle heure est le dernier bus? |
| how do I get to the airport? | comment est-ce que je fais pour aller à l'aéroport? |
| where's the nearest underground/subway (US) station? | où est la station de métro la plus proche? |
| can you call me a taxi, please? | pouvez-vous m'appeler un taxi, s'il vous plaît? |
| take the first turning right | prenez la première rue à droite |
| turn left at the traffic lights | prenez à gauche aux feux |
| just past the church | juste après l'église |
| I'll take a taxi | je vais prendre un taxi |

## ❷ Food and drink

| Booking a restaurant | Réserver une table |
|---|---|
| can you recommend a good restaurant? | pouvez-vous me recommander un bon restaurant? |
| I'd like to reserve a table for four | je voudrais réserver une table pour quatre personnes |
| a reservation for tomorrow evening at eight o'clock | une réservation pour demain soir à huit heures |
| I booked a table for two | j'ai réservé une table pour deux |

| Ordering | Passer commande |
|---|---|
| could we see the menu/wine list? | est-ce qu'on pourrait voir la carte/la carte des vins? |
| do you have a vegetarian/children's menu? | est-ce que vous avez un menu végétarien/enfant? |
| could we have some more bread/chips? | est-ce qu'on pourrait avoir un peu plus de pain/frites? |
| could I have the bill/check (US)? | je pourrais avoir l'addition? |
| we'd like something to drink first | on voudrait d'abord boire quelque chose |
| a bottle/glass of mineral water, please | une bouteille/un verre d'eau minérale, s'il vous plaît |
| a black/white coffee | un café/un café crème |
| we'd like to pay separately | on voudrait payer séparément |

| Reading a menu | Lire la carte |
|---|---|
| starters/soups/salads | entrées/soupes/salades |
| main dishes | plat principal |
| dish/soup of the day | plat/soupe du jour |
| seafood | fruits de mer |
| choice of vegetables | légumes d'accompagnement |
| meat/game and poultry | viande/gibier et volaille |
| side dishes | plats d'accompagnement |
| desserts | desserts |
| drinks | boissons |

## Boire et manger 2

| Any complaints? | Des réclamations? |
| --- | --- |
| there's a mistake in the bill/ check (US) | il y a une erreur dans l'addition |
| the meat isn't cooked/ is overdone | la viande n'est pas assez cuite/ est trop cuite |
| that's not what I ordered | ce n'est pas ce que j'ai commandé |
| I asked for a small portion | j'ai demandé une petite portion |
| we are waiting to be served | on attend d'être servis |
| we are still waiting for our drinks | on attend toujours les boissons |
| my coffee is cold | mon café est froid |
| the wine is not chilled | le vin n'est pas assez frais |

| Food shopping | Faire les courses |
| --- | --- |
| where is the nearest supermarket? | où est le supermarché le plus proche ? |
| is there a baker's/butcher's near here? | y a-t-il une boulangerie/ boucherie près d'ici ? |
| can I have a carrier bag? | est-ce que je peux avoir un sac? |
| how much is it? | combien ça coûte ? |
| I'll have that one/this one | je prends celui-là/celui-ci |

| On the shopping list | Sur la liste de courses |
| --- | --- |
| I'd like some bread | je voudrais du pain |
| that's all, thank you | ce sera tout, merci |
| a bit more/less, please | un peu plus/moins, s'il vous plaît |
| 100 grams of cheese | 100 grammes de fromage |
| half a kilo of tomatoes | une livre de tomates |
| a packet of tea | un paquet de thé |
| a carton/litre of milk | une brique/un litre de lait |
| a can/bottle of beer | une boîte/canette de bière |

## ❸ Places to stay

| Camping | Camper |
|---|---|
| can we pitch our tent here? | est-ce qu'on peut planter notre tente ici ? |
| can we park our caravan here? | est-ce qu'on peut mettre notre caravane ici ? |
| what are the facilities like? | le camping est-il bien équipé ? |
| how much is it per night? | c'est combien par nuit ? |
| where do we park the car? | où est-ce qu'on peut garer la voiture ? |
| we're looking for a campsite | on cherche un camping |
| this is a list of local campsites | c'est une liste des campings de la région |
| we go on a camping holiday every year | nous partons camper chaque année pour les vacances |

| At the hotel | À l'hôtel |
|---|---|
| I'd like a double/single room with bath | je voudrais une chambre double/simple avec bain |
| we have a reservation in the name of Milne | nous avons une réservation au nom de Milne |
| we'll be staying three nights, from Friday to Sunday | nous resterons trois nuits, de vendredi à dimanche |
| how much does the room cost? | combien coûte la chambre ? |
| I'd like to see the room, please | je voudrais voir la chambre, s'il vous plaît |
| what time is breakfast? | à quelle heure est le petit déjeuner ? |
| bed and breakfast | chambres d'hôtes |
| we'd like to stay another night | on voudrait rester une nuit de plus |
| please call me at 7:30 | réveillez-moi à 7h30 |
| are there any messages for me? | est-ce qu'il y a des messages pour moi ? |

| Hostels | Auberges de jeunesse |
| --- | --- |
| could you tell me where the youth hostel is? | pourriez-vous me dire où se trouve l'auberge de jeunesse? |
| what time does the hostel close? | à quelle heure ferme l'auberge de jeunesse? |
| I'm staying in a hostel | je loge à l'auberge de jeunesse |
| I know a really good hostel in Dublin | je connais une très bonne auberge de jeunesse à Dublin |
| I'd like to go backpacking in Australia | j'aimerais bien aller faire de la randonnée en Australie |

| Rooms to let | Locations |
| --- | --- |
| I'm looking for a room with a reasonable rent | je cherche une chambre à louer avec un loyer raisonnable |
| I'd like to rent an apartment for a few weeks | je voudrais louer un appartement pendant quelques semaines |
| where do I find out about rooms to let? | où est-ce que je peux me renseigner sur des chambres à louer ? |
| what's the weekly rent? | quel est le montant du loyer pour la semaine ? |
| I'm staying with friends at the moment | je loge chez des amis pour le moment |
| I rent an apartment on the outskirts of town | je loue un appartement en banlieue |
| the room's fine – I'll take it | la chambre est bien – je la prends |
| the deposit is one month's rent in advance | l'acompte correspond à un mois de loyer payable d'avance |

## 4 Shopping and money

| At the bank | À la banque |
|---|---|
| I'd like to change some money | je voudrais changer de l'argent |
| I want to change some euros into pounds | je veux changer des euros en livres |
| do you take Eurocheques? | acceptez-vous les Eurochèques? |
| what's the exchange rate today? | quel est le taux de change aujourd'hui ? |
| I prefer traveller's cheques/ traveler's checks (US) to cash | je préfère les chèques de voyage à l'argent liquide |
| I'd like to transfer some money from my account | je voudrais retirer de l'argent sur mon compte |
| I'll get some money from the cash machine | je vais retirer de l'argent au distributeur |
| I usually pay by direct debit | d'habitude, je paye par prélèvement automatique |

| Finding the right shop | Trouver le bon magasin |
|---|---|
| where's the main shopping district? | où se trouve le principal quartier commerçant ? |
| where's a good place to buy sunglasses/shoes? | quel est le meilleur endroit pour acheter des lunettes de soleil/chaussures ? |
| where can I buy batteries/ postcards? | où est-ce que je peux acheter des piles/cartes postales ? |
| where's the nearest chemist/ bookshop? | où est la pharmacie/librairie la plus proche ? |
| is there a good food shop around here? | est-ce qu'il y a une bonne épicerie près d'ici ? |
| what time do the shops open/ close? | à quelle heure ouvrent/ ferment les magasins ? |
| where did you get those? | où les avez-vous trouvés ? |
| I'm looking for presents for my family | je cherche des cadeaux pour ma famille |
| we'll do all our shopping on Saturday | nous ferons toutes nos courses samedi |
| I love shopping | j'adore faire les magasins |

## Achats et argent 4

| Are you being served? | On s'occupe de vous ? |
|---|---|
| how much does that cost? | combien ça coûte ? |
| can I try it on? | est-ce que je peux l'essayer ? |
| can you keep it for me? | pouvez-vous me le/la garder ? |
| do you have this in another colour/color (US)? | est-ce que vous avez ce modèle-ci dans une autre couleur ? |
| I'm just looking | je regarde |
| I'll think about it | je vais réfléchir |
| I need a bigger/smaller size | il me faut une taille au-dessus/ au-dessous |
| I take a size 10/a medium | je fais du 38/il me faut une taille moyenne |
| it doesn't suit me | ça ne me va pas |
| could you wrap it for me, please? | pourriez-vous l'emballer, s'il vous plaît ? |
| do you take credit cards? | est-ce que vous acceptez les cartes de crédit? |
| can I pay by cheque/check (US)? | est-ce que je peux payer par chèque ? |
| I'm sorry, I don't have any change | je suis désolé/-e mais je n'ai pas de monnaie |
| I'd like a receipt, please | je voudrais un reçu, s'il vous plaît |

| Changing things | Faire un échange |
|---|---|
| can I have a refund? | j'aimerais être remboursé/-e |
| can you mend it for me? | est-ce que vous pouvez me le/ la réparer ? |
| can I speak to the manager? | je voudrais parler au responsable |
| it doesn't work | ça ne marche pas |
| I'd like to change it, please | je voudrais l'échanger, s'il vous plaît |
| I bought this here yesterday | je l'ai acheté/-e ici hier |

## 5 Sport and leisure

| Keeping fit | Rester en bonne santé |
|---|---|
| where can we play football/squash? | où est-ce qu'on peut jouer au football/squash? |
| where is the sports centre/center (US)? | où se trouve le centre sportif? |
| what's the charge per day? | quel est le prix pour la journée? |
| is there a reduction for children/a student discount? | est-ce qu'il y a des réductions enfants/étudiants ? |
| I'm looking for a swimming pool/tennis court | je cherche une piscine/un court de tennis |
| you have to be a member | vous devez être membre |
| I play tennis on Mondays | je joue au tennis le lundi |
| I would like to go fishing/riding | je voudrais aller à la pêche/monter à cheval |
| I want to do aerobics | je veux faire de l'aérobic |
| I love swimming/snowboarding | j'adore nager/faire du surf des neiges |
| we want to hire skis/rollerblades | nous voulons louer des skis/rollers |

| Watching sport | Le sport en spectateur |
|---|---|
| is there a football match on Saturday? | est-ce qu'il y a un match de foot samedi ? |
| which teams are playing? | quelles sont les équipes qui jouent ? |
| where can I get tickets? | où est-ce que je peux acheter des billets ? |
| I'd like to see a rugby/football match | je voudrais voir un match de rugby/foot |
| my favourite/favorite (US) team is... | mon équipe préférée est... |
| let's watch the match on TV | regardons le match à la télé |

| Going to the cinema/theatre/club | Aller au cinéma/théâtre/en boîte |
|---|---|
| what's on? | qu'est-ce qu'il y a au programme ? |
| when does the box office open/close? | à quelle heure ouvre/ferme le guichet ? |
| what time does the concert/performance start? | à quelle heure commence le concert/ la représentation ? |
| when does it finish? | à quelle heure ça finit? |
| are there any seats left for tonight? | est-ce qu'il y a encore des places pour ce soir ? |
| how much are the tickets? | combien coûtent les billets ? |
| where can I get a programme/program (US)? | où est-ce que je peux me procurer un programme ? |
| I want to book tickets for tonight's performance | je veux réserver des places pour la représentation de ce soir |
| I'll book seats in the circle/in the stalls | je vais réserver des places au balcon/à l'orchestre |
| we'd like to go to a club | on voudrait aller en boîte |
| I go clubbing every weekend | je vais en boîte tous les week-ends |

| Hobbies | Passe-temps |
|---|---|
| do you have any hobbies? | est-ce que vous avez des passe-temps ? |
| what do you do at the weekend? | que faites-vous le week-end ? |
| I like yoga/listening to music | j'aime le yoga/écouter de la musique |
| I spend a lot of time surfing the Net | je passe beaucoup de temps à surfer sur l' Internet |
| I read a lot | je lis beaucoup |
| I collect comic strips | je collectionne les bandes dessinées |

## ❻ Good timing

| Telling the time | Exprimer l'heure |
|---|---|
| could you tell me the time? | pourriez-vous me dire l'heure ? |
| what time is it? | quelle heure est-il ? |
| it's 2 o'clock | il est 2 heures |
| at about 8 o'clock | vers 8 heures |
| at 9 o'clock tomorrow | à 9 heures demain |
| from 10 o'clock onwards | à partir de 10 heures |
| it starts at 8 p.m. | ça commence à 20 heures |
| at 5 o'clock in the morning/ afternoon | à 5 heures du matin/de l'après-midi |
| it's five past/quarter past/ half past one | il est une heure cinq/et quart/ et demie |
| it's twenty-five to/quarter to/ five to one | il est une heure moins vingt-cinq/le quart/cinq |
| a quarter of an hour | un quart d'heure |

| Days and dates | Jours et dates |
|---|---|
| Sunday, Monday, Tuesday, Wednesday, Thursday, Friday, Saturday | dimanche, lundi, mardi, mercredi, jeudi, vendredi, samedi |
| January, February, March, April, May, June, July, August, September, October, November, December | janvier, février, mars, avril, mai, juin, juillet, août, septembre, octobre, novembre, décembre |
| what's the date today ? | on est le combien aujourd'hui ? |
| it's the second of June | on est le deux juin |
| what day is it? it's Monday | on est quel jour ? on est lundi |
| we meet up every Monday | on se réunit tous les lundis |
| she comes on Tuesdays | elle vient le mardi |
| we're going away in August | nous partons en août |
| on November 8th | le 8 novembre |

## ❷ Food and drink

| Booking a restaurant | Réserver une table |
|---|---|
| can you recommend a good restaurant? | pouvez-vous me recommander un bon restaurant? |
| I'd like to reserve a table for four | je voudrais réserver une table pour quatre personnes |
| a reservation for tomorrow evening at eight o'clock | une réservation pour demain soir à huit heures |
| I booked a table for two | j'ai réservé une table pour deux |

| Ordering | Passer commande |
|---|---|
| could we see the menu/wine list? | est-ce qu'on pourrait voir la carte/la carte des vins? |
| do you have a vegetarian/ children's menu? | est-ce que vous avez un menu végétarien/enfant? |
| could we have some more bread/chips? | est-ce qu'on pourrait avoir un peu plus de pain/frites? |
| could I have the bill/check (US)? | je pourrais avoir l'addition? |
| we'd like something to drink first | on voudrait d'abord boire quelque chose |
| a bottle/glass of mineral water, please | une bouteille/un verre d'eau minérale, s'il vous plaît |
| a black/white coffee | un café/un café crème |
| we'd like to pay separately | on voudrait payer séparément |

| Reading a menu | Lire la carte |
|---|---|
| starters/soups/salads | entrées/soupes/salades |
| main dishes | plat principal |
| dish/soup of the day | plat/soupe du jour |
| seafood | fruits de mer |
| choice of vegetables | légumes d'accompagnement |
| meat/game and poultry | viande/gibier et volaille |
| side dishes | plats d'accompagnement |
| desserts | desserts |
| drinks | boissons |

| | |
|---|---|
| what time do I have to check in? | à quelle heure est-ce que je dois me présenter à l'enregistrement? |
| where do I check in? | où est le comptoir d'enregistrement? |
| I'd like to confirm my flight | je voudrais confirmer mon vol |
| I'd like a window seat/an aisle seat | je voudrais une place côté fenêtre/côté couloir |
| I want to change/cancel my reservation | je voudrais modifier/annuler ma réservation |

| Getting there | Trouver son chemin |
|---|---|
| could you tell me the way to the castle? | pourriez-vous m'indiquer la route pour aller au château ? |
| how long will it take to get there? | combien de temps est-ce qu'il faut pour y arriver? |
| how far is it from here? | c'est loin d'ici? |
| which bus do I take for the cathedral? | quel bus est-ce que je dois prendre pour aller à la cathédrale? |
| can you tell me where to get off? | pouvez-vous me dire où je dois descendre ? |
| how much is the fare to the town centre/center (US)? | quel est le prix d'un billet pour le centre-ville? |
| what time is the last bus? | à quelle heure est le dernier bus? |
| how do I get to the airport? | comment est-ce que je fais pour aller à l'aéroport? |
| where's the nearest underground/subway (US) station? | où est la station de métro la plus proche? |
| can you call me a taxi, please? | pouvez-vous m'appeler un taxi, s'il vous plaît? |
| take the first turning right | prenez la première rue à droite |
| turn left at the traffic lights | prenez à gauche aux feux |
| just past the church | juste après l'église |
| I'll take a taxi | je vais prendre un taxi |

## En temps et en heure 6

| Public holidays and special days | Jours fériés |
|---|---|
| Bank holiday | jour férié |
| long weekend | week-end prolongé |
| New Year's Day (1 Jan) | le Jour de l'an |
| St Valentine's Day (14 Feb) | la Saint-Valentin |
| Shrove Tuesday/Pancake Day | Mardi gras |
| Ash Wednesday | le mercredi des Cendres |
| Mother's Day | la fête des Mères |
| Palm Sunday | le dimanche des Rameaux |
| Good Friday | vendredi saint |
| Easter Day | Pâques |
| Easter Monday | le lundi de Pâques |
| Ascension Day | l'Ascension |
| Pentecost/Whitsun | la Pentecôte |
| Whit Monday | le lundi de Pentecôte |
| Father's Day | la fête des Pères |
| St John the Baptist's Day (24 Jun) | la Saint-Jean |
| Independence day (4 Jul) | la fête de l'Indépendance (aux États-Unis) |
| Bastille day (14 July) | le 14 juillet |
| Halloween (31 Oct) | Halloween (soir des fantômes et des sorcières) |
| All Saints' Day (1 Nov) | la Toussaint |
| Guy Fawkes Day/Bonfire Night (5 Nov) | fête de la Conspiration des Poudres avec feux de joie et feux d'artifice |
| Remembrance Sunday | le jour du Souvenir |
| Thanksgiving | le jour d'Action de grâces |
| Christmas Day (25 Dec) | Noël |
| Boxing Day (26 Dec) | le lendemain de Noël |
| New Year's Eve (31 Dec) | la Saint-Sylvestre |

## 7 Keeping in touch

| On the phone | Au téléphone |
|---|---|
| where can I buy a phone card? | où est-ce que je peux acheter une carte de téléphone? |
| may I use your phone? | est-ce que je peux utiliser votre téléphone? |
| do you have a mobile? | avez-vous un portable? |
| what is the code for Lyons/ St Albans? | quel est l'indicatif pour Lyon/ St Albans? |
| I want to make a phone call | je veux téléphoner |
| I'd like to reverse the charges/ to call collect (US) | je voudrais appeler en PCV |
| the line's engaged/busy (US) | la ligne est occupée |
| there's no answer | ça ne répond pas |
| hello, this is Danielle | allô, c'est Danielle |
| is Alistair there, please? | est-ce qu'Alistair est là, s'il vous plaît? |
| who's calling? | qui est à l'appareil? |
| sorry, wrong number | désolé/-e, vous faites erreur |
| just a moment, please | un instant, s'il vous plaît |
| would you like to hold? | vous patientez? |
| please tell him/her I called | pourriez-vous lui dire que j'ai appelé? |
| I'd like to leave a message for him/her | j'aimerais lui laisser un message |
| I'll try again later | je réessaierai plus tard |
| can he/she ring me back? | est-ce qu'il/elle peut me rappeler? |
| my home number is... | mon numéro personnel est le... |
| my business number is... | mon numéro professionnel est le... |
| my fax number is... | mon numéro de télécopie est le... |
| we were cut off | on a été coupé |

| Writing | Écrire |
|---|---|
| what's your address? | quelle est votre adresse? |
| here's my business card | voici ma carte de visite |
| where is the nearest post office? | où est le bureau de poste le plus proche ? |
| could I have a stamp for France/Italy, please? | je voudrais un timbre pour la France/l'Italie, s'il vous plaît |
| I'd like to send a parcel/ a telegram | je voudrais envoyer un paquet/ un télégramme |

| On line | En ligne |
|---|---|
| are you on the Internet? | êtes-vous sur Internet ? |
| what's your e-mail address? | quelle est votre adresse électronique ? |
| we could send it by e-mail | nous pourrions l'envoyer par courrier électronique |
| I'll e-mail it to you on Thursday | je vous l'envoie jeudi par courrier électronique |
| I looked it up on the Internet | j'ai vérifié sur Internet |
| the information is on their website | l'information se trouve sur leur site Internet |

| Meeting up | Se retrouver |
|---|---|
| what shall we do this evening? | qu'est-ce qu'on fait ce soir ? |
| where shall we meet? | où est-ce qu'on se retrouve ? |
| I'll see you outside the café at 6 o'clock | on se retrouve à 6 heures devant le café |
| see you later | à tout à l'heure |
| I can't today, I'm busy | je ne peux pas aujourd'hui, je suis occupé/-e |

'Vous' is used when being generally polite (e.g. a child to a teacher, a customer to a shopkeeper, a tourist asking directions). When speaking to a friend or a member of the family, 'tu' replaces 'vous'.

## ❽ Conversion charts/Conversion

### Length/Longueur

| inches/pouces | 0.39 | 3.9 | 7.8 | 11.7 | 15.6 | 19.7 | 39 |
|---|---|---|---|---|---|---|---|
| cm/centimètres | 1 | 10 | 20 | 30 | 40 | 50 | 100 |

### Distance/Distance

| miles/miles | 0.62 | 6.2 | 12.4 | 18.6 | 24.9 | 31 | 62 |
|---|---|---|---|---|---|---|---|
| km/kilomètres | 1 | 10 | 20 | 30 | 40 | 50 | 100 |

### Weight/Poids

| pounds/livres | 2.2 | 22 | 44 | 66 | 88 | 110 | 220 |
|---|---|---|---|---|---|---|---|
| kg/kilogrammes | 1 | 10 | 20 | 30 | 40 | 50 | 100 |

### Capacity/Contenance

| gallons/gallons | 0.22 | 2.2 | 4.4 | 6.6 | 8.8 | 11 | 22 |
|---|---|---|---|---|---|---|---|
| litres/litres | 1 | 10 | 20 | 30 | 40 | 50 | 100 |

### Temperature/Température

| °C | 0 | 5 | 10 | 15 | 20 | 25 | 30 | 37 | 38 | 40 |
|---|---|---|---|---|---|---|---|---|---|---|
| °F | 32 | 41 | 50 | 59 | 68 | 77 | 86 | 98.4 | 100 | 104 |

### Clothing and shoe sizes/Tailles et pointures

Women's clothing sizes/Tailles femme

| UK | 8 | 10 | 12 | 14 | 16 | 18 |
|---|---|---|---|---|---|---|
| US | 6 | 8 | 10 | 12 | 14 | 16 |
| France | 36 | 38 | 40 | 42 | 44 | 46 |

Men's clothing sizes/Tailles homme

| UK/US | 36 | 38 | 40 | 42 | 44 | 46 |
|---|---|---|---|---|---|---|
| France | 46 | 48 | 50 | 52 | 54 | 56 |

Men's and women's shoes/Pointures homme et femme

| UK women | 4 | 5 | 6 | 7 | 7.5 | 8 | | | |
|---|---|---|---|---|---|---|---|---|---|
| UK men | | | | 6 | 7 | 8 | 9 | 10 | 11 |
| US | 6.5 | 7.5 | 8.5 | 9.5 | 10.5 | 11.5 | 12.5 | 13.5 | 14.5 |
| France | 37 | 38 | 39 | 40 | 41 | 42 | 43 | 44 | 45 |

# English–French Dictionary

# Aa

**a** /eɪ, ə/ *determiner*

**an** avant voyelle ou h muet.

⇨ For expressions such as **make a noise, make a fortune** ⇒**noise, fortune**.

····➤ un/une; ~ **tree** un arbre; ~ **chair** une chaise.

····➤ (per) **ten francs** ~ **kilo** dix francs le kilo; **three times** ~ **day** trois fois par jour.

! When talking about what people do or are, **a** is not translated into French: **she's a teacher** *elle est professeur*; **he's a widower** *il est veuf*.

**aback** /ə'bæk/ *adv* **taken** ~ déconcerté.

**abandon** /ə'bændən/ *vt* abandonner. ● *n* abandon *m*.

**abate** /ə'beɪt/ *vi* (*flood, fever*) baisser; (*storm*) se calmer. ● *vt* diminuer.

**abbey** /'æbɪ/ *n* abbaye *f*.

**abbot** /'æbət/ *n* abbé *m*.

**abbreviate** /ə'bri:vɪeɪt/ *vt* abréger. **abbreviation** *n* abréviation *f*.

**abdicate** /'æbdɪkeɪt/ *vt/i* abdiquer.

**abdomen** /'æbdəmən/ *n* abdomen *m*.

**abduct** /æb'dʌkt/ *vt* enlever. **abductor** *n* ravisseur/-euse *m/f*.

**abhor** /əb'hɔ:(r)/ *vt* (*pt* **abhorred**) exécrer.

**abide** /ə'baɪd/ *vt* supporter; ~ **by** respecter.

**ability** /ə'bɪlətɪ/ *n* capacité *f* (**to do** à faire); (talent) talent *m*.

**abject** /'æbdʒekt/ *a* (*state*) misérable; (*coward*) abject.

**ablaze** /ə'bleɪz/ *a* en feu.

**able** /'eɪbl/ *a* (skilled) compétent; **be** ~ **to do** pouvoir faire; (know how to) savoir faire. **ably** *adv* avec compétence.

**abnormal** /æb'nɔ:ml/ *a* anormal. **abnormality** *n* anomalie *f*.

**aboard** /ə'bɔ:d/ *adv* à bord. ● *prep* à bord de.

**abode** /ə'bəud/ *n* demeure *f*; **of no fixed** ~ sans domicile fixe.

**abolish** /ə'bɒlɪʃ/ *vt* abolir.

**Aborigine** /æbə'rɪdʒənɪ/ *n* aborigène *mf* (d'Australie).

**abort** /ə'bɔ:t/ *vt* faire avorter; (Comput) abandonner. ● *vi* avorter.

**abortion** /ə'bɔ:ʃn/ *n* avortement *m*; **have an** ~ se faire avorter.

**abortive** /ə'bɔ:tɪv/ *a* (*attempt*) avorté; (*coup*) manqué.

**about** /ə'baut/ *adv* (approximately) environ; ~ **the same** à peu près pareil; **there was no-one** ~ il n'y avait personne. ● *prep* **it's** ~ ... il s'agit de ...; **what I like** ~ **her is** ce que j'aime chez elle c'est; **to wander** ~ **the streets** errer dans les rues; **how/what** ~ **some tea?** et si on prenait un thé?; **what** ~ **you?** et toi? ● *adj* **be** ~ **to do** être sur le point de faire; **be up and** ~ être

debout. **~-face**, **~-turn** *n* (fig) volte-face *f inv*.

**above** /ə'bʌv/ *prep* au-dessus de; **he is not ~ lying** il n'est pas incapable de mentir; **~ all** surtout. ● *adv* **the apartment ~** l'appartement du dessus; **see ~** voir ci-dessus. **~-board** *a* honnête. **~-mentioned** *a* susmentionné.

**abrasive** /ə'breɪsɪv/ *a* abrasif; (*manner*) mordant. ● *n* abrasif *m*.

**abreast** /ə'brest/ *adv* de front; **keep ~ of** se tenir au courant de.

**abroad** /ə'brɔ:d/ *adv* à l'étranger.

**abrupt** /ə'brʌpt/ *a* (sudden, curt) brusque; (steep) abrupt. **abruptly** *adv* (suddenly) brusquement; (curtly) avec brusquerie.

**abscess** /'æbses/ *n* abcès *m*.

**abseil** /'æbseɪl/ *vi* descendre en rappel.

**absence** /'æbsəns/ *n* absence *f*; (lack) manque *m*; **in the ~ of** faute de.

**absent** /'æbsənt/ *a* absent.

**absentee** /æbsən'ti:/ *n* absent/-e *m/f*.

**absent-minded** *a* distrait.

**absolute** /'æbsəlu:t/ *a* (*monarch, majority*) absolu; (*chaos, idiot*) véritable. **absolutely** *adv* absolument.

**absolve** /əb'zɒlv/ *vt* **~ sb of sth** décharger qn de qch.

**absorb** /əb'sɔ:b/ *vt* absorber.

**abstain** /əb'steɪn/ *vi* s'abstenir (**from** de).

**abstract¹** /'æbstrækt/ *a* abstrait. ● *n* (summary) résumé *m*; **in the ~** dans l'abstrait.

**abstract²** /əb'strækt/ *vt* tirer.

**absurd** /əb'sɜ:d/ *a* absurde.

**abundance** /ə'bʌndəns/ *n* abondance *f*. **abundant** *a* abondant.

**abundantly** *adv* (entirely) tout à fait.

**abuse¹** /ə'bju:z/ *vt* (*position*) abuser de; (*person*) maltraiter; (insult) injurier.

**abuse²** /ə'bju:s/ *n* (misuse) abus *m* (**of** de); (cruelty) mauvais traitement *m*; (insults) injures *fpl*.

**abusive** /ə'bju:sɪv/ *a* (*person*) grossier; (*language*) injurieux.

**abysmal** /ə'bɪzməl/ *a* épouvantable.

**abyss** /ə'bɪs/ *n* abîme *m*.

**academic** /ækə'demɪk/ *a* (*career*) universitaire; (*year*) académique; (scholarly) intellectuel; (theoretical) théorique. ● *n* universitaire *mf*.

**academy** /ə'kædəmɪ/ *n* (school) école *f*; (society) académie *f*.

**accelerate** /ək'seləreɪt/ *vi* (speed up) s'accélérer; (Auto) accélérer. **accelerator** *n* accélérateur *m*.

**accent¹** /'æksənt/ *n* accent *m*.

**accent²** /æk'sent/ *vt* accentuer.

**accept** /ək'sept/ *vt* accepter. **acceptable** *a* acceptable. **acceptance** *n* (of offer) acceptation *f*; (of proposal) approbation *f*.

**access** /'ækses/ *n* accès *m*. **accessible** *a* accessible.

**accessory** /ək'sesərɪ/ *a* accessoire. ● *n* (Jur) complice *mf* (**to** de).

**accident** /'æksɪdənt/ *n* accident *m*; (chance) hasard *m*; **by ~** par hasard. **accidental** *a* (*death*) accidentel; (*meeting*) fortuit. **accidentally** *adv* accidentellement; (by chance) par hasard.

**acclaim** /ə'kleɪm/ *vt* applaudir. ● *n* louanges *fpl*.

**acclimatize** /ə'klaɪmətaɪz/ *vt/i* (s')acclimater (**to** à).

**accommodate** /ə'kɒmədeɪt/ *vt* loger; (adapt to) s'adapter à; (satisfy) satisfaire. **accommodating** *a*

accommodant. **accommodation** *n* logement *m*.

**accompaniment** /ə'kʌmpənɪmənt/ *n* accompagnement *m*. **accompany** *vt* accompagner.

**accomplice** /ə'kʌmplɪs/ *n* complice *mf* (**in, to** de).

**accomplish** /ə'kʌmplɪʃ/ *vt* accomplir; (*objective*) réaliser. **accomplished** *a* très compétent. **accomplishment** *n* (feat) réussite *f*; (talent) talent *m*.

**accord** /ə'kɔ:d/ *vi* concorder (**with** avec). ● *vt* accorder (**sb sth** qch à qn). ● *n* accord *m*; **of my own ~** de moi-même.

**accordance** /ə'kɔ:dəns/ *n* **in ~ with** conformément à.

**according** /ə'kɔ:dɪŋ/ *adv* **~ to** (*principle, law*) selon; (*person, book*) d'après. **accordingly** *adv* en conséquence.

**accordion** /ə'kɔ:dɪən/ *n* accordéon *m*.

**accost** /ə'kɒst/ *vt* aborder.

**account** /ə'kaʊnt/ *n* (Comm) compte *m*; (description) compte-rendu *m*; **on ~ of** à cause de; **on no ~** en aucun cas; **take into ~** tenir compte de; **it's of no ~** peu importe. □ **~ for** (explain) expliquer; (represent) représenter. **accountability** *n* responsabilité *f*. **accountable** *a* responsable (**for** de; **to** envers).

**accountancy** /ə'kaʊntənsɪ/ *n* comptabilité *f*. **accountant** *n* comptable *mf*. **accounts** *npl* comptabilité *f*, comptes *mpl*.

**accumulate** /ə'kju:mjʊleɪt/ *vt/i* (s')accumuler.

**accuracy** /'ækjərəsɪ/ *n* (of figures) justesse *f*; (of aim) précision *f*; (of forecast) exactitude *f*. **accurate** *a* juste, précis. **accurately** *adv* exactement, précisément.

**accusation** /ækju:'zeɪʃn/ *n* accusation *f*.

**accuse** /ə'kju:z/ *vt* accuser; **the ~d** l'accusé/-e *m/f*.

**accustomed** /ə'kʌstəmd/ *a* accoutumé; **become ~ to** s'accoutumer à.

**ace** /eɪs/ *n* (card, person) as *m*.

**ache** /eɪk/ *n* douleur *f*. ● *vi* (*person*) avoir mal; **my leg ~s** ma jambe me fait mal.

**achieve** /ə'tʃi:v/ *vt* (*aim*) atteindre; (*result*) obtenir; (*ambition*) réaliser. **achievement** *n* (feat) réussite *f*; (fulfilment) réalisation *f* (**of** de).

**acid** /'æsɪd/ *a & n* acide (*m*). **acidity** *n* acidité *f*. **~ rain** *n* pluies *fpl* acides.

**acknowledge** /ək'nɒlɪdʒ/ *vt* (*error, authority*) reconnaître; (*letter*) accuser réception de. **acknowledgement** *n* reconnaissance *f*.

**acne** /'æknɪ/ *n* acné *f*.

**acorn** /'eɪkɔ:n/ *n* (Bot) gland *m*.

**acoustic** /ə'ku:stɪk/ *a* acoustique. **acoustics** *npl* acoustique *f*.

**acquaint** /ə'kweɪnt/ *vt* **~ sb with sth** mettre qn au courant de qch; **be ~ed with** (*person*) connaître; (*fact*) savoir. **acquaintance** *n* connaissance *f*.

**acquire** /ə'kwaɪə(r)/ *vt* acquérir; (*habit*) prendre.

**acquit** /ə'kwɪt/ *vt* (*pt* **acquitted**) (Jur) acquitter. **acquittal** *n* acquittement *m*.

**acre** /'eɪkə(r)/ *n* acre *f*, ≈ demi-hectare *m*.

**acrid** /'ækrɪd/ *a* âcre.

**acrimonious** /ækrɪ'məʊnɪəs/ *a* acrimonieux.

**acrobat** /'ækrəbæt/ *n* acrobate *mf*. **acrobatics** *npl* acrobaties *fpl*.

**acronym** /'ækrənɪm/ *n* acronyme *m*.

**across** /ə'krɒs/ *adv & prep* (side to side) d'un côté à l'autre (de); (on other side) de l'autre côté (**from** de); **go** *or* **walk** ~ traverser; **lie** ~ **the bed** se coucher en travers du lit; ~ **the world** partout dans le monde.

**act** /ækt/ *n* acte *m*; (Jur, Pol) loi *f*; **put on an** ~ jouer la comédie. ● *vi* agir; (Theat) jouer; ~ **as** servir de. ● *vt* (*part, role*) jouer.

**acting** /'æktɪŋ/ *n* (Theat) jeu *m*. ● *a* (temporary) intérimaire.

**action** /'ækʃn/ *n* action *f*; (Mil) combat *m*; **out of** ~ hors service; **take** ~ agir.

**activate** /'æktɪveɪt/ *vt* (*machine*) faire démarrer; (*alarm*) déclencher.

**active** /'æktɪv/ *a* actif; (*volcano*) en activité; **take an** ~ **interest in** s'intéresser activement à. **activist** *n* activiste *mf*. **activity** *n* activité *f*.

**actor** /'æktə(r)/ *n* acteur *m*. **actress** *n* actrice *f*.

**actual** /'æktʃʊəl/ *a* réel; **the** ~ **words** les mots exacts; **in the** ~ **house** (the house itself) dans la maison elle-même. **actuality** *n* réalité *f*. **actually** *adv* (in fact) en fait; (really) vraiment.

**acute** /ə'kju:t/ *a* (*anxiety*) vif; (*illness*) aigu; (*shortage*) grave; (*mind*) pénétrant.

**ad** /æd/ *n* (TV) pub *f* Ⓘ; **small** ~ petite annonce *f*.

**AD** *abbr* (**Anno domini**) ap. J.-C.

**adamant** /'ædəmənt/ *a* catégorique.

**adapt** /ə'dæpt/ *vt/i* (s')adapter (**to** à). **adaptability** *n* adaptabilité *f*. **adaptable** *a* souple. **adaptation** *n* adaptation *f*. **adaptor** *n* (Electr) adaptateur *m*.

**add** /æd/ *vt/i* ajouter (**to** à); (in maths) additionner. □ ~ **up** (*facts, figures*) s'accorder; ~ **sth up** additionner qch; ~ **up to** s'élever à.

**adder** /'ædə(r)/ *n* vipère *f*.

**addict** /'ædɪkt/ *n* toxicomane *mf*; (fig) accro *mf* Ⓘ.

**addicted** /ə'dɪktɪd/ *a* **be** ~ avoir une dépendance (**to** à); (fig) être accro Ⓘ (**to** à). **addiction** *n* (Med) dépendance *f* (**to** à); passion *f* (**to** pour). **addictive** *a* qui crée une dépendance.

**addition** /ə'dɪʃn/ *n* (item) ajout *m*; (in maths) addition *f*; **in** ~ en plus. **additional** *a* supplémentaire.

**additive** /'ædɪtɪv/ *n* additif *m*.

**address** /ə'dres/ *n* adresse *f*; (speech) discours *m*. ● *vt* (*letter*) mettre l'adresse sur; (*crowd*) s'adresser à; ~ **sth to** adresser qch à. **addressee** *n* destinataire *mf*.

**adequate** /'ædɪkwət/ *a* suffisant; (satisfactory) satisfaisant.

**adhere** /əd'hɪə(r)/ *vi* (lit, fig) adhérer (**to** à); ~ **to** (*policy*) observer.

**adjacent** /ə'dʒeɪsnt/ *a* contigu; ~ **to** attenant à.

**adjective** /'ædʒɪktɪv/ *n* adjectif *m*.

**adjoin** /ə'dʒɔɪn/ *vt* être contigu à. **adjoining** *a* (*room*) voisin.

**adjourn** /ə'dʒɜ:n/ *vt* (*trial*) ajourner; **the session was** ~**ed** la séance a été levée. ● *vi* s'arrêter; (*Parliament*) lever la séance; ~ **to** passer à.

**adjust** /ə'dʒʌst/ *vt* (*level, speed*) régler; (*price*) ajuster; (*clothes*) rajuster. ● *vt/i* ~ **(oneself) to** s'adapter à. **adjustable** *a* réglable. **adjustment** *n* (of rates) rajustement *m*; (of control) réglage *m*; (of person) adaptation *f*.

**ad lib** /æd'lɪb/ *vt/i* (*pt* **ad libbed**) improviser.

**administer** /ad'mɪnɪstə(r)/ *vt* administrer.

**administration** /ədmɪnɪ'streɪʃn/ *n* administration *f*. **administrative** *a* administratif. **administrator** *n* administrateur/-trice *m/f*.

**admiral** /'ædmərəl/ *n* amiral *m*.

**admiration** /ædmə'reɪʃn/ *n* admiration *f*. **admire** *vt* admirer. **admirer** *n* admirateur/-trice *m/f*.

**admission** /əd'mɪʃn/ *n* (to a place) entrée *f*; (confession) aveu *m*.

**admit** /əd'mɪt/ *vt* (*pt* **admitted**) (acknowledge) reconnaître, admettre; (*crime*) avouer; (*new member*) admettre; **~ to** reconnaître. **admittance** *n* entrée *f*. **admittedly** *adv* il est vrai.

**ado** /ə'du:/ *n* **without more ~** sans plus de cérémonie.

**adolescence** /ædə'lesns/ *n* adolescence *f*. **adolescent** *n & a* adolescent/-e (*m/f*).

**adopt** /ə'dɒpt/ *vt* adopter. **adopted** *a* (*child*) adoptif. **adoption** *n* adoption *f*. **adoptive** *a* adoptif.

**adorable** /ə'dɔ:rəbl/ *a* adorable. **adoration** *n* adoration *f*. **adore** *vt* adorer.

**adorn** /ə'dɔ:n/ *vt* orner.

**adrift** /ə'drɪft/ *a & adv* à la dérive.

**adult** /'ædʌlt/ *a & n* adulte (*mf*).

**adultery** /ə'dʌltərɪ/ *n* adultère *m*.

**adulthood** /'ædʌlthʊd/ *n* âge *m* adulte.

**advance** /əd'vɑ:ns/ *vt* (*sum*) avancer; (*tape, career*) faire avancer; (*interests*) servir. ● *vi* (lit) avancer; (progress) progresser. ● *n* avance *f*; (progress) progrès *m*; **in ~** à l'avance. **advanced** *a* avancé; (*studies*) supérieur.

**advantage** /əd'vɑ:ntɪdʒ/ *n* avantage *m*; **take ~ of** profiter de; (*person*) exploiter. **advantageous** *a* avantageux.

**adventure** /əd'ventʃə(r)/ *n* aventure *f*. **adventurer** *n* aventurier/-ière *m/f*. **adventurous** *a* aventureux.

**adverb** /'ædvɜ:b/ *n* adverbe *m*.

**adverse** /'ædvɜ:s/ *a* défavorable.

**advert** /'ædvɜ:t/ *n* annonce *f*; (TV) pub *f* [I].

**advertise** /'ædvətaɪz/ *vt* faire de la publicité pour; (*car, house, job*) mettre une annonce pour. ● *vi* faire de la publicité; (for staff) passer une annonce. **advertisement** *n* publicité *f*; (in newspaper) annonce *f*. **advertiser** *n* annonceur *m*. **advertising** *n* publicité *f*.

**advice** /əd'vaɪs/ *n* conseils *mpl*; **some ~, a piece of ~** un conseil.

**advise** /əd'vaɪz/ *vt* conseiller; (inform) aviser; **~ against** déconseiller. **adviser** *n* conseiller/-ère *m/f*. **advisory** *a* consultatif.

**advocate**[1] /'ædvəkət/ *n* (Jur) avocat *m*; (supporter) partisan *m*.

**advocate**[2] /'ædvəkeɪt/ *vt* recommander.

**aerial** /'eərɪəl/ *a* aérien. ● *n* antenne *f*.

**aerobics** /eə'rəʊbɪks/ *n* aérobic *m*.

**aeroplane** /'eərəpleɪn/ *n* avion *m*.

**aerosol** /'eərəsɒl/ *n* bombe *f* aérosol.

**aesthetic** /i:s'θetɪk/ *a* esthétique.

**afar** /ə'fɑ:(r)/ *adv* **from ~** de loin.

**affair** /ə'feə(r)/ *n* (matter) affaire *f*; (romance) liaison *f*.

**affect** /ə'fekt/ *vt* affecter.

**affection** /ə'fekʃn/ *n* affection *f*. **affectionate** *a* affectueux.

**affinity** /ə'fɪnətɪ/ *n* affinité *f*.

**afflict** /ə'flɪkt/ *vt* affliger.

**affluence** /'æfluəns/ *n* richesse *f*.

**afford** /ə'fɔ:d/ *vt* avoir les moyens d'acheter; (provide) fournir; **can you ~ the time?** avez-vous le temps?

**afloat** /ə'fləʊt/ *adj & adv* (*boat*) à flot.

**afoot** /ə'fʊt/ *adv* **sth is ~** il se prépare qch.

**afraid** /ə'freɪd/ *a* **be ~** (frightened) avoir peur (**of, to** de; **that** que); (worried) craindre (**that** que); **I'm ~ I can't come** je suis désolé mais je ne peux pas venir.

**Africa** /'æfrɪkə/ *n* Afrique *f*.

**African** /'æfrɪkən/ *n* Africain/-e *m*/*f*. ● *a* africain.

**after** /'ɑ:ftə(r)/ *adv & prep* après; **soon ~** peu après; **be ~ sth** rechercher qch; **~ all** après tout. ● *conj* après que; **~ doing** après avoir fait.

**aftermath** /'ɑ:ftəmɑ:θ/ *n* conséquences *fpl* (**of** de).

**afternoon** /ɑ:ftə'nu:n/ *n* après-midi *m or f inv*; **in the ~** (dans) l'après-midi.

**after**: **~shave** *n* après-rasage *m*. **~thought** *n* pensée *f* après coup.

**afterwards** /'ɑ:ftəwədz/ *adv* après, par la suite.

**again** /ə'gen/ *adv* encore; **~ and ~** à plusieurs reprises; **start ~** recommencer; **she never saw him ~** elle ne l'a jamais revu.

**against** /ə'genst/ *prep* contre; **~ the law** illégal.

**age** /eɪdʒ/ *n* âge *m*; (era) ère *f*, époque *f*; **I've been waiting for ~s** j'attends depuis des heures. ● *vt*/*i* (*pres p* **ageing**) vieillir.

**aged**[1] /eɪdʒd/ *a* **~ six** âgé de six ans.

**aged**[2] /'eɪdʒɪd/ *a* âgé.

**ageism** /'eidʒɪzəm/ *n* discrimination *f* en raison de l'âge.

**agency** /'eɪdʒənsɪ/ *n* agence *f*.

**agenda** /ə'dʒendə/ *n* ordre *m* du jour; (fig) programme *m*.

**agent** /'eɪdʒənt/ *n* agent *m*.

**aggravate** /'ægrəveɪt/ *vt* (make worse) aggraver; (annoy) exaspérer. **aggravation** *n* (worsening) aggravation *f*; (annoyance) ennuis *mpl*.

**aggression** /ə'greʃn/ *n* agression *f*. **aggressive** *a* agressif. **aggressiveness** *n* agressivité *f*. **aggressor** *n* agresseur *m*.

**ago** /ə'gəʊ/ *adv* il y a; **a month ~** il y a un mois; **long ~** il y a longtemps; **how long ~?** il y a combien de temps?

**agonize** /'ægənaɪz/ *vi* se tourmenter (**over** à propos de). **agonized** *a* angoissé. **agonizing** *a* déchirant. **agony** *n* douleur *f* atroce; (mental) angoisse *f*.

**agree** /ə'gri:/ *vi* être d'accord (**on** sur; **with** avec); **~ to** consentir à; **~ with** (approve of) approuver. ● *vt* être d'accord (**that** sur le fait que); (admit) convenir (**that** que); (*date, solution*) se mettre d'accord sur.

**agreeable** /ə'gri:əbl/ *a* agréable; **be ~** (willing) être d'accord.

**agreed** /ə'gri:d/ *a* (*time, place*) convenu; **we're ~** nous sommes d'accord.

**agreement** /ə'gri:mənt/ *n* accord *m*; **in ~** d'accord.

**agricultural** /ægrɪ'kʌltʃərəl/ *a* agricole. **agriculture** *n* agriculture *f*.

**aground** /ə'graʊnd/ *adv* **run ~** (*ship*) s'échouer.

**ahead** /ə'hed/ *adv* (in front) en avant, devant; (in advance) à l'avance; **be 10 points ~** avoir 10 points d'avance; **~ of time** en avance; **go ~!** allez-y!

**aid** /eɪd/ *vt* aider. ● *n* aide *f*; **in ~ of** au profit de.

**aide** /eɪd/ *n* aide *mf*.

**Aids** /eɪdz/ *n* (Med) sida *m*.

**aim** /eɪm/ *vt* (*gun*) braquer (**at** sur); **be ~ed at sb** (*campaign, remark*) viser qn. ● *vi* **~ for/at sth** viser qch; **~ to do** avoir l'intention de faire. ● *n* but *m*; **take ~** viser. **aimless** *a* sans but.

**air** /eə(r)/ *n* air *m*; **by ~** par avion; **on the ~** à l'antenne. ● *vt* aérer; (*views*) exprimer. ● *a* (*base, disaster*) aérien; (*pollution, pressure*) atmosphérique. **~-bed** *n* matelas *m* pneumatique. **~-conditioning** *n* climatisation *f*. **~craft** *n inv* avion *m*. **~craft carrier** *n* porte-avions *m inv*. **~field** *n* terrain *m* d'aviation. **~ force** *n* armée *f* de l'air. **~ freshener** *n* désodorisant *m* d'atmosphère. **~ hostess** *n* hôtesse *f* de l'air. **~lift** *vt* transporter par pont aérien. **~line** *n* compagnie *f* aérienne. **~liner** *n* avion *m* de ligne. **~lock** *n* (in pipe) bulle *f* d'air; (chamber) sas *m*. **~mail** *n* **(by) ~mail** par avion. **~plane** *n* (US) avion *m*. **~port** *n* aéroport *m*. **~ raid** *n* attaque *f* aérienne. **~tight** *a* hermétique. **~ traffic controller** *n* contrôleur/-euse *m/f* aérien/-ne. **~waves** *npl* ondes *fpl*.

**airy** /'eərɪ/ *a* (**-ier, -iest**) (*room*) clair et spacieux.

**aisle** /aɪl/ *n* (of church) allée *f* centrale; (in train) couloir *m*.

**ajar** /ə'dʒɑ:(r)/ *adv & a* entrouvert.

**akin** /ə'kɪn/ *a* **~ to** semblable à.

**alarm** /ə'lɑ:m/ *n* alarme *f*; (clock) réveil *m*; (feeling) frayeur *f*. ● *vt* inquiéter. **~-clock** *n* réveil *m*.

**alas** /ə'læs/ *interj* hélas.

**Albania** /æl'beɪnɪə/ *n* Albanie *f*.

**album** /'ælbəm/ *n* album *m*.

**alcohol** /'ælkəhɒl/ *n* alcool *m*.

**alcoholic** /ælkə'hɒlɪk/ *a* alcoolique; (*drink*) alcoolisé. ● *n* alcoolique *mf*.

**ale** /eɪl/ *n* bière *f*.

**alert** /ə'lɜ:t/ *a* alerte; (watchful) vigilant. ● *n* alerte *f*; **on the ~** sur le qui-vive. ● *vt* alerter; **~ sb to** prévenir qn de. **alertness** *n* vivacité *f*; vigilance *f*.

**A-level** /'eɪlevl/ *n* ≈ baccalauréat *m*.

**algebra** /'ældʒɪbrə/ *n* algèbre *f*.

**Algeria** /æl'dʒɪərɪə/ *n* Algérie *f*.

**alias** /'eɪlɪəs/ *n* (*pl* **~es**) faux nom *m*. ● *prep* alias.

**alibi** /'ælɪbaɪ/ *n* alibi *m*.

**alien** /'eɪlɪən/ *n & a* étranger/-ère (*m/f*) (**to** à).

**alienate** /'eɪlɪəneɪt/ *vt* éloigner.

**alight** /ə'laɪt/ *a* en feu, allumé.

**alike** /ə'laɪk/ *a* semblable. ● *adv* de la même façon; **look ~** se ressembler.

**alive** /ə'laɪv/ *a* vivant; **~ to** conscient de; **~ with** grouillant de.

---

**all** /ɔ:l/

● *pronoun*

···► (everything) tout; **is that ~?** c'est tout?; **that was ~ (that) he said** c'est tout ce qu'il a dit; **I ate it ~** j'ai tout mangé.

> ! Use the translation **tous** for a group of masculine or mixed gender people or objects and **toutes** for a group of feminine gender: **we were all delighted** *nous étions tous ravis*; **'where are the cups?'—'they're all in the kitchen'** *'où sont les*

*tasses?'—'elles sont toutes dans la cuisine'.*

● *determiner*

····➤ tout/toute/tous/toutes; ~ **the time** tout le temps; ~ **his life** toute sa vie; ~ **of us** nous tous; ~ **(the) women** toutes les femmes.

● *adverb*

····➤ (completely) tout; **they were ~ alone** ils étaient tout seuls; **tell me ~ about it** raconte-moi tout; ~ **for** tout à fait pour; **not ~ that well** pas si bien que ça; ~ **too** bien trop.

! When the adjective that follows is in the feminine and begins with a consonant, the translation is *toute*/*toutes*: **she was all alone** *elle était toute seule*.

**allege** /ə'ledʒ/ *vt* prétendre. **allegedly** *adv* prétendument.

**allergic** /ə'lɜ:dʒɪk/ *a* allergique (**to** à). **allergy** *n* allergie *f.*

**alleviate** /ə'li:vɪeɪt/ *vt* alléger.

**alley** /'ælɪ/ *n* (street) ruelle *f.*

**alliance** /ə'laɪəns/ *n* alliance *f.*

**allied** /'ælaɪd/ *a* allié.

**alligator** /'ælɪgeɪtə(r)/ *n* alligator *m.*

**allocate** /'æləkeɪt/ *vt* (*funds*) affecter; (*time*) accorder; (*task*) assigner.

**allot** /ə'lɒt/ *vt* (*pt* **allotted**) (*money*) attribuer; (*task*) assigner. **allotment** *n* attribution *f*; (land) parcelle *f* de terre.

**all-out** /'ɔ:laʊt/ *a* (*effort*) acharné; (*strike*) total.

**allow** /ə'laʊ/ *vt* (authorize) autoriser à; (let) laisser; (enable) permettre; (concede) accorder; ~ **for** tenir compte de.

**allowance** /ə'laʊəns/ *n* allocation *f*; **make ~s for sth** tenir compte de qch; **make ~s for sb** essayer de comprendre qn.

**alloy** /'ælɔɪ/ *n* alliage *m.*

**all right** /ɔ:l'raɪt/ *a* (not bad) pas mal; **are you ~?** ça va?; **is it ~ if ...?** est-ce que ça va si ...? ● *adv* (*see*) bien; (*function*) comme il faut. ● *interj* d'accord.

**ally**[1] /'ælaɪ/ *n* allié/-e *m*/*f.*

**ally**[2] /ə'laɪ/ *vt* allier; ~ **oneself with** s'allier avec.

**almighty** /ɔ:l'maɪtɪ/ *a* tout-puissant; (very great) formidable.

**almond** /'ɑ:mənd/ *n* amande *f.* ~ **tree** *n* amandier *m.*

**almost** /'ɔ:lməʊst/ *adv* presque; **he ~ died** il a failli mourir.

**alone** /ə'ləʊn/ *a & adv* seul.

**along** /ə'lɒŋ/ *prep* le long de; **walk ~ the beach** marcher sur la plage. ● *adv* **come ~** venir; **walk ~** marcher; **push/pull sth ~** pousser/tirer qch; **all ~** (time) depuis le début; ~ **with** avec.

**alongside** /əlɒŋ'saɪd/ *adv* à côté; **come ~** (Naut) accoster. ● *prep* (next to) à côté de; (all along) le long de.

**aloof** /ə'lu:f/ *a* distant.

**aloud** /ə'laʊd/ *adv* à haute voix.

**alphabet** /'ælfəbet/ *n* alphabet *m.* **alphabetical** *a* alphabétique.

**alpine** /'ælpaɪn/ *a* (*landscape*) alpestre; (*climate*) alpin.

**already** /ɔ:l'redɪ/ *adv* déjà.

**alright** /ɔ:l'raɪt/ *a & adv* = ALL RIGHT.

**Alsatian** /æl'seɪʃn/ *n* (dog) berger *m* allemand.

**also** /'ɔ:lsəʊ/ *adv* aussi.

**altar** /'ɔ:ltə(r)/ *n* autel *m.*

**alter** /'ɔ:ltə(r)/ *vt/i* changer; (*building*) transformer; (*garment*) retoucher. **alteration** *n* changement *m*; (to building) transformation *f*; (to garment) retouche *f*.

**alternate¹** /'ɔ:ltəneɪt/ *vt/i* alterner.

**alternate²** /ɔ:l'tɜ:nət/ *a* en alternance; **on ~ days** un jour sur deux. **alternately** *adv* alternativement.

**alternative** /ɔ:l'tɜ:nətɪv/ *a* autre; (*solution*) de rechange. ● *n* (specified option) alternative *f*; (possible option) choix *m*. **alternatively** *adv* sinon.

**alternator** /'ɔ:ltəneɪtə(r)/ *n* alternateur *m*.

**although** /ɔ:l'ðəʊ/ *conj* bien que.

**altitude** /'æltɪtju:d/ *n* altitude *f*.

**altogether** /ɔ:ltə'geðə(r)/ *adv* (completely) tout à fait; (on the whole) tout compte fait.

**aluminium** /ælju'mɪnɪəm/ *n* aluminium *m*.

**always** /'ɔ:lweɪz/ *adv* toujours.

**am** /æm/ ⇒BE.

**a.m.** /eɪ'em/ *adv* du matin.

**amalgamate** /ə'mælgəmeɪt/ *vt/i* (merge) fusionner; (*metals*) (s')amalgamer.

**amateur** /'æmətə(r)/ *n & a* amateur (*m*)

**amaze** /ə'meɪz/ *vt* stupéfaire. **amazed** *a* stupéfait. **amazement** *n* stupéfaction *f*. **amazing** *a* stupéfiant; (great) exceptionnel.

**ambassador** /æm'bæsədə(r)/ *n* ambassadeur *m*.

**amber** /'æmbə(r)/ *n* ambre *m*; (Auto) orange *m*.

**ambiguity** /æmbɪ'gju:ətɪ/ *n* ambiguïté *f*. **ambiguous** *a* ambigu.

**ambition** /æm'bɪʃn/ *n* ambition *f*. **ambitious** *a* ambitieux.

**ambulance** /'æmbjʊləns/ *n* ambulance *f*.

**ambush** /'æmbʊʃ/ *n* embuscade *f*. ● *vt* tendre une embuscade à.

**amenable** /ə'mi:nəbl/ *a* obligeant; **~ to** (responsive) sensible à.

**amend** /ə'mend/ *vt* modifier. **amendment** *n* (to rule) amendement *m*.

**amends** /ə'mendz/ *npl* **make ~** réparer son erreur.

**amenities** /ə'mi:nətɪz/ *npl* équipements *mpl*.

**America** /ə'merɪkə/ *n* Amérique *f*.

**American** /ə'merɪkən/ *n* Américain/-e *m*/*f*. ● *a* américain.

**amiable** /'eɪmɪəbl/ *a* aimable.

**amicable** /'æmɪkəbl/ *a* amical.

**amid(st)** /ə'mɪd(st)/ *prep* au milieu de.

**amiss** /ə'mɪs/ *a* **there is something ~** il y a quelque chose qui ne va pas.

**ammonia** /ə'məʊnɪə/ *n* (gas) ammoniac *m*; (solution) ammoniaque *f*.

**ammunition** /æmjʊ'nɪʃn/ *n* munitions *fpl*.

**amnesty** /'æmnəstɪ/ *n* amnistie *f*.

**among(st)** /ə'mʌŋ(st)/ *prep* parmi; (affecting a group) chez; **be ~ the poorest** être un des plus pauvres; **be ~ the first** être dans les premiers.

**amorous** /'æmərəs/ *a* amoureux.

**amount** /ə'maʊnt/ *n* quantité *f*; (total) montant *m*; (sum of money) somme *f*. ● *vi* **~ to** (add up to) s'élever à; (be equivalent to) revenir à.

**amp** /æmp/ *n* ampère *m*.

**amphibian** /æm'fɪbɪən/ *n* amphibie *m*.

**ample** /'æmpl/ *a* (*resources*) largement suffisant; (*proportions*) généreux.

**amplifier** /'æmplɪfaɪə(r)/ *n* amplificateur *m.*

**amputate** /'æmpjʊteɪt/ *vt* amputer.

**amuse** /ə'mju:z/ *vt* amuser.

**amusement** /ə'mju:zmənt/ *n* (mirth) amusement *m*; (diversion) distraction *f.* ~ **arcade** *n* salle *f* de jeux.

**an** /æn, ən/ ⇒A.

**anaemia** /ə'ni:mɪə/ *n* anémie *f.*

**anaesthetic** /ænɪs'θetɪk/ *n* anesthésique *m.*

**analyse** /'ænəlaɪz/ *vt* analyser. **analysis** *n* (*pl* **-yses** /-əsi:z/) analyse *f.* **analyst** *n* analyste *mf.*

**anarchist** /'ænəkɪst/ *n* anarchiste *mf.*

**anatomical** /ænə'tɒmɪkl/ *a* anatomique. **anatomy** *n* anatomie *f.*

**ancestor** /'ænsestə(r)/ *n* ancêtre *m.*

**anchor** /'æŋkə(r)/ *n* ancre *f.* ● *vt* mettre à l'ancre. ● *vi* jeter l'ancre.

**anchovy** /'æntʃəvɪ/ *n* anchois *m.*

**ancient** /'eɪnʃənt/ *a* ancien.

**ancillary** /æn'sɪlərɪ/ *a* auxiliaire.

**and** /ænd, ən(d)/ *conj* et; **two hundred** ~ **sixty** deux cent soixante; **go** ~ **see him** allez le voir; **richer** ~ **richer** de plus en plus riche.

**anew** /ə'nju:/ *adv* (once more) encore, de nouveau; (in a new way) à nouveau.

**angel** /'eɪndʒl/ *n* ange *m.*

**anger** /'æŋgə(r)/ *n* colère *f.* ● *vt* mettre en colère, fâcher.

**angle** /'æŋgl/ *n* angle *m.* ● *vi* pêcher (à la ligne); ~ **for** (fig) quêter. **angler** *n* pêcheur/-euse *m/f.*

**Anglo-Saxon** /'æŋgləʊ'sæksn/ *a* anglo-saxon. ● *n* Anglo-Saxon/-ne *m/f.*

**angry** /'æŋgrɪ/ *a* (**-ier, -iest**) fâché, en colère; **get** ~ se fâcher, se mettre en colère (**with** contre); **make sb** ~ mettre qn en colère.

**anguish** /'æŋgwɪʃ/ *n* angoisse *f.*

**animal** /'ænɪml/ *n & a* animal (*m*).

**animate**[1] /'ænɪmət/ *a* (*person*) vivant; (*object*) animé.

**animate**[2] /'ænɪmeɪt/ *vt* animer.

**aniseed** /'ænɪsi:d/ *n* anis *m.*

**ankle** /'æŋkl/ *n* cheville *f.* ~ **sock** *n* socquette *f.*

**annex** /ə'neks/ *vt* annexer.

**anniversary** /ænɪ'vɜ:sərɪ/ *n* anniversaire *m.*

**announce** /ə'naʊns/ *vt* annoncer (**that** que). **announcement** *n* (spoken) annonce *f*; (written) avis *m.* **announcer** *n* (radio, TV) speaker/-ine *m/f.*

**annoy** /ə'nɔɪ/ *vt* agacer, ennuyer. **annoyance** *n* contrariété *f.* **annoyed** *a* fâché (**with** contre); **get** ~**ed** se fâcher. **annoying** *a* ennuyeux.

**annual** /'ænjʊəl/ *a* annuel. ● *n* publication *f* annuelle. **annually** *adv* (*earn, produce*) par an; (*do, inspect*) tous les ans.

**annul** /ə'nʌl/ *vt* (*pt* **annulled**) annuler.

**anonymity** /ænə'nɪmətɪ/ *n* anonymat *m.* **anonymous** *a* anonyme.

**anorak** /'ænəræk/ *n* anorak *m.*

**another** /ə'nʌðə(r)/ *det & pron* un/-e autre; ~ **coffee** (one more) encore un café; ~ **ten minutes** encore dix minutes, dix minutes de plus; **can I have** ~**?** est-ce que je peux en avoir un autre?

**answer** /'ɑ:nsə(r)/ *n* réponse *f*; (solution) solution *f*; (phone) **there's no** ~ ça ne répond pas. ● *vt* répondre à; (*prayer*) exaucer; ~ **the door** ouvrir la porte. ● *vi*

répondre. □ ~ **back** répondre; ~ **for** répondre de; ~ **to** (*superior*) dépendre de; (*description*) répondre à. **answerable** *a* responsable (**for** de; **to** devant). **answering machine** *n* répondeur *m*.

**ant** /ænt/ *n* fourmi *f*.

**antagonism** /æn'tægənɪzəm/ *n* antagonisme *m*. **antagonize** *vt* provoquer l'hostilité de.

**Antarctic** /æn'tɑ:ktɪk/ *n* **the** ~ l'Antarctique *m*. ● *a* antarctique.

**antenatal** /'æntɪneɪtl/ *a* prénatal.

**antenna** /æn'tenə/ *n* (*pl* **-ae** /-i:/) (of insect) antenne *f*; (*pl* **-as**; aerial; US) antenne *f*.

**anthem** /'ænθəm/ *n* (Relig) motet *m*; (of country) hymne *m* national.

**antibiotic** /æntɪbaɪ'ɒtɪk/ *n* & *a* antibiotique (*m*).

**antibody** /'æntɪbɒdɪ/ *n* anticorps *m*.

**anticipate** /æn'tɪsɪpeɪt/ *vt* (foresee, expect) prévoir, s'attendre à; (forestall) devancer.

**anticipation** /æntɪsɪ'peɪʃn/ *n* attente *f*; **in** ~ **of** en prévision *or* attente de.

**anticlimax** /æntɪ'klaɪmæks/ *n* (let-down) déception *f*.

**anticlockwise** /æntɪ'klɒkwaɪz/ *adv* & *a* dans le sens inverse des aiguilles d'une montre.

**antics** /'æntɪks/ *npl* pitreries *fpl*.

**antifreeze** /'æntɪfri:z/ *n* antigel *m*.

**antiquated** /'æntɪkweɪtɪd/ *a* (*idea*) archaïque; (*building*) vétuste.

**antique** /æn'ti:k/ *a* (old) ancien; (old-style) à l'ancienne. ● *n* objet *m* ancien, antiquité *f*. ~ **dealer** *n* antiquaire *mf*. ~ **shop** *n* magasin *m* d'antiquités.

**anti-Semitic** /æntɪsɪ'mɪtɪk/ *a* antisémite.

**antiseptic** /æntɪ'septɪk/ *a* & *n* antiseptique (*m*).

**antisocial** /æntɪ'səʊʃl/ *a* asocial, antisocial; (reclusive) sauvage.

**antlers** /'æntləz/ *npl* bois *mpl*.

**anxiety** /æŋ'zaɪətɪ/ *n* (worry) anxiété *f*; (eagerness) impatience *f*.

**anxious** /'æŋkʃəs/ *a* (troubled) anxieux; (eager) impatient (**to** de).

**any** /'enɪ/ *det* (some) du, de l', de la, des; (after negative) de, d'; (every) tout; (no matter which) n'importe quel; **at** ~ **moment** à tout moment; **have you** ~ **water?** avez-vous de l'eau? ● *pron* (no matter which one) n'importe lequel; (any amount of it or them) en; **I do not have** ~ je n'en ai pas; **did you see** ~ **of them?** en avez-vous vu? ● *adv* (a little) un peu; **do you have** ~ **more?** en avez-vous encore?; **do you have** ~ **more tea?** avez-vous encore du thé?; **I don't do it** ~ **more** je ne le fais plus.

**anybody** /'enɪbɒdɪ/ *pron* (no matter who) n'importe qui; (somebody) quelqu'un; (after negative) personne; **he did not see** ~ il n'a vu personne.

**anyhow** /'enɪhaʊ/ *adv* (anyway) de toute façon; (carelessly) n'importe comment.

**anyone** /'enɪwʌn/ *pron* = ANYBODY.

**anything** /'enɪθɪŋ/ *pron* (no matter what) n'importe quoi; (something) quelque chose; (after negative) rien; **he did not see** ~ il n'a rien vu; ~ **but** nullement; ~ **you do** tout ce que tu fais.

**anyway** /'enɪweɪ/ *adv* de toute façon.

**anywhere** /'enɪweə(r)/ *adv* (no matter where) n'importe où; (somewhere) quelque part; (after negative) nulle part; **he does not go** ~ il ne

va nulle part; ~ **you go** partout où tu vas, où que tu ailles; ~ **else** partout ailleurs.

**apart** /ə'pɑ:t/ *adv* (on or to one side) à part; (separated) séparé; (into pieces) en pièces; ~ **from** à part, excepté; **ten metres** ~ à dix mètres l'un de l'autre; **come** ~ (break) tomber en morceaux; (*machine*) se démonter; **legs** ~ les jambes écartées; **keep** ~ séparer; **take** ~ démonter.

**apartment** /ə'pɑ:tmənt/ *n* (US) appartement *m.*

**ape** /eɪp/ *n* singe *m.* ● *vt* singer.

**aperitif** /ə'perətɪf/ *n* apéritif *m.*

**apex** /'eɪpeks/ *n* sommet *m.*

**apologetic** /əpɒlə'dʒetɪk/ *a* (*tone*) d'excuse; **be** ~ s'excuser. **apologetically** *adv* en s'excusant.

**apologize** /ə'pɒlədʒaɪz/ *vi* s'excuser (**for** de; **to** auprès de).

**apology** /ə'pɒlədʒɪ/ *n* excuses *fpl.*

**apostrophe** /ə'pɒstrəfɪ/ *n* apostrophe *f.*

**appal** /ə'pɔ:l/ *vt* (*pt* **appalled**) horrifier. **appalling** *a* épouvantable.

**apparatus** /æpə'reɪtəs/ *n* appareil *m.*

**apparent** /ə'pærənt/ *a* apparent. **apparently** *adv* apparemment.

**appeal** /ə'pi:l/ *n* appel *m*; (attractiveness) attrait *m*, charme *m.* ● *vi* (Jur) faire appel; ~ **to sb** (beg) faire appel à qn; (attract) plaire à qn; ~ **to sb for sth** demander qch à qn. **appealing** *a* (attractive) attirant.

**appear** /ə'pɪə(r)/ *vi* apparaître; (arrive) se présenter; (seem, be published) paraître; (Theat) jouer; ~ **on TV** passer à la télé. **appearance** *n* apparition *f*; (aspect) apparence *f.*

**appease** /ə'pi:z/ *vt* apaiser.

**appendix** /ə'pendɪks/ *n* (*pl* **-ices** /-ɪsi:z/) appendice *m.*

**appetite** /'æpɪtaɪt/ *n* appétit *m.*

**appetizer** /'æpɪtaɪzə(r)/ *n* (snack) amuse-gueule *m inv*; (drink) apéritif *m.*

**appetizing** /'æpɪtaɪzɪŋ/ *a* appétissant.

**applaud** /ə'plɔ:d/ *vt*/*i* applaudir; (*decision*) applaudir à. **applause** *n* applaudissements *mpl.*

**apple** /'æpl/ *n* pomme *f.* **~-tree** *n* pommier *m.*

**appliance** /ə'plaɪəns/ *n* appareil *m.*

**applicable** /'æplɪkəbl/ *a* valable; **if** ~ le cas échéant.

**applicant** /'æplɪkənt/ *n* candidat/-e *m*/*f* (**for** à).

**application** /æplɪ'keɪʃn/ *n* application *f*; (request, form) demande *f*; (for job) candidature *f.*

**apply** /ə'plaɪ/ *vt* appliquer. ● *vi* ~ **to** (refer) s'appliquer à; (ask) s'adresser à; ~ **for** (*job*) postuler pour; (*grant*) demander; ~ **oneself to** s'appliquer à.

**appoint** /ə'pɔɪnt/ *vt* (to post) nommer; (fix) désigner; **well-~ed** bien équipé.

**appointment** /ə'pɔɪntmənt/ *n* nomination *f*; (meeting) rendez-vous *m inv*; (job) poste *m*; **make an** ~ prendre rendez-vous (**with** avec).

**appraisal** /ə'preɪzl/ *n* évaluation *f.* **appraise** *vt* évaluer.

**appreciate** /ə'pri:ʃɪeɪt/ *vt* (like) apprécier; (understand) comprendre; (be grateful for) être reconnaissant de. ● *vi* prendre de la valeur. **appreciation** *n* appréciation *f*; (gratitude) reconnaissance *f*; (rise) augmentation *f.* **appreciative** *a* reconnaissant; (*audience*) enthousiaste.

**apprehend** /æprɪ'hend/ *vt* (arrest) appréhender; (understand) com-

prendre. **apprehension** *n* (arrest) appréhension *f*; (fear) crainte *f*.

**apprehensive** /æprɪ'hensɪv/ *a* inquiet; **be ~ of** craindre.

**apprentice** /ə'prentɪs/ *n* apprenti *m*. ● *vt* mettre en apprentissage.

**approach** /ə'prəʊtʃ/ *vt* (s')approcher de; (accost) aborder; (with request) s'adresser à. ● *vi* (s')approcher. ● *n* approche *f*; **an ~ to** (*problem*) une façon d'aborder; (*person*) une démarche auprès de. **approachable** *a* abordable.

**appropriate**[1] /ə'prəʊprɪeɪt/ *vt* s'approprier.

**appropriate**[2] /ə'prəʊprɪət/ *a* approprié, propre. **appropriately** *adv* à propos

**approval** /ə'pru:vl/ *n* approbation *f*; **on ~** à *or* sous condition.

**approve** /ə'pru:v/ *vt* approuver. ● *vi* **~ of** approuver. **approving** *a* approbateur.

**approximate**[1] /ə'prɒksɪmeɪt/ *vi* **~ to** se rapprocher de.

**approximate**[2] /ə'prɒksɪmət/ *a* approximatif. **approximately** *adv* environ. **approximation** *n* approximation *f*.

**apricot** /'eɪprɪkɒt/ *n* abricot *m*.

**April** /'eɪprəl/ *n* avril *m*. **~ Fools Day** *n* le premier avril.

**apron** /'eɪprən/ *n* tablier *m*.

**apt** /æpt/ *a* (suitable) approprié; **be ~ to** avoir tendance à.

**aptitude** /'æptɪtju:d/ *n* aptitude *f*.

**aptly** /'æptlɪ/ *adv* à propos.

**Aquarius** /ə'kweərɪəs/ *n* Verseau *m*.

**aquatic** /ə'kwætɪk/ *a* aquatique; (Sport) nautique.

**Arab** /'ærəb/ *n* Arabe *mf*. ● *a* arabe.

**Arabian** /ə'reɪbɪən/ *a* d'Arabie.

**Arabic** /'ærəbɪk/ *a* & *n* (Ling) arabe (*m*).

**arbitrary** /'ɑ:bɪtrərɪ/ *a* arbitraire.

**arbitrate** /'ɑ:bɪtreɪt/ *vi* arbitrer. **arbitration** *n* arbitrage *m*. **arbitrator** *n* médiateur/-trice *m/f*.

**arcade** /ɑ:'keɪd/ *n* (shops) galerie *f*; (arches) arcades *fpl*.

**arch** /ɑ:tʃ/ *n* arche *f*; (of foot) voûte *f* plantaire. ● *vt/i* (s')arquer. ● *a* (playful) malicieux.

**archaeological** /ɑ:kɪə'lɒdʒɪkl/ *a* archéologique. **archaeologist** *n* archéologue *mf*. **archaeology** *n* archéologie *f*.

**archbishop** /ɑ:tʃ'bɪʃəp/ *n* archevêque *m*.

**archery** /'ɑ:tʃərɪ/ *n* tir *m* à l'arc.

**architect** /'ɑ:kɪtekt/ *n* architecte *mf*; (of plan) artisan *m*. **architectural** *a* architectural. **architecture** *n* architecture *f*.

**archives** /'ɑ:kaɪvz/ *npl* archives *fpl*.

**archway** /'ɑ:tʃweɪ/ *n* voûte *f*.

**Arctic** /'ɑ:ktɪk/ *n* **the ~** l'Arctique *m*. ● *a* (*climate*) arctique; (*expedition*) polaire; (*conditions*) glacial.

**ardent** /'ɑ:dnt/ *a* ardent.

**are** /ɑ:(r)/ ⇒BE.

**area** /'eərɪə/ *n* (region) région *f*; (district) quartier *m*; (fig) domaine *m*; (in geometry) aire *f*; **parking/picnic ~** aire *f* de parking/de pique-nique.

**arena** /ə'ri:nə/ *n* arène *f*.

**aren't** /ɑ:nt/ = ARE NOT

**Argentina** /ɑ:dʒən'ti:nə/ *n* Argentine *f*.

**arguable** /'ɑ:gjʊəbl/ *a* discutable. **arguably** *adv* selon certains.

**argue** /'ɑ:gju:/ *vi* (quarrel) se disputer; (reason) argumenter. ● *vt* (debate) discuter; **~ that** alléguer que.

**argument** /'ɑ:gjʊmənt/ *n* dispute *f*; (reasoning) argument *m*; (discussion)

débat *m*. **argumentative** *a* ergoteur.

**Aries** /'eəri:z/ *n* Bélier *m*.

**arise** /ə'raɪz/ *vi* (*pt* **arose**; *pp* **risen**) (*problem*) survenir; (*question*) se poser; ~ **from** résulter de.

**aristocrat** /'ærɪstəkræt/ *n* aristocrate *mf*.

**arithmetic** /ə'rɪθmətɪk/ *n* arithmétique *f*.

**ark** /ɑ:k/ *n* (Relig) arche *f*.

**arm** /ɑ:m/ *n* bras *m*; ~ **in arm** bras dessus bras dessous. ● *vt* armer; ~**ed robbery** vol *m* à main armée.

**armament** /'ɑ:məmənt/ *n* armement *m*.

**arm**: ~**-band** *n* brassard *m*. ~**chair** *n* fauteuil *m*.

**armour** /'ɑ:mə(r)/ *n* armure *f*. **armoured** *a* blindé. **armoury** *n* arsenal *m*.

**armpit** /'ɑ:mpɪt/ *n* aisselle *f*.

**arms** /ɑ:mz/ *npl* (weapons) armes *fpl*. ~ **dealer** *n* trafiquant *m* d'armes.

**army** /'ɑ:mɪ/ *n* armée *f*.

**aroma** /ə'rəʊmə/ *n* arôme *m*. **aromatic** *a* aromatique.

**arose** /ə'rəʊz/ ⇒ARISE.

**around** /ə'raʊnd/ *adv* (tout) autour; (here and there) çà et là. ● *prep* autour de; ~ **here** par ici.

**arouse** /ə'raʊz/ *vt* (awaken, cause) éveiller; (excite) exciter.

**arrange** /ə'reɪndʒ/ *vt* arranger; (*time, date*) fixer; ~ **to** s'arranger pour.

**arrangement** /ə'reɪndʒmənt/ *n* arrangement *m*; (agreement) entente *f*; **make** ~**s** prendre des dispositions.

**array** /ə'reɪ/ *n* **an** ~ **of** (display) un étalage impressionnant de.

**arrears** /ə'rɪəz/ *npl* arriéré *m*; **in** ~ (*rent*) arriéré; **he is in** ~ il a des retards dans ses paiements.

**arrest** /ə'rest/ *vt* arrêter; (attention) retenir. ● *n* arrestation *f*; **under** ~ en état d'arrestation.

**arrival** /ə'raɪvl/ *n* arrivée *f*; **new** ~ nouveau venu *m*, nouvelle venue *f*.

**arrive** /ə'raɪv/ *vi* arriver; ~ **at** (*destination*) arriver à; (*decision*) parvenir à.

**arrogance** /'ærəgəns/ *n* arrogance *f*.

**arrow** /'ærəʊ/ *n* flèche *f*.

**arse** /ɑ:s/ *n* ⊠ cul *m* ⊠.

**arson** /'ɑ:sn/ *n* incendie *m* criminel. **arsonist** *n* incendiaire *mf*.

**art** /ɑ:t/ *n* art *m*; (fine arts) beaux-arts *mpl*.

**artery** /'ɑ:tərɪ/ *n* artère *f*.

**art gallery** *n* (public) musée *m* (*d'art*); (private) galerie *f* (*d'art*).

**arthritis** /ɑ:'θraɪtɪs/ *n* arthrite *f*.

**artichoke** /'ɑ:tɪtʃəʊk/ *n* artichaut *m*.

**article** /'ɑ:tɪkl/ *n* article *m*; ~ **of clothing** vêtement *m*.

**articulate** /ɑ:'tɪkjʊlət/ *a* (*person*) capable de s'exprimer clairement; (*speech*) distinct.

**articulated lorry** *n* semi-remorque *m*.

**artificial** /ɑ:tɪ'fɪʃl/ *a* artificiel.

**artist** /'ɑ:tɪst/ *n* artiste *mf*.

**arts** /ɑ:ts/ *npl* **the** ~ les arts *mpl*; (Univ) lettres *fpl*.

**artwork** /'a:twɜ:k/ *n* (of book) illustrations *fpl*.

**as** /æz, əz/ *conj* comme; (while) pendant que; (over gradual period of time) au fur et à mesure que; ~ **she grew older** au fur et à mesure qu'elle vieillissait; **do** ~ **I say** fais ce que je dis; ~ **usual** comme d'habitude. ● *prep* ~ **a mother** en tant que mère; ~ **a gift** en cadeau; ~ **from**

Monday à partir de lundi; ~ **for**, ~ to quant à; ~ **if** comme si; **you look ~ if you're tired** vous avez l'air (d'être) fatigué. ● *adv* ~ **tall** ~ aussi grand que; ~ **much** ~, ~ **many** ~ autant que; ~ **soon** ~ aussitôt que; ~ **well** ~ aussi bien que; ~ **wide** ~ **possible** aussi large que possible.

**asbestos** /æz'bestɒs/ *n* amiante *f*.

**ascend** /ə'send/ *vt* gravir. ● *vi* monter.

**ascertain** /æsə'teɪn/ *vt* établir (that que).

**ash** /æʃ/ *n* cendre *f*; ~**(-tree)** frêne *m*.

**ashamed** /ə'ʃeɪmd/ *a* **be** ~ avoir honte (of de).

**ashore** /ə'ʃɔ:(r)/ *adv* à terre.

**ashtray** /'æʃtreɪ/ *n* cendrier *m*.

**Asia** /'eɪʃə/ *n* Asie *f*.

**Asian** /'eɪʃn/ *n* Asiatique *mf*. ● *a* asiatique.

**aside** /ə'saɪd/ *adv* de côté; ~ **from** à part. ● *n* aparté *m*.

**ask** /ɑ:sk/ *vt/i* demander; (*a question*) poser; (invite) inviter; ~ **sb sth** demander qch à qn; ~ **sb to do** demander à qn de faire; ~ **about** (*thing*) se renseigner sur; (*person*) demander des nouvelles de; ~ **for** demander.

**asleep** /ə'sli:p/ *a* endormi; (numb) engourdi. ● *adv* **fall** ~ s'endormir.

**asparagus** /ə'spærəgəs/ *n* (plant) asperge *f*; (Culin) asperges *fpl*.

**aspect** /'æspekt/ *n* aspect *m*; (direction) orientation *f*.

**asphyxiate** /əs'fɪksɪeɪt/ *vt/i* (s')asphyxier.

**aspire** /əs'paɪə(r)/ *vi* aspirer (to à; to do à faire).

**aspirin** /'æsprɪn/ *n* aspirine® *f*.

**ass** /æs/ *n* âne *m*; (person 🅘) idiot/-e *m/f*.

**assail** /ə'seɪl/ *vt* attaquer. **assailant** *n* agresseur *m*.

**assassin** /ə'sæsɪn/ *n* assassin *m*. **assassinate** *vt* assassiner. **assassination** *n* assassinat *m*.

**assault** /ə'sɔ:lt/ *n* (Mil) assaut *m*; (Jur) agression *f*. ● *vt* (*person*: Jur) agresser.

**assemble** /ə'sembl/ *vt* (construct) assembler; (gather) rassembler. ● *vi* se rassembler.

**assembly** /ə'semblɪ/ *n* assemblée *f*. ~ **line** *n* chaîne *f* de montage.

**assent** /ə'sent/ *n* assentiment *m*. ● *vi* consentir.

**assert** /ə'sɜ:t/ *vt* affirmer; (*rights*) revendiquer. **assertion** *n* affirmation *f*. **assertive** *a* assuré.

**assess** /ə'ses/ *vt* évaluer; (*payment*) déterminer le montant de. **assessment** *n* évaluation *f*. **assessor** *n* (valuer) expert *m*.

**asset** /'æset/ *n* (advantage) atout *m*; (financial) bien *m*; ~**s** (Comm) actif *m*.

**assign** /ə'saɪn/ *vt* (allot) assigner; ~ **sb to** (appoint) affecter qn à.

**assignment** /ə'saɪnmənt/ *n* (task) mission *f*; (diplomatic) poste *m*; (academic) devoir *m*.

**assist** /ə'sɪst/ *vt/i* aider. **assistance** *n* aide *f*.

**assistant** /ə'sɪstənt/ *n* aide *mf*; (in shop) vendeur/-euse *m/f*. ● *a* (manager) adjoint.

**associate**[1] /ə'səʊʃɪət/ *n & a* associé/-e (*m/f*).

**associate**[2] /ə'səʊʃɪeɪt/ *vt* associer. ● *vi* ~ **with** fréquenter. **association** *n* association *f*.

**assorted** /ə'sɔ:tɪd/ *a* divers; (*foods*) assorti.

**assortment** /ə'sɔ:tmənt/ *n* assortiment *m*; (of people) mélange *m*.

**assume** /ə'sju:m/ *vt* supposer; (*power, attitude*) prendre; (*role, burden*) assumer.

**assurance** /ə'ʃʊərəns/ *n* assurance *f.*

**assure** /ə'ʃʊə(r)/ *vt* assurer.

**asterisk** /'æstərɪsk/ *n* astérisque *m.*

**asthma** /'æsmə/ *n* asthme *m.*

**astonish** /ə'stɒnɪʃ/ *vt* étonner.

**astound** /ə'staʊnd/ *vt* stupéfier.

**astray** /ə'streɪ/ *adv* **go ~** s'égarer; **lead ~** égarer.

**astride** /ə'straɪd/ *adv & prep* à califourchon (sur).

**astrologer** /ə'strɒlədʒə(r)/ *n* astrologue *mf.* **astrology** *n* astrologie *f.*

**astronaut** /'æstrənɔ:t/ *n* astronaute *mf.*

**astronomer** /ə'strɒnəmə(r)/ *n* astronome *mf.*

**asylum** /ə'saɪləm/ *n* asile *m.*

**at** /æt, ət/ *preposition*

⇒ For expressions such as **laugh at, look at** ⇒**laugh, look.**

- (in position or place) à; **he's ~ his desk** il est à son bureau; **she's ~ work/school** elle est au travail/à l'école.
- (at someone's house or business) chez; **~ Mary's/the dentist's** chez Mary/le dentiste.
- (in times, ages) à; **~ four o'clock** à quatre heures; **~ two years of age** à l'âge de deux ans.

**ate** /et/ ⇒EAT.

**atheist** /'eɪθɪɪst/ *n* athée *mf.*

**athlete** /'æθli:t/ *n* athlète *mf.* **athletic** *a* athlétique. **athletics** *npl* athlétisme *m*; (US) sports *mpl.*

**Atlantic** /ət'læntɪk/ *a* atlantique. ● *n* **the ~ (Ocean)** l'Atlantique *m.*

**atlas** /'ætləs/ *n* atlas *m.*

**atmosphere** /'ætməsfɪə(r)/ *n* (air) atmosphère *f*; (mood) ambiance *f.* **atmospheric** *a* atmosphérique; d'ambiance.

**atom** /'ætəm/ *n* atome *m.*

**atrocious** /ə'trəʊʃəs/ *a* atroce.

**atrocity** /ə'trɒsətɪ/ *n* atrocité *f.*

**attach** /ə'tætʃ/ *vt/i* (s')attacher; (*letter*) joindre (**to** à).

**attaché** /ə'tæʃeɪ/ *n* (Pol) attaché/-e *m/f.* **~ case** *n* attaché-case *m.*

**attached** /ə'tætʃt/ *a* **be ~ to** (like) être attaché à; **the ~ letter** la lettre ci-jointe.

**attachment** /ə'tætʃmənt/ *n* (accessory) accessoire *m*; (affection) attachement *m*; (e-mail) pièces *fpl* jointes.

**attack** /ə'tæk/ *n* attaque *f*; (Med) crise *f.* ● *vt* attaquer.

**attain** /ə'teɪn/ *vt* atteindre (à); (gain) acquérir.

**attempt** /ə'tempt/ *vt* tenter. ● *n* tentative *f*; **an ~ on sb's life** un attentat contre qn.

**attend** /ə'tend/ *vt* assister à; (*class*) suivre; (*school, church*) aller à. ● *vi* assister; **~ (to)** (look after) s'occuper de. **attendance** *n* présence *f*; (people) assistance *f.*

**attendant** /ə'tendənt/ *n* employé/-e *m/f.* ● *a* associé.

**attention** /ə'tenʃn/ *n* attention *f*; **~!** (Mil) garde-à-vous!; **pay ~** faire *or* prêter attention (**to** à).

**attentive** /ə'tentɪv/ *a* attentif; (considerate) attentionné. **attentively** *adv* attentivement. **attentiveness** *n* attention *f.*

**attest** /ə'test/ *vt/i* **~ (to)** attester.

**attic** /'ætɪk/ *n* grenier *m.*

**attitude** /'ætɪtju:d/ *n* attitude *f.*

**attorney** /ə'tɜ:nɪ/ *n* (US) avocat/-e *m*/*f*.

**attract** /ə'trækt/ *vt* attirer. **attraction** *n* attraction *f*; (charm) attrait *m*.

**attractive** /ə'træktɪv/ *a* attrayant, séduisant. **attractively** *adv* agréablement. **attractiveness** *n* attrait *m*, beauté *f*.

**attribute**[1] /ə'trɪbju:t/ *vt* ~ **to** attribuer à.

**attribute**[2] /'ætrɪbju:t/ *n* attribut *m*.

**aubergine** /'əʊbəʒi:n/ *n* aubergine *f*.

**auction** /'ɔ:kʃn/ *n* vente *f* aux enchères. ● *vt* vendre aux enchères. **auctioneer** *n* commissaire-priseur *m*.

**audacious** /ɔ:'deɪʃəs/ *a* audacieux.

**audience** /'ɔ:dɪəns/ *n* (theatre, radio) public *m*; (interview) audience *f*.

**audiovisual** /ɔ:dɪəʊ'vɪʒʊəl/ *a* audiovisuel.

**audit** /'ɔ:dɪt/ *n* vérification *f* des comptes. ● *vt* vérifier

**audition** /ɔ:'dɪʃn/ *n* audition *f*. ● *vt*/*i* auditionner (**for** pour).

**auditor** /'ɔ:dɪtə(r)/ *n* commissaire *m* aux comptes.

**August** /'ɔ:gəst/ *n* août *m*.

**aunt** /ɑ:nt/ *n* tante *f*.

**auspicious** /ɔ:'spɪʃəs/ *a* favorable.

**Australia** /ɒ'streɪlɪə/ *n* Australie *f*.

**Australian** /ɒ'streɪlɪən/ *n* Australien/-ne *m*/*f*. ● *a* australien.

**Austria** /'ɒstrɪə/ *n* Autriche *f*.

**Austrian** /'ɒstrɪən/ *n* Autrichien/-ne *m*/*f*. ● *a* autrichien.

**authentic** /ɔ:'θentɪk/ *a* authentique.

**author** /'ɔ:θə(r)/ *n* auteur *m*.

**authoritarian** /ɔ:θɒrɪ'teərɪən/ *a* autoritaire.

**authoritative** /ɔ:'θɒrɪtətɪv/ *a* (credible) qui fait autorité; (*manner*) autoritaire.

**authority** /ɔ:'θɒrətɪ/ *n* autorité *f*; (permission) autorisation *f*.

**authorization** /ɔ:θəraɪ'zeɪʃn/ *n* autorisation *f*. **authorize** *vt* autoriser.

**autistic** /ɔ:'tɪstɪk/ *a* (*person*) autiste; (*response*) autistique.

**autograph** /'ɔ:təgrɑ:f/ *n* autographe *m*. ● *vt* signer, dédicacer.

**automate** /'ɔ:təmeɪt/ *vt* automatiser.

**automatic** /ɔ:tə'mætɪk/ *a* automatique. ● *n* (Auto) voiture *f* automatique.

**automobile** /'ɔ:təməbi:l/ *n* (US) auto(mobile) *f*.

**autonomous** /ɔ:'tɒnəməs/ *a* autonome.

**autumn** /'ɔ:təm/ *n* automne *m*.

**auxiliary** /ɔ:g'zɪlɪərɪ/ *a* & *n* auxiliaire (*mf*); ~ **(verb)** auxiliaire *m*.

**avail** /ə'veɪl/ *vt* ~ **oneself of** profiter de. ● *n* **of no** ~ inutile; **to no** ~ sans résultat.

**availability** /əveɪlə'bɪlətɪ/ *n* disponibilité *f*. **available** *a* disponible.

**avenge** /ə'vendʒ/ *vt* venger; ~ **oneself** se venger (**on** de).

**avenue** /'ævənju:/ *n* avenue *f*; (line of approach: fig) voie *f*.

**average** /'ævərɪdʒ/ *n* moyenne *f*; **on** ~ en moyenne. ● *a* moyen. ● *vt* faire la moyenne de; (produce, do) faire en moyenne.

**aviary** /'eɪvɪərɪ/ *n* volière *f*.

**avocado** /ævə'kɑ:dəʊ/ *n* avocat *m*.

**avoid** /ə'vɔɪd/ *vt* éviter. **avoidance** *n* (of injuries) prévention *f*; (of responsibility) refus *m*.

**await** /ə'weɪt/ *vt* attendre.

**awake** /ə'weɪk/ *vt/i* (*pt* **awoke**; *pp* **awoken**) (s')éveiller. ● *a* **be ~** ne pas dormir, être (r)éveillé.

**award** /ə'wɔ:d/ *vt* (*grant*) attribuer; (*prize*) décerner; (*points*) accorder. ● *n* récompense *f*, prix *m*; (scholarship) bourse *f*; **pay ~** augmentation *f* (de salaire).

**aware** /ə'weə(r)/ *a* (well-informed) averti; **be ~ of** (*danger*) être conscient de; (*fact*) savoir; **become ~ of** prendre conscience de. **awareness** *n* conscience *f*.

**away** /ə'weɪ/ *adv* (far) (au) loin; (absent) absent, parti; **~ from** loin de; **move ~** s'écarter; (to new home) déménager; **six kilometres ~** à six kilomètres (de distance); **take ~** emporter; **he was snoring ~** il ronflait. ● *a & n* **~ (match)** match *m* à l'extérieur.

**awe** /ɔ:/ *n* crainte *f* (révérencielle).

**awe-inspiring** /'ɔ:ɪnspaɪrɪŋ/ *a* impressionnant.

**awesome** /'ɔ:səm/ *a* redoutable.

**awful** /'ɔ:fl/ *a* affreux. **awfully** *adv* (badly) affreusement; (very 🄸) rudement.

**awkward** /'ɔ:kwəd/ *a* difficile; (inconvenient) inopportun; (clumsy) maladroit; (embarrassing) gênant; (embarrassed) gêné. **awkwardly** *adv* maladroitement; avec gêne. **awkwardness** *n* maladresse *f*; (discomfort) gêne *f*.

**awning** /'ɔ:nɪŋ/ *n* auvent *m*; (of shop) store *m*.

**awoke**, **awoken** /ə'wəʊk, ə'wəʊkən/ ⇒AWAKE.

**axe** /æks/ *n* hache *f*. ● *vt* (*pres p* **axing**) réduire; (eliminate) supprimer; (employee) renvoyer.

**axis** /'æksɪs/ *n* (*pl* **axes** /-si:z/) axe *m*.

**axle** /'æksl/ *n* essieu *m*.

# Bb

**BA** *abbr* ⇒BACHELOR OF ARTS.

**babble** /'bæbl/ *vi* babiller; (*stream*) gazouiller. ● *n* babillage *m*.

**baby** /'beɪbɪ/ *n* bébé *m*. **~ carriage** *n* (US) voiture *f* d'enfant. **~-sit** *vi* faire du babysitting, garder des enfants. **~-sitter** *n* baby-sitter *mf*.

**bachelor** /'bætʃələ(r)/ *n* célibataire *m*. **B~ of Arts** licencié/-e *m/f* ès lettres.

**back** /bæk/ *n* (of person, hand, page, etc.) dos *m*; (of house) derrière *m*; (of vehicle) arrière *m*; (of room) fond *m*; (of chair) dossier *m*; (in football) arrière *m*; **at the ~ of the book** à la fin du livre; **in ~ of** (US) derrière. ● *a* (*leg, wheel*) arrière *inv*; (*door, gate*) de derrière; (*taxes*) arriéré. ● *adv* en arrière; (returned) de retour, rentré; **come ~** revenir; **give ~** rendre; **take ~** reprendre; **I want it ~** je veux le récupérer. ● *vt* (support) appuyer; (bet on) miser sur; (*vehicle*) faire reculer. ● *vi* (of person, vehicle) reculer. □ **~ down** céder; **~ out** se désister; (Auto) sortir en marche arrière; **~ up** (support) appuyer. **~ache** *n* mal *m* de dos. **~-bencher** *n* (Pol) député *m*. **~bone** *n* colonne *f* vertébrale. **~date** *vt* antidater. **~fire** *vi* (Auto) pétarader; (fig) mal tourner. **~gammon** *n* trictrac *m*.

**background** /'bækgraʊnd/ *n* fond *m*, arrière-plan *m*; (context) contexte *m*; (environment) milieu *m*; (ex-

perience) formation *f*. ● *a* (*music, noise*) de fond.

**backhand** /'bækhænd/ *n* revers *m*. **backhander** *n* (bribe) pot-de-vin *m*.

**backing** /'bækɪŋ/ *n* soutien *m*.

**back**: **~lash** *n* retour *m* de bâton; réaction *f* violente (**against** contre). **~log** *n* retard *m*. **~number** *n* vieux numéro *m*. **~pack** *n* sac *m* à dos. **~side** *n* (buttocks [!]) derrière *m*. **~stage** *a & adv* dans les coulisses. **~stroke** *n* dos *m* crawlé. **~track** *vi* rebrousser chemin; (change one's opinion) faire marche arrière.

**back-up** *n* soutien *m*; (Comput) sauvegarde *f*. ● *a* de secours; (Comput) de sauvegarde.

**backward** /'bækwəd/ *a* (*step etc.*) en arrière; (retarded) arriéré.

**backwards** /'bækwədz/ *adv* en arrière; (*walk*) à reculons; (*read*) à l'envers; **go ~ and forwards** aller et venir.

**bacon** /'beɪkən/ *n* lard *m*; (in rashers) bacon *m*.

**bacteria** /bæk'tɪərɪə/ *npl* bactéries *fpl*.

**bad** /bæd/ *a* (**worse**, **worst**) mauvais; (wicked) méchant; (ill) malade; (*accident*) grave; (*food*) gâté; **feel ~** se sentir mal; **go ~** se gâter; **~ language** gros mots *mpl*; **too ~!** tant pis!; (I'm sorry) dommage!

**badge** /bædʒ/ *n* badge *m*; (coat of arms) insigne *m*.

**badger** /'bædʒə(r)/ *n* blaireau *m*. ● *vt* harceler.

**badly** /'bædlɪ/ *adv* mal; (*hurt*) gravement; **want ~** avoir grande envie de.

**badminton** /'bædmɪntən/ *n* badminton *m*.

**bad-tempered** *a* irritable.

**baffle** /'bæfl/ *vt* déconcerter.

**bag** /bæg/ *n* sac *m*; **~s** (luggage) bagages *mpl*; (under eyes [!]) valises *fpl*; **~s of** plein de.

**baggage** /'bægɪdʒ/ *n* bagages *mpl*; **~ reclaim** réception *f* des bagages.

**baggy** /'bægɪ/ *a* large.

**bagpipes** /'bægpaɪps/ *npl* cornemuse *f*.

**bail** /beɪl/ *n* caution *f*; **on ~** sous caution; (cricket) bâtonnet *m*. ● *vt* mettre en liberté provisoire.

**bailiff** /'beɪlɪf/ *n* huissier *m*.

**bait** /beɪt/ *n* appât *m*. ● *vt* appâter; (fig) tourmenter.

**bake** /beɪk/ *vt* faire cuire au four; **~ a cake** faire un gâteau. ● *vi* cuire; (*person*) faire du pain. **baked beans** *npl* haricots *mpl* blancs à la tomate. **baked potato** *n* pomme *f* de terre en robe des champs. **baker** *n* boulanger/-ère *m/f*. **bakery** *n* boulangerie *f*.

**balance** /'bæləns/ *n* équilibre *m*; (scales) balance *f*; (outstanding sum: Comm) solde *m*; (of payments, of trade) balance *f*; (remainder) restant *m*. ● *vt* mettre en équilibre; (weigh up *also* Comm) balancer; (*budget*) équilibrer; (to compensate) contrebalancer. ● *vi* être en équilibre.

**balcony** /'bælkənɪ/ *n* balcon *m*.

**bald** /bɔːld/ *a* chauve; (*tyre*) lisse; (fig) simple.

**balk** /bɔːk/ *vt* contrecarrer. ● *vi* **~ at** reculer devant.

**ball** /bɔːl/ *n* (golf, tennis, etc.) balle *f*; (football) ballon *m*; (billiards) bille *f*; (of wool) pelote *f*; (sphere) boule *f*; (dance) bal *m*.

**ballet** /'bæleɪ/ *n* ballet *m*.

**balloon** /bə'luːn/ *n* ballon *m*.

**ballot** /'bælət/ *n* scrutin *m*. ● *vt* consulter par vote (**on** sur). **~-box** *n* urne *f*. **~-paper** *n* bulletin *m* de vote.

**ballpoint pen** *n* stylo *m* (à) bille.

**ban** /bæn/ *vt* (*pt* **banned**) interdire; ~ **sb from** exclure qn de; ~ **sb from doing** interdire à qn de faire. ● *n* interdiction *f* (**on** de).

**banal** /bəˈnɑːl/ *a* banal.

**banana** /bəˈnɑːnə/ *n* banane *f*.

**band** /bænd/ *n* (strip, group of people) bande *f*; (pop group) groupe *m*; (brass band) fanfare *f*. ● *vi* ~ **together** se réunir.

**bandage** /ˈbændɪdʒ/ *n* bandage *m*. ● *vt* bander.

**B and B** *abbr* ⇒BED AND BREAKFAST.

**bandit** /ˈbændɪt/ *n* bandit *m*.

**bandstand** /ˈbændstænd/ *n* kiosque *m* à musique.

**bang** /bæŋ/ *n* (blow, noise) coup *m*; (explosion) détonation *f*; (of door) claquement *m*. ● *vt*/*i* taper; (*door*) claquer; ~ **one's head** se cogner la tête. ● *interj* vlan. ● *adv* [I] ~ **in the middle** en plein milieu; ~ **on time** à l'heure pile.

**banger** /ˈbæŋə(r)/ *n* (*firework*) pétard *m*; (Culin) saucisse *f*; **(old)** ~ (*car* [I]) guimbarde *f*.

**banish** /ˈbænɪʃ/ *vt* bannir.

**banister**/ˈbænɪstə/ *n* rampe *f* d'escalier.

**bank** /bæŋk/ *n* (Comm) banque *f*; (of river) rive *f*; (of sand) banc *m*. ● *vt* mettre en banque. ● *vi* (Aviat) virer; ~ **with** avoir un compte à; ~ **on** compter sur. ~ **account** *n* compte *m* en banque. ~ **card** *n* carte *f* bancaire. ~ **holiday** *n* jour *m* férié.

**banking** /ˈbæŋkɪŋ/ *n* opérations *fpl* bancaires; (as career) la banque.

**banknote** /ˈbæŋknəʊt/ *n* billet *m* de banque.

**bankrupt** /ˈbæŋkrʌpt/ *a* **be** ~ être en faillite; **go** ~ faire faillite. ● *n* failli/-e *m*/*f*. ● *vt* mettre en faillite. **bankruptcy** *n* faillite *f*.

**bank statement** *n* relevé *m* de compte.

**banner** /ˈbænə(r)/ *n* bannière *f*.

**baptism** /ˈbæptɪzəm/ *n* baptême *m*. **baptize** *vt* baptiser.

**bar** /bɑː(r)/ *n* (of metal) barre *f*; (on window, cage) barreau *m*; (of chocolate) tablette *f*; (pub) bar *m*; (counter) comptoir *m*; (Mus) mesure *f*; (fig) obstacle *m*; ~ **of soap** savonnette *f*; **the** ~ (Jur) le barreau. ● *vt* (*pt* **barred**) (obstruct) barrer; (prohibit) interdire; (exclude) exclure. ● *prep* sauf.

**barbecue** /ˈbɑːbɪkjuː/ *n* barbecue *m*. ● *vt* faire au barbecue.

**barbed wire** /bɑːbdˈwaɪə(r)/ *n* fil *m* de fer barbelé.

**barber** /ˈbɑːbə(r)/ *n* coiffeur *m* (*pour hommes*).

**bar code** *n* code *m* (à) barres.

**bare** /beə(r)/ *a* nu; (*cupboard*) vide. ● *vt* mettre à nu. ~**foot** *a* nu-pieds *inv*, pieds nus. **barely** *adv* à peine.

**bargain** /ˈbɑːgɪn/ *n* (deal) marché *m*; (cheap thing) occasion *f*. ● *vi* négocier; (haggle) marchander; **not** ~ **for** ne pas s'attendre à.

**barge** /bɑːdʒ/ *n* péniche *f*. ● *vi* ~ **in** interrompre; (into room) faire irruption.

**bark** /bɑːk/ *n* (of tree) écorce *f*; (of dog) aboiement *m*. ● *vi* aboyer.

**barley** /ˈbɑːlɪ/ *n* orge *f*.

**bar**: ~**maid** *n* serveuse *f*. ~**man** *n* (*pl* **-men**) barman *m*.

**barn** /bɑːn/ *n* grange *f*.

**barracks** /ˈbærəks/ *npl* caserne *f*.

**barrel** /ˈbærəl/ *n* tonneau *m*; (of oil) baril *m*; (of gun) canon *m*.

**barren** /ˈbærən/ *a* stérile.

**barricade** /bærɪˈkeɪd/ *n* barricade *f*. ● *vt* barricader.

**barrier** /ˈbærɪə(r)/ *n* barrière *f*; **ticket ~** guichet *m*.

**barrister** /ˈbærɪstə(r)/ *n* avocat *m*.

**bartender** /ˈbɑːtendə(r)/ *n* (US) barman *m*.

**barter** /ˈbɑːtə(r)/ *n* troc *m*. ● *vt* troquer (**for** contre).

**base** /beɪs/ *n* base *f*. ● *vt* baser (**on** sur; **in** à). ● *a* ignoble. **baseball** *n* base-ball *m*.

**basement** /ˈbeɪsmənt/ *n* sous-sol *m*.

**bash** /bæʃ/ 🅸 *vt* cogner; **~ed in** enfoncé. ● *n* coup *m* violent; **have a ~ at** s'essayer à.

**basic** /ˈbeɪsɪk/ *a* fondamental, élémentaire; **the ~s** l'essentiel *m*. **basically** *adv* au fond.

**basil** /ˈbæzɪl/ *n* basilic *m*.

**basin** /ˈbeɪsn/ *n* (for liquids) cuvette *f*; (for food) bol *m*; (for washing) lavabo *m*; (of river) bassin *m*.

**basis** /ˈbeɪsɪs/ *n* (*pl* **bases** /-siːz/) base *f*.

**bask** /bɑːsk/ *vi* se prélasser (**in** à).

**basket** /ˈbɑːskɪt/ *n* corbeille *f*; (with handle) panier *m*. **basketball** *n* basket(-ball) *m*.

**Basque** /bɑːsk/ *n* (person) Basque *mf*; (Ling) basque *m*. ● *a* basque.

**bass**[1] /beɪs/ *a* (*voice, part*) de basse; (*sound, note*) grave. ● *n* (*pl* **basses**) basse *f*.

**bass**[2] /bæs/ *n inv* (freshwater fish) perche *f*; (sea) bar *m*.

**bassoon** /bəˈsuːn/ *n* basson *m*.

**bastard** /ˈbɑːstəd/ *n* (illegitimate) bâtard/-e *m*/*f*; (insult ☒) salaud *m* ☒.

**bat** /bæt/ *n* (cricket etc.) batte *f*; (table tennis) raquette *f*; (animal) chauve-souris *f*. ● *vt* (*pt* **batted**) (ball) frapper; **not ~ an eyelid** ne pas sourciller.

**batch** /bætʃ/ *n* (of cakes, people) fournée *f*; (of goods, text *also* Comput) lot *m*.

**bath** /bɑːθ/ *n* (*pl* **-s** /bɑːðz/) bain *m*; (tub) baignoire *f*; **have a ~** prendre un bain; **(swimming) ~s** piscine *f*. ● *vt* donner un bain à.

**bathe** /beɪð/ *vt* baigner. ● *vi* se baigner; (US) prendre un bain.

**bathing** /ˈbeɪðɪŋ/ *n* baignade *f*. **~-costume** *n* maillot *m* de bain.

**bath**: **~robe** *n* (US) robe *f* de chambre. **~room** *n* salle *f* de bains.

**baton** /ˈbætən/ *n* (policeman's) matraque *f*; (Mus) baguette *f*.

**batter** /ˈbætə(r)/ *vt* battre. ● *n* (Culin) pâte *f* (à frire).

**battery** /ˈbætərɪ/ *n* (Mil, Auto) batterie *f*; (of torch, radio) pile *f*.

**battle** /ˈbætl/ *n* bataille *f*; (fig) lutte *f*. ● *vi* se battre. **~field** *n* champ *m* de bataille.

**baulk** /bɔːk/ *vt*/*i* = BALK.

**bay** /beɪ/ *n* (Bot) laurier *m*; (Geog, Archit) baie *f*; (area) aire *f*; (bark) aboiement *m*; **keep** *or* **hold at ~** tenir à distance. ● *vi* aboyer. **~-leaf** *n* feuille *f* de laurier. **~ window** *n* fenêtre *f* en saillie.

**bazaar** /bəˈzɑː(r)/ *n* (shop, market) bazar *m*; (sale) vente *f*.

**BC** *abbr* (**before Christ**) avant J.-C.

**BBS** *abbr* (**Bulletin Board System**) (Internet) babillard *m* électronique, BBS *m*.

**be** /biː/

*present* **am**, **is**, **are**; *past* **was**, **were**; *past participle* **been**.

● *intransitive verb*

····➤ être; **I am tired** je suis fatigué; **it's me** c'est moi.

····➤ (feelings) avoir; **I am hot** j'ai chaud; **he is hungry/thirsty** il a faim/soif; **her hands are cold** elle a froid aux mains.

····➤ (age) avoir; **I am 15** j'ai 15 ans.

····➤ (weather) faire; **it's warm** il fait chaud; **it's 25** il fait 25.

····➤ (health) aller; **how are you?** comment allez-vous *or* comment vas-tu?

····➤ (visit) aller; **I've never been to Italy** je ne suis jamais allé en Italie.

● *auxiliary verb*

····➤ (in tenses) **I am working** je travaille; **he was writing to his mother** il écrivait à sa mère; **she is to do it at once** (obligation) elle doit le faire tout de suite.

····➤ (in passives) **he was killed** il a été tué; **the window has been fixed** on a réparé la fenêtre.

····➤ (in tag questions) **their house is lovely, isn't it?** leur maison est très jolie, n'est-ce pas?

····➤ (in short answers) **'I am a painter'—'are you?'** 'je suis peintre'—'ah oui?'; **'are you a doctor?'—'yes, I am'** 'êtes-vous médecin?'—'oui'; **'you're not going out'—'yes I am'** 'tu ne sors pas'—'si'.

**beach** /bi:tʃ/ *n* plage *f*.

**beacon** /'bi:kən/ *n* (lighthouse) phare *m*; (marker) balise *f*.

**bead** /bi:d/ *n* perle *f*.

**beak** /bi:k/ *n* bec *m*.

**beaker** /'bi:kə(r)/ *n* gobelet *m*.

**beam** /bi:m/ *n* (timber) poutre *f*; (of light) rayon *m*; (of torch) faisceau *m*. ● *vi* rayonner. ● *vt* (broadcast) transmettre.

**bean** /bi:n/ *n* haricot *m*.

**bear** /beə(r)/ *n* ours *m*. ● *vt* (*pt* **bore**; *pp* **borne**) (carry, show, feel) porter; (endure, sustain) supporter; (*child*) mettre au monde. ● *vi* ~ **left** (go) prendre à gauche; ~ **in mind** tenir compte de. □ ~ **out** confirmer; ~ **up** tenir le coup. **bearable** *a* supportable.

**beard** /bɪəd/ *n* barbe *f*.

**bearer** /beərə(r)/ *n* porteur/-euse *m*/*f*.

**bearing** /'beərɪŋ/ *n* (behaviour) maintien *m*; (relevance) rapport *m*; **get one's** ~**s** s'orienter.

**beast** /bi:st/ *n* bête *f*; (*person*) brute *f*.

**beat** /bi:t/ *vt*/*i* (*pt* **beat**; *pp* **beaten**) battre; ~ **a retreat** battre en retraite; ~ **it!** dégage! 🅸; **it** ~**s me** 🅸 ça me dépasse. ● *n* (of drum, heart) battement *m*; (Mus) mesure *f*; (of policeman) ronde *f*. □ ~ **off** repousser; ~ **up** tabasser. **beating** *n* raclée *f*.

**beautiful** /'bju:tɪfl/ *a* beau.

**beauty** /'bju:tɪ/ *n* beauté *f*. ~ **parlour** *n* institut *m* de beauté. ~ **spot** *n* grain *m* de beauté; (place) site *m* pittoresque.

**beaver** /'bi:və(r)/ *n* castor *m*.

**became** /bɪ'keɪm/ ⇨BECOME.

**because** /bɪ'kɒz/ *conj* parce que; ~ **of** à cause de.

**become** /bɪ'kʌm/ *vt*/*i* (*pt* **became**; *pp* **become**) devenir; (befit) convenir à; **what has** ~ **of her?** qu'est-ce qu'elle est devenue?

**bed** /bed/ *n* lit *m*; (layer) couche *f*; (of sea) fond *m*; (of flowers) parterre *m*; **go to** ~ (aller) se coucher. ● *vi* (*pt* **bedded**) ~ **down** se coucher. **bed and breakfast** *n* chambre *f* avec petit déjeuner, chambre *f* d'hôte. ~**bug** *n* punaise *f*. ~**clothes** *npl* couvertures *fpl*.

**bedding** /'bedɪŋ/ *n* literie *f*.

**bed**: **~ridden** *a* cloué au lit. **~room** *n* chambre *f* (à coucher). **~side** *n* chevet *m*. **~sit**, **~sitter** *n* chambre *f* meublée, studio *m*. **~spread** *n* dessus *m* de lit. **~time** *n* heure *f* du coucher.

**bee** /bi:/ *n* abeille *f*; **make a ~-line for** aller tout droit vers.

**beech** /bi:tʃ/ *n* hêtre *m*.

**beef** /bi:f/ *n* bœuf *m*. **~burger** *n* hamburger *m*.

**beehive** /'bi:haɪv/ *n* ruche *f*.

**been** /bi:n/ ⇒BE.

**beer** /bɪə(r)/ *n* bière *f*.

**beetle** /'bi:tl/ *n* scarabée *m*.

**beetroot** /'bi:tru:t/ *n inv* betterave *f*.

**before** /bɪ'fɔ:(r)/ *prep* (time) avant; (place) devant; **the day ~ yesterday** avant-hier. ● *adv* avant; (already) déjà; **the day ~** la veille. ● *conj* **~ leaving** avant de partir; **~ I forget** avant que j'oublie. **beforehand** *adv* à l'avance.

**beg** /beg/ *vt* (*pt* **begged**) (*food, money, favour*) demander (**from** à); **~ sb to do** supplier qn de faire. ● *vi* mendier; **it is going ~ging** personne n'en veut.

**began** /bɪ'gæn/ ⇒BEGIN.

**beggar** /'begə(r)/ *n* mendiant/-e *m/f*.

**begin** /bɪ'gɪn/ *vt/i* (*pt* **began**, *pp* **begun**, *pres p* **beginning**) commencer (**to do** à faire). **beginner** *n* débutant/-e *m/f*. **beginning** *n* commencement *m*, début *m*.

**begun** /bɪ'gʌn/ ⇒BEGIN.

**behalf** /bɪ'hɑ:f/ *n* **on ~ of** (*act, speak, campaign*) pour; (*phone, write*) de la part de.

**behave** /bɪ'heɪv/ *vi* se conduire; **~ (oneself)** se conduire bien.

**behaviour**, (US) **behavior** /bɪ'heɪvjə(r)/ *n* comportement *m* (**towards** envers).

**behead** /bɪ'hed/ *vt* décapiter.

**behind** /bɪ'haɪnd/ *prep* derrière; (in time) en retard sur. ● *adv* derrière; (late) en retard; **leave ~** oublier. ● *n* (buttocks [I]) derrière *m* [I].

**beige** /beɪʒ/ *a & n* beige (*m*).

**being** /'bi:ɪŋ/ *n* (person) être *m*.

**belch** /beltʃ/ *vi* avoir un renvoi. ● *vt* **~ out** (*smoke*) s'échapper. ● *n* renvoi *m*.

**Belgian** /'beldʒən/ *n* Belge *mf*. ● *a* belge. **Belgium** *n* Belgique *f*.

**belief** /bɪ'li:f/ *n* conviction *f*; (trust) confiance *f*; (faith: Relig) foi *f*.

**believe** /bɪ'li:v/ *vt/i* croire; **~ in** croire à; (*deity*) croire en. **believer** *n* croyant/-e *m/f*.

**bell** /bel/ *n* cloche *f*; (small) clochette *f*; (on door) sonnette *f*.

**belly** /'belɪ/ *n* ventre *m*. **~ button** *n* nombril *m*.

**belong** /bɪ'lɒŋ/ *vi* **~ to** appartenir à; (*club*) être membre de.

**belongings** /bɪ'lɒŋɪŋz/ *npl* affaires *fpl*.

**beloved** /bɪ'lʌvɪd/ *a & n* bien-aimé/-e (*m/f*).

**below** /bɪ'ləʊ/ *prep* sous, au-dessous de; (fig) indigne de. ● *adv* en dessous; (on page) ci-dessous.

**belt** /belt/ *n* ceinture *f*; (Tech) courroie *f*; (fig) zone *f*. ● *vt* (hit [I]) rosser. ● *vi* (rush [I]) **~ in/out** entrer/sortir à toute vitesse.

**beltway** /'beltweɪ/ *n* (US) périphérique *m*.

**bemused** /bɪ'mju:zd/ *a* perplexe.

**bench** /bentʃ/ *n* banc *m*; **the ~** (Jur) la magistrature (assise).

**bend** /bend/ *vt* (*pt* **bent**) (*knee, arm, wire*) plier; (*head, back*) courber. ● *vi* (*road*) tourner; (*person*)

~ **down/over** se pencher. ● *n* courbe *f*; (in road) virage *m*; (of arm, knee) pli *m*.

**beneath** /bɪ'ni:θ/ *prep* sous, au-dessous de; (fig) indigne de. ● *adv* en dessous.

**benefactor** /'benɪfæktə(r)/ *n* bienfaiteur/-trice *m/f*.

**beneficial** /benɪ'fɪʃl/ *a* bénéfique.

**benefit** /'benɪfɪt/ *n* avantage *m*; (allowance) allocation *f*. ● *vt* (be useful to) profiter à; (do good to) faire du bien à. ● *vi* profiter; ~ **from** tirer profit de.

**benign** /bɪ'naɪn/ *a* (kindly) bienveillant; (Med) bénin.

**bent** /bent/ ⇒BEND. ● *n* (talent) aptitude *f*; (inclination) penchant *m*. ● *a* tordu; ▣ corrompu; ~ **on doing** décidé à faire.

**bequest** /bɪ'kwest/ *n* legs *m*.

**bereaved** /bɪ'ri:vd/ *a* endeuillé; **the** ~ la famille endeuillée. **bereavement** *n* deuil *m*.

**berry** /'berɪ/ *n* baie *f*.

**berserk** /bə'sɜ:k/ *a* fou furieux.

**berth** /bɜ:θ/ *n* (in train, ship) couchette *f*; (anchorage) mouillage *m*; **give a wide** ~ **to** éviter. ● *vi* mouiller.

**beside** /bɪ'saɪd/ *prep* à côté de; ~ **oneself** hors de soi; ~ **the point** sans rapport.

**besides** /bɪ'saɪdz/ *prep* en plus de. ● *adv* en plus.

**besiege** /bɪ'si:dʒ/ *vt* assiéger.

**best** /best/ *a* meilleur; **the** ~ **book** le meilleur livre; **the** ~ **part of** la plus grande partie de; **the** ~ **thing is to** le mieux est de. ● *adv* **(the)** ~ (*behave, play*) le mieux. ● *n* **the** ~ le meilleur, la meilleure; **do one's** ~ faire de son mieux; **make the** ~ **of** s'accommoder de. ~ **man** *n* témoin. ~**-seller** *n* bestseller *m*, livre *m* à succès.

**bet** /bet/ *n* pari *m*. ● *vt/i* (*pt* **bet** *or* **betted**, *pres p* **betting**) parier (**on** sur).

**betray** /bɪ'treɪ/ *vt* trahir.

**better** /'betə(r)/ *a* meilleur; **the** ~ **part of** la plus grande partie de; **get** ~ s'améliorer; (recover) se remettre. ● *adv* mieux; **I had** ~ **go** je ferais mieux de partir. ● *vt* (improve) améliorer; (do better than) surpasser. ● *n* **get the** ~ **of** l'emporter sur; **so much the** ~ tant mieux. ~ **off** *a* (richer) plus riche; **he is/would be** ~ **off at home** il est/serait mieux chez lui.

**betting-shop** /'betɪŋʃɒp/ *n* bureau *m* du PMU.

**between** /bɪ'twi:n/ *prep* entre. ● *adv* **in** ~ au milieu.

**beverage** /'bevərɪdʒ/ *n* boisson *f*.

**beware** /bɪ'weə(r)/ *vi* prendre garde (**of** à).

**bewilder** /bɪ'wɪldə(r)/ *vt* déconcerter.

**beyond** /bɪ'jɒnd/ *prep* au-delà de; (*control, reach*) hors de; (besides) excepté. ● *adv* au-delà; **it is** ~ **me** ça me dépasse.

**bias** /'baɪəs/ *n* (inclination) tendance *f*; (prejudice) parti *m* pris. ● *vt* (*pt* **biased**) influer sur. **biased** *a* partial.

**bib** /bɪb/ *n* bavoir *m*.

**Bible** /'baɪbl/ *n* Bible *f*.

**biceps** /'baɪseps/ *n* biceps *m*.

**bicycle** /'baɪsɪkl/ *n* vélo *m*, bicyclette *f*. ● *a* (*bell, chain*) de vélo; (*pump, clip*) à vélo.

**bid** /bɪd/ *n* (at auction) enchère *f*; (attempt) tentative *f*. ● *vt/i* (*pt* **bade** /bæd/, *pp* **bidden** *or* **bid**, *pres p* **bidding**) (offer) offrir, mettre une enchère (de) (**for** pour); ~ **sb good morning** dire bonjour à qn; ~ **sb farewell** faire ses adieux à qn.

**bidding** /ˈbɪdɪŋ/ *n* (at auction) enchères *fpl*; **he did my ~** il a fait ce que je lui ai dit.

**bifocals** /baɪˈfəʊklz/ *npl* verres *mpl* à double foyer.

**big** /bɪg/ *a* (**bigger**, **biggest**) grand; (in bulk) gros.

**bike** /baɪk/ *n* vélo *m*.

**bikini** /bɪˈkiːnɪ/ *n* bikini *m*.

**bilberry** /ˈbɪlbərɪ/ *n* myrtille *f*.

**bilingual** /baɪˈlɪŋgwəl/ *a* bilingue.

**bill** /bɪl/ *n* (invoice) facture *f*; (in hotel, for gas) note *f*; (in restaurant) addition *f*; (of sale) acte *m*; (Pol) projet *m* de loi; (banknote: US) billet *m* de banque; (Theat) **on the ~** à l'affiche; (of bird) bec *m*. ● *vt* (person: Comm) envoyer la facture à. **~board** *n* panneau *m* d'affichage.

**billet** /ˈbɪlɪt/ *n* cantonnement *m*. ● *vt* (*pt* **billeted**) cantonner (**on** chez).

**billiards** /ˈbɪljədz/ *n* billard *m*.

**billion** /ˈbɪljən/ *n* billion *m*; (US) milliard *m*.

**bin** /bɪn/ *n* (for rubbish) poubelle *f*; (for storage) casier *m*.

**bind** /baɪnd/ *vt* (*pt* **bound**) attacher; (book) relier; **be bound by** être tenu par. ● *n* (bore) corvée *f*.

**binding** /ˈbaɪndɪŋ/ *n* reliure *f*. ● *a* (agreement, contract) qui lie.

**binge** /bɪndʒ/ *n* (drinking) beuverie *f*; (eating) gueuleton *m*.

**binoculars** /bɪˈnɒkjʊləz/ *npl* jumelles *fpl*.

**biochemistry** /baɪəʊˈkemɪstrɪ/ *n* biochimie *f*.

**biodegradable** /baɪəʊdɪˈgreɪdəbl/ *a* biodégradable.

**biographer** /baɪˈɒgrəfə(r)/ *n* biographe *mf*. **biography** *n* biographie *f*.

**biological** /baɪəˈlɒdʒɪkl/ *a* biologique.

**biologist** /baɪˈɒlədʒɪst/ *n* biologiste *mf*.

**biology** /baɪˈɒlədʒɪ/ *n* biologie *f*.

**birch** /bɜːtʃ/ *n* (tree) bouleau *m*; (whip) fouet *m*.

**bird** /bɜːd/ *n* oiseau *m*; (girl ☐) nana *f*.

**Biro**® /ˈbaɪərəʊ/ *n* stylo *m* à bille, bic® *m*.

**birth** /bɜːθ/ *n* naissance *f*; **give ~** accoucher. **~ certificate** *n* acte *m* de naissance. **~-control** *n* contraception *f*. **~day** *n* anniversaire *m*. **~mark** *n* tache *f* de naissance. **~-rate** *n* taux *m* de natalité.

**biscuit** /ˈbɪskɪt/ *n* biscuit *m*; (US) petit pain *m* (au lait).

**bisect** /baɪˈsekt/ *vt* couper en deux.

**bishop** /ˈbɪʃəp/ *n* évêque *m*.

**bit** /bɪt/ ⇒BITE. ● *n* morceau *m*; (of horse) mors *m*; (of tool) mèche *f*; **a ~** (a little) un peu; (Comput) bit *m*.

**bitch** /bɪtʃ/ *n* chienne *f*; (woman ☒) garce *f* ☒. ● *vi* dire du mal (**about** de).

**bite** /baɪt/ *vt/i* (*pt* **bit**; *pp* **bitten**) mordre; **~ one's nails** se ronger les ongles. ● *n* morsure *f*; (by insect) piqûre *f*; (mouthful) bouchée *f*; **have a ~** manger un morceau.

**bitter** /ˈbɪtə(r)/ *a* amer; (weather) glacial. ● *n* bière *f*. **bitterly** *adv* amèrement; **it is ~ly cold** il fait un temps glacial.

**bizarre** /bɪˈzɑː(r)/ *a* bizarre.

**black** /blæk/ *a* noir; **~ and blue** couvert de bleus. ● *n* (colour) noir *m*; **B~** (person) Noir/-e *m/f*. ● *vt* noircir; (goods) boycotter. **~berry** *n* mûre *f*. **~bird** *n* merle *m*. **~board** *n* tableau *m* noir. **~currant** *n* cassis *m*.

**blacken** /ˈblækən/ *vt/i* noircir.

**black**: ~ **eye** *n* œil *m* poché. ~**head** *n* point *m* noir. ~ **ice** *n* verglas *m*. ~**leg** *n* jaune *m*.

**blacklist** /ˈblæklɪst/ *n* liste *f* noire. ● *vt* mettre à l'index.

**blackmail** /ˈblækmeɪl/ *n* chantage *m*. ● *vt* faire chanter. **blackmailer** *n* maître-chanteur *m*.

**black**: ~ **market** *n* marché *m* noir. ~**out** *n* panne *f* de courant; (Med) syncope *f*. ~ **pudding** *n* boudin *m*. ~ **sheep** *n* brebis *f* galeuse. ~**smith** *n* forgeron *m*. ~ **spot** *n* point *m* noir.

**bladder** /ˈblædə(r)/ *n* vessie *f*.

**blade** /bleɪd/ *n* (of knife) lame *f*; (of propeller, oar) pale *f*; ~ **of grass** brin *m* d'herbe.

**blame** /bleɪm/ *vt* accuser; ~ **sb for sth** reprocher qch à qn; **he is to** ~ il est responsable (**for** de). ● *n* responsabilité *f* (**for** de).

**bland** /blænd/ *a* (insipid) fade.

**blank** /blæŋk/ *a* (*page*) blanc; (*screen*) vide; (*cheque*) en blanc; **to look** ~ avoir l'air ébahi. ● *n* blanc *m*; ~ **(cartridge)** cartouche *f* à blanc.

**blanket** /ˈblæŋkɪt/ *n* couverture *f*; (layer) couche *f*.

**blasphemous** /ˈblæsfəməs/ *a* blasphématoire; (*person*) blasphémateur.

**blast** /blɑːst/ *n* explosion *f*; (wave of air) souffle *m*; (of wind) rafale *f*; (noise from siren etc.) coup *m*. ● *vt* (blow up) faire sauter. □ ~ **off** décoller. ~ **furnace** *n* haut-fourneau *m*. ~-**off** *n* lancement *m*.

**blatant** /ˈbleɪtnt/ *a* (obvious) flagrant; (shameless) éhonté.

**blaze** /bleɪz/ *n* feu *m*; (accident) incendie *m*. ● *vt* ~ **a trail** faire œuvre de pionnier. ● *vi* (*fire*) brûler; (*sky, eyes*) flamboyer.

**bleach** /bliːtʃ/ *n* (for cleaning) eau *f* de Javel; (for hair, fabric) décolorant *m*. ● *vt*/*i* blanchir; (*hair*) décolorer.

**bleak** /bliːk/ *a* (*landscape*) désolé; (*outlook, future*) sombre.

**bleed** /bliːd/ *vt*/*i* (*pt* **bled**) saigner.

**bleep** /bliːp/ *n* bip *m*.

**blemish** /ˈblemɪʃ/ *n* imperfection *f*; (on fruit, reputation) tache *f*. ● *vt* entacher.

**blend** /blend/ *vt* mélanger. ● *vi* se fondre ensemble; **to** ~ **with** se marier à. ● *n* mélange *m*. **blender** *n* mixeur *n*, mixer *n*.

**bless** /bles/ *vt* bénir; **be** ~**ed with** jouir de; ~ **you!** à vos souhaits! **blessed** *a* (holy) saint; (damned 🄸) sacré. **blessing** *n* bénédiction *f*; (benefit) avantage *m*; (stroke of luck) chance *f*.

**blew** /bluː/ ⇒BLOW.

**blight** /blaɪt/ *n* (disease: Bot) rouille *f*; (fig) plaie *f*.

**blind** /blaɪnd/ *a* aveugle (**to** à); (*corner, bend*) sans visibilité. ● *vt* aveugler. ● *n* (on window) store *m*; **the** ~ les aveugles *mpl*.

**blindfold** /ˈblaɪndfəʊld/ *a* **be** ~ avoir les yeux bandés. ● *adv* les yeux bandés. ● *n* bandeau *m*. ● *vt* bander les yeux à.

**blindness** /ˈblaɪndnɪs/ *n* (Med) cécité *f*; (fig) aveuglement *m*.

**blind spot** *n* (Auto) angle *m* mort.

**blink** /blɪŋk/ *vi* cligner des yeux; (*light*) clignoter.

**bliss** /blɪs/ *n* délice *m*. **blissful** *a* délicieux.

**blister** /ˈblɪstə(r)/ *n* ampoule *f*; (on paint) cloque *f*. ● *vi* cloquer.

**blitz** /blɪts/ *n* (Aviat) raid *m* éclair. ● *vt* bombarder.

**blob** /blɒb/ *n* (drop) (grosse) goutte *f*; (stain) tache *f*.

**border** /ˈbɔːdə(r)/ *n* (edge) bord *m*; (frontier) frontière *f*; (in garden) bordure *f*. ● *vi* ~ **on** être voisin de, avoisiner.

**bore** /bɔː(r)/ *vt* ennuyer; **be ~d** s'ennuyer; ⇒BEAR. ● *vi* (Tech) forer. ● *n* raseur/-euse *m*/*f*; (thing) ennui *m*. **boredom** *n* ennui *m*. **boring** *a* ennuyeux.

**born** /bɔːn/ *a* né; **be ~** naître.

**borne** /bɔːn/ ⇒BEAR.

**borough** /ˈbʌrə/ *n* municipalité *f*.

**borrow** /ˈbɒrəʊ/ *vt* emprunter (**from** à).

**Bosnia** /ˈbɒznɪə/ *n* Bosnie *f*.

**Bosnian** /ˈbɒznɪən/ *a* bosniaque. ● *n* Bosniaque.

**bosom** /ˈbʊzəm/ *n* poitrine *f*; **~ friend** ami/-e *m*/*f* intime.

**boss** /bɒs/ *n* [!] patron/-ne *m*/*f*. ● *vt* **~ (about)** [!] mener par le bout du nez.

**bossy** /ˈbɒsɪ/ *a* autoritaire.

**botch** /bɒtʃ/ *vt* bâcler, saboter.

**both** /bəʊθ/ *det* les deux; **~ the books** les deux livres. ● *pron* tous/toutes (les) deux, l'un/-e et l'autre; **we ~ agree** nous sommes tous les deux d'accord; **I bought ~ (of them)** j'ai acheté les deux; **I saw ~ of you** je vous ai vus tous les deux; **~ Paul and Anne** (et) Paul et Anne. ● *adv* à la fois.

**bother** /ˈbɒðə(r)/ *vt* (annoy, worry) ennuyer; (disturb) déranger. ● *vi* se déranger; **don't ~ (calling)** ce n'est pas la peine (d'appeler); **don't ~ about us** ne t'inquiète pas pour nous; **I can't be ~ed** j'ai la flemme [!]. ● *n* ennui *m*; (effort) peine *f*; **it's no ~** ce n'est rien.

**bottle** /ˈbɒtl/ *n* bouteille *f*; (for baby) biberon *m*. ● *vt* mettre en bouteille. □ **~ up** contenir. **~ bank** *n* collecteur *m* (*de verre usagé*). **~neck** *n* (traffic jam) embouteillage *m*. **~-opener** *n* ouvre-bouteilles *m inv*.

**bottom** /ˈbɒtəm/ *n* fond *m*; (of hill, page, etc.) bas *m*; (buttocks) derrière *m* [!]. ● *a* inférieur, du bas.

**bought** /bɔːt/ ⇒BUY.

**bounce** /baʊns/ *vi* rebondir; (*person*) faire des bonds, bondir; (*cheques* [✖]) être refusé. ● *vt* faire rebondir. ● *n* rebond *m*.

**bound** /baʊnd/ *vi* (leap) bondir; **~ed by** limité par; ⇒BIND. ● *n* bond *m*. ● *a* **be ~ for** être en route pour, aller vers; **~ to** (obliged) obligé de; (certain) sûr de.

**boundary** /ˈbaʊndrɪ/ *n* limite *f*.

**bounds** /baʊndz/ *npl* limites *fpl*; **out of ~** être interdit d'accès.

**bout** /baʊt/ *n* période *f*; (Med) accès *m*; (boxing) combat *m*.

**bow¹** /bəʊ/ *n* (weapon) arc *m*; (of violin) archet *m*; (knot) nœud *m*.

**bow²** /baʊ/ *n* salut *m*; (of ship) proue *f*. ● *vt*/*i* (s')incliner.

**bowels** /ˈbaʊəlz/ *npl* intestins *mpl*; (fig) profondeurs *fpl*.

**bowl** /bəʊl/ *n* (for washing) cuvette *f*; (for food) bol *m*; (for soup) assiette *f* creuse. ● *vt*/*i* (cricket) lancer; **~ over** bouleverser.

**bowler** /ˈbəʊlə(r)/ *n* (cricket) lanceur *m*; **~ (hat)** (chapeau) melon *m*.

**bowling** /ˈbəʊlɪŋ/ *n* (ten-pin) bowling *m*; (on grass) jeu *m* de boules. **~-alley** *n* bowling *m*.

**bow-tie** /bəʊˈtaɪ/ *n* nœud *m* papillon.

**box** /bɒks/ *n* boîte *f*; (*cardboard*) carton *m*; (Theat) loge *f*; **the ~** [!] la télé. ● *vt* mettre en boîte; (Sport) boxer; **~ sb's ears** gifler qn; **~ in** enfermer.

**boxing** /'bɒksɪŋ/ *n* boxe *f*. ● *a* de boxe. **B~ Day** *n* le lendemain de Noël.

**box office** /'bɒks ɒfɪs/ *n* guichet *m*.

**boy** /bɔɪ/ *n* garçon *m*.

**boycott** /'bɔɪkɒt/ *vt* boycotter. ● *n* boycottage *m*.

**boyfriend** *n* (petit) ami *m*.

**bra** /brɑː/ *n* soutien-gorge *m*.

**brace** /breɪs/ *n* (fastener) attache *f*; (dental) appareil *m*; (tool) vilbrequin *m*; **~s** (for trousers) bretelles *fpl*. ● *vt* soutenir; **~ oneself** rassembler ses forces.

**bracket** /'brækɪt/ *n* (for shelf etc.) tasseau *m*, support *m*; (group) tranche *f*; **in ~s** entre parenthèses. ● *vt* mettre entre parenthèses *or* crochets.

**braid** /breɪd/ *n* (trimming) galon *m*; (of hair) tresse *f*.

**brain** /breɪn/ *n* cerveau *m*; **~s** (fig) intelligence *f*. ● *vt* assommer. **brainless** *a* stupide. **~wash** *vt* faire subir un lavage de cerveau à. **~wave** *n* idée *f* géniale, trouvaille *f*. **brainy** *a* (**-ier**, **-iest**) doué.

**brake** /breɪk/ *n* (Auto *also* fig) frein *m*. ● *vt/i* freiner. **~ light** *n* feu *m* stop.

**bran** /bræn/ *n* son *m*.

**branch** /brɑːntʃ/ *n* (of tree) branche *f*; (of road) embranchement *m*; (Comm) succursale *f*; (of bank) agence *f*. ● *vi* **~ (off)** bifurquer.

**brand** /brænd/ *n* marque *f*. ● *vt* **~ sb as** désigner qn comme qch.

**brand-new** /brænd'njuː/ *a* tout neuf.

**brandy** /'brændɪ/ *n* cognac *m*.

**brass** /brɑːs/ *n* cuivre *m*; **get down to ~ tacks** en venir aux choses sérieuses; **the ~** (Mus) les cuivres *mpl*; **top ~** [✱] galonnés *mpl*.

**brat** /bræt/ *n* [!] môme *mf* [!].

**brave** /breɪv/ *a* courageux; (*smile*) brave. ● *n* (American Indian) brave *m*. ● *vt* braver. **bravery** *n* courage *m*.

**brawl** /brɔːl/ *n* bagarre *f*. ● *vi* se bagarrer.

**Brazil** /brə'zɪl/ *n* Brésil *m*.

**breach** /briːtʃ/ *n* (of copyright, privilege) violation *f*; (in relationship) rupture *f*; (gap) brèche *f*. ● *vt* ouvrir une brèche dans.

**bread** /bred/ *n* pain *m*; **~ and butter** tartine *f*. **~-bin**, (US) **~-box** *n* boîte *f* à pain. **~crumbs** *npl* chapelure *f*.

**breadth** /bretθ/ *n* largeur *f*.

**bread-winner** /'bredwɪnə(r)/ *n* soutien *m* de famille.

**break** /breɪk/ *vt* (*pt* **broke**, *pp* **broken**) casser; (smash into pieces) briser; (*vow, silence, rank, etc.*) rompre; (*law*) violer; (*a record*) battre; (*news*) révéler; (*journey*) interrompre; (*heart, strike, ice*) briser; **~ one's arm** se casser le bras. ● *vi* (se) casser; se briser. ● *n* cassure *f*, rupture *f*; (in relationship, continuity) rupture *f*; (interval) interruption *f*; (at school) récréation *f*, récré *f*; (for coffee) pause *f*; (luck [!]) chance *f*. □ **~ away from** se détacher; **~ down** *vi* (collapse) s'effondrer; (*negotiations*) échouer; (machine) tomber en panne; *vt* (*door*) enfoncer; (analyse) analyser; **~ even** rentrer dans ses frais; **~ into** cambrioler; **~ off** (se) détacher; (suspend) rompre; (stop talking) s'interrompre; **~ out** (*fire, war, etc.*) éclater; **~ up** (end) (faire) cesser; (*couple*) rompre; (*marriage*) (se) briser; (*crowd*) (se) disperser; (*schools*) être en vacances. **breakable** *a* fragile. **breakage** *n* casse *f*.

**breakdown** /ˈbreɪkdaʊn/ *n* (Tech) panne *f*; (Med) dépression *f*; (of figures) analyse *f*. ● *a* (Auto) de dépannage.

**breakfast** /ˈbrekfəst/ *n* petit déjeuner *m*.

**break**: **~-in** *n* cambriolage *m*. **~through** *n* percée *f*.

**breast** /brest/ *n* sein *m*; (chest) poitrine *f*. **~-feed** *vt* (*pt* **-fed**) allaiter. **~-stroke** *n* brasse *f*.

**breath** /breθ/ *n* souffle *m*, haleine *f*; **out of ~** à bout de souffle; **under one's ~** tout bas.

**breathalyser**® /ˈbreθəlaɪzə(r)/ *n* alcootest *m*.

**breathe** /bri:ð/ *vt*/*i* respirer. □ **~ in** inspirer; **~ out** expirer.

**breathless** /ˈbreθlɪs/ *a* à bout de souffle.

**breathtaking** /ˈbreθteɪkɪŋ/ *a* à vous couper le souffle.

**bred** /bred/ ⇒BREED.

**breed** /bri:d/ *vt* (*pt* **bred**) élever; (give rise to) engendrer. ● *vi* se reproduire. ● *n* race *f*.

**breeze** /bri:z/ *n* brise *f*.

**brew** /bru:/ *vt* (*beer*) brasser; (*tea*) faire infuser. ● *vi* (*beer*) fermenter; (*tea*) infuser; (fig) se préparer. ● *n* décoction *f*. **brewer** *n* brasseur *m*. **brewery** *n* brasserie *f*.

**bribe** /braɪb/ *n* pot-de-vin *m*. ● *vt* soudoyer. **bribery** *n* corruption *f*.

**brick** /brɪk/ *n* brique *f*. **~layer** *n* maçon *m*.

**bridal** /ˈbraɪdl/ *a* (*dress*) de mariée; (*car, chamber*) des mariés.

**bride** /braɪd/ *n* mariée *f*. **~groom** *n* marié *m*. **~smaid** *n* demoiselle *f* d'honneur.

**bridge** /brɪdʒ/ *n* pont *m*; (Naut) passerelle *f*; (of nose) arête *f*; (card game) bridge *m*. ● *vt* **~ a gap** combler une lacune.

**bridle** /ˈbraɪdl/ *n* bride *f*. ● *vt* brider. **~-path** *n* piste *f* cavalière.

**brief** /bri:f/ *a* bref. ● *n* instructions *fpl*; (Jur) dossier *m*. ● *vt* donner des instructions à.

**briefcase** /ˈbri:fkeɪs/ *n* serviette *f*.

**briefs** /bri:fs/ *npl* slip *m*.

**bright** /braɪt/ *a* brillant, vif; (*day, room*) clair; (cheerful) gai; (clever) intelligent.

**brighten** /ˈbraɪtn/ *vt* égayer. ● *vi* (*weather*) s'éclaircir; (*face*) s'éclairer.

**brilliant** /ˈbrɪljənt/ *a* (*student, career*) brillant; (*light*) éclatant; (very good ⓘ) super.

**brim** /brɪm/ *n* bord *m*. ● *vi* (*pt* **brimmed**); **~ over** déborder (**with** de).

**bring** /brɪŋ/ *vt* (*pt* **brought**) (*thing*) apporter; (*person, vehicle*) amener; **~ to bear** (*pressure etc.*) exercer. □ **~ about** provoquer; **~ back** (return with) rapporter; (*colour, shine*) redonner; **~ down** faire tomber; (shoot down, knock down) abattre; **~ forward** avancer; **~ off** réussir; **~ out** (take out) sortir; (show) faire ressortir; (book) publier; **~ round** faire revenir à soi; **~ up** (*child*) élever; (Med) vomir; (*question*) aborder.

**brink** /brɪŋk/ *n* bord *m*.

**brisk** /brɪsk/ *a* vif.

**bristle** /ˈbrɪsl/ *n* poil *m*. ● *vi* se hérisser; **bristling with** hérissé de.

**Britain** /ˈbrɪtn/ *n* Grande-Bretagne *f*.

**British** /ˈbrɪtɪʃ/ *a* britannique; **the ~** les Britanniques *mpl*.

**Briton** /ˈbrɪtn/ *n* Britannique *mf*.

**Brittany** /ˈbrɪtənɪ/ *n* Bretagne *f*.

**brittle** /ˈbrɪtl/ *a* fragile.

**broad** /brɔ:d/ *a* large; (*choice, range*) grand.

**broadcast** /'brɔ:dkɑ:st/ *vt/i* (*pt* **broadcast**) diffuser; (person) parler à la télévision *or* à la radio. ● *n* émission *f*.

**broadly** /'brɔ:dlɪ/ *adv* en gros.

**broad-minded** /brɔ:d'maɪndɪd/ *a* large d'esprit.

**broccoli** /'brɒkəlɪ/ *n inv* brocoli *m*.

**brochure** /'brəʊʃə(r)/ *n* brochure *f*.

**broke** /brəʊk/ ⇒BREAK. ● *a* (penniless ⊠) fauché.

**broken** /'brəʊkən/ ⇒BREAK. ● *a* ~ **English** mauvais anglais *m*.

**bronchitis** /brɒŋ'kaɪtɪs/ *n* bronchite *f*.

**bronze** /brɒnz/ *n* bronze *m*.

**brooch** /brəʊtʃ/ *n* broche *f*.

**brood** /bru:d/ *n* nichée *f*, couvée *f*. ● *vi* méditer tristement.

**broom** /bru:m/ *n* balai *m*.

**broth** /brɒθ/ *n* bouillon *m*.

**brothel** /'brɒθl/ *n* maison *f* close.

**brother** /'brʌðə(r)/ *n* frère *m*. **~hood** *n* fraternité *f*. **~-in-law** *n* (*pl* **~s-in-law**) beau-frère *m*.

**brought** /brɔ:t/ ⇒BRING.

**brow** /braʊ/ *n* front *m*; (of hill) sommet *m*.

**brown** /braʊn/ *a* (*object*) marron; (*hair*) brun; ~ **bread** pain *m* complet; ~ **sugar** sucre *m* roux. ● *n* marron *m*; brun *m*. ● *vt/i* brunir; (Culin) (faire) dorer.

**Brownie** /'braʊnɪ/ *n* jeannette *f*.

**browse** /braʊz/ *vi* flâner; (*animal*) brouter. ● *vt* (Comput) naviguer. **browser** *n* (Comput) navigateur *m*.

**bruise** /bru:z/ *n* bleu *m*. ● *vt* (*knee, arm etc.*) faire un bleu à; (*fruit*) abîmer.

**brush** /brʌʃ/ *n* brosse *f*; (skirmish) accrochage *m*; (bushes) broussailles *fpl*. ● *vt* brosser. □ ~ **against** frôler; ~ **aside** (dismiss) repousser; (move) écarter; ~ **up (on)** se remettre à.

**Brussels** /'brʌslz/ *n* Bruxelles. ~ **sprouts** *npl* choux *mpl* de Bruxelles.

**brutal** /'bru:tl/ *a* brutal.

**brute** /bru:t/ *n* brute *f*; **by ~ force** par la force.

**BSE** *abbr* (**bovine spongiform encephalopathy**) encéphalopathie *f* spongiforme bovine, ESB *f*.

**bubble** /'bʌbl/ *n* bulle *f*; **blow ~s** faire des bulles. ● *vi* bouillonner; ~ **over** déborder. ~ **bath** *n* bain *m* moussant.

**buck** /bʌk/ *n* mâle *m*; (US, ⊠) dollar *m*; **pass the ~** rejeter la responsabilité (**to** sur). ● *vi* (*horse*) ruer; ~ **up** ⊠ prendre courage; (hurry ⊠) se grouiller ⓘ.

**bucket** /'bʌkɪt/ *n* seau *m* (**of** de).

**buckle** /'bʌkl/ *n* boucle *f*. ● *vt/i* (fasten) (se) boucler; (bend) voiler.

**bud** /bʌd/ *n* bourgeon *m*. ● *vi* (*pt* **budded**) bourgeonner.

**Buddhism** /'bʊdɪzəm/ *n* bouddhisme *m*.

**budding** /'bʌdɪŋ/ *a* (*talent*) naissant; (*athlete*) en herbe.

**budge** /bʌdʒ/ *vt/i* (faire) bouger.

**budgerigar** /'bʌdʒərɪgɑ:(r)/ *n* perruche *f*.

**budget** /'bʌdʒɪt/ *n* budget *m*. ● *vi* ~ **for** prévoir (dans son budget).

**buff** /bʌf/ *n* (colour) chamois *m*; ⓘ fanatique *mf*.

**buffalo** /'bʌfələʊ/ *n* (*pl* **-oes** *or* **-o**) buffle *m*; (US) bison *m*.

**buffer** /'bʌfə(r)/ *n* tampon *m*; ~ **zone** zone *f* tampon.

**buffet**[1] /'bʊfeɪ/ *n* (meal, counter) buffet *m*; ~ **car** buffet *m*.

**buffet²** /ˈbʌfɪt/ *n* (blow) soufflet *m*. ● *vt* (*pt* **buffeted**) souffleter.

**bug** /bʌg/ *n* (bedbug) punaise *f*; (any small insect) bestiole *f*; (germ) microbe *m*; (stomachache [I]) ennuis *mpl* gastriques; (device) micro *m*; (defect) défaut *m*; (Comput) bogue *f*, bug *m*. ● *vt* (*pt* **bugged**) mettre des micros dans; ⊠ embêter.

**buggy** /ˈbʌgɪ/ *n* poussette *f*.

**build** /bɪld/ *vt*/*i* (*pt* **built**) bâtir, construire. ● *n* carrure *f*. □ **~ up** (increase) augmenter, monter; (accumulate) (s')accumuler. **builder** *n* entrepreneur *m* en bâtiment; (workman) ouvrier *m* du bâtiment.

**building** /ˈbɪldɪŋ/ *n* (structure) bâtiment *m*; (dwelling) immeuble *m*. **~ society** *n* caisse *f* d'épargne.

**build-up** /ˈbɪldʌp/ *n* accumulation *f*; (fig) publicité *f*.

**built** /bɪlt/ ⇒BUILD.

**built-in** *a* encastré.

**built-up area** *a* agglomération *f*, zone *f* urbanisée.

**bulb** /bʌlb/ *n* (Bot) bulbe *m*; (Electr) ampoule *f*.

**Bulgaria** /bʌlˈgeərɪə/ *n* Bulgarie *f*.

**Bulgarian** /bʌlˈgeərɪən/ *n* (person) Bulgare *mf*; (Ling) bulgare *m*. ● *a* bulgare.

**bulge** /bʌldʒ/ *n* renflement *m*. ● *vi* se renfler, être renflé; **be bulging with** être gonflé *or* bourré de.

**bulimia** /bju:ˈlɪmɪə/ *n* boulimie *f*.

**bulk** /bʌlk/ *n* volume *f*; **in ~** (*buy, sell*) en gros; (transport) en vrac; **the ~ of** la majeure partie de.

**bull** /bʊl/ *n* taureau *m*. **~dog** *n* bouledogue *m*. **~doze** *vt* raser au bulldozer.

**bullet** /ˈbʊlɪt/ *n* balle *f*.

**bulletin** /ˈbʊlətɪn/ *n* bulletin *m*.

**bullet-proof** /ˈbʊlɪtpruf/ *a* (*vest*) pare-balles *inv*; (*vehicle*) blindé.

**bullfight** /ˈbʊlfaɪt/ *n* corrida *f*.

**bullion** /ˈbʊljən/ *n* or *m or* argent *m* en lingots.

**bullring** /ˈbʊlrɪŋ/ *n* arène *f*.

**bull's-eye** /ˈbʊlzaɪ/ *n* mille *m*.

**bully** /ˈbʊlɪ/ *n* (child) petite brute *f*; (adult) tyran *m*. ● *vt* maltraiter.

**bum** /bʌm/ *n* ⊠ derrière *m* [I]; (US, ⊠) vagabond/-e *m*/*f*.

**bumble-bee** /ˈbʌmblbi:/ *n* bourdon *m*.

**bump** /bʌmp/ *n* (swelling) bosse *f*; (on road) bosse *f*. ● *vt*/*i* cogner, heurter. □ **~ along** cahoter; **~ into** (hit) rentrer dans; (meet) tomber sur.

**bumper** /ˈbʌmpə(r)/ *n* pare-chocs *m inv*. ● *a* exceptionnel.

**bumpy** /ˈbʌmpɪ/ *a* (*road*) accidenté.

**bun** /bʌn/ *n* (cake) petit pain *m*; (hair) chignon *m*.

**bunch** /bʌntʃ/ *n* (of flowers) bouquet *m*; (of keys) trousseau *m*; (of people) groupe *m*; (of bananas) régime *m*; **~ of grapes** grappe *f* de raisin.

**bundle** /ˈbʌndl/ *n* paquet *m*. ● *vt* mettre en paquet; (push) fourrer.

**bung** /bʌŋ/ *n* bouchon *m*. ● *vt* (stop up) boucher; (throw ⊠) flanquer [I]

**bunion** /ˈbʌnjən/ *n* (Med) oignon *m*.

**bunk** /bʌŋk/ *n* (on ship, train) couchette *f*. **~-beds** *npl* lits *mpl* superposés.

**buoy** /bɔɪ/ *n* bouée *f*. ● *vt* **~ up** (hearten) soutenir, encourager.

**buoyancy** /ˈbɔɪənsɪ/ *n* (of floating object) flottabilité *f*; (cheerfulness) gaieté *f*.

**burden** /ˈbɜ:dn/ *n* fardeau *m*. ● *vt* ennuyer (**with** de).

**bureau** /ˈbjʊərəʊ/ *n* (*pl* **-eaux** /-əʊz/) bureau *m*.

**bureaucracy** /bjʊəˈrɒkrəsɪ/ *n* bureaucratie *f*.

**burglar** /ˈbɜ:glə(r)/ *n* cambrioleur *m*; **~ alarm** alarme *f*. **burglarize**

*vt* (US) cambrioler. **burglary** *n* cambriolage *m*. **burgle** *vt* cambrioler.

**Burgundy** /'bɜ:gəndɪ/ *n* (wine) bourgogne *m*.

**burial** /'berɪəl/ *n* enterrement *m*.

**burn** /bɜ:n/ *vt*/*i* (*pt* **burned** *or* **burnt**) brûler. ● *n* brûlure *f*. □ ~ **down** être réduit en cendres. **burning** *a* en flammes; (fig) brûlant.

**burnt** /bɜ:nt/ ⇒BURN.

**burp** /bɜ:p/ *n* [I] rot *m*. ● *vi* [I] roter.

**burrow** /'bʌrəʊ/ *n* terrier *m*. ● *vt* creuser.

**bursar** /'bɜ:sə(r)/ *n* intendant/-e *m*/*f*. **bursary** *n* bourse *f*.

**burst** /bɜ:st/ *vt*/*i* (*pt* **burst**) (*balloon, bubble*) crever; (*pipe*) (faire) éclater. ● *n* explosion *f*; (of laughter) éclat *m*; (surge) élan *m*. □ ~ **into** (*room*) faire interruption dans; ~ **into tears** fondre en larmes; ~ **out** ~ **out laughing** éclater de rire; ~ **with be** ~**ing with** déborder de.

**bury** /'berɪ/ *vt* (*person etc.*) enterrer; (hide, cover) enfouir; (engross, thrust) plonger.

**bus** /bʌs/ *n* (*pl* **buses**) (auto)bus *m*. ● *vt* transporter en bus. ● *vi* (*pt* **bussed**) prendre l'autobus.

**bush** /bʊʃ/ *n* (shrub) buisson *m*; (land) brousse *f*.

**business** /'bɪznɪs/ *n* (task, concern) affaire *f*; (commerce) affaires *fpl*; (line of work) métier *m*; (shop) commerce *m*; **he has no** ~ **to** il n'a pas le droit de; **mean** ~ être sérieux; **that's none of your** ~! ça ne vous regarde pas! ~**like** *a* sérieux. ~**man** *n* homme *m* d'affaires.

**busker** /'bʌskə(r)/ *n* musicien/-ne *m*/*f* des rues.

**bus-stop** /'bʌstɒp/ *n* arrêt *m* d'autobus.

**bust** /bʌst/ *n* (statue) buste *m*; (bosom) poitrine *f*. ● *vt*/*i* (*pt* **busted** *or* **bust**) (burst ⊠) crever; (break ⊠) (se) casser. ● *a* (broken, finished ⊠) fichu; **go** ~ ⊠ faire faillite.

**bustle** /'bʌsl/ *vi* s'affairer. ● *n* affairement *m*, remue-ménage *m*.

**busy** /'bɪzɪ/ *a* (**-ier**, **-iest**) (*person*) occupé; (*street*) animé; (*day*) chargé. ● *vt* ~ **oneself with** s'occuper à.

**but** /bʌt, bət/ *conj* mais. ● *prep* sauf; ~ **for** sans; **nobody** ~ personne d'autre que; **nothing** ~ rien que. ● *adv* (only) seulement.

**butcher** /'bʊtʃə(r)/ *n* boucher *m*. ● *vt* massacrer.

**butler** /'bʌtlə(r)/ *n* maître *m* d'hôtel.

**butt** /bʌt/ *n* (of gun) crosse *f*; (of cigarette) mégot *m*; (of joke) cible *f*; (barrel) tonneau *m*; (US, [I]) derrière *m* [I]. ● *vi* ~ **in** interrompre.

**butter** /'bʌtə(r)/ *n* beurre *m*. ● *vt* beurrer. ~**-bean** *n* haricot *m* blanc. ~**cup** *n* bouton-d'or *m*.

**butterfly** /'bʌtəflaɪ/ *n* papillon *m*.

**buttock** /'bʌtək/ *n* fesse *f*.

**button** /'bʌtn/ *n* bouton *m*. ● *vt*/*i* ~ **(up)** (se) boutonner.

**buttonhole** /'bʌtnhəʊl/ *n* boutonnière *f*. ● *vt* accrocher.

**buy** /baɪ/ *vt* (*pt* **bought**) acheter (**from** à); ~ **sth for sb** acheter qch à qn, prendre qch pour qn; (believe ⊠) croire, avaler.

**buzz** /bʌz/ *n* bourdonnement *m*. ● *vi* bourdonner. **buzzer** *n* sonnerie *f*.

**by** /baɪ/ *prep* par, de; (near) à côté de; (before) avant; (means) en, à, par; ~ **bike** à vélo; ~ **car** en auto; ~ **day** de jour; ~ **the kilo** au kilo; ~ **running** en courant; ~ **sea** par mer; ~ **that time** à ce moment-là; ~ **the way** à propos; ~ **oneself** tout seul. ● *adv*

close ~ tout près; ~ **and large** dans l'ensemble.

**bye(-bye)** /haɪ('baɪ)/ *interj* ⓘ au revoir, salut ⓘ.

**by-election** *n* élection *f* partielle.

**Byelorussia** /bjeləʊ'rʊʃə/ *n* Biélorussie *f*.

**by-law** *n* arrêté *m* municipal.

**bypass** /'baɪpɑ:s/ *n* (Auto) rocade *f*; (Med) pontage *m*. ● *vt* contourner.

**by-product** *n* dérivé *m*; (fig) conséquence *f*.

**byte** /baɪt/ *n* octet *m*.

# Cc

**cab** /kæb/ *n* taxi *m*; (of lorry, train) cabine *f*.

**cabbage** /'kæbɪdʒ/ *n* chou *m*.

**cabin** /'kæbɪn/ *n* (hut) cabane *f*; (in ship, aircraft) cabine *f*.

**cabinet** /'kæbɪnɪt/ *n* petit placard *m*; (glass-fronted) vitrine *f*; (Pol) cabinet *m*.

**cable** /'keɪbl/ *n* câble *m*. ● *vt* câbler. ~**-car** *n* téléphérique *m*. ~ **television** *n* télévision *f* par câble.

**cache** /kæʃ/ *n* (hoard) cache *f*; (place) cachette *f*.

**cackle** /'kækl/ *n* (of hen) caquet *m*; (laugh) ricanement *m*. ● *vi* caqueter; (laugh) ricaner.

**cactus** /'kæktəs/ *n* (*pl* **-ti** /-taɪ/ *or* ~**es**) cactus *m*.

**cadet** /kə'det/ *n* élève *m* officier.

**Caesarean** /sɪ'zeərɪən/ *a* ~ **(section)** césarienne *f*.

**café** /'kæfeɪ/ *n* café *m*, snack-bar *m*.

**caffeine** /'kæfi:n/ *n* caféine *f*.

**cage** /keɪdʒ/ *n* cage *f*. ● *vt* mettre en cage.

**cagey** /'keɪdʒɪ/ *a* réticent.

**cagoule** /kə'gu:l/ *n* K-way® *m*.

**cajole** /kə'dʒəʊl/ *vt* ~ **sb into doing sth** amener qn à faire qch par la cajolerie.

**cake** /keɪk/ *n* gâteau *m*; (of soap) pain *m*. ● *vi* former une croûte (**on** sur).

**calculate** /'kælkjʊleɪt/ *vt* calculer; (estimate) évaluer. **calculated** *a* délibéré; (*risk*) calculé. **calculating** *a* calculateur. **calculation** *n* calcul *m*. **calculator** *n* calculatrice *f*.

**calculus** /'kælkjʊləs/ *n* (*pl* **-li** /-laɪ/ *or* ~**es**) calcul *m*.

**calendar** /'kælɪndə(r)/ *n* calendrier *m*.

**calf** /kɑ:f/ *n* (*pl* **calves**) (young cow or bull) veau *m*; (of leg) mollet *m*.

**calibre** /'kælɪbə(r)/ *n* calibre *m*.

**call** /kɔ:l/ *vt/i* appeler; (loudly) crier; **he's ~ed John** il s'appelle John; ~ **sb stupid** traiter qn d'imbécile. ● *n* appel *m*; (of bird) cri *m*; (visit) visite *f*; **make/pay a ~ on** rendre visite à; **be on ~** être de garde; ~ **box** cabine *f* téléphonique. □ ~ **back** rappeler; (visit) repasser; ~ **for** (*help*) appeler à; (demand) demander; (require) exiger; (collect) passer prendre; ~ **in** passer; ~ **off** annuler; ~ **on** (visit) rendre visite à; (urge) demander à (**to do** de faire); ~ **out** (**to**) appeler; ~ **round** venir; ~ **up** appeler.

**calling** /'kɔ:lɪŋ/ *n* vocation *f*.

**callous** /'kæləs/ *a* inhumain.

**calm** /kɑ:m/ *a* calme. ● *n* calme *m*. ● *vt/i* ~ **(down)** (se) calmer.

**calorie** /'kælərɪ/ *n* calorie *f.*

**camcorder** /'kæmkɔ:də(r)/ *n* caméscope® *m.*

**came** /keɪm/ ⇨COME.

**camel** /'kæml/ *n* chameau *m.*

**camera** /'kæmərə/ *n* appareil(-photo) *m*; (TV, cinema) caméra *f*; **in ~** à huis clos. **~man** *n* (*pl* **-men**) cadreur *m*, cameraman *m.*

**camouflage** /'kæməflɑ:ʒ/ *n* camouflage *m.* ● *vt* camoufler.

**camp** /kæmp/ *n* camp *m.* ● *vi* camper.

**campaign** /kæm'peɪn/ *n* campagne *f.* ● *vi* faire campagne.

**camper** /'kæmpə(r)/ *n* campeur/-euse *m/f.* **~(-van)** *n* camping-car *m.*

**camping** /'kæmpɪŋ/ *n* camping *m*; **go ~** faire du camping.

**campsite** /'kæmpsaɪt/ *n* camping *m.*

**campus** /'kæmpəs/ *n* (*pl* **~es**) campus *m.*

---

**can¹** /kæn, kən/

*infinitive* **be able to**; *present* **can**; *present negative* **can't**, **cannot** (*formal*); *past* **could**; *past participle* **been able to**

● *auxiliary verb*

····➤ pouvoir; **where ~ I buy stamps?** où est-ce que je peux acheter des timbres?; **she can't come** elle ne peut pas venir.

····➤ (be allowed to) pouvoir; **~ I smoke?** est-ce que je peux fumer?

····➤ (know how to) savoir; **she ~ swim** elle sait nager; **he can't drive** il ne sait pas conduire.

····➤ (with verbs of perception) **I ~ hear you** je t'entends; **~ they see us?** est-ce qu'ils nous voient?

---

**can²** /kæn/ *n* (for food) boîte *f*; (of petrol) bidon *m.* ● *vt* (*pt* **canned**) mettre en conserve.

**Canada** /'kænədə/ *n* Canada *m.*

**Canadian** /kə'neɪdɪən/ *n* Canadien/-ne *m/f.* ● *a* canadien.

**canal** /kə'næl/ *n* canal *m.*

**canary** /kə'neərɪ/ *n* canari *m.*

**cancel** /'kænsl/ *vt/i* (*pt* **cancelled**) (call off, revoke) annuler; (cross out) barrer; (a stamp) oblitérer; **~ out** (se) neutraliser. **cancellation** *n* annulation *f.*

**cancer** /'kænsə(r)/ *n* cancer *m*; **have ~** avoir un cancer.

**Cancer** /'kænsə(r)/ *n* Cancer *m.*

**cancerous** /'kænsərəs/ *a* cancéreux.

**candid** /'kændɪd/ *a* franc.

**candidate** /'kændɪdət/ *n* candidat/-e *m/f.*

**candle** /'kændl/ *n* bougie *f*; (in church) cierge *m.* **~stick** *n* bougeoir *m.*

**candy** /'kændɪ/ *n* (US) bonbon(s) *m(pl).* **~-floss** *n* barbe *f* à papa.

**cane** /keɪn/ *n* canne *f*; (for baskets) rotin *m*; (for punishment) badine *f.* ● *vt* donner des coups de badine à.

**canister** /'kænɪstə(r)/ *n* boîte *f.*

**cannabis** /'kænəbɪs/ *n* cannabis *m.*

**cannibal** /'kænɪbl/ *n* cannibale *mf.*

**cannon** /'kænən/ *n* (*pl* **~** *or* **~s**) canon *m.* **~-ball** *n* boulet *m* de canon.

**cannot** /'kænət/ = CAN NOT.

**canoe** /kə'nu:/ *n* canoë *m.* ● *vi* faire du canoë. **canoeist** *n* canoéiste *mf.*

**canon** /'kænən/ *n* (clergyman) chanoine *m*; (rule) canon *m*.

**can-opener** *n* ouvre-boîtes *m inv*.

**canopy** /'kænəpɪ/ *n* dais *m*; (for bed) baldaquin *m*.

**can't** /kɑ:nt/ = CAN NOT.

**canteen** /kæn'ti:n/ *n* (restaurant) cantine *f*; (flask) bidon *m*.

**canter** /'kæntə(r)/ *n* petit galop *m*. ● *vi* aller au petit galop.

**canvas** /'kænvəs/ *n* toile *f*.

**canvass** /'kænvəs/ *vt/i* (Comm, Pol) faire du démarchage (auprès de); ~ **opinion** sonder l'opinion.

**canyon** /'kænjən/ *n* cañon *m*.

**cap** /kæp/ *n* (hat) casquette *f*; (of bottle, tube) bouchon *m*; (of beer or milk bottle) capsule *f*; (of pen) capuchon *m*; (for toy gun) amorce *f*. ● *vt* (*pt* **capped**) couronner.

**capability** /keɪpə'bɪlətɪ/ *n* capacité *f*.

**capable** /'keɪpəbl/ *a* (person) compétent; ~ **of doing** capable de faire.

**capacity** /kə'pæsətɪ/ *n* capacité *f*; **in my** ~ **as a doctor** en ma qualité de médecin.

**cape** /keɪp/ *n* (cloak) cape *f*; (Geog) cap *m*.

**caper** /'keɪpə(r)/ *vi* gambader. ● *n* (leap) cabriole *f*; (funny film) comédie *f*; (Culin) câpre *f*.

**capital** /'kæpɪtl/ *a* (*letter*) majuscule; (*offence*) capital. ● *n* (town) capitale *f*; (money) capital *m*; ~ **(letter)** majuscule *f*.

**capitalism** /'kæpɪtəlɪzəm/ *n* capitalisme *m*.

**capitalize** /'kæpɪtəlaɪz/ *vi* ~ **on** tirer parti de.

**capitulate** /kə'pɪtʃʊleɪt/ *vi* capituler.

**Capricorn** /'kæprɪkɔ:n/ *n* Capricorne *m*.

**capsize** /kæp'saɪz/ *vt/i* (faire) chavirer.

**capsule** /'kæpsju:l/ *n* capsule *f*.

**captain** /'kæptɪn/ *n* capitaine *m*.

**caption** /'kæpʃn/ *n* (under photo) légende *f*; (subtitle) sous-titre *m*.

**captivate** /'kæptɪveɪt/ *vt* captiver.

**captive** /'kæptɪv/ *a & n* captif/-ive (*m/f*). **captivity** *n* captivité *f*.

**capture** /'kæptʃə(r)/ *vt* (*person, animal*) capturer; (*moment, likeness*) saisir. ● *n* capture *f*.

**car** /kɑ:(r)/ *n* voiture *f*. ● *a* (*industry, insurance*) automobile; (*accident, phone*) de voiture; (*journey, chase*) en voiture.

**caravan** /'kærəvæn/ *n* caravane *f*.

**carbohydrate** /kɑ:bəʊ'haɪdreɪt/ *n* hydrate *m* de carbone.

**carbon** /'kɑ:bən/ *n* carbone *m*.

**carburettor** /kɑ:bjʊ'retə(r)/ *n* carburateur *m*.

**card** /kɑ:d/ *n* carte *f*.

**cardboard** /'kɑ:dbɔ:d/ *n* carton *m*.

**cardiac** /'kɑ:dɪæk/ *a* cardiaque; ~ **arrest** arrêt *m* du cœur.

**cardigan** /'kɑ:dɪgən/ *n* cardigan *m*.

**cardinal** /'kɑ:dɪnl/ *a* (*sin*) capital; (*rule*) fondamental; (*number*) cardinal. ● *n* cardinal *m*.

**card-index** *n* fichier *m*.

**care** /keə(r)/ *n* (attention) soin *m*, attention *f*; (worry) souci *m*; (looking after) soins *mpl*; **take** ~ **of** (deal with) s'occuper de; (be careful with) prendre soin de; **take** ~ **to do sth** faire bien attention à faire qch. ● *vi* ~ **about** s'intéresser à; ~ **for** s'occuper de; (invalid) soigner; ~ **to do** vouloir faire; **I don't** ~ ça m'est égal.

**career** /kə'rɪə(r)/ *n* carrière *f*. ● *vi* ~ **in/out** entrer/sortir à toute vitesse.

**carefree** /'keəfri:/ *a* insouciant

**careful** /'keəfl/ *a* prudent; (*research, work*) méticuleux; **(be)** ~! (fais) attention! **carefully** *adv* avec soin; (cautiously) prudemment.

**careless** /'keəlɪs/ *a* négligent; (work) bâclé.

**caress** /kə'res/ *n* caresse *f*. ● *vt* caresser.

**caretaker** /'keəteɪkə(r)/ *n* concierge *mf*. ● *a* (*president*) par intérim.

**car ferry** *n* ferry *m*.

**cargo** /'kɑ:gəʊ/ *n* (*pl* ~**es**) chargement *m*; (Naut) cargaison *f*.

**Caribbean** /kærɪ'bi:ən/ *a* des Caraïbes, des Antilles. ● *n* **the** ~ (sea) la mer des Antilles; (islands) les Antilles *fpl*.

**caring** /'keərɪŋ/ *a* affectueux.

**carnation** /kɑ:'neɪʃn/ *n* œillet *m*.

**carnival** /'kɑ:nɪvl/ *n* carnaval *m*.

**carol** /'kærəl/ *n* chant *m* de Noël.

**carp** /kɑ:p/ *n inv* carpe *f*. ● *vi* maugréer.

**car-park** *n* parc *m* de stationnement, parking *m*.

**carpenter** /'kɑ:pɪntə(r)/ *n* (joiner) menuisier *m*; (builder) charpentier *m*. **carpentry** *n* menuiserie *f*; (structural) charpenterie *f*.

**carpet** /'kɑ:pɪt/ *n* (fitted) moquette *f*; (loose) tapis *m*. ● *vt* (*pt* **carpeted**) mettre de la moquette dans.

**carriage** /'kærɪdʒ/ *n* (rail ) wagon *m*; (ceremonial) carrosse *m*; (of goods) transport *m*; (cost) port *m*.

**carriageway** /'kærɪdʒweɪ/ *n* chaussée *f*.

**carrier** /'kærɪə(r)/ *n* transporteur *m*; (Med) porteur/-euse *m/f*; ~ **(bag)** sac *m* en plastique.

**carrot** /'kærət/ *n* carotte *f*.

**carry** /'kærɪ/ *vt/i* porter; (*goods*) transporter; (*involve*) comporter; (*motion*) voter; **be carried away** s'emballer. □ ~ **off** emporter; (prize) remporter; ~ **on** (continue) continuer; (*business*) conduire; (*conversation*) mener; ~ **out** (*order, plan*) exécuter; (*duty*) remplir; (*experiment, operation, repair*) effectuer. ~**-cot** *n* porte-bébé *m*.

**car sharing** *n* covoiturage *m*.

**cart** /kɑ:t/ *n* charrette *f*. ● *vt* (*heavy bag* [I]) trimballer [I].

**carton** /'kɑ:tn/ *n* (box) boîte *f*; (of yoghurt, cream) pot *m*; (of cigarettes) cartouche *f*.

**cartoon** /kɑ:'tu:n/ *n* dessin *m* humoristique; (cinema) dessin *m* animé; (strip cartoon) bande *f* dessinée.

**cartridge** /'kɑ:trɪdʒ/ *n* cartouche *f*.

**carve** /kɑ:v/ *vt* tailler; (meat) découper.

**car-wash** *n* lavage *m* automatique.

**cascade** /kæs'keɪd/ *n* cascade *f*. ● *vi* tomber en cascade.

**case** /keɪs/ *n* cas *m*; (Jur) affaire *f*; (suitcase) valise *f*; (crate) caisse *f*; (for spectacles) étui *m*; **(just) in** ~ au cas où; **in** ~ **he comes** au cas où il viendrait; **in** ~ **of fire** en cas d'incendie; **in any** ~ de toute façon; **the** ~ **for sth** les arguments *mpl* en faveur de qch; **the** ~ **for the defence** la défense.

**cash** /kæʃ/ *n* espèces *fpl*, argent *m*; **in** ~ en espèces. ● *a* (*price*) comptant. ● *vt* encaisser; ~ **in (on)** profiter (de). ~**-back** *n* retrait *m* d'argent à la caisse. ~ **desk** *n*

caisse *f.* ~ **dispenser** *n* distributeur *m* de billets.

**cashew** /'kæʃu:/ *n* cajou *m.*

**cash-flow** *n* marge *f* brute d'autofinancement.

**cashier** /kæ'ʃɪə(r)/ *n* caissier/-ière *m/f.*

**cashmere** /'kæʃmɪə(r)/ *n* cachemire *m.*

**cash**: ~ **point** *n* distributeur *m* de billets. ~ **point card** *n* carte *f* de retrait. ~ **register** *n* caisse *f* enregistreuse.

**casino** /kə'si:nəʊ/ *n* casino *m.*

**casket** /'kɑ:skɪt/ *n* (box) coffret *m*; (coffin) cercueil *m.*

**casserole** /'kæsərəʊl/ *n* (pan) daubière *f*; (food) ragoût *m.*

**cassette** /kə'set/ *n* cassette *f.*

**cast** /kɑ:st/ *vt* (*pt* **cast**) (*object, glance*) jeter; (*shadow*) projeter; (*metal*) couler; ~ **(off)** (shed) se dépouiller de; ~ **one's vote** voter; ~ **iron** fonte *f.* ● *n* (cinema, Theat, TV) distribution *f*; (mould) moule *m*; (Med) plâtre *m.*

**castaway** /'kɑ:stəweɪ/ *n* naufragé/-e *m/f.*

**cast-iron** *a* de fonte; (fig) en béton.

**castle** /'kɑ:sl/ *n* château *m*; (chess) tour *f.*

**cast-offs** *npl* vieux vêtements *mpl.*

**castor** /'kɑ:stə(r)/ *n* (wheel) roulette *f.*

**castrate** /kæ'streɪt/ *vt* châtrer.

**casual** /'kæʒʊəl/ *a* (informal) décontracté; (*remark*) désinvolte; (*acquaintance*) de passage; (*work*) temporaire. **casually** *adv* (*remark*) d'un air détaché; (*dress*) simplement.

**casualty** /'kæʒʊəltɪ/ *n* victime *f*; (part of hospital) urgences *fpl.*

**cat** /kæt/ *n* chat *m*; (feline) félin *m.*

**catalogue** /'kætəlɒg/ *n* catalogue *m.* ● *vt* dresser un catalogue de.

**catalyst** /'kætəlɪst/ *n* catalyseur *m.*

**catalytic** /kætə'lɪtɪk/ *a* ~ **converter** pot *m* catalytique.

**catapult** /'kætəpʌlt/ *n* lance-pierres *m inv.* ● *vt* projeter.

**cataract** /'kætərækt/ *n* (Med, Geog) cataracte *f.*

**catarrh** /kə'tɑ:(r)/ *n* catarrhe *m.*

**catastrophe** /kə'tæstrəfɪ/ *n* catastrophe *f.*

**catch** /kætʃ/ *vt* (*pt* **caught**) attraper; (*bus, plane*) prendre; (understand) saisir; ~ **sb doing** surprendre qn en train de faire; ~ **fire** prendre feu; ~ **sight of** apercevoir; ~ **sb's attention/eye** attirer l'attention de qn. ● *vi* (get stuck) se prendre (*in* dans); (start to burn) prendre. ● *n* (*fastening*) fermeture *f*; (drawback) piège *m*; (in sport) prise *f.* □ ~ **on** devenir populaire; ~ **out** prendre de court; ~ **up** rattraper son retard; ~ **up with sb** rattraper qn.

**catching** /'kætʃɪŋ/ *a* contagieux.

**catchment** /'kætʃmənt/ *n* ~ **area** (School) secteur *m.*

**catch-phrase** *n* formule *f* favorite.

**catchy** /'kætʃɪ/ *a* entraînant.

**category** /'kætɪgərɪ/ *n* catégorie *f.*

**cater** /'keɪtə(r)/ *vi* organiser des réceptions; ~ **for/to** (*guests*) accueillir; (*needs*) pourvoir à; (*reader*) s'adresser à. **caterer** *n* traiteur *m.*

**caterpillar** /'kætəpɪlə(r)/ *n* chenille *f.*

**cathedral** /kə'θi:drəl/ *n* cathédrale *f.*

**catholic** /ˈkæθəlɪk/ *a* éclectique. **Catholic** *a & n* catholique (*mf*). **Catholicism** *n* catholicisme *m*.

**Catseye**® *n* plot *m* rétroréfléchissant.

**cattle** /ˈkætl/ *npl* bétail *m*.

**caught** /kɔ:t/ ⇒CATCH.

**cauliflower** /ˈkɒlɪflaʊə(r)/ *n* chou-fleur *m*.

**cause** /kɔ:z/ *n* cause *f*; (reason) raison *f*, motif *m*. ● *vt* causer; ~ **sth to grow/move** faire pousser/bouger qch.

**causeway** /ˈkɔ:zweɪ/ *n* chaussée *f*.

**caution** /ˈkɔ:ʃn/ *n* prudence *f*; (warning) avertissement *m*. ● *vt* avertir. **cautious** *a* prudent. **cautiously** *adv* prudemment.

**cave** /keɪv/ *n* grotte *f*. ● *vi* ~ **in** s'effondrer; (agree) céder. ~**man** *n* (*pl* **-men**) homme *m* des cavernes.

**cavern** /ˈkævən/ *n* caverne *f*.

**caviare** /ˈkævɪɑ:(r)/ *n* caviar *m*.

**caving** /ˈkeɪvɪŋ/ *n* spéléologie *f*.

**CCTV** *abbr* (**closed circuit television**) télévision *f* en circuit fermé.

**CD** *abbr* (**compact disc**) disque *m* compact, CD *m*.

**CD-ROM** /si:di:ˈrɒm/ *n* disque *m* optique compact, CD-ROM *m*.

**cease** /si:s/ *vt/i* cesser. ~**-fire** *n* cessez-le-feu *m inv*.

**cedilla** /sɪˈdɪlə/ *n* cédille *f*.

**ceiling** /ˈsi:lɪŋ/ *n* plafond *m*.

**celebrate** /ˈselɪbreɪt/ *vt* (*occasion*) fêter; (*Easter, mass*) célébrer. ● *vi* faire la fête. **celebrated** *a* célèbre. **celebration** *n* fête *f*.

**celebrity** /sɪˈlebrətɪ/ *n* célébrité *f*.

**celery** /ˈselərɪ/ *n* céleri *m*.

**cell** /sel/ *n* cellule *f*.

**cellar** /ˈselə(r)/ *n* cave *f*.

**cellist** /ˈtʃelɪst/ *n* violoncelliste *mf*. **cello** *n* violoncelle *m*.

**Celt** /kelt/ *n* Celte *mf*.

**cement** /sɪˈment/ *n* ciment *m*. ● *vt* cimenter. ~**-mixer** *n* bétonnière *f*.

**cemetery** /ˈsemətrɪ/ *n* cimetière *m*.

**censor** /ˈsensə(r)/ *n* censeur *m*. ● *vt* censurer.

**censure** /ˈsenʃə(r)/ *n* censure *f*. ● *vt* critiquer.

**census** /ˈsensəs/ *n* recensement *m*.

**cent** /sent/ *n* (coin) cent *m*.

**centenary** /senˈti:nərɪ/ *n* centenaire *m*.

**centigrade** /ˈsentɪgreɪd/ *a* centigrade.

**centilitre**, (US) **centiliter** /ˈsentɪli:tə(r)/ *n* centilitre *m*.

**centimetre**, (US) **centimeter** /ˈsentɪmi:tə(r)/ *n* centimètre *m*.

**centipede** /ˈsentɪpi:d/ *n* mille-pattes *m inv*.

**central** /ˈsentrəl/ *a* central; ~ **heating** chauffage *m* central; ~ **locking** fermeture *f* centralisée des portes. **centralize** *vt* centraliser. **centrally** *adv* (situated) au centre.

**centre**, (US) **center** /ˈsentə(r)/ *n* centre *m*. ● *vt* (*pt* **centred**) centrer. ● *vi* ~ **on** tourner autour de.

**century** /ˈsentʃərɪ/ *n* siècle *m*.

**ceramic** /sɪˈræmɪk/ *a* (*art*) céramique; (*object*) en céramique.

**cereal** /ˈsɪərɪəl/ *n* céréale *f*.

**ceremonial** /serɪˈməʊnɪəl/ *a* (*dress*) de cérémonie. ● *n* cérémonial *m*. **ceremony** *n* cérémonie *f*.

**certain** /ˈsɜ:tn/ *a* certain; **for** ~ avec certitude; **make** ~ **of** s'assurer de. **certainly** *adv* certainement. **certainty** *n* certitude *f*.

**certificate** /sə'tɪfɪkət/ *n* certificat *m*.

**certify** /'sɜ:tɪfaɪ/ *vt* certifier.

**cesspit**, **cesspool** /'sespɪt, 'sespu:l/ *n* fosse *f* d'aisances.

**chafe** /tʃeɪf/ *vt/i* frotter (contre).

**chagrin** /'ʃægrɪn/ *n* dépit *m*.

**chain** /tʃeɪn/ *n* chaîne *f*; **~ reaction** réaction *f* en chaîne; **~ store** magasin *m* à succursales multiples. ● *vt* enchaîner. **~-smoke** *vi* fumer sans arrêt.

**chair** /tʃeə(r)/ *n* chaise *f*; (armchair) fauteuil *m*; (Univ) chaire *f*; (chairperson) président/-e *m/f*. ● *vt* (preside over) présider. **~man** *n* (*pl* **-men**) président/-e *m/f*. **~woman** *n* (*pl* **-women**) présidente *f*

**chalk** /tʃɔ:k/ *n* craie *f*.

**challenge** /'tʃælɪndʒ/ *n* défi *m*, (opportunity) challenge *m*. ● *vt* (summon) défier (**to do** de faire); (question truth of) contester. **challenger** *n* (Sport) challenger *m*. **challenging** *a* stimulant.

**chamber** /'tʃeɪmbə(r)/ *n* (old use) chambre *f*. **~maid** *n* femme *f* de chambre. **~ music** *n* musique *f* de chambre. **~-pot** *n* pot *m* de chambre.

**champagne** /ʃæm'peɪn/ *n* champagne *m*.

**champion** /'tʃæmpɪən/ *n* champion/-ne *m/f*. ● *vt* défendre. **championship** *n* championnat *m*.

**chance** /tʃɑ:ns/ *n* (luck) hasard *m*; (opportunity) occasion *f*; (likelihood) chances *fpl*; (risk) risque *m*; **by ~** par hasard; **by any ~** par hasard; **~s are that** il est probable que. ● *a* fortuit. ● *vt* **~ doing** prendre le risque de faire; **~ it** tenter sa chance.

**chancellor** /'tʃɑ:nsələ(r)/ *n* chancelier *m*; **C~ of the Exchequer** Chancelier de l'Échiquier.

**chandelier** /ʃændə'lɪə(r)/ *n* lustre *m*.

**change** /tʃeɪndʒ/ *vt* (alter) changer; (exchange) échanger (**for** contre); (*money*) changer; **~ trains/one's dress** changer de train/de robe; **~ one's mind** changer d'avis. ● *vi* changer; (change clothes) se changer; **~ into** se transformer en; **~ over** passer (**to** à). ● *n* changement *m*; (money) monnaie *f*; **a ~ for the better** une amélioration; **a ~ for the worse** un changement en pire; **a ~ of clothes** des vêtements de rechange; **for a ~** pour changer. **changeable** *a* changeant. **changing room** *n* (in shop) cabine *f* d'essayage; (Sport) vestiaire *m*.

**channel** /'tʃænl/ *n* (for liquid, information) canal *m*; (TV) chaîne *f*; (groove) rainure *f*. ● *vt* (*pt* **channelled**) canaliser. **C~** *n* **the (English) C~** la Manche; **the C~ tunnel** le tunnel sous la Manche; **the C~ Islands** les îles *fpl* Anglo-Normandes

**chant** /tʃɑ:nt/ *n* (Relig) mélopée *f*; (of demonstrators) chant *m* scandé. ● *vt/i* scander; (Relig) psalmodier.

**chaos** /'keɪɒs/ *n* chaos *m*.

**chap** /tʃæp/ *n* (man 🄸) type *m* 🄸.

**chapel** /'tʃæpl/ *n* chapelle *f*.

**chaplain** /'tʃæplɪn/ *n* aumônier *m*.

**chapped** /tʃæpt/ *a* gercé.

**chapter** /'tʃæptə(r)/ *n* chapitre *m*.

**char** /tʃɑ:(r)/ *vt* (*pt* **charred**) carboniser.

**character** /'kærəktə(r)/ *n* caractère *m*; (in novel, play) personnage *m*; **of good ~** de bonne réputation.

**characteristic** /kærəktə'rɪstɪk/ *a & n* caractéristique (*f*).

**charcoal** /'tʃɑ:kəʊl/ *n* charbon *m* de bois; (art) fusain *m*.

**charge** /tʃɑ:dʒ/ *n* (fee) frais *mpl*; (Mil) charge *f*; (Jur) inculpation *f*; (task, custody) charge *f*; **in ~ of** responsable de; **take ~ of** prendre en charge, se charger de. ● *vt* (*customer*) faire payer; (*enemy, gun*) charger; (Jur) inculper (**with** de); **~ £20 an hour** prendre 20 livres de l'heure; **~ card** carte *f* d'achat. ● *vi* faire payer; (*bull*) foncer; (*person*) se précipiter.

**charisma** /kə'rɪzmə/ *n* charisme *m*. **charismatic** *a* charismatique.

**charitable** /'tʃærɪtəbl/ *a* charitable. **charity** *n* charité *f*; (organization) organisation *f* caritative.

**charm** /tʃɑ:m/ *n* charme *m*; (trinket) amulette *f*. ● *vt* charmer. **charming** *a* charmant.

**chart** /tʃɑ:t/ *n* (graph) graphique *m*; (table) tableau *m*; (map) carte *f*. ● *vt* (route) porter sur la carte.

**charter** /'tʃɑ:tə(r)/ *n* charte *f*; **~ (flight)** charter *m*. ● *vt* affréter; **~ed accountant** expert-comptable *m*.

**chase** /tʃeɪs/ *vt* poursuivre; **~ away** *or* **off** chasser. ● *vi* courir (**after** après). ● *n* chasse *f*.

**chassis** /'ʃæsɪ/ *n* châssis *m*.

**chastise** /tʃæ'staɪz/ *vt* châtier.

**chat** /tʃæt/ *n* conversation *f*; (on Internet) causette *f*, bavardage *m*, chat *m*; **have a ~** bavarder; **~room** *n* salle *f* de causette, salle *f* de bavardage. **~ show** *n* talk-show *m*. ● *vi* (*pt* **chatted**) bavarder. □ **~ up** Ⓘ draguer Ⓘ.

**chatter** /'tʃætə(r)/ *n* bavardage *m*. ● *vi* bavarder; **his teeth are ~ing** il claque des dents. **~box** *n* bavard/-e *m/f*.

**chatty** /'tʃætɪ/ *a* bavard.

**chauffeur** /'ʃəʊfə(r)/ *n* chauffeur *m*.

**chauvinist** /'ʃəʊvɪnɪst/ *n* chauvin/-e *m/f*, macho *m*.

**cheap** /tʃi:p/ *a* bon marché *inv*; (*fare, rate*) réduit; (*joke, gimmick*) facile; **~er** meilleur marché *inv*. **cheapen** *vt* déprécier. **cheaply** *adv* à bas prix.

**cheat** /'tʃi:t/ *vi* tricher. ● *vt* tromper. ● *n* tricheur/-euse *m/f*.

**check** /tʃek/ *vt/i* vérifier; (*tickets, rises, inflation*) contrôler; (stop) arrêter; (tick off: US) cocher. ● *n* contrôle *m*; (curb) frein *m*; (chess) échec *m*; (pattern) carreaux *mpl*; (bill: US) addition *f*; (cheque: US) chèque *m*. □ **~ in** remplir la fiche; (at airport) enregistrer; **~ out** partir; **~ sth out** vérifier qch; **~ up** vérifier; **~ up on** (*story*) vérifier; (*person*) faire une enquête sur.

**check**: **~-in** *n* enregistrement *m*. **checking account** *n* (US) compte *m* courant. **~-list** *n* liste *f* de contrôle. **~mate** *n* échec *m* et mat. **~-out** *n* caisse *f*. **~-point** *n* contrôle *m*. **~-up** *n* examen *m* médical.

**cheek** /tʃi:k/ *n* joue *f*; (impudence) culot *m* Ⓘ. **cheeky** *a* effronté.

**cheer** /tʃɪə(r)/ *n* gaieté *f*; **~s** acclamations *fpl*; (when drinking) à la vôtre. ● *vt/i* applaudir; **~ sb (up)** (gladden) remonter le moral à qn; **~ up** prendre courage. **cheerful** *a* joyeux. **cheerfulness** *n* gaieté *f*.

**cheerio** /tʃɪərɪ'əʊ/ *interj* salut.

**cheese** /tʃi:z/ *n* fromage *m*.

**cheetah** /'tʃi:tə/ *n* guépard *m*.

**chef** /ʃef/ *n* chef *m*.

**chemical** /'kemɪkl/ *a* chimique. ● *n* produit *m* chimique.

**chemist** /'kemɪst/ *n* pharmacien/-ne *m/f*; (scientist) chimiste *mf*; **~'s (shop)** pharmacie *f*. **chemistry** *n* chimie *f*.

**cheque** /tʃek/ *n* chèque *m*. **~-book** *n* chéquier *m*. **~ card** *n* carte *f* bancaire.

**chequered** /ˈtʃekəd/ *a* (pattern) à damiers; (fig) en dents de scie.

**cherish** /ˈtʃerɪʃ/ *vt* chérir; (hope) caresser.

**cherry** /ˈtʃerɪ/ *n* cerise *f*; (tree, wood) cerisier *m*.

**chess** /tʃes/ *n* échecs *mpl*. **~-board** *n* échiquier *m*.

**chest** /tʃest/ *n* (Anat) poitrine *f*; (box) coffre *m*; **~ of drawers** commode *f*.

**chestnut** /ˈtʃesnʌt/ *n* (nut) marron *m*, châtaigne *f*; (tree) marronnier *m*; (sweet) châtaignier *m*.

**chew** /tʃu:/ *vt* mâcher.

**chic** /ʃi:k/ *a* chic *inv*.

**chick** /tʃɪk/ *n* poussin *m*.

**chicken** /ˈtʃɪkɪn/ *n* poulet *m*. ● *a* ⊠ froussard. ● *vi* **~ out** ⊠ se dégonfler. **~-pox** *n* varicelle *f*.

**chick-pea** /ˈtʃɪkpi:/ *n* pois *m* chiche

**chicory** /ˈtʃɪkərɪ/ *n* (for salad) endive *f*; (in coffee) chicorée *f*.

**chief** /tʃi:f/ *n* chef *m*. ● *a* principal. **chiefly** *adv* principalement.

**chilblain** /ˈtʃɪlbleɪn/ *n* engelure *f*.

**child** /tʃaɪld/ *n* (*pl* **children** /ˈtʃɪldrən/) enfant *mf*. **~birth** *n* accouchement *m*. **childhood** *n* enfance *f*. **childish** *a* puéril. **childless** *a* sans enfants. **childlike** *a* enfantin. **~-minder** *n* nourrice *f*.

**Chile** /ˈtʃɪlɪ/ *n* Chili *m*.

**chill** /tʃɪl/ *n* froid *m*; (Med) refroidissement *m*. ● *a* froid. ● *vt* (*person*) faire frissonner; (*wine*) rafraîchir; (*food*) mettre à refroidir.

**chilli** /ˈtʃɪlɪ/ *n* (*pl* **~es**) piment *m*.

**chilly** /ˈtʃɪlɪ/ *a* froid; **it's ~** il fait froid.

**chime** /tʃaɪm/ *n* carillon *m*. ● *vt/i* carillonner.

**chimney** /ˈtʃɪmnɪ/ *n* cheminée *f*. **~-sweep** *n* ramoneur *m*.

**chimpanzee** /tʃɪmpænˈzi:/ *n* chimpanzé *m*.

**chin** /tʃɪn/ *n* menton *m*.

**china** /ˈtʃaɪnə/ *n* porcelaine *f*.

**China** /ˈtʃaɪnə/ *n* Chine *f*.

**Chinese** /tʃaɪˈni:z/ *n* (person) Chinois/-e *m/f*; (Ling) chinois *m*. ● *a* chinois.

**chip** /tʃɪp/ *n* (on plate) ébréchure *f*; (piece) éclat *m*; (of wood) copeau *m*; (Culin) frite *f*; (Comput) puce *f*, **(potato) ~s** (US) chips *fpl*. ● *vt/i* (*pt* **chipped**) (s')ébrécher; **~ in** 🅸 dire son mot; (with money) contribuer.

**chiropodist** /kɪˈrɒpədɪst/ *n* pédicure *mf*.

**chirp** /tʃɜ:p/ *n* pépiement *m*. ● *vi* pépier. **chirpy** *a* gai.

**chisel** /ˈtʃɪzl/ *n* ciseau *m*. ● *vt* (*pt* **chiselled**) ciseler.

**chit** /tʃɪt/ *n* note *f*; (voucher) bon *m*.

**chitchat** /ˈtʃɪttʃæt/ *n* 🅸 bavardage *m*.

**chivalrous** /ˈʃɪvəlrəs/ *a* galant.

**chives** /tʃaɪvz/ *npl* ciboulette *f*.

**chlorine** /ˈklɔ:ri:n/ *n* chlore *m*.

**choc-ice** /ˈtʃɒkaɪs/ *n* esquimau *m*.

**chock-a-block** /tʃɒkəˈblɒk/ *a* plein à craquer.

**chocolate** /ˈtʃɒklət/ *n* chocolat *m*.

**choice** /tʃɔɪs/ *n* choix *m*. ● *a* de choix.

**choir** /ˈkwaɪə(r)/ *n* chœur *m*. **~boy** *n* jeune choriste *m*.

**choke** /tʃəʊk/ *vt/i* (s')étrangler; **~ (up)** boucher. ● *n* starter *m*.

**cholesterol** /kəˈlestərɒl/ *n* cholestérol *m*.

**choose** /tʃu:z/ *vt/i* (*pt* **chose**; *pp* **chosen**) choisir; ~ **to do** décider de faire. **choosy** *a* difficile.

**chop** /tʃɒp/ *vt/i* (*pt* **chopped**) (*wood*) couper; (*food*) hacher; **chopping board** planche *f* à découper; ~ **down** abattre. ● *n* (meat) côtelette *f*. **chopper** *n* hachoir *m*; [!] hélico *m* [!].

**choppy** /'tʃɒpɪ/ *a* (*sea*) agité.

**chopstick** /'tʃɒpstɪk/ *n* baguette *f* (*chinoise*).

**chord** /kɔ:d/ *n* (Mus) accord *m*.

**chore** /tʃɔ:(r)/ *n* (routine) tâche *f*; (unpleasant) corvée *f*.

**chortle** /'tʃɔ:tl/ *n* gloussement *m*. ● *vi* glousser.

**chorus** /'kɔ:rəs/ *n* chœur *m*; (of song) refrain *m*.

**chose**, **chosen** /tʃəʊz, 'tʃəʊzn/ ⇒CHOOSE.

**Christ** /kraɪst/ *n* le Christ.

**christen** /'krɪsn/ *vt* baptiser. **christening** *n* baptême *m*.

**Christian** /'krɪstʃən/ *a* & *n* chrétien/-ne (*m/f*); ~ **name** nom *m* de baptême. **Christianity** *n* christianisme *m*.

**Christmas** /'krɪsməs/ *n* Noël *m*; ~ **Day/Eve** le jour/la veille de Noël. ● *a* (*card, tree*) de Noël.

**chronic** /'krɒnɪk/ *a* (*situation, disease*) chronique; (bad [!]) nul.

**chronicle** /'krɒnɪkl/ *n* chronique *f*.

**chronological** /krɒnə'lɒdʒɪkl/ *a* chronologique.

**chrysanthemum** /krɪ'sænθəməm/ *n* chrysanthème *m*.

**chubby** /'tʃʌbɪ/ *a* (**-ier**, **-iest**) potelé.

**chuck** /tʃʌk/ *vt* [!] lancer; ~ **away** *or* **out** [!] balancer.

**chuckle** /'tʃʌkl/ *n* gloussement *m*. ● *vi* glousser.

**chuffed** /tʃʌft/ *a* [!] vachement content [!].

**chunk** /tʃʌŋk/ *n* morceau *m*. **chunky** *a* (*sweater, jewellery*) gros; (*person*) costaud.

**church** /'tʃɜ:tʃ/ *n* église *f*. ~**goer** *n* pratiquant/-e *m/f*. ~**yard** *n* cimetière *m*.

**churn** /'tʃɜ:n/ *n* baratte *f*; (milk-can) bidon *m*. ● *vt* baratter; ~ **out** produire en série.

**chute** /ʃu:t/ *n* toboggan *m*; (for rubbish) vide-ordures *m inv*.

**chutney** /'tʃʌtnɪ/ *n* condiment *m* aigre-doux.

**cider** /'saɪdə(r)/ *n* cidre *m*.

**cigar** /sɪ'gɑ:(r)/ *n* cigare *m*.

**cigarette** /sɪgə'ret/ *n* cigarette *f*; ~ **end** mégot *m*.

**cinder** /'sɪndə(r)/ *n* cendre *f*.

**cinema** /'sɪnəmə/ *n* cinéma *m*.

**cinnamon** /'sɪnəmən/ *n* cannelle *f*.

**circle** /'sɜ:kl/ *n* cercle *m*; (Theat) balcon *m*. ● *vt* (go round) tourner autour de; (word, error) encercler. ● *vi* tourner en rond.

**circuit** /'sɜ:kɪt/ *n* circuit *m*. ~ **board** *n* carte *f* de circuit imprimé. ~**-breaker** *n* disjoncteur *m*.

**circuitous** /sɜ:'kju:ɪtəs/ *a* indirect.

**circular** /'sɜ:kjʊlə(r)/ *a* & *n* circulaire (*f*).

**circulate** /'sɜ:kjʊleɪt/ *vt/i* (faire) circuler. **circulation** *n* circulation *f*; (of newspaper) tirage *m*.

**circumcise** /'sɜ:kəmsaɪz/ *vt* circoncire.

**circumference** /sɜ:'kʌmfərəns/ *n* circonférence *f*.

**circumflex** /'sɜ:kəmfleks/ *n* circonflexe *m*.

**circumstance** /'sɜ:kəmstəns/ *n* circonstance *f*; **~s** (financial) situation *f*; **under no ~s** en aucun cas.

**circus** /'sɜ:kəs/ *n* cirque *m*.

**cistern** /'sɪstən/ *n* réservoir *m*.

**citation** /saɪ'teɪʃn/ *n* citation *f*. **cite** *vt* citer.

**citizen** /'sɪtɪzn/ *n* citoyen/-ne *m*/*f*; (of town) habitant/-e *m*/*f*. **citizenship** *n* nationalité *f*.

**citrus** /'sɪtrəs/ *a* **~ fruit(s)** agrumes *mpl*; **~ tree** citrus *m*.

**city** /'sɪtɪ/ *n* (grande) ville *f*.

**civic** /'sɪvɪk/ *a* (*official*) municipal; (*pride, duty*) civique.

**civil** /'sɪvl/ *a* civil. **~ disobedience** *n* résistance *f* passive. **~ engineer** *n* ingénieur *m* des travaux publics.

**civilian** /sɪ'vɪlɪən/ *a* & *n* civil/-e (*m*/*f*).

**civilization** /sɪvəlaɪ'zeɪʃn/ *n* civilisation *f*. **civilize** *vt* civiliser.

**civil**: **~ law** *n* droit *m* civil. **~ liberties** *npl* libertés *fpl* individuelles. **~ rights** *npl* droits *mpl* civils. **~ servant** *n* fonctionnaire *mf*. **~ service** *n* fonction *f* publique. **~ war** *n* guerre *f* civile.

**clad** /klæd/ *a* **~ in** vêtu de.

**claim** /kleɪm/ *vt* (demand) revendiquer; (assert) prétendre. ● *n* revendication *f*; (assertion) affirmation *f*; (for insurance) réclamation *f*; (right) droit *m*. **claimant** *n* (of benefits) demandeur/-euse *m*/*f*.

**clairvoyant** /kleə'vɔɪənt/ *n* voyant/-e *m*/*f*.

**clam** /klæm/ *n* palourde *f*.

**clamber** /'klæmbə(r)/ *vi* grimper.

**clammy** /'klæmɪ/ *a* (**-ier**, **-iest**) moite.

**clamour** /'klæmə(r)/ *n* clameur *f*. ● *vi* **~ for** réclamer.

**clamp** /klæmp/ *n* valet *m*; (Med) pince *f*; **(wheel) ~** sabot *m* de Denver. ● *vt* cramponner; (*jaw*) serrer; (*car*) mettre un sabot de Denver à; **~ down on** faire de la répression contre.

**clan** /klæn/ *n* clan *m*.

**clang** /klæŋ/ *n* son *m* métallique.

**clap** /klæp/ *vt*/*i* (*pt* **clapped**) applaudir; (put forcibly) mettre; **~ one's hands** frapper dans ses mains. ● *n* applaudissement *m*; (of thunder) coup *m*.

**claret** /'klærət/ *n* bordeaux *m* rouge.

**clarification** /klærɪfɪ'keɪʃn/ *n* clarification *f*. **clarify** *vt*/*i* (se) clarifier.

**clarinet** /klærɪ'net/ *n* clarinette *f*.

**clarity** /'klærətɪ/ *n* clarté *f*.

**clash** /klæʃ/ *n* choc *m*; (fig) conflit *m*. ● *vi* (*metal objects*) s'entrechoquer; (*armies*) s'affronter; (*interests*) être incompatibles, (*meetings*) avoir lieu en même temps; (*colours*) jurer.

**clasp** /klɑ:sp/ *n* (fastener) fermoir *m*. ● *vt* serrer.

**class** /klɑ:s/ *n* classe *f*. ● *vt* classer; **~ sb/sth as** assimiler qn/qch à.

**classic** /'klæsɪk/ *a* & *n* classique (*m*); **~s** (Univ) lettres *fpl* classiques. **classical** *a* classique.

**classified** /'klæsɪfaɪd/ *a* (*information*) secret; **~ (ad)** petite annonce *f*.

**classroom** /'klɑ:srʊm/ *n* salle *f* de classe.

**clatter** /'klætə(r)/ *n* cliquetis *m*. ● *vi* cliqueter.

**clause** /klɔ:z/ *n* clause *f*; (Gram) proposition *f*.

**claw** /klɔː/ *n* (of animal, small bird) griffe *f*; (of bird of prey) serre *f*; (of lobster) pince *f*. ● *vt* griffer.

**clay** /kleɪ/ *n* argile *f*.

**clean** /kliːn/ *a* propre; (shape, stroke) net. ● *adv* complètement. ● *vt* nettoyer; ~ **one's teeth** se brosser les dents. ● *vi* ~ **up** faire le nettoyage. **cleaner** *n* (at home) femme *f* de ménage; (industrial) agent *m* de nettoyage; (of clothes) teinturier/-ière *m/f*. **cleanliness** *n* propreté *f*. **cleanly** *adv* proprement; (sharply) nettement.

**cleanse** /klenz/ *vt* nettoyer; (fig) purifier.

**clean-shaven** *a* glabre.

**clear** /klɪə(r)/ *a* (*explanation*) clair; (*need, sign*) évident; (*glass*) transparent; (*profit*) net; (*road*) dégagé; **make sth** ~ être très clair sur qch; ~ **of** (away from) à l'écart de. ● *adv* complètement; **stand** ~ **of** s'éloigner de. ● *vt* (free) dégager (**of** de); (*table*) débarrasser; (*building*) évacuer; (*cheque*) compenser; (jump over) franchir; (*debt*) liquider; (Jur) disculper. ● *vi* (*fog*) se dissiper; (*cheque*) être compensé. □ ~ **away** *or* **off** (remove) enlever; ~ **off** *or* **out** 🄸 décamper; ~ **out** (clean) nettoyer; ~ **up** (tidy) ranger; (*mystery*) éclaircir; (*weather*) s'éclaircir.

**clearance** /ˈklɪərəns/ *n* (permission) autorisation *f*; (space) espace *m*; ~ **sale** liquidation *f*.

**clear-cut** *a* net.

**clearing** /ˈklɪərɪŋ/ *n* clairière *f*.

**clearly** /ˈklɪəlɪ/ *adv* clairement.

**clef** /klef/ *n* (Mus) clé *f*.

**cleft** /kleft/ *n* fissure *f*.

**clench** /klentʃ/ *vt* serrer.

**clergy** /ˈklɜːdʒɪ/ *n* clergé *m*. **~man** *n* (*pl* **-men**) ecclésiastique *m*.

**cleric** /ˈklerɪk/ *n* clerc *m*. **clerical** *a* (Relig) clérical; (*staff, work*) de bureau.

**clerk** /klɑːk/ *n* employé/-e *m/f* de bureau; (US) **(sales)** ~ vendeur/-euse *m/f*.

**clever** /ˈklevə(r)/ *a* intelligent; (skilful) habile.

**click** /klɪk/ *n* déclic *m*; (Comput) clic *m*. ● *vi* faire un déclic; (people 🄸) sympathiser; (Comput) cliquer (**on** sur). ● *vt* (*heels, tongue*) faire claquer.

**client** /ˈklaɪənt/ *n* client/-e *m/f*.

**clientele** /kliːənˈtel/ *n* clientèle *f*.

**cliff** /klɪf/ *n* falaise *f*.

**climate** /ˈklaɪmɪt/ *n* climat *m*.

**climax** /ˈklaɪmæks/ *n* (of story, contest) point *m* culminant.

**climb** /klaɪm/ *vt* grimper; (*steps*) monter; (*tree, ladder*) grimper à; (*mountain*) faire l'ascension de. ● *vi* grimper; ~ **into** (*car*) monter dans; ~ **into bed** se mettre au lit. ● *n* (of mountain) escalade *f*; (steep hill, rise) montée *f*. □ ~ **down** (fig) reculer. **climber** *n* alpiniste *mf*.

**clinch** /klɪntʃ/ *vt* (*deal*) conclure; (*victory, order*) décrocher.

**cling** /klɪŋ/ *vi* (*pt* **clung**) se cramponner (**to** à); (stick) coller. **~-film** *n* scellofrais® *m*.

**clinic** /ˈklɪnɪk/ *n* centre *m* médical; (private) clinique *f*. **clinical** *a* clinique.

**clink** /klɪŋk/ *n* tintement *m*. ● *vt/i* (faire) tinter.

**clip** /klɪp/ *n* (for paper) trombone *m*; (for hair) barrette *f*; (for tube) collier *m*; (of film) extrait *m*. ● *vt* (*pt* **clipped**) (fasten) attacher (**to** à); (cut) couper.

**clippers** /ˈklɪpəz/ *npl* tondeuse *f*; (for nails) coupe-ongles *m inv*.

**clipping** /'klɪpɪŋ/ *n* (from press) coupure *f* de presse.

**cloak** /kləʊk/ *n* cape *f*; (man's) houppelande *f*. **~room** *n* vestiaire *m*; (toilet) toilettes *fpl*.

**clobber** /'klɒbə(r)/ *n* [I] attirail *m*. ● *vt* (hit [I]) tabasser [I].

**clock** /klɒk/ *n* pendule *f*; (large) horloge *f*. ● *vi* ~ **on/in** *or* **off/out** pointer; ~ **up** (*miles*) faire. **~-tower** *n* beffroi *m*. **~wise** *a* & *adv* dans le sens des aiguilles d'une montre.

**clockwork** /'klɒkwɜ:k/ *n* mécanisme *m*. ● *a* mécanique.

**clog** /klɒg/ *n* sabot *m*. ● *vt/i* (*pt* **clogged**) (se) boucher.

**cloister** /'klɔɪstə(r)/ *n* cloître *m*.

**clone** /kləʊn/ *n* clone *m*. ● *vt* cloner.

**close**[1] /kləʊs/ *a* (*friend, relative*) proche (**to** de); (*link, collaboration*) étroit; (*examination*) minutieux; (*result, match*) serré; (*weather*) lourd; ~ **together** (crowded) serrés; ~ **by**, ~ **at hand** tout près; **have a** ~ **shave** l'échapper belle; **keep a** ~ **watch on** surveiller de près. ● *adv* près. ● *n* (street) impasse *f*

**close**[2] /kləʊz/ *vt* fermer; (*meeting, case*) mettre fin à. ● *vi* se fermer; (*shop*) fermer; (*meeting, play*) prendre fin. ● *n* fin *f*.

**closely** /'kləʊslɪ/ *adv* (follow) de près. **closeness** *n* proximité *f*.

**closet** /'klɒzɪt/ *n* (US) placard *m*.

**close-up** *n* gros plan *m*.

**closure** /'kləʊʒə(r)/ *n* fermeture *f*.

**clot** /klɒt/ *n* (of blood) caillot *m*; (in sauce) grumeau *m*. ● *vt/i* (*pt* **clotted**) (se) coaguler.

**cloth** /klɒθ/ *n* (fabric) tissu *m*; (duster) chiffon *m*; (table-cloth) nappe *f*.

**clothe** /kləʊð/ *vt* vêtir.

**clothes** /kləʊðz/ *npl* vêtements *mpl*. **~-hanger** *n* cintre *m*. **~-line** *n* corde *f* à linge.

**clothing** /'kləʊðɪŋ/ *n* vêtements *mpl*.

**cloud** /klaʊd/ *n* nuage *m*. ● *vi* ~ **(over)** se couvrir (de nuages); (*face*) s'assombrir. **cloudy** *a* (*sky*) couvert; (*liquid*) trouble.

**clout** /klaʊt/ *n* (blow) coup *m* de poing; (power) influence *f*. ● *vt* frapper.

**clove** /kləʊv/ *n* clou *m* de girofle; ~ **of garlic** gousse *f* d'ail.

**clover** /'kləʊvə(r)/ *n* trèfle *m*.

**clown** /klaʊn/ *n* clown *m*.

**club** /klʌb/ *n* (group) club *m*; (weapon) massue *f*; **(golf)** ~ club *m* (de golf); **~s** (cards) trèfle *m*. ● *vt/i* (*pt* **clubbed**) matraquer. □ ~ **together** cotiser.

**clue** /klu:/ *n* indice *m*; (in crossword) définition *f*; **I haven't a** ~ [I] je n'en ai pas la moindre idée.

**clump** /klʌmp/ *n* massif *m*.

**clumsy** /'klʌmzɪ/ *a* (**-ier, -iest**) maladroit; (*tool*) peu commode.

**clung** /klʌŋ/ ⇒CLING.

**cluster** /'klʌstə(r)/ *n* (of people, islands) groupe *m*; (of flowers, berries) grappe *f*. ● *vi* se grouper.

**clutch** /klʌtʃ/ *vt* (hold) serrer fort; (grasp) saisir. ● *vi* ~ **at** (try to grasp) essayer de saisir. ● *n* (Auto) embrayage *m*; (of eggs) couveé *f*; (of people) groupe *m*.

**clutter** /'klʌtə(r)/ *n* désordre *m*. ● *vt* ~ **(up)** encombrer.

**coach** /kəʊtʃ/ *n* autocar *m*; (of train) wagon *m*; (horse-drawn) carrosse *m*; (Sport) entraîneur/-euse *m/f*. ● *vt* (*team*) entraîner; (*pupil*) donner des leçons particulières à.

**coal** /kəʊl/ *n* charbon *m*. **~field** *n* bassin *m* houiller. **~-mine** *n* mine *f* de charbon.

**coarse** /kɔ:s/ *a* grossier.

**coast** /kəʊst/ *n* côte *f*. ● *vi* (car, bicycle) descendre en roue libre. **coastal** *a* côtier.

**coast**: **~guard** *n* (person) garde-côte *m*; (organization) gendarmerie *f* maritime. **~line** *n* littoral *m*.

**coat** /kəʊt/ *n* manteau *m*; (of animal) pelage *m*; (of paint) couche *f*; **~ of arms** armoiries *fpl*. ● *vt* enduire, couvrir; (with chocolate) enrober (with de). **coating** *n* couche *f*.

**coax** /kəʊks/ *vt* cajoler.

**cob** /kɒb/ *n* (of corn) épi *m*.

**cobbler** /'kɒblə(r)/ *n* cordonnier *m*.

**cobblestones** /'kɒblstəʊnz/ *npl* pavés *mpl*.

**cobweb** /'kɒbweb/ *n* toile *f* d'araignée.

**cocaine** /kəʊ'keɪn/ *n* cocaïne *f*.

**cock** /kɒk/ *n* (rooster) coq *m*; (oiseau) mâle *m*. ● *vt* (*gun*) armer; (*ears*) dresser.

**cockerel** /'kɒkərəl/ *n* jeune coq *m*.

**cockle** /'kɒkl/ *n* (Culin) coque *f*.

**cock**: **~pit** *n* poste *m* de pilotage. **~roach** *n* cafard *m*. **~tail** *n* cocktail *m*.

**cocky** /'kɒkɪ/ *a* (**-ier**, **-iest**) trop sûr de soi.

**cocoa** /'kəʊkəʊ/ *n* cacao *m*.

**coconut** /'kəʊkənʌt/ *n* noix *f* de coco.

**COD** *abbr* (**cash on delivery**) envoi *m* contre remboursement.

**cod** /kɒd/ *n inv* morue *f*; **~-liver oil** huile *f* de foie de morue.

**code** /kəʊd/ *n* code *m*. ● *vt* coder.

**coerce** /kəʊ'ɜ:s/ *vt* contraindre.

**coexist** /kəʊɪg'zɪst/ *vi* coexister.

**coffee** /'kɒfɪ/ *n* café *m*. **~ bar** *n* café *m*. **~-bean** *n* grain *m* de café. **~-pot** *n* cafetière *f*. **~-table** *n* table *f* basse.

**coffin** /'kɒfɪn/ *n* cercueil *m*.

**cog** /kɒg/ *n* pignon *m*; (fig) rouage *m*.

**cognac** /'kɒnjæk/ *n* cognac *m*.

**coil** /kɔɪl/ *vt/i* (s')enrouler. ● *n* (of rope) rouleau *m*; (of snake) anneau *m*; (contraceptive) stérilet *m*.

**coin** /kɔɪn/ *n* pièce *f* (*de monnaie*). ● *vt* (*word*) inventer.

**coincide** /kəʊɪn'saɪd/ *vi* coïncider. **coincidence** *n* coïncidence *f*. **coincidental** *a* dû à une coïncidence.

**colander** /'kʌləndə(r)/ *n* passoire *f*.

**cold** /kəʊld/ *a* froid; (*person*) **be** *or* **feel ~** avoir froid; **it is ~** il fait froid; **get ~ feet** avoir les jetons ⓘ; **~-blooded** (lit) à sang froid; (fig) sans pitié. ● *n* froid *m*; (Med) rhume *m*; **~ sore** bouton *m* de fièvre. **coldness** *n* froideur *f*.

**coleslaw** /'kəʊlslɔ:/ *n* salade *f* de chou cru.

**colic** /'kɒlɪk/ *n* coliques *fpl*.

**collaborate** /kə'læbəreɪt/ *vi* collaborer.

**collapse** /kə'læps/ *vi* s'effondrer; (*person*) s'écrouler; (fold) se plier. ● *n* effondrement *m*.

**collar** /'kɒlə(r)/ *n* col *m*; (of dog) collier *m*. **~-bone** *n* clavicule *f*.

**collateral** /kə'lætərəl/ *n* nantissement *m*.

**colleague** /'kɒli:g/ *n* collègue *mf*.

**collect** /kə'lekt/ *vt* rassembler; (pick up) ramasser; (call for) passer prendre; (*money, fare*) encaisser; (*taxes, rent*) percevoir; (as hobby) collectionner. ● *vi* se rassembler;

(*dust*) s'amasser. ● *adv* **call ~** (US) appeler en PCV. **collection** *n* collection *f*; (of money) collecte *f*; (in church) quête *f*; (of mail) levée *f*.

**collective** /kə'lektɪv/ *a* collectif.

**collector** /kə'lektə(r)/ *n* (as hobby) collectionneur/-euse *m/f*; (of taxes) percepteur *m*; (of rent, debt) encaisseur *m*.

**college** /'kɒlɪdʒ/ *n* (for higher education) établissement *m* d'enseignement supérieur; (within university) collège *m*; **be at ~** faire des études supérieures.

**collide** /kə'laɪd/ *vi* entrer en collision (**with** avec).

**colliery** /'kɒlɪərɪ/ *n* houillère *f*.

**collision** /kə'lɪʒn/ *n* collision *f*.

**colloquial** /kə'ləʊkwɪəl/ *a* familier. **colloquialism** *n* expression *f* familière.

**Colombia** /kə'læmbɪə/ *n* Colombie *f*.

**colon** /'kəʊlən/ *n* (Gram) deux-points *m inv*; (Anat) côlon *m*.

**colonel** /'kɜ:nl/ *n* colonel *m*.

**colonial** /kə'ləʊnɪəl/ *a* & *n* colonial/-e (*m/f*).

**colour**, (US) **color** /'kʌlə(r)/ *n* couleur *f*; **~-blind** daltonien. ● *a* (*photo*) en couleur; (*TV set*) couleur *inv*. ● *vt* colorer; (with crayon) colorier. **coloured** *a* de couleur. **colourful** *a* aux couleurs vives; (fig) haut en couleur. **colouring** *n* (of skin) teint *m*; (in food) colorant *m*.

**colt** /kəʊlt/ *n* poulain *m*.

**column** /'kɒləm/ *n* colonne *f*.

**coma** /'kəʊmə/ *n* coma *m*.

**comb** /kəʊm/ *n* peigne *m*. ● *vt* peigner; **~ one's hair** se peigner; **~ a place** passer un lieu au peigne fin.

**combat** /'kɒmbæt/ *n* combat *m*. ● *vt* (*pt* **combated**) combattre.

**combination** /kɒmbɪ'neɪʃn/ *n* combinaison *f*.

**combine**[1] /kəm'baɪn/ *vt/i* (se) combiner, (s')unir.

**combine**[2] /'kɒmbaɪn/ *n* (Comm) groupe *m*; **~ (harvester)** moissonneuse-batteuse *f*.

**come** /kʌm/ *vi* (*pt* **came**; *pp* **come**) venir; (*bus, letter*) arriver; (*postman*) passer; **~ and look!** viens voir!; **~ in** (*size, colour*) exister en; **when it ~s to** lorsqu'il s'agit de. □ **~ about** survenir; **~ across** (*meaning*) passer; **~ across sth** tomber sur qch; **~ away** (leave) partir; (come off) se détacher; **~ back** revenir; **~ by** obtenir; **~ down** descendre; (*price*) baisser; **~ forward** se présenter; **~ in** entrer; **~ in useful** être utile; **~ in for** recevoir; **~ into** (money) hériter de; **~ off** (succeed) réussir; (fare) s'en tirer; (detach) se détacher; **~ on** (actor) entrer en scène; (light) s'allumer; (improve) faire des progrès; **~ on!** allez!; **~ out** sortir; **~ round** reprendre connaissance; (change mind) changer d'avis; **~ through** s'en tirer; **~ to** reprendre connaissance; **~ to sth** (*amount*) revenir à qch; (*decision, conclusion*) arriver à qch; **~ up** (*problem*) être soulevé; (*opportunity*) se présenter; (*sun*) se lever; **~ up against** se heurter à; **~ up with** trouver.

**comedian** /kə'mi:dɪən/ *n* comique *m*.

**comedy** /'kɒmədɪ/ *n* comédie *f*.

**comfort** /'kʌmfət/ *n* confort *m*; (consolation) réconfort *m*. ● *vt* consoler. **comfortable** *a* (*chair, car*) confortable; (*person*) à l'aise; (wealthy) aisé.

**comfortably** /'kʌmftəblɪ/ *adv* confortablement; **~ off** aisé.

**comfy** /ˈkʌmfɪ/ *a* [!] = COMFORTABLE.

**comic** /ˈkɒmɪk/ *a* comique. ● *n* (person) comique *m*; ~ **(book)**, ~ **strip** bande *f* dessinée.

**coming** /ˈkʌmɪŋ/ *n* arrivée *f*; ~**s and goings** allées et venues *fpl*. ● *a* à venir.

**comma** /ˈkɒmə/ *n* virgule *f*.

**command** /kəˈmɑːnd/ *n* (authority) commandement *m*; (order) ordre *m*; (mastery) maîtrise *f*. ● *vt* ordonner à (**to do** de faire); (be able to use) disposer de; (*respect*) inspirer. **commandeer** *vt* réquisitionner. **commander** *n* commandant *m*. **commanding** *a* imposant. **commandment** *n* commandement *m*.

**commando** /kəˈmɑːndəʊ/ *n* commando *m*.

**commemorate** /kəˈmeməreɪt/ *vt* commémorer.

**commence** /kəˈmens/ *vt/i* commencer.

**commend** /kəˈmend/ *vt* (praise) louer; (entrust) confier.

**commensurate** /kəˈmenʃərət/ *a* proportionné.

**comment** /ˈkɒment/ *n* commentaire *m*. ● *vi* faire des commentaires; ~ **on** commenter. **commentary** *n* commentaire *m*; (radio, TV) reportage *m*. **commentate** *vi* faire un reportage. **commentator** *n* commentateur/-trice *m/f*.

**commerce** /ˈkɒmɜːs/ *n* commerce *m*.

**commercial** /kəˈmɜːʃl/ *a* commercial; (*traveller*) de commerce. ● *n* publicité *f*.

**commiserate** /kəˈmɪzəreɪt/ *vi* compatir (**with** avec).

**commission** /kəˈmɪʃn/ *n* commission *f*; (order for work) commande *f*; **out of** ~ hors service. ● *vt* (order) commander; (Mil) nommer officier; ~ **to do** charger de faire. **commissioner** *n* préfet *m* (de police); (in EC) membre *m* de la Commission européenne.

**commit** /kəˈmɪt/ *vt* (*pt* **committed**) commettre; (entrust) confier; ~ **oneself** s'engager; ~ **perjury** se parjurer; ~ **suicide** se suicider; ~ **to memory** apprendre par cœur. **commitment** *n* engagement *m*.

**committee** /kəˈmɪtɪ/ *n* comité *m*.

**commodity** /kəˈmɒdətɪ/ *n* article *m*.

**common** /ˈkɒmən/ *a* (shared by all) commun (**to** à); (usual) courant; (vulgar) vulgaire, commun; **in** ~ en commun; ~ **people** le peuple; ~ **sense** bon sens *m*. ● *n* terrain *m* communal; **the C~s** Chambre *f* des Communes.

**commoner** /ˈkɒmənə(r)/ *n* roturier/-ière *m/f*.

**common law** *n* droit *m* coutumier.

**commonly** /ˈkɒmənlɪ/ *adv* communément.

**commonplace** /ˈkɒmənpleɪs/ *a* banal. ● *n* banalité *f*.

**common-room** *n* salle *f* de détente.

**Commonwealth** /ˈkɒmənwelθ/ *n* **the** ~ le Commonwealth *m*.

**commotion** /kəˈməʊʃn/ *n* (noise) vacarme *m*; (disturbance) agitation *f*.

**communal** /ˈkɒmjʊnl, kəˈmjuːnl/ *a* (shared) commun; (*life*) collectif.

**commune** /ˈkɒmjuːn/ *n* (group) communauté *f*.

**communicate** /kəˈmjuːnɪkeɪt/ *vt/i* communiquer. **communication** *n* communication *f*. **communicative** *a* communicatif.

**communion** /kəˈmjuːnɪən/ *n* communion *f*.

**Communism** /'kɒmjʊnɪzəm/ *n* communisme *m*. **Communist** *a* & *n* communiste (*mf*).

**community** /kə'mju:nətɪ/ *n* communauté *f*.

**commute** /kə'mju:t/ *vi* faire la navette. ● *vt* (Jur) commuer. **commuter** *n* navetteur/-euse *m*/*f*.

**compact** /kəm'pækt/ *a* compact; (lady's case) poudrier *m*.

**compact disc** *n* disque *m* compact. ~ **player** *n* platine *f* laser.

**companion** /kəm'pænjən/ *n* compagnon/-agne *m*/*f*. **companionship** *n* camaraderie *f*.

**company** /'kʌmpənɪ/ *n* (companionship, firm) compagnie *f*; (guests) invités/-es *m*/*fpl*.

**comparative** /kəm'pærətɪv/ *a* (*study, form*) comparatif; (*comfort*) relatif.

**compare** /kəm'peə(r)/ *vt* comparer (**with, to** à); ~**d with** par rapport à. ● *vi* être comparable. **comparison** *n* comparaison *f*.

**compartment** /kəm'pɑ:tmənt/ *n* compartiment *m*.

**compass** /'kʌmpəs/ *n* (for direction) boussole *f*; (scope) portée *f*; **a pair of** ~**es** compas *m*

**compassionate** /kəm'pæʃənət/ *a* compatissant.

**compatible** /kəm'pætəbl/ *a* compatible.

**compel** /kəm'pel/ *vt* (*pt* **compelled**) contraindre. **compelling** *a* irrésistible.

**compensate** /'kɒmpənseɪt/ *vt*/*i* (financially) dédommager (**for** de); ~ **for sth** compenser qch. **compensation** *n* compensation *f*; (financial) dédommagement *m*.

**compete** /kəm'pi:t/ *vi* concourir; ~ **with** rivaliser avec.

**competent** /'kɒmpɪtənt/ *a* compétent.

**competition** /kɒmpə'tɪʃn/ *n* (contest) concours *m*; (Sport) compétition *f*; (Comm) concurrence *f*.

**competitive** /kəm'petətɪv/ *a* (*prices*) compétitif; (*person*) qui a l'esprit de compétition.

**competitor** /kəm'petɪtə(r)/ *n* concurrent/-e *m*/*f*.

**compile** /kəm'paɪl/ *vt* (*list*) dresser; (*book*) rédiger.

**complacency** /kəm'pleɪsnsɪ/ *n* suffisance *f*.

**complain** /kəm'pleɪn/ *vi* se plaindre (**about, of** de). **complaint** *n* plainte *f*; (official) réclamation *f*; (illness) maladie *f*.

**complement** /'kɒmplɪmənt/ *n* complément *m*. ● *vt* compléter. **complementary** *a* complémentaire.

**complete** /kəm'pli:t/ *a* complet; (finished) achevé; (downright) parfait. ● *vt* achever; (*a form*) remplir. **completely** *adv* complètement. **completion** *n* achèvement *m*.

**complex** /'kɒmpleks/ *a* complexe. ● *n* (Psych) complexe *m*.

**complexion** /kəm'plekʃn/ *n* (of face) teint *m*; (fig) caractère *m*.

**compliance** /kəm'plaɪəns/ *n* (agreement) conformité *f*.

**complicate** /'kɒmplɪkeɪt/ *vt* compliquer. **complicated** *a* compliqué. **complication** *n* complication *f*.

**compliment** /'kɒmplɪmənt/ *n* compliment *m*. ● *vt* complimenter. **complimentary** *a* (offert) à titre gracieux; (praising) flatteur.

**comply** /kəm'plaɪ/ *vi* ~ **with** se conformer à, obéir à.

**component** /kəm'pəʊnənt/ *n* (of machine) pièce *f*; (chemical substance)

composant *m*; (element: fig) composante *f*. ● *a* constituant.

**compose** /kəm'pəʊz/ *vt* composer; ~ **oneself** se calmer. **composed** *a* calme. **composer** *n* (Mus) compositeur *m*. **composition** *n* composition *f*.

**composure** /kəm'pəʊʒə(r)/ *n* calme *m*.

**compound** /'kɒmpaʊnd/ *n* (substance, word) composé *m*; (enclosure) enclos *m*. ● *a* composé.

**comprehend** /kɒmprɪ'hend/ *vt* comprendre. **comprehension** *n* compréhension *f*.

**comprehensive** /kɒmprɪ'hensɪv/ *a* étendu, complet; (*insurance*) tous risques *inv*. ~ **school** *n* collège *m* d'enseignement secondaire.

**compress** /kəm'pres/ *vt* comprimer.

**comprise** /kəm'praɪz/ *vt* comprendre, inclure.

**compromise** /'kɒmprəmaɪz/ *n* compromis *m*. ● *vt* compromettre. ● *vi* transiger, arriver à un compromis.

**compulsive** /kəm'pʌlsɪv/ *a* (Psych) compulsif; (*liar, smoker*) invétéré.

**compulsory** /kəm'pʌlsərɪ/ *a* obligatoire.

**computer** /kəm'pju:tə(r)/ *n* ordinateur *m*; ~ **science** informatique *f*. **computerize** *vt* informatiser.

**comrade** /'kɒmreɪd/ *n* camarade *mf*.

**con**[1] /kɒn/ *vt* (*pt* **conned**) ⊠ rouler ⊡, escroquer (**out of** de). ● *n* ⊠ escroquerie *f*.

**con**[2] /kɒn/ ⇒PRO.

**conceal** /kən'si:l/ *vt* dissimuler (**from** à).

**concede** /kən'si:d/ *vt* concéder. ● *vi* céder.

**conceited** /kən'si:tɪd/ *a* vaniteux.

**conceive** /kən'si:v/ *vt/i* concevoir; ~ **of** concevoir.

**concentrate** /'kɒnsntreɪt/ *vt/i* (se) concentrer. **concentration** *n* concentration *f*.

**concept** /'kɒnsept/ *n* concept *m*.

**conception** /kən'sepʃn/ *n* conception *f*.

**concern** /kən'sɜ:n/ *n* (interest, business) affaire *f*; (worry) inquiétude *f*; (firm: Comm) entreprise *f*, affaire *f*. ● *vt* concerner; ~ **oneself with, be ~ed with** s'occuper de. **concerned** *a* inquiet. **concerning** *prep* en ce qui concerne.

**concert** /'kɒnsət/ *n* concert *m*.

**concession** /kən'seʃn/ *n* concession *f*.

**conciliation** /kənsɪlɪ'eɪʃn/ *n* conciliation *f*.

**concise** /kən'saɪs/ *a* concis.

**conclude** /kən'klu:d/ *vt* conclure. ● *vi* se terminer. **conclusion** *n* conclusion *f*. **conclusive** *a* concluant.

**concoct** /kən'kɒkt/ *vt* confectionner; (invent: fig) fabriquer. **concoction** *n* mélange *m*.

**concourse** /'kɒŋkɔ:s/ *n* (Rail) hall *m*.

**concrete** /'kɒŋkri:t/ *n* béton *m*. ● *a* de béton; (fig) concret. ● *vt* bétonner.

**concur** /kən'kɜ:(r)/ *vi* (*pt* **concurred**) être d'accord.

**concurrently** /kən'kʌrəntlɪ/ *adv* simultanément.

**concussion** /kən'kʌʃn/ *n* commotion *f* (cérébrale).

**condemn** /kən'dem/ *vt* condamner.

**condensation** /kɒnden'seɪʃn/ *n* (on walls) condensation *f*; (on windows) buée *f*. **condense** *vt*/*i* (se) condenser.

**condition** /kən'dɪʃn/ *n* condition *f*; **on ~ that** à condition que. ● *vt* conditionner. **conditional** *a* conditionnel.

**conditioner** /kən'dɪʃənə(r)/ *n* après-shampooing *m*.

**condolences** /kən'dəʊlənsɪz/ *npl* condoléances *fpl*.

**condom** /'kɒndɒm/ *n* préservatif *m*.

**condone** /kən'dəʊn/ *vt* pardonner, fermer les yeux sur.

**conducive** /kən'dju:sɪv/ *a* **~ to** favorable à.

**conduct¹** /'kɒndʌkt/ *n* conduite *f*.

**conduct²** /kən'dʌkt/ *vt* conduire; (*orchestra*) diriger. **conductor** *n* chef *m* d'orchestre; (of bus) receveur *m*; (on train, US) chef *m* de train; (Electr) conducteur *m*. **conductress** *n* receveuse *f*.

**cone** /kəʊn/ *n* cône *m*; (of ice-cream) cornet *m*.

**confectioner** /kən'fekʃənə(r)/ *n* confiseur/-euse *m*/*f*. **confectionery** *n* confiserie *f*.

**confer** /kən'fɜ:(r)/ *vt*/*i* (*pt* **conferred**) conférer.

**conference** /'kɒnfərəns/ *n* conférence *f*.

**confess** /kən'fes/ *vt*/*i* avouer; (Relig) (se) confesser. **confession** *n* confession *f*; (of crime) aveu *m*.

**confide** /kən'faɪd/ *vt* confier. ● *vi* **~ in** se confier à.

**confidence** /'kɒnfɪdəns/ *n* (trust) confiance *f*; (boldness) confiance *f* en soi; (secret) confidence *f*; **in ~** en confidence. **confident** *a* sûr.

**confidential** /kɒnfɪ'denʃl/ *a* confidentiel.

**confine** /kən'faɪn/ *vt* enfermer; (limit) limiter; **~d space** espace *m* réduit; **~d to** limité à.

**confirm** /kən'fɜ:m/ *vt* confirmer. **confirmed** *a* (*bachelor*) endurci; (*smoker*) invétéré.

**confiscate** /'kɒnfɪskeɪt/ *vt* confisquer.

**conflict¹** /'kɒnflɪkt/ *n* conflit *m*.

**conflict²** /kən'flɪkt/ *vi* (*statements, views*) être en contradiction (**with** avec); (*appointments*) tomber en même temps (**with** que). **conflicting** *a* contradictoire.

**conform** /kən'fɔ:m/ *vt*/*i* (se) conformer.

**confound** /kən'faʊnd/ *vt* confondre.

**confront** /kən'frʌnt/ *vt* affronter; **~ with** confronter avec.

**confuse** /kən'fju:z/ *vt* (bewilder) troubler; (mistake, confound) confondre; **become ~d** s'embrouiller; **I am ~d** je m'y perds. **confusing** *a* déroutant. **confusion** *n* confusion *f*.

**congeal** /kən'dʒi:l/ *vt*/*i* (se) figer.

**congested** /kən'dʒestɪd/ *a* (*road*) embouteillé; (*passage*) encombré; (Med) congestionné. **congestion** *n* (traffic) encombrement(s) *m*(*pl*); (Med) congestion *f*.

**congratulate** /kən'grætjʊleɪt/ *vt* féliciter (**on** de). **congratulations** *npl* félicitations *fpl*.

**congregate** /'kɒŋgrɪgeɪt/ *vi* se rassembler. **congregation** *n* assemblée *f*.

**congress** /'kɒŋgres/ *n* congrès *m*; **C~** (US) le Congrès.

**conjugate** /'kɒndʒʊgeɪt/ *vt* conjuguer. **conjugation** *n* conjugaison *f*.

**conjunction** /kən'dʒʌŋkʃn/ *n* (Ling) conjonction *f*; **in ~ with** conjointement avec.

**conjunctivitis** /kɒndʒʌŋktɪ'vaɪtɪs/ *n* conjonctivite *f*.

**conjure** /'kʌndʒə(r)/ *vi* faire des tours de passe-passe. ● *vt* ~ **up** faire apparaître. **conjuror** *n* prestidigitateur/-trice *m/f*.

**con man** *n* ▣ escroc *m*.

**connect** /kə'nekt/ *vt/i* (se) relier; (in mind) faire le rapport entre; (install, wire up to mains) brancher; ~ **with** (of train) assurer la correspondance avec; ~**ed** (*idea, event*) lié; **be** ~**ed with** avoir rapport à.

**connection** /kə'nekʃn/ *n* rapport *m*; (Rail) correspondance *f*; (phone call) communication *f*; (Electr) contact *m*; (joining piece) raccord *m*; ~**s** (Comm) relations *fpl*.

**connive** /kə'naɪv/ *vi* ~ **at** se faire le complice de.

**conquer** /'kɒŋkə(r)/ *vt* vaincre; (country) conquérir. **conqueror** *n* conquérant *m*.

**conquest** /'kɒŋkwest/ *n* conquête *f*.

**conscience** /'kɒnʃəns/ *n* conscience *f*. **conscientious** *a* consciencieux.

**conscious** /'kɒnʃəs/ *a* conscient; (deliberate) voulu. **consciously** *adv* consciemment. **consciousness** *n* conscience *f*; (Med) connaissance *f*.

**conscript** /'kɒnskrɪpt/ *n* appelé *m*.

**consecutive** /kən'sekjʊtɪv/ *a* consécutif.

**consensus** /kən'sensəs/ *n* consensus *m*.

**consent** /kən'sent/ *vi* consentir (**to** à). ● *n* consentement *m*.

**consequence** /'kɒnsɪkwəns/ *n* conséquence *f*. **consequently** *adv* par conséquent.

**conservation** /kɒnsə'veɪʃn/ *n* préservation *f*; ~ **area** zone *f* protégée. **conservationist** *n* défenseur *m* de l'environnement.

**conservative** /kən'sɜ:vətɪv/ *a* conservateur; (*estimate*) minimal.

**Conservative Party** *n* parti *m* conservateur.

**conservatory** /kən'sɜ:vətrɪ/ *n* (greenhouse) serre *f*; (room) véranda *f*.

**conserve** /kən'sɜ:v/ *vt* conserver; (*energy*) économiser.

**consider** /kən'sɪdə(r)/ *vt* considérer; (allow for) tenir compte de; (*possibility*) envisager (**doing** de faire).

**considerable** /kən'sɪdərəbl/ *a* considérable; (much) beaucoup de.

**considerate** /kən'sɪdərət/ *a* prévenant, attentionné. **consideration** *n* considération *f*; (respect) égard(s) *m(pl)*.

**considering** /kən'sɪdərɪŋ/ *prep* compte tenu de.

**consignment** /kən'saɪnmənt/ *n* envoi *m*.

**consist** /kən'sɪst/ *vi* consister (**of** en; **in doing** à faire).

**consistency** /kən'sɪstənsɪ/ *n* (of liquids) consistance *f*; (of argument) cohérence *f*.

**consistent** /kən'sɪstənt/ *a* cohérent; ~ **with** conforme à.

**consolation** /kɒnsə'leɪʃn/ *n* consolation *f*.

**consolidate** /kən'sɒlɪdeɪt/ *vt/i* (se) consolider.

**consonant** /'kɒnsənənt/ *n* consonne *f*.

**conspicuous** /kən'spɪkjʊəs/ *a* (easily seen) en évidence; (showy) voyant; (noteworthy) remarquable.

**conspiracy** /kən'spɪrəsɪ/ *n* conspiration *f*.

**constable** /'kʌnstəbl/ *n* agent *m* de police, gendarme *m*.

**constant** /'kɒnstənt/ *a* (*questions*) incessant; (unchanging) constant; (*friend*) fidèle. ● *n* constante *f*. **constantly** *adv* constamment.

**constellation** /kɒnstə'leɪʃn/ *n* constellation *f*.

**constipation** /kɒnstɪ'peɪʃn/ *n* constipation *f*.

**constituency** /kən'stɪtjʊənsɪ/ *n* circonscription *f* électorale.

**constituent** /kən'stɪtjʊənt/ *a* constitutif. ● *n* élément *m* constitutif; (Pol) électeur/-trice *m/f*.

**constitution** /kɒnstɪ'tju:ʃn/ *n* constitution *f*.

**constrain** /kən'streɪn/ *vt* contraindre. **constraint** *n* contrainte *f*.

**constrict** /kən'strɪkt/ *vt* (*flow*) comprimer; (*movement*) gêner.

**construct** /kən'strʌkt/ *vt* construire. **construction** *n* construction *f*. **constructive** *a* constructif.

**consulate** /'kɒnsjʊlət/ *n* consulat *m*.

**consult** /kən'sʌlt/ *vt* consulter. ● *vi* ~ **with** conférer avec. **consultant** *n* conseiller/-ère *m/f*; (Med) spécialiste *mf*. **consultation** *n* consultation *f*.

**consume** /kən'sju:m/ *vt* consommer; (destroy) consumer. **consumer** *n* consommateur/-trice *m/f*.

**consummate** /'kɒnsəmeɪt/ *vt* consommer.

**consumption** /kən'sʌmpʃn/ *n* consommation *f*; (Med) phtisie *f*.

**contact** /'kɒntækt/ *n* contact *m*; (person) relation *f*. ● *vt* contacter. ~ **lenses** *npl* lentilles *fpl* (de contact).

**contagious** /kən'teɪdʒəs/ *a* contagieux.

**contain** /kən'teɪn/ *vt* contenir; ~ **oneself** se contenir. **container** *n* récipient *m*; (for transport) container *m*.

**contaminate** /kən'tæmɪneɪt/ *vt* contaminer.

**contemplate** /'kɒntəmpleɪt/ *vt* (gaze at) contempler; (think about) envisager.

**contemporary** /kən'temprərɪ/ *a* & *n* contemporain/-e (*m/f*).

**contempt** /kən'tempt/ *n* mépris *m*. **contemptible** *a* méprisable. **contemptuous** *a* méprisant.

**contend** /kən'tend/ *vt* soutenir. ● *vi* ~ **with** (compete) rivaliser avec; (face) faire face à. **contender** *n* adversaire *mf*.

**content¹** /'kɒntent/ *n* (of letter) contenu *m*; (amount) teneur *f*; ~**s** contenu *m*.

**content²** /kən'tent/ *a* satisfait. ● *vt* contenter. **contented** *a* satisfait. **contentment** *n* contentement *m*.

**contest¹** /'kɒntest/ *n* (competition) concours *m*; (struggle) lutte *f*.

**contest²** /kən'test/ *vt* contester; (compete for or in) disputer. **contestant** *n* concurrent/-e *m/f*.

**context** /'kɒntekst/ *n* contexte *m*.

**continent** /'kɒntɪnənt/ *n* continent *m*; the C~ l'Europe *f* (continentale). **continental** *a* continental, européen. **continental quilt** *n* couette *f*.

**contingency** /kən'tɪndʒənsɪ/ *n* éventualité *f*; ~ **plan** plan *m* d'urgence.

**continual** /kən'tɪnjʊəl/ *a* continuel.

**continuation** /kəntɪnjʊ'eɪʃn/ *n* continuation *f*; (after interruption) reprise *f*; (new episode) suite *f*.

**continue** /kən'tɪnju:/ *vt/i* continuer; (resume) reprendre. **continued** *a* continu.

**continuous** /kən'tɪnjʊəs/ *a* continu. **continuously** *adv* (without a break) sans interruption; (repeatedly) continuellement.

**contort** /kən'tɔ:t/ *vt* tordre; **~ oneself** se contorsionner.

**contour** /'kɒntʊə(r)/ *n* contour *m*.

**contraband** /'kɒntrəbænd/ *n* contrebande *f*.

**contraception** /kɒntrə'sepʃn/ *n* contraception *f*. **contraceptive** *a* & *n* contraceptif (*m*).

**contract¹** /'kɒntrækt/ *n* contrat *m*.

**contract²** /kən'trækt/ *vt/i* (se) contracter. **contraction** *n* contraction *f*.

**contractor** /kən'træktə(r)/ *n* entrepreneur/-euse *m/f*.

**contradict** /kɒntrə'dɪkt/ *vt* contredire. **contradictory** *a* contradictoire.

**contrary¹** /'kɒntrərɪ/ *a* contraire (to à). ● *n* contraire *m*; **on the ~** au contraire. ● *adv* **~ to** contrairement à.

**contrary²** /kən'treərɪ/ *a* entêté.

**contrast¹** /'kɒntrɑ:st/ *n* contraste *m*.

**contrast²** /kən'trɑ:st/ *vt/i* contraster.

**contravention** /kɒntrə'venʃn/ *n* infraction *f*.

**contribute** /kən'trɪbju:t/ *vt* donner. ● *vi* **~ to** contribuer à; (take part) participer à; (newspaper) collaborer à. **contribution** *n* contribution *f*. **contributor** *n* collaborateur/-trice *m/f*.

**contrive** /kən'traɪv/ *vt* imaginer; **~ to do** trouver moyen de faire.

**control** /kən'trəʊl/ *vt* (*pt* **controlled**) (*firm*) diriger; (check) contrôler; (restrain) maîtriser. ● *n* contrôle *m*; (mastery) maîtrise *f*; **~s** commandes *fpl*; (knobs) boutons *mpl*; **have under ~** (*event*) avoir en main; **in ~ of** maître de. **~ tower** *n* tour *f* de contrôle.

**controversial** /kɒntrə'vɜ:ʃl/ *a* discutable, discuté. **controversy** *n* controverse *f*.

**conurbation** /kɒnɜ:'beɪʃn/ *n* agglomération *f*, conurbation *f*.

**convalesce** /kɒnvə'les/ *vi* être en convalescence.

**convene** /kən'vi:n/ *vt* convoquer. ● *vi* se réunir.

**convenience** /kən'vi:nɪəns/ *n* commodité *f*; **~s** toilettes *fpl*; **all modern ~s** tout le confort moderne; **at your ~** quand cela vous conviendra, à votre convenance. **~ foods** *npl* plats *mpl* tout préparés.

**convenient** /kən'vi:nɪənt/ *a* commode, pratique; (*time*) bien choisi; **be ~ for** convenir à.

**convent** /'kɒnvənt/ *n* couvent *m*.

**convention** /kən'venʃn/ *n* (assembly, agreement) convention *f*; (custom) usage *m*. **conventional** *a* conventionnel.

**conversation** /kɒnvə'seɪʃn/ *n* conversation *f*. **conversational** *a* (*tone*) de la conversation; (*French*) de tous les jours.

**converse¹** /kən'vɜ:s/ *vi* s'entretenir, converser (**with** avec).

**converse²** /'kɒnvɜ:s/ *a* & *n* inverse (*m*). **conversely** *adv* inversement.

**conversion** /kən'vɜ:ʃn/ *n* conversion *f*.

**convert¹** /kən'vɜ:t/ *vt* convertir; (*house*) aménager. ● *vi* **~ into** se transformer en.

**convert²** /'kɒnvɜːt/ *n* converti/-e *m/f*.

**convertible** /kən'vɜːtəbl/ *a* convertible. ● *n* (car) décapotable *f*.

**convey** /kən'veɪ/ *vt* (*wishes, order*) transmettre; (*goods, people*) transporter; (*idea, feeling*) communiquer. **conveyor belt** *n* tapis *m* roulant.

**convict¹** /kən'vɪkt/ *vt* déclarer coupable.

**convict²** /'kɒnvɪkt/ *n* prisonnier/-ière *m/f*.

**conviction** /kən'vɪkʃn/ *n* (Jur) condamnation *f*; (opinion) conviction *f*.

**convince** /kən'vɪns/ *vt* convaincre.

**convoke** /kən'vəʊk/ *vt* convoquer.

**convoy** /'kɒnvɔɪ/ *n* convoi *m*.

**convulse** /kən'vʌls/ *vt* convulser; (fig) bouleverser; **be ~d with laughter** se tordre de rire.

**cook** /kʊk/ *vt/i* (faire) cuire; (of person) faire la cuisine; **~ up** ⊡ fabriquer. ● *n* cuisinier/-ière *m/f*. **cooker** *n* (stove) cuisinière *f*. **cookery** *n* cuisine *f*.

**cookie** /'kʊkɪ/ *n* (US) biscuit *m*.

**cooking** /'kʊkɪŋ/ *n* cuisine *f*. ● *a* de cuisine.

**cool** /kuːl/ *a* frais; (calm) calme; (unfriendly) froid. ● *n* fraîcheur *f*; (calmness ⊠) sang-froid *m*; **in the ~** au frais. ● *vt/i* rafraîchir. **~ box** *n* glacière *f*.

**coolly** /'kuːllɪ/ *adv* calmement; froidement.

**coop** /kuːp/ *n* poulailler *m*. ● *vt* **~ up** enfermer.

**co-operate** /kəʊ'ɒpəreɪt/ *vi* coopérer. **co-operation** *n* coopération *f*.

**co-operative** /kəʊ'ɒpərətɪv/ *a* coopératif. ● *n* coopérative *f*.

**co-ordinate** /kəʊ'ɔːdɪneɪt/ *vt* coordonner.

**cop** /kɒp/ *vt* (*pt* **copped**) ⊠ piquer. ● *n* (policeman ⊠) flic *m*. □ **~ out** ⊠ se dérober.

**cope** /kəʊp/ *vi* s'en sortir ⊡, se débrouiller; **~ with** (*problem*) faire face à.

**copper** /'kɒpə(r)/ *n* cuivre *m*; (coin) sou *m*; ⊠ flic *m*. ● *a* de cuivre.

**copulate** /'kɒpjʊleɪt/ *vi* s'accoupler.

**copy** /'kɒpɪ/ *n* copie *f*; (of book, newspaper) exemplaire *m*; (print: Photo) épreuve *f*. ● *vt/i* copier.

**copyright** /'kɒpɪraɪt/ *n* droit *m* d'auteur, copyright *m*.

**copy-writer** *n* rédacteur-concepteur *m*, rédactrice-conceptrice *f*

**cord** /kɔːd/ *n* (petite) corde *f*; (of curtain, pyjamas) cordon *m*; (Electr) cordon *m* électrique; (fabric) velours *m* côtelé.

**cordial** /'kɔːdɪəl/ *a* cordial. ● *n* (drink) sirop *m*.

**corduroy** /'kɔːdərɔɪ/ *n* velours *m* côtelé.

**core** /kɔː(r)/ *n* (of apple) trognon *m*; (of problem) cœur *m*; (Tech) noyau *m*. ● *vt* (*apple*) évider.

**cork** /kɔːk/ *n* liège *m*; (for bottle) bouchon *m*. ● *vt* boucher. **corkscrew** *n* tire-bouchon *m*.

**corn** /kɔːn/ *n* blé *m*; (maize: US) maïs *m*; (seed) grain *m*; (hard skin) cor *m*.

**cornea** /'kɔːnɪə/ *n* cornée *f*.

**corner** /'kɔːnə(r)/ *n* coin *m*; (bend in road) virage *m*; (football) corner *m*. ● *vt* coincer, acculer; (*market*) accaparer. ● *vi* prendre un virage.

**cornflour** /'kɔːnflaʊə(r)/ *n* farine *f* de maïs.

**cornice** /'kɔːnɪs/ *n* corniche *f*.

**corny** /'kɔ:nɪ/ *a* (**-ier**, **-iest**) (*joke*) éculé.

**corollary** /kə'rɒlərɪ/ *n* corollaire *m*.

**coronary** /'kɒrənərɪ/ *n* infarctus *m*.

**coronation** /kɒrə'neɪʃn/ *n* couronnement *m*.

**corporal** /'kɔ:pərəl/ *n* caporal *m*. **~ punishment** *n* châtiment *m* corporel.

**corporate** /'kɔ:pərət/ *a* (*ownership*) en commun; (*body*) constitué.

**corporation** /kɔ:pə'reɪʃn/ *n* (Comm) société *f*.

**corpse** /kɔ:ps/ *n* cadavre *m*.

**corpuscle** /'kɔ:pʌsl/ *n* globule *m*.

**correct** /kə'rekt/ *a* (right) exact, juste, correct; (proper) correct; **you are ~** vous avez raison. ● *vt* corriger.

**correction** /kə'rekʃn/ *n* correction *f*.

**correlate** /'kɒrəleɪt/ *vt/i* (faire) correspondre.

**correspond** /kɒrɪ'spɒnd/ *vi* correspondre. **correspondence** *n* correspondance *f*.

**corridor** /'kɒrɪdɔ:(r)/ *n* couloir *m*.

**corrode** /kə'rəʊd/ *vt/i* (se) corroder.

**corrugated** /'kɒrəgeɪtɪd/ *a* ondulé; **~ iron** tôle *f* ondulée.

**corrupt** /kə'rʌpt/ *a* corrompu. ● *vt* corrompre. **corruption** *n* corruption *f*.

**Corsica** /'kɔ:sɪkə/ *n* Corse *f*.

**cosh** /kɒʃ/ *n* matraque *f*. ● *vt* matraquer.

**cosmetic** /kɒz'metɪk/ *n* produit *m* de beauté. ● *a* cosmétique; (fig, pej) superficiel. **~ surgery** *n* chirurgie *f* esthétique

**cosmopolitan** /kɒzmə'pɒlɪt(ə)n/ *a & n* cosmopolite (*mf*).

**cosmos** /'kɒzmɒs/ *n* cosmos *m*.

**cost** /kɒst/ *vt* (*pt* **cost**) coûter; (*pt* **costed**) établir le prix de. ● *n* coût *m*; **~s** (Jur) dépens *mpl*; **at all ~s** à tout prix; **to one's ~** à ses dépens; **~ price** prix *m* de revient; **~ of living** coût *m* de la vie. **~-effective** *a* rentable.

**costly** /'kɒstlɪ/ *a* (**-ier**, **-iest**) coûteux; (valuable) précieux.

**costume** /'kɒstju:m/ *n* costume *m*; (for swimming) maillot *m*. **~ jewellery** *npl* bijoux *mpl* de fantaisie

**cosy** /'kəʊzɪ/ *a* (**-ier**, **-iest**) confortable, intime.

**cot** /kɒt/ *n* lit *m* d'enfant; (camp-bed: US) lit *m* de camp.

**cottage** /'kɒtɪdʒ/ *n* petite maison *f* de campagne; (thatched) chaumière *f*. **~ pie** *n* hachis *m* Parmentier

**cotton** /'kɒtn/ *n* coton *m*; (for sewing) fil *m* (à coudre). ● *vi* **~ on** ⊠ piger. **~ wool** *n* coton *m* hydrophile.

**couch** /kaʊtʃ/ *n* canapé *m*. ● *vt* (express) formuler.

**cough** /kɒf/ *vi* tousser. ● *n* toux *f*. □ **~ up** ⊠ cracher, payer.

**could** /kʊd/ ⇨CAN.

**couldn't** /'kʊdnt/ = COULD NOT.

**council** /'kaʊnsl/ *n* conseil *m*. **~ house** *n* maison *f* louée par la municipalité, ≈ H.L.M. *m or f*.

**councillor** /'kaʊnsələ(r)/ *n* conseiller/-ère *m/f* municipal/-e.

**counsel** /'kaʊnsl/ *n* conseil *m*. ● *n inv* (Jur) avocat/-e *m/f*. **counsellor** *n* conseiller/-ère *m/f*.

**count** /kaʊnt/ *vt/i* compter. ● *n* (numerical record) décompte *m*; (nobleman) comte *m*. □ **~ on** compter sur.

**counter** /'kaʊntə(r)/ *n* comptoir *m*; (in bank) guichet *m*; (token) jeton *m*. ● *adv* ~ **to** à l'encontre de. ● *a* opposé. ● *vt* opposer; (blow) parer. ● *vi* riposter.

**counteract** /kaʊntər'ækt/ *vt* neutraliser.

**counterbalance** /'kaʊntəbæləns/ *n* contrepoids *m*. ● *vt* contrebalancer.

**counterfeit** /'kaʊntəfɪt/ *a* & *n* faux (*m*). ● *vt* contrefaire.

**counterfoil** /'kaʊntəfɔɪl/ *n* souche *f*.

**counter-productive** /kaʊntəprə'dʌktɪv/ *a* qui produit l'effet contraire.

**countess** /'kaʊntɪs/ *n* comtesse *f*.

**countless** /'kaʊntlɪs/ *a* innombrable.

**country** /'kʌntrɪ/ *n* (land, region) pays *m*; (homeland) patrie *f*; (countryside) campagne *f*.

**countryman** /'kʌntrɪmən/ *n* (*pl* **-men**) campagnard *m*; (fellow citizen) compatriote *m*.

**countryside** /'kʌntrɪsaɪd/ *n* campagne *f*.

**county** /'kaʊntɪ/ *n* comté *m*.

**coup** /ku:/ *n* (achievement) joli coup *m*; (Pol) coup *m* d'état.

**couple** /'kʌpl/ *n* (people, animals) couple *m*; **a** ~ **(of)** (two or three) deux ou trois. ● *vt*/*i* (s')accoupler.

**coupon** /'ku:pɒn/ *n* coupon *m*; (for shopping) bon *m* *or* coupon *m* de réduction.

**courage** /'kʌrɪdʒ/ *n* courage *m*.

**courgette** /kʊə'ʒet/ *n* courgette *f*.

**courier** /'kʊrɪə(r)/ *n* messager/-ère *m*/*f*; (for tourists) guide *m*.

**course** /kɔ:s/ *n* cours *m*; (for training) stage *m*; (series) série *f*; (Culin) plat *m*; (for golf) terrain *m*; (at sea) itinéraire *m*; **change** ~ changer de cap; ~ **(of action)** façon *f* de faire; **during the** ~ **of** pendant; **in due** ~ en temps utile; **of** ~ bien sûr.

**court** /kɔ:t/ *n* cour *f*; (tennis) court *m*; **go to** ~ aller devant les tribunaux. ● *vt* faire la cour à; (*danger*) rechercher.

**courteous** /'kɜ:tɪəs/ *a* courtois.

**courtesy** /'kɜ:təsɪ/ *n* courtoisie *f*; **by** ~ **of** avec la permission de.

**court-house** *n* (US) palais *m* de justice.

**court-martial** *vt* (*pt* **-martialled**) faire passer en conseil de guerre. ● *n* cour *f* martiale.

**court**: ~**room** *n* salle *f* de tribunal. ~**shoe** *n* escarpin *m*. ~**yard** *n* cour *f*.

**cousin** /'kʌzn/ *n* cousin/-e *m*/*f*; **first** ~ cousin/-e *m*/*f* germain/-e.

**cove** /kəʊv/ *n* anse *f*, crique *f*.

**covenant** /'kʌvənənt/ *n* convention *f*.

**cover** /'kʌvə(r)/ *vt* couvrir. ● *n* (for bed, book) couverture *f*; (lid) couvercle *m*; (for furniture) housse *f*; (shelter) abri *m*; **take** ~ se mettre à l'abri. □ ~ **up** cacher; (*crime*) couvrir; ~ **up for** couvrir.

**coverage** /'kʌvərɪdʒ/ *n* reportage *m*.

**covering** /'kʌvərɪŋ/ *n* enveloppe *f*; ~ **letter** lettre *f* d'accompagnement.

**covert** /'kʌvət/ *a* (*activity*) secret; (*threat*) voilé; (*look*) dérobé.

**cover-up** *n* opération *f* de camouflage.

**cow** /kaʊ/ *n* vache *f*.

**coward** /'kaʊəd/ *n* lâche *mf*.

**cowboy** /'kaʊbɔɪ/ *n* cow-boy *m*.

**cowshed** /'kaʊʃed/ *n* étable *f*.

**coy** /kɔɪ/ *a* (faussement) timide, qui fait le *or* la timide.

**cozy** /'kəʊzɪ/ US = COSY.

**crab** /kræb/ *n* crabe *m*. **~-apple** *n* pomme *f* sauvage.

**crack** /kræk/ *n* fente *f*; (in glass) fêlure *f*; (noise) craquement *m*; (joke ☒) plaisanterie *f*. ● *a* ☐ d'élite. ● *vt*/*i* (break partially) (se) fêler; (split) (se) fendre; (*nut*) casser; (*joke*) raconter; (*problem*) résoudre; **get ~ing** ☐ s'y mettre. □ **~ down on** ☐ sévir contre; **~ up** ☐ craquer.

**cracker** /'krækə(r)/ *n* (Culin) biscuit *m* (salé); (for Christmas) diablotin *f*.

**crackle** /'krækl/ *vi* crépiter. ● *n* crépitement *m*.

**cradle** /'kreɪdl/ *n* berceau *m*. ● *vt* bercer.

**craft** /krɑ:ft/ *n* métier *m* artisanal; (technique) art *m*; (boat) bateau *m*. **craftsman** *n* (*pl* **-men**) artisan *m*. **craftsmanship** *n* art *m*.

**crafty** /'krɑ:ftɪ/ *a* (**-ier**, **-iest**) rusé.

**crag** /kræg/ *n* rocher *m* à pic.

**cram** /kræm/ *vt*/*i* (*pt* **crammed**); (for an exam) bachoter (**for** pour); **~ into** (pack) (s')entasser dans; **~ with** (fill) bourrer de.

**cramp** /kræmp/ *n* crampe *f*.

**cramped** /kræmpt/ *a* à l'étroit.

**cranberry** /'krænbərɪ/ *n* canneberge *f*.

**crane** /kreɪn/ *n* grue *f*. ● *vt* (*neck*) tendre.

**crank** /kræŋk/ *n* excentrique *mf*; (Tech) manivelle *f*.

**crap** /kræp/ *n* (nonsense ☒) conneries *fpl* ☒; (faeces ☒) merde *f* ☒.

**crash** /kræʃ/ *n* accident *m*; (noise) fracas *m*; (of thunder) coup *m*; (of firm) faillite *f*. ● *vt*/*i* avoir un accident (avec); (of plane) s'écraser; (two vehicles) se percuter; **~ into** rentrer dans. **~ course** *n* cours *m* intensif. **~-helmet** *n* casque *m* (antichoc). **~-land** *vi* atterrir en catastrophe.

**crate** /kreɪt/ *n* cageot *m*.

**cravat** /krə'væt/ *n* foulard *m*.

**crave** /kreɪv/ *vt*/*i* **~ (for)** désirer ardemment. **craving** *n* envie *f* irrésistible.

**crawl** /krɔ:l/ *vi* (*insect*) ramper; (*vehicle*) se traîner; **be ~ing with** grouiller de. ● *n* (pace) pas *m*; (swimming) crawl *m*.

**crayfish** /'kreɪfɪʃ/ *n inv* écrevisse *f*.

**crayon** /'kreɪən/ *n* craie *f* grasse.

**craze** /kreɪz/ *n* engouement *m*.

**crazy** /'kreɪzɪ/ *a* (**-ier**, **-iest**) fou; **~ about** (person) fou de; (thing) fana *or* fou de.

**creak** /kri:k/ *n* grincement *m*. ● *vi* grincer.

**cream** /kri:m/ *n* crème *f*. ● *a* crème *inv*. ● *vt* écrémer.

**crease** /kri:s/ *n* pli *m*. ● *vt*/*i* (se) froisser.

**create** /kri:'eɪt/ *vt* créer. **creation** *n* création *f*. **creative** *a* (*person*) créatif; (*process*) créateur. **creator** *n* créateur/-trice *m*/*f*.

**creature** /'kri:tʃə(r)/ *n* créature *f*.

**crèche** /kreʃ/ *n* garderie *f*.

**credentials** /krɪ'denʃlz/ *npl* (identity) pièces *fpl* d'identité; (competence) références *fpl*.

**credibility** /kredə'bɪlətɪ/ *n* crédibilité *f*.

**credit** /'kredɪt/ *n* (credence) crédit *m*; (honour) honneur *m*; **in ~** créditeur; **~s** (cinema) générique *m*. ● *a* (*balance*) créditeur. ● *vt* croire; (Comm) créditer; **~ sb with** attribuer à qn. **~ card** *n* carte *f* de crédit. **~ note** *n* avoir *m*.

**creditor** /'kredɪtə(r)/ *n* créancier/-ière *m*/*f*.

**credit-worthy** *a* solvable.

**creed** /kri:d/ *n* credo *m*.

**creek** /kri:k/ *n* (US) ruisseau *m*; **up the ~** ⊠ dans le pétrin ⊡.

**creep** /kri:p/ *vi* (*pt* **crept**) (*insect, cat*) ramper; (fig) se glisser. ● *n* (person ⊠) pauvre type *m* ⊡; **give sb the ~s** faire frissonner qn. **creeper** *n* liane *f*.

**cremate** /krɪ'meɪt/ *vt* incinérer. **cremation** *n* incinération *f*. **crematorium** *n* (*pl* **-ia**) crématorium *m*.

**crêpe** /kreɪp/ *n* crêpe *m*. **~ paper** *n* papier *m* crêpon.

**crept** /krept/ ⇒CREEP.

**crescent** /'kresnt/ *n* croissant *m*; (of houses) rue *f* en demi-lune.

**cress** /kres/ *n* cresson *m*.

**crest** /krest/ *n* crète *f*; (coat of arms) armoiries *fpl*.

**cretin** /'kretɪn/ *n* crétin/-e *m/f*.

**crevice** /'krevɪs/ *n* fente *f*.

**crew** /kru:/ *n* (of plane, ship) équipage *m*; (gang) équipe *f*. **~ cut** *n* coupe *f* en brosse. **~ neck** *n* (col) ras du cou *m*.

**crib** /krɪb/ *n* lit *m* d'enfant. ● *vt/i* (*pl* **cribbed**) copier.

**cricket** /'krɪkɪt/ *n* (Sport) cricket *m*; (insect) grillon *m*.

**crime** /kraɪm/ *n* crime *m*; (minor) délit *m*; (acts) criminalité *f*.

**criminal** /'krɪmɪnl/ *a* & *n* criminel/-le (*m/f*).

**crimson** /'krɪmzn/ *a* & *n* cramoisi (*m*).

**cringe** /krɪndʒ/ *vi* reculer; (fig) s'humilier.

**crinkle** /'krɪŋkl/ *vt/i* (se) froisser. ● *n* pli *m*.

**cripple** /'krɪpl/ *n* infirme *mf*. ● *vt* estropier; (fig) paralyser.

**crisis** /'kraɪsɪs/ *n* (*pl* **crises** /-si:z/) crise *f*.

**crisp** /krɪsp/ *a* (Culin) croquant; (air, reply) vif. **crisps** *npl* chips *fpl*.

**criss-cross** /'krɪskrɒs/ *a* entrecroisé. ● *vt/i* (s')entrecroiser.

**criterion** /kraɪ'tɪərɪən/ *n* (*pl* **-ia**) critère *m*.

**critic** /'krɪtɪk/ *n* critique *m*. **critical** *a* critique. **critically** *adv* d'une manière critique; (*ill*) gravement.

**criticism** /'krɪtɪsɪzəm/ *n* critique *f*.

**criticize** /'krɪtɪsaɪz/ *vt/i* critiquer.

**croak** /krəʊk/ *n* (*bird*) croassement *m*; (*frog*) coassement *m*. ● *vi* croasser; coasser.

**Croatia** /krəʊ'eɪʃə/ *n* Croatie *f*.

**Croatian** /krəʊ'eɪʃn/ *n* Croate *mf*. ● *a* Croate.

**crochet** /'krəʊʃeɪ/ *n* crochet *m*. ● *vt* faire du crochet.

**crockery** /'krɒkərɪ/ *n* vaisselle *f*.

**crocodile** /'krɒkədaɪl/ *n* crocodile *m*.

**crook** /krʊk/ *n* (criminal ⊡) escroc *m*; (stick) houlette *f*.

**crooked** /'krʊkɪd/ *a* tordu; (winding) tortueux; (askew) de travers; (dishonest: fig) malhonnête.

**crop** /krɒp/ *n* récolte *f*; (fig) quantité *f*. ● *vt* (*pt* **cropped**) couper. ● *vi* **~ up** se présenter.

**cross** /krɒs/ *n* croix *f*; (hybrid) hybride *m*. ● *vt/i* traverser; (*legs, animals*) croiser; (*cheque*) barrer; (*paths*) se croiser; **~ sb's mind** venir à l'esprit de qn. ● *a* en colère, fâché (**with** contre); **talk at ~ purposes** parler sans se comprendre. □ **~ off** *or* **out** rayer. **~-check** *vt* vérifier (pour confirmer). **~-country** (**running**) *n* cross *m*. **~-examine** *vt* faire subir un contre-interrogatoire à. **~-eyed** *a* **be ~-eyed** loucher. **~fire** *n* feux *mpl* croisés.

**crossing** /'krɒsɪŋ/ *n* (by boat) traversée *f*; (on road) passage *m* clouté.

**crossly** /'krɒslɪ/ *adv* avec colère.

**cross**: **~-reference** *n* renvoi *m*. **~roads** *n* carrefour *m*. **~word** *n* mots *mpl* croisés.

**crotch** /krɒtʃ/ *n* (of garment) entre-jambes *m inv*.

**crouch** /kraʊtʃ/ *vi* s'accroupir.

**crow** /krəʊ/ *n* corbeau *m*; **as the ~ flies** à vol d'oiseau. ● *vi* (of cock) chanter; (fig) jubiler. **~bar** *n* pied-de-biche *m*.

**crowd** /kraʊd/ *n* foule *f*. **crowded** *a* plein.

**crown** /kraʊn/ *n* couronne *f*; (top part) sommet *m*. ● *vt* couronner.

**Crown Court** *n* Cour *f* d'assises.

**crucial** /'kru:ʃl/ *a* crucial.

**crucifix** /'kru:sɪfɪks/ *n* crucifix *m*.

**crucify** /'kru:sɪfaɪ/ *vt* crucifier.

**crude** /kru:d/ *a* (raw) brut; (rough, vulgar) grossier.

**cruel** /krʊəl/ *a* (**crueller**, **cruellest**) cruel.

**cruise** /kru:z/ *n* croisière *f*. ● *vi* (*ship*) croiser; (*tourists*) faire une croisière; (*vehicle*) rouler; **cruising speed** vitesse *f* de croisière.

**crumb** /krʌm/ *n* miette *f*.

**crumble** /'krʌmbl/ *vt/i* (s')effriter; (*bread*) (s')émietter; (collapse) s'écrouler.

**crumple** /'krʌmpl/ *vt/i* (se) froisser.

**crunch** /krʌntʃ/ *vt* croquer. ● *n* (event) moment *m* critique; **when it comes to the ~** quand ça devient sérieux.

**crusade** /kru:'seɪd/ *n* croisade *f*. **crusader** *n* (knight) croisé *m*; (fig) militant/-e *m/f*.

**crush** /krʌʃ/ *vt* écraser; (*clothes*) froisser. ● *n* (crowd) presse *f*; **a ~ on** ▣ le béguin pour.

**crust** /krʌst/ *n* croûte *f*. **crusty** *a* croustillant.

**crutch** /krʌtʃ/ *n* béquille *f*; (crotch) entrejambes *m inv*.

**crux** /krʌks/ *n* **the ~ of** (problem) le point crucial de.

**cry** /kraɪ/ *n* cri *m*. ● *vi* (weep) pleurer; (call out) crier. □ **~ off** se décommander.

**crying** /'kraɪɪŋ/ *a* (*need*) urgent; **a ~ shame** une vraie honte. ● *n* pleurs *mpl*.

**cryptic** /'krɪptɪk/ *a* énigmatique.

**crystal** /'krɪstl/ *n* cristal *m*. **~-clear** *a* parfaitement clair.

**cub** /kʌb/ *n* petit *m*; **Cub (Scout)** louveteau *m*.

**Cuba** /'kju:bə/ *n* Cuba *f*.

**cube** /kju:b/ *n* cube *m*. **cubic** *a* cubique; (*metre*) cube.

**cubicle** /'kju:bɪkl/ *n* (in room, hospital) box *m*; (at swimming-pool) cabine *f*.

**cuckoo** /'kʊku:/ *n* coucou *m*.

**cucumber** /'kju:kʌmbə(r)/ *n* concombre *m*.

**cuddle** /'kʌdl/ *vt* câliner. ● *vi* **(kiss and) ~** s'embrasser. ● *n* caresse *f*. **cuddly** *a* câlin; **cuddly toy** peluche *f*.

**cue** /kju:/ *n* signal *m*; (Theat) réplique *f*; (billiards) queue *f*.

**cuff** /kʌf/ *n* manchette *f*; (US: on trousers) revers *m*; **off the ~** impromptu. ● *vt* gifler. **~-link** *n* bouton *m* de manchette.

**cul-de-sac** /'kʌldəsæk/ *n* (*pl* **culs-de-sac**) impasse *f*.

**cull** /kʌl/ *vt* (select) choisir; (kill) massacrer.

**culminate** /'kʌlmɪneɪt/ *vi* **~ in** se terminer par. **culmination** *n* point *m* culminant.

**culprit** /'kʌlprɪt/ *n* coupable *mf*.

**cult** /kʌlt/ *n* culte *m*.

**cultivate** /'kʌltɪveɪt/ *vt* cultiver. **cultivation** *n* culture *f*.

**cultural** /ˈkʌltʃərəl/ *a* culturel.

**culture** /ˈkʌltʃə(r)/ *n* culture *f*. **cultured** *a* cultivé.

**cumbersome** /ˈkʌmbəsəm/ *a* encombrant.

**cunning** /ˈkʌnɪŋ/ *a* rusé. ● *n* astuce *f*, ruse *f*.

**cup** /kʌp/ *n* tasse *f*; (prize) coupe *f*; **Cup final** finale *f* de la coupe.

**cupboard** /ˈkʌbəd/ *n* placard *m*.

**cup-tie** *n* match *m* de coupe.

**curate** /ˈkjʊərət/ *n* vicaire *m*.

**curator** /kjʊəˈreɪtə(r)/ *n* (of museum) conservateur *m*.

**curb** /kɜːb/ *n* (restraint) frein *m*; (of path) (US) bord *m* du trottoir. ● *vt* (desires) refréner; (price increase) freiner.

**cure** /kjʊə(r)/ *vt* guérir; (fig) éliminer; (Culin) fumer; (in brine) saler. ● *n* (recovery) guérison *f*; (remedy) remède *m*.

**curfew** /ˈkɜːfjuː/ *n* couvre-feu *m*.

**curiosity** /kjʊərɪˈɒsətɪ/ *n* curiosité *f*. **curious** *a* curieux.

**curl** /kɜːl/ *vt/i* (*hair*) boucler. ● *n* boucle *f*. □ ~ **up** se pelotonner; (shrivel) se racornir.

**curler** /ˈkɜːlə(r)/ *n* bigoudi *m*.

**curly** /ˈkɜːlɪ/ *a* (**-ier**, **-iest**) bouclé.

**currant** /ˈkʌrənt/ *n* raisin *m* de Corinthe.

**currency** /ˈkʌrənsɪ/ *n* (money) monnaie *f*; (of word) fréquence *f*; **foreign** ~ devises *fpl* étrangères.

**current** /ˈkʌrənt/ *a* (*term, word*) usité; (topical) actuel; (*year*) en cours. ● *n* courant *m*. ~ **account** *n* compte *m* courant. ~ **events** *npl* l'actualité *f*.

**currently** /ˈkʌrəntlɪ/ *adv* actuellement.

**curriculum** /kəˈrɪkjʊləm/ *n* (*pl* **-la**) programme *m* scolaire. ~ **vitae** *n* curriculum vitae *m*.

**curry** /ˈkʌrɪ/ *n* curry *m*. ● *vt* ~ **favour with** chercher les bonnes grâces de.

**curse** /kɜːs/ *n* (spell) malédiction *f*; (swearword) juron *m*. ● *vt* maudire. ● *vi* (swear) jurer.

**cursor** /ˈkɜːsə(r)/ *n* curseur *m*.

**curt** /kɜːt/ *a* brusque.

**curtain** /ˈkɜːtn/ *n* rideau *m*.

**curve** /kɜːv/ *n* courbe *f*. ● *vi* (*line*) s'incurver; (*edge*) se recourber; (*road*) faire une courbe. ● *vt* courber.

**cushion** /ˈkʊʃn/ *n* coussin *m*. ● *vt* (a blow) amortir; (fig) protéger.

**custard** /ˈkʌstəd/ *n* crème *f* anglaise; (set) flan *m*.

**custody** /ˈkʌstədɪ/ *n* (of child) garde *f*; (Jur) détention *f* préventive.

**custom** /ˈkʌstəm/ *n* coutume *f*; (patronage: Comm) clientèle *f*. **customary** *a* habituel.

**customer** /ˈkʌstəmə(r)/ *n* client/-e *m/f*; (person [I]) type *m*.

**customize** /ˈkʌstəmaɪz/ *vt* personnaliser.

**custom-made** *a* fait sur mesure.

**customs** /ˈkʌstəmz/ *npl* douane *f*. ● *a* douanier. ~ **officer** *n* douanier *m*.

**cut** /kʌt/ *vt/i* (*pt* **cut**; *pres p* **cutting**) *vt* couper; (*hedge*) tailler; (*prices*) réduire. ● *vi* couper. ● *n* (wound) coupure *f*; (of clothes) coupe *f*; (in surgery) incision *f*; (share) part *f*; (in prices) réduction *f*. □ ~ **back** *vi* faire des économies; *vt* réduire. ~ **down (on)** réduire; ~ **in** (in conversation) intervenir; ~ **off** couper; (*tide, army*) isoler; ~ **out** *vt* découper; (leave out) supprimer; *vi* (*engine*) s'arrêter. ~ **short** (visit) écourter; ~ **up** couper; (carve) découper.

**cut-back** *n* réduction *f*.

**cute** /kju:t/ *a* ▣ mignon.

**cutlery** /'kʌtlərɪ/ *n* couverts *mpl.*

**cutlet** /'kʌtlɪt/ *n* côtelette *f.*

**cut-price** *a* à prix réduit.

**cutting** /'kʌtɪŋ/ *a* cinglant. ● *n* (from newspaper) coupure *f*; (plant) bouture *f.*

**CV** *abbr* ⇒CURRICULUM VITAE.

**cyanide** /'saɪənaɪd/ *n* cyanure *m.*

**cyberspace** /'saɪbəspeɪs/ *n* cyberespace *m.*

**cycle** /'saɪkl/ *n* cycle *m*; (bicycle) vélo *m.* ● *vi* aller à vélo.

**cycling** /'saɪklɪŋ/ *n* cyclisme *m.* ~ **shorts** *npl* cycliste *m.*

**cyclist** /'saɪkɪst/ *n* cycliste *mf.*

**cylinder** /'sɪlɪndə(r)/ *n* cylindre *m.*

**cymbal** /'sɪmbl/ *n* cymbale *f.*

**cynic** /'sɪnɪk/ *n* cynique *mf.* **cynical** *a* cynique. **cynicism** *n* cynisme *m.*

**cypress** /'saɪprəs/ *n* cyprès *m.*

**Cypriot** /'sɪprɪət/ *n* Cypriote *mf.* ● *a* cypriote.

**Cyprus** /'sɪprəs/ *n* Chypre *f.*

**cyst** /sɪst/ *n* kyste *m.*

**czar** /zɑ:(r)/ *n* tsar *m.*

**Czech** /tʃek/ *n* (person) Tchèque *mf*; (Ling) tchèque *m.* ~ **Republic** *n* République *f* tchèque.

# Dd

**dab** /dæb/ *vt* (*pt* **dabbed**) tamponner; ~ **sth on** appliquer qch par petites touches. ● *n* touche *f.*

**dabble** /'dæbl/ *vi* ~ **in sth** faire qch en amateur.

**dad** /dæd/ *n* ▣ papa *m.* **daddy** *n* ▣ papa *m.*

**daffodil** /'dæfədɪl/ *n* jonquille *f.*

**daft** /dɑ:ft/ *a* bête.

**dagger** /'dægə(r)/ *n* poignard *m.*

**daily** /'deɪlɪ/ *a* quotidien. ● *adv* tous les jours. ● *n* (newspaper) quotidien *m.*

**dainty** /'deɪntɪ/ *a* (**-ier, -iest**) (*lace, food*) délicat; (*shoe, hand*) mignon.

**dairy** /'deərɪ/ *n* (on farm) laiterie *f*; (shop) crémerie *f.* ● *a* (*farm, cow, product*) laitier; (*butter*) fermier.

**daisy** /'deɪzɪ/ *n* pâquerette *f.*

**dam** /dæm/ *n* barrage *m.*

**damage** /'dæmɪdʒ/ *n* (to property) dégâts *mpl*; (Med) lésions *fpl*; **to do sth** ~ (cause, trade) porter atteinte à; ~**s** (Jur) dommages-intérêts *mpl.* ● *vt* (*property*) endommager; (*health*) nuire à; (*reputation*) porter atteinte à. **damaging** *a* (to health) nuisible; (to reputation) préjudiciable.

**damn** /dæm/ *vt* (Relig) damner; (condemn: fig) condamner. ● *interj* ▣ zut ▣, merde ▣. ● *n* **not give/care a** ~ **about** se ficher de ▣. ● *a* fichu ▣. ● *adv* franchement.

**damp** /dæmp/ *n* humidité *f.* ● *a* humide. **dampen** *vt* (lit) humecter; (fig) refroidir. **dampness** *n* humidité *f.*

**dance** /dɑ:ns/ *vt/i* danser. ● *n* danse *f*; (gathering) bal *m*; ~ **hall** dancing *m.* **dancer** *n* danseur/-euse *m/f.*

**dandelion** /'dændɪlaɪən/ *n* pissenlit *m.*

**dandruff** /'dændrʌf/ *n* pellicules *fpl.*

**Dane** /deɪn/ *n* Danois/-e *m/f.*

**danger** /'deɪndʒə(r)/ *n* danger *m*; (risk) risque *m*; **be in ~ of** risquer de. **dangerous** *a* dangereux.

**dangle** /'dæŋgl/ *vt* (*object*) balancer; (*legs*) laisser pendre. ● *vi* (*object*) se balancer (**from** à).

**Danish** /'deɪnɪʃ/ *n* (Ling) danois *m*. ● *a* danois.

**dare** /deə(r)/ *vt* oser (**(to) do** faire); **~ sb to do** défier qn de faire. ● *n* défi *m*. **daring** *a* audacieux.

**dark** /dɑ:k/ *a* (*day, colour, suit, mood, warning*) sombre; (*hair, eyes, skin*) brun; (*secret, thought*) noir. ● *n* noir *m*; (nightfall) tombée *f* de la nuit; **in the ~** (fig) dans le noir. **darken** *vt/i* (*sky*) (s')obscurcir; (*colour*) (se) foncer; (*mood*) (s')assombrir. **darkness** *n* obscurité *f*. **~-room** *n* chambre *f* noire.

**darling** /'dɑ:lɪŋ/ *a & n* chéri/-e (*m/f*).

**dart** /dɑ:t/ *n* fléchette *f*; **~s** (game) fléchettes *fpl*. ● *vi* **~ in/away** entrer/filer comme une flèche.

**dash** /dæʃ/ *vi* se précipiter; **~ off** se sauver. ● *vt* (*hope*) anéantir; **~ sth against** projeter qch contre. ● *n* course *f* folle; (of liquid) goutte *f*; (of colour) touche *f*; (in punctuation) tiret *m*.

**dashboard** /'dæʃbɔ:d/ *n* tableau *m* de bord.

**data** /'deɪtə/ *npl* données *fpl*. **~base** *n* base *f* de données. **~ capture** *n* saisie *f* de données. **~ processing** *n* traitement *m* des données. **~ protection** *n* protection *f* de l'information.

**date** /deɪt/ *n* date *f*; (meeting) rendez-vous *m*; (fruit) datte *f*; **out of ~** (old-fashioned) démodé; (*passport*) périmé; **to ~** à ce jour; **up to ~** (modern) moderne; (*list*) à jour. ● *vt/i* dater; (go out with) sortir avec; **~ from** dater de. **dated** *a* démodé.

**daughter** /'dɔ:tə(r)/ *n* fille *f*. **~-in-law** *n* (*pl* **~s-in-law**) belle-fille *f*.

**daunt** /dɔ:nt/ *vt* décourager.

**dawdle** /'dɔ:dl/ *vi* traînasser [I].

**dawn** /dɔ:n/ *n* aube *f*. ● *vi* (*day*) se lever; **it ~ed on me that** je me suis rendu compte que.

**day** /deɪ/ *n* jour *m*; (whole day) journée *f*; (period) époque *f*; **the ~ before** la veille; **the following** *or* **next ~** le lendemain. **~break** *n* aube *f*.

**daydream** *n* rêves *mpl*. ● *vi* rêvasser (**about** de).

**day ~light** *n* jour *m*. **~time** *n* journée *f*. **~ trader** *n* spéculateur *m* à la journée, scalper *m*.

**daze** /deɪz/ *n* **in a ~** (from blow) étourdi; (from drug) hébété. **dazed** *a* (by blow) abasourdi; (by news) ahuri.

**dazzle** /'dæzl/ *vt* éblouir.

**dead** /ded/ *a* mort; (numb) engourdi. ● *adv* complètement; **in ~ centre** au beau milieu; **stop ~** s'arrêter net. ● *n* **in the ~ of** au cœur de; **the ~** les morts. **deaden** *vt* (*sound, blow*) amortir; (*pain*) calmer. **~ end** *n* impasse *f*. **~line** *n* date *f* limite. **~lock** *n* impasse *f*.

**deadly** /'dedlɪ/ *a* (**-ier, -iest**) mortel; (*weapon*) meurtrier.

**deaf** /def/ *a* sourd. **deafen** *vt* assourdir. **deafness** *n* surdité *f*.

**deal** /di:l/ *vt* (*pt* **dealt**) donner; (*blow*) porter. ● *vi* (trade) être en activité; **~ in** être dans le commerce de. ● *n* affaire *f*; (cards) donne *f*; **a great** *or* **good ~** beaucoup (**of** de). □ **~ with** (handle, manage) s'occuper de; (be about) traiter de. **dealer** *n* marchand/-e *m/f*; (agent) concessionnaire *mf*. **dealings** *npl* relations *fpl*.

**dear** /dɪə(r)/ *a* cher; **~ Sir/Madam** Monsieur/Madame. ● *n* **(my) ~**

mon chéri/ma chérie *m/f.* ● *adv* cher. ● *interj* **oh ~!** oh mon Dieu!

**death** /deθ/ *n* mort *f*; **~ penalty** peine *f* de mort.

**debase** /dɪ'beɪs/ *vt* avilir.

**debatable** /dɪ'beɪtəbl/ *a* discutable.

**debate** /dɪ'beɪt/ *n* (formal) débat *m*; (informal) discussion *f*. ● *vt* (formally) débattre de; (informally) discuter.

**debit** /'debɪt/ *n* débit *m*. ● *a* (*balance*) débiteur. ● *vt* (*pt* **debited**) débiter.

**debris** /'deɪbri:/ *n* débris *mpl*; (rubbish) déchets *mpl*.

**debt** /det/ *n* dette *f*; **be in ~** avoir des dettes.

**debug** /di:'bʌg/ *vt* déboguer.

**decade** /'dekeɪd/ *n* décennie *f*.

**decadent** /'dekədənt/ *a* décadent.

**decaffeinated** /di:'kæfɪneɪtɪd/ *a* décaféiné.

**decay** /dɪ'keɪ/ *vi* (*vegetation*) pourrir; (*tooth*) se carier; (fig) décliner. ● *n* pourriture *f*; (of tooth) carie *f*; (fig) déclin *m*.

**deceased** /dɪ'si:st/ *a* décédé. ● *n* défunt/-e *m/f*.

**deceit** /dɪ'si:t/ *n* tromperie *f*. **deceitful** *a* trompeur.

**deceive** /dɪ'si:v/ *vt* tromper.

**December** /dɪ'sembə(r)/ *n* décembre *m*.

**decent** /'di:snt/ *a* (respectable) comme il faut; (adequate) convenable; (good) bon; (kind) gentil; (not indecent) décent. **decently** *adv* convenablement.

**deception** /dɪ'sepʃn/ *n* tromperie *f*. **deceptive** *a* trompeur.

**decide** /dɪ'saɪd/ *vt/i* décider **(to do** de faire); (question) régler; **~ on** se décider pour. **decided** *a* (firm) résolu; (clear) net. **decidedly** *adv* nettement.

**decimal** /'desɪml/ *a* décimal. ● *n* décimale *f*; **~ point** virgule *f*.

**decipher** /dɪ'saɪfə(r)/ *vt* déchiffrer.

**decision** /dɪ'sɪʒn/ *n* décision *f*.

**decisive** /dɪ'saɪsɪv/ *a* (conclusive) décisif; (firm) décidé.

**deck** /dek/ *n* pont *m*; (of cards: US) jeu *m*; (of bus) étage *m*. **~-chair** *n* chaise *f* longue.

**declaration** /deklə'reɪʃn/ *n* déclaration *f*. **declare** *vt* déclarer.

**decline** /dɪ'klaɪn/ *vt/i* refuser; (fall) baisser. ● *n* (waning) déclin *m*; (drop) baisse *f*; **in ~** sur le déclin.

**decode** /di:'kəʊd/ *vt* décoder.

**decommission** /ˌdi:kə'mɪʃn/ *vt* (arms) mettre hors service; (reactor) démanteler.

**decompose** /di:kəm'pəʊz/ *vt/i* (se) décomposer.

**decor** /'deɪkɔ:(r)/ *n* décor *m*.

**decorate** /'dekəreɪt/ *vt* décorer; (*room*) refaire, peindre. **decoration** *n* décoration *f*. **decorative** *a* décoratif.

**decorator** /'dekəreɪtə(r)/ *n* peintre *m*; **(interior) ~** décorateur/-trice *m/f*.

**decoy** /'di:kɔɪ/ *n* (person, vehicle) leurre *m*; (for hunting) appeau *m*.

**decrease**[1] /dɪ'kri:s/ *vt/i* diminuer.

**decrease**[2] /'di:kri:s/ *n* diminution *f*.

**decree** /dɪ'kri:/ *n* (Pol, Relig) décret *m*; (Jur) jugement *m*. ● *vt* (*pt* **decreed**) décréter.

**decrepit** /dɪ'krepɪt/ *a* (building) délabré; (person) décrépit.

**dedicate** /'dedɪkeɪt/ *vt* dédier; **~ oneself to** se consacrer à.

**dedicated** /'dedɪkeɪtɪd/ *a* dévoué; **~ line** (Internet) ligne *f* spécialisée.

**dedication** /'dedɪkeɪʃn/ *n* dévouement *m*; (in book) dédicace *f*.

**deduce** /dɪ'dju:s/ *vt* déduire.

**deduct** /dɪ'dʌkt/ *vt* déduire; (from wages) retenir.

**deed** /di:d/ *n* acte *m*.

**deem** /di:m/ *vt* considérer.

**deep** /di:p/ *a* profond; (*mud, carpet*) épais. ● *adv* profondément; ~ **in thought** absorbé dans ses pensées. **deepen** *vt/i* (*admiration, concern*) augmenter.

**deep-freeze** *n* congélateur *m*. ● *vt* congeler.

**deep vein thrombosis** *n* thrombose *f* veineuse profonde.

**deer** /dɪə(r)/ *n inv* cerf *m*; (doe) biche *f*.

**deface** /dɪ'feɪs/ *vt* dégrader.

**default** /dɪ'fɔ:lt/ *vi* (Jur) ~ **(on payments)** ne pas régler ses échéances. ● *n* (on payments) non-remboursement *m*; **by** ~ par défaut; **win by** ~ gagner par forfait. ● *a* (Comput) par défaut.

**defeat** /dɪ'fi:t/ *vt* vaincre; (thwart) faire échouer. ● *n* défaite *f*.

**defect**[1] /'di:fekt/ *n* défaut *m*.

**defect**[2] /dɪ'fekt/ *vi* faire défection; ~ **to** passer à.

**defective** /dɪ'fektɪv/ *a* défectueux.

**defector** /dɪ'fektə(r)/ *n* transfuge *mf*.

**defence** /dɪ'fens/ *n* défense *f*.

**defend** /dɪ'fend/ *vt* défendre. **defendant** *n* (Jur) accusé/-e *m*/*f*. **defender** défenseur *m*.

**defensive** /dɪ'fensɪv/ *a* défensif. ● *n* défensive *f*.

**defer** /dɪ'fɜ:(r)/ *vt* (*pt* **deferred**) (postpone) reporter; (*judgement*) suspendre; (*payment*) différer.

**deference** /'defərəns/ *n* déférence *f*. **deferential** *a* déférent.

**defiance** /dɪ'faɪəns/ *n* défi *m*; **in** ~ **of** contre. **defiant** *a* rebelle. **defiantly** *adv* avec défi.

**deficiency** /dɪ'fɪʃənsɪ/ *n* insuffisance *f*; (fault) défaut *m*.

**deficient** /dɪ'fɪʃnt/ *a* insuffisant; **be** ~ **in** manquer de.

**deficit** /'defɪsɪt/ *n* déficit *m*.

**define** /dɪ'faɪn/ *vt* définir.

**definite** /'defɪnɪt/ *a* (exact) précis; (obvious) net; (firm) ferme; (certain) certain. **definitely** *adv* certainement; (clearly) nettement.

**definition** /defɪ'nɪʃn/ *n* définition *f*.

**deflate** /dɪ'fleɪt/ *vt* dégonfler.

**deflect** /dɪ'flekt/ *vt* (*missile*) dévier; (*criticism*) détourner.

**deforestation** /di:fɒrɪ'steɪʃn/ *n* déforestation *f*.

**deform** /dɪ'fɔ:m/ *vt* déformer.

**defraud** /dɪ'frɔ:d/ *vt* (*client, employer*) escroquer; (*state, customs*) frauder; ~ **sb of sth** escroquer qch à qn.

**defrost** /di:'frɒst/ *vt* dégivrer.

**deft** /deft/ *a* adroit.

**defunct** /dɪ'fʌŋkt/ *a* défunt.

**defuse** /di:'fju:z/ *vt* désamorcer.

**defy** /dɪ'faɪ/ *vt* défier; (*attempts*) résister à.

**degenerate**[1] /dɪ'dʒenəreɪt/ *vi* dégénérer (**into** en).

**degenerate**[2] /dɪ'dʒenərət/ *a* & *n* dégénéré/-e (*m*/*f*).

**degrade** /dɪ'greɪd/ *vt* (humiliate) humilier; (damage) dégrader.

**degree** /dɪ'gri:/ *n* degré *m*; (Univ) diplôme *m* universitaire; (Bachelor's degree) licence *f*; **to such a** ~ **that** à tel point que.

**dehydrate** /di:'haɪdreɪt/ *vt/i* (se) déshydrater.

**deign** /deɪn/ *vt* ~ **to do** daigner faire.

**dejected** /dɪ'dʒektɪd/ *a* découragé.

**delay** /dɪ'leɪ/ *vt* (*flight*) retarder; (*decision*) différer; ~ **doing** attendre pour faire. ● *n* (of plane, post) retard *m*; (time lapse) délai *m*.

**delegate¹** /'delɪgət/ *n* délégué/-e *m/f*.

**delegate²** /'delɪgeɪt/ *vt* déléguer. **delegation** *n* délégation *f*.

**delete** /dɪ'li:t/ *vt* supprimer; (Comput) effacer; (with pen) barrer. **deletion** *n* suppression *f*; (with line) rature *f*.

**deliberate¹** /dɪ'lɪbəreɪt/ *vi* délibérer.

**deliberate²** /dɪ'lɪbərət/ *a* délibéré; (*steps, manner*) mesuré. **deliberately** *adv* (*do, say*) exprès; (*sarcastically, provocatively*) délibérément.

**delicacy** /'delɪkəsɪ/ *n* délicatesse *f*; (food) mets *m* raffiné.

**delicate** /'delɪkət/ *a* délicat.

**delicatessen** /delɪkə'tesn/ *n* épicerie *f* fine.

**delicious** /dɪ'lɪʃəs/ *a* délicieux.

**delight** /dɪ'laɪt/ *n* joie *f*, plaisir *m*. ● *vt* ravir. ● *vi* ~ **in** prendre plaisir à. **delighted** *a* ravi. **delightful** *a* charmant/-e.

**delinquent** /dɪ'lɪŋkwənt/ *a* & *n* délinquant/-e (*m/f*).

**delirious** /dɪ'lɪrɪəs/ *a* délirant.

**deliver** /dɪ'lɪvə(r)/ *vt* (*message*) remettre; (*goods*) livrer; (*speech*) faire; (*baby*) mettre au monde; (rescue) délivrer. **delivery** *n* (of goods) livraison *f*; (of mail) distribution *f*; (of baby) accouchement *m*.

**delude** /dɪ'lu:d/ *vt* tromper; ~ **oneself** se faire des illusions.

**deluge** /'delju:dʒ/ *n* déluge *m*. ● *vt* submerger (**with** de).

**delusion** /dɪ'lu:ʒn/ *n* illusion *f*.

**delve** /delv/ *vi* fouiller.

**demand** /dɪ'mɑ:nd/ *vt* (request, require) demander; (forcefully) exiger. ● *n* (request) demande *f*; (pressure) exigence *f*; **in** ~ très demandé; **on** ~ à la demande. **demanding** *a* exigeant.

**demean** /dɪ'mi:n/ *vt* ~ **oneself** s'abaisser.

**demeanour**, (US) **demeanor** /dɪ'mi:nə(r)/ *n* comportement *m*.

**demented** /dɪ'mentɪd/ *a* fou.

**demise** /dɪ'maɪz/ *n* disparition *f*.

**demo** /'deməʊ/ *n* (demonstration 🄸) manif *f* 🄸.

**democracy** /dɪ'mɒkrəsɪ/ *n* démocratie *f*.

**democrat** /'deməkræt/ *n* démocrate *mf*. **democratic** *a* démocratique.

**demolish** /dɪ'mɒlɪʃ/ *vt* démolir.

**demon** /'di:mən/ *n* démon *m*.

**demonstrate** /'demənstreɪt/ *vt* démontrer; (*concern, skill*) manifester. ● *vi* (Pol) manifester. **demonstration** *n* démonstration *f*; (Pol) manifestation *f*. **demonstrative** *a* démonstratif. **demonstrator** *n* manifestant/-e *m/f*.

**demoralize** /dɪ'mɒrəlaɪz/ *vt* démoraliser.

**demote** /dɪ'məʊt/ *vt* rétrograder.

**den** /den/ *n* (of lion) antre *m*; (room) tanière *f*.

**denial** /dɪ'naɪəl/ *n* (of rumour) démenti *m*; (of rights) négation *f*; (of request) rejet *m*.

**denim** /'denɪm/ *n* jean *m*; ~**s** (jeans) jean *m*.

**Denmark** /'denmɑ:k/ *n* Danemark *m*.

**denomination** /dɪnɒmɪ'neɪʃn/ *n* (Relig) confession *f*; (money) valeur *f*.

**denounce** /dɪ'naʊns/ *vt* dénoncer.

**dense** /dens/ *a* dense. **densely** *adv* (*packed*) très. **density** *n* densité *f*.

**dent** /dent/ *n* bosse *f*. ● *vt* cabosser.

**dental** /'dentl/ *a* dentaire; ~ **floss** fil *m* dentaire; ~ **surgeon** chirurgien-dentiste *m*.

**dentist** /'dentɪst/ *n* dentiste *mf*. **dentistry** *n* médecine *f* dentaire.

**dentures** /'dentʃəz/ *npl* dentier *m*.

**deny** /dɪ'naɪ/ *vt* nier (**that** que); (*rumour*) démentir; ~ **sb sth** refuser qch à qn.

**deodorant** /di:'əʊdərənt/ *n* déodorant *m*.

**depart** /dɪ'pɑ:t/ *vi* partir; ~ **from** (deviate) s'éloigner de.

**department** /dɪ'pɑ:tmənt/ *n* (in shop) rayon *m*; (in hospital, office) service *m*; (Univ) département *m*; **D~ of Health** ministère *m* de la santé; ~ **store** grand magasin *m*.

**departure** /dɪ'pɑ:tʃə(r)/ *n* départ *m*; **a** ~ **from** (*custom, truth*) une entorse à.

**depend** /dɪ'pend/ *vi* dépendre (**on** de); ~ **on** (rely on) compter sur; **it (all)** ~**s** ça dépend, ~**ing on the season** suivant la saison. **dependable** *a* (*person*) digne de confiance. **dependant** *n* personne *f* à charge. **dependence** *n* dépendance *f*.

**dependent** /dɪ'pendənt/ *a* dépendant; **be** ~ **on** dépendre de.

**depict** /dɪ'pɪkt/ *vt* (describe) dépeindre; (in picture) représenter.

**deplete** /dɪ'pli:t/ *vt* réduire.

**deport** /dɪ'pɔ:t/ *vt* expulser.

**depose** /dɪ'pəʊz/ *vt* déposer.

**deposit** /dɪ'pɒzɪt/ *vt* (*pt* **deposited**) déposer. ● *n* (in bank) dépôt *m*; (on house) versement *m* initial; (on holiday) acompte *m*; (against damage) caution *f*; (on bottle) consigne *f*; (of mineral) gisement *m*; ~ **account** compte *m* de dépôt. **depositor** *n* (Comm) déposant/-e *m/f*.

**depot** /'depəʊ/ *n* dépôt *m*; (US) gare *f*.

**depreciate** /dɪ'pri:ʃɪeɪt/ *vt/i* (se) déprécier.

**depress** /dɪ'pres/ *vt* déprimer. **depressing** *a* déprimant. **depression** *n* dépression *f*; (Econ) récession *f*.

**deprivation** /deprɪ'veɪʃn/ *n* privation *f*.

**deprive** /dɪ'praɪv/ *vt* ~ **of** priver de. **deprived** *a* démuni.

**depth** /depθ/ *n* profondeur *f*; (of knowledge, ignorance) étendue *f*; (of colour, emotion) intensité *f*.

**deputize** /'depjʊtaɪz/ *vi* ~ **for** remplacer.

**deputy** /'depjʊtɪ/ *n* adjoint/-e *m/f*. ● *a* adjoint; ~ **chairman** vice-président *m*.

**derail** /dɪ'reɪl/ *vt* faire dérailler. **derailment** *n* déraillement *m*.

**deranged** /dɪ'reɪndʒd/ *a* dérangé,

**derelict** /'derəlɪkt/ *a* abandonné.

**deride** /dɪ'raɪd/ *vt* ridiculiser. **derision** *n* moqueries *fpl*. **derisory** *a* dérisoire.

**derivative** /dɪ'rɪvətɪv/ *a* & *n* dérivé (*m*).

**derive** /dɪ'raɪv/ *vt* ~ **sth from** tirer qch de. ● *vi* ~ **from** découler de.

**derogatory** /dɪ'rɒgətrɪ/ *a* (*word*) péjoratif; (*remark*) désobligeant.

**descend** /dɪ'send/ *vt/i* descendre; **be** ~**ed from** descendre de. **descendant** *n* descendant/-e *m/f*.

**descent** *n* descente *f*; (lineage) origine *f*.

**describe** /dɪ'skraɪb/ *vt* décrire; ~ **sb as sth** qualifier qn de qch. **description** *n* description *f*. **descriptive** *a* descriptif.

**desert¹** /'dezət/ *n* désert *m*.

**desert²** /dɪ'zɜ:t/ *vt/i* abandonner; (*cause*) déserter. **deserted** *a* désert. **deserter** *n* déserteur *m*.

**deserts** /dɪ'zɜ:ts/ *npl* **get one's ~** avoir ce qu'on mérite.

**deserve** /dɪ'zɜ:v/ *vt* mériter (**to** de). **deservedly** *adv* à juste titre. **deserving** *a* (*person*) méritant; (*action*) louable.

**design** /dɪ'zaɪn/ *n* (sketch) plan *m*; (idea) conception *f*; (pattern) motif *m*; (art of designing) design *m*; (aim) dessein *m*. ● *vt* (sketch) dessiner; (devise, intend) concevoir.

**designate** /'dezɪgneɪt/ *vt* désigner.

**designer** /dɪ'zaɪnə(r)/ *n* concepteur/-trice *m/f*; (of fashion, furniture) créateur/-trice *m/f*. ● *a* (*clothes*) de haute couture; (*sunglasses, drink*) de dernière mode.

**desirable** /dɪ'zaɪərəbl/ *a* (*outcome*) souhaitable; (*person*) désirable.

**desire** /dɪ'zaɪə(r)/ *n* désir *m*. ● *vt* désirer.

**desk** /desk/ *n* bureau *m*; (of pupil) pupitre *m*; (in hotel) réception *f*; (in bank) caisse *f*.

**desolate** /'desələt/ *a* (place) désolé; (*person*) affligé.

**despair** /dɪ'speə(r)/ *n* désespoir *m*. ● *vi* désespérer (**of** de).

**desperate** /'despərət/ *a* désespéré; (criminal) prêt à tout; **be ~ for** avoir désespérément besoin de. **desperately** *adv* désespérément; (*worried*) terriblement; (*ill*) gravement.

**desperation** /despə'reɪʃn/ *n* désespoir *m*; **in ~** en désespoir de cause.

**despicable** /dɪ'spɪkəbl/ *a* méprisable.

**despise** /dɪ'spaɪz/ *vt* mépriser.

**despite** /dɪ'spaɪt/ *prep* malgré.

**despondent** /dɪ'spɒndənt/ *a* découragé.

**dessert** /dɪ'zɜ:t/ *n* dessert *m*. **~spoon** *n* cuillère *f* à dessert

**destination** /destɪ'neɪʃn/ *n* destination *f*.

**destiny** /'destɪnɪ/ *n* destin *m*.

**destitute** /'destɪtju:t/ *a* sans ressources.

**destroy** /dɪ'strɔɪ/ *vt* détruire; (*animal*) abattre. **destroyer** *n* (warship) contre-torpilleur *m*.

**destruction** /dɪ'strʌkʃn/ *n* destruction *f*. **destructive** *a* destructeur.

**detach** /dɪ'tætʃ/ *vt* détacher; **~ed house** maison *f* (individuelle).

**detail** /'di:teɪl/ *n* détail *m*; **go into ~** entrer dans les détails. ● *vt* (*plans*) exposer en détail.

**detain** /dɪ'teɪn/ *vt* retenir; (in prison) placer en détention. **detainee** *n* détenu/-e *m/f*.

**detect** /dɪ'tekt/ *vt* (*error, trace*) déceler; (*crime, mine, sound*) détecter. **detection** *n* détection *f*. **detective** *n* inspecteur/-trice *m/f*; (private) détective *m*.

**detention** /dɪ'tenʃn/ *n* détention *f*; (School) retenue *f*.

**deter** /dɪ'tɜ:(r)/ *vt* (*pt* **deterred**) dissuader (**from** de).

**detergent** /dɪ'tɜ:dʒənt/ *a & n* détergent (*m*).

**deteriorate** /dɪ'tɪərɪəreɪt/ *vi* se détériorer.

**determine** /dɪ'tɜ:mɪn/ *vt* déterminer; **~ to do** résoudre de faire. **determined** *a* (*person*) décidé; (*air*) résolu.

**deterrent** /dɪ'terənt/ *n* moyen *m* de dissuasion. ● *a* (*effect*) dissuasif.

**detest** /dɪ'test/ *vt* détester.

**detonate** /'detəneɪt/ *vt/i* (faire) détoner. **detonation** *n* détonation *f.* **detonator** *n* détonateur *m.*

**detour** /'di:tʊə(r)/ *n* détour *m.*

**detract** /dɪ'trækt/ *vi* **~ from** (*success, value*) porter atteinte à; (*pleasure*) diminuer.

**detriment** /'detrɪmənt/ *n* **to the ~ of** au détriment de. **detrimental** *a* nuisible (**to** à).

**devalue** /di:'vælju:/ *vt* dévaluer.

**devastate** /'devəsteɪt/ *vt* (*place*) ravager; (*person*) accabler.

**develop** /dɪ'veləp/ *vt* (*plan*) élaborer; (*mind, body*) développer; (*land*) mettre en valeur; (*illness*) attraper; (*habit*) prendre. ● *vi* (*child, country, plot, business*) se développer; (*hole, crack*) se former.

**development** /dɪ'veləpmənt/ *n* développement *m*; (**housing**) ~ lotissement *m*; (**new**) **~** fait *m* nouveau.

**deviate** /'di:vɪeɪt/ *vi* dévier; **~ from** (*norm*) s'écarter de.

**device** /dɪ'vaɪs/ *n* appareil *m*; (means) moyen *m*; (bomb) engin *m* explosif.

**devil** /'devl/ *n* diable *m.*

**devious** /'di:vɪəs/ *a* (*person*) retors.

**devise** /dɪ'vaɪz/ *vt* (*scheme*) concevoir; (*product*) inventer.

**devoid** /dɪ'vɔɪd/ *a* **~ of** dépourvu de.

**devolution** /di:və'lu:ʃn/ *n* (Pol) régionalisation *f.*

**devote** /dɪ'vəʊt/ *vt* consacrer (**to** à). **devoted** *a* dévoué. **devotion** *n* dévouement *m*; (Relig) dévotion *f.*

**devour** /dɪ'vaʊə(r)/ *vt* dévorer.

**devout** /dɪ'vaʊt/ *a* fervent.

**dew** /dju:/ *n* rosée *f.*

**diabetes** /daɪə'bi:ti:z/ *n* diabète *m.*

**diabolical** /daɪə'bɒlɪkl/ *a* diabolique; (bad ◻) atroce.

**diagnose** /'daɪəgnəʊz/ *vt* diagnostiquer. **diagnosis** *n* (*pl* **-oses** /-si:z/) diagnostic *m.*

**diagonal** /daɪ'ægənl/ *a* diagonal. ● *n* diagonale *f.*

**diagram** /'daɪəgræm/ *n* schéma *m.*

**dial** /'daɪəl/ *n* cadran *m.* ● *vt* (*pt* **dialled**) (*number*) faire; (*person*) appeler; **dialling code** indicatif *m*; **dialling tone** tonalité *f.*

**dialect** /'daɪəlekt/ *n* dialecte *m.*

**dialogue** /'daɪəlɒg/ *n* dialogue *m.*

**diameter** /daɪ'æmɪtə(r)/ *n* diamètre *m.*

**diamond** /'daɪəmənd/ *n* diamant *m*; (shape) losange *m*; (baseball) terrain *m*, **~s** (cards) carreau *m.*

**diaper** /'daɪəpə(r)/ *n* (US) couche *f.*

**diaphragm** /'daɪəfræm/ *n* diaphragme *m.*

**diarrhoea**, (US) **diarrhea** /daɪə'rɪə/ *n* diarrhée *f.*

**diary** /'daɪərɪ/ *n* (for appointments) agenda *m*; (journal) journal *m* intime.

**dice** /daɪs/ *n inv* dé *m.* ● *vt* (*food*) couper en dés.

**dictate** /dɪk'teɪt/ *vt/i* dicter.

**dictation** /dɪk'teɪʃn/ *n* dictée *f.*

**dictator** /dɪk'teɪtə(r)/ *n* dictateur *m.* **dictatorship** *n* dictature *f.*

**dictionary** /'dɪkʃənrɪ/ *n* dictionnaire *m.*

**did** /dɪd/ ⇨DO.

**didn't** /'dɪdnt/ = DID NOT.

**die** /daɪ/ *vi* (*pres p* **dying**) mourir; (*plant*) crever; **be dying to do** mourir d'envie de faire. ◻ **~ down** diminuer; **~ out** disparaître.

**diesel** /'di:zl/ *n* gazole *m*; **~ engine** moteur *m* diesel.

**diet** /'daɪət/ *n* (usual food) alimentation *f*; (restricted) régime *m*. ● *vi* être au régime. **dietary** *a* alimentaire. **dietician** *n* diététicien(ne) *m/f*.

**differ** /'dɪfə(r)/ *vi* différer (**from** de).

**difference** /'dɪfrəns/ *n* différence *f*; (disagreement) différend *m*. **different** *a* différent (**from, to** de).

**differentiate** /dɪfə'renʃɪeɪt/ *vt* différencier. ● *vi* faire la différence (**between** entre).

**differently** /'dɪfrəntlɪ/ *adv* différemment (**from** de).

**difficult** /'dɪfɪkəlt/ *a* difficile. **difficulty** *n* difficulté *f*.

**diffuse[1]** /dɪ'fju:s/ *a* diffus.

**diffuse[2]** /dɪ'fju:z/ *vt* diffuser.

**dig** /dɪg/ *vt/i* (*pt* **dug**; *pres p* **digging**) (excavate) creuser; (in garden) bêcher. ● *n* (poke) coup *m* de coude; (remark) pique *f* [!]; (Archeol) fouilles *fpl*. □ ~ **up** déterrer.

**digest** /dɪ'dʒest/ *vt/i* digérer. **digestible** *a* digestible. **digestion** *n* digestion *f*.

**digger** /'dɪgə(r)/ *n* excavateur *m*.

**digit** /'dɪdʒɪt/ *n* chiffre *m*.

**digital** /'dɪdʒɪtl/ *a* (*clock*) à affichage numérique; (*display, recording*) numérique. ~ **audio tape** *n* cassette *f* audionumérique. ~ **camera** *n* appareil *m* photo numérique.

**dignified** /'dɪgnɪfaɪd/ *a* digne.

**dignitary** /'dɪgnɪtərɪ/ *n* dignitaire *m*.

**dignity** /'dɪgnɪtɪ/ *n* dignité *f*.

**digress** /daɪ'gres/ *vi* faire une digression.

**dilapidated** /dɪ'læpɪdeɪtɪd/ *a* délabré.

**dilate** /daɪ'leɪt/ *vt/i* (se) dilater.

**dilemma** /dɪ'lemə/ *n* dilemme *m*.

**diligent** /'dɪlɪdʒənt/ *a* appliqué.

**dilute** /daɪ'lju:t/ *vt* diluer.

**dim** /dɪm/ *a* (**dimmer**, **dimmest**) (weak) faible; (dark) sombre; (indistinct) vague; [!] stupide. ● *vt/i* (*pt* **dimmed**) (*light*) baisser.

**dime** /daɪm/ *n* (US) (pièce *f* de) dix cents.

**dimension** /daɪ'menʃn/ *n* dimension *f*.

**diminish** /dɪ'mɪnɪʃ/ *vt/i* diminuer.

**dimple** /'dɪmpl/ *n* fossette *f*.

**din** /dɪn/ *n* vacarme *m*.

**dine** /daɪn/ *vi* dîner. **diner** *n* dîneur/-euse *m/f*; (US) restaurant *m* à service rapide.

**dinghy** /'dɪŋgɪ/ *n* dériveur *m*.

**dingy** /'dɪndʒɪ/ *a* (**-ier**, **-iest**) miteux, minable.

**dining room** /'daɪnɪŋrʊm/ *n* salle *f* à manger.

**dinner** /'dɪnə(r)/ *n* (evening meal) dîner *m*; (lunch) déjeuner *m*; **have** ~ dîner. **~-jacket** *n* smoking *m*. ~ **party** *n* dîner *m*.

**dinosaur** /'daɪnəsɔ:(r)/ *n* dinosaure *m*.

**dip** /dɪp/ *vt/i* (*pt* **dipped**) plonger; ~ **into** (*book*) feuilleter; (*savings*) puiser dans; ~ **one's headlights** se mettre en code. ● *n* (slope) déclivité *f*; (in sea) bain *m* rapide.

**diploma** /dɪ'pləʊmə/ *n* diplôme *m*.

**diplomacy** /dɪ'pləʊməsɪ/ *n* diplomatie *f*. **diplomat** *n* diplomate *mf*. **diplomatic** *a* (Pol) diplomatique; (tactful) diplomate.

**dire** /daɪə(r)/ *a* affreux; (*need, poverty*) extrême.

**direct** /dɪ'rekt/ *a* direct. ● *adv* directement. ● *vt* diriger; (*letter, remark*) adresser; (*a play*) mettre en scène; ~ **sb to** indiquer à qn le chemin de; (order) signifier à qn de.

**direction** /dɪ'rekʃn/ *n* direction *f*; (Theat) mise *f* en scène; **~s** indications *fpl*; **ask ~s** demander le chemin; **~s for use** mode *m* d'emploi.

**directly** /dɪ'rektlɪ/ *adv* directement; (at once) tout de suite. ● *conj* dès que.

**director** /dɪ'rektə(r)/ *n* directeur/-trice *m/f*; (Theat) metteur *m* en scène.

**directory** /dɪ'rektərɪ/ *n* (phone book) annuaire *m*. **~ enquiries** *npl* renseignements *mpl* téléphoniques.

**dirt** /dɜ:t/ *n* saleté *f*; (earth) terre *f*; **~ cheap** ☒ très bon marché *inv*. **~-track** *n* (Sport) cendrée *f*.

**dirty** /'dɜ:tɪ/ *a* (**-ier**, **-iest**) sale; (word) grossier; **get ~** se salir. ● *vt/i* (se) salir.

**disability** /dɪsə'bɪlətɪ/ *n* handicap *m*.

**disable** /dɪs'eɪbl/ *vt* rendre infirme. **disabled** *a* handicapé.

**disadvantage** /dɪsəd'vɑ:ntɪdʒ/ *n* désavantage *m*. **disadvantaged** *a* défavorisé.

**disagree** /dɪsə'gri:/ *vi* ne pas être d'accord (**with** avec); **~ with sb** (*food, climate*) ne pas convenir à qn. **disagreement** *n* désaccord *m*; (quarrel) différend *m*.

**disappear** /dɪsə'pɪə(r)/ *vi* disparaître. **disappearance** *n* disparition *f* (**of** de).

**disappoint** /dɪsə'pɔɪnt/ *vt* décevoir. **disappointment** *n* déception *f*.

**disapproval** /dɪsə'pru:vl/ *n* désapprobation *f* (**of** de).

**disapprove** /dɪsə'pru:v/ *vi* **~ (of)** désapprouver.

**disarm** /dɪs'ɑ:m/ *vt/i* désarmer. **disarmament** *n* désarmement *m*.

**disarray** /dɪsə'reɪ/ *n* désordre *m*.

**disaster** /dɪ'zɑ:stə(r)/ *n* désastre *m*. **disastrous** *a* désastreux.

**disband** /dɪs'bænd/ *vi* disperser. ● *vt* dissoudre.

**disbelief** /dɪsbɪ'li:f/ *n* incrédulité *f*.

**disc** /dɪsk/ *n* disque *m*; (Comput) = DISK.

**discard** /dɪ'skɑ:d/ *vt* se débarrasser de; (*beliefs*) abandonner.

**discharge** /dɪs'tʃɑ:dʒ/ *vt* (unload) décharger; (*liquid*) déverser; (*duty*) remplir; (dismiss) renvoyer; (*prisoner*) libérer. ● *vi* (of pus) s'écouler.

**disciple** /dɪ'saɪpl/ *n* disciple *m*.

**disciplinary** /'dɪsɪplɪnərɪ/ *a* disciplinaire.

**discipline** /'dɪsɪplɪn/ *n* discipline *f*. ● *vt* discipliner; (punish) punir.

**disc jockey** *n* disc jockey *m*, animateur *m*.

**disclaimer** /dɪs'kleɪmə(r)/ *n* démenti *m*.

**disclose** /dɪs'kləʊz/ *vt* révéler. **disclosure** *n* révélation *f* (**of** de).

**disco** /'dɪskəʊ/ *n* (club ☐) discothèque *f*, (event) soirée *f* disco.

**discolour** /dɪs'kʌlə(r)/ *vt/i* (se) décolorer.

**discomfort** /dɪs'kʌmfət/ *n* gêne *f*.

**disconcert** /dɪskən'sɜ:t/ *vt* déconcerter.

**disconnect** /dɪskə'nekt/ *vt* détacher; (unplug) débrancher; (cut off) couper.

**discontent** /dɪskən'tent/ *n* mécontentement *m*.

**discontinue** /dɪskən'tɪnju:/ *vt* (*service*) supprimer; (*production*) arrêter.

**discord** /'dɪskɔ:d/ *n* discorde *f*; (Mus) discordance *f*.

**discount**[1] /'dɪskaʊnt/ *n* remise *f*; (on minor purchase) rabais *m*.

**discount**[2] /dɪs'kaʊnt/ *vt* (*advice*) ne pas tenir compte de; (*possibility*) écarter.

**discourage** /dɪ'skʌrɪdʒ/ *vt* décourager.

**discourse** /'dɪskɔ:s/ *n* discours *m*.

**discourteous** /dɪs'kɜ:tɪəs/ *a* peu courtois.

**discover** /di'skʌvə(r)/ *vt* découvrir. **discovery** *n* découverte *f*.

**discreet** /dɪ'skri:t/ *a* discret.

**discrepancy** /dɪ'skrepənsɪ/ *n* divergence *f*.

**discretion** /dɪ'skreʃn/ *n* discrétion *f*.

**discriminate** /dɪ'skrɪmɪneɪt/ *vt*/*i* distinguer; ~ **against** faire de la discrimination contre. **discriminating** *a* qui a du discernement. **discrimination** *n* discernement *m*; (bias) discrimination *f*.

**discus** /'dɪskəs/ *n* disque *m*.

**discuss** /dɪ'skʌs/ *vt* (talk about) discuter de; (in writing) examiner. **discussion** *n* discussion *f*.

**disdain** /dɪs'deɪn/ *n* dédain *m*.

**disease** /dɪ'zi:z/ *n* maladie *f*.

**disembark** /dɪsɪm'bɑ:k/ *vt*/*i* débarquer.

**disenchanted** /dɪsɪn'tʃɑ:ntɪd/ *a* désabusé.

**disentangle** /dɪsɪn'tæŋgl/ *vt* démêler.

**disfigure** /dɪs'fɪgə(r)/ *vt* défigurer.

**disgrace** /dɪs'greɪs/ *n* (shame) honte *f*; (disfavour) disgrâce *f*. ● *vt* déshonorer. **disgraced** *a* (in disfavour) disgracié. **disgraceful** *a* honteux.

**disgruntled** /dɪs'grʌntld/ *a* mécontent.

**disguise** /dɪs'gaɪz/ *vt* déguiser. ● *n* déguisement *m*; **in** ~ déguisé.

**disgust** /dɪs'gʌst/ *n* dégoût *m*. ● *vt* dégoûter.

**dish** /dɪʃ/ *n* plat *m*; **the** ~**es** (crockery) la vaisselle. ● *vt* ~ **out** Ⓘ distribuer; ~ **up** servir.

**dishcloth** /'dɪʃklɒθ/ *n* lavette *f*; (for drying) torchon *m*.

**dishearten** /dɪs'hɑ:tn/ *vt* décourager.

**dishevelled** /dɪ'ʃevld/ *a* échevelé.

**dishonest** /dɪs'ɒnɪst/ *a* malhonnête.

**dishonour**, (US) **dishonor** /dɪs'ɒnə(r)/ *n* déshonneur *m*.

**dishwasher** /'dɪʃwɒʃə(r)/ *n* lave-vaisselle *m inv*.

**disillusion** /dɪsɪ'lu:ʒn/ *vt* désabuser. **disillusionment** *n* désillusion *f*.

**disincentive** /dɪsɪn'sentɪv/ *n* **be a** ~ **to** décourager.

**disinclined** /dɪsɪn'klaɪnd/ *a* ~ **to** peu disposé à.

**disinfect** /dɪsɪn'fekt/ *vt* désinfecter. **disinfectant** *n* désinfectant *m*.

**disintegrate** /dɪs'ɪntɪgreɪt/ *vt*/*i* (se) désintégrer.

**disinterested** /dɪs'ɪntrəstɪd/ *a* désintéressé.

**disjointed** /dɪs'dʒɔɪntɪd/ *a* (talk) décousu.

**disk** /dɪsk/ *n* (US) = DISC; (Comput) disque *m*. ~ **drive** *n* drive *m*, lecteur *m* de disquettes.

**diskette** /dɪ'sket/ *n* disquette *f*.

**dislike** /dɪs'laɪk/ *n* aversion *f*. ● *vt* ne pas aimer.

**dislocate** /'dɪsləkeɪt/ *vt* (limb) disloquer.

**dislodge** /dɪs'lɒdʒ/ *vt* (move) déplacer; (drive out) déloger.

**disloyal** /dɪs'lɔɪəl/ *a* déloyal (**to** envers).

**dismal** /'dɪzməl/ *a* morne, triste.

**dismantle** /dɪs'mæntl/ *vt* démonter, défaire.

**dismay** /dɪs'meɪ/ *n* consternation *f* (at devant). ● *vt* consterner.

**dismiss** /dɪs'mɪs/ *vt* renvoyer; (*appeal*) rejeter; (from mind) écarter. **dismissal** *n* renvoi *m*.

**dismount** /dɪs'maʊnt/ *vi* descendre, mettre pied à terre.

**disobedient** /dɪsə'bi:dɪənt/ *a* désobéissant.

**disobey** /dɪsə'beɪ/ *vt* désobéir à. ● *vi* désobéir.

**disorder** /dɪs'ɔ:də(r)/ *n* désordre *m*; (ailment) trouble(s) *m(pl)*. **disorderly** *a* désordonné.

**disorganized** /dɪs'ɔ:gənaɪzd/ *a* désorganisé.

**disown** /dɪs'əʊn/ *vt* renier.

**disparaging** /dɪ'spærɪdʒɪŋ/ *a* désobligeant.

**dispassionate** /dɪ'spæʃənət/ *a* impartial; (unemotional) calme.

**dispatch** /dɪ'spætʃ/ *vt* (send, complete) expédier; (troops) envoyer. ● *n* expédition *f*, envoi *m*; (report) dépêche *f*.

**dispel** /dɪ'spel/ *vt* (*pt* **dispelled**) dissiper.

**dispensary** /dɪ'spensərɪ/ *n* (in hospital) pharmacie *f*, (in chemist's) officine *f*.

**dispense** /dɪ'spens/ *vt* distribuer; (*medicine*) préparer. ● *vi* ~ **with** se passer de. **dispenser** *n* (container) distributeur *m*.

**disperse** /dɪ'spɜ:s/ *vt/i* (se) disperser.

**display** /dɪ'spleɪ/ *vt* montrer, exposer; (*feelings*) manifester. ● *n* exposition *f*, manifestation *f*; (Comm) étalage *m*; (of computer) visuel *m*.

**displeased** /dɪs'pli:zd/ *a* mécontent (**with** de).

**disposable** /dɪ'spəʊzəbl/ *a* jetable.

**disposal** /dɪ'spəʊzl/ *n* (of waste) évacuation *f*; **at sb's** ~ à la disposition de qn.

**dispose** /dɪ'spəʊz/ *vt* disposer. ● *vi* ~ **of** se débarrasser de; **well ~d to** bien disposé envers.

**disposition** /dɪspə'zɪʃn/ *n* disposition *f*; (character) naturel *m*.

**disprove** /dɪs'pru:v/ *vt* réfuter.

**dispute** /dɪ'spju:t/ *vt* contester. ● *n* discussion *f*; (Pol) conflit *m*; **in** ~ contesté.

**disqualify** /dɪs'kwɒlɪfaɪ/ *vt* rendre inapte; (Sport) disqualifier; ~ **from driving** retirer le permis à.

**disquiet** /dɪs'kwaɪət/ *n* inquiétude *f*. **disquieting** *a* inquiétant.

**disregard** /dɪsrɪ'gɑ:d/ *vt* ne pas tenir compte de. ● *n* indifférence *f* (**for** à).

**disrepair** /dɪsrɪ'peə(r)/ *n* délabrement *m*.

**disreputable** /dɪs'repjʊtəbl/ *a* peu recommendable.

**disrepute** /dɪsrɪ'pju:t/ *n* discrédit *m*.

**disrespect** /dɪsrɪ'spekt/ *n* manque *m* de respect. **disrespectful** *a* irrespectueux.

**disrupt** /dɪs'rʌpt/ *vt* (disturb, break up) perturber; (*plans*) déranger. **disruption** *n* perturbation *f*. **disruptive** *a* perturbateur.

**dissatisfied** /dɪ'sætɪsfaɪd/ *a* mécontent.

**dissect** /dɪ'sekt/ *vt* disséquer.

**disseminate** /dɪ'semɪneɪt/ *vt* diffuser.

**dissent** /dɪ'sent/ *vi* différer (**from** de). ● *n* dissentiment *m*.

**dissertation** /dɪsə'teɪʃn/ *n* mémoire *m*.

**disservice** /dɪs'sɜ:vɪs/ *n* **do a** ~ **to sb** rendre un mauvais service à qn.

**dissident** /ˈdɪsɪdənt/ *a & n* dissident/-e (*m/f*).

**dissimilar** /dɪˈsɪmɪlə(r)/ *a* dissemblable, différent.

**dissipate** /ˈdɪsɪpeɪt/ *vt/i* (se) dissiper. **dissipated** *a* (person) dissolu.

**dissolve** /dɪˈzɒlv/ *vt/i* (se) dissoudre.

**dissuade** /dɪˈsweɪd/ *vt* dissuader.

**distance** /ˈdɪstəns/ *n* distance *f*; **from a ~** de loin; **in the ~** au loin. **distant** *a* éloigné, lointain; (*relative*) éloigné; (aloof) distant.

**distaste** /dɪsˈteɪst/ *n* dégoût *m*. **distasteful** *a* désagréable.

**distil** /dɪˈstɪl/ *vt* (*pt* **distilled**) distiller.

**distinct** /dɪˈstɪŋkt/ *a* distinct; (definite) net; **as ~ from** par opposition à. **distinction** *n* distinction *f*; (in exam) mention *f* très bien. **distinctive** *a* distinctif.

**distinguish** /dɪˈstɪŋgwɪʃ/ *vt/i* distinguer.

**distort** /dɪˈstɔːt/ *vt* déformer. **distortion** *n* distorsion *f*; (of facts) déformation *f*.

**distract** /dɪˈstrækt/ *vt* distraire. **distracted** *a* (distraught) éperdu. **distracting** *a* gênant. **distraction** *n* (lack of attention, entertainment) distraction *f*.

**distraught** /dɪˈstrɔːt/ *a* éperdu.

**distress** /dɪˈstres/ *n* douleur *f*; (poverty, danger) détresse *f*. ● *vt* peiner. **distressing** *a* pénible.

**distribute** /dɪˈstrɪbjuːt/ *vt* distribuer.

**district** /ˈdɪstrɪkt/ *n* région *f*; (of town) quartier *m*.

**distrust** /dɪsˈtrʌst/ *n* méfiance *f*. ● *vt* se méfier de.

**disturb** /dɪˈstɜːb/ *vt* déranger; (alarm, worry) troubler. **disturbance** *n* dérangement *m* (**of** de); (noise) tapage *m*. **disturbances** *npl* (Pol) troubles *mpl*. **disturbed** *a* troublé; (psychologically) perturbé. **disturbing** *a* troublant.

**disused** /dɪsˈjuːzd/ *a* désaffecté.

**ditch** /dɪtʃ/ *n* fossé *m*. ● *vt* ▣ abandonner.

**ditto** /ˈdɪtəʊ/ *adv* idem.

**dive** /daɪv/ *vi* plonger; (rush) se précipiter. ● *n* plongeon *m*; (of plane) piqué *m*; (place ▣) bouge *m*. **diver** *n* plongeur/-euse *m/f*.

**diverge** /daɪˈvɜːdʒ/ *vi* diverger. **divergent** *a* divergent.

**diverse** /daɪˈvɜːs/ *a* divers.

**diversion** /daɪˈvɜːʃn/ *n* détournement *m*; (distraction) diversion *f*; (of traffic) déviation *f*. **divert** *vt* détourner; (*traffic*) dévier.

**divide** /dɪˈvaɪd/ *vt/i* (se) diviser.

**dividend** /ˈdɪvɪdend/ *n* dividende *m*.

**divine** /dɪˈvaɪn/ *a* divin.

**diving**: **~-board** *n* plongeoir *m*. **~-suit** *n* scaphandre *m*.

**division** /dɪˈvɪʒn/ *n* division *f*.

**divorce** /dɪˈvɔːs/ *n* divorce *m* (**from** avec). ● *vt/i* divorcer (d'avec).

**divulge** /daɪˈvʌldʒ/ *vt* divulguer.

**DIY** *abbr* ⇒DO-IT-YOURSELF.

**dizziness** /ˈdɪzɪnɪs/ *n* vertige *m*.

**dizzy** /ˈdɪzɪ/ *a* (**-ier**, **-iest**) vertigineux; **be** *or* **feel ~** avoir le vertige.

**do** /duː/

*present* **do, does**; *present negative* **don't, do not**; *past* **did**; *past participle* **done**

● *transitive and intransitive verb*

····➤ faire; **she is doing her homework** elle fait ses devoirs.

····➤(progress, be suitable) aller; **how are you doing?** comment ça va?

····➤(be enough) suffire; **will five dollars ~?** cinq dollars, ça suffira?

● *auxiliary verb*

····➤(in questions) **~ you like Mozart?** aimes-tu Mozart?, est-ce que tu aimes Mozart?; **did your sister phone?** est-ce que ta sœur a téléphoné?, ta sœur a-t-elle téléphoné?

····➤(in negatives) **I don't like Mozart** je n'aime pas Mozart.

····➤(emphatic uses) **I ~ like your dress** j'aime beaucoup ta robe; **I ~ think you should go** je pense vraiment que tu devrais y aller.

····➤(referring back to another verb) **I live in Oxford and so does Lily** j'habite à Oxford et Lily aussi; **she gets paid more than I ~** elle est payée plus que moi; **'I don't like carrots'–'neither ~ I'** 'je n'aime pas les carottes'–'moi non plus'.

····➤(imperatives) **don't shut the door** ne ferme pas la porte; **~ be quiet** tais-toi!

····➤(short questions and answers) **you like fish, don't you?** tu aimes le poisson, n'est-ce pas?; **Lola didn't phone, did she?** Lola n'a pas téléphoné par hasard?; **'does he play tennis?'—'no he doesn't/yes he does'** 'est-ce qu'il joue au tennis?—'non/oui'; **'Marion didn't say that'—'yes she did'** 'Marion n'a pas dit ça'—'si'.

□ **do away with** supprimer;

**do up** (fasten) fermer; (*house*) refaire;

**do with it's to ~ with** c'est à propos de; **it's nothing to ~ with** ça n'a rien à voir avec;

**do without** se passer de.

**docile** /'dəʊsaɪl/ *a* docile.

**dock** /dɒk/ *n* (Jur) banc *m* des accusés; dock *m*. ● *vi* arriver au port. ● *vt* mettre à quai; (*wages*) faire une retenue sur.

**doctor** /'dɒktə(r)/ *n* médecin *m*, docteur *m*; (Univ) docteur *m*. ● *vt* (*cat*) châtrer; (fig) altérer.

**doctorate** /'dɒktərət/ *n* doctorat *m*.

**document** /'dɒkjʊmənt/ *n* document *m*. **documentary** *a* & *n* documentaire (*m*). **documentation** *n* documentation *f*.

**dodge** /dɒdʒ/ *vt* esquiver. ● *vi* faire un saut de côté. ● *n* mouvement *m* de côté.

**dodgems** /'dɒdʒəmz/ *npl* autos *fpl* tamponneuses.

**dodgy** /'dɒdʒɪ/ *a* (**-ier, -iest**) (I: difficult) épineux, délicat; (untrustworthy) louche I.

**doe** /dəʊ/ *n* (deer) biche *f*.

**does** /dʌz/ ⇒DO.

**doesn't** /'dʌznt/ = DOES NOT.

**dog** /dɒg/ *n* chien *m*. ● *vt* (*pt* **dogged**) poursuivre. **~-collar** *n* col *m* romain. **~-eared** *a* écorné.

**dogged** /'dɒgɪd/ *a* obstiné.

**dogma** /'dɒgmə/ *n* dogme *m*. **dogmatic** *a* dogmatique.

**dogsbody** /'dɒgzbɒdɪ/ *n* bonne *f* à tout faire.

**do-it-yourself** *n* bricolage *m*.

**doldrums** /'dɒldrəmz/ *npl* **be in the ~** (person) avoir le cafard.

**dole** /dəʊl/ *vt* **~ out** distribuer. ● *n* I indemnité *f* de chômage; **on the ~** I au chômage.

**doll** /dɒl/ *n* poupée *f*. ● *vt* **~ up** I bichonner.

**dollar** /'dɒlə(r)/ *n* dollar *m*.

**dollop** /'dɒləp/ *n* (of food I) gros morceau *m*.

**dolphin** /'dɒlfɪn/ *n* dauphin *m*.

**domain** /də'meɪn/ *n* domaine *m*.

**dome** /dəʊm/ *n* dôme *m*.

**domestic** /də'mestɪk/ *a* familial; (*trade, flights*) intérieur; (*animal*) domestique. **domesticated** *a* (*animal*) domestiqué.

**domestic science** *n* arts *mpl* ménagers.

**dominant** /'dɒmɪnənt/ *a* dominant.

**dominate** /'dɒmɪneɪt/ *vt/i* dominer. **domination** *n* domination *f*.

**domineering** /dɒmɪ'nɪərɪŋ/ *a* dominateur.

**domino** /'dɒmɪnəʊ/ *n* (*pl* **~es**) domino *m*.

**donate** /dəʊ'neɪt/ *vt* faire don de. **donation** *n* don *m*.

**done** /dʌn/ ⇒DO.

**donkey** /'dɒŋkɪ/ *n* âne *m*. **~ work** *n* travail *m* pénible.

**donor** /'dəʊnə(r)/ *n* donateur/-trice *m/f*; (of blood) donneur/-euse *m/f*.

**don't** /dəʊnt/ = DO NOT.

**doodle** /'du:dl/ *vi* griffonner.

**doom** /du:m/ *n* (ruin) ruine *f*; (fate) destin *m*. ● *vt* **be ~ed to** être destiné *or* condamné à; **~ed (to failure)** voué à l'échec.

**door** /dɔ:(r)/ *n* porte *f*; (of vehicle) portière *f*, porte *f*. **~bell** *n* sonnette *f*. **~man** *n* (*pl* **-men**) portier *m*. **~mat** *n* paillasson *m*. **~step** *n* pas *m* de (la) porte, seuil *m*. **~way** *n* porte *f*.

**dope** /dəʊp/ *n* ⊡ cannabis *m*; (idiot ⊠) imbécile *mf*. ● *vt* doper. **dopey** *a* (foolish ⊠) imbécile.

**dormant** /'dɔ:mənt/ *a* en sommeil.

**dormitory** /'dɔ:mɪtrɪ/ *n* dortoir *m*; (Univ, US) résidence *f*.

**dosage** /'dəʊsɪdʒ/ *n* dose *f*; (on label) posologie *f*.

**dose** /dəʊs/ *n* dose *f*.

**dot** /dɒt/ *n* point *m*; **on the ~** ⊡ à l'heure pile.

**dot-com** /dɒt'kɒm/ *n* (société) point com *f*. **~ millionaire** *n* millionnaire *mf* de l'Internet. **~ shares** *npl* actions *fpl* des sociétés point com.

**dote** /dəʊt/ *vi* **~ on** adorer.

**dot-matrix** *a* (printer) matriciel.

**dotted** /dɒtɪd/ *a* (*fabric*) à pois; **~ line** pointillé *m*; **~ with** parsemé de.

**double** /'dʌbl/ *a* double; (*room, bed*) pour deux personnes; **~ the size** deux fois plus grand. ● *adv* deux fois; **pay ~** payer le double. ● *n* double *m*; (stuntman) doublure *f*; **~s** (tennis) double *m*; **at** or **on the ~** au pas de course. ● *vt/i* doubler; (fold) plier en deux. **~-bass** *n* (Mus) contrebasse *f*. **~-check** *vt* revérifier. **~ chin** *n* double menton *m*. **~-cross** *vt* tromper. **~-decker** *n* autobus *m* à impériale. **~ Dutch** *n* de l'hébreu *m*.

**doubt** /daʊt/ *n* doute *m*. ● *vt* douter de; **~ if** *or* **that** douter que. **doubtful** *a* incertain, douteux; (*person*) qui a des doutes. **doubtless** *adv* sans doute.

**dough** /dəʊ/ *n* pâte *f*; (money ⊠) fric *m* ⊡.

**doughnut** /'dəʊnʌt/ *n* beignet *m*.

**douse** /daʊs/ *vt* arroser; (*light, fire*) éteindre.

**dove** /dʌv/ *n* colombe *f*.

**Dover** /'dəʊvə(r)/ *n* Douvres.

**dowdy** /'daʊdɪ/ *a* (**-ier**, **-iest**) (*clothes*) sans chic, monotone; (*person*) sans élégance.

**down** /daʊn/ *adv* en bas; (of sun) couché; (lower) plus bas; **come** *or* **go ~** descendre; **go ~ to the post office** aller à la poste; **~ under** aux

antipodes; ~ **with** à bas. ● *prep* en bas de; (along) le long de. ● *vt* (knock down, shoot down) abattre; (drink) vider. ● *n* (fluff) duvet *m*.

**down**: **~-and-out** *n* clochard/-e *m/f*. **~cast** *a* démoralisé. **~fall** *n* chute *f*. **~grade** *vt* déclasser. **~-hearted** *a* découragé.

**downhill** /daʊn'hɪl/ *adv* **go ~** descendre; (pej) baisser.

**down**: **~load** *n* (Comput) télécharger. **~-market** *a* bas de gamme. **~ payment** *n* acompte *m*. **~pour** *n* grosse averse *f*.

**downright** /'daʊnraɪt/ *a* (utter) véritable; (honest) franc. ● *adv* carrément.

**downsize** /'daʊnsaɪz/ *vt/i* dégraisser.

**downstairs** /daʊn'steəz/ *adv* en bas. ● *a* d'en bas.

**down**. **~stream** *adv* en aval. **~-to-earth** *a* pratique.

**downtown** /'daʊntaʊn/ *a* (US) du centre-ville; ~ **Boston** le centre de Boston.

**downtrodden** /'daʊntrɒdn/ *a* tyrannisé.

**downward** /'daʊnwəd/ *a* & *adv*, **downwards** *adv* vers le bas.

**doze** /dəʊz/ *vi* somnoler; **~ off** s'assoupir. ● *n* somme *m*

**dozen** /'dʌzn/ *n* douzaine *f*; **a ~ eggs** une douzaine d'œufs; **~s of** [I] des dizaines de.

**Dr** *abbr* (**Doctor**) Docteur.

**drab** /dræb/ *a* terne.

**draft** /drɑ:ft/ *n* (outline) brouillon *m*; (Comm) traite *f*; **the ~** (Mil, US) la conscription; **a ~ treaty** un projet de traité; (US) = DRAUGHT. ● *vt* faire le brouillon de; (draw up) rédiger.

**drag** /dræg/ *vt/i* (*pt* **dragged**) traîner; (*river*) draguer; (pull away) arracher; **~ on** s'éterniser. ● *n* (task [I]) corvée *f*; (person [I]) raseur/-euse *m/f*; **in ~** en travesti.

**dragon** /'drægən/ *n* dragon *m*.

**drain** /dreɪn/ *vt* (*land*) drainer; (*vegetables*) égoutter; (*tank, glass*) vider; (use up) épuiser; **~ (off)** (*liquid*) faire écouler. ● *vi* **~ (off)** (of liquid) s'écouler. ● *n* (sewer) égout *m*; **~(-pipe)** tuyau *m* d'écoulement; **a ~ on** une ponction sur. **draining-board** *n* égouttoir *m*.

**drama** /'drɑ:mə/ *n* art *m* dramatique, théâtre *m*; (play, event) drame *m*. **dramatic** *a* (situation) dramatique; (increase) spectaculaire. **dramatist** *n* dramaturge *m*. **dramatize** *vt* adapter pour la scène; (fig) dramatiser.

**drank** /dræŋk/ ⇒DRINK.

**drape** /dreɪp/ *vt* draper. **drapes** *npl* (US) rideaux *mpl*.

**drastic** /'dræstɪk/ *a* sévère.

**draught** /drɑ:ft/ *n* courant *m* d'air; **~s** (game) dames *fpl*. **~ beer** *n* bière *f* pression.

**draughty** /'drɑ:ftɪ/ *a* plein de courants d'air.

**draw** /drɔ:/ *vt* (*pt* **drew**; *pp* **drawn**) (*picture*) dessiner; (*line*) tracer; (pull) tirer; (attract) attirer. ● *vi* dessiner; (Sport) faire match nul; (come, move) venir. ● *n* (Sport) match *m* nul; (in lottery) tirage *m* au sort. **~ back** reculer; **~ near** (s')approcher (**to** de); **~ out** (*money*) retirer; **~ up** *vi* (stop) s'arrêter; *vt* (*document*) dresser; (*chair*) approcher.

**drawback** /'drɔ:bæk/ *n* inconvénient *m*.

**drawer** /drɔ:(r)/ *n* tiroir *m*.

**drawing** /'drɔ:ɪŋ/ *n* dessin *m*. **~-board** *n* planche *f* à dessin. **~-pin** *n* punaise *f*. **~-room** *n* salon *m*.

**drawl** /drɔ:l/ *n* voix *f* traînante.

**drawn** /drɔ:n/ ⇒DRAW. ● *a* (*features*) tiré; (*match*) nul.

**dread** /dred/ *n* terreur *f*, crainte *f*. ● *vt* redouter. **dreadful** *a* épouvantable, affreux. **dreadfully** *adv* terriblement.

**dream** /dri:m/ *n* rêve *m*. ● *vt*/*i* (*pt* **dreamed** *or* **dreamt**) rêver; ~ **up** imaginer. ● *a* (ideal) de ses rêves.

**dreary** /'drɪərɪ/ *a* (**-ier**, **-iest**) triste; (boring) monotone.

**dredge** /dredʒ/ *vt* (*river*) draguer; ~ **sth up** (fig) exhumer.

**dregs** /dregz/ *npl* lie *f*.

**drench** /drentʃ/ *vt* tremper.

**dress** /dres/ *n* robe *f*; (clothing) tenue *f*. ● *vt*/*i* (s')habiller; (*food*) assaisonner; (*wound*) panser; ~ **up as** se déguiser en; **get** ~**ed** s'habiller. ~ **circle** *n* premier balcon *m*.

**dresser** /'dresə(r)/ *n* (furniture) buffet *m*; **be a stylish** ~ s'habiller avec chic.

**dressing** /'dresɪŋ/ *n* (sauce) assaisonnement *m*; (bandage) pansement *m*. ~**-gown** *n* robe *f* de chambre. ~**-room** *n* (Sport) vestiaire *m*; (Theat) loge *f*. ~**-table** *n* coiffeuse *f*.

**dressmaker** /'dresmeɪkə(r)/ *n* couturière *f*. **dressmaking** *n* couture *f*.

**dress rehearsal** *n* répétition *f* générale.

**dressy** /'dresɪ/ *a* (**-ier**, **-iest**) chic *inv*.

**drew** /dru:/ ⇒DRAW.

**dribble** /'drɪbl/ *vi* (*liquid*) dégouliner; (*person*) baver; (football) dribbler.

**dried** /draɪd/ *a* (fruit) sec.

**drier** /'draɪə(r)/ *n* séchoir *m*.

**drift** /drɪft/ *vi* aller à la dérive; (pile up) s'amonceler; ~ **towards** glisser vers. ● *n* dérive *f*; amoncellement *m*; (of events) tournure *f*; (meaning) sens *m*; **snow** ~ congère *f*. **driftwood** *n* bois *m* flotté.

**drill** /drɪl/ *n* (tool) perceuse *f*; (for teeth) roulette *f*; (training) exercice *m*; (procedure 🅸) marche *f* à suivre; (**pneumatic**) ~ marteau *m* piqueur. ● *vt* percer; (train) entraîner. ● *vi* être à l'exercice.

**drink** /drɪŋk/ *vt*/*i* (*pt* **drank**; *pp* **drunk**) boire. ● *n* (liquid) boisson *f*; (glass of alcohol) verre *m*; **a** ~ **of water** un verre d'eau. **drinking water** *n* eau *f* potable.

**drip** /drɪp/ *vi* (*pt* **dripped**) (é)goutter; (washing) s'égoutter. ● *n* goutte *f*; (person 🅧) lavette *f*.

**drip-dry** *vt* laisser égoutter. ● *a* sans essorage.

**drive** /draɪv/ *vt* (*pt* **drove**; *pp* **driven**) (*vehicle*) conduire; (sb somewhere) chasser, pousser; (*machine*) actionner; ~ **mad** rendre fou. ● *vi* conduire. ● *n* promenade *f* en voiture; (private road) allée *f*; (fig) énergie *f*; (Psych) instinct *m*; (Pol) campagne *f*; (Auto) traction *f*; (golf, Comput) drive *m*; **it's a two-hour** ~ il y a deux heures de route; **left-hand** ~ conduite *f* à gauche. □ ~ **at** en venir à.

**drivel** /'drɪvl/ *n* bêtises *fpl*.

**driver** /'draɪvə(r)/ *n* conducteur/-trice *m*/*f*, chauffeur *m*. ~**'s license** *n* (US) permis *m* de conduire.

**driving** /'draɪvɪŋ/ *n* conduite *f*; **take one's** ~ **test** passer son permis. ● *a* (*rain*) battant; (*wind*) cinglant. ~ **licence** *n* permis *m* de conduire. ~ **school** *n* auto-école *f*.

**drizzle** /'drɪzl/ *n* bruine *f*. ● *vi* bruiner.

**drone** /drəʊn/ *n* (of engine) ronronnement *m*; (of insects) bourdonne-

ment *m.* ● *vi* ronronner; bourdonner.

**drool** /dru:l/ *vi* baver (**over** sur).

**droop** /dru:p/ *vi* pencher, tomber.

**drop** /drɒp/ *n* goutte *f*; (fall, lowering) chute *f*. ● *vt/i* (*pt* **dropped**) (laisser) tomber; (decrease, lower) baisser; ~ **(off)** (*person from car*) déposer; ~ **a line** écrire un mot (**to** à). □ ~ **in** passer (**on** chez); ~ **off** (doze) s'assoupir; ~ **out** se retirer (**of** de); (of student) abandonner.

**drop-out** *n* marginal/-e *m/f*, raté/-e *m/f*.

**droppings** /'drɒpɪŋz/ *npl* crottes *fpl*.

**drought** /draʊt/ *n* sécheresse *f*.

**drove** /drəʊv/ ⇒DRIVE.

**droves** /drəʊvz/ *npl* foules *fpl*.

**drown** /draʊn/ *vt/i* (se) noyer.

**drowsy** /'draʊzɪ/ *a* somnolent; **be** *or* **feel** ~ avoir envie de dormir.

**drug** /drʌg/ *n* drogue *f*; (Med) médicament *m*. ● *vt* (*pt* **drugged**) droguer. ~ **addict** *n* drogué/-e *m/f* **drugstore** *n* (US) drugstore *m*.

**drum** /drʌm/ *n* tambour *m*; (for oil) bidon *m*; ~**s** batterie *f*. ● *vi* (*pt* **drummed**) tambouriner. ● *vt* ~ **into sb** répéter sans cesse à qn; ~ **up** (*support*) susciter; (*business*) créer. **drummer** *n* tambour *m*, (in pop group) batteur *m*.

**drumstick** /'drʌmstɪk/ *n* baguette *f* de tambour; (of chicken) pilon *m*.

**drunk** /drʌŋk/ ⇒DRINK. ● *a* ivre; **get** ~ s'enivrer. ● *n* ivrogne/-esse *m/f*. **drunken** *a* ivre. **drunkenness** *n* ivresse *f*.

**dry** /draɪ/ *a* (**drier**, **driest**) sec; (*day*) sans pluie; **be** *or* **feel** ~ avoir soif. ● *vt/i* (faire) sécher; ~ **up** (dry dishes) essuyer la vaisselle; (of supplies) (se) tarir; (be silent Ⓘ) se taire. ~**-clean** *vt* nettoyer à sec. ~**-cleaner** *n* teinturier *m*. ~ **run** *n* galop *m* d'essai.

**dual** /'dju:əl/ *a* double. ~ **carriageway** *n* route *f* à quatre voies. ~**-purpose** *a* qui fait double emploi.

**dub** /dʌb/ *vt* (*pt* **dubbed**) (film) doubler (**into** en); (nickname) surnommer.

**dubious** /'dju:bɪəs/ *a* douteux; **be** ~ **about** avoir des doutes sur.

**duck** /dʌk/ *n* canard *m*. ● *vi* se baisser subitement. ● *vt* (*head*) baisser; (*person*) plonger dans l'eau.

**duct** /dʌkt/ *n* conduit *m*.

**dud** /dʌd/ *a* (*tool* ⊠) mal fichu; (*coin* ⊠) faux; (*cheque* ⊠) sans provision. ● *n* **be a** ~ (not work ⊠) ne pas marcher.

**due** /dju:/ *a* (owing) dû; (expected) attendu; (proper) qui convient; ~ **to** à cause de; (caused by) dû à; **she's** ~ **to leave now** il est prévu qu'elle parte maintenant; **in** ~ **course** (at the right time) en temps voulu; (later) plus tard. ● *adv* ~ **east** droit vers l'est. ● *n* dû *m*; ~**s** droits *mpl*; (of club) cotisation *f*.

**duel** /'dju:əl/ *n* duel *m*.

**duet** /dju:'et/ *n* duo *m*.

**dug** /dʌg/ ⇒DIG.

**duke** /dju:k/ *n* duc *m*.

**dull** /dʌl/ *a* ennuyeux; (*colour*) terne; (*weather*) maussade; (*sound*) sourd. ● *vt* (*pain*) atténuer; (*shine*) ternir.

**duly** /'dju:lɪ/ *adv* comme il convient; (as expected) comme prévu.

**dumb** /dʌm/ *a* muet; (stupid Ⓘ) bête. ● *vt* ~ **down** (*course, TV coverage*) baisser le niveau intellectuel de.

**dumbfound** /dʌm'faʊnd/ *vt* sidérer, ahurir.

**dummy** /'dʌmɪ/ *n* (of tailor) mannequin *m*; (of baby) sucette *f*. ● *a* factice. ~ **run** *n* galop *m* d'essai.

**dump** /dʌmp/ *vt* déposer; (get rid of [!]) se débarrasser de. ● *n* tas *m* d'ordures; (refuse tip) décharge *f*; (Mil) dépôt *m*; (dull place [!]) trou *m* [!]; **be in the ~s** [!] avoir le cafard.

**dune** /dju:n/ *n* dune *f*.

**dung** /dʌŋ/ *n* (excrement) bouse *f*, crotte *f*; (manure) fumier *m*.

**dungarees** /dʌŋgə'ri:z/ *npl* salopette *f*.

**dungeon** /'dʌndʒən/ *n* cachot *m*.

**duplicate¹** /'dju:plɪkət/ *n* double *m*. ● *a* identique.

**duplicate²** /'dju:plɪkeɪt/ *vt* faire un double de; (on machine) polycopier.

**durable** /'djʊərəbl/ *a* (tough) résistant; (enduring) durable.

**duration** /djʊ'reɪʃn/ *n* durée *f*.

**during** /'djʊərɪŋ/ *prep* pendant.

**dusk** /dʌsk/ *n* crépuscule *m*.

**dusky** /'dʌskɪ/ *a* (**-ier, -iest**) foncé.

**dust** /dʌst/ *n* poussière *f*. ● *vt/i* épousseter; (sprinkle) saupoudrer (with de). **~bin** *n* poubelle *f*.

**duster** /'dʌstə(r)/ *n* chiffon *m*.

**dust**: **~man** *n* (*pl* **-men**) éboueur *m*. **~pan** *n* pelle *f* (à poussière).

**dusty** /'dʌstɪ/ *a* (**-ier, -iest**) poussiéreux.

**Dutch** /dʌtʃ/ *a* néerlandais; **go ~** partager les frais. ● *n* (Ling) néerlandais *m*. **~man** *n* Néerlandais *m*. **~woman** *n* Néerlandaise *f*.

**dutiful** /'dju:tɪfl/ *a* obéissant.

**duty** /'dju:tɪ/ *n* devoir *m*; (tax) droit *m*; (of official) fonction *f*. **on ~** de service. **~-free** *a* hors-taxe.

**duvet** /'du:veɪ/ *n* couette *f*.

**dwarf** /dwɔ:f/ *n* nain/-e *m/f*. ● *vt* rapetisser.

**dwell** /dwel/ *vi* (*pt* **dwelt**) demeurer; **~ on** s'étendre sur. **dweller** *n* habitant/-e *m/f*. **dwelling** *n* habitation *f*.

**dwindle** /'dwɪndl/ *vi* diminuer.

**dye** /daɪ/ *vt* teindre. ● *n* teinture *f*.

**dying** /'daɪɪŋ/ *a* mourant; (*art*) qui se perd.

**dynamic** /daɪ'næmɪk/ *a* dynamique.

**dynamite** /'daɪnəmaɪt/ *n* dynamite *f*.

**dysentery** /'dɪsəntrɪ/ *n* dysenterie *f*.

**dyslexia** /dɪs'leksɪə/ *n* dyslexie *f*. **dyslexic** *a* & *n* dyslexique (*mf*).

**each** /i:tʃ/ *det* chaque *inv*; **~ one** chacun/-e *m/f*. ● *pron* chacun/-e *m/f*; **oranges at 30p ~** des oranges à 30 pence pièce.

**each other** *pron* l'un/l'une l'autre, les uns/les unes les autres; **know ~** se connaître; **love ~** s'aimer.

**eager** /'i:gə(r)/ *a* impatient (**to** de); (*person, acceptance*) enthousiaste; **~ for** avide de.

**eagle** /'i:gl/ *n* aigle *m*.

**ear** /ɪə(r)/ *n* oreille *f*; (of corn) épi *m*. **~ache** *n* mal *m* à l'oreille. **~-drum** *n* tympan *m*.

**earl** /ɜ:l/ *n* comte *m*.

**early** /'ɜ:lɪ/ (**-ier, -iest**) *adv* tôt, de bonne heure; (ahead of time) en avance; **as I said earlier** comme je l'ai déjà dit. ● *a* (*attempt, years*) premier; (*hour*) matinal; (*fruit*)

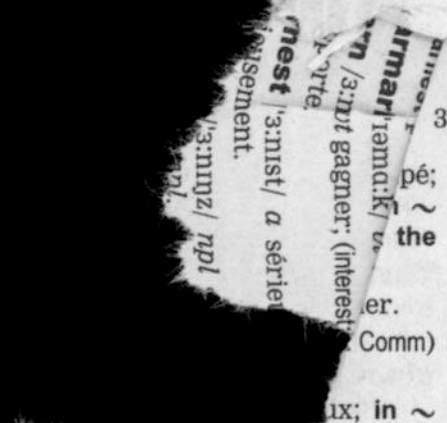

pé;
~
the
er.
Comm)
ux; in ~
sérieu
**earnings** salaire *m*; (profits) gains *m*
**ear**: **~phones** *npl* casque *m*. **~-ring** *n* boucle *f* d'oreille. **~shot** *n* **within/in ~shot** à portée de voix.
**earth** /3:θ/ *n* terre *f*; **why/how/where on ~...?** pourquoi/comment/où diable...? ● *vt* (Electr) mettre à la terre. **earthenware** *n* faïence *f*. **~quake** *n* tremblement *m* de terre.
**ease** /i:z/ *n* facilité *f*; (comfort) bien-être *m*; **at ~** à l'aise; (Mil) au repos; **with ~** facilement. ● *vt* (*pain, pressure*) atténuer; (*congestion*) réduire; (*transition*) faciliter. ● *vi* (*pain, pressure*) s'atténuer; (*congestion, rain*) diminuer.
**easel** /ˈi:zl/ *n* chevalet *m*.
**east** /i:st/ *n* est *m*; **the E~** (Orient) l'Orient *m*. ● *a* (*side, coast*) est; (*wind*) d'est. ● *adv* à l'est.
**Easter** /ˈi:stə(r)/ *n* Pâques *m*; **~ egg** œuf *m* de Pâques.
**easterly** /ˈi:stəlɪ/*a* (*wind*) d'est; (*direction*) de l'est.
**eastern** /ˈi:stən/ de l'est; **~ France** l'est de la France.
**-astward** /ˈi:stwəd/ *a* (*side*) est (*journey*) vers l'est.
ˈi:zɪ/ *a* (**-ier**, **-iest**) facile; **go** y aller doucement avec; te fatigue pas. **~going** nt.
**ate**; *pp* **eaten**)
er.

**eavesdrop** /ˈi:vzdrɒp/ *vi* (*pt* **-dropped**) écouter aux portes.
**ebb** /eb/ *n* reflux *m*. ● *vi* descendre; (fig) décliner.
**EC** *abbr* (**European Community**) CE *f*.
**eccentric** /ɪkˈsentrɪk/ *a* & *n* excentrique (*mf*).
**echo** /ˈekəʊ/ *n* (*pl* **-oes**) écho *m*. ● *vt* répercuter; (*idea, opinion*) reprendre. ● *vi* retentir, résonner.
**eclipse** /ɪˈklɪps/ *n* éclipse *f*. ● *vt* éclipser.
**ecological** /i:kəˈlɒdʒɪkl/ *a* écologique.
**ecology** /i:ˈkɒlədʒɪ/ *n* écologie *f*.
**e-commerce** /ˈi:kɒmɜ:s/ *n* commerce *m* électronique, commerce *m* en ligne.
**economic** /i:kəˈnɒmɪk/ *a* économique; (profitable) rentable. **economical** *a* économique; (person) économe. **economics** *n* économie *f*, sciences *fpl* économiques. **economist** *n* économiste *mf*.
**economize** /ɪˈkɒnəmaɪz/ *vi* **~ (on)** économiser.
**economy** /ɪˈkɒnəmɪ/ *n* économie *f*. **~ -class syndrome** *n* syndrome *m* de la classe économique.
**ecosystem** /ˈikəʊsɪstəm/ *n* écosystème *m*.
**ecstasy** /ˈekstəsɪ/ *n* extase *f*; (drug) ecstasy *m*.
**eczema** /ˈeksɪmə/ *n* eczéma *m*.
**edge** /edʒ/ *n* bord *m*; (of town) abords *mpl*; (of knife) tranchant *m*; **have the ~ on** [I] l'emporter sur; **on ~** énervé. ● *vt* (trim) border. ● *vi* **~ forward** avancer doucement.
**edgeways** /ˈedʒweɪz/ *adv* **I can't get a word in ~** je n'arrive pas à placer un mot.
**edgy** /ˈedʒɪ/ *a* énervé.
**edible** /ˈedɪbl/ *a* comestible.

**edit** /'edɪt/ *vt* (*pt* **ed**... *paper, page*) être le ré... rédactrice de; (check) réviser; ... couper; (TV, cinema) monter.

**edition** /ɪ'dɪʃn/ *n* édition *f*.

**editor** /'edɪtə(r)/ *n* (writer) rédacteur/-trice *m/f*; (of works, anthology) éditeur/-trice *m/f*; (TV, cinema) monteur/-teuse *m/f*; **the ~ (in chief)** le rédacteur en chef.

**editorial** /edɪ'tɔ:rɪəl/ *a* de la rédaction. ● *n* éditorial *m*.

**educate** /'edʒʊkeɪt/ *vt* instruire; (mind, public) éduquer. **educated** *a* instruit. **education** *n* éducation *f*; (schooling) études *fpl*. **educational** *a* éducatif; (*establishment, method*) d'enseignement.

**eel** /i:l/ *n* anguille *f*.

**eerie** /'ɪərɪ/ *a* (**-ier, -iest**) sinistre.

**effect** /ɪ'fekt/ *n* effet *m*; **come into ~** entrer en vigueur; **in ~** effectivement; **take ~** agir. ● *vt* effectuer.

**effective** /ɪ'fektɪv/ *a* efficace; (actual) effectif. **effectively** *adv* efficacement; (in effect) en réalité. **effectiveness** *n* efficacité *f*.

**effeminate** /ɪ'femɪnət/ *a* efféminé.

**effervescent** /efə'vesnt/ *a* effervescent.

**efficiency** /ɪ'fɪʃnsɪ/ *n* efficacité *f*; (of machine) rendement *m*. **efficient** *a* efficace. **efficiently** *adv* efficacement.

**effort** /'efət/ *n* efforts *mpl*; **make an ~** faire un effort; **be worth the ~** en valoir la peine. **effortless** *a* facile.

**effusive** /ɪ'fju:sɪv/ *a* expansif.

**e.g.** /i:'dʒi:/ *abbr* par ex.

**egg** /eg/ *n* œuf *m*. ● *vt* **~ on** pousser. **~-cup** *n* coquetier *m*. **~-plant** *n* (US) aubergine *f*. **~shell** *n* coquille *f* d'œuf.

**el**...
*n*.

**eight** ...
**teen** *a* ...
& *n* h...
quatre-v...

**either** /'a...(r)... & *pron* l'un/une ou l'autre; (with negative) ni l'un/une ni l'autre; **you can take ~** tu peux prendre n'importe lequel/laquelle. ● *adv* non plus. ● *conj* **~...or** ou (bien)... ou (bien); (with negative) ni...ni.

**eject** /ɪ'dʒekt/ *vt* (*troublemaker*) expulser; (*waste*) rejeter.

**elaborate**[1] /ɪ'læbərət/ *a* compliqué.

**elaborate**[2] /ɪ'læbəreɪt/ *vt* élaborer. ● *vi* préciser; **~ on** s'étendre sur.

**elastic** /ɪ'læstɪk/ *a* & *n* élastique (*m*); **~ band** élastique *m*. **elasticity** *n* élasticité *f*.

**elated** /ɪ'leɪtɪd/ *a* transporté de joie.

**elbow** /'elbəʊ/ *n* coude *m*; **~ room** espace *m* vital.

**elder** /'eldə(r)/ *a* & *n* aîné/-e (*m/f*); (tree) sureau *m*.

**elderly** /'eldəlɪ/ *a* âgé; **the ~** les personnes *fpl* âgées.

**eldest** /'eldɪst/ *a* & *n* aîné/-e (*m/f*).

**elect** /ɪ'lekt/ *vt* élire; **~ to do** choisir de faire. ● *a* (president etc) futur. **election** *n* élection... **elector** *n* électeur/-trice... **electoral** *a* électoral. ... **ate** *n* électorat *m*.

**electric** /ɪ'lektrɪk/ ... **blanket** couvert... **electrical** *a* ... **cian** *n* élec...

...té *f*. **electrify** *vt* (...e) électriser. **elec-**...te *vt* électrocuter.
...**lectronic** /ɪlek'trɒnɪk/ *a* électronique. ~ **publishing** *n* éditique *f*. **electronics** *n* électronique *f*.
**elegance** /'elɪgəns/ *n* élégance *f*.
**element** /'elɪmənt/ *n* élément *m*; (of heater etc.) résistance *f*. **elementary** *a* élémentaire.
**elephant** /'elɪfənt/ *n* éléphant *m*.
**elevate** /'elɪveɪt/ *vt* élever. **elevation** *n* élévation *f*. **elevator** *n* (US) ascenseur *m*.
**eleven** /ɪ'levn/ *a* & *n* onze (*m*). **eleventh** *a* & *n* onzième (*mf*).
**elicit** /ɪ'lɪsɪt/ *vt* obtenir (from de).
**eligible** /'elɪdʒəbl/ *a* admissible (for à); be ~ for avoir droit à.
**eliminate** /ɪ'lɪmɪneɪt/ *vt* éliminer.
**elm** /elm/ *n* orme *m*.
**elongate** /'i:lɒŋgeɪt/ *vt* allonger.
**elope** /ɪ'ləʊp/ *vi* s'enfuir (with avec). **elopement** *n* fugue *f* (amoureuse).
**eloquence** /'eləkwəns/ *n* éloquence *f*.
**else** /els/ *adv* d'autre; somebody/nothing ~ quelqu'un/rien d'autre; everybody ~ tous les autres; somewhere/something ~ autre part/chose; or ~ ou bien. **elsewhere** *adv* ailleurs.
**elude** /ɪ'lu:d/ *vt* échapper à.
**elusive** /ɪ'lu:sɪv/ *a* insaisissable.
**e-mail** /'i:meɪl/ *n* (medium) courrier *m* électronique; (item) e-mail *m*, mél *m*. ● *vt* ~ **sb** envoyer un e-mail à qn; ~ **sth** envoyer qch par courrier électronique.
...**mancipate** /ɪ'mænsɪpeɪt/ *vt* ...nciper.
...**nkment** /ɪm'bæŋkmənt/ *n* ...quai *m*; (of railway) remblai
**embark** /ɪm'bɑ:k/ *vt* embarquer. ● *vi* (Naut) embarquer; ~ **on** (*journey*) entreprendre; (*campaign, career*) se lancer dans.
**embarrass** /ɪm'bærəs/ *vt* plonger dans l'embarras; be/feel ~**ed** être/se sentir gêné. **embarrassment** *n* confusion *f*, gêne *f*.
**embassy** /'embəsɪ/ *n* ambassade *f*.
**embed** /ɪm'bed/ *vt* (*pt* **embedded**) enfoncer (in dans).
**embellish** /ɪm'belɪʃ/ *vt* embellir.
**embers** /'embəz/ *npl* braises *fpl*.
**embezzle** /ɪm'bezl/ *vt* détourner (from de). **embezzlement** *n* détournement *m* de fonds.
**emblem** /'embləm/ *n* emblème *m*.
**embodiment** /ɪm'bɒdɪmənt/ *n* incarnation *f*. **embody** *vt* incarner; (legally) incorporer.
**emboss** /ɪm'bɒs/ *vt* (metal) repousser; (paper) gaufrer.
**embrace** /ɪm'breɪs/ *vt* (*person*) étreindre; (*religion*) embrasser; (include) comprendre. ● *n* étreinte *f*.
**embroider** /ɪm'brɔɪdə(r)/ *vt* broder. **embroidery** *n* broderie *f*.
**embryo** /'embrɪəʊ/ *n* embryon *m*.
**emerald** /'emərəld/ *n* émeraude *f*.
**emerge** /ɪ'mɜ:dʒ/ *vi* (*person*) sortir (from de); it ~**d that** il est apparu que. **emergence** *n* apparition *f*.
**emergency** /ɪ'mɜ:dʒənsɪ/ *n* (crisis) crise *f*; (urgent case: Med) urgence *f*; **in an** ~ en cas d'urgence. ● *a* d'urgence; ~ **exit** *n* sortie *f* de secours. ~ **landing** *n* atterrissage *m* forcé. ~ **room** *n* (US) salle *f* des urgences.
**emigrant** /'emɪgrənt/ *n* émigrant/-e *m/f*. **emigrate** *vi* émigrer.
**eminence** /'emɪnəns/ *n* éminence *f*. **eminent** *a* éminent.

**emission** /ɪ'mɪʃn/ *n* émission *f*.

**emit** /ɪ'mɪt/ *vt* (*pt* **emitted**) émettre.

**emotion** /ɪ'məʊʃn/ *n* émotion *f*. **emotional** *a* (*development*) émotif; (*reaction*) émotionnel; (*film, scene*) émouvant.

**emotive** /ɪ'məʊtɪv/ *a* qui soulève les passions.

**emperor** /'empərə(r)/ *n* empereur *m*.

**emphasis** /'emfəsɪs/ *n* accent *m*; **lay ~ on** mettre l'accent sur. **emphasize** *vt* mettre l'accent sur. **emphatic** *a* catégorique; (manner) énergique.

**empire** /'empaɪə(r)/ *n* empire *m*.

**employ** /ɪm'plɔɪ/ *vt* employer. **employee** *n* employé/-e *m/f*. **employer** *n* employeur/-euse *m/f*.

**employment** /ɪm'plɔɪmənt/ *n* emploi *m*; **find ~** trouver du travail.

**empower** /ɪm'paʊə(r)/ *vt* autoriser (**to do** à faire).

**empty** /'emptɪ/ *a* (**-ier, -iest**) vide; (*street*) désert; (promise) vain; **on an ~ stomach** à jeun. ● *vt*/*i* (se) vider. **~-handed** *a* les mains vides.

**emulate** /'emjʊleɪt/ *vt* imiter.

**enable** /ɪ'neɪbl/ *vt* **~ sb to** permettre à qn de.

**enamel** /ɪ'næml/ *n* émail *m*. ● *vt* (*pt* **enamelled**) émailler.

**encampment** /ɪn'kæmpmənt/ *n* campement *m*.

**encase** /ɪn'keɪs/ *vt* revêtir, recouvrir (**in** de).

**enchant** /ɪn'tʃɑ:nt/ *vt* enchanter.

**enclose** /ɪn'kləʊz/ *vt* entourer; (land) clôturer; (with letter) joindre. **enclosed** *a* (space) clos; (with letter) ci-joint. **enclosure** *n* enceinte *f*; (with letter) pièce *f* jointe.

**encompass** /ɪn'kʌmpəs/ *vt* inclure.

**encore** /'ɒŋkɔ:(r)/ *int* & *n* bis (*m*).

**encounter** /ɪn'kaʊntə(r)/ *vt* rencontrer. ● *n* rencontre *f*.

**encourage** /ɪn'kʌrɪdʒ/ *vt* encourager.

**encroach** /ɪn'krəʊtʃ/ *vi* **~ upon** empiéter sur.

**encyclopaedia** /ɪnsaɪklə'pi:dɪə/ *n* encyclopédie *f*. **encyclopaedic** *a* encyclopédique.

**end** /end/ *n* fin *f*; (farthest part) bout *m*; **come to an ~** prendre fin; **~-product** produit *m* fini; **in the ~** finalement; **no ~ of** Ⓔ énormément de; **on ~** (upright) debout; (in a row) de suite; **put an ~ to** mettre fin à. ● *vt* (*marriage*) mettre fin à; **~ one's days** finir ses jours. ● *vi* se terminer; **~ up doing** finir par faire.

**endanger** /ɪn'deɪndʒə(r)/ *vt* mettre en danger.

**endearing** /ɪn'dɪərɪŋ/ *a* attachant.

**endeavour** (US) **endeavor** /ɪn'devə(r)/ *n* (attempt) tentative *f*; (hard work) effort *m*. ● *vi* faire tout son possible (**to do** pour faire).

**ending** /'endɪŋ/ *n* fin *f*.

**endive** /'endɪv/ *n* chicorée *f*.

**endless** /'endlɪs/ *a* interminable; (*supply*) inépuisable; (*patience*) infini.

**endorse** /ɪn'dɔ:s/ *vt* (*candidate, decision*) appuyer; (*product, claim*) approuver; (*cheque*) endosser.

**endurance** /ɪn'djʊərəns/ *n* endurance *f*.

**endure** /ɪn'djʊə(r)/ *vt* supporter. ● *vi* durer. **enduring** *a* durable.

**enemy** /'enəmɪ/ *n* & *a* ennemi/-e (*m/f*).

**energetic** /enə'dʒetɪk/ *a* énergique. **energy** *n* énergie *f*.

...t (*staff*) en-
...retenir; **be ~d in**
... **~ in** se livrer à.
...fiancé; (busy) occupé;
...ancer. **engagement** *n*
...es *fpl*; (meeting) rendez-
... (undertaking) engagement *m*.
...**ing** /ɪn'geɪdʒɪŋ/ *a* atta-
..., engageant.
...**ne** /'endʒɪn/ *n* moteur *m*; (of
...n) locomotive *f*; (of ship) ma-
...ines *fpl*. **~-driver** *n* mécanicien
...

...**gineer** /endʒɪ'nɪə(r)/ *n* ingé-
...ieur *m*; (repairman) technicien *m*;
...on ship) mécanicien *m*. ● *vt* (con-
...rive) manigancer.

...**ngineering** /endʒɪ'nɪərɪŋ/ *n* ingénierie *f*; (industry) mécanique *f*; **civil ~** génie *m* civil.

**England** /'ɪŋglənd/ *n* Angleterre *f*.

**English** /'ɪŋglɪʃ/ *a* anglais. ● *n* (Ling) anglais *m*; **the ~** les Anglais *mpl*. **~man** *n* Anglais *m*. **~-speaking** *a* anglophone. **~woman** *n* Anglaise *f*.

**engrave** /ɪn'greɪv/ *vt* graver.

**engrossed** /ɪn'grəʊst/ *a* absorbé (**in** dans).

**engulf** /ɪn'gʌlf/ *vt* engouffrer.

**enhance** /ɪn'hɑ:ns/ *vt* (*prospects, status*) améliorer; (*price, value*) augmenter.

**enjoy** /ɪn'dʒɔɪ/ *vt* aimer (**doing** faire); (benefit from) jouir de; **~ oneself** s'amuser; **~ your meal!** bon appétit! **enjoyable** *a* agréable. **enjoyment** *n* plaisir *m*.

**enlarge** /ɪn'lɑ:dʒ/ *vt* agrandir. ● *vi* s'agrandir; (*pupil*) se dilater; **~ on** s'étendre sur. **enlargement** *n* agrandissement *m*.

...n'laɪtn/ *vt* éclairer (**on**
...**htenment** *n* instruc-
tion *f*; (information) éclaircissement *m*.

**enlist** /ɪn'lɪst/ *vt* (*person*) recruter; (fig) obtenir. ● *vi* s'engager.

**enmity** /'enmətɪ/ *n* inimitié *f*.

**enormous** /ɪ'nɔ:məs/ *a* énorme. **enormously** *adv* énormément.

**enough** /ɪ'nʌf/ *adv & n* assez; **have ~ of** en avoir assez de. ● *det* assez de; **~ glasses/time** assez de verres/de temps.

**enquire** /ɪn'kwaɪə(r)/ ⇒INQUIRE. **enquiry** ⇒INQUIRY.

**enrage** /ɪn'reɪdʒ/ *vt* mettre en rage, rendre furieux.

**enrol** /ɪn'rəʊl/ *vt/i* (*pt* **enrolled**) (s')inscrire. **enrolment** *n* inscription *f*.

**ensure** /ɪn'ʃʊə(r)/ *vt* garantir; **~ that** (ascertain) s'assurer que.

**entail** /ɪn'teɪl/ *vt* entraîner.

**entangle** /ɪn'tæŋgl/ *vt* emmêler.

**enter** /'entə(r)/ *vt* (*room, club, phase*) entrer dans; (note down, register) inscrire; (data) entrer, saisir. ● *vi* entrer (**into** dans); **~ for** s'inscrire à.

**enterprise** /'entəpraɪz/ *n* entreprise *f*; (boldness) initiative *f*. **enterprising** *a* entreprenant.

**entertain** /entə'teɪn/ *vt* amuser, divertir; (guests) recevoir; (ideas) considérer. **entertainer** *n* artiste *mf*. **entertaining** *a* divertissant. **entertainment** *n* divertissement *m*; (performance) spectacle *m*.

**enthral** /ɪn'θrɔ:l/ *vt* (*pt* **enthralled**) captiver.

**enthusiasm** /ɪn'θju:zɪæzəm/ *n* enthousiasme *m* (**for** pour).

**enthusiast** /ɪn'θju:zɪæst/ *n* passionné/-e *m/f* (**for** de). **enthusiastic** *a* (supporter) enthousiaste; **be**

~ic about être enti

**enthusiastically**

enthousiasme.

**entice** /ɪn'taɪs/ *vt* attirer; ~ **to do** entraîner à faire.

**entire** /ɪn'taɪə(r)/ *a* entier. **entirely** *adv* entièrement. **entirety** *n* **in its ~ty** en entier.

**entitle** /ɪn'taɪtl/ *vt* donner droit à (**to sth** à qch; **to do** de faire); **~d** (book) intitulé; **be ~d to sth** avoir droit à qch.

**entrance**[1] /'entrəns/ *n* (entering, way in) entrée *f* (**to** de); (right to enter) admission *f*. ● *a* (charge, exam) d'entrée.

**entrance**[2] /ɪn'trɑ:ns/ *vt* transporter.

**entrant** /'entrənt/ *n* (Sport) concurrent/-e *m/f*; (in exam) candidat/-e *m/f*.

**entrenched** /ɪn'trentʃt/ *a* (*opinion*) inébranlable; (Mil) retranché.

**entrepreneur** /ɒntrəprə'nɜ:(r)/ *n* entrepreneur/-euse *m/f*.

**entrust** /ɪn'trʌst/ *vt* confier; ~ **sb with sth** confier qch à qn.

**entry** /'entrɪ/ *n* entrée *f*; ~ **form** fiche *f* d'inscription.

**envelop** /ɪn'veləp/ *vt* (*pt* **enveloped**) envelopper.

**envelope** /'envələʊp/ *n* enveloppe *f*.

**envious** /'envɪəs/ *a* envieux (**of** de).

**environment** /ɪn'vaɪərənmənt/ *n* (ecological) environnement *m*; (social) milieu *m*. **environmental** *a* du milieu; de l'environnement. **environmentalist** *n* écologiste *mf*.

**envisage** /ɪn'vɪzɪdʒ/ *vt* prévoir (**doing** de faire).

**envoy** /'envɔɪ/ *n* envoyé/-e *m/f*.

**epidemic**

*f*.

**epilepsy** /'epɪle

**episode** /'epɪsəʊd/

**epitome** /ɪ'pɪtəmɪ/ *n*

**epitomize** *vt* incarner.

**equal** /'i:kwəl/ *a* & *n* égal

~ **opportunities/rights** ég

chances/droits; ~ **to** (*ta*

hauteur de. ● *vt* (*pt* **equ**

égaler. **equality** *n* éga

**equalize** *vt/i* égaliser. **equ**

*n* (goal) but *m* égalisateur. **eq**

*adv* (*divide*) en parts égales; (j

tout aussi

**equanimity** /ekwə'nɪmətɪ/ *n* s

nité *f*.

**equate** /ɪ'kweɪt/ *vt* assimiler (w

à). **equation** *n* équation *f*.

**equator** /ɪ'kweɪtə(r)/ *n* équateu

*m*.

**equilibrium** /i:kwɪ'lɪbrɪəm/ *n* équilibre *m*.

**equip** /ɪ'kwɪp/ *vt* (*pt* **equipped**) équiper (**with** de). **equipment** *n* équipement *m*.

**equity** /'ekwətɪ/ *n* équité *f*.

**equivalence** /ɪ'kwɪvələns/ *n* équivalence *f*.

**era** /'ɪərə/ *n* ère *f*, époque *f*.

**eradicate** /ɪ'rædɪkeɪt/ *vt* éliminer; (*disease*) éradiquer.

**erase** /ɪ'reɪz/ *vt* effacer. **eraser** *n* (rubber) gomme *f*.

**erect** /ɪ'rekt/ *a* droit. ● *vt* ériger. **erection** *n* érection *f*.

**erode** /ɪ'rəʊd/ *vt* éroder; (fig) saper. **erosion** *n* érosion *f*.

**erotic** /ɪ'rɒtɪk/ *a* érotique.

**errand** /'erənd/ *n* commission *f*, course *f*.

...ler. ...*prices*) **escalation** *n* ...*f*. **escalator** *n* ...écanique, escalator®

**...e** /eskə'peɪd/ *n* frasque *f*.

**...cape** /ɪ'skeɪp/ *vt* échapper à. *vi* s'enfuir, s'évader; (*gas*) fuir. ● *n* fuite *f*, évasion *f*; (of gas etc.) fuite *f*; **have a lucky** *or* **narrow ~** l'échapper belle.

**escapism** /ɪ'skeɪpɪzəm/ *n* évasion *f* (*du réel*).

**escort**[1] /'eskɔ:t/ *n* (guard) escorte *f*; (companion) compagnon/compagne *m*/*f*.

**escort**[2] /ɪ'skɔ:t/ *vt* escorter.

**Eskimo** /'eskɪməʊ/ *n* Esquimau/-de *m*/*f*.

**especially** /ɪ'speʃəlɪ/ *adv* en particulier.

**espionage** /'espɪənɑ:ʒ/ *n* espionnage *m*.

**espresso** /e'spresəʊ/ *n* (café) express *m*.

**essay** /'eseɪ/ *n* essai *m*; (School) rédaction *f*; (Univ) dissertation *f*.

**essence** /'esns/ *n* essence *f*.

**essential** /ɪ'senʃl/ *a* essentiel; **the ~s** l'essentiel *m*. **essentially** *adv* essentiellement.

**establish** /ɪ'stæblɪʃ/ *vt* établir; (business) fonder.

**establishment** /ɪ'stæblɪʃmənt/ *n* (process) instauration *f*; (institution) établissement *m*; **the E~** l'ordre *m* établi.

**...sthetic** /...e... ...THETIC.

**estimate**[1] /'estɪmət/ *n* ... estimation *f*; (Comm) devis ...

**estimate**[2] /'estɪmeɪt/ *vt* éva... **~ that** estimer que. **estimation** ... (esteem) estime *f*; (judgment) opinion *f*.

**Estonia** /ɪstəʊnɪə/ *n* Estonie *f*.

**estuary** /'estʃʊərɪ/ *n* estuaire *m*.

**eternal** /ɪ'tɜ:nl/ *a* éternel.

**eternity** /ɪ'tɜ:nətɪ/ *n* éternité *f*.

**ethic** /'eθɪk/ *n* éthique *f*; **~s** moralité *f*. **ethical** *a* éthique.

**ethnic** /'eθnɪk/ *a* ethnique. **~ cleansing** *n* nettoyage *m* ethnique.

**ethos** /'i:θɒs/ *n* philosophie *f*.

**EU** *abbr* (**European Union**) UE *f*, Union *f* européenne.

**euphoria** /ju:'fɔ:rɪə/ *n* euphorie *f*.

**euro** /'jʊərəʊ/ *n* euro *m*. **~ zone** *n* zone *f* euro.

**Euroland** /'jʊərəʊlænd/ *n* euroland *m*.

**Europe** /'jʊərəp/ *n* Europe *f*.

**European** /jʊərə'pɪən/ *a* & *n* européen/-ne (*m*/*f*).

**eurosceptic** /'jʊərəʊskɛptɪk/ *n* eurosceptique *mf*.

**euthanasia** /ju:θə'neɪzɪə/ *n* euthanasie *f*.

**evacuate** /ɪ'vækjʊeɪt/ *vt* évacuer.

**evade** /ɪ'veɪd/ *vt* (*blow*) esquiver; (*question*) éluder.

**evaporate** /ɪ'væpəreɪt/ *vi* s'évaporer; **~d milk** lait *m* condensé.

**evasion** /ɪ'veɪʒn/ *n* fuite *f* (**of** devant); (excuse) faux-fuyant *m*; **tax ~** évasion *f* fiscale. **evasive** *a* évasif.

…tc.; ~ so qua…
…out (*differences*) s'atté…
… sth out (*inequalities*)
…e qch; ~ **up** équilibrer.
…ning /'i:vnɪŋ/ *n* soir *m*; (whole evening, event) soirée *f*.
**evenly** /'i:vnlɪ/ *adv* (*spread, apply*) uniformément; (*breathe*) régulièrement; (equally) en parts égales.
**event** /ɪ'vent/ *n* événement *m*; (Sport) épreuve *f*; **in the ~ of** en cas de. **eventful** *a* mouvementé.
**eventual** /ɪ'ventʃʊəl/ *a* (*outcome, decision*) final; (*aim*) à long terme. **eventuality** *n* éventualité *f*. **eventually** *adv* finalement; (in future) un jour ou l'autre.
**ever** /'evə(r)/ *adv* jamais; (at all times) toujours.
**evergreen** /'evəgri:n/ *n* arbre *m* à feuilles persistantes.
**everlasting** /evə'lɑ:stɪŋ/ *a* éternel.
**ever since** *prep & adv* depuis.
**every** /'evrɪ/ *a* ~ **house/window** toutes les maisons/les fenêtres; ~ **time/minute** chaque fois/minute; ~ **day** tous les jours; ~ **other day** tous les deux jours. **everybody** *pron* tout le monde. **everyday** *a* quotidien. **everyone** *pron* tout le monde. **everything** *pron* tout. **everywhere** *adv* partout; ~**where he goes** partout où il va.
**evict** /ɪ'vɪkt/ *vt* expulser (**from** de).
**evidence** /'evɪdəns/ *n* (proof) preuves *fpl* (**that** que; **of, for** de); (testimony) témoignage *m*; (traces) trace *f* (**of** de); **give ~** témoigner; **be in ~** être visible. **evident** *a* manifeste. **evidently** *adv* (appar-

ev…
élabo…
**ewe** /ju:/ *n* b…
**ex-** /eks/ *pref* ex-, a…
**exact** /ɪg'zækt/ *a* … **opposite** exactement … ● *vt* exiger (**from** de). **exactly** … exactement.
**exaggerate** /ɪg'zædʒəreɪt/ *vt/i* exagérer.
**exalted** /ɪg'zɔ:ltɪd/ *a* élevé.
**exam** /ɪg'zæm/ *n* ⓘ examen *m*.
**examination** /ɪgzæmɪ'neɪʃn/ *n* examen *m*.
**examine** /ɪg'zæmɪn/ *vt* examiner; (witness) interroger. **examiner** *n* examinateur/-trice *m/f*.
**example** /ɪg'zɑ:mpl/ *n* exemple *m*; **for ~** par exemple; **make an ~ of** punir pour l'exemple.
**exasperate** /ɪg'zæspəreɪt/ *vt* exaspérer.
**excavate** /'ekskəveɪt/ *vt* fouiller. **excavations** *npl* fouilles *fpl*.
**exceed** /ɪk'si:d/ *vt* dépasser. **exceedingly** *adv* extrêmement.
**excel** /ɪk'sel/ *vi* (*pt* **excelled**) exceller (**at, in** en; **at doing** à faire). ● *vt* surpasser.
**excellence** /'eksələns/ *n* excellence *f*. **excellent** *a* excellent.
**except** /ɪk'sept/ *prep* sauf, excepté; ~ **for** à part. ● *vt* excepter. **excepting** *prep* sauf, excepté.
**exception** /ɪk'sepʃn/ *n* exception *f*; **take ~ to** s'offusquer. **exceptional** *a* exceptionnel.
**excerpt** /'eksɜ:pt/ *n* extrait *m*.

*a* excessif.

...ndʒ/ *vt* échan-... *n* échange *m*; ...hange *m*; **~ rate** ...ge; **telephone ~** ...phonique.

...**hequer** /ɪks'tʃekə(r)/ *n* (Pol) ...inistère *m* britannique des finances.

**excise** /'eksaɪz/ *n* excise *f*, taxe *f*.

**excite** /ɪk'saɪt/ *vt* exciter; (enthuse) enthousiasmer. **excited** *a* excité; **get ~d** s'exciter. **excitement** *n* excitation *f*. **exciting** *a* passionnant.

**exclaim** /ɪk'skleɪm/ *vt* s'exclamer.

**exclamation** /eksklə'meɪʃn/ *n* exclamation *f*; **~ mark** *or* **point** (US) point *m* d'exclamation.

**exclude** /ɪk'sklu:d/ *vt* exclure.

**exclusive** /ɪk'sklu:sɪv/ *a* (*club*) fermé; (*rights*) exclusif; (*news item*) en exclusivité; **~ of meals** repas non compris. **exclusively** *adv* exclusivement.

**excruciating** /ɪk'skru:ʃɪeɪtɪŋ/ *a* atroce.

**excursion** /ɪk'skɜ:ʃn/ *n* excursion *f*.

**excuse**[1] /ɪk'skju:z/ *vt* excuser; **~ from** (exempt) dispenser de; **~ me!** excusez-moi!, pardon!

**excuse**[2] /ɪk'skju:s/ *n* (reason) excuse *f*; (pretext) prétexte *m* (**for sth** à qch; **for doing** pour faire).

**ex-directory** /eksdɪ'rektərɪ/ *a* sur liste rouge.

**execute** /'eksɪkju:t/ *vt* exécuter. **executioner** *n* bourreau *m*.

**exec**... ...zekjʊtɪv/ *n* (person) cadre... (com)mittee) exécutif *m*. ● *a* exécu...

**exemplary** /ɪg'zemplərɪ/ *a* exemplaire.

**exemplify** /ɪg'zemplɪfaɪ/ *vt* illustrer.

**exempt** /ɪg'zempt/ *a* exempt (**from** de). ● *vt* exempter.

**exercise** /'eksəsaɪz/ *n* exercice *m*; **~ book** cahier *m*. ● *vt* exercer; (*restraint, patience*) faire preuve de. ● *vi* faire de l'exercice.

**exert** /ɪg'zɜ:t/ *vt* exercer; **~ oneself** se fatiguer. **exertion** *n* effort *m*.

**exhaust** /ɪg'zɔ:st/ *vt* épuiser. ● *n* (Auto) pot *m* d'échappement.

**exhaustive** /ɪg'zɔ:stɪv/ *a* exhaustif.

**exhibit** /ɪg'zɪbɪt/ *vt* exposer; (fig) manifester. ● *n* objet *m* exposé.

**exhibition** /eksɪ'bɪʃn/ *n* exposition *f*; (of skill) démonstration *f*. **exhibitionist** *n* exhibitionniste *mf*.

**exhibitor** /ɪg'zɪbɪtə(r)/ *n* exposant/-e *m*/*f*.

**exhilarate** /ɪg'zɪləreɪt/ *vt* griser.

**exile** /'eksaɪl/ *n* exil *m*; (person) exilé/-e *m*/*f*. ● *vt* exiler.

**exist** /ɪg'zɪst/ *vi* exister. **existence** *n* existence *f*; **be in ~ence** exister. **existing** *a* actuel.

**exit** /'eksɪt/ *n* sortie *f*. ● *vt*/*i* (*also* Comput) sortir (de).

**exodus** /'eksədəs/ *n* exode *m*.

**exonerate** /ɪg'zɒnəreɪt/ *vt* disculper.

**exotic** /ɪg'zɒtɪk/ *a* exotique.

**expand** /ɪk'spænd/ *vt* développer; (*workforce*) accroître. ● *vi* se développer; (*population*) s'accroître; (*metal*) se dilater.

**expanse** /ɪk'spæns/ *n* étendue *f*.

**expansion** /ɪk'sp... cès ... loppement *m*; (Pol... sion *f*.

**expatriate** /eks'pætrɪət/ ... expatrié/-e (*m*/*f*).

**expect** /ɪk'spekt/ *vt* s'attendre à; (suppose) supposer; (demand) exiger; (*baby*) attendre.

**expectancy** /ɪk'spektənsɪ/ *n* attente *f*.

**expectant** /ɪk'spektənt/ *a* ~ mother future maman *f*.

**expectation** /ekspek'teɪʃn/ *n* (assumption) prévision *f*; (hope) aspiration *f*; (demand) exigence *f*.

**expedient** /ɪk'spi:dɪənt/ *a* opportun. ● *n* expédient *m*.

**expedition** /ekspɪ'dɪʃn/ *n* expédition *f*.

**expel** /ɪk'spel/ *vt* (*pt* **expelled**) expulser; (*pupil*) renvoyer.

**expend** /ɪk'spend/ *vt* consacrer.

**expenditure** /ɪk'spendɪtʃə(r)/ *n* dépenses *fpl*.

**expense** /ɪk'spens/ *n* frais *mpl*; **at sb's ~** aux frais de qn; **~ account** frais *mpl* de représentation. **expensive** *a* cher; (*tastes*) de luxe. **expensively** *adv* luxueusement.

**experience** /ɪk'spɪərɪəns/ *n* expérience *f*. ● *vt* (undergo) connaître; (feel) éprouver; **~d** expérimenté.

**experiment** /ɪk'sperɪment/ *n* expérience *f*. ● *vi* expérimenter, faire des essais.

**expert** /'ekspɜ:t/ *n* spécialiste *mf*. ● *a* spécialisé, expert. **expertise** *n* compétence *f*. **expertly** *adv* de manière experte.

**expire** /ɪk'spaɪə(r)/ *vi* expirer; **~d** périmé. **expiry** *n* expiration *f*.

**explain** /ɪk'spleɪn/ *vt* expliquer. **explanation** *n* explication *f*. **explanatory** *a* explicatif.

**explicit** /ɪk'splɪsɪt/ *a* explicite.

...

**exploratio**... ploration *f*. ... exploratoire. ... (fig) étudier. ... rateur/-trice *m*...

**explosion** /ɪk'sp... sion *f*. **explosive** *a* & *n* ... (*m*).

**exponent** /ɪk'spəʊnənt/ *n* avocat/-e *m*/*f* (of de).

**export**[1] /ɪk'spɔ:t/ *vt* exporter.

**export**[2] /'ekspɔ:t/ *n* (process) exportation *f*; (product) produit *m* d'exportation.

**expose** /ɪk'spəʊz/ *vt* exposer; (disclose) révéler.

**exposure** /ɪk'spəʊʒə(r)/ *n* révélation *f*; (Photo) pose *f*; **die of ~** mourir de froid.

**express** /ɪk'spres/ *vt* exprimer. ● *a* exprès. ● *adv* **send sth ~** envoyer qch en exprès. ● *n* (train) rapide *m*. **expression** *n* expression *f*. **expressive** *a* expressif. **expressly** *adv* expressément.

**exquisite** /'ekskwɪzɪt/ *a* exquis.

**extend** /ɪk'stend/ *vt* (visit) prolonger; (*house*) agrandir; (*range*) élargir; (*arm, leg*) étendre. ● *vi* (stretch) s'étendre; (in time) se prolonger. **extension** *n* (of line, road) prolongement *m*; (of visa, loan) prorogation *f*; (building) addition *f*; (phone number) poste *m*; (cable) rallonge *f*.

**extensive** /ɪk'stensɪv/ *a* vaste; (study) approfondi; (damage) considérable. **extensively** *adv* (much) beaucoup; (very) très.

**extent** /ɪk'stent/ *n* (size, scope) étendue *f*; (degree) mesure *f*; **to some ~** dans une certaine mesure; **to such an ~ that** à tel point que.

…enjʊeɪtɪŋ/ *a*

…ə(r)/ *a & n* exté-…

… /ɪk'stɜ:mɪneɪt/ *vt*

… /ɪk'stɜ:nl/ *a* extérieur; (medical use) externe.

…**ct** /ɪk'stɪŋkt/ *a* (species) disparu; (volcano, passion) éteint.

**extinguish** /ɪk'stɪŋgwɪʃ/ *vt* éteindre. **extinguisher** *n* extincteur *m*.

**extol** /ɪk'stəʊl/ *vt* (*pt* **extolled**) louer, chanter les louanges de.

**extort** /ɪk'stɔ:t/ *vt* extorquer (**from** à). **extortion** *n* (Jur) extorsion *f*. **extortionate** *a* exorbitant.

**extra** /'ekstrə/ *a* supplémentaire; **~ charge** supplément *m*; **~ time** (football) prolongation *f*; **~ strong** extra-fort. ● *adv* encore; plus. ● *n* supplément *m*; (cinema) figurant/-e *m/f*.

**extract¹** /ɪk'strækt/ *vt* sortir (**from** de); (*tooth*) extraire; (*promise*) arracher.

**extract²** /'ekstrækt/ *n* extrait *m*.

**extra-curricular** /ekstrəkə'rɪkjʊlə(r)/ *a* parascolaire.

**extradite** /'ekstrədaɪt/ *vt* extrader.

**extramarital** /ekstrə'mærɪtl/ *a* extraconjugal.

**extramural** /ekstrə'mjʊərəl/ *a* (Univ) hors faculté.

**extraordinary** /ɪk'strɔ:dnrɪ/ *a* extraordinaire.

**extravagance** /ɪk'strævəgəns/ *n* prodigalité *f*. **extravagant** *a* (*person*) dépensier; (*claim*) extravagant.

**extreme** /ɪk'stri:m/ *a & n* extrême (*m*). **extremely** *adv* extrêmement. **extremist** *n* extrémiste *mf*.

**extremity** *n* extrémité *f*.

**extricate** /'ekstrɪkeɪt/ *vt* dégager.

**extrovert** /'ekstrəvɜ:t/ *n* extraverti/-e *m/f*.

**exuberance** /ɪg'zju:bərəns/ *n* exubérance *f*.

**exude** /ɪg'zju:d/ *vt* (*charm*) respirer; (*smell*) exhaler.

**eye** /aɪ/ *n* œil *m* (*pl* yeux); **keep an ~ on** surveiller. ● *vt* (*pt* **eyed**; *pres p* **eyeing**) regarder. **~ball** *n* globe *m* oculaire. **~brow** *n* sourcil *m*. **~-catching** *a* attrayant. **~lash** *n* cil *m*. **~lid** *n* paupière *f*. **~-opener** *n* révélation *f*. **~-shadow** *n* ombre *f* à paupières. **~sight** *n* vue *f*. **~sore** *n* horreur *f*. **~witness** *n* témoin *m* oculaire.

# Ff

**fable** /'feɪbl/ *n* fable *f*.

**fabric** /'fæbrɪk/ *n* (cloth) tissu *m*.

**fabulous** /'fæbjʊləs/ *a* fabuleux; (marvellous Ⓘ) formidable.

**face** /feɪs/ *n* visage *m*, figure *f*; (expression) air *m*; (appearance, dignity) face *f*; (of clock) cadran *m*; (Geol) face *f*; (of rock) paroi *f*; **in the ~ of** face à; **make a (funny) ~** faire la grimace; **~ to ~** face à face. ● *vt* être en face de; (*risk*) devoir affronter; (confront) faire face à; (deal with) **I can't ~ him** je n'ai pas le courage de le voir. ● *vi* (*person*) regarder; (*chair*) être tourné vers; (*window*) donner sur; **~ up to** faire face à; **~d with** face à.

**face-lift** /'feɪslɪft/ *n* lifting *m*; **give a ~ to** donner un coup de neuf à.

**face value** *n* valeur *f* nominale; **take sth at ~** prendre qch au pied de la lettre.

**facial** /'feɪʃl/ *a* (*hair*) du visage; (*injury*) au visage. ● *n* soin *m* du visage.

**facility** /fə'sɪlətɪ/ *n* (building) complexe *m*; (feature) fonction *f*; **facilities** (equipment) équipements *mpl*.

**facsimile** /fæk'sɪməlɪ/ *n* facsimilé *m*.

**fact** /fækt/ *n* fait *m*; **as a matter of ~, in ~** en fait; **know for a ~ that** savoir de source sûre que; **owing/due to the ~ that** étant donné que.

**factor** /'fæktə(r)/ *n* facteur *m*.

**factory** /'fæktərɪ/ *n* usine *f*.

**factual** /'fæktʃʊəl/ *a* (*account, description*) basé sur les faits; (*evidence*) factuel.

**faculty** /'fækltɪ/ *n* faculté *f*.

**fade** /feɪd/ *vi* (*sound*) s'affaiblir; (*memory*) s'effacer; (*flower*) se faner; (*material*) se décolorer; (*colour*) passer.

**fail** /feɪl/ *vi* échouer; (grow weak) s'affaiblir; (run short) manquer; (*engine*) tomber en panne. ● *vt* (*exam*) échouer à; **~ to do** (not do) ne pas faire; (not be able) ne pas réussir à faire; **without ~** à coup sûr.

**failing** /'feɪlɪŋ/ *n* défaut *m*; **~ that/this** sinon.

**failure** /'feɪljə(r)/ *n* échec *m*; (person) raté/-e *m/f*; (breakdown) panne *f*; **~ to do** (inability) incapacité *f* de faire.

**faint** /feɪnt/ *a* léger, faible; **feel ~** (ill) se sentir mal; **I haven't the ~est idea** je n'en ai pas la moindre idée. ● *vi* s'évanouir. ● *n* évanouissement *m*. **~-hearted** *a* timide.

**fair** /feə(r)/ *n* foire *f*. ● *a* (*hair, person*) blond; (*skin*) clair; (*weather*) beau; (*amount, quality*) raisonnable; (just) juste, équitable. ● *adv* (*play*) loyalement.

**fair-ground** *n* champ *m* de foire.

**fairly** /'feəlɪ/ *adv* (justly) équitablement; (rather) assez.

**fairness** /'feənɪs/ *n* justice *f*.

**fairy** /'feərɪ/ *n* fée *f*. **~ story, ~-tale** *n* conte *m* de fées.

**faith** /feɪθ/ *n* (belief) foi *f*; (confidence) confiance *f*.

**faithful** /'feɪθfl/ *a* fidèle.

**fake** /feɪk/ *n* (forgery) faux *m*; (person) imposteur *m*; **it is a ~** c'est un faux. ● *a* faux. ● *vt* (*signature*) contrefaire; (*results*) falsifier; (*illness*) feindre.

**falcon** /'fɔ:lkən/ *n* faucon *m*.

**fall** /fɔ:l/ *vi* (*pt* **fell**; *pp* **fallen**) tomber; **~ short** être insuffisant. ● *n* chute *f*; (autumn: US) automne *m*; **Niagara F~s** chutes *fpl* du Niagara. □ **~ back on** se rabattre sur; **~ behind** prendre du retard; **~ down** *or* **off** tomber; **~ for** (*person* [I]) tomber amoureux de; (*a trick* [I]) se laisser prendre à; **~ in** (Mil) se mettre en rangs; **~ off** (decrease) diminuer; **~ out** se brouiller (**with** avec); **~ over** tomber (par terre); **~ through** (*plans*) tomber à l'eau.

**fallacy** /'fæləsɪ/ *n* erreur *f*.

**false** /fɔ:ls/ *a* faux. **~ teeth** *npl* dentier *m*.

**falter** /'fɔ:ltə(r)/ *vi* (*economy*) fléchir; (*courage*) faiblir; (when speaking) bafouiller [I].

**fame** /feɪm/ *n* renommée *f*. **famed** *a* célèbre (**for** pour).

**familiar** /fə'mɪlɪə(r)/ *a* familier; **be ~ with** connaître.

**family** /'fæməlɪ/ *n* famille *f*. ● *a* de famille, familial.

**famine** /'fæmɪn/ *n* famine *f*.

**famished** /'fæmɪʃt/ *a* affamé.

…) …m/f; …/f, passion- … (*pt* **fanned**) …, (fig) attiser. ● *vi* ~ …yer en éventail.

…: /fəˈnætɪk/ *n* fanatique *mf*.

…**belt** *n* courroie *f* de ventilateur.

**fancy** /ˈfænsɪ/ *n* (whim, fantasy) fantaisie *f*; **take a ~ to sb** se prendre d'affection pour qn; **it took my ~** ça m'a plu. ● *a* (*buttons etc.*) fantaisie *inv*; (*prices*) extravagant; (impressive) impressionnant. ● *vt* s'imaginer; (want I) avoir envie de; (like I) aimer. ~ **dress** *n* déguisement *m*.

**fang** /fæŋ/ *n* (of dog) croc *m*; (of snake) crochet *m*.

**fantasize** /ˈfæntəsaɪz/ *vi* fantasmer.

**fantastic** /fænˈtæstɪk/ *a* fantastique.

**fantasy** /ˈfæntəsɪ/ *n* fantaisie *f*; (daydream) fantasme *m*.

**fanzine** /ˈfænziːn/ *n* magazine *m* des fans, fanzine *m*.

**FAQ** *abbr* (**Frequently Asked Questions**) (Internet) FAQ *f*, foire *f* aux questions.

**far** /fɑː(r)/ *adv* loin; (much) beaucoup; (very) très; ~ **away**, ~ **off** au loin; **as ~ as** (up to) jusqu'à; **as ~ as I know** autant que je sache; **by ~** de loin; ~ **from** loin de. ● *a* lointain; (end, side) autre. **~away** *a* lointain.

**farce** /fɑːs/ *n* farce *f*.

**fare** /feə(r)/ *n* (prix du) billet *m*; (food) nourriture *f*. ● *vi* (progress) aller; (manage) se débrouiller.

**Far East** *n* Extrême-Orient *m*.

…**l** /feəˈwel/ *interj* & *n* adieu …*m*).

…**arm** /fɑːm/ *n* ferme *f*. ● *vt* cultiver; ~ **out** céder en sous-traitance. ● *vi* être fermier. **farmer** *n* fermier *m*. **~house** *n* ferme *f*. **farming** *n* agriculture *f*. **~yard** *n* basse-cour *f*.

**farther** /ˈfɑːðə(r)/ *adv* plus loin. ● *a* plus éloigné.

**farthest** /fɑːðɪst/ *adv* le plus loin. ● *a* le plus éloigné.

**fascinate** /ˈfæsɪneɪt/ *vt* fasciner.

**Fascism** /ˈfæʃɪzəm/ *n* fascisme *m*.

**fashion** /ˈfæʃn/ *n* (current style) mode *f*; (manner) façon *f*; **in ~** à la mode; **out of ~** démodé. ● *vt* façonner. **fashionable** *a* à la mode.

**fast** /fɑːst/ *a* rapide; (colour) grand teint *inv*; (firm) fixe, solide; **be ~** (of a clock) avancer. ● *adv* vite; (firmly) ferme; **be ~ asleep** dormir d'un sommeil profond. ● *vi* jeûner. ● *n* jeûne *m*.

**fasten** /ˈfɑːsn/ *vt*/*i* (s')attacher. **fastener**, **fastening** *n* attache *f*, fermeture *f*.

**fast food** *n* fast-food *m*; restauration *f* rapide.

**fat** /fæt/ *n* graisse *f*; (on meat) gras *m*. ● *a* (**fatter**, **fattest**) gros, gras; (*meat*) gras; (*profit*) gros; **a ~ lot** I bien peu (**of** de).

**fatal** /ˈfeɪtl/ *a* mortel; (fateful, disastrous) fatal. **fatality** *n* mort *m*. **fatally** *adv* mortellement.

**fate** /feɪt/ *n* sort *m*. **fateful** *a* fatidique.

**father** /ˈfɑːðə(r)/ *n* père *m*. **~hood** *n* paternité *f*. **~-in-law** *n* (*pl* **~s-in-law**) beau-père *m*.

**fathom** /ˈfæðəm/ *vt* comprendre.

**fatigue** /fəˈtiːg/ *n* épuisement *m*; (Tech) fatigue *f*. ● *vt* fatiguer.

**fatten** /ˈfætn/ *vt*/*i* engraisser. **fattening** *a* qui fait grossir.

**fatty** /ˈfætɪ/ *a* (*food*) gras; (...) adipeux.

**faucet** /ˈfɔːsɪt/ *n* (US) robinet *m*.

**fault** /fɔːlt/ *n* (defect, failing) défaut *m*; (blame) faute *f*; (Geol) faille *f*; **at ~** fautif; **find ~ with** critiquer. ● *vt* **~ sth/sb** prendre en défaut qn/qch. **faulty** *a* défectueux.

**favour**, (US) **favor** /ˈfeɪvə(r)/ *n* faveur *f*; **do sb a ~** rendre service à qn; **in ~ of** pour. ● *vt* favoriser; (support) être en faveur de; (prefer) préférer. **favourable** *a* favorable.

**favourite** /ˈfeɪvərɪt/ *a* & *n* favori/-te (*m*/*f*).

**fawn** /fɔːn/ *n* (animal) faon *m*; (colour) beige *m* foncé. ● *vi* **~ on** flagorner.

**fax** /fæks/ *n* fax *m*, télécopie *f*. ● *vt* faxer, envoyer par télécopie. **~ machine** *n* fax *m*; télécopieur *m*; (for public use) Publifax® *m*.

**FBI** *abbr* (**Federal Bureau of Investigation**) (US) Police *f* judiciaire fédérale.

**fear** /fɪə(r)/ *n* crainte *f*, peur *f*; (fig) risque *m*; **for ~ of/that** de peur de/que. ● *vt* craindre.

**feasible** /ˈfiːzəbl/ *a* faisable; (likely) plausible.

**feast** /fiːst/ *n* festin *m*; (Relig) fête *f*. ● *vi* festoyer. ● *vt* régaler (**on** de).

**feat** /fiːt/ *n* exploit *m*.

**feather** /ˈfeðə(r)/ *n* plume *f*. ● *vt* **~ one's nest** s'enrichir.

**feature** /ˈfiːtʃə(r)/ *n* caractéristique *f*; (of person, face) trait *m*; (film) long métrage *m*; (article) article *m* de fond. ● *vt* (*advert*) représenter; (give prominence to) mettre en vedette. ● *vi* figurer (**in** dans).

**February** /ˈfebrʊərɪ/ *n* février *m*.

**fed** /fed/ ⇨FEED. ● *a* **be ~ up** [I] en avoir marre [I] (**with** de).

**federal** /ˈfedərəl/ *a* fédéral.

(...)

**feeb...**

**feed** /fiːd/ *v*... donner à manger à... (supply) alimenter. ●... (on de); **~ in information** ... des données. ● *n* nourriture *f*; (of baby) tétée *f*.

**feedback** /ˈfiːdbæk/ *n* réaction(s) *f*(*pl*); (Med, Tech) feed-back *m*.

**feel** /fiːl/ *vt* (*pt* **felt**) (touch) tâter; (be conscious of) sentir; (*emotion*) ressentir; (experience) éprouver; (think) estimer. ● *vi* (*tired, lonely*) se sentir; **~ hot/thirsty** avoir chaud/soif; **~ as if** avoir l'impression que; **~ awful** (ill) se sentir malade; **~ like** (want [I]) avoir envie de.

**feeler** /ˈfiːlə(r)/ *n* antenne *f*; **put out ~s** tâter le terrain.

**feeling** /ˈfiːlɪŋ/ *n* (emotion) sentiment *m*; (physical) sensation *f*; (impression) impression *f*.

**feet** /fiːt/ ⇨FOOT.

**feign** /feɪn/ *vt* feindre.

**fell** /fel/ ⇨FALL. ● *vt* (cut down) abattre.

**fellow** /ˈfeləʊ/ *n* compagnon *m*, camarade *m*; (of society) membre *m*; (man [I]) type *m* [I]. **~-countryman** *n* compatriote *m*. **~-passenger** *n* compagnon *m* de voyage.

**fellowship** /ˈfeləʊʃɪp/ *n* camaraderie *f*; (group) association *f*.

**felony** /ˈfelənɪ/ *n* crime *m*.

**felt** /felt/ ⇨FEEL. ● *n* feutre *m*. **~-tip** *n* feutre *m*.

**female** /ˈfiːmeɪl/ *a* (*animal*) femelle; (*voice, sex*) féminin. ● *n* femme *f*; (animal) femelle *f*.

**feminine** /ˈfemənɪn/ *a* & *n* féminin (*m*). **femininity** *n* féminité *f*.

**feminist** *n* féministe *mf*.

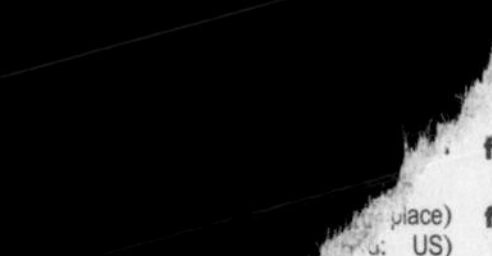

place)
US)

n ferment *m*;
ation *f*.

ment/ *vt*/*i* (faire) fer-

/fɜ:n/ *n* fougère *f*.

**rocious** /fəˈrəʊʃəs/ *a* féroce.

**ferret** /ˈferɪt/ *n* (animal) furet *m*. ● *vi* **~ about** fureter. ● *vt* **~ out** dénicher.

**ferry** /ˈferɪ/ *n* (long-distance) ferry *m*; (short-distance) bac *m*. ● *vt* transporter.

**fertile** /ˈfɜ:taɪl/ *a* fertile; (*person, animal*) fécond. **fertilizer** *n* engrais *m*.

**festival** /ˈfestɪvl/ *n* festival *m*; (Relig) fête *f*.

**festive** /ˈfestɪv/ *a* de fête, gai; **~ season** période *f* des fêtes. **festivity** *n* réjouissances *fpl*.

**fetch** /fetʃ/ *vt* (go for) aller chercher; (bring person) amener; (bring thing) apporter; (be sold for) rapporter.

**fête** /feɪt/ *n* fête *f*; (church) kermesse *f*. ● *vt* fêter.

**fetish** /ˈfetɪʃ/ *n* (object) fétiche *m*; (Psych) obsession *f*.

**feud** /fju:d/ *n* querelle *f*.

**fever** /ˈfi:və(r)/ *n* fièvre *f*. **feverish** *a* fiévreux.

**few** /fju:/ *det* peu de; **a ~ houses** quelques maisons; **quite a ~ people** un bon nombre de per-

ies. ● *pron* quelques-uns/ iques-unes.

**ver** /ˈfju:ə(r)/ *det* moins de; **be ~** tre moins nombreux (**than** que). **fewest** *det* le moins de.

**fiancé** /fɪˈɒnseɪ/ *n* fiancé *m*. **fiancée** *n* fiancée *f*.

**fibre**, (US) **fiber** /ˈfaɪbə(r)/ *n* fibre *f*. **~glass** *n* fibre *f* de verre.

**fiction** /ˈfɪkʃn/ *n* fiction *f*; **(works of) ~** romans *mpl*. **fictional** *a* fictif.

**fiddle** /ˈfɪdl/ *n* 🄸 violon *m*; (swindle 🄸) combine *f*. ● *vi* ☒ frauder. ● *vt* 🄸 falsifier; **~ with** 🄸 tripoter 🄸.

**fidget** /ˈfɪdʒɪt/ *vi* gigoter sans cesse.

**field** /fi:ld/ *n* champ *m*; (Sport) terrain *m*; (fig) domaine *m*. ● *vt* (*ball*: cricket) bloquer.

**fierce** /fɪəs/ *a* féroce; (*storm, attack*) violent.

**fiery** /ˈfaɪərɪ/ *a* (**-ier**, **-iest**) (hot) ardent; (spirited) fougueux.

**fifteen** /fɪfˈti:n/ *a* & *n* quinze (*m*).

**fifth** /fɪfθ/ *a* & *n* cinquième (*mf*).

**fifty** /ˈfɪftɪ/ *a* & *n* cinquante (*m*).

**fig** /fɪg/ *n* figue *f*.

**fight** /faɪt/ *vi* (*pt* **fought**) se battre; (struggle: fig) lutter; (quarrel) se disputer. ● *vt* se battre avec; (*evil*: fig) lutter contre. ● *n* (struggle) lutte *f*; (quarrel) dispute *f*; (brawl) bagarre *f*; (Mil) combat *m*. □ **~ back** se défendre (**against** contre); **~ off** surmonter; **~ over** se disputer qch. **fighter** *n* (determined person) lutteur/-euse *m*/*f*; (plane) avion *m* de chasse. **fighting** *n* combats *mpl*.

**figment** /ˈfɪgmənt/ *n* **a ~ of the imagination** un produit de l'imagination.

**figure** /ˈfɪgə(r)/ *n* (number) chiffre *m*; (diagram) figure *f*; (shape) forme *f*;

(body) ligne *f*; **~s** arithmétiqu
● *vt* s'imaginer. ● *vi* (appear) fig
rer; **that ~s** (US, 🄸) c'est logique
**~ out** comprendre. **~ of speech**
*n* façon *f* de parler.

**file** /faɪl/ *n* (tool) lime *f*; dossier *m*, classeur *m*; (Comput) fichier *m*; (row) file *f*. ● *vt* limer; (*papers*) classer; (Jur) déposer. □ **~ in** entrer en file; **~ past** défiler devant.

**filing cabinet** *n* classeur *m*.

**fill** /fɪl/ *vt*/*i* (se) remplir. ● *n* **have had one's ~** en avoir assez. □ **~ in** (*form*) remplir; **~ out** prendre du poids; **~ up** (Auto) faire le plein (de carburant); (*bath, theatre*) (se) remplir.

**fillet** /'fɪlɪt, US fɪ'leɪ/ *n* filet *m*. ● *vt* découper en filets.

**filling** /'fɪlɪŋ/ *n* (of tooth) plombage *m*; (of sandwich) garniture *f*. **~ station** *n* station-service *f*.

**film** /fɪlm/ *n* film *m*; (Photo) pellicule *f*. ● *vt* filmer. **~-goer** *n* cinéphile *mf*. **~ star** *n* vedette *f* de cinéma.

**filter** /'fɪltə(r)/ *n* filtre *m*; (traffic signal) flèche *f*. ● *vt*/*i* filtrer; (of traffic) suivre la flèche. **~ coffee** *n* café *m* filtre.

**filth** /fɪlθ/ *n* crasse *f*. **filthy** *a* crasseux.

**fin** /fɪn/ *n* (of fish, seal) nageoire *f*; (of shark) aileron *m*.

**final** /'faɪnl/ *a* dernier; (conclusive) définitif. ● *n* (Sport) finale *f*.

**finale** /fɪ'nɑːlɪ/ *n* (Mus) finale *m*.

**finalize** /'faɪnəlaɪz/ *vt* mettre au point, fixer.

**finally** /'faɪnəlɪ/ *adv* (lastly, at last) enfin, finalement; (once and for all) définitivement.

**finance** /'faɪnæns/ *n* finance *f*. ● *a* financier. ● *vt* financer. **financial** *a* financier.

**find** /faɪnd/ *vt* (*pt* **found**) trouver; (*sth lost*) retrouver. ● *n* trouvaille

**fing**
palpe
*n* emprein
*m* du doigt.

**finish** /'fɪnɪʃ/ *v*
finir de faire; **~ up** d
faire; **~ up in** se retro
fin *f*; (of race) arrivée *f*; (a
finition *f*.

**finite** /'faɪnaɪt/ *a* fini.

**Finland** /'fɪnlənd/ *n* Finlande *f*. **Finn** *n* Finlandais/-e *m*/*f*.

**Finnish** /'fɪnɪʃ/ *a* finlandais. ● *n* (Ling) finnois *m*.

**fir** /fɜː(r)/ *n* sapin *m*.

**fire** /'faɪə(r)/ *n* (element) feu *m*; (blaze) incendie *m*; (heater) radiateur *m*; **set ~ to** mettre le feu à. ● *vt* (bullet) tirer; (dismiss) renvoyer; (fig) enflammer. ● *vi* tirer (**at** sur); **~ a gun** tirer un coup de revolver/de fusil. **~ alarm** *n* alarme *f* incendie. **~arm** *n* arme *f* à feu. **~ brigade** *n* pompiers *mpl*. **~ engine** *n* voiture *f* de pompiers. **~ escape** *n* escalier *m* de secours. **~ extinguisher** *n* extincteur *m*. **~man** *n* (*pl* **-men**) pompier *m*. **~place** *n* cheminée *f*. **~ station** *n* caserne *f* de pompiers. **~wall** *n* mur *m* coupe-feu; (Internet) pare-feu *m inv*. **~wood** *n* bois *m* de chauffage. **~work** *n* feu *m* d'artifice.

**firing-squad** *n* peloton *m* d'exécution.

**firm** /fɜːm/ *n* entreprise *f*, société *f*. ● *a* ferme; (*belief*) solide.

**first** /fɜːst/ *a* premier; **at ~ hand** de première main, **at ~ sight** à pre-

mière vue; ~ **of all** tout d'abord. ● *n* premier/-ière *m/f.* ● *adv* d'abord, premièrement; (arrive) le premier, la première; **at** ~ d'abord. ~ **aid** *n* premiers soins *mpl.* ~**-class** *a* de première [illegible]asse. ~ **floor** *n* premier étage *m*; [illegible]) rez-de-chaussée *m inv.* ~ [illegible]**r** *n* première (vitesse) *f.* **F**~ [illegible] *n* (US) épouse *f* du Président. [illegible] /'fɜ:stlɪ/ *adv* premièrement. **[illegible]me** *n* prénom *m.*

**fish** /fɪʃ/ *n* poisson *m*; ~ **shop** poissonnerie *f.* ● *vi* pêcher; ~ **for** (*cod*) pêcher; ~ **out** (from water) repêcher; (take out ⓘ) sortir. **fisherman** *n* (*pl* **-men**) *n* pêcheur *m.*

**fishing** /'fɪʃɪŋ/ *n* pêche *f*; **go** ~ aller à la pêche. ~ **rod** *n* canne *f* à pêche.

**fishmonger** /'fɪʃmʌŋgə(r)/ *n* poissonnier/-ière *m/f.*

**fist** /fɪst/ *n* poing *m.*

**fit** /fɪt/ *n* accès *m*, crise *f*; **be a good** ~ (*dress*) être à la bonne taille. ● *a* (**fitter**, **fittest**) en bonne santé; (proper) convenable; (good enough) bon; (able) capable; **in no** ~ **state to do** pas en état de faire. ● *vt/i* (*pt* **fitted**) (into space) aller; (install) poser. □ ~ **in** *vt* caser; *vi* (*newcomer*) s'intégrer; ~ **out**, ~ **up** équiper.

**fitness** /'fɪtnɪs/ *n* forme *f*; (of remark) justesse *f.*

**fitted** /'fɪtɪd/ *a* (*wardrobe*) encastré. ~ **carpet** *n* moquette *f.*

**fitting** /'fɪtɪŋ/ *a* approprié. ● *n* essayage *m.* ~ **room** *n* cabine *f* d'essayage.

**five** /faɪv/ *a* & *n* cinq (*m*).

**fix** /fɪks/ *vt* (make firm, attach, decide) fixer; (mend) réparer; (deal with) arranger; ~ **sb up with sth** trouver qch à qn.

**fixture** /'fɪkstʃə(r)/ *n* (Sport) match *m*; ~**s** (in house) installations *fpl.*

**fizz** /fɪz/ *vi* pétiller. ● *n* pétillement *m.* **fizzy** *a* gazeux.

**flabbergast** /'flæbəgɑ:st/ *vt* sidérer.

**flabby** /'flæbɪ/ *a* flasque.

**flag** /flæg/ *n* drapeau *m*; (Naut) pavillon *m.* ● *vt* (*pt* **flagged**) ~ **(down)** faire signe de s'arrêter à. ● *vi* (weaken) faiblir; (*sick person*) s'affaiblir. ~**-pole** *n* mât *m.* ~**stone** *n* dalle *f.*

**flake** /fleɪk/ *n* flocon *m*; (of paint, metal) écaille *f.* ● *vi* s'écailler.

**flamboyant** /flæm'bɔɪənt/ *a* (*colour*) éclatant; (*manner*) extravagant.

**flame** /fleɪm/ *n* flamme *f*; **burst into** ~**s** exploser; **go up in** ~**s** brûler. ● *vi* flamber.

**flamingo** /flə'mɪŋgəʊ/ *n* flamant *m* (rose).

**flammable** /'flæməbl/ *a* inflammable.

**flan** /flæn/ *n* tarte *f*; (custard tart) flan *m.*

**flank** /flæŋk/ *n* flanc *m.* ● *vt* flanquer.

**flannel** /'flænl/ *n* (material) flannelle *f*; (for face) gant *m* de toilette.

**flap** /flæp/ *vi* (*pt* **flapped**) battre. ● *vt* ~ **its wings** battre des ailes. ● *n* (of pocket) rabat *m*; (of table) abattant *m.*

**flare** /fleə(r)/ *vi* ~ **up** (fighting) éclater. ● *n* flamboiement *m*; (Mil) fusée *f* éclairante; (in skirt) évasement *m.* **flared** *a* évasé.

**flash** /flæʃ/ *vi* briller; (on and off) clignoter; ~ **past** passer à toute vitesse. ● *vt* faire briller; (aim torch) diriger (**at** sur); (flaunt) étaler; ~ **one's headlights** faire un appel de phares. ● *n* (of news, camera) flash *m*; **in a** ~ en un éclair. ~**back** *n*

retour *m* en arrière. **~light** *n* lampe *f* de poche.

**flask** /flɑ:sk/ *n* (for chemicals) flacon *m*; (for drinks) thermos® *m or f inv*.

**flat** /flæt/ *a* (**flatter**, **flattest**) plat; (*tyre*) à plat; (*refusal*) catégorique; (*fare, rate*) fixe. ● *adv* (*say*) carrément. ● *n* (rooms) appartement *m*; (tyre ⓘ) crevaison *f*; (Mus) bémol *m*.

**flat out** *adv* (*drive*) à toute vitesse; (*work*) d'arrache-pied.

**flatten** /'flætn/ *vt*/*i* (s')aplatir.

**flatter** /'flaetə(r)/ *vt* flatter.

**flaunt** /flɔ:nt/ *vt* étaler, afficher.

**flavour**, (US) **flavor** /'fleɪvə(r)/ *n* goût *m*; (of ice-cream) parfum *m*. ● *vt* parfumer (**with** à), assaisonner (**with** de). **flavouring** *n* arôme *m* artificiel.

**flaw** /flɔ:/ *n* défaut *m*

**flea** /fli:/ *n* puce *f* ~ **market** *n* marché *m* aux puces.

**fleck** /flek/ *n* petite tache *f*.

**fled** /fled/ ⇒FLEE.

**flee** /fli:/ *vt*/*i* fuir.

**fleece** /fli:s/ *n* toison *f*; (garment) polaire *f*. ● *vt* plumer.

**fleet** /fli:t/ *n* (Naut, Aviat) flotte *f*; **a ~ of vehicles** (in reserve) parc *m*, (on road) convoi *m*.

**fleeting** /'fli:tɪŋ/ *a* très bref.

**Flemish** /'flemɪʃ/ *a* flamand. ● *n* (Ling) flamand *m*.

**flesh** /fleʃ/ *n* chair *f*; **one's (own) ~ and blood** la chair de sa chair.

**flew** /flu:/ ⇒FLY.

**flex** /fleks/ *vt* (*knee*) fléchir; (*muscle*) faire jouer. ● *n* (Electr) fil *m*.

**flexible** /'fleksəbl/ *a* flexible.

**flexitime** /'fleksɪtaɪm/ *n* horaire *m* variable.

**flick** /flɪk/ *n* petit coup *m*. ● *vt* donner un petit coup à; **~ through** feuilleter.

**flight** /flaɪt/ *n* (of bird, plane) vol *m*; **~ of stairs** escalier *m*; (fleeing) fuite *f*; **take ~** prendre la fuite. **~-deck** *n* poste *m* de pilotage.

**flimsy** /'flɪmzɪ/ *a* (**-ier**, **-iest**) (pej) mince, peu solide.

**flinch** /flɪntʃ/ *vi* (wince) broncher; (draw back) reculer.

**fling** /flɪŋ/ *vt* (*pt* **flung**) jeter.

**flint** /flɪnt/ *n* (rock) silex *m*.

**flip** /flɪp/ *vt* (*pt* **flipped**) donner un petit coup à; **~ through** feuilleter. ● *n* chiquenaude *f*.

**flippant** /'flɪpənt/ *a* désinvolte.

**flipper** /'flɪpə(r)/ *n* (of seal) nageoire *f*; (of swimmer) palme *f*

**flirt** /flɜ:t/ *vi* flirter. ● *n* flirteur/-euse *m*/*f*.

**float** /fləʊt/ *vt*/*i* (faire) flotter. ● *n* flotteur *m*; (cart) char *m*.

**flock** /flɒk/ *n* (of sheep) troupeau *m*; (of people) foule *f*. ● *vi* affluer.

**flog** /flɒg/ *vt* (*pt* **flogged**) (beat) fouetter; (sell ⓘ) vendre.

**flood** /flʌd/ *n* inondation *f*; (fig) flot *m*. ● *vt* inonder. ● *vi* (*building*) être inondé; (*river*) déborder; (*people*: fig) affluer.

**floodlight** /'flʌdlaɪt/ *n* projecteur *m*. ● *vt* (*pt* **floodlit**) illuminer.

**floor** /flɔ:(r)/ *n* sol *m*, plancher *m*; (for dancing) piste *f*; (storey) étage *m*. ● *vt* (knock down) terrasser; (baffle) stupéfier. **~-board** *n* planche *f*.

**flop** /flɒp/ *vi* (*pt* **flopped**) (drop) s'affaler; (fail ⓘ) échouer; (*head*) tomber. ● *n* ⓘ échec *m*, fiasco *m*.

**floppy** /'flɒpɪ/ *a* lâche, flasque. **~ (disk)** *n* disquette *f*.

**florist** /'flɒrɪst/ *n* fleuriste *mf*.

**flounder** /'flaʊndə(r)/ *vi* (*animal, person*) se débattre (**in** dans); (*economy*) stagner. ● *n* flet *m*; (US) poisson *m* plat.

**flour** /'flaʊə(r)/ *n* farine *f*.

**flourish** /'flʌrɪʃ/ *vi* prospérer. ● *vt* brandir. ● *n* geste *m* élégant; (curve) fioriture *f*.

**flout** /flaʊt/ *vt* se moquer de.

**flow** /fləʊ/ *vi* couler; (circulate) circuler; (*traffic*) s'écouler; (hang loosely) flotter; ~ **in** affluer; ~ **into** (of river) se jeter dans. ● *n* (of liquid, traffic) écoulement *m*; (of tide) flux *m*; (of orders, words: fig) flot *m*. ~ **chart** *n* organigramme *m*.

**flower** /'flaʊə(r)/ *n* fleur *f*. ● *vi* fleurir.

**flown** /fləʊn/ ⇒FLY.

**flu** /flu:/ *n* grippe *f*.

**fluctuate** /'flʌktʃʊeɪt/ *vi* varier.

**fluent** /'flu:ənt/ *a* (*style*) aisé; **be ~ (in a language)** parler (une langue) couramment.

**fluff** /flʌf/ *n* peluche(s) *f(pl)*; (down) duvet *m*.

**fluid** /'flu:ɪd/ *a* & *n* fluide (*m*).

**fluke** /flu:k/ *n* coup *m* de chance.

**flung** /flʌŋ/ ⇒FLING.

**fluoride** /'flʊəraɪd/ *n* fluor *m*.

**flush** /flʌʃ/ *vi* rougir. ● *vt* nettoyer à grande eau; ~ **the toilet** tirer la chasse d'eau. ● *n* (blush) rougeur *f*; (fig) excitation *f*. ● *a* ~ **with** (level with) au ras de. □ ~ **out** chasser.

**fluster** /'flʌstə(r)/ *vt* énerver.

**flute** /flu:t/ *n* flûte *f*.

**flutter** /'flʌtə(r)/ *vi* voleter; (of wings) battre. ● *n* (*wings*) battement *m*; (fig) agitation *f*; (bet Ⓘ) pari *m*.

**flux** /flʌks/ *n* changement *m* continuel.

**fly** /flaɪ/ *n* mouche *f*; (of trousers) braguette *f*. ● *vi* (*pt* **flew**; *pp* **flown**) voler; (*passengers*) voyager en avion; (*flag*) flotter; (rush) filer. ● *vt* (*aircraft*) piloter; (*passengers, goods*) transporter par avion; (*flag*) arborer. □ ~ **off** s'envoler.

**flyer** /'flaɪə(r)/ *n* (person) aviateur *m*; (circular) prospectus *m*.

**flying** /'flaɪɪŋ/ *a* (*saucer*) volant; **with ~ colours** haut la main; ~ **start** excellent départ *m*; ~ **visit** visite *f* éclair (*a inv*). ● *n* (activity) aviation *f*.

**flyover** /'flaɪəʊvə(r)/ *n* pont *m* (routier).

**foal** /fəʊl/ *n* poulain *m*.

**foam** /fəʊm/ *n* écume *f*, mousse *f*; ~ **(rubber)** caoutchouc *m* mousse. ● *vi* écumer, mousser.

**focus** /'fəʊkəs/ *n* (*pl* **~es** *or* **-ci** /-saɪ/) foyer *m*; (fig) centre *m*; **be in/out of ~** être/ne pas être au point. ● *vt/i* (faire) converger; (*instrument*) mettre au point; (with camera) faire la mise au point (**on** sur); (fig) (se) concentrer. ~ **group** *n* groupe *m* de discussion.

**fodder** /'fɒdə(r)/ *n* fourrage *m*.

**foetus** /'fi:təs/ *n* fœtus *m*.

**fog** /fɒg/ *n* brouillard *m*. ● *vt/i* (*pt* **fogged**) (*window*) (s')embuer.

**foggy** /'fɒgɪ/ *a* brumeux; **it is ~** il fait du brouillard.

**foil** /fɔɪl/ *n* (tin foil) papier *m* d'aluminium; (deterrent) repoussoir *m*. ● *vt* (thwart) déjouer.

**fold** /fəʊld/ *vt/i* (*paper, clothes*) (se) plier; (*arms*) croiser; (fail) s'effondrer. ● *n* pli *m*; (for sheep) parc *m* à moutons; (Relig) bercail *m*. **folder** *n* (file) chemise *f*; (leaflet) dépliant *m*. **folding** *a* pliant.

**foliage** /'fəʊlɪɪdʒ/ *n* feuillage *m*.

**folk** /fəʊk/ *n* gens *mpl*; **~s** parents *mpl*. ● *a* (*dance*) folklorique; (*music*) folk.

**folklore** /ˈfəʊklɔ:(r)/ *n* folklore *m*.

**follow** /ˈfɒləʊ/ *vt/i* suivre; **it ~s that** il s'ensuit que; **~ suit** en faire autant. **~ up** (*letter*) donner suite à. **follower** *n* partisan *m*.

**following** /ˈfɒləʊɪŋ/ *n* partisans *mpl*. ● *a* suivant. ● *prep* à la suite de.

**fond** /fɒnd/ *a* (loving) affectueux; (*hope*) cher; **be ~ of** aimer.

**fondle** /ˈfɒndl/ *vt* caresser.

**fondness** /ˈfɒndnɪs/ *n* affection *f*; (for things) attachement *m*.

**food** /fu:d/ *n* nourriture *f*; **French ~** la cuisine française. ● *a* alimentaire. **~ processor** *n* robot *m* (ménager).

**fool** /fu:l/ *n* idiot/-e *m/f*. ● *vt* duper. ● *vi* **~ around** faire l'idiot. **foolish** *a* idiot.

**foot** /fʊt/ *n* (*pl* **feet**) pied *m*; (measure) pied *m* (=30.48 cm); (*of stairs, page*) bas *m*; **on ~** à pied; **on or to one's feet** debout; **under sb's feet** dans les jambes de qn. ● *vt* (*bill*) payer.

**footage** /ˈfʊtɪdʒ/ *n* métrage *m*.

**foot-and-mouth disease** *n* fièvre *f* aphteuse.

**football** /ˈfʊtbɔ:l/ *n* (ball) ballon *m*; (game) football *m*. **footballer** *n* footballeur *m*.

**foot**: **~-bridge** *n* passerelle *f*. **~hold** *n* prise *f*.

**footing** /ˈfʊtɪŋ/ *n* **on an equal ~** sur un pied d'égalité; **be on a friendly ~ with sb** avoir des rapports amicaux avec qn; **lose one's ~** perdre pied.

**foot**: **~note** *n* note *f* (*en bas de la page*). **~path** *n* (in countryside) sentier *m*; (in town) chemin *m*. **~print** *n* empreinte *f* (*de pied*). **~step** *n* pas *m*. **~wear** *n* chaussures *fpl*.

**for** /fɔ:(r), fə(r)/

● *preposition*

····➤ pour; **~ me** pour moi; **music ~ dancing** de la musique pour danser; **what is it ~?** ça sert à quoi?

····➤ (with a time period that is still continuing) depuis; **I've been waiting ~ two hours** j'attends depuis deux heures; **I haven't seen him ~ ten years** je ne l'ai pas vu depuis dix ans.

····➤ (with a time period that has ended) pendant; **I waited ~ two hours** j'ai attendu pendant deux heures.

····➤ (with a future time period) pour; **I'm going to Paris ~ six weeks** je vais à Paris pour six semaines.

····➤ (with distances) pendant; **I drove ~ 50 kilometres** j'ai roulé pendant 50 kilomètres.

**forbade** /fəˈbæd/ →FORBID.

**forbid** /fəˈbɪd/ *vt* (*pt* **forbade**; *pp* **forbidden**) interdire, défendre (**sb to do** à qn de faire); **~ sb sth** interdire *or* défendre qch à qn; **you are forbidden to leave** il vous est interdit de partir. **forbidding** *a* menaçant.

**force** /fɔ:s/ *n* force *f*; **come into ~** entrer en vigueur; **the ~s** les forces *fpl* armées. ● *vt* forcer. **~ into** faire entrer de force; **~ on** imposer à. **forced** *a* forcé.

**force-feed** *vt* (*pt* **-fed**) (*person*) nourrir de force; (*animal*) gaver.

**forceful** /ˈfɔ:sfl/ *a* énergique.

**ford** /fɔ:d/ *n* gué *m*.

**forearm** /ˈfɔ:rɑ:m/ *n* avant-bras *m inv*.

**forecast** /ˈfɔ:kɑ:st/ *vt* (*pt* **forecast**) prévoir. ● *n* **weather ~** météo *f*.

**forecourt** /ˈfɔːkɔːt/ *n* (of garage) devant *m*; (of station) cour *f*.

**forefinger** /ˈfɔːfɪŋgə(r)/ *n* index *m*.

**forefront** /ˈfɔːfrʌnt/ *n* **at/in the ~ of** à la pointe de.

**foregone** /ˈfɔːgɒn/ *a* **it's a ~ conclusion** c'est couru d'avance.

**foreground** /ˈfɔːgraʊnd/ *n* premier plan *m*.

**forehead** /ˈfɒrɪd/ *n* front *m*.

**foreign** /ˈfɒrən/ *a* étranger; (*trade*) extérieur; (*travel*) à l'étranger. **foreigner** *n* étranger/-ère *m/f*.

**foreman** /ˈfɔːmən/ *n* (*pl* **-men**) contremaître *m*.

**foremost** /ˈfɔːməʊst/ *a* le plus éminent. ● *adv* **first and ~** tout d'abord.

**forensic** /fəˈrensɪk/ *a* médico-légal; **~ medicine** médecine *f* légale.

**foresee** /fɔːˈsiː/ *vt* (*pt* **-saw**; *pp* **-seen**) prévoir.

**forest** /ˈfɒrɪst/ *n* forêt *f*. **forestry** *n* sylviculture *f*.

**foretaste** /ˈfɔːteɪst/ *n* avant-goût *m*.

**forever** /fəˈrevə(r)/ *adv* toujours.

**foreword** /ˈfɔːwɜːd/ *n* avant-propos *m inv*.

**forfeit** /ˈfɔːfɪt/ *n* (penalty) peine *f*; (in game) gage *m*. ● *vt* perdre.

**forgave** /fəˈgeɪv/ ⇒FORGIVE.

**forge** /fɔːdʒ/ *n* forge *f*. ● *vt* (*metal, friendship*) forger; (copy) contrefaire, falsifier. ● *vi* **~ ahead** aller de l'avant, avancer. **forger** *n* faussaire *m*. **forgery** *n* faux *m*, contrefaçon *f*.

**forget** /fəˈget/ *vt/i* (*pt* **forgot**; *pp* **forgotten**) oublier; **~ oneself** s'oublier. **forgetful** *a* distrait. **~-me-not** *n* myosotis *m*.

**forgive** /fəˈgɪv/ *vt* (*pt* **forgave**; *pp* **forgiven**) pardonner (**sb for sth** qch à qn).

**fork** /fɔːk/ *n* fourchette *f*; (for digging) fourche *f*; (in road) bifurcation *f*. ● *vi* (*road*) bifurquer; **~ out** 🄸 payer. **forked** *a* fourchu. **~-lift truck** *n* chariot *m* élévateur.

**form** /fɔːm/ *n* forme *f*; (document) formulaire *m*; (School) classe *f*; **on ~** en forme. ● *vt/i* (se) former.

**formal** /ˈfɔːml/ *a* officiel, en bonne et due forme; (*person*) compassé, cérémonieux; (*dress*) de cérémonie; (*denial, grammar*) formel; (*language*) soutenu. **formality** *n* cérémonial *m*; (requirement) formalité *f*.

**format** /ˈfɔːmæt/ *n* format *m*. ● *vt* (*pt* **formatted**) (*disk*) formater.

**former** /ˈfɔːmə(r)/ *a* ancien; (first of two) premier. ● *n* **the ~** celui-là, celle-là. **formerly** *adv* autrefois.

**formula** /ˈfɔːmjʊlə/ *n* (*pl* **-ae** /-iː/ *or* **-as**) formule *f*. **formulate** *vt* formuler.

**fort** /fɔːt/ *n* (Mil) fort *m*; **to hold the ~** s'occuper de tout.

**forth** /fɔːθ/ *adv* **from this day ~** à partir d'aujourd'hui; **and so ~** et ainsi de suite; **go back and ~** aller et venir.

**forthcoming** /fɔːθˈkʌmɪŋ/ *a* à venir, prochain; (sociable 🄸) communicatif.

**forthright** /ˈfɔːθraɪt/ *a* direct.

**forthwith** /fɔːθˈwɪθ/ *adv* sur-le-champ.

**fortnight** /ˈfɔːtnaɪt/ *n* quinze jours *mpl*, quinzaine *f*.

**fortnightly** /ˈfɔːtnaɪtlɪ/ *a* bimensuel. ● *adv* tous les quinze jours.

**fortunate** /ˈfɔːtʃənət/ *a* heureux; **be ~** avoir de la chance. **fortunately** *adv* heureusement.

**fortune** /ˈfɔːtʃuːn/ *n* fortune *f*; **make a ~** faire fortune; **have the good ~ to** avoir la chance de. **~-teller** *n* diseur/-euse *m/f* de bonne aventure.

**forty** /ˈfɔːtɪ/ *a & n* quarante (*m*); **~ winks** un petit somme.

**forward** /ˈfɔːwəd/ *a* en avant; (advanced) précoce; (bold) effronté. ● *n* (Sport) avant *m*. ● *adv* en avant; **come ~** se présenter; **go ~** avancer. ● *vt* (*letter, e-mail*) faire suivre; (*goods*) expédier; (fig) favoriser. **forwardness** *n* précocité *f*. **forwards** *adv* en avant.

**fossil** /ˈfɒsl/ *n & a* fossile (*m*).

**foster** /ˈfɒstə(r)/ *vt* (promote) encourager; (*child*) élever. ● *a* (*child, parent*) adoptif; (*family, home*) de placement.

**fought** /fɔːt/ ⇒FIGHT.

**foul** /faʊl/ *a* (*smell, weather*) infect; (*place, action*) immonde; (*language*) ordurier. ● *n* (*football*) faute *f*. ● *vt* souiller, encrasser; **~ up** 🅸 gâcher **~-mouthed** *a* grossier.

**found** /faʊnd/ ⇒FIND. ● *vt* fonder. **foundation** *n* fondation *f*; (basis) fondement *m*; (make-up) fond *m* de teint. **founder** *n* fondateur/-trice *m/f*.

**fountain** /ˈfaʊntɪn/ *n* fontaine *f*. **~-pen** *n* stylo *m* à encre.

**four** /fɔː(r)/ *a & n* quatre (*m*).

**fourteen** /fɔːˈtiːn/ *a & n* quatorze (*m*).

**fourth** /ˈfɔːθ/ *a & n* quatrième (*mf*).

**four-wheel drive** *n* (car) quatre-quatre *m*.

**fowl** /faʊl/ *n* (one bird) poulet *m*; (group) volaille *f*.

**fox** /fɒks/ *n* renard *m*. ● *vt* (baffle) mystifier; (deceive) tromper.

**fraction** /ˈfrækʃn/ *n* fraction *f*.

**fracture** /ˈfræktʃə(r)/ *n* fracture *f*. ● *vt/i* (se) fracturer.

**fragile** /ˈfrædʒaɪl/ *a* fragile.

**fragment** /ˈfrægmənt/ *n* fragment *m*.

**fragrance** /ˈfreɪgrəns/ *n* parfum *m*.

**frail** /freɪl/ *a* frêle.

**frame** /freɪm/ *n* (of building, boat) charpente *f*; (of picture) cadre *m*; (of window) châssis *m*; (of spectacles) monture *f*; **~ of mind** humeur *f*. ● *vt* encadrer; (fig) formuler; (Jur, 🅸) monter un coup contre. **~work** *n* structure *f*; (context) cadre *m*.

**France** /frɑːns/ *n* France *f*.

**franchise** /ˈfræntʃaɪz/ *n* (Pol) droit *m* de vote; (Comm) franchise *f*.

**frank** /fræŋk/ *a* franc. ● *vt* affranchir. **frankly** *adv* franchement.

**frantic** /ˈfræntɪk/ *a* frénétique; **~ with** fou de.

**fraternity** /frəˈtɜːnətɪ/ *n* (bond) fraternité *f*; (group, club) confrérie *f*.

**fraud** /frɔːd/ *n* (deception) fraude *f*; (person) imposteur *m*. **fraudulent** *a* frauduleux.

**fray** /freɪ/ *n* **the ~** la bataille. ● *vt/i* (s')effilocher.

**freckle** /ˈfrekl/ *n* tache *f* de rousseur.

**free** /friː/ *a* libre; (gratis) gratuit; (lavish) généreux; **~ (of charge)** gratuit(ement); **a ~ hand** carte *f* blanche. ● *vt* (*pt* **freed**) libérer; (clear) dégager.

**freedom** /ˈfriːdəm/ *n* liberté *f*.

**free**: **~ enterprise** *n* la libre entreprise. **~kick** *n* coup *m* franc. **~lance** *a & n* free-lance (*mf*), indépendant/-e (*m/f*).

**freely** /ˈfriːlɪ/ *adv* librement.

**Freemason** /ˈfriːmeɪsn/ *n* franc-maçon *m*.

**Freenet** /ˈfri:net/ *n* (Comput) Libertel *m*.

**free**: ~ **phone**, ~ **number** *n* numéro *m* vert. **~-range** *a* (*eggs*) de ferme.

**Freeware** /ˈfri:weə(r)/ *n* (Comput) Gratuiciel *m*.

**freeway** *n* (US) autoroute *f*.

**freeze** /fri:z/ *vt/i* (*pt* **froze**; *pp* **frozen**) geler; (Culin) (se) congeler; (*wages*) bloquer. ● *n* gel *m*; blocage *m*. **~-dried** *a* lyophilisé.

**freezer** /ˈfrɪ:zə(r)/ *n* congélateur *m*.

**freezing** /ˈfrizɪŋ/ *a* glacial; **below** ~ au-dessous de zéro.

**freight** /freɪt/ *n* fret *m*.

**French** /frentʃ/ *a* français. ● *n* (Ling) français *m*; **the** ~ les Français *mpl*. ~ **bean** *n* haricot *m* vert. ~ **fries** *npl* frites *fpl*. **~man** *n* Français *m*. **~-speaking** *a* francophone. ~ **window** *n* porte-fenêtre *f*. **~woman** *n* Française *f*.

**frenzied** /ˈfrenzɪd/ *a* frénétique. **frenzy** *n* frénésie *f*.

**frequent**[1] /ˈfri:kwənt/ *a* fréquent.

**frequent**[2] /frɪˈkwent/ *vt* fréquenter.

**fresco** /ˈfreskəʊ/ *n* fresque *f*.

**fresh** /freʃ/ *a* frais; (different, additional) nouveau; (cheeky Ⓘ) culotté.

**freshen** /ˈfreʃn/ *vi* (*weather*) fraîchir; ~ **up** (*person*) se rafraîchir.

**freshly** /ˈfreʃlɪ/ *adv* nouvellement.

**freshness** /ˈfreʃnɪs/ *n* fraîcheur *f*.

**freshwater** /ˈfreʃwɔ:tə(r)/ *a* d'eau douce.

**friction** /ˈfrɪkʃn/ *n* friction *f*.

**Friday** /ˈfraɪdɪ/ *n* vendredi *m*.

**fridge** /frɪdʒ/ *n* frigo *m*.

**fried** /fraɪd/ ⇒FRY. ● *a* frit; ~ **eggs** œufs *mpl* sur le plat.

**friend** /frend/ *n* ami/-e *m/f*. **friendly** *a* (**-ier**, **-iest**) amical, gentil. **friendship** *n* amitié *f*.

**frieze** /fri:z/ *n* frise *f*.

**fright** /fraɪt/ *n* peur *f*; (person, thing) horreur *f*.

**frighten** /ˈfraɪtn/ *vt* effrayer; ~ **off** faire fuir; **frightened** *a* effrayé; **be ~ed** avoir peur (of de). **frightening** *a* effrayant.

**frill** /frɪl/ *n* (trimming) fanfreluche *f*; **with no ~s** très simple.

**fringe** /frɪndʒ/ *n* (edging, hair) frange *f*; (of area) bordure *f*; (of society) marge *f*. ~ **benefits** *npl* avantages *mpl* sociaux.

**frisk** /frɪsk/ *vt* (search) fouiller.

**fritter** /ˈfrɪtə(r)/ *n* beignet *m*. ● *vt* ~ **away** gaspiller.

**frivolity** /frɪˈvɒlətɪ/ *n* frivolité *f*.

**frizzy** /ˈfrɪzɪ/ *a* crépu.

**fro** /frəʊ/ ⇒TO AND FRO.

**frog** /frɒg/ *n* grenouille *f*; **a ~ in one's throat** un chat dans la gorge.

**frolic** /ˈfrɒlɪk/ *vi* (*pt* **frolicked**) s'ébattre. ● *n* ébats *mpl*.

**from** /frɒm/ *prep* de; (with time, prices) à partir de, de; (*habit, conviction*) par; (according to) d'après; **take ~ sb** prendre à qn; **take ~ one's pocket** prendre dans sa poche.

**front** /frʌnt/ *n* (of car, train) avant *m*; (of garment, building) devant *m*; (Mil, Pol) front *m*; (of book, pamphlet) début *m*; (appearance: fig) façade *f*. ● *a* de devant, avant *inv*; (first) premier; ~ **door** porte *f* d'entrée; **in ~ (of)** devant. **frontage** *n* façade *f*.

**frontier** /ˈfrʌntɪə(r)/ *n* frontière *f*.

**frost** /frɒst/ *n* gel *m*, gelée *f*; (on glass) givre *m*. ● *vt/i* (se) givrer. **~-bite** *n* gelure *f*.

**frosty** /ˈfrɒstɪ/ *a* (*weather, welcome*) glacial; (*window*) givré.

**froth** /frɒθ/ *n* (on beer) mousse *f*; (on water) écume *f*. ● *vi* mousser, écumer.

**frown** /fraʊn/ *vi* froncer les sourcils; ~ **on** désapprouver. ● *n* froncement *m* de sourcils.

**froze** /frəʊz/ ⇒FREEZE.

**frozen** /'frəʊzn/ ⇒FREEZE. ● *a* congelé.

**fruit** /fruːt/ *n* fruit *m*; (collectively) fruits *mpl*. **fruitful** *a* (*discussions*) fructueux. ~ **machine** *n* machine *f* à sous.

**frustrate** /frʌ'streɪt/ *vt* (*plan*) faire échouer; (*person*: Psych) frustrer; (upset ①) exaspérer. **frustration** *n* (Psych) frustration *f*; (disappointment) déception *f*.

**fry** /fraɪ/ *vt/i* (*pt* **fried**) (faire) frire. **frying-pan** *n* poêle *f* (à frire).

**FTP** *abbr* (**File Transfer Protocol**) (Internet) protocole *m* FTP.

**fudge** /fʌdʒ/ *n* caramel *m* mou. ● *vt* (*issue*) esquiver.

**fuel** /'fjuːəl/ *n* combustible *m*; (for car engine) carburant *m*. ● *vt* (*pt* **fuelled**) alimenter en combustible.

**fugitive** /'fjuːdʒətɪv/ *n* & *a* fugitif/-ive (*m*/*f*).

**fulfil** /fʊl'fɪl/ *vt* (*pt* **fulfilled**) accomplir, réaliser; (*condition*) remplir; ~ **oneself** s'épanouir. **fulfilling** *a* satisfaisant. **fulfilment** *n* réalisation *f*, épanouissement *m*.

**full** /fʊl/ *a* plein (**of** de); (*bus, hotel*) complet; (*programme*) chargé; (*skirt*) ample; **be** ~ **(up)** n'avoir plus faim; **at** ~ **speed** à toute vitesse. ● *n* **in** ~ intégralement; **to the** ~ complètement. ~ **back** *n* (Sport) arrière *m*. ~ **moon** *n* pleine lune *f*. ~ **name** *n* nom *m* et prénom *m*. ~**-scale** *a* (*drawing etc.*) grandeur nature *inv*; (fig) de grande envergure. ~ **stop** *n* point *m*. ~**-time** *a* & *adv* à plein temps.

**fully** /'fʊlɪ/ *adv* complètement; ~ **fledged** (*member, citizen*) à part entière.

**fume** /fjuːm/ *vi* rager. **fumes** *npl* émanations *fpl*, vapeurs *fpl*.

**fun** /fʌn/ *n* amusement *m*; **be** ~ être chouette; **for** ~ pour rire; **make** ~ **of** se moquer de.

**function** /'fʌŋkʃn/ *n* (purpose, duty) fonction *f*; (event) réception *f*. ● *vi* fonctionner.

**fund** /fʌnd/ *n* fonds *m*. ● *vt* fournir les fonds pour.

**fundamental** /fʌndə'mentl/ *a* fondamental. **fundamentalist** *n* intégriste *m/f*.

**funeral** /'fjuːnərəl/ *n* enterrement *m*. ● *a* funèbre.

**fun-fair** *n* fête *f* foraine.

**fungus** /'fʌŋgəs/ *n* (*pl* **-gi** /-gaɪ/) (plant) champignon *m*; (mould) moisissure *f*.

**funnel** /'fʌnl/ *n* (for pouring) entonnoir *m*; (of ship) cheminée *f*.

**funny** /'fʌnɪ/ *a* (**-ier**, **-iest**) drôle; (odd) bizarre.

**fur** /fɜː(r)/ *n* (for garment) fourrure *f*; (on animal) poils *mpl*; (in kettle) tartre *m*.

**furious** /'fjʊərɪəs/ *a* furieux.

**furnace** /'fɜːnɪs/ *n* fourneau *m*.

**furnish** /'fɜːnɪʃ/ *vt* (*room*) meubler; (supply) fournir. **furnishings** *npl* ameublement *m*.

**furniture** /'fɜːnɪtʃə(r)/ *n* meubles *mpl*, mobilier *m*.

**furry** /'fɜːrɪ/ *a* (*animal*) à fourrure; (*toy*) en peluche.

**further** /'fɜːðə(r)/ *a* plus éloigné; (additional) supplémentaire. ● *adv* plus loin; (more) davantage. ● *vt* avancer. ~ **education** *n* formation *f* continue.

**furthermore** /'fɜ:ðəmɔ:(r)/ *adv* en outre, de plus.

**furthest** /'fɜ:ðɪst/ *a* le plus éloigné. ● *adv* le plus loin.

**fury** /'fjʊərɪ/ *n* fureur *f*.

**fuse** /fju:z/ *vt*/*i* (melt) fondre; (unite: fig) fusionner; ~ **the lights** faire sauter les plombs. ● *n* (of plug) fusible *m*; (of bomb) amorce *f*.

**fuss** /fʌs/ *n* (when upset) histoire(s) *f(pl)*; (when excited) agitation *f*; **make a ~** faire des histoires; s'agiter; (about food) faire des chichis; **make a ~ of** faire grand cas de. ● *vi* s'agiter. **fussy** *a* (finicky) tatillon; (hard to please) difficile.

**future** /'fju:tʃə(r)/ *a* futur. ● *n* avenir *m*; (Gram) futur *m*; **in ~** à l'avenir.

**fuzzy** /'fʌzɪ/ *a* (*hair*) crépu; (*photograph*) flou.

# Gg

**Gaelic** /'geɪlɪk/ *n* gaélique *m*.

**gag** /gæg/ *n* (on mouth) bâillon *m*; (joke) blague *f*. ● *vt* (*pt* **gagged**) bâillonner.

**gain** /geɪn/ *vt* (*respect, support*) gagner; (*speed, weight*) prendre. ● *vi* (of clock) avancer. ● *n* (increase) augmentation *f* (**in** de); (profit) gain *m*.

**galaxy** /'gæləksɪ/ *n* galaxie *f*.

**gale** /geɪl/ *n* tempête *f*.

**gallery** /'gælərɪ/ *n* galerie *f*; (art) ~ musée *m*.

**Gallic** /'gælɪk/ *a* français.

**gallon** /'gælən/ *n* gallon *m* (*imperial = 4.546 litres*; *Amer. = 3.785 litres*).

**gallop** /'gæləp/ *n* galop *m*. ● *vi* (*pt* **galloped**) galoper.

**galore** /gə'lɔ:(r)/ *adv* (*prizes, bargains*) en abondance; (*drinks, sandwiches*) à gogo Ⓘ.

**gamble** /'gæmbl/ *vt*/*i* jouer; ~ **on** miser sur. ● *n* (venture) entreprise *f* risquée; (bet) pari *m*; (risk) risque *m*. **gambling** *n* jeu *m*.

**game** /geɪm/ *n* jeu *m*; (football) match *m*; (tennis) partie *f*; (animals, birds) gibier *m*. ● *a* (brave) courageux; ~ **for** prêt à. ~**keeper** *n* garde-chasse *m*.

**gammon** /'gæmən/ *n* jambon *m*.

**gang** /gæŋ/ *n* (of youths) bande *f*; (of workmen) équipe *f*. ● *vi* ~ **up** se liguer (**on, against** contre).

**gangway** /'gæŋweɪ/ *n* passage *m*; (aisle) allée *f*; (of ship) passerelle *f*.

**gaol** /dʒeɪl/ *n* & *vt* = JAIL.

**gap** /gæp/ *n* trou *m*, vide *m*; (in time) intervalle *m*; (in education) lacune *f*; (difference) écart *m*. ~ **year** *n* année *f* de coupure (avant d'entrer à l'université).

**gape** /geɪp/ *vi* rester bouche bée. **gaping** *a* béant.

**garage** /'gærɑ:ʒ/ *n* garage *m*.

**garbage** /'gɑ:bɪdʒ/ *n* (US) ordures *fpl*.

**garden** /'gɑ:dn/ *n* jardin *m*. ● *vi* jardiner. **gardener** *n* jardinier/-ière *m*/*f*. **gardening** *n* jardinage *m*.

**gargle** /'gɑ:gl/ *vi* se gargariser.

**garish** /'geərɪʃ/ *a* (*clothes*) tape-à-l'œil; (*light*) cru.

**garland** /'gɑ:lənd/ *n* guirlande *f*.

**garlic** /'gɑ:lɪk/ *n* ail *m*.

**garment** /'gɑ:mənt/ *n* vêtement *m*.

**garnish** /'gɑ:nɪʃ/ *vt* garnir (**with** de). ● *n* garniture *f*.

**garter** /'gɑ:tə(r)/ *n* jarretière *f*.

**gas** /gæs/ *n* (*pl* **~es**) gaz *m*; (Med) anesthésie *m*; (petrol: US) essence *f*. ● *a* (*mask, pipe*) à gaz. ● *vt* asphyxier; (Mil) gazer. ● *vi* 🄸 bavarder.

**gash** /gæʃ/ *n* entaille *f*. ● *vt* entailler.

**gasoline** /'gæsəli:n/ *n* (petrol: US) essence *f*.

**gasp** /gɑ:sp/ *vi* haleter; (in surprise: fig) avoir le souffle coupé. ● *n* halètement *m*.

**gate** /geɪt/ *n* (in garden, airport) porte *f*; (of field) barrière *f*. **~way** *n* porte *f*; (Internet) passerelle *f*.

**gather** /'gæðə(r)/ *vt* (*people, objects*) rassembler; (pick up) ramasser; (*flowers*) cueillir; (fig) comprendre; **~ speed** prendre de la vitesse; (sewing) froncer. ● *vi* (*people*) se rassembler; (pile up) s'accumuler. **gathering** *n* réunion *m*.

**gauge** /geɪdʒ/ *n* jauge *f*, indicateur *m*. ● *vt* (*speed, distance*) jauger; (*reaction, mood*) évaluer.

**gaunt** /gɔ:nt/ *a* décharné.

**gauze** /gɔ:z/ *n* gaze *f*.

**gave** /geɪv/ ⇨GIVE.

**gay** /geɪ/ *a* (joyful) gai; (homosexual) gay *inv*. ● *n* gay *mf*.

**gaze** /geɪz/ *vi* **~ (at)** regarder (fixement). ● *n* regard *m* (fixe).

**gazette** /gə'zet/ *n* journal *m* (officiel).

**GB** *abbr* ⇨GREAT BRITAIN.

**gear** /gɪə(r)/ *n* (equipment) matériel *m*; (Tech) engrenage *m*; (Auto) vitesse *f*; **in ~** en prise, **out of ~** au point mort. ● *vt* **to be geared to** s'adresser à. **~box** *n* (Auto) boîte *f* de vitesses. **~-lever** (US) **~-shift** *n* levier *m* de vitesse.

**geese** /gi:s/ ⇨GOOSE.

**gel** /dʒel/ *n* (for hair) gel *m*.

**gem** /dʒem/ *n* pierre *f* précieuse.

**Gemini** /'dʒemɪnaɪ/ *n* Gémeaux *mpl*.

**gender** /'dʒendə(r)/ *n* (Ling) genre *m*; (of person) sexe *m*.

**gene** /dʒi:n/ *n* gène *m*. **~ library** *n* génothèque *f*.

**general** /'dʒenrəl/ *a* général. ● *n* général *m*; **in ~** en général.

**general election** *n* élections *fpl* législatives.

**generalization** /dʒenrəlaɪ'zeɪʃn/ *n* généralisation *f*. **generalize** *vt*/*i* généraliser.

**general practitioner** *n* (Med) généraliste *m*.

**generate** /'dʒenəreɪt/ *vt* produire.

**generation** /dʒenə'reɪʃn/ *n* génération *f*.

**generator** /'dʒenəreɪtə(r)/ *n* (Electr) groupe *m* électrogène.

**generosity** /dʒenə'rɒsətɪ/ *n* générosité *f*. **generous** *a* généreux, (plentiful) copieux.

**genetics** /dʒɪ'netɪks/ *n* génétique *f*.

**Geneva** /dʒɪ'ni:və/ *n* Genève.

**genial** /'dʒi:nɪəl/ *a* affable, sympathique.

**genitals** /'dʒenɪtlz/ *npl* organes *mpl* génitaux.

**genius** /'dʒi:nɪəs/ *n* (*pl* **~es**) génie *m*.

**genome** *n* /'dʒi:nəʊm/ *n* génome *m*.

**gentle** /'dʒentl/ *a* (mild, kind) doux; (*pressure, breeze*) léger; (*reminder, hint*) discret.

**gentleman** /'dʒentlmən/ *n* (*pl* **-men**) (man) monsieur *m*; (well-bred) gentleman *m*.

**gently** /'dʒentlɪ/ *adv* doucement.

**gents** /dʒents/ *npl* (toilets) toilettes *fpl*; (on sign) 'Messieurs'

**genuine** /ˈdʒenjʊɪn/ *a* (*reason, motive*) vrai; (*jewel, substance*) véritable; (*person, belief*) sincère.

**geography** /dʒɪˈɒgrəfɪ/ *n* géographie *f.*

**geology** /dʒɪˈɒlədʒɪ/ *n* géologie *f*.

**geometry** /dʒɪˈɒmətrɪ/ *n* géométrie *f.*

**geriatric** /dʒerɪˈætrɪk/ *a* gériatrique.

**germ** /dʒɜ:m/ *n* (Med) microbe *m.*

**German** /ˈdʒɜ:mən/ *n* (person) Allemand/-e *m*/*f*; (Ling) allemand *m.* ● *a* allemand. **Germanic** *a* germanique.

**German measles** *n* rubéole *f.*

**Germany** /ˈdʒɜ:mənɪ/ *n* Allemagne *f.*

**gesture** /ˈdʒestʃə(r)/ *n* geste *m.*

**get** /get/

*past* **got**; *past participle* **got, gotten** (US); *present participle* **getting**

● *transitive verb*

····➤ recevoir; **we got a letter** nous avons reçu une lettre.

····➤ (obtain) **I got a job in Paris** j'ai trouvé un travail à Paris; **I'll ~ sth to eat at the airport** je mangerai qch à l'aéroport.

····➤ (buy) acheter; **~ sb a present** acheter un cadeau à qn.

····➤ (achieve) obtenir; **he got it right** il a obtenu le bon résultat; **~ good grades** avoir de bonnes notes.

····➤ (fetch) chercher; **go and ~ a chair** va chercher une chaise.

····➤ (transport) prendre; **we can ~ the bus** on peut prendre le bus.

····➤ (understand ⊡) comprendre; **now let me ~ this right** alors si je comprends bien...

····➤ (experience) **~ a surprise** être surpris; **~ a shock** avoir un choc.

····➤ (illness) **~ measles** attraper la rougeole; **~ a cold** s'enrhumer.

····➤ (ask or persuade) **~ him to call me** dis-lui de m'appeler; **I'll ~ her to help me** je lui demanderai de m'aider.

····➤ (cause to be done) **~ a TV repaired** faire réparer une télévision; **~ one's hair cut** se faire couper les cheveux.

● *intransitive verb*

····➤ devenir; **he's getting old** il vieillit; **it's getting late** il se fait tard.

····➤ (in passives) **~ married** se marier; **~ hurt** être blessé.

····➤ (arrive) arriver; **~ to the airport** arriver à l'aéroport.

□ **get about** (*person*) se déplacer.
**get along** (manage) se débrouiller; (progress) avancer.
**get along with** s'entendre avec.
**get at** (reach) atteindre; (imply) vouloir dire.
**get away** partir; (escape) s'échapper.
**get back** *vi* revenir. *vt* récupérer.
**get by** *vi* (manage) se débrouiller. *vt* (pass) passer.
**get down** *vt*/*i* déscendre. *vt* (depress) déprimer.
**get in** entrer.
**get into** (*car*) monter dans; (*dress*) mettre.
**get off** *vt* (*bus*) descendre; (remove) enlever. *vi* (from bus) descendre; (leave) partir; (Jur) être acquitté.

**get on** *vi* (to bus) monter; (succeed) réussir. *vt* (*bus*) monter.

**get on with** (*person*) s'entendre avec; (*job*) attaquer.

**get out** sortir.

**get out of** (fig) se soustraire.

**get over** (*illness*) se remettre de.

**get round** (*rule*) contourner; (*person*) entortiller.

**get through** *vi* passer; (on phone) ~ **through to sb** avoir qn. *vt* traverser.

**get up** se lever.

**get up to** faire.

**getaway** /'getəweɪ/ *n* fuite *f*.

**ghastly** /'gɑ:stlɪ/ *a* (**-ier**, **-iest**) affreux.

**gherkin** /'gɜ:kɪn/ *n* cornichon *m*.

**ghetto** /'getəʊ/ *n* ghetto *m*.

**ghost** /gəʊst/ *n* fantôme *m*.

**giant** /'dʒaɪənt/ *n* & *a* géant (*m*).

**gibberish** /'dʒɪbərɪʃ/ *n* baragouin *m*, charabia *m*.

**giblets** /'dʒɪblɪts/ *npl* abats *mpl*.

**giddy** /'gɪdɪ/ *a* (**-ier**, **-iest**) vertigineux; **be** *or* **feel** ~ avoir le vertige.

**gift** /gɪft/ *n* (present) cadeau *m*; (ability) don *m*.

**gifted** /'gɪftɪd/ *a* doué.

**gift-wrap** *n* paquet-cadeau *m*.

**gigantic** /dʒaɪ'gæntɪk/ *a* gigantesque.

**giggle** /'gɪgl/ *vi* ricaner (sottement), glousser. ● *n* ricanement *m*; **the ~s** le fou rire.

**gimmick** /'gɪmɪk/ *n* truc *m*.

**gin** /dʒɪn/ *n* gin *m*.

**ginger** /'dʒɪndʒə(r)/ *n* gingembre *m*. ● *a* (*hair*) roux. ~ **beer** *n* boisson *f* gazeuse au gingembre. **~bread** *n* pain *m* d'épices.

**gingerly** /'dʒɪndʒəlɪ/ *adv* avec précaution.

**giraffe** /dʒɪ'rɑ:f/ *n* girafe *f*.

**girl** /gɜ:l/ *n* (child) (petite) fille *f*; (young woman) (jeune) fille *f*. **~friend** *n* amie *f*; (of boy) petite amie *f*.

**giro** /'dʒaɪərəʊ/ *n* virement *m* bancaire; (cheque) mandat *m*.

**gist** /dʒɪst/ *n* essentiel *m*.

**give** /gɪv/ *vt* (*pt* **gave**; *pp* **given**) donner; (*gesture*) faire; (*laugh, sigh*) pousser; ~ **sb sth** donner qch à qn. ● *vi* donner; (yield) céder; (stretch) se détendre. ● *n* élasticité *f*. □ ~ **away** donner; (*secret*) trahir; ~ **back** rendre; ~ **in** (yield) céder (to à); ~ **off** (*heat, fumes*) dégager; (*signal, scent*) émettre; ~ **out** *vt* distribuer; ~ **over** (devote) consacrer; (stop ⊞) cesser; ~ **up** *vt*/*i* (renounce) renoncer (à); (yield) céder, ~ **oneself up** se rendre; ~ **way** céder; (collapse) s'effondrer.

**given** /'gɪvn/ ⇒GIVE. ● *a* donné. ~ **name** *n* prénom *m*.

**glad** /glæd/ *a* content. **gladly** *adv* avec plaisir.

**glamorous** /'glæmərəs/ *a* séduisant, ensorcelant.

**glamour**, (US) **glamor** /'glæmə(r)/ *n* enchantement *m*, séduction *f*.

**glance** /glɑ:ns/ *n* coup *m* d'œil. ● *vi* ~ **at** jeter un coup d'œil à.

**gland** /glænd/ *n* glande *f*.

**glare** /gleə(r)/ *vi* briller très fort; ~ **at** regarder d'un air furieux. ● *n* (of lights) éclat *m* (aveuglant); (stare: fig) regard *m* furieux. **glaring** *a* (dazzling) éblouissant; (obvious) flagrant.

**glass** /glɑ:s/ *n* verre *m*. **glasses** *npl* (spectacles) lunettes *fpl*.

**glaze** /gleɪz/ *vt* (door) vitrer; (pottery) vernisser. ● *n* vernis *m*.

**gleam** /gli:m/ *n* lueur *f*. ● *vi* luire.

**glide** /glaɪd/ *vi* glisser; (of plane) planer. **glider** *n* planeur *m*.

**glimpse** /glɪmps/ *n* (insight) aperçu *m*; **catch a ~ of** entrevoir.

**glitter** /'glɪtə(r)/ *vi* scintiller. ● *n* scintillement *m*.

**global** /'gləʊbl/ *a* (world-wide) mondial; (all-embracing) global. **~ warming** *n* réchauffement *m* de la planète. **globalization** *n* mondialisation *f*.

**globe** /gləʊb/ *n* globe *m*.

**gloom** /glu:m/ *n* obscurité *f*; (sadness: fig) tristesse *f*. **gloomy** *a* triste; (pessimistic) pessimiste.

**glorious** /'glɔ:rɪəs/ *a* splendide; (*deed, hero*) glorieux.

**glory** /'glɔ:rɪ/ *n* gloire *f*; (beauty) splendeur *f*.

**gloss** /glɒs/ *n* lustre *m*, brillant *m*. ● *a* brillant. ● *vi* **~ over** (make light of) glisser sur; (cover up) dissimuler.

**glossary** /'glɒsərɪ/ *n* glossaire *m*.

**glossy** /'glɒsɪ/ *a* brillant.

**glove** /glʌv/ *n* gant *m*. **~ compartment** *n* (Auto) boîte *f* à gants.

**glow** /gləʊ/ *vi* (*fire*) rougeoyer; (*person, eyes*) rayonner. ● *n* rougeoiement *m*, éclat *m*. **glowing** *a* (*report*) enthousiaste.

**glue** /glu:/ *n* colle *f*. ● *vt* (*pres p* **gluing**) coller.

**GM** *abbr* (**genetically modified**) transgénique.

**gnaw** /nɔ:/ *vt*/*i* ronger.

**GNP** *abbr* (**Gross National Product**) produit *m* national brut, PNB *m*.

**go** /gəʊ/

⇨ *present* **go**, **goes**; *past* **went**; *past participle* **gone**

● *intransitive verb*

····➤ aller; **~ to school/town/market** aller à l'école/en ville/au marché; **~ for a swim/walk/coffee** aller nager/se promener/prendre un café.

····➤ (leave) s'en aller; **I must be ~ing** il faut que je m'en aille.

····➤ (vanish) **the money's gone** il n'y a plus d'argent; **my bike's gone** mon vélo n'est plus là.

····➤ (work, function) marcher; **is the car ~ing?** est-ce que la voiture marche?

····➤ (become) devenir; **~ blind** devenir aveugle; **~ pale/red** pâlir/rougir.

····➤ (turn out, progress) aller; **how's it going?** comment ça va?; **how did the exam ~?** comment s'est passé l'examen?

····➤ (in future tenses) **be ~ing to do** aller faire.

● *noun*

····➤ (turn) tour *m*; (try) essai *m*; **have a ~!** essaie!; **full of ~** Ⓘ dynamique.

□ **go across** traverser.

**go after** poursuivre.

**go away** partir; **~ away!** va-t'en!, allez-vous-en!

**go back** retourner; **~ back in** rentrer; **~ back to work** reprendre le travail.

**go down** (*quality, price*) baisser; (*person*) descendre; (*sun*) se coucher.

**go in** entrer.

**go in for** (*exam*) se présenter à.

**go off** (leave) partir; (*bomb*) exploser; (*alarm clock*) sonner; (*milk*) tourner; (*light*) s'éteindre.

**go on** (continue) continuer; (*light*) s'allumer; **~ on doing** continuer à faire; **what's ~ing on?** qu'est-ce qui se passe?

**go out** sortir; (*light, fire*) s'éteindre.

**go over** vérifier.

**go round** (be enough) être assez; **~ round to see sb** passer voir qn.

**go through** (check) examiner; (search) fouiller; **~ through a difficult time** traverser une période difficile.

**go together** aller ensemble.

**go under** (sink) couler; (fail) échouer.

**go up** (*person*) monter; (*price, salary*) augmenter.

**go without** se passer de.

---

**go-ahead** /'gəʊəhed/ *n* feu *m* vert. ● *a* dynamique.

**goal** /gəʊl/ *n* but *m*. **~keeper** *n* gardien *m* de but. **~-post** *n* poteau *m* de but.

**goat** /gəʊt/ *n* chèvre *f*.

**gobble** /'gɒbl/ *vt* engouffrer.

**go-between** *n* intermédiaire *m/f*.

**god** /gɒd/ *n* dieu *m*. **~child** *n* (*pl* **-children**) filleul/-e *m/f*. **~daughter** *n* filleule *f*.

**goddess** /'gɒdɪs/ *n* déesse *f*.

**god**: **~father** *n* parrain *m*. **~mother** *n* marraine *f*. **~send** *n* aubaine *f*. **~son** *n* filleul *m*.

**goggles** /'gɒglz/ *npl* lunettes *fpl* (protectrices).

**going** /'gəʊɪŋ/ *n* **it is slow/hard ~** c'est lent/difficile. ● *a* (*price, rate*) actuel.

**go-kart** *n* kart *m*.

**gold** /gəʊld/ *n* or *m*. ● *a* en or, d'or.

**golden** /'gəʊldən/ *a* en or, d'or; (in colour) doré; (opportunity) unique.

**gold**: **~fish** *n* poisson *m* rouge. **~-plated** *a* plaqué or. **~smith** *n* orfèvre *m*.

**golf** /gɒlf/ *n* golf *m*. **~-course** *n* terrain *m* de golf.

**gone** /gɒn/ ⇒GO. ● *a* parti; **~ six o'clock** six heures passées; **the butter's all ~** il n'y a plus de beurre.

**good** /gʊd/ *a* (**better**, **best**) bon; (weather) beau; (well-behaved) sage; **as ~ as** (almost) pratiquement; **that's ~ of you** c'est gentil (de ta part); **be ~ with** savoir s'y prendre avec; **feel ~** se sentir bien; **it is ~ for you** ça vous fait du bien. ● *n* bien *m*; **do ~** faire du bien; **is it any ~?** est-ce que c'est bien?; **it's no ~** ça ne vaut rien; **it is no ~ shouting** ça ne sert à rien de crier; **for ~** pour toujours. **~ afternoon** *interj* bonjour. **~bye** *interj & n* au revoir (*m inv*). **~ evening** *interj* bonsoir. **G~ Friday** *n* Vendredi *m* saint. **~-looking** *a* beau. **~ morning** *interj* bonjour. **~-natured** *a* gentil.

**goodness** /'gʊdnɪs/ *n* bonté *f*; **my ~!** mon Dieu!

**good-night** *interj* bonsoir, bonne nuit.

**goods** /gʊdz/ *npl* marchandises *fpl*.

**goodwill** /gʊd'wɪl/ *n* bonne volonté *f*.

**goose** /gu:s/ *n* (*pl* **geese**) oie *f*. **gooseberry** *n* groseille *f* à maquereau. **~-pimples** *npl* chair *f* de poule.

**gorge** /gɔ:dʒ/ *n* (Geog) gorge *f*. ● *vt* **~ oneself** se gaver (**on** de).

**gorgeous** /'gɔ:dʒəs/ *a* magnifique, splendide, formidable.

**gorilla** /gə'rɪlə/ *n* gorille *m*.

**gory** /'gɔ:rɪ/ *a* (**-ier**, **-iest**) sanglant; (horrific: fig) horrible.

**gospel** /'gɒspl/ *n* évangile *m*; **the G~** l'Évangile *m*.

**gossip** /ˈgɒsɪp/ *n* bavardages *mpl*, commérages *mpl*; (person) bavard/-e *m/f*. ● *vi* bavarder.

**got** /gɒt/ ⇒GET. ● **have ~** avoir; **have ~ to do** devoir faire.

**govern** /ˈgʌvn/ *vt/i* gouverner. **governess** *n* gouvernante *f*. **government** *n* gouvernement *m*. **governor** *n* gouverneur *m*.

**gown** /gaʊn/ *n* robe *f*; (of judge, teacher) toge *f*.

**GP** *abbr* ⇒GENERAL PRACTITIONER.

**grab** /græb/ *vt* (*pt* **grabbed**) saisir.

**grace** /greɪs/ *n* grâce *f*. ● *vt* (honour) honorer; (adorn) orner. **graceful** *a* gracieux.

**gracious** /ˈgreɪʃəs/ *a* (kind) bienveillant; (elegant) élégant.

**grade** /greɪd/ *n* catégorie *f*; (of goods) qualité *f*; (on scale) grade *m*; (school mark) note *f*; (class: US) classe *f*. ● *vt* classer; (school work) noter. **~ school** *n* (US) école *f* primaire.

**gradual** /ˈgrædʒʊəl/ *a* progressif, graduel. **gradually** *adv* progressivement, peu à peu.

**graduate**[1] /ˈgrædʒʊət/ *n* (Univ) diplômé/-e *m/f*.

**graduate**[2] /ˈgrædʒʊeɪt/ *vi* obtenir son diplôme. ● *vt* graduer. **graduation** *n* remise *f* des diplômes.

**graffiti** /grəˈfi:ti:/ *npl* graffiti *mpl*.

**graft** /grɑ:ft/ *n* (Med, Bot) greffe *f*; (work) boulot *m*. ● *vt* greffer (**on to** sur); (work) trimer.

**grain** /greɪn/ *n* (seed, quantity, texture) grain *m*; (in wood) fibre *f*.

**gram** /græm/ *n* gramme *m*.

**grammar** /ˈgræmə(r)/ *n* grammaire *f*.

**grand** /grænd/ *a* magnifique; (*duke, chorus*) grand.

**grandad** /ˈgrændæd/ *n* Ⓘ papy *m*.

**grand**: **~child** *n* (girl) petite-fille *f*; (boy) petit-fils *m*; **her ~children** ses petits-enfants *mpl*. **~daughter** *n* petite-fille *f*. **~father** *n* grand-père *m*. **~ma** *n* = GRANNY. **~mother** *n* grand-mère *f*. **~parents** *npl* grands-parents *mpl*. **~ piano** *n* piano *m* à queue. **~son** *n* petit-fils *m*. **~stand** *n* tribune *f*.

**granny** /ˈgrænɪ/ *n* Ⓘ mémé *f*, mamie *f*.

**grant** /grɑ:nt/ *vt* (*permission*) accorder; (*request*) accéder à; (admit) admettre (**that** que); **take sth for ~ed** considérer qch comme une chose acquise. ● *n* subvention *f*; (Univ) bourse *f*.

**granule** /ˈgrænju:l/ *n* (*of sugar, salt*) grain *m*; (*of coffee*) granulé *m*.

**grape** /greɪp/ *n* grain *m* de raisin; **~s** raisin(s) *m(pl)*.

**grapefruit** /ˈgreɪpfru:t/ *n inv* pamplemousse *m*.

**graph** /grɑ:f/ *n* graphique *m*.

**graphic** /ˈgræfɪk/ *a* (*arts*) graphique; (fig) vivant, explicite. **graphics** *npl* (Comput) graphiques *mpl*.

**grasp** /grɑ:sp/ *vt* saisir. ● *n* (hold) prise *f*; (strength of hand) poigne *f*; (reach) portée *f*; (fig) compréhension *f*.

**grass** /grɑ:s/ *n* herbe *f*. **~hopper** *n* sauterelle *f*. **~land** *n* prairie *f*.

**grass roots** *npl* peuple *m*. ● *a* (*movement*) populaire; (*support*) de base.

**grate** /greɪt/ *n* (hearth) âtre *m*; (fire basket) grille *f*. ● *vt* râper. ● *vi* grincer.

**grateful** /ˈgreɪtfl/ *a* reconnaissant.

**grater** /ˈgreɪtə(r)/ *n* râpe *f*.

**gratified** /ˈgrætɪfaɪd/ *a* très heureux. **gratify** *vt* faire plaisir à.

**grating** /ˈgreɪtɪŋ/ *n* (bars) grille *f*; (noise) grincement *m*.

**gratitude** /ˈgrætɪtju:d/ *n* reconnaissance *f*.

**gratuity** /grəˈtju:ətɪ/ *n* (tip) pourboire *m*; (bounty: Mil) prime *f*.

**grave**[1] /greɪv/ *n* tombe *f*. ● *a* (serious) grave.

**grave**[2] /grɑ:v/ *a* ~ **accent** accent *m* grave.

**gravel** /ˈgrævl/ *n* graviers *mpl*.

**grave**: ~**stone** *n* pierre *f* tombale. ~**yard** *n* cimetière *m*.

**gravity** /ˈgrævətɪ/ *n* (seriousness) gravité *f*; (force) pesanteur *f*.

**gravy** /ˈgreɪvɪ/ *n* jus *m* (de viande).

**gray** /greɪ/ (US) *a* & *n* = GREY.

**graze** /greɪz/ *vi* (eat) paître. ● *vt* (touch) frôler; (scrape) écorcher. ● *n* écorchure *f*.

**grease** /gri:s/ *n* graisse *f*. ● *vt* graisser. **greasy** *a* graisseux.

**great** /greɪt/ *a* grand; (very good Ⓘ) génial Ⓘ, formidable Ⓘ, (*grandfather, grandmother*) arrière.

**Great Britain** *n* Grande-Bretagne *f*.

**greatly** /ˈgreɪtlɪ/ *adv* (very) très; (much) beaucoup.

**Greece** /gri:s/ *n* Grèce *f*.

**greed** /gri:d/ *n* avidité *f*; (for food) gourmandise *f*. **greedy** *a* avide; gourmand.

**Greek** /gri:k/ *n* (person) Grec/-que *m/f*; (Ling) grec *m*. ● *a* grec.

**green** /gri:n/ *a* vert; (fig) naïf. ● *n* vert *m*; (grass) pelouse *f*; (golf) green *m*; ~**s** légumes *mpl* verts. ~**grocer** *n* marchand/-e *m/f* de fruits et légumes.

**green house** *n* serre *f*; ~ **effect** effet *m* de serre.

**greet** /gri:t/ *vt* (welcome) accueillir; (address politely) saluer. **greeting** *n* accueil *m*.

**greetings** /ˈgri:tɪŋs/ *interj* salutations! ● *npl* (*Christmas*) vœux *mpl*. ~ **card** *n* carte *f* de vœux.

**grew** /gru:/ ⇨GROW.

**grey** /greɪ/ *a* gris; (fig) triste; **go** ~ (*hair, person*) grisonner. ● *n* gris *m*. ~**hound** *n* lévrier *m*.

**grid** /grɪd/ *n* grille *f*; (network: Electr) réseau *m*.

**grief** /gri:f/ *n* chagrin *m*; **come to** ~ (*person*) avoir un malheur; (fail) tourner mal.

**grievance** /ˈgri:vns/ *n* griefs *mpl*.

**grieve** /gri:v/ *vt/i* (s')affliger; ~ **for** pleurer.

**grill** /grɪl/ *n* (cooking device) gril *m*; (food) grillade *f*; (Auto) calandre *f*. ● *vt/i* (faire) griller; (interrogate) mettre sur la sellette.

**grim** /grɪm/ *a* sinistre.

**grimace** /grɪˈmeɪs/ *n* grimace *f*. ● *vi* grimacer.

**grime** /graɪm/ *n* crasse *f*.

**grin** /grɪn/ *vi* (*pt* **grinned**) sourire. ● *n* (large) sourire *m*.

**grind** /graɪnd/ *vt* (*pt* **ground**) (*grain*) écraser; (*coffee*) moudre; (sharpen) aiguiser; ~ **one's teeth** grincer des dents. ● *vi* ~ **to a halt** s'immobiliser. ● *n* corvée *f*.

**grip** /grɪp/ *vt* (*pt* **gripped**) saisir; (interest) passionner. ● *n* prise *f*; (strength of hand) poigne *f*; **come to** ~**s with** en venir aux prises avec.

**grisly** /ˈgrɪzlɪ/ *a* (**-ier**, **-iest**) (*remains*) macabre; (*sight*) horrible.

**gristle** /ˈgrɪsl/ *n* cartilage *m*.

**grit** /grɪt/ *n* (for roads) sable *m*; (fig) courage *m*. ● *vt* (*pt* **gritted**) (*road*) sabler; (*teeth*) serrer.

**groan** /grəʊn/ *vi* gémir. ● *n* gémissement *m*.

**grocer** /ˈgrəʊsə(r)/ *n* (person) épicier/-ière *m/f*; (shop) épicerie *f*.

**groceries** *npl* (shopping) courses *fpl*; (goods) épicerie *f*. **grocery** *n* (shop) épicerie *f*.

**groin** /grɔɪn/ *n* aine *f*.

**groom** /gru:m/ *n* marié *m*; (for horses) palefrenier/-ière *m/f*. ● *vt* (*horse*) panser; (fig) préparer.

**groove** /gru:v/ *n* (for door etc.) rainure *f*; (in record) sillon *m*.

**grope** /grəʊp/ *vi* tâtonner; **~ for** chercher à tâtons.

**gross** /grəʊs/ *a* (*behaviour*) vulgaire; (Comm) brut. ● *n inv* grosse *f*.

**grotto** /'grɒtəʊ/ *n* (*pl* **~es**) grotte *f*.

**grouch** /graʊtʃ/ *vi* (grumble ⓘ) rouspéter, râler.

**ground**[1] /graʊnd/ *n* terre *f*, sol *m*; (area) terrain *m*; (reason) raison *f*; (Electr, US) masse *f*; **~s** terres *fpl*, parc *m*; (of coffee) marc *m*; **on the ~** par terre; **lose ~** perdre du terrain. ● *vt/i* (Naut) échouer; (aircraft) retenir au sol.

**ground**[2] /graʊnd/ ⇒GRIND. ● *a* **~ beef** (US) bifteck *m* haché.

**ground**: **~ floor** *n* rez-de-chaussée *m inv*. **~work** *n* travail *m* préparatoire.

**group** /gru:p/ *n* groupe *m*. ● *vt/i* (se) grouper. **~ware** *n* (Comput) logiciel *m* de groupe.

**grovel** /'grɒvl/ *vi* (*pt* **grovelled**) ramper.

**grow** /grəʊ/ *vi* (*pt* **grew**; *pp* **grown**) (*person*) grandir; (*plant*) pousser; (become) devenir; (*crime*) augmenter. ● *vt* cultiver; **~ up** devenir adulte, grandir. **grower** *n* cultivateur/-trice *m/f*.

**growl** /graʊl/ *vi* (*dog*) gronder; (*person*) grogner. ● *n* grognement *m*.

**grown** /grəʊn/ ⇒GROW. ● *a* adulte. **~-up** *a* & *n* adulte (*mf*).

**growth** /grəʊθ/ *n* (of person, plant) croissance *f*; (in numbers) accroissement *m*; (of hair, tooth) pousse *f*; (Med) grosseur *f*, tumeur *f*.

**grudge** /grʌdʒ/ *vt* **~ doing** faire à contrecœur; **~ sb sth** (*success, wealth*) en vouloir à qn de qch. ● *n* rancune *f*; **have a ~ against** en vouloir à.

**grumble** /'grʌmbl/ *vi* ronchonner, grogner (**at** après).

**grumpy** /'grʌmpɪ/ *a* (**-ier**, **-iest**) grincheux, grognon.

**grunt** /grʌnt/ *vi* grogner. ● *n* grognement *m*.

**guarantee** /gærən'ti:/ *n* garantie *f*. ● *vt* garantir.

**guard** /gɑ:d/ *vt* protéger; (watch) surveiller. ● *vi* **~ against** se protéger contre. ● *n* (Mil) garde *f*; (person) garde *m*; (on train) chef *m* de train.

**guardian** /'gɑ:dɪən/ *n* gardien/-ne *m/f*; (of orphan) tuteur/-trice *m/f*.

**guess** /ges/ *vt/i* deviner; (suppose) penser. ● *n* conjecture *f*.

**guest** /gest/ *n* invité/-e *m/f*; (in hotel) client/-e *m/f*. **~-house** *n* pension *f*. **~-room** *n* chambre *f* d'amis.

**guidance** /'gaɪdns/ *n* (advice) conseils *mpl*; (information) information *f*.

**guide** /gaɪd/ *n* (person, book) guide *m*; (girl) guide *f*. ● *vt* guider. **~book** *n* guide *m*. **~-dog** *n* chien *m* d'aveugle. **~line** *n* indication *f*; (advice) conseils *mpl*.

**guillotine** /'gɪləti:n/ *n* (for execution) guillotine *f*; (for paper) massicot *m*.

**guilt** /gɪlt/ *n* culpabilité *f*. **guilty** *a* coupable.

**guinea-pig** /'gɪnɪpɪg/ *n* (animal) cochon *m* d'Inde; (fig) cobaye *m*.

**guitar** /gɪ'tɑ:(r)/ *n* guitare *f*.

**gulf** /gʌlf/ *n* (part of sea) golfe *m*; (hollow) gouffre *m*.

**gull** /gʌl/ *n* mouette *f*, (larger) goéland *m*.

**gullible** /'gʌləbl/ *a* crédule.

**gully** /'gʌlɪ/ *n* (ravine) ravin *m*; (drain) rigole *f*.

**gulp** /gʌlp/ *vt* ~ **(down)** avaler en vitesse. ● *vi* (from fear etc.) avoir la gorge serrée. ● *n* gorgée *f*.

**gum** /gʌm/ *n* (Anat) gencive *f*; (glue) colle *f*; (for chewing) chewing-gum *m*. ● *vt* (*pt* **gummed**) gommer.

**gun** /gʌn/ *n* (pistol) revolver *m*; (rifle) fusil *m*; (large) canon *m*. ● *vt* (*pt* **gunned**) ~ **down** abattre. ~**fire** *n* fusillade *f*. ~**powder** *n* poudre *f* à canon. ~**shot** *n* coup *m* de feu.

**gurgle** /'gɜ:gl/ *n* (of water) gargouillement *m*; (of baby) gazouillis *m*. ● *vi* (*water*) gargouiller; (*baby*) gazouiller.

**gush** /gʌʃ/ *vi* ~ **(out)** jaillir. ● *n* jaillissement *m*.

**gust** /gʌst/ *n* rafale *f*; (of smoke) bouffée *f*.

**gut** /gʌt/ *n* (belly 🅸) ventre *m*. ● *vt* (*pt* **gutted**) (*fish*) vider; (of fire) dévaster. **gutted** *a* 🅸 abattu.

**guts** /gʌts/ *npl* 🅸 (insides of human) tripes *fpl* 🅸; (insides of animal, building) entrailles *fpl*; (courage) cran *m* 🅸.

**gutter** /'gʌtə(r)/ *n* (on roof) gouttière *f*; (in street) caniveau *m*.

**guy** /gaɪ/ *n* (man 🅸) type *m*.

**gym** /dʒɪm/ *n* (place) gymnase *m*; (activity) gym(nastique) *f*.

**gymnasium** /dʒɪm'neɪzɪəm/ *n* gymnase *m*.

**gymnastics** /dʒɪm'næstɪks/ *npl* gymnastique *f*.

**gynaecologist** /gaɪnɪ'kɒlədʒɪst/ *n* gynécologue *mf*.

**gypsy** /'dʒɪpsɪ/ *n* bohémien/-ne *m/f*.

# Hh

**habit** /'hæbɪt/ *n* habitude *f*; (costume: Relig) habit *m*; **be in/get into the ~ of** avoir/prendre l'habitude de.

**habitual** /hə'bɪtʃʊəl/ *a* (usual) habituel; (*smoker, liar*) invétéré.

**hack** /hæk/ *n* (writer) écrivaillon *m*. ● *vi* (Comput) pirater; ~ **into** s'introduire dans. ● *vt* tailler. **hacker** *n* (Comput) pirate *m* informatique.

**hackneyed** /'hæknɪd/ *a* rebattu.

**had** /hæd/ ⇒HAVE.

**haddock** /'hædək/ *n inv* églefin *m*.

**haemorrhage** /'hemərɪdʒ/ *n* hémorragie *f*.

**haggard** /'hægəd/ *a* (*person*) exténué; (*face, look*) défait.

**haggle** /'hægl/ *vi* marchander; ~ **over sth** discuter du prix de qch.

**hail** /heɪl/ *n* grêle *f*. ● *vt* (greet) saluer; (*taxi*) héler. ● *vi* grêler; ~ **from** venir de. ~**stone** *n* grêlon *m*.

**hair** /heə(r)/ *n* (on head) cheveux *mpl*; (on body, of animal) poils *mpl*; (single strand on head) cheveu *m*; (on body) poil *m*. ~**brush** *n* brosse *f* à cheveux. ~**cut** *n* coupe *f* de cheveux. ~**do** *n* 🅸 coiffure *f*. ~**dresser** *n* coiffeur/-euse *m/f*. ~**-drier** *n* séchoir *m* (à cheveux). ~**pin** *n* épingle *f* à cheveux. ~ **remover** *n* dépilatoire *m*. ~**-style** *n* coiffure *f*.

**hairy** /'heərɪ/ *a* (**-ier, -iest**) poilu; (terrifying 🅸) horrifiant.

**half** /hɑ:f/ *n* (*pl* **halves**) (part) moitié *f*, (fraction) demi *m*; ~ **a dozen** une demi-douzaine; ~ **an hour** une demi-heure, **four and**

**a ~** quatre et demi; **an hour and a ~** une heure et demie; **~ and half** moitié moitié; **in ~** en deux. ● *a* demi; **~ price** à moitié prix. ● *adv* à moitié. **~-back** *n* (Sport) demi *m*. **~-hearted** *a* tiède. **~-mast** *n* **at ~-mast** en berne. **~-term** *n* vacances *fpl* de demi-trimestre. **~-time** *n* mi-temps *f*. **~-way** *adv* à mi-chemin. **~-wit** *n* imbécile *mf*.

**hall** /hɔ:l/ *n* (in house) entrée *f*; (corridor) couloir *m*; (in airport) hall *m*; (for events) salle *f*; **~ of residence** résidence *f* universitaire.

**hallmark** /'hɔ:lmɑ:k/ *n* (on gold) poinçon *m*; (fig) caractéristique *f*.

**hallo** /hə'ləʊ/ = HELLO.

**Hallowe'en** /hæləʊ'i:n/ *n* la veille de la Toussaint.

**halt** /hɔ:lt/ *n* arrêt *m*; (temporary) suspension *f*; (Mil) halte *f*. ● *vt* (*proceedings*) interrompre; (*arms sales, experiments*) mettre fin à. ● *vi* (*vehicle*) s'arrêter; (*army*) faire halte.

**halve** /hɑ:v/ *vt* (*time*) réduire de moitié; (*fruit*) couper en deux.

**ham** /hæm/ *n* jambon *m*.

**hamburger** /'hæmbɜ:gə(r)/ *n* hamburger *m*.

**hammer** /'hæmə(r)/ *n* marteau *m*. ● *vt/i* marteler; **~ sth into sth** enfoncer qch dans qch; **~ sth out** (*agreement*) parvenir à qch.

**hammock** /'hæmək/ *n* hamac *m*.

**hamper** /'hæmpə(r)/ *n* panier *m*. ● *vt* gêner.

**hamster** /'hæmstə(r)/ *n* hamster *m*.

**hand** /hænd/ *n* main *f*; (of clock) aiguille *f*; (writing) écriture *f*; (worker) ouvrier/-ière *m/f*; (cards) jeu *m*; **give sb a ~** donner un coup de main à qn; **at ~** proche; **on ~** disponible; **on the one ~...on the other ~** d'une part...d'autre part; **to ~** à portée de la main. ● *vt* **~ sb sth, ~ sth to sb** donner qch à qn. ▫ **~ in** *or* **over** remettre; **~ out** distribuer. **~bag** *n* sac *m* à main. **~-baggage** *n* bagages *mpl* à main. **~book** *n* manuel *m*. **~brake** *n* frein *m* à main. **~cuffs** *npl* menottes *fpl*.

**handicap** /'hændɪkæp/ *n* handicap *m*. ● *vt* (*pt* **handicapped**) handicaper.

**handkerchief** /'hæŋkətʃɪf/ *n* (*pl* **~s**) mouchoir *m*.

**handle** /'hændl/ *n* (of door, bag) poignée *f*; (of implement) manche *m*; (of cup, bucket) anse *f*; (of frying pan) queue *f*. ● *vt* (manage) manier; (deal with) traiter; (touch) manipuler.

**hand**: **~-out** *n* document *m*; (leaflet) prospectus *m*; (money) aumône *f*. **~shake** *n* poignée *f* de main.

**handsome** /'hænsəm/ *a* (good looking) beau; (generous) généreux.

**handwriting** /'hændraɪtɪŋ/ *n* écriture *f*.

**handy** /'hændɪ/ *a* (**-ier**, **-iest**) (*book, skill*) utile; (*size, shape, tool*) pratique; (*person*) doué. **~man** *n* (*pl* **-men**) bricoleur *m*, homme *m* à tout faire.

**hang** /hæŋ/ *vt* (*pt* **hung**) (from hook, hanger) accrocher; (from rope) suspendre; (*pt* **hanged**) (*person*) pendre. ● *vi* (from hook) être accroché; (from rope) être suspendu; (*person*) être pendu. ● *n* **get the ~ of doing** 🅸 piger comment faire 🅸. ▫ **~about** traîner; **~ on** 🅸 (hold out) tenir; (wait) attendre; **~ on to sth** s'agripper à qch; **~ out** *vi* 🅸 (live) crécher 🅸; (spend time) passer son temps; *vt* (*washing*) étendre; **~ up** (telephone) raccrocher.

**hanger** /'hæŋə(r)/ *n* (for clothes) cintre *m*.

**hang-gliding** *n* vol *m* libre.

**hangover** /ˈhæŋəʊvə(r)/ *n* gueule *f* de bois [!].

**hang-up** *n* [!] complexe *m*.

**hankering** /ˈhæŋkərɪŋ/ *n* envie *f*.

**haphazard** /hæpˈhæzəd/ *a* peu méthodique.

**happen** /ˈhæpən/ *vi* arriver, se passer; **~ to sb** arriver à qn; **it so ~s that** il se trouve que.

**happily** /ˈhæpɪlɪ/ *adv* joyeusement; (fortunately) heureusement.

**happiness** /ˈhæpɪnɪs/ *n* bonheur *m*.

**happy** /ˈhæpɪ/ *a* (**-ier**, **-iest**) heureux; **I'm not ~ about it** je ne suis pas content; **~ with sth** satisfait de qch; **~ medium** juste milieu *m*.

**harass** /ˈhærəs/ *vt* harceler. **harassment** *n* harcèlement *m*.

**harbour**, (US) **harbor** /ˈhɑːbə(r)/ *n* port *m*. ● *vt* (shelter) héberger.

**hard** /hɑːd/ *a* dur; (difficult) difficile, dur; (*evidence, fact*) solide; **find it ~ to do** avoir du mal à faire; **~ on sb** dur envers qn. ● *adv* (work) dur; (pull, hit, cry) fort; (think, study) sérieusement. **~board** *n* aggloméré *m*. **~ copy** *n* (Comput) tirage *m*. **~ disk** *n* disque *m* dur.

**hardly** /ˈhɑːdlɪ/ *adv* à peine; (*expect, hope*) difficilement; **~ ever** presque jamais.

**hardship** /ˈhɑːdʃɪp/ *n* (poverty) privations *fpl*; (ordeal) épreuve *f*.

**hard**: **~ shoulder** *n* bande *f* d'arrêt d'urgence. **~ up** *a* [!] fauché [!]. **~ware** *n* (Comput) matériel *m*, hardware *m*; (goods) quincaillerie *f*. **~-working** *a* travailleur.

**hardy** /ˈhɑːdɪ/ *a* (**-ier**, **-iest**) résistant.

**hare** /heə(r)/ *n* lièvre *m*. ● *vi* **~ around** courir partout.

**harm** /hɑːm/ *n* mal *m*; **there is no ~ in** il n'y a pas de mal à. ● *vt* (*person*) faire du mal à; (*object*) endommager. **harmful** *a* nuisible. **harmless** *a* inoffensif.

**harmony** /ˈhɑːmənɪ/ *n* harmonie *f*.

**harness** /ˈhɑːnɪs/ *n* harnais *m*. ● *vt* (*horse*) harnacher; (use) exploiter.

**harp** /hɑːp/ *n* harpe *f*. ● *vi* **~ on (about)** rabâcher.

**harrowing** /ˈhærəʊɪŋ/ *a* (*experience*) atroce; (*story*) déchirant.

**harsh** /hɑːʃ/ *a* (*punishment*) sévère; (*person*) dur; (*light*) cru; (*voice*) rude; (*chemical*) corrosif. **harshness** *n* dureté *f*.

**harvest** /ˈhɑːvɪst/ *n* récolte *f*; **the wine ~** les vendanges *fpl*. ● *vt* (*corn*) moissonner; (*vegetables*) récolter.

**has** /hæz/ ⇒HAVE.

**hassle** /ˈhæsl/ *n* complications *fpl*. ● *vt* [F] talonner (**about** à propos de); (worry) stresser.

**haste** /heɪst/ *n* hâte *f*; **in ~** à la hâte; **make ~** se dépêcher.

**hasty** /ˈheɪstɪ/ *a* (**-ier**, **-iest**) précipité.

**hat** /hæt/ *n* chapeau *m*.

**hatch** /hætʃ/ *n* (Aviat) panneau *m* mobile; (Naut) écoutille *f*; (for food) passe-plats *m inv*. ● *vt/i* (*eggs*) (faire) éclore.

**hate** /heɪt/ *n* haine *f*. ● *vt* détester; (violently) haïr; (*sport, food*) avoir horreur de.

**hatred** /ˈheɪtrɪd/ *n* haine *f*.

**haughty** /ˈhɔːtɪ/ *a* (**-ier**, **-iest**) hautain.

**haul** /hɔːl/ *vt* tirer. ● *n* (by thieves) butin *m*; (by customs) saisie *f*; **it will be a long ~** l'étape sera longue; **long/short ~** (*transport*) long/court courrier *m*. **haulage** *n*

transport *m* routier. **haulier** *n* (firm) société *f* de transports routiers.

**haunt** /hɔ:nt/ *vt* hanter. ● *n* lieu *m* de prédilection.

**have** /hæv/

*present* **have, has**; *past* **had**; *past participle* **had**

● *transitive verb*

····➤ (possess) avoir; **I ~ (got) a car** j'ai une voiture; **they ~ (got) problems** ils ont des problèmes.

····➤ (do sth) **~ a try** essayer; **~ a bath** prendre un bain.

····➤ **~ sth done** faire faire qch; **~ your hair cut** se faire couper les cheveux.

● *auxiliary verb*

····➤ (in perfect tenses) avoir; être; **I ~ seen him** je l'ai vu; **she had fallen** elle était tombée.

····➤ (in tag questions) **you've seen her, haven't you?** tu l'as vue, n'est-ce pas?; **you haven't seen her, ~ you?** tu ne l'as pas vue, par hasard?

····➤ (in short answers) **'you've never met him'—'yes I ~'** 'tu ne l'as jamais rencontré'—'mais si!'

····➤ (must) **~ to** devoir; **I ~ to go** je dois partir; **you don't ~ to do it** tu n'es pas obligé de le faire.

⇨ For expressions such as **have a walk, have dinner** ⇨**walk, dinner**.

**haven** /'heɪvn/ *n* refuge *m*; (fig) havre *m*.

**havoc** /'hævək/ *n* dévastation *f*.

**hawk** /hɔ:k/ *n* faucon *m*.

**hay** /heɪ/ *n* foin *m*; **~ fever** rhume *m* des foins.

**haywire** /'heɪwaɪə(r)/ *a* **go ~** (*plans*) dérailler; (*machine*) se détraquer.

**hazard** /'hæzəd/ *n* risque *m*; **~ (warning) lights** feux *mpl* de détresse. ● *vt* hasarder.

**haze** /heɪz/ *n* brume *f*.

**hazel** /'heɪzl/ *n* (bush) noisetier *m*. **~nut** *n* noisette *f*.

**hazy** /'heɪzɪ/ *a* (**-ier**, **-iest**) (misty) brumeux; (fig) vague.

**he** /hi:/ *pron* il; (emphatic) lui; **here ~ is** le voici.

**head** /hed/ *n* tête *f*; (leader) chef *m*; (of beer) mousse *f*; **~s or tails?** pile ou face? ● *vt* (*list*) être en tête de; (*team*) être à la tête de; (*chapter*) intituler; **~ the ball** faire une tête. ● *vi* **~ for** se diriger vers.

**headache** /'hedeɪk/ *n* mal *m* de tête; **have a ~** avoir mal à la tête.

**heading** /'hedɪŋ/ *n* titre *m*; (subject category) rubrique *f*.

**head**: **~lamp**, **~light** *n* phare *m*. **~line** *n* gros titre *m*. **~master** *n* directeur *m*. **~mistress** *n* directrice *f*. **~ office** *n* siège *m* social. **~-on** *a & adv* de front. **~phones** *npl* casque *m*. **~quarters** *npl* siège *m* social; (Mil) quartier *m* général. **~ rest** *n* (Auto) repose-tête *m inv*. **~strong** *a* têtu.

**heal** /hi:l/ *vt*/*i* guérir.

**health** /helθ/ *n* santé *f*. **~ centre** *n* centre *m* médico-social. **~ food** *n* produits *mpl* diététiques. **~ insurance** *n* assurance *f* maladie.

**healthy** /'helθɪ/ *a* (*person, plant, skin, diet*) sain; (*air*) salutaire.

**heap** /hi:p/ *n* tas *m*; **~s of** 🄸 un tas de. ● *vt* **~ (up)** entasser.

**hear** /hɪə(r)/ *vt* (*pt* **heard**) entendre; (*news, rumour*) apprendre; (*lecture, broadcast*)

écouter. ● *vi* entendre; ~ **from** recevoir des nouvelles de; ~ **of** *or* **about** entendre parler de.

**hearing** /ˈhɪərɪŋ/ *n* ouïe *f*; (of case) audience *f*; **give sb a** ~ écouter qn. ~**-aid** *n* prothèse *f* auditive.

**hearse** /hɜːs/ *n* corbillard *m*.

**heart** /hɑːt/ *n* cœur *m*; ~**s** (cards) cœur *m*; **at** ~ au fond; **by** ~ par cœur; **be** ~**-broken** avoir le cœur brisé; **lose** ~ perdre courage. ~ **attack** *n* crise *f* cardiaque. ~**burn** *n* brûlures *fpl* d'estomac. ~**felt** *a* sincère.

**hearth** /hɑːθ/ *n* foyer *m*.

**heartily** /ˈhɑːtɪlɪ/ *adv* (*greet*) chaleureusement; (*laugh, eat*) de bon cœur.

**hearty** /ˈhɑːtɪ/ *a* (**-ier**, **-iest**) (sincere) chaleureux; (*meal*) solide.

**heat** /hiːt/ *n* chaleur *f*; (contest) épreuve *f* éliminatoire. ● *vt* (*house*) chauffer; ~ **(up)** (*food*) faire chauffer; (reheat) réchauffer. **heated** *a* (fig) passionné; (lit) (*pool*) chauffé. **heater** *n* appareil *m* de chauffage.

**heather** /ˈheðə(r)/ *n* bruyère *f*.

**heating** /ˈhiːtɪŋ/ *n* chauffage *m*.

**heave** /hiːv/ *vt* (lift) hisser; (pull) traîner péniblement; ~ **a sigh** pousser un soupir. ● *vi* (*pull*) tirer de toutes ses forces; (retch) avoir un haut-le-cœur.

**heaven** /ˈhevn/ *n* ciel *m*.

**heavily** /ˈhevɪlɪ/ *adv* lourdement; (smoke, drink) beaucoup.

**heavy** /ˈhevɪ/ *a* (**-ier**, **-iest**) lourd; (*cold, work*) gros; (*traffic*) dense. ~ **goods vehicle** *n* poids *m* lourd. ~**-handed** *a* maladroit. ~**weight** *n* poids *m* lourd.

**Hebrew** /ˈhiːbruː/ *n* (person) Hébreu *m*; (Ling) hébreu *m*. ● *a* hébreu; (Ling) hébraïque.

**hectic** /ˈhektɪk/ *a* (*activity*) intense; (*period, day*) mouvementé.

**hedge** /hedʒ/ *n* haie *f*. ● *vi* (in answering) se dérober.

**hedgehog** /ˈhedʒhɒg/ *n* hérisson *m*.

**heel** /hiːl/ *n* talon *m*.

**hefty** /ˈheftɪ/ *a* (**-ier**, **-iest**) (*person*) costaud Ⓘ; (*object*) pesant.

**height** /haɪt/ *n* hauteur *f*; (of person) taille *f*; (of plane, mountain) altitude *f*; (of fame, glory) apogée *m*; (of joy, folly, pain) comble *m*.

**heir** /eə(r)/ *n* héritier/-ière *m/f*. **heiress** *n* héritière *f*. **heirloom** *n* objet *m* de famille.

**held** /held/ ⇒HOLD.

**helicopter** /ˈhelɪkɒptə(r)/ *n* hélicoptère *m*.

**hell** /hel/ *n* enfer *m*.

**hello** /həˈləʊ/ *interj* bonjour!; (on phone) allô!

**helmet** /ˈhelmɪt/ *n* casque *m*.

**help** /help/ *vt/i* aider (**to do** à faire); ~ **(sb) with a bag/the housework** aider qn à porter un sac/à faire le ménage; ~ **oneself** se servir; **he can't** ~ **it** ce n'est pas de sa faute. ● *n* aide *f* ● *interj* au secours! **helper** *n* aide *m/f*. **helpful** *a* utile; (*person*) serviable. **helping** *n* portion *f*. **helpless** *a* impuissant.

**hem** /hem/ *n* ourlet *m*. ● *vt* (*pt* **hemmed**) faire un ourlet à; ~ **in** cerner.

**hen** /hen/ *n* poule *f*.

**hence** /hens/ *adv* (for this reason) d'où; (from now) d'ici. **henceforth** *adv* désormais.

**hepatitis** /hepəˈtaɪtɪs/ *n* hépatite *f*.

**her** /hɜː(r)/ *pron* la, l'; (indirect object) lui; **it's** ~ c'est elle; **for** ~ pour elle. ● *a* son, sa; *pl* ses.

**herb** /hɜ:b/ *n* herbe *f*; **~s** (Culin) fines herbes *fpl*.

**herd** /hɜ:d/ *n* troupeau *m*.

**here** /hɪə(r)/ *adv* ici; **~!** (take this) tiens!; tenez!; **~ is, ~ are** voici; **I'm ~** je suis là. **hereabouts** *adv* par ici. **hereafter** *adv* après; (in book) ci-après. **hereby** *adv* par le présent acte; (in letter) par la présente.

**herewith** /hɪə'wɪð/ *adv* ci-joint.

**heritage** /'herɪtɪdʒ/ *n* patrimoine *m*.

**hernia** /'hɜ:nɪə/ *n* hernie *f*.

**hero** /'hɪərəʊ/ *n* (*pl* **~es**) héros *m*.

**heroic** /hɪ'rəʊɪk/ *a* héroïque.

**heroin** /'herəʊɪn/ *n* héroïne *f*.

**heroine** /'herəʊɪn/ *n* héroïne *f*.

**heron** /'herən/ *n* héron *m*.

**herring** /'herɪŋ/ *n* hareng *m*.

**hers** /hɜ:z/ *pron* le sien, la sienne, les sien(ne)s; **it is ~** c'est à elle *or* le sien *or* la sienne.

**herself** /hɜ:'self/ *pron* (emphatic) elle-même; (reflexive) se; **proud of ~** fière d'elle; **by ~** toute seule.

**hesitate** /'hezɪteɪt/ *vi* hésiter. **hesitation** *n* hésitation *f*.

**heterosexual** /hetərəʊ'seksjʊəl/ *a & n* hétérosexuel/-le (*m*/*f*).

**hexagon** /'heksəgən/ *n* hexagone *m*.

**heyday** /'heɪdeɪ/ *n* apogée *m*.

**HGV** *abbr* ⇒HEAVY GOODS VEHICLE.

**hi** /haɪ/ *interj* [I] salut! [I].

**hiccup** /'hɪkʌp/ *n* hoquet *m*; **(the) ~s** le hoquet. ● *vi* hoqueter.

**hide** /haɪd/ *vt* (*pt* **hid**; *pp* **hidden**) cacher (**from** à). ● *vi* se cacher (**from** de); **go into hiding** se cacher. ● *n* (skin) peau *f*.

**hideous** /'hɪdɪəs/ *a* (*monster, object*) hideux; (*noise*) affreux.

**hiding** /'haɪdɪŋ/ *n* **go into ~** se cacher; **give sb a ~** administrer une correction à qn.

**hierarchy** /'haɪərɑ:kɪ/ *n* hiérarchie *f*.

**hi-fi** /haɪ'faɪ/ *n* (chaîne *f*) hi-fi *f inv*.

**high** /haɪ/ *a* haut; (*price, number*) élevé; (*priest, speed*) grand; (*voice*) aigu; **in the ~ season** en pleine saison. ● *n* **a (new) ~** un niveau record. ● *adv* haut. **~brow** *a & n* intellectuel/-le (*m*/*f*). **~ chair** *n* chaise *f* haute. **~ court** *n* cour *f* suprême. **higher education** *n* enseignement *m* supérieur. **~-jump** *n* saut *m* en hauteur. **~-level** *a* à haut niveau.

**highlight** /'haɪlaɪt/ *n* (best moment) point *m* fort; **~s** (in hair) reflet *m*; (artificial) mèches *fpl*; (Sport) résumé *m*. ● *vt* (emphasize) souligner.

**highly** /'haɪlɪ/ *adv* extrêmement; (paid) très bien; **speak/think ~ of** dire/penser beaucoup de bien de.

**Highness** /'haɪnɪs/ *n* Altesse *f*.

**high**: **~-rise** (**building**) *n* tour *f*. **~ school** *n* lycée *m*. **~-speed** *a* (*train*) à grande vitesse; (*film*) ultrarapide. **~ street** *n* rue *f* principale. **~-tech** *a* de pointe.

**highway** /'haɪweɪ/ *n* route *f* nationale; (US) autoroute *f*; **~ code** code *m* de la route.

**hijack** /'haɪdʒæk/ *vt* détourner. ● *n* détournement *m*. **hijacker** *n* pirate *m* (de l'air).

**hike** /haɪk/ *n* randonnée *f*; **price ~** hausse *f* de prix. ● *vi* faire de la randonnée.

**hilarious** /hɪ'leərɪəs/ *a* désopilant.

**hill** /hɪl/ *n* colline *f*; (slope) côte *f*. **hilly** *a* vallonné.

**him** /hɪm/ *pron* le, l'; (indirect object) lui; **it's ~** c'est lui; **for ~** pour lui.

**himself** /hɪm'self/ *pron* (emphatic) lui-même; (reflexive) se; **proud of ~** fier de lui; **by ~** tout seul.

**hind** /haɪnd/ *a* de derrière.

**hinder** /'hɪndə(r)/ *vt* (hamper) gêner; (prevent) empêcher.

**hindsight** /'haɪndsaɪt/ *n* **with ~** rétrospectivement.

**Hindu** /hɪn'du:/ *n* Hindou/-e *m/f*. ● *a* hindou.

**hinge** /hɪndʒ/ *n* charnière *f*. ● *vi* **~ on** dépendre de.

**hint** /hɪnt/ *n* allusion *f*; (of spice, accent) pointe *f*; (of colour) touche *f*; (advice) conseil *m*. ● *vt* laisser entendre. ● *vi* **~ at** faire allusion à.

**hip** /hɪp/ *n* hanche *f*.

**hippopotamus** /hɪpə'pɒtəməs/ *n* (*pl* **~es**) hippopotame *m*.

**hire** /'haɪə(r)/ *vt* (*thing*) louer; (*person*) engager. ● *n* location *f*. **~-car** *n* voiture *f* de location. **~-purchase** *n* achat *m* à crédit.

**his** /hɪz/ *a* son, sa, *pl* ses. ● *pron* le sien, la sienne, les sien(ne)s; **it is ~** c'est à lui *or* le sien *or* la sienne.

**hiss** /hɪs/ *n* sifflement *m*. ● *vt/i* siffler.

**history** /'hɪstərɪ/ *n* histoire *f*; **make ~** entrer dans l'histoire.

**hit** /hɪt/ *vt* (*pt* **hit**; *pres p* **hitting**) frapper; (collide with) heurter; (find) trouver; (affect, reach) toucher. ● *vi* **~ on** (find) tomber sur; **~ it off** s'entendre bien (**with** avec). ● *n* (blow) coup *m*; (fig) succès *m*; (song) tube *m* Ⓘ; (on Internet) (visit) visite *f*, accès *m*; (result) page *f* trouvée, résultat *m*.

**hitch** /hɪtʃ/ *vt* (fasten) accrocher; **~ up** remonter. ● *n* (snag) anicroche *f*. **~-hike** *vi* faire du stop Ⓘ. **~-hiker** *n* auto-stoppeur/-euse *m/f*.

**hi-tech** /haɪ'tek/ *a & n* = HIGH-TECH.

**hitherto** /hɪðə'tu:/ *adv* jusqu'ici.

**HIV** *abbr* (**human immunodeficiency virus**) VIH *m*.

**hive** /haɪv/ *n* ruche *f*. ● *vt* **~ off** séparer; (*industry*) céder.

**HIV-positive** *a* séropositif.

**hoard** /hɔ:d/ *vt* amasser; (*supplies*) stocker. ● *n* trésor *m*; (of provisions) provisions *fpl*.

**hoarse** /hɔ:s/ *a* enroué.

**hoax** /həʊks/ *n* canular *m*.

**hobby** /'hɒbɪ/ *n* passe-temps *m inv*.

**hockey** /'hɒkɪ/ *n* hockey *m*.

**hog** /hɒg/ *n* cochon *m*. ● *vt* (*pt* **hogged**) Ⓘ monopoliser.

**hold** /həʊld/ *vt* (*pt* **held**) tenir; (contain) contenir; (*conversation, opinion*) avoir; (*shares, record, person*) détenir; **~ (the line), please** ne quittez pas. ● *vi* (*rope, weather*) tenir. ● *n* prise *f*; **get ~ of** attraper; (*ticket*) se procurer; (*person*) (by phone) joindre; **on ~** en attente. □ **~ back** (contain) retenir; (hide) cacher; **~ down** (*job*) garder; (*person*) tenir; (*costs*) limiter; **~ on** (stand firm) tenir bon; (wait) attendre; **~ on to** (keep) garder; (cling to) se cramponner à; **~ out** *vt* (offer) offrir; *vi* (resist) tenir le coup; **~ up** (support) soutenir; (delay) retarder; (rob) attaquer.

**holder** /'həʊldə(r)/ *n* détenteur/-trice *m/f*; (of passport, post) titulaire *mf*; (for object) support *m*.

**hold-up** *n* retard *m*; (of traffic) embouteillage *m*; (robbery) hold-up *m inv*.

**hole** /həʊl/ *n* trou *m*.

**holiday** /'hɒlədeɪ/ *n* vacances *fpl*; (public) jour *m* férié; (time off) congé *m*. ● *vi* passer ses vacances. ● *a* de vacances. **~-maker** *n* vacancier/-ière *m/f*.

**Holland** /'hɒlənd/ *n* Hollande *f*.

**hollow** /ˈhɒləʊ/ *a* creux; (fig) faux. ● *n* creux *m*. ● *vt* creuser.

**holly** /ˈhɒlɪ/ *n* houx *m*.

**holy** /ˈhəʊlɪ/ *a* (**-ier**, **-iest**) saint; (water) bénit; **H~ Ghost, H~ Spirit** Saint-Esprit *m*.

**homage** /ˈhɒmɪdʒ/ *n* hommage *m*.

**home** /həʊm/ *n* (place to live) logement *m*; maison *f*; (institution) maison *f*; (family base) foyer *m*; (country) pays *m*. ● *a* de la maison, du foyer; (of family) de famille; (Pol) intérieur; (*match, visit*) à domicile. ● *adv* **(at) ~** à la maison, chez soi; **come** *or* **go ~** rentrer; (from abroad) rentrer dans son pays; **feel at ~ with** être à l'aise avec. **~ computer** *n* ordinateur *m*, PC *m*.

**homeless** /ˈhəʊmlɪs/ *a* sans abri. ● *n* **the ~** les sans-abri *mpl*.

**homely** /ˈhəʊmlɪ/ *a* (**-ier**, **-iest**) (cosy) accueillant; (simple) sans prétention; (person: US) sans attraits.

**home**: **~-made** *a* (fait) maison. **H~ Office** *n* ministère *m* de l'Intérieur. **~ page** *n* (Internet) page *f* d'accueil. **H~ Secretary** *n* Ministre *m* de l'Intérieur. **~sick** *a* **be ~sick** avoir le mal du pays. **~work** *n* devoirs *mpl*.

**homosexual** /hɒməˈsekʃʊəl/ *a* & *n* homosexuel/-le (*m*/*f*).

**honest** /ˈɒnɪst/ *a* (truthful) intègre; (trustworthy) honnête; (sincere) franc. **honestly** *adv* honnêtement; franchement. **honesty** *n* honnêteté *f*.

**honey** /ˈhʌnɪ/ *n* miel *m*; (person Ⓘ) chéri/-e *m*/*f*. **~moon** *n* voyage *m* de noces; (fig) lune *f* de miel.

**honk** /hɒŋk/ *vi* klaxonner.

**honorary** /ˈɒnərərɪ/ *a* (*person*) honoraire; (*degree*) honorifique.

**honour**, (US) **honor** /ˈɒnə(r)/ *n* honneur *m*. ● *vt* honorer.

**hood** /hʊd/ *n* capuchon *m*; (on car, pram) capote *f*; (car engine cover: US) capot *m*.

**hoof** /hu:f/ *n* (*pl* **~s**) sabot *m*.

**hook** /hʊk/ *n* crochet *m*; (on garment) agrafe *f*; (for fishing) hameçon *m*; **off the ~** tiré d'affaire; (phone) décroché. ● *vt* accrocher.

**hoot** /hu:t/ *n* (of owl) (h)ululement *m*; (of car) coup *m* de klaxon. ● *vi* (*owl*) (h)ululer; (*car*) klaxonner; (jeer) huer.

**hoover** /ˈhuvə(r)/ *vt* **~ a room** passer l'aspirateur dans une pièce.

**Hoover**® /ˈhu:və(r)/ *n* aspirateur *m*.

**hop** /hɒp/ *vi* (*pt* **hopped**) sauter (à cloche-pied); **~ in!** Ⓘ vas-y, monte! ● *n* bond *m*; **~s** houblon *m*.

**hope** /həʊp/ *n* espoir *m*. ● *vt*/*i* espérer; **~ for** espérer avoir; **I ~ so** je l'espère.

**hopeful** /ˈhəʊpfl/ *a* (*news, sign*) encourageant; (*person*) plein d'espoir; (*mood*) optimiste. **hopefully** *adv* (with luck) avec un peu de chance; (with hope) avec optimisme.

**hopeless** /ˈhəʊplɪs/ *a* désespéré; (useless: fig) nul Ⓘ.

**horizon** /həˈraɪzn/ *n* horizon *m*.

**horizontal** /hɒrɪˈzɒntl/ *a* horizontal.

**hormone** /ˈhɔ:məʊn/ *n* hormone *f*.

**horn** /hɔ:n/ *n* corne *f*; (of car) klaxon® *m*; (Mus) cor *m*.

**horoscope** /ˈhɒrəskəʊp/ *n* horoscope *m*.

**horrible** /ˈhɒrəbl/ *a* horrible.

**horrid** /ˈhɒrɪd/ *a* horrible.

**horrific** /həˈrɪfɪk/ *a* horrifiant.

**horrify** /ˈhɒrɪfaɪ/ *vt* horrifier.

**horror** /ˈhɒrə(r)/ *n* horreur *f*. ● *a* (*film, story*) d'épouvante.

**horse** /hɔ:s/ *n* cheval *m*. **~back** *n* **on ~back** à cheval. **~-chestnut** *n*

marron *m* (d'Inde). **~man** *n* (*pl* **-men**) cavalier *m*. **~power** *n* puissance *f* (en chevaux). **~-race** *n* course *f* de chevaux. **~-radish** *n* raifort *m*. **~shoe** *n* fer *m* à cheval. **~show** *n* concours *m* hippique.

**hose** /həʊz/ *n* tuyau *m*. ● *vt* arroser. **~-pipe** *n* tuyau *m*.

**hospitable** /hɒ'spɪtəbl/ *a* hospitalier.

**hospital** /'hɒspɪtl/ *n* hôpital *m*.

**host** /həʊst/ *n* (to guests) hôte *m*; (on TV) animateur *m*, (Internet) ordinateur *m* hôte; **a ~ of** une foule de; (Relig) hostie *f*.

**hostage** /'hɒstɪdʒ/ *n* otage *m*; **hold sb ~** garder qn en otage.

**hostel** /'hɒstl/ *n* foyer *m*; **(youth) ~** auberge *f* (de jeunesse).

**hostess** /'həʊstɪs/ *n* hôtesse *f*.

**hostile** /'hɒstaɪl/ *a* hostile.

**hot** /hɒt/ *a* (**hotter**, **hottest**) chaud; (Culin) épicé; **be** *or* **feel ~** avoir chaud; **it is ~** il fait chaud; **in ~ water** ☐ dans le pétrin. ● *vt*/*i* (*pt* **hotted**) **~ up** ☐ chauffer. **~ air balloon** *n* montgolfière *f*. **~ dog** *n* hot-dog *m*.

**hotel** /həʊ'tel/ *n* hôtel *m*.

**hot**: **~headed** *a* impétueux. **~ list** *n* (Internet) signets *mpl* favoris. **~plate** *n* plaque *f* chauffante. **~ water bottle** *n* bouillotte *f*.

**hound** /haʊnd/ *n* chien *m* de chasse. ● *vt* poursuivre.

**hour** /'aʊə(r)/ *n* heure *f*.

**hourly** /'aʊəlɪ/ *a* horaire; **on an ~ basis** à l'heure. ● *adv* toutes les heures.

**house¹** /haʊs/ *n* maison *f*; (Pol) Chambre *f*; **on the ~** aux frais de la maison.

**house²** /haʊz/ *vt* loger; (of building) abriter.

**household** /'haʊshəʊld/ *n* (house, family) ménage *m*. ● *a* ménager.

**house**: **~keeper** *n* gouvernante *f*. **~-proud** *a* méticuleux. **~-warming** *n* pendaison *f* de crémaillère. **~wife** *n* (*pl* **-wives**) ménagère *f*. **~work** *n* travaux *mpl* ménagers.

**housing** /'haʊzɪŋ/ *n* logement *m*; **~ association** service *m* de logement; **~ development** cité *f*; (smaller) lotissement *m*.

**hover** /'hɒvə(r)/ *vi* (*bird*) voleter; (vacillate) vaciller. **hovercraft** *n* aéroglisseur *m*.

**how** /haʊ/ *adv* comment; **~ are you?** comment allez-vous?; **~ long/tall is...?** quelle est la longueur/hauteur de...?; **~ many?**, **~ much?** combien?; **~ pretty!** comme *or* que c'est joli!; **~ about a walk?** si on faisait une promenade?; **~ do you do?** (greeting) enchanté.

**however** /haʊ'evə(r)/ *adv* (nevertheless) cependant; **~ hard I try** j'ai beau essayer; **~ much it costs** quel que soit le prix; **~ young/poor he is** si jeune/pauvre soit-il; **~ you like** comme tu veux.

**howl** /haʊl/ *n* hurlement *m*. ● *vi* hurler.

**HP** *abbr* ⇒HIRE-PURCHASE.

**hp** *abbr* ⇒HORSEPOWER.

**HQ** *abbr* ⇒HEADQUARTERS.

**hub** /hʌb/ *n* moyeu *m*; (fig) centre *m*.

**hug** /hʌg/ *vt* (*pt* **hugged**) serrer dans ses bras. ● *n* étreinte *f*; **give sb a ~** serrer qn dans ses bras.

**huge** /hju:dʒ/ *a* énorme.

**hull** /hʌl/ *n* (of ship) coque *f*.

**hum** /hʌm/ *vt*/*i* (*pt* **hummed**) (*person*) fredonner; (*insect*) bourdonner; (*engine*) ronronner. ● *n* bourdonnement *m*; ronronnement *m*.

**human** /'hju:mən/ *a* humain. ● *n* humain *m*. ~ **being** *n* être *m* humain.

**humane** /hju:'meɪn/ *a* (*person*) humain; (*act*) d'humanité; (*killing*) sans cruauté.

**humanitarian** /hju:mænɪ'teərɪən/ *a* humanitaire.

**humanity** /hju:'mænətɪ/ *n* humanité *f*.

**humble** /'hʌmbl/ *a* humble.

**humid** /'hju:mɪd/ *a* humide.

**humiliate** /hju:'mɪlɪeɪt/ *vt* humilier.

**humorous** /'hju:mərəs/ *a* humoristique; (*person*) plein d'humour.

**humour**, (US) **humor** /'hju:mə(r)/ *n* humour *m*; (mood) humeur *f*. ● *vt* amadouer.

**hump** /hʌmp/ *n* bosse *f*. ● *vt* 🄸 porter.

**hunchback** /'hʌntʃbæk/ *n* bossu/-e *m/f*.

**hundred** /'hʌndrəd/ *a* & *n* cent (*m*); **two** ~ **and one** deux cent un; ~**s of** des centaines de. **hundredth** *a* & *n* centième (*mf*).

**hung** /hʌŋ/ ⇒HANG.

**Hungarian** /hʌŋ'geərɪən/ *n* (person) Hongrois/-e *m/f*; (Ling) hongrois *m*. ● *a* hongrois. **Hungary** *n* Hongrie *f*.

**hunger** /'hʌŋgə(r)/ *n* faim *f*. ● *vi* ~ **for** avoir faim de.

**hungry** /'hʌŋgrɪ/ *a* (**-ier**, **-iest**) affamé; **be** ~ avoir faim.

**hunt** /hʌnt/ *vt/i* chasser; ~ **for** chercher. ● *n* chasse *f*. **hunter** *n* chasseur *m*. **hunting** *n* chasse *f*.

**hurdle** /'hɜ:dl/ *n* (Sport) haie *f*; (fig) obstacle *m*.

**hurricane** /'hʌrɪkən/ *n* ouragan *m*.

**hurry** /'hʌrɪ/ *vi* se dépêcher; ~ **out** sortir précipitamment. ● *vt* (*work*) terminer à la hâte; (*person*) bousculer. ● *n* hâte *f*; **in a** ~ pressé.

**hurt** /hɜ:t/ *vt/i* (*pt* **hurt**) faire mal (à); (injure, offend) blesser. ● *a* blessé. ● *n* blessure *f*.

**hurtle** /'hɜ:tl/ *vi* ~ **down** dévaler; ~ **along a road** foncer sur une route.

**husband** /'hʌzbənd/ *n* mari *m*.

**hush** /hʌʃ/ *vt* faire taire; ~ **up** (*news*) étouffer. ● *n* silence *m*. ● *interj* chut!

**husky** /'hʌskɪ/ *a* (**-ier**, **-iest**) enroué. ● *n* husky *m*.

**hustle** /'hʌsl/ *vt* (push, rush) bousculer. ● *vi* (hurry) se dépêcher; (work: US) se démener. ● *n* ~ **and bustle** agitation *f*.

**hut** /hʌt/ *n* cabane *f*.

**hyacinth** /'haɪəsɪnθ/ *n* jacinthe *f*.

**hydrant** /'haɪdrənt/ *n* (**fire**) ~ bouche *f* d'incendie.

**hydraulic** /haɪ'drɔ:lɪk/ *a* hydraulique.

**hydroelectric** /haɪdrəʊɪ'lektrɪk/ *a* hydroélectrique.

**hydrogen** /'haɪdrədʒən/ *n* hydrogène *m*; ~ **bomb** bombe *f* à hydrogène.

**hyena** /haɪ'i:nə/ *n* hyène *f*.

**hygiene** /'haɪdʒi:n/ *n* hygiène *f*. **hygienic** *a* hygiénique.

**hymn** /hɪm/ *n* cantique *m*; (fig) hymne *m*.

**hype** /haɪp/ *n* 🄸 battage *m* publicitaire. ● *vt* ~ **(up)** (*film, book*) faire du battage pour.

**hyperactive** /haɪpər'æktɪv/ *a* hyperactif.

**hyperlink** /'haɪpərlɪnk/ *n* hyperlien *m*.

**hypermarket** /'haɪpəmɑ:kɪt/ *n* hypermarché *m*.

**hypertext** /'haɪpətekst/ *n* hypertexte *m*.

**hyphen** /ˈhaɪfn/ *n* trait *m* d'union.

**hypnosis** /hɪpˈnəʊsɪs/ *n* hypnose *f*.

**hypocrisy** /hɪˈpɒkrəsɪ/ *n* hypocrisie *f*. **hypocrite** *n* hypocrite *mf*. **hypocritical** *a* hypocrite.

**hypothesis** /haɪˈpɒθəsɪs/ *n* (*pl* **-ses**) hypothèse *f*.

**hysteria** /hɪˈstɪərɪə/ *n* hystérie *f*. **hysterical** *a* hystérique.

**hysterics** /hɪˈsterɪks/ *npl* crise *f* de nerfs; **be in ~** rire aux larmes.

**I** /aɪ/ *pron* je, j'; (stressed) moi.

**ice** /aɪs/ *n* glace *f*; (on road) verglas *m*. ● *vt* (*cake*) glacer. ● *vi* **~ (up)** (*window*) se givrer, (*river*) geler. **~box** *n* (US) réfrigérateur *m*. **~-cream** *n* glace *f*. **~-cube** *n* glaçon *m*. **~ hockey** *n* hockey *m* sur glace.

**Iceland** /ˈaɪslənd/ *n* Islande *f*. **Icelander** *n* Islandais/-e *m/f*. **Icelandic** *a* & *n* islandais (*m*).

**ice**: **~ lolly** *n* glace *f* (*sur bâtonnet*). **~ rink** *n* patinoire *f*. **~ skate** *n* patin *m* à glace.

**icicle** /ˈaɪsɪkl/ *n* stalactite *f* (de glace).

**icing** /ˈaɪsɪŋ/ *n* (sugar) glaçage *m*.

**icy** /ˈaɪsɪ/ *a* (**-ier**, **-iest**) (*hands, wind*) glacé; (*road*) verglacé; (*manner, welcome*) glacial.

**ID** *n* pièce *f* d'identité; **~ card** carte *f* d'identité.

**idea** /aɪˈdɪə/ *n* idée *f*.

**ideal** /aɪˈdɪəl/ *a* idéal. ● *n* idéal *m*.

**identical** /aɪˈdentɪkl/ *a* identique.

**identification** /aɪdentɪfɪˈkeɪʃn/ *n* identification *f*; (papers) pièce *f* d'identité.

**identify** /aɪˈdentɪfaɪ/ *vt* identifier. ● *vi* **~ with** s'identifier à.

**identikit** /aɪˈdentɪkɪt/ *n* **~ picture** portrait-robot *m*.

**identity** /aɪˈdentətɪ/ *n* identité *f*.

**ideological** /aɪdɪəˈlɒdʒɪkl/ *a* idéologique.

**idiom** /ˈɪdɪəm/ *n* (phrase) idiome *m*; (language) parler *m*, langue *f*. **idiomatic** *a* idiomatique.

**idiosyncrasy** /ɪdɪəˈsɪŋkrəsɪ/ *n* particularité *f*.

**idiot** /ˈɪdɪət/ *n* idiot/-e *m/f*. **idiotic** *a* idiot.

**idle** /ˈaɪdl/ *a* (lazy) paresseux; (doing nothing) oisif; (*boast, threat*) vain. ● *vi* (*engine*) tourner au ralenti. ● *vt* **~ away** gaspiller.

**idol** /ˈaɪdl/ *n* idole *f*. **idolize** *vt* idolâtrer.

**idyllic** /ɪˈdɪlɪk/ *a* idyllique.

**i.e.** *abbr* c-à-d, c'est-à-dire.

**if** /ɪf/ *conj* si.

**ignite** /ɪɡˈnaɪt/ *vt/i* (s')enflammer.

**ignition** /ɪɡˈnɪʃn/ *n* (Auto) allumage *m*; **~ (switch)** contact *m*; **~ key** clé *f* de contact.

**ignorance** /ˈɪɡnərəns/ *n* ignorance *f*. **ignorant** *a* ignorant (of de). **ignorantly** *adv* par ignorance.

**ignore** /ɪɡˈnɔː(r)/ *vt* (*person*) ignorer; (*mistake, remark*) ne pas relever; (*feeling, fact*) ne pas tenir compte de.

**ill** /ɪl/ *a* malade. ● *adv* mal. ● *n* mal *m*. **~-advised** *a* malavisé. **~ at ease** *a* mal à l'aise. **~-bred** *a* mal élevé.

**illegal** /ɪˈliːɡl/ *a* illégal.

**illegible** /ɪˈledʒəbl/ *a* illisible.

**illegitimate** /ɪlɪ'dʒɪtɪmət/ *a* illégitime.

**ill**: **~-fated** *a* malheureux. **~ feeling** *n* ressentiment *m*.

**illiterate** /ɪ'lɪtərət/ *a & n* analphabète (*mf*).

**illness** /'ɪlnɪs/ *n* maladie *f*.

**ill-treat** *vt* maltraiter.

**illuminate** /ɪ'lu:mɪneɪt/ *vt* éclairer; (decorate with lights) illuminer. **illumination** *n* éclairage *m*.

**illusion** /ɪ'lu:ʒn/ *n* illusion *f*.

**illustrate** /'ɪləstreɪt/ *vt* illustrer. **illustration** *n* illustration *f*. **illustrative** *a* qui illustre.

**image** /'ɪmɪdʒ/ *n* image *f*; (of firm, person) image *f* de marque. **imagery** *n* images *fpl*.

**imaginable** /ɪ'mædʒɪnəbl/ *a* imaginable. **imaginary** *a* imaginaire. **imagination** *n* imagination *f*. **imaginative** *a* plein d'imagination.

**imagine** /ɪ'mædʒɪn/ *vt* (s')imaginer (**that** que); **~ being rich** s'imaginer riche.

**imbalance** /ɪm'bæləns/ *n* déséquilibre *m*.

**imitate** /'ɪmɪteɪt/ *vt* imiter.

**immaculate** /ɪ'mækjʊlət/ *a* impeccable.

**immaterial** /ɪmə'tɪərɪəl/ *a* sans importance (**to** pour; **that** que).

**immature** /ɪmə'tjʊə(r)/ *a* (*person*) immature; (*plant*) qui n'est pas arrivé à maturité.

**immediate** /ɪ'mi:dɪət/ *a* immédiat.

**immediately** /ɪ'mi:dɪətlɪ/ *adv* immédiatement. ● *conj* dès que.

**immense** /ɪ'mens/ *a* immense. **immensely** *adv* extrêmement, immensément.

**immerse** /ɪ'mɜ:s/ *vt* plonger (**in** dans). **immersion** *n* immersion *f*; **immersion heater** chauffe-eau *m inv* électrique.

**immigrant** /'ɪmɪgrənt/ *n & a* immigré/-e (*m/f*); (newly-arrived) immigrant/-e (*m/f*). **immigrate** *vi* immigrer. **immigration** *n* immigration *f*.

**imminent** /'ɪmɪnənt/ *a* imminent.

**immobilizer** /ɪ'məʊbɪlaizə(r)/ *n* système *m* antidémarrage.

**immoral** /ɪ'mɒrəl/ *a* immoral.

**immortal** /ɪ'mɔ:tl/ *a* immortel.

**immune** /ɪ'mju:n/ *a* immunisé (**from, to** contre); (*reaction, system*) immunitaire. **immunity** *n* immunité *f*. **immunization** *n* immunisation *f*. **immunize** *vt* immuniser.

**impact** /'ɪmpækt/ *n* impact *m*.

**impair** /ɪm'peə(r)/ *vt* (*performance*) affecter; (*ability*) affaiblir.

**impart** /ɪm'pɑ:t/ *vt* communiquer, transmettre.

**impartial** /ɪm'pɑ:ʃl/ *a* impartial.

**impassable** /ɪm'pɑ:səbl/ *a* (*barrier*) infranchissable; (*road*) impraticable.

**impassive** /ɪm'pæsɪv/ *a* impassible.

**impatience** /ɪm'peɪʃns/ *n* impatience *f*. **impatient** *a* impatient; **get impatient** s'impatienter. **impatiently** *adv* impatiemment.

**impeccable** /ɪm'pekəbl/ *a* impeccable.

**impede** /ɪm'pi:d/ *vt* entraver.

**impediment** /ɪm'pedɪmənt/ *n* entrave *f*; **speech ~** défaut *m* d'élocution.

**impending** /ɪm'pendɪŋ/ *a* imminent.

**imperative** /ɪm'perətɪv/ *a* urgent. ● *n* impératif *m*.

**imperfect** /ɪm'pɜ:fɪkt/ *a* incomplet; (faulty) défectueux. ● *n* (Gram)

imparfait *m*. **imperfection** *n* imperfection *f*.

**imperial** /ɪm'pɪərɪəl/ *a* impérial; (measure) conforme aux normes britanniques. **imperialism** *n* impérialisme *m*.

**impersonal** /ɪm'pɜ:sənl/ *a* impersonnel.

**impersonate** /ɪm'pɜ:səneɪt/ *vt* se faire passer pour; (mimic) imiter.

**impertinent** /ɪm'pɜ:tɪnənt/ *a* impertinent.

**impervious** /ɪm'pɜ:vɪəs/ *a* imperméable (to à).

**impetuous** /ɪm'petʃʊəs/ *a* impétueux.

**impetus** /'ɪmpɪtəs/ *n* impulsion *f*.

**impinge** /ɪm'pɪndʒ/ *vi* ~ **on** affecter; (encroach) empiéter sur.

**implement** /'ɪmplɪmənt/ *n* instrument *m*; (tool) outil *m*. ● *vt* exécuter, mettre en application; (*software*) implanter.

**implicit** /ɪm'plɪsɪt/ *a* (implied) implicite (in dans); (unquestioning) absolu.

**imply** /ɪm'plaɪ/ *vt* (assume, mean) impliquer; (insinuate) laisser entendre.

**impolite** /ɪmpə'laɪt/ *a* impoli.

**import**[1] /ɪm'pɔ:t/ *vt* importer.

**import**[2] /'ɪmpɔ:t/ *n* (*article*) importation *f*; (*meaning*) signification *f*.

**importance** /ɪm'pɔ:tns/ *n* importance *f*. **important** *a* important.

**impose** /ɪm'pəʊz/ *vt* imposer (**on sb** à qn; **on sth** sur qch). ● *vi* s'imposer; ~ **on sb** abuser de la bienveillance de qn. **imposing** *a* imposant. **imposition** *n* dérangement *m*; (tax) imposition *f*.

**impossible** /ɪm'pɒsəbl/ *a* impossible. ● *n* **the** ~ l'impossible *m*.

**impotent** /'ɪmpətənt/ *a* impuissant.

**impound** /ɪm'paʊnd/ *vt* confisquer, saisir.

**impoverish** /ɪm'pɒvərɪʃ/ *vt* appauvrir.

**impractical** /ɪm'præktɪkl/ *a* peu réaliste.

**impregnable** /ɪm'pregnəbl/ *a* imprenable.

**impress** /ɪm'pres/ *vt* impressionner; ~ **sth on sb** faire bien comprendre qch à qn. **impression** *n* impression *f*. **impressionable** *a* impressionnable. **impressive** *a* impressionnant.

**imprint**[1] /'ɪmprɪnt/ *n* empreinte *f*.

**imprint**[2] /ɪm'prɪnt/ *vt* (fix) graver (on dans); (print) imprimer.

**imprison** /ɪm'prɪzn/ *vt* emprisonner.

**improbable** /ɪm'prɒbəbl/ *a* (not likely) improbable; (incredible) invraisemblable.

**improper** /ɪm'prɒpə(r)/ *a* (unseemly) malséant; (dishonest) irrégulier.

**improve** /ɪm'pru:v/ *vt*/*i* (s')améliorer. **improvement** *n* amélioration *f*.

**improvise** /'ɪmprəvaɪz/ *vt*/*i* improviser.

**impudent** /'ɪmpjʊdənt/ *a* impudent.

**impulse** /'ɪmpʌls/ *n* impulsion *f*; **on** ~ sur un coup de tête. **impulsive** *a* impulsif. **impulsively** *adv* par impulsion.

**impurity** /ɪm'pjʊərətɪ/ *n* impureté *f*.

**in** /ɪn/ *prep* (inside, within) dans; (expressing place, position) à, en; (expressing time) en, dans; ~ **the box/garden** dans la boîte/le jardin; ~ **Paris/school** à Paris/l'école; ~ **town** en ville; ~ **the country** à la campagne; ~ **English** en anglais; ~ **India** en Inde; ~ **Japan** au Japon; ~ **winter** en hiver; ~ **spring** au printemps;

~ **an hour** (at end of) au bout d'une heure, ~ **an hour('s time)** dans une heure; ~ **(the space of) an hour** en une heure; ~ **doing** en faisant; ~ **the evening** le soir; **one** ~ **ten** un sur dix; ~ **between** entre les deux; (time) entretemps; ~ **a firm voice** d'une voix ferme; ~ **blue** en bleu; ~ **ink** à l'encre; ~ **uniform** en uniforme; ~ **a skirt** en jupe; ~ **a whisper** en chuchotant; ~ **a loud voice** d'une voix forte; **the best** ~ le meilleur de; **we are** ~ **for** on va avoir; **have it** ~ **for sb** 🄸 avoir qn dans le collimateur. ● *adv* (inside) dedans; (at home) là, à la maison; (in fashion) à la mode; **come** ~ entrer; **run** ~ entrer en courant.

**inability** /ɪnəˈbɪlətɪ/ *n* incapacité *f* (**to do** de faire).

**inaccessible** /ɪnækˈsesəbl/ *a* inaccessible.

**inaccurate** /ɪnˈækjərət/ *a* inexact.

**inactive** /ɪnˈæktɪv/ *a* inactif. **inactivity** *n* inaction *f*.

**inadequate** /ɪnˈædɪkwət/ *a* insuffisant.

**inadvertently** /ɪnədˈvɜːtəntlɪ/ *adv* par mégarde.

**inadvisable** /ɪnədˈvaɪzəbl/ *a* inopportun, à déconseiller.

**inane** /ɪˈneɪn/ *a* idiot, débile.

**inanimate** /ɪnˈænɪmət/ *a* inanimé.

**inappropriate** /ɪnəˈprəʊprɪət/ *a* inopportun; (*term*) inapproprié.

**inarticulate** /ɪnɑːˈtɪkjʊlət/ *a* qui a du mal à s'exprimer.

**inasmuch as** /ɪnəzˈmʌtʃəz/ *adv* dans la mesure où; (because) vu que.

**inaugurate** /ɪˈnɔːgjʊreɪt/ *vt* (open, begin) inaugurer; (*person*) investir.

**inborn** /ɪnˈbɔːn/ *a* inné.

**inbred** /ɪnˈbred/ *a* (inborn) inné.

**Inc.** *abbr* (**incorporated**) S.A.

**incapable** /ɪnˈkeɪpəbl/ *a* incapable (**of doing** de faire).

**incapacitate** /ɪnkəˈpæsɪteɪt/ *vt* immobiliser.

**incense¹** /ˈɪnsens/ *n* encens *m*.

**incense²** /ɪnˈsens/ *vt* mettre en fureur.

**incentive** /ɪnˈsentɪv/ *n* motivation *f*; (payment) prime *f*.

**incessant** /ɪnˈsesnt/ *a* incessant. **incessantly** *adv* sans cesse.

**incest** /ˈɪnsest/ *n* inceste *m*. **incestuous** *a* incestueux.

**inch** /ɪntʃ/ *n* pouce *m* (=*2.54 cm.*). ● *vi* ~ **towards** se diriger petit à petit vers.

**incidence** /ˈɪnsɪdəns/ *n* fréquence *f*.

**incident** /ˈɪnsɪdənt/ *n* incident *m*. **incidental** *a* secondaire. **incidentally** *adv* à propos; (by chance) par la même occasion.

**incinerate** /ɪnˈsɪnəreɪt/ *vt* incinérer. **incinerator** *n* incinérateur *m*.

**incite** /ɪnˈsaɪt/ *vt* inciter, pousser.

**inclination** /ɪnklɪˈneɪʃn/ *n* (tendency) tendance *f*; (desire) envie *f*.

**incline¹** /ɪnˈklaɪn/ *vt*/*i* (s')incliner; **be** ~**d to** avoir tendance à.

**incline²** /ˈɪnklaɪn/ *n* pente *f*.

**include** /ɪnˈkluːd/ *vt* comprendre, inclure. **including** *prep* (y) compris. **inclusion** *n* inclusion *f*.

**inclusive** /ɪnˈkluːsɪv/ *a & adv* inclus; ~ **of delivery** livraison comprise.

**income** /ˈɪnkʌm/ *n* revenus *mpl*; ~ **tax** impôt *m* sur le revenu.

**incoming** /ˈɪnkʌmɪŋ/ *a* (*tide*) montant; (*tenant, government*) nouveau; (*call*) qui vient de l'extérieur.

**incompatible** /ɪnkəm'pætəbl/ *a* incompatible.

**incompetent** /ɪn'kɒmpɪtənt/ *a* incompétent.

**incomplete** /ɪnkəm'pli:t/ *a* incomplet.

**incomprehensible** /ɪnkɒmprɪ'hensəbl/ *a* incompréhensible.

**inconceivable** /ɪnkən'si:vəbl/ *a* inconcevable.

**inconclusive** /ɪnkən'klu:sɪv/ *a* peu concluant.

**incongruous** /ɪn'kɒŋgrʊəs/ *a* déconcertant, surprenant.

**inconsiderate** /ɪnkən'sɪdərət/ *a* (*person*) peu attentif à autrui; (*act*) maladroit.

**inconsistent** /ɪnkən'sɪstənt/ *a* (*argument*) incohérent; (*performance*) inégal; (*behaviour*) changeant; ~ **with** en contradiction avec.

**inconspicuous** /ɪnkən'spɪkjʊəs/ *a* qui passe inaperçu.

**incontinent** /ɪn'kɒntɪnənt/ *a* incontinent.

**inconvenience** /ɪnkən'vi:nɪəns/ *n* dérangement *m*; (drawback) inconvénient *m* ● *vt* déranger. **inconvenient** *a* incommode; **if it's not inconvenient for you** *si* cela ne vous dérange pas.

**incorporate** /ɪn'kɔ:pəreɪt/ *vt* incorporer (**into** dans); (contain) comporter.

**incorrect** /ɪnkə'rekt/ *a* incorrect.

**increase¹** /'ɪnkri:s/ *n* augmentation *f* (**in, of** de); **be on the** ~ être en progression.

**increase²** /ɪn'kri:s/ *vt/i* augmenter. **increasing** *a* croissant. **increasingly** *adv* de plus en plus.

**incredible** /ɪn'kredəbl/ *a* incroyable.

**incriminate** /ɪn'krɪmɪneɪt/ *vt* incriminer. **incriminating** *a* compromettant.

**incubate** /'ɪnkjʊbeɪt/ *vt* (eggs) couver. **incubation** *n* incubation *f*. **incubator** *n* couveuse *f*.

**incur** /ɪn'kɜ:(r)/ *vt* (*pt* **incurred**) (*penalty, anger*) encourir; (*debts*) contracter.

**indebted** /ɪn'detɪd/ *a* ~ **to sb** redevable à qn (**for** de); (grateful) reconnaissant à qn.

**indecent** /ɪn'di:snt/ *a* indécent.

**indecisive** /ɪndɪ'saɪsɪv/ *a* indécis; (ending) peu concluant.

**indeed** /ɪn'di:d/ *adv* en effet; (emphatic) vraiment.

**indefinite** /ɪn'defɪnɪt/ *a* vague; (period, delay) illimité. **indefinitely** *adv* indéfiniment.

**indelible** /ɪn'deləbl/ *a* indélébile.

**indemnity** /ɪn'demnətɪ/ *n* (protection) assurance *f*; (payment) indemnité *f*.

**indent** /ɪn'dent/ *vt* (text) renfoncer. **indentation** *n* (dent) marque *f*.

**independence** /ɪndɪ'pendəns/ *n* indépendance *f*. **independent** *a* indépendant. **independently** *adv* de façon indépendante; **independently of** indépendamment de.

**index** /'ɪndeks/ *n* (*pl* ~**es**) (in book) index *m*; (in library) catalogue *m*; (in economy) indice *m*; ~ **card** fiche *f*; ~ **(finger)** index *m*. ● *vt* classer. ~**-linked** *a* indexé.

**India** /'ɪndɪə/ *n* Inde *f*.

**Indian** /'ɪndɪən/ *n* Indien/-ne *m/f*. ● *a* indien.

**indicate** /'ɪndɪkeɪt/ *vt* indiquer. **indication** *n* indication *f*.

**indicative** /ɪn'dɪkətɪv/ *a* & *n* indicatif (*m*).

**indicator** /ˈɪndɪkeɪtə(r)/ *n* (pointer) aiguille *f*; (on vehicle) clignotant *m*; (board) tableau *m*.

**indict** /ɪnˈdaɪt/ *vt* inculper. **indictment** *n* accusation *f*.

**indifferent** /ɪnˈdɪfrənt/ *a* indifférent; (not good) médiocre.

**indigenous** /ɪnˈdɪdʒɪnəs/ *a* indigène.

**indigestible** /ɪndɪˈdʒestəbl/ *a* indigeste. **indigestion** *n* indigestion *f*.

**indignant** /ɪnˈdɪgnənt/ *a* indigné.

**indirect** /ɪndɪˈrekt/ *a* indirect. **indirectly** *adv* indirectement.

**indiscreet** /ɪndɪˈskri:t/ *a* indiscret. **indiscretion** *n* indiscrétion *f*.

**indiscriminate** /ɪndɪˈskrɪmɪnət/ *a* sans distinction. **indiscriminately** *adv* sans distinction.

**indisputable** /ɪndɪˈspju:təbl/ *a* indiscutable.

**individual** /ɪndɪˈvɪdʒʊəl/ *a* individuel; (*tuition*) particulier. ● *n* individu *m*. **individualist** *n* individualiste *mf*. **individuality** *n* individualité *f*. **individually** *adv* individuellement.

**indoctrinate** /ɪnˈdɒktrɪneɪt/ *vt* endoctriner. **indoctrination** *n* endoctrinement *m*.

**indolent** /ˈɪndələnt/ *a* indolent.

**Indonesia** /ɪndəʊˈni:zɪə/ *n* Indonésie *f*.

**indoor** /ˈɪndɔ:(r)/ *a* (*clothes*) d'intérieur; (pool, court) couvert. **indoors** *adv* à l'intérieur.

**induce** /ɪnˈdju:s/ *vt* (influence) persuader; (stronger) inciter (**to do** à faire). **inducement** *n* (financial) récompense *f*; (incentive) motivation *f*.

**induction** /ɪnˈdʌkʃn/ *n* (Electr) induction *f*; (inauguration) installation *f*.

**indulge** /ɪnˈdʌldʒ/ *vt* (*person, whim*) céder à; (*child*) gâter. ● *vi* ~ **in** se livrer à. **indulgence** *n* indulgence *f*; (treat) plaisir *m*. **indulgent** *a* indulgent.

**industrial** /ɪnˈdʌstrɪəl/ *a* industriel; (accident) du travail; ~ **action** grève *f*; ~ **dispute** conflit *m* social. **industrialist** *n* industriel/-le *m/f*. **industrialized** *a* industrialisé.

**industrious** /ɪnˈdʌstrɪəs/ *a* diligent.

**industry** /ˈɪndəstrɪ/ *n* industrie *f*; (zeal) zèle *m*.

**inebriated** /ɪˈni:brɪeɪtɪd/ *a* ivre.

**inedible** /ɪnˈedɪbl/ *a* immangeable.

**ineffective** /ɪnɪˈfektɪv/ *a* inefficace.

**inefficient** /ɪnɪˈfɪʃnt/ *a* inefficace; (person) incompétent.

**ineligible** /ɪnˈelɪdʒəbl/ *a* inéligible; **be** ~ **for** ne pas avoir droit à.

**inept** /ɪˈnept/ *a* incompétent; (tactless) maladroit.

**inequality** /ɪnɪˈkwɒlətɪ/ *n* inégalité *f*.

**inescapable** /ɪnɪˈskeɪpəbl/ *a* indéniable.

**inevitable** /ɪnˈevɪtəbl/ *a* inévitable.

**inexcusable** /ɪnɪkˈskju:zəbl/ *a* inexcusable.

**inexhaustible** /ɪnɪgˈzɔ:stəbl/ *a* inépuisable.

**inexpensive** /ɪnɪkˈspensɪv/ *a* pas cher.

**inexperience** /ɪnɪkˈspɪərɪəns/ *n* inexpérience *f*. **inexperienced** *a* inexpérimenté.

**infallible** /ɪnˈfæləbl/ *a* infaillible.

**infamous** /ˈɪnfəməs/ *a* (*person*) tristement célèbre; (*deed*) infâme.

**infancy** /ˈɪnfənsɪ/ *n* petite enfance *f*; **in its** ~ (fig) à ses débuts *mpl*.

**infant** *n* (baby) bébé *m*; (at school) enfant *m*. **infantile** *a* infantile.

**infatuated** /ɪn'fætʃʊeɪtɪd/ *a* ~ with entiché de. **infatuation** *n* engouement *m*.

**infect** /ɪn'fekt/ *vt* contaminer; ~ sb with sth transmettre qch à qn. **infection** *n* infection *f*. **infectious** *a* contagieux.

**infer** /ɪn'fɜ:(r)/ *vt* (*pt* **inferred**) (deduce) déduire.

**inferior** /ɪn'fɪərɪə(r)/ *a* inférieur (to à); (*work, product*) de qualité inférieure. ● *n* inférieur/-e *m/f*. **inferiority** *n* infériorité *f*.

**inferno** /ɪn'fɜ:nəʊ/ *n* (hell) enfer *m*; (blaze) brasier *m*.

**infertile** /ɪn'fɜ:taɪl/ *a* infertile.

**infest** /ɪn'fest/ *vt* infester (with de).

**infidelity** /ɪnfɪ'delətɪ/ *n* infidélité *f*.

**infighting** /'ɪnfaɪtɪŋ/ *n* conflits *mpl* internes.

**infinite** /'ɪnfɪnət/ *a* infini. **infinitely** *adv* infiniment. **infinitive** *n* infinitif *m*. **infinity** *n* infinité *f*.

**infirm** /ɪn'fɜ:m/ *a* infirme. **infirmary** *n* hôpital *m*; (sick-bay) infirmerie *f*. **infirmity** *n* infirmité *f*.

**inflame** /ɪn'fleɪm/ *vt* enflammer. **inflammable** *a* inflammable. **inflammation** *n* inflammation *f*. **inflammatory** *a* incendiaire.

**inflatable** /ɪn'fleɪtəbl/ *a* gonflable. **inflate** *vt* (lit, fig) gonfler.

**inflation** /ɪn'fleɪʃn/ *n* inflation *f*.

**inflection** /ɪn'flekʃn/ *n* (of word root) flexion *f*; (of vowel, voice) inflexion *f*.

**inflict** /ɪn'flɪkt/ *vt* infliger (on à).

**influence** /'ɪnflʊəns/ *n* influence *f*; under the ~ (drunk Ⓘ) éméché. ● *vt* (*person*) influencer; (*choice*) influer sur. **influential** *a* (powerful) influent; (*theory, artist*) très suivi.

**influenza** /ɪnflʊ'enzə/ *n* grippe *f*.

**influx** /'ɪnflʌks/ *n* afflux *m*.

**inform** /ɪn'fɔ:m/ *vt* informer (of de); keep ~ed tenir au courant.

**informal** /ɪn'fɔ:ml/ *a* (simple) simple, sans façons; (unofficial) officieux; (colloquial) familier. **informality** *n* simplicité *f*. **informally** *adv* (*dress*) en tenue décontractée; (*speak*) en toute simplicité.

**informant** /ɪn'fɔ:mənt/ *n* indicateur/-trice *m/f*.

**information** /ɪnfə'meɪʃn/ *n* renseignements *mpl*, informations *fpl*; some ~ un renseignement. ~ **superhighway** *n* autoroute *f* de l'information. ~ **technology** *n* informatique *f*.

**informative** /ɪn'fɔ:mətɪv/ *a* (*book*) riche en renseignements; (*visit*) instructif.

**informer** /ɪn'fɔ:mə(r)/ *n* indicateur/-trice *m/f*.

**infrequent** /ɪn'fri:kwənt/ *a* rare.

**infringe** /ɪn'frɪndʒ/ *vt* (*rule*) enfreindre; (*rights*) ne pas respecter. **infringement** *n* infraction *f*.

**infuriate** /ɪn'fjʊərɪeɪt/ *vt* exaspérer.

**ingenuity** /ɪndʒɪ'nju:ətɪ/ *n* ingéniosité *f*

**ingot** /'ɪŋgət/ *n* lingot *m*.

**ingrained** /ɪn'greɪnd/ *a* (*hatred*) enraciné; (*dirt*) bien incrusté

**ingratiate** /ɪn'greɪʃɪeɪt/ *vt* ~ oneself with se faire bien voir de.

**ingredient** /ɪn'gri:dɪənt/ *n* ingrédient *m*.

**inhabit** /ɪn'hæbɪt/ *vt* habiter. **inhabitable** *a* habitable. **inhabitant** *n* habitant/-e *m/f*.

**inhale** /ɪn'heɪl/ *vt* inhaler; (smoke) avaler. **inhaler** *n* inhalateur *m*.

**inherent** /ɪn'hɪərənt/ *a* inhérent (in à). **inherently** *adv* en soi, par sa nature.

**inherit** /ɪn'herɪt/ *vt* hériter de; ~ **sth from sb** hériter qch de qn. **inheritance** *n* héritage *m*.

**inhibit** /ɪn'hɪbɪt/ *vt* (restrain) inhiber; (prevent) entraver.

**inhospitable** /ɪnhɒ'spɪtəbl/ *a* inhospitalier.

**inhuman** /ɪn'hju:mən/ *a* inhumain.

**initial** /ɪ'nɪʃl/ *n* initiale *f*. ● *vt* (*pt* **initialled**) parapher. ● *a* initial.

**initiate** /ɪ'nɪʃɪeɪt/ *vt* (*project*) mettre en œuvre; (*talks*) amorcer; (*person*) initier (**into** à). **initiation** *n* initiation *f*; (start) amorce *f*.

**initiative** /ɪ'nɪʃətɪv/ *n* initiative *f*.

**inject** /ɪn'dʒekt/ *vt* injecter (**into** dans); (*new element*: fig) insuffler (**into** à). **injection** *n* injection *f*, piqûre *f*.

**injure** /'ɪndʒə(r)/ *vt* blesser; (damage) nuire à. **injury** *n* blessure *f*.

**injustice** /ɪn'dʒʌstɪs/ *n* injustice *f*.

**ink** /ɪŋk/ *n* encre *f*.

**inkling** /'ɪŋklɪŋ/ *n* petite idée *f*.

**inland** /'ɪnlənd/ *a* intérieur; **I~ Revenue** service *m* des impôts britannique.

**in-laws** /'ɪnlɔ:z/ *npl* (parents) beaux-parents *mpl*; (family) belle-famille *f*.

**inlay**[1] /ɪn'leɪ/ *vt* (*pt* **inlaid**) incruster (**with** de); (on wood) marqueter.

**inlay**[2] /'ɪnleɪ/ *n* incrustation *f*; (on wood) marqueterie *f*.

**inlet** /'ɪnlet/ *n* bras *m* de mer; (Tech) arrivée *f*.

**inmate** /'ɪnmeɪt/ *n* (of asylum) interné/-e *m/f*; (of prison) détenu/-e *m/f*.

**inn** /ɪn/ *n* auberge *f*.

**innate** /ɪ'neɪt/ *a* inné.

**inner** /'ɪnə(r)/ *a* intérieur; ~ **city** quartiers *mpl* déshérités; ~ **tube** chambre *f* à air.

**innocent** /'ɪnəsnt/ *a* & *n* innocent/-e (*m/f*).

**innocuous** /ɪ'nɒkjʊəs/ *a* inoffensif.

**innovate** /'ɪnəveɪt/ *vi* innover.

**innuendo** /ɪnju:'endəʊ/ *n* (*pl* **~es**) insinuations *fpl*; (sexual) allusions *fpl* grivoises.

**innumerable** /ɪ'nju:mərəbl/ *a* innombrable.

**inoculate** /ɪ'nɒkjʊleɪt/ *vt* vacciner (**against** contre).

**inopportune** /ɪn'ɒpətju:n/ *a* inopportun.

**in-patient** *n* malade *mf* hospitalisé/-e.

**input** /'ɪnpʊt/ *n* (of energy) alimentation *f* (**of** en); (contribution) contribution *f*; (data) données *fpl*; (computer process) saisie *f* des données. ● *vt* (*data*) saisir.

**inquest** /'ɪnkwest/ *n* enquête *f*.

**inquire** /ɪn'kwaɪə(r)/ *vi* se renseigner (**about, into** sur). ● *vt* demander.

**inquiry** /ɪn'kwaɪərɪ/ *n* demande *f* de renseignements; (inquest) enquête *f*.

**inquisitive** /ɪn'kwɪzətɪv/ *a* curieux.

**inroad** /'ɪnrəʊd/ *n* **make ~s into** faire une avancée sur.

**insane** /ɪn'seɪn/ *a* fou; (Jur) aliéné. **insanity** *n* folie *f*; (Jur) aliénation *f* mentale.

**inscribe** /ɪn'skraɪb/ *vt* inscrire. **inscription** *n* inscription *f*.

**inscrutable** /ɪn'skru:təbl/ *a* énigmatique.

**insect** /'ɪnsekt/ *n* insecte *m*. **insecticide** *n* insecticide *m*.

**insecure** /ɪnsɪ'kjʊə(r)/ *a* (*person*) qui manque d'assurance; (job) précaire; (*lock, property*) peu sûr. **insecurity** *n* (of person) manque *m*

d'assurance; (of situation) insécurité *f*.

**insensitive** /ɪn'sensətɪv/ *a* insensible; (*remark*) indélicat.

**inseparable** /ɪn'seprəbl/ *a* inséparable (**from** de).

**insert** /ɪn'sɜ:t/ *vt* insérer (**in** dans).

**in-service** /'ɪnsɜ:vɪs/ *a* (training) continu.

**inshore** /ɪn'ʃɔ:(r)/ *a* côtier.

**inside** /ɪn'saɪd/ *n* intérieur *m*; **~s** ⊡ entrailles *fpl*. ● *a* intérieur. ● *adv* à l'intérieur; **go ~** entrer. ● *prep* à l'intérieur de; (of time) en moins de; **~ out** à l'envers; (thoroughly) à fond.

**insight** /'ɪnsaɪt/ *n* (perception) perspicacité *f*; (idea) aperçu *m*.

**insignia** /ɪn'sɪgnɪə/ *npl* insigne *m*.

**insignificant** /ɪnsɪg'nɪfɪkənt/ *a* (*cost, difference*) négligeable; (*person*) insignifiant.

**insincere** /ɪnsɪn'sɪə(r)/ *a* peu sincère.

**insinuate** /ɪn'sɪnjʊeɪt/ *vt* insinuer.

**insist** /ɪn'sɪst/ *vt/i* insister (**that** pour *que*); **~ on** exiger, **~ on doing** vouloir à *tout* prix faire. **insistence** *n* insistance *f* **insistent** *a* insistant. **insistently** *adv* avec insistance.

**insofar as** /ɪnsəʊ'fɑ:əz/ *adv* dans la mesure où.

**insolent** /'ɪnsələnt/ *a* insolent.

**insolvent** /ɪn'sɒlvənt/ *a* insolvable.

**insomnia** /ɪn'sɒmnɪə/ *n* insomnie *f*. **insomniac** *n* insomniaque *mf*.

**inspect** /ɪn'spekt/ *vt* (*school, machinery*) inspecter; (*tickets*) contrôler. **inspection** *n* inspection *f*; (of passport, ticket) contrôle *m*. **inspector** *n* inspecteur/-trice *m/f*; (on bus) contrôleur/-euse *m/f*.

**inspiration** /ɪnspə'reɪʃn/ *n* inspiration *f*. **inspire** *vt* inspirer.

**install** /ɪn'stɔ:l/ *vt* installer.

**instalment** /ɪn'stɔ:lmənt/ *n* (payment) versement *m*; (of serial) épisode *m*.

**instance** /'ɪnstəns/ *n* exemple *m*; (case) cas *m*; **for ~** par exemple; **in the first ~** en premier lieu.

**instant** /'ɪnstənt/ *a* immédiat; (*food*) instantané. ● *n* instant *m*. **instantaneous** *a* instantané. **instantly** *adv* immédiatement.

**instead** /ɪn'sted/ *adv* plutôt; **~ of doing** au lieu de faire; **~ of sb** à la place de qn.

**instep** /'ɪnstep/ *n* cou-de-pied *m*.

**instigate** /'ɪnstɪgeɪt/ *vt* (*attack*) lancer; (*proceedings*) engager.

**instil** /ɪn'stɪl/ *vt* (*pt* **instilled**) inculquer; (*fear*) insuffler.

**instinct** /'ɪnstɪŋkt/ *n* instinct *m*. **instinctive** *a* instinctif.

**institute** /'ɪnstɪtju:t/ *n* institut *m*. ● *vt* instituer; (*proceedings*) engager. **institution** *n* institution *f*; (school, hospital) établissement *m*.

**instruct** /ɪn'strʌkt/ *vt* (teach) instruire; (order) ordonner; **~ sb in sth** enseigner qch à qn; **~ sb to do** donner l'ordre à qn de faire. **instruction** *n* instruction *f*. **instructions** *npl* (for use) mode *m* d'emploi. **instructive** *a* instructif. **instructor** *n* (skiing, driving) moniteur/-trice *m/f*.

**instrument** /'ɪnstrʊmənt/ *n* instrument *m*.

**instrumental** /ɪnstrʊ'mentl/ *a* instrumental; **be ~ in** contribuer à. **instrumentalist** *n* instrumentiste *mf*.

**insubordinate** /ɪnsə'bɔ:dɪnət/ *a* insubordonné.

**insufficient** /ɪnsə'fɪʃnt/ *a* insuffisant.

**insular** /ˈɪnsjʊlə(r)/ *a* (Geog) insulaire; (mind, person: fig) borné.

**insulate** /ˈɪnsjʊleɪt/ *vt* (room, wire) isoler.

**insulin** /ˈɪnsjʊlɪn/ *n* insuline *f*.

**insult**[1] /ɪnˈsʌlt/ *vt* insulter.

**insult**[2] /ˈɪnsʌlt/ *n* insulte *f*.

**insurance** /ɪnˈʃʊərəns/ *n* assurance *f* (**against** contre).

**insure** /ɪnˈʃʊə(r)/ *vt* assurer; ~ **that** (US) s'assurer que.

**intact** /ɪnˈtækt/ *a* intact.

**intake** /ˈɪnteɪk/ *n* (of food) consommation *f*; (School, Univ) admissions *fpl*.

**integral** /ˈɪntɪgrəl/ *a* intégral (**to** à).

**integrate** /ˈɪntɪgreɪt/ *vt/i* (s')intégrer (**with** à; **into** dans).

**integrity** /ɪnˈtegrətɪ/ *n* intégrité *f*.

**intellect** /ˈɪntəlekt/ *n* intelligence *f*. **intellectual** *a* & *n* intellectuel/-le (*m/f*).

**intelligence** /ɪnˈtelɪdʒəns/ *n* intelligence *f*; (Mil) renseignements *mpl*. **intelligent** *a* intelligent. **intelligently** *adv* intelligemment.

**intend** /ɪnˈtend/ *vt* (*outcome*) vouloir; ~ **to do** avoir l'intention de faire. **intended** *a* (*result*) voulu; (*visit*) projeté.

**intense** /ɪnˈtens/ *a* intense; (person) sérieux. **intensely** *adv* (very) extrêmement.

**intensify** /ɪnˈtensɪfaɪ/ *vt/i* (s')intensifier.

**intensive** /ɪnˈtensɪv/ *a* intensif; **in ~ care** en réanimation.

**intent** /ɪnˈtent/ *n* intention *f*. ● *a* absorbé; ~ **on doing** résolu à faire.

**intention** /ɪnˈtenʃn/ *n* intention *f*. **intentional** *a* intentionnel.

**intently** /ɪnˈtentlɪ/ *adv* attentivement.

**interact** /ɪntəˈrækt/ *vi* (*factors*) agir l'un sur l'autre; (*people*) communiquer. **interactive** *a* (*TV, video*) interactif.

**intercept** /ɪntəˈsept/ *vt* intercepter.

**interchange** /ˈɪntətʃeɪndʒ/ *n* (road junction) échangeur *m*; (exchange) échange *m*.

**interchangeable** /ɪntəˈtʃeɪndʒəbl/ *a* interchangeable.

**intercom** /ˈɪntəkɒm/ *n* interphone® *m*.

**interconnected** /ɪntəkəˈnektɪd/ *a* (*parts*) raccordé; (*problems*) lié.

**intercourse** /ˈɪntəkɔ:s/ *n* rapports *mpl*.

**interest** /ˈɪntrəst/ *n* intérêt *m*; ~ **rate** taux *m* d'intérêt. ● *vt* intéresser (**in** à). **interested** *a* intéressé; **be ~ed in** s'intéresser à. **interesting** *a* intéressant.

**interfere** /ɪntəˈfɪə(r)/ *vi* se mêler des affaires des autres; ~ **in** se mêler de; ~ **with** (*freedom*) empiéter sur; (tamper with) toucher. **interference** *n* ingérence *f*; (sound, light waves) brouillage *m*; (radio) parasites *mpl*.

**interim** /ˈɪntərɪm/ *n* **in the ~** entretemps. ● *a* (*government*) provisoire; (*payment*) intermédiaire.

**interior** /ɪnˈtɪərɪə(r)/ *n* intérieur *m*. ● *a* intérieur.

**interjection** /ɪntəˈdʒekʃn/ *n* interjection *f*.

**interlock** /ɪntəˈlɒk/ *vt/i* (Tech) (s')emboîter, (s')enclencher.

**interlude** /ˈɪntəlu:d/ *n* intervalle *m*; (Theat, Mus) intermède *m*.

**intermediary** /ɪntəˈmi:dɪərɪ/ *a* & *n* intermédiaire (*mf*).

**intermediate** /ɪntəˈmi:dɪət/ *a* intermédiaire; (*exam, level*) moyen.

**intermission** /ɪntəˈmɪʃn/ *n* (Theat) entracte *m*.

**intermittent** /ɪntəˈmɪtnt/ *a* intermittent.

**intern¹** /ɪnˈtɜːn/ *vt* interner.

**intern²** /ˈɪntɜːn/ *n* (US) stagiaire *mf*; (Med) interne *mf*.

**internal** /ɪnˈtɜːnl/ *a* interne; (domestic: Pol) intérieur; **I~ Revenue** (US) service *m* des impôts américain.

**international** /ɪntəˈnæʃnəl/ *a* international.

**Internet** /ˈɪntənet/ *n* Internet *m*; **on the ~** sur Internet; **~ access** accès à Internet; **~ service provider** fournisseur *m* d'accès Internet.

**interpret** /ɪnˈtɜːprɪt/ *vt* interpréter (**as** comme). ● *vi* faire l'interprète. **interpretation** *n* interprétation *f*. **interpretor** *n* interprète *mf*.

**interrelated** /ɪntərɪˈleɪtɪd/ *a* interdépendant, lié.

**interrogate** /ɪnˈterəgeɪt/ *vt* interroger. **interrogative** *a* & *n* (Ling) interrogatif (*m*).

**interrupt** /ɪntəˈrʌpt/ *vt*/*i* interrompre. **interruption** *n* interruption *f*.

**intersect** /ɪntəˈsekt/ *vt*/*i* (lines, roads) (se) croiser. **intersection** *n* intersection *f*.

**interspersed** /ɪntəˈspɜːst/ *a* parsemé (**with** de).

**intertwine** /ɪntəˈtwaɪn/ *vt*/*i* (s')entrelacer.

**interval** /ˈɪntəvl/ *n* intervalle *m*; (Theat) entracte *m*.

**intervene** /ɪntəˈviːn/ *vi* intervenir; (of time) s'écouler (**between** entre); (happen) arriver.

**interview** /ˈɪntəvjuː/ *n* (for job) entretien *m*; (by a journalist) interview *f*. ● *vt* (*candidate*) faire passer un entretien à; (*celebrity*) interviewer.

**intestine** /ɪnˈtestɪn/ *n* intestin *m*.

**intimacy** /ˈɪntɪməsɪ/ *n* intimité *f*.

**intimate¹** /ˈɪntɪmeɪt/ *vt* (state) annoncer; (hint) laisser entendre.

**intimate²** /ˈɪntɪmət/ *a* intime. **intimately** *adv* intimement.

**intimidate** /ɪnˈtɪmɪdeɪt/ *vt* intimider.

**into** /ˈɪntuː, ˈɪntə/ *prep* (put, go, fall) dans; (divide, translate, change) en; **be ~ jazz** être fana du jazz [I]; **8 ~ 24 is 3** 24 divisé par 8 égale 3.

**intolerant** /ɪnˈtɒlərənt/ *a* intolérant.

**intonation** /ɪntəˈneɪʃn/ *n* intonation *f*.

**intoxicate** /ɪnˈtɒksɪkeɪt/ *vt* enivrer. **intoxicated** *a* ivre. **intoxication** *n* ivresse *f*.

**intractable** /ɪnˈtræktəbl/ *a* (*person*) intraitable; (*problem*) rebelle.

**Intranet** /ˈɪntrənet/ *n* (Comput) Intranet *m*.

**intransitive** /ɪnˈtrænsətɪv/ *a* intransitif.

**intravenous** /ɪntrəˈviːnəs/ *a* (Med) intraveineux.

**intricate** /ˈɪntrɪkət/ *a* complexe.

**intrigue** /ɪnˈtriːg/ *vt* intriguer. ● *n* intrigue *f*. **intriguing** *a* fascinant; (curious) curieux.

**intrinsic** /ɪnˈtrɪnsɪk/ *a* intrinsèque (**to** *à*).

**introduce** /ɪntrəˈdjuːs/ *vt* (*person, idea, programme*) présenter; (*object, law*) introduire (**into** *dans*). **introduction** *n* introduction *f*; (of person) présentation *f*. **introductory** *a* (words) préliminaire.

**introvert** /ˈɪntrəvɜːt/ *n* introverti/-e *m*/*f*.

**intrude** /ɪnˈtruːd/ *vi* (person) s'imposer (**on sb** à qn), déranger. **intruder** *n* intrus/-e *m*/*f*.

**intrusion** *n* intrusion *f*.

**intuition** /ɪntju:'ɪʃn/ *n* intuition *f*. **intuitive** *a* intuitif.

**inundate** /'ɪnʌndeɪt/ *vt* inonder (with de).

**invade** /ɪn'veɪd/ *vt* envahir.

**invalid**[1] /'ɪnvəlɪd/ *n* malade *mf*; (disabled) infirme *mf*.

**invalid**[2] /ɪn'vælɪd/ *a* (*passport*) pas valable; (*claim*) sans fondement. **invalidate** *vt* (*argument*) infirmer; (*claim*) annuler.

**invaluable** /ɪn'væljʊəbl/ *a* inestimable.

**invariable** /ɪn'veərɪəbl/ *a* invariable. **invariably** *adv* invariablement.

**invasion** /ɪn'veɪʒn/ *n* invasion *f*.

**invent** /ɪn'vent/ *vt* inventer. **invention** *n* invention *f*. **inventive** *a* inventif. **inventor** *n* inventeur/-trice *m/f*.

**inventory** /'ɪnvəntrɪ/ *n* inventaire *m*.

**invert** /ɪn'vɜ:t/ *vt* (*order*) intervertir; (*image, values*) renverser; **~ed commas** guillemets *mpl*.

**invest** /ɪn'vest/ *vt* investir; (time, effort) consacrer. ● *vi* faire un investissement; **~ in** (buy) s'acheter.

**investigate** /ɪn'vestɪgeɪt/ *vt* examiner; (*crime*) enquêter sur. **investigation** *n* investigation *f*. **investigator** *n* (police) enquêteur/-euse *m/f*.

**investment** /ɪn'vestmənt/ *n* investissement *m*; **emotional ~** engagement *m* personnel. **investor** *n* investisseur/-euse *m/f*; (in shares) actionnaire *mf*.

**invigilate** /ɪn'vɪdʒɪleɪt/ *vi* (*exam*) surveiller. **invigilator** *n* surveillant/-e *m/f*.

**invigorate** /ɪn'vɪgəreɪt/ *vt* revigorer.

**invisible** /ɪn'vɪzəbl/ *a* invisible.

**invitation** /ɪnvɪ'teɪʃn/ *n* invitation *f*. **invite** *vt* inviter; (ask for) demander. **inviting** *a* engageant.

**invoice** /'ɪnvɔɪs/ *n* facture *f*. ● *vt* facturer.

**involuntary** /ɪn'vɒləntrɪ/ *a* involontaire.

**involve** /ɪn'vɒlv/ *vt* impliquer; (*person*) faire participer (**in** à). **involved** *a* (complex) compliqué; (at stake) en jeu; **be ~d in** (*work*) participer à; (*crime*) être mêlé à. **involvement** *n* participation *f* (**in** à).

**inward** /'ɪnwəd/ *a* (*feeling*) intérieur. **inwardly** *adv* intérieurement. **inwards** *adv* vers l'intérieur.

**iodine** /'aɪədi:n/ *n* iode *m*; (antiseptic) teinture *f* d'iode.

**iota** /aɪ'əʊtə/ *n* iota *m*; **not one ~ of** pas un grain de.

**IOU** *abbr* (**I owe you**) reconnaissance *f* de dette.

**IQ** *abbr* (**intelligence quotient**) QI *m*.

**Iran** /ɪ'rɑ:n/ *n* Iran *m*.

**Iraq** /ɪ'rɑ:k/ *n* Irak *m*.

**irate** /aɪ'reɪt/ *a* furieux.

**IRC** *abbrev* (**Internet Relay Chat**) (Internet) conversation *f* IRC.

**Ireland** /'aɪələnd/ *n* Irlande *f*.

**Irish** /'aɪərɪʃ/ *n & a* irlandais (*m*). **~man** *n* Irlandais *m*. **~woman** *n* Irlandaise *f*.

**iron** /'aɪən/ *n* fer *m*; (appliance) fer *m* (à repasser). ● *a* (*will*) de fer; (*bar*) en fer. ● *vt* repasser; **~ out** (fig) aplanir.

**ironic(al)** /aɪ'rɒnɪk(l)/ *a* ironique.

**iron**: **ironing-board** *n* planche *f* à repasser. **~monger** *n* quincaillier *m*.

**irony** /'aɪərənɪ/ *n* ironie *f*.

**irrational** /ɪ'ræʃənl/ *a* irrationnel; (person) pas raisonnable.

**irregular** /ɪ'regjʊlə(r)/ *a* irrégulier.

**irrelevant** /ɪ'reləvənt/ *a* hors de propos.

**irreplaceable** /ɪrɪ'pleɪsəbl/ *a* irremplaçable.

**irresistible** /ɪrɪ'zɪstəbl/ *a* irrésistible.

**irrespective** /ɪrɪ'spektɪv/ *a* ~ **of** sans tenir compte de.

**irresponsible** /ɪrɪ'spɒnsəbl/ *a* irresponsable.

**irreverent** /ɪ'revərənt/ *a* irrévérencieux.

**irreversible** /ɪrɪ'vɜ:səbl/ *a* irréversible.

**irrigate** /'ɪrɪgeɪt/ *vt* irriguer.

**irritable** /'ɪrɪtəbl/ *a* irritable.

**irritate** /'ɪrɪteɪt/ *vt* irriter. **irritating** *a* irritant.

**is** /ɪz/ ⇒BE.

**ISDN** *abbr* (integrated services digital network) RNIS *m*, réseau *m* numérique à intégration de services.

**Islam** /'ɪzlɑ:m/ *n* (faith) Islam *m*; (Muslims) Islam *m*. **Islamic** *a* islamique.

**island** /'aɪlənd/ *n* île *f*.

**isle** /aɪl/ *n* île *f*.

**isolate** /'aɪsəleɪt/ *vt* isoler. **isolation** *n* isolement *m*.

**Israel** /'ɪzreɪl/ *n* Israël *m*.

**Israeli** /ɪz'reɪlɪ/ *n* Israélien/-ne *m*/*f*. ● *a* israélien.

**issue** /'ɪʃu:/ *n* question *f*; (outcome) résultat *m*; (of magazine) numéro *m*; (of stamps) émission *f*; (offspring) descendance *f*; **at** ~ en cause. ● *vt* distribuer; (stamps) émettre; (*book*) publier; (*order*) délivrer. ● *vi* ~ **from** provenir de.

**it** /ɪt/

● *pronoun*

⋯➤ (subject) il, elle; **'where's the book/chair?'—'~'s in the kitchen'** 'où est le livre/la chaise?'—'il/elle est dans la cuisine'.

⋯➤ (object) le, la, l'; **~'s my book and I want ~** c'est mon livre et je le veux; **I liked his shirt, did you notice ~?** sa chemise m'a plu, l'as-tu remarquée?; **give ~ to me** donne-le-moi.

⋯➤ (with preposition) **we talked a lot about ~** on en a beaucoup parlé; **Elliott went to ~** Elliott y est allé.

⋯➤ (impersonal) il; **~'s raining** il pleut; **~ will snow** il va neiger.

**IT** *abbr* ⇒INFORMATION TECHNOLOGY.

**Italian** /ɪ'tælɪən/ *n* (person) Italien/-ne *m*/*f*; (Ling) italien *m*. ● *a* italien.

**italics** /ɪ'tælɪks/ *npl* italique *m*.

**Italy** /'ɪtəlɪ/ *n* Italie *f*.

**itch** /ɪtʃ/ *n* démangeaison *f*. ● *vi* démanger; **my arm ~es** j'ai le bras qui me démange; **be ~ing to do** mourir d'envie de faire.

**item** /'aɪtəm/ *n* article *m*; (on agenda) point *m*.

**itemize** /'aɪtəmaɪz/ *vt* détailler; **~d bill** facture *f* détaillée.

**itinerary** /aɪ'tɪnərərɪ/ *n* itinéraire *m*.

**its** /ɪts/ *det* son, sa; *pl* ses.

**it's** /ɪts/ = IT IS, IT HAS.

**itself** /ɪt'self/ *pron* lui-même, elle-même; (reflexive) se.

**ivory** /'aɪvərɪ/ *n* ivoire *m*; **~ tower** tour *f* d'ivoire.

**ivy** /'aɪvɪ/ *n* lierre *m*.

# Jj

**jab** /dʒæb/ *vt* (*pt* **jabbed**) ~ **sth into sth** planter qch dans qch. ● *n* coup *m*; (injection) piqûre *f*.

**jack** /dʒæk/ *n* (Auto) cric *m*; (cards) valet *m*; (Electr) jack *m*. ● *vt* ~ **up** soulever avec un cric.

**jackal** /ˈdʒækɔːl/ *n* chaçal *m*.

**jacket** /ˈdʒækɪt/ *n* veste *f*, veston *m*; (of book) jaquette *f*.

**jack-knife** /ˈdʒæknaɪf/ *n* couteau *m* pliant. ● *vi* (lorry) se mettre en portefeuille.

**jackpot** /ˈdʒækpɒt/ *n* gros lot *m*; **hit the** ~ gagner le gros lot.

**jade** /dʒeɪd/ *n* (stone) jade *m*.

**jaded** /ˈdʒeɪdɪd/ *a* (tired) fatigué; (bored) blasé.

**jagged** /ˈdʒægɪd/ *a* (*rock*) déchiqueté; (*knife*) dentelé.

**jail** /dʒeɪl/ *n* prison *f*. ● *vt* mettre en prison.

**jam** /dʒæm/ *n* confiture *f*; **(traffic)** ~ embouteillage *m*. ● *vt/i* (*pt* **jammed**) (wedge) (se) coincer; (cram) (s')entasser; (*street*) encombrer; (*radio*) brouiller.

**Jamaica** /dʒəˈmeɪkə/ *n* Jamaïque *f*.

**jam-packed** *a* 🄸 bondé; ~ **with** bourré de.

**jangle** /ˈdʒæŋgl/ *n* tintement *m*. ● *vt/i* (faire) tinter.

**janitor** /ˈdʒænɪtə(r)/ *n* (US) gardien *m*.

**January** /ˈdʒænjʊərɪ/ *n* janvier *m*.

**Japan** /dʒəˈpæn/ *n* Japon *m*.

**Japanese** /dʒæpəˈniːʒ/ *n* (person) Japonais/-e *m*/*f*; (Ling) japonais *m*. ● *a* japonais.

**jar** /dʒɑː(r)/ *n* pot *m*, bocal *m*. ● *vi* (*pt* **jarred**) rendre un son discordant; (*colours*) détonner. ● *vt* ébranler.

**jargon** /ˈdʒɑːgən/ *n* jargon *m*.

**jaundice** /ˈdʒɔːndɪs/ *n* jaunisse *f*.

**javelin** /ˈdʒævlɪn/ *n* javelot *m*.

**jaw** /dʒɔː/ *n* mâchoire *f*.

**jay** /dʒeɪ/ *n* geai *m*.

**jazz** /dʒæz/ *n* jazz *m*. ● *vt* ~ **up** (*dress*) rajeunir; (*event*) ranimer.

**jealous** /ˈdʒeləs/ *a* jaloux. **jealousy** *n* jalousie *f*.

**jeans** /dʒiːnz/ *npl* jean *m*.

**jeer** /dʒɪə(r)/ *vt*/*i* ~ **(at)** huer. ● *n* huée *f*.

**jelly** /ˈdʒelɪ/ *n* gelée *f*. ~**fish** *n* méduse *f*.

**jeopardize** /ˈdʒepədaɪz/ *vt* (*career, chance*) compromettre; (*lives*) mettre en péril.

**jerk** /dʒɜːk/ *n* secousse *f*; (fool 🅇) crétin *m* 🄸. ● *vt* tirer brusquement. ● *vi* tressaillir. **jerky** *a* saccadé.

**jersey** /ˈdʒɜːzɪ/ *n* (garment) pull-over *m*; (fabric) jersey *m*.

**jet** /dʒet/ *n* (plane, stream) jet *m*; (mineral) jais *m*; ~ **lag** décalage *m* horaire.

**jettison** /ˈdʒetɪsn/ *vt* jeter par-dessus bord; (Aviat) larguer; (fig) rejeter.

**jetty** /ˈdʒetɪ/ *n* jetée *f*.

**Jew** /dʒuː/ *n* juif/juive *m*/*f*.

**jewel** /ˈdʒuːəl/ *n* bijou *m*. **jeweller** *n* bijoutier/-ière *m*/*f*. **jeweller('s)** *n* (shop) bijouterie *f*. **jewellery** *n* bijoux *mpl*.

**Jewish** /ˈdʒuːɪʃ/ *a* juif.

**jibe** /dʒaɪb/ *n* moquerie *f*.

**jigsaw** /'dʒɪgsɔ:/ *n* puzzle *m*.

**jingle** /'dʒɪŋgl/ *vt/i* (faire) tinter. ● *n* tintement *m*; (advertising) refrain *m* publicitaire, sonal *m*.

**jinx** /dʒɪŋks/ *n* (person) porte-malheur *m inv*; (curse) sort *m*.

**jitters** /'dʒɪtəz/ *npl* **have the ~** 🅘 être nerveux. **jittery** *a* nerveux.

**job** /dʒɒb/ *n* emploi *m*; (post) poste *m*; **out of a ~** sans emploi; **it is a good ~ that** heureusement que; **just the ~** tout à fait ce qu'il faut. **~ centre** *n* bureau *m* des services nationaux de l'emploi. **jobless** *a* sans emploi.

**jockey** /'dʒɒkɪ/ *n* jockey *m*.

**jog** /dʒɒg/ *n* **go for a ~** aller faire un jogging. ● *vt* (*pt* **jogged**) heurter; (*memory*) rafraîchir. ● *vi* faire du jogging. **jogging** *n* jogging *m*.

**join** /dʒɔɪn/ *vt* (attach) réunir, joindre; (*club*) devenir membre de; (*company*) entrer dans; (*army*) s'engager dans; (*queue*) se mettre dans; **~ sb** (in activity) se joindre à qn; (meet) rejoindre qn. ● *vi* (become member) adhérer; (*pieces*) se joindre; (*roads*) se rejoindre. ● *n* raccord *m*. ■ **~ in** participer; **~ in sth** participer à qch; **~ up** (Mil) s'engager; **~ sth up** relier qch. **joiner** *n* menuisier/-ière *m/f*.

**joint** /dʒɔɪnt/ *a* (*action*) collectif; (*measures, venture*) commun; (*winner*) ex aequo *inv*; (*account*) joint; **~ author** coauteur *m*. ● *n* (join) joint *m*; (Anat) articulation *f*; (Culin) rôti *m*; **out of ~** déboîté.

**joke** /dʒəʊk/ *n* plaisanterie *f*; (trick) farce *f*; **it's no ~** ce n'est pas drôle. ● *vi* plaisanter. **joker** *n* blagueur/-euse *m/f*; (cards) joker *m*.

**jolly** /'dʒɒlɪ/ *a* (**-ier, -iest**) (*person*) enjoué; (*tune*) joyeux. ● *adv* 🅘 drôlement.

**jolt** /dʒəʊlt/ *vt* secouer. ● *vi* cahoter. ● *n* secousse *f*; (shock) choc *m*.

**jostle** /'dʒɒsl/ *vt/i* (se) bousculer.

**jot** /dʒɒt/ *vt* (*pt* **jotted**) **~ (down)** noter.

**journal** /'dʒɜ:nl/ *n* journal *m*. **journalism** *n* journalisme *m*. **journalist** *n* journaliste *mf*.

**journey** /'dʒɜ:nɪ/ *n* (trip) voyage *m*; (short or habitual) trajet *m*. ● *vi* voyager.

**joy** /dʒɔɪ/ *n* joie *f*. **joyful** *a* joyeux.

**joy**: **~riding** *n* rodéo *m* à la voiture volée. **~stick** *n* (Comput) manette *f*; (Aviat) manche *m* à balai.

**jubilant** /'dʒu:bɪlənt/ *a* (*person*) exultant; (*mood*) réjoui.

**Judaism** /'dʒu:deɪɪzəm/ *n* judaïsme *m*.

**judge** /dʒʌdʒ/ *n* juge *m*. ● *vt* juger; (*distance*) estimer; **judging by/from** à en juger par. **judg(e)ment** *n* jugement *m*.

**judicial** /dʒu:'dɪʃl/ *a* judiciaire. **judiciary** *n* magistrature *f*.

**judo** /'dʒu:dəʊ/ *n* judo *m*.

**jug** /dʒʌg/ *n* (glass) carafe *f*; (pottery) pichet *m*.

**juggernaut** /'dʒʌgənɔ:t/ *n* (lorry) poids *m* lourd.

**juggle** /'dʒʌgl/ *vt/i* jongler (avec). **juggler** *n* jongleur/-euse *m/f*.

**juice** /dʒu:s/ *n* jus *m*. **juicy** *a* juteux, (*details* 🅘) croustillant.

**jukebox** /'dʒu:kbɒks/ *n* juke-box *m*.

**July** /dʒu:'laɪ/ *n* juillet *m*.

**jumble** /'dʒʌmbl/ *vt* mélanger. ● *n* (of objects) tas *m*; (of ideas) fouillis *m*; **~ sale** vente *f* de charité.

**jumbo** /'dʒʌmbəʊ/ *n* (also **~ jet**) gros-porteur *m*.

**jump** /dʒʌmp/ *vt* sauter; **~ the lights** passer au feu rouge; **~ the queue** passer devant tout le

monde. ● *vi* sauter; (in surprise) sursauter; (*price*) monter en flèche; ~ **at** (*opportunity*) sauter sur. ● *n* saut *m*, bond *m*; (increase) bond *m*.

**jumper** /'dʒʌmpə(r)/ *n* pull(-over) *m*; (dress: US) robe *f* chasuble.

**jump-leads** *npl* câbles *mpl* de démarrage.

**jumpy** /'dʒʌmpɪ/ *a* nerveux.

**junction** /'dʒʌŋkʃn/ *n* (of roads) carrefour *m*; (on motorway) échangeur *m*.

**June** /dʒu:n/ *n* juin *m*.

**jungle** /'dʒʌŋgl/ *n* jungle *f*.

**junior** /'dʒu:nɪə(r)/ *a* (young) jeune; (in rank) subalterne; (school) primaire. ● *n* cadet/-te *m/f*; (School) élève *mf* du primaire.

**junk** /dʒʌŋk/ *n* bric-à-brac *m inv*; (poor quality) camelote *f*; ~ **food** nourriture *f* industrielle.

**junkie** /'dʒʌŋkɪ/ *n* ▣ drogué/-e *m/f*.

**junk**: ~ **mail** *n* prospectus *mpl*. ~**-shop** *n* boutique *f* de bric-à-brac.

**jurisdiction** /dʒʊərɪs'dɪkʃn/ *n* compétence *f*; (Jur) juridiction *f*.

**juror** /'dʒʊərə(r)/ *n* juré *m*.

**jury** /'dʒʊərɪ/ *n* jury *m*.

**just** /dʒʌst/ *a* (fair) juste. ● *adv* (immediately, slightly) juste; (simply) tout simplement; (exactly) exactement; **he has/had** ~ **left** il vient/venait de partir; **have** ~ **missed** avoir manqué de peu; **I'm** ~ **leaving** je suis sur le point de partir; **it's** ~ **a cold** ce n'est qu'un rhume; ~ **as tall/well as** tout aussi grand/bien que; ~ **listen!** écoutez donc!; **it's** ~ **ridiculous** c'est vraiment ridicule.

**justice** /'dʒʌstɪs/ *n* justice *f*; **J**~ **of the Peace** juge *m* de paix.

**justification** /dʒʌstɪfɪ'keɪʃn/ *n* justification *f*. **justify** *vt* justifier.

**jut** /dʒʌt/ *vi* (*pt* **jutted**) ~ **(out)** s'avancer en saillie.

**juvenile** /'dʒu:vənaɪl/ *a* (childish) puéril; (*offender*) mineur; (*delinquent*) jeune. ● *n* jeune *mf*; (Jur) mineur/-e *m/f*.

**juxtapose** /dʒʌkstə'pəʊz/ *vt* juxtaposer.

# Kk

**kangaroo** /kæŋgə'ru:/ *n* kangourou *m*.

**karate** /kə'rɑ:tɪ/ *n* karaté *m*.

**kebab** /kə'bæb/ *n* brochette *f*.

**keel** /ki:l/ *n* (of ship) quille *f*. ● *vi* ~ **over** (*bateau*) chavirer; (*person*) s'écrouler.

**keen** /ki:n/ *a* (*interest, wind, feeling*) vif; (*mind, analysis*) pénétrant; (*edge, appetite*) aiguisé; (eager) enthousiaste; **be** ~ **on** être passionné de; **be** ~ **to do** *or* **on doing** tenir beaucoup à faire. **keenly** *adv* vivement. **keenness** *n* enthousiasme *m*.

**keep** /ki:p/ *vt* (*pt* **kept**) garder; (*promise, shop, diary*) tenir; (*family*) faire vivre; (*animals*) élever; (*rule*) respecter; (celebrate) célébrer; (delay) retenir; ~ **sth clean/warm** garder qch propre/au chaud; ~ **sb in/out** empêcher qn de sortir/d'entrer; ~ **sb from doing** empêcher qn de faire. ● *vi* (*food*) se conserver; ~ **(on)** continuer (**doing** à faire). ● *n* pension *f*; (of castle) donjon *m*. □ ~ **down** rester allongé; ~ **sth down** limiter qch; ~ **your voice down!** baisse la voix!; ~ **to** (*road*) ne pas s'écarter de;

(*rules*) respecter; ~ **up** (*car, runner*) suivre; (*rain*) continuer; ~ **up with sb** (in speed) aller aussi vite que; (*class, inflation, fashion, news*) suivre.

**keeper** /'ki:pə(r)/ *n* gardien/-ne *m/f*.

**keepsake** /'ki:pseɪk/ *n* souvenir *m*.

**kennel** /'kenl/ *n* niche *f*.

**kept** /kept/ ⇒KEEP.

**kerb** /kɜ:b/ *n* bord *m* du trottoir.

**kernel** /'kɜ:nl/ *n* amande *f*; ~ **of truth** fond *m* de vérité.

**kettle** /'ketl/ *n* bouilloire *f*.

**key** /ki:/ *n* clé *f*; (of computer, piano) touche *f* ● *a* (*industry, figure*) clé (*inv*). ● *vt* ~ (in) saisir. ~**board** *n* clavier *m*. ~**hole** *n* trou *m* de serrure. ~**-pad** *n* (of telephone) clavier *m* numérique. ~**-ring** *n* porte-clés *m inv*. ~**stroke** *n* (Comput) frappe *f*.

**khaki** /'kɑ:kɪ/ *a* kaki *inv*.

**kick** /kɪk/ *vt/i* donner un coup de pied (à); (*horse*) botter. ● *n* coup *m* de pied; (of gun) recul *m*; **get a ~ out of doing** [I] prendre plaisir à faire. □ ~ **out** [I] virer [I].

**kick-off** *n* coup *m* d'envoi.

**kid** /kɪd/ *n* (*goat, leather*) chevreau *m*; (child [I]) gosse *mf* [I]. ● *vt/i* (*pt* **kidded**) blaguer.

**kidnap** /'kɪdnæp/ *vt* (*pt* **kidnapped**) enlever. **kidnapping** *n* enlèvement *m*.

**kidney** /'kɪdnɪ/ *n* rein *m*; (Culin) rognon *m*.

**kill** /kɪl/ *vt* tuer; (*rumour*: fig) arrêter. ● *n* mise *f* à mort. **killer** *n* tueur/-euse *m/f*. **killing** *n* meurtre *m*.

**kiln** /kɪln/ *n* four *m*.

**kilo** /'ki:ləʊ/ *n* kilo *m*.

**kilobyte** /'kɪləbaɪt/ *n* kilo-octet *m*.

**kilogram** /'kɪləgræm/ *n* kilogramme *m*.

**kilometre**, (US) **kilometer** /kɪ'lɒmɪtə(r)/ *n* kilomètre *m*.

**kilowatt** /'kɪləwɒt/ *n* kilowatt *m*.

**kin** /kɪn/ *n* parents *mpl*.

**kind** /kaɪnd/ *n* genre *m*, sorte *f*; **in** ~ en nature; ~ **of** (somewhat [I]) assez. ● *a* gentil, bon.

**kindergarten** /'kɪndəgɑ:tn/ *n* jardin *m* d'enfants.

**kindle** /'kɪndl/ *vt/i* (s')allumer.

**kindly** /'kaɪndlɪ/ *a* (**-ier**, **-iest**) (*person*) gentil; (*interest*) bienveillant. ● *adv* avec gentillesse; **would you ~ do** auriez-vous l'amabilité de faire

**kindness** /'kaɪndnɪs/ *n* bonté *f*.

**king** /kɪŋ/ *n* roi *m*. **kingdom** *n* royaume *m*; (Bot) règne *m*. ~**fisher** *n* martin-pêcheur *m*. ~**-size(d)** *a* géant.

**kiosk** /'ki:ɒsk/ *n* kiosque *m*; **telephone ~** cabine *f* téléphonique; (Internet) borne *f* interactive, kiosque *m*.

**kiss** /kɪs/ *n* baiser *m*. ● *vt/i* (s')embrasser.

**kit** /kɪt/ *n* (clothing) affaires *fpl*; (set of tools) trousse *f*; (for assembly) kit *m*. ● *vt* (*pt* **kitted**) ~ **out** équiper.

**kitchen** /'kɪtʃɪn/ *n* cuisine *f*.

**kite** /kaɪt/ *n* (toy) cerf-volant *m*; (bird) milan *m*.

**kitten** /'kɪtn/ *n* chaton *m*.

**kitty** /'kɪtɪ/ *n* (fund) cagnotte *f*.

**knack** /næk/ *n* tour *m* de main (**of doing** pour faire).

**knead** /ni:d/ *vt* pétrir.

**knee** /ni:/ *n* genou *m*. ~**cap** *n* rotule *f*.

**kneel** /ni:l/ *vi* (*pt* **knelt**) ~ **(down)** se mettre à genoux; (in prayer) s'agenouiller.

**knew** /nju:/ ⇒KNOW.

**knickers** /'nɪkəz/ *npl* petite culotte *f*, slip *m*.

**knife** /naɪf/ *n* (*pl* **knives**) couteau *m*. ● *vt* poignarder.

**knight** /naɪt/ *n* chevalier *m*; (chess) cavalier *m*. ● *vt* anoblir. **~hood** *n* titre *m* de chevalier.

**knit** /nɪt/ *vt/i* (*pt* **knitted** *or* **knit**) tricoter; (*bones*) (se) souder. **knitting** *n* tricot *m*. **knitwear** *n* tricots *mpl*.

**knob** /nɒb/ *n* bouton *m*.

**knock** /nɒk/ *vt/i* cogner; (criticize [I]) critiquer; **~ sth off/out** faire tomber qch. ● *n* coup *m*. □ **~ down** (*chair, pedestrian*) renverser; (demolish) abattre; (reduce) baisser; **~ off** (stop work [I]) arrêter de travailler; **~ £10 off** faire une réduction de 10 livres; **~ it off!** [I] ça suffit!; **~ out** assommer; **~ over** renverser; **~ up** (*meal*) préparer en vitesse.

**knock-out** *n* (boxing) knock-out *m*.

**knot** /nɒt/ *n* nœud *m*. ● *vt* (*pt* **knotted**) nouer.

**know** /nəʊ/ *vt/i* (*pt* **knew**; *pp* **known**) (*answer, reason, language*) savoir (**that** que); (*person, place, name, rule, situation*) connaître; (recognize) reconnaître; **~ how to do** savoir faire; **~ about** (*event*) être au courant de; (*subject*) s'y connaître en; **~ of** (from experience) connaître; (from information) avoir entendu parler de. **~-how** *n* savoir-faire *m inv*.

**knowingly** /'nəʊɪŋlɪ/ *adv* (intentionally) délibérément; (meaningfully) d'un air entendu.

**knowledge** /'nɒlɪdʒ/ *n* connaissance *f*; (learning) connaissances *fpl*. **knowledgeable** *a* savant.

**knuckle** /'nʌkl/ *n* jointure *f*, articulation *f*.

**Koran** /kə'rɑ:n/ *n* Coran *m*.

**Korea** /kə'rɪə/ *n* Corée *f*.

**kosher** /'kəʊʃə(r)/ *a* casher *inv*.

# Ll

**lab** /læb/ *n* [I] labo *m*.

**label** /'leɪbl/ *n* étiquette *f*. ● *vt* (*pt* **labelled**) étiqueter.

**laboratory** /lə'bɒrətrɪ/ *n* laboratoire *m*.

**laborious** /lə'bɔ:rɪəs/ *a* laborieux.

**labour**, (US) **labor** /'leɪbə(r)/ *n* travail *m*; (workers) main-d'œuvre *f*; **in ~** en train d'accoucher. ● *vi* peiner (**to do** à faire). ● *vt* trop insister sur.

**Labour** /'leɪbə(r)/ *n* le parti travailliste. ● *a* travailliste.

**laboured** /'leɪbəd/ *a* laborieux.

**labourer** /'leɪbərə(r)/ *n* ouvrier/-ière *m/f*; (on farm) ouvrier/-ière *m/f* agricole.

**lace** /leɪs/ *n* dentelle *f*; (of shoe) lacet *m*. ● *vt* (*shoe*) lacer; (*drink*) arroser.

**lacerate** /'læsəreɪt/ *vt* lacérer.

**lack** /læk/ *n* manque *m*; **for ~ of** faute de. ● *vt* manquer de; **be ~ing** manquer (**in** de).

**lad** /læd/ *n* garçon *m*, gars *m*.

**ladder** /'lædə(r)/ *n* échelle *f*; (in stocking) maille *f* filée. ● *vt/i* (*stocking*) filer.

**laden** /'leɪdn/ *a* chargé (**with** de).

**ladle** /'leɪdl/ *n* louche *f*.

**lady** /'leɪdɪ/ *n* (*pl* **ladies**) dame *f*; **ladies and gentlemen** mesdames et

messieurs; **young** ~ jeune femme *or* fille *f*. ~**bird** *n* coccinelle *f*.

**ladylike** /ˈleɪdɪlaɪk/ *a* distingué.

**lag** /læg/ *vi* (*pt* **lagged**) traîner. ● *vt* (*pipes*) calorifuger. ● *n* (interval) décalage *m*.

**lager** /ˈlɑ:gə(r)/ *n* bière *f* blonde.

**lagoon** /ləˈgu:n/ *n* lagune *f*.

**laid** /leɪd/ ⇒LAY¹. ~ **back** *a* décontracté.

**lain** /leɪn/ ⇒LIE².

**lake** /leɪk/ *n* lac *m*.

**lamb** /læm/ *n* agneau *m*; **leg of** ~ gigot *m* d'agneau.

**lame** /leɪm/ *a* boiteux.

**lament** /ləˈment/ *n* lamentation *f*. ● *vt/i* se lamenter (sur).

**laminated** /ˈlæmɪneɪtɪd/ *a* laminé.

**lamp** /læmp/ *n* lampe *f*. ~**post** *n* réverbère *m*. ~**shade** *n* abat-jour *m inv*.

**lance** /lɑ:ns/ *vt* (Med) inciser.

**land** /lænd/ *n* terre *f*; (plot) terrain *m*; (country) pays *m*. ● *a* terrestre, (*policy, reform*) agraire. ● *vt/i* débarquer; (*aircraft*) (se) poser, (faire) atterrir; (fall) tomber; (obtain) décrocher; (*a blow*) porter; ~ **up** se retrouver.

**landing** /ˈlændɪŋ/ *n* débarquement *m*; (Aviat) atterrissage *m*, (top of stairs) palier *m*. ~**-stage** *n* débarcadère *m*.

**land**~**lady** *n* propriétaire *f*; (of pub) patronne *f*. ~**lord** *n* propriétaire *m*; (of pub) patron *m*. ~**mark** *n* (point de) repère *m*. ~**mine** *n* mine *f* terrestre.

**landscape** /ˈlæn(d)skeɪp/ *n* paysage *m*. ● *vt* aménager.

**landslide** /ˈlændslaɪd/ *n* glissement *m* de terrain; (Pol) raz-de-marée *m inv* (électoral).

**lane** /leɪn/ *n* (path, road) chemin *m*; (strip of road) voie *f*; (of traffic) file *f*; (Aviat) couloir *m*.

**language** /ˈlæŋgwɪdʒ/ *n* langue *f*; (speech, style) langage *m*. ~ **engineering** *n* ingénierie *f* des langues. ~ **laboratory** *n* laboratoire *m* de langue.

**lank** /læŋk/ *a* (*hair*) plat.

**lanky** /ˈlæŋkɪ/ *a* (**-ier, -iest**) grand et maigre.

**lantern** /ˈlæntən/ *n* lanterne *f*.

**lap** /læp/ *n* genoux *mpl*; (Sport) tour *m* (de piste). ● *vi* (*pt* **lapped**) (*waves*) clapoter. □ ~ **up** laper.

**lapel** /ləˈpel/ *n* revers *m*.

**lapse** /læps/ *vi* (decline) se dégrader; (expire) se périmer; ~ **into** retomber dans. ● *n* défaillance *f*, erreur *f*; (of time) intervalle *m*.

**laptop** /ˈlæptɒp/ *n* (Comput) portable *m*.

**lard** /lɑ:d/ *n* saindoux *m*.

**larder** /ˈlɑ:də(r)/ *n* garde-manger *m inv*.

**large** /lɑ:dʒ/ *a* grand, gros; **at** ~ en liberté; **by and** ~ en général. **largely** *adv* en grande mesure.

**lark** /lɑ:k/ *n* (bird) alouette *f*, (bit of fun 🄸) rigolade *f*. ● *vi* 🄸 rigoler.

**larva** /ˈlɑ:və/ *n* (*pl* **-vae** /-vi:/) larve *f*.

**laryngitis** /lærɪnˈdʒaɪtɪs/ *n* laryngite *f*.

**laser** /ˈleɪzə(r)/ *n* laser *m*. ~ **printer** *n* imprimante *f* laser. ~ **treatment** *n* (Med) laserothérapie *f*.

**lash** /læʃ/ *vt* fouetter. ● *n* coup *m* de fouet; (eyelash) cil *m*. □ ~ **out** (spend) dépenser follement; ~ **out against** a[illegible]mer.

**lass** /læs/ *n* jeune [illegible] *f*.

**lasso** /læˈsu:/ *n* lasso *m*.

**last** /lɑ:st/ *a* dernier; **the ~ straw** le comble, **the ~ word** le mot de la fin; **on its ~ legs** sur le point de rendre l'âme; **~ night** hier soir. ● *adv* en dernier; (most recently) la dernière fois. ● *n* dernier/-ière *m/f*; (remainder) reste *m*; **at (long) ~** enfin. ● *vi* durer. **~-ditch** *a* ultime. **lasting** *a* durable. **lastly** *adv* en dernier lieu. **~-minute** *a* de dernière minute.

**latch** /lætʃ/ *n* loquet *m*.

**late** /leɪt/ *a* (not on time) en retard; (former) ancien; (*hour, fruit*) tardif; **the ~ Mrs X** feu Mme X. ● *adv* (not early) tard; (not on time) en retard; **in ~ July** fin juillet; **of ~** dernièrement. **lately** *adv* dernièrement. **latest** *a* ⇒LATE; (last) dernier.

**lathe** /leɪð/ *n* tour *m*.

**lather** /'lɑ:ðə(r)/ *n* mousse *f*. ● *vt* savonner. ● *vi* mousser.

**Latin** /'lætɪn/ *n* (Ling) latin *m*. ● *a* latin. **~ America** *n* Amérique *f* latine.

**latitude** /'lætɪtju:d/ *n* latitude *f*.

**latter** /'lætə(r)/ *a* dernier. ● *n* **the ~** celui-ci, celle-ci.

**Latvia** /'lætvɪə/ *n* Lettonie *f*.

**laudable** /'lɔ:dəbl/ *a* louable.

**laugh** /lɑ:f/ *vi* rire (**at** de). ● *n* rire *m*. **laughable** *a* ridicule.

**laughing stock** *n* risée *f*.

**laughter** /'lɑ:ftə(r)/ *n* (act) rire *m*; (sound of laughs) rires *mpl*.

**launch** /lɔ:ntʃ/ *vt* (*rocket*) lancer; (*boat*) mettre à l'eau; **~ (out) into** se lancer dans. ● *n* lancement *m*; (boat) vedette *f*. **launching pad** *n* aire *f* de lancement

**launderette** /lɔ:n'dret/ *n* laverie *f* automatique.

**laundry** /'lɔ:ndrɪ/ *n* (place) blanchisserie *f*; (clothes) linge *m*.

**laurel** /'lɒrəl/ *n* laurier *m*.

**lava** /'lɑ:və/ *n* lave *f*.

**lavatory** /'lævətrɪ/ *n* toilettes *fpl*.

**lavender** /'lævəndə(r)/ *n* lavande *f*.

**lavish** /'lævɪʃ/ *a* (*person*) généreux; (lush) somptueux. ● *vt* prodiguer (**on** à). **lavishly** *adv* luxueusement.

**law** /lɔ:/ *n* loi *f*; (profession, subject of study) droit *m*; **~ and order** l'ordre public. **~-abiding** *a* respectueux des lois. **~court** *n* tribunal *m*.

**lawful** /'lɔ:fl/ *a* légal.

**lawn** /lɔ:n/ *n* pelouse *f*, gazon *m*. **~-mower** *n* tondeuse *f* à gazon.

**lawsuit** /'lɔ:su:t/ *n* procès *m*.

**lawyer** /'lɔ:jə(r)/ *n* avocat *m*.

**lax** /læks/ *a* (*government*) laxiste; (*security*) relâché.

**laxative** /'læksətɪv/ *n* laxatif *m*.

**lay**[1] /leɪ/ *a* (non-clerical) laïque; (*worker*) non-initié. ● *vt* (*pt* **laid**) poser, mettre; (*trap*) tendre; (*table*) mettre; (*plan*) former; (*eggs*) pondre. ● *vi* pondre; **~ waste** ravager. □ **~ aside** mettre de côté; **~ down** (dé)poser; (condition) (im-)poser; **~ off** *vt* (*worker*) licencier; *vi* 🅸 arrêter; **~ on** (provide) fournir; **~ out** (design) dessiner; (display) disposer; (*money*) dépenser.

**lay**[2] /leɪ/ ⇒LIE[2].

**lay-by** /'leɪbaɪ/ *n* (*pl* **~s**) aire *f* de repos.

**layer** /'leɪə(r)/ *n* couche *f*.

**layman** /'leɪmən/ *n* (*pl* **-men**) profane *m*.

**layout** /'leɪaʊt/ *n* disposition *f*.

**laze** /leɪz/ *vi* paresser. **laziness** *n* paresse *f*. **lazy** *a* (**-ier, -iest**) paresseux.

**lead**[1] /li:d/ *vt/i* (*pt* **led**) mener; (*team*) diriger; (*life*) mener; (induce) amener; **~ to** conduire à, mener à. ● *n* avance *f*; (clue) indice *m*; (leash)

laisse *f*; (Theat) premier rôle *m*; (wire) fil *m*; **in the ~** en tête. □ **~ away** emmener; **~ up to** (come to) en venir à; (precede) précéder.

**lead²** /led/ *n* plomb *m*; (of pencil) mine *f*.

**leader** /'li:də(r)/ *n* chef *m*; (of country, club) dirigeant/-e *m*/*f*; (leading article) éditorial *m*. **leadership** *n* direction *f*.

**lead-free** *a* (*petrol*) sans plomb.

**leading** /'li:dɪŋ/ *a* principal.

**leaf** /li:f/ *n* (*pl* **leaves**) feuille *f*; (of table) rallonge *f*. ● *vi* **~ through** feuilleter.

**leaflet** /'li:flɪt/ *n* prospectus *m*.

**leafy** /'li:fɪ/ *a* feuillu.

**league** /li:g/ *n* ligue *f*; (Sport) championnat *m*; **in ~ with** de mèche avec.

**leak** /li:k/ *n* fuite *f*. ● *vi* fuir; (news: fig) s'ébruiter. ● *vt* répandre; (fig) divulguer.

**lean¹** /li:n/ *a* maigre. ● *n* (of meat) maigre *m*.

**lean²** /li:n/ *vt*/*i* (*pt* **leaned** *or* **leant** /lent/) (rest) (s')appuyer; (slope) pencher. □ **~ out** se pencher à l'extérieur; **~ over** (of person) se pencher.

**leaning** /'li:nɪŋ/ *a* penché. ● *n* tendance *f*.

**leap** /li:p/ *vi* (*pt* **leaped** *or* **leapt** /lept/) bondir. ● *n* bond *m*. **~ year** *n* année *f* bissextile.

**learn** /lɜ:n/ *vt*/*i* (*pt* **learned** *or* **learnt**) apprendre (**to do** à faire). **learned** *a* érudit. **learner** *n* débutant/-e *m*/*f*.

**lease** /li:s/ *n* bail *m*. ● *vt* louer à bail.

**leash** /li:ʃ/ *n* laisse *f*.

**least** /li:st/ *a* **the ~** (smallest amount of) le moins de; (slightest) le *or* la moindre. ● *n* le moins. ● *adv* le moins; (with adjective) le *or* la moins; **at ~** au moins.

**leather** /'leðə(r)/ *n* cuir *m*.

**leave** /li:v/ *vt* (*pt* **left**) laisser; (depart from) quitter; (*person*) laisser tranquille; **be left (over)** rester. ● *n* (holiday) congé *m*; (consent) permission *f*; **take one's ~** prendre congé (of de); **on ~** (Mil) en permission. □ **~ alone** (*thing*) ne pas toucher; (*person*) laisser tranquille; **~ behind** laisser; **~ out** omettre.

**Lebanon** /'lebənən/ *n* Liban *m*.

**lecture** /'lektʃə(r)/ *n* cours *m*, conférence *f*; (rebuke) réprimande *f*. ● *vt*/*i* faire un cours *or* une conférence (à); (rebuke) réprimander. **lecturer** *n* conférencier/-ière *m*/*f*; (Univ) enseignant/-e *m*/*f*.

**led** /led/ ⇨LEAD¹.

**ledge** /ledʒ/ *n* (window) rebord *m*; (rock) saillie *f*.

**ledger** /'ledʒə(r)/ *n* grand livre *m*.

**leech** /li:tʃ/ *n* sangsue *f*.

**leek** /li:k/ *n* poireau *m*.

**leer** /lɪə(r)/ *vi* **~ (at)** lorgner. ● *n* regard *m* sournois.

**leeway** /'li:weɪ/ *n* (fig) liberté *f* d'action; (Naut) dérive *f*.

**left** /left/ ⇨LEAVE. ● *a* gauche. ● *adv* à gauche. ● *n* gauche *f*. **~-hand** *a* à *or* de gauche. **~-handed** *a* gaucher.

**left luggage (office)** *n* consigne *f*.

**left-overs** *npl* restes *mpl*

**left-wing** *a* de gauche

**leg** /leg/ *n* jambe *f*; (of animal) patte *f*; (of table) pied *m*; (of chicken) cuisse *f*; (of lamb) gigot *m*; (of journey) étape *f*.

**legacy** /'legəsɪ/ *n* legs *m*.

**legal** /'li:gl/ *a* légal; (affairs) juridique.

**legend** /'ledʒənd/ *n* légende *f*.

**lock** /lɒk/ *n* (of door) serrure *f*; (on canal) écluse *f*; (of hair) mèche *f*. ● *vt/i* fermer à clef; (wheels: Auto) (se) bloquer. □ ~ **in** *or* **up** (*person*) enfermer; ~ **out** (by mistake) enfermer dehors.

**locker** /'lɒkə(r)/ *n* casier *m*.

**locket** /'lɒkɪt/ *n* médaillon *m*.

**locksmith** /'lɒksmɪθ/ *n* serrurier *m*.

**locum** /'ləʊkəm/ *n* (doctor) remplaçant/-e *m/f*.

**lodge** /lɒdʒ/ *n* (house) pavillon *m* (de gardien *or* de chasse); (of porter) loge *f*. ● *vt* (accommodate) loger; (*money, complaint*) déposer. ● *vi* être logé (**with** chez); (become fixed) se loger. **lodger** *n* locataire *mf*, pensionnaire *mf*. **lodgings** *n* logement *m*.

**loft** /lɒft/ *n* grenier *m*.

**lofty** /'lɒftɪ/ *a* (**-ier**, **-iest**) (tall, noble) élevé; (haughty) hautain.

**log** /lɒg/ *n* (of wood) bûche *f*; ~**(-book)** (Naut) journal *m* de bord; (Auto) ≈ carte *f* grise. ● *vt* (*pt* **logged**) noter; (distance) parcourir. □ ~ **on** (Comput) se connecter; ~ **off** (Comput) se déconnecter.

**logic** /'lɒdʒɪk/ *a* logique. **logical** *a* logique.

**logistics** /lə'dʒɪstɪks/ *n* logistique *f*.

**loin** /lɔɪn/ *n* (Culin) filet *m*; ~**s** reins *mpl*.

**loiter** /'lɔɪtə(r)/ *vi* traîner.

**loll** /lɒl/ *vi* se prélasser.

**lollipop** /'lɒlɪpɒp/ *n* sucette *f*.

**London** /'lʌndən/ *n* Londres. **Londoner** *n* Londonien/-ne *m/f*.

**lone** /ləʊn/ *a* solitaire.

**lonely** /'ləʊnlɪ/ (**-ier**, **-iest**) solitaire; (person) seul, solitaire.

**long** /lɒŋ/ *a* long; **how** ~ **is?** quelle est la longueur de?; (in time) quelle est la durée de?; **how** ~**?** combien de temps?; **a** ~ **time** longtemps. ● *adv* longtemps; **he will not be** ~ il n'en a pas pour longtemps; **as** *or* **so** ~ **as** pourvu que; **before** ~ avant peu; **I no** ~**er do** je ne fais plus. ● *vi* avoir bien *or* très envie (**for**, **to** de); ~ **for sb** (pine for) se languir de qn. ~**-distance** *a* (*flight*) sur long parcours; (*phone call*) interurbain; (*runner*) de fond. ~ **face** *n* grimace *f*. ~**hand** *n* écriture *f* courante.

**longing** /'lɒŋɪŋ/ *n* envie *f* (**for** de); (nostalgia) nostalgie *f* (**for** de).

**longitude** /'lɒndʒɪtju:d/ *n* longitude *f*.

**long**: ~ **jump** *n* saut *m* en longueur. ~**-range** *a* (*missile*) à longue portée; (*forecast*) à long terme. ~**-sighted** *a* presbyte. ~**-standing** *a* de longue date. ~**-term** *a* à long terme. ~ **wave** *n* grandes ondes *fpl*. ~**-winded** *a* verbeux.

**loo** /lu:/ *n* 🅸 toilettes *fpl*.

**look** /lʊk/ *vi* regarder; (seem) avoir l'air; ~ **like** ressembler à, avoir l'air de. ● *n* regard *m*; (appearance) air *m*, aspect *m*; **(good)** ~**s** beauté *f*. □ ~ **after** s'occuper de, soigner; ~ **at** regarder; ~ **back on** repenser à; ~ **down on** mépriser; ~ **for** chercher; ~ **forward to** attendre avec impatience; ~ **in on** passer voir; ~ **into** examiner; ~ **out** faire attention; ~ **out for** (*person*) guetter; (*symptoms*) guetter l'apparition de; ~ **round** se retourner; ~ **up** (*word*) chercher; (visit) passer voir; ~ **up to** respecter.

**look-out** /'lʊkaʊt/ *n* (Mil) poste *m* de guet; (person) guetteur *m*; **be on the** ~ **for** rechercher.

**loom** /lu:m/ *vi* surgir; (*war*) menacer; (*interview*) être imminent. ● *n* métier *m* à tisser.

**loony** /'lu:nɪ/ *n* & *a* 🅸 fou, folle (*mf*).

**loop** /lu:p/ *n* boucle *f*. ● *vt* boucler. **~hole** *n* lacune *f*.

**loose** /lu:s/ *a* (*knot*) desserré; (*page*) détaché; (*clothes*) ample, lâche; (*tooth*) qui bouge; (lax) relâché; (not packed) en vrac; (inexact) vague; (pej) immoral; **at a ~ end** désœuvré; **come ~** bouger. **loosely** *adv* sans serrer; (roughly) vaguement. **loosen** *vt* (slacken) desserrer; (untie) défaire.

**loot** /lu:t/ *n* butin *m*. ● *vt* piller.

**lord** /lɔ:d/ *n* seigneur *m*; (British title) lord *m*; **the L~** le Seigneur.

**lorry** /'lɒrɪ/ *n* camion *m*.

**lose** /lu:z/ *vt/i* (*pt* **lost**) perdre; **get lost** se perdre. **loser** *n* perdant/-e *m/f*.

**loss** /lɒs/ *n* perte *f*; **be at a ~** être perplexe; **be at a ~ to** être incapable de; **heat ~** déperdition *f* de chaleur.

**lost** /lɒst/ ⇨LOSE. ● *a* perdu. **~ property** *n* objets *mpl* trouvés.

**lot** /lɒt/ *n* **the ~** (le) tout *m*; (people) tous *mpl*, toutes *fpl*; **a ~ (of)**, **~s (of)** 🄸 beaucoup (de); **quite a ~ (of)** 🄸 pas mal (de); (fate) sort *m*; (at auction) lot *m*; (land) lotissement *m*.

**lotion** /'ləʊʃn/ *n* lotion *f*.

**lottery** /'lɒtərɪ/ *n* loterie *f*.

**loud** /laʊd/ *a* bruyant, fort. ● *adv* fort; **out ~** tout haut. **loudly** *adv* fort. **~speaker** *n* haut-parleur *m*.

**lounge** /laʊndʒ/ *vi* paresser. ● *n* salon *m*.

**louse** /laʊs/ *n* (*pl* **lice**) pou *m*.

**lousy** /'laʊzɪ/ *a* (**-ier**, **-iest**) 🄸 infect.

**lout** /laʊt/ *n* rustre *m*.

**lovable** /'lʌvəbl/ *a* adorable.

**love** /lʌv/ *n* amour *m*; (tennis) zéro *m*; **in ~** amoureux (**with** de); **make ~** faire l'amour. ● *vt* (*person*) aimer; (like greatly) aimer (beaucoup) (**to do** faire). **~ affair** *n* liaison *f* amoureuse. **~ life** *n* vie *f* amoureuse.

**lovely** /'lʌvlɪ/ *a* (**-ier**, **-iest**) joli; (delightful 🄸) très agréable.

**lover** /'lʌvə(r)/ *n* (male) amant *m*; (female) maîtresse *f*; (devotee) amateur *m* (**of** de).

**loving** /'lʌvɪŋ/ *a* affectueux.

**low** /ləʊ/ *a & adv* bas; **~ in sth** à faible teneur en qch. ● *n* (low pressure) dépression *f*; **reach a (new) ~** atteindre son niveau le plus bas. ● *vi* meugler. **~-calorie** *a* basses-calories. **~-cut** *a* décolleté.

**lower** /'ləʊə(r)/ *a & adv* ⇨LOW. ● *vt* baisser; **~ oneself** s'abaisser.

**low**: **~-fat** *a* (*diet*) sans matières grasses; (*cheese*) allégé. **~-key** *a* modéré; (discreet) discret. **~lands** *npl* plaine(s) *f(pl)*. **~-lying** *a* à faible altitude.

**loyal** /'lɔɪəl/ *a* loyal (**to** envers).

**loyalty** /'lɔɪəltɪ/ *n* fidélité *f*. **~ card** *n* carte *f* de fidélité.

**lozenge** /'lɒzɪndʒ/ *n* (shape) losange *m*; (tablet) pastille *f*.

**Ltd.** *abbr* (**Limited**) SA.

**lubricant** /'lu:brɪkənt/ *n* lubrifiant *m*. **lubricate** *vt* lubrifier.

**luck** /lʌk/ *n* chance *f*; **bad ~** malchance *f*; **good ~!** bonne chance!

**luckily** /'lʌkɪlɪ/ *adv* heureusement.

**lucky** /'lʌkɪ/ *a* (**-ier**, **-iest**) qui a de la chance, heureux; (event) heureux; (number) qui porte bonheur; **it's ~ that** heureusement que.

**ludicrous** /'lu:dɪkrəs/ *a* ridicule.

**lug** /lʌg/ *vt* (*pt* **lugged**) traîner.

**luggage** /'lʌgɪdʒ/ *n* bagages *mpl*. **~-rack** *n* porte-bagages *m inv*.

**lukewarm** /'lu:kwɔ:m/ *a* tiède.

**lull** /lʌl/ *vt* **he ~ed them into thinking that** il leur a fait croire que. ● *n* accalmie *f*.

**lullaby** /'lʌləbaɪ/ *n* berceuse *f*.

**lumber** /'lʌmbə(r)/ *n* bois *m* de charpente. ● *vt* 🅸 **~ sb with** (*chore*) coller à qn 🅸. **~jack** *n* bûcheron *m*.

**luminous** /'lu:mɪnəs/ *a* lumineux.

**lump** /lʌmp/ *n* morceau *m*; (swelling on body) grosseur *f*; (in liquid) grumeau *m*. ● *vt* **~ together** réunir. **~ sum** *n* somme *f* globale.

**lunacy** /'lu:nəsɪ/ *n* folie *f*.

**lunar** /'lu:nə(r)/ *a* lunaire.

**lunatic** /'lu:nətɪk/ *n* fou/ folle *m/f*.

**lunch** /lʌntʃ/ *n* déjeuner *m*. ● *vi* déjeuner.

**luncheon** /'lʌntʃən/ *n* déjeuner *m*. **~ voucher** *n* chèque-repas *m*.

**lung** /lʌŋ/ *n* poumon *m*.

**lunge** /lʌndʒ/ *vi* bondir (**at** sur; **forward** en avant).

**lurch** /lɜ:tʃ/ *n* **leave in the ~** planter là, laisser en plan. ● *vi* (*person*) tituber.

**lure** /lʊə(r)/ *vt* appâter, attirer. ● *n* (attraction) attrait *m*, appât *m*.

**lurid** /'lʊərɪd/ *a* choquant, affreux; (gaudy) voyant.

**lurk** /lɜ:k/ *vi* se cacher; (in ambush) s'embusquer; (prowl) rôder; (*suspicion, danger*) menacer.

**luscious** /'lʌʃəs/ *a* appétissant.

**lush** /lʌʃ/ *a* luxuriant.

**lust** /lʌst/ *vi* **~ after** convoiter.

**Luxemburg** /'lʌksəmbɜ:g/ *n* Luxembourg *m*.

**luxurious** /lʌg'ʒʊərɪəs/ *a* luxueux.

**luxury** /'lʌkʃərɪ/ *n* luxe *m*. ● *a* de luxe.

**lying** /'laɪɪŋ/ ⇒LIE[1], LIE[2]. ● *n* mensonges *mpl*.

**lyric** /'lɪrɪk/ *a* lyrique. **lyrical** *a* lyrique. **lyrics** *npl* paroles *fpl*.

# Mm

**MA** *abbr* ⇒MASTER OF ARTS.

**mac** /mæk/ *n* 🅸 imper *m*.

**machine** /mə'ʃi:n/ *n* machine *f*. ● *vt* (sew) coudre à la machine; (Tech) usiner. **~-gun** *n* mitrailleuse *f*.

**mackerel** /'mækrəl/ *n inv* maquereau *m*.

**mackintosh** /'mækɪntɒʃ/ *n* imperméable *m*.

**mad** /mæd/ *a* (**madder, maddest**) fou; (foolish) insensé; (*dog*) enragé; (angry 🅸) furieux; **be ~ about** se passionner pour; (*person*) être fou de; **drive sb ~** exaspérer qn; **like ~** comme un fou. **~ cow disease** *n* maladie *f* de la vache folle.

**madam** /'mædəm/ *n* madame *f*; (unmarried) mademoiselle *f*.

**made** /meɪd/ ⇒MAKE.

**madly** /'mædlɪ/ *adv* (*interested, in love*) follement; (frantically) comme un fou.

**madman** /'mædmən/ *n* (*pl* **-men**) fou *m*.

**madness** /'mædnɪs/ *n* folie *f*.

**magazine** /mægə'zi:n/ *n* revue *f*, magazine *m*; (of gun) magasin *m*.

**maggot** /'mægət/ *n* (in fruit) ver *m*, (for fishing) asticot *m*.

**magic** /'mædʒɪk/ *n* magie *f*. ● *a* magique.

**magician** /mə'dʒɪʃn/ *n* magicien/ -ne *m/f*.

**magistrate** /'mædʒɪstreɪt/ *n* magistrat *m*.

**magnet** /'mægnɪt/ *n* aimant *m*. **magnetic** *a* magnétique.

**magnificent** /mæg'nɪfɪsnt/ *a* magnifique.

**magnify** /'mægnɪfaɪ/ *vt* grossir; (*sound*) amplifier; (fig) exagérer. **magnifying glass** *n* loupe *f*.

**magpie** /'mægpaɪ/ *n* pie *f*.

**mahogany** /mə'hɒgənɪ/ *n* acajou *m*.

**maid** /meɪd/ *n* (servant) bonne *f*; (in hotel) femme *f* de chambre.

**maiden** /'meɪdn/ *n* (old use) jeune fille *f*. ● *a* (*aunt*) célibataire; (*voyage*) premier. **~ name** *n* nom *m* de jeune fille.

**mail** /meɪl/ *n* (postal service) poste *f*; (letters) courrier *m*; (armour) cotte *f* de mailles. ● *a* (*bag, van*) postal. ● *vt* envoyer par la poste. **~ box** *n* boîte *f* aux lettres; (Comput) boîte *f* aux lettres électronique. **mailing list** *n* liste *f* d'adresses. **~man** *n* (*pl* **-men**) (US) facteur *m*. **~ order** *n* vente *f* par correspondance. **~shot** *n* publipostage *m*.

**main** /meɪn/ *a* principal; **a ~ road** une grande route. ● *n* **(water/gas) ~** conduite *f* d'eau/de gaz; **the ~s** (Electr) le secteur; **in the ~** en général. **~frame** *n* unité *f* centrale. **~land** *n* continent *m*. **~stream** *n* tendance *f* principale, ligne *f*.

**maintain** /meɪn'teɪn/ *vt* (continue, keep, assert) maintenir; (*house, machine, family*) entretenir; (*rights*) soutenir.

**maintenance** /'meɪntənəns/ *n* (care) entretien *m*; (continuation) maintien *m*; (allowance) pension *f* alimentaire.

**maisonette** /meɪzə'net/ *n* duplex *m*.

**maize** /meɪz/ *n* maïs *m*.

**majestic** /mə'dʒestɪk/ *a* majestueux.

**majesty** /'mædʒəstɪ/ *n* majesté *f*.

**major** /'meɪdʒə(r)/ *a* majeur. ● *n* commandant *m*. ● *vi* **~ in** (Univ, US) se spécialiser en.

**majority** /mə'dʒɒrətɪ/ *n* majorité *f*; **the ~ of people** la plupart des gens. ● *a* majoritaire.

**make** /meɪk/ *vt/i* (*pt* **made**) faire; (manufacture) fabriquer; (*friends*) se faire; (*money*) gagner; (*decision*) prendre; (*place, position*) arriver à; (cause to be) rendre; **~ sb do sth** faire faire qch à qn; (force) obliger qn à faire qch; **be made of** être fait de; **~ oneself at home** se mettre à l'aise; **~ sb happy** rendre qn heureux; **~ it** arriver; (succeed) réussir; **I ~ it two o'clock** j'ai deux heures; **I ~ it 150** d'après moi, ça fait 150; **I cannot ~ anything of it** je n'y comprends rien; **can you ~ Friday?** vendredi, c'est possible?; **~ as if to** faire mine de. ● *n* (brand) marque *f*. □ **~ do** (manage) se débrouiller (**with** avec); **~ for** se diriger vers; (cause) tendre à créer; **~ good** *vi* réussir; *vt* compenser; (repair) réparer; **~ off** filer (**with** avec); **~ out** distinguer; (understand) comprendre; (draw up) faire; (assert) prétendre; **~ up** *vt* faire, former; (*story*) inventer; (*deficit*) combler; *vi* se réconcilier; **~ up (one's face)** se maquiller; **~ up for** compenser; (*time*) rattraper; **~ up one's mind** se décider; **~ up to** se concilier les bonnes grâces de.

**make-believe** *a* feint, illusoire. ● *n* fantaisie *f*.

**maker** /'meɪkə(r)/ *n* fabricant *m*.

**makeshift** /'meɪkʃɪft/ *a* improvisé.

**make-up** /ˈmeɪkʌp/ *n* maquillage *m*; (of object) constitution *f*; (Psych) caractère *m*.

**malaria** /məˈleərɪə/ *n* paludisme *m*.

**Malaysia** /məˈleɪzɪə/ *n* Malaisie *f*.

**male** /meɪl/ *a* (*voice, sex*) masculin; (Bot, Tech) mâle. ● *n* mâle *m*.

**malfunction** /mælˈfʌŋkʃn/ *n* mauvais fonctionnement *m*. ● *vi* mal fonctionner.

**malice** /ˈmælɪs/ *n* méchanceté *f*. **malicious** *a* méchant.

**malignant** /məˈlɪgnənt/ *a* malveillant; (*tumour*) malin.

**mall** /mɔːl/ *n* **(shopping) ~** (in suburbs) centre *m* commercial; (in town) galerie *f* marchande.

**malnutrition** /mælnjuːˈtrɪʃn/ *n* sous-alimentation *f*.

**Malta** /ˈmɔːltə/ *n* Malte *f*.

**mammal** /ˈmæml/ *n* mammifère *m*.

**mammoth** /ˈmæməθ/ *n* mammouth *m*. ● *a* (*task*) gigantesque; (*organization*) géant.

**man** /mæn/ *n* (*pl* **men**) homme *m*; (in sports team) joueur *m*; (chess) pièce *f*; **~ to man** d'homme à homme. ● *vt* (*pt* **manned**) (*desk*) tenir; (*ship*) armer; (*guns*) servir; (be on duty at) être de service à.

**manage** /ˈmænɪdʒ/ *vt* (*project, organization*) diriger; (*shop, affairs*) gérer; (handle) manier; **I could ~ another drink** 🄸 je prendrais bien encore un verre; **can you ~ Friday?** vendredi, c'est possible? ● *vi* se débrouiller; **~ to do** réussir à faire. **manageable** *a* (*tool, size, person*) maniable; (*job*) faisable.

**management** /ˈmænɪdʒmənt/ *n* (managers) direction *f*; (of shop) gestion *f*.

**manager** /ˈmænɪdʒə(r)/ *n* directeur/-trice *m/f*; (of shop) gérant/-e *m/f*; (of actor) impresario *m*.

**mandate** /ˈmændeɪt/ *n* mandat *m*.

**mandatory** /ˈmændətrɪ/ *a* obligatoire.

**mane** /meɪn/ *n* crinière *f*.

**mango** /ˈmæŋgəʊ/ *n* (*pl* **~es**) mangue *f*.

**manhandle** /ˈmænhændl/ *vt* maltraiter, malmener.

**man**: **~hole** *n* regard *m*. **~hood** *n* âge *m* d'homme; (quality) virilité *f*.

**maniac** /ˈmeɪnɪæk/ *n* maniaque *mf*, fou *m*, folle *f*.

**manicure** /ˈmænɪkjʊə(r)/ *n* manucure *f*. ● *vt* soigner, manucurer.

**manifest** /ˈmænɪfest/ *a* manifeste. ● *vt* manifester.

**manipulate** /məˈnɪpjʊleɪt/ *vt* (*tool, person*) manipuler.

**mankind** /mænˈkaɪnd/ *n* genre *m* humain.

**manly** /ˈmænlɪ/ *a* viril.

**man-made** *a* (*fibre*) synthétique; (*pond*) artificiel; (*disaster*) d'origine humaine.

**manned** /mænd/ *a* (*spacecraft*) habité.

**manner** /ˈmænə(r)/ *n* manière *f*; (attitude) attitude *f*; (kind) sorte *f*; **~s** (social behaviour) manières *fpl*.

**mannerism** /ˈmænərɪzəm/ *n* particularité *f*; (quirk) manie *f*.

**manoeuvre** /məˈnuːvə(r)/ *n* manœuvre *f*. ● *vt/i* manœuvrer.

**manor** /ˈmænə(r)/ *n* manoir *m*.

**manpower** /ˈmænpaʊə(r)/ *n* main-d'œuvre *f*.

**mansion** /ˈmænʃn/ *n* (in countryside) demeure *f*; (in town) hôtel *m* particulier.

**manslaughter** /ˈmænslɔːtə(r)/ *n* homicide *m* involontaire.

**mantelpiece** /'mæntlpi:s/ *n* (manteau *m* de) cheminée.

**manual** /'mænjʊəl/ *a* (*labour*) manuel; (*typewriter*) mécanique. ● *n* (handbook) manuel *m*.

**manufacture** /mænjʊ'fæktʃə(r)/ *vt* fabriquer. ● *n* fabrication *f*.

**manure** /mə'njʊə(r)/ *n* fumier *m*.

**many** /'menɪ/ *a* & *n* beaucoup (de); **a great** *or* **good** ~ un grand nombre (de); ~ **a** bien des.

**map** /mæp/ *n* carte *f*; (of streets) plan *m*. ● *vt* (*pt* **mapped**) faire la carte de; ~ **out** (*route*) tracer; (arrange) organiser.

**mar** /mɑ:(r)/ *vt* (*pt* **marred**) gâcher.

**marble** /'mɑ:bl/ *n* marbre *m*; (for game) bille *f*.

**March** /mɑ:tʃ/ *n* mars *m*.

**march** /mɑ:tʃ/ *vi* (Mil) marcher (au pas). ● *vt* ~ **off** (lead away) emmener. ● *n* marche *f*.

**margin** /'mɑ:dʒɪn/ *n* marge *f*.

**marginal** /'mɑ:dʒɪnl/ *a* marginal; (*increase*) léger, faible; (*seat*: Pol) disputé.

**marinate** /'mærɪneɪt/ *vt* faire mariner (**in** dans)

**marine** /mə'ri:n/ *a* marin. ● *n* (shipping) marine *f*; (sailor) fusilier *m* marin.

**marital** /'mærɪtl/ *a* conjugal. ~ **status** *n* situation *f* de famille.

**mark** /mɑ:k/ *n* (currency) mark *m*; (stain) tache *f*; (trace) marque *f*; (School) note *f*; (target) but *m*. ● *vt* marquer; (*exam*) corriger; ~ **out** délimiter; (*person*) désigner; ~ **time** marquer le pas.

**marker** /'mɑ:kə(r)/ *n* (pen) marqueur *m*; (tag) repère *m*; (School, Univ) examinateur/-trice *m*/*f*.

**market** /'mɑ:kɪt/ *n* marché *m*; **on the** ~ en vente. ● *vt* (sell) vendre; (launch) commercialiser. ~ **research** *n* étude *f* de marché.

**marmalade** /'mɑ:məleɪd/ *n* confiture *f* d'oranges.

**maroon** /mə'ru:n/ *n* bordeaux *m inv*. ● *a* bordeaux *inv*.

**marooned** /mə'ru:nd/ *a* abandonné; (snow-bound) bloqué.

**marquee** /mɑ:'ki:/ *n* grande tente *f*; (of circus) chapiteau *m*; (awning: US) auvent *m*.

**marriage** /'mærɪdʒ/ *n* mariage *m* (**to** avec).

**married** /'mærɪd/ *a* marié (**to** à); (life) conjugal; **get** ~ se marier (**to** avec).

**marrow** /'mærəʊ/ *n* (of bone) moelle *f*; (vegetable) courge *f*.

**marry** /'mærɪ/ *vt* épouser; (give or unite in marriage) marier. ● *vi* se marier.

**marsh** /mɑ:ʃ/ *n* marais *m*.

**marshal** /'mɑ:ʃl/ *n* maréchal *m*; (at event) membre *m* du service d'ordre. ● *vt* (*pt* **marshalled**) rassembler.

**martyr** /'mɑ:tə(r)/ *n* martyr/-e *m*/*f*. ● *vt* martyriser.

**marvel** /'mɑ:vl/ *n* merveille *f*. ● *vi* (*pt* **marvelled**) s'émerveiller (**at** de).

**marvellous** /'mɑ:vələs/ *a* merveilloux.

**marzipan** /'mɑ:zɪpæn/ *n* pâte *f* d'amandes.

**masculine** /'mæskjʊlɪn/ *a* & *n* masculin (*m*).

**mash** /mæʃ/ *n* (potatoes ⊞) purée *f*. ● *vt* écraser. **mashed potatoes** *npl* purée *f* (de pommes de terre).

**mask** /mɑ:sk/ *n* masque *m*. ● *vt* masquer.

**Mason** /'meɪsn/ *n* franc-maçon *m*.

**masonry** /'meɪsənrɪ/ *n* maçonnerie *f*.

**mass** /mæs/ *n* (Relig) messe *f*; masse *f*; **the ~es** les masses *fpl*. ● *vt*/*i* (se) masser.

**massacre** /ˈmæsəkə(r)/ *n* massacre *m*. ● *vt* massacrer.

**massage** /ˈmæsɑːʒ/ *n* massage *m*. ● *vt* masser.

**massive** /ˈmæsɪv/ *a* (large) énorme; (heavy) massif.

**mass media** *n* médias *mpl*.

**mass-produce** *vt* fabriquer en série.

**mast** /mɑːst/ *n* (on ship) mât *m*; (for radio, TV) pylône *m*.

**master** /ˈmɑːstə(r)/ *n* maître *m*; (in secondary school) professeur *m*; **M~ of Arts** titulaire *mf* d'une maîtrise ès lettres. ● *vt* maîtriser.

**masterpiece** /ˈmɑːstəpiːs/ *n* chef-d'œuvre *m*.

**mastery** /ˈmɑːstərɪ/ *n* maîtrise *f*.

**mat** /mæt/ *n* (petit) tapis *m*; (at door) paillasson *m*.

**match** /mætʃ/ *n* (for lighting fire) allumette *f*; (Sport) match *m*; (equal) égal/-e *m*/*f*; (marriage) mariage *m*; (sb to marry) parti *m*; **be a ~ for** pouvoir tenir tête à. ● *vt* opposer; (go with) aller avec; (*cups*) assortir; (equal) égaler. ● *vi* (be alike) être assorti. **matchbox** *n* boîte *f* à allumettes.

**matching** /ˈmætʃɪŋ/ *a* assorti.

**mate** /meɪt/ *n* camarade *mf*; (of animal) compagnon *m*, compagne *f*; (assistant) aide *mf*; (chess) mat *m*. ● *vt*/*i* (s')accoupler (**with** avec).

**material** /məˈtɪərɪəl/ *n* matière *f*; (fabric) tissu *m*; (documents, for building) matériau(x) *m*(*pl*); **~s** (equipment) matériel *m*. ● *a* matériel; (fig) important. **materialistic** *a* matérialiste.

**materialize** /məˈtɪərɪəlaɪz/ *vi* se matérialiser, se réaliser.

**maternal** /məˈtɜːnl/ *a* maternel.

**maternity** /məˈtɜːnətɪ/ *n* maternité *f*. ● *a* (*clothes*) de grossesse. **~ hospital** *n* maternité *f*. **~ leave** *n* congé *m* maternité.

**mathematics** /mæθəˈmætɪks/ *n* & *npl* mathématiques *fpl*.

**maths**, (US) **math** /mæθs/ *n* maths *fpl*.

**mating** /ˈmeɪtɪŋ/ *n* accouplement *m*.

**matrimony** /ˈmætrɪmənɪ/ *n* mariage *m*.

**matron** /ˈmeɪtrən/ *n* (married, elderly) dame *f* âgée; (in hospital) infirmière *f* en chef.

**matt** /mæt/ *a* mat.

**matter** /ˈmætə(r)/ *n* (substance) matière *f*; (affair) affaire *f*; **as a ~ of fact** en fait; **what is the ~?** qu'est-ce qu'il y a? ● *vi* importer; **it does not ~** ça ne fait rien; **no ~ what happens** quoi qu'il arrive.

**mattress** /ˈmætrɪs/ *n* matelas *m*.

**mature** /məˈtjʊə(r)/ *a* (psychologically) mûr; (*plant*) adulte. ● *vt*/*i* (se) mûrir. **maturity** *n* maturité *f*.

**mauve** /məʊv/ *a* & *n* mauve (*m*).

**maverick** /ˈmævərɪk/ *n* non-conformiste *mf*.

**maximize** /ˈmæksɪmaɪz/ *vt* porter au maximum.

**maximum** /ˈmæksɪməm/ *a* & *n* (*pl* **-ima**) maximum (*m*).

---

**may** /meɪ/

*past* **might**

● *auxiliary verb*

····➤ (possibility) **they ~ be able to come** ils pourront peut-être venir; **she ~ not have seen him** elle ne l'a peut-être pas vu; **it ~ rain** il risque de pleuvoir; **'will you**

come?'—'**I might**' 'tu viendras?'—'peut-être'.

····➤ (permission) **you ~ leave** vous pouvez partir; **~ I smoke?** puis-je fumer?

····➤ (wish) **~ he be happy** qu'il soit heureux.

**May** /meɪ/ *n* mai *m*.

**maybe** /'meɪbi:/ *adv* peut-être.

**mayhem** /'meɪhem/ *n* (havoc) ravages *mpl*.

**mayonnaise** /meɪə'neɪz/ *n* mayonnaise *f*.

**mayor** /meə(r)/ *n* maire *m*.

**maze** /meɪz/ *n* labyrinthe *m*.

**Mb** *abbr* (**megabyte**) (Comput) Mo.

**me** /mi:/ *pron* me, m'; (after prep.) moi; (indirect object) me, m'; **he knows ~** il me connaît.

**meadow** /'medəʊ/ *n* pré *m*.

**meagre** /'mi:gə(r)/ *a* maigre.

**meal** /mi:l/ *n* repas *m*; (grain) farine *f*.

**mean** /mi:n/ *a* (poor) misérable; (miserly) avare; (unkind) méchant; (average) moyen. ● *n* milieu *m*; (average) moyenne *f*; **in the ~ time** en attendant. ● *vt* (*pt* **meant**) vouloir dire, signifier; (involve) entraîner; **I ~ that!** je suis sérieux; **be meant for** être destiné à; **~ to do** avoir l'intention de faire.

**meaning** /'mi:nɪŋ/ *n* sens *m*, signification *f*. **meaningful** *a* significatif. **meaningless** *a* dénué de sens.

**means** /mi:nz/ *n* moyen(s) *m(pl)*; **by ~ of sth** au moyen de qch. ● *npl* (wealth) moyens *mpl* financiers; **by all ~** certainement; **by no ~** nullement.

**meant** /ment/ ⇒MEAN.

**meantime** /'mi:ntaɪm/, **meanwhile** /'mi:nwaɪl/ *adv* en attendant.

**measles** /'mi:zlz/ *n* rougeole *f*.

**measure** /'meʒə(r)/ *n* mesure *f*; (ruler) règle *f*. ● *vt/i* mesurer; **~ up to** être à la hauteur de.

**meat** /mi:t/ *n* viande *f*. **meaty** *a* de viande; (fig) substantiel.

**mechanic** /mɪ'kænɪk/ *n* mécanicien/-ne *m/f*.

**mechanical** /mɪ'kænɪkl/ *a* mécanique.

**mechanism** /'mekənɪzəm/ *n* mécanisme *m*.

**medal** /'medl/ *n* médaille *f*.

**meddle** /'medl/ *vi* (interfere) se mêler (**in** de); (tinker) toucher (**with** à).

**media** /'mi:dɪə/ *n* ⇒MEDIUM. ● *npl* **the ~** les média *mpl*; **talk to the ~** parler à la presse.

**median** /'mi:dɪən/ *a* médian. ● *n* médiane *f*.

**mediate** /'mi:dɪeɪt/ *vi* servir d'intermédiaire.

**medical** /'medɪkl/ *a* médical; (student) en médecine. ● *n* visite *f* médicale.

**medication** /medɪ'keɪʃn/ *n* médicaments *mpl*.

**medicine** /'medsn/ *n* (science) médecine *f*; (substance) médicament *m*.

**medieval** /medɪ'i:vl/ *a* médiéval.

**mediocre** /mi:dɪ'əʊkə(r)/ *a* médiocre.

**meditate** /'medɪteɪt/ *vt/i* méditer.

**Mediterranean** /medɪtə'reɪnɪən/ *a* méditerranéen. ● *n* **the ~** la Méditerranée *f*.

**medium** /'mi:dɪəm/ *n* (*pl* **media**) (mid-point) milieu *m*; (for transmitting data) support *m*; (*pl* **mediums**) (person) médium *m*. ● *a* moyen.

**medley** /ˈmedlɪ/ *n* mélange *m*; (Mus) pot-pourri *m*.

**meet** /miːt/ *vt* (*pt* **met**) rencontrer; (see again) retrouver; (be introduced to) faire la connaissance de; (face) faire face à; (*requirement*) satisfaire. ● *vi* se rencontrer; (see each other again) se retrouver; (in session) se réunir.

**meeting** /ˈmiːtɪŋ/ *n* réunion *f*; (between two people) rencontre *f*.

**megabyte** /ˈmegəbaɪt/ *n* (Comput) mégaoctet *m*.

**melancholy** /ˈmelənkəlɪ/ *n* mélancolie *f*. ● *a* mélancolique.

**mellow** /ˈmeləʊ/ *a* (*fruit*) mûr; (*sound, colour*) moelleux, doux; (*person*) mûri. ● *vt/i* (mature) mûrir; (soften) (s')adoucir.

**melody** /ˈmelədɪ/ *n* mélodie *f*.

**melon** /ˈmelən/ *n* melon *m*.

**melt** /melt/ *vt/i* (faire) fondre.

**member** /ˈmembə(r)/ *n* membre *m*. **M～ of Parliament** *n* député *m*. **membership** *n* adhésion *f*; (members) membres *mpl*; (fee) cotisation *f*.

**memento** /mɪˈmentəʊ/ *n* (*pl* **～es**) (object) souvenir *m*.

**memo** /ˈmeməʊ/ *n* note *f*.

**memoir** /ˈmemwɑː(r)/ *n* (record, essay) mémoire *m*.

**memorandum** /meməˈrændəm/ *n* note *f*.

**memorial** /mɪˈmɔːrɪəl/ *n* monument *m*. ● *a* commémoratif.

**memorize** /ˈmeməraɪz/ *vt* apprendre par cœur.

**memory** /ˈmemərɪ/ *n* (mind, in computer) mémoire *f*; (thing remembered) souvenir *m*; **from ～** de mémoire; **in ～ of** à la mémoire de.

**men** /men/ ⇒MAN.

**menace** /ˈmenəs/ *n* menace *f*; (nuisance) peste *f*. ● *vt* menacer.

**mend** /mend/ *vt* réparer; (darn) raccommoder; **～ one's ways** s'amender. ● *n* raccommodage *m*; **on the ～** en voie de guérison.

**meningitis** /menɪnˈdʒaɪtɪs/ *n* méningite *f*.

**menopause** /ˈmenəpɔːz/ *n* ménopause *f*.

**mental** /ˈmentl/ *a* mental; (*hospital*) psychiatrique.

**mentality** /menˈtælətɪ/ *n* mentalité *f*.

**mention** /ˈmenʃn/ *vt* mentionner; **don't ～ it!** il n'y a pas de quoi!, je vous en prie! ● *n* mention *f*.

**menu** /ˈmenjuː/ *n* (food, on computer) menu *m*; (list) carte *f*.

**MEP** *abbr* (**member of the European Parliament**) député *m* au Parlement européen.

**mercenary** /ˈmɜːsɪnərɪ/ *a* & *n* mercenaire (*m*).

**merchandise** /ˈmɜːtʃəndaɪz/ *n* marchandises *fpl*.

**merchant** /ˈmɜːtʃənt/ *n* marchand *m*. ● *a* (*ship, navy*) marchand. **～ bank** *n* banque *f* de commerce.

**merciful** /ˈmɜːsɪfl/ *a* miséricordieux.

**mercury** /ˈmɜːkjʊrɪ/ *n* mercure *m*.

**mercy** /ˈmɜːsɪ/ *n* pitié *f*; **at the ～ of** à la merci de.

**mere** /mɪə(r)/ *a* simple. **merest** *a* moindre.

**merge** /mɜːdʒ/ *vt/i* (se) mêler (**with** à); (*companies*: Comm) fusionner. **merger** *n* fusion *f*.

**mermaid** /ˈmɜːmeɪd/ *n* sirène *f*.

**merrily** /ˈmerɪlɪ/ *adv* (happily) joyeusement; (unconcernedly) avec insouciance.

**merry** /ˈmerɪ/ *a* (**-ier**, **-iest**) gai; **make ～** faire la fête. **～-go-round** *n* manège *m*.

**mesh** /meʃ/ *n* maille *f*; (fabric) tissu *m* à mailles; (network) réseau *m*.

**mesmerize** /'mezməraɪz/ *vt* hypnotiser.

**mess** /mes/ *n* désordre *m*, gâchis *m*; (dirt) saleté *f*; (Mil) mess *m*; **make a ~ of** gâcher. ● *vt* **~ up** gâcher. ● *vi* **~ about** s'amuser; (dawdle) traîner; **~ with** (tinker with) tripoter.

**message** /'mesɪdʒ/ *n* message *m*.

**messenger** /'mesɪndʒə(r)/ *n* messager/-ère *m/f*.

**messy** /'mesɪ/ *a* (**-ier**, **-iest**) en désordre; (dirty) sale.

**met** /met/ ⇒MEET.

**metal** /'metl/ *n* métal *m*. ● *a* de métal. **metallic** *a* métallique; (paint, colour) métallisé.

**metallurgy** /mɪ'tælədʒɪ/ *n* métallurgie *f*.

**metaphor** /'metəfə(r)/ *n* métaphore *f*.

**meteor** /'mi:tɪə(r)/ *n* météore *m*.

**meteorite** /'mi:tɪəraɪt/ *n* météorite *m*.

**meteorology** /mi:tɪə'rɒlədʒɪ/ *n* météorologie *f*.

**meter** /'mi:tə(r)/ *n* compteur *m*; (US) = METRE.

**method** /'meθəd/ *n* méthode *f*.

**methylated spirit(s)** /'meθɪleɪtɪd 'spɪrɪt(s)/ *n* alcool *m* à brûler.

**meticulous** /mɪ'tɪkjʊləs/ *a* méticuleux.

**metre**, (US) **meter** /'mi:tə(r)/ *n* mètre *m*.

**metric** /'metrɪk/ *a* métrique.

**metropolis** /mə'trɒpəlɪs/ *n* métropole *f*. **metropolitan** *a* métropolitain.

**mew** /mju:/ *n* miaulement *m*. ● *vi* miauler.

**mews** /mju:z/ *npl* appartements *mpl* chic aménagés dans d'anciennes écuries.

**Mexico** /'meksɪkəʊ/ *n* Mexique *m*.

**miaow** /mi:'aʊ/ *n* & *vi* = MEW.

**mice** /maɪs/ ⇒MOUSE.

**mickey** /'mɪkɪ/ *n* **take the ~ out of** 🅸 se moquer de.

**microchip** /'maɪkrəʊtʃɪp/ *n* puce *f*; circuit *m* intégré.

**microlight** /'maɪkrəʊlaɪt/ *n* ULM *m*.

**microprocessor** /maɪkrəʊ'prəʊsesə(r)/ *n* microprocesseur *m*.

**microscope** /'maɪkrəskəʊp/ *n* microscope *m*.

**microwave** /'maɪkrəʊweɪv/ *n* micro-onde *f*; **~ (oven)** four *m* à micro-ondes. ● *vt* passer au four à micro-ondes.

**mid** /mɪd/ *a* **in ~ air** en plein ciel; **in ~ March** à la mi-mars; **~ afternoon** milieu *m* de l'après-midi; **he's in his ~ twenties** il a environ vingt-cinq ans.

**midday** /mɪd'deɪ/ *n* midi *m*.

**middle** /'mɪdl/ *a* (*door*, *shelf*) du milieu; (*size*) moyen. ● *n* milieu *m*; **in the ~ of** au milieu de. **~-aged** *a* d'âge mûr. **M~ Ages** *n* Moyen Âge *m*. **~ class** *n* classe *f* moyenne. **M~ East** *n* Moyen-Orient *m*.

**midge** /mɪdʒ/ *n* moucheron *m*.

**midget** /'mɪdʒɪt/ *n* nain/-e *m/f*. ● *a* minuscule.

**midnight** /'mɪdnaɪt/ *n* minuit *f*; **it's ~** il est minuit.

**midst** /mɪdst/ *n* **in the ~ of** au beau milieu de; **in our ~** parmi nous.

**midsummer** /mɪd'sʌmə(r)/ *n* milieu *m* de l'été; (solstice) solstice *m* d'été.

**midway** /mɪdweɪ/ *adv* **~ between/along** à mi-chemin entre/le long de.

**midwife** /'mɪdwaɪf/ *n* (*pl* **-wives**) sage-femme *f*.

**might**[1] /maɪt/ *v aux* **I ~ have been killed!** j'aurais pu être tué; **you ~ try doing sth** vous pourriez faire qch; ⇒MAY.

**might**[2] /maɪt/ *n* puissance *f*.

**mighty** /'maɪtɪ/ *a* puissant; (huge Ⓘ) énorme. ● *adv* Ⓘ vachement Ⓘ.

**migrant** /'maɪgrənt/ *a* & *n* (*bird*) migrateur (*m*); (*worker*) migrant/-e (*m*/*f*).

**migrate** /maɪ'greɪt/ *vi* émigrer. **migration** *n* migration *f*.

**mild** /maɪld/ *a* (*surprise, taste, tobacco, attack*) léger; (*weather, cheese, soap, person*) doux; (*case, infection*) bénin.

**mile** /maɪl/ *n* mile *m* (= *1.6 km*); **walk for ~s** marcher pendant des kilomètres; **~s better** Ⓘ bien meilleur. **mileage** *n* nombre *m* de miles, kilométrage *m*.

**milestone** /'maɪlstəʊn/ *n* (lit) borne *f*; (fig) étape *f* importante.

**military** /'mɪlɪtrɪ/ *a* militaire.

**militia** /mɪ'lɪʃə/ *n* milice *f*.

**milk** /mɪlk/ *n* lait *m*. ● *vt* (*cow*) traire; (fig) pomper.

**milkman** /'mɪlkmən/ *n* (*pl* **-men**) laitier *m*.

**milky** /'mɪlkɪ/ *a* (*skin, colour*) laiteux; (*tea*) au lait; **M~ Way** Voie *f* lactée.

**mill** /mɪl/ *n* moulin *m*; (factory) usine *f*. ● *vt* moudre. ● *vi* **~ around** grouiller.

**millennium** /mɪ'lenɪəm/ *n* (*pl* **~s**) millénaire *m*.

**millimetre**, (US) **millimeter** /'mɪlɪmi:tə(r)/ *n* millimètre *m*.

**million** /'mɪljən/ *n* million *m*; **a ~ pounds** un million de livres. **millionaire** *n* millionnaire *m*.

**millstone** /'mɪlstəʊn/ *n* meule *f*; (fig) boulet *m*.

**mime** /maɪm/ *n* (actor) mime *mf*; (art) mime *m*. ● *vt*/*i* mimer.

**mimic** /'mɪmɪk/ *vt* (*pt* **mimicked**) imiter. ● *n* imitateur/-trice *m*/*f*.

**mince** /mɪns/ *vt* hacher; **not to ~ matters** ne pas mâcher ses mots. ● *n* viande *f* hachée.

**mind** /maɪnd/ *n* esprit *m*; (sanity) raison *f*; (opinion) avis *m*; **be on sb's ~** préoccuper qn; **bear that in ~** ne l'oubliez pas; **change one's ~** changer d'avis; **make up one's ~** se décider (**to** à). ● *vt* (have charge of) s'occuper de; (heed) faire attention à; **I do not ~ the noise** le bruit ne me dérange pas; **I don't ~** ça m'est égal; **would you ~ checking?** je peux vous demander de vérifier?

**minder** /'maɪndə(r)/ *n* (bodyguard) garde *m* de corps; (**child**) **~** nourrice *f*.

**mindless** /'maɪndlɪs/ *a* (*programme*) bête; (*work*) abrutissant; (*vandalism*) gratuit.

**mine** /maɪn/ *n* mine *f*. ● *vt* extraire; (Mil) miner. ● *pron* le mien, la mienne, les mien(ne)s; **the blue car is ~** la voiture bleue est la mienne *or* à moi.

**minefield** /'maɪnfi:ld/ *n* (lit) champ *m* de mines; (fig) terrain *m* miné.

**miner** /'maɪnə(r)/ *n* mineur *m*.

**mineral** /'mɪnərəl/ *n* & *a* minéral (*m*); **~ water** eau *f* minérale.

**minesweeper** /'maɪnswi:pə(r)/ *n* (ship) dragueur *m* de mines.

**mingle** /'mɪŋgl/ *vt*/*i* (se) mêler (**with** à).

**minibus** /'mɪnɪbʌs/ *n* minibus *m*.

**minicab** /'mɪnɪkæb/ *n* taxi *m* (*non agréé*).

**minimal** /'mɪnɪml/ *a* minimal.

**minimize** /'mɪnɪmaɪz/ *vt* minimiser; (Comput) réduire.

**minimum** /'mɪnɪməm/ *a & n* (*pl* **-ima**) minimum (*m*).

**minister** /'mɪnɪstə(r)/ *n* ministre *m*. **ministerial** *a* ministériel. **ministry** *n* ministère *m*.

**mink** /mɪŋk/ *n* vison *m*.

**minor** /'maɪnə(r)/ *a* (*change, surgery*) mineur; (*injury, burn*) léger; (*road*) secondaire. ● *n* (Jur) mineur/-e *m/f*.

**minority** /maɪ'nɒrətɪ/ *n* minorité *f*; **in the ~** en minorité. ● *a* minoritaire.

**mint** /mɪnt/ *n* (Bot, Culin) menthe *f*; (sweet) bonbon *m* à la menthe; (fortune [I]) fortune *f*. ● *vt* frapper; **in ~ condition** à l'état neuf.

**minus** /'maɪnəs/ *prep* moins; (without [I]) sans. ● *n* moins *m*; (drawback) inconvénient *m*.

**minute¹** /'mɪnɪt/ *n* minute *f*; **~s** (of meeting) compte-rendu *m*.

**minute²** /maɪ'nju:t/ *a* (*object*) minuscule; (*risk, variation*) minime.

**miracle** /'mɪrəkl/ *n* miracle *m*.

**mirror** /'mɪrə(r)/ *n* miroir *m*, glace *f*; (Auto) rétroviseur. ● *vt* refléter.

**misbehave** /mɪsbɪ'heɪv/ *vi* se conduire mal.

**miscalculation** /mɪskælkjʊ'leɪʃn/ *n* (lit) erreur *f* de calcul; (fig) mauvais calcul *m*.

**miscarriage** /'mɪskærɪdʒ/ *n* fausse couche *f*; **~ of justice** erreur *f* judiciaire.

**miscellaneous** /mɪsə'leɪnɪəs/ *a* divers.

**mischief** /'mɪstʃɪf/ *n* (playfulness) espièglerie *f*; (by children) bêtises *fpl*. **mischievous** *a* espiègle; (malicious) méchant.

**misconduct** /mɪs'kɒndʌkt/ *n* mauvaise conduite *f*.

**misconstrue** /mɪskən'stru:/ *vt* mal interpréter.

**misdemeanour**, (US) **misdemeanor** /mɪsdɪ'mi:nə(r)/ *n* (Jur) délit *m*.

**miser** /'maɪzə(r)/ *n* avare *mf*.

**miserable** /'mɪzrəbl/ *a* (sad) malheureux; (wretched) misérable; (*performance, result*) lamentable.

**misery** /'mɪzərɪ/ *n* (unhappiness) souffrance *f*; (misfortune) misère *f*; (person [I]) rabat-joie *mf inv*.

**misfit** /'mɪsfɪt/ *n* inadapté/-e *m/f*.

**misfortune** /mɪs'fɔ:tʃu:n/ *n* malheur *m*.

**misgiving** /mɪs'gɪvɪŋ/ *n* (doubt) doute *m*; (apprehension) crainte *f*.

**misguided** /mɪs'gaɪdɪd/ *a* (foolish) imprudent; (mistaken) erroné; **be ~** (*person*) se tromper.

**mishap** /'mɪshæp/ *n* incident *m*.

**misjudge** /mɪs'dʒʌdʒ/ *vt* (*distance, speed*) mal évaluer; (*person*) mal juger.

**mislay** /mɪs'leɪ/ *vt* (*pt* **mislaid**) égarer.

**mislead** /mɪs'li:d/ *vt* (*pt* **misled**) tromper. **misleading** *a* trompeur

**misplace** /mɪs'pleɪs/ *vt* mal ranger; (lose) égarer. **misplaced** *a* (*fear, criticism*) déplacé.

**misprint** /'mɪsprɪnt/ *n* coquille *f*, faute *f* typographique.

**misread** /mɪs'ri:d/ *vt* (*pt* **misread** /mɪs'red/) mal lire; (*intentions*) mal interpréter.

**miss** /mɪs/ *vt/i* manquer; (*bus*) rater; **he ~es her/Paris** elle/Paris lui manque; **you're ~ing the point** tu n'as rien compris; **~ sth out** omettre qch; **~ out on sth** laisser passer qch. ● *n* coup *m* manqué; **it was a near ~** on l'a échappé belle.

**Miss** /mɪs/ *n* Mademoiselle *f*; ~ **Smith** (written) Mlle Smith.

**misshapen** /mɪs'ʃeɪpən/ *a* difforme.

**missile** /'mɪsaɪl/ *n* (Mil) missile *m*; (thrown) projectile *m*.

**mission** /'mɪʃn/ *n* mission *f*. **missionary** *n* missionnaire *mf*.

**misspell** /mɪs'spel/ *vt* (*pt* **misspelt** *or* **misspelled**) mal écrire.

**mist** /mɪst/ *n* brume *f*; (on window) buée *f*. ● *vt/i* (s')embuer.

**mistake** /mɪ'steɪk/ *n* erreur *f*; **by** ~ par erreur; **make a** ~ faire une erreur. ● *vt* (*pt* **mistook**; *pp* **mistaken**) (*meaning*) mal interpréter; ~ **for** prendre pour.

**mistaken** /mɪ'steɪkən/ *a* (*enthusiasm*) mal placé; **be** ~ avoir tort.

**mistletoe** /'mɪsltəʊ/ *n* gui *m*.

**mistreat** /mɪs'tri:t/ *vt* maltraiter.

**mistress** /'mɪstrɪs/ *n* maîtresse *f*.

**misty** /'mɪstɪ/ *a* (**-ier**, **-iest**) brumeux; (*window*) embué.

**misunderstanding** /mɪsʌndə'stændɪŋ/ *n* malentendu *m*.

**misuse** /mɪs'ju:z/ *vt* (*word*) mal employer; (*power*) abuser de; (*equipment*) faire mauvais usage de.

**mitten** /'mɪtn/ *n* moufle *f*.

**mix** /mɪks/ *n* mélange *m*. ● *vt* mélanger; (*drink*) préparer; (*cement*) malaxer. ● *vi* se mélanger (**with** avec, à); (socially) être sociable; ~ **with sb** fréquenter qn. □ ~ **up** (confuse) confondre; (jumble up) mélanger; **get** ~**ed up in** se trouver mêlé à.

**mixed** /mɪkst/ *a* (*school*) mixte; (*collection, diet*) varié; (*nuts, sweets*) assorti.

**mixer** /'mɪksə(r)/ *n* (Culin) batteur *m* électrique; **be a good** ~ être sociable; ~ **tap** mélangeur *m*.

**mixture** /'mɪkstʃə(r)/ *n* mélange *m*.

**mix-up** *n* confusion *f* (**over** sur).

**moan** /məʊn/ *n* gémissement *m*. ● *vi* gémir; (complain 🄸) râler 🄸.

**mob** /mɒb/ *n* (crowd) foule *f*; (gang) gang *m*; **the M**~ la Mafia. ● *vt* (*pt* **mobbed**) assaillir.

**mobile** /'məʊbaɪl/ *a* mobile; ~ **phone** téléphone *m* portable. ● *n* mobile *m*.

**mobilize** /'məʊbɪlaɪz/ *vt/i* mobiliser.

**mock** /mɒk/ *vt/i* se moquer (de). ● *a* faux.

**mockery** /'mɒkərɪ/ *n* moquerie *f*; **a** ~ **of** une parodie de.

**mock-up** *n* maquette *f*.

**mode** /məʊd/ *n* mode *m*.

**model** /'mɒdl/ *n* (Comput, Auto) modèle *m*; (scale representation) maquette *f*; (person showing clothes) mannequin *m*. ● *a* modèle; (*car*) modèle réduit *inv*; (*railway*) miniature. ● *vt* (*pt* **modelled**) modeler; (*clothes*) présenter. ● *vi* être mannequin; (pose) poser. **modelling** *n* métier *m* de mannequin.

**modem** /'məʊdem/ *n* modem *m*.

**moderate** /'mɒdərət/ *a* & *n* modéré/-e (*m/f*).

**moderation** /mɒdə'reɪʃn/ *n* modération *f*; **in** ~ avec modération.

**modern** /'mɒdn/ *a* moderne; ~ **languages** langues *fpl* vivantes. **modernize** *vt* moderniser.

**modest** /'mɒdɪst/ *a* modeste. **modesty** *n* modestie *f*.

**modification** /mɒdɪfɪ'keɪʃn/ *n* modification *f*. **modify** *vt* modifier.

**module** /'mɒdju:l/ *n* module *m*.

**moist** /mɔɪst/ *a* (*soil*) humide; (*skin, palms*) moite; (*cake*) moelleux. **moisten** *vt* humecter. **moisture** *n* humidité *f*. **moisturizer** *n* crème *f* hydratante.

**molar** /'məʊlə(r)/ *n* molaire *f*.

**mold** /məʊld/ (US) = MOULD.

**mole** /məʊl/ *n* grain *m* de beauté; (animal) taupe *f*.

**molecule** /'mɒlɪkju:l/ *n* molécule *f*.

**molest** /mə'lest/ *vt* (pester) importuner; (sexually) agresser sexuellement.

**moment** /'məʊmənt/ *n* (short time) instant *m*; (point in time) moment *m*. **momentarily** *adv* momentanément; (soon: US) très bientôt. **momentary** *a* momentané.

**momentum** /mə'mentəm/ *n* élan *m*.

**monarch** /'mɒnək/ *n* monarque *m*. **monarchy** *n* monarchie *f*.

**Monday** /'mʌndɪ/ *n* lundi *m*.

**monetary** /'mʌnɪtrɪ/ *a* monétaire.

**money** /'mʌnɪ/ *n* argent *m*; **make** ~ (*person*) gagner de l'argent; (*business*) rapporter de l'argent. **~-box** *n* tirelire *f*. ~ **order** *n* mandat *m* postal.

**monitor** /'mɒnɪtə(r)/ *n* dispositif *m* de surveillance; (Comput) moniteur *m*. ● *vt* surveiller; (*broadcast*) être à l'écoute de.

**monk** /mʌŋk/ *n* moine *m*.

**monkey** /'mʌŋkɪ/ *n* singe *m*.

**monopolize** /mə'nɒpəlaɪz/ *vt* monopoliser. **monopoly** *n* monopole *m*.

**monotonous** /mə'nɒtənəs/ *a* monotone. **monotony** *n* monotonie *f*.

**monsoon** /mɒn'su:n/ *n* mousson *f*.

**monster** /'mɒnstə(r)/ *n* monstre *m*. **monstrous** *a* monstrueux.

**month** /mʌnθ/ *n* mois *m*.

**monthly** /'mʌnθlɪ/ *a* mensuel. ● *adv* (*pay*) au mois; (*publish*) tous les mois. ● *n* (periodical) mensuel *m*.

**monument** /'mɒnjʊmənt/ *n* monument *m*.

**moo** /mu:/ *vi* meugler.

**mood** /mu:d/ *n* humeur *f*; **in a good/bad** ~ de bonne/mauvaise humeur. **moody** *a* d'humeur changeante.

**moon** /mu:n/ *n* lune *f*.

**moonlight** /'mu:nlaɪt/ *n* clair *m* de lune. **moonlighting** *n* 🄸 travail *m* au noir.

**moor** /mʊə(r)/ *n* lande *f*. ● *vt* amarrer.

**mop** /mɒp/ *n* balai *m* à franges; ~ **of hair** crinière *f* 🄸. ● *vt* (*pt* **mopped**) ~ **(up)** éponger.

**moped** /'məʊped/ *n* vélomoteur *m*.

**moral** /'mɒrəl/ *a* moral. ● *n* morale *f*; **~s** moralité *f*.

**morale** /mə'rɑ:l/ *n* moral *m*.

**morbid** /'mɔ:bɪd/ *a* morbide.

**more** /mɔ:(r)/ *adv* plus; ~ **serious** plus sérieux; **work** ~ travailler plus; **sleep ~ and ~** dormir de plus en plus; **once** ~ une fois de plus; **I don't go there any** ~ je n'y vais plus; ~ **or less** plus ou moins. ● *det* plus de; **a little ~ wine** un peu plus de vin; ~ **bread** encore un peu de pain; **there's no ~ bread** il n'y a plus de pain; **nothing** ~ rien de plus. ● *pron* plus; **cost ~ than** coûter plus cher que; **I need ~ of it** il m'en faut davantage.

**moreover** /mɔ:'rəʊvə(r)/ *adv* de plus.

**morning** /'mɔ:nɪŋ/ *n* matin *m*; (whole morning) matinée *f*.

**Morocco** /mə'rɒkəʊ/ *n* Maroc *m*.

**morsel** /'mɔ:sl/ *n* morceau *m*.

**mortal** /'mɔ:tl/ *a* & *n* mortel/-le (*m*/*f*).

**mortgage** /'mɔ:gɪdʒ/ *n* emprunt-logement *m*. ● *vt* hypothéquer.

**mortuary** /'mɔ:tʃərɪ/ *n* morgue *f*.

**mosaic** /məʊ'zeɪɪk/ *n* mosaïque *f*.

**mosque** /mɒsk/ *n* mosquée *f*.

**mosquito** /mə'ski:təʊ/ *n* (*pl* **~es**) moustique *m*.

**moss** /mɒs/ *n* mousse *f*.

**most** /məʊst/ *det* (nearly all) la plupart de; **~ people** la plupart des gens; **the ~ votes/money** le plus de voix/d'argent. ● *n* le plus. ● *pron* la plupart; **~ of us** la plupart d'entre nous; **~ of the money** la plus grande partie de l'argent; **the ~ I can do is ...** tout ce que je peux faire c'est ... ● *adv* **the ~ beautiful house/hotel in Oxford** la maison la plus belle/l'hôtel le plus beau d'Oxford; **~ interesting** très intéressant; **what I like ~ (of all) is** ce que j'aime le plus c'est. **mostly** *adv* surtout.

**moth** /mɒθ/ *n* papillon *m* de nuit; (in cloth) mite *f*.

**mother** /'mʌðə(r)/ *n* mère *f*. ● *vt* (lit) materner; (fig) dorloter. **motherhood** *n* maternité *f*. **~-in-law** *n* (*pl* **~s-in-law**) belle-mère *f*. **~-of-pearl** *n* nacre *f*. **M~'s Day** *n* la fête des mères. **~-to-be** *n* future maman *f*. **~ tongue** *n* langue *f* maternelle.

**motion** /'məʊʃn/ *n* mouvement *m*; (proposal) motion *f*; **~ picture** (US) film *m*. ● *vt*/*i* **~ (to) sb to** faire signe à qn de. **motionless** *a* immobile.

**motivate** /'məʊtɪveɪt/ *vt* motiver.

**motive** /'məʊtɪv/ *n* motif *m*; (Jur) mobile *m*.

**motor** /'məʊtə(r)/ *n* moteur *m*; (car) auto *f*. ● *a* (*industry, insurance, vehicle*) automobile; (*activity, disorder*: Med) moteur. **~bike** *n* moto *f*. **~ car** *n* auto *f*. **~-cyclist** *n* motocycliste *mf*. **~ home** *n* autocaravane *f*.

**motorist** /'məʊtərɪst/ *n* automobiliste *mf*.

**motorway** /'məʊtəweɪ/ *n* autoroute *f*.

**mottled** /'mɒtld/ *a* tacheté.

**motto** /'mɒtəʊ/ *n* (*pl* **~es**) devise *f*.

**mould** /məʊld/ *n* (shape) moule *m*; (fungus) moisissure *f*. ● *vt* mouler; (influence) former. **moulding** *n* moulure *f*. **mouldy** *a* moisi.

**mount** /maʊnt/ *n* (hill) mont *m*; (horse) monture *f*. ● *vt* (*stairs*) gravir; (*platform, horse, bike*) monter sur; (*jewel, picture, campaign, exhibit*) monter. ● *vi* monter; (*number, toll*) augmenter; (*concern*) grandir.

**mountain** /'maʊntɪn/ *n* montagne *f*; **~ bike** (vélo) tout terrain *m*, VTT *m*. **mountaineer** *n* alpiniste *mf*.

**mourn** /mɔ:n/ *vt*/*i* **~ (for)** pleurer. **mournful** *a* mélancolique. **mourning** *n* deuil *m*.

**mouse** /maʊs/ *n* (*pl* **mice**) souris *f*. **~trap** *n* souricière *f*.

**mouth** /maʊθ/ *n* bouche *f*; (of dog, cat) gueule *f*; (of cave, tunnel) entrée *f*. **mouthful** *n* bouchée *f*. **~wash** *n* eau *f* dentifrice. **~watering** *a* appétissant.

**move** /mu:v/ *vt* (*object*) déplacer; (*limb, head*) bouger; (emotionally) émouvoir; **~ house** déménager. ● *vi* bouger; (*vehicle*) rouler; (change address) déménager; (act)

agir. ● *n* mouvement *m*; (in game) coup *m*; (player's turn) tour *m*; (step, act) manœuvre *f*; (house change) déménagement *m*; **on the ~** en mouvement. □ **~ back** reculer; **~ in** emménager; **~ in with** s'installer avec; **~ on** (*person*) se mettre en route; (*vehicle*) repartir; (*time*) passer; **~ sth on** faire avancer qch; **~ sb on** faire circuler qn; **~ over** *or* **up** se pousser.

**movement** /'mu:vmənt/ *n* mouvement *m*.

**movie** /'mu:vɪ/ *n* (US) film *m*; **the ~s** le cinéma.

**moving** /'mu:vɪŋ/ *a* (*vehicle*) en marche; (*part, target*) mobile; (*staircase*) roulant; (touching) émouvant.

**mow** /məʊ/ *vt* (*pp* **mowed** *or* **mown**) (*lawn*) tondre; (*hay*) couper; **~ down** faucher. **mower** *n* tondeuse *f*.

**MP** *abbr* ⇒MEMBER OF PARLIAMENT

**Mr** /'mɪstə(r)/ *n* (*pl* **Messrs**) **~ Smith** Monsieur *or* M. Smith; **~ President** Monsieur le Président.

**Mrs** /'mɪsɪz/ *n* (*pl* **Mrs**) **~ Smith** Madame *or* Mme Smith.

**Ms** /mɪz/ *n* Mme.

**much** /mʌtʃ/ *adv* beaucoup; **too ~** trop; **very ~** beaucoup; **I like them as ~ as you (do)** je les aime autant que toi. ● *pron* beaucoup; **not ~** pas grand-chose; **he didn't say ~** il n'a pas dit grand-chose; **I ate so ~ that** j'ai tellement mangé que. ● *det* beaucoup de; **too ~ money** trop d'argent; **how ~ time is left?** combien de temps reste-t-il?

**muck** /mʌk/ *n* saletés *fpl*; (manure) fumier *m*. □ **~ about** 🅸 faire l'imbécile. **mucky** *a* sale.

**mud** /mʌd/ *n* boue *f*.

**muddle** /'mʌdl/ *n* (mix-up) malentendu *m*; (mess) pagaille *f* 🅸; **get into a ~** s'embrouiller. □ **~ through** se débrouiller; **~ up** embrouiller.

**muddy** /'mʌdɪ/ *a* couvert de boue.

**muffle** /'mʌfl/ *vt* emmitoufler; (*bell*) assourdir; (*voice*) étouffer.

**mug** /mʌg/ *n* grande tasse *f*; (for beer) chope *f*; (face 🅸) gueule *f* ☒; (fool 🅸) poire *f* 🅸. ● *vt* (*pt* **mugged**) agresser. **mugger** *n* agresseur *m*.

**muggy** /'mʌgɪ/ *a* lourd.

**mule** /mju:l/ *n* mulet *m*.

**multicoloured** /'mʌltɪkʌləd/ *a* multicolore.

**multiple** /'mʌltɪpl/ *a* & *n* multiple (*m*); **~ sclerosis** sclérose *f* en plaques.

**multiplication** /mʌltɪplɪ'keɪʃn/ *n* multiplication *f*. **multiply** *vt*/*i* (se) multiplier.

**multistorey** /mʌltɪ'stɔ:rɪ/ *a* (*car park*) à niveaux multiples.

**mum** /mʌm/ *n* 🅸 maman *f*.

**mumble** /'mʌmbl/ *vt*/*i* marmonner.

**mummy** /'mʌmɪ/ *n* (mother 🅸) maman *f*; (embalmed body) momie *f*.

**mumps** /mʌmps/ *n* oreillons *mpl*.

**munch** /mʌntʃ/ *vt* mâcher.

**mundane** /mʌn'deɪn/ *a* terre-à-terre.

**municipal** /mju:'nɪsɪpl/ *a* municipal.

**mural** /'mjʊərəl/ *a* mural. ● *n* peinture *f* murale.

**murder** /'mɜ:də(r)/ *n* meurtre *m*. ● *vt* assassiner. **murderer** *n* meurtrier *m*, assassin *m*.

**murky** /'mɜ:kɪ/ *a* (**-ier**, **-iest**) (*water*) glauque; (*past*) trouble.

**murmur** /'mɜ:mə(r)/ *n* murmure *m*. ● *vt*/*i* murmurer.

**muscle** /'mʌsl/ *n* muscle *m*. ● *vi* **~ in** 🅸 s'imposer (**on** dans).

**muscular** /'mʌskjʊlə(r)/ *a* (*tissue, disease*) musculaire; (*body, person*) musclé.

**museum** /mju:'zɪəm/ *n* musée *m*.

**mushroom** /'mʌʃrʊm/ *n* champignon *m*. ● *vi* (*town*) proliférer; (*demand*) s'accroître rapidement.

**music** /'mju:zɪk/ *n* musique *f*.

**musical** /'mju:zɪkl/ *a* (*person*) musicien; (*voice*) mélodieux; (*accompaniment*) musical; (*instrument*) de musique. ● *n* comédie *f* musicale.

**musician** /mju:'zɪʃn/ *n* musicien/-ne *m/f*.

**Muslim** /'mʊzlɪm/ *n* Musulman/-e *m/f*. ● *a* musulman.

**mussel** /'mʌsl/ *n* moule *f*.

**must** /mʌst/ *v aux* devoir; **you ~ go** vous devez partir, il faut que vous partiez; **she ~ be consulted** il faut la consulter; **he ~ be old** il doit être vieux; **I ~ have done it** j'ai dû le faire. ● *n* **be a ~** 🄸 être indispensable.

**mustard** /'mʌstəd/ *n* moutarde *f*.

**musty** /'mʌstɪ/ *a* (**-ier, -iest**) (*room*) qui sent le renfermé; (*smell*) de moisi.

**mute** /mju:t/ *a* & *n* muet/-te (*m/f*). **muted** *a* (*colour*) sourd; (*response*) tiède; (*celebration*) mitigé.

**mutilate** /'mju:tɪleɪt/ *vt* mutiler.

**mutter** /'mʌtə(r)/ *vt/i* marmonner.

**mutton** /'mʌtn/ *n* mouton *m*.

**mutual** /'mju:tʃʊəl/ *a* (reciprocal) réciproque; (common) commun; (*consent*) mutuel. **mutually** *adv* mutuellement.

**muzzle** /'mʌzl/ *n* (snout) museau *m*; (device) muselière *f*; (of gun) canon *m*. ● *vt* museler.

**my** /maɪ/ *a* mon, ma, *pl* mes.

**myself** /maɪ'self/ *pron* (reflexive) me, m'; **I've hurt ~** je me suis fait mal; (emphatic) moi-même; **I did it ~** je l'ai fait moi-même; (after preposition) moi, moi-même; **I am proud of ~** je suis fier de moi.

**mysterious** /mɪ'stɪərɪəs/ *a* mystérieux.

**mystery** /'mɪstərɪ/ *n* mystère *m*.

**mystic** /'mɪstɪk/ *a* & *n* mystique (*mf*). **mystical** *a* mystique.

**myth** /mɪθ/ *n* mythe *m*. **mythical** *a* mythique. **mythology** *n* mythologie *f*.

# Nn

**nag** /næg/ *vt/i* (*pt* **nagged**) critiquer; (pester) harceler. **nagging** *a* persistant.

**nail** /neɪl/ *n* clou *m*; (of finger, toe) ongle *m*; **on the ~** sans tarder, tout de suite. ● *vt* clouer. **~ polish** *n* vernis *m* à ongles.

**naïve** /naɪ'i:v/ *a* naïf.

**naked** /'neɪkɪd/ *a* nu; **to the ~ eye** à l'œil nu.

**name** /neɪm/ *n* nom *m*; (fig) réputation *f*. ● *vt* nommer; (*terms*) fixer; **be ~d after** porter le nom de.

**namely** /'neɪmlɪ/ *adv* à savoir.

**nanny** /'nænɪ/ *n* nurse *f*.

**nap** /næp/ *n* somme *m*.

**nape** /neɪp/ *n* nuque *f*.

**napkin** /'næpkɪn/ *n* serviette *f*.

**nappy** /'næpɪ/ *n* couche *f*.

**narcotic** /nɑ:'kɒtɪk/ *a* & *n* narcotique (*m*).

**narrative** /'nærətɪv/ *n* récit *m*.

**narrator** *n* narrateur/-trice *m/f*.

**narrow** /ˈnærəʊ/ *a* étroit. ● *vt/i* (se) rétrécir; (limit) (se) limiter; **~ down the choices** limiter les choix. **~-minded** *a* à l'esprit étroit; (*ideas*) étroit.

**nasal** /ˈneɪzl/ *a* nasal.

**nasty** /ˈnɑːstɪ/ *a* (**-ier**, **-iest**) mauvais, désagréable; (malicious) méchant.

**nation** /ˈneɪʃn/ *n* nation *f*.

**national** /ˈnæʃnəl/ *a* national. ● *n* ressortissant/-e *m/f*.

**nationality** /næʃəˈnælətɪ/ *n* nationalité *f*.

**nationalize** /ˈnæʃnəlaɪz/ *vt* nationaliser.

**nationally** /ˈnæʃnəlɪ/ *adv* à l'échelle nationale.

**native** /ˈneɪtɪv/ *n* (local inhabitant) autochtone *mf*; (non-European) indigène *mf*; **be a ~ of** être originaire de. ● *a* indigène; (*country*) natal; (inborn) inné; **~ language** langue *f* maternelle; **~ speaker of French** personne *f* de langue maternelle française.

**natural** /ˈnætʃrəl/ *a* naturel.

**naturally** /ˈnætʃrəlɪ/ *adv* (normally, of course) naturellement; (by nature) de nature.

**nature** /ˈneɪtʃə(r)/ *n* nature *f*.

**naughty** /ˈnɔːtɪ/ *a* (**-ier**, **-iest**) vilain, méchant; (indecent) grivois.

**nausea** /ˈnɔːsɪə/ *n* nausée *f*. **nauseous** *a* (*smell*) écœurant.

**nautical** /ˈnɔːtɪkl/ *a* nautique.

**naval** /ˈneɪvl/ *a* (*battle*) naval; (*officer*) de marine.

**navel** /ˈneɪvl/ *n* nombril *m*.

**navigate** /ˈnævɪgeɪt/ *vt* (*sea*) naviguer sur; (*ship*) piloter. ● *vi* naviguer. **navigation** *n* navigation *f*.

**navy** /ˈneɪvɪ/ *n* marine *f*. ● *a* **~ (blue)** bleu *inv* marine.

**near** /nɪə(r)/ *adv* près; **draw ~** (s')approcher (**to** de). ● *prep* près de. ● *a* proche; **~ to** près de. ● *vt* approcher de.

**nearby** /nɪəˈbaɪ/ *a* proche. ● *adv* à proximité.

**nearly** /ˈnɪəlɪ/ *adv* presque; **I ~ forgot** j'ai failli oublier; **not ~ as pretty as** loin d'être aussi joli que.

**nearness** /ˈnɪənɪs/ *n* proximité *f*.

**nearside** /ˈnɪəsaɪd/ *a* (Auto) du côté du passager.

**neat** /niːt/ *a* soigné, net; (*room*) bien rangé; (clever) habile; (*drink*) sec. **neatly** *adv* avec soin; habilement. **neatness** *n* netteté *f*.

**necessarily** /nesəˈserəlɪ/ *adv* nécessairement.

**necessary** /ˈnesəsərɪ/ *a* nécessaire.

**necessitate** /nɪˈsesɪteɪt/ *vt* nécessiter.

**necessity** /nɪˈsesətɪ/ *n* nécessité *f*; (thing) chose *f* indispensable.

**neck** /nek/ *n* cou *m*; (of dress) encolure *f*. **~ and neck** *a* à égalité. **~lace** *n* collier *m*. **~line** *n* encolure *f*. **~tie** *n* cravate *f*.

**nectarine** /ˈnektərɪn/ *n* brugnon *m*, nectarine *f*.

**need** /niːd/ *n* besoin *m*. ● *vt* avoir besoin de; (demand) demander; **you ~ not come** vous n'êtes pas obligé de venir.

**needle** /ˈniːdl/ *n* aiguille *f*.

**needless** /ˈniːdlɪs/ *a* inutile.

**needlework** /ˈniːdlwɜːk/ *n* couture *f*; (object) ouvrage *m* (à l'aiguille).

**needy** /ˈniːdɪ/ *a* (**-ier**, **-iest**) nécessiteux. ● *n* **the ~** les indigents.

**negative** /ˈnegətɪv/ *a* négatif. ● *n* (of photograph) négatif *m*; (word: Gram) négation *f*; **in the ~** (answer) par la

négative; (Gram) à la forme négative.

**neglect** /nɪ'glekt/ *vt* négliger, laisser à l'abandon; ~ **to do** négliger de faire. ● *n* manque *m* de soins; **(state of)** ~ abandon *m*.

**negligent** /'neglɪdʒənt/ *a* négligent.

**negotiate** /nɪ'gəʊʃɪeɪt/ *vt/i* négocier. **negotiation** *n* négociation *f*.

**neigh** /neɪ/ *n* hennissement *m*. ● *vi* hennir.

**neighbour**, (US) **neighbor** /'neɪbə(r)/ *n* voisin/-e *m/f*. **neighbourhood** *n* voisinage *m*, quartier *m*; **in the ~hood of** aux alentours de. **neighbouring** *a* voisin. **neighbourly** *a* amical.

**neither** /'naɪðə(r)/ *a* & *pron* aucun/-e des deux, ni l'un/-e ni l'autre. ● *adv* ni; ~ **big nor small** ni grand ni petit. ● *conj* (ne) non plus.

**nephew** /'nevju:/ *n* neveu *m*.

**nerve** /nɜ:v/ *n* nerf *m*; (courage) courage *m*; (calm) sang-froid *m*; (impudence 🄸) culot *m*; **~s** (before exams) trac *m*. **~-racking** *a* éprouvant.

**nervous** /'nɜ:vəs/ *a* nerveux; **be** *or* **feel** ~ (afraid) avoir peur; ~ **breakdown** dépression *f* nerveuse. **nervousness** *n* nervosité *f*; (fear) crainte *f*.

**nest** /nest/ *n* nid *m*. ● *vi* nicher. **~-egg** *n* pécule *m*.

**nestle** /'nesl/ *vi* se blottir.

**net** /net/ *n* filet *m*; (Comput) net *m*, Internet *m*. ● *vt* (*pt* **netted**) prendre au filet. ● *a* (weight) net. **~ball** *n* netball *m*.

**Netherlands** /'neðələndz/ *n* **the** ~ les Pays-Bas *mpl*.

**netiquette** /'netɪket/ *n* nétiquette *f*.

**Netsurfer** /'netsɜ:fər/ *n* Internaute *mf*.

**nettle** /'netl/ *n* ortie *f*.

**network** /'netwɜ:k/ *n* réseau *m*.

**neurotic** /njʊə'rɒtɪk/ *a* & *n* névrosé/-e (*m/f*).

**neuter** /'nju:tə(r)/ *a* & *n* neutre (*m*). ● *vt* (castrate) castrer.

**neutral** /'nju:trəl/ *a* neutre; ~ **(gear)** (Auto) point *m* mort.

**never** /'nevə(r)/ *adv* (ne) jamais; **he ~ refuses** il ne refuse jamais; **I ~ saw him** 🄸 je ne l'ai pas vu; ~ **again** plus jamais; ~ **mind** (don't worry) ne vous en faites pas; (it doesn't matter) peu importe.

**nevertheless** /nevəðə'les/ *adv* néanmoins, toutefois.

**new** /nju:/ *a* nouveau; (brand-new) neuf. **~-born** *a* nouveau-né. **~comer** *n* nouveau venu *m*, nouvelle venue *f*.

**newly** /'nju:lɪ/ *adv* nouvellement. **~weds** *npl* jeunes mariés *mpl*.

**news** /nju:z/ *n* nouvelle(s) *f(pl)*; (radio, press) informations *fpl*; (TV) actualités *fpl*, informations *fpl*. ~ **agency** *n* agence *f* de presse. **~agent** *n* marchand/-e *m/f* de journaux. **~caster** *n* présentateur/-trice *m/f*. **~group** *n* (Internet) forum *m* de discussion. **~letter** *n* bulletin *m*. **~paper** *n* journal *m*.

**new year** *n* nouvel an *m*. **New Year's Day** *n* le jour de l'an. **New Year's Eve** *n* la Saint-Sylvestre.

**New Zealand** /nju:'zi:lənd/ *n* Nouvelle-Zélande *f*.

**next** /nekst/ *a* prochain; (adjoining) voisin; (following) suivant; ~ **to** à côté de; ~ **door** à côté (**to** de). ● *adv* la prochaine fois; (afterwards) ensuite. ● *n* suivant/-e *m/f*; (*e-mail*) message *m* suivant. **~-door** *a* d'à côté. ~ **of kin** *n* parent *m* le plus proche.

**nib** /nɪb/ *n* plume *f*.

**nibble** /'nɪbl/ *vt/i* grignoter.

**nice** /naɪs/ *a* agréable, bon; (kind) gentil; (pretty) joli; (respectable) bien *inv*; (subtle) délicat. **nicely** *adv* agréablement; gentiment; (well) bien.

**nicety** /'naɪsətɪ/ *n* subtilité *f*.

**niche** /ni:ʃ/ *n* (recess) niche *f*; (fig) place *f*, situation *f*.

**nick** /nɪk/ *n* petite entaille *f*; **be in good/bad ~** être en bon/mauvais état. ● *vt* (steal, arrest 🅸) piquer.

**nickel** /'nɪkl/ *n* (metal) nickel *m*; (US) pièce *f* de cinq cents.

**nickname** /'nɪkneɪm/ *n* surnom *m*. ● *vt* surnommer.

**nicotine** /'nɪkəti:n/ *n* nicotine *f*.

**niece** /ni:s/ *n* nièce *f*.

**niggling** /'nɪglɪŋ/ *a* (*person*) tatillon; (*detail*) insignifiant.

**night** /naɪt/ *n* nuit *f*; (evening) soir *m*. ● *a* de nuit. **~-cap** *n* boisson *f* (*avant d'aller se coucher*). **~-club** *n* boîte *f* de nuit. **~-dress** *n* chemise *f* de nuit. **~fall** *n* tombée *f* de la nuit. **nightie** *n* chemise *f* de nuit.

**nightingale** /'naɪtɪŋgeɪl/ *n* rossignol *m*.

**nightly** /'naɪtlɪ/ *a* & *adv* (de) chaque nuit *or* soir.

**night: ~mare** *n* cauchemar *m*. **~-time** *n* nuit *f*.

**nil** /nɪl/ *n* (Sport) zéro *m*. ● *a* (*chances, risk*) nul.

**nimble** /'nɪmbl/ *a* agile.

**nine** /naɪn/ *a* & *n* neuf (*m*).

**nineteen** /naɪn'ti:n/ *a* & *n* dix-neuf (*m*).

**ninety** /'naɪntɪ/ *a* & *n* quatre-vingt-dix (*m*).

**ninth** /'naɪnθ/ *a* & *n* neuvième (*mf*).

**nip** /nɪp/ *vt/i* (*pt* **nipped**) (pinch) pincer; (rush 🅸) courir; **~ out/back** sortir/rentrer rapidement. ● *n* pincement *m*.

**nipple** /'nɪpl/ *n* mamelon *m*; (of baby's bottle) tétine *f*.

**nippy** /'nɪpɪ/ *a* (**-ier**, **-iest**) (*air*) piquant; (*car*) rapide.

**nitrogen** /'naɪtrədʒən/ *n* azote *m*.

**no** /nəʊ/ *det* aucun/-e; pas de; **~ man** aucun homme; **~ money/time** pas d'argent/de temps; **~ one** = NOBODY; **~ smoking/entry** défense de fumer/d'entrer; **~ way!** 🅸 pas question! ● *adv* non. ● *n* (*pl* **noes**) non *m inv*.

**nobility** /nəʊ'bɪlɪtɪ/ *n* noblesse *f*.

**noble** /'nəʊbl/ *a* noble.

**nobody** /'nəʊbədɪ/ *pron* (ne) personne; **he knows ~** il ne connaît personne. ● *n* nullité *f*.

**nocturnal** /nɒk'tɜ:nl/ *a* nocturne.

**nod** /nɒd/ *vt/i* (*pt* **nodded**); **~ (one's head)** faire un signe de tête; **~ off** s'endormir. ● *n* signe *m* de tête.

**noise** /nɔɪz/ *n* bruit *m*; **make a ~** faire du bruit. **noisily** *adv* bruyamment. **noisy** *a* (**-ier**, **-iest**) bruyant.

**no man's land** *n* no man's land *m*.

**nominal** /'nɒmɪnl/ *a* symbolique, nominal; (*value*) nominal.

**nominate** /'nɒmɪneɪt/ *vt* nommer; (put forward) proposer.

**none** /nʌn/ *pron* aucun/-e; **~ of us** aucun/-e de nous; **I have ~** je n'en ai pas.

**non-existent** /nɒnɪg'zɪstənt/ *a* inexistant.

**nonplussed** /nɒn'plʌst/ *a* perplexe.

**nonsense** /'nɒnsəns/ *n* absurdités *fpl*.

**non-smoker** /nɒn'sməʊkə(r)/ *n* non-fumeur *m*.

**non-stick** *a* antiadhésif.

**non-stop** /nɒn'stɒp/ *a* (*train, flight*) direct. ● *adv* sans arrêt.

**noodles** /'nu:dlz/ *npl* nouilles *fpl.*

**noon** /nu:n/ *n* midi *m.*

**nor** /nɔ:(r)/ *adv* ni. ● *conj* (ne) non plus; ~ **shall I come** je ne viendrai pas non plus.

**norm** /nɔ:m/ *n* norme *f.*

**normal** /'nɔ:ml/ *a* normal.

**Norman** /'nɔ:mən/ *n* Normand/-e *m/f.* ● *a* (*village*) normand; (*arch*) roman.

**north** /nɔ:θ/ *n* nord *m.* ● *a* nord *inv*, du nord. ● *adv* vers le nord.

**North America** *n* Amérique *f* du Nord.

**north-east** /nɔ:θ'i:st/ *n* nord-est *m.*

**northerly** /'nɔ:ðəlɪ/ *a* (*wind, area*) du nord; (*point*) au nord.

**northern** /'nɔ:ðən/ *a* (*accent*) du nord; (*coast*) nord. **northerner** *n* habitant/-e *m/f* du nord.

**northward** /'nɔ:θwəd/ *a* (*side*) nord *inv*; (*journey*) vers le nord.

**north-west** /nɔ:θ'west/ *n* nord-ouest *m.*

**Norway** /'nɔ:weɪ/ *n* Norvège *f.*

**Norwegian** /nɔ:'wi:dʒən/ *n* (*person*) Norvégien/-ne *m/f*; (*language*) norvégien *m.* ● *a* norvégien.

**nose** /nəʊz/ *n* nez *m.* ● *vi* ~ **about** fouiner.

**nosedive** /'nəʊzdaɪv/ *n* piqué *m.* ● *vi* descendre en piqué.

**nostalgia** /nɒ'stældʒə/ *n* nostalgie *f.*

**nostril** /'nɒstrəl/ *n* narine *f*; (of horse) naseau *m.*

**nosy** /'nəʊzɪ/ *a* (**-ier, -iest**) ⊡ curieux, indiscret.

**not** /nɒt/ *adv* (ne) pas; **I do ~ know** je ne sais pas; ~ **at all** pas du tout; ~ **yet** pas encore; **I suppose ~** je suppose que non.

**notably** /'nəʊtəblɪ/ *adv* notamment.

**notch** /nɒtʃ/ *n* entaille *f.* ● *vt* ~ **up** (score) marquer.

**note** /nəʊt/ *n* note *f*; (banknote) billet *m*; (short letter) mot *m.* ● *vt* noter; (notice) remarquer. ~**book** *n* carnet *m.*

**nothing** /'nʌθɪŋ/ *pron* (ne) rien; **he eats ~** il ne mange rien; ~ **else** rien d'autre; ~ **much** pas grand-chose; **for ~** pour rien, gratis. ● *n* rien *m*; (person) nullité *f.* ● *adv* nullement.

**notice** /'nəʊtɪs/ *n* avis *m*, annonce *f*; (poster) affiche *f*; **(advance)** ~ préavis *m*; **at short** ~ dans des délais très brefs; **give in one's** ~ donner sa démission; **take** ~ faire attention (**of** à). ● *vt* remarquer, observer. **noticeable** *a* visible. ~**-board** *n* tableau *m* d'affichage.

**notify** /'nəʊtɪfaɪ/ *vt* (inform) aviser; (make known) notifier.

**notion** /'nəʊʃn/ *n* idée *f*, notion *f.*

**notorious** /nəʊ'tɔ:rɪəs/ *a* (*criminal*) notoire; (*district*) mal famé; (*case*) tristement célèbre.

**notwithstanding** /nɒtwɪθ'stændɪŋ/ *prep* malgré. ● *adv* néanmoins.

**nought** /nɔ:t/ *n* zéro *m.*

**noun** /naʊn/ *n* nom *m.*

**nourish** /'nʌrɪʃ/ *vt* nourrir. **nourishing** *a* nourrissant. **nourishment** *n* nourriture *f.*

**novel** /'nɒvl/ *n* roman *m.* ● *a* nouveau. **novelist** *n* romancier/-ière *m/f.* **novelty** *n* nouveauté *f.*

**November** /nəʊ'vembə(r)/ *n* novembre *m.*

**now** /naʊ/ *adv* maintenant. ● *conj* maintenant que; **just** ~ maintenant; (a moment ago) tout à l'heure; ~ **and again**, ~ **and then** de temps à autre.

**nowadays** /ˈnaʊədeɪz/ *adv* de nos jours.

**nowhere** /ˈnəʊweə(r)/ *adv* nulle part.

**nozzle** /ˈnɒzl/ *n* (tip) embout *m*; (of hose) jet *m*.

**nuclear** /ˈnju:klɪə(r)/ *a* nucléaire.

**nude** /nju:d/ *a* nu. ● *n* nu/-e *m/f*; **in the ~** tout nu.

**nudge** /nʌdʒ/ *vt* pousser du coude. ● *n* coup *m* de coude.

**nudism** /ˈnju:dɪzəm/ *n* nudisme *m*. **nudity** *n* nudité *f*.

**nuisance** /ˈnju:sns/ *n* (thing, event) ennui *m*; (person) peste *f*; **be a ~** être embêtant.

**null** /nʌl/ *a* nul.

**numb** /nʌm/ *a* engourdi (**with** par). ● *vt* engourdir.

**number** /ˈnʌmbə(r)/ *n* nombre *m*; (of ticket, house, page) numéro *m*; (written figure) chiffre *m*; **a ~ of people** plusieurs personnes. ● *vt* numéroter; (count, include) compter. **~-plate** *n* plaque *f* d'immatriculation.

**numeral** /ˈnju:mərəl/ *n* chiffre *m*.

**numerate** /ˈnju:mərət/ *a* qui sait compter.

**numerical** /nju:ˈmerɪkl/ *a* numérique.

**numerous** /ˈnju:mərəs/ *a* nombreux.

**nun** /nʌn/ *n* religieuse *f*.

**nurse** /nɜ:s/ *n* infirmier/-ière *m/f*; (nanny) nurse *f*. ● *vt* soigner; (*hope*) nourrir.

**nursery** /ˈnɜ:sərɪ/ *n* (room) chambre *f* d'enfants; (for plants) pépinière *f*; **(day) ~** crèche *f*. **~ rhyme** *n* comptine *f*. **~ school** *n* (école) maternelle *f*.

**nursing home** *n* maison *f* de retraite.

**nut** /nʌt/ *n* (walnut, Brazil nut) noix *f*; (hazelnut) noisette *f*; (peanut) cacahuète *f*; (Tech) écrou *m*. **~crackers** *npl* casse-noix *m inv*.

**nutmeg** /ˈnʌtmeg/ *n* muscade *f*.

**nutrient** /ˈnju:trɪənt/ *n* substance *f* nutritive.

**nutritious** /nju:ˈtrɪʃəs/ *a* nutritif.

**nuts** /nʌts/ *a* (crazy Ⓘ) cinglé.

**nutshell** /ˈnʌtʃel/ *n* coquille *f* de noix; **in a ~** en un mot.

**nylon** /ˈnaɪlɒn/ *n* nylon *m*.

# Oo

**oak** /əʊk/ *n* chêne *m*.

**OAP** *abbr* (**old-age pensioner**) retraité/-e *m/f*.

**oar** /ɔ:(r)/ *n* rame *f*.

**oath** /əʊθ/ *n* (promise) serment *m*; (swear-word) juron *m*.

**oats** /əʊts/ *npl* avoine *f*.

**obedience** /əˈbi:dɪəns/ *n* obéissance *f*. **obedient** *a* obéissant. **obediently** *adv* docilement.

**obese** /əʊˈbi:s/ *a* obèse.

**obey** /əˈbeɪ/ *vt/i* obéir (à).

**object**[1] /ˈɒbdʒɪkt/ *n* (thing) objet *m*; (aim) but *m*; (Gram) complément *m* d'objet; **money is no ~** l'argent n'est pas un problème.

**object**[2] /əbˈdʒekt/ *vi* protester. ● *vt* **~ that** objecter que; **~ to** (*behaviour*) désapprouver; (*plan*) protester contre. **objection** *n* objection *f*; (drawback) inconvénient *m*.

**objective** /əbˈdʒektɪv/ *a* & *n* objectif (*m*).

**obligation** /ɒblɪ'geɪʃn/ *n* devoir *m*.

**obligatory** /ə'blɪgətrɪ/ *a* obligatoire.

**oblige** /ə'blaɪdʒ/ *vt* obliger (**to do** à faire).

**oblivion** /ə'blɪvɪən/ *n* oubli *m*. **oblivious** *a* inconscient (**to, of** de).

**oblong** /'ɒblɒŋ/ *a* oblong. ● *n* rectangle *m*.

**obnoxious** /əb'nɒkʃəs/ *a* odieux.

**oboe** /'əʊbəʊ/ *n* hautbois *m*.

**obscene** /əb'si:n/ *a* obscène.

**obscure** /əb'skjʊə(r)/ *a* obscur. ● *vt* obscurcir; (conceal) cacher.

**observance** /əb'zɜ:vəns/ *n* (of law) respect *m*; (of sabbath) observance *f*. **observant** *a* observateur.

**observation** /ɒbzə'veɪʃn/ *n* observation *f*.

**observe** /əb'zɜ:v/ *vt* observer; (remark) remarquer.

**obsess** /əb'ses/ *vt* obséder. **obsession** *n* obsession *f*. **obsessive** *a* (*person*) maniaque; (*thought*) obsédant; (*illness*) obsessionnel.

**obsolete** /'ɒbsəli:t/ *a* dépassé.

**obstacle** /'ɒbstəkl/ *n* obstacle *m*.

**obstinate** /'ɒbstɪnət/ *a* obstiné.

**obstruct** /əb'strʌkt/ *vt* (*road*) bloquer; (*view*) cacher; (*progress*) gêner. **obstruction** *n* (act) obstruction *f*; (thing) obstacle *m*; (in traffic) encombrement *m*.

**obtain** /əb'teɪn/ *vt* obtenir. ● *vi* avoir cours. **obtainable** *a* disponible.

**obvious** /'ɒbvɪəs/ *a* évident. **obviously** *adv* manifestement.

**occasion** /ə'keɪʒn/ *n* occasion *f*; (big event) événement *m*; **on ~** à l'occasion.

**occasional** /ə'keɪʒənl/ *a* (*event*) qui a lieu de temps en temps; **the ~ letter** une lettre de temps en temps. **occasionally** *adv* de temps à autre.

**occupation** /ɒkjʊ'peɪʃn/ *n* (activity) occupation *f*; (job) métier *m*, profession *f*. **occupational therapy** *n* ergothérapie *f*.

**occupier** /'ɒkjʊpaɪə(r)/ *n* occupant/-e *m*/*f*.

**occupy** /'ɒkjʊpaɪ/ *vi* occuper.

**occur** /ə'kɜ:(r)/ *vi* (*pt* **occurred**) se produire; (arise) se présenter; **~ to sb** venir à l'esprit de qn.

**occurrence** /ə'kʌrəns/ *n* (event) fait *m*; (instance) occurrence *f*.

**ocean** /'əʊʃn/ *n* océan *m*.

**Oceania** /əʊʃɪ'eɪnɪə/ *n* Océanie *f*.

**o'clock** /ə'klɒk/ *adv* **it is six ~** il est six heures; **at one ~** à une heure.

**October** /ɒk'təʊbə(r)/ *n* octobre *m*.

**octopus** /'ɒktəpəs/ *n* (*pl* **~es**) pieuvre *f*.

**odd** /ɒd/ *a* bizarre; (*number*) impair; (left over) qui reste; (*sock*) dépareillé; **write the ~ article** écrire un article de temps en temps; **~ jobs** menus travaux *mpl*; **twenty ~** vingt et quelques. **oddity** *n* bizarrerie *f*.

**odds** /ɒdz/ *npl* chances *fpl*; (in betting) cote *f* (**on** de); **at ~** en désaccord; **it makes no ~** ça ne fait rien; **~ and ends** des petites choses.

**odour**, (US) **odor** /'əʊdə(r)/ *n* odeur *f*. **odourless** *a* inodore.

**of** /ɒv/

⇨ For expressions such as **of course, consist of** ⇨**course, consist.**

● *preposition*

····➤ de; **a photo ~ the dog** une photo du chien; **the king ~ the beasts** le roi des animaux; **(made) ~ gold** en or; **it's kind ~ you** c'est très gentil de votre part; **some ~ us** quelques-uns d'entre nous; **~ it/them** en; **have you heard ~ it?** est-ce que tu en as entendu parler?

**off** /ɒf/ *adv* **be ~** partir, s'en aller; **I'm ~** je m'en vais; **30 metres ~** à 30 mètres; **a month ~** dans un mois. ● *a* (*gas, water*) coupé; (*tap*) fermé; (*light, TV*) éteint; (*party, match*) annulé; (bad) (*food*) avarié; (*milk*) tourné; **Friday is my day ~** je ne travaille pas le vendredi; **25% ~** 25% de remise. ● *prep* **3 metres ~ the ground** 3 mètres (au-dessus) du sol; **just ~ the kitchen** juste à côté de la cuisine.

**offence** /ə'fens/ *n* (Jur) infraction *f*; **give ~ to** offenser; **take ~** s'offenser (**at** de).

**offend** /ə'fend/ *vt* offenser; **be ~ed** s'offenser (**at** de). ● *vi* (Jur) commettre une infraction. **offender** *n* délinquant/-e *m/f*.

**offensive** /ə'fensɪv/ *a* (*remark*) injurieux; (*language*) grossier; (*smell*) repoussant; (*weapon*) offensif. ● *n* offensive *f*.

**offer** /'ɒfə(r)/ *vt* (*pt* **offered**) offrir. ● *n* offre *f*; **on ~** en promotion.

**offhand** /ɒf'hænd/ *a* désinvolte. ● *adv* à l'improviste.

**office** /'ɒfɪs/ *n* bureau *m*; (duty) fonction *f*; **in ~** au pouvoir. ● *a* de bureau.

**officer** /'ɒfɪsə(r)/ *n* (army) officier *m*; **(police) ~** policier *m*; **(government) ~** fonctionnaire *mf*.

**official** /ə'fɪʃl/ *a* officiel. ● *n* (civil servant) fonctionnaire *mf*; (of party, union) officiel/-le *m/f*; (of police, customs) agent *m*.

**off**: **~-licence** *n* magasin *m* de vins et spiritueux. **~-line** *a* autonome; (switched off) déconnecté; (Comput) hors connexion. **~-load** *vt* (*stock*) écouler; (Comput) décharger. **~-peak** *a* (*call*) au tarif réduit; (*travel*) en période creuse. **~-putting** *a* rebutant. **~set** *vt* (*pt* **-set**; *pres p* **-setting**) compenser. **~shore** *a* (*waters*) du large; (*funds*) hors-lieu *inv*. **~side** *a* (Sport) hors jeu *inv*; (Auto) du côté du conducteur. **~spring** *n inv* progéniture *f*. **~-white** *a* blanc cassé *inv*.

**often** /'ɒfn/ *adv* souvent; **how ~ do you meet?** vous vous voyez tous les combien?; **every so ~** de temps en temps.

**oil** /ɔɪl/ *n* (for lubrication, cooking) huile *f*; (for fuel) pétrole *m*; (for heating) mazout *m*. ● *vt* huiler. **~field** *n* gisement *m* pétrolifère. **~-painting** *n* peinture *f* à l'huile. **~skins** *npl* ciré *m*. **~-tanker** *n* pétrolier *m*.

**oily** /'ɔɪlɪ/ *a* graisseux.

**ointment** /'ɔɪntmənt/ *n* pommade *f*.

**OK**, **okay** /əʊ'keɪ/ *a* d'accord; **is it ~ if...?** ça va si...?; **feel ~** aller bien.

**old** /əʊld/ *a* vieux; (*person*) vieux, âgé; (former) ancien; **how ~ is he?** quel âge a-t-il?; **he is eight years ~** il a huit ans; **~er, ~est** aîné. **~ age** *n* vieillesse *f*. **~-age pensioner** *n* retraité/-e *m/f*. **~-fashioned** *a* démodé; (person) vieux jeu *inv*. **~ man** *n* vieillard *m*, vieux *m*. **~ woman** *n* vieille *f*.

**olive** /'ɒlɪv/ *n* olive *f*; **~ oil** huile *f* d'olive. ● *a* olive *inv*.

**Olympic** /ə'lımpık/ *a* olympique. ~ **Games** *npl* Jeux *mpl* olympiques.

**omelette** /'ɒmlıt/ *n* omelette *f*.

**omen** /'əʊmen/ *n* augure *m*.

**ominous** /'ɒmınəs/ *a* (*presence, cloud*) menaçant; (*sign*) de mauvais augure.

**omission** /ə'mıʃn/ *n* omission *f*. **omit** *vt* (*pt* **omitted**) omettre.

**on** /ɒn/ *prep* sur; ~ **the table** sur la table; **put the key** ~ **it** mets la clé dessus; ~ **22 March** le 22 mars; ~ **Monday** lundi; ~ **TV** à la télé; ~ **video** en vidéo; **be** ~ **steroids** prendre des stéroïdes; ~ **arriving** en arrivant. ● *a* (*TV, oven, light*) allumé; (*dishwasher, radio*) en marche; (*tap*) ouvert; (*lid*) mis; **the match is still** ~ le match aura lieu quand même; **the news is** ~ **in 10 minutes** les informations sont dans 10 minutes. ● *adv* **have sth** ~ porter qch; **20 years** ~ 20 ans plus tard; **from that day** ~ à partir de ce jour-là; **further** ~ plus loin; ~ **and off** (occasionally) de temps en temps; **go** ~ **and** ~ (*person*) parler pendant des heures.

**once** /wʌns/ *adv* une fois; (formerly) autrefois. ● *conj* une fois que; **all at** ~ tout d'un coup.

**oncoming** /'ɒnkʌmıŋ/ *a* (*vehicle*) qui approche.

**one** /wʌn/ *det & n* un/-e (*m/f*). ● *pron* un/-e *m/f*; (impersonal) on; ~ **(and only)** seul (et unique); **a big** ~ un grand/une grande; **this/that** ~ celui-ci/-là, celle-ci/-là; ~ **another** l'un/-e l'autre. ~**-off** *a* ⊡ unique, exceptionnel. ~**self** *pron* soi-même; (reflexive) se. ~**-way** *a* (*street*) à sens unique; (*ticket*) simple.

**ongoing** /'ɒngəʊıŋ/ *a* (*process*) continu; **be** ~ être en cours.

**onion** /'ʌnjən/ *n* oignon *m*.

**on-line** /ɒn'laın/ *a & adv* en ligne.

**onlooker** /'ɒnlʊkə(r)/ *n* spectateur/-trice *m/f*.

**only** /'əʊnlı/ *a* seul; ~ **son** fils unique. ● *adv & conj* seulement; **he is** ~ **six** il n'a que six ans.

**onset** /'ɒnset/ *n* début *m*.

**onward(s)** /'ɒnwəd(z)/ *adv* en avant.

**open** /'əʊpən/ *a* ouvert; (*view*) dégagé; (free to all) public; (undisguised) manifeste; (*question*) en attente; **in the** ~ **air** en plein air. ● *vt/i* (*door*) (s')ouvrir; (*shop, play*) ouvrir; ~ **out** *or* **up** (s')ouvrir. ~**-ended** *a* (*stay*) de durée indéterminée; (*debate, question*) ouvert. ~**-heart** *a* (*surgery*) à cœur ouvert.

**opening** /'əʊpənıŋ/ *n* (of book) début *m*; (of exhibition, shop) ouverture *f*; (of film) première *f*; (in market) débouché *m*; (job) poste *m* (disponible).

**open**: ~**-minded** *a* **be** ~**-minded** avoir l'esprit ouvert. ~**-plan** *a* paysagé.

**opera** /'ɒpərə/ *n* opéra *m*.

**operate** /'ɒpəreıt/ *vt/i* opérer; (Tech) (faire) fonctionner; ~ **on** (Med) opérer; **operating theatre** salle *f* d'opération.

**operation** /ɒpə'reıʃn/ *n* opération *f*; **have an** ~ se faire opérer; **in** ~ (*plan*) en vigueur; (*mine*) en service.

**operative** /'ɒpərətıv/ *n* employé/-e *m/f*. ● *a* (*law*) en vigueur.

**operator** /'ɒpəreıtə(r)/ *n* opérateur/-trice *m/f*; (telephonist) standardiste *mf*.

**opinion** /ə'pınjən/ *n* opinion *f*, avis *m*. **opinionated** *a* qui a des avis sur tout.

**opponent** /ə'pəʊnənt/ *n* adversaire *mf.*

**opportunity** /ɒpə'tju:nətɪ/ *n* occasion *f* (**to do** de faire).

**oppose** /ə'pəʊz/ *vt* s'opposer à; **as ~d to** par opposition à. **opposing** *a* opposé.

**opposite** /'ɒpəzɪt/ *a* (*direction, side*) opposé; (*building*) d'en face. ● *n* contraire *m.* ● *adv* en face. ● *prep* **~ (to)** en face de.

**opposition** /ɒpə'zɪʃn/ *n* opposition *f.*

**oppress** /ə'pres/ *vt* opprimer. **oppressive** *a* (cruel) oppressif; (*heat*) oppressant.

**opt** /ɒpt/ *vi* **~ for** opter pour; **~ out** refuser de participer (**of** à); **~ to do** choisir de faire.

**optical** /'ɒptɪkl/ *a* optique. **~ illusion** *n* illusion *f* d'optique. **~ scanner** *n* lecteur *m* optique.

**optician** /ɒp'tɪʃn/ *n* opticien/-ne *m/f.*

**optimism** /'ɒptɪmɪzəm/ *n* optimisme *m.* **optimist** *n* optimiste *mf.* **optimistic** *a* optimiste.

**option** /'ɒpʃn/ *n* option *f*; (choice) choix *m*

**optional** /'ɒpʃənl/ *a* facultatif; **~ extras** accessoires *mpl* en option.

**or** /ɔ:(r)/ *conj* ou; (with negative) ni.

**oral** /'ɔ:rəl/ *n & a* oral (*m*).

**orange** /'ɒrɪndʒ/ *n* (fruit) orange *f*; (*colour*) orange *m.* ● *a* (colour) orange *inv.*

**orbit** /'ɔ:bɪt/ *n* orbite *f.* ● *vt* décrire une orbite autour de.

**orchard** /'ɔ:tʃəd/ *n* verger *m.*

**orchestra** /'ɔ:kɪstrə/ *n* orchestre *m.*

**orchid** /'ɔ:kɪd/ *n* orchidée *f.*

**ordeal** /ɔ:'di:l/ *n* épreuve *f.*

**order** /'ɔ:də(r)/ *n* ordre *m*; (Comm) commande *f*; **in ~** (tidy) en ordre; (*document*) en règle; **in ~ that** pour que; **in ~ to** pour. ● *vt* ordonner; (*goods*) commander; **~ sb to** ordonner à qn de.

**orderly** /'ɔ:dəlɪ/ *a* (tidy) ordonné; (not unruly) discipliné. ● *n* (Mil) planton *m*; (Med) aide-soignant/-e *m/f.*

**ordinary** /'ɔ:dɪnrɪ/ *a* (usual) ordinaire; (average) moyen.

**ore** /ɔ:(r)/ *n* minerai *m.*

**organ** /'ɔ:gən/ *n* organe *m*; (Mus) orgue *m.*

**organic** /ɔ:'gænɪk/ *a* organique; (*produce*) biologique.

**organization** /ɔ:gənaɪ'zeɪʃn/ *n* organisation *f.*

**organize** /'ɔ:gənaɪz/ *vt* organiser.

**organizer** /'ɔ:gənaɪzə(r)/ *n* organisateur/-trice *m/f*; **electronic ~** agenda *m* électronique.

**orgasm** /'ɔ:gæzəm/ *n* orgasme *m.*

**Orient** /'ɔ:rɪənt/ *n* **the ~** l'Orient *m.* **oriental** *a* oriental.

**origin** /'ɒrɪdʒɪn/ *n* origine *f.*

**original** /ə'rɪdʒənl/ *a* original; (*inhabitant*) premier; (*member*) originaire. **originality** *n* originalité *f.* **originally** *adv* (at the outset) à l'origine.

**originate** /ə'rɪdʒɪneɪt/ *vi* (plan) prendre naissance; **~ from** provenir de; (person) venir de. ● *vt* être l'auteur de. **originator** *n* (of idea) auteur *m*; (of invention) créateur/-trice *m/f.*

**ornament** /'ɔ:nəmənt/ *n* (decoration) ornement *m*; (object) objet *m* décoratif.

**orphan** /'ɔ:fn/ *n* orphelin/-e *m/f.* ● *vt* rendre orphelin. **orphanage** *n* orphelinat *m.*

**orthopaedic** /ɔ:θə'pi:dɪk/ *a* orthopédique.

**ostentatious** /ɒsten'teɪʃəs/ *a* tape-à-l'œil *inv.*

**osteopath** /ˈɒstɪəpæθ/ *n* ostéopathe *mf*.

**ostrich** /ˈɒstrɪtʃ/ *n* autruche *f*.

**other** /ˈʌðə(r)/ *a* autre; **the ~ one** l'autre *mf*. ● *n & pron* autre *mf*; **(some) ~s** d'autres. ● *adv* **~ than** (apart from) à part; (otherwise than) autrement que. **otherwise** *adv* autrement.

**otter** /ˈɒtə(r)/ *n* loutre *f*.

**ouch** /aʊtʃ/ *interj* aïe!

**ought** /ɔːt/ *v aux* devoir; **you ~ to stay** vous devriez rester; **he ~ to succeed** il devrait réussir; **I ~ to have done it** j'aurais dû le faire.

**ounce** /aʊns/ *n* once *f* (= *28.35 g*).

**our** /ˈaʊə(r)/ *a* notre, *pl* nos.

**ours** /ˈaʊəz/ *poss* le *or* la nôtre, les nôtres.

**ourselves** /aʊəˈselvz/ *pron* (reflexive) nous; (emphatic) nous-mêmes; (after preposition) **for ~** pour nous, pour nous-mêmes.

**out** /aʊt/ *adv* dehors; **he's ~** il est sorti; **further ~** plus loin; **be ~** (*book*) être publié; (*light*) être éteint; (*sun*) briller; (*flower*) être épanoui; (*tide*) être bas; (*player*) être éliminé; **~ of** hors de; **go/walk/get ~ of** sortir de; **~ of pity** par pitié; **made ~ of** fait de; **5 ~ of 6** 5 sur 6. **~break** *n* (of war) déclenchement *m*; (of violence, boils) éruption *f*. **~burst** *n* explosion *f*. **~cast** *n* paria *m*. **~class** *vt* surclasser. **~come** *n* résultat *m*. **~cry** *n* tollé *m*. **~dated** *a* démodé. **~door** *a* (*activity*) de plein air; (*pool*) en plein air. **~doors** *adv* dehors.

**outer** /ˈaʊtə(r)/ *a* extérieur; **~ space** espace *m* extra-atmosphérique.

**outfit** /ˈaʊtfɪt/ *n* (clothes) tenue *f*.

**outgoing** /ˈaʊtgəʊɪŋ/ *a* (*minister, tenant*) sortant; (sociable) ouvert. **outgoings** *npl* dépenses *fpl*.

**outgrow** /aʊtˈgrəʊ/ *vt* (*pt* **-grew**; *pp* **-grown**) (*clothes*) devenir trop grand pour; (*habit*) dépasser.

**outing** /ˈaʊtɪŋ/ *n* sortie *f*.

**outlaw** /ˈaʊtlɔː/ *n* hors-la-loi *m inv*. ● *vt* déclarer illégal.

**outlet** /ˈaʊtlet/ *n* (for water, gas) tuyau *m* de sortie; (for goods) débouché *m*; (for feelings) exutoire *m*.

**outline** /ˈaʊtlaɪn/ *n* contour *m*; (of plan) grandes lignes *fpl*; (of essay) plan *m*. ● *vt* tracer le contour de; (summarize) exposer brièvement.

**out**: **~live** *vt* survivre à. **~look** *n* perspective *f*. **~number** *vt* surpasser en nombre. **~ of date** *a* démodé; (expired) périmé. **~ of hand** *a* incontrôlable. **~ of order** *a* en panne. **~ of work** *a* sans travail. **~patient** *n* malade *mf* externe.

**output** /ˈaʊtpʊt/ *n* rendement *m*; (Comput) sortie *f*. ● *vt/i* (Comput) sortir.

**outrage** /ˈaʊtreɪdʒ/ *n* (anger) indignation *f*; (atrocity) attentat *m*; (scandal) outrage *m*. ● *vt* (*morals*) outrager; (*person*) scandaliser. **outrageous** *a* scandaleux.

**outright** /aʊtˈraɪt/ *adv* (completely) catégoriquement; (killed) sur le coup. ● *a* (*majority*) absolu; (*ban*) catégorique; (*hostility*) pur et simple.

**outset** /ˈaʊtset/ *n* début *m*.

**outside** /aʊtˈsaɪd, ˈaʊtsaɪd/ *n* extérieur *m*. ● *adv* dehors. ● *prep* en dehors de; (in front of) devant. ● *a* extérieur. **outsider** *n* étranger/-ère *m/f*; (Sport) outsider *m*.

**out**: **~skirts** *npl* périphérie *f*. **~spoken** *a* franc. **~standing** *a*

exceptionnel; (not settled) en suspens.

**outward** /'aʊtwəd/ *a & adv* vers l'extérieur; (*sign*) extérieur; (*journey*) d'aller. **outwards** *adv* vers l'extérieur.

**oval** /'əʊvl/ *n & a* ovale (*m*).

**ovary** /'əʊvərɪ/ *n* ovaire *m*.

**oven** /'ʌvn/ *n* four *m*.

**over** /'əʊvə(r)/ *prep* (across) par-dessus; (above) au-dessus de; (covering) sur; (more than) plus de; **it's ~ the road** c'est de l'autre côté de la rue; **~ here/there** par ici/là; **children ~ six** les enfants de plus de six ans; **~ the weekend** pendant le week-end; **all ~ the house** partout dans la maison. ● *a, adv* (*term*) terminé; (*war*) fini; **get sth ~ with** en finir avec qch; **ask sb ~** inviter qn; **~ and ~ (again)** à plusieurs reprises; **five times ~** cinq fois de suite.

**overall** /əʊvər'ɔːl/ *a* global, d'ensemble; (*length*) total. ● *adv* globalement.

**overalls** /'əʊvərɔːlz/ *npl* combinaison *f*.

**over**: **~board** *adv* par-dessus bord. **~cast** *a* couvert **~charge** *vt* faire payer trop cher à. **~coat** *n* pardessus *m*.

**overcome** /əʊvə'kʌm/ *vt* (*pt* **-came**; *pp* **-come**) (*enemy*) vaincre; (*difficulty, fear*) surmonter; **~ by** accablé de.

**overcrowded** /əʊvə'kraʊdɪd/ *a* bondé; (*country*) surpeuplé.

**overdo** /əʊvə'duː/ *vt* (*pt* **-did**; *pp* **-done**) (Culin) trop cuire; **~ it** (overwork) en faire trop.

**over**: **~dose** *n* surdose *f*, overdose *f*. **~draft** *n* découvert *m*. **~draw** *vt* (*pt* **-drew**; *pp* **-drawn**) faire un découvert sur. **~due** *a* en retard; (*bill*) impayé.

**overflow¹** /əʊvə'fləʊ/ *vi* déborder.

**overflow²** /'əʊvəfləʊ/ *n* (outlet) trop-plein *m*.

**overhaul** /əʊvə'hɔːl/ *vt* réviser.

**overhead¹** /əʊvə'hed/ *adv* au-dessus; (in sky) dans le ciel.

**overhead²** /'əʊvəhed/ *a* aérien; **~ projector** rétroprojecteur *m*. **overheads** *npl* frais *mpl* généraux.

**over**: **~hear** *vt* (*pt* **-heard**) entendre par hasard. **~lap** *vt/i* (*pt* **-lapped**) (se) chevaucher. **~leaf** *adv* au verso. **~load** *vt* surcharger. **~look** *vt* (*window*) donner sur; (miss) ne pas voir.

**overnight¹** /əʊvə'naɪt/ *adv* dans la nuit; (instantly: fig) du jour au lendemain.

**overnight²** /'əʊvənaɪt/ *a* (*train*) de nuit; (*stay*) d'une nuit; (fig) soudain.

**over**: **~power** *vt* (*thief*) maîtriser; (*army*) vaincre; (fig) accabler. **~priced** *a* trop cher. **~rate** *vt* surestimer. **~react** *vi* réagir de façon excessive. **~riding** *a* (*consideration*) numéro un; (*importance*) primordial. **~rule** *vt* (*decision*) annuler.

**overrun** /əʊvə'rʌn/ *vt* (*pt* **-ran**; *pp* **-run**; *pres p* **-running**) (*country*) envahir; (*budget*) dépasser. ● *vi* (meeting) durer plus longtemps que prévu.

**overseas** /əʊvə'siːz/ *a* étranger. ● *adv* outre-mer, à l'étranger.

**over**: **~see** *vt* (*pt* **-saw**; *pp* **-seen**) surveiller. **~sight** *n* omission *f*. **~sleep** *vi* (*pt* **-slept**) se réveiller trop tard. **~take** *vt/i* (*pt* **-took**; *pp* **-taken**) dépasser; (fig) frapper. **~time** *n* heures *fpl* supplémentaires. **~turn** *vt/i* (se) renverser. **~weight** *a* trop gros.

**overwhelm** /əʊvə'welm/ *vt* (*enemy*) écraser; (*shame*) accabler.

**overwhelmed** *a* (with offers, calls) submergé (**with, by** de); (with shame, work) accablé; (by sight) ébloui. **overwhelming** *a* (*heat, grief*) accablant; (*defeat, victory*) écrasant; (*urge*) irrésistible.

**overwork** /əʊvə'wɜ:k/ *vt/i* (se) surmener. ● *n* surmenage *m*.

**owe** /əʊ/ *vt* devoir. **owing** *a* dû; **owing to** en raison de.

**owl** /aʊl/ *n* hibou *m*.

**own** /əʊn/ *a* propre. ● *pron* **my ~** le mien, la mienne; **a house of one's ~** sa propre maison; **on one's ~** tout seul. ● *vt* posséder; **~ up (to)** [I] avouer. **owner** *n* propriétaire *mf*. **ownership** *n* propriété *f*; (of land) possession *f*.

**oxygen** /'ɒksɪdʒən/ *n* oxygène *m*.

**oyster** /'ɔɪstə(r)/ *n* huître *f*.

**ozone** /'əʊzəʊn/ *n* ozone *m*; **~ layer** couche *f* d'ozone.

# Pp

**PA** *abbr* ⇒PERSONAL ASSISTANT.

**pace** /peɪs/ *n* pas *m*; (speed) allure *f*; **keep ~ with** suivre. ● *vt* (*room*) arpenter. ● *vi* **~ (up and down)** faire les cent pas.

**Pacific** /pə'sɪfɪk/ *n* **~ (Ocean)** océan *m* Pacifique.

**pack** /pæk/ *n* paquet *m*; (Mil) sac *m*; (of hounds) meute *f*; (of thieves) bande *f*; (of lies) tissu *m*. ● *vt* (into case) mettre dans une valise; (into box, crate) emballer; (for sale) conditionner; (*crowd*) remplir complètement; **~ one's suitcase** faire sa valise. ● *vi* faire ses valises; **~ into** (cram) s'entasser dans; **~ off** expédier; **send ~ing** envoyer promener.

**package** /'pækɪdʒ/ *n* paquet *m*; (Comput) progiciel *m*; **~ deal** offre *f* globale; **~ holiday** voyage *m* organisé. ● *vt* empaqueter.

**packed** /'pækt/ *a* (crowded) bondé; **~ lunch** repas *m* froid.

**packet** /'pækɪt/ *n* paquet *m*.

**packing** /'pækɪŋ/ *n* (action, material) emballage *m*.

**pad** /pæd/ *n* (of paper) bloc *m*; (to protect) protection *f*; (for ink) tampon *m*; **(launch) ~** rampe *f* de lancement. ● *vt* (*pt* **padded**) rembourrer; (text: fig) délayer. ● *vi* (*pt* **padded**) (walk) marcher à pas feutrés. **padding** *n* rembourrage *m*.

**paddle** /'pædl/ *n* pagaie *f*. ● *vt* **~ a canoe** pagayer. ● *vi* patauger.

**padlock** /'pædlɒk/ *n* cadenas *m*. ● *vt* cadenasser.

**paediatrician** /pi:dɪə'trɪʃn/ *n* pédiatre *mf*.

**pagan** /'peɪgən/ *a & n* païen/-ne (*m/f*).

**page** /peɪdʒ/ *n* (of book) page *f*. ● *vt* (on pager) rechercher; (over speaker) faire appeler. **pager** *n* radiomessageur *m*.

**pain** /peɪn/ *n* douleur *f*; **~s** efforts *mpl*; **be in ~** souffrir; **take ~s to** se donner du mal pour. ● *vt* (grieve) peiner. **painful** *a* douloureux; (laborious) pénible. **~-killer** *n* analgésique *m*. **painless** *a* (*operation*) indolore; (*death*) sans souffrance; (trouble-free) sans peine. **painstaking** *a* minutieux.

**paint** /peɪnt/ *n* peinture *f*; **~s** (in tube, box) couleurs *fpl*. ● *vt/i* peindre. **~brush** *n* pinceau *m*. **painter** *n* peintre *m*. **painting** *n* peinture *f*. **~work** *n* peintures *fpl*.

**pair** /peə(r)/ *n* paire *f*; (of people) couple *m*; **a ~ of trousers** un pantalon. ● *vi* **~ off** former un couple.

**pajamas** /pəˈdʒɑːməz/ *npl* (US) = PYJAMAS.

**Pakistan** /pækɪˈstɑːn/ *n* Pakistan *m*.

**palace** /ˈpælɪs/ *n* palais *m*.

**palatable** /ˈpælətəbl/ *a* (*food*) savoureux; (*solution*) acceptable.

**palate** *n* palais *m*.

**pale** /peɪl/ *a* pâle. ● *vi* pâlir.

**Palestine** /ˈpæləstaɪn/ *n* Palestine *f*.

**pallid** /ˈpælɪd/ *a* pâle.

**palm** /pɑːm/ *n* (of hand) paume *f*; (tree) palmier *m*; (symbol) palme *f*. □ **~ off** [I] **~ sth off as** faire passer qch pour; **~ sth off on sb** refiler qch à qn [I].

**palpitate** /ˈpælpɪteɪt/ *vi* palpiter.

**paltry** /ˈpɔːltrɪ/ *a* (**-ier, -iest**) dérisoire, piètre.

**pamper** /ˈpæmpə(r)/ *vt* choyer.

**pamphlet** /ˈpæmflɪt/ *n* brochure *f*.

**pan** /pæn/ *n* casserole *f*; (for frying) poêle *f*.

**pancake** /ˈpænkeɪk/ *n* crêpe *f*.

**pandemonium** /pændɪˈməʊnɪəm/ *n* tohu-bohu *m*.

**pander** /ˈpændə(r)/ *vi* **~ to** (*person, taste*) flatter bassement.

**pane** /peɪn/ *n* carreau *m*, vitre *f*.

**panel** /ˈpænl/ *n* (of door) panneau *m*; (of experts, judges) commission *f*; (on discussion programme) invités *mpl*; (**instrument**) **~** tableau *m* de bord.

**pang** /pæŋ/ *n* serrement *m* au cœur; **~s of conscience** remords *mpl*.

**panic** /ˈpænɪk/ *n* panique *f*. ● *vt/i* (*pt* **panicked**) (s')affoler. **~-stricken** *a* pris de panique, affolé.

**pansy** /ˈpænzɪ/ *n* (Bot) pensée *f*.

**pant** /pænt/ *vi* haleter.

**panther** /ˈpænθə(r)/ *n* panthère *f*.

**pantomime** /ˈpæntəmaɪm/ *n* (show) spectacle *m* de Noël; (mime) mime *m*.

**pantry** /ˈpæntrɪ/ *n* garde-manger *m inv*.

**pants** /pænts/ *npl* (underwear) slip *m*; (trousers: US) pantalon *m*.

**paper** /ˈpeɪpə(r)/ *n* papier *m*; (newspaper) journal *m*; (exam) épreuve *f*; (essay) exposé *m*; (wallpaper) papier *m* peint; (identity) **~s** papiers *mpl* (d'identité); **on ~** par écrit. ● *vt* (*room*) tapisser. **~back** *n* livre *m* de poche. **~-clip** *n* trombone *m*. **~ feed tray** *n* (Comput) bac *m* d'alimentation en papier. **~work** *n* (work) travail *m* administratif; (documentation) documents *mpl*.

**par** /pɑː(r)/ *n* **be below ~** ne pas être en forme; **on a ~ with** (*performance*) comparable à; (*person*) l'égal de; (golf) par *m*.

**parachute** /ˈpærəʃuːt/ *n* parachute *m*. ● *vi* descendre en parachute.

**parade** /pəˈreɪd/ *n* (procession) parade *f*, (Mil) défilé *m*. ● *vi* défiler. ● *vt* faire étalage de.

**paradise** /ˈpærədaɪs/ *n* paradis *m*.

**paradox** /ˈpærədɒks/ *n* paradoxe *m*.

**paraffin** /ˈpærəfɪn/ *n* pétrole *m* (*lampant*); (wax) paraffine *f*.

**paragliding** /ˈpærəglaɪdɪŋ/ *n* parapente *m*.

**paragon** /ˈpærəgən/ *n* modèle *m*.

**paragraph** /ˈpærəgrɑːf/ *n* paragraphe *m*.

**parallel** /ˈpærəlel/ *a* parallèle. ● *n* parallèle *m*; (maths) parallèle *f*.

**paralyse** /ˈpærəlaɪz/ *vt* paralyser.

**paralysis** *n* paralysie *f*.

**paramedic** /pærə'medɪk/ *n* auxiliaire *mf* médical/-e.

**paramount** /'pærəmaʊnt/ *a* suprême.

**paranoia** /pærə'nɔɪə/ *n* paranoïa *f*. **paranoid** *a* paranoïaque; (Psych) paranoïde.

**paraphernalia** /pærəfə'neɪlɪə/ *n* attirail *m*.

**parasol** /'pærəsɒl/ *n* ombrelle *f*; (on table, at beach) parasol *m*.

**paratrooper** /'pærətru:pə(r)/ *n* (Mil) parachutiste *mf*.

**parcel** /'pɑ:sl/ *n* paquet *m*.

**parchment** /'pɑ:tʃmənt/ *n* parchemin *m*.

**pardon** /'pɑ:dn/ *n* pardon *m*; (Jur) grâce *f*; **I beg your ~** je vous demande pardon. ● *vt* (*pt* **pardoned**) pardonner (**sb for sth** qch à qn); (Jur) gracier.

**parent** /'peərənt/ *n* parent *m*.

**parenthesis** /pə'renθəsɪs/ *n* (*pl* **-theses** /-si:z/) parenthèse *f*.

**parenthood** /'peərənthʊd/ *n* (fatherhood) paternité *f*; (motherhood) maternité *f*.

**Paris** /'pærɪs/ *n* Paris.

**parish** /'pærɪʃ/ *n* (Relig) paroisse *f*; (municipal) commune *f*.

**park** /pɑ:k/ *n* parc *m*. ● *vt/i* (se) garer; (remain parked) stationner. **~ and ride** *n* parc *m* relais.

**parking** /'pɑ:kɪŋ/ *n* stationnement *m*; **no ~** stationnement interdit. **~-lot** *n* (US) parking *m*. **~-meter** *n* parcmètre *m*. **~ ticket** *n* (fine) contravention *f*, PV *m* ⓘ.

**parliament** /'pɑ:ləmənt/ *n* parlement *m*. **parliamentary** *a* parlementaire.

**parlour**, (US) **parlor** /'pɑ:lə(r)/ *n* salon *m*.

**parody** /'pærədɪ/ *n* parodie *f*. ● *vt* parodier.

**parole** /pə'rəʊl/ *n* **on ~** en liberté conditionnelle.

**parrot** /'pærət/ *n* perroquet *m*.

**parry** /'pærɪ/ *vt* (Sport) parer; (*question*) éluder. ● *n* parade *f*.

**parsley** /'pɑ:slɪ/ *n* persil *m*.

**parsnip** /'pɑ:snɪp/ *n* panais *m*.

**part** /pɑ:t/ *n* partie *f*; (of serial) épisode *m*; (of machine) pièce *f*; (Theat) rôle *m*; (side in dispute) parti *m*; **in ~** en partie; **on the ~ of** de la part de; **take ~ in** participer à. ● *a* partiel. ● *adv* en partie. ● *vt/i* (separate) (se) séparer; **~ with** se séparer de.

**part-exchange** *n* reprise *f*; **take sth in ~** reprendre qch.

**partial** /'pɑ:ʃl/ *a* partiel; (biased) partial; **be ~ to** avoir un faible pour.

**participant** /pɑ:'tɪsɪpənt/ *n* participant/-e *m/f*. **participate** *vi* participer (**in** à). **participation** *n* participation *f*.

**participle** /'pɑ:tɪsɪpl/ *n* participe *m*.

**particular** /pə'tɪkjʊlə(r)/ *n* détail *m*; **~s** détails *mpl*; **in ~** en particulier. ● *a* particulier; (fussy) difficile; (careful) méticuleux; **that ~ man** cet homme-là. **particularly** *adv* particulièrement.

**parting** /'pɑ:tɪŋ/ *n* séparation *f*; (in hair) raie *f*. ● *a* d'adieu.

**partition** /pɑ:'tɪʃn/ *n* (of room) cloison *f*; (Pol) partition *f*. ● *vt* (*room*) cloisonner; (*country*) partager.

**partly** /'pɑ:tlɪ/ *adv* en partie.

**partner** /'pɑ:tnə(r)/ *n* (professional) associé/-e *m/f*; (economic, sporting) partenaire *mf*; (spouse) époux/-se *m/f*; (unmarried) partenaire *mf*. **partnership** *n* association *f*.

**partridge** /'pɑ:trɪdʒ/ *n* perdrix *f*.

**part-time** *a & adv* à temps partiel.

**party** /'pɑ:tɪ/ *n* fête *f*; (formal) réception *f*; (group) groupe *m*; (Pol) parti *m*; (Jur) partie *f*.

**pass** /pɑ:s/ *vt/i* (*pt* **passed**) passer; (overtake) dépasser; (in exam) réussir; (approve) (*candidate*) admettre; (*invoice*) approuver; (*remark*) faire; (*judgement*) prononcer; (*law, bill*) adopter; ~ **(by)** (*building*) passer devant; (*person*) croiser. ● *n* (permit) laisser-passer *m inv*; (ticket) carte *f* d'abonnement; (Geog) col *m*; (Sport) passe *f*; ~ **(mark)** (in exam) moyenne *f*. □ ~ **away** mourir; ~ **out** (faint) s'évanouir; ~ **sth out** distribuer qch; ~ **over** (overlook) délaisser; ~ **up** (forego) laisser passer.

**passage** /'pæsɪdʒ/ *n* (way through, text) passage *m*; (voyage) traversée *f*; (corridor) couloir *m*.

**passenger** /'pæsɪndʒə(r)/ *n* (in car, plane, ship) passager/-ère *m/f*; (in train, bus, tube) voyageur/-euse *m/f*.

**passer-by** /pɑ:sə'baɪ/ *n* (*pl* **passers-by**) passant/-e *m/f*.

**passing** /'pɑ:sɪŋ/ *a* (*motorist*) qui passe, (*whim*) passager; (*reference*) en passant.

**passion** /'pæʃn/ *n* passion *f*. **passionate** *a* passionné.

**passive** /'pæsɪv/ *a* passif.

**passport** /'pɑ:spɔ:t/ *n* passeport *m*.

**password** /'pɑ:swɜ:d/ *n* mot *m* de passe.

**past** /pɑ:st/ *a* (*times, problems*) passé; (*president*) ancien; **the** ~ **months** ces derniers mois. ● *n* passé *m*. ● *prep* (beyond) après; **walk/go** ~ **sth** passer devant qch; **10** ~ **6** six heures dix; **it's** ~ **11** il est 11 heures passées. ● *adv* **go/walk** ~ passer.

**pasta** /'pæstə/ *n* pâtes *fpl* (alimentaires).

**paste** /peɪst/ *n* (glue) colle *f*; (dough) pâte *f*; (of fish, meat) pâté *m*; (jewellery) strass *m*. ● *vt* coller.

**pasteurize** /'pæstʃəraɪz/ *vt* pasteuriser.

**pastime** /'pɑ:staɪm/ *n* passe-temps *m inv*.

**pastry** /'peɪstrɪ/ *n* (dough) pâte *f*; (tart) pâtisserie *f*.

**pat** /pæt/ *vt* (*pt* **patted**) tapoter. ● *n* petite tape *f*.

**patch** /pætʃ/ *n* pièce *f*; (over eye) bandeau *m*; (spot) tache *f*; (of snow, ice) plaque *f*; (of vegetables) carré *m*; **bad** ~ période *f* difficile. □ ~ **up** (*trousers*) rapiécer; (*quarrel*) résoudre.

**patent** /'peɪtnt/ *a* (obvious) manifeste; (patented) breveté; ~ **leather** cuir *m* verni. ● *n* brevet *m*. ● *vt* faire breveter.

**path** /pɑ:θ/ *n* (*pl* **-s** /pɑ:ðz/) sentier *m*, chemin *m*; (in park) allée *f*; (of rocket) trajectoire *f*.

**pathetic** /pə'θetɪk/ *a* misérable; (bad film) lamentable.

**patience** /'peɪʃns/ *n* patience *f*.

**patient** /'peɪʃnt/ *a* patient. ● *n* patient/-e *m/f*. **patiently** *adv* patiemment.

**patriotic** /peɪtrɪ'ɒtɪk/ *a* patriotique; (*person*) patriote.

**patrol** /pə'trəʊl/ *n* patrouille *f*; ~ **car** voiture *f* de police. ● *vt/i* patrouiller (dans).

**patron** /'peɪtrən/ *n* (of the arts) mécène *m*; (customer) client/-e *m/f*. **patronage** *n* clientèle *f*; (support) patronage *m*. **patronize** *vt* (*person*) traiter avec condescendance; (*establishment*) fréquenter.

**patter** /'pætə(r)/ *n* (of steps) bruit *m*; (of rain) crépitement *m*.

**pattern** /'pætn/ *n* motif *m*, dessin *m*; (for sewing) patron *m*; (for knitting) modèle *m*.

**paunch** /pɔ:ntʃ/ *n* ventre *m*.

**pause** /pɔ:z/ *n* pause *f*. ● *vi* faire une pause; (hesitate) hésiter.

**pave** /peɪv/ *vt* paver; ~ **the way** ouvrir la voie (**for** à).

**pavement** /ˈpeɪvmənt/ *n* trottoir *m*; (US) chaussée *f*.

**paving stone** *n* pavé *m*.

**paw** /pɔ:/ *n* patte *f*. ● *vt* (*animal*) donner des coups de patte à.

**pawn** /pɔ:n/ *n* pion *m*. ● *vt* mettre en gage. **~broker** *n* prêteur/-euse *m*/*f* sur gages. **~-shop** *n* mont-de-piété *m*.

**pay** /peɪ/ *vt* (*pt* **paid**) payer; (*interest*) rapporter; (*compliment, attention*) faire; (*visit, homage*) rendre. ● *vi* payer; (*business*) rapporter; ~ **for sth** payer qch. ● *n* salaire *m*; ~ **rise** augmentation *f* (*de salaire*). □ ~ **back** rembourser; ~ **in** déposer; ~ **off** (*loan*) rembourser; (*worker*) congédier; (succeed) être payant; ~ **out** payer, débourser.

**payable** /ˈpeɪəbl/ *a* payable; ~ **to** (*cheque*) à l'ordre de.

**payment** /ˈpeɪmənt/ *n* paiement *m*; (regular) versement *m*; (reward) récompense *f*.

**payroll** /ˈpeɪrəʊl/ *n* fichier *m* des salaires; **be on the ~ of** être employé par.

**PC** *abbr* ⇒PERSONAL COMPUTER.

**PDA** *abbr* (**personal digital assistant**) assistant *m* personnel numérique.

**PE** *abbr* (**physical education**) éducation *f* physique, EPS *f*.

**pea** /pi:/ *n* (petit) pois *m*.

**peace** /pi:s/ *n* paix *f*; ~ **of mind** tranquillité *f* d'esprit. **peaceful** *a* (tranquil) paisible; (peaceable) pacifique.

**peach** /pi:tʃ/ *n* pêche *f*.

**peacock** /ˈpi:kɒk/ *n* paon *m*.

**peak** /pi:k/ *n* (of mountain) pic *m*; (of cap) visière *f*; (maximum) maximum *m*; (on graph) sommet *m*; (of career) apogée *m*; (of fitness) meilleur *m*; ~ **hours** heures *fpl* de pointe.

**peal** /pi:l/ *n* (of bells) carillon *m*; (of laughter) éclat *m*.

**peanut** /ˈpi:nʌt/ *n* cacahuète *f*; **~s** (money ▣) clopinettes *fpl* ▣.

**pear** /peə(r)/ *n* poire *f*.

**pearl** /pɜ:l/ *n* perle *f*.

**peasant** /ˈpeznt/ *n* paysan/-ne *m*/*f*.

**peat** /pi:t/ *n* tourbe *f*.

**pebble** /ˈpebl/ *n* caillou *m*; (on beach) galet *m*.

**peck** /pek/ *vt*/*i* (*food*) picorer; (attack) donner des coups de bec (à). ● *n* coup *m* de bec; **a ~ on the cheek** une bise.

**peckish** /ˈpekɪʃ/ *a* **be ~** ▣ avoir faim.

**peculiar** /pɪˈkju:lɪə(r)/ *a* (odd) bizarre; (special) particulier (**to** à). **peculiarity** *n* bizarrerie *f*.

**pedal** /ˈpedl/ *n* pédale *f*. ● *vi* pédaler.

**pedantic** /pɪˈdæntɪk/ *a* pédant.

**peddle** /ˈpedl/ *vt* colporter; (*drugs*) faire du trafic de.

**pedestrian** /pɪˈdestrɪən/ *n* piéton *m*. ● *a* (*precinct, street*) piétonnier; (fig) prosaïque; ~ **crossing** passage *m* pour piétons.

**pedigree** /ˈpedɪgri:/ *n* (of animal) pedigree *m*; (of person) ascendance *f*. ● *a* (*dog*) de pure race.

**peek** /pi:k/ *vi* & *n* = PEEP.

**peel** /pi:l/ *n* (on fruit) peau *m*; (removed) épluchures *fpl*. ● *vt* (*fruit, vegetables*) éplucher; (*prawn*) décortiquer. ● *vi* (of skin) peler; (of paint) s'écailler.

**peep** /pi:p/ *vi* jeter un coup d'œil (furtif) (**at** à). ● *n* coup *m* d'œil (furtif). **~hole** *n* judas *m*.

**peer** /pɪə(r)/ *vi* ~ **(at)** regarder fixement. ● *n* (equal, noble) pair *m*; (contemporary) personne *f* de la même génération. **peerage** *n* pairie *f*.

**peg** /peg/ *n* (for clothes) pince *f* à linge; (to hang coats) patère *f*; (for tent) piquet *m*. ● *vt* (*pt* **pegged**) (*clothes*) accrocher avec des pinces; (*prices*) indexer.

**pejorative** /pɪ'dʒɒrətɪv/ *a* péjoratif.

**pelican** /'pelɪkən/ *n* pélican *m*; ~ **crossing** passage *m* pour piétons.

**pellet** /'pelɪt/ *n* (round mass) boulette *f*; (for gun) plomb *m*.

**pelt** /pelt/ *vt* bombarder (**with** de). ● *n* (skin) peau *f*.

**pelvis** /'pelvɪs/ *n* (Anat) bassin *m*.

**pen** /pen/ *n* stylo *m*; (for sheep) enclos *m*; (for baby, cattle) parc *m*.

**penal** /'pi:nl/ *a* pénal. **penalize** *vt* pénaliser.

**penalty** /'penltɪ/ *n* peine *f*, (fine) amende *f*; (in football) penalty *m*.

**penance** /'penəns/ *n* pénitence *f*.

**pence** /pens/ ⇒PENNY.

**pencil** /'pensl/ *n* crayon *m*. ● *vt* (*pt* **pencilled**) crayonner; ~ **in** noter provisoirement. ~ **sharpener** *n* taille-crayons *m inv*.

**pending** /'pendɪŋ/ *a* (*matter*) en souffrance; (Jur) en instance. ● *prep* (until) en attendant.

**penetrate** /'penɪtreɪt/ *vt* pénetrer; (*silence, defences*) percer; (*organization*) infiltrer. ● *vi* pénétrer. **penetrating** *a* pénétrant.

**pen-friend** *n* correspondant/-e *m*/*f*.

**penguin** /'peŋgwɪn/ *n* manchot *m*, pingouin *m*.

**pen**: ~**knife** *n* (*pl* **-knives**) canif *m*. ~**-name** *n* pseudonyme *m*.

**penniless** /'penɪlɪs/ *a* sans le sou.

**penny** /'penɪ/ *n* (*pl* **pennies** *or* **pence**) (unit of currency) penny *m*; (small amount) centime *m*.

**pension** /'penʃn/ *n* (from state) pension *f*; (from employer) retraite *f*; ~ **scheme** plan *m* de retraite. ● *vt* ~ **off** mettre à la retraite. **pensioner** *n* retraité/-e *m*/*f*.

**pensive** /'pensɪv/ *a* songeur.

**penthouse** /'penthaus/ *n* appartement *m* de luxe (*au dernier étage*).

**penultimate** /pen'ʌltɪmət/ *a* avant-dernier.

**people** /'pi:pl/ *npl* gens *mpl*, personnes *fpl*; **English** ~ les Anglais *mpl*; ~ **say** on dit. ● *n* peuple *m*. ● *vt* peupler. ~ **carrier** *n* monospace *m*.

**pepper** /'pepə(r)/ *n* poivre *m*; (vegetable) poivron *m*. ● *vt* (Culin) poivrer.

**peppermint** /'pepəmɪnt/ *n* (plant) menthe *f* poivrée; (sweet) bonbon *m* à la menthe.

**per** /pɜ:(r)/ *prep* par; ~ **annum** par an; ~ **cent** pour cent; ~ **kilo** le kilo; **ten km** ~ **hour** dix km à l'heure.

**percentage** /pə'sentɪdʒ/ *n* pourcentage *m*.

**perception** /pə'sepʃn/ *n* perception *f*. **perceptive** *a* perspicace.

**perch** /pɜ:tʃ/ *n* (of bird) perchoir *m*. ● *vi* (se) percher.

**perennial** /pə'renɪəl/ *a* perpétuel; (*plant*) vivace.

**perfect**[1] /pə'fekt/ *vt* perfectionner.

**perfect**[2] /'pɜ:fɪkt/ *a* parfait. ● *n* (Ling) parfait *m*. **perfectly** *adv* parfaitement.

**perfection** /pə'fekʃn/ *n* perfection *f*; **to** ~ à la perfection.

**perforate** /'pɜ:fəreɪt/ *vt* perforer.

**perform** /pə'fɔ:m/ *vt* (*task*) exécuter; (*function*) remplir; (*operation*)

procéder à; (*play*) jouer; (*song*) chanter. ● *vi* (*actor, musician, team*) jouer; ~ **well/badly** (*candidate, business*) avoir de bons/de mauvais résultats. **performance** *n* interprétation *f*; (of car, team) performance *f*; (show) représentation *f*; (fuss) histoire *f*. **performer** *n* artiste *mf*.

**perfume** /'pɜ:fju:m/ *n* parfum *m*.

**perhaps** /pə'hæps/ *adv* peut-être.

**peril** /'perəl/ *n* péril *m*. **perilous** *a* périlleux.

**perimeter** /pə'rɪmɪtə(r)/ *n* périmètre *m*.

**period** /'pɪərɪəd/ *n* période *f*; (era) époque *f*; (lesson) cours *m*; (Gram) point *m*; (Med) règles *fpl*. ● *a* d'époque. **periodical** *n* périodique *m*.

**peripheral** /pə'rɪfərəl/ *a* (*vision, suburb*) périphérique; (*issue*) annexe. ● *n* (Comput) périphérique *m*.

**perish** /'perɪʃ/ *vi* périr; (*rubber*) se détériorer.

**perjury** /'pɜ:dʒərɪ/ *n* faux témoignage *m*.

**perk** /pɜ:k/ *n* ⊞ avantage *m*. ● *vt/i* ~ **up** ⊞ (se) remonter. **perky** *a* ⊞ gai.

**perm** /pɜ:m/ *n* permanente *f*. ● *vt* **have one's hair ~ed** se faire faire une permanente.

**permanent** /'pɜ:mənənt/ *a* permanent. **permanently** *adv* (*happy*) en permanence; (*employed*) de façon permanente.

**permissible** /pə'mɪsəbl/ *a* permis.

**permission** /pə'mɪʃn/ *n* permission *f*.

**permissive** /pə'mɪsɪv/ *a* libéral; (pej) permissif.

**permit¹** /pə'mɪt/ *vt* (*pt* **permitted**) permettre (**sb to** à qn de), autoriser (**sb to** qn à).

**permit²** /'pɜ:mɪt/ *n* permis *m*.

**perpendicular** /pɜ:pən'dɪkjʊlə(r)/ *a* perpendiculaire.

**perpetrator** /'pɜ:pɪtreɪtə(r)/ *n* auteur *m*.

**perpetuate** /pə'petʃʊeɪt/ *vt* perpétuer.

**perplexed** /pə'plekst/ *a* perplexe.

**persecute** /'pɜ:sɪkju:t/ *vt* persécuter.

**perseverance** /pɜ:sɪ'vɪərəns/ *n* persévérance *f*. **persevere** *vi* persévérer.

**persist** /pə'sɪst/ *vi* persister (**in doing** à faire). **persistence** *n* persistance *f*. **persistent** *a* (*cough, snow*) persistant; (obstinate) obstiné; (*noise, pressure*) continuel.

**person** /'pɜ:sn/ *n* personne *f*; **in ~** en personne.

**personal** /'pɜ:sənl/ *a* (*life, problem, opinion*) personnel; (*safety, freedom, insurance*) individuel. **~ ad** *n* petite annonce *f*. **~ assistant** *n* secrétaire *mf* de direction. **~ computer** *n* ordinateur *m* (personnel), micro-ordinateur *m*.

**personality** /pɜ:sə'nælətɪ/ *n* personnalité *f*; (star) vedette *f*.

**personal**: **~ organizer** *n* agenda *m*. **~ stereo** *n* baladeur *m*.

**personnel** /pɜ:sə'nel/ *n* personnel *m*.

**perspiration** /pəspɪ'reɪʃn/ *n* (sweat) sueur *f*; (sweating) transpiration *f*. **perspire** *vi* transpirer.

**persuade** /pə'sweɪd/ *vt* persuader (**to** de). **persuasion** *n* persuasion *f*. **persuasive** *a* persuasif.

**pertinent** /'pɜ:tɪnənt/ *a* pertinent.

**perturb** /pə'tɜ:b/ *vt* troubler.

**Peru** /pə'ru:/ *n* Pérou *m*.

**pervasive** /pə'veɪsɪv/ *a* (*smell*) pénétrant; (*feeling*) envahissant.

**perverse** /pə'vɜ:s/ *a* (*desire*) pervers; (*refusal, attitude*) illogique. **perversion** *n* perversion *f*.

**pervert¹** /pə'vɜ:t/ *vt* (*truth*) travestir; (*values*) fausser; (*justice*) entraver.

**pervert²** /'pɜ:vɜ:t/ *n* pervers/-e *m/f*.

**pessimist** /'pesɪmɪst/ *n* pessimiste *mf*. **pessimistic** *a* pessimiste.

**pest** /pest/ *n* (insect) insecte *m* nuisible, (animal) animal *m* nuisible; (person [I]) enquiquineur/-euse *m/f* [I].

**pester** /'pestə(r)/ *vt* harceler.

**pet** /pet/ *n* animal *m* de compagnie; (favourite) chouchou/-te *m/f*. ● *a* (*theory, charity*) favori; ~ **hate** bête *f* noire; ~ **name** petit nom *m*. ● *vi* (*pt* **petted**) caresser; (spoil) chouchouter [I].

**petal** /'petl/ *n* pétale *m*.

**peter** /'pi:tə(r)/ *vi* ~ **out** (*conversation*) tarir; (*supplies*) s'épuiser.

**petite** /pə'ti:t/ *a* (*woman*) menue.

**petition** /pɪ'tɪʃn/ *n* pétition *f*. ● *vt* adresser une pétition à.

**petrol** /'petrəl/ *n* essence *f* ~ **bomb** *n* cocktail *m* molotov. ~ **station** *n* station-service *f*. ~ **tank** *n* réservoir *m* d'essence.

**petticoat** /'petɪkəʊt/ *n* jupon *m*.

**petty** /'petɪ/ *a* (**-ier**, **-iest**) (minor) petit; (mean) mesquin; ~ **cash** petite caisse *f*.

**pew** /pju:/ *n* banc *m* (d'église).

**pharmacist** /'fɑ:məsɪst/ *n* pharmacien/-ne *m/f*. **pharmacy** *n* pharmacie *f*.

**phase** /feɪz/ *n* phase *f*. ● *vt* ~ **in/out** introduire/supprimer peu à peu.

**PhD** *abbr* (**Doctor of Philosophy**) doctorat *m*.

**pheasant** /'feznt/ *n* faisan/-e *m/f*.

**phenomenon** /fə'nɒmɪnən/ *n* (*pl* **-ena**) phénomène *m*.

**phew** /fju:/ *interj* ouf.

**philosopher** /fɪ'lɒsəfə(r)/ *n* philosophe *mf*. **philosophical** *a* philosophique; (resigned) philosophe. **philosophy** *n* philosophie *f*.

**phlegm** /flem/ *n* (Med) mucosité *f*.

**phobia** /'fəʊbɪə/ *n* phobie *f*.

**phone** /fəʊn/ *n* téléphone *m*; **on the** ~ au téléphone. ● *vt* (person) téléphoner à; ~ **England** téléphoner en Angleterre. ● *vi* téléphoner; ~ **back** rappeler. ~ **book** *n* annuaire *m*. ~ **booth**, ~ **box** *n* cabine *f* téléphonique. ~ **call** *n* coup *m* de fil [I]. ~**card** *n* télécarte *f*. ~**-in** *n* émission *f* à ligne ouverte. ~ **number** *n* numéro *m* de téléphone.

**phonetic** /fə'netɪk/ *a* phonétique.

**phoney** /'fəʊnɪ/ *a* (**-ier**, **-iest**) [I] faux. ● *n* [I] (person) charlatan *m*; **it's a** ~ c'est un faux.

**photocopier** /'fəʊtəʊkɒpɪə(r)/ *n* photocopieuse *f*.

**photocopy** /'fəʊtəʊkɒpɪ/ *n* photocopie *f*. ● *vt* photocopier.

**photograph** /'fəʊtəgrɑ:f/ *n* photographie *f*. ● *vt* photographier. **photographer** *n* photographe *mf*.

**phrase** /freɪz/ *n* expression *f*; (idiom) locution *f*. ● *vt* exprimer, formuler. ~**-book** *n* guide *m* de conversation.

**physical** /'fɪzɪkl/ *a* physique.

**physicist** /'fɪzɪsɪst/ *n* physicien/-ne *m/f*.

**physics** /'fɪzɪks/ *n* physique *f*.

**physiotherapist** /fɪzɪəʊ'θerəpɪst/ *n* kinésithérapeute *mf*. **physiotherapy** *n* kinésithérapie *f*.

**physique** /fɪ'zi:k/ *n* physique *m*.

**piano** /pɪ'ænəʊ/ *n* piano *m*.

**pick** /pɪk/ *n* choix *m*; (best) meilleur/-e *m/f*; (tool) pioche *f*. ● *vt* choisir; (*flower*) cueillir; (*lock*) crocheter; **~ a quarrel with** chercher querelle à; **~ one's nose** se curer le nez. □ **~ on** harceler; **~ out** choisir; (identify) distinguer; **~ up** *vt* ramasser; (*sth fallen*) relever; (*weight*) soulever; (*habit, passenger, speed*) prendre; (learn) apprendre; *vi* s'améliorer.

**pickaxe** /'pɪkæks/ *n* pioche *f*.

**picket** /'pɪkɪt/ *n* (striker) gréviste *mf*; (stake) piquet *m*; **~ (line)** piquet *m* de grève. ● *vt* (*pt* **picketed**) installer un piquet de grève devant.

**pickle** /'pɪkl/ *n* conserves *fpl* au vinaigre; (gherkin) cornichon *m*. ● *vt* conserver dans du vinaigre.

**pick-up** /'pɪkʌp/ *n* (stylus-holder) lecteur *m*; (on guitar) capteur *m*; (collection) ramassage *m*; (improvement) reprise *f*.

**picnic** /'pɪknɪk/ *n* pique-nique *m*. ● *vi* (*pt* **picnicked**) pique-niquer.

**pictorial** /pɪk'tɔ:rɪəl/ *a* (*magazine*) illustré; (*record*) graphique.

**picture** /'pɪktʃə(r)/ *n* image *f*; (painting) tableau *m*; (photograph) photo *f*; (drawing) dessin *m*; (film) film *m*; (fig) description *f*; **the ~s** le cinéma. ● *vt* s'imaginer; **be ~d** (shown) être représenté.

**picturesque** /pɪktʃə'resk/ *a* pittoresque.

**pie** /paɪ/ *n* (sweet) tarte *f*; (savoury) tourte *f*.

**piece** /pi:s/ *n* morceau *m*; (of string, ribbon) bout *m*; (of currency, machine) pièce *f*; **a ~ of advice/furniture** un conseil/meuble; **go to ~s** (fig) s'effondrer; **take to ~s** démonter.

**pier** /pɪə(r)/ *n* jetée *f*.

**pierce** /pɪəs/ *vt* percer.

**pig** /pɪg/ *n* porc *m*, cochon *m*.

**pigeon** /'pɪdʒən/ *n* pigeon *m*. **~-hole** *n* casier *m*.

**pig-headed** *a* entêté.

**pigsty** /'pɪgstaɪ/ *n* porcherie *f*.

**pigtail** /'pɪgteɪl/ *n* natte *f*.

**pike** /paɪk/ *n inv* (fish) brochet *m*.

**pile** /paɪl/ *n* (heap) tas *m*; (stack) pile *f*; (of carpet) poil *m*; **~s of** Ⓘ un tas de Ⓘ. ● *vt* **~ (up)** entasser. ● *vi* **~ into** s'engouffrer dans; **~ up** (*snow, leaves*) s'entasser; (*debts, work*) s'accumuler. **~-up** *n* (Auto) carambolage *m*.

**pilgrim** /'pɪlgrɪm/ *n* pèlerin *m*. **pilgrimage** *n* pèlerinage *m*.

**pill** /pɪl/ *n* pilule *f*.

**pillar** /'pɪlə(r)/ *n* pilier *m*. **~-box** *n* boîte *f* aux lettres.

**pillion** /'pɪljən/ *n* siège *m* de passager; **ride ~** monter en croupe.

**pillow** /'pɪləʊ/ *n* oreiller *m*. **~case** *n* taie *f* d'oreiller.

**pilot** /'paɪlət/ *n* pilote *m*. ● *a* pilote. ● *vt* (*pt* **piloted**) piloter. **~-light** *n* veilleuse *f*.

**pimple** /'pɪmpl/ *n* bouton *m*.

**pin** /pɪn/ *n* épingle *f*; (of plug) fiche *f*; (for wood, metal) goujon *m*; (in surgery) broche *f*; **have ~s and needles** avoir des fourmis. ● *vt* (*pt* **pinned**) épingler, attacher; (trap) coincer; **~ sb down** (fig) forcer qn à se décider; **~ up** accrocher.

**pinafore** /'pɪnəfɔ:(r)/ *n* tablier *m*.

**pincers** /'pɪnsəz/ *npl* tenailles *fpl*.

**pinch** /pɪntʃ/ *vt* pincer; (steal Ⓘ) piquer. ● *vi* (be too tight) serrer. ● *n* (mark) pinçon *m*; (of salt) pincée *f*; **at a ~** à la rigueur.

**pine** /paɪn/ *n* (tree) pin *m*. ● *vi* ~ (away) dépérir; ~ **for** languir après.

**pineapple** /ˈpaɪnæpl/ *n* ananas *m*.

**pinecone** *n* pomme *f* de pin.

**pink** /pɪŋk/ *a* & *n* rose (*m*).

**pinpoint** /ˈpɪnpɔɪnt/ *vt* (*problem, cause, location*) indiquer; (*time*) déterminer.

**pint** /paɪnt/ *n* pinte *f* (GB = *0.57 litre*; US = *0.47 litre*).

**pin-up** /ˈpɪnʌp/ *n* 🅸 pin-up *f inv* 🅸.

**pioneer** /paɪəˈnɪə(r)/ *n* pionnier *m*. ● *vt* ~ **the use of** être le premier à utiliser.

**pious** /ˈpaɪəs/ *a* pieux.

**pip** /pɪp/ *n* (seed) pépin *m*; (sound) top *m*.

**pipe** /paɪp/ *n* tuyau *m*; (to smoke) pipe *f*; (Mus) chalumeau *m*; ~**s** cornemuse *f*. ● *vt* transporter par tuyau. □ ~ **down** se taire.

**pipeline** /ˈpaɪplaɪn/ *n* oléoduc *m*; **in the** ~ en cours.

**piping** /ˈpaɪpɪŋ/ *n* tuyauterie *f*; ~ **hot** fumant.

**pirate** /ˈpaɪərət/ *n* pirate *m*. ● *vt* pirater.

**Pisces** /ˈpaɪsi:z/ *n* Poissons *mpl*.

**pistol** /ˈpɪstl/ *n* pistolet *m*.

**pit** /pɪt/ *n* fosse *f*; (mine) puits *m*; (quarry) carrière *f*; (for orchestra) fosse *f*; (of stomach) creux *m*; (of cherry: US) noyau *m*. ● *vt* (*pt* **pitted**) marquer; (fig) opposer; ~ **oneself against** se mesurer à. ~ **stop** *n* arrêt *m* mécanique.

**pitch** /pɪtʃ/ *n* (Sport) terrain *m*; (of voice, note) hauteur *f*; (degree) degré *m*; (Mus) ton *m*; (tar) brai *m*. ● *vt* jeter; (*tent*) planter. ● *vi* (*ship*) tanguer. □ ~ **in** 🅸 contribuer.

**pitfall** /ˈpɪtfɔ:l/ *n* écueil *m*.

**pitiful** /ˈpɪtɪfl/ *a* pitoyable. **pitiless** *a* impitoyable.

**pittance** /ˈpɪtns/ *n* **earn a** ~ gagner trois fois rien.

**pity** /ˈpɪtɪ/ *n* pitié *f*; (regrettable fact) dommage *m*; **take** ~ **on** avoir pitié de; **what a** ~! quel dommage! ● *vt* avoir pitié de.

**pivot** /ˈpɪvət/ *n* pivot *m*. ● *vi* (*pt* **pivoted**) pivoter.

**placard** /ˈplækɑ:d/ *n* affiche *f*.

**place** /pleɪs/ *n* endroit *m*, lieu *m*; (house) maison *f*; (seat, rank) place *f*; **at** *or* **to my** ~ chez moi; **change** ~**s** changer de place; **in the first** ~ d'abord; **out of** ~ déplacé; **take** ~ avoir lieu. ● *vt* placer; (*order*) passer; (remember) situer; **be** ~**d** (in race) se placer. ~**-mat** *n* set *m*.

**placid** /ˈplæsɪd/ *a* placide.

**plagiarism** /ˈpleɪdʒərɪzəm/ *n* plagiat *m*. **plagiarize** *vt*/*i* plagier.

**plague** /pleɪg/ *n* (bubonic) peste *f*; (epidemic) épidémie *f*; (of ants, locusts) invasion *f*. ● *vt* harceler.

**plaice** /pleɪs/ *n inv* carrelet *m*.

**plain** /pleɪn/ *a* (obvious) clair; (candid) franc; (simple) simple; (not pretty) sans beauté; (not patterned) uni; ~ **chocolate** chocolat *m* noir; **in** ~ **clothes** en civil. ● *adv* franchement. ● *n* plaine *f*. **plainly** *adv* clairement; franchement; simplement.

**plaintiff** /ˈpleɪntɪf/ *n* plaignant/-e *m*/*f*.

**plaintive** /ˈpleɪntɪv/ *a* plaintif.

**plait** /plæt/ *vt* tresser. ● *n* natte *f*.

**plan** /plæn/ *n* projet *m*, plan *m*; (diagram) plan *m*. ● *vt* (*pt* **planned**) projeter (**to do** de faire); (*timetable, day*) organiser; (*economy, work*) planifier. ● *vi* prévoir; ~ **on** s'attendre à.

**plane** /pleɪn/ *n* (level) plan *m*; (aeroplane) avion *m*; (tool) rabot *m*. ● *a* plan. ● *vt* raboter.

**planet** /ˈplænɪt/ *n* planète *f*.

**plank** /plæŋk/ *n* planche *f*.

**planning** /ˈplænɪŋ/ *n* (of economy, work) planification *f*; (of holiday, party) organisation *f*; (of town) urbanisme *m*; **family ~** planning *m* familial; **~ permission** permis *m* de construire.

**plant** /plɑːnt/ *n* plante *f*; (Tech) matériel *m*; (factory) usine *f*. ● *vt* planter; (*bomb*) placer.

**plaster** /ˈplɑːstə(r)/ *n* plâtre *m*; (adhesive) sparadrap *m*. ● *vt* plâtrer; (cover) couvrir (**with** de).

**plastic** /ˈplæstɪk/ *a* en plastique; (*art, substance*) plastique; **~ surgery** chirurgie *f* esthétique. ● *n* plastique *m*.

**plate** /pleɪt/ *n* assiette *f*; (of metal) plaque *f*; (silverware) argenterie *f*; (in book) gravure *f*. ● *vt* (*metal*) plaquer.

**plateau** /ˈplætəʊ/ *n* (*pl* **~x** /-z/) plateau *m*; (fig) palier *m*.

**platform** /ˈplætfɔːm/ *n* (stage) estrade *f*; (for speaking) tribune *f*; (Rail) quai *m*; (Pol) plate-forme *f*.

**platoon** /pləˈtuːn/ *n* (Mil) section *f*.

**play** /pleɪ/ *vt*/*i* jouer; (*instrument*) jouer de; (*record*) mettre; (*game*) jouer à; (*opponent*) jouer contre; (*match*) disputer; **~ safe** ne pas prendre de risques. ● *n* jeu *m*; (Theat) pièce *f*. □ **~ down** minimiser; **~ on** (*fears*) exploiter; **~ up** [!] commencer à faire des siennes [!]; **~ up sth** mettre l'accent sur qch.

**playful** /ˈpleɪfl/ *a* (*remark*) taquin; (*child*) joueur.

**play**: **~ground** *n* cour *f* de récréation. **~-group**, **~-school** *n* garderie *f*.

**playing** /ˈpleɪɪŋ/ *n* (Sport) jeu *m*; (Theat) interprétation *f*. **~-card** *n* carte *f* à jouer. **~-field** *n* terrain *m* de sport.

**play**: **~-pen** *n* parc *m* (pour bébé). **~wright** *n* auteur *m* dramatique.

**plc** *abbr* (**public limited company**) SA.

**plea** /pliː/ *n* (for mercy, tolerance) appel *m*; (for food, money) demande *f*; (reason) excuse *f*; **make a ~ of guilty** plaider coupable.

**plead** /pliːd/ *vt*/*i* supplier; (Jur) plaider.

**pleasant** /ˈpleznt/ *a* agréable.

**please** /pliːz/ *vt*/*i* plaire (à), faire plaisir (à); **~ oneself, do as one ~s** faire ce qu'on veut. ● *adv* s'il vous *or* te plaît. **pleased** *a* content (**with** de). **pleasing** *a* agréable.

**pleasure** /ˈpleʒə(r)/ *n* plaisir *m*; **with ~** avec plaisir; **my ~** je vous en prie.

**pleat** /pliːt/ *n* pli *m*. ● *vt* plisser.

**pledge** /pledʒ/ *n* (token) gage *m*; (promise) promesse *f*. ● *vt* promettre; (pawn) mettre en gage.

**plentiful** /ˈplentɪfl/ *a* abondant.

**plenty** /ˈplentɪ/ *n* abondance *f*; **~ (of)** (a great deal) beaucoup (de); (enough) assez (de).

**pliers** /ˈplaɪəz/ *npl* pinces *fpl*.

**plight** /plaɪt/ *n* détresse *f*.

**plinth** /plɪnθ/ *n* socle *m*.

**plod** /plɒd/ *vi* (*pt* **plodded**) avancer péniblement.

**plonk** /plɒŋk/ *n* [!] pinard *m* [!].

**plot** /plɒt/ *n* (*conspiracy*) complot *m*; (of novel) intrigue *f*; **~ (of land)** terrain *m*. ● *vt*/*i* (*pt* **plotted**) (plan) comploter; (mark out) tracer.

**plough** /plaʊ/ *n* charrue *f*. ● *vt*/*i* labourer. □ **~ back** réinvestir; **~ through** avancer péniblement dans.

**plow** /plaʊ/ *n* & *vt*/*i* (US) = PLOUGH.

**ploy** /plɔɪ/ *n* stratagème *m*.

**pluck** /plʌk/ *vt* (*flower, fruit*) cueillir; (*bird*) plumer; (*eyebrows*)

épiler; (*strings*: Mus) pincer; **~ up courage** prendre son courage à deux mains. **plucky** *a* courageux.

**plug** /plʌg/ *n* (for sink) bonde *f*; (Electr) fiche *f*, prise *f*. ● *vt* (*pt* **plugged**) (*hole*) boucher; (publicize 🅸) faire du battage autour de. □ **~ in** brancher. **~-hole** *n* bonde *f*.

**plum** /plʌm/ *n* prune *f*; **~ pudding** (plum-)pudding *m*.

**plumber** /ˈplʌmə(r)/ *n* plombier *m*.

**plume** /pluːm/ *n* (of feathers) panache *m*.

**plummet** /ˈplʌmɪt/ *vi* tomber, plonger.

**plump** /plʌmp/ *a* potelé, dodu.

**plunge** /plʌndʒ/ *vt/i* (dive, thrust) plonger; (fall) tomber. ● *n* plongeon *m*; (fall) chute *f*; **take the ~** se jeter à l'eau. **plunger** *n* (for sink) ventouse *f*.

**plural** /ˈplʊərəl/ *a* pluriel; (*noun*) au pluriel; (*ending*) du pluriel. ● *n* pluriel *m*.

**plus** /plʌs/ *prep* plus; **ten ~** plus de dix. ● *a* (Electr & fig) positif. ● *n* signe *m* plus; (fig) atout *m*.

**ply** /plaɪ/ *vt* (*tool*) manier; (*trade*) exercer. ● *vi* faire la navette; **~ sb with drink** offrir continuellement à boire à qn.

**plywood** /ˈplaɪwʊd/ *n* contreplaqué *m*.

**p.m.** /piːˈem/ *adv* de l'après-midi *or* du soir.

**pneumatic drill** /njuːˈmætɪk drɪl/ *n* marteau-piqueur *m*.

**pneumonia** /njuːˈməʊnɪə/ *n* pneumonie *f*.

**PO** *abbr* ⇒POST OFFICE.

**poach** /pəʊtʃ/ *vt/i* (*game*) braconner; (*staff*) débaucher; (Culin) pocher.

**PO Box** *n* boîte *f* postale.

**pocket** /ˈpɒkɪt/ *n* poche *f*; **be out of ~** avoir perdu de l'argent. ● *a* de poche. ● *vt* empocher. **~-book** *n* (notebook) carnet *m*; (wallet: US) portefeuille *m*; (handbag: US) sac *m* à main. **~-money** *n* argent *m* de poche.

**pod** /pɒd/ *n* (peas) cosse *f*; (vanilla) gousse *f*.

**podgy** /ˈpɒdʒɪ/ *a* (**-ier**, **-iest**) dodu.

**poem** /ˈpəʊɪm/ *n* poème *m*. **poet** *n* poète *m*. **poetic** *a* poétique. **poetry** *n* poésie *f*.

**point** /pɔɪnt/ *n* (position) point *m*; (tip) pointe *f*; (decimal point) virgule *f*; (remark) remarque *f*; **good ~s** qualités *fpl*; **on the ~ of** sur le point de; **~ in time** moment *m*; **~ of view** point *m* de vue; **to the ~** pertinent; **what is the ~?** à quoi bon? ● *vt* (aim) braquer; (show) indiquer; **~ out** signaler. ● *vi* indiquer du doigt; **~ out that, make the ~ that** faire remarquer que. **~-blank** *a* & *adv* à bout portant.

**pointed** /ˈpɔɪntɪd/ *a* (sharp) pointu; (window) en pointe; (*remark*) lourd de sens.

**pointless** /ˈpɔɪntlɪs/ *a* inutile.

**poise** /pɔɪz/ *n* (confidence) assurance *f*; (physical elegance) aisance *f*.

**poison** /ˈpɔɪzn/ *n* poison *m*. ● *vt* empoisonner. **poisonous** *a* (*substance*) toxique; (*plant*) vénéneux; (*snake*) venimeux.

**poke** /pəʊk/ *vt/i* (push) pousser; (*fire*) tisonner; (thrust) fourrer; **~ fun at** se moquer de. ● *n* (petit) coup *m*. □ **~ out** (*head*) sortir.

**poker** /ˈpəʊkə(r)/ *n* (for fire) tisonnier *m*; (cards) poker *m*.

**Poland** /ˈpəʊlənd/ *n* Pologne *f*.

**polar** /ˈpəʊlə(r)/ *a* polaire.

**pole** /pəʊl/ *n* (stick) perche *f*; (for flag) mât *m*; (Geog) pôle *m*.

**Pole** /pəʊl/ *n* Polonais/-e *m/f*.

**pole-vault** *n* saut *m* à la perche.

**police** /pə'li:s/ *n* police *f*. ● *vt* faire la police dans. ~ **constable** *n* agent *m* de police. ~**man** *n* (*pl* **-men**) agent *m* de police. ~ **station** *n* commissariat *m* de police. ~**woman** *n* (*pl* **-women**) femme-agent *f*.

**policy** /'pɒlɪsɪ/ *n* politique *f*; (*insurance*) police *f* (d'assurance).

**polish** /'pɒlɪʃ/ *vt* polir; (*shoes, floor*) cirer. ● *n* (for shoes) cirage *m*; (for floor) encaustique *f*; (for nails) vernis *m*; (shine) poli *m*; (fig) raffinement *m*. □ ~ **off** finir en vitesse; ~ **up** (*language*) perfectionner.

**Polish** /'pəʊlɪʃ/ *a* polonais. ● *n* (Ling) polonais *m*.

**polished** /'pɒlɪʃt/ *a* raffiné.

**polite** /pə'laɪt/ *a* poli.

**political** /pə'lɪtɪkl/ *a* politique.

**politician** /pɒlɪ'tɪʃn/ *n* homme *m* politique, femme *f* politique.

**politics** /'pɒlətɪks/ *n* politique *f*.

**poll** /pəʊl/ *n* (vote casting) scrutin *m*; (survey) sondage *m*; **go to the** ~**s** aller aux urnes. ● *vt* (*votes*) obtenir.

**pollen** /'pɒlən/ *n* pollen *m*.

**polling booth** *n* isoloir *m*.

**polling station** *n* bureau *m* de vote.

**pollution** /pə'lu:ʃn/ *n* pollution *f*.

**polo** /'pəʊləʊ/ *n* polo *m*. ~ **neck** *n* col *m* roulé.

**pomegranate** /'pɒmɪgrænɪt/ *n* grenade *f*.

**pomp** /pɒmp/ *n* pompe *f*.

**pompous** /'pɒmpəs/ *a* pompeux.

**pond** /pɒnd/ *n* étang *m*; (artificial) bassin *m*; (stagnant) mare *f*.

**ponder** /'pɒndə(r)/ *vt/i* réfléchir (à), méditer (sur).

**pong** /pɒŋ/ *n* (stink 🅃) puanteur *f*. ● *vi* 🅃 puer.

**pony** /'pəʊnɪ/ *n* poney *m*. ~**tail** *n* queue *f* de cheval.

**poodle** /'pu:dl/ *n* caniche *m*.

**pool** /pu:l/ *n* (puddle) flaque *f*; (pond) étang *m*; (of blood) mare *f*; (for swimming) piscine *f*; (fund) fonds *m* commun; (of ideas) réservoir *m*; (snooker) billard *m* américain; ~**s** pari *m* mutuel sur le football. ● *vt* mettre en commun.

**poor** /pɔ:(r)/ *a* (not wealthy) pauvre; (not good) médiocre, mauvais.

**poorly** /'pɔ:lɪ/ *a* malade. ● *adv* mal.

**pop** /pɒp/ *n* (noise) pan *m*; (music) pop *m*. ● *a* pop *inv*. ● *vt/i* (*pt* **popped**) (burst) crever; (put) mettre; ~ **in**/**out**/**off** entrer/sortir/partir. □ ~ **up** surgir.

**pope** /pəʊp/ *n* pape *m*.

**poppy** /'pɒpɪ/ *n* pavot *m*; (wild) coquelicot *m*.

**popular** /'pɒpjʊlə(r)/ *a* populaire; (in fashion) en vogue; **be** ~ **with** plaire à.

**population** /pɒpjʊ'leɪʃn/ *n* population *f*.

**porcelain** /'pɔ:səlɪn/ *n* porcelaine *f*.

**porcupine** /'pɔ:kjʊpaɪn/ *n* porc-épic *m*.

**pork** /pɔ:k/ *n* porc *m*.

**pornography** /pɔ:'nɒgrəfɪ/ *n* pornographie *f*.

**port** /pɔ:t/ *n* (harbour) port *m*; (left: Naut) bâbord *m*; ~ **of call** escale *f*; (wine) porto *m*.

**portable** /'pɔ:təbl/ *a* portable.

**porter** /'pɔ:tə(r)/ *n* (carrier) porteur *m*; (door-keeper) portier *m*.

**portfolio** /pɔ:t'fəʊlɪəʊ/ *n* (Pol, Comm) portefeuille *m*.

**portion** /'pɔ:ʃn/ *n* (at meal) portion *f*; (part) partie *f*.

**portrait** /'pɔ:trɪt/ *n* portrait *m*.

**portray** /pɔ:'treɪ/ *vt* représenter.

**Portugal** /'pɔ:tjʊgl/ *n* Portugal *m*.

**Portuguese** /pɔ:tʃʊ'gi:z/ *n* (Ling) portugais *m*; (*person*) Portugais/-e *m/f*. ● *a* portugais.

**pose** /pəʊz/ *vt/i* poser; ~ **as** (*expert*) se poser en. ● *n* pose *f*.

**poser** /'pəʊzə(r)/ *n* (person) frimeur/-euse *m/f*; (puzzle) colle *f*.

**posh** /pɒʃ/ *a* ▣ chic *inv*.

**position** /pə'zɪʃn/ *n* position *f*; (job, state) situation *f*. ● *vt* placer.

**positive** /'pɒzətɪv/ *a* positif; (sure) sûr, certain; (real) réel, vrai.

**possess** /pə'zes/ *vt* posséder.

**possession** /pə'zeʃn/ *n* possession *f*; **take ~ of** prendre possession de.

**possessive** /pə'zesɪv/ *a* possessif.

**possible** /'pɒsəbl/ *a* possible.

**possibly** /'pɒsəblɪ/ *adv* peut-être; **if I ~ can** si cela m'est possible; **I cannot ~ leave** il m'est impossible de partir.

**post** /pəʊst/ *n* (pole) poteau *m*; (station, job) poste *m*; (mail service) poste *f*; (letters) courrier *m*. ● *a* postal. ● *vt* (*letter*) poster; **keep ~ed** tenir au courant; ~ **(up)** (a notice) afficher; (appoint) affecter.

**postage** /'pəʊstɪdʒ/ *n* affranchissement *m*; tarif *m* postal.

**postal** /'pəʊstl/ *a* postal. ~ **order** *n* mandat *m*.

**post**: **~box** *n* boîte *f* aux lettres. **~card** *n* carte *f* postale. **~ code** *n* code *m* postal.

**poster** /'pəʊstə(r)/ *n* (for information) affiche *f*; (for decoration) poster *m*.

**postgraduate** /pəʊst'grædʒʊət/ *n* étudiant/-e *m/f* de troisième cycle.

**posthumous** /'pɒstjʊməs/ *a* posthume.

**post**: **~man** *n* (*pl* **-men**) facteur *m*. **~mark** *n* cachet *m* de la poste.

**post-mortem** /pəʊst'mɔ:təm/ *n* autopsie *f*.

**post office** *n* poste *f*.

**postpone** /pə'spəʊn/ *vt* remettre.

**postscript** /'pəʊskrɪpt/ *n* (to letter) post-scriptum *m inv*.

**posture** /'pɒstʃə(r)/ *n* posture *f*. ● *vi* prendre des poses.

**pot** /pɒt/ *n* pot *m*; (drug ▣) hasch *m*; **go to ~** ▣ aller à la ruine; **take ~ luck** tenter sa chance. ● *vt* (*plants*) mettre en pot.

**potato** /pə'teɪtəʊ/ *n* (*pl* **~es**) pomme *f* de terre.

**pot-belly** *n* bedaine *f*.

**potential** /pə'tenʃl/ *a* & *n* potentiel (*m*).

**pot-hole** /'pɒthəʊl/ *n* (in rock) caverne *f*; (in road) nid *m* de poule. **pot-holing** *n* spéléologie *f*.

**potter** /'pɒtə(r)/ *n* potier *m*. ● *vi* bricoler. **pottery** *n* (art) poterie *f*; (objects) poteries *fpl*.

**potty** /'pɒtɪ/ *a* (**-ier, -iest**) (crazy ▣) toqué. ● *n* pot *m*.

**pouch** /paʊtʃ/ *n* poche *f*; (for tobacco) blague *f*.

**poultry** /'pəʊltrɪ/ *n* volailles *fpl*.

**pounce** /paʊns/ *vi* bondir (**on** sur). ● *n* bond *m*.

**pound** /paʊnd/ *n* (weight) livre *f* (= *454 g*); (money) livre *f*; (for dogs, cars) fourrière *f*. ● *vt* (crush) piler; (bombard) pilonner. ● *vi* frapper fort; (of heart) battre fort; (walk) marcher à pas lourds.

**pour** /pɔ:(r)/ *vt* verser. ● *vi* couler, ruisseler (**from** de); (rain) pleuvoir à torrents. □ ~ **in/out** (*people*) arriver/sortir en masse; ~ **off** *or* **out** vider. **pouring rain** *n* pluie *f* torrentielle.

**pout** /paʊt/ *vi* faire la moue.

**poverty** /'pɒvətɪ/ *n* misère *f*, pauvreté *f*.

**powder** /ˈpaʊdə(r)/ *n* poudre *f.* ● *vt* poudrer.

**power** /ˈpaʊə(r)/ *n* (strength) puissance *f*; (control) pouvoir *m*; (energy) énergie *f*; (Electr) courant *m.* ● *vt* (*engine*) faire marcher; (*plane*) propulser; **~ed by** (*engine*) propulsé par; (*generator*) alimenté par. **~ cut** *n* coupure *f* de courant.

**powerful** /ˈpaʊəfl/ *a* puissant.

**powerless** /ˈpaʊəlɪs/ *a* impuissant.

**power**: **~ point** *n* prise *f* de courant. **~-station** *n* centrale *f* électrique.

**practical** /ˈpræktɪkl/ *a* pratique. **~ joke** *n* farce *f*.

**practice** /ˈpræktɪs/ *n* (procedure) pratique *f*; (of profession) exercice *m*; (Sport) entraînement *m*; **in ~** (in fact) en pratique; (well-trained) en forme; **out of ~** rouillé; **put into ~** mettre en pratique.

**practise** /ˈpræktɪs/ *vt*/*i* (*musician, typist*) s'exercer (à); (Sport) s'entraîner (à); (put into practice) pratiquer; (*profession*) exercer.

**praise** /preɪz/ *vt* faire l'éloge de; (*God*) louer. ● *n* éloges *mpl*, louanges *fpl*.

**pram** /præm/ *n* landau *m*.

**prance** /prɑːns/ *vi* caracoler.

**prawn** /prɔːn/ *n* crevette *f* rose.

**pray** /preɪ/ *vi* prier. **prayer** *n* prière *f*.

**preach** /priːtʃ/ *vt*/*i* prêcher; **~ at** or **to** prêcher.

**precarious** /prɪˈkeərɪəs/ *a* précaire.

**precaution** /prɪˈkɔːʃn/ *n* précaution *f*.

**precede** /prɪˈsiːd/ *vt* précéder.

**precedence** /ˈpresɪdəns/ *n* (in importance) priorité *f*; (in rank) préséance *f*.

**precedent** /ˈpresɪdənt/ *n* précédent *m*.

**precinct** /ˈpriːsɪŋkt/ *n* quartier *m* commerçant; (pedestrian area) zone *f* piétonne; (district: US) circonscription *f*.

**precious** /ˈpreʃəs/ *a* précieux.

**precipitate** /prɪˈsɪpɪteɪt/ *vt* (*person, event, chemical*) précipiter.

**précis** /ˈpreɪsiː/ *n* résumé *m*.

**precise** /prɪˈsaɪs/ *a* précis; (careful) méticuleux. **precision** *n* précision *f*.

**precocious** /prɪˈkəʊʃəs/ *a* précoce.

**preconceived** /priːkənˈsiːvd/ *a* préconçu.

**predator** /ˈpredətə(r)/ *n* prédateur *m*.

**predicament** /prɪˈdɪkəmənt/ *n* situation *f* difficile.

**predict** /prɪˈdɪkt/ *vt* prédire. **predictable** *a* prévisible. **prediction** *n* prédiction *f*.

**predispose** /priːdɪˈspəʊz/ *vt* prédisposer (**to do** à faire).

**predominant** /prɪˈdɒmɪnənt/ *a* prédominant.

**pre-empt** /priːˈempt/ *vt* (anticipate) anticiper; (*person*) devancer.

**preface** /ˈprefɪs/ *n* (to book) préface *f*; (to speech) préambule *m*.

**prefect** /ˈpriːfekt/ *n* (pupil) élève *m*/*f* chargé/-e de la discipline; (official) préfet *m*.

**prefer** /prɪˈfɜː(r)/ *vt* (*pt* **preferred**) préférer (**to do** faire). **preferably** *adv* de préférence. **preference** *n* préférence *f*. **preferential** *a* préférentiel.

**prefix** /ˈpriːfɪks/ *n* préfixe *m*.

**pregnancy** /ˈpregnənsɪ/ *n* grossesse *f*. **pregnant** *a* (*woman*) enceinte; (*animal*) pleine; (*pause*) éloquent.

**prehistoric** /pri:hɪ'stɒrɪk/ *a* préhistorique.

**prejudge** /pri:'dʒʌdʒ/ *vt* (*issue*) préjuger de; (*person*) juger d'avance.

**prejudice** /'predʒʊdɪs/ *n* préjugé(s) *m(pl)*; (harm) préjudice *m*. ● *vt* (*claim*) porter préjudice à; (*person*) léser. **prejudiced** *a* partial; (person) qui a des préjugés.

**premature** /'premətjʊə(r)/ *a* prématuré.

**premeditated** /pri:'medɪteɪtɪd/ *a* prémédité.

**premises** /'premɪsɪz/ *npl* locaux *mpl*; **on the ~** sur les lieux.

**premium** /'pri:mɪəm/ *n* (*insurance*) prime *f*; **be at a ~** être précieux.

**preoccupied** /pri:'ɒkjʊpaɪd/ *a* préoccupé.

**preparation** /prepə'reɪʃn/ *n* préparation *f*; **~s** préparatifs *mpl*.

**preparatory** /prɪ'pærətrɪ/ *a* préparatoire. **~ school** *n* école *f* primaire privée; (US) école *f* secondaire privée.

**prepare** /prɪ'peə(r)/ *vt*/*i* (se) préparer (**for** à); **be ~d for** (expect) s'attendre à; **~d to** prêt à.

**preposition** /prepə'zɪʃn/ *n* préposition *f*.

**preposterous** /prɪ'pɒstərəs/ *a* absurde, ridicule.

**prep school** *n* = PREPARATORY SCHOOL.

**prerequisite** /pri:'rekwɪzɪt/ *n* condition *f* préalable.

**prescribe** /prɪ'skraɪb/ *vt* prescrire.

**prescription** /prɪ'skrɪpʃn/ *n* (Med) ordonnance *f*.

**presence** /'prezns/ *n* présence *f*; **~ of mind** présence *f* d'esprit.

**present¹** /'preznt/ *a* présent. ● *n* présent *m*; (gift) cadeau *m*; **at ~** à présent; **for the ~** pour le moment.

**present²** /prɪ'zent/ *vt* présenter; (*film, concert*) donner; **~ sb with** offrir à qn. **presentation** *n* présentation *f*. **presenter** *n* présentateur/-trice *m*/*f*.

**preservation** /prezə'veɪʃn/ *n* (of food) conservation *f*; (of wildlife) préservation *f*.

**preservative** /prɪ'zɜ:vətɪv/ *n* (Culin) agent *m* de conservation.

**preserve** /prɪ'zɜ:v/ *vt* préserver; (Culin) conserver. ● *n* réserve *f*; (fig) domaine *m*; (jam) confiture *f*.

**presidency** /'prezɪdənsɪ/ *n* présidence *f*.

**president** /'prezɪdənt/ *n* président/-e *m*/*f*.

**press** /pres/ *vt*/*i* (*button*) appuyer (sur); (squeeze) presser; (iron) repasser; (pursue) poursuivre; **be ~ed for** (*time*) manquer de; **~ for sth** faire pression pour avoir qch; **~ sb to do sth** pousser qn à faire qch; **~ on** continuer (**with sth** qch). ● *n* (newspapers, machine) presse *f*; (for wine) pressoir *m*. **~ cutting** *n* coupure *f* de presse.

**pressing** /'presɪŋ/ *a* pressant.

**press**: **~ release** *n* communiqué *m* de presse. **~-stud** *n* bouton-pression *m*. **~-up** *n* pompe *f*.

**pressure** /'preʃə(r)/ *n* pression *f*. ● *vt* faire pression sur. **~-cooker** *n* cocotte-minute *f*. **~ group** *n* groupe *m* de pression.

**pressurize** /'preʃəraɪz/ *vt* (*cabin*) pressuriser; (*person*) faire pression sur.

**prestige** /pre'sti:ʒ/ *n* prestige *m*.

**presumably** /prɪ'zju:məblɪ/ *adv* vraisemblablement.

**presume** /prɪ'zju:m/ *vt* (suppose) présumer.

**pretence**, (US) **pretense** /prɪ'tens/ *n* feinte *f*, simulation *f*; (claim) prétention *f*; (pretext) prétexte *m*.

**pretend** /prɪ'tend/ *vt/i* faire semblant (**to do** de faire); ~ **to** (lay claim to) prétendre à.

**pretentious** /prɪ'tenʃəs/ *a* prétentieux.

**pretext** /'pri:tekst/ *n* prétexte *m*.

**pretty** /'prɪtɪ/ *a* (**-ier**, **-iest**) joli. ● *adv* assez; ~ **much** presque.

**prevail** /prɪ'veɪl/ *vi* (be usual) prédominer; (win) prévaloir; ~ **on** persuader (**to do** de faire). **prevailing** *a* actuel; (*wind*) dominant.

**prevalent** /'prevələnt/ *a* répandu.

**prevent** /prɪ'vent/ *vt* empêcher (**from doing** de faire). **prevention** *n* prévention *f*. **preventive** *a* préventif.

**preview** /'pri:vju:/ *n* avant-première *f*; (fig) aperçu *m*.

**previous** /'pri:vɪəs/ *a* précédent, antérieur; ~ **to** avant. **previously** *adv* auparavant.

**prey** /preɪ/ *n* proie *f*; **bird of** ~ rapace *m*. ● *vi* ~ **on** faire sa proie de; (worry) préoccuper.

**price** /praɪs/ *n* prix *m*. ● *vt* fixer le prix de. **priceless** *a* inestimable; (amusing [I]) impayable [I].

**prick** /prɪk/ *vt* (with pin) piquer; ~ **up one's ears** dresser l'oreille.

**prickle** /'prɪkl/ *n* piquant *m*.

**pride** /praɪd/ *n* orgueil *m*; (satisfaction) fierté *f*; ~ **of place** place *f* d'honneur. ● *vpr* ~ **oneself on** s'enorgueillir de.

**priest** /pri:st/ *n* prêtre *m*.

**prim** /prɪm/ *a* (**primmer**, **primmest**) guindé, méticuleux.

**primarily** /'praɪmərəlɪ/ *adv* essentiellement.

**primary** /'praɪmərɪ/ *a* (*school, elections*) primaire; (chief, basic) premier, fondamental. ● *n* (Pol: US) primaire *f*.

**prime** /praɪm/ *a* principal, premier; (first-rate) excellent. ● *vt* (*pump, gun*) amorcer; (*surface*) apprêter. **P~ Minister** *n* Premier Ministre *m*.

**primitive** /'prɪmɪtɪv/ *a* primitif.

**primrose** /'prɪmrəʊz/ *n* primevère *f* (*jaune*).

**prince** /prɪns/ *n* prince *m*. **princess** *n* princesse *f*.

**principal** /'prɪnsəpl/ *a* principal. ● *n* (of school) directeur/-trice *m/f*.

**principle** /'prɪnsəpl/ *n* principe *m*; **in/on** ~ en/par principe.

**print** /prɪnt/ *vt* imprimer; (write in capitals) écrire en majuscules; ~**ed matter** imprimés *mpl*. ● *n* (of foot) empreinte *f*; (letters) caractères *mpl*; (photograph) épreuve *f*; (engraving) gravure *f*; **in** ~ disponible; **out of** ~ épuisé. **printer** *n* (person) imprimeur *m*; (Comput) imprimante *f*.

**prion** /'pri:ɒn/ *n* prion *m*.

**prior** /'praɪə(r)/ *a* précédent. ● *n* (Relig) prieur *m*. ~ **to** *prep* avant (de).

**priority** /praɪ'ɒrətɪ/ *n* priorité *f*; **take** ~ avoir la priorité (**over** sur).

**prise** /praɪz/ *vt* forcer; ~ **open** ouvrir en forçant.

**prison** /'prɪzn/ *n* prison *f*. **prisoner** *n* prisonnier/-ière *m/f*. ~ **officer** *n* gardien/-ne *m/f* de prison.

**pristine** /'prɪsti:n/ *a* **be in ~ condition** être comme neuf.

**privacy** /'prɪvəsɪ/ *n* intimité *f*, solitude *f*.

**private** /'praɪvɪt/ *a* privé; (confidential) personnel; (*lessons, house*) particulier; (*ceremony*) intime; **in** ~ en privé; (of ceremony) dans l'intimité.

● *n* (soldier) simple soldat *m*. **privately** *adv* en privé; dans l'intimité; (inwardly) intérieurement.

**privilege** /'prɪvəlɪdʒ/ *n* privilège *m*. **privileged** *a* privilégié; **be ~d to** avoir le privilège de.

**prize** /praɪz/ *n* prix *m*. ● *a* (*entry*) primé; (*fool*) parfait. ● *vt* (value) priser.

**pro** /prəʊ/ *n* **the ~s and cons** le pour et le contre.

**probable** /'prɒbəbl/ *a* probable. **probably** *adv* probablement.

**probation** /prə'beɪʃn/ *n* (testing) essai *m*; (Jur) liberté *f* surveillée.

**probe** /prəʊb/ *n* (device) sonde *f*; (fig) enquête *f*. ● *vt* sonder. ● *vi* **~ into** sonder.

**problem** /'prɒbləm/ *n* problème *m*. ● *a* difficile. **problematic** *a* problématique.

**procedure** /prə'si:dʒə(r)/ *n* procédure *f*; (way of doing sth) démarche *f* à suivre.

**proceed** /prə'si:d/ *vi* (go) aller, avancer; (pass) passer (**to** à); (act) procéder; **~ (with)** continuer; **~ to do** se mettre à faire.

**proceedings** /prə'si:dɪŋz/ *npl* (discussions) débats *mpl*; (meeting) réunion *f*; (report) actes *mpl*; (Jur) poursuites *fpl*.

**proceeds** /'prəʊsi:dz/ *npl* (profits) produit *m*, bénéfices *mpl*.

**process** /'prəʊses/ *n* processus *m*; (method) procédé *m*; **in ~** en cours; **in the ~ of doing** en train de faire. ● *vt* (*material, data*) traiter.

**procession** /prə'seʃn/ *n* défilé *m*.

**procrastinate** /prə'kræstɪneɪt/ *vi* différer, tergiverser.

**procure** /prə'kjʊə(r)/ *vt* obtenir.

**prod** /prɒd/ *vt*/*i* (*pt* **prodded**) pousser doucement. ● *n* petit coup *m*.

**prodigy** /'prɒdɪdʒɪ/ *n* prodige *m*.

**produce¹** /'prɒdju:s/ *n* produits *mpl*.

**produce²** /prə'dju:s/ *vt*/*i* produire; (bring out) sortir; (show) présenter; (cause) provoquer; (Theat, TV) mettre en scène; (radio) réaliser; (cinema) produire. **producer** *n* metteur *m* en scène; réalisateur *m*; producteur *m*.

**product** /'prɒdʌkt/ *n* produit *m*.

**production** /prə'dʌkʃn/ *n* production *f*; (Theat, TV) mise *f* en scène; (radio) réalisation *f*.

**productive** /prə'dʌktɪv/ *a* productif. **productivity** *n* productivité *f*.

**profession** /prə'feʃn/ *n* profession *f*.

**professional** /prə'feʃənl/ *a* professionnel; (of high quality) de professionnel; (*person*) qui exerce une profession libérale. ● *n* professionnel/-le *m*/*f*.

**professor** /prə'fesə(r)/ *n* professeur *m* (*titulaire d'une chaire*).

**proficient** /prə'fɪʃnt/ *a* compétent.

**profile** /'prəʊfaɪl/ *n* (of face) profil *m*; (of body, mountain) silhouette *f*; (by journalist) portrait *m*.

**profit** /'prɒfɪt/ *n* profit *m*, bénéfice *m*. ● *vi* **~ by** tirer profit de. **profitable** *a* rentable.

**profound** /prə'faʊnd/ *a* profond.

**profusely** /prə'fju:slɪ/ *adv* (*bleed*) abondamment; (*apologize*) avec effusion. **profusion** *n* profusion *f*.

**program** /'prəʊgræm/ *n* (US) = PROGRAMME; **(computer) ~** programme *m*. ● *vt* (*pt* **programmed**) programmer.

**programme** /'prəʊgræm/ *n* programme *m*; (broadcast) émission *f*.

**programmer** /'prəʊgræmə(r)/ *n* programmeur/-euse *m/f*.

**programming** /'prəʊgræmɪŋ/ *n* (Comput) programmation *f*.

**progress**[1] /'prəʊgres/ *n* progrès *m(pl)*; **in ~** en cours; **make ~** faire des progrès; **~ report** compte-rendu *m*.

**progress**[2] /prə'gres/ *vi* (advance, improve) progresser.

**progressive** /prə'gresɪv/ *a* progressif; (reforming) progressiste.

**prohibit** /prə'hɪbɪt/ *vt* interdire (**sb from doing** à qn de faire).

**project**[1] /prə'dʒekt/ *vt* projeter. ● *vi* (jut out) être en saillie.

**project**[2] /'prɒdʒekt/ *n* (plan) projet *m*; (undertaking) entreprise *f*; (School) dossier *m*.

**projection** /prə'dʒekʃn/ *n* projection *f*; saillie *f*; (estimate) prévision *f*.

**projector** /prə'dʒektə(r)/ *n* projecteur *m*.

**proliferate** /prə'lɪfəreɪt/ *vi* proliférer.

**prolong** /prə'lɒŋ/ *vt* prolonger.

**prominent** /'prɒmɪnənt/ *a* (projecting) proéminent; (conspicuous) bien en vue; (fig) important.

**promiscuous** /prə'mɪskjʊəs/ *a* de mœurs faciles.

**promise** /'prɒmɪs/ *n* promesse *f*. ● *vt/i* promettre. **promising** *a* prometteur, (*person*) qui promet.

**promote** /prə'məʊt/ *vt* promouvoir; (advertise) faire la promotion de. **promotion** *n* promotion *f*.

**prompt** /prɒmpt/ *a* rapide; (punctual) à l'heure, ponctuel. ● *adv* (on the dot) pile. ● *vt* inciter; (cause) provoquer; (Theat) souffler à. ● *n* (Comput) message *m* guide-opérateur. **prompter** *n* souffleur/-euse *m/f*. **promptly** *adv* rapidement; ponctuellement.

**prone** /prəʊn/ *a* **~ to** sujet à.

**pronoun** /'prəʊnaʊn/ *n* pronom *m*.

**pronounce** /prə'naʊns/ *vt* prononcer. **pronunciation** *n* prononciation *f*.

**proof** /pru:f/ *n* (evidence) preuve *f*; (test, trial copy) épreuve *f*; (of alcohol) teneur *f* en alcool. ● *a* **~ against** à l'épreuve de.

**prop** /prɒp/ *n* support *m*; (Theat) accessoire *m*. ● *vt* (*pt* **propped**) **~ (up)** (support) étayer; (lean) appuyer.

**propaganda** /prɒpə'gændə/ *n* propagande *f*.

**propel** /prə'pel/ *vt* (*pt* **propelled**) (*vehicle, ship*) propulser; (*person*) pousser.

**propeller** /prə'pelə(r)/ *n* hélice *f*.

**proper** /'prɒpə(r)/ *a* correct, bon; (adequate) convenable; (real) vrai; (thorough Ⓘ) parfait. **properly** *adv* correctement, comme il faut; (adequately) convenablement.

**proper noun** *n* nom *m* propre.

**property** /'prɒpətɪ/ *n* (house) propriété *f*; (things owned) biens *mpl*, propriété *f*. ● *a* immobilier, foncier.

**prophecy** /'prɒfəsɪ/ *n* prophétie *f*.

**prophet** /'prɒfɪt/ *n* prophète *m*.

**proportion** /prə'pɔ:ʃn/ *n* (ratio, dimension) proportion *f*; (amount) partie *f*.

**proposal** /prə'pəʊzl/ *n* proposition *f*; (of marriage) demande *f* en mariage.

**propose** /prə'pəʊz/ *vt* proposer. ● *vi* faire une demande en mariage; **~ to do** se proposer de faire.

**proposition** /prɒpə'zɪʃn/ *n* proposition *f*; (matter Ⓘ) affaire *f*. ● *vt* Ⓘ faire des propositions malhonnêtes à.

**proprietor** /prə'praɪətə(r)/ *n* propriétaire *mf.*

**propriety** /prə'praɪətɪ/ *n* (correct behaviour) bienséance *f.*

**prose** /prəʊz/ *n* prose *f*; (translation) thème *m.*

**prosecute** /'prɒsɪkju:t/ *vt* poursuivre en justice. **prosecution** *n* poursuites *fpl.* **prosecutor** *n* procureur *m.*

**prospect**[1] /'prɒspekt/ *n* (outlook) perspective *f*; (chance) espoir *m.*

**prospect**[2] /prə'spekt/ *vt/i* prospecter.

**prospective** /prə'spektɪv/ *a* (future) futur; (possible) éventuel.

**prospectus** /prə'spektəs/ *n* brochure *f*; (Univ) livret *m* de l'étudiant.

**prosperity** /prɒ'sperɪtɪ/ *n* prospérité *f.* **prosperous** *a* prospère.

**prostitute** /'prɒstɪtju:t/ *n* prostituée *f.*

**prostrate** /'prɒstreɪt/ *a* (prone) à plat ventre; (exhausted) prostré.

**protect** /prə'tekt/ *vt* protéger. **protection** *n* protection *f.* **protective** *a* protecteur; (*clothes*) de protection.

**protein** /'prəʊti:n/ *n* protéine *f.*

**protest**[1] /'prəʊtest/ *n* protestation *f*; **under ~** en protestant.

**protest**[2] /prə'test/ *vt/i* protester.

**Protestant** /'prɒtɪstənt/ *a & n* protestant/-e (*m/f*).

**protester** /prə'testə(r)/ *n* manifestant/-e *m/f.*

**protocol** /'prəʊtəkɒl/ *n* protocole *m.*

**protrude** /prə'tru:d/ *vi* dépasser.

**proud** /praʊd/ *a* fier, orgueilleux.

**prove** /pru:v/ *vt* prouver. ● *vi* **~ (to be) easy** se révéler facile; **~ oneself** faire ses preuves. **proven** *a* éprouvé.

**proverb** /'prɒvɜ:b/ *n* proverbe *m.*

**provide** /prə'vaɪd/ *vt* fournir (**sb with sth** qch à qn). ● *vi* **~ for** (allow for) prévoir; (guard against) parer à; (*person*) pourvoir aux besoins de.

**provided** /prə'vaɪdɪd/ *conj* **~ that** à condition que.

**providing** /prə'vaɪdɪŋ/ *conj* = PROVIDED.

**province** /'prɒvɪns/ *n* province *f*; (fig) compétence *f.*

**provision** /prə'vɪʒn/ *n* (stock) provision *f*; (supplying) fourniture *f*; (stipulation) dispositions *fpl*; **~s** (food) provisions *fpl.*

**provisional** /prə'vɪʒənl/ *a* provisoire.

**provocative** /prə'vɒkətɪv/ *a* provocant.

**provoke** /prə'vəʊk/ *vt* provoquer.

**prow** /praʊ/ *n* proue *f.*

**prowess** /'praʊɪs/ *n* prouesses *fpl.*

**prowl** /praʊl/ *vi* rôder.

**proxy** /'prɒksɪ/ *n* **by ~** par procuration.

**prudish** /'pru:dɪʃ/ *a* pudibond, prude.

**prune** /pru:n/ *n* pruneau *m.* ● *vt* (cut) tailler.

**pry** /praɪ/ *vi* **~ into** mettre son nez dans.

**psalm** /sɑ:m/ *n* psaume *m.*

**pseudonym** /'sju:dənɪm/ *n* pseudonyme *m.*

**psychiatric** /saɪkɪ'ætrɪk/ *a* psychiatrique. **psychiatrist** *n* psychiatre *mf.* **psychiatry** *n* psychiatrie *f.*

**psychic** /'saɪkɪk/ *a* (*phenomenon*) métapsychique; (*person*) doué de télépathie.

**psychoanalyse** /saɪkəʊ'ænəlaɪz/ *vt* psychanalyser.

**psychological** /saɪkə'lɒdʒɪkl/ *a* psychologique. **psychologist** *n*

psychologue *mf*. **psychology** *n* psychologie *f*.

**PTO** *abbr* (**please turn over**) TSVP.

**pub** /pʌb/ *n* pub *m*.

**puberty** /'pju:bətɪ/ *n* puberté *f*.

**public** /'pʌblɪk/ *a* public; (*library*) municipal; **in ~** en public.

**publican** /'pʌblɪkən/ *n* patron/-ne *m/f* de pub.

**publication** /pʌblɪ'keɪʃn/ *n* publication *f*.

**public house** *n* pub *m*.

**publicity** /pʌb'lɪsətɪ/ *n* publicité *f*.

**publicize** /'pʌblɪsaɪz/ *vt* faire connaître au public.

**public**: **~ relations** *n* relations *fpl* publiques. **~ school** *n* école *f* privée; (US) école *f* publique. **~ transport** *n* transports *mpl* en commun.

**publish** /'pʌblɪʃ/ *vt* publier. **publisher** *n* éditeur *m*. **publishing** *n* édition *f*.

**pudding** /'pʊdɪŋ/ *n* dessert *m*; (steamed) pudding *m*.

**puddle** /'pʌdl/ *n* flaque *f* d'eau.

**puff** /pʌf/ *n* (of smoke) bouffée *f*; (of breath) souffle *m*. ● *vt/i* souffler. □ **~ at** (*cigar*) tirer sur. **~ out** (swell) (se) gonfler.

**pull** /pʊl/ *vt/i* tirer; (*muscle*) se froisser; **~ a face** faire une grimace; **~ one's weight** faire sa part du travail; **~ sb's leg** faire marcher qn. ● *n* traction *f*; (fig) attraction *f*; (influence) influence *f*; **give a ~** tirer. □ **~ away** (Auto) démarrer; **~ back** *or* **out** (withdraw) (se) retirer; **~ down** (*building*) démolir; **~ in** (enter) entrer; (stop) s'arrêter; **~ off** enlever; (fig) réussir; **~ out** (from bag) sortir; (extract) arracher; (Auto) déboîter; **~ over** (Auto) se ranger (sur le côté); **~ through** s'en tirer; **~ oneself together** se ressaisir.

**pull-down menu** *n* (Comput) menu *m* déroulant.

**pulley** /'pʊlɪ/ *n* poulie *f*.

**pullover** /'pʊləʊvə(r)/ *n* pull(-over) *m*.

**pulp** /pʌlp/ *n* (of fruit) pulpe *f*; (for paper) pâte *f* à papier.

**pulpit** /'pʊlpɪt/ *n* chaire *f*.

**pulsate** /pʌl'seɪt/ *vi* battre.

**pulse** /pʌls/ *n* (Med) pouls *m*.

**pump** /pʌmp/ *n* pompe *f*; (plimsoll) chaussure *f* de sport. ● *vt/i* pomper; (*person*) soutirer des renseignements à; **~ up** gonfler.

**pumpkin** /'pʌmpkɪn/ *n* citrouille *f*.

**pun** /pʌn/ *n* jeu *m* de mots.

**punch** /pʌntʃ/ *vt* donner un coup de poing à; (*ticket*) poinçonner. ● *n* coup *m* de poing; (vigour ⊞) punch *m*; (device) poinçonneuse *f*; (drink) punch *m*. **~-line** *n* chute *f*.

**punctual** /'pʌŋktʃʊəl/ *a* à l'heure; (habitually) ponctuel.

**punctuation** /pʌŋktʃʊ'eɪʃn/ *n* ponctuation *f*.

**puncture** /'pʌŋktʃə(r)/ *n* crevaison *f*. ● *vt/i* crever.

**pungent** /'pʌndʒənt/ *a* âcre.

**punish** /'pʌnɪʃ/ *vt* punir (**for sth** de qch). **punishment** *n* punition *f*.

**punk** /pʌŋk/ *n* (music, fan) punk *m*; (US: ⊞) voyou *m*.

**punt** /pʌnt/ *n* (boat) barque *f*; (Irish pound) livre *f* irlandaise.

**puny** /'pju:nɪ/ *a* (**-ier**, **-iest**) chétif.

**pupil** /'pju:pl/ *n* (person) élève *mf*; (of eye) pupille *f*.

**puppet** /'pʌpɪt/ *n* marionnette *f*.

**puppy** /'pʌpɪ/ *n* chiot *m*.

**purchase** /'pɜ:tʃəs/ *vt* acheter (**from sb** à qn). ● *n* achat *m*.

**pure** /pjʊə(r)/ *a* pur.

**purgatory** /'pɜ:gətrɪ/ *n* purgatoire *m*.

**purge** /pɜ:dʒ/ *vt* purger (**of** de). ● *n* purge *f.*

**purification** /pjʊərɪfɪ'keɪʃn/ *n* (of water, air) épuration *f*; (Relig) purification *f*. **purify** *vt* épurer; purifier.

**puritan** /'pjʊərɪtən/ *n* puritain/-e *m/f.*

**purity** /'pjʊərətɪ/ *n* pureté *f.*

**purple** /'pɜ:pl/ *a* & *n* violet (*m*).

**purpose** /'pɜ:pəs/ *n* but *m*; (determination) résolution *f*; **on ~** exprès; **to no ~** sans résultat.

**purr** /pɜ:(r)/ *n* ronronnement *m.* ● *vi* ronronner.

**purse** /pɜ:ʃ/ *n* porte-monnaie *m inv*; (handbag: US) sac *m* à main. ● *vt* (*lips*) pincer.

**pursue** /pə'sju:/ *vt* poursuivre.

**pursuit** /pə'sju:t/ *n* poursuite *f*; (hobby) activité *f*, occupation *f.*

**pus** /pʌs/ *n* pus *m.*

**push** /pʊʃ/ *vt/i* pousser; (*button*) appuyer sur; (thrust) enfoncer; (recommend Ⓘ) proposer avec insistance; **be ~ed for** (*time*) manquer de; **be ~ing thirty** Ⓘ friser la trentaine; **~ sb around** bousculer qn. ● *n* poussée *f*; (effort) gros effort *m*; (drive) dynamisme *m*; **give the ~ to** Ⓘ flanquer à la porte Ⓘ. □ **~ in** resquiller; **~ on** continuer; **~ up** (lift) relever; (*prices*) faire monter.

**pushchair** *n* poussette *f.*

**pusher** /'pʊʃə(r)/ *n* revendeur/-euse *m/f* (de drogue).

**push-up** *n* pompe *f.*

**put** /pʊt/ *vt/i* (*pt* **put**; *pres p* **putting**) mettre, placer, poser; (*question*) poser; **~ the damage at a million** estimer les dégâts à un million; **~ sth tactfully** dire qch avec tact. □ **~ across** communiquer; **~ away** ranger; (in hospital, prison) enfermer; **~ back** (postpone) remettre; (delay) retarder; **~ down** (dé)poser; (write) inscrire; (pay) verser; (suppress) réprimer; **~ forward** (*plan*) soumettre; **~ in** (insert) introduire; (fix) installer; (submit) soumettre; **~ in for** faire une demande de; **~ off** (postpone) renvoyer à plus tard; (disconcert) déconcerter; (displease) rebuter; **~ sb off sth** dégoûter qn de qch; **~ on** (*clothes, radio*) mettre; (*light*) allumer; (*accent, weight*) prendre; **~ out** sortir; (stretch) (é)tendre; (extinguish) éteindre; (disconcert) déconcerter; (inconvenience) déranger; **~ up** lever, remonter; (*building*) construire; (*notice*) mettre; (*price*) augmenter; (*guest*) héberger; (*offer*) offrir; **~ up with** supporter.

**putty** /'pʌtɪ/ *n* mastic *m.*

**puzzle** /'pʌzl/ *n* énigme *f*; (game) casse-tête *m inv*; (jigsaw) puzzle *m.* ● *vt* rendre perplexe. ● *vi* se creuser la tête.

**pyjamas** /pə'dʒɑ:məz/ *npl* pyjama *m.*

**pylon** /'paɪlɒn/ *n* pylône *m.*

# Qq

**quack** /kwæk/ *n* (of duck) coin-coin *m inv*; (doctor) charlatan *m.*

**quadrangle** /'kwɒdræŋgl/ (of college) *n* cour *f.*

**quadruple** /kwɒ'dru:pl/ *a* & *n* quadruple (*m*). ● *vt/i* quadrupler.

**quail** /kweɪl/ *n* (bird) caille *f.*

**quaint** /kweɪnt/ *a* pittoresque; (old) vieillot; (odd) bizarre.

**qualification** /kwɒlɪfɪ'keɪʃn/ *n* diplôme *m*; (ability) compétence *f*; (fig) réserve *f*, restriction *f.*

**qualified** /ˈkwɒlɪfaɪd/ *a* diplômé; (able) qualifié (**to do** pour faire); (fig) conditionnel.

**qualify** /ˈkwɒlɪfaɪ/ *vt* qualifier; (modify) mettre des réserves à; (*statement*) nuancer. ● *vi* obtenir son diplôme (**as** de); (Sport) se qualifier; ~ **for** remplir les conditions requises pour.

**quality** /ˈkwɒlətɪ/ *n* qualité *f*.

**qualm** /kwɑːm/ *n* scrupule *m*.

**quantity** /ˈkwɒntətɪ/ *n* quantité *f*.

**quarantine** /ˈkwɒrəntiːn/ *n* quarantaine *f*.

**quarrel** /ˈkwɒrəl/ *n* dispute *f*, querelle *f*. ● *vi* (*pt* **quarrelled**) se disputer.

**quarry** /ˈkwɒrɪ/ *n* (excavation) carrière *f*; (prey) proie *f*. ● *vt* extraire.

**quart** /kwɔːt/ *n* ≈ litre *m*.

**quarter** /ˈkwɔːtə(r)/ *n* quart *m*; (of year) trimestre *m*; (25 cents: US) quart *m* de dollar; (district) quartier *m*; ~**s** logement *m*; **from all** ~**s** de toutes parts. ● *vt* diviser en quatre; (*troops*) cantonner.

**quarterly** /ˈkwɔːtəlɪ/ *a* trimestriel. ● *adv* tous les trois mois.

**quartet** /kwɔːˈtet/ *n* quatuor *m*.

**quartz** /kwɔːts/ *n* quartz *m*. ● *a* (*watch*) à quartz.

**quash** /kwɒʃ/ *vt* (suppress) étouffer; (Jur) annuler.

**quaver** /ˈkweɪvə(r)/ *vi* trembler, chevroter. ● *n* (Mus) croche *f*.

**quay** /kiː/ *n* (Naut) quai *m*.

**queasy** /ˈkwiːzɪ/ *a* **feel** ~ avoir mal au cœur.

**queen** /kwiːn/ *n* reine *f*; (cards) dame *f*.

**queer** /kwɪə(r)/ *a* étrange; (dubious) louche; ☒ homosexuel.

**quench** /kwentʃ/ *vt* éteindre; (*thirst*) étancher; (*desire*) étouffer.

**query** /ˈkwɪərɪ/ *n* question *f*. ● *vt* mettre en question.

**quest** /kwest/ *n* recherche *f*.

**question** /ˈkwestʃən/ *n* question *f*; **in** ~ en question; **out of the** ~ hors de question. ● *vt* interroger; (doubt) mettre en question, douter de. ~ **mark** *n* point *m* d'interrogation.

**questionnaire** /kwestʃəˈneə(r)/ *n* questionnaire *m*.

**queue** /kjuː/ *n* queue *f*. ● *vi* (*pres p* **queuing**) faire la queue.

**quibble** /ˈkwɪbl/ *vi* ergoter.

**quick** /kwɪk/ *a* rapide; (clever) vif/vive; **be** ~ (hurry) se dépêcher. ● *adv* vite. ● *n* **cut to the** ~ piquer au vif. **quicken** *vt/i* (s')accélérer. **quickly** *adv* rapidement, vite. ~**sand** *n* sables *mpl* mouvants.

**quid** /kwɪd/ *n inv* ☐ livre *f* sterling.

**quiet** /ˈkwaɪət/ *a* (calm, still) tranquille; (silent) silencieux; (gentle) doux; (discreet) discret; **keep** ~ se taire. ● *n* tranquillité *f*; **on the** ~ en cachette. **quieten** *vt/i* (se) calmer. **quietly** *adv* (*speak*) doucement; (*sit*) en silence.

**quilt** /kwɪlt/ *n* édredon *m*; **(continental)** ~ couette *f*.

**quirk** /kwɜːk/ *n* bizarrerie *f*.

**quit** /kwɪt/ *vt* (*pt* **quitted**) quitter; (*smoking*) arrêter de. ● *vi* abandonner; (resign) démissionner; ~ **doing** (US) cesser de faire.

**quite** /kwaɪt/ *adv* tout à fait, vraiment; (rather) assez; ~ **a few** un bon nombre (de).

**quits** /kwɪts/ *a* quitte (**with** envers); **call it** ~ en rester là.

**quiver** /ˈkwɪvə(r)/ *vi* trembler.

**quiz** /kwɪz/ *n* (*pl* **quizzes**) test *m*; (game) jeu-concours *m*. ● *vt* (*pt* **quizzed**) questionner.

**quotation** /kwəʊˈteɪʃn/ *n* citation *f*; (price) devis *m*; (stock exchange)

cotation *f*; ~ **marks** guillemets *mpl*.

**quote** /kwəʊt/ *vt* citer; (*reference, number*) rappeler; (*price*) indiquer; (*share price*) coter. ● *vi* ~ **for** faire un devis pour; ~ **from** citer. ● *n* (quotation) citation *f*; (estimate) devis *m*; **in ~s** ⊡ entre guillemets.

# Rr

**rabbi** /'ræbaɪ/ *n* rabbin *m*.

**rabbit** /'ræbɪt/ *n* lapin *m*.

**rabies** /'reɪbi:z/ *n* (disease) rage *f*.

**race** /reɪs/ *n* (contest) course *f*; (group) race *f*. ● *a* racial; ~ **relations** relations *fpl* inter-raciales. ● *vt* (compete with) faire la course avec; (*horse*) faire courir. ● *vi* courir; (*pulse*) battre précipitamment; (*engine*) s'emballer. **~course** *n* champ *m* de courses. **~horse** *n* cheval *m* de course. **~-track** *n* piste *f*; (for horses) champ *m* de courses.

**racing** /'reɪsɪŋ/ *n* courses *fpl*; ~ **car** voiture *f* de course.

**racism** /'reɪsɪzəm/ *n* racisme *m*. **racist** *a* & *n* raciste (*mf*).

**rack** /ræk/ *n* (shelf) étagère *f*; (for clothes) portant *m*; (for luggage) compartiment *m* à bagages; (for dishes) égouttoir *m*. ● *vt* ~ **one's brains** se creuser la cervelle.

**racket** /'rækɪt/ *n* (Sport) raquette *f*; (noise) vacarme *m*; (swindle) escroquerie *f*; (crime) trafic *m*.

**radar** /'reɪdɑ:(r)/ *n* & *a* radar (*m*).

**radial** /'reɪdɪəl/ *n* ~ **(tyre)** pneu *m* radial.

**radiate** /'reɪdɪeɪt/ *vt* (*happiness*) rayonner de; (*heat*) émettre. ● *vi* rayonner (**from** de). **radiation** *n* (radioactivity) radiation *f*. **radiator** *n* radiateur *m*.

**radical** /'rædɪkl/ *n* & *a* radical/-e (*m*/*f*).

**radio** /'reɪdɪəʊ/ *n* radio *f*; **on the ~** à la radio. ● *vt* (*message*) envoyer par radio; (*person*) appeler par radio.

**radioactive** /reɪdɪəʊ'æktɪv/ *a* radioactif.

**radiographer** /reɪdɪ'ɒgrəfə(r)/ *n* manipulateur/-trice *m*/*f* radiographe.

**radish** /'rædɪʃ/ *n* radis *m*.

**radius** /'reɪdɪəs/ *n* (*pl* **-dii** /-dɪaɪ/) rayon *m*.

**raffle** /'ræfl/ *n* tombola *f*.

**rag** /ræg/ *n* chiffon *m*; **~s** loques *fpl*.

**rage** /reɪdʒ/ *n* rage *f*, colère *f*; **be all the ~** faire fureur. ● *vi* (*person*) tempêter; (*storm, battle*) faire rage.

**ragged** /'rægɪd/ *a* (*clothes*) en loques; (*person*) dépenaillé.

**raid** /reɪd/ *n* (Mil, on stock market) raid *m*; (by police) rafle *f*; (by criminals) hold-up *m inv*. ● *vt* faire un raid *or* une rafle *or* un hold-up dans. **raider** *n* (thief) pillard *m*; (Mil) commando *m*; (corporate) raider *m*.

**rail** /reɪl/ *n* (on balcony) balustrade *f*; (stairs) rampe *f*; (for train) rail *m*; (for curtain) tringle *f*; **by ~** par chemin de fer.

**railing** /'reɪlɪŋ/ *n* (*also* **~s**) grille *f*.

**railway**, (US) **railroad** /'reɪlweɪ/ *n* chemin *m* de fer. ~ **line** *n* voie *f* ferrée. ~ **station** *n* gare *f*.

**rain** /reɪn/ *n* pluie *f*. ● *vi* pleuvoir. **~bow** *n* arc-en-ciel *m*. **~coat** *n* imperméable *m*. **~fall** *n* précipitation *f*. ~ **forest** *n* forêt *f* tropicale.

**rainy** /ˈreɪnɪ/ *a* (**-ier**, **-iest**) pluvieux; (*season*) des pluies.

**raise** /reɪz/ *vt* (*barrier, curtain*) lever; (*child, cattle*) élever; (*question*) soulever; (*price, salary*) augmenter. ● *n* (US) augmentation *f*.

**raisin** /ˈreɪzn/ *n* raisin *m* sec.

**rake** /reɪk/ *n* râteau *m*. ● *vt* (*garden*) ratisser; (search) fouiller dans. □ **~ in** (*money*) amasser; **~ up** (*past*) remuer.

**rally** /ˈrælɪ/ *vt/i* (se) rallier; (*strength*) reprendre; (after illness) aller mieux; **~ round** venir en aide. ● *n* rassemblement *m*; (Auto) rallye *m*; (tennis) échange *m*.

**ram** /ræm/ *n* bélier *m*. ● *vt* (*pt* **rammed**) (thrust) enfoncer; (crash into) rentrer dans.

**RAM** /ræm/ *abbr* (**random access memory**) RAM *f*.

**ramble** /ˈræmbl/ *n* randonnée *f*. ● *vi* faire une randonnée. □ **~ on** discourir.

**ramp** /ræmp/ *n* (slope) rampe *f*; (in garage) pont *m* de graissage.

**rampage¹** /ræmˈpeɪdʒ/ *vi* se déchaîner (**through** dans).

**rampage²** /ˈræmpeɪdʒ/ *n* **go on the ~** tout saccager.

**ran** /ræn/ ⇒RUN.

**rancid** /ˈrænsɪd/ *a* rance.

**random** /ˈrændəm/ *a* (fait) au hasard. ● *n* **at ~** au hasard.

**rang** /ræŋ/ ⇒RING².

**range** /reɪndʒ/ *n* (of prices, products) gamme *f*; (of people, beliefs) variété *f*; (of radar, weapon) portée *f*; (of aircraft) autonomie *f*; (of mountains) chaîne *f*. ● *vi* aller; (vary) varier.

**rank** /ræŋk/ *n* rang *m*; (Mil) grade *m*. ● *vt/i* **~ among** (se) classer parmi.

**ransack** /ˈrænsæk/ *vt* (search) fouiller; (pillage) mettre à sac.

**ransom** /ˈrænsəm/ *n* rançon *f*.

**rap** /ræp/ *n* coup *m* sec; (Mus) rap *m*. ● *vi* (*pt* **rapped**) donner des coups secs (**on** sur).

**rape** /reɪp/ *vt* violer. ● *n* viol *m*.

**rapid** /ˈræpɪd/ *a* rapide.

**rapist** /ˈreɪpɪst/ *n* violeur *m*.

**rapturous** /ˈræptʃərəs/ *a* (*delight*) extasié; (*welcome*) enthousiaste.

**rare** /reə(r)/ *a* rare; (Culin) saignant. **rarely** *adv* rarement.

**rascal** /ˈrɑːskl/ *n* coquin/-e *m/f*.

**rash** /ræʃ/ *n* (Med) rougeurs *fpl*. ● *a* irréfléchi.

**raspberry** /ˈrɑːzbrɪ/ *n* framboise *f*.

**rat** /ræt/ *n* rat *m*. ● *vi* (*pt* **ratted**) **~ on** (desert) lâcher; (inform on) dénoncer.

**rate** /reɪt/ *n* (ratio, level) taux *m*; (speed) rythme *m*; (price) tarif *m*; (of exchange) taux *m*; **at any ~** en tout cas. ● *vt* (value) estimer; (deserve) mériter; **~ sth highly** admirer beaucoup qch. ● *vi* **~ as** être considéré comme.

**rather** /ˈrɑːðə(r)/ *adv* (by preference) plutôt; (fairly) assez, plutôt; (a little) un peu; **I would ~ go** j'aimerais mieux partir; **~ than go** plutôt que de partir.

**rating** /ˈreɪtɪŋ/ *n* (score, value) cote *f*; **the ~s** (TV) l'indice *m* d'écoute, l'audimat® *m*.

**ratio** /ˈreɪʃɪəʊ/ *n* proportion *f*.

**ration** /ˈræʃn/ *n* ration *f*. ● *vt* rationner.

**rational** /ˈræʃənl/ *a* rationnel; (*person*) sensé.

**rationalize** /ˈræʃənəlaɪz/ *vt* justifier; (organize) rationaliser.

**rattle** /ˈrætl/ *vi* (*bottles, chains*) s'entrechoquer; (*window*) vibrer. ● *vt* (*bottles, chains*) faire s'entrechoquer; (fig, Ⓘ) énerver. ● *n* cliquetis *m*; (toy) hochet *m*.

**~snake** *n* serpent *m* à sonnette, crotale *m*.

**rave** /reɪv/ *vi* (enthuse) s'emballer; (in fever) délirer; (in anger) tempêter.

**ravenous** /'rævənəs/ *a* **be ~** avoir une faim de loup.

**ravine** /rə'vi:n/ *n* ravin *m*.

**raving** /'reɪvɪŋ/ *a* **~ lunatic** fou *m* furieux, folle *f* furieuse.

**ravishing** /'rævɪʃɪŋ/ *a* ravissant.

**raw** /rɔ:/ *a* cru; (not processed) brut; (*wound*) à vif; (immature) inexpérimenté; **get a ~ deal** être mal traité; **~ material** matière *f* première.

**ray** /reɪ/ *n* (of light) rayon *m*; **~ of hope** lueur *f* d'espoir.

**razor** /'reɪzə(r)/ *n* rasoir *m*. **~-blade** *n* lame *f* de rasoir.

**re** /ri:/ *prep* au sujet de; (at top of letter) objet.

**reach** /ri:tʃ/ *vt* (*place, level*) atteindre; (*decision*) arriver à; (contact) joindre; (*audience, market*) toucher. ● *vi* **~ up/down** lever/baisser le bras; **~ across** étendre le bras. ● *n* portée *f*; **within ~ of** à portée de; (close to) à proximité de.

**react** /rɪ'ækt/ *vi* réagir. **reaction** *n* réaction *f*. **reactor** *n* réacteur *m*.

**read** /ri:d/ *vt*/*i* (*pt* **read** /red/) lire; (study) étudier; (*instrument*) indiquer; **~ about sb** lire quelque chose sur qn; **~ out** lire à haute voix. **reader** *n* lecteur/-trice *m*/*f*. **reading** *n* lecture *f*; (measurement) indication *f*; (interpretation) interprétation *f*.

**readjust** /ri:ə'dʒʌst/ *vt* rajuster. ● *vi* se réadapter (**to** à).

**read-only memory**, **ROM** *n* mémoire *f* morte.

**ready** /'redɪ/ *a* (**-ier**, **-iest**) prêt; (quick) prompt. **~-made** *a* tout fait. **~-to-wear** *a* prêt-à-porter.

**real** /rɪəl/ *a* (not imaginary) véritable, réel; (not artificial) vrai; **it's a ~ shame** c'est vraiment dommage. **~ estate** *n* biens *mpl* immobiliers.

**realism** /'rɪəlɪzəm/ *n* réalisme *m*. **realistic** *a* réaliste.

**reality** /rɪ'ælətɪ/ *n* réalité *f*. **~ TV** *n* télé-réalité *f*.

**realize** /'rɪəlaɪz/ *vt* se rendre compte de, comprendre; (fulfil, turn into cash) réaliser; (*price*) atteindre.

**really** /'rɪəlɪ/ *adv* vraiment.

**reap** /ri:p/ *vt* (*crop*) recueillir; (*benefits*) récolter.

**reappear** /ri:ə'pɪə(r)/ *vi* reparaître.

**rear** /rɪə(r)/ *n* arrière *m*; (of person) derrière *m* Ⓘ. ● *a* (*seat*) arrière *inv*; (*entrance*) de derrière. ● *vt* élever. ● *vi* (*horse*) se cabrer. **~-view mirror** *n* rétroviseur *m*.

**reason** /'ri:zn/ *n* raison *f* (**to do, for doing** de faire); **within ~** dans la limite du raisonnable. ● *vi* **~ with sb** raisonner qn.

**reasonable** /'ri:znəbl/ *a* raisonnable.

**reassurance** /ri:ə'ʃɔ:rəns/ *n* réconfort *m*. **reassure** *vt* rassurer.

**rebate** /'ri:beɪt/ *n* (refund) remboursement *m*; (discount) remise *f*.

**rebel**[1] /'rebl/ *n* & *a* rebelle (*mf*).

**rebel**[2] /rɪ'bel/ *vi* (*pt* **rebelled**) se rebeller. **rebellion** *n* rébellion *f*.

**rebound**[1] /rɪ'baʊnd/ *vi* rebondir; **~ on** (backfire) se retourner contre.

**rebound**[2] /'ri:baʊnd/ *n* *n* rebond *m*.

**rebuke** /rɪ'bju:k/ *vt* réprimander. ● *n* réprimande *f*.

**recall** /rɪ'kɔ:l/ *vt* (remember) se souvenir de; (call back) rappeler. ● *n*

(memory) mémoire *f*; (Comput, Mil) rappel *m*.

**recap** /'ri:kæp/ *vt/i* (*pt* **recapped**) récapituler. ● *n* récapitulation *f*.

**recede** /rɪ'si:d/ *vi* s'éloigner; **his hair is receding** son front se dégarnit.

**receipt** /rɪ'si:t/ *n* (written) reçu *m*; (of letter) réception *f*; **~s** (Comm) recettes *fpl*.

**receive** /rɪ'si:v/ *vt* recevoir; (*stolen goods*) receler. **receiver** *n* (telephone) combiné *m*; (TV) récepteur *m*.

**recent** /'ri:snt/ *a* récent. **recently** *adv* récemment.

**receptacle** /rɪ'septəkl/ *n* récipient *m*.

**reception** /rɪ'sepʃn/ *n* réception *f*; **give sb a warm ~** donner un accueil chaleureux à qn.

**recess** /rɪ'ses/ *n* (alcove) alcôve *m*; (for door) embrasure *f*; (Jur, Pol) vacances *fpl*; (School, US) récréation *f*.

**recession** /rɪ'seʃn/ *n* récession *f*.

**recharge** /ri:'tʃɑ:dʒ/ *vt* recharger.

**recipe** /'resəpɪ/ *n* recette *f*.

**recipient** /rɪ'sɪpɪənt/ *n* (of honour) récipiendaire *mf*; (of letter) destinataire *mf*.

**reciprocate** /rɪ'sɪprəkeɪt/ *vt* (*compliment*) retourner; (*kindness*) payer de retour. ● *vi* en faire autant.

**recite** /rɪ'saɪt/ *vi* réciter.

**reckless** /'reklɪs/ *a* imprudent.

**reckon** /'rekən/ *vt/i* calculer; (judge) considérer; (think) penser; **~ on/with** compter sur/avec. **reckoning** *n* (guess) estimation *f*; (calculation) calculs *mpl*.

**reclaim** /rɪ'kleɪm/ *vt* récupérer; (*flooded land*) assécher.

**recline** /rɪ'klaɪn/ *vi* s'allonger; (*seat*) s'incliner.

**recluse** /rɪ'klu:s/ *n* reclus/-e *m/f*.

**recognition** /rekəg'nɪʃn/ *n* reconnaissance *f*; **beyond ~** méconnaissable; **gain ~** être reconnu.

**recognize** /'rekəgnaɪz/ *vt* reconnaître.

**recollect** /rekə'lekt/ *vt* se souvenir de, se rappeler. **recollection** *n* souvenir *m*.

**recommend** /rekə'mend/ *vt* recommander. **recommendation** *n* recommandation *f*.

**reconcile** /'rekənsaɪl/ *vt* (*people*) réconcilier; (*facts*) concilier; **~ oneself to** se résigner à.

**recondition** /ri:kən'dɪʃn/ *vt* remettre à neuf.

**reconsider** /ri:kən'sɪdə(r)/ *vt* réexaminer. ● *vi* réfléchir.

**reconstruct** /ri:kən'strʌkt/ *vt* reconstruire; (*crime*) faire une reconstitution de.

**record¹** /rɪ'kɔ:d/ *vt/i* (in register, on tape) enregistrer; (in diary) noter; **~ that** rapporter que.

**record²** /'rekɔ:d/ *n* (of events) compte-rendu *m*; (official) procès-verbal *m*; (personal, administrative) dossier *m*; (historical) archives *fpl*; (past history) réputation *f*; (Mus) disque *m*; (Sport) record *m*; **(criminal) ~** casier *m* judiciaire; **off the ~** officieusement. ● *a* record *inv*.

**recorder** /rɪ'kɔ:də(r)/ *n* (Mus) flûte *f* à bec.

**recording** /rɪ'kɔ:dɪŋ/ *n* enregistrement *m*.

**record-player** *n* tourne-disque *m*.

**recover** /rɪ'kʌvə(r)/ *vt* récupérer. ● *vi* se remettre; (*economy*) se redresser. **recovery** *n* (Med) rétablissement *m*; (of economy) relance *f*.

**recreation** /rekrɪ'eɪʃn/ *n* récréation *f*.

**recruit** /rɪ'kru:t/ *n* recrue *f*. ● *vt* recruter. **recruitment** *n* recrutement *m*.

**rectangle** /'rektæŋgl/ *n* rectangle *m*.

**rectify** /'rektɪfaɪ/ *vt* rectifier.

**recuperate** /rɪ'kju:pəreɪt/ *vt* récupérer. ● *vi* se rétablir.

**recur** /rɪ'kɜ:(r)/ *vi* (*pt* **recurred**) se reproduire.

**recycle** /ri:'saɪkl/ *vt* recycler.

**red** /red/ *a* (**redder**, **reddest**) rouge; (*hair*) roux. ● *n* rouge *m*; **in the ~** en déficit. **R~ Cross** *n* Croix-Rouge *f*. **~currant** *n* groseille *f*.

**redecorate** /ri:'dekəreɪt/ *vt* repeindre, refaire.

**redeploy** /ri:dɪ'plɔɪ/ *vt* réorganiser; (*troops*) répartir.

**red**: **~-handed** *a* en flagrant délit. **~-hot** *a* brûlant.

**redirect** /ri:daɪə'rekt/ *vt* (*traffic*) dévier; (*letter*) faire suivre.

**redness** /'rednɪs/ *n* rougeur *f*.

**redo** /ri:'du:/ *vt* (*pt* **-did**; *pp* **-done**) refaire.

**redress** /rɪ'dres/ *vt* (*wrong*) redresser; (*balance*) rétablir. ● *n* réparation *f*.

**reduce** /rɪ'dju:s/ *vt* réduire; (*temperature*) faire baisser. **reduction** *n* réduction *f*.

**redundancy** /rɪ'dʌndənsɪ/ *n* licenciement *m*.

**redundant** /rɪ'dʌndənt/ *a* superflu; (*worker*) licencié; **make ~** licencier.

**reed** /ri:d/ *n* (plant) roseau *m*.

**reef** /ri:f/ *n* récif *m*, écueil *m*.

**reel** /ri:l/ *n* (of thread) bobine *f*; (of film) bande *f*; (winding device) dévidoir *m*. ● *vi* chanceler. ● *vt* **~ off** réciter.

**refectory** /rɪ'fektərɪ/ *n* réfectoire *m*.

**refer** /rɪ'fɜ:(r)/ *vt/i* (*pt* **referred**) **~ to** (allude to) faire allusion à; (concern) s'appliquer à; (consult) consulter; (direct) renvoyer à.

**referee** /refə'ri:/ *n* (Sport) arbitre *m*. ● *vt* (*pt* **refereed**) arbitrer.

**reference** /'refrəns/ *n* référence *f*; (mention) allusion *f*; (person) personne *f* pouvant fournir des références; **in** *or* **with ~ to** en ce qui concerne; (Comm) suite à.

**referendum** /refə'rendəm/ *n* (*pl* **~s**) référendum *m*.

**refill**[1] /ri:'fɪl/ *vt* (*glass*) remplir à nouveau; (*pen*) recharger.

**refill**[2] /'ri:fɪl/ *n* recharge *f*.

**refine** /rɪ'faɪn/ *vt* raffiner.

**reflect** /rɪ'flekt/ *vt* refléter; (*heat, light*) renvoyer. ● *vi* réfléchir (**on** à); **~ well/badly on sb** faire honneur/du tort à qn.

**reflection** /rɪ'flekʃn/ *n* réflexion *f*; (image) reflet *m*; **on ~** à la réflexion.

**reflective** /rɪ'flektɪv/ *a* (*surface*) réfléchissant; (*person*) réfléchi.

**reflector** /rɪ'flektə(r)/ *n* (on car) catadioptre *m*.

**reflex** /'ri:fleks/ *a* & *n* réflexe (*m*).

**reflexive** /rɪ'fleksɪv/ *a* (Gram) réfléchi.

**reform** /rɪ'fɔ:m/ *vt* réformer. ● *vi* (*person*) s'amender. ● *n* réforme *f*.

**refrain** /rɪ'freɪn/ *n* refrain *m*. ● *vi* s'abstenir (**from** de).

**refresh** /rɪ'freʃ/ *vt* (*drink*) rafraîchir; (*rest*) reposer. **refreshments** *npl* rafraîchissements *mpl*.

**refrigerate** /rɪ'frɪdʒəreɪt/ *vt* réfrigérer. **refrigerator** *n* réfrigérateur *m*.

**refuel** /ri:'fju:əl/ *vt/i* (*pt* **refuelled**) (se) ravitailler.

**refuge** /'refju:dʒ/ *n* refuge *m*; **take ~** se réfugier. **refugee** *n* réfugié/-e *m/f*.

**refund[1]** /rɪ'fʌnd/ *vt* rembourser.

**refund[2]** /'ri:fʌnd/ *n* remboursement *m*.

**refurbish** /ri:'fɜ:bɪʃ/ *vt* remettre à neuf.

**refuse[1]** /rɪ'fju:z/ *vt/i* refuser.

**refuse[2]** /'refju:s/ *n* ordures *fpl*.

**regain** /rɪ'geɪn/ *vt* retrouver; (*lost ground*) regagner.

**regard** /rɪ'gɑ:d/ *vt* considérer; **as ~s** en ce qui concerne. ● *n* égard *m*, estime *f*; **in this ~** à cet égard; **~s** amitiés *fpl*. **regarding** *prep* en ce qui concerne.

**regardless** /rɪ'gɑ:dlɪs/ *adv* malgré tout; **~ of** sans tenir compte de.

**regime** /reɪ'ʒi:m/ *n* régime *m*.

**regiment** /'redʒɪmənt/ *n* régiment *m*.

**region** /'ri:dʒən/ *n* région *f*; **in the ~ of** environ.

**register** /'redʒɪstə(r)/ *n* registre *m*. ● *vt* (record) enregistrer; (*vehicle*) faire immatriculer; (*birth*) déclarer; (*letter*) recommander; (indicate) indiquer; (express) exprimer. ● *vi* (enrol) s'inscrire; (at hotel) se présenter; (fig) être compris.

**registrar** /redʒɪ'strɑ:(r)/ *n* officier *m* de l'état civil; (Univ) responsable *m* du bureau de la scolarité.

**registration** /redʒɪ'streɪʃn/ *n* (of voter, student) inscription *f*; (of birth) déclaration *f*; **~ (number)** (Auto) numéro *m* d'immatriculation.

**registry office** *n* bureau *m* de l'état civil.

**regret** /rɪ'gret/ *n* regret *m*. ● *vt* (*pt* **regretted**) regretter (**to do** de faire). **regretfully** *adv* à regret.

**regular** /'regjʊlə(r)/ *a* régulier; (usual) habituel. ● *n* habitué/-e *m/f*. **regularity** *n* régularité *f*. **regularly** *adv* régulièrement.

**regulate** /'regjʊleɪt/ *vt* régler. **regulation** *n* (rule) règlement *m*; (process) réglementation *f*.

**rehabilitate** /ri:ə'bɪlɪteɪt/ *vt* (in public esteem) réhabiliter; (prisoner) réinsérer.

**rehearsal** /rɪ'hɜ:sl/ *n* répétition *f*. **rehearse** *vt/i* répéter.

**reign** /reɪn/ *n* règne *m*. ● *vi* régner (**over** sur).

**reimburse** /ri:ɪm'bɜ:s/ *vt* rembourser.

**reindeer** /'reɪndɪə(r)/ *n inv* renne *m*.

**reinforce** /ri:ɪn'fɔ:s/ *vt* renforcer. **reinforcement** *n* renforcement *m*; **~s** renforts *mpl*.

**reinstate** /ri:ɪn'steɪt/ *vt* (*person*) réintégrer; (*law*) rétablir.

**reject[1]** /'ri:dʒekt/ *n* marchandise *f* de deuxième choix.

**reject[2]** /rɪ'dʒekt/ *vt* (*offer, plea*) rejeter; (*goods*) refuser. **rejection** *n* (personal) rejet *m*; (of candidate, work) refus *m*.

**rejoice** /rɪ'dʒɔɪs/ *vi* se réjouir.

**relapse** /rɪ'læps/ *n* rechute *f*. ● *vi* rechuter; **~ into** retomber dans.

**relate** /rɪ'leɪt/ *vt* raconter; (associate) associer. ● *vi* **~ to** se rapporter à; (get on with) s'entendre avec. **related** *a* apparenté; **we are ~** nous sommes parents.

**relation** /rɪ'leɪʃn/ *n* rapport *m*; (person) parent/-e *m/f*. **relationship** *n* relations *fpl*; (link) rapport *m*.

**relative** /'relətɪv/ *n* parent/-e *m/f*. ● *a* relatif; (respective) respectif.

**relax** /rɪ'læks/ *vt* (*grip*) relâcher; (*muscle*) décontracter; (*discipline*)

assouplir. ● *vi* (*person*) se détendre; (*grip*) se relâcher. **relaxation** *n* détente *f*. **relaxing** *a* délassant.

**relay**[1] /'ri:leɪ/ *n* (also ~ **race**) course *f* de relais.

**relay**[2] /rɪ'leɪ/ *vt* relayer.

**release** /rɪ'li:s/ *vt* (*prisoner*) libérer; (*fastening*) faire jouer; (*object, hand*) lâcher; (*film*) faire sortir; (*news*) publier. ● *n* libération *f*; (of film) sortie *f*; (new record, film) nouveauté *f*.

**relevance** /'reləvəns/ *n* pertinence *f*, intérêt *m*.

**relevant** /'reləvənt/ *a* pertinent; **be ~ to** avoir rapport à.

**reliability** /rɪlaɪə'bɪlətɪ/ *n* (of firm) sérieux *m*; (of car) fiabilité *f*; (of person) honnêteté *f*. **reliable** *a* (*firm*) sérieux; (*person, machine*) fiable.

**reliance** /rɪ'laɪəns/ *n* dépendance *f*.

**relic** /'relɪk/ *n* vestige *m*; (object) relique *f*.

**relief** /rɪ'li:f/ *n* soulagement *m* (**from à**); (assistance) secours *m*; (outline) relief *m*; ~ **road** route *f* de délestage.

**relieve** /rɪ'li:v/ *vt* soulager; (help) secourir; (take over from) relayer.

**religion** /rɪ'lɪdʒən/ *n* religion *f*. **religious** *a* religieux.

**relish** /'relɪʃ/ *n* plaisir *m*; (Culin) condiment *m*. ● *vt* (*food*) savourer; (*idea*) se réjouir de.

**relocate** /ri:ləʊ'keɪt/ *vt* muter. ● *vi* (*company*) déménager; (*worker*) être muté.

**reluctance** /rɪ'lʌktəns/ *n* répugnance *f*.

**reluctant** /rɪ'lʌktənt/ *a* (*person*) peu enthousiaste; (*consent*) accordé à contrecœur; ~ **to** peu disposé à. **reluctantly** *adv* à contrecœur.

**rely** /rɪ'laɪ/ *vi* ~ **on** (count) compter sur; (be dependent) dépendre de.

**remain** /rɪ'meɪn/ *vi* rester. **remainder** *n* reste *m*.

**remand** /rɪ'mɑ:nd/ *vt* mettre en détention provisoire. ● *n* **on** ~ en détention provisoire.

**remark** /rɪ'mɑ:k/ *n* remarque *f*. ● *vt* remarquer. ● *vi* ~ **on** faire des remarques sur. **remarkable** *a* remarquable.

**remedy** /'remədɪ/ *n* remède *m*. ● *vt* remédier à.

**remember** /rɪ'membə(r)/ *vt* se souvenir de, se rappeler; ~ **to do** ne pas oublier de faire. **remembrance** *n* souvenir *m*.

**remind** /rɪ'maɪnd/ *vt* rappeler (**sb of sth** qch à qn); ~ **sb to do** rappeler à qn de faire. **reminder** *n* rappel *m*.

**reminisce** /remɪ'nɪs/ *vi* évoquer ses souvenirs.

**remission** /rɪ'mɪʃn/ *n* (Med) rémission *f*; (Jur) remise *f*.

**remnant** /'remnənt/ *n* reste *m*; (trace) vestige *m*; (of cloth) coupon *m*.

**remodel** /ri:'mɒdel/ *vt* (*pt* **remodelled**) remodeler.

**remorse** /rɪ'mɔ:s/ *n* remords *m*.

**remote** /rɪ'məʊt/ *a* (*place, time*) lointain; (*person*) distant; (slight) vague; ~ **control** télécommande *f*.

**removable** /rɪ'mu:vəbl/ *a* amovible.

**removal** /rɪ'muvl/ *n* (of employee) renvoi *m*; (of threat) suppression *f*; (of troops) retrait *m*; (of stain) détachage *m*; (from house) déménagement *m*; ~ **men** déménageurs *mpl*.

**remove** /rɪ'mu:v/ *vt* enlever; (dismiss) renvoyer; (do away with) supprimer; (Comput) effacer.

**remunerate** /rɪ'mju:nəreɪt/ *vt* rémunérer. **remuneration** *n* rémunération *f*.

**render** /'rendə(r)/ *vt* rendre.

**renegade** /'renɪgeɪd/ *n* renégat/-e *m*/*f*.

**renew** /rɪ'nju:/ *vt* renouveler; (resume) reprendre. **renewable** *a* renouvelable.

**renounce** /rɪ'naʊns/ *vt* renoncer à; (disown) renier.

**renovate** /'renəveɪt/ *vt* rénover.

**renown** /rɪ'naʊn/ *n* renommée *f*.

**rent** /rent/ *n* loyer *m*. ● *vt* louer; **for ~** à louer. **rental** *n* prix *m* de location.

**reopen** /ri:'əʊpən/ *vt*/*i* rouvrir.

**reorganize** /ri:'ɔ:gənaɪz/ *vt* réorganiser.

**rep** /rep/ *n* (Comm) représentant/-e *m*/*f*.

**repair** /rɪ'peə(r)/ *vt* réparer. ● *n* réparation *f*; **in good/bad ~** en bon/mauvais état.

**repatriate** /ri:'pætrɪeɪt/ *vt* rapatrier. **repatriation** *n* rapatriement *m*.

**repay** /ri:'peɪ/ *vt* (*pt* **repaid**) rembourser; (reward) récompenser. **repayment** *n* remboursement *m*.

**repeal** /rɪ'pi:l/ *vt* abroger. ● *n* abrogation *f*.

**repeat** /rɪ'pi:t/ *vt*/*i* répéter; (renew) renouveler; **~ itself**, **~ oneself** se répéter. ● *n* répétition *f*; (broadcast) reprise *f*.

**repel** /rɪ'pel/ *vt* (*pt* **repelled**) repousser.

**repent** /rɪ'pent/ *vi* se repentir (**of** de).

**repercussion** /ri:pə'kʌʃn/ *n* répercussion *f*.

**repetition** /repɪ'tɪʃn/ *n* répétition *f*.

**replace** /rɪ'pleɪs/ *vt* (put back) remettre; (take the place of) remplacer. **replacement** *n* remplacement *m* (**of** de); (person) remplaçant/-e *m*/*f*; (new part) pièce *f* de rechange.

**replay** /'ri:pleɪ/ *n* (Sport) match *m* rejoué; (recording) répétition *f* immédiate.

**replenish** /rɪ'plenɪʃ/ *vt* (refill) remplir; (renew) renouveler.

**replica** /'replɪkə/ *n* copie *f* exacte.

**reply** /rɪ'plaɪ/ *vt*/*i* répondre. ● *n* réponse *f*.

**report** /rɪ'pɔ:t/ *vt* rapporter, annoncer (**that** que); (notify) signaler; (denounce) dénoncer. ● *vi* faire un rapport; **~** (**on**) (*news item*) faire un reportage sur; **~ to** (go) se présenter chez. ● *n* rapport *m*; (in press) reportage *m*; (School) bulletin *m*. **reporter** *n* reporter *m*.

**repossess** /ri:pə'zes/ *vt* reprendre.

**represent** /reprɪ'zent/ *vt* représenter.

**representation** /reprɪzen'teɪʃn/ *n* représentation *f*; **make ~s to** protester auprès de.

**representative** /reprɪ'zentətɪv/ *a* représentatif, typique (**of** de). ● *n* représentant/-e *m*/*f*.

**repress** /rɪ'pres/ *vt* réprimer.

**reprieve** /rɪ'pri:v/ *n* (delay) sursis *m*; (pardon) grâce *f*. ● *vt* accorder un sursis à; gracier.

**reprimand** /'reprɪmɑ:nd/ *vt* réprimander. ● *n* réprimande *f*.

**reprisals** /rɪ'praɪzlz/ *npl* représailles *fpl*.

**reproach** /rɪ'prəʊtʃ/ *vt* reprocher (**sb for sth** qch à qn). ● *n* reproche *m*.

**reproduce** /riːprəˈdjuːs/ *vt/i* (se) reproduire. **reproduction** *n* reproduction *f*. **reproductive** *a* reproducteur.

**reptile** /ˈreptaɪl/ *n* reptile *m*.

**republic** /rɪˈpʌblɪk/ *n* république *f*. **republican** *a* & *n* républicain/-e (*m*/*f*).

**repudiate** /rɪˈpjuːdɪeɪt/ *vt* répudier; (*contract*) refuser d'honorer.

**reputable** /ˈrepjʊtəbl/ *a* honorable, de bonne réputation.

**reputation** /repjʊˈteɪʃn/ *n* réputation *f*.

**repute** /rɪˈpjuːt/ *n* réputation *f*.

**request** /rɪˈkwest/ *n* demande *f*. ● *vt* demander (**of, from** à).

**require** /rɪˈkwaɪə(r)/ *vt* (of thing) demander; (of person) avoir besoin de; (demand, order) exiger. **required** *a* requis. **requirement** *n* exigence *f*; (condition) condition *f* (requise).

**rescue** /ˈreskjuː/ *vt* sauver. ● *n* sauvetage *m* (**of** de); (help) secours *m*.

**research** /rɪˈsɜːtʃ/ *n* recherche(s) *f*(*pl*). ● *vt/i* faire des recherches (sur). **researcher** *n* chercheur/-euse *m*/*f*.

**resemblance** /rɪˈzembləns/ *n* ressemblance *f*. **resemble** *vt* ressembler à.

**resent** /rɪˈzent/ *vt* être indigné de, s'offenser de. **resentment** *n* ressentiment *m*.

**reservation** /rezəˈveɪʃn/ *n* (doubt) réserve *f*; (booking) réservation *f*; (US) réserve *f* (indienne); **make a ~** réserver.

**reserve** /rɪˈzɜːv/ *vt* réserver. ● *n* (*stock, land*) réserve *f*; (Sport) remplaçant/-e *m*/*f*; **in ~** en réserve; **the ~s** (Mil) les réserves *fpl*. **reserved** *a* (*person, room*) réservé.

**reshuffle** /riːˈʃʌfl/ *vt* (Pol) remanier. ● *n* (Pol) remaniement *m* (ministériel).

**residence** /ˈrezɪdəns/ *n* résidence *f*; (of students) foyer *m*; **in ~** (*doctor*) résidant.

**resident** /ˈrezɪdənt/ *a* résidant; **be ~** résider. ● *n* habitant/-e *m*/*f*; (foreigner) résident/-e *m*/*f*; (in hotel) pensionnaire *mf*. **residential** *a* résidentiel.

**resign** /rɪˈzaɪn/ *vt* abandonner; (*job*) démissionner de. ● *vi* démissionner; **~ oneself to** se résigner à. **resignation** *n* résignation *f*; (from job) démission *f*. **resigned** *a* résigné.

**resilience** /rɪˈzɪlɪəns/ *n* élasticité *f*; ressort *m*.

**resin** /ˈrezɪn/ *n* résine *f*.

**resist** /rɪˈzɪst/ *vt/i* résister (à). **resistance** *n* résistance *f*. **resistant** *a* (Med) rebelle; (*metal*) résistant.

**resolution** /rezəˈluːʃn/ *n* résolution *f*.

**resolve** /rɪˈzɒlv/ *vt* résoudre (**to do** de faire). ● *n* résolution *f*.

**resort** /rɪˈzɔːt/ *vi* **~ to** avoir recours à. ● *n* (recourse) recours *m*; (place) station *f*; **in the last ~** en dernier ressort.

**resource** /rɪˈsɔːs/ *n* ressource *f*; **~s** (wealth) ressources *fpl*. **resourceful** *a* ingénieux.

**respect** /rɪˈspekt/ *n* respect *m*; (aspect) égard *m*; **with ~ to** à l'égard de, relativement à. ● *vt* respecter.

**respectability** /rɪspektəˈbɪlətɪ/ *n* respectabilité *f*. **respectable** *a* respectable.

**respectful** /rɪˈspektfl/ *a* respectueux.

**respective** /rɪˈspektɪv/ *a* respectif.

**respite** /ˈresp(a)ɪt/ *n* répit *m*.

**respond** /rɪ'spɒnd/ *vi* répondre (**to** à); **~ to** (react to) réagir à. **response** *n* réponse *f*.

**responsibility** /rɪspɒnsə'bɪlətɪ/ *n* responsabilité *f*. **responsible** *a* responsable; (*job*) qui comporte des responsabilités.

**responsive** /rɪ'spɒnsɪv/ *a* réceptif.

**rest** /rest/ *vt/i* (se) reposer; (lean) (s')appuyer (**on** sur); (be buried, lie) reposer; (remain) demeurer. ● *n* repos *m*; (support) support *m*; **have a ~** se reposer; **the ~** (remainder) le reste (**of** de); (other people) les autres.

**restaurant** /'restərɒnt/ *n* restaurant *m*.

**restless** /'restlɪs/ *a* agité.

**restoration** /restə'reɪʃn/ *n* rétablissement *m*; restauration *f*.

**restore** /rɪ'stɔ:(r)/ *vt* rétablir; (*building*) restaurer; **~ sth to sb** restituer qch à qn.

**restrain** /rɪ'streɪn/ *vt* contenir; **~ sb from** retenir qn de. **restrained** *a* (moderate) mesuré; (in control of self) maître de soi.

**restrict** /rɪ'strɪkt/ *vt* restreindre.

**rest room** *n* (US) toilettes *fpl*.

**result** /rɪ'zʌlt/ *n* résultat *m*. ● *vi* résulter; **~ in** aboutir à.

**resume** /rɪ'zju:m/ *vt/i* reprendre.

**résumé** /'rezju:meɪ/ *n* résumé *m*; (of career: US) CV *m*, curriculum vitae *m*.

**resurrect** /rezə'rekt/ *vt* ressusciter.

**resuscitate** /rɪ'sʌsɪteɪt/ *vt* réanimer.

**retail** /'ri:teɪl/ *n* détail *m*. ● *a & adv* au détail. ● *vt/i* (se) vendre (au détail). **retailer** *n* détaillant/-e *m/f*.

**retain** /rɪ'teɪn/ *vt* (hold back, remember) retenir; (keep) conserver.

**retaliate** /rɪ'tælɪeɪt/ *vi* riposter. **retaliation** *n* représailles *fpl*.

**retch** /retʃ/ *vi* avoir un haut-le-cœur.

**retire** /rɪ'taɪə(r)/ *vi* (from work) prendre sa retraite; (withdraw) se retirer; (go to bed) se coucher. **retired** *a* retraité. **retirement** *n* retraite *f*.

**retort** /rɪ'tɔ:t/ *vt/i* répliquer. ● *n* réplique *f*.

**retrace** /ri:'treɪs/ *vt* **~ one's steps** revenir sur ses pas.

**retract** /rɪ'trækt/ *vt/i* (se) rétracter.

**retrain** /ri:'treɪn/ *vt/i* (se) recycler.

**retreat** /rɪ'tri:t/ *vi* (Mil) battre en retraite. ● *n* retraite *f*.

**retrieval** /rɪ'tri:vl/ *n* (Comput) extraction *f*. **retrieve** *vt* (*object*) récupérer; (*situation*) redresser; (*data*) extraire.

**retrospect** /'retrəspekt/ *n* **in ~** rétrospectivement.

**return** /rɪ'tɜ:n/ *vi* (come back) revenir; (go back) retourner; (go home) rentrer. ● *vt* (give back) rendre; (bring back) rapporter; (send back) renvoyer; (put back) remettre. ● *n* retour *m*; (yield) rapport *m*; **~s** (Comm) bénéfices *mpl*; **in ~ for** en échange de. **~ ticket** *n* aller-retour *m*.

**reunion** /ri:'ju:nɪən/ *n* réunion *f*.

**reunite** /ri:ju:'naɪt/ *vt* réunir.

**rev** /rev/ *n* (Auto [!]) tour *m*. ● *vt/i* (*pt* **revved**) **~ (up)** (engine [!]) (s')emballer.

**reveal** /rɪ'vi:l/ *vt* révéler; (allow to appear) laisser voir.

**revelation** /revə'leɪʃn/ *n* révélation *f*.

**revenge** /rɪ'vendʒ/ *n* vengeance *f*. ● *vt* venger.

**revenue** /'revənju:/ *n* revenu *m*.

**reverberate** /rɪ'vɜ:bəreɪt/ *vi* (*sound, light*) se répercuter.

**reverend** /'revərənd/ *a* révérend.

**reversal** /rɪ'vɜ:sl/ *n* renversement *m*; (of view) revirement *m*.

**reverse** /rɪ'vɜ:s/ *a* contraire, inverse. ● *n* contraire *m*; (back) revers *m*, envers *m*; (gear) marche *f* arrière. ● *vt* (*situation, bracket*) renverser; (*order*) inverser; (*decision*) annuler; ~ **the charges** appeler en PCV. ● *vi* (Auto) faire marche arrière.

**review** /rɪ'vju:/ *n* (inspection, magazine) revue *f*; (of book) critique *f*. ● *vt* passer en revue; (situation) réexaminer; faire la critique de. **reviewer** *n* critique *m*.

**revise** /rɪ'vaɪz/ *vt* réviser; (*text*) revoir. **revision** *n* révision *f*.

**revival** /rɪ'vaɪvl/ *n* (of economy) reprise *f*; (of interest) regain *m*.

**revive** /rɪ'vaɪv/ *vt* (person, hopes) ranimer; (custom) rétablir. ● *vi* se ranimer.

**revoke** /rɪ'vəʊk/ *vt* révoquer.

**revolt** /rɪ'vəʊlt/ *vt*/*i* (se) révolter. ● *n* révolte *f*. **revolting** *a* dégoûtant.

**revolution** /revə'lu:ʃn/ *n* révolution *f*.

**revolve** /rɪ'vɒlv/ *vi* tourner.

**revolver** /rɪ'vɒlvə(r)/ *n* revolver *m*.

**revolving door** *n* porte *f* à tambour.

**reward** /rɪ'wɔ:d/ *n* récompense *f*. ● *vt* récompenser (**for** de). **rewarding** *a* rémunérateur; (worthwhile) qui (en) vaut la peine.

**rewind** /ri:'waɪnd/ *vt* (*pt* **rewound**) rembobiner.

**rewire** /ri:'waɪə(r)/ *vt* refaire l'installation électrique de.

**rhetorical** /rɪ'tɒrɪkl/ *a* (de) rhétorique; (*question*) de pure forme.

**rheumatism** /'ru:mətɪzəm/ *n* rhumatisme *m*.

**rhinoceros** /raɪ'nɒsərəs/ *n* (*pl* **~es**) rhinocéros *m*.

**rhubarb** /'ru:bɑ:b/ *n* rhubarbe *f*.

**rhyme** /raɪm/ *n* rime *f*; (poem) vers *mpl*. ● *vt*/*i* (faire) rimer.

**rhythm** /'rɪðəm/ *n* rythme *m*. **rhythmic(al)** *a* rythmique.

**rib** /rɪb/ *n* côte *f*.

**ribbon** /'rɪbən/ *n* ruban *m*; **in ~s** en lambeaux.

**rice** /raɪs/ *n* riz *m*. ~ **pudding** *n* riz *m* au lait.

**rich** /rɪtʃ/ *a* riche.

**rid** /rɪd/ *vt* (*pt* **rid**; *pres p* **ridding**) débarrasser (**of** de); **get ~ of** se débarrasser de.

**ridden** /'rɪdn/ ⇒RIDE.

**riddle** /'rɪdl/ *n* énigme *f*. ● *vt* ~ **with** (*bullets*) cribler de; (*mistakes*) bourrer de.

**ride** /raɪd/ *vi* (*pt* **rode**; *pp* **ridden**) aller (à bicyclette, à cheval); (in car) rouler; (on a horse as sport) monter à cheval. ● *vt* (a particular horse) monter; (distance) parcourir. ● *n* promenade *f*, tour *m*; (distance) trajet *m*; **give sb a ~** (US) prendre qn en voiture; **go for a ~** aller faire un tour (à bicyclette, à cheval). **rider** *n* cavalier/-ière *m*/*f*; (in horse race) jockey *m*; (cyclist) cycliste *mf*; (motorcyclist) motocycliste *mf*.

**ridge** /rɪdʒ/ *n* arête *f*, crête *f*.

**ridiculous** /rɪ'dɪkjʊləs/ *a* ridicule.

**riding** /'raɪdɪŋ/ *n* équitation *f*.

**rifle** /'raɪfl/ *n* fusil *m*. ● *vt* (rob) dévaliser.

**rift** /rɪft/ *n* (crack) fissure *f*; (between people) désaccord *m*.

**rig** /rɪg/ *vt* (*pt* **rigged**) (equip) équiper; (*election, match*) truquer.

● *n* (for oil) derrick *m*. □ ~ **out** habiller; ~ **up** (arrange) arranger.

**right** /raɪt/ *a* (morally) bon; (fair) juste; (best) bon, qu'il faut; (not left) droit; **be** ~ (person) avoir raison (**to** de); (calculation, watch) être exact; **put** ~ arranger, rectifier. ● *n* (entitlement) droit *m*; (not left) droite *f*; (not evil) le bien; **be in the** ~ avoir raison; **on the** ~ à droite. ● *vt* (a wrong, sth fallen) redresser. ● *adv* (not left) à droite; (directly) tout droit; (exactly) bien, juste; (completely) tout (à fait); ~ **away** tout de suite; ~ **now** (at once) tout de suite; (at present) en ce moment.

**righteous** /'raɪtʃəs/ *a* vertueux.

**rightful** /'raɪtfl/ *a* légitime.

**right-handed** *a* droitier.

**rightly** /'raɪtlɪ/ *adv* correctement; (with reason) à juste titre.

**right of way** *n* (Auto) priorité *f*.

**right wing** *a* de droite.

**rigid** /'rɪdʒɪd/ *a* rigide.

**rigorous** /'rɪgərəs/ *a* rigoureux.

**rim** /rɪm/ *n* bord *m*.

**rind** /raɪnd/ *n* (on cheese) croûte *f*; (on bacon) couenne *f*; (on fruit) écorce *f*.

**ring**[1] /rɪŋ/ *n* (hoop) anneau *m*; (jewellery) bague *f*; (circle) cercle *m*; (boxing) ring *m*; **(wedding)** ~ alliance *f*. ● *vt* entourer; (word in text) entourer d'un cercle.

**ring**[2] /rɪŋ/ *vt*/*i* (*pt* **rang**; *pp* **rung**) sonner; (of words) retentir; ~ **the bell** sonner. ● *n* sonnerie *f*; **give sb a** ~ donner un coup de fil à qn. □ ~ **back** rappeler; ~ **off** raccrocher; ~ **up** téléphoner (à).

**ring road** *n* périphérique *m*.

**rink** /rɪŋk/ *n* patinoire *f*.

**rinse** /rɪns/ *vt* rincer; ~ **out** rincer. ● *n* rinçage *m*.

**riot** /'raɪət/ *n* émeute *f*; (of colours) profusion *f*; **run** ~ se déchaîner. ● *vi* faire une émeute.

**rip** /rɪp/ *vt*/*i* (*pt* **ripped**) (se) déchirer; **let** ~ (not check) laisser courir; ~ **off** ⊠ rouler. ● *n* déchirure *f*.

**ripe** /raɪp/ *a* mûr. **ripen** *vt*/*i* mûrir.

**rip-off** *n* [I] vol *m*; arnaque *f* [I].

**ripple** /'rɪpl/ *n* ride *f*, ondulation *f*. ● *vt*/*i* (*water*) (se) rider.

**rise** /raɪz/ *vi* (*pt* **rose**; *pp* **risen**) (go upwards, increase) monter, s'élever; (stand up, get up from bed) se lever; (rebel) se soulever; (*sun*) se lever; (*water*) monter; ~ **up** se soulever. ● *n* (slope) pente *f*; (increase) hausse *f*; (in pay) augmentation *f*; (progress, boom) essor *m*; **give** ~ **to** donner lieu à.

**risk** /rɪsk/ *n* risque *m*; **at** ~ menacé. ● *vt* risquer; **doing** (venture) se risquer à faire. **risky** *a* risqué.

**rite** /raɪt/ *n* rite *m*; **last** ~**s** derniers sacrements *mpl*.

**rival** /'raɪvl/ *n* rival/-e *m*/*f*. ● *a* rival; (*claim*) opposé. ● *vt* (*pt* **rivalled**) rivaliser avec.

**river** /'rɪvə(r)/ *n* rivière *f*; (flowing into sea) fleuve *m*. ● *a* (*fishing, traffic*) fluvial.

**rivet** /'rɪvɪt/ *n* (bolt) rivet *m*. ● *vt* (*pt* **riveted**) river, riveter.

**Riviera** /rɪvɪ'eərə/ *n* **the (French)** ~ la Côte d'Azur.

**road** /rəʊd/ *n* route *f*; (in town) rue *f*; (small) chemin *m*; **the** ~ **to** (*glory*: fig) le chemin de. ● *a* (*sign, safety*) routier. ~**-map** *n* carte *f* routière. ~ **rage** *n* violence *f* au volant. ~**worthy** *a* en état de marche.

**roam** /rəʊm/ *vi* errer. ● *vt* (*streets, seas*) parcourir.

**roar** /rɔː(r)/ *n* hurlement *m*; (of lion, wind) rugissement *m*; (of lorry, thunder) grondement *m*. ● *vt*/*i* hurler;

(*lion, wind*) rugir; (*lorry, thunder*) gronder; ~ **with laughter** rire aux éclats.

**roast** /rəʊst/ *vt/i* rôtir. ● *n* (meat) rôti *m*. ● *a* rôti. ~ **beef** *n* rôti *m* de bœuf.

**rob** /rɒb/ *vt* (*pt* **robbed**) voler (**sb of sth** qch à qn); (*bank, house*) dévaliser; (deprive) priver (**of** de). **robber** *n* voleur/-euse *m/f*. **robbery** *n* vol *m*.

**robe** /rəʊb/ *n* (of judge) robe *f*; (dressing-gown) peignoir *m*.

**robin** /'rɒbɪn/ *n* rouge-gorge *m*.

**robot** /'rəʊbɒt/ *n* robot *m*.

**robust** /rəʊ'bʌst/ *a* robuste.

**rock** /rɒk/ *n* roche *f*; (rock face, boulder) rocher *m*; (hurled stone) pierre *f*; (sweet) sucre *m* d'orge; (Mus) rock *m*; **on the ~s** (*drink*) avec des glaçons; (*marriage*) en crise. ● *vt/i* (se) balancer; (shake) (faire) trembler; (*child*) bercer. **~-climbing** *n* varappe *f*.

**rocket** /'rɒkɪt/ *n* fusée *f*.

**rocking-chair** *n* fauteuil *m* à bascule.

**rocky** /'rɒkɪ/ *a* (**-ier**, **-iest**) (*ground*) rocailleux; (*hill*) rocheux; (shaky: fig) branlant.

**rod** /rɒd/ *n* (metal) tige *f*; (wooden) baguette *f*; (for fishing) canne *f* à pêche.

**rode** /rəʊd/ ⇒RIDE.

**roe** /rəʊ/ *n* œufs *mpl* de poisson.

**rogue** /rəʊg/ *n* (dishonest) bandit *m*; (mischievous) coquin/-e *m/f*.

**role** /rəʊl/ *n* rôle *m*.

**roll** /rəʊl/ *vt/i* rouler; ~ **(about)** (*child, dog*) se rouler; **be ~ing (in money)** 🅸 rouler sur l'or. ● *n* rouleau *m*; (list) liste *f*; (bread) petit pain *m*; (of drum, thunder) roulement *m*; (of ship) roulis *m*. □ ~ **out** étendre; **~over** se retourner; ~ **up** (*sleeves*) retrousser.

**roll-call** *n* appel *m*.

**roller** /'rəʊlə(r)/ *n* rouleau *m*. **~blade** *n* patin *m* en ligne, roller *m*. **~-coaster** *n* montagnes *fpl* russes. **~-skate** *n* patin *m* à roulettes.

**ROM** (*abbr*) (**read-only memory**) mémoire *f* morte.

**Roman** /'rəʊmən/ *a* & *n* romain/-e (*m/f*). ~ **Catholic** *a* & *n* catholique (*mf*).

**romance** /rə'mæns/ *n* (novel) roman *m* d'amour; (love) amour *m*; (affair) idylle *f*; (fig) poésie *f*.

**Romania** /rəʊ'meɪnɪə/ *n* Roumanie *f*.

**Romanian** /rəʊ'meɪnɪən/ *a* roumain. ● *n* (person) Roumain/-e *m/f*; (language) roumain *m*.

**romantic** /rə'mæntɪk/ *a* (*love*) romantique; (of the imagination) romanesque.

**roof** /ru:f/ *n* toit *m*; (of mouth) palais *m*. ● *vt* recouvrir. **~-rack** *n* galerie *f*. **~-top** *n* toit *m*.

**room** /ru:m/ *n* pièce *f*; (bedroom) chambre *f*; (large hall) salle *f*; (space) place *f*; ~ **for manoeuvre** marge *f* de manœuvre. **~-mate** *n* camarade *mf* de chambre.

**roomy** /'ru:mɪ/ *a* spacieux; (*clothes*) ample.

**root** /ru:t/ *n* racine *f*; (source) origine *f*; **take** ~ prendre racine. ● *vt/i* (s')enraciner. □ ~ **about** fouiller; ~ **for** (US 🅸) encourager; ~ **out** extirper.

**rope** /rəʊp/ *n* corde *f*; **know the ~s** être au courant. ● *vt* attacher; ~ **in** (*person*) enrôler.

**rose** /rəʊz/ *n* rose *f*. ● ⇒RISE.

**rosé** /'rəʊzeɪ/ *n* rosé *m*.

**rosy** /'rəʊzɪ/ *a* (**-ier**, **-iest**) rose; (hopeful) plein d'espoir.

**rot** /rɒt/ *vt*/*i* (*pt* **rotted**) pourrir. ● *n* pourriture *f*.

**rota** /ˈrəʊtə/ *n* liste *f* (de service).

**rotate** /rəʊˈteɪt/ *vt*/*i* (faire) tourner; (change round) alterner.

**rotten** /ˈrɒtn/ *a* pourri; (*tooth*) gâté; (bad Ⓘ) mauvais, sale.

**rough** /rʌf/ *a* (*manners*) rude; (to touch) rugueux; (*ground*) accidenté; (violent) brutal; (bad) mauvais; (*estimate*) approximatif. ● *adv* (*live*) à la dure; (*play*) brutalement.

**roughage** /ˈrʌfɪdʒ/ *n* fibres *fpl*.

**roughly** /ˈrʌflɪ/ *adv* rudement; (approximately) à peu près.

**round** /raʊnd/ *a* rond. ● *n* (circle) rond *m*; (slice) tranche *f*; (of visits, drinks) tournée *f*; (competition) partie *f*, manche *f*; (boxing) round *m*; (of talks) série *f*; ~ **of applause** applaudissements *mpl*; **go the ~s** circuler. ● *prep* autour de; **she lives ~ here** elle habite par ici; **~ the clock** vingt-quatre heures sur vingt quatre. ● *adv* autour; **~ about** (nearby) par ici; (fig) à peu près; **go** *or* **come ~ to** (*a friend*) passer chez; **enough to go ~** assez pour tout le monde. ● *vt* (*object*) arrondir; (*corner*) tourner. □ **~ off** terminer; **~ up** rassembler

**roundabout** /ˈraʊndəbaʊt/ *n* (in fairground) manège *m*; (for traffic) rond-point *m*. ● *a* indirect.

**round trip** *n* voyage *m* aller-retour.

**round-up** *n* rassemblement *m*; (of suspects) rafle *f*.

**route** /ruːt/ *n* itinéraire *m*, parcours *m*; (Naut, Aviat) route *f*.

**routine** /ruːˈtiːn/ *n* routine *f*. ● *a* de routine.

**row¹** /rəʊ/ *n* rangée *f*, rang *m*; **in a ~** (consecutive) consécutif. ● *vi* ramer; (Sport) faire de l'aviron. ● *vt* **~ a boat up the river** remonter la rivière à la rame.

**row²** /raʊ/ *n* (noise Ⓘ) tapage *m*; (quarrel Ⓘ) dispute *f*. ● *vi* Ⓘ se disputer.

**rowdy** /ˈraʊdɪ/ *a* (**-ier**, **-iest**) tapageur.

**rowing** /ˈrəʊɪŋ/ *n* aviron *m*. **~-boat** *n* bateau *m* à rames.

**royal** /ˈrɔɪəl/ *a* royal. **royalty** *n* famille *f* royale; **royalties** droits *mpl* d'auteur

**RSI** *abbr* (**repetitive strain injury**) **TMS** *m*, trouble *m* musculo-squelettique.

**rub** /rʌb/ *vt*/*i* (*pt* **rubbed**) frotter; **~ it in** insister, en rajouter. ● *n* friction *f*. □ **~ out** (s')effacer.

**rubber** /ˈrʌbə(r)/ *n* caoutchouc *m*; (eraser) gomme *f*. **~ band** *n* élastique *m*. **~ stamp** *n* tampon *m*.

**rubbish** /ˈrʌbɪʃ/ *n* (refuse) ordures *fpl*; (junk) saletés *fpl*; (fig) bêtises *fpl*.

**rubble** /ˈrʌbl/ *n* décombres *mpl*.

**ruby** /ˈruːbɪ/ *n* rubis *m*.

**rucksack** /ˈrʌksæk/ *n* sac *m* à dos.

**rude** /ruːd/ *a* impoli, grossier; (improper) indécent; (*blow*) brutal.

**ruffle** /ˈrʌfl/ *vt* (*hair*) ébouriffer; (*clothes*) froisser; (*person*) contrarier. ● *n* (frill) ruche *f*.

**rug** /rʌg/ *n* petit tapis *m*.

**rugby** /ˈrʌgbɪ/ *n* rugby *m*.

**rugged** /ˈrʌgɪd/ *a* (*surface*) rude, rugueux; (*ground*) accidenté; (*character, features*) rude.

**ruin** /ˈruːɪn/ *n* ruine *f*. ● *vt* (destroy) ruiner; (damage) abîmer; (spoil) gâter.

**rule** /ruːl/ *n* règle *f*; (regulation) règlement *m*; (Pol) gouvernement *m*; **as a ~** en règle générale. ● *vt* gouverner; (master) dominer; (decide) décider; **~ out** exclure. ● *vi*

régner. **ruler** *n* dirigeant/-e *m/f*, gouvernant *m*; (measure) règle *f*.

**ruling** /'ru:lɪŋ/ *a* (*class*) dirigeant; (*party*) au pouvoir. ● *n* décision *f*.

**rum** /rʌm/ *n* rhum *m*.

**rumble** /rʌmbl/ *vi* gronder; (*stomach*) gargouiller. ● *n* grondement *m*; gargouillement *m*.

**rumour**, (US) **rumor** /'ru:mə(r)/ *n* bruit *m*, rumeur *f*; **there's a ~ that** le bruit court que.

**rump** /rʌmp/ *n* (of animal) croupe *f*; (of bird) croupion *m*; (steak) romsteck *m*.

**run** /rʌn/ *vi* (*pt* **ran**; *pp* **run**; *pres p* **running**) courir; (flow) couler; (pass) passer; (function) marcher; (melt) fondre; (extend) s'étendre; (of bus) circuler; (of play) se jouer; (last) durer; (of colour in washing) déteindre; (in election) être candidat. ● *vt* (manage) diriger; (*event*) organiser; (*risk, race*) courir; (*house*) tenir; (*temperature, errand*) faire; (Comput) exécuter. ● *n* course *f*; (journey) parcours *m*; (outing) promenade *f*; (rush) ruée *f*; (series) série *f*; (for chickens) enclos *m*; (in cricket) point *m*; **in the long ~** avec le temps; **on the ~** en fuite. □ **~ across** rencontrer par hasard; **~ away** s'enfuir; **~ down** descendre en courant; (of vehicle) renverser; (*production*) réduire progressivement; (belittle) dénigrer; **~ into** (hit) heurter; **~ off** (*copies*) tirer; **~ out** (be used up) s'épuiser; (of lease) expirer; **~ out of** manquer de; **~ over** (of vehicle) écraser; (*details*) revoir; **~ through** regarder qch rapidement; **~ sth through sth** passer qch à travers qch; **~ up** (*bill*) accumuler.

**runaway** /'rʌnəweɪ/ *n* fugitif/-ive *m/f*. ● *a* fugitif; (*horse, vehicle*) fou; (*inflation*) galopant.

**rung** /rʌŋ/ ⇒RING². ● *n* (of ladder) barreau *m*.

**runner** /'rʌnə(r)/ *n* coureur/-euse *m/f*. **~ bean** *n* haricot *m* d'Espagne. **~-up** *n* second/-e *m/f*.

**running** /'rʌnɪŋ/ *n* course *f* à pied; (of business) gestion *f*; (of machine) marche *f*; **be in the ~ for** être sur les rangs pour. ● *a* (*commentary*) suivi; (*water*) courant; **four days ~** quatre jours de suite.

**runway** /'rʌnweɪ/ *n* piste *f*.

**rural** /'rʊərəl/ *a* rural.

**rush** /rʌʃ/ *vi* (move) se précipiter; (be in a hurry) se dépêcher. ● *vt* (*person*) bousculer; (Mil) prendre d'assaut; **~ to** envoyer d'urgence à. ● *n* ruée *f*; (haste) bousculade *f*; (plant) jonc *m*; **in a ~** pressé. **~-hour** *n* heure *f* de pointe.

**Russia** /'rʌʃə/ *n* Russie *f*.

**Russian** /'rʌʃən/ *a* russe. ● *n* (person) Russe *mf*; (language) russe.

**rust** /rʌst/ *n* rouille *f*. ● *vt/i* rouiller.

**rustle** /'rʌsl/ *vt/i* (*papers*) froisser.

**rusty** /'rʌstɪ/ *a* rouillé.

**ruthless** /'ru:θlɪs/ *a* impitoyable.

**rye** /raɪ/ *n* seigle *m*.

# Ss

**sabbath** /'sæbəθ/ *n* (Jewish) sabbat *m*; (Christian) jour *m* du seigneur.

**sabbatical** /sə'bætɪkl/ *a* (Univ) sabbatique.

**sabotage** /'sæbətɑ:ʒ/ *n* sabotage *m*. ● *vt* saboter.

**saccharin** /'sækərɪn/ *n* saccharine *f*.

**sack** /sæk/ *n* (bag) sac *m*; **get the ~** Ⓘ être renvoyé. ● *vt* Ⓘ renvoyer; (plunder) saccager. **sacking** *n* (cloth) toile *f* à sac; (dismissal Ⓘ) renvoi *m*.

**sacrament** /'sækrəmənt/ *n* sacrement *m*.

**sacred** /'seɪkrɪd/ *a* sacré.

**sacrifice** /'sækrɪfaɪs/ *n* sacrifice *m*. ● *vt* sacrifier.

**sad** /sæd/ *a* (**sadder**, **saddest**) triste.

**saddle** /'sædl/ *n* selle *f*. ● *vt* (*horse*) seller.

**sadist** /'seɪdɪst/ *n* sadique *mf*. **sadistic** *a* sadique.

**sadly** /'sædlɪ/ *adv* tristement; (unfortunately) malheureusement.

**sadness** /'sædnɪs/ *n* tristesse *f*.

**safe** /seɪf/ *a* (not dangerous) sans danger; (reliable) sûr; (out of danger) en sécurité; (after accident) sain et sauf; **~ from** à l'abri de. ● *n* coffre-fort *m*.

**safeguard** /'seɪfgɑ:d/ *n* sauvegarde *f*. ● *vt* sauvegarder.

**safely** /'seɪflɪ/ *adv* sans danger; (in safe place) en sûreté.

**safety** /'seɪftɪ/ *n* sécurité *f*. **~-belt** *n* ceinture *f* de sécurité. **~-pin** *n* épingle *f* de sûreté. **~-valve** *n* soupape *f* de sûreté.

**saffron** /'sæfrən/ *n* safran *m*.

**sag** /sæg/ *vi* (*pt* **sagged**) (*beam, mattress*) s'affaisser; (*flesh*) être flasque.

**sage** /seɪdʒ/ *n* (herb) sauge *f*.

**Sagittarius** /sædʒɪ'teərɪəs/ *n* Sagittaire *m*.

**said** /sed/ ⇒SAY.

**sail** /seɪl/ *n* voile *f*; (journey) tour *m* en bateau. ● *vi* (*person*) voyager en bateau; (as sport) faire de la voile; (set off) prendre la mer; **~ across** traverser. ● *vt* (*boat*) piloter; (*sea*) traverser. **sailing-boat**, **sailing-ship** *n* voilier *m*.

**sailor** /'seɪlə(r)/ *n* marin *m*.

**saint** /seɪnt/ *n* saint/-e *m*/*f*.

**sake** /seɪk/ *n* **for the ~ of** pour.

**salad** /'sæləd/ *n* salade *f*.

**salaried** /'sælərɪd/ *a* salarié.

**salary** /'sælərɪ/ *n* salaire *m*.

**sale** /seɪl/ *n* vente *f*; **for ~** à vendre; **on ~** en vente; (reduced) en solde; **~s** (reductions) soldes *mpl*; **~s assistant**, (US) **~s clerk** vendeur/-euse *m*/*f*.

**salesman** /'seɪlzmən/ *n* (*pl* **-men**) (in shop) vendeur *m*; (traveller) représentant *m*.

**saline** /'seɪlaɪn/ *a* salin. ● *n* sérum *m* physiologique.

**saliva** /sə'laɪvə/ *n* salive *f*.

**salmon** /'sæmən/ *n inv* saumon *m*.

**salon** /'sælɒn/ *n* salon *m*.

**saloon** /sə'lu:n/ *n* (on ship) salon *m*; **~ (car)** berline *f*.

**salt** /sɔ:lt/ *n* sel *m*. ● *vt* saler. **salty** *a* salé.

**salutary** /'sæljʊtrɪ/ *a* salutaire.

**salute** /sə'lu:t/ *n* salut *m*. ● *vt* saluer. ● *vi* faire un salut.

**salvage** /'sælvɪdʒ/ *n* sauvetage *m*; (of waste) récupération *f*. ● *vt* sauver; (for re-use) récupérer.

**same** /seɪm/ *a* même (**as** que). ● *pron* **the ~** le même, la même, les mêmes; **at the ~ time** en même temps; **the ~ (thing)** la même chose.

**sample** /'sɑ:mpl/ *n* échantillon *m*; (of blood) prélèvement *m*. ● *vt* essayer; (*food*) goûter.

**sanctimonious** /sæŋktɪ'məʊnɪəs/ *a* (pej) supérieur.

**sanction** /'sæŋkʃn/ *n* sanction *f*. ● *vt* sanctionner.

**sanctity** /'sæŋktətɪ/ *n* sainteté *f*.

**sanctuary** /'sæŋktʃʊərɪ/ *n* (safe place) refuge *m*; (Relig) sanctuaire *m*; (for animals) réserve *f*.

**sand** /sænd/ *n* sable *m*; **~s** (beach) plage *f*.

**sandal** /'sændl/ *n* sandale *f*.

**sandpaper** /'sændpeɪpə(r)/ *n* papier *m* de verre. ● *vt* poncer.

**sandpit** /'sændpɪt/ *n* bac *m* à sable.

**sandwich** /'sænwɪdʒ/ *n* sandwich *m*; **~ course** cours *m* avec stage pratique.

**sandy** /'sændɪ/ *a* (*beach*) de sable; (*soil*) sablonneux; (hair) blond roux *inv*.

**sane** /seɪn/ *a* (*view*) sensé; (*person*) sain d'esprit.

**sang** /sæŋ/ ⇒SING.

**sanitary** /'sænɪtrɪ/ *a* (clean) hygiénique; (*system*) sanitaire; **~ towel** serviette *f* hygiénique.

**sanitation** /sænɪ'teɪʃn/ *n* installations *fpl* sanitaires.

**sanity** /'sænətɪ/ *n* équilibre *m* mental; (sense) bon sens *m*.

**sank** /sæŋk/ ⇒SINK.

**Santa** (**Claus**) /'sæntəklɔːz/ *n* le père Noël.

**sapphire** /'sæfaɪə(r)/ *n* saphir *m*.

**sarcasm** /'sɑːkæzəm/ *n* sarcasme *m*. **sarcastic** *a* sarcastique.

**sash** /sæʃ/ *n* (on uniform) écharpe *f*; (on dress) ceinture *f*.

**sat** /sæt/ ⇒SIT.

**satchel** /'sætʃl/ *n* cartable *m*.

**satellite** /'sætəlaɪt/ *n* & *a* satellite (*m*); **~ dish** antenne *f* parabolique.

**satire** /'sætaɪə(r)/ *n* satire *f*. **satirical** *a* satirique.

**satisfaction** /sætɪs'fækʃn/ *n* satisfaction *f*.

**satisfactory** /sætɪs'fæktərɪ/ *a* satisfaisant.

**satisfy** /'sætɪsfaɪ/ *vt* satisfaire; (convince) convaincre.

**saturate** /'sætʃəreɪt/ *vt* saturer. **saturated** *a* (wet) trempé.

**Saturday** /'sætədɪ/ *n* samedi *m*.

**sauce** /sɔːs/ *n* sauce *f*.

**saucepan** /'sɔːspən/ *n* casserole *f*.

**saucer** /'sɔːsə(r)/ *n* soucoupe *f*.

**Saudi Arabia** /saʊdɪə'reɪbɪə/ *n* Arabie *f* saoudite.

**sausage** /'sɒsɪdʒ/ *n* (for cooking) saucisse *f*; (ready to eat) saucisson *m*.

**savage** /'sævɪdʒ/ *a* (*blow, temper*) violent; (*attack*) sauvage. ● *n* sauvage *mf*. ● *vt* attaquer sauvagement.

**save** /seɪv/ *vt* sauver; (*money*) économiser; (*time*) gagner; (keep) garder; **~ (sb) doing sth** éviter (à qn) de faire qch. ● *n* (football) arrêt *m*. **saver** *n* épargnant/-e *m*/*f*. **saving** *n* économie *f*. **savings** *npl* économies *fpl*.

**saviour**, (US) **savior** /'seɪvɪə(r)/ *n* sauveur *m*.

**savour**, (US) **savor** /'seɪvə(r)/ *n* saveur *f*. ● *vt* savourer. **savoury** *a* (tasty) savoureux; (Culin) salé.

**saw** /sɔː/ ⇒SEE. ● *n* scie *f*. ● *vt* (*pt* **sawed**; *pp* **sawn** /sɔːn/ *or* **sawed**) scier.

**sawdust** /'sɔːdʌst/ *n* sciure *f*.

**saxophone** /'sæksəfəʊn/ *n* saxophone *m*.

**say** /seɪ/ *vt*/*i* (*pt* **said** /sed/) dire; (*prayer*) faire. ● *n* **have a ~** dire son mot; (in decision) avoir voix au chapitre. **saying** *n* proverbe *m*.

**scab** /skæb/ *n* croûte *f*.

**scaffolding** /'skæfəʊldɪŋ/ *n* échafaudage *m*.

**scald** /skɔːld/ *vt* (injure, cleanse) ébouillanter. ● *n* brûlure *f*.

**scale** /skeɪl/ *n* (for measuring) échelle *f*; (extent) étendue *f*; (Mus) gamme *f*;

(on fish) écaille *f*; **on a small ~** sur une petite échelle; **~ model** maquette *f*. ● *vt* (climb) escalader; **~ down** réduire. **scales** *npl* (for weighing) balance *f*.

**scallop** /'skɒləp/ *n* coquille *f* Saint-Jacques.

**scalp** /skælp/ *n* cuir *m* chevelu.

**scampi** /'skæmpɪ/ *npl* (fresh) langoustines *fpl*; (breaded) scampi *mpl*.

**scan** /skæn/ *vt* (*pt* **scanned**) scruter; (quickly) parcourir. ● *n* (ultrasound) échographie *f*; (CAT) scanner *m*.

**scandal** /'skændl/ *n* scandale *m*; (gossip) potins *mpl* 🄸.

**Scandinavia** /skændɪ'neɪvɪə/ *n* Scandinavie *f*.

**scanty** /'skæntɪ/ *a* (**-ier**, **-iest**) maigre; (*clothing*) minuscule.

**scapegoat** /'skeɪpgəʊt/ *n* bouc *m* émissaire.

**scar** /skɑ:(r)/ *n* cicatrice *f*. ● *vt* (*pt* **scarred**) marquer.

**scarce** /skeəs/ *a* rare. **scarcely** *adv* à peine.

**scare** /'skeə(r)/ *vt* faire peur à; **be ~d** avoir peur. ● *n* peur *f*; **bomb ~** alerte *f* à la bombe. **scarecrow** *n* épouvantail *m*.

**scarf** /skɑ:f/ *n* (*pl* **scarves**) écharpe *f*; (over head) foulard *m*.

**scarlet** /'skɑ:lət/ *a* écarlate; **~ fever** scarlatine *f*.

**scary** /'skeərɪ/ *a* (**-ier**, **-iest**) 🄸 qui fait peur.

**scathing** /'skeɪðɪŋ/ *a* cinglant.

**scatter** /'skætə(r)/ *vt* (throw) éparpiller, répandre; (disperse) disperser. ● *vi* se disperser.

**scavenge** /'skævɪndʒ/ *vi* fouiller (dans les ordures). **scavenger** *n* (animal) charognard *m*.

**scene** /si:n/ *n* scène *f*; (of accident, crime) lieu *m*; (sight) spectacle *m*; behind the **~s** en coulisse. **scenery** *n* paysage *m*; (Theat) décors *mpl*. **scenic** *a* panoramique.

**scent** /sent/ *n* (perfume) parfum *m*; (trail) piste *f*. ● *vt* flairer; (make fragrant) parfumer.

**sceptic** /'skeptɪk/ *n* sceptique *mf*. **sceptical** *a* sceptique. **scepticism** *n* scepticisme *m*.

**schedule** /'ʃedju:l, US 'skedʒʊl/ *n* horaire *m*; (for job) planning *m*; **behind ~** en retard; **on ~** dans les temps. ● *vt* prévoir; **~d flight** vol *m* régulier.

**scheme** /ski:m/ *n* projet *m*; (dishonest) combine *f*; **pension ~** plan *m* de retraite. ● *vi* comploter.

**schizophrenic** /skɪtsəʊ'frenɪk/ *a* & *n* schizophrène (*mf*).

**scholar** /'skɒlə(r)/ *n* érudit/-e *m*/*f*.

**school** /sku:l/ *n* école *f*; **go to ~** aller à l'école. ● *a* (*age, year, holidays*) scolaire. **~boy** *n* élève *m*. **~girl** *n* élève *f*. **schooling** *n* scolarité *f*. **~teacher** *n* (primary) instituteur/-trice *m*/*f*; (secondary) professeur *m*.

**science** /'saɪəns/ *n* science *f*; **teach ~** enseigner les sciences. **scientific** *a* scientifique. **scientist** *n* scientifique *mf*.

**scissors** /'sɪzəz/ *npl* ciseaux *mpl*.

**scold** /skəʊld/ *vt* gronder.

**scoop** /sku:p/ *n* (shovel) pelle *f*; (measure) mesure *f*; (for ice cream) cuillère *f* à glace; (news) exclusivité *f*.

**scooter** /'sku:tə(r)/ *n* (child's) trottinette *f*; (motor cycle) scooter *m*.

**scope** /skəʊp/ *n* étendue *f*; (competence) compétence *f*; (opportunity) possibilité *f*.

**scorch** /skɔ:tʃ/ *vt* brûler; (*iron*) roussir.

**score** /skɔ:(r)/ *n* score *m*; (Mus) partition *f*; **on that ~** à cet égard.

● *vt* marquer; (*success*) remporter. ● *vi* marquer un point; (football) marquer un but; (keep score) marquer les points. **scorer** *n* (Sport) marqueur *m*.

**scorn** /skɔ:n/ *n* mépris *m*. ● *vt* mépriser.

**Scorpio** /'skɔ:pɪəʊ/ *n* Scorpion *m*.

**Scot** /skɒt/ *n* Écossais/-e *m/f*.

**Scotland** /'skɒtlənd/ *n* Écosse *f*.

**Scottish** /'skɒtɪʃ/ *a* écossais.

**scoundrel** /'skaʊndrəl/ *n* gredin *m*.

**scour** /'skaʊə(r)/ *vt* (*pan*) récurer; (search) parcourir. **scourer** *n* tampon *m* à récurer.

**scourge** /skɜ:dʒ/ *n* fléau *m*.

**scout** /skaʊt/ *n* éclaireur *m*. ● *vi* ~ **around for** rechercher.

**scowl** /skaʊl/ *n* air *m* renfrogné. ● *vi* prendre un air renfrogné.

**scramble** /'skræmbl/ *vi* (clamber) grimper. ● *vt* (*eggs*) brouiller. ● *n* (rush) course *f*.

**scrap** /skræp/ *n* petit morceau *m*; ~**s** (of metal, fabric) déchets *mpl*; (of food) restes *mpl*; (fight Ⓘ) bagarre *f*. ● *vt* (*pt* **scrapped**) abandonner; (*car*) détruire.

**scrape** /skreɪp/ *vt* gratter; (damage) érafler. ● *vi* ~ **against** érafler. □ ~ **through** réussir de justesse.

**scrap**: ~**-paper** *n* papier *m* brouillon. ~ **yard** *n* casse *f*.

**scratch** /skrætʃ/ *vt/i* (se) gratter; (with claw, nail) griffer; (graze) érafler; (mark) rayer. ● *n* (on body) égratignure *f*; (on surface) éraflure *f*; **start from** ~ partir de zéro; **up to** ~ à la hauteur. ~ **card** *n* jeu *m* de grattage.

**scrawl** /skrɔ:l/ *n* gribouillage *m*. ● *vt/i* gribouiller.

**scrawny** /'skrɔ:nɪ/ *a* (**-ier**, **-iest**) décharné.

**scream** /skri:m/ *vt/i* crier. ● *n* cri *m* (perçant).

**screech** /skri:tʃ/ *vi* (scream) hurler; (*tyres*) crisser. ● *n* cri *m* strident; (of tyres) crissement *m*.

**screen** /skri:n/ *n* écran *m*; (folding) paravent *m*. ● *vt* masquer; (protect) protéger; (*film*) projeter; (*candidates*) filtrer; (Med) faire subir un test de dépistage. **screening** *n* (cinema) projection *f*; (Med) dépistage *m*.

**screen**: ~**play** *n* scénario *m*. ~ **saver** *n* protecteur *m* d'écran.

**screw** /skru:/ *n* vis *f*. ● *vt* visser; ~ **up** (*eyes*) plisser; (ruin Ⓘ) cafouiller Ⓘ. ~**driver** *n* tournevis *m*.

**scribble** /'skrɪbl/ *vt/i* griffonner. ● *n* griffonnage *m*.

**script** /skrɪpt/ *n* script *m*; (of play) texte *m*.

**scroll** /skrəʊl/ *n* rouleau *m*. ● *vt/i* (Comput) (faire) défiler. ~ **bar** *n* barre *f* de défilement.

**scrounge** /skraʊndʒ/ Ⓘ *vt* (*favour*) quémander; (*cigarette*) piquer Ⓘ; ~ **money from sb** taper de l'argent à qn. ● *vi* ~ **off sb** vivre sur le dos de qn.

**scrub** /skrʌb/ *n* (land) broussailles *fpl*. ● *vt/i* (*pt* **scrubbed**) nettoyer (à la brosse), frotter.

**scruffy** /'skrʌfɪ/ *a* (**-ier**, **-iest**) Ⓘ dépenaillé.

**scrum** /skrʌm/ *n* (rugby) mêlée *f*.

**scruple** /'skru:pl/ *n* scrupule *m*.

**scrutinize** /'skru:tɪnaɪz/ *vt* scruter. **scrutiny** *n* examen *m* minutieux.

**scuba-diving** /'sku:bədaɪvɪŋ/ *n* plongée *f* sous-marine.

**scuffle** /'skʌfl/ *n* bagarre *f*.

**sculpt** /skʌlpt/ *vt/i* sculpter. **sculptor** *n* sculpteur *m*.

**sculpture** /'skʌlptʃə(r)/ *n* sculpture *f*.

**scum** /skʌm/ *n* (on liquid) mousse *f*; (people: pej) racaille *f*.

**scurry** /'skʌrɪ/ *vi* se précipiter, courir (**for** pour chercher); **~ off** se sauver.

**sea** /si:/ *n* mer *f*; **at ~** en mer; **by ~** par mer. ● *a* (*air*) marin; (*bird*) de mer; (*voyage*) par mer. **~food** *n* fruits *mpl* de mer. **~gull** *n* mouette *f*.

**seal** /si:l/ *n* (animal) phoque *m*; (insignia) sceau *m*; (with wax) cachet *m*. ● *vt* sceller; cacheter; (stick down) coller. □ **~ off** (*area*) boucler.

**seam** /si:m/ *n* (in cloth) couture *f*; (of coal) veine *f*.

**search** /sɜ:tʃ/ *vt*/*i* (examine) fouiller, (seek) chercher; (study) examiner; (Comput) rechercher. ● *n* fouille *f*; (quest) recherches *fpl*; (Comput) recherche *f*; **in ~ of** à la recherche de. **~ engine** *n* (Internet) moteur *m* de recherche. **~light** *n* projecteur *m*. **~-warrant** *n* mandat *m* de perquisition.

**sea**: **~shell** *n* coquillage *m*. **~shore** *n* (coast) littoral *m*; (beach) plage *f*.

**seasick** /'si:sɪk/ *a* **be ~** avoir le mal de mer.

**seaside** /'si:saɪd/ *n* bord *m* de la mer.

**season** /'si:zn/ *n* saison *f*; **~ ticket** carte *f* d'abonnement. ● *vt* assaisonner. **seasonal** *a* saisonnier. **seasoning** *n* assaisonnement *m*.

**seat** /si:t/ *n* siège *m*; (place) place *f*; (of trousers) fond *m*; **take a ~** asseyez-vous. ● *vt* (put) placer; **the room ~s 30** la salle peut accueillir 30 personnes. **~-belt** *n* ceinture *f* (*de sécurité*).

**seaweed** /'si:wi:d/ *n* algue *f* marine.

**secluded** /sɪ'klu:dɪd/ *a* retiré.

**seclusion** /sɪ'klu:ʒn/ *n* isolement *m*.

**second**[1] /'sekənd/ *a* deuxième, second; **a ~ chance** une nouvelle chance; **have ~ thoughts** avoir des doutes. ● *n* deuxième *mf*, second/-e *m*/*f*; (unit of time) seconde *f*; **~s** (food) rab *m* 🅸. ● *adv* (in race) deuxième; (secondly) deuxièmement. ● *vt* (*proposal*) appuyer.

**second**[2] /sɪ'kɒnd/ *vt* (transfer) détacher (**to** à).

**secondary** /'sekəndrɪ/ *a* secondaire; **~ school** lycée *m*, école *f* secondaire.

**second-best** *n* pis-aller *m*.

**second-class** *a* (Rail) de deuxième classe; (*post*) au tarif lent.

**second hand** *n* (on clock) trotteuse *f*.

**second-hand** *a & adv* (*article*) d'occasion; (*information*) de seconde main.

**secondly** /'sekəndlɪ/ *adv* deuxièmement.

**second-rate** *a* médiocre.

**secrecy** /'si:krəsɪ/ *n* secret *m*.

**secret** /'si:krɪt/ *a* secret. ● *n* secret *m*; **in ~** en secret.

**secretarial** /sekrə'teərɪəl/ *a* (*work*) de secrétaire.

**secretary** /'sekrətrɪ/ *n* secrétaire *mf*; **S~ of State** ministre *m*; (US) ministre *m* des Affaires étrangères.

**secrete** /sɪ'kri:t/ *vt* (Med) sécréter; (hide) cacher.

**secretive** /'si:krətɪv/ *a* secret. **secretly** *adv* secrètement.

**sect** /sekt/ *n* secte *f*. **sectarian** *a* sectaire.

**section** /'sekʃn/ *n* partie *f*; (in store) rayon *m*; (of newspaper) rubrique *f*; (of book) passage *m*.

**sector** /'sektə(r)/ *n* secteur *m*.

**secular** /'sekjʊlə(r)/ *a* (*school*) laïque; (*art, music*) profane.

**secure** /sɪ'kjʊə(r)/ *a* (safe) sûr; (*job, marriage*) stable; (*knot, lock*) solide; (*window*) bien fermé; (*feeling*) de sécurité; (*person*) sécurisé. ● *vt* attacher; (obtain) s'assurer; (ensure) assurer.

**security** /sɪ'kjʊərətɪ/ *n* (safety) sécurité *f*; (for loan) caution *f*; **~ guard** vigile *m*.

**sedate** /sɪ'deɪt/ *a* calme. ● *vt* donner un sédatif à. **sedative** *n* sédatif *m*.

**seduce** /sɪ'dju:s/ *vt* séduire. **seducer** *n* séducteur/-trice *m/f*. **seduction** *n* séduction *f*. **seductive** *a* séduisant.

**see** /si:/ *vt/i* (*pt* **saw**; *pp* **seen**) voir; **see you (soon)!** à bientôt!; **~ing that** vu que. □ **~ out** (*person*) raccompagner à la porte; **~ through** (*deception*) déceler; (*person*) percer à jour; **~ sth through** mener qch à bonne fin; **~ to** s'occuper de; **~ to it that** veiller à ce que.

**seed** /si:d/ *n* graine *f*; (collectively) graines *fpl*; (origin: fig) germe *m*; (tennis) tête *f* de série. **seedling** *n* plant *m*.

**seek** /si:k/ *vt* (*pt* **sought**) chercher.

**seem** /si:m/ *vi* sembler; **he ~s to think** il a l'air de croire.

**seen** /si:n/ ⇒SEE.

**seep** /si:p/ *vi* suinter; **~ into** s'infiltrer dans.

**see-saw** /'si:sɔ:/ *n* tapecul *m*. ● *vt* osciller.

**seethe** /si:ð/ *vi* **~ with** (*anger*) bouillir de; (*people*) grouiller de.

**segment** /'segmənt/ *n* segment *m*; (of orange) quartier *m*.

**segregate** /'segrɪgeɪt/ *vt* séparer.

**seize** /si:z/ *vt* saisir; (*territory, prisoner*) s'emparer de. ● *vi* **~ on** (*chance*) saisir; **~ up** (*engine*) se gripper.

**seizure** /'si:ʒə(r)/ *n* (Med) crise *f*.

**seldom** /'seldəm/ *adv* rarement.

**select** /sɪ'lekt/ *vt* sélectionner. ● *a* privilégié. **selection** *n* sélection *f*. **selective** *a* sélectif.

**self** /self/ *n* (*pl* **selves**) moi *m*; (on cheque) moi-même. **~-assured** *a* plein d'assurance. **~-catering** *a* (*holiday*) en location. **~-centred**, (US) **~-centered** *a* égocentrique. **~-confident** *a* sûr de soi. **~-conscious** *a* timide. **~-contained** *a* (*flat*) indépendant. **~-control** *n* sang-froid *m*. **~-defence** *n* autodéfense *f*; (Jur) légitime défense *f*. **~-employed** *a* qui travaille à son compte. **~-esteem** *n* amour-propre *m*. **~-governing** *a* autonome. **~-indulgent** *a* complaisant. **~-interest** *n* intérêt *m* personnel.

**selfish** /'selfɪʃ/ *a* égoïste.

**selfless** /'selflɪs/ *a* désintéressé.

**self**: **~-portrait** *n* autoportrait *m*. **~-reliant** *a* autosuffisant. **~-respect** *n* respect *m* de soi. **~-righteous** *a* satisfait de soi. **~-sacrifice** *n* abnégation *f*. **~-satisfied** *a* satisfait de soi. **~-seeking** *a* égoïste. **~-service** *n* & *a* libre-service (*m*).

**sell** /sel/ *vt/i* (*pt* **sold**) vendre; **~ well** se vendre bien. □ **~ off** liquider; **~ out** (*items*) se vendre; **have sold out** avoir tout vendu.

**Sellotape**® /'seləʊteɪp/ *n* scotch® *m*.

**sell-out** *n* (betrayal) 🄸 revirement *m*; **be a ~** (*show*) afficher complet.

**semester** /sɪ'mestə(r)/ *n* (Univ) semestre *m*.

**semicircle** /'semɪsɜ:kl/ *n* demi-cercle *m*.

**semicolon** /semɪ'kəʊlən/ *n* point-virgule *m*.

**semi-detached** /semɪ'dɪtætʃt/ *a* ~ **house** maison *f* jumelée.

**semifinal** /semɪ'faɪnl/ *n* demi-finale *f*.

**seminar** /'semɪnɑ:(r)/ *n* séminaire *m*.

**semolina** /semə'li:nə/ *n* semoule *f*.

**senate** /'senɪt/ *n* sénat *m*. **senator** *n* sénateur *m*.

**send** /send/ *vt*/*i* (*pt* **sent**) envoyer. □ ~ **away** (dismiss) renvoyer; ~ (**away** *or* **off**) **for** commander (par la poste); ~ **back** renvoyer; ~ **for** (*person, help*) envoyer chercher; ~ **up** Ⓘ parodier.

**senile** /'si:naɪl/ *a* sénile.

**senior** /'si:nɪə(r)/ *a* plus âgé (**to** que); (in rank) haut placé; **be ~ to sb** être le supérieur de qn. ● *n* aîné/-e *m*/*f*. ~ **citizen** *n* personne *f* âgée. ~ **school** *n* lycée *m*.

**sensation** /sen'seɪʃn/ *n* sensation *f*. **sensational** *a* sensationnel.

**sense** /sens/ *n* sens *m*; (mental impression) sentiment *m*; (common sense) bon sens *m*; **~s** (mind) raison *f*; **there's no ~ in doing** cela ne sert à rien de faire; **make ~** avoir un sens; **make ~ of** comprendre. ● *vt* (pres)sentir. **senseless** *a* insensé; (Med) sans connaissance.

**sensible** /'sensəbl/ *a* raisonnable; (*clothing*) pratique.

**sensitive** /'sensətɪv/ *a* sensible (**to** à); (*issue*) difficile.

**sensory** /'sensərɪ/ *a* sensoriel.

**sensual** /'senʃʊəl/ *a* sensuel. **sensuality** *n* sensualité *f*.

**sensuous** /'senʃʊəs/ *a* sensuel.

**sent** /sent/ ⇒SEND.

**sentence** /'sentəns/ *n* phrase *f*; (punishment: Jur) peine *f*. ● *vt* ~ **to** condamner à.

**sentiment** /'sentɪmənt/ *n* sentiment *m*. **sentimental** *a* sentimental.

**sentry** /'sentrɪ/ *n* sentinelle *f*.

**separate**[1] /'seprət/ *a* (*piece*) à part; (*issue*) autre; (*sections*) différent; (*organizations*) distinct.

**separate**[2] /'sepəreɪt/ *vt*/*i* (se) séparer.

**separately** /'seprətlɪ/ *adv* séparément.

**separation** /sepə'reɪʃn/ *n* séparation *f*.

**September** /sep'tembə(r)/ *n* septembre *m*.

**septic** /'septɪk/ *a* (*wound*) infecté; ~ **tank** fosse *f* septique.

**sequel** /'si:kwəl/ *n* suite *f*.

**sequence** /'si:kwəns/ *n* (order) ordre *m*; (series) suite *f*; (in film) séquence *f*.

**Serb** /'sɜ:b/ *a* serbe. ● *n* (person) Serbe *mf*; (Ling) serbe *m*.

**Serbia** /'sɜ:bɪə/ *n* Serbie *f*.

**sergeant** /'sɑ:dʒənt/ *n* (Mil) sergent *m*; (policeman) brigadier *m*.

**serial** /'sɪərɪəl/ *n* feuilleton *m*. ● *a* (Comput) série *inv*.

**series** /'sɪərɪz/ *n inv* série *f*.

**serious** /'sɪərɪəs/ *a* sérieux; (*accident, crime*) grave.

**seriously** /'sɪərɪəslɪ/ *adv* sérieusement; (*ill*) gravement; **take ~** prendre au sérieux.

**sermon** /'sɜ:mən/ *n* sermon *m*.

**serpent** /'sɜ:pənt/ *n* serpent *m*.

**serrated** /sɪ'reɪtɪd/ *a* dentelé.

**serum** /'sɪərəm/ *n* sérum *m*.

**servant** /'sɜ:vənt/ *n* domestique *mf*.

**serve** /sɜ:v/ *vt/i* servir; faire; (*transport, hospital*) desservir; ~ **as/to** servir de/à; ~ **a purpose** être utile; ~ **a sentence** (Jur) purger une peine. ● *n* (tennis) service *m*.

**server** /sɜ:və(r)/ *n* serveur *m*; **remote** ~ téléserveur *m*.

**service** /'sɜ:vɪs/ *n* service *m*; (maintenance) révision *f*; (Relig) office *m*; ~**s** (Mil) forces *fpl* armées. ● *vt* (*car*) réviser. ~ **area** *n* (Auto) aire *f* de services. ~ **charge** *n* service *m*. ~ **station** *n* station-service *f*.

**session** /'seʃn/ *n* séance *f*; **be in** ~ (Jur) tenir séance.

**set** /set/ *vt* (*pt* **set**; *pres p* **setting**) placer; (*table*) mettre; (*limit*) fixer; (*clock*) mettre à l'heure; (*example, task*) donner; (TV, cinema) situer; ~ **fire to** mettre le feu à; ~ **free** libérer; ~ **to music** mettre en musique. ● *vi* (*sun*) se coucher; (*jelly*) prendre; ~ **sail** partir. ● *n* (of chairs, stamps) série *f*; (of knives, keys) jeu *m*; (of people) groupe *m*; (TV, radio) poste *m*; (Theat) décor *m*; (tennis) set *m*; (mathematics) ensemble *m*. ● *a* (*time, price*) fixe; (*procedure*) bien determiné; (*meal*) à prix fixe; (*book*) au programme; ~ **against sth** opposé à; **be** ~ **on doing** tenir absolument à faire. □ ~ **about** se mettre à; ~ **back** (delay) retarder; (cost **I**) coûter; ~ **in** (take hold) s'installer, commencer; ~ **off** *or* **out** partir; ~ **off** (*panic, riot*) déclencher; (*bomb*) faire exploser; ~ **out** (state) présenter; (arrange) disposer; ~ **out to do sth** chercher à faire qch; ~ **up** (*stall*) monter; (*equipment*) assembler; (*experiment*) préparer; (*company*) créer; (*meeting*) organiser. ~**-back** *n* revers *m*.

**settee** /se'ti:/ *n* canapé *m*.

**setting** /'setɪŋ/ *n* cadre *m*; (on dial) position *f*.

**settle** /'setl/ *vt* (arrange, pay) régler; (*date*) fixer; (*nerves*) calmer. ● *vi* (come to rest) (*bird*) se poser; (*dust*) se déposer; (live) s'installer. □ ~ **down** se calmer; (marry etc.) se ranger; ~ **for** accepter; ~ **in** s'installer; ~ **up** (**with**) régler.

**settlement** /'setlmənt/ *n* règlement *m* (**of** de); (agreement) accord *m*; (place) colonie *f*.

**settler** /'setlə(r)/ *n* colon *m*.

**seven** /'sevn/ *a* & *n* sept (*m*).

**seventeen** /sevn'ti:n/ *a* & *n* dix-sept (*m*).

**seventh** /'sevnθ/ *a* & *n* septième (*mf*).

**seventy** /'sevntɪ/ *a* & *n* soixante-dix (*m*).

**sever** /'sevə(r)/ *vt* (cut) couper; (*relations*) rompre.

**several** /'sevrəl/ *a* & *pron* plusieurs; ~ **of us** plusieurs d'entre nous.

**severe** /sɪ'vɪə(r)/ *a* (harsh) sévère; (serious) grave.

**sew** /səʊ/ *vt/i* (*pt* **sewed**; *pp* **sewn** *or* **sewed**) coudre.

**sewage** /'sju:ɪdʒ/ *n* eaux *fpl* usées.

**sewer** /'su:ə(r)/ *n* égout *m*.

**sewing** /'səʊɪŋ/ *n* couture *f*. ~**-machine** *n* machine *f* à coudre.

**sewn** /səʊn/ ⇒SEW.

**sex** /seks/ *n* sexe *m*; **have** ~ avoir des rapports (sexuels). ● *a* sexuel. **sexist** *a* & *n* sexiste (*mf*). **sexual** *a* sexuel.

**shabby** /'ʃæbɪ/ *a* (**-ier**, **-iest**) (*place, object*) miteux; (*person*) habillé de façon miteuse; (*treatment*) mesquin.

**shack** /ʃæk/ *n* cabane *f*.

**shade** /ʃeɪd/ *n* ombre *f*; (of colour, opinion) nuance *f*; (for lamp) abat-jour *m inv*; **a** ~ **bigger** légèrement plus

grand. ● *vt* (*tree*) ombrager; (*hat*) projeter une ombre sur.

**shadow** /ˈʃædəʊ/ *n* ombre *f.* ● *vt* (follow) filer. **S~ Cabinet** *n* cabinet *m* fantôme.

**shady** /ˈʃeɪdɪ/ *a* (**-ier**, **-iest**) ombragé; (dubious) véreux.

**shaft** /ʃɑːft/ *n* (of tool) manche *m*; (of arrow) tige *f*; (in machine) axe *m*; (of mine) puits *m*; (of light) rayon *m*.

**shake** /ʃeɪk/ *vt* (*pt* **shook**; *pp* **shaken**) secouer; (*bottle*) agiter; (*belief*) ébranler; **~ hands with** serrer la main à; **~ one's head** dire non de la tête. ● *vi* trembler. ● *n* secousse *f*; **give sth a ~** secouer qch. □ **~ off** se débarrasser de. **~-up** *n* (Pol) remaniement *m*.

**shaky** /ˈʃeɪkɪ/ *a* (**-ier**, **-iest**) (*hand, voice*) tremblant; (*ladder*) branlant; (weak: fig) instable.

**shall** /ʃæl, ʃ(ə)l/ *v aux* **I ~ do** je ferai; **we ~ see** nous verrons; **~ we go . . .?** si on allait . . .?

**shallow** /ˈʃæləʊ/ *a* peu profond; (fig) superficiel.

**shame** /ʃeɪm/ *n* honte *f*; **it's a ~** c'est dommage. ● *vt* faire honte à.

**shampoo** /ʃæmˈpuː/ *n* shampooing *m*. ● *vt* faire un shampooing à.

**shandy** /ˈʃændɪ/ *n* panaché *m*.

**shan't** /ʃɑːnt/ = SHALL NOT.

**shanty** /ˈʃæntɪ/ *n* (shack) baraque *f*; **~ town** bidonville *m*.

**shape** /ʃeɪp/ *n* forme *f*. ● *vt* (*clay*) modeler; (*rock*) façonner; (*future*: fig) déterminer; **~ sth into balls** faire des boules avec qch. ● *vi* **~ up** (*plan*) prendre tournure; (*person*) faire des progrès.

**share** /ʃeə(r)/ *n* part *f*; (Comm) action *f*. ● *vt/i* partager; (*feature*) avoir en commun. **~holder** *n* actionnaire *mf*. **~ware** *n* (Comput) logiciel *m* contributif.

**shark** /ʃɑːk/ *n* requin *m*.

**sharp** /ʃɑːp/ *a* (*knife*) tranchant; (*pin*) pointu; (*point, angle, cry*) aigu; (*person, mind*) vif; (*tone*) acerbe. ● *adv* (*stop*) net; (*sing, play*) trop haut; **six o'clock ~** six heures pile. ● *n* (Mus) dièse *m*.

**sharpen** /ˈʃɑːpən/ *vt* aiguiser; (*pencil*) tailler.

**shatter** /ˈʃætə(r)/ *vt* (*glass*) fracasser; (*hope*) briser. ● *vi* (*glass*) voler en éclats.

**shave** /ʃeɪv/ *vt/i* (se) raser. ● *n* **have a ~** se raser. **shaver** *n* rasoir *m* électrique.

**shaving** /ˈʃeɪvɪŋ/ *n* (of wood) copeau *m*. ● *a* (*cream, foam, gel*) à raser.

**shawl** /ʃɔːl/ *n* châle *m*.

**she** /ʃiː/ *pron* elle. ● *n* (animal) femelle *f*.

**shear** /ʃɪə(r)/ *vt* (*pp* **shorn** *or* **sheared**) (*sheep*) tondre; **~ off** se détacher.

**shears** /ʃɪəz/ *npl* cisaille *f*.

**shed** /ʃed/ *n* remise *f*. ● *vt* (*pt* **shed**; *pres p* **shedding**) perdre; (*light, tears*) répandre.

**sheen** /ʃiːn/ *n* lustre *m*.

**sheep** /ʃiːp/ *n inv* mouton *m*. **~-dog** *n* chien *m* de berger.

**sheepish** /ˈʃiːpɪʃ/ *a* penaud.

**sheepskin** /ˈʃiːpskɪn/ *n* peau *f* de mouton.

**sheer** /ʃɪə(r)/ *a* pur; (steep) à pic; (*fabric*) très fin. ● *adv* à pic.

**sheet** /ʃiːt/ *n* drap *m*; (of paper) feuille *f*; (of glass, ice) plaque *f*.

**shelf** /ʃelf/ *n* (*pl* **shelves**) étagère *f*; (in shop, fridge) rayon *m*; (in oven) plaque *f*.

**shell** /ʃel/ *n* coquille *f*; (on beach) coquillage *m*; (of building) carcasse *f*;

(explosive) obus *m*. ● *vt* (*nut*) décortiquer; (*peas*) écosser; (Mil) bombarder.

**shellfish** /'ʃelfɪʃ/ *npl* (lobster etc.) crustacés *mpl*; (mollusc) coquillages *mpl*.

**shelter** /'ʃeltə(r)/ *n* abri *m*. ● *vt/i* (s')abriter; (give lodging to) donner asile à.

**shelve** /ʃelv/ *vt* (*plan*) mettre en suspens.

**shepherd** /'ʃepəd/ *n* berger *m*; **~'s pie** hachis *m* Parmentier. ● *vt* (*people*) guider.

**sherry** /'ʃerɪ/ *n* xérès *m*.

**shield** /ʃi:ld/ *n* bouclier *m*; (screen) écran *m*. ● *vt* protéger.

**shift** /ʃɪft/ *vt/i* (se) déplacer, bouger; (exchange, alter) changer de. ● *n* changement *m*; (workers) équipe *f*; (work) poste *m*; **~ work** travail *m* posté, travail *m* par roulement.

**shifty** /'ʃɪftɪ/ *a* (**-ier**, **-iest**) louche.

**shimmer** /'ʃɪmə(r)/ *vi* chatoyer. ● *n* chatoiement *m*.

**shin** /ʃɪn/ *n* tibia *m*.

**shine** /ʃaɪn/ *vt* (*pt* **shone** /ʃɒn/) (*torch*) braquer (**on** sur). ● *vi* (*light, sun, hair*) briller; (*brass*) reluire. ● *n* lustre *m*.

**shingle** /'ʃɪŋgl/ *n* (pebbles) galets *mpl*; (on roof) bardeau *m*.

**shingles** /'ʃɪŋglz/ *npl* (Med) zona *m*.

**shiny** /'ʃaɪnɪ/ *a* (**-ier**, **-iest**) brillant.

**ship** /ʃɪp/ *n* bateau *m*, navire *m*. ● *vt* (*pt* **shipped**) transporter. **shipment** *n* (by sea) cargaison *f*; (by air, land) chargement *m*. **shipping** *n* (ships) navigation *f*. **~wreck** *n* épave *f*; (event) naufrage *m*.

**shirt** /ʃɜ:t/ *n* chemise *f*; (woman's) chemisier *m*.

**shiver** /'ʃɪvə(r)/ *vi* frissonner. ● *n* frisson *m*.

**shock** /ʃɒk/ *n* choc *m*; (Electr) décharge *f*; **in ~** en état de choc; **~ absorber** amortisseur *m*. ● *a* (*result*) choc *inv*; (*tactics*) de choc. ● *vt* choquer.

**shoddy** /'ʃɒdɪ/ *a* (**-ier**, **-iest**) mal fait; (*behaviour*) mesquin.

**shoe** /ʃu:/ *n* chaussure *f*; (of horse) fer *m*; **(brake) ~** sabot *m* (*de frein*). ● *vt* (*pt* **shod** /ʃɒd/; *pres p* **shoeing**) (*horse*) ferrer. **~lace** *n* lacet *m*. **~ size** *n* pointure *f*.

**shone** /ʃɒn/ ⇒SHINE.

**shook** /ʃʊk/ ⇒SHAKE.

**shoot** /ʃu:t/ *vt* (*pt* **shot**) (*gun*) tirer un coup de; (*bullet*) tirer; (*missile, glance*) lancer; (*person*) tirer sur; (kill) abattre; (execute) fusiller; (*film*) tourner. ● *vi* tirer (**at** sur). ● *n* (Bot) pousse *f*. □ **~ down** abattre; **~ out** (rush) sortir en vitesse; **~ up** (spurt) jaillir; (grow) pousser vite.

**shooting** /'ʃu:tɪŋ/ *n* (killing) meurtre *m* (*par arme à feu*); **hear ~** entendre des coups de feu.

**shop** /ʃɒp/ *n* magasin *m*; (small) boutique *f*; (workshop) atelier *m*. ● *vi* (*pt* **shopped**) faire ses courses; **~ around** comparer les prix. **~ assistant** *n* vendeur/-euse *m/f*. **~-floor** *n* (workers) ouvriers *mpl*. **~keeper** *n* commerçant/-e *m/f*. **~lifter** *n* voleur/-euse *m/f* à l'étalage.

**shopper** /'ʃɒpə(r)/ *n* acheteur/-euse *m/f*.

**shopping** /'ʃɒpɪŋ/ *n* (goods) achats *mpl*; **go ~** (for food) faire les courses; (for clothes etc.) faire les magasins. **~ bag** *n* sac *m* à provisions. **~ centre**, (US) **~ center** *n* centre *m* commercial.

**shop window** *n* vitrine *f*.

**shore** /ʃɔ:(r)/ *n* côte *f*, rivage *m*; **on ~** à terre.

**short** /ʃɔ:t/ *a* court; (*person*) petit; (brief) court, bref; (curt) brusque; **be ~ (of)** manquer (de); **everything ~ of** tout sauf; **nothing ~ of** rien de moins que; **cut ~** écourter; **cut sb ~** interrompre qn; **fall ~ of** ne pas arriver à; **he is called Tom for ~** son diminutif est Tom; **in ~** en bref. ● *adv* (*stop*) net. ● *n* (Electr) court-circuit *m*; (film) court-métrage *m*; **~s** (trousers) short *m*.

**shortage** /ˈʃɔ:tɪdʒ/ *n* manque *m*.

**short**: **~bread** *n* sablé *m*. **~-change** *vt* (cheat) rouler Ⓘ. **~ circuit** *n* court-circuit *m*. **~coming** *n* défaut *m*. **~ cut** *n* raccourci *m*.

**shorten** /ˈʃɔ:tn/ *vt* raccourcir.

**shortfall** /ˈʃɔ:tfɔ:l/ *n* déficit *m*.

**shorthand** /ˈʃɔ:thænd/ *n* sténographie *f*; **~ typist** sténodactylo *f*.

**short**: **~ list** *n* liste *f* des candidats choisis. **~-lived** *a* de courte durée.

**shortly** /ˈʃɔ:tlɪ/ *adv* bientôt.

**short**: **~-sighted** *a* myope. **~-staffed** *a* à court de personnel; **~ story** *n* nouvelle *f*. **~-term** *a* à court terme.

**shot** /ʃɒt/ ⇒SHOOT. ● *n* (firing, attempt) coup *m* de feu; (person) tireur *m*; (bullet) balle *f*; (photograph) photo *f*; (injection) piqûre *f*; **like a ~** sans hésiter. **~-gun** *n* fusil *m* de chasse.

**should** /ʃʊd, ʃəd/ *v aux* devoir; **you ~ help me** vous devriez m'aider; **I ~ have stayed** j'aurais dû rester; **I ~ like to** j'aimerais bien; **if he ~ come** s'il venait.

**shoulder** /ˈʃəʊldə(r)/ *n* épaule *f*. ● *vt* (*responsibility*) endosser; (*burden*) se charger de. **~-bag** *n* sac *m* à bandoulière. **~-blade** *n* omoplate *f*.

**shout** /ʃaʊt/ *n* cri *m*. ● *vt/i* crier (**at** après); **~ sth out** lancer qch à haute voix.

**shove** /ʃʌv/ *n* **give sth a ~** pousser qch. ● *vt/i* pousser; **~ off!** Ⓘ tire-toi! Ⓘ.

**shovel** /ˈʃʌvl/ *n* pelle *f*. ● *vt* (*pt* **shovelled**) pelleter.

**show** /ʃəʊ/ *vt* (*pt* **showed**; *pp* **shown**) montrer; (*dial, needle*) indiquer; (put on display) exposer; (*film*) donner; (conduct) conduire; **~ sb in/out** faire entrer/sortir qn. ● *vi* (be visible) se voir. ● *n* (exhibition) exposition *f*, salon *m*; (Theat) spectacle *m*; (cinema) séance *f*; (of strength) démonstration *f*; **for ~** pour l'effet; **on ~** exposé. □ **~ off** faire le fier/la fière; **~ sth/sb off** exhiber qch/qn; **~ up** se voir; (appear) se montrer; **~ sb up** Ⓘ faire honte à qn.

**shower** /ˈʃaʊə(r)/ *n* douche *f*; (of rain) averse *f*. ● *vt* **~ with** couvrir de. ● *vi* se doucher.

**showing** /ˈʃəʊɪŋ/ *n* performance *f*; (cinema) séance *f*.

**show-jumping** *n* concours *m* hippique.

**shown** /ʃəʊn/ ⇒SHOW.

**show**: **~-off** *n* m'as-tu-vu *mf inv* Ⓘ. **~room** *n* salle *f* d'exposition.

**shrank** /ʃræŋk/ ⇒SHRINK.

**shrapnel** /ˈʃræpn(ə)l/ *n* éclats *mpl* d'obus.

**shred** /ʃred/ *n* lambeau *m*; (least amount; fig) parcelle *f*. ● *vt* (*pt* **shredded**) déchiqueter; (Culin) râper.

**shrewd** /ʃru:d/ *a* (*person*) habile; (*move*) astucieux.

**shriek** /ʃri:k/ *n* hurlement *m*. ● *vt/i* hurler.

**shrill** /ʃrɪl/ *a* (*voice*) perçant; (*tone*) strident.

**shrimp** /ʃrɪmp/ *n* crevette *f*.

**shrine** /ʃraɪn/ *n* (place) lieu *m* de pèlerinage.

**shrink** /ʃrɪŋk/ *vt/i* (*pt* **shrank**; *pp* **shrunk**) rétrécir; (lessen) diminuer; ~ **from** reculer devant.

**shrivel** /ˈʃrɪvl/ *vt/i* (*pt* **shrivelled**) (se) ratatiner.

**shroud** /ʃraʊd/ *n* linceul *m*. ● *vt* (veil) envelopper.

**Shrove Tuesday** *n* mardi *m* gras.

**shrub** /ʃrʌb/ *n* arbuste *m*.

**shrug** /ʃrʌg/ *vt* (*pt* **shrugged**) ~ **one's shoulders** hausser les épaules; ~ **sth off** ignorer qch.

**shrunk** /ʃrʌŋk/ ⇒SHRINK.

**shudder** /ˈʃʌdə(r)/ *vi* frémir. ● *n* frémissement *m*.

**shuffle** /ˈʃʌfl/ *vt* (*feet*) traîner; (*cards*) battre. ● *vi* traîner les pieds.

**shun** /ʃʌn/ *vt* (*pt* **shunned**) fuir.

**shut** /ʃʌt/ *vt* (*pt* **shut**; *pres p* **shutting**) fermer. ● *vi* (*door*) se fermer; (*shop*) fermer. □ ~ **in** *or* **up** enfermer; ~ **up** Ⓘ se taire; ~ **sb up** faire taire qn.

**shutter** /ˈʃʌtə(r)/ *n* volet *m*; (Photo) obturateur *m*.

**shuttle** /ˈʃʌtl/ *n* (bus) navette *f*; ~ **service** navette *f*. ● *vi* faire la navette. ● *vt* transporter.

**shuttlecock** /ˈʃʌtlkɒk/ *n* (badminton) volant *m*.

**shy** /ʃaɪ/ *a* timide. ● *vi* ~ **away from** se tenir à l'écart de.

**sibling** /ˈsɪblɪŋ/ *n* frère/sœur *m/f*.

**sick** /sɪk/ *a* malade; (*humour*) macabre; (*mind*) malsain; **be** ~ (vomit) vomir; **be** ~ **of** Ⓘ en avoir assez *or* marre de Ⓘ; **feel** ~ avoir mal au cœur. ~**-leave** *n* congé *m* de maladie.

**sickly** /ˈsɪklɪ/ *a* (**-ier**, **-iest**) (*person*) maladif; (*taste, smell*) écœurant.

**sickness** /ˈsɪknɪs/ *n* maladie *f*.

**sick-pay** *n* indemnité *f* de maladie.

**side** /saɪd/ *n* côté *m*; (of road, river) bord *m*; (of hill, body) flanc *m*; (Sport) équipe *f*; (TV Ⓘ) chaîne *f*; ~ **by** ~ côte à côte. ● *a* latéral. ● *vi* ~ **with** se ranger du côté de. ~**board** *n* buffet *m*. ~**-effect** *n* effet *m* secondaire. ~**light** *n* (Auto) feu *m* de position. ~**line** *n* activité *f* secondaire. ~**-show** *n* attraction *f*. ~**-step** *vt* (*pt* **-stepped**) éviter. ~**-street** *n* rue *f* latérale. ~**-track** *vt* fourvoyer. ~**walk** *n* (US) trottoir *m*.

**sideways** /ˈsaɪdweɪz/ *a* (*look*) de travers. ● *adv* (*move*) latéralement; (*look at*) de travers.

**siding** /ˈsaɪdɪŋ/ *n* voie *f* de garage.

**sidle** /ˈsaɪdl/ *vi* s'avancer furtivement (**up to** vers).

**siege** /siːdʒ/ *n* siège *m*.

**siesta** /sɪˈestə/ *n* sieste *f*.

**sieve** /sɪv/ *n* tamis *m*; (for liquids) passoire *f*. ● *vt* tamiser.

**sift** /sɪft/ *vt* tamiser. ● *vi* ~ **through** examiner.

**sigh** /saɪ/ *n* soupir *m*. ● *vt/i* soupirer.

**sight** /saɪt/ *n* vue *f*; (scene) spectacle *m*; (on gun) mire *f*; **at** *or* **on** ~ à vue; **catch** ~ **of** apercevoir; **in** ~ visible; **lose** ~ **of** perdre de vue. ● *vt* apercevoir.

**sightseeing** /ˈsaɪtsiːɪŋ/ *n* tourisme *m*.

**sign** /saɪn/ *n* signe *m*; (notice) panneau *m*. ● *vt/i* signer. □ ~ **on** (as unemployed) pointer au chômage; ~ **up** (s')engager.

**signal** /ˈsɪgnəl/ *n* signal *m*. ● *vt* (*pt* **signalled**) (gesture) faire signe (**that** que); (indicate) indiquer.

**signatory** /ˈsɪgnətrɪ/ *n* signataire *mf*.

**signature** /'sɪgnətʃə(r)/ *n* signature *f*; ~ **tune** indicatif *m*.

**significance** /sɪg'nɪfɪkəns/ *n* importance *f*; (meaning) signification *f*. **significant** *a* important; (meaningful) significatif. **significantly** *adv* (much) sensiblement.

**signify** /'sɪgnɪfaɪ/ *vt* signifier.

**signpost** /'saɪnpəʊst/ *n* panneau *m* indicateur.

**silence** /'saɪləns/ *n* silence *m*. ● *vt* faire taire.

**silent** /'saɪlənt/ *a* silencieux; (*film*) muet. **silently** *adv* silencieusement.

**silhouette** /sɪlu:'et/ *n* silhouette *f*. ● *vt* **be** ~**d against** se profiler contre.

**silicon** /'sɪlɪkən/ *n* silicium *m*; ~ **chip** puce *f* électronique.

**silk** /sɪlk/ *n* soie *f*.

**silly** /'sɪlɪ/ *a* (**-ier**, **-iest**) bête, idiot.

**silver** /'sɪlvə(r)/ *n* argent *m*; (silverware) argenterie *f*. ● *a* en argent.

**similar** /'sɪmɪlə(r)/ *a* semblable (**to** à). **similarity** *n* ressemblance *f*. **similarly** *adv* de même.

**simile** /'sɪmɪlɪ/ *n* comparaison *f*.

**simmer** /'sɪmə(r)/ *vt*/*i* (*soup*) mijoter; (*water*) (laisser) frémir.

**simple** /'sɪmpl/ *a* simple

**simplicity** /sɪm'plɪsətɪ/ *n* simplicité *f*.

**simplify** /'sɪmplɪfaɪ/ *vt* simplifier.

**simplistic** /sɪm'plɪstɪk/ *a* simpliste.

**simply** /'sɪmplɪ/ *adv* simplement; (absolutely) absolument.

**simulate** /'sɪmjʊleɪt/ *vt* simuler.

**simultaneous** /sɪml'teɪnɪəs/ *a* simultané.

**sin** /sɪn/ *n* péché *m*. ● *vi* (*pt* **sinned**) pécher.

**since** /sɪns/

● *preposition*

····➤ depuis; **I haven't seen him ~ Monday** je ne l'ai pas vu depuis lundi; **I've been waiting ~ yesterday** j'attends depuis hier; **she had been living in Paris ~ 1985** elle habitait Paris depuis 1985.

● *conjunction*

····➤ (in time expressions) depuis que; **~ she's been working here** depuis qu'elle travaille ici; **~ she left** depuis qu'elle est partie *or* depuis son départ.

····➤ (because) comme; **~ he was ill, he couldn't go** comme il était malade, il ne pouvait pas y aller.

● *adverb*

····➤ depuis; **he hasn't been seen ~** on ne l'a pas vu depuis.

**sincere** /sɪn'sɪə(r)/ *a* sincère. **sincerely** *adv* sincèrement. **sincerity** *n* sincérité *f*

**sinful** /'sɪnfl/ *a* immoral; ~ **man** pécheur *m*.

**sing** /sɪŋ/ *vt*/*i* (*pt* **sang**; *pp* **sung**) chanter.

**singe** /sɪndʒ/ *vt* (*pres p* **singeing**) brûler légèrement; (with iron) roussir.

**singer** /'sɪŋə(r)/ *n* chanteur/-euse *m*/*f*.

**single** /'sɪŋgl/ *a* seul; (not double) simple; (unmarried) célibataire; (*room, bed*) pour une personne; (*ticket*) simple; **in ~ file** en file indienne. ● *n* (ticket) aller simple *m*; (record) 45 tours *m inv*; **~s** (tennis) simple *m*. ● *vt* **~ out** choisir. **~-handed** *a* tout seul. **~-minded**

*a* tenace. ~ **parent** *n* parent *m* isolé.

**singular** /ˈsɪŋgjʊlə(r)/ *n* singulier *m*. ● *a* (strange) singulier; (*noun*) au singulier.

**sinister** /ˈsɪnɪstə(r)/ *a* sinistre.

**sink** /sɪŋk/ *vt* (*pt* **sank**; *pp* **sunk**) (*boat*) couler; (*well*) forer; (*post*) enfoncer. ● *vi* (*boat*) couler; (*sun*, *level*) baisser; (*wall*) s'effondrer. ● *n* (in kitchen) évier *m*; (wash-basin) lavabo *m*. □ ~ **in** (*news*) faire son chemin.

**sinner** /ˈsɪnə(r)/ *n* pécheur/-eresse *m/f*.

**sip** /sɪp/ *n* petite gorgée *f*. ● *vt* (*pt* **sipped**) boire à petites gorgées.

**siphon** /ˈsaɪfn/ *n* siphon *m*. ● *vt* ~ **off** siphonner.

**sir** /sɜ:(r)/ *n* Monsieur *m*.

**siren** /ˈsaɪərən/ *n* sirène *f*.

**sirloin** /ˈsɜ:lɔɪn/ *n* aloyau *m*.

**sister** /ˈsɪstə(r)/ *n* sœur *f*; (nurse) infirmière *f* en chef. ~**-in-law** *n* (*pl* ~**s-in-law**) belle-sœur *f*.

**sit** /sɪt/ *vt/i* (*pt* **sat**; *pres p* **sitting**) (s')asseoir; (*committee*) siéger; ~ **(for)** (exam) se présenter à; **be** ~**ting** être assis. □ ~ **around** ne rien faire; ~ **down** s'asseoir.

**site** /saɪt/ *n* emplacement *m*; **(building)** ~ chantier *m*. ● *vt* construire.

**sitting** /ˈsɪtɪŋ/ *n* séance *f*; (in restaurant) service *m*. ~**-room** *n* salon *m*.

**situate** /ˈsɪtʃʊeɪt/ *vt* situer; **be** ~**d** être situé. **situation** *n* situation *f*.

**six** /sɪks/ *a* & *n* six (*m*).

**sixteen** /sɪkˈsti:n/ *a* & *n* seize (*m*).

**sixth** /sɪksθ/ *a* & *n* sixième (*mf*).

**sixty** /ˈsɪkstɪ/ *a* & *n* soixante (*m*).

**size** /saɪz/ *n* dimension *f*; (of person, garment) taille *f*; (of shoes) pointure *f*; (of sum, salary) montant *m*; (extent) ampleur *f*. □ ~ **up** (*person*) se faire une opinion de; (*situation*) évaluer. **sizeable** *a* assez grand.

**skate** /skeɪt/ *n* patin *m*; (fish) raie *f*. ● *vi* patiner.

**skateboard** /ˈskeɪtbɔ:d/ *n* skateboard *m*, planche *f* à roulettes. ● *vi* faire du skateboard.

**skating** /ˈskeɪtɪŋ/ *n* patinage *m*.

**skeletal** /ˈskelɪtl/ *a* squelettique.

**skeleton** /ˈskelɪtən/ *n* squelette *m*; ~ **staff** effectifs *mpl* minimums.

**sketch** /sketʃ/ *n* esquisse *f*; (hasty) croquis *m*; (Theat) sketch *m*. ● *vt* faire une esquisse *or* un croquis de. ● *vi* faire des esquisses.

**sketchy** /ˈsketʃɪ/ *a* (**-ier**, **-iest**) insuffisant; (*memory*) vague.

**skewer** /ˈskjʊə(r)/ *n* brochette *f*.

**ski** /ski:/ *n* ski *m*. ● *a* de ski. ● *vi* (*pt* **ski'd** *or* **skied**; *pres p* **skiing**) skier; (go skiing) faire du ski.

**skid** /skɪd/ *vi* (*pt* **skidded**) déraper. ● *n* dérapage *m*.

**skier** /ˈski:ə(r)/ *n* skieur/-euse *m/f*.

**skiing** /ˈski:ɪŋ/ *n* ski *m*.

**ski jump** *n* saut *m* à ski.

**skilful** /ˈskɪlfl/ *a* habile.

**ski lift** *n* remontée *f* mécanique.

**skill** /skɪl/ *n* habileté *f*; (craft) compétence *f*; ~**s** connaissances *fpl*. **skilled** *a* (*worker*) qualifié; (talented) consommé.

**skim** /skɪm/ *vt* (*pt* **skimmed**) écumer; (*milk*) écrémer; (pass over) effleurer. ● *vi* ~ **through** parcourir.

**skimpy** /ˈskɪmpɪ/ *a* (*clothes*) étriqué; (*meal*) chiche.

**skin** /skɪn/ *n* peau *f*. ● *vt* (*pt* **skinned**) (*animal*) écorcher.

**skinny** /ˈskɪnɪ/ *a* (**-ier**, **-iest**) Ⓘ maigre.

**skip** /skɪp/ *vi* (*pt* **skipped**) sautiller; (with rope) sauter à la corde.

● *vt* (*page, class*) sauter. ● *n* petit saut *m*; (container) benne *f*.

**skipper** /'skɪpə(r)/ *n* capitaine *m*.

**skirmish** /'skɜ:mɪʃ/ *n* escarmouche *f*, accrochage *m*.

**skirt** /skɜ:t/ *n* jupe *f*. ● *vt* contourner. **skirting-board** *n* plinthe *f*.

**skittle** /'skɪtl/ *n* quille *f*.

**skull** /skʌl/ *n* crâne *m*.

**sky** /skaɪ/ *n* ciel *m*. **~-blue** *a & n* bleu ciel *m inv*. **~scraper** *n* gratte-ciel *m inv*.

**slab** /slæb/ *n* (of stone) dalle *f*.

**slack** /slæk/ *a* (not tight) détendu; (*person*) négligent; (*period*) creux. ● *n* (in rope) mou *m*. ● *vi* se relâcher.

**slacken** /'slækən/ *vt* (*rope*) donner du mou à; (*grip*) relâcher; (*pace*) réduire. ● *vi* (*grip, rope*) se relâcher; (*activity*) ralentir; (*rain*) se calmer.

**slam** /slæm/ *vt/i* (*pt* **slammed**) (*door*) claquer; (throw) flanquer; (criticize Ⓘ) critiquer. ● *n* (noise) claquement *m*.

**slander** /'slɑ:ndə(r)/ *n* (offence) diffamation *f*; (statement) calomnie *f*. ● *vt* calomnier; (Jur) diffamer. **slanderous** *a* diffamatoire.

**slang** /slæŋ/ *n* argot *m*.

**slant** /slɑ:nt/ *vt/i* (faire) pencher; (*news*) présenter sous un certain jour. ● *n* inclinaison *f*; (bias) angle *m*. **slanted** *a* (biased) orienté; (sloping) en pente.

**slap** /slæp/ *vt* (*pt* **slapped**) (strike) donner une tape à; (*face*) gifler; (put) flanquer Ⓘ. ● *n* claque *f*; (on face) gifle *f*. ● *adv* tout droit.

**slapdash** /'slæpdæʃ/ *a* (*person*) brouillon Ⓘ; (*work*) baclé Ⓘ.

**slash** /slæʃ/ *vt* (*picture, tyre*) taillader; (*face*) balafrer; (*throat*) couper; (fig) réduire (radicalement). ● *n* lacération *f*.

**slat** /slæt/ *n* (in blind) lamelle *f*; (on bed) latte *f*.

**slate** /sleɪt/ *n* ardoise *f*. ● *vt* Ⓘ taper sur Ⓘ.

**slaughter** /'slɔ:tə(r)/ *vt* massacrer; (*animal*) abattre. ● *n* massacre *m*; abattage *m*.

**slave** /sleɪv/ *n* esclave *mf*. ● *vi* trimer Ⓘ. **slavery** *n* esclavage *m*.

**sleazy** /'sli:zɪ/ *a* (**-ier**, **-iest**) Ⓘ (*story*) scabreux; (*club*) louche.

**sledge** /sledʒ/ *n* luge *f*; (horse-drawn) traîneau *m*.

**sleek** /sli:k/ *a* (*hair*) lisse, brillant; (*shape*) élégant.

**sleep** /sli:p/ *n* sommeil *m*; **go to ~** s'endormir. ● *vi* (*pt* **slept**) dormir; (spend the night) coucher; **~ in** faire la grasse matinée. ● *vt* loger.

**sleeper** /'sli:pə(r)/ *n* (Rail) (berth) couchette *f*; (on track) traverse *f*.

**sleeping-bag** *n* sac *m* de couchage.

**sleeping-pill** *n* somnifère *m*.

**sleep-walker** *n* somnambule *mf*.

**sleepy** /'sli:pɪ/ *a* (**-ier**, **-iest**) somnolent; **be ~** avoir sommeil.

**sleet** /sli:t/ *n* neige *f* fondue.

**sleeve** /sli:v/ *n* manche *f*; (of record) pochette *f*; **up one's ~** en réserve.

**sleigh** /sleɪ/ *n* traîneau *m*.

**slender** /'slendə(r)/ *a* (*person*) mince; (*majority*) faible.

**slept** /slept/ ⇒SLEEP.

**slice** /slaɪs/ *n* tranche *f*. ● *vt* couper (en tranches).

**slick** /slɪk/ *a* (adept) habile; (insincere) roublard Ⓘ. ● *n* **(oil) ~** marée *f* noire.

**slide** /slaɪd/ *vt/i* (*pt* **slid**) glisser; **~ into** (go silently) se glisser dans. ● *n* glissade *f*; (fall: fig) baisse *f*; (in

playground) toboggan *m*; (for hair) barrette *f*; (Photo) diapositive *f*.

**sliding** /'slaɪdɪŋ/ *a* (*door*) coulissant; ~ **scale** échelle *f* mobile.

**slight** /slaɪt/ *a* petit, léger; (slender) mince; (frail) frêle. ● *vt* (insult) offenser. ● *n* affront *m*. **slightest** *a* moindre. **slightly** *adv* légèrement, un peu.

**slim** /slɪm/ *a* (**slimmer**, **slimmest**) mince. ● *vi* (*pt* **slimmed**) maigrir.

**slime** /slaɪm/ *n* dépôt *m* gluant; (on river-bed) vase *f*. **slimy** *a* visqueux; (fig) servile.

**sling** /slɪŋ/ *n* (weapon, toy) fronde *f*; (bandage) écharpe *f*. ● *vt* (*pt* **slung**) jeter, lancer.

**slip** /slɪp/ *vt*/*i* (*pt* **slipped**) glisser; ~**ped disc** hernie *f* discale; ~ **sb's mind** échapper à qn. ● *n* (mistake) erreur *f*; (petticoat) combinaison *f*; (paper) bout *m* de papier; ~ **of the tongue** lapsus *m*. □ ~ **away** s'esquiver; ~ **into** (go) se glisser dans; (*clothes*) mettre; ~ **up** 🄸 faire une gaffe 🄸.

**slipper** /'slɪpə(r)/ *n* pantoufle *f*.

**slippery** /'slɪpərɪ/ *a* glissant.

**slip road** *n* bretelle *f*.

**slit** /slɪt/ *n* fente *f*. ● *vt* (*pt* **slit**; *pres p* **slitting**) déchirer; ~ **sth open** ouvrir qch; ~ **sb's throat** égorger qn.

**slither** /'slɪðə(r)/ *vi* glisser.

**sliver** /'slɪvə(r)/ *n* (of glass) éclat *m*; (of soap) reste *m*.

**slobber** /'slɒbə(r)/ *vi* 🄸 baver.

**slog** /slɒg/ 🄸 *vt* (*pt* **slogged**) (hit) frapper dur. ● *vi* (work) bosser 🄸. ● *n* (work) travail *m* dur.

**slogan** /'sləʊgən/ *n* slogan *m*.

**slope** /sləʊp/ *vi* être en pente; (*handwriting*) pencher. ● *n* pente *f*; (of mountain) flanc *m*.

**sloppy** /'slɒpɪ/ *a* (**-ier**, **-iest**) (*food*) liquide; (*work*) négligé; (*person*) négligent.

**slosh** /slɒʃ/ *vt* 🄸 répandre; (hit 🄸) frapper. ● *vi* clapoter.

**slot** /slɒt/ *n* fente *f*. ● *vt*/*i* (*pt* **slotted**) (s')insérer.

**sloth** /sləʊθ/ *n* paresse *f*.

**slot-machine** *n* distributeur *m* automatique; (for gambling) machine *f* à sous.

**slouch** /slaʊtʃ/ *vi* être avachi.

**Slovakia** /slə'vækɪə/ *n* Slovaquie *f*.

**Slovenia** /slə'vi:nɪə/ *n* Slovénie *f*.

**slovenly** /'slʌvnlɪ/ *a* débraillé.

**slow** /sləʊ/ *a* lent; **be** ~ (*clock*) retarder; **in** ~ **motion** au ralenti. ● *adv* lentement. ● *vt*/*i* ralentir. **slowly** *adv* lentement. **slowness** *n* lenteur *f*.

**sludge** /slʌdʒ/ *n* vase *f*.

**slug** /slʌg/ *n* (mollusc) limace *f*; (bullet 🄸) balle *f*; (blow 🄸) coup *m*.

**sluggish** /'slʌgɪʃ/ *a* (*person*) léthargique; (*circulation*) lent.

**slum** /slʌm/ *n* taudis *m*.

**slump** /slʌmp/ *n* (Econ) effondrement *m*; (in support) baisse *f*. ● *vi* (*demand, trade*) chuter; (*economy*) s'effondrer; (*person*) s'affaler.

**slung** /slʌŋ/ ⇒SLING.

**slur** /slɜ:(r)/ *vt*/*i* (*pt* **slurred**) (*words*) mal articuler. ● *n* calomnie *f* (**on** sur).

**slush** /slʌʃ/ *n* (snow) neige *f* fondue. ~ **fund** *n* caisse *f* noire.

**sly** /slaɪ/ *a* (crafty) rusé; (secretive) sournois. ● *n* **on the** ~ en cachette.

**smack** /smæk/ *n* tape *f*; (on face) gifle *f*. ● *vt* donner une tape à; gifler. ● *vi* ~ **of sth** sentir qch. ● *adv* 🄸 tout droit.

**small** /smɔ:l/ *a* petit. ● *n* ~ **of the back** creux *m* des reins. ● *adv* (*cut*)

menu. ~ **ad** *n* petite annonce *f*. ~ **business** *n* petite entreprise *f*. ~ **change** *n* petite monnaie *f*. ~ **pox** *n* variole *f*. ~ **print** *n* petits caractères *mpl*. ~ **talk** *n* banalités *fpl*.

**smart** /smɑ:t/ *a* élégant; (clever Ⓘ) malin, habile; (*restaurant*) chic *inv*; (Comput) intelligent. ● *vi* (*wound*) brûler.

**smarten** /ˈsmɑ:tn/ *vt/i* ~ **(up)** embellir; ~ **(oneself) up** s'arranger.

**smash** /smæʃ/ *vt/i* (se) briser, (se) fracasser; (*opponent, record*) pulvériser. ● *n* (noise) fracas *m*; (blow) coup *m*; (car crash) collision *f*; (hit record Ⓘ) tube *m* Ⓘ.

**smashing** /ˈsmæʃɪŋ/ *a* Ⓘ épatant.

**SME** *abbr* (**small and medium enterprises**) PME.

**smear** /smɪə(r)/ *vt* (stain) tacher; (coat) enduire; (discredit: fig) diffamer. ● *n* tache *f*; (effort to discredit) propos *m* diffamatoire; ~ **(test)** frottis *m*.

**smell** /smel/ *n* odeur *f*; (sense) odorat *m*. ● *vt/i* (*pt* **smelt** *or* **smelled**) sentir; ~ **of** sentir. **smelly** *a* qui sent mauvais.

**smelt** /smelt/ →SMELL.

**smile** /smaɪl/ *n* sourire *m*. ● *vi* sourire.

**smiley** /ˈsmaɪlɪ/ *n* (Internet) binette *f*.

**smirk** /smɜ:k/ *n* petit sourire *m* satisfait.

**smitten** /ˈsmɪtn/ *a* (in love) fou d'amour.

**smog** /smɒg/ *n* smog *m*.

**smoke** /sməʊk/ *n* fumée *f*; **have a** ~ fumer. ● *vt/i* fumer. **smoked** *a* fumé. **smokeless** *a* (*fuel*) non polluant. **smoker** *n* fumeur/-euse *m/f*. **smoky** *a* (*air*) enfumé.

**smooth** /smu:ð/ *a* lisse; (*movement*) aisé; (*manners*) onctueux; (*flight*) sans heurts. ● *vt* lisser; (*process*) faciliter.

**smoothly** /ˈsmu:ðlɪ/ *adv* (*move, flow*) doucement; (*brake, start*) en douceur; **go** ~ marcher bien.

**smother** /ˈsmʌðə(r)/ *vt* (stifle) étouffer; (cover) couvrir.

**smoulder** /ˈsməʊldə(r)/ *vi* (lit) se consumer; (fig) couver.

**smudge** /smʌdʒ/ *n* trace *f*. ● *vt/i* (*ink*) (s')étaler.

**smug** /smʌg/ *a* (**smugger, smuggest**) suffisant.

**smuggle** /ˈsmʌgl/ *vt* passer (en contrebande). **smuggler** *n* contrebandier/-ière *m/f*. **smuggling** *n* contrebande *f*.

**smutty** /ˈsmʌtɪ/ *a* grivois.

**snack** /snæk/ *n* casse-croûte *m inv*.

**snag** /snæg/ *n* inconvénient *m*; (in cloth) accroc *m*.

**snail** /sneɪl/ *n* escargot *m*.

**snake** /sneɪk/ *n* serpent *m*.

**snap** /snæp/ *vt/i* (*pt* **snapped**) (*whip, fingers*) (faire) claquer; (break) (se) casser net; (say) dire sèchement. ● *n* claquement *m*; (Photo) photo *f*. ● *a* soudain. □ ~ **up** (buy) sauter sur.

**snapshot** /ˈsnæpʃɒt/ *n* photo *f*.

**snare** /sneə(r)/ *n* piège *m*.

**snarl** /snɑ:l/ *vi* gronder (en montrant les dents). ● *n* grondement *m*. ~**-up** *n* embouteillage *m*.

**snatch** /snætʃ/ *vt* (grab) attraper; (steal) voler; (*opportunity*) saisir; ~ **sth from sb** arracher qch à qn. ● *n* (theft) vol *m*; (short part) fragment *m*.

**sneak** /sni:k/ *vi* aller furtivement. ● *n* Ⓘ rapporteur/-euse *m/f*.

**sneer** /snɪə(r)/ *n* sourire *m* méprisant. ● *vi* sourire avec mépris.

**sneeze** /sni:z/ *n* éternuement *m*. ● *vi* éternuer.

**snide** /snaɪd/ *a* narquois.

**sniff** /snɪf/ *vt/i* renifler. ● *n* reniflement *m*.

**snigger** /'snɪgə(r)/ *n* ricanement *m*. ● *vi* ricaner.

**snip** /snɪp/ *vt* (*pt* **snipped**) couper.

**sniper** /'snaɪpə(r)/ *n* tireur *m* embusqué.

**snippet** /'snɪpɪt/ *n* bribe *f*.

**snivel** /'snɪvl/ *vi* (*pt* **snivelled**) pleurnicher.

**snob** /snɒb/ *n* snob *mf*.

**snooker** /'snu:kə(r)/ *n* snooker *m*.

**snoop** /snu:p/ *vi* ▣ fourrer son nez partout.

**snooty** /'snu:tɪ/ *a* (**-ier**, **-iest**) ▣ snob *inv*, hautain.

**snooze** /snu:z/ *n* petit somme *m*. ● *vi* sommeiller.

**snore** /snɔ:(r)/ *n* ronflement *m*. ● *vi* ronfler.

**snorkel** /'snɔ:kl/ *n* tuba *m*.

**snort** /snɔ:t/ *n* grognement *m*. ● *vi* (*person*) grogner; (*horse*) s'ébrouer.

**snout** /snaʊt/ *n* museau *m*.

**snow** /snəʊ/ *n* neige *f*. ● *vi* neiger; **be ~ed under with** être submergé de.

**snowball** /'snəʊbɔ:l/ *n* boule *f* de neige. ● *vi* faire boule de neige.

**snow**: **~boarding** *n* surf *m* des neiges. **~-bound** *a* bloqué par la neige. **~-drift** *n* congère *f*. **~drop** *n* perce-neige *m or f inv*. **~flake** *n* flocon *m* de neige. **~man** *n* (*pl* **-men**) bonhomme *m* de neige. **~-plough** *n* chasse-neige *m inv*.

**snub** /snʌb/ *vt* (*pt* **snubbed**) rembarrer. ● *n* rebuffade *f*.

**snuffle** /'snʌfl/ *vi* renifler.

**snug** /snʌg/ *a* (**snugger**, **snuggest**) (cosy) confortable; (tight) bien ajusté.

**snuggle** /'snʌgl/ *vi* se pelotonner.

**so** /səʊ/ *adv* si, tellement; (thus) ainsi; **~ am I** moi aussi; **~ good as** aussi bon que; **that is ~** c'est ça; **I think ~** je pense que oui; **five or ~** environ cinq; **~ as to** de manière à; **~ far** jusqu'ici; **~ long!** ▣ à bientôt!; **~ many**, **~ much** tant (de); **~ that** pour que. ● *conj* donc, alors.

**soak** /səʊk/ *vt/i* (faire) tremper (**in** dans). □ **~ in** pénétrer; **~ up** absorber. **soaking** *a* trempé.

**soap** /səʊp/ *n* savon *m*. ● *vt* savonner. **~ opera** *n* feuilleton *m*. **~ powder** *n* lessive *f*.

**soar** /sɔ:(r)/ *vi* monter (en flèche).

**sob** /sɒb/ *n* sanglot *m*. ● *vi* (*pt* **sobbed**) sangloter.

**sober** /'səʊbə(r)/ *a* qui n'a pas bu d'alcool; (serious) sérieux. ● *vi* **~ up** dessoûler.

**soccer** /'sɒkə(r)/ *n* football *m*.

**sociable** /'səʊʃəbl/ *a* sociable.

**social** /'səʊʃl/ *a* social. ● *n* réunion *f* (amicale), fête *f*.

**socialism** /'səʊʃəlɪzəm/ *n* socialisme *m*. **socialist** *a & n* socialiste (*mf*).

**socialize** /'səʊʃəlaɪz/ *vi* se mêler aux autres; **~ with** fréquenter.

**socially** /'səʊʃəlɪ/ *adv* socialement; (*meet*) en société.

**social**: **~ security** *n* aide *f* sociale. **~ worker** *n* travailleur/-euse *m/f* social/-e.

**society** /sə'saɪətɪ/ *n* société *f*.

**sociological** /səʊsɪə'lɒdʒɪkl/ *a* sociologique. **sociologist** *n* sociologue *mf*. **sociology** *n* sociologie *f*.

**sock** /sɒk/ *n* chaussette *f.* ● *vt* (hit Ⓘ) flanquer un coup (de poing) à.

**socket** /'sɒkɪt/ *n* (for lamp) douille *f*; (Electr) prise *f* (de courant); (of eye) orbite *f.*

**soda** /'səʊdə/ *n* soude *f*; **~(-water)** eau *f* de Seltz.

**sodden** /'sɒdn/ *a* détrempé.

**sofa** /'səʊfə/ *n* canapé *m.* **~ bed** *n* canapé-lit *m.*

**soft** /sɒft/ *a* (gentle, lenient) doux; (not hard) doux, mou; (*heart, wood*) tendre; (silly) ramolli. **~ drink** *n* boisson *f* non alcoolisée.

**soften** /'sɒfn/ *vt/i* (se) ramollir; (tone down, lessen) (s')adoucir.

**soft spot** *n* **to have a ~ for sb** avoir un faible pour qn.

**software** /'sɒftweə(r)/ *n* logiciel *m.*

**soggy** /'sɒgɪ/ *a* (**-ier**, **-iest**) (*ground*) détrempé; (*food*) ramolli.

**soil** /sɔɪl/ *n* sol *m*, terre *f.* ● *vt/i* (se) salir.

**sold** /səʊld/ ⇒SELL. ● *a* **~ out** épuisé.

**solder** /'sɒldə(r)/ *n* soudure *f.* ● *vt* souder.

**soldier** /'səʊldʒə(r)/ *n* soldat *m.* ● *vi* **~ on** Ⓘ persévérer.

**sole** /səʊl/ *n* (of foot) plante *f*; (of shoe) semelle *f*; (fish) sole *f.* ● *a* unique, seul. **solely** *adv* uniquement.

**solemn** /'sɒləm/ *a* solennel.

**solicitor** /sə'lɪsɪtə(r)/ *n* notaire *m*; (for court and police work) ≈ avocat/-e *m/f.*

**solid** /'sɒlɪd/ *a* solide; (not hollow) plein; (*gold*) massif; (*mass*) compact; (*meal*) substantiel. ● *n* solide *m*; **~s** (food) aliments *mpl* solides.

**solidarity** /sɒlɪ'dærətɪ/ *n* solidarité *f.*

**solidify** /sə'lɪdɪfaɪ/ *vt/i* (se) solidifier.

**solitary** /'sɒlɪtrɪ/ *a* (alone) solitaire; (only) seul.

**solo** /'səʊləʊ/ *n* solo *m.* ● *a* (Mus) solo *inv*; (*flight*) en solitaire.

**soluble** /'sɒljʊbl/ *a* soluble.

**solution** /sə'lu:ʃn/ *n* solution *f.*

**solve** /sɒlv/ *vt* résoudre.

**solvent** /'sɒlvənt/ *a* (Comm) solvable. ● *n* (dis)solvant *m.*

**some** /sʌm, səm/

● *determiner*

➤ (unspecified amount) du/de l'/de la/des; **I have to buy ~ bread** je dois acheter du pain; **have ~ water** prenez de l'eau; **~ sweets** des bonbons.

➤ (certain) certains/certaines; **~ people say that** certains disent que.

➤ (unknown) un/une; **~ man came to the house** un homme est venu à la maison.

➤ (considerable amount) **we stayed there for ~ time** nous sommes restés là assez longtemps; **it will take ~ doing** ça ne va pas être facile à faire.

**!** In front of a plural adjective *des* changes to *de*: **some pretty dresses** *de jolies robes*.

● *pronoun*

➤ en; **he wants ~** il en veut; **have ~ more** reprenez-en.

➤ (certain) certains/certaines; **~ are expensive** certains sont chers.

● *adverb*

➤ environ; **~ 20 people** environ 20 personnes.

**somebody** /'sʌmbədɪ/ *pron* quelqu'un. ● *n* **be a ~** être quelqu'un.

**somehow** /'sʌmhaʊ/ *adv* d'une manière ou d'une autre; (for some reason) je ne sais pas pourquoi.

**someone** /'sʌmwʌn/ *pron & n* = SOMEBODY.

**someplace** /'sʌmpleɪs/ *adv* (US) = SOMEWHERE.

**somersault** /'sʌməsɔ:lt/ *n* roulade *f*. ● *vi* faire une roulade.

**something** /'sʌmθɪŋ/ *pron & n* quelque chose (*m*); **~ good** quelque chose de bon; **~ like** un peu comme.

**sometime** /'sʌmtaɪm/ *adv* un jour; **~ in June** en juin. ● *a* (former) ancien.

**sometimes** /'sʌmtaɪmz/ *adv* quelquefois, parfois.

**somewhat** /'sʌmwɒt/ *adv* quelque peu, un peu.

**somewhere** /'sʌmweə(r)/ *adv* quelque part.

**son** /sʌn/ *n* fils *m*.

**song** /sɒŋ/ *n* chanson *f*; (of bird) chant *m*.

**son-in-law** /'sʌnɪnlɔ:/ *n* (*pl* **sons-in-law**) gendre *m*.

**soon** /su:n/ *adv* bientôt; (early) tôt; **I would ~er stay** j'aimerais mieux rester; **~ after** peu après; **~er or later** tôt ou tard.

**soot** /sʊt/ *n* suie *f*.

**soothe** /su:ð/ *vt* calmer.

**sophisticated** /sə'fɪstɪkeɪtɪd/ *a* raffiné; (*machine*) sophistiqué.

**sopping** /'sɒpɪŋ/ *a* trempé.

**soppy** /'sɒpɪ/ *a* (**-ier**, **-iest**) ⓘ sentimental.

**sorcerer** /'sɔ:sərə(r)/ *n* sorcier *m*.

**sordid** /'sɔ:dɪd/ *a* sordide.

**sore** /'sɔ:(r)/ *a* douloureux; (vexed) en rogne (**at, with** contre). ● *n* plaie *f*.

**sorely** /'sɔ:lɪ/ *adv* fortement.

**sorrow** /'sɒrəʊ/ *n* chagrin *m*.

**sorry** /'sɒrɪ/ *a* (**-ier**, **-iest**) (regretful) désolé (**to** de; **that** que); (wretched) triste; **feel ~ for** plaindre; **~!** pardon!

**sort** /sɔ:t/ *n* genre *m*, sorte *f*, espèce *f*; (person ⓘ) type *m*; **what ~ of?** quel genre de?; **be out of ~s** ne pas être dans son assiette. ● *vt* **~ (out)** (classify) trier; **~ out** (tidy) ranger; (arrange) arranger; (*problem*) régler.

**so-so** /səʊ'səʊ/ *a & adv* comme ci comme ça.

**sought** /sɔ:t/ ⇒SEEK.

**soul** /səʊl/ *n* âme *f*.

**sound** /saʊnd/ *n* son *m*, bruit *m*. ● *a* solide; (healthy) sain; (sensible) sensé. ● *vt/i* sonner; (seem) sembler (**as if** que); (test) sonder; **~ out** sonder; **~ a horn** klaxonner; **~ like** sembler être. **~ asleep** *a* profondément endormi. **~ barrier** *n* mur *m* du son.

**soundly** /'saʊndlɪ/ *adv* (*sleep*) à poings fermés; (*built*) solidement.

**sound-proof** /'saʊndpru:f/ *a* insonorisé. ● *vt* insonoriser.

**sound-track** /'saʊndtræk/ *n* bande *f* sonore.

**soup** /su:p/ *n* soupe *f*, potage *m*.

**sour** /'saʊə(r)/ *a* aigre. ● *vt/i* (s')aigrir.

**source** /sɔ:s/ *n* source *f*.

**south** /saʊθ/ *n* sud *m*. ● *a* sud *inv*, du sud. ● *adv* vers le sud.

**South Africa** *n* Afrique *f* du Sud.

**South America** *n* Amérique *f* du Sud.

**south-east** *n* sud-est *m*.

**southern** /'sʌðən/ *a* du sud. **southerner** *n* habitant/-e *m/f* du sud.

**southward** /'saʊθwəd/ *a* (*side*) sud *inv*; (*journey*) vers le sud.

**south-west** *n* sud-ouest *m*.

**souvenir** /su:və'nɪə(r)/ *n* souvenir *m*.

**sovereign** /'sɒvrɪn/ *n* & *a* souverain/-e (*m/f*).

**sow**[1] /səʊ/ *vt* (*pt* **sowed**; *pp* **sowed** *or* **sown**) (*seed*) semer; (*land*) ensemencer.

**sow**[2] /saʊ/ *n* (pig) truie *f*.

**soya** /'sɔɪə/ *n* soja *m*. ~ **sauce** *n* sauce *f* soja.

**spa** /spɑ:/ *n* station *f* thermale.

**space** /speɪs/ *n* espace *m*; (room) place *f*; (period) période *f*. ● *a* (*research*) spatial. ● *vt* ~ **(out)** espacer. ~**craft** *n inv*, ~**ship** *n* engin *m* spatial. ~**suit** *n* combinaison *f* spatiale.

**spacious** /'speɪʃəs/ *a* spacieux.

**spade** /speɪd/ *n* (for garden) bêche *f*; (child's) pelle *f*; (cards) pique *m* ~**work** *n* (fig) travail *m* préparatoire.

**spaghetti** /spə'getɪ/ *n* spaghetti *mpl*.

**Spain** /speɪn/ *n* Espagne *f*.

**spam** /spæm/ *n* (Comput) multipostage *m* abusif.

**span** /spæn/ *n* (of arch) portée *f*; (of wings) envergure *f*; (of time) durée *f*. ● *vt* (*pt* **spanned**) enjamber; (in time) embrasser.

**Spaniard** /'spænɪəd/ *n* Espagnol/-e *m/f*.

**spaniel** /'spænɪəl/ *n* épagneul *m*.

**Spanish** /'spænɪʃ/ *a* espagnol. ● *n* espagnol *m*.

**spank** /spæŋk/ *vt* donner une fessée à.

**spanner** /'spænə(r)/ *n* (tool) clé *f* (plate); (adjustable) clé *f* à molette.

**spare** /speə(r)/ *vt* (treat leniently) épargner; (do without) se passer de; (afford to give) donner, accorder. ● *a* en réserve; (surplus) de trop; (*tyre, shoes*) de rechange; (*room, bed*) d'ami; **are there any ~ tickets?** y a-t-il encore des places? ● *n* ~ (part) pièce *f* de rechange. ~ **time** *n* loisirs *mpl*.

**sparing** /'speərɪŋ/ *a* frugal. **sparingly** *adv* en petite quantité.

**spark** /spɑ:k/ *n* étincelle *f*. ● *vt* ~ **off** (initiate) provoquer.

**sparkle** /'spɑ:kl/ *vi* étinceler. ● *n* étincellement *m*. **sparkling** *a* (*wine*) mousseux, pétillant; (*eyes*) brillant.

**spark-plug** *n* bougie *f*.

**sparrow** /'spærəʊ/ *n* moineau *m*.

**sparse** /spɑ:s/ *a* clairsemé. **sparsely** *adv* (*furnished*) peu.

**spasm** /'spæzəm/ *n* (of muscle) spasme *m*; (of coughing, anger) accès *m*.

**spat** /spæt/ ⇒SPIT.

**spate** /speɪt/ *n* **a ~ of** (*letters*) une avalanche de.

**spatter** /'spætə(r)/ *vt* éclabousser (with de).

**spawn** /spɔ:n/ *n* frai *m*, œufs *mpl*. ● *vt* pondre. ● *vi* frayer.

**speak** /spi:k/ *vi* (*pt* **spoke**; *pp* **spoken**) parler. ● *vt* (say) dire; (*language*) parler. □ ~ **up** parler plus fort.

**speaker** /'spi:kə(r)/ *n* (in public) orateur *m*; (Pol) président *m*; (loudspeaker) baffle *m*; **be a French/a good ~** parler français/bien.

**spear** /spɪə(r)/ *n* lance *f*.

**spearmint** /'spɪəmɪnt/ *n* menthe *f* verte.

**special** /'speʃl/ *a* spécial; (exceptional) exceptionnel.

**specialist** /'speʃəlɪst/ *n* spécialiste *mf.*

**speciality**, (US) **specialty** /speʃɪ'ælətɪ/ *n* spécialité *f.*

**specialize** /'speʃəlaɪz/ *vi* se spécialiser (**in** en).

**specially** /'speʃəlɪ/ *adv* spécialement.

**species** /'spi:ʃɪz/ *n inv* espèce *f.*

**specific** /spə'sɪfɪk/ *a* précis, explicite.

**specification** /spesɪfɪ'keɪʃn/ *n* (of design) spécification *f*; (of car equipment) caractéristiques *fpl.* **specify** *vt* spécifier.

**specimen** /'spesɪmɪn/ *n* spécimen *m*, échantillon *m.*

**speck** /spek/ *n* (stain) (petite) tache *f*; (particle) grain *m.*

**specs** /speks/ *npl* ☐ lunettes *fpl.*

**spectacle** /'spektəkl/ *n* spectacle *m.* **spectacles** *n* lunettes *fpl.* **spectacular** *a* spectaculaire.

**spectator** /spek'teɪtə(r)/ *n* spectateur/-trice *m/f.*

**spectrum** /'spektrəm/ *n* (*pl* **-tra**) spectre *m*; (of ideas) gamme *f.*

**speculate** /'spekjʊleɪt/ *vi* s'interroger (**about** sur); (Comm) spéculer. **speculation** *n* conjectures *fpl*; (Comm) spéculation *f.* **speculator** *n* spéculateur/-trice *m/f.*

**speech** /spi:tʃ/ *n* (faculty) parole *f*; (diction) élocution *f*; (dialect) langage *m*; (address) discours *m.* **speechless** *a* muet (**with** de).

**speed** /spi:d/ *n* (of movement) vitesse *f*; (swiftness) rapidité *f.* ● *vi* (*pt* **sped** /sped/) aller vite; (*pt* **speeded**) (drive too fast) aller trop vite. ☐ ~ **up** accélérer; (of pace) s'accélérer.

**speedboat** /'spi:dbəʊt/ *n* vedette *f.*

**speeding** /'spi:dɪŋ/ *n* excès *m* de vitesse.

**speed limit** *n* limitation *f* de vitesse.

**speedometer** /spi:'dɒmɪtə(r)/ *n* compteur *m* (de vitesse).

**spell** /spel/ *n* (magic) charme *m*, sortilège *m*; (curse) sort *m*; (of time) (courte) période *f.* ● *vt/i* (*pt* **spelled** *or* **spelt**) écrire; (mean) signifier; ~ **out** épeler; (explain) expliquer. **~checker** *n* correcteur *m* orthographique.

**spelling** /'spelɪŋ/ *n* orthographe *f.* ● *a* (*mistake*) d'orthographe.

**spend** /spend/ *vt* (*pt* **spent**) (*money*) dépenser (**on** pour); (*time, holiday*) passer; (*energy*) consacrer (**on** à). ● *vi* dépenser.

**spent** /spent/ ⇒SPEND. ● *a* (used) utilisé; (*person*) épuisé.

**sperm** /spɜ:m/ *n* (*pl* **sperms** *or* **sperm**) sperme *m.*

**sphere** /sfɪə(r)/ *n* sphère *f.*

**spice** /spaɪs/ *n* épice *f*; (fig) piquant *m.*

**spick-and-span** *a* impeccable.

**spicy** /'spaɪsɪ/ *a* épicé; piquant.

**spider** /'spaɪdə(r)/ *n* araignée *f.*

**spike** /spaɪk/ *n* pointe *f.*

**spill** /spɪl/ *vt* (*pt* **spilled** *or* **spilt**) renverser, répandre. ● *vi* se répandre; ~ **over** déborder.

**spin** /spɪn/ *vt/i* (*pt* **spun**; *pres p* **spinning**) (*wool, web*) filer; (turn) (faire) tourner; (*story*) débiter; ~ **out** faire durer. ● *n* (movement, excursion) tour *m.*

**spinach** /'spɪnɪdʒ/ *n* épinards *mpl.*

**spinal** /'spaɪnl/ *a* vertébral. ~ **cord** *n* moelle *f* épinière.

**spin-drier** *n* essoreuse *f.*

**spine** /spaɪn/ *n* colonne *f* vertébrale; (prickle) piquant *m.*

**spin-off** *n* avantage *m* accessoire; (by-product) dérivé *m*.

**spinster** /'spɪnstə(r)/ *n* célibataire *f*; (pej) vieille fille *f*.

**spiral** /'spaɪərəl/ *a* en spirale; (*staircase*) en colimaçon. ● *n* spirale *f*. ● *vi* (*pt* **spiralled**) (*prices*) monter (en flèche).

**spire** /'spaɪə(r)/ *n* flèche *f*.

**spirit** /'spɪrɪt/ *n* esprit *m*; (boldness) courage *m*; **~s** (morale) moral *m*; (drink) spiritueux *mpl*. ● *vt* **~ away** faire disparaître. **spirited** *a* fougueux. **~-level** *n* niveau *m* à bulle.

**spiritual** /'spɪrɪtʃʊəl/ *a* spirituel.

**spit** /spɪt/ *vt*/*i* (*pt* **spat** *or* **spit**; *pres p* **spitting**) cracher; (of rain) crachiner; **~ out** cracher; **the ~ting image of** le portrait craché *or* vivant de. ● *n* crachat(s) *m*(*pl*); (for meat) broche *f*.

**spite** /spaɪt/ *n* rancune *f*; **in ~ of** malgré. ● *vt* contrarier.

**splash** /splæʃ/ *vt* éclabousser. ● *vi* faire des éclaboussures; **~ (about)** patauger. ● *n* (act, mark) éclaboussure *f*; (sound) plouf *m*; (of colour) tache *f*.

**spleen** /spli:n/ *n* (Anat) rate *f*.

**splendid** /'splendɪd/ *a* magnifique, splendide.

**splint** /splɪnt/ *n* (Med) attelle *f*.

**splinter** /'splɪntə(r)/ *n* éclat *m*; (in finger) écharde *f*. **~ group** *n* groupe *m* dissident.

**split** /splɪt/ *vt*/*i* (*pt* **split**; *pres p* **splitting**) (cut) fendre; (tear) (se) déchirer; (divide) (se) diviser; (share) partager; **~ one's sides** se tordre (de rire). ● *n* fente *f*; déchirure *f*; (share [I]) part *f*, partage *m*; (quarrel) rupture *f*; (Pol) scission *f*. □ **~ up** (*couple*) rompre. **~ second** *n* fraction *f* de seconde.

**splutter** /'splʌtə(r)/ *vi* crachoter; (stammer) bafouiller; (*engine*) tousser.

**spoil** /spɔɪl/ *vt* (*pt* **spoilt** *or* **spoiled**) (pamper) gâter; (ruin) abîmer; (mar) gâcher, gâter. ● *n* **~(s)** butin *m*. **~-sport** *n* trouble-fête *mf inv*.

**spoke**[1] /spəʊk/ *n* rayon *m*.

**spoke**[2], **spoken** /spəʊk, 'spəʊkən/ ⇒SPEAK.

**spokesman** /'spəʊksmən/ *n* (*pl* **-men**) porte-parole *m inv*.

**sponge** /spʌndʒ/ *n* éponge *f*. ● *vt* éponger. ● *vi* **~ on** vivre aux crochets de. **~-bag** *n* trousse *f* de toilette. **~-cake** *n* génoise *f*.

**sponsor** /'spɒnsə(r)/ *n* (of concert) parrain *m*, sponsor *m*; (surety) garant *m*; (for membership) parrain *m*, marraine *f*. ● *vt* parrainer, sponsoriser; (*member*) parrainer. **sponsorship** *n* patronage *m*; parrainage *m*.

**spontaneous** /spɒn'teɪnɪəs/ *a* spontané.

**spoof** /spu:f/ *n* [I] parodie *f*.

**spoon** /spu:n/ *n* cuiller *f*, cuillère *f*.

**spoonful** /'spu:nfʊl/ *n* (*pl* **~s**) cuillerée *f*.

**sport** /spɔ:t/ *n* sport *m*; **(good) ~** (person [I]) chic type *m*; **~s car/coat** voiture/veste *f* de sport. ● *vt* (display) exhiber, arborer.

**sporting** /'spɔ:tɪŋ/ *a* sportif; **a ~ chance** une assez bonne chance.

**sportsman** /'spɔ:tsmən/ *n* (*pl* **-men**) sportif *m*.

**sporty** /'spɔ:tɪ/ *a* [I] sportif.

**spot** /spɒt/ *n* (mark, stain) tache *f*; (dot) point *m*; (in pattern) pois *m*; (drop) goutte *f*; (place) endroit *m*; (pimple) bouton *m*; **a ~ of** [I] un peu de; **on the ~** sur place; (without delay) sur le coup. ● *vt* (*pt* **spotted**) [I]

apercevoir. ~ **check** *n* contrôle *m* surprise.

**spotless** /'spɒtlɪs/ *a* impeccable.

**spotlight** /'spɒtlaɪt/ *n* (lamp) projecteur *m*, spot *m*.

**spotty** /'spɒtɪ/ *a* (*skin*) boutonneux.

**spouse** /spaʊs/ *n* époux *m*, épouse *f*.

**spout** /spaʊt/ *n* (of teapot) bec *m*; (of liquid) jet *m*; **up the** ~ (ruined 🄸) fichu. ● *vi* jaillir.

**sprain** /spreɪn/ *n* entorse *f*, foulure *f*. ● *vt* ~ **one's wrist** se fouler le poignet.

**sprang** /spræŋ/ ⇒SPRING.

**sprawl** /sprɔ:l/ *vi* (*town, person*) s'étaler. ● *n* étalement *m*.

**spray** /spreɪ/ *n* (of flowers) gerbe *f*; (water) gerbe *f* d'eau; (from sea) embruns *mpl*; (device) bombe *f*, atomiseur *m*. ● *vt* (*surface, insecticide, plant)* vaporiser; (*person*) asperger; (*crops*) traiter.

**spread** /spred/ *vt/i* (*pt* **spread**) (stretch, extend) (s')étendre; (*news, fear*) (se) répandre; (*illness*) (se) propager; (*butter*) (s')étaler. ● *n* propagation *f*; (of population) distribution *f*; (paste) pâte *f* à tartiner; (food) belle table *f*. ~**-eagled** *a* bras et jambes écartés. ~**sheet** *n* tableur *m*.

**spree** /spri:/ *n* **go on a** ~ (have fun 🄸) faire la noce.

**sprig** /sprɪg/ *n* petite branche *f*.

**sprightly** /'spraɪtlɪ/ *a* (**-ier**, **-iest**) alerte, vif.

**spring** /sprɪŋ/ *vi* (*pt* **sprang**; *pp* **sprung**) bondir. ● *vt* ~ **sth on sb** annoncer qch de but en blanc à qn. ● *n* bond *m*; (device) ressort *m*; (season) printemps *m*; (of water) source *f*. □ ~ **from** provenir de; ~ **up** surgir. ~**board** *n* tremplin *m*. ~ **onion** *n* oignon *m* blanc.

**springy** /'sprɪŋɪ/ *a* (**-ier**, **-iest**) élastique.

**sprinkle** /'sprɪŋkl/ *vt* (with liquid) arroser (**with** de); (with salt, flour) saupoudrer (**with** de); (*sand*) répandre. **sprinkler** *n* (in garden) arroseur *m*; (for fires) extincteur *m* (à déclenchement) automatique.

**sprint** /sprɪnt/ *vi* (Sport) sprinter. ● *n* sprint *m*.

**sprout** /spraʊt/ *vt/i* pousser. ● *n* (on plant) pousse *f*; **(Brussels)** ~**s** choux *mpl* de Bruxelles.

**spruce** /spru:s/ *a* pimpant. ● *vt* ~ **oneself up** se faire beau. ● *n* (tree) épicéa *m*.

**sprung** /sprʌŋ/ ⇒SPRING.

**spud** /spʌd/ *n* 🄸 patate *f*.

**spun** /spʌn/ ⇒SPIN.

**spur** /spɜ:(r)/ *n* (of rider) éperon *m*; (stimulus) aiguillon *m*; **on the** ~ **of the moment** sous l'impulsion du moment. ● *vt* (*pt* **spurred**) éperonner.

**spurious** /'spjʊərɪəs/ *a* faux.

**spurn** /spɜ:n/ *vt* repousser.

**spurt** /spɜ:t/ *vi* jaillir; (fig) accélérer. ● *n* jet *m*; (of energy) sursaut *m*.

**spy** /spaɪ/ *n* espion/-ne *m/f*. ● *vi* espionner. ● *vt* apercevoir.

**squabble** /'skwɒbl/ *vi* se chamailler. ● *n* chamaillerie *f*.

**squad** /skwɒd/ *n* (of soldiers) escouade *f*; (Sport) équipe *f*.

**squadron** /'skwɒdrən/ *n* (Mil) escadron *m*; (Aviat) escadrille *f*.

**squalid** /'skwɒlɪd/ *a* sordide.

**squander** /'skwɒndə(r)/ *vt* (*money, time*) gaspiller.

**square** /skweə(r)/ *n* carré *m*; (open space in town) place *f*. ● *a* carré; (honest) honnête; (*meal*) solide; (boring 🄸) ringard; **(all)** ~ (quits) quitte;

~ **metre** mètre *m* carré. ● *vt* (settle) régler; ~ **up to** faire face à.

**squash** /skwɒʃ/ *vt* écraser; (crowd) serrer. ● *n* (game) squash *m*; (marrow: US) courge *f*; **lemon** ~ citronnade *f*; **orange** ~ orangeade *f*.

**squat** /skwɒt/ *vi* (*pt* **squatted**) s'accroupir; ~ **in a house** squatteriser une maison. ● *a* (dumpy) trapu. **squatter** *n* squatter *m*.

**squawk** /skwɔ:k/ *n* cri *m* rauque. ● *vi* pousser un cri rauque.

**squeak** /skwi:k/ *n* petit cri *m*; (of door) grincement *m*. ● *vi* crier; grincer.

**squeal** /skwi:l/ *n* cri *m* aigu. ● *vi* pousser un cri aigu. ~ **on** (inform on Ⓘ) dénoncer.

**squeamish** /'skwi:mɪʃ/ *a* (trop) délicat.

**squeeze** /skwi:z/ *vt* presser; (*hand, arm*) serrer; (extract) exprimer (**from** de); (extort) soutirer (**from** à). ● *vi* (force one's way) se glisser. ● *n* pression *f*; (Comm) restrictions *fpl* de crédit.

**squid** /skwɪd/ *n* calmar *m*.

**squint** /skwɪnt/ *vi* loucher; (with half-shut eyes) plisser les yeux. ● *n* (Med) strabisme *m*.

**squirm** /skwɜ:m/ *vi* se tortiller.

**squirrel** /'skwɪrəl/ *n* écureuil *m*.

**squirt** /skwɜ:t/ *vt/i* (faire) jaillir ● *n* jet *m*.

**stab** /stæb/ *vt* (*pt* **stabbed**) (with knife) poignarder. ● *n* coup *m* (de couteau), **have a** ~ **at sth** essayer de faire qch.

**stability** /stə'bɪlətɪ/ *n* stabilité *f*. **stabilize** *vt* stabiliser.

**stable** /'steɪbl/ *a* stable. ● *n* écurie *f*. ~**-boy** *n* lad *m*.

**stack** /stæk/ *n* tas *m*. ● *vt* ~ **(up)** entasser, empiler.

**stadium** /'steɪdɪəm/ *n* stade *m*.

**staff** /stɑ:f/ *n* personnel *m*; (in school) professeurs *mpl*; (Mil) état-major *m*; (stick) bâton *m*. ● *vt* pourvoir en personnel.

**stag** /stæg/ *n* cerf *m*.

**stage** /steɪdʒ/ *n* (Theat) scène *f*; (phase) stade *m*, étape *f*; (platform in hall) estrade *f*; **go on the** ~ faire du théâtre. ● *vt* mettre en scène; (fig) organiser. ~ **door** *n* entrée *f* des artistes. ~ **fright** *n* trac *m*.

**stagger** /'stægə(r)/ *vi* chanceler. ● *vt* (shock) stupéfier; (*payments*) échelonner. **staggering** *a* stupéfiant.

**stagnate** /stæg'neɪt/ *vi* stagner.

**stag night** *n* soirée *f* pour enterrer une vie de garçon.

**staid** /steɪd/ *a* sérieux.

**stain** /steɪn/ *vt* tacher; (*wood*) colorer. ● *n* tache *f*; (colouring) colorant *m*. **stained glass window** *n* vitrail *m*

**stainless steel** *n* acier *m* inoxydable.

**stain remover** *n* détachant *m*

**stair** /steə(r)/ *n* marche *f*; **the** ~**s** l'escalier *m*. ~**case**, ~**way** *n* escalier *m*.

**stake** /steɪk/ *n* (post) pieu *m*, (wager) enjeu *m*; **at** ~ en jeu. ● *vt* (*area*) jalonner; (*wager*) jouer; ~ **a claim to** revendiquer.

**stale** /steɪl/ *a* pas frais; (*bread*) rassis; (*smell*) de renfermé.

**stalk** /stɔ:k/ *n* (of plant) tige *f*. ● *vi* marcher de façon guindée. ● *vt* (*hunter*) chasser; (*murderer*) suivre.

**stall** /stɔ:l/ *n* (in stable) stalle *f*; (in market) éventaire *m*; ~**s** (Theat) orchestre *m*. ● *vt/i* (Auto) caler; ~ **(for time)** temporiser.

**stallion** /'stæljən/ *n* étalon *m*.

**stamina** /'stæmɪnə/ *n* résistance *f*.

**stammer** /ˈstæmə(r)/ *vt/i* bégayer. ● *n* bégaiement *m*.

**stamp** /stæmp/ *vt/i* ~ **(one's foot)** taper du pied. ● *vt* (*letter*) timbrer. ● *n* (for postage, marking) timbre *m*; (mark: fig) sceau *m*. □ ~ **out** supprimer. **~-collecting** *n* philatélie *f*.

**stampede** /stæmˈpiːd/ *n* fuite *f* désordonnée; (rush: fig) ruée *f*. ● *vi* s'enfuir en désordre; se ruer.

**stand** /stænd/ *vi* (*pt* **stood**) être *or* se tenir (debout); (rise) se lever; (be situated) se trouver; (Pol) être candidat (**for** à); ~ **in line** (US) faire la queue; ~ **to reason** être logique. ● *vt* mettre (debout); (tolerate) supporter; ~ **a chance** avoir une chance. ● *n* (stance) position *f*; (Mil) résistance *f*; (for lamp) support *m*; (at fair) stand *m*; (in street) kiosque *m*; (for spectators) tribune *f*; (Jur, US) barre *f*; **make a** ~ prendre position. □ ~ **back** reculer; ~ **by** *or* **around** ne rien faire; ~ **by** (be ready) se tenir prêt; (*promise, person*) rester fidèle à; ~ **down** se désister; ~ **for** représenter; 🄸 supporter; ~ **in for** remplacer; ~ **out** ressortir; ~ **up** se lever; ~ **up for** défendre; ~ **up to** résister à.

**standard** /ˈstændəd/ *n* norme *f*; (level) niveau *m* (voulu); (flag) étendard *m*; ~ **of living** niveau *m* de vie; **~s** (morals) principes *mpl*. ● *a* ordinaire.

**standard of living** *n* niveau *m* de vie.

**stand-by** /ˈstændbaɪ/ *a* de réserve. ● *n* **be a** ~ être de réserve.

**stand-in** /ˈstændɪn/ *n* remplaçant/-e *m/f*.

**standing** /ˈstændɪŋ/ *a* debout *inv*. ● *n* réputation *f*; (duration) durée *f*. ~ **order** *n* prélèvement *m* bancaire.

**standpoint** /ˈstændpɔɪnt/ *n* point *m* de vue.

**standstill** /ˈstændstɪl/ *n* **at a** ~ immobile; **bring/come to a** ~ (s')immobiliser.

**stank** /stæŋk/ ⇒STINK.

**staple** /ˈsteɪpl/ *n* agrafe *f*. ● *vt* agrafer. ● *a* principal, de base.

**stapler** *n* agrafeuse *f*.

**star** /stɑː(r)/ *n* étoile *f*; (person) vedette *f*. ● *vt* (*pt* **starred**) (*film*) avoir pour vedette. ● *vi* ~ **in** être la vedette de.

**starch** /stɑːtʃ/ *n* amidon *m*; (in food) fécule *f*. ● *vt* amidonner.

**stardom** /ˈstɑːdəm/ *n* célébrité *f*.

**stare** /steə(r)/ *vi* ~ **at** regarder fixement. ● *n* regard *m* fixe.

**starfish** /ˈstɑːfɪʃ/ *n* étoile *f* de mer.

**stark** /stɑːk/ *a* (desolate) désolé; (severe) austère; (utter) complet; (*fact*) brutal. ● *adv* complètement.

**starling** /ˈstɑːlɪŋ/ *n* étourneau *m*.

**start** /stɑːt/ *vt/i* commencer; (*machine*) (se) mettre en marche; (*fashion*) lancer; (cause) provoquer; (jump) sursauter; (of vehicle) démarrer; ~ **to do** commencer *or* se mettre à faire; **~ing tomorrow** à partir de demain. ● *n* commencement *m*, début *m*; (of race) départ *m*; (lead) avance *f*; (jump) sursaut *m*. □ ~ **off** commencer (**doing** par faire); ~ **out** partir; ~ **up** (*business*) lancer. **starter** *n* (Auto) démarreur *m*; (runner) partant *m*; (Culin) entrée *f*.

**starting point** *n* point *m* de départ.

**startle** /ˈstɑːtl/ *vt* (make jump) faire tressaillir; (shock) alarmer.

**starvation** /stɑːˈveɪʃn/ *n* faim *f*.

**starve** /stɑːv/ *vi* mourir de faim. ● *vt* affamer; (deprive) priver.

**stash** /stæʃ/ *vt* cacher.

**state** /steɪt/ *n* état *m*; (pomp) apparat *m*; **S~** État *m*; **the S~s** les États-Unis; **get into a ~** s'affoler. ● *a* d'État, de l'État; (*school*) public. ● *vt* affirmer (**that** que); (*views*) exprimer; (fix) fixer.

**stately** /ˈsteɪtlɪ/ *a* (**-ier**, **-iest**) majestueux. **~ home** *n* château *m*.

**statement** /ˈsteɪtmənt/ *n* déclaration *f*; (of account) relevé *m*.

**statesman** /ˈsteɪtsmən/ *n* (*pl* **-men**) homme *m* d'État.

**static** /ˈstætɪk/ *a* statique. ● *n* (radio, TV) parasites *mpl*.

**station** /ˈsteɪʃn/ *n* (Rail) gare *f*; (TV) chaîne *f*; (Mil) poste *m*; (rank) condition *f*. ● *vt* poster, placer; **~ed at** *or* **in** (Mil) en garnison à.

**stationary** /ˈsteɪʃənrɪ/ *a* immobile, stationnaire; (*vehicle*) à l'arrêt.

**stationery** /ˈsteɪʃnərɪ/ *n* papeterie *f*.

**station wagon** *n* (US) break *m*.

**statistic** /stəˈtɪstɪk/ *n* statistique *f*; **~s** statistique *f*.

**statue** /ˈstætʃu:/ *n* statue *f*.

**status** /ˈsteɪtəs/ *n* (*pl* **~es**) situation *f*, statut *m*; (prestige) standing *m*.

**statute** /ˈstætʃu:t/ *n* loi *f*; **~s** (rules) statuts *mpl*. **statutory** *a* statutaire; (*holiday*) légal.

**staunch** /stɔ:ntʃ/ *a* loyal, fidèle.

**stave** /steɪv/ *n* (Mus) portée *f*. ● *vt* **~ off** écarter, conjurer.

**stay** /steɪ/ *vi* rester; (spend time) séjourner; (reside) loger. ● *vt* (*hunger*) tromper. ● *n* séjour *m*. □ **~ away from** (*school*) ne pas aller à; **~ behind** *or* **~ on** rester; **~ in** rester à la maison; **~ up** veiller, se coucher tard.

**stead** /sted/ *n* **stand sb in good ~** être utile à qn.

**steadfast** /ˈstedfɑ:st/ *a* ferme.

**steady** /ˈstedɪ/ *a* (**-ier**, **-iest**) stable; (*hand, voice*) ferme; (regular) régulier; (staid) sérieux. ● *vt* maintenir, assurer; (calm) calmer.

**steak** /steɪk/ *n* steak *m*, bifteck *m*; (of fish) darne *f*.

**steal** /sti:l/ *vt*/*i* (*pt* **stole**; *pp* **stolen**) voler (**from sb** à qn).

**steam** /sti:m/ *n* vapeur *f*; (on glass) buée *f*. ● *vt* (cook) cuire à la vapeur. ● *vi* fumer. **~-engine** *n* locomotive *f* à vapeur

**steamer** /ˈsti:mə(r)/ *n* (Culin) cuit-vapeur *m*; (boat) (bateau à) vapeur *m*.

**steel** /sti:l/ *n* acier *m*; **~ industry** sidérurgie *f*. ● *vpr* **~ oneself** s'endurcir, se cuirasser.

**steep** /sti:p/ *a* raide, rapide; (*price*: [I]) excessif. ● *vt* (soak) tremper; **~ed in** (fig) imprégné de.

**steeple** /ˈsti:pl/ *n* clocher *m*.

**steer** /stɪə(r)/ *vt* diriger; (*ship*) gouverner; (fig) guider. ● *vi* (in ship) gouverner; **~ clear of** éviter.

**steering-wheel** *n* volant *m*.

**stem** /stem/ *n* tige *f*; (of glass) pied *m*. ● *vi* (*pt* **stemmed**) **~ from** provenir de. ● *vt* (*pt* **stemmed**) (check, stop) endiguer, contenir. **~ cell** *n* cellule *f* souche.

**stench** /stentʃ/ *n* puanteur *f*.

**stencil** /ˈstensl/ *n* pochoir *m*. ● *vt* (*pt* **stencilled**) décorer au pochoir.

**step** /step/ *vi* (*pt* **stepped**) marcher, aller. ● *n* pas *m*; (stair) marche *f*; (of train) marchepied *m*; (action) mesure *f*; **~s** (ladder) escabeau *m*; **in ~** au pas; (fig) conforme (**with** à). □ **~ down** (resign) démissionner; (from ladder) descendre; **~ forward** faire un pas en avant; **~ in** (intervene) intervenir; **~ up** (pressure)

augmenter. **~brother** *n* demi-frère *m*. **~daughter** *n* belle-fille *f*. **~father** *n* beau-père *m*. **~-ladder** *n* escabeau *m*. **~mother** *n* belle-mère *f*. **stepping-stone** *n* (fig) tremplin *m*. **~sister** *n* demi-sœur *f*. **~son** *n* beau-fils *m*.

**stereo** /'sterɪəʊ/ *n* stéréo *f*; (record-player) chaîne *f* stéréo. ● *a* stéréo *inv*.

**stereotype** /'sterɪətaɪp/ *n* stéréotype *m*. **stereotyped** *a* stéréotypé.

**sterile** /'steraɪl, US 'sterəl/ *a* stérile. **sterility** *n* stérilité *f*.

**sterilize** /'sterəlaɪz/ *vt* stériliser.

**sterling** /'stɜ:lɪŋ/ *n* livre(s) *f(pl)* sterling. ● *a* sterling *inv*; (*silver*) fin; (fig) excellent.

**stern** /stɜ:n/ *a* sévère. ● *n* (of ship) arrière *m*.

**steroid** /'sterɔɪd/ *n* stéroïde *m*.

**stew** /stju:/ *vt/i* cuire à la casserole; **~ed fruit** compote *f*; **~ed tea** thé *m* trop infusé. ● *n* ragoût *m*.

**steward** /'stjʊəd/ *n* (of club) intendant *m*; (on ship) steward *m*. **stewardess** *n* hôtesse *f*.

**stick** /stɪk/ *vt* (*pt* **stuck**) (glue) coller; (put Ⓘ) mettre; (endure Ⓘ) supporter. ● *vi* (adhere) coller, adhérer; (to pan) attacher; (remain Ⓘ) rester; (be jammed) être coincé; **be stuck with sb** Ⓘ se farcir qn. ● *n* bâton *m*; (for walking) canne *f*. □ **~ at** persévérer dans; **~ out** *vt* (*head*) sortir; (*tongue*) tirer; *vi* (protrude) dépasser; **~ to** (*promise*) rester fidèle à; **~ up for** Ⓘ défendre.

**sticker** /'stɪkə(r)/ *n* autocollant *m*.

**sticky** /'stɪkɪ/ *a* (**-ier**, **-iest**) poisseux; (*label, tape*) adhésif.

**stiff** /stɪf/ *a* raide; (*limb, joint*) ankylosé; (tough) dur; (*drink*) fort; (*price*) élevé; (*manner*) guindé; **~ neck** torticolis *m*.

**stifle** /'staɪfl/ *vt/i* étouffer.

**stiletto** /stɪ'letəʊ/ *a* & *n* **~s**, **~ heels** talons *mpl* aiguille.

**still** /stɪl/ *a* immobile; (quiet) calme, tranquille; **keep ~!** arrête de bouger! ● *n* silence *m*. ● *adv* encore, toujours; (even) encore; (nevertheless) tout de même.

**stillborn** /'stɪlbɔ:n/ *a* mort-né.

**still life** *n* nature *f* morte.

**stimulate** /'stɪmjʊleɪt/ *vt* stimuler. **stimulation** *n* stimulation *f*.

**stimulus** /'stɪmjʊləs/ *n* (*pl* **-li** /-laɪ/) (spur) stimulant *m*.

**sting** /stɪŋ/ *n* piqûre *f*; (of insect) aiguillon *m*. ● *vt/i* (*pt* **stung**) piquer.

**stingy** /'stɪndʒɪ/ *a* (**-ier**, **-iest**) avare (**with** de).

**stink** /stɪŋk/ *n* puanteur *f*. ● *vi* (*pt* **stank** *or* **stunk**; *pp* **stunk**) **~ (of)** puer.

**stipulate** /'stɪpjʊleɪt/ *vt* stipuler.

**stir** /stɜ:(r)/ *vt/i* (*pt* **stirred**) (move) remuer; (excite) exciter; **~ up** (*trouble*) provoquer. ● *n* agitation *f*.

**stirrup** /'stɪrəp/ *n* étrier *m*.

**stitch** /stɪtʃ/ *n* point *m*; (in knitting) maille *f*; (Med) point *m* de suture; (muscle pain) point *m* de côté; **be in ~es** Ⓘ avoir le fou rire. ● *vt* coudre.

**stock** /stɒk/ *n* réserve *f*; (Comm) stock *m*; (financial) valeurs *fpl*; (family) souche *f*; (soup) bouillon *m*; **we're out of ~** il n'y en a plus; **take ~** (fig) faire le point; **in ~** en stock. ● *a* (goods) courant. ● *vt* (*shop*) approvisionner; (sell) vendre. ● *vi* **~ up** s'approvisionner (**with** de). **~ broker** *n* agent *m* de change. **~ cube** *n* bouillon-cube *m*. **S~ Exchange** *n* Bourse *f*.

**stocking** /'stɒkɪŋ/ *n* bas *m*.

**stock market** *n* Bourse *f*.

**stockpile** /'stɒkpaɪl/ *n* stock *m*. ● *vt* stocker; (*arms*) amasser.

**stock-taking** *n* (Comm) inventaire *m*.

**stocky** /'stɒkɪ/ *a* (**-ier**, **-iest**) trapu.

**stodgy** /'stɒdʒɪ/ *a* lourd.

**stole**, **stolen** /stəʊl, 'stəʊlən/ ⇒STEAL.

**stomach** /'stʌmək/ *n* estomac *m*; (abdomen) ventre *m*. ● *vt* (put up with) supporter. **~-ache** *n* mal *m* à l'estomac *or* au ventre.

**stone** /stəʊn/ *n* pierre *f*; (pebble) caillou *m*; (in fruit) noyau *m*; (weight) 6,350 kg. ● *a* de pierre; **~-cold/-deaf** complètement froid/sourd. ● *vt* (throw stones) lapider; (*fruit*) dénoyauter.

**stony** /'stəʊnɪ/ *a* pierreux.

**stood** /stʊd/ ⇒STAND.

**stool** /stu:l/ *n* tabouret *m*.

**stoop** /stu:p/ *vi* (bend) se baisser; (condescend) s'abaisser. ● *n* **have a ~** être voûté.

**stop** /stɒp/ *vt*/*i* (*pt* **stopped**) arrêter (**doing** de faire), (*moving, talking*) s'arrêter; (prevent) empêcher (**from** de); (*hole, leak*) boucher; (*pain, noise*) cesser; (stay 🅸) rester. ● *n* arrêt *m*; (full stop) point *m*; **~(-over)** halte *f*; (port of call) escale *f*. □ **~ off** s'arrêter; **~ up** boucher.

**stopgap** /'stɒpgæp/ *n* bouche-trou *m*. ● *a* intérimaire.

**stoppage** /'stɒpɪdʒ/ *n* arrêt *m*; (of work) arrêt *m* de travail; (of pay) retenue *f*.

**stopper** /'stɒpə(r)/ *n* bouchon *m*.

**stop-watch** *n* chronomètre *m*.

**storage** /'stɔ:rɪdʒ/ *n* (of goods, food) emmagasinage *m*. **~ heater** *n* radiateur *m* électrique à accumulation.

**store** /stɔ:(r)/ *n* réserve *f*; (warehouse) entrepôt *m*; (shop) grand magasin *m*; (US) magasin *m*; **have in ~ for** réserver à; **set ~ by** attacher du prix à. ● *vt* (for future) mettre en réserve; (in warehouse, mind) emmagasiner. **~-room** *n* réserve *f*.

**storey** /'stɔ:rɪ/ *n* étage *m*.

**stork** /stɔ:k/ *n* cigogne *f*.

**storm** /stɔ:m/ *n* tempête *f*, orage *m*. ● *vt* prendre d'assaut. ● *vi* (rage) tempêter.

**story** /'stɔ:rɪ/ *n* histoire *f*; (in press) article *m*; (storey: US) étage *m*. **~-teller** *n* conteur/-euse *m*/*f*.

**stout** /staʊt/ *a* corpulent; (strong) solide. ● *n* bière *f* brune.

**stove** /stəʊv/ *n* cuisinière *f*.

**stow** /stəʊ/ *vt* **~ away** (put away) ranger; (hide) cacher. ● *vi* voyager clandestinement.

**straddle** /'strædl/ *vt* être à cheval sur, enjamber.

**straggler** /'stræglə(r)/ *n* traînard/-e *m*/*f*.

**straight** /streɪt/ *a* droit; (tidy) en ordre; (frank) franc; **~ face** visage *m* sérieux; **get sth ~** mettre qch au clair. ● *adv* (in straight line) droit; (direct) tout droit; **~ ahead** *or* **on** tout droit; **~ away** tout de suite; **~ off** 🅸 sans hésiter. ● *n* (Sport) ligne *f* droite.

**straighten** /'streɪtn/ *vt* (*nail, situation*) redresser; (tidy) arranger.

**straightforward** /streɪt'fɔ:wəd/ *a* honnête; (easy) simple.

**straight off** *a* 🅸 sans hésiter.

**strain** /streɪn/ *vt* (*rope, ears*) tendre; (*limb*) fouler; (*eyes*) fatiguer; (*muscle*) froisser; (filter) passer; (*vegetables*) égoutter; (fig) mettre à l'épreuve. ● *vi* fournir des efforts. ● *n* tension *f*; (fig) effort *m*; (breed) race *f*; (of virus) variété *f*; **~s**

(tune: Mus) accents *mpl.* **strained** *a* forcé; (*relations*) tendu. **strainer** *n* passoire *f.*

**strait** /streɪt/ *n* détroit *m*; **~s** détroit *m*; **be in dire ~s** être aux abois. **~-jacket** *n* camisole *f* de force.

**strand** /strænd/ *n* (thread) fil *m*, brin *m*; (of hair) mèche *f.*

**stranded** /'strændɪd/ *a* (*person*) en rade; (*ship*) échoué.

**strange** /streɪndʒ/ *a* étrange; (unknown) inconnu. **stranger** *n* inconnu/-e *m/f.*

**strangle** /'stræŋgl/ *vt* étrangler.

**stranglehold** /'stræŋglhəʊld/ *n* **have a ~ on** tenir à la gorge.

**strap** /stræp/ *n* (of leather) courroie *f*; (of dress) bretelle *f*; (of watch) bracelet *m*. ● *vt* (*pt* **strapped**) attacher.

**strategic** /strə'ti:dʒɪk/ *a* stratégique. **strategy** *n* stratégie *f.*

**straw** /strɔ:/ *n* paille *f*; **the last ~** le comble.

**strawberry** /'strɔ:brɪ/ *n* fraise *f.*

**stray** /streɪ/ *vi* s'égarer; (deviate) s'écarter. ● *a* perdu; (isolated) isolé. ● *n* animal *m* perdu.

**streak** /stri:k/ *n* raie *f*, bande *f*; (trace) trace *f*; (period) période *f*; (tendency) tendance *f*. ● *vt* (mark) strier. ● *vi* filer à toute allure.

**stream** /stri:m/ *n* ruisseau *m*; (current) courant *m*; (flow) flot *m*; (in school) classe *f* (de niveau). ● *vi* ruisseler (**with** de); (*eyes, nose*) couler.

**streamline** /'stri:mlaɪn/ *vt* rationaliser. **streamlined** *a* (*shape*) aérodynamique.

**street** /stri:t/ *n* rue *f*. **~car** *n* (US) tramway *m*. **~ lamp** *n* réverbère *m*. **~ map** *n* indicateur *m* des rues.

**strength** /streŋθ/ *n* force *f*; (of wall, fabric) solidité *f*; **on the ~ of** en vertu de. **strengthen** *vt* renforcer, fortifier.

**strenuous** /'strenjʊəs/ *a* (*exercise*) énergique; (*work*) ardu.

**stress** /stres/ *n* (emphasis) accent *m*; (pressure) pression *f*; (Med) stress *m*. ● *vt* souligner, insister sur.

**stretch** /stretʃ/ *vt* (pull taut) tendre; (*arm, leg*) étendre; (*neck*) tendre; (*clothes*) étirer; (*truth*) forcer; **~ one's legs** se dégourdir les jambes. ● *vi* s'étendre; (*person*) s'étirer; (*clothes*) se déformer. ● *n* étendue *f*; (period) période *f*; (of road) tronçon *m*; **at a ~** d'affilée. ● *a* (*fabric*) extensible.

**stretcher** /'stretʃə(r)/ *n* brancard *m*.

**strew** /stru:/ *vt* (*pt* **strewed**; *pp* **strewed** *or* **strewn**) (scatter) répandre; (cover) joncher.

**strict** /strɪkt/ *a* strict.

**stride** /straɪd/ *vi* (*pt* **strode**; *pp* **stridden**) faire de grands pas. ● *n* grand pas *m*.

**strife** /straɪf/ *n* conflit(s) *m(pl)*.

**strike** /straɪk/ *vt* (*pt* **struck**) frapper; (*blow*) donner; (*match*) frotter; (*gold*) trouver. ● *vi* faire grève; (attack) attaquer; (*clock*) sonner. ● *n* (of workers) grève *f*; (Mil) attaque *f*; (find) découverte *f*; **on ~** en grève. □ **~ off** *or* **out** rayer; **~ up** (*a friendship*) lier amitié (**with** avec). **striker** *n* gréviste *mf*; (football) attaquant/-e *m/f*. **striking** *a* frappant.

**string** /strɪŋ/ *n* ficelle *f*; (of violin, racket) corde *f*; (of pearls) collier *m*; (of lies) chapelet *m*; **the ~s** (Mus) les cordes; **pull ~s** faire jouer ses relations. ● *vt* (*pt* **strung**) (thread) enfiler. **stringed** *a* (*instrument*) à cordes.

**stringent** /ˈstrɪndʒənt/ *a* rigoureux, strict.

**stringy** /ˈstrɪŋɪ/ *a* filandreux.

**strip** /strɪp/ *vt/i* (*pt* **stripped**) (undress) (se) déshabiller; (deprive) dépouiller. ● *n* bande *f*.

**stripe** /straɪp/ *n* rayure *f*, raie *f*. **striped** *a* rayé.

**strip light** *n* néon *m*.

**stripper** /ˈstrɪpə(r)/ *n* strip-teaseur/-euse *m/f*; (solvent) décapant .

**strip-tease** *n* strip-tease *m*.

**strive** /straɪv/ *vi* (*pt* **strove**; *pp* **striven**) s'efforcer (**to** de).

**strode** /strəʊd/ ⇒STRIDE.

**stroke** /strəʊk/ *vt* (with hand) caresser. ● *n* coup *m*; (of pen) trait *m*; (swimming) nage *f*; (Med) attaque *f*, congestion *f*; **at a ~** d'un seul coup

**stroll** /strəʊl/ *vi* flâner; **~ in** entrer tranquillement. ● *n* petit tour *m*. **stroller** *n* (US) poussette *f*.

**strong** /strɒŋ/ *a* fort; (*shoes, fabric*) solide; **be fifty ~** être fort de cinquante personnes. **~hold** *n* bastion *m*.

**strongly** /ˈstrɒŋlɪ/ *adv* (greatly) fortement; (with energy) avec force; (deeply) profondément.

**strove** /strəʊv/ ⇒STRIVE.

**struck** /strʌk/ ⇒STRIKE.

**structure** /ˈstrʌktʃə(r)/ *n* (of cell, poem) structure *f*; (building) construction *f*.

**struggle** /ˈstrʌgl/ *vi* lutter, se battre. ● *n* lutte *f*; (effort) effort *m*; **have a ~ to** avoir du mal à.

**strum** /strʌm/ *vt* (*pt* **strummed**) gratter de.

**strung** /strʌŋ/ ⇒STRING. ● *a* **~ up** (tense) nerveux.

**strut** /strʌt/ *n* (support) étai *m*. ● *vi* (*pt* **strutted**) se pavaner.

**stub** /stʌb/ *n* bout *m*; (counterfoil) talon *m*. ● *vt* (*pt* **stubbed**) **~ one's toe** se cogner le doigt de pied. □ **~ out** écraser.

**stubble** /ˈstʌbl/ *n* (on chin) barbe *f* de plusieurs jours; (remains of wheat) chaume *m*.

**stubborn** /ˈstʌbən/ *a* obstiné.

**stuck** /stʌk/ ⇒STICK. ● *a* (jammed) coincé; **I'm ~** (for answer) je sèche. **~-up** *a* 🄸 prétentieux.

**stud** /stʌd/ *n* (on jacket) clou *m*; (for collar) bouton *m*; (stallion) étalon *m*; (horse farm) haras *m*. ● *vt* (*pt* **studded**) clouter.

**student** /ˈstju:dnt/ *n* (Univ) étudiant/-e *m/f*; (School) élève *mf*. ● *a* (*restaurant, life*) universitaire.

**studio** /ˈstju:dɪəʊ/ *n* studio *m*.

**studious** /ˈstju:dɪəs/ *a* (*person*) studieux; (deliberate) étudié.

**study** /ˈstʌdɪ/ *n* étude *f*; (office) bureau *m*. ● *vt/i* étudier.

**stuff** /stʌf/ *n* substance *f*; 🄸 chose(s) *f(pl)*. ● *vt* rembourrer; (*animal*) empailler; (cram) bourrer; (Culin) farcir; (block up) boucher; (put) fourrer. **stuffing** *n* bourre *f*; (Culin) farce *f*.

**stuffy** /ˈstʌfɪ/ *a* (**-ier**, **-iest**) mal aéré; (dull 🄸) vieux jeu *inv*.

**stumble** /ˈstʌmbl/ *vi* trébucher; **~ across** *or* **on** tomber sur. **stumbling-block** *n* obstacle *m*.

**stump** /stʌmp/ *n* (of tree) souche *f*; (of limb) moignon *m*; (of pencil) bout *m*.

**stumped** /stʌmpt/ *a* embarrassé.

**stun** /stʌn/ *vt* (*pt* **stunned**) étourdir; (bewilder) stupéfier.

**stung** /stʌŋ/ ⇒STING.

**stunk** /stʌŋk/ ⇒STINK.

**stunning** /ˈstʌnɪŋ/ *a* (delightful 🄸) sensationnel.

**stunt** /stʌnt/ *vt* (*growth*) retarder. ● *n* (feat 🄸) tour *m* de force; (trick 🄸) truc *m*; (dangerous) cascade *f*.

**stupid** /'stju:pɪd/ *a* stupide, bête. **stupidity** *n* stupidité *f*.

**sturdy** /'stɜ:dɪ/ *a* (**-ier**, **-iest**) robuste.

**stutter** /'stʌtə(r)/ *vi* bégayer. ● *n* bégaiement *m*.

**sty** /staɪ/ *n* (pigsty) porcherie *f*; (on eye) orgelet *m*.

**style** /staɪl/ *n* style *m*; (fashion) mode *f*; (sort) genre *m*; (pattern) modèle *m*; **do sth in ~** faire qch avec classe. ● *vt* (design) créer; **~ sb's hair** coiffer qn.

**stylish** /'staɪlɪʃ/ *a* élégant.

**stylist** /'staɪlɪst/ *n* (of hair) coiffeur/-euse *m*/*f*.

**suave** /swɑ:v/ *a* (urbane) courtois; (smooth: pej) doucereux.

**subconscious** /sʌb'kɒnʃəs/ *a* & *n* inconscient (*m*), subconscient (*m*).

**subcontract** /sʌbkən'trækt/ *vt* sous-traiter.

**subdue** /səb'dju:/ *vt* (*feeling*) maîtriser; (*country*) subjuguer. **subdued** *a* (*person, mood*) morose; (*light*) tamisé; (*criticism*) contenu.

**subject**[1] /'sʌbdʒɪkt/ *a* (*state*) soumis; **~ to** soumis à; (liable to, dependent on) sujet à. ● *n* sujet *m*; (focus) objet *m*; (School, Univ) matière *f*; (citizen) ressortissant/-e *m*/*f*, sujet/-te *m*/*f*.

**subject**[2] /səb'dʒekt/ *vt* soumettre.

**subjective** /səb'dʒektɪv/ *a* subjectif.

**subject-matter** *n* contenu *m*.

**subjunctive** /səb'dʒʌŋktɪv/ *a* & *n* subjonctif (*m*).

**sublet** /sʌb'let/ *vt* sous-louer.

**submarine** /sʌbmə'ri:n/ *n* sous-marin *m*.

**submerge** /səb'mɜ:dʒ/ *vt* submerger. ● *vi* plonger.

**submissive** /səb'mɪsɪv/ *a* soumis.

**submit** /səb'mɪt/ *vt*/*i* (*pt* **submitted**) (se) soumettre (**to** à).

**subordinate** /sə'bɔ:dɪnət/ *a* subalterne; (Gram) subordonné. ● *n* subordonné/-e *m*/*f*.

**subpoena** /səb'pi:nə/ *n* (Jur) citation *f*, assignation *f*.

**subscribe** /səb'skraɪb/ *vt*/*i* verser (de l'argent) (**to** à); **~ to** (*loan, theory*) souscrire à; (*newspaper*) s'abonner à, être abonné à. **subscriber** *n* abonné/-e *m*/*f*. **subscription** *n* abonnement *m*; (membership dues) cotisation *f*.

**subsequent** /'sʌbsɪkwənt/ *a* (later) ultérieur; (next) suivant. **subsequently** *adv* par la suite.

**subside** /səb'saɪd/ *vi* (*land*) s'affaisser; (*flood, wind*) baisser.

**subsidiary** /səb'sɪdɪərɪ/ *a* accessoire. ● *n* (Comm) filiale *f*.

**subsidize** /'sʌbsɪdaɪz/ *vt* subventionner. **subsidy** *n* subvention *f*.

**substance** /'sʌbstəns/ *n* substance *f*.

**substandard** /sʌb'stændəd/ *a* de qualité inférieure.

**substantial** /səb'stænʃl/ *a* considérable; (*meal*) substantiel.

**substitute** /'sʌbstɪtju:t/ *n* succédané *m*; (person) remplaçant/-e *m*/*f*. ● *vt* substituer (**for** à).

**subtitle** /'sʌbtaɪtl/ *n* sous-titre *m*.

**subtle** /'sʌtl/ *a* subtil.

**subtract** /səb'trækt/ *vt* soustraire.

**suburb** /'sʌbɜ:b/ *n* faubourg *m*, banlieue *f*; **~s** banlieue *f*. **suburban** *a* de banlieue. **suburbia** *n* la banlieue.

**subway** /'sʌbweɪ/ *n* passage *m* souterrain; (US) métro *m*.

**succeed** /sək'si:d/ *vi* réussir (**in doing** à faire). ● *vt* (follow) succéder à.

**success** /sək'ses/ *n* succès *m*, réussite *f*.

**successful** /sək'sesfl/ *a* réussi, couronné de succès; (favourable) heureux; (in exam) reçu; **be ~ in doing** réussir à faire.

**succession** /sək'seʃn/ *n* succession *f*; **in ~** de suite.

**successive** /sək'sesɪv/ *a* successif; **six ~ days** six jours consécutifs.

**successor** /sək'sesə(r)/ *n* successeur *m*.

**such** /sʌtʃ/ *det & pron* tel(le), tel(le)s; (so much) tant (de). ● *adv* si; **~ a book** un tel livre; **~ books** de tels livres; **~ courage** tant de courage; **~ a big house** une si grande maison; **~ as** comme, tel que; **as ~** en tant que tel; **there's no ~ thing** ça n'existe pas. **~-and-~** *a* tel ou tel.

**suck** /sʌk/ *vt* sucer. □ **~ in** *or* **up** aspirer. **sucker** *n* (rubber pad) ventouse *f*; (person ⊡) dupe *f*.

**suction** /'sʌkʃn/ *n* succion *f*.

**sudden** /'sʌdn/ *a* soudain, subit; **all of a ~** tout à coup. **suddenly** *adv* subitement, brusquement.

**sue** /su:/ *vt* (*pres p* **suing**) poursuivre (en justice).

**suede** /sweɪd/ *n* daim *m*.

**suffer** /'sʌfə(r)/ *vt/i* souffrir; (*loss, attack*) subir. **sufferer** *n* victime *f*, malade *mf*. **suffering** *n* souffrance(s) *f(pl)*.

**sufficient** /sə'fɪʃnt/ *a* (enough) suffisamment de; (big enough) suffisant.

**suffix** /'sʌfɪks/ *n* suffixe *m*.

**suffocate** /'sʌfəkeɪt/ *vt/i* suffoquer.

**sugar** /'ʃʊgə(r)/ *n* sucre *m*. ● *vt* sucrer.

**suggest** /sə'dʒest/ *vt* suggérer. **suggestion** *n* suggestion *f*.

**suicidal** /su:ɪ'saɪdl/ *a* suicidaire.

**suicide** /'su:ɪsaɪd/ *n* suicide *m*; **commit ~** se suicider.

**suit** /su:t/ *n* (man's) costume *m*; (woman's) tailleur *m*; (cards) couleur *f*. ● *vt* convenir à; (*garment, style*) aller à; (adapt) adapter.

**suitable** /'su:təbl/ *a* qui convient (**for** à), convenable. **suitably** *adv* convenablement.

**suitcase** /'su:tkeɪs/ *n* valise *f*.

**suite** /swi:t/ *n* (rooms) suite *f*; (furniture) mobilier *m*.

**suited** /'su:tɪd/ *a* **(well) ~** (matched) bien assorti; **~ to** fait pour, apte à.

**sulk** /sʌlk/ *vi* bouder.

**sullen** /'sʌlən/ *a* maussade.

**sultana** /sʌl'tɑ:nə/ *n* raisin *m* de Smyrne, raisin *m* sec.

**sultry** /'sʌltrɪ/ *a* (**-ier, -iest**) étouffant, lourd; (fig) sensuel.

**sum** /sʌm/ *n* somme *f*; (in arithmetic) calcul *m*. ● *vt/i* (*pt* **summed**) **~ up** résumer, récapituler; (assess) évaluer.

**summarize** /'sʌməraɪz/ *vt* résumer.

**summary** /'sʌmərɪ/ *n* résumé *m*. ● *a* sommaire.

**summer** /'sʌmə(r)/ *n* été *m*. ● *a* d'été. **~time** *n* (season) été *m*.

**summery** /'sʌmərɪ/ *a* estival.

**summit** /'sʌmɪt/ *n* sommet *m*; **~ (conference)** (Pol) (conférence *f* au) sommet *m*.

**summon** /'sʌmən/ *vt* appeler; **~ sb to a meeting** convoquer qn à une réunion; **~ up** (*strength, courage*) rassembler.

**summons** /'sʌmənz/ *n* (Jur) assignation *f*. ● *vt* assigner.

**sun** /sʌn/ *n* soleil *m*. ● *vt* (*pt* **sunned**) **~ oneself** se chauffer au soleil. **~burn** *n* coup *m* de soleil.

**Sunday** /'sʌndɪ/ *n* dimanche *m*. **~ school** *n* catéchisme *m*.

**sundry** /ˈsʌndrɪ/ *a* divers; **sundries** articles *mpl* divers; **all and ~** tout le monde.

**sunflower** /ˈsʌnflaʊə(r)/ *n* tournesol *m*.

**sung** /sʌŋ/ ⇒SING.

**sun-glasses** *npl* lunettes *fpl* de soleil.

**sunk** /sʌŋk/ ⇒SINK.

**sunken** /ˈsʌŋkən/ *a* (*ship*) submergé; (*eyes*) creux.

**sunlight** /ˈsʌnlaɪt/ *n* soleil *m*.

**sunny** /ˈsʌnɪ/ *a* (**-ier**, **-iest**) ensoleillé.

**sun**: **~rise** *n* lever *m* du soleil. **~-roof** *n* toit *m* ouvrant. **~screen** *n* filtre *m* solaire. **~set** *n* coucher *m* du soleil. **~shine** *n* soleil *m*. **~stroke** *n* insolation *f*.

**sun-tan** /ˈsʌntæn/ *n* bronzage *m*. **~ lotion** *n* lotion *f* solaire. **~ oil** *n* huile *f* solaire.

**super** /ˈsu:pə(r)/ *a* [I] formidable.

**superb** /su:ˈpɜ:b/ *a* superbe.

**superficial** /su:pəˈfɪʃl/ *a* superficiel.

**superfluous** /su:ˈpɜ:flʊəs/ *a* superflu.

**superimpose** /su:pərɪmˈpəʊz/ *vt* superposer (**on** à).

**superintendent** /su:pərɪnˈtendənt/ *n* directeur/-trice *m/f*; (of police) commissaire *m*.

**superior** /su:ˈpɪərɪə(r)/ *a* & *n* supérieur/-e (*m/f*).

**superlative** /su:ˈpɜ:lətɪv/ *a* suprême. ● *n* (Gram) superlatif *m*.

**supermarket** /ˈsu:pəmɑ:kɪt/ *n* supermarché *m*.

**supersede** /su:pəˈsi:d/ *vt* remplacer, supplanter.

**superstition** /su:pəˈstɪʃn/ *n* superstition *f*. **superstitious** *a* superstitieux.

**superstore** /ˈsu:pəstɔ:(r)/ *n* hypermarché *m*.

**supervise** /ˈsu:pəvaɪz/ *vt* surveiller, diriger. **supervision** *n* surveillance *f*. **supervisor** *n* surveillant/-e *m/f*; (shop) chef *m* de rayon; (firm) chef *m* de service.

**supper** /ˈsʌpə(r)/ *n* dîner *m*; (late at night) souper *m*.

**supple** /ˈsʌpl/ *a* souple.

**supplement¹** /ˈsʌplɪmənt/ *n* supplément *m*. **supplementary** *a* supplémentaire.

**supplement²** /ˈsʌplɪment/ *vt* compléter.

**supplier** /səˈplaɪə(r)/ *n* fournisseur *m*.

**supply** /səˈplaɪ/ *vt* fournir; (equip) pourvoir; (feed) alimenter (**with** en). ● *n* provision *f*; (of gas) alimentation *f*; **supplies** (food) vivres *mpl*; (material) fournitures *fpl*.

**support** /səˈpɔ:t/ *vt* soutenir; (*family*) assurer la subsistance de. ● *n* soutien *m*, appui *m*; (Tech) support *m*. **supporter** *n* partisan/-e *m/f*; (Sport) supporter *m*. **supportive** *a* qui soutient et encourage.

**suppose** /səˈpəʊz/ *vt/i* supposer; **be ~d to do** être censé faire, devoir faire; **supposing he comes** supposons qu'il vienne. **supposedly** *adv* soi-disant, prétendument.

**suppress** /səˈpres/ *vt* (put an end to) supprimer; (restrain) réprimer; (stifle) étouffer.

**supreme** /su:ˈpri:m/ *a* suprême.

**surcharge** /ˈsɜ:tʃɑ:dʒ/ *n* supplément *m*; (tax) surtaxe *f*.

**sure** /ʃɔ:(r)/ *a* sûr; **make ~ of** s'assurer de; **make ~ that** vérifier que. ● *adv* (US [I]) pour sûr. **surely** *adv* sûrement.

**surf** /sɜ:f/ *n* ressac *m*. ● *vi* faire du surf; (*Internet*) surfer.

**surface** /ˈsɜːfɪs/ *n* surface *f*. ● *a* superficiel. ● *vt* revêtir. ● *vi* faire surface; (fig) réapparaître.

**surfer** /ˈsɜːfə(r)/ *n* surfeur/-euse *m/f*; (*Internet*) internaute *mf*.

**surge** /sɜːdʒ/ *vi* (*waves, crowd*) déferler; (increase) monter. ● *n* (wave) vague *f*; (rise) montée *f*.

**surgeon** /ˈsɜːdʒən/ *n* chirurgien *m*.

**surgery** /ˈsɜːdʒərɪ/ *n* chirurgie *f*; (office) cabinet *m*; (session) consultation *f*; **need ~** devoir être opéré.

**surgical** /ˈsɜːdʒɪkl/ *a* chirurgical. **~ spirit** *n* alcool *m* à 90 degrés.

**surly** /ˈsɜːlɪ/ *a* (**-ier**, **-iest**) bourru.

**surname** /ˈsɜːneɪm/ *n* nom *m* de famille.

**surplus** /ˈsɜːpləs/ *n* surplus *m*. ● *a* en surplus.

**surprise** /səˈpraɪz/ *n* surprise *f*. ● *vt* surprendre. **surprised** *a* surpris (at de). **surprising** *a* surprenant.

**surrender** /səˈrendə(r)/ *vi* se rendre. ● *vt* (hand over) remettre; (Mil) rendre. ● *n* (Mil) reddition *f*; (of passport) remise *f*.

**surround** /səˈraʊnd/ *vt* entourer; (Mil) encercler. **surrounding** *a* environnant. **surroundings** *npl* environs *mpl*; (setting) cadre *m*.

**surveillance** /sɜːˈveɪləns/ *n* surveillance *f*.

**survey¹** /səˈveɪ/ *vt* (review) passer en revue; (inquire into) enquêter sur; (*building*) inspecter.

**survey²** /ˈsɜːveɪ/ *n* (inquiry) enquête *f*; inspection *f*; (general view) vue *f* d'ensemble.

**surveyor** /səˈveɪə(r)/ *n* expert *m* (géomètre).

**survival** /səˈvaɪvl/ *n* survie *f*.

**survive** /səˈvaɪv/ *vt/i* survivre (à). **survivor** *n* survivant/-e *m/f*.

**susceptible** /səˈseptəbl/ *a* sensible (**to** à); **~ to** (prone to) prédisposé à.

**suspect¹** /səˈspekt/ *vt* soupçonner; (doubt) douter de.

**suspect²** /ˈsʌspekt/ *n & a* suspect/-e (*m/f*).

**suspend** /səˈspend/ *vt* (hang, stop) suspendre; (*licence*) retirer provisoirement. **suspended sentence** *n* condamnation *f* avec sursis.

**suspender** /səˈspendə(r)/ *n* jarretelle *f*; **~s** (braces: US) bretelles *fpl*. **~ belt** *n* porte-jarretelles *m*.

**suspension** /səˈspenʃn/ *n* suspension *f*; retrait *m* provisoire.

**suspicion** /səˈspɪʃn/ *n* soupçon *m*; (distrust) méfiance *f*.

**suspicious** /səsˈpɪʃəs/ *a* soupçonneux; (causing suspicion) suspect; **be ~ of** se méfier de. **suspiciously** *adv* de façon suspecte.

**sustain** /səsˈteɪn/ *vt* supporter; (*effort*) soutenir; (suffer) subir.

**sustenance** /ˈsʌstɪnəns/ *n* (food) nourriture *f*; (nourishment) valeur *f* nutritive.

**swallow** /ˈswɒləʊ/ *vt/i* avaler; **~ up** (absorb, engulf) engloutir. ● *n* hirondelle *f*.

**swam** /swæm/ ⇒SWIM.

**swamp** /swɒmp/ *n* marais *m*. ● *vt* (flood, overwhelm) submerger.

**swan** /swɒn/ *n* cygne *m*.

**swap** /swɒp/ *vt/i* (*pt* **swapped**) [!] échanger. ● *n* [!] échange *m*.

**swarm** /swɔːm/ *n* essaim *m*. ● *vi* fourmiller; **~ into** *or* **round** (*crowd*) envahir.

**swat** /swɒt/ *vt* (*pt* **swatted**) (*fly*) écraser.

**sway** /sweɪ/ *vt/i* (se) balancer; (influence) influencer. ● *n* balancement *m*; (rule) empire *m*.

**swear** /sweə(r)/ *vt/i* (*pt* **swore**; *pp* **sworn**) jurer (**to sth** de qch); ~ **at** injurier; ~ **by sth** 🅸 ne jurer que par qch. **~-word** *n* juron *m*.

**sweat** /swet/ *n* sueur *f*. ● *vi* suer.

**sweater** /'swetə(r)/ *n* pull-over *m*.

**sweat-shirt** *n* sweat-shirt *m*.

**swede** /swi:d/ *n* rutabaga *m*.

**Swede** /swi:d/ *n* Suédois/-e *m/f*. **Sweden** *n* Suède *f*.

**Swedish** /'swi:dɪʃ/ *a* suédois. ● *n* (Ling) suédois *m*.

**sweep** /swi:p/ *vt/i* (*pt* **swept**) (*floor*) balayer; (carry away) emporter, entraîner; (*chimney*) ramoner. ● *n* coup *m* de balai; (curve) courbe *f*; (mouvement) geste *m*, mouvement *m*; (for chimneys) ramoneur *m*. □ ~ **by** passer rapidement *or* majestueusement. **sweeper** *n* (for carpet) balai *m* mécanique; (football) libero *m*.

**sweet** /swi:t/ *a* (not sour, pleasant) doux; (not savoury) sucré; (charming 🅸) gentil; **have a ~ tooth** aimer les sucreries. ● *n* bonbon *m*; (dish) dessert *m*. **~corn** *n* maïs *m*.

**sweeten** /'swi:tn/ *vt* sucrer; (fig) adoucir. **sweetener** *n* édulcorant *m*.

**sweetheart** /'swi:thɑ:t/ *n* petit/-e ami/-e *m/f*; (term of endearment) chéri/-e *m/f*.

**sweetly** /'swi:tlɪ/ *adv* gentiment.

**sweetness** /'swi:tnɪs/ *n* douceur *f*; goût *m* sucré.

**sweet pea** *n* pois *m* de senteur.

**swell** /swel/ *vt/i* (*pt* **swelled**; *pp* **swollen** *or* **swelled**) (increase) grossir; (expand) (se) gonfler; (*hand, face*) enfler. ● *n* (of sea) houle *f*. **swelling** *n* (Med) enflure *f*.

**sweltering** /'sweltərɪŋ/ *a* étouffant.

**swept** /swept/ ⇒SWEEP.

**swerve** /swɜ:v/ *vi* faire un écart.

**swift** /swɪft/ *a* rapide. ● *n* (bird) martinet *m*.

**swim** /swɪm/ *vi* (*pt* **swam**; *pp* **swum**; *pres p* **swimming**) nager; (be dizzy) tourner. ● *vt* traverser à la nage; (*distance*) nager. ● *n* baignade *f*; **go for a ~** aller se baigner. **swimmer** *n* nageur/-euse *m/f*. **swimming** *n* natation *f*.

**swimming-pool** *n* piscine *f*.

**swim-suit** *n* maillot *m* (de bain).

**swindle** /'swɪndl/ *vt* escroquer. ● *n* escroquerie *f*.

**swine** /swaɪn/ *npl* (pigs) pourceaux *mpl*. ● *n inv* (person 🅸) salaud *m*.

**swing** /swɪŋ/ *vt/i* (*pt* **swung**) (se) balancer; (turn round) tourner; (*pendulum*) osciller. ● *n* balancement *m*; (seat) balançoire *f*; (of opinion) revirement *m* (**towards** en faveur de); (Mus) rythme *m*; **be in full ~** battre son plein. □ ~ **round** (*person*) se retourner.

**swipe** /swaɪp/ *vt* (hit 🅸) frapper; (steal 🅸) piquer.

**swirl** /swɜ:l/ *vi* tourbillonner. ● *n* tourbillon *m*.

**Swiss** /swɪs/ *a* suisse. ● *n inv* Suisse *mf*.

**switch** /swɪtʃ/ *n* bouton *m* (électrique), interrupteur *m*; (shift) changement *m*, revirement *m*. ● *vt* (transfer) transférer; (exchange) échanger (**for** contre); (reverse positions of) changer de place; ~ **trains** (change) changer de train. ● *vi* changer. □ ~ **off** éteindre; ~ **on** mettre, allumer.

**switchboard** /'swɪtʃbɔ:d/ *n* standard *m*.

**Switzerland** /'swɪtsələnd/ *n* Suisse *f*.

**swivel** /'swɪvl/ *vt/i* (*pt* **swivelled**) (faire) pivoter.

**swollen** /'swəʊlən/ ⇒SWELL.

**swoop** /swu:p/ *vi* (*bird*) fondre; (*police*) faire une descente, foncer. ● *n* (police raid) descente *f*.

**sword** /sɔ:d/ *n* épée *f*.

**swore** /swɔ:(r)/ ⇒SWEAR.

**sworn** /swɔ:n/ ⇒SWEAR. ● *a* (*enemy*) juré; (*ally*) dévoué.

**swot** /swɒt/ *vt*/*i* (*pt* **swotted**) (study 🅸) bûcher 🅸. ● *n* 🅸 bûcheur/-euse *m*/*f* 🅸.

**swum** /swʌm/ ⇒SWIM.

**swung** /swʌŋ/ ⇒SWING.

**syllabus** /'sɪləbəs/ *n* (*pl* ~**es**) (School, Univ) programme *m*.

**symbol** /'sɪmbl/ *n* symbole *m*. **symbolic(al)** *a* symbolique. **symbolize** *vt* symboliser.

**symmetrical** /sɪ'metrɪkl/ *a* symétrique.

**sympathetic** /sɪmpə'θetɪk/ *a* compatissant; (fig) compréhensif.

**sympathize** /'sɪmpəθaɪz/ *vi* ~ with (pity) plaindre; (fig) comprendre les sentiments de. **sympathizer** *n* sympathisant/-e *m*/*f*.

**sympathy** /'sɪmpəθɪ/ *n* (pity) compassion *f*; (fig) compréhension *f*; (solidarity) solidarité *f*; (condolences) condoléances *fpl*; (affinity) affinité *f*; **be in ~ with** comprendre, être en accord avec.

**symptom** /'sɪmptəm/ *n* symptôme *m*.

**synagogue** /'sɪnəgɒg/ *n* synagogue *f*.

**synonym** /'sɪnənɪm/ *n* synonyme *m*.

**synopsis** /sɪ'nɒpsɪs/ *n* (*pl* **-opses** /-si:z/) résumé *m*.

**syntax** /'sɪntæks/ *n* syntaxe *f*.

**synthesis** /'sɪnθəsɪs/ *n* (*pl* **-theses** /-si:z/) synthèse *f*.

**synthetic** /sɪn'θetɪk/ *a* synthétique.

**syringe** /sɪ'rɪndʒ/ *n* seringue *f*.

**syrup** /'sɪrəp/ *n* (liquid) sirop *m*; (treacle) mélasse *f* raffinée.

**system** /'sɪstəm/ *n* système *m*; (body) organisme *m*; (order) méthode *f*. **systematic** *a* systématique.

**systems analyst** *n* analyste-programmeur/-euse *m*/*f*.

# Tt

**tab** /tæb/ *n* (on can) languette *f*; (on garment) patte *f*; (label) étiquette *f*; (US 🅸) addition *f*; (Comput) tabulatrice *f*; (setting) tabulation *f*.

**table** /'teɪbl/ *n* table *f*; **at (the) ~** à table; **lay** *or* **set the ~** mettre la table. ● *vt* (*motion*) présenter. **~-cloth** *n* nappe *f*. **~-mat** *n* set *m* de table. **~spoon** *n* cuillère *f* de service.

**tablet** /'tæblɪt/ *n* (of stone) plaque *f*; (drug) comprimé *m*.

**table tennis** *n* tennis *m* de table; ping-pong® *m*.

**taboo** /tə'bu:/ *n* & *a* tabou (*m*).

**tacit** /'tæsɪt/ *a* tacite.

**tack** /tæk/ *n* (nail) clou *m*; (stitch) point *m* de bâti; (course of action) voie *f*. ● *vt* (nail) clouer; (stitch) bâtir; (add) ajouter. ● *vi* (Naut) louvoyer.

**tackle** /'tækl/ *n* équipement *m*; (in soccer) tacle *m*; (in rugby) plaquage *m*. ● *vt* (*problem*) s'attaquer à; (*player*) tacler, plaquer.

**tact** /tækt/ *n* tact *m*. **tactful** *a* plein de tact.

**tactics** /'tæktɪks/ *npl* tactique *f*.

**tadpole** /'tædpəʊl/ *n* têtard *m*.

**tag** /tæg/ *n* (label) étiquette *f*. ● *vt* (*pt* **tagged**) (label) étiqueter. ● *vi* ~ **along** Ⓘ suivre.

**tail** /teɪl/ *n* queue *f*; ~**s** (coat) habit *m*; ~**s!** (on coin) pile! ● *vt* (follow) filer. ● *vi* ~ **away** *or* **off** diminuer. ~**-back** *n* bouchon *m*. ~**-gate** *n* hayon *m*.

**tailor** /'teɪlə(r)/ *n* tailleur *m*. ● *vt* (*garment*) façonner; (fig) adapter. ~**-made** *a* fait sur mesure.

**take** /teɪk/ *vt/i* (*pt* **took**; *pp* **taken**) prendre (**from sb** à qn); (carry) emporter, porter (**to** à); (escort) emmener; (contain) contenir; (tolerate) supporter; (accept) accepter; (*prize*) remporter; (*exam*) passer; (*precedence*) avoir; (*view*) adopter; ~ **sb home** ramener qn chez lui; **be taken by** *or* **with** être impressionné par; **be taken ill** tomber malade; **it** ~**s time** il faut du temps pour. □ ~ **after** tenir de; ~ **apart** démonter; (fig) descendre en flammes Ⓘ; ~ **away** (*object*) enlever; (*person*) emmener; (*pain*) supprimer; ~ **back** reprendre; (return) rendre; (accompany) raccompagner; (*statement*) retirer; ~ **down** (*object*) descendre; (*notes*) prendre; ~ **in** (*object*) rentrer; (include) inclure; (cheat) tromper; ~ **off** (Aviat) décoller; ~ **sth off** enlever qch; ~ **sb off** imiter qn; ~ **on** (*task, staff, passenger*) prendre; (*challenger*) relever le défi de; ~ **out** sortir; (*stain*) enlever; ~ **over** *vt* (*country, firm*) prendre le contrôle de; *vi* prendre le pouvoir; ~ **over from** remplacer; ~ **part** participer (**in** à); ~ **place** avoir lieu; ~ **to** se prendre d'amitié pour; (*activity*) prendre goût à; ~ **to doing** se mettre à faire; ~ **up** (*object*) monter; (*hobby*) se mettre à; (occupy) prendre; (resume) reprendre; ~ **up with** se lier avec. ~**-away** *n* (meal) repas *m* à emporter. ~**-off** *n* (Aviat) décollage *m*. ~**over** *n* (Pol) prise *f* de pouvoir; (Comm) rachat *m*.

**tale** /teɪl/ *n* conte *m*; (report) récit *m*; (lie) histoire *f*.

**talent** /'tælənt/ *n* talent *m*. **talented** *a* doué.

**talk** /tɔ:k/ *vt/i* parler; (chat) bavarder; ~ **sb into doing** persuader qn de faire; ~ **sth over** discuter de qch. ● *n* (talking) propos *mpl*; (conversation) conversation *f*; (lecture) exposé *m*.

**talkative** /'tɔ:kətɪv/ *a* bavard.

**tall** /tɔ:l/ *a* (high) haut; (*person*) grand.

**tame** /teɪm/ *a* apprivoisé; (dull) insipide. ● *vt* apprivoiser; (*lion*) dompter.

**tamper** /'tæmpə(r)/ *vi* ~ **with** (*lock, machine*) tripoter; (*accounts, evidence*) trafiquer.

**tan** /tæn/ *vt/i* (*pt* **tanned**) bronzer; (*hide*) tanner. ● *n* bronzage *m*.

**tangerine** /tændʒə'ri:n/ *n* mandarine *f*.

**tangle** /'tæŋgl/ *vt/i* ~ **(up)** s'emmêler. ● *n* enchevêtrement *m*.

**tank** /tæŋk/ *n* réservoir *m*; (vat) cuve *f*; (for fish) aquarium *m*; (Mil) char *m* (de combat).

**tanker** /'tæŋkə(r)/ *n* (lorry) camion-citerne *m*; (ship) navire-citerne *m*; **oil/petrol** ~ pétrolier *m*.

**tantrum** /'tæntrəm/ *n* crise *f* (de colère).

**tap** /tæp/ *n* (for water) robinet *m*; (knock) petit coup *m*; **on** ~ disponible. ● *vt* (*pt* **tapped**) (knock) taper (doucement); (*resources*) exploiter; (*phone*) mettre sur écoute.

**tape** /teɪp/ *n* bande *f* (magnétique); (cassette) cassette *f*; (video) cassette *f* vidéo; (fabric) ruban *m*; (sticky) scotch® *m*. ● *vt* (record) enre-

gistrer; ~ **sth to sth** coller qch à qch. ~**-measure** *n* mètre *m* ruban. ~ **recorder** *n* magnétophone *m*.

**tapestry** /'tæpɪstrɪ/ *n* tapisserie *f*.

**tar** /tɑ:(r)/ *n* goudron *m*. ● *vt* (*pt* **tarred**) goudronner.

**target** /'tɑ:gɪt/ *n* cible *f*; (objective) objectif *m*. ● *vt* (*city*) prendre pour cible; (*weapon*) diriger; (in marketing) viser.

**tariff** /'tærɪf/ *n* (price list) tarif *m*; (on imports) droit *m* de douane.

**tarmac**, **Tarmac®** /'tɑ:mæk/ *n* macadam *m*; (runway) piste *f*.

**tarpaulin** /tɑ:'pɔ:lɪn/ *n* bâche *f*.

**tarragon** /'tærəgən/ *n* estragon *m*.

**tart** /tɑ:t/ *n* tarte *f*. ● *a* aigrelet.

**task** /tɑ:sk/ *n* tâche *f*.

**taste** /teɪst/ *n* goût *m*; (experience) aperçu *m*. ● *vt* (eat, enjoy) goûter à; (try) goûter; (perceive taste of) sentir (le goût de). ● *vi* ~ **of** *or* **like** avoir un goût de. **tasteful** *a* de bon goût.

**tattoo** /tə'tu:/ *vt* tatouer. ● *n* tatouage *m*.

**tatty** /'tætɪ/ *a* (**-ier**, **-iest**) 🄸 miteux.

**taught** /tɔ:t/ ⇒TEACH.

**taunt** /tɔ:nt/ *vt* railler. ● *n* raillerie *f*.

**Taurus** /'tɔ:rəs/ *n* Taureau *m*.

**tax** /tæks/ *n* (on goods, services) taxe *f*; (on income) impôt *m*. ● *vt* imposer; (put to test: fig) mettre à l'épreuve. **taxable** *a* imposable. **taxation** *n* imposition *f*; (taxes) impôts *mpl*.

**tax**: ~**-collector** *n* percepteur *m*. ~**-deductible** *a* déductible des impôts. ~ **disc** *n* vignette *f*. ~**-free** *a* exempt d'impôts. ~ **haven** *n* paradis *m* fiscal.

**taxi** /'tæksɪ/ *n* taxi *m*. ~ **rank** *n* station *f* de taxi.

**tax**: ~**payer** *n* contribuable *mf*. ~ **relief** *n* dégrèvement *m* fiscal. ~ **return** *n* déclaration *f* d'impôts.

**tea** /ti:/ *n* (drink, meal) thé *m*; (children's snack) goûter *m*; ~ **bag** sachet *m* de thé.

**teach** /ti:tʃ/ *vt* (*pt* **taught**) apprendre (**sb sth** qch à qn); (in school) enseigner (**sb sth** qch à qn). ● *vi* enseigner. **teacher** *n* enseignant/-e *m*/*f*; (secondary) professeur *m*; (primary) instituteur/-trice *m*/*f*.

**team** /ti:m/ *n* équipe *f*; (of animals) attelage *m*. ● *vi* ~ **up** faire équipe (**with** avec).

**teapot** /'ti:pɒt/ *n* théière *f*.

**tear**[1] /teə(r)/ *vt*/*i* (*pt* **tore**; *pp* **torn**) (se) déchirer; (snatch) arracher (**from** à); (rush) aller à toute vitesse. ● *n* déchirure *f*.

**tear**[2] /tɪə(r)/ *n* larme *f*; **in** ~**s** en larmes. ~**-gas** *n* gaz *m* lacrymogène.

**tease** /ti:z/ *vt* taquiner. ● *n* taquin/-e *m*/*f*.

**tea**: ~**-shop** *n* salon *m* de thé. ~**spoon** *n* petite cuillère *f*.

**teat** /ti:t/ *n* tétine *f*.

**tea-towel** *n* torchon *m*.

**technical** /'teknɪkl/ *a* technique.

**technician** /tek'nɪʃn/ *n* technicien/-ne *m*/*f*.

**technique** /tek'ni:k/ *n* technique *f*.

**techno** /'teknəʊ/ *n* (Mus) techno *f*.

**technology** /tek'nɒlədʒɪ/ *n* technologie *f*.

**teddy** /'tedɪ/ *a* ~ **bear** ours *m* en peluche.

**tedious** /'ti:dɪəs/ *a* ennuyeux.

**tee** /ti:/ *n* (golf) tee *m*.

**teenage** /ˈti:neɪdʒ/ *a* (*girl, boy*) adolescent; (*fashion*) des adolescents. **teenager** *n* jeune *mf*, adolescent/-e *m/f*.

**teens** /ti:nz/ *npl* **in one's ~** adolescent.

**teeth** /ti:θ/ ⇒TOOTH.

**teethe** /ti:ð/ *vi* faire ses dents.

**teetotaller** /ti:ˈtəʊtlə(r)/ *n* personne *f* qui ne boit pas d'alcool.

**telecommunications** /telɪkəmju:nɪˈkeɪʃnz/ *npl* télécommunications *fpl*.

**telecommuting** /telɪkəˈmju:tɪŋ/ *n* télétravail *m*.

**teleconferencing** /telɪˈkɒnfərənsɪŋ/ *n* téléconférence *f*.

**telegram** /ˈtelɪgræm/ *n* télégramme *m*.

**telegraph** /ˈtelɪgrɑ:f/ *n* télégraphe *m*. ● *a* télégraphique.

**telephone** /ˈtelɪfəʊn/ *n* téléphone *m*. ● *vt* (*person*) téléphoner à; (*message*) téléphoner. ● *vi* téléphoner. **~ book** annuaire *m*. **~ booth**, **~-box** *n* cabine *f* téléphonique. **~ call** *n* coup *m* de téléphone. **~ number** *n* numéro *m* de téléphone.

**telephoto** /telɪˈfəʊtəʊ/ *a* **~ lens** téléobjectif *m*.

**telescope** /ˈtelɪskəʊp/ *n* télescope *m*. ● *vt/i* (se) télescoper.

**teletext** /ˈtelɪtekst/ *n* télétexte *m*.

**televise** /ˈtelɪvaɪz/ *vt* téléviser.

**television** /ˈtelɪvɪʒn/ *n* télévision *f*; **~ set** poste *m* de télévision, téléviseur *m*.

**teleworking** /ˈtelɪwɜ:kɪŋ/ *n* télétravail *m*.

**telex** /ˈteleks/ *n* télex *m*. ● *vt* envoyer par télex.

**tell** /tel/ *vt* (*pt* **told**) dire (**sb sth** qch à qn); (*story*) raconter; (distinguish) distinguer; **~ sb to do sth** dire à qn de faire qch; **~ sth from sth** voir la différence entre qch et qch. ● *vi* (show) avoir un effet; (know) savoir. □ **~ off** Ⓘ gronder.

**temp** /temp/ *n* intérimaire *mf*. ● *vi* faire de l'intérim.

**temper** /ˈtempə(r)/ *n* humeur *f*; (anger) colère *f*; **lose one's ~** se mettre en colère.

**temperament** /ˈtemprəmənt/ *n* tempérament *m*. **temperamental** *a* capricieux.

**temperature** /ˈtemprətʃə(r)/ *n* température *f*; **have a ~** avoir de la fièvre *or* de la température.

**temple** /ˈtempl/ *n* temple *m*; (of head) tempe *f*.

**temporary** /ˈtemprərɪ/ *a* temporaire, provisoire.

**tempt** /tempt/ *vt* tenter; **~ sb to do** donner envie à qn de faire.

**ten** /ten/ *a* & *n* dix (*m*).

**tenacious** /tɪˈneɪʃəs/ *a* tenace.

**tenancy** /ˈtenənsɪ/ *n* location *f*. **tenant** *n* locataire *mf*.

**tend** /tend/ *vt* s'occuper de. ● *vi* **~ to** (be apt to) avoir tendance à; (look after) s'occuper de. **tendency** *n* tendance *f*.

**tender** /ˈtendə(r)/ *a* tendre; (sore, painful) sensible. ● *vt* offrir, donner. ● *vi* faire une soumission. ● *n* (Comm) soumission *f*; **be legal ~** (money) avoir cours.

**tendon** /ˈtendən/ *n* tendon *m*.

**tennis** /ˈtenɪs/ *n* tennis *m*. ● *a* (*court, match*) de tennis.

**tenor** /ˈtenə(r)/ *n* (Mus) ténor *m*.

**tense** /tens/ *n* (Gram) temps *m*. ● *a* tendu. ● *vt* (*muscles*) tendre, raidir. ● *vi* (*face*) se crisper.

**tension** /ˈtenʃn/ *n* tension *f*.

**tent** /tent/ *n* tente *f*.

**tentative** /ˈtentətɪv/ *a* provisoire; (hesitant) timide.

**tenth** /tenθ/ *a & n* dixième (*mf*).

**tepid** /ˈtepɪd/ *a* tiède.

**term** /tɜ:m/ *n* (word, limit) terme *m*; (of imprisonment) temps *m*; (School) trimestre *m*; **~s** conditions *fpl*; **on good/bad ~s** en bons/mauvais termes; **in the short/long ~** à court/long terme; **come to ~s with sth** accepter qch; **~ of office** (Pol) mandat *m*. ● *vt* appeler.

**terminal** /ˈtɜ:mɪnl/ *a* (*point*) terminal; (*illness*) incurable. ● *n* (oil, computer) terminal *m*; (Rail) terminus *m*; (Electr) borne *f*; (**air**) **~** aérogare *f*.

**terminate** /ˈtɜ:mɪneɪt/ *vt* mettre fin à. ● *vi* prendre fin.

**terminus** /ˈtɜ:mɪnəs/ *n* (*pl* **-ni** /-naɪ/) (station) terminus *m*.

**terrace** /ˈterəs/ *n* terrasse *f*; (houses) rangée *f* de maisons contiguës; **the ~s** (Sport) les gradins *mpl*.

**terracotta** /terəˈkɒtə/ *n* terre *f* cuite.

**terrible** /ˈterəbl/ *a* affreux, atroce.

**terrific** /təˈrɪfɪk/ *a* (huge) énorme; (great Ⓣ) formidable.

**terrify** /ˈterɪfaɪ/ *vt* terrifier; **be terrified of** avoir très peur de.

**territory** /ˈterɪtərɪ/ *n* territoire *m*.

**terror** /ˈterə(r)/ *n* terreur *f*.

**terrorism** /ˈterərɪzəm/ *n* terrorisme *m*. **terrorist** *n* terroriste *mf*.

**test** /test/ *n* épreuve *f*; (written exam) contrôle *m*; (of machine, product) essai *m*; (of sample) analyse *f*; **driving ~** examen *m* du permis de conduire. ● *vt* évaluer; (School) contrôler; (*machine, product*) essayer; (*sample*) analyser; (*patience, strength*) mettre à l'épreuve. ● *vi* **~ for** faire une recherche de.

**testament** /ˈtestəmənt/ *n* testament *m*; **Old/New T~** Ancien/Nouveau Testament *m*.

**testicle** /ˈtestɪkl/ *n* testicule *m*.

**testify** /ˈtestɪfaɪ/ *vt*/*i* témoigner (**to** de; **that** que).

**testimony** /ˈtestɪmənɪ/ *n* témoignage *m*.

**test tube** *n* éprouvette *f*.

**tetanus** /ˈtetənəs/ *n* tétanos *m*.

**text** /tekst/ *n* texte *m*. ● *vt* **~sb** envoyer un message texte à qn. **~book** *n* manuel *m*. **~ message** *n* message *m* texte.

**texture** /ˈtekstʃə(r)/ *n* (of paper) grain *m*; (of fabric) texture *f*.

**than** /ðæn, ðən/ *conj* que, qu'; (with numbers) de; **more/less ~ ten** plus/moins de dix.

**thank** /θæŋk/ *vt* remercier; **~ you!**, **~s!** merci! **thankful** *a* reconnaissant (**for** de). **thanks** *npl* remerciements *mpl*; **~s to** grâce à. **Thanksgiving** (**Day**) *n* (US) jour *m* d'Action de Grâces.

---

**that** /ðæt/ *pl* **those**

● *determiner*

····➤ ce, cet, cette, ces; **~ dog** ce chien; **~ man** cet homme; **~ woman** cette femme; **those books** ces livres; **at ~ moment** à ce moment-là.

! To distinguish from **this** and **these**, you need to add -là after the noun: **I prefer that car** *je préfère cette voiture-là.*

● *pronoun*

····➤ cela, ça, ce; **what's ~?**, **what are those?** qu'est-ce que c'est (que ça)?; **who's ~?** qui est-ce?; **~ is my brother** c'est *or* voilà mon frère; **those are my parents** ce sont mes parents.

····➤ (emphatic) celui-là, celle-là, ceux-là, celles-là; **all the dresses**

**are** [illegible] **but I like ~/those best** toutes les [illegible] jolies mais je préfère celle-là/[illegible]

● *relative pronoun*

····➤ (for subject) qui; **the man ~ stole the car** l'homme qui a volé la voiture.

····➤ (for object) que; **the girl ~ I met** la fille que j'ai rencontrée.

! With a preposition, use *lequel*/*laquelle*/*lesquels*/*lesquelles*: **the chair ~ I was sitting on** *la chaise sur laquelle j'étais assis.*

! With a preposition that translates as *à*, use *auquel*/*à laquelle*/*auxquels*/*auxquelles*: **the girls ~ I was talking to** *les filles auxquelles je parlais.*

! With a preposition that translates as *de*, use *dont*: **the people ~ I've talked about** *les personnes dont j'ai parlé.*

● *conjunction* que; **she said ~ she would do it** elle a dit qu'elle le ferait.

**thatched** /θætʃd/ *a* de chaume; **~ cottage** chaumière *f*.

**thaw** /θɔ:/ *vt*/*i* (faire) dégeler; (*snow*) (faire) fondre. ● *n* dégel *m*.

**the** /ðə, ði:/ *determiner*

····➤ le, l', la, les; **~ dog** le chien; **~ tree** l'arbre; **~ chair** la chaise; **to ~ shops** aux magasins.

! With a preposition that translates as *à*: *à* + *le* = *au* and *à* + *les* = *aux*.

**theatre** /'θɪətə(r)/ *n* théâtre *m*.

**theft** /θeft/ *n* vol *m*.

**their** /ðeə(r)/ *a* leur, *pl* leurs.

**theirs** /ðeəz/ *pron* le *or* la leur, les [illegible]

**them** /[illegible] ðəm/ *pron* les; (after preposition) eux, [illegible]; **(to) ~** leur; **phone ~!** téléphone[illegible]; **I know ~** je les connais; **both of** [illegible] toutes les deux.

**themselves** /ðəm'selvz/ *pron* eux-mêmes, elles-mêmes; (reflexive) se; (after preposition) eux, elles.

**then** /ðen/ *adv* alors; (next) ensuite, puis; (therefore) alors, donc. ● *a* d'alors; **from ~ on** dès lors.

**theology** /θɪ'ɒlədʒɪ/ *n* théologie *f*.

**theory** /'θɪərɪ/ *n* théorie *f*.

**therapy** /'θerəpɪ/ *n* thérapie *f*.

**there** /ðeə(r)/ *adv* là; (with verb) y; (over there) là-bas; **he goes ~** il y va; **on ~** là-dessus; **~ is, ~ are** il y a; (pointing) voilà. ● *interj*; **~, ~!** allons, allons!

**therefore** /'ðeəfɔ:(r)/ *adv* donc.

**thermal** /'θɜ:ml/ *a* thermique.

**thermometer** /θə'mɒmɪtə(r)/ *n* thermomètre *m*.

**Thermos®** /'θɜ:məs/ *n* thermos® *m or f inv*.

**thermostat** /'θɜ:məstæt/ *n* thermostat *m*.

**thesaurus** /θɪ'sɔ:rəs/ *n* (*pl* **-ri** /-raɪ/) dictionnaire *m* de synonymes.

**these** /ði:z/ ⇒THIS.

**thesis** /'θi:sɪs/ *n* (*pl* **theses** /-si:z/) thèse *f*.

**they** /ðeɪ/ *pron* ils, elles; (emphatic) eux, elles; (people in general) on.

**thick** /θɪk/ *a* épais; (stupid) bête; **be 6 cm ~** avoir 6 cm d'épaisseur.

**thief** /θi:f/ *n* (*pl* **thieves**) voleur/-euse *m*/*f*.

**thigh** /θaɪ/ *n* cuisse *f*.

**thin** /θɪn/ *a* (**thinner**, **thinnest**) mince; (*person*) maigre, mince; (sparse) clairsemé; (fine) fin. ● *vt/i* (*pt* **thinned**) ~ (**down**) (*paint*) diluer; (*soup*) allonger.

**thing** /θɪŋ/ *n* chose *f*; **~s** (belongings) affaires *fpl*; **the best ~ is to** le mieux est de; **the (right) ~** ce qu'il faut (**for sb** à qn).

**think** /θɪŋk/ *vt/i* (*pt* **thought**) penser (**about**, **of** à); (carefully) réfléchir (**about**, **of** à); (believe) croire; **I ~ so** je crois que oui; **~ of doing** envisager de faire. □ **~ over** bien réfléchir à; **~ up** inventer.

**third** /θɜ:d/ *a* troisième. ● *n* troisième *mf*; (fraction) tiers *m*. **T~ World** *n* tiers-monde *m*.

**thirst** /θɜ:st/ *n* soif *f*.

**thirsty** /ˈθɜ:stɪ/ *a* **be ~** avoir soif; **make ~** donner soif à.

**thirteen** /θɜ:ˈti:n/ *a* & *n* treize (*m*).

**thirty** /ˈθɜ:tɪ/ *a* & *n* trente (*m*).

**this** /ðɪs/ *pl* **these**

● *determiner*

⋯➤ ce/cet/cette/ces; **~ dog** ce chien; **~ man** cet homme; **~ woman** cette femme; **these books** ces livres.

> ! To distinguish from **that** and **those**, you need to add *-ci* after the noun: **I prefer this car** *je préfère cette voiture-ci*.

● *pronoun*

⋯➤ ce; **what's ~?**, **what are these?** qu'est-ce que c'est?; **who is ~?** qui est-ce?; **~ is the kitchen** voici la cuisine; **~ is Sophie** je te *or* vous présente Sophie; **these are your things** ce sont tes affaires.

⋯➤ (emphatic) celui-ci/celle-ci/ceux-ci/celles-ci; **all the dresses are nice but I like ~/these best** toutes les robes sont jolies mais je préfère celle-ci/celles-ci.

**thistle** /ˈθɪsl/ *n* chardon *m*.

**thorn** /θɔ:n/ *n* épine *f*.

**thorough** /ˈθʌrə/ *a* (detailed) approfondi; (meticulous) minutieux. **thoroughly** *adv* (*clean*, *study*) à fond; (very) tout à fait.

**those** /ðəʊz/ ⇒THAT.

**though** /ðəʊ/ *conj* bien que. ● *adv* quand même.

**thought** /θɔ:t/ ⇒THINK. ● *n* pensée *f*, idée *f*. **thoughtful** *a* pensif; (kind) prévenant.

**thousand** /ˈθaʊznd/ *a* & *n* mille (*m inv*); **~s of** des milliers de. **thousandth** *a* & *n* millième (*mf*).

**thread** /θred/ *n* (yarn & fig) fil *m*; (of screw) pas *m*. ● *vt* enfiler; **~ one's way** se faufiler.

**threat** /θret/ *n* menace *f*. **threaten** *vt/i* menacer (**with** de).

**three** /θri:/ *a* & *n* trois (*m*).

**threw** /θru:/ ⇒THROW.

**thrill** /θrɪl/ *n* frisson *m*; (pleasure) plaisir *m*. ● *vt* transporter (de joie); **be ~ed** être ravi. ● *vi* frissonner (de joie).

**thrive** /θraɪv/ *vi* (*pt* **thrived** *or* **throve**; *pp* **thrived** *or* **thriven**) prospérer; **he ~s on it** cela lui réussit.

**throat** /θrəʊt/ *n* gorge *f*; **have a sore ~** avoir mal à la gorge.

**throb** /θrɒb/ *vi* (*pt* **throbbed**) (*heart*) battre; (*engine*) vibrer. ● *n* (pain) élancement *m*; (of engine) vibration *f*. **throbbing** *a* (*pain*) lancinant.

**throne** /θrəʊn/ *n* trône *m*.

**through** /θru:/ *prep* à travers; (during) pendant; (by means or way of, out

of) par; ([illegible] reason of) grâce à, à cause de. ● *adv* à travers; (entirely) jusqu'au bout. ● *a* ([illegible]) direct; **be ~** (finished) avoir fini; **co[illegible]** ~ (cross, pierce) traverser; **I'm putting you ~** je vous passe votre correspondant.

**throughout** /θruː'aʊt/ *prep* **~ the country** dans tout le pays; **~ the day** pendant toute la journée. ● *adv* (place) partout; (time) tout le temps.

**throw** /θrəʊ/ *vt* (*pt* **threw**; *pp* **thrown**) jeter, lancer; (baffle) déconcerter; **~ a party** faire une fête. ● *n* jet *m*; (of dice) coup *m*. □ **~ away** jeter; **~ off** (get rid of) se débarrasser de; **~ out** jeter; (*person*) expulser; (reject) rejeter; **~ up** (*arms*) lever; (vomit 🅸) vomir.

**thrust** /θrʌst/ *vt* (*pt* **thrust**) pousser. ● *n* poussée *f*.

**thud** /θʌd/ *n* bruit *m* sourd.

**thug** /θʌg/ *n* voyou *m*.

**thumb** /θʌm/ *n* pouce *m*. ● *vt* (*book*) feuilleter; **~ a lift** faire de l'auto-stop. **~-index** *n* répertoire *m* à onglets.

**thump** /θʌmp/ *vt*/*i* cogner (sur); (*heart*) battre fort. ● *n* coup *m*.

**thunder** /'θʌndə(r)/ *n* tonnerre *m*. ● *vi* (*weather, person*) tonner. **~storm** *n* orage *m*.

**Thursday** /'θɜːzdɪ/ *n* jeudi *m*.

**thus** /ðʌs/ *adv* ainsi.

**thwart** /θwɔːt/ *vt* contrecarrer.

**thyme** /taɪm/ *n* thym *m*.

**tick** /tɪk/ *n* (sound) tic-tac *m*; (mark) coche *f*; (moment 🅸) instant *m*; (insect) tique *f*. ● *vi* faire tic-tac. ● *vt* **~ (off)** cocher. □ **~ over** tourner au ralenti.

**ticket** /'tɪkɪt/ *n* billet *m*; (for bus, cloakroom) ticket *m*; (label) étiquette *f*. **~-collector** *n* contrôleur/-euse *m*/*f*. **~-office** *n* guichet *m*.

**tickle** /'tɪkl/ *vt* chatouiller; (amuse: fig) amuser. ● *n* chatouillement *m*.

**tidal** /'taɪdl/ *a* (*river*) à marées; **~ wave** raz-de-marée *m inv*.

**[illegible]** /taɪd/ *n* marée *f*; (of events) cours [illegible]

**tidy** /'taɪdɪ/ *a* ([illegible] **-iest**) (*room*) bien rangé; (*appe[illegible] work*) soigné; (methodical) ordonné; ([illegible]nt 🅸) joli. ● *vt*/*i* **~ (up)** faire du rangement; **~ sth (up)** ranger qch; **~ oneself up** s'arranger.

**tie** /taɪ/ *vt* (*pres p* **tying**) attacher; (*knot*) faire; (*scarf*) nouer; (link) lier. ● *vi* (in football) faire match nul; (in race) être ex aequo. ● *n* (necktie) cravate *f*; (fastener) attache *f*; (link) lien *m*; (draw) match *m* nul. □ **~ down** attacher; **~ in with** être lié à; **~ up** attacher; (*money*) immobiliser; (occupy) occuper.

**tier** /tɪə(r)/ *n* étage *m*, niveau *m*; (in stadium) gradin *m*.

**tiger** /'taɪgə(r)/ *n* tigre *m*.

**tight** /taɪt/ *a* (*clothes, budget*) serré; (*grip*) ferme; (*rope*) tendu; (*security*) strict; (*angle*) aigu. ● *adv* (*hold, sleep*) bien; (*squeeze*) fort.

**tighten** /'taɪtn/ *vt*/*i* (se) tendre; (*bolt*) (se) resserrer; (*control*) renforcer.

**tights** /taɪts/ *npl* collant *m*.

**tile** /taɪl/ *n* (on wall, floor) carreau *m*; (on roof) tuile *f*. ● *vt* carreler; couvrir de tuiles.

**till** /tɪl/ *n* caisse *f* (enregistreuse). ● *vt* (*land*) cultiver. ● *prep & conj* = UNTIL.

**timber** /'tɪmbə(r)/ *n* bois *m* (de construction); (trees) arbres *mpl*.

**time** /taɪm/ *n* temps *m*; (moment) moment *m*; (epoch) époque *f*; (by clock) heure *f*; (occasion) fois *f*; (rhythm) mesure *f*; **~s** (multiplying) fois *fpl*; **any ~** n'importe quand; **for the ~ being** pour le moment;

**from ~ to ~** de temps en temps; **have a good ~** s'amuser; **in no ~** en un rien de temps; **in ~** à temps; (eventually) avec le temps; **a long ~** longtemps; **on ~** à l'heure; **what's the ~?** quelle heure est-il?; **~ off** du temps libre. ● *vt* choisir le moment de; (measure) minuter; (Sport) chronométrer. **~-limit** *n* délai *m*.

**timer** /ˈtaɪmə(r)/ *n* minuterie *f*; (for cooker) minuteur *m*.

**time: ~-scale** *n* délais *mpl*. **~table** *n* horaire *m*. **~ zone** *n* fuseau *m* horaire.

**timid** /ˈtɪmɪd/ *a* timide; (fearful) peureux.

**tin** /tɪn/ *n* étain *m*; (container) boîte *f*; **~(plate)** fer-blanc *m*. ● *vt* (*pt* **tinned**) mettre en boîte. **~ foil** *n* papier *m* d'aluminium.

**tingle** /ˈtɪŋgl/ *vi* picoter. ● *n* picotement *m*.

**tin-opener** *n* ouvre-boîtes *m inv*.

**tint** /tɪnt/ *n* teinte *f*; (for hair) shampooing *m* colorant. ● *vt* teinter.

**tiny** /ˈtaɪnɪ/ *a* (**-ier**, **-iest**) tout petit.

**tip** /tɪp/ *n* (of stick, pen, shoe, ski) pointe *f*; (of nose, finger, wing) bout *m*; (gratuity) pourboire *m*; (advice) tuyau *m*; (for rubbish) décharge *f*. ● *vt*/*i* (*pt* **tipped**) (tilt) pencher; (overturn) (faire) basculer; (pour) verser; (empty) déverser; (give money) donner un pourboire à. □ **~ off** prévenir

**tiptoe** /ˈtɪptəʊ/ *n* **on ~** sur la pointe des pieds.

**tire** /ˈtaɪə(r)/ *vt*/*i* (se) fatiguer; **~ of** se lasser de. ● *n* (US) pneu *m*.

**tired** /ˈtaɪəd/ *a* fatigué; **be ~ of** en avoir assez de.

**tiring** /ˈtaɪərɪŋ/ *a* fatigant.

**tissue** /ˈtɪʃuː/ *n* tissu *m*; (handkerchief) mouchoir *m* en papier; **~ (paper)** papier *m* de soie.

**tit** /tɪt/ *n* (bird) mésange *f*; **give ~ for tat** rendre coup pour coup.

**title** /ˈtaɪtl/ *n* titre *m*. **~ deed** *n* titre *m* de propriété.

---

**to** /tuː, tə/

● *preposition*

····➤ à; **~ Paris** à Paris; **give the book ~ Jane** donne le livre à Jane; **~ the office** au bureau; **~ the shops** aux magasins.

····➤ (with feminine countries) en; **~ France** en France.

····➤ (to + personal pronoun) me/te/lui/nous/vous/leur; **she gave it ~ them** elle le leur a donné; **I'll say it ~ her** je vais le lui dire

**!** *à + le = au*
*à + les = aux.*

● *in infinitive*

*to* is not normally translated (**to go** *aller*; **to sing** *chanter*)

····➤ (in order to) pour; **he's gone into town ~ buy a shirt** il est parti en ville pour acheter une chemise.

····➤ (after adjectives) à; de; **be easy/difficult ~ read** être facile/difficile à lire; **it's easy/difficult to read her writing** c'est facile/difficile de lire son écriture.

➡ For verbal expressions using the infinitive 'to' such as **tell sb to do sth**, **help sb to do sth** ⇨**tell**, **help**.

---

**toad** /təʊd/ *n* crapaud *m*.

**toast** /təʊst/ *n* pain *m* grillé, toast *m*; (drink) toast *m*. ● *vt* (*bread*) faire

griller; (*drink to*) porter un toast à. **toaster** *n* grille-pain *m inv*.

**tobacco** /tə'bækəʊ/ *n* tabac *m*.

**tobacconist** /tə'bækənɪst/ marchand/-e *m/f* de tabac; **~'s (shop)** tabac *m*.

**toboggan** /tə'bɒgən/ *n* toboggan *m*, luge *f*.

**today** /tə'deɪ/ *n & adv* aujourd'hui (*m*).

**toddler** /'tɒdlə(r)/ *n* bébé *m* (*qui fait ses premiers pas*).

**toe** /təʊ/ *n* orteil *m*; (of shoe) bout *m*; **on one's ~s** vigilant. ● *vt* **~ the line** se conformer.

**together** /tə'geðə(r)/ *adv* ensemble; (at same time) à la fois; **~ with** avec.

**toilet** /'tɔɪlɪt/ *n* toilettes *fpl*.

**toiletries** /'tɔɪlɪtrɪz/ *npl* articles *mpl* de toilette.

**token** /'təʊkən/ *n* (symbol) témoignage *m*; (voucher) bon *m*; (coin) jeton *m*. ● *a* symbolique.

**told** /təʊld/ ⇒TELL.

**tolerance** /'tɒlərəns/ *n* tolérance *f*.

**tolerate** /'tɒləreɪt/ *vt* tolérer.

**toll** /təʊl/ *n* péage *m*; **death ~** nombre *m* de morts; **take its ~** faire des ravages. ● *vi* (*bell*) sonner.

**tomato** /tə'mɑ:təʊ/ *n* (*pl* **~es**) tomate *f*.

**tomb** /tu:m/ *n* tombeau *m*.

**tomorrow** /tə'mɒrəʊ/ *n & adv* demain (*m*); **~ morning/night** demain matin/soir; **the day after ~** après-demain.

**ton** /tʌn/ *n* tonne *f* ( = *1016 kg*); **(metric) ~** tonne *f* ( = *1000 kg*); **~s of** ▣ des masses de.

**tone** /təʊn/ *n* ton *m*; (of radio, telephone) tonalité *f*. ● *vt* **~ down** atténuer. ● *vi* **~ (in)** s'harmoniser **(with** avec).

**tongs** /tɒŋz/ *npl* (for coal) pincettes *fpl*; (for sugar) pince *f*; (for hair) fer *m*.

**tongue** /tʌŋ/ *n* langue *f*.

**tonic** /'tɒnɪk/ *n* (Med) tonique *m*. ● *a* (*effect, dose*) tonique; **~ (water)** tonic *m*, Schweppes® *m*.

**tonight** /tə'naɪt/ *n & adv* (evening) ce soir; (night) cette nuit.

**tonsil** /'tɒnsl/ *n* amygdale *f*.

**too** /tu:/ *adv* trop; (also) aussi; **~ many people** trop de gens; **I've got ~ much/many** j'en ai trop; **me ~** moi aussi.

**took** /tʊk/ ⇒TAKE.

**tool** /tu:l/ *n* outil *m*. **~bar** *n* barre *f* d'outils. **~-box** *n* boîte *f* à outils.

**toot** /tu:t/ *n* coup *m* de klaxon®. ● *vt/i* **~ (the horn)** klaxonner.

**tooth** /tu:θ/ *n* (*pl* **teeth**) dent *f*. **~ache** *n* mal *m* de dents. **~brush** *n* brosse *f* à dents. **~paste** *n* dentifrice *m*. **~pick** *n* cure-dents *m inv*.

**top** /tɒp/ *n* (highest point) sommet *m*; (upper part) haut *m*; (upper surface) dessus *m*; (lid) couvercle *m*; (of bottle, tube) bouchon *m*; (of beer bottle) capsule *f*; (of list) tête *f*; **on ~ of** sur; (fig) en plus de. ● *a* (*shelf*) du haut; (*step, floor*) dernier; (in rank) premier; (best) meilleur; (distinguished) éminent; (maximum) maximum. ● *vt* (*pt* **topped**) (exceed) dépasser; (list) venir en tête de; **~ up** remplir; **~ped with** (*dome*) surmonté de; (*cream*) recouvert de.

**topic** /'tɒpɪk/ *n* sujet *m*.

**topless** /'tɒplɪs/ *a* aux seins nus.

**torch** /tɔ:tʃ/ *n* (electric) lampe *f* de poche; (flaming) torche *f*.

**tore** /tɔ:(r)/ ⇒TEAR[1].

**torment** /tɔ:'ment/ *vt* tourmenter.

**torn** /tɔ:n/ ⇒TEAR[1].

**torrent** /'tɒrənt/ *n* torrent *m*.

**tortoise** /'tɔ:təs/ *n* tortue *f*. **~shell** *n* écaille *f*.

**torture** /'tɔ:tʃə(r)/ *n* torture *f*; (fig) supplice *m*. ● *vt* torturer.

**Tory** /'tɔ:rɪ/ *n* & *a* tory (*mf*), conservateur/-trice (*m*/*f*).

**toss** /tɒs/ *vt* lancer; (*salad*) tourner; (*pancake*) faire sauter. ● *vi* se retourner; **~ a coin**, **~ up** tirer à pile ou face (**for** pour).

**tot** /tɒt/ *n* petit/-e enfant *m*/*f*; (drink) petit verre *m*.

**total** /'təʊtl/ *n* & *a* total (*m*). ● *vt* (*pt* **totalled**) (add up) additionner; (amount to) se monter à.

**touch** /tʌtʃ/ *vt* toucher; (tamper with) toucher à. ● *vi* se toucher. ● *n* (sense) toucher *m*; (contact) contact *m*; (of artist, writer) touche *f*; **a ~ of** (small amount) un petit peu de; **get in ~ with** se mettre en contact avec; **out of ~ with** déconnecté de. □ **~ down** (Aviat) atterrir; **~ up** retoucher. **~down** *n* atterrissage *m*; (Sport) essai *m*. **~-line** *n* ligne *f* de touche. **~-tone** *a* (*phone*) à touches.

**tough** /tʌf/ *a* (*negotiator*) coriace; (*law*) sévère; (*time*) difficile; (robust) robuste.

**tour** /tʊə(r)/ *n* voyage *m*; (visit) visite *f*; (by team) tournée *f*; **on ~** en tournée. ● *vt* visiter.

**tourist** /'tʊərɪst/ *n* touriste *mf*. ● *a* touristique. **~ office** *n* syndicat *m* d'initiative.

**tournament** /'tɔ:nəmənt/ *n* tournoi *m*.

**tout** /taʊt/ *vi* **~ (for)** racoler. ● *vt* (sell) revendre. ● *n* racoleur/-euse *m*/*f*; revendeur/-euse *m*/*f*.

**tow** /təʊ/ *vt* remorquer. ● *n* remorque *f*; **on ~** en remorque.

**toward(s)** /tə'wɔ:d(z)/ *prep* vers; (of attitude) envers.

**towel** /'taʊəl/ *n* serviette *f*.

**tower** /'taʊə(r)/ *n* tour *f*. ● *vi* **~ above** dominer.

**town** /taʊn/ *n* ville *f*; **in ~** en ville. **~ council** *n* conseil *m* municipal. **~ hall** *n* mairie *f*.

**tow**: **~-path** *n* chemin *m* de halage. **~ truck** *n* dépanneuse *f*.

**toxic** /'tɒksɪk/ *a* toxique.

**toy** /tɔɪ/ *n* jouet *m*. ● *vi* **~ with** (object) jouer avec; (idea) caresser.

**trace** /treɪs/ *n* trace *f*. ● *vt* (*person*) retrouver; (*cause*) déterminer; (*life*) retracer; (draw) tracer; (with tracing paper) décalquer.

**track** /træk/ *n* (of person, car) traces *fpl*; (of missile) trajectoire *f*; (path) sentier *m*; (Sport) piste *f*; (Rail) voie *f*; (on disc) morceau *m*; **keep ~ of** suivre. ● *vt* suivre la trace *or* la trajectoire de. □ **~ down** retrouver. **~ suit** *n* survêtement *m*.

**tractor** /'træktə(r)/ *n* tracteur *m*.

**trade** /treɪd/ *n* commerce *m*; (job) métier *m*; (swap) échange *m*. ● *vi* faire du commerce; **~ on** exploiter. ● *vt* échanger. ● *a* (*route*, *deficit*) commercial. **~-in** *n* reprise *f*. **~ mark** *n* marque *f* (de fabrique); (registered) marque *f* déposée.

**trader** /'treɪdə(r)/ *n* commerçant/-e *m*/*f*; (on stockmarket) opérateur/-trice *m*/*f*.

**trade union** *n* syndicat *m*.

**trading** /'treɪdɪŋ/ *n* commerce *m*; (on stockmarket) transactions *fpl* (boursières).

**tradition** /trə'dɪʃn/ *n* tradition *f*.

**traffic** /'træfɪk/ *n* trafic *m*; (on road) circulation *f*. ● *vi* (*pt* **trafficked**) faire du trafic (**in** de). **~ jam** *n* embouteillage *m*. **~-lights** *npl* feux *mpl* (de circulation). **~ warden** contractuel/-le *m*/*f*.

**trail** /treɪl/ *vt/i* traîner; (*plant*) ramper; (track) suivre; ~ **behind** traîner. ● *n* (of powder) traînée *f*; (track) piste *f*; (path) sentier *m*.

**trailer** /ˈtreɪlə(r)/ *n* remorque *f*; (caravan) caravane *f*; (film) bande-annonce *f*.

**train** /treɪn/ *n* (Rail) train *m*; (underground) rame *f*; (procession) file *f*; (of dress) traîne *f*. ● *vt* (instruct, develop) former; (*sportsman*) entraîner; (*animal*) dresser; (*ear*) exercer; (*aim*) braquer. ● *vi* être formé, étudier; (Sport) s'entraîner. **trained** *a* (skilled) qualifié; (*doctor*) diplômé. **trainee** *n* stagiaire *mf*. **trainer** *n* (Sport) entraîneur/-euse *m/f*. **trainers** *npl* (shoes) chaussures *fpl* de sport. **training** *n* formation *f*; (Sport) entraînement *m*.

**tram** /træm/ *n* tram(way) *m*.

**tramp** /træmp/ *vi* marcher (d'un pas lourd). ● *vt* parcourir. ● *n* (vagrant) clochard/-e *m/f*; (sound) bruit *m*.

**trample** /ˈtræmpl/ *vt/i* ~ **(on)** piétiner; (fig) fouler aux pieds.

**tranquil** /ˈtræŋkwɪl/ *a* tranquille. **tranquillizer** *n* tranquillisant *m*.

**transact** /træn'zækt/ *vt* négocier. **transaction** *n* transaction *f*.

**transcript** /ˈtrænskrɪpt/ *n* transcription *f*.

**transfer**[1] /træns'fɜ:(r)/ *vt* (*pt* **transferred**) transférer; (*power*) céder; (*employee*) muter. ● *vi* être transféré; (*employee*) être muté.

**transfer**[2] /ˈtrænsfɜ:(r)/ *n* transfert *m*; (of employee) mutation *f*; (image) décalcomanie *f*.

**transform** /træns'fɔ:m/ *vt* transformer.

**transitive** /ˈtrænsətɪv/ *a* transitif.

**translate** /trænz'leɪt/ *vt* traduire. **translation** *n* traduction *f*. **translator** *n* traducteur/-trice *m/f*.

**transmit** /trænz'mɪt/ *vt* (*pt* **transmitted**) transmettre. **transmitter** *n* émetteur *m*.

**transparency** /træns'pærənsɪ/ *n* transparence *f*; (Photo) diapositive *f*.

**transplant** /ˈtrænsplɑ:nt/ *n* transplantation *f*; (Med) greffe *f*.

**transport**[1] /træn'spɔ:t/ *vt* transporter.

**transport**[2] /ˈtrænspɔ:t/ *n* transport *m*.

**trap** /træp/ *n* piège *m*. ● *vt* (*pt* **trapped**) (jam, pin down) coincer; (cut off) bloquer; (snare) prendre au piège.

**trash** /træʃ/ *n* (refuse) ordures *fpl*; (nonsense) idioties *fpl*. **~-can** *n* (US) poubelle *f*.

**trauma** /ˈtrɔ:mə/ *n* traumatisme *m*. **traumatic** *a* traumatisant.

**travel** /ˈtrævl/ *vi* (*pt* **travelled**, US **traveled**) voyager; (*vehicle, bullet*) aller. ● *vt* parcourir. ● *n* voyages *mpl*. ~ **agency** *n* agence *f* de voyages.

**traveller**, (US) **traveler** /ˈtrævlə(r)/ *n* voyageur/-euse *m/f*; **~'s cheque** chèque *m* de voyage.

**trawler** /ˈtrɔ:lə(r)/ *n* chalutier *m*.

**tray** /treɪ/ *n* plateau *m*; (on office desk) corbeille *f*.

**treacle** /ˈtri:kl/ *n* mélasse *f*.

**tread** /tred/ *vi* (*pt* **trod**; *pp* **trodden**) marcher (**on** sur). ● *vt* fouler. ● *n* (sound) pas *m*; (of tyre) chape *f*.

**treasure** /ˈtreʒə(r)/ *n* trésor *m*. ● *vt* (*gift, memory*) chérir; (*friendship, possession*) tenir beaucoup à.

**treasury** /ˈtreʒərɪ/ *n* trésorerie *f*; **the T~** le ministère des Finances.

**treat** /tri:t/ *vt* traiter; ~ **sb to sth** offrir qch à qn. ● *n* (pleasure) plaisir

*m*; (food) gâterie *f*. **treatment** *n* traitement *m*.

**treaty** /'tri:tɪ/ *n* traité *m*.

**treble** /'trebl/ *a* triple; ~ **clef** clé *f* de sol. ● *vt/i* tripler. ● *n* (voice) soprano *m*.

**tree** /tri:/ *n* arbre *m*.

**trek** /trek/ *n* randonnée *f*. ● *vi* (*pt* **trekked**) ~ **across/through** traverser péniblement; **go ~king** faire de la randonnée.

**tremble** /'trembl/ *vi* trembler.

**tremendous** /trɪ'mendəs/ *a* énorme; (excellent) formidable.

**tremor** /'tremə(r)/ *n* tremblement *m*; (**earth**) ~ secousse *f*.

**trench** /trentʃ/ *n* tranchée *f*.

**trend** /trend/ *n* tendance *f*; (fashion) mode *f*. **trendy** *a* 🄸 branché 🄸.

**trespass** /'trespəs/ *vi* s'introduire illégalement (**on** dans). **trespasser** *n* intrus/-e *m/f*.

**trial** /'traɪəl/ *n* (Jur) procès *m*; (test) essai *m*; (ordeal) épreuve *f*; **go on** ~ passer en jugement; **by ~ and error** par expérience.

**triangle** /'traɪæŋgl/ *n* triangle *m*.

**tribe** /traɪb/ *n* tribu *f*.

**tribunal** /traɪ'bju:nl/ *n* tribunal *m*.

**tributary** /'trɪbjʊtərɪ/ *n* affluent *m*.

**tribute** /'trɪbju:t/ *n* tribut *m*; **pay ~ to** rendre hommage à.

**trick** /trɪk/ *n* tour *m*; (dishonest) combine *f*; (knack) astuce *f*; **do the ~** 🄸 faire l'affaire. ● *vt* tromper. **trickery** *n* ruse *f*.

**trickle** /'trɪkl/ *vi* dégouliner; ~ **in/out** arriver or partir en petit nombre. ● *n* filet *m*; (fig) petit nombre *m*.

**tricky** /'trɪkɪ/ *a* (*task*) difficile; (*question*) épineux; (*person*) malin.

**trifle** /'traɪfl/ *n* bagatelle *f*; (cake) diplomate *m*; **a ~** (small amount) un peu. ● *vi* ~ **with** jouer avec.

**trigger** /'trɪgə(r)/ *n* (of gun) gâchette *f*; (of machine) manette *f*. ● *vt* ~ (**off**) (initiate) déclencher.

**trim** /trɪm/ *a* (**trimmer**, **trimmest**) soigné; (figure) svelte. ● *vt* (*pt* **trimmed**) (*hair*, *grass*) couper; (*budget*) réduire; (decorate) décorer. ● *n* (cut) coupe *f* d'entretien; (decoration) garniture *f*; **in ~** en forme.

**trinket** /'trɪŋkɪt/ *n* babiole *f*.

**trip** /trɪp/ *vt/i* (*pt* **tripped**) (faire) trébucher. ● *n* (journey) voyage *m*; (outing) excursion *f*.

**triple** /'trɪpl/ *a* triple. ● *vt/i* tripler. **triplets** *npl* triplés/-es *m/fpl*.

**tripod** /'traɪpɒd/ *n* trépied *m*.

**trite** /traɪt/ *a* banal.

**triumph** /'traɪəmf/ *n* triomphe *m*. ● *vi* triompher (**over** de).

**trivial** /'trɪvɪəl/ *a* insignifiant.

**trod**, **trodden** /trɒd, 'trɒdn/ ⇒TREAD.

**trolley** /'trɒlɪ/ *n* chariot *m*.

**trombone** /trɒm'bəʊn/ *n* (Mus) trombone *m*.

**troop** /tru:p/ *n* bande *f*; **~s** (Mil) troupes *fpl*. ● *vi* ~ **in/out** entrer/sortir en bande.

**trophy** /'trəʊfɪ/ *n* trophée *m*.

**tropic** /'trɒpɪk/ *n* tropique *m*; **~s** tropiques *mpl*.

**trot** /trɒt/ *n* trot *m*; **on the ~** 🄸 coup sur coup. ● *vi* (*pt* **trotted**) trotter.

**trouble** /'trʌbl/ *n* problèmes *mpl*; ennuis *mpl*; (pains, effort) peine *f*; **be in ~** avoir des ennuis; **go to a lot of ~** se donner du mal; **what's the ~?** quel est le problème? ● *vt* (bother) déranger; (worry) tracasser. ● *vi* ~ (**oneself**) **to do** se donner la peine de faire. **~maker** *n* provocateur/

-trice m/f. ~shooter n conciliateur/-trice m/f; (Tech) expert m.

**troublesome** /'trʌblsəm/ a ennuyeux.

**trousers** /'traʊzəz/ *npl* pantalon *m*; **short ~** short *m*.

**trout** /traʊt/ *n inv* truite *f*.

**trowel** /'traʊəl/ *n* (garden) déplantoir *m*; (for mortar) truelle *f*.

**truant** /'tru:ənt/ *n* (School) élève *mf* qui fait l'école buissonnière; **play ~** sécher les cours.

**truce** /tru:s/ *n* trève *f*.

**truck** /trʌk/ *n* (lorry) camion *m*; (cart) chariot *m*; (Rail) wagon *m* de marchandises. **~-driver** *n* routier *m*.

**true** /tru:/ *a* vrai; (accurate) exact; (faithful) fidèle.

**truffle** /'trʌfl/ *n* truffe *f*.

**truly** /'tru:lɪ/ *adv* vraiment; (faithfully) fidèlement; (truthfully) sincèrement.

**trumpet** /'trʌmpɪt/ *n* trompette *f*.

**trunk** /trʌŋk/ *n* (of tree, body) tronc *m*; (of elephant) trompe *f*; (box) malle *f*; (Auto, US) coffre *m*; **~s** (for swimming) slip *m* de bain.

**trust** /trʌst/ *n* confiance *f*; (association) trust *m*; **in ~** en dépôt. ● *vt* avoir confiance en; **~ sb with** confier à qn. ● *vi* **~ in** *or* **to** s'en remettre à. **trustee** *n* administrateur/-trice *m/f*. **trustworthy** *a* digne de confiance.

**truth** /tru:θ/ *n* (*pl* **-s** /tru:ðz/) vérité *f*. **truthful** *a* (*account*) véridique; (*person*) qui dit la vérité.

**try** /traɪ/ *vt/i* (*pt* **tried**) essayer; (be a strain on) éprouver; (Jur) juger; **~ on** *or* **out** essayer; **~ to do** essayer de faire. ● *n* (attempt) essai *m*; (rugby) essai *m*.

**T-shirt** /'ti:ʃɜ:t/ *n* tee-shirt *m*.

**tub** /tʌb/ *n* (for flowers) bac *m*; (of ice cream) pot *m*; (bath) baignoire *f*.

**tube** /tju:b/ *n* tube *m*; **the ~** ▣ le métro.

**tuberculosis** /tju:bɜ:kjʊ'ləʊsɪs/ *n* tuberculose *f*.

**tuck** /tʌk/ *n* pli *m*. ● *vt* (put away, place) ranger; (hide) cacher. ● *vi* **~ in** *or* **into** ▣ attaquer. **~ in** (shirt) rentrer; (blanket, person) border.

**Tuesday** /'tju:zdɪ/ *n* mardi *m*.

**tug** /tʌg/ *vt* (*pt* **tugged**) tirer. ● *vi* **~ at/on** tirer sur. ● *n* (boat) remorqueur *m*.

**tuition** /tju:'ɪʃn/ *n* cours *mpl*; (fee) frais *mpl* pédagogiques.

**tulip** /'tju:lɪp/ *n* tulipe *f*.

**tumble** /'tʌmbl/ *vi* (fall) dégringoler. ● *n* chute *f*. **~-drier** *n* sèche-linge *m inv*.

**tumbler** /'tʌmblə(r)/ *n* verre *m* droit.

**tummy** /'tʌmɪ/ *n* ▣ ventre *m*.

**tumour** /'tju:mə(r)/ *n* tumeur *f*.

**tuna** /'tju:nə/ *n inv* thon *m*.

**tune** /tju:n/ *n* air *m*; **be in ~/out of ~** (instrument) être/ne pas être en accord; (singer) chanter juste/faux. ● *vt* (*engine*) régler; (Mus) accorder. ● *vi* **~ in (to)** (radio, TV) écouter. □ **~ up** s'accorder.

**Tunisia** /tju:'nɪzɪə/ *n* Tunisie *f*.

**tunnel** /'tʌnl/ *n* tunnel *m*; (in mine) galerie *f*. ● *vi* (*pt* **tunnelled**) creuser un tunnel (**into** dans).

**turf** /tɜ:f/ *n* (*pl* **turf** *or* **turves**) gazon *m*; **the ~** (racing) le turf. ● *vt* **~ out** ▣ jeter dehors.

**Turk** /tɜ:k/ *n* Turc *m*, Turque *f*. **Turkey** *n* Turquie *f*.

**turkey** /'tɜ:kɪ/ *n* dinde *f*.

**Turkish** /'tɜ:kɪʃ/ *a* turc. ● *n* (Ling) turc *m*.

**turn** /tɜ:n/ *vt/i* tourner; (*person*) se tourner; (to other side) retourner;

(change) (se) transformer (**into** en); (become) devenir; (deflect) détourner; (milk) tourner. ● *n* tour *m*; (in road) tournant *m*; (of mind, events) tournure *f*; **do a good ~** rendre service; **in ~** à tour de rôle; **take ~s** se relayer. □ **~ against** se retourner contre; **~ away** *vi* se détourner; *vt* (avert) détourner; (refuse) refuser; (send back) renvoyer; **~ back** *vi* (return) retourner; (*vehicle*) faire demi-tour; *vt* (fold) rabattre; **~ down** refuser; (fold) rabattre; (reduce) baisser; **~ off** (*light*) éteindre; (*engine*) arrêter; (*tap*) fermer; (of driver) tourner; **~ on** (*light*) allumer; (*engine*) allumer; (*tap*) ouvrir; **~ out** *vt* (*light*) eteindre; (empty) vider; (produce) produire; *vi* **it ~s out that** il se trouve que; **~ out well/badly** bien/mal se terminer; **~ over** (se) retourner; **~ round** (person) se retourner; **~ up** *vi* arriver; (be found) se retrouver; *vt* (find) déterrer; (collar) remonter.

**turning** /'tɜ:nɪŋ/ *n* rue *f*; (bend) virage *m*.

**turnip** /'tɜ:nɪp/ *n* navet *m*.

**turn**: **~-out** *n* assistance *f*. **~over** *n* (pie) chausson *m*; (money) chiffre *m* d'affaires. **~table** *n* (for record) platine *f*.

**turquoise** /'tɜ:kwɔɪz/ *a* turquoise *inv*.

**turtle** /'tɜ:tl/ *n* tortue *f* (de mer). **~-neck** *n* col *m* montant.

**tutor** /'tju:tə(r)/ *n* (private) professeur *m* particulier; (Univ) (GB) chargé/-e *m/f* de travaux dirigés.

**tutorial** /tju:'tɔ:rɪəl/ *n* (Univ) classe *f* de travaux dirigés.

**tuxedo** /tʌk'si:dəʊ/ *n* (US) smoking *m*.

**TV** /ti:'vi:/ *n* télé *f*.

**tweezers** /'twi:zəz/ *npl* pince *f* (à épiler).

**twelfth** /twelfθ/ *a* & *n* douzième (*mf*).

**twelve** /twelv/ *a* & *n* douze (*m*); **~ (o'clock)** midi *m or* minuit *m*.

**twentieth** /'twentɪəθ/ *a* & *n* vingtième (*mf*).

**twenty** /'twentɪ/ *a* & *n* vingt (*m*).

**twice** /twaɪs/ *adv* deux fois.

**twig** /twɪg/ *n* brindille *f*.

**twilight** /'twaɪlaɪt/ *n* crépuscule *m*. ● *a* crépusculaire.

**twin** /twɪn/ *n* & *a* jumeau/-elle (*m/f*). ● *vt* (*pt* **twinned**) jumeler.

**twinge** /twɪndʒ/ *n* (of pain) élancement *m*; (of conscience, doubt) accès *m*.

**twinkle** /'twɪŋkl/ *vi* (*star*) scintiller; (*eye*) pétiller. ● *n* scintillement *m*; pétillement *m*.

**twinning** /'twɪnɪŋ/ *n* jumelage *m*.

**twist** /twɪst/ *vt* tordre; (weave together) entortiller; (roll) enrouler; (distort) déformer. ● *vi* (*rope*) s'entortiller; (*road*) zigzaguer. ● *n* torsion *f*; (in rope) tortillon *m*; (in road) tournant *m*; (in play, story) coup *m* de théâtre.

**twitch** /twɪtʃ/ *vi* (*person*) trembloter; (*mouth*) trembler; (*string*) vibrer. ● *n* (tic) tic *m*; (jerk) secousse *f*.

**two** /tu:/ *a* & *n* deux (*m*); **in ~s** par deux; **break in ~** casser en deux.

**tycoon** /taɪ'ku:n/ *n* magnat *m*.

**type** /taɪp/ *n* type *m*, genre *m*; (print) caractères *mpl*. ● *vt/i* (write) taper (à la machine). **~face** *n* police *f* (de caractères). **~writer** *n* machine *f* à écrire.

**typical** /'tɪpɪkl/ *a* typique.

**typist** /'taɪpɪst/ *n* dactylo *mf*.

**tyrant** /'taɪərənt/ *n* tyran *m*.

**tyre** /'taɪə(r)/ *n* pneu *m*.

# Uu

**udder** /'ʌdə(r)/ *n* pis *m*, mamelle *f*.

**UFO** /'ju:fəʊ/ *n* OVNI *m inv*.

**UHT** *abbr* (**ultra heat treated**) **~ milk** lait *m* longue conservation.

**ugly** /'ʌglɪ/ *a* (**-ier**, **-iest**) laid.

**UK** *abbr* ⇒UNITED KINGDOM.

**Ukraine** /ju:'kreɪn/ *n* Ukraine *f*.

**ulcer** /'ʌlsə(r)/ *n* ulcère *m*.

**ulterior** /ʌl'tɪərɪə(r)/ *a* ultérieur; **~ motive** arrière-pensée *f*.

**ultimate** /'ʌltɪmət/ *a* dernier, ultime; (definitive) définitif; (basic) fondamental.

**ultrasound** /'ʌltrəsaʊnd/ *n* ultra-son *m*.

**umbilical cord** /ʌm'bɪlɪkl kɔ:d/ *n* cordon *m* ombilical.

**umbrella** /ʌm'brelə/ *n* parapluie *m*.

**umpire** /'ʌmpaɪə(r)/ *n* arbitre *m*. ● *vt* arbitrer.

**umpteenth** /ʌmp'ti:nθ/ *a* [I] énième.

**UN** *abbr* (**United Nations**) ONU *f*.

**unable** /ʌn'eɪbl/ *a* incapable; (through circumstances) dans l'impossibilité (**to do** de faire).

**unacceptable** /ʌnək'septəbl/ *a* (*suggestion*) inacceptable; (*behaviour*) inadmissible.

**unanimous** /ju:'nænɪməs/ *a* unanime. **unanimously** *adv* à l'unanimité.

**unattended** /ʌnə'tendɪd/ *a* sans surveillance.

**unattractive** /ʌnə'træktɪv/ *a* (*idea*) peu attrayant; (*person*) peu attirant.

**unauthorized** /ʌn'ɔ:θəraɪzd/ *a* non autorisé.

**unavoidable** /ʌnə'vɔɪdəbl/ *a* inévitable.

**unbearable** /ʌn'beərəbl/ *a* insupportable.

**unbelievable** /ʌnbɪ'li:vəbl/ *a* incroyable.

**unbiased** /ʌn'baɪəst/ *a* impartial.

**unblock** /ʌn'blɒk/ *vt* déboucher.

**unborn** /ʌn'bɔ:n/ *a* (*child*) à naître; (*generation*) à venir.

**uncalled-for** /ʌn'kɔ:ldfɔ:(r)/ *a* injustifié, déplacé.

**uncanny** /ʌn'kænɪ/ *a* (**-ier**, **-iest**) étrange, troublant.

**uncivilized** /ʌn'sɪvɪlaɪzd/ *a* barbare.

**uncle** /'ʌŋkl/ *n* oncle *m*.

**uncomfortable** /ʌn'kʌmftəbl/ *a* (*chair*) inconfortable; (*feeling*) pénible; **feel** *or* **be ~** (person) être mal à l'aise.

**uncommon** /ʌn'kɒmən/ *a* rare.

**unconscious** /ʌn'kɒnʃəs/ *a* sans connaissance, inanimé; (not aware) inconscient (**of** de). ● *n* inconscient *m*.

**unconventional** /ʌnkən'venʃənl/ *a* peu conventionnel.

**uncouth** /ʌn'ku:θ/ *a* grossier.

**uncover** /ʌn'kʌvə(r)/ *vt* découvrir.

**undecided** /ʌndɪ'saɪdɪd/ *a* indécis.

**under** /'ʌndə(r)/ *prep* sous; (less than) moins de; (according to) selon. ● *adv* au-dessous; **~ it/there** là-dessous. **~ age** *a* mineur. **~cover** *a* secret. **~cut** *vt* (*pt* **-cut**; *pres p* **-cutting**) (Comm)

vendre moins cher que. **~dog** *n* (Pol) opprimé/-e *m/f*; (socially) déshérité/-e *m/f*. **~done** *a* pas assez cuit. **~estimate** *vt* sous-estimer. **~fed** *a* sous-alimenté. **~go** *vt* (*pt* **-went**; *pp* **-gone**) subir. **~graduate** *n* étudiant/-e *m/f* (*qui prépare la licence*).

**underground** /'ʌndəgraʊnd/ *a* souterrain; (secret) clandestin. ● *adv* sous terre. ● *n* (rail) métro *m*.

**under**: **~line** *vt* souligner. **~mine** *vt* saper.

**underneath** /ʌndə'ni:θ/ *prep* sous. ● *adv* (en) dessous.

**under**: **~pants** *npl* slip *m*. **~rate** *vt* sous-estimer.

**understand** /ʌndə'stænd/ *vt/i* (*pt* **-stood**) comprendre.

**understanding** /ʌndə'stændɪŋ/ *a* compréhensif. ● *n* compréhension *f*; (agreement) entente *f*.

**undertake** /ʌndə'teɪk/ *vt* (*pt* **-took**; *pp* **-taken**) entreprendre. **~taker** *n* entrepreneur *m* de pompes funèbres. **~taking** *n* (task) entreprise *f*; (promise) promesse *f*.

**underwater** /ʌndə'wɔ:tə(r)/ *a* sous-marin. ● *adv* sous l'eau.

**under**: **~wear** *n* sous-vêtements *mpl*. **~world** *n* (of crime) milieu *m*, pègre *f*.

**undo** /ʌn'du:/ *vt* (*pt* **-did**; *pp* **-done** /-dʌn/) défaire, détacher; (*wrong*) réparer; (Comput) annuler.

**undress** /ʌn'dres/ *vt/i* (se) déshabiller; **get ~ed** se déshabiller

**undue** /ʌn'dju:/ *a* excessif.

**unearth** /ʌn'ɜ:θ/ *vt* déterrer.

**uneasy** /ʌn'i:zɪ/ *a* (ill at ease) mal à l'aise; (worried) inquiet; (*situation*) difficile.

**uneducated** /ʌn'edʒʊkeɪtɪd/ *a* (*person*) inculte; (*speech*) populaire.

**unemployed** /ʌnɪm'plɔɪd/ *a* en chômage. ● *npl* **the ~** les chômeurs *mpl*.

**unemployment** /ʌnɪm'plɔɪmənt/ *n* chômage *m*; **~ benefit** allocations *fpl* de chômage.

**uneven** /ʌn'i:vn/ *a* inégal.

**unexpected** /ʌnɪk'spektɪd/ *a* inattendu, imprévu. **unexpectedly** *adv* (*arrive*) à l'improviste; (*small*, *fast*) étonnamment.

**unfair** /ʌn'feə(r)/ *a* injuste.

**unfaithful** /ʌn'feɪθfl/ *a* infidèle.

**unfit** /ʌn'fɪt/ *a* (Med) pas en forme; (ill) malade; (unsuitable) impropre (**for** à); **~ to** (unable) pas en état de.

**unfold** /ʌn'fəʊld/ *vt* déplier; (expose) exposer. ● *vi* se dérouler.

**unforeseen** /ʌnfɔ:'si:n/ *a* imprévu.

**unforgettable** /ʌnfə'getəbl/ *a* inoubliable.

**unfortunate** /ʌn'fɔ:tʃʊnət/ *a* malheureux; (*event*) fâcheux.

**ungrateful** /ʌn'greɪtfl/ *a* ingrat.

**unhappy** /ʌn'hæpɪ/ *a* (**-ier**, **-iest**) (*person*) malheureux; (*face*) triste; (not pleased) mécontent (**with** de).

**unharmed** /ʌn'hɑ:md/ *a* indemne, sain et sauf.

**unhealthy** /ʌn'helθɪ/ *a* (**-ier**, **-iest**) (*climate*) malsain, (*person*) en mauvaise santé.

**unheard-of** /ʌn'hɜ:dɒv/ *a* inouï.

**unhurt** /ʌn'hɜ:t/ *a* indemne.

**uniform** /'ju:nɪfɔ:m/ *n* uniforme *m*. ● *a* uniforme.

**unify** /'ju:nɪfaɪ/ *vt* unifier.

**unintentional** /ʌnɪn'tenʃənl/ *a* involontaire.

**uninterested** /ʌn'ɪntrəstɪd/ *a* indifférent (**in** à).

**union** /'ju:nɪən/ *n* union *f*; (trade union) syndicat *m*; **U~ Jack** drapeau *m* du Royaume-Uni.

**unique** /ju:'ni:k/ *a* unique.

**unit** /'ju:nɪt/ *n* unité *f*; (of furniture) élément *m*; ~ **trust** ≈ SICAV *f*.

**unite** /ju:'naɪt/ *vt/i* (s')unir.

**United Kingdom** *n* Royaume-Uni *m*.

**United Nations** *npl* Nations *fpl* Unies.

**United States (of America)** *npl* États-Unis *mpl* (d'Amérique).

**unity** /'ju:nətɪ/ *n* unité *f*.

**universal** /ju:nɪ'vɜ:sl/ *a* universel.

**universe** /'ju:nɪvɜ:s/ *n* univers *m*.

**university** /ju:nɪ'vɜ:sətɪ/ *n* université *f*. ● *a* universitaire; (*student, teacher*) d'université.

**unkind** /ʌn'kaɪnd/ *a* pas gentil, méchant.

**unknown** /ʌn'nəʊn/ *a* inconnu. ● *n* the ~ l'inconnu *m*.

**unleaded** /ʌn'ledɪd/ *a* sans plomb.

**unless** /ən'les/ *conj* à moins que.

**unlike** /ʌn'laɪk/ *a* différent. ● *prep* contrairement à; (different from) différent de.

**unlikely** /ʌn'laɪklɪ/ *a* improbable.

**unload** /ʌn'ləʊd/ *vt* décharger.

**unlock** /ʌn'lɒk/ *vt* ouvrir.

**unlucky** /ʌn'lʌkɪ/ *a* (**-ier**, **-iest**) malheureux; (*number*) qui porte malheur.

**unmarried** /ʌn'mærɪd/ *a* célibataire.

**unnatural** /ʌn'nætʃrəl/ *a* pas naturel, anormal.

**unnecessary** /ʌn'nesəsərɪ/ *a* inutile.

**unnoticed** /ʌn'nəʊtɪst/ *a* inaperçu.

**unofficial** /ʌnə'fɪʃl/ *a* officieux.

**unpack** /ʌn'pæk/ *vt* (*suitcase*) défaire; (*contents*) déballer. ● *vi* défaire sa valise.

**unpleasant** /ʌn'pleznt/ *a* désagréable (**to** avec).

**unplug** /ʌn'plʌg/ *vt* débrancher.

**unpopular** /ʌn'pɒpjʊlə(r)/ *a* impopulaire; ~ **with** mal vu de.

**unprofessional** /ʌnprə'feʃənl/ *a* peu professionnel.

**unqualified** /ʌn'kwɒlɪfaɪd/ *a* non diplômé; (*success*) total; **be** ~ **to** ne pas être qualifié pour.

**unravel** /ʌn'rævl/ *vt* (*pt* **unravelled**) démêler.

**unreasonable** /ʌn'ri:znəbl/ *a* irréaliste.

**unrelated** /ʌnrɪ'leɪtɪd/ *a* sans rapport (**to** avec).

**unreliable** /ʌnrɪ'laɪəbl/ *a* peu sérieux; (*machine*) peu fiable.

**unrest** /ʌn'rest/ *n* troubles *mpl*.

**unroll** /ʌn'rəʊl/ *vt* dérouler.

**unruly** /ʌn'ru:lɪ/ *a* indiscipliné.

**unsafe** /ʌn'seɪf/ *a* (dangerous) dangereux; (*person*) en danger.

**unscheduled** /ʌn'ʃedju:ld, US ʌn'skedju:ld/ *a* pas prévu.

**unscrupulous** /ʌn'skru:pjʊləs/ *a* sans scrupules, malhonnête.

**unsettled** /ʌn'setld/ *a* instable.

**unsightly** /ʌn'saɪtlɪ/ *a* laid.

**unskilled** /ʌn'skɪld/ *a* (worker) non qualifié.

**unsound** /ʌn'saʊnd/ *a* (*roof*) en mauvais état; (*investment*) douteux.

**unsteady** /ʌn'stedɪ/ *a* (*step*) chancelant; (*ladder*) instable; (*hand*) mal assuré.

**unsuccessful** /ʌnsək'sesfl/ *a* (*result, candidate*) malheureux; (*attempt*) infructueux; **be** ~ ne pas réussir (**in doing** à faire).

**unsuitable** /ʌn'su:təbl/ *a* inapproprié; **be** ~ ne pas convenir.

**unsure** /ʌn'ʃɔ:(r)/ *a* incertain.

**untidy** /ʌn'taɪdɪ/ *a* (**-ier**, **-iest**) (*person*) désordonné; (*room*) en désordre; (*work*) mal soigné.

**untie** /ʌn'taɪ/ *vt* (*knot, parcel*) défaire; (*person*) détacher.

**until** /ən'tɪl/ *prep* jusqu'à; **not ~** pas avant. ● *conj* jusqu'à ce que; **not ~** pas avant que.

**untrue** /ʌn'tru:/ *a* faux.

**unused** /ʌn'ju:zd/ *a* (new) neuf; (not in use) inutilisé.

**unusual** /ʌn'ju:ʒʊəl/ *a* exceptionnel; (strange) insolite, étrange.

**unwanted** /ʌn'wɒntɪd/ *a* (useless) superflu; (*child*) non désiré.

**unwelcome** /ʌn'welkəm/ *a* fâcheux; (*guest*) importun.

**unwell** /ʌn'wel/ *a* souffrant.

**unwilling** /ʌn'wɪlɪŋ/ *a* peu disposé (**to** à); (*accomplice*) malgré soi.

**unwind** /ʌn'waɪnd/ *vt/i* (*pt* **unwound** /ʌn'waʊnd/) (se) dérouler; (relax 🄸) se détendre.

**unwise** /ʌn'waɪz/ *a* imprudent.

**unwrap** /ʌn'ræp/ *vt* déballer.

**up** /ʌp/ *adv* en haut, en l'air; (*sun, curtain*) levé; (out of bed) levé, debout; (finished) fini; **be ~** (*level, price*) avoir monté. ● *prep* (a hill) en haut de; (a tree) dans; (a ladder) sur; **come** *or* **go ~** monter; **~ in the bedroom** là-haut dans la chambre; **~ there** là-haut; **~ to** jusqu'à; (*task*) à la hauteur de; **it is ~ to you** ça dépend de vous (**to** de); **be ~ to sth** (able) être capable de qch; (plot) préparer qch; **be ~ to** (in book) en être à; **be ~ against** faire face à; **~ to date** moderne; (*news*) récent. ● *n* **~s and downs** les hauts et les bas *mpl*.

**up-and-coming** *a* prometteur.

**upbringing** /'ʌpbrɪŋɪŋ/ *n* éducation *f*.

**update** /ʌp'deɪt/ *vt* mettre à jour.

**upgrade** /ʌp'greɪd/ *vt* améliorer; (*person*) promouvoir.

**upheaval** /ʌp'hi:vl/ *n* bouleversement *m*.

**uphill** /ʌp'hɪl/ *a* qui monte; (fig) difficile. ● *adv* **go ~** monter.

**upholstery** /ʌp'həʊlstərɪ/ *n* rembourrage *m*; (in vehicle) garniture *f*.

**upkeep** /'ʌpki:p/ *n* entretien *m*.

**up-market** *a* haut-de-gamme.

**upon** /ə'pɒn/ *prep* sur.

**upper** /'ʌpə(r)/ *a* supérieur; **have the ~ hand** avoir le dessus. ● *n* (of shoe) empeigne *f*. **~ class** *n* aristocratie *f*. **~most** *a* (highest) le plus haut.

**upright** /'ʌpraɪt/ *a* droit. ● *n* (post) montant *m*.

**uprising** /'ʌpraɪzɪŋ/ *n* soulèvement *m*.

**uproar** /'ʌprɔ:(r)/ *n* tumulte *m*.

**uproot** /ʌp'ru:t/ *vt* déraciner.

**upset**[1] /ʌp'set/ *vt* (*pt* **upset**; *pres p* **upsetting**) (overturn) renverser; (*plan, stomach*) déranger; (*person*) contrarier, affliger. ● *a* peiné.

**upset**[2] /'ʌpset/ *n* dérangement *m*; (distress) chagrin *m*.

**upside-down** /ʌpsaɪd'daʊn/ *adv* (lit) à l'envers; (fig) sens dessus dessous.

**upstairs** /ʌp'steəz/ *adv* en haut. ● *a* (*flat*) du haut.

**uptight** /ʌp'taɪt/ *a* 🄸 tendu, coincé 🄸.

**up-to-date** *a* à la mode; (*records*) à jour.

**upward** /'ʌpwəd/ *a* & *adv*, **upwards** *adv* vers le haut.

**urban** /'ɜ:bən/ *a* urbain.

**urge** /ɜ:dʒ/ *vt* conseiller vivement (**to do** de faire); **~ on** encourager. ● *n* forte envie *f*.

**urgency** /'ɜ:dʒənsɪ/ *n* urgence *f*; (of request, tone) insistance *f*. **urgent** *a* urgent; (*request*) pressant.

**urinal** /jʊə'raɪnl/ *n* urinoir *m*.

**urine** /'jʊərɪn/ *n* urine *f*.

**us** /ʌs, əs/ *pron* nous; **(to)** ~ nous; **both of** ~ tous/toutes les deux.

**US** *abbr* ⇒UNITED STATES.

**USA** *abbr* ⇒UNITED STATES OF AMERICA.

**use¹** /ju:z/ *vt* se servir de, utiliser; (consume) consommer; ~ **up** épuiser.

**use²** /ju:s/ *n* usage *m*, emploi *m*; **in** ~ en usage; **it is no** ~ **doing** ça ne sert à rien de faire; **make** ~ **of** se servir de; **of** ~ utile.

**used¹** /ju:zd/ *a* (*car*) d'occasion.

**used²** /ju:st/ *v aux* **he** ~ **to smoke** il fumait (autrefois). ● *a* ~ **to** habitué à.

**useful** /'ju:sfl/ *a* utile.

**useless** /'ju:slɪs/ *a* inutile; (*person*) incompétent.

**user** /'ju:zə(r)/ *n* (of road, service) usager *m*; (of product) utilisateur/-trice *m/f*. ~**-friendly** *a* facile d'emploi; (Comput) convivial.

**usual** /'ju:ʒʊəl/ *a* habituel, normal; **as** ~ comme d'habitude. **usually** *adv* d'habitude.

**utility** /ju:'tɪlətɪ/ *n* utilité *f*; **(public)** ~ service *m* public.

**utmost** /'ʌtməʊst/ *a* (furthest, most intense) extrême; **the** ~ **care** le plus grand soin. ● *n* **do one's** ~ faire tout son possible.

**utter** /'ʌtə(r)/ *a* complet, absolu. ● *vt* prononcer.

**U-turn** /'ju:tɜ:n/ *n* demi-tour *m*; (fig) volte-face *f inv*.

# Vv

**vacancy** /'veɪkənsɪ/ *n* (post) poste *m* vacant; (room) chambre *f* disponible.

**vacant** /'veɪkənt/ *a* (*post*) vacant; (*seat*) libre; (*look*) vague.

**vacate** /və'keɪt/ *vt* quitter.

**vacation** /veɪ'keɪʃn/ *n* vacances *fpl*.

**vaccinate** /'væksɪneɪt/ *vt* vacciner.

**vacuum** /'vækjʊəm/ *n* vide *m*. ~ **cleaner** *n* aspirateur *m*. ~**-packed** *a* emballé sous vide.

**vagina** /və'dʒaɪnə/ *n* vagin *m*.

**vagrant** /'veɪgrənt/ *n* vagabond/-e *m/f*.

**vague** /veɪg/ *a* vague; (*outline*) flou; **be** ~ **about** ne pas préciser.

**vain** /veɪn/ *a* (conceited) vaniteux; (useless) vain; **in** ~ en vain.

**valentine** /'væləntaɪn/ *n* ~ **(card)** carte *f* de la Saint-Valentin.

**valid** /'vælɪd/ *a* (*argument, ticket*) valable; (*passport*) valide.

**valley** /'vælɪ/ *n* vallée *f*.

**valuable** /'væljʊəbl/ *a* (object) de valeur; (*help*) précieux. **valuables** *npl* objets *mpl* de valeur.

**valuation** /væljʊ'eɪʃn/ *n* (of painting) expertise *f*; (of house) évaluation *f*.

**value** /'vælju:/ *n* valeur *f*; ~ **added tax** taxe *f* à la valeur ajoutée, TVA *f*. ● *vt* (appraise) évaluer; (cherish) attacher de la valeur à.

**valve** /vælv/ *n* (Tech) soupape *f*; (of tyre) valve *f*; (Med) valvule *f*.

**van** /væn/ *n* camionnette *f*.

**vandal** /'vændl/ *n* vandale *mf*.

**vanguard** /'vængɑ:d/ *n* **in the ~ of** à l'avant-garde *f* de.

**vanilla** /və'nɪlə/ *n* vanille *f*.

**vanish** /'vænɪʃ/ *vi* disparaître.

**vapour** /'veɪpə(r)/ *n* vapeur *f*.

**variable** /'veərɪəbl/ *a* variable.

**varicose** /'værɪkəʊs/ *a* **~ veins** varices *fpl*.

**varied** /'veərɪd/ *a* varié.

**variety** /və'raɪətɪ/ *n* variété *f*; (entertainment) variétés *fpl*.

**various** /'veərɪəs/ *a* divers.

**varnish** /'vɑ:nɪʃ/ *n* vernis *m*. ● *vt* vernir.

**vary** /'veərɪ/ *vt/i* varier.

**vase** /vɑ:z/ *n* vase *m*.

**vast** /vɑ:st/ *a* (*space*) vaste; (in quantity) énorme.

**vat** /væt/ *n* cuve *f*.

**VAT** /vi:eɪ'ti:, væt/ *abbr* (**value added tax**) TVA *f*.

**vault** /vɔ:lt/ *n* (roof) voûte *f*; (in bank) chambre *f* forte; (tomb) caveau *m*; (jump) saut *m*. ● *vt/i* sauter.

**VCR** *abbr* ⇒VIDEO CASSETTE RECORDER.

**VDU** *abbr* ⇒VISUAL DISPLAY UNIT.

**veal** /vi:l/ *n* veau *m*.

**vegan** /'vi:gən/ *a & n* végétalien/-ne (*m/f*).

**vegetable** /'vedʒtəbl/ *n* légume *m*. ● *a* végétal.

**vegetarian** /vedʒɪ'teərɪən/ *a & n* végétarien/-ne (*m/f*).

**vehicle** /'vi:ɪkl/ *n* véhicule *m*.

**veil** /veɪl/ *n* voile *m*.

**vein** /veɪn/ *n* (in body, rock) veine *f*; (on leaf) nervure *f*.

**velvet** /'velvɪt/ *n* velours *m*.

**vending-machine** /'vendɪŋməʃi:n/ *n* distributeur *m* automatique.

**veneer** /və'nɪə(r)/ *n* (on wood) placage *m*; (fig) vernis *m*.

**venereal** /və'nɪərɪəl/ *a* vénérien.

**venetian** /və'ni:ʃn/ *a* **~ blind** jalousie *f*.

**vengeance** /'vendʒəns/ *n* vengeance *f*; **with a ~** de plus belle.

**venison** /'venɪzn/ *n* venaison *f*.

**venom** /'venəm/ *n* venin *m*.

**vent** /vent/ *n* bouche *f*, conduit *m*; (in coat) fente *f*. ● *vt* (*anger*) décharger (**on** sur).

**ventilate** /'ventɪleɪt/ *vt* ventiler. **ventilator** *n* ventilateur *m*.

**venture** /'ventʃə(r)/ *n* entreprise *f*. ● *vt/i* (se) risquer.

**venue** /'venju:/ *n* lieu *m*.

**verb** /vɜ:b/ *n* verbe *m*.

**verbal** /'vɜ:bl/ *a* verbal.

**verbatim** /vɜ:'beɪtɪm/ *a & adv* mot pour mot.

**verdict** /'vɜ:dɪkt/ *n* verdict *m*.

**verge** /vɜ:dʒ/ *n* bord *m*; **on the ~ of doing** sur le point de faire. ● *vi* **~ on** friser, frôler.

**verify** /'verɪfaɪ/ *vt* vérifier.

**vermin** /'vɜ:mɪn/ *n* vermine *f*.

**versatile** /'vɜ:sətaɪl/ *a* (*person*) aux talents variés; (*mind*) souple.

**verse** /vɜ:s/ *n* strophe *f*; (of Bible) verset *m*; (poetry) vers *mpl*.

**version** /'vɜ:ʃn/ *n* version *f*.

**versus** /'vɜ:səs/ *prep* contre.

**vertebra** /'vɜ:tɪbrə/ *n* (*pl* **-brae** /-bri:/) vertèbre *f*.

**vertical** /'vɜ:tɪkl/ *a* vertical.

**vertigo** /'vɜ:tɪgəʊ/ *n* vertige *m*.

**very** /'verɪ/ *adv* très. ● *a* (actual) même; **the ~ day** le jour même; **at the ~ end** tout à la fin; **the ~ first** le tout premier; **~ much** beaucoup.

**vessel** /'vesl/ *n* vaisseau *m*.

**vest** /vest/ *n* maillot *m* de corps; (waistcoat: US) gilet *m*.

**vet** /vet/ *n* vétérinaire *mf.* ● *vt* (*pt* **vetted**) (*candidate*) examiner (de près).

**veteran** /'vetərən/ *n* vétéran *m*; (war) ~ ancien combattant *m.*

**veterinary** /'vetərɪnərɪ/ *a* vétérinaire; ~ **surgeon** vétérinaire *mf.*

**veto** /'vi:təʊ/ *n* (*pl* ~**es**) veto *m*; (right) droit *m* de veto. ● *vt* mettre son veto à.

**via** /'vaɪə/ *prep* via, par.

**vibrate** /vaɪ'breɪt/ *vt/i* (faire) vibrer.

**vicar** /'vɪkə(r)/ *n* pasteur *m.*

**vice** /vaɪs/ *n* (depravity) vice *m*; (Tech) étau *m.*

**vicinity** /vɪ'sɪnətɪ/ *n* environs *mpl*; **in the** ~ **of** à proximité de.

**vicious** /'vɪʃəs/ *a* (spiteful) méchant; (violent) brutal; ~ **circle** cercle *m* vicieux.

**victim** /'vɪktɪm/ *n* victime *f.*

**victor** /'vɪktə(r)/ *n* vainqueur *m.* **victory** *n* victoire *f.*

**video** /'vɪdɪəʊ/ *a* (*game, camera*) vidéo *inv.* ● *n* (recorder) magnétoscope *m*; (film) vidéo *f*; ~ **(cassette)** cassette *f* vidéo. ● *vt* enregistrer.

**videotape** /'vɪdɪəʊteɪp/ *n* bande *f* vidéo. ● *vt* (*programme*) enregistrer; (*wedding*) filmer avec une caméra vidéo.

**view** /vju:/ *n* vue *f*; **in my** ~ à mon avis; **in** ~ **of** compte tenu de; **on** ~ exposé; **with a** ~ **to** dans le but de. ● *vt* (watch) regarder; (consider) considérer (**as** comme); (*house*) visiter. **viewer** *n* (TV) téléspectateur/-trice *m/f.*

**view**: ~**finder** *n* viseur *m.* ~**point** *n* point *m* de vue.

**vigilant** /'vɪdʒɪlənt/ *a* vigilant.

**vigour**, (US) **vigor** /'vɪgə(r)/ *n* vigueur *f.*

**vile** /vaɪl/ *a* (base) vil; (bad) abominable.

**villa** /'vɪlə/ *n* pavillon *m*; (for holiday) villa *f.*

**village** /'vɪlɪdʒ/ *n* village *m.*

**villain** /'vɪlən/ *n* scélérat *m*, bandit *m*; (in story) méchant *m.*

**vindictive** /vɪn'dɪktɪv/ *a* vindicatif.

**vine** /vaɪn/ *n* vigne *f.*

**vinegar** /'vɪnɪgə(r)/ *n* vinaigre *m.*

**vineyard** /'vɪnjəd/ *n* vignoble *m.*

**vintage** /'vɪntɪdʒ/ *n* (year) année *f*, millésime *m.* ● *a* (*wine*) de grand cru; (*car*) d'époque.

**viola** /vɪ'əʊlə/ *n* (Mus) alto *m.*

**violate** /'vaɪəleɪt/ *vt* violer.

**violence** /'vaɪələns/ *n* violence *f.* **violent** *a* violent.

**violet** /'vaɪələt/ *n* (Bot) violette *f*; (colour) violet *m.*

**violin** /vaɪə'lɪn/ *n* violon *m.*

**VIP** *abbr* (**very important person**) personnalité *f*, VIP *m.*

**virgin** /'vɜ:dʒɪn/ *n* (woman) vierge *f.*

**Virgo** /'vɜ:gəʊ/ *n* Vierge *f.*

**virtual** /'vɜ:tʃʊəl/ *a* quasi-total; (Comput) virtuel. **virtually** *adv* pratiquement.

**virtue** /'vɜ:tʃu:/ *n* vertu *f*; (advantage) mérite *m*; **by** ~ **of** en raison de.

**virus** /'vaɪərəs/ *n* virus *m.*

**visa** /'vi:zə/ *n* visa *m.*

**visibility** /vɪzə'bɪlətɪ/ *n* visibilité *f.* **visible** *a* visible.

**vision** /'vɪʒn/ *n* vision *f.*

**visit** /'vɪzɪt/ *vt* (*pt* **visited**) (*person*) rendre visite à; (*place*) visiter. ● *vi* être en visite. ● *n* (tour, call) visite *f*; (stay) séjour *m.* **visitor** *n* visiteur/-euse *m/f*; (guest) invité/-e *m/f.*

**visual** /'vɪʒʊəl/ *a* visuel. ~ **display unit** *n* visuel *m*, console *f* de visualisation.

**visualize** /'vɪʒʊəlaɪz/ *vt* se représenter; (foresee) envisager.

**vital** /'vaɪtl/ *a* vital.

**vitamin** /'vɪtəmɪn/ *n* vitamine *f*.

**vivacious** /vɪ'veɪʃəs/ *a* plein de vivacité.

**vivid** /'vɪvɪd/ *a* (*colour, imagination*) vif; (*description, dream*) frappant.

**vivisection** /vɪvɪ'sekʃn/ *n* vivisection *f*.

**vocabulary** /və'kæbjʊlərɪ/ *n* vocabulaire *m*.

**vocal** /'vəʊkl/ *a* vocal; (*person*) qui s'exprime franchement. ~ **cords** *npl* cordes *fpl* vocales.

**vocation** /və'keɪʃn/ *n* vocation *f*. **vocational** *a* professionnel.

**voice** /vɔɪs/ *n* voix *f*. ● *vt* (express) formuler. ~ **mail** *n* messagerie *f* vocale.

**void** /vɔɪd/ *a* vide (**of** de); (not valid) nul. ● *n* vide *m*.

**volatile** /'vɒlətaɪl/ *a* (*person*) versatile; (*situation*) explosif.

**volcano** /vɒl'keɪnəʊ/ *n* (*pl* ~**es**) volcan *m*.

**volley** /'vɒlɪ/ *n* (of blows, in tennis) volée *f*; (of gunfire) salve *f*.

**volt** /vəʊlt/ *n* (Electr) volt *m*. **voltage** *n* tension *f*.

**volume** /'vɒlju:m/ *n* volume *m*.

**voluntary** /'vɒləntərɪ/ *a* volontaire; (unpaid) bénévole.

**volunteer** /vɒlən'tɪə(r)/ *n* volontaire *mf*. ● *vi* s'offrir (**to do** pour faire); (Mil) s'engager comme volontaire. ● *vt* offrir.

**vomit** /'vɒmɪt/ *vt/i* (*pt* **vomited**) vomir. ● *n* vomi *m*.

**vote** /vəʊt/ *n* vote *m*; (right) droit *m* de vote. ● *vt/i* voter; ~ **sb in** élire qn. **voter** *n* électeur/-trice *m/f*. **voting** *n* vote *m* (**of** de); (poll) scrutin *m*.

**vouch** /vaʊtʃ/ *vi* ~ **for** se porter garant de.

**voucher** /'vaʊtʃə(r)/ *n* bon *m*.

**vowel** /'vaʊəl/ *n* voyelle *f*.

**voyage** /'vɔɪɪdʒ/ *n* voyage *m* (en mer).

**vulgar** /'vʌlgə(r)/ *a* vulgaire.

**vulnerable** /'vʌlnərəbl/ *a* vulnérable.

# Ww

**wad** /wɒd/ *n* (pad) tampon *m*; (bundle) liasse *f*.

**wade** /weɪd/ *vi* ~ **through** (*mud*) patauger dans; (*book*: fig) avancer péniblement dans.

**wafer** /'weɪfə(r)/ *n* (biscuit) gaufrette *f*.

**waffle** /'wɒfl/ *n* (talk [I]) verbiage *m*; (cake) gaufre *f*. ● *vi* [I] divaguer.

**wag** /wæg/ *vt/i* (*pt* **wagged**) (tail) remuer.

**wage** /weɪdʒ/ *vt* (campaign) mener; ~ **war** faire la guerre. ● *n* (weekly, daily) salaire *m*; ~**s** salaire *m*. ~**-earner** *n* salarié/-e *m/f*.

**wagon** /'wægən/ *n* (horse-drawn) chariot *m*; (Rail) wagon *m* (de marchandises).

**wail** /weɪl/ *vi* gémir. ● *n* gémissement *m*.

**waist** /weɪst/ *n* taille *f*. ~**coat** *n* gilet *m*.

**wait** /weɪt/ *vt/i* attendre; **I can't** ~ **to start** j'ai hâte de commencer; **let's** ~ **and see** attendons voir;

~ **for** [illegible]ndre; ~ **on** servir. ● *n* attente *f*.

**waiter** /'weɪtə(r)/ [illegible] garçon *m*, serveur *m*.

**waiting-list** *n* liste *f* d'attente.

**waiting-room** *n* salle *f* d'attente.

**waitress** /'weɪtrɪs/ *n* serveuse *f*.

**waive** /weɪv/ *vt* renoncer à.

**wake** /weɪk/ *vt*/*i* (*pt* **woke**; *pp* **woken**) ~ **(up)** (se) réveiller. ● *n* (track) sillage *m*; **in the ~ of** (after) à la suite de. ~ **up call** *n* réveil *m* téléphoné.

**Wales** /weɪlz/ *n* pays *m* de Galles.

**walk** /wɔ:k/ *vi* marcher; (not ride) aller à pied; (stroll) se promener. ● *vt* (*streets*) parcourir; (distance) faire à pied; (*dog*) promener. ● *n* promenade *f*, tour *m*; (gait) démarche *f*; (pace) marche *f*, pas *m*; (path) allée *f*; **have a ~** faire une promenade. □ ~ **out** (go away) partir; (worker) faire grève; ~ **out on** abandonner.

**walkie-talkie** /wɔ:kɪ'tɔ:kɪ/ *n* talkie-walkie *m*.

**walking** /'wɔ:kɪŋ/ *n* marche *f* (à pied). ● *a* (*corpse, dictionary*: fig) ambulant.

**walkman®** /'wɔ:kmən/ *n* walkman® *m*, baladeur *m*.

**walk**: ~**-out** *n* grève *f* surprise. ~**-over** *n* victoire *f* facile.

**wall** /wɔ:l/ *n* mur *m*; (of tunnel, stomach) paroi *f*. ● *a* mural. **walled** *a* (*city*) fortifié.

**wallet** /'wɒlɪt/ *n* portefeuille *m*.

**wallpaper** /'wɔ:lpeɪpə(r)/ *n* papier *m* peint. ● *vt* tapisser.

**walnut** /'wɔ:lnʌt/ *n* (nut) noix *f*; (tree) noyer *m*.

**waltz** /wɔ:ls/ *n* valse *f*. ● *vi* valser.

**wander** /'wɒndə(r)/ *vi* errer; (stroll) flâner; (digress) s'écarter du sujet; (in mind) divaguer.

**wane** /weɪn/ *vi* décroître.

**want** /wɒnt/ *vt* vouloir (**to do** faire); (need) avoir besoin de (**doing** d'être fait); (ask for) demander; **I ~ you to do it** je veux que vous le [illegible]siez. ● *vi* ~ **for** manquer de. ● *n* ([illegible] poverty) besoin *m*; (desire) désir *m*; ([illegible]) manque *m*; **for ~ of** faute de. **wan[illegible]** *a* (*criminal*) recherché par la poli[illegible]

**war** /wɔ:(r)/ *n* guerre *f*; **at** [illegible] guerre; **on the ~path** sur le sentier de la guerre.

**ward** /wɔ:d/ *n* (in hospital) salle *f*; (minor: Jur) pupille *mf*; (Pol) division *f* électorale. ● *vt* ~ **off** (*danger*) prévenir.

**warden** /'wɔ:dn/ *n* directeur/-trice *m*/*f*; (of park) gardien/-ne *m*/*f*; **(traffic)** ~ contractuel/-le *m*/*f*.

**wardrobe** /'wɔ:drəʊb/ *n* (furniture) armoire *f*; (clothes) garde-robe *f*.

**warehouse** /'weəhaʊs/ *n* entrepôt *m*.

**wares** /weəz/ *npl* marchandises *fpl*.

**warfare** /'wɔ:feə(r)/ *n* guerre *f*.

**warm** /wɔ:m/ *a* chaud; (hearty) chaleureux; **be** *or* **feel** ~ avoir chaud; **it is** ~ il fait chaud. ● *vt*/*i* ~ **(up)** (se) réchauffer; (*food*) chauffer; (liven up) (s')animer; (exercise) s'échauffer.

**warmth** /wɔ:mθ/ *n* chaleur *f*.

**warn** /wɔ:n/ *vt* avertir, prévenir; ~ **sb off sth** (advise against) mettre qn en garde contre qch; (forbid) interdire qch à qn.

**warning** /'wɔ:nɪŋ/ *n* avertissement *m*; (notice) avis *m*; **without ~** sans prévenir. ~ **light** *n* voyant *m*. ~ **triangle** *n* triangle *m* de sécurité.

**warp** /wɔ:p/ *vt*/*i* (*wood*) (se) voiler; (pervert) pervertir; (*judgment*) fausser.

**warrant** /ˈwɒrənt/ *n* (for arrest) mandat *m* (d'arrêt); (Comm) autorisation *f.* ● *vt* justifier.

**warranty** /ˈwɒrəntɪ/ *n* garantie *f.*

**wart** /wɔːt/ *n* verrue *f.*

**wartime** /ˈwɔːtaɪm/ *n* **in ~** en temps de guerre.

**wary** /ˈweərɪ/ *a* (**-ier**, **-iest**) prudent.

**was** /wɒz, wəz/ ⇒BE.

**wash** /wɒʃ/ *vt*/*i* (se) laver; (flow over) baigner; **~ one's hands of** se laver les mains de. ● *n* lavage *m*; (clothes) lessive *f*; **have a ~** se laver. □ **~ up** faire la vaisselle; (US) se laver. **~-basin** *n* lavabo *m.*

**washer** /ˈwɒʃə(r)/ *n* rondelle *f.*

**washing** /ˈwɒʃɪŋ/ *n* lessive *f.* **~-machine** *n* machine *f* à laver. **~-powder** *n* lessive *f.*

**washing-up** *n* vaisselle *f.* **~ liquid** *n* liquide *m* vaisselle.

**wash**: **~-out** *n* [I] fiasco *m.* **~-room** *n* (US) toilettes *fpl.*

**wasp** /wɒsp/ *n* guêpe *f.*

**wastage** /ˈweɪstɪdʒ/ *n* gaspillage *m.*

**waste** /weɪst/ *vt* gaspiller; (*time*) perdre. ● *vi* **~ away** dépérir. ● *a* superflu; **~ products** *or* **matter** déchets *mpl.* ● *n* gaspillage *m*; (of time) perte *f*; (rubbish) déchets *mpl*; **lay ~** dévaster. **wasteful** *a* peu économique; (*person*) gaspilleur.

**waste**: **~ land** *n* (desolate) terre *f* désolée; (unused) terre *f* inculte, (in town) terrain *m* vague. **~ paper** *n* vieux papiers *mpl.* **~-paper basket** *n* corbeille *f* (à papier).

**watch** /wɒtʃ/ *vt*/*i* (*television*) regarder; (observe) observer; (guard, spy on) surveiller, (be careful about) faire attention à. ● *n* (for telling time) montre *f*; (Naut) quart *m*; **be on the ~** guetter; **keep ~ on** surveiller. □ **~ out** (take care) faire attention (for à); **~ out for** (keep watch) guetter.

**water** /ˈwɔːtə(r)/ *n* eau *f*; **by ~** en bateau. ● *vt* arroser. ● *vi* (*eyes*) larmoyer; **my/his mouth ~s** l'eau me/lui vient à la bouche. □ **~ down** couper (d'eau); (tone down) édulcorer. **~-colour** *n* (painting) aquarelle *f.* **~cress** *n* cresson *m* (de fontaine). **~fall** *n* chute *f* d'eau, cascade *f.* **~ heater** *n* chauffe-eau *m.* **watering-can** *n* arrosoir *m.* **~-lily** *n* nénuphar *m.* **~-melon** *n* pastèque *f.* **~proof** *a* (*material*) imperméable. **~shed** *n* (in affairs) tournant *m* décisif. **~-skiing** *n* ski *m* nautique. **~tight** *a* étanche. **~way** *n* voie *f* navigable.

**watery** /ˈwɔːtərɪ/ *a* (*colour*) délavé; (*eyes*) humide; (*soup*) trop liquide.

**wave** /weɪv/ *n* vague *f*; (in hair) ondulation *f*; (radio) onde *f*; (sign) signe *m.* ● *vt* agiter. ● *vi* faire signe (de la main); (move in wind) flotter.

**waver** /ˈweɪvə(r)/ *vi* vaciller.

**wavy** /ˈweɪvɪ/ *a* (*line*) onduleux; (*hair*) ondulé.

**wax** /wæks/ *n* cire *f*; (for skis) fart *m.* ● *vt* cirer; farter; (*car*) lustrer.

**way** /weɪ/ *n* (road, path) chemin *m* (to de); (distance) distance *f*; (direction) direction *f*; (manner) façon *f*; (means) moyen *m*; **~s** (habits) habitudes *fpl*; **be in the ~** bloquer le passage; (hindrance: fig) gêner (qn); **be on one's** *or* **the ~** être sur son *or* le chemin; **by the ~** à propos; **by the ~side** au bord de la route; **by ~ of** comme; (via) par; **go out of one's ~** se donner du mal; **in a ~** dans un sens; **make one's ~ somewhere** se rendre quelque part; **push one's ~ through** se frayer un passage; **that ~** par là; **this ~** par ici; **~ in** entrée *f*; **~ out** sortie *f.* ● *adv* [I] loin.

**we** /wiː/ *pron* nous.

**weak** /wi:k/ *a* faible; (delicate) fragile.

**weakness** /'wi:knɪs/ *n* faiblesse *f*; (fault) point *m* faible; **a ~ for** (liking) un faible pour.

**wealth** /welθ/ *n* richesse *f*; (riches, resources) richesses *fpl*; (quantity) profusion *f*.

**wealthy** /'welθɪ/ *a* (**-ier**, **-iest**) riche. ● *n* **the ~** les riches *mpl*.

**wean** /wi:n/ *vt* (*baby*) sevrer.

**weapon** /'wepən/ *n* arme *f*.

**wear** /weə(r)/ *vt* (*pt* **wore**; *pp* **worn**) porter; (put on) mettre; (*expression*) avoir. ● *vi* (last) durer; **~ (out)** (s')user. ● *n* (use) usage *m*; (damage) usure *f*. □ **~ down** user; **~ off** (*colour, pain*) passer; **~ out** (exhaust) épuiser.

**weary** /'wɪərɪ/ *a* (**-ier**, **-iest**) fatigué, las. ● *vi* **~ of** se lasser de.

**weather** /'weðə(r)/ *n* temps *m*; **under the ~** patraque. ● *a* météorologique. ● *vt* (survive) réchapper de *or* à. **~ forecast** *n* météo *f*.

**weave** /wi:v/ *vt/i* (*pt* **wove**; *pp* **woven**) tisser; (*basket*) tresser; (move) se faufiler. ● *n* tissage *m*.

**web** /web/ *n* (of spider) toile *f*; (on foot) palmure *f*.

**Web** /web/ *n* (Comput) Web *m*. **~ cam** *n* webcam *f*. **~ site** *n* site *m* Internet. **~master** *n* administrateur *m* de site Internet. **~ page** *n* page *f* Web. **~ search** *n* recherche *f* sur le Web.

**wedding** /'wedɪŋ/ *n* mariage *m*. **~-ring** *n* alliance *f*.

**wedge** /wedʒ/ *n* (of wood) coin *m*; (under wheel) cale *f*. ● *vt* caler; (push) enfoncer; (crowd) coincer.

**Wednesday** /'wenzdɪ/ *n* mercredi *m*.

**weed** /wi:d/ *n* mauvaise herbe *f*. ● *vt/i* désherber; **~ out** extirper.

**week** /wi:k/ *n* semaine *f*; **a ~ today/tomorrow** aujourd'hui/demain en huit. **~day** *n* jour *m* de semaine. **~end** *n* week-end *m*, fin *f* de semaine.

**weekly** /'wi:klɪ/ *adv* toutes les semaines. ● *a* & *n* (periodical) hebdomadaire (*m*).

**weep** /wi:p/ *vt/i* (*pt* **wept**) pleurer (**for sb** qn).

**weigh** /weɪ/ *vt/i* peser; **~ anchor** lever l'ancre. □ **~ down** lester (avec un poids); (bend) faire plier; (fig) accabler; **~ up** calculer.

**weight** /weɪt/ *n* poids *m*; **lose/put on ~** perdre/prendre du poids. **~-lifting** *n* haltérophilie *f*. **~ training** *n* musculation *f* en salle.

**weird** /wɪəd/ *a* bizarre.

**welcome** /'welkəm/ *a* agréable; (timely) opportun; **be ~** être le *or* la bienvenu(e), être les bienvenu(e)s; **you're ~!** il n'y a pas de quoi!; **~ to do** libre de faire. ● *interj* soyez le *or* la bienvenu(e), soyez les bienvenu(e)s. ● *n* accueil *m*. ● *vt* accueillir; (as greeting) souhaiter la bienvenue à; (fig) se réjouir de.

**weld** /weld/ *vt* souder. ● *n* soudure *f*.

**welfare** /'welfeə(r)/ *n* bien-être *m*; (aid) aide *f* sociale. **W~ State** *n* État-providence *m*.

**well**[1] /wel/ *n* puits *m*.

**well**[2] /wel/ *adv* (**better**, **best**) bien; **do ~** (succeed) réussir; **~ done!** bravo! ● *a* bien *inv*; **as ~** aussi; **be ~** (healthy) aller bien. ● *interj* eh bien; (surprise) tiens.

**well**: **~-behaved** *a* sage. **~-being** *n* bien-être *m inv*.

**wellington** /'welɪŋtən/ *n* (boot) botte *f* de caoutchouc.

**well**: **~-known** *a* (bien) connu. **~-meaning** *a* bien intentionné. **~ off** aisé, riche. **~-read** *a*

instruit. **~-to-do** *a* riche. **~-wisher** *n* admirateur/-trice *m/f*.

**Welsh** /welʃ/ *a* gallois. ● *n* (Ling) gallois *m*.

**went** /went/ ⇒GO.

**wept** /wept/ ⇒WEEP.

**were** /wɜ:(r), wə(r)/ ⇒BE.

**west** /west/ *n* ouest *m*; **the W~** (Pol) l'Occident *m*. ● *a* d'ouest. ● *adv* vers l'ouest.

**western** /'westən/ *a* de l'ouest; (Pol) occidental. ● *n* (film) western *m*. **westerner** *n* occidental/-e *m/f*.

**West Indies** /west'ɪndi:z/ *n* Antilles *fpl*.

**westward** /'westwəd/ *a* (*side*) ouest *inv*; (*journey*) vers l'ouest.

**wet** /wet/ *a* (**wetter**, **wettest**) mouillé; (damp, rainy) humide; (*paint*) frais; **get ~** se mouiller. ● *vt* (*pt* **wetted**) mouiller. ● *n* **the ~** l'humidité *f*; (rain) la pluie *f*. **~ suit** *n* combinaison *f* de plongée.

**whale** /weɪl/ *n* baleine *f*.

**wharf** /wɔ:f/ *n* quai *m*.

**what** /wɒt/

● *pronoun*

····➤ (in questions as object pronoun) qu'est-ce que?; **~ are we going to do?** qu'est-ce que nous allons faire?

····➤ (in questions as subject pronoun) qu'est-ce qui?; **~ happened?** qu'est-ce qui s'est passé?

····➤ (introducing clause as object) ce que; **I don't know ~ he wants** je ne sais pas ce qu'il veut.

····➤ (introducing clause as subject) ce qui; **tell me ~ happened** raconte-moi ce qui s'est passé.

····➤ (with prepositions) quoi; **~ are you thinking about?** à quoi penses-tu?

● *determiner*

····➤ quel/quelle/quels/quelles; **~ train did you catch?** quel train as-tu pris?; **~ time is it?** quelle heure est-il?

**whatever** /wɒt'evə(r)/ *a* **~ book** quel que soit le livre. ● *pron* (no matter what) quoi que, quoi qu'; (anything that) tout ce qui; (object) tout ce que *or* qu'. **~ happens** quoi qu'il arrive; **~ happened?** qu'est-ce qui est arrivé?; **~ the problems** quels que soient les problèmes; **~ you want** tout ce que vous voulez; **nothing ~** rien du tout.

**whatsoever** /wɒtsəʊ'evər/ *a* & *pron* = WHATEVER.

**wheat** /wi:t/ *n* blé *m*, froment *m*.

**wheel** /wi:l/ *n* roue *f*; **at the ~** (of vehicle) au volant; (helm) au gouvernail. ● *vt* pousser. ● *vi* tourner; **~ and deal** faire des combines. **~barrow** *n* brouette *f*. **~chair** *n* fauteuil *m* roulant.

**when** /wen/ *adv* & *pron* quand. ● *conj* quand, lorsque; **the day/moment ~** le jour/moment où.

**whenever** /wen'evə(r)/ *conj* & *adv* (at whatever time) quand; (every time that) chaque fois que.

**where** /weə(r)/ *adv*, *conj* & *pron* où; (whereas) alors que; (the place that) là où.

**whereabouts** /'weərəbaʊts/ *adv* (à peu près) où. ● *n* **sb's ~** l'endroit où se trouve qn

**whereas** /weər'æz/ *conj* alors que.

**wherever** /weər'evə(r)/ *conj* & *adv* où que; (everywhere) partout où; (anywhere) (là) où; (emphatic where) où donc.

**whether** /'weðə(r)/ *conj* si; **not know ~** ne pas savoir si; **~ I go or not** que j'aille ou non.

**which** /wɪtʃ/

● *pronoun*

····➤ (in questions) lequel/laquelle/ lesquels/lesquelles; **there are three peaches, ~ do you want?** il y a trois pêches, laquelle veux-tu?

····➤ (in questions with superlative adjective) quel/quelle/quels/quelles; **~ (apple) is the biggest?** quelle est la plus grosse?

····➤ (in relative clauses as subject) qui; **the book ~ is on the table** le livre qui est sur la table.

····➤ (in relative clauses as object) que; **the book ~ Tina is reading** le livre que lit Tina.

● *determiner*

····➤ quel/quelle/quels/quelles; **~ car did you choose?** quelle voiture as-tu choisie?

**whichever** /wɪtʃ'evə(r)/ *a* **~ book** quel que soit le livre que *or* qui; **take ~ book you wish** prenez le livre que vous voulez. ● *pron* celui/celle/ceux/celles qui *or* que.

**while** /waɪl/ *n* moment *m*. ● *conj* (when) pendant que; (although) bien que; (as long as) tant que. ● *vt* **~ away** (*time*) passer.

**whilst** /waɪlst/ *conj* = WHILE.

**whim** /wɪm/ *n* caprice *m*.

**whine** /waɪn/ *vi* gémir, se plaindre. ● *n* gémissement *m*.

**whip** /wɪp/ *n* fouet *m*. ● *vt* (*pt* **whipped**) fouetter; (Culin) fouetter, battre; (seize) enlever brusquement. ● *vi* (move) aller en vitesse. □ **~ up** exciter; (cause) provoquer; (*meal* Ⓘ) préparer.

**whirl** /wɜ:l/ *vt/i* (faire) tourbillonner. ● *n* tourbillon *m*. **~pool** *n* tourbillon *m*. **~wind** *n* tourbillon *m* (de vent).

**whisk** /wɪsk/ *vt* (snatch) enlever *or* emmener brusquement; (Culin) fouetter. ● *n* (Culin) fouet *m*.

**whiskers** /'wɪskəz/ *npl* (of animal) moustaches *fpl*; (of man) favoris *mpl*.

**whisper** /'wɪspə(r)/ *vt/i* chuchoter. ● *n* chuchotement *m*; (rumour: fig) rumeur *f*, bruit *m*.

**whistle** /'wɪsl/ *n* sifflement *m*; (instrument) sifflet *m*. ● *vt/i* siffler; **~ at** *or* **for** siffler.

**white** /waɪt/ *a* blanc. ● *n* blanc *m*; (person) blanc/-che *m/f*. **~ coffee** *n* café *m* au lait. **~-collar worker** *n* employé/-e *m/f* de bureau. **~ elephant** *n* projet *m* coûteux et peu rentable. **~ lie** *n* pieux mensonge *m*. **W~ Paper** *n* livre *m* blanc.

**whitewash** /'waɪtwɒʃ/ *n* blanc *m* de chaux. ● *vt* blanchir à la chaux; (*person*: fig) blanchir.

**Whitsun** /'wɪtsn/ *n* la Pentecôte.

**whiz** /wɪz/ *vi* (*pt* **whizzed**) (through air) fendre l'air; (hiss) siffler; (rush) aller à toute vitesse. **~-kid** *n* jeune prodige *m*.

**who** /hu:/ *pron* qui.

**whoever** /hu:'evə(r)/ *pron* (no matter who) qui que ce soit qui *or* que; (the one who) quiconque; **tell ~ you want** dites-le à qui vous voulez.

**whole** /həʊl/ *a* entier; (intact) intact; **the ~ house** toute la maison. ● *n* totalité *f*; (unit) tout *m*; **on the ~** dans l'ensemble. **~foods** *npl* aliments *mpl* naturels et diététiques. **~-hearted** *a* sans réserve. **~meal** *a* complet.

**wholesale** /'həʊlseɪl/ *a* (*firm*) de gros; (fig) systématique. ● *adv* (in large quantities) en gros; (fig) en masse.

**wholesome** /'həʊlsəm/ *a* sain.

**wholly** /'həʊlɪ/ *adv* entièrement.

**whom** /hu:m/ *pron* (that) que, qu'; (after prepositions & in questions) qui; **of ~** dont; **with ~** avec qui.

**whooping cough** /'hu:pɪŋkɒf/ *n* coqueluche *f.*

**whose** /hu:z/ *pron & a* à qui, de qui; **~ hat is this?, ~ is this hat?** à qui est ce chapeau?; **~ son are you?** de qui êtes-vous le fils?; **the man ~ hat I see** l'homme dont je vois le chapeau.

**why** /waɪ/ *adv* pourquoi; **the reason ~** la raison pour laquelle.

**wicked** /'wɪkɪd/ *a* méchant, mauvais, vilain.

**wide** /waɪd/ *a* large; (*ocean*) vaste. ● *adv* (*fall*) loin du but; **open ~** ouvrir tout grand; **~ open** grand ouvert; **~ awake** éveillé. **widely** *adv* (*spread, space*) largement; (*travel*) beaucoup; (generally) généralement; (extremely) extrêmement.

**widespread** /'waɪdspred/ *a* très répandu.

**widow** /'wɪdəʊ/ *n* veuve *f.* **widowed** *a* (*man*) veuf; (*woman*) veuve. **widower** *n* veuf *m.*

**width** /wɪdθ/ *n* largeur *f.*

**wield** /wi:ld/ *vt* (*axe*) manier; (*power*: fig) exercer.

**wife** /waɪf/ *n* (*pl* **wives**) femme *f*, épouse *f.*

**wig** /wɪg/ *n* perruque *f.*

**wiggle** /'wɪgl/ *vt/i* remuer; (*hips*) tortiller; (*worm*) se tortiller.

**wild** /waɪld/ *a* sauvage; (*sea, enthusiasm*) déchaîné; (mad) fou; (angry) furieux. ● *adv* (*grow*) à l'état sauvage; **run ~** (free) courir en liberté.

**wildlife** /'waɪldlaɪf/ *n* faune *f.*

**will¹** /wɪl/

*present* **will**; *present negative* **won't, will not**; *past* **would**

● *auxiliary verb*

····> (in future tense) **he'll come** il viendra; **it ~ be sunny tomorrow** il va faire du soleil demain.

····> (inviting and requesting) **~ you have some coffee?** est-ce que vous voulez du café?

····> (making assumptions) **they won't know what's happened** ils ne doivent pas savoir ce qui s'est passé.

····> (in short questions and answers) **you'll come again, won't you?** tu reviendras, n'est-ce pas?; **'they won't forget'—'yes they ~'** 'ils n'oublieront pas'—'si'.

····> (capacity) **the lift ~ hold 12** l'ascenseur peut transporter 12 personnes.

····> (ability) **the car won't start** la voiture ne veut pas démarrer.

● *transitive verb*

····> **~ sb's death** souhaiter ardemment la mort de qn.

**will²** /wɪl/ *n* volonté *f*; (document) testament *m*; **at ~** quand *or* comme on veut.

**willing** /'wɪlɪŋ/ *a* (*help, offer*) spontané; (*helper*) bien disposé; **~ to** disposé à. **willingly** *adv* (with pleasure) volontiers; (not forced) volontairement. **willingness** *n* empressement *m* (**to do** à faire).

**willow** /'wɪləʊ/ *n* saule *m.*

**will-power** /'wɪlpaʊə(r)/ *n* volonté *f.*

**win** /wɪn/ *vt/i* (*pt* **won**; *pres p* **winning**) gagner; (*victory, prize*) remporter; (*fame, fortune*) acquérir, trouver; **~ round** convaincre. ● *n* victoire *f.*

**winch** /wɪntʃ/ *n* treuil *m.* ● *vt* hisser au treuil.

**wind¹** /[illegible]nd/ *n* vent *m*; (breath) souffle *m*; **ge**[illegible]**of** avoir vent de; **in the ~** dans l'air. ● [illegible]ssouffler. **~ farm** *n* ferme *f* d'éolien[illegible]

**wind²** /waɪnd/ *vt*/*i* (*pt* **wou**[illegible]) (s')enrouler; (of path, river) serpenter; **~ (up)** (*clock*) remonter; **~ up** (end) (se) terminer; **~ up in hospital** finir à l'hôpital.

**windmill** /ˈwɪndmɪl/ *n* moulin *m* à vent.

**window** /ˈwɪndəʊ/ *n* fenêtre *f*; (glass pane) vitre *f*; (in vehicle, train) vitre *f*; (in shop) vitrine *f*; (counter) guichet *m*; (Comput) fenêtre *f*. **~-box** *n* jardinière *f*. **~-cleaner** *n* laveur *m* de carreaux. **~-dresser** *n* étalagiste *mf*. **~-ledge** *n* rebord *m* de (la) fenêtre. **~-shopping** *n* lèche-vitrines *m*. **~-sill** *n* (inside) appui *m* de (la) fenêtre; (outside) rebord *m* de (la) fenêtre.

**windscreen** /ˈwɪndskriːn/ *n* pare-brise *m inv*. **~ wiper** *n* essuie-glace *m*.

**windshield** /ˈwɪndʃiːld/ *n* (US) = WINDSCREEN.

**windsurfing** /ˈwɪndsɜːfɪŋ/ *n* planche *f* à voile.

**windy** /ˈwɪndɪ/ *a* (**-ier**, **-iest**) venteux; **it is ~** il y a du vent.

**wine** /waɪn/ *n* vin *m*. **~-cellar** *n* cave *f* (*à vin*). **~glass** *n* verre *m* à vin. **~-grower** *n* viticulteur *m*. **~ list** *n* carte *f* des vins. **~-tasting** *n* dégustation *f* de vins.

**wing** /wɪŋ/ *n* aile *f*; **~s** (Theat) coulisses *fpl*; **under one's ~** sous son aile. **~ mirror** *n* rétroviseur *m* extérieur.

**wink** /wɪŋk/ *vi* faire un clin d'œil; (*light, star*) clignoter. ● *n* clin *m* d'œil; clignotement *m*.

**winner** /ˈwɪnə(r)/ *n* (of game) gagnant/-e *m*/*f*; (of fight) vainqueur *m*.

**winning** /ˈwɪnɪŋ/ ⇒WIN. ● *a* (*number, horse*) gagnant; (*team*) victorieux; (*smile*) engageant. **winnings** *npl* gains *mpl*.

**winter** /ˈwɪntə(r)/ *n* hiver *m*.

**wi**[illegible] /waɪp/ *vt* essuyer. ● *vi* **~ up** essuye[illegible]aisselle. ● *n* coup *m* de torchon *or* d'[illegible]ge. □ **~ out** (destroy) anéantir; (rem[illegible]) [illegible]ffacer.

**wire** /ˈwaɪə(r)/ *n* fil *m*; ([illegible]) [illegible]légramme *m*.

**wiring** /ˈwaɪərɪŋ/ *n* (Electr) installation *f* électrique.

**wisdom** /ˈwɪzdəm/ *n* sagesse *f*.

**wise** /waɪz/ *a* prudent, sage.

**wish** /wɪʃ/ *n* (specific) souhait *m*, vœu *m*; (general) désir *m*; **best ~es** (in letter) amitiés *fpl*; (on greeting card) meilleurs vœux *mpl*. ● *vt* souhaiter, vouloir, désirer (**to do** faire); (bid) souhaiter. ● *vi* **~ for** souhaiter; **I ~ he'd leave** je voudrais bien qu'il parte.

**wishful** /ˈwɪʃfl/ *a* **it's ~ thinking** c'est prendre ses désirs pour des réalités.

**wistful** /ˈwɪstfl/ *a* mélancolique.

**wit** /wɪt/ *n* intelligence *f*; (humour) esprit *m*; (person) homme *m* d'esprit, femme *f* d'esprit.

**witch** /wɪtʃ/ *n* sorcière *f*.

**with** /wɪð/ *prep* avec; (having) à; (because of) de; (at house of) chez; **the man ~ the beard** l'homme à la barbe; **fill ~** remplir de; **pleased**/**shaking ~** content/frémissant de.

**withdraw** /wɪðˈdrɔː/ *vt*/*i* (*pt* **withdrew**; *pp* **withdrawn**) (se) retirer. **withdrawal** *n* retrait *m*.

**wither** /ˈwɪðə(r)/ *vt*/*i* (se) flétrir.

**withhold** /wɪðˈhəʊld/ *vt* (*pt* **withheld**) refuser (de donner); (retain) retenir; (conceal) cacher (**from** à).

**within** /wɪ'ðɪn/ *prep & adv* à l'intérieur (de); (in distances) à moins de; ~ **a month** (before) avant un mois; ~ **sight** en vue.

**without** /wɪ'ðaʊt/ *prep* sans; ~ **my knowing** sans que je sache.

**withstand** /wɪð'stænd/ *vt* (*pt* **withstood**) résister à.

**witness** /'wɪtnɪs/ *n* témoin *m*; (evidence) témoignage *m*; **bear** ~ **to** témoigner de. ● *vt* être le témoin de, voir. ~ **box**, ~ **stand** *n* barre *f* des témoins.

**witty** /'wɪtɪ/ *a* (**-ier**, **-iest**) spirituel.

**wives** /waɪvz/ ⇨WIFE.

**wizard** /'wɪzəd/ *n* magicien *m*; (genius: fig) génie *m*.

**woke**, **woken** /wəʊk, 'wəʊkən/ ⇨WAKE.

**wolf** /wʊlf/ *n* (*pl* **wolves**) loup *m*. ● *vt* (*food*) engloutir.

**woman** /'wʊmən/ *n* (*pl* **women**) femme *f*; ~ **doctor** femme *f* médecin; ~ **driver** femme *f* au volant.

**women** /'wɪmɪn/ ⇨WOMAN.

**won** /wʌn/ ⇨WIN.

**wonder** /'wʌndə(r)/ *n* émerveillement *m*; (thing) merveille *f*; **it is no** ~ ce *or* il n'est pas étonnant (**that** que). ● *vt* se demander (**if** si). ● *vi* s'étonner (**at** de); (reflect) songer (**about** à).

**wonderful** /'wʌndəfl/ *a* merveilleux.

**won't** /wəʊnt/ = WILL NOT.

**wood** /wʊd/ *n* bois *m*.

**wooden** /'wʊdn/ *a* en *or* de bois; (stiff: fig) raide, comme du bois.

**wood**: ~**wind** *n* (Mus) bois *mpl*. ~**work** *n* (craft, objects) menuiserie *f*.

**wool** /wʊl/ *n* laine *f*. **woollen** *a* de laine. **woollens** *npl* lainages *mpl*.

**woolly** /'wʊlɪ/ *a* laineux; (vague) nébuleux. ● *n* (garment ⊡) lainage *m*.

**word** /wɜ:d/ *n* mot *m*; (spoken) parole *f*, mot *m*; (promise) parole *f*; (news) nouvelles *fpl*; **by** ~ **of mouth** de vive voix; **give/keep one's** ~ donner/tenir sa parole; **have a** ~ **with** parler à; **in other** ~**s** autrement dit. ● *vt* rédiger. **wording** *n* termes *mpl*.

**word processing** *n* traitement *m* de texte. **word processor** *n* machine *f* à traitement de texte.

**wore** /wɔ:(r)/ ⇨WEAR.

**work** /wɜ:k/ *n* travail *m*; (product, book) œuvre *f*, ouvrage *m*; (building work) travaux *mpl*; ~**s** (Tech) mécanisme *m*; (factory) usine *f*. ● *vi* (*person*) travailler; (drug) agir; (Tech) fonctionner, marcher. ● *vt* (Tech) faire fonctionner, faire marcher; (*land, mine*) exploiter; (shape, hammer) travailler; ~ **sb** (make work) faire travailler qn. □ ~ **out** *vt* (solve) résoudre; (calculate) calculer; (elaborate) élaborer; *vi* (succeed) marcher; (Sport) s'entraîner; ~ **up** *vt* développer; *vi* (to climax) monter vers. ~**ed up** (*person*) énervé.

**workaholic** /wɜ:kə'hɒlɪk/ *n* ⊡ bourreau *m* de travail.

**worker** /'wɜ:kə(r)/ *n* travailleur/-euse *m/f*; (manual) ouvrier/-ière *m/f*.

**work-force** *n* main-d'œuvre *f*.

**working** /'wɜ:kɪŋ/ *a* (*day, lunch*) de travail. ~**s** mécanisme *m*; **in** ~ **order** en état de marche.

**working class** *n* classe *f* ouvrière. ● *a* ouvrier.

**workman** /'wɜ:kmən/ *n* (*pl* **-men**) ouvrier *m*.

**work**: **~out** *n* séance *f* de mise en forme. **~shop** *n* atelier *m*. **~-station** *n* poste *m* de travail.

**world** /wɜ:ld/ *n* monde *m*. **best in the ~** meilleur au monde. ● *a* (*power*) mondial; (*record*) du monde.

**world-wide** *a* universel.

**World Wide Web, WWW** *n* World Wide Web *m*, réseau *m* des réseaux.

**worm** /wɜ:m/ *n* ver *m*. ● *vt* **~ one's way into** s'insinuer dans.

**worn** /wɔ:n/ ⇒WEAR. ● *a* usé. **~-out** *a* (*thing*) complètement usé; (*person*) épuisé.

**worried** /'wʌrɪd/ *a* inquiet.

**worry** /'wʌrɪ/ *vt*/*i* (s')inquiéter. ● *n* souci *m*.

**worse** /wɜ:s/ *a* pire, plus mauvais; **be ~ off** perdre. ● *adv* plus mal. ● *n* pire *m*. **worsen** *vt*/*i* empirer.

**worship** /'wɜ:ʃɪp/ *n* (adoration) culte *m*. ● *vt* (*pt* **worshipped**) adorer. ● *vi* faire ses dévotions.

**worst** /wɜ:st/ *a* pire, plus mauvais. ● *adv* **(the) ~** (*sing*) le plus mal. ● *n* **the ~ (one)** (person, object) le *or* la pire; **the ~ (thing)** le pire.

**worth** /wɜ:θ/ *a* **be ~** valoir; **it is ~ waiting** ça vaut la peine d'attendre; **it is ~ (one's) while** ça (en) vaut la peine. ● *n* valeur *f*; **ten pence ~ of** (pour) dix pence de. **worthless** *a* qui ne vaut rien. **worthwhile** *a* qui (en) vaut la peine.

**worthy** /'wɜ:ðɪ/ *a* (**-ier, -iest**) digne (**of** de); (laudable) louable.

**would** /wʊd, wəd/ *v aux* **he ~ do/you ~ sing** (conditional tense) il ferait/tu chanterais; **he ~ have done** il aurait fait; **I ~ come every day** (used to) je venais chaque jour; **I ~ like some tea** je voudrais du thé; **~ you come here?** voulez-vous venir ici?; **he wouldn't come** il a refusé de venir. **~-be** *a* soi-disant.

**wound**[1] /wu:nd/ *n* blessure *f*. ● *vt* blesser; **the ~ed** les blessés *mpl*.

**wound**[2] /waʊnd/ ⇒WIND[2].

**wove, woven** /wəʊv, 'wəʊvn/ ⇒WEAVE.

**wrap** /ræp/ *vt* (*pt* **wrapped**) **~ (up)** envelopper. ● *vi* **~ up** (dress warmly) se couvrir; **~ped up in** (engrossed) absorbé dans.

**wrapping** /'ræpɪŋ/ *n* emballage *m*.

**wreak** /ri:k/ *vt* **~ havoc** faire des ravages.

**wreath** /ri:θ/ *n* (of flowers, leaves) couronne *f*.

**wreck** /rek/ *n* (sinking) naufrage *m*; (ship, remains, person) épave *f*; (vehicle) voiture *f* accidentée *or* délabrée. ● *vt* détruire; (*ship*) provoquer le naufrage de. **wreckage** *n* (pieces) débris *mpl*; (wrecked building) décombres *mpl*.

**wrestle** /'resl/ *vi* lutter, se débattre (**with** contre).

**wrestling** /'reslɪŋ/ *n* lutte *f*; **(all-in) ~** catch *m*.

**wriggle** /'rɪgl/ *vt*/*i* (se) tortiller.

**wring** /rɪŋ/ *vt* (*pt* **wrung**) (twist) tordre; (*clothes*) essorer; **~ out of** (obtain from) arracher à.

**wrinkle** /'rɪŋkl/ *n* (crease) pli *m*; (on skin) ride *f*. ● *vt*/*i* (se) rider.

**wrist** /rɪst/ *n* poignet *m*.

**write** /raɪt/ *vt*/*i* (*pt* **wrote**; *pp* **written**) écrire. □ **~ back** répondre; **~ down** noter; **~ off** (*debt*) passer aux profits et pertes; (*vehicle*) considérer bon pour la casse; **~ up** (from notes) rédiger.

**write-off** /'raɪtɒf/ *n* perte *f* totale.

**writer** /'raɪtə(r)/ *n* auteur *m*, écrivain *m*; **~ of** auteur de.

**write-up** /'raɪtʌp/ *n* compte-rendu *m*.

**writing** /'raɪtɪŋ/ *n* écriture *f*; **~(s)** (works) écrits *mpl*; **in ~** par écrit. **~-paper** *n* papier *m* à lettres.

**written** /'rɪtn/ ⇒WRITE.

**wrong** /rɒŋ/ *a* (incorrect, mistaken) faux, mauvais; (unfair) injuste; (amiss) qui ne va pas; (*clock*) pas à l'heure; **be ~** (*person*) avoir tort (**to** de); (be mistaken) se tromper; **go ~** (err) se tromper; (turn out badly) mal tourner; **it is ~ to** (morally) c'est mal de; **what's ~?** qu'est-ce qui ne va pas?; **what is ~ with you?** qu'est-ce que vous avez? ● *adv* mal. ● *n* injustice *f*; (evil) mal *m*; **be in the ~** avoir tort. ● *vt* faire (du) tort à. **wrongful** *a* injustifié, injuste. **wrongfully** *adv* à tort. **wrongly** *adv* mal; (*blame*) à tort.

**wrote** /rəʊt/ ⇒WRITE.

**wrought iron** /rɔːt'aɪən/ *n* fer *m* forgé.

**wrung** /rʌŋ/ ⇒WRING.

**Xmas** /'krɪsməs/ *n* Noël *m*.

**X-ray** /'eksreɪ/ *n* rayon *m* X; (photograph) radio(graphie) *f*. ● *vt* radiographier.

**yank** /jæŋk/ *vt* tirer brusquement. ● *n* coup *m* brusque.

**yard** /jɑːd/ *n* (measure) yard *m* (= *0.9144 metre*); (of house) cour *f*; (garden: US) jardin *m*; (for storage) chantier *m*, dépôt *m*. **~stick** *n* mesure *f*.

**yawn** /jɔːn/ *vi* bâiller. ● *n* bâillement *m*.

**year** /jɪə(r)/ *n* an *m*, année *f*; **school/tax ~** année scolaire/fiscale; **be ten ~s old** avoir dix ans.

**yearly** /'jɪəlɪ/ *a* annuel. ● *adv* annuellement.

**yearn** /jɜːn/ *vi* avoir bien *or* très envie (**for, to** de).

**yeast** /jiːst/ *n* levure *f*.

**yell** /jel/ *vt/i* hurler. ● *n* hurlement *m*.

**yellow** /'jeləʊ/ *a* jaune; (cowardly 🄸) froussard. ● *n* jaune *m*.

**yes** /jes/ *adv* oui; (as answer to negative question) si. ● *n* oui *m inv*.

**yesterday** /'jestədeɪ/ *n & adv* hier (*m*).

**yet** /jet/ *adv* encore; (already) déjà. ● *conj* pourtant, néanmoins.

**yield** /jiːld/ *vt* (produce) produire rendre; (*profit*) rapporter; (surrender) céder. ● *n* rendement *m*.

**yoga** /'jəʊgə/ *n* yoga *m*.

**yoghurt** /'jɒgət/ *n* yaourt *m*.

**yolk** /jəʊk/ *n* jaune *m* (d'œuf).

**you** /juː/ *pron* (familiar form) tu, *pl* vous; (polite form) vous; (object) te, t', *pl* vous; (polite) vous; (after prep.) toi *pl* vous; (polite) vous; (indefinite) on; (object) vous; (**to**) **~** te, t', *pl* vous;

(polite) vous. **I gave ~ a pen** je vous ai donné un stylo. **I know ~** je te connais *or* je vous connais.

**young** /jʌŋ/ *a* jeune. ● *n* (people) jeunes *mpl*; (of animals) petits *mpl*.

**your** /jɔ:(r)/ *a* (familiar form) ton, ta, *pl* tes; (polite form, & familiar form pl.) votre, *pl* vos.

**yours** /jɔ:z/ *pron* (familiar form) le tien, la tienne, les tien(ne)s; (polite form, & familiar form pl.) le *or* la vôtre, les vôtres; **~ faithfully/sincerely** je vous prie d'agréer mes salutations les meilleures.

**yourself** /jɔ:'self/ *pron* (familiar form) toi-même; (polite form) vous-même; (reflexive & after prepositions) te, t'; vous; **proud of ~** fier de toi. **yourselves** *pron* vous-mêmes; (reflexive) vous.

**youth** /ju:θ/ *n* jeunesse *f*; (young man) jeune *m*. **~ hostel** *n* auberge *f* de jeunesse.

**Yugoslav** /ju:gəʊ'slɑ:v/ *a* yougoslave. ● *n* Yougoslave *mf*.

**Yugoslavia** /ju:gəʊ'slɑ:vɪə/ *n* Yougoslavie *f*.

# Zz

**zap** /zæp/ *vt* Ⅱ (kill) descendre; (Comput) enlever.

**zeal** /zi:l/ *n* zèle *m*.

**zebra** /'zebrə/ *n* zèbre *m*. **~ crossing** *n* passage *m* pour piétons.

**zero** /'zɪərəʊ/ *n* zéro *m*.

**zest** /zest/ *n* (gusto) entrain *m*; (spice: fig) piment *m*; (of orange or lemon peel) zeste *m*.

**zip** /zɪp/ *n* (vigour) allant *m*; **~(-fastener)** fermeture *f* éclair®. ● *vt* (*pt* **zipped**) fermer avec une fermeture éclair®; (Comput) compresser. **Zip code** (US) *n* code *m* postal.

**zodiac** /'zəʊdɪæk/ *n* zodiaque *m*.

**zone** /zəʊn/ *n* zone *f*.

**zoo** /zu:/ *n* zoo *m*.

**zoom** /zu:m/ *vi* (rush) se précipiter. □ **~ off** *or* **past** filer (comme une flèche). **~ lens** *n* zoom *m*.

**zucchini** /zu:'ki:nɪ/ *n inv* (US) courgette *f*.

# 1 chanter

### Present indicative

| | |
|---|---|
| je | chante |
| tu | chantes |
| il | chante |
| nous | chantons |
| vous | chantez |
| ils | chantent |

### Future indicative

| | |
|---|---|
| je | chanterai |
| tu | chanteras |
| il | chantera |
| nous | chanterons |
| vous | chanterez |
| ils | chanteront |

### Imperfect indicative

| | |
|---|---|
| je | chantais |
| tu | chantais |
| il | chantait |
| nous | chantions |
| vous | chantiez |
| ils | chantaient |

### Perfect indicative

| | | |
|---|---|---|
| j' | ai | chanté |
| tu | as | chanté |
| il | a | chanté |
| elle | a | chanté |
| nous | avons | chanté |
| vous | avez | chanté |
| ils | ont | chanté |
| elles | ont | chanté |

### Present subjunctive

| | | |
|---|---|---|
| (que) | je | chante |
| (que) | tu | chantes |
| (qu') | il | chante |
| (que) | nous | chantions |
| (que) | vous | chantiez |
| (qu') | ils | chantent |

### Present conditional

| | |
|---|---|
| je | chanterais |
| tu | chanterais |
| il | chanterait |
| nous | chanterions |
| vous | chanteriez |
| ils | chanteraient |

### Past participle

chanté/chantée

### Pluperfect indicative

| | | |
|---|---|---|
| j' | avais | chanté |
| tu | avais | chanté |
| il | avait | chanté |
| elle | avait | chanté |
| nous | avions | chanté |
| vous | aviez | chanté |
| ils | avaient | chanté |
| elles | avaient | chanté |

## 2 finir

**Present indicative**

| | |
|---|---|
| je | finis |
| tu | finis |
| il | finit |
| nous | finissons |
| vous | finissez |
| ils | finissent |

**Future indicative**

| | |
|---|---|
| je | finirai |
| tu | finiras |
| il | finira |
| nous | finirons |
| vous | finirez |
| ils | finiront |

**Imperfect indicative**

| | |
|---|---|
| je | finissais |
| tu | finissais |
| il | finissait |
| nous | finissions |
| vous | finissiez |
| ils | finissaient |

**Perfect indicative**

| | | |
|---|---|---|
| j' | ai | fini |
| tu | as | fini |
| il | a | fini |
| elles | a | fini |
| nous | avons | fini |
| vous | avez | fini |
| ils | ont | fini |
| elles | ont | fini |

**Present subjunctive**

| | | |
|---|---|---|
| (que) | je | finisse |
| (que) | tu | finisses |
| (qu') | il | finisse |
| (que) | nous | finissions |
| (que) | vous | finissiez |
| (qu') | ils | finissent |

**Present conditional**

| | |
|---|---|
| je | finirais |
| tu | finirais |
| il | finirait |
| nous | finirions |
| vous | finiriez |
| ils | finiraient |

**Past participle**

fini/finie

**Pluperfect indicative**

| | | |
|---|---|---|
| j' | avais | fini |
| tu | avais | fini |
| il | avait | fini |
| elle | avait | fini |
| nous | avions | fini |
| vous | aviez | fini |
| ils | avaient | fini |
| elles | avaient | fini |

## 3 attendre

### Present indicative

| | |
|---|---|
| j' | attends |
| tu | attends |
| il | attend |
| nous | attendons |
| vous | attendez |
| ils | attendent |

### Future indicative

| | |
|---|---|
| j' | attendrai |
| tu | attendras |
| il | attendra |
| nous | attendrons |
| vous | attendrez |
| ils | attendront |

### Imperfect indicative

| | |
|---|---|
| j' | attendais |
| tu | attendais |
| il | attendait |
| nous | attendions |
| vous | attendiez |
| ils | attendaient |

### Perfect indicative

| | | |
|---|---|---|
| j' | ai | attendu |
| tu | as | attendu |
| il | a | attendu |
| elle | a | attendu |
| nous | avons | attendu |
| vous | avez | attendu |
| ils | ont | attendu |
| elles | ont | attendu |

### Present subjunctive

| | | |
|---|---|---|
| (que) | j' | attende |
| (que) | tu | attendes |
| (qu') | il | attende |
| (que) | nous | attendions |
| (que) | vous | attendiez |
| (qu') | ils | attendent |

### Present conditional

| | |
|---|---|
| j' | attendrais |
| tu | attendrais |
| il | attendrait |
| nous | attendrions |
| vous | attendriez |
| ils | attendraient |

### Past participle

attendu/attendue

### Pluperfect indicative

| | | |
|---|---|---|
| j' | avais | attendu |
| tu | avais | attendu |
| il | avait | attendu |
| elle | avait | attendu |
| nous | avions | attendu |
| vous | aviez | attendu |
| ils | avaient | attendu |
| elles | avaient | attendu |

# 4 être

**Present indicative**

| | |
|---|---|
| je | suis |
| tu | es |
| il | est |
| nous | sommes |
| vous | êtes |
| ils | sont |

**Future indicative**

| | |
|---|---|
| je | serai |
| tu | seras |
| il | sera |
| nous | serons |
| vous | serez |
| ils | seront |

**Imperfect indicative**

| | |
|---|---|
| j' | étais |
| tu | étais |
| il | était |
| nous | étions |
| vous | étiez |
| ils | étaient |

**Perfect indicative**

| | | |
|---|---|---|
| j' | ai | été |
| tu | as | été |
| il | a | été |
| elle | a | été |
| nous | avons | été |
| vous | avez | été |
| ils | ont | été |
| elles | ont | été |

**Present subjunctive**

| | | |
|---|---|---|
| (que) | je | sois |
| (que) | tu | sois |
| (qu') | il | soit |
| (que) | nous | soyons |
| (que) | vous | soyez |
| (qu') | ils | soient |

**Present conditional**

| | |
|---|---|
| je | serais |
| tu | serais |
| il | serait |
| nous | serions |
| vous | seriez |
| ils | seraient |

**Past participle**

été (*invariable*)

**Pluperfect indicative**

| | | |
|---|---|---|
| j' | avais | été |
| tu | avais | été |
| il | avait | été |
| elle | avait | été |
| nous | avions | été |
| vous | aviez | été |
| ils | avaient | été |
| elles | avaient | été |

# 5 avoir

**Present indicative**

| | |
|---|---|
| j' | ai |
| tu | as |
| il | a |
| nous | avons |
| vous | avez |
| ils | ont |

**Future indicative**

| | |
|---|---|
| j' | aurai |
| tu | auras |
| il | aura |
| nous | aurons |
| vous | aurez |
| ils | auront |

**Imperfect indicative**

| | |
|---|---|
| j' | avais |
| tu | avais |
| il | avait |
| nous | avions |
| vous | aviez |
| ils | avaient |

**Perfect indicative**

| | | |
|---|---|---|
| j' | ai | eu |
| tu | as | eu |
| il | a | eu |
| elle | a | eu |
| nous | avons | eu |
| vous | avez | eu |
| ils | ont | eu |
| elles | ont | eu |

**Present subjunctive**

| | | |
|---|---|---|
| (que) | j' | aie |
| (que) | tu | aies |
| (qu') | il | ait |
| (que) | nous | ayons |
| (que) | vous | ayez |
| (qu') | ils | aient |

**Present conditional**

| | |
|---|---|
| j' | aurais |
| tu | aurais |
| il | aurait |
| nous | aurions |
| vous | auriez |
| ils | auraient |

**Past participle**

eu/eue

**Pluperfect indicative**

| | | |
|---|---|---|
| j' | avais | eu |
| tu | avais | eu |
| il | avait | eu |
| elle | avait | eu |
| nous | avions | eu |
| vous | aviez | eu |
| ils | avaient | eu |
| elles | avaient | eu |

**[6] acheter**
**1** j'achète **2** j'achèterai **3** j'achetais **4** que j'achète **5** acheté

**[7] acquérir**
**1** j'acquiers, nous acquérons, ils acquièrent **2** j'acquerrai **3** j'acquérais **4** que j'acquière **5** acquis

**[8] aller**
**1** je' vais, tu vas, il va, nous allons, vous allez, ils vont **2** j'irai **3** j'allais **4** que j'aille, que nous allions, qu'ils aillent **5** allé

**[9] asseoir**
**1** j'assieds, tu assieds, il assied. nou asseyons, vous asseyez, il asseyent *or* j'assois, tu assois, il assoit, nous assoyons, vous assoyez, ils assoient **2** j'assiérai *or* j'assoirai **3** j'assiérai *or* j'assoyais **4** que j'asseye, que nous asseyions, qu'ils asseyent *or* que j'assoie, que nous assoyions, qu'ils assoient **5** assis

**[10] avancer**
**1** nous avançons **3** j'avançais

**[11] battre**
**1** je bats, il bat, nous battons **2** je battrai **3** je battais **4** que je batte **5** battu

**[12] boire**
**1** je bois, il boit, nous buvons, ils boivent **2** je boirai **3** je buvais **4** que je boive **5** bu

**[13] bouillir**
**1** je bous, il bout, nous bouillons, ils bouillent **2** je bouillirai **3** je bouillais **4** que je bouille **5** bouilli

**[14] céder**
**1** je cède, nous cédons, ils cèdent **2** je céderai **3** je cédais **4** que je cède **5** cédé

**[15] créer**
**1** je crée, nous créons **2** je créerai **3** je créais **4** que je crée **5** créé

**[16] conclure**
**1** je conclus, il conclut, nous concluons, ils concluent **2** je conclurai **3** je concluais **4** que je conclue **5** conclu (*but* inclus)

**[17] conduire**
**1** je conduis, nous conduisons, **2** je conduirai **3** je conduisais **4** que je conduise **5** conduit (*but* lui, nui)

**[18] connaître**
**1** je connais, il connaît, nous connaissons **2** je connaîtrai **3** je connaissais **4** que je connaisse **5** connu

**[19] coudre**
**1** je couds, il coud, nous cousons, ils cousent **2** je coudrai **3** je cousais **4** que je couse **5** cousu

**[20] courir**

**1** je cours, il court, nous courons, ils courent **2** je courrai **3** je courais **4** que je coure **5** couru

**[21] couvrir**
**1** je couvre **2** je couvrirai **3** je couvrais **4** que je couvre **5** couvert

**[22] craindre**
**1** je crains, il craint, nous craignons, ils craignent **2** je craindrai **3** je craignais **4** que je craigne **5** craint

**[23] croire**
**1** je crois, il croit, nous croyons, ils croient **2** je croirai **3** je croyais, nous croyions **4** que je croie, que nous croyions **5** cru

**[24] croître**
**1** je croîs, il croît, nous croissons **2** je croîtrai **3** je croissais **4** que je croisse **5** crû/crue (*but* accru, décru)

**[25] cueillir**
**1** je cueille **2** je cueillerai **3** je cueillais **4** que je cueille **5** cueilli

**[26] devoir**
**1** je dois, il doit, nous devons, ils doivent **2** je devrai **3** je devais **4** que je doive, que nous devions **5** dû/due

**[27] dire**
**1** je dis, il dit, nous disons, vous dites, ils disent **2** je dirai **3** je disais **4** que je dise **5** dit

**[28] dissoudre**
**1** je dissous, il dissout, nous dissolvons, ils dissolvent **2** je dissoudrai **3** je dissolvais **4** que je dissolve **5** dissous/dissoute

**[29] distraire**
**1** je distrais, il distrait, nous distrayons **2** je distrairai **3** je distrayais **4** que je distraie **5** distrait

**[30] écrire**
**1** j'écris, il écrit, nous écrivons **2** j'écrirai **3** j'écrivais **4** que j'écrive **5** écrit

**[31] employer**
**1** j'emploie, nous employons, ils emploient **2** j'emploierai **3** j'employais, nous employions **4** que j'emploie, que nous employions **5** employé

**[32] envoyer**
**1** j'envoie, nous envoyons, ils envoient **2** j'enverrai **3** j'envoyais, nous envoyions **4** que j'envoie, que nous envoyions **5** envoyé

**[33] faire**
**1** je fais, nous faisons (*say* /fəzɔ̃/), vous faites, ils font **2** je ferai **3** je faisais (*say* /fəzɛ/) **4** que je fasse, que nous fassions **5** fait

**[34] falloir** (*impersonal*)
**1** il faut **2** il faudra **3** il fallait **4** qu'il faille **5** fallu

**[35] fuir**
**1** je fuis, nous fuyons **2** je fuirai **3** je fuyais, nous fuyions **4** que je fuie, que nous fuyions **5** fui

**[36] haïr**
**1** je hais, il hait, nous haïssons, ils haïssent **2** je haïrai **3** je haïssais **4** que je haïsse **5** haï

**[37] interdire**
**1** j'interdis, vous interdisez **2** j'interdirai **3** j'interdisais **4** que j'interdise **5** interdit

**[38] jeter**
**1** je jette, nous jetons, ils jettent **2** je jetterai **3** je jetais **4** que je jette **5** jeté

**[39] lire**
**1** je lis, il lit, nous lisons **2** je lirai **3** je lisais **4** que je lise **5** lu

**[40] manger**
**1** je mange, nous mangeons **2** je mangerai **3** je mangeais **4** que je mange, que nous mangions **5** mangé

**[41] maudire**
**1** je maudis, il maudit, nous maudissons **2** je maudirai **3** je maudissais **4** que je maudisse **5** maudit

**[42] mettre**
**1** je mets, tu mets, nous mettons **2** je mettrai **3** je mettais **4** que je mette **5** mis

**[43] mourir**
**1** je meurs, il meurt, nous mourons **2** je mourrai **3** je mourais **4** que je meure **5** mort

**[44] naître**
**1** je nais, il naît, nous naissons **2** je naîtrai **3** je naissais **4** que je naisse **5** né

**[45] oublier**
**1** j'oublie, nous oublions, ils oublient **2** j'oublierai **3** j'oubliais, nous oubliions, vous oubliiez **4** que nous oubliions, que vous oubliiez **5** oublié

**[46] partir**
**1** je pars, nous partons **2** je partirai **3** je partais **4** que je parte **5** parti

**[47] plaire**
**1** je plais, il plaît (*but* il tait), nous plaisons **2** je plairai **3** je plaisais **4** que je plaise **5** plu

**[48] pleuvoir** (*impersonal*)
**1** il pleut **2** il pleuvra **3** il pleuvait **4** qu'il pleuve **5** plu

**[49] pouvoir**
**1** je peux, il peut, nous pouvons, ils peuvent **2** je pourrai **3** je pouvais **4** que je puisse, que nous puissions **5** pu

**[50] prendre**
**1** je prends, il prend, nous prenons **2** je prendrai **3** je prenais **4** que je prenne **5** pris

---

**1** Present Indicative **2** Future Indicative **3** Imperfect Indicative **4** Present Subjunctive **5** Past Participle

[51] **prévoir**
**1** je prévois, il prévoit, nous prévoyons, ils prévoient **2** je prévoirai **3** je prévoyais, nous prévoyions **4** que je prévoie, que nous prévoyions **5** prévu

[52] **recevoir**
**1** je reçois, il reçoit, nous recevons, ils reçoivent **2** je recevrai **3** je recevais **4** que je reçoive, que nous recevions **5** reçu

[53] **résoudre**
**1** je résous, il résout, nous résolvons, ils résolvent **2** je résoudrai **3** je résolvais **4** que je résolve **5** résolu

[54] **rire**
**1** je ris, nous rions, ils rient **2** je rirai **3** je riais, nous riions **4** que je rie, que nous riions **5** ri

[55] **savoir**
**1** je sais, il sait, nous savons, ils savent **2** je saurai **3** je savais **4** que je sache, que nous sachions **5** su

[56] **suffire**
**1** il suffit, ils suffisent **2** il suffira **3** il suffisait **4** qu'il suffise **5** suffi (*but* frit)

[57] **suivre**
**1** je suis, il suit, nous suivons **2** je suivrai **3** je suivais **4** que je suive **5** suivi

[58] **tenir**
**1** je tiens, il tient, nous tenons, ils tiennent **2** je tiendrai **3** je tenais **4** que je tienne, que nous tenions **5** tenu

[59] **vaincre**
**1** je vaincs, il vainc, nous vainquons, ils vainquent **2** je vaincrai **3** je vainquais **4** que je vainque **5** vaincu

[60] **valoir**
**1** je vaux, il vaut, nous valons **2** je vaudrai **3** je valais **4** que je vaille, que nous valions **5** valu

[61] **vêtir**
**1** je vêts, il vêt, nous vêtons **2** je vêtirai **3** je vêtais **4** que je vête **5** vêtu

[62] **vivre**
**1** je vis, il vit, nous vivons, ils vivent **2** je vivrai **3** je vivais **4** que je vive **5** vécu

[63] **voir**
**1** je vois, nous voyons, ils voient **2** je verrai **3** je voyais, nous voyions **4** que je voie, que nous voyions **5** vu

[64] **vouloir**
**1** je veux, il veut, nous voulons, ils veulent **2** je voudrai **3** je voulais **4** que je veuille, que nous voulions **5** voulu

---

**1** Present Indicative **2** Future Indicative **3** Imperfect Indicative **4** Present Subjunctive **5** Past Participle

## What are the equivalent tenses in English?

**Present indicative**
je chante = *I sing, I'm singing*

**Future indicative**
je chanterai = *I will sing*

**Imperfect indicative**
je chantais = *I was singing*

**Perfect indicative**
j'ai chanté = *I sang, I have sung*

**Pluperfect indicative**
j'avais chanté = *I had sung*

**Present subjunctive**
bien que je chante = *although I sing*

**Present conditional**
si je pouvais, je chanterais = *if I could, I would sing*

**Past participle**
chanté/chantée = *sung*

## How to conjugate a reflexive verb

**Present indicative and other simple tenses**

je me lave
tu te laves
il se lave
elle se lave
nous nous lavons
vous vous lavez
ils se lavent
elles se lavent

**in the negative form**

je ne me lave pas
tu ne te laves pas
il ne se lave pas
elle ne se lave pas
nous ne nous lavons pas
vous ne vous lavez pas
ils ne se lavent pas
elles ne se lavent pas

**Perfect indicative and other compound tenses**
*(always with auxiliary* ***être****)*

je me suis lavé
tu t'es lavé
il s'est lavé
elle s'est lavée
nous nous sommes lavés
vous vous êtes lavés
ils se sont lavés
elles se sont lavées

**in the negative form**

je ne me suis pas lavé
tu ne t'es pas lavé
il ne s'est pas lavé
elle ne s'est pas lavée
nous ne nous sommes pas lavés
vous ne vous êtes pas lavés
ils ne se sont pas lavés
elles ne se sont pas lavées

# Verbes irréguliers anglais

| Infinitif | Prétérit | Participe passé |
|---|---|---|
| **be** | was | been |
| **bear** | bore | borne |
| **beat** | beat | beaten |
| **become** | became | become |
| **begin** | began | begun |
| **bend** | bent | bent |
| **bet** | bet, betted | bet, betted |
| **bid** | bade, bid | bidden, bid |
| **bind** | bound | bound |
| **bite** | bit | bitten |
| **bleed** | bled | bled |
| **blow** | blew | blown |
| **break** | broke | broken |
| **breed** | bred | bred |
| **bring** | brought | brought |
| **build** | built | built |
| **burn** | burnt, burned | burnt, burned |
| **burst** | burst | burst |
| **buy** | bought | bought |
| **catch** | caught | caught |
| **choose** | chose | chosen |
| **cling** | clung | clung |
| **come** | came | come |
| **cost** | cost, costed (*vt*) | cost, costed |
| **cut** | cut | cut |
| **deal** | dealt | dealt |
| **dig** | dug | dug |
| **do** | did | done |
| **draw** | drew | drawn |
| **dream** | dreamt, dreamed | dreamt, dreamed |
| **drink** | drank | drunk |
| **drive** | drove | driven |
| **eat** | ate | eaten |
| **fall** | fell | fallen |
| **feed** | fed | fed |
| **feel** | felt | felt |
| **fight** | fought | fought |
| **find** | found | found |
| **flee** | fled | fled |
| **fly** | flew | flown |
| **freeze** | froze | frozen |
| **get** | got | got, gotten US |
| **give** | gave | given |
| **go** | went | gone |
| **grow** | grew | grown |
| **hang** | hung, hanged (*vt*) | hung, hanged |
| **have** | had | had |
| **hear** | heard | heard |
| **hide** | hid | hidden |
| **hit** | hit | hit |
| **hold** | held | held |
| **hurt** | hurt | hurt |
| **keep** | kept | kept |
| **kneel** | knelt | knelt |
| **know** | knew | known |
| **lay** | laid | laid |
| **lead** | led | led |
| **lean** | leaned, leant | leaned, leant |
| **learn** | learnt, learned | learnt, learned |
| **leave** | left | left |

| Infinitif | Prétérit | Participe passé |
|---|---|---|
| **lend** | lent | lent |
| **let** | let | let |
| **lie** | lay | lain |
| **lose** | lost | lost |
| **make** | made | made |
| **mean** | meant | meant |
| **meet** | met | met |
| **pay** | paid | paid |
| **put** | put | put |
| **read** | read | read |
| **ride** | rode | ridden |
| **ring** | rang | rung |
| **rise** | rose | risen |
| **run** | ran | run |
| **say** | said | said |
| **see** | saw | seen |
| **seek** | sought | sought |
| **sell** | sold | sold |
| **send** | sent | sent |
| **set** | set | set |
| **sew** | sewed | sewn, sewed |
| **shake** | shook | shaken |
| **shine** | shone | shone |
| **shoe** | shod | shod |
| **shoot** | shot | shot |
| **show** | showed | shown |
| **shut** | shut | shut |
| **sing** | sang | sung |
| **sink** | sank | sunk |
| **sit** | sat | sat |
| **sleep** | slept | slept |
| **sling** | slung | slung |
| **smell** | smelt, smelled | smelt, smelled |

| Infinitif | Prétérit | Participe passé |
|---|---|---|
| **speak** | spoke | spoken |
| **spell** | spelled, spelt | spelled, spelt |
| **spend** | spent | spent |
| **spit** | spat | spat |
| **spoil** | spoilt, spoiled | spoilt, spoiled |
| **spread** | spread | spread |
| **spring** | sprang | sprung |
| **stand** | stood | stood |
| **steal** | stole | stolen |
| **stick** | stuck | stuck |
| **sting** | stung | stung |
| **stride** | strode | stridden |
| **strike** | struck | struck |
| **swear** | swore | sworn |
| **sweep** | swept | swept |
| **swell** | swelled | swollen, swelled |
| **swim** | swam | swum |
| **swing** | swung | swung |
| **take** | took | taken |
| **teach** | taught | taught |
| **tear** | tore | torn |
| **tell** | told | told |
| **think** | thought | thought |
| **throw** | threw | thrown |
| **thrust** | thrust | thrust |
| **tread** | trod | trodden |
| **under-stand** | under-stood | understood |
| **wake** | woke | woken |
| **wear** | wore | worn |
| **win** | won | won |
| **write** | wrote | written |

# Numbers/Les nombres

## Cardinal numbers/ Les nombres cardinaux

0 zero **zéro**
1 one **un**
2 two **deux**
3 three **trois**
4 four **quatre**
5 five **cinq**
6 six **six**
7 seven **sept**
8 eight **huit**
9 nine **neuf**
10 ten **dix**
11 eleven **onze**
12 twelve **douze**
13 thirteen **treize**
14 fourteen **quatorze**
15 fifteen **quinze**
16 sixteen **seize**
17 seventeen **dix-sept**
18 eighteen **dix-huit**
19 nineteen **dix-neuf**
20 twenty **vingt**
21 twenty-one **vingt et un**
22 twenty-two **vingt-deux**
30 thirty **trente**
40 forty **quarante**
50 fifty **cinquante**
60 sixty **soixante**
70 seventy **soixante-dix**
80 eighty **quatre-vingt**
90 ninety **quatre-vingt dix**
100 a hundred **cent**
101 a hundred and one **cent un**
110 a hundred and ten **cent dix**
200 two hundred **deux cents**
250 two hundred and fifty **deux cent cinquante**
1,000 one thousand **mille**
1,001 one thousand and one **mille un**
2,000 two thousand **deux mille**
10,000 ten thousand **dix mille**
100,000 a hundred thousand **cent mille**
1,000,000 a million **un million**

## Ordinal numbers/ Les nombres ordinaux

1st first **premier**
2nd second **deuxième**
3rd third **troisième**
4th fourth **quatrième**
5th fifth **cinquième**
6th sixth **sixième**
7th seventh **septième**
8th eighth **huitième**
9th ninth **neuvième**
10th tenth **dixième**
11th eleventh **onzième**
12th twelfth **douzième**
13th thirteenth **treizième**
14th fourteenth **quatorzième**
15th fifteenth **quinzième**
16th sixteenth **seizième**

17th seventeenth **dix-septième**

18th eighteenth **dix-huitième**

19th nineteenth **dix-neuvième**

20th twentieth **vingtième**

21st twenty-first **vingt et unième**

22nd twenty-second **vingt-deuxième**

30th thirtieth **trentième**

40th fortieth **quarantième**

50th fiftieth **cinquantième**

60th sixtieth **soixantième**

70th seventieth **soixante-dixième**

80th eightieth **quatre-vingtième**

90th ninetieth **quatre-vingt-dixième**

100th hundredth **centième**

101st hundred and first **cent unième**

110th hundred and tenth **cent dixième**

200th two hundredth **deux centième**

250th two hundred and fiftieth **deux cent cinquantième**

1,000th thousandth **millième**

1,001st thousand and first **mille et unième**

2,000th two thousandth **deux millième**

10,000th ten thousandth **dix millième**

100,000th hundred thousandth **cent millième**

1,000,000th millionth **millionième**

## Fractions/Les fractions

½ a half **un demi**

⅓ a third **un tiers**

¼ a quarter **un quart**

⅒ a tenth **un dixième**

⅔ two-thirds **deux tiers**

⅝ five-eighths **cinq huitièmes**

1/100 one hundredth **un centième**

1 ½ one and a half **un et demi**

2 ¼ two and a quarter **deux et un quart**

## Decimals/Les décimaux

0.1 point one **zéro virgule un**

0.25 point two five **zéro virgule vingt-cinq**

1.2 one point two **un virgule deux**

1.46 one point four six **un virgule quarante-six**

## Percentages/Pourcentages

25% twenty-five per cent **vingt-cinq pour cent**

50% fifty per cent **cinquante pour cent**

100% a hundred per cent **cent pour cent**

365% three hundred and sixty-five per cent **trois cent soixante-cinq pour cent**

4.25% four point two five per cent **quatre virgule vingt-cinq pour cent**